M000016809

STUDIES IN ANCIENT ORIENTAL CIVILIZATION • NO. 58

THE ORIENTAL INSTITUTE OF THE UNIVERSITY OF CHICAGO

Edward F. Wente

GOLD OF PRAISE

STUDIES ON ANCIENT EGYPT IN HONOR OF EDWARD F. WENTE

edited by

EMILY TEETER *and* JOHN A. LARSON

THE ORIENTAL INSTITUTE OF THE UNIVERSITY OF CHICAGO
STUDIES IN ANCIENT ORIENTAL CIVILIZATION • NO. 58
CHICAGO • ILLINOIS

Library of Congress Catalog Card Number: 99-67192
ISBN: 1-885923-09-0
ISSN: 0081-7554

The Oriental Institute, Chicago

Published 1999. Printed in the United States of America.

Cover Illustration

After *Kheruef*, pl. 36

Printed by McNaughton & Gunn, Saline, Michigan

The paper used in this publication meets the minimum requirements of American National Standard for Information Services — Permanence of Paper for Printed Library Materials, ANSI Z39.48-1984.

TABLE OF CONTENTS

LIST OF ABBREVIATIONS

Bibliographical Abbreviations

CT 1	*The Egyptian Coffin Texts,* Volume 1: *Texts of Spells 1–75.* A. de Buck. Oriental Institute Publications 34. Chicago: University of Chicago Press, 1935
CT 2	*The Egyptian Coffin Texts,* Volume 2: *Texts of Spells 76–163.* A. de Buck. Oriental Institute Publications 49. Chicago: University of Chicago Press, 1938
CT 3	*The Egyptian Coffin Texts,* Volume 3: *Texts of Spells 164–267.* A. de Buck. Oriental Institute Publications 64. Chicago: University of Chicago Press, 1947
CT 4	*The Egyptian Coffin Texts,* Volume 4: *Texts of Spells 268–354.* A. de Buck. Oriental Institute Publications 67. Chicago: University of Chicago Press, 1951
CT 5	*The Egyptian Coffin Texts,* Volume 5: *Texts of Spells 355–471.* A. de Buck. Oriental Institute Publications 73. Chicago: University of Chicago Press, 1954
CT 6	*The Egyptian Coffin Texts,* Volume 6: *Texts of Spells 472–786.* A. de Buck. Oriental Institute Publications 81. Chicago: University of Chicago Press, 1956
CT 7	*The Egyptian Coffin Texts,* Volume 7: *Texts of Spells 787–1185.* A. de Buck. Oriental Institute Publications 87. Chicago: University of Chicago Press, 1961
Kheruef	*The Tomb of Kheruef: Theban Tomb 192.* The Epigraphic Survey. Oriental Institute Publications 102. Chicago: Oriental Institute, 1980
KRI	*Ramesside Inscriptions: Historical and Biographical.* 8 Volumes. K. A. Kitchen. Oxford: B. H. Blackwell, 1968–
LÄ	*Lexikon der Ägyptologie.* Wolfgang Helck, Eberhard Otto, and Wolfhart Westendorf, eds. Wiesbaden: Otto Harrassowitz, 1975–
LD	*Denkmäler aus Aegypten und Aethiopien.* 12 volumes. R. Lepsius. Reprint (Originally published Berlin: Nicholaische Buchhandlung, 1849–1913). Geneva: Éditions de Belles-Lettres, 1972–73
MH 1	*Medinet Habu,* Volume 1: *Earlier Historical Records of Ramses III.* The Epigraphic Survey. Oriental Institute Publications 8. Chicago: University of Chicago Press, 1930
MH 2	*Medinet Habu,* Volume 2: *Later Historical Records of Ramses III.* The Epigraphic Survey. Oriental Institute Publications 9. Chicago: University of Chicago Press, 1932
MH 4	*Medinet Habu,* Volume 4: *Festival Scenes of Ramses III.* The Epigraphic Survey. Oriental Institute Publications 51. Chicago: University of Chicago Press, 1940
PM 1/1	*Topographic Bibliography of Ancient Egyptian Hieroglyphic Texts, Reliefs, and Paintings,* Volume 1: *The Theban Necropolis,* Part 1: *Private Tombs.* Bertha Porter and Rosalind L. B. Moss. Second edition. Oxford: Clarendon Press, 1960
PM 1/2	*Topographic Bibliography of Ancient Egyptian Hieroglyphic Texts, Reliefs, and Paintings,* Volume 1: *The Theban Necropolis,* Part 2: *Royal Tombs and Smaller Cemeteries.* Bertha Porter and Rosalind L. B. Moss. Second edition. Oxford: Clarendon Press, 1964

PM 2	*Topographic Bibliography of Ancient Egyptian Hieroglyphic Texts, Reliefs, and Paintings,* Volume 2: *Theban Temples.* Bertha Porter and Rosalind L. B. Moss. Second edition. Oxford: Clarendon Press, 1972
PM 3/1	*Topographic Bibliography of Ancient Egyptian Hieroglyphic Texts, Reliefs, and Paintings,* Volume 3: *Memphis,* Part 1: *Abû Rawâsh to Abûṣîr.* Bertha Porter and Rosalind L. B. Moss; Jaromír Málek, editor. Second edition. Oxford: Clarendon Press, 1974
PM 3/2	*Topographic Bibliography of Ancient Egyptian Hieroglyphic Texts, Reliefs, and Paintings,* Volume 3: *Memphis,* Part 2: *Ṣaqqâra to Dahshûr.* Bertha Porter and Rosalind L. B. Moss; Jaromír Málek, editor. Second edition. Oxford: Griffith Institute, Ashmolean Museum, 1981
PM 5	*Topographic Bibliography of Ancient Egyptian Hieroglyphic Texts, Reliefs, and Paintings,* Volume 5: *Upper Egypt: Sites (Deir Rîfa to Aswân, Excluding Thebes and the Temples of Abydos, Dendera, Esna, Edfu, Kôm Ombo, and Philae).* Bertha Porter and Rosalind L. B. Moss. Oxford: Clarendon Press, 1937
PM 6	*Topographic Bibliography of Ancient Egyptian Hieroglyphic Texts, Reliefs, and Paintings,* Volume 6: *Upper Egypt: Chief Temples (Excluding Thebes), Abydos, Dendera, Esna, Edfu, Kôm Ombo, and Philae.* Bertha Porter and Rosalind L. B. Moss. Oxford: Clarendon Press, 1939
PM 7	*Topographic Bibliography of Ancient Egyptian Hieroglyphic Texts, Reliefs, and Paintings,* Volume 7: *Nubia, the Deserts, and Outside Egypt.* Bertha Porter and Rosalind L. B. Moss. Oxford: Clarendon Press, 1951
RIK 3	*Reliefs and Inscriptions at Karnak,* Volume 3: *Bubastite Portal.* The Epigraphic Survey. Oriental Institute Publications 74. Chicago: University of Chicago Press, 1954
RIK 4	*Reliefs and Inscriptions at Karnak,* Volume 4: *The Battle Reliefs of King Sety I.* The Epigraphic Survey. Oriental Institute Publications 107. Chicago: Oriental Institute, 1986
Urk. 1	*Urkunden des Alten Reiches.* Kurt Sethe. Urkunden des ägyptischen Altertums 1. Leipzig: J. C. Hinrichs, 1933
Urk. 3	*Urkunden des älteren Aethiopenkönige.* Kurt Sethe. Urkunden des ägyptischen Altertums 3. Leipzig: J. C. Hinrichs, 1905
Urk. 4	*Urkunden der 18. Dynastie.* Kurt Sethe. Urkunden des ägyptischen Altertums 4. Leipzig: J. C. Hinrichs, 1906–09
Urk. 7	*Historische-biographische Urkunden des Mittleren Reiches.* Kurt Sethe. Urkunden des ägyptischen Altertums 7. Leipzig: J. C. Hinrichs, 1935
Wb.	*Wörterbuch der ägyptischen Sprache.* A. Erman and H. Grapow. Leipzig: J. C. Hinrichs, 1926–51
Wb. Belegstellen	*Wörterbuch der aegyptischen Sprache: Die Belegstellen.* 5 volumes. Edited by A. Erman and H. Grapow. Berlin: Akademie-Verlag, 1953–55

Other Abbreviations

O.	Ostracon
BD	Book of the Dead (quoted by spell)
Berlin	Prefix for registration number of object in the Berlin Museum, Berlin
BM	Prefix for registration number of object in the British Museum, London
Brooklyn	Prefix for registration number of object in the Brooklyn Museum of Art, Brooklyn

ca.	*circa*, about, approximately
Cairo	Prefix for registration number of object in the Egyptian Museum, Cairo
Carter no.	Prefix for registration number of object from tomb of Tutankhamun in the Egyptian Museum, Cairo
CFETK	Centre Franco-égyptien d'Études des Temples de Karnak
CG	Prefix for registration number of object in the Catalogue général des antiquités égyptiennes du Musée, Cairo
col(s).	column(s)
cont.	continued
DM	Deir el-Medina
DN	divine name
e.g.	*exempli gratia,* for example
ed(s).	edition, editor(s)
et al.	*et alii,* and others
f(f).	and the following page(s)
fig(s).	figure(s)
fn(s).	footnote(s)
frag(s).	fragment(s)
Guide	Prefix for Maspero's numbering system for Egyptian Museum, Cairo
i.e.	*id est*, that is
JE	Journal d'Entrée, Egyptian Museum, Cairo
KV	Kings' Valley
l(l).	line(s)
Louvre	Prefix for registration number of object in the Musée du Louvre, Paris
MMA	Prefix for registration number of object in the Metropolitan Museum of Art, New York
n(n).	note(s)
no(s).	number(s)
n.p.	no publisher
NYP	not yet published, forthcoming, in press
OIM	Prefix for registration number of object in the Oriental Institute Museum, University of Chicago, Chicago
p(p).	page(s)
P.	papyrus
pers. comm.	personal communication
pl(s).	plate(s)
PN	personal name

Pushkin	Prefix for registration number of object in the Pushkin Museum of Fine Arts, Moscow
RN	royal name
s.v.	*sub verbo, sub voce,* under the word
sc.	*scilicet,* that is to say
TT	Theban Tomb
Turin	Prefix for registration number of object in the Museo Egizio, Turin
University Museum	Prefix for registration number of object in the University of Pennsylvania Museum of Archaeology and Anthropology
viz.	*videlicet,* namely
« »	to be omitted

LIST OF FIGURES

FRONTISPIECE. EDWARD F. WENTE

1. A MONUMENT OF KHAEMWASET HONORING IMHOTEP. *James P. Allen*

4. INVENTORY OFFERING LISTS AND THE NOMENCLATURE FOR BOXES AND CHESTS IN THE OLD KINGDOM. *Edward Brovarski*

LIST OF TABLES

PREFACE

Edward F. Wente is a rare individual in the field of Egyptology. He is a man of interests that range from grammar to studies of chronology, iconography, and religion. In each of these fields he has made significant and lasting contributions, easily on par with colleagues who have a single, more restricted focus.

His publications have become classic references. *Late Ramesside Letters*, *The Literature of Ancient Egypt*, *An X-Ray Atlas of the Royal Mummies*, and *Letters from Ancient Egypt* are basic tools for teaching as well as for research. His study of mysticism in ancient Egypt, his chronology of the New Kingdom, and the discussion of succession and the genealogy of the royal family at the end of the Twentieth Dynasty, are still the basic works against which future remarks must be directed. These publications are a fitting legacy for a full and accomplished academic life, yet his greatest legacy may be the fact that the majority of Egyptologists in major American institutions received their training from Professor Wente. Their own vast body of publications, and in turn their own students, can be taken as yet another tribute not only to his intellect but also to his commitment to teaching. The fact that the contributions in this volume come from the United States, Europe, and the Middle East is an indication of the high regard in which Professor Wente is held by his colleagues.

Among Professor Wente's epigraphic challenges were the texts in the tomb of Kheruef at Thebes. In the inscriptions in that tomb that refer to the first jubilee of Amenhotep III, the king bestows rewards upon his loyal followers. Among those honors was "Gold of Praise." We hope that this Gold of Praise bestowed by his many colleagues and admirers throughout the world will serve to honor Professor Wente for his many contributions to the field of Egyptology on the occasion of his retirement in December 1995, and to wish him a productive, happy, and healthy future.

Emily Teeter
Editor

John A. Larson
Co-Editor

ACKNOWLEDGMENTS

The editors wish to acknowledge the great amount of assistance that we received from many of our colleagues here at the Oriental Institute: Professors Robert D. Biggs, Peter F. Dorman, Janet H. Johnson, and Robert K. Ritner; Steve Vinson, Research Associate for the Demotic Dictionary Project; Charles E. Jones, Bibliographer of the Oriental Institute Research Archives; Jean Grant, Photographer, Oriental Institute Museum; Thomas Dousa and François Gaudard, Research Assistants for the Demotic Dictionary Project; Simrit Dhesi, Blane Conklin, and Kathleen Mineck, graduate students in the Department of Near Eastern Languages and Civilizations; Joan Curry, Project Assistant; and, in the Publications Office, Thomas A. Holland and especially Thomas G. Urban, who worked indefatigably on the preparation of this complex manuscript. We also thank Professor Lorelei Corcoran of the University of Memphis for instigating the project so many years ago. To the authors, we extend our thanks for their continued patience during the gestation period of this volume, and we hope that they are happy with the result.

EDWARD F. WENTE

Edward Frank Wente was born in New York City on October 7, 1930. Later, the family moved to Summit, New Jersey, where Wente graduated from high school in 1948. Wente was accepted at the University of Chicago, where he completed the requirements for an A.B. degree in three years, and graduated with honors on June 20, 1951. In the autumn quarter of 1951, Wente began graduate studies in Egyptology in the Department of Oriental Languages and Civilizations, taking classes in the Oriental Institute. The Egyptology faculty in those days consisted of Professors John A. Wilson, William F. Edgerton, and Keith C. Seele; some of his colleagues included Klaus Baer, Frederick J. Giles, Nicholas B. Millet, and William A. Ward. It was during his days as a graduate student that Wente met Leila Ibrahim, who was to become his wife in 1970, and who was to have her own successful teaching career specializing in Graeco-Roman and Coptic art. Wente was awarded University Fellowships for the academic years 1953/54 and 1954/55. Prof. Edgerton thought so highly of Wente's demonstrated abilities and potential that he moved quickly to counter an offer from Richard A. Parker, who hoped that Wente would transfer to Brown University in Providence.

On June 7, 1954, Wente passed his preliminary examinations in the Department and later that year he was admitted to candidacy for the Ph.D. That summer, he was a Fellow of the American Numismatic Society in New York. While working on his dissertation, Wente was a Fulbright Exchange Student at Cairo University during the academic years of 1955/56 and 1956/57. The following year, he served as director of the Cairo office of the American Research Center in Egypt, at which time he contributed a series of reports about current activities of Egyptological interest to the A.R.C.E. newsletters.

Wente returned to the University of Chicago in the autumn of 1958 and completed his dissertation under the supervision of Edgerton, receiving his Ph.D. in 1959 on the basis of his thesis entitled "The Syntax of Verbs of Motion in Egyptian." Since that day, now more than forty years ago, the University of Chicago has been the focal point of Wente's professional career in Egyptology.

Wente's appointments at the University of Chicago include Research Associate of the Oriental Institute (1959–1963) and subsequently Assistant Professor (1963–1965), Associate Professor (1965–1970), and Professor of Egyptology (1970–1996) in the Department of Near Eastern Languages and Civilizations. Since his retirement from teaching in 1996, Wente has served as Professor Emeritus, which has given him more time for research and travel with Leila to Egypt.

Wente's purely academic duties were augmented by fieldwork. From 1959 to 1968, Wente served as an epigrapher with the Epigraphic Survey of the Oriental Institute headquartered at Chicago House in Luxor, Egypt. In 1961, Wente was seconded to the Oriental Institute Nubian Expedition as epigrapher to record the inscriptions and decoration in the temple of Ramesses II at Beit el-Wali. During the field season of 1972/73, Wente returned to Luxor as field director of the Epigraphic Survey. Upon his return to Chicago, Wente taught a full range of graduate courses in Egyptology, including most stages of the Egyptian language, surveys and seminars on history and chronology, and coveted seminars on religious texts and theological issues. Many of the professional Egyptologists working today, as well as many of the contributors to this volume, were Wente's students during that period, and their heartfelt individual comments are a testament to the impact of his teaching and personality.

In addition to his teaching responsibilities, Wente served as chairman of the Department of Near Eastern Languages and Civilizations at the University of Chicago from 1975 to 1979; he was acting chairman during the summer of 1971 and again during the summer of 1986.

Outside the Oriental Institute, Wente's contributions to Egyptology have included his work as technical advisor to the Seattle Art Museum for the Treasures of Tutankhamun exhibition in 1977, and his membership on a number of committees, among which are the Grants Committee of the American Research Center in Egypt, 1977–1979; the Archeology Advisory Council, Smithsonian Institution, 1979–1983; the Editorial Board, Writings from the Ancient World, Society of Biblical Literature, 1986–1992; and the Visiting Committee, Department of Egyptian Art, The Metropolitan Museum of Art, 1988–1999. Wente has been a member of the American Research Center in Egypt since 1957.

The range of Wente's interests and activities in the field of Egyptology is documented by his regular contributions to the Individual Research Projects section of Oriental Institute annual reports since 1972/73. Wente is well known for his expertise in the areas of epigraphy, Egyptian philology, and the history of the New Kingdom; his memory for bibliographic references is phenomenal.

His interest in railroading, which he shared with his friend Klaus Baer, is manifested in his collection of model trains. Ever since his student days Wente has been active in the Lutheran Church.

This happy occasion — the presentation of a volume of collected studies in honor of our teacher, mentor, colleague and friend — reminds us all that for five decades Edward F. Wente has absorbed, nurtured, developed, and transmitted the intellectual heritage of Egyptology at the University of Chicago. We hope that he will find these contributions both interesting and stimulating, and we look forward with eager anticipation to the steady growth of his own bibliography during the coming years.

PUBLICATIONS AND COMMUNICATIONS OF EDWARD F. WENTE

THROUGH OCTOBER 1999

Charles E. Jones

1956

"An Egyptologist in Egypt." *American Research Center in Egypt Newsletter* 22, pages 3–4.

1957

"Letters from Egypt." *American Research Center in Egypt Newsletter* 24, pages 1–11.

"[Letter from Egypt]." *American Research Center in Egypt Newsletter* 25, pages 1–3.

"Letters from Egypt." *American Research Center in Egypt Newsletter* 26, pages 2–7.

1958

"[Letters from Egypt]." *American Research Center in Egypt Newsletter* 27, pages 1–4.

"[Letters from Egypt]." *American Research Center in Egypt Newsletter* 28, pages 1–4.

"[Letter from Egypt]." *American Research Center in Egypt Newsletter* 30, pages 1–2.

1959

The Syntax of Verbs of Motion in Egyptian. A Dissertation Submitted to the Faculty of the Division of the Humanities in Candidacy for the Degree of Doctor of Philosophy, Department of Near Eastern Languages and Civilizations. Chicago: University of Chicago, August 1959. Supervised by William F. Edgerton.

1961

"*iwiw.f sḏm* in Late Egyptian." *Journal of Near Eastern Studies* 20, pages 120–23.

"A Letter of Complaint to the Vizier To." *Journal of Near Eastern Studies* 20, pages 252–57.

1962

Ostraca Michaelides. With Hans Goedicke. Wiesbaden: Otto Harrassowitz.

"Egyptian 'Make Merry' Songs Reconsidered." *Journal of Near Eastern Studies* 21, pages 118–28, plates 16–19.

"The Late Egyptian Conjunctive as a Past Continuative." *Journal of Near Eastern Studies* 21, pages 304–11.

1963

Medinet Habu, Volume 6*: The Temple Proper,* Part 2: *The Re Chapel, the Royal Mortuary Complex, and Adjacent Rooms with Miscellaneous Material from the Pylons, the Forecourts, and the First Hypostyle Hall, Plates 363–482*. Epigraphic Survey. Participating co-author. Oriental Institute Publications 84. Chicago: University of Chicago Press.

"Shekelesh or Shasu?" *Journal of Near Eastern Studies* 22, pages 167–72.

"Two Ramesside Stelas Pertaining to the Cult of Amenophis I." *Journal of Near Eastern Studies* 22, pages 30–36.

Review of *The Kadesh Inscriptions of Ramesses II*, by Sir Alan Gardiner. *Journal of Near Eastern Studies* 22, pages 204–07.

Review of *The Conflict of Horus and Seth from Egyptian and Classical Sources*, by J. Gwyn Griffiths. *Journal of Near Eastern Studies* 22, pages 273–76.

1964

Medinet Habu, Volume 7: *The Third Hypostyle Hall and All Rooms Accessible from It with Friezes of Scenes from the Roof Terraces and Exterior Walls of the Temple, Plates 483–590.* Epigraphic Survey. Participating co-author. Oriental Institute Publications 93. Chicago: University of Chicago Press.

1965

"A Note on 'The Eloquent Peasant,' B I, 13–15." *Journal of Near Eastern Studies* 24, pages 105–09.

Review of *Papyrus Reisner I: The Records of a Building Project in the Reign of Sesostris I*, by William Kelly Simpson. *Journal of Near Eastern Studies* 24, pages 127–29.

Review of *Ägyptische Grammatik*, by C. E. Sander-Hansen. *Bibliotheca Orientalis* 22, pages 148–50.

1966

"The Suppression of the High Priest." *Journal of Near Eastern Studies* 25, pages 73–87, figure 1 (on unnumbered page), plates 7–10.

1967

The Beit El-Wali Temple of Ramesses II. With Herbert Ricke and George R. Hughes. Oriental Institute Nubian Expedition 1. Chicago: University of Chicago Press.

Late Ramesside Letters. Studies in Ancient Oriental Civilization 33. Chicago: University of Chicago Press.

"On the Chronology of the Twenty-First Dynasty." *Journal of Near Eastern Studies* 26, pages 155–76.

"The Superimposed Cartouches in the Entrance Hall." In *The Beit El-Wali Temple of Ramesses II*, with Herbert Ricke and George R. Hughes, pages 34–38. Oriental Institute Nubian Expedition 1. Chicago: University of Chicago Press.

"Translations of the Texts." In *The Beit El-Wali Temple of Ramesses II*, with Herbert Ricke and George R. Hughes, pages 10–33. Oriental Institute Nubian Expedition 1. Chicago: University of Chicago Press.

Review of *Hieratic Inscriptions from the Tomb of Tutʿankhamūn*, by Jaroslav Černý. Tutʿankhamūn's Tomb Series II. *Journal of the American Research Center in Egypt* 6, page 169.

Review of *Papyrus Reisner II: Accounts of the Dockyard Workshop at This in the Reign of Sesostris I*, by William Kelly Simpson. *Journal of Near Eastern Studies* 26, pages 63–64.

Review of *Untersuchungen zu altägyptischen Bestattungsdarstellungen*, by Jürgen Settgast. Abhandlungen des Deutschen archäologischen Instituts Kairo, Ägyptologische Reihe 3. *Journal of the American Research Center in Egypt* 6, pages 173–74.

1968

Review of *Horemhab et la reine Moutnedjemet ou la fin d'une dynastie*, by Robert Hari. *Journal of the American Oriental Society* 88, pages 547–48.

Review of *Non-Verbal Sentence Patterns in Late Egyptian*, by Sara Israelit Groll. *Bibliotheca Orientalis* 25, pages 183–84.

1969

"Hathor at the Jubilee." In *Studies in Honor of John A. Wilson, September 12, 1969*, edited by Gerald E. Kadish, pages 83–91. Studies in Ancient Oriental Civilization 35. Chicago: University of Chicago Press.

"A Late Egyptian Emphatic Tense." *Journal of Near Eastern Studies* 28, pages 1–14.

Review of *History and Chronology of the Eighteenth Dynasty of Egypt: Seven Studies*, by Donald B. Redford. *Journal of Near Eastern Studies* 28, pages 273–80.

1970

Medinet Habu, Volume 8: *The Eastern High Gate with Translations of Texts, Plates 591–660*. Epigraphic Survey. Participating co-author. Oriental Institute Publications 94. Chicago: University of Chicago Press.

1971

Review of *Die Ritualszenen auf der Umfassungsmauer Ramses' II. in Karnak*, by Wolfgang Helck. Ägyptologische Abhandlungen 18. *Journal of Near Eastern Studies* 30, pages 315–18.

1972

The Literature of Ancient Egypt: An Anthology of Stories, Instructions, and Poetry. With R. O. Faulkner and William Kelly Simpson. New Haven: Yale University Press.

Review of *Papyrus Reisner III: The Records of a Building Project in the Early Twelfth Dynasty*, by William Kelly Simpson. *Journal of Near Eastern Studies* 31, pages 138–39.

Review of *Ikhnaton: Legend and History*, by Frederick J. Giles. *Journal of Near Eastern Studies* 31, pages 139–40.

Review of *Introduction to Ancient History*, by Hermann Bengtson, translated from the sixth edition by R. I. Frank and Frank D. Gulliard. *Journal of Near Eastern Studies* 31, pages 140–41.

1973

The Literature of Ancient Egypt: An Anthology of Stories, Instructions, and Poetry. New edition. With R. O. Faulkner and William Kelly Simpson. New Haven: Yale University Press.

"The Epigraphic Survey." In *The Oriental Institute of the University of Chicago: Report 1972/73*, edited by John A. Brinkman, pages 5–7. Chicago: Oriental Institute.

"Individual Research." In *The Oriental Institute of the University of Chicago: Report 1972/73*, edited by John A. Brinkman, page 38. Chicago: Oriental Institute.

"Late Ramesside Letters." In *Textes et languages de l'Égypte pharaonique: Cent cinquant années de recherches, 1822–1972: Hommages à Jean-François Champollion* 2, pages 103–06. Bibliothèque d'étude 64/2. Cairo: Institut français d'archéologie orientale.

"Letter from Egypt." *The Oriental Institute Archaeological Newsletter* 8, pages 1–2.

"A Prince's Tomb in the Valley of the Kings." *Journal of Near Eastern Studies* 32, pages 223–34.

"Report on the Work of the Epigraphic Survey, The Oriental Institute, Luxor, Egypt for the Season 1972–1973." *American Research Center in Egypt Newsletter* 86, pages 30–32.

Review of *Egypt: The Amarna Period and the End of the Eighteenth Dynasty*, by Cyril Aldred. Cambridge Ancient History, Volume 2, Chapter 19. Revised edition. *Journal of Near Eastern Studies* 32, pages 247–48.

Review of *Die Lehre des Dwꜣ-H̱tjj*, by Wolfgang Helck. Kleine ägyptische Texte. *Journal of the American Oriental Society* 93, page 397.

1974

"The Application of Cluster Analysis to the Identification of the 'Elder Woman' in the Tomb of Amenhotep II." With James E. Harris and Charles Kowalski. *American Research Center in Egypt Newsletter* 91, page 29.

"Egypt, History of, II: From the Beginning of the 18th Dynasty to c. 330 BC." In *The New Encyclopaedia Britannica. Macropaedia*, Volume 6, pages 471–81. 15th edition. Chicago: Encyclopaedia Britannica.

"Individual Research Projects." In *The Oriental Institute of the University of Chicago: Report 1973/74*, edited by John A. Brinkman, pages 65–66. Chicago: Oriental Institute.

"A Misplaced Letter to the Dead." *Oriental Institute News & Notes* 10, page 3.

"Revising Chronology." In *The Oriental Institute of the University of Chicago: Report 1973/74*, edited by John A. Brinkman, pages 52–54. Chicago: Oriental Institute.

1975

"Individual Research." In *The Oriental Institute of the University of Chicago: Report for 1974/75*, edited by John A. Brinkman, pages 51–52. Chicago: Oriental Institute.

"Thutmose III's Accession and the Beginning of the New Kingdom." *Journal of Near Eastern Studies* 34, pages 265–72.

"Was Paiankh Herihor's Son?" *Drevnii Vostok* 1, pages 36–38.

1976

Studies in Honor of George R. Hughes, January 12, 1977. Edited with Janet H. Johnson. Studies in Ancient Oriental Civilization 39. Chicago: University of Chicago Press.

"Individual Research." In *The Oriental Institute Annual Report 1975/76*, edited by John A. Brinkman, pages 53–54. Chicago: Oriental Institute.

"A Misplaced Letter to the Dead." *Orientalia Lovaniensia Periodica* 6/7, pages 595–600.

Review of *The Third Intermediate Period in Egypt (1100–650 B.C.)*, by Kenneth A. Kitchen. *Journal of Near Eastern Studies* 35, pages 275–78.

Review of *Hathor and Toth: Two Key Figures of the Ancient Egyptian Religion*, by C. J. Bleeker. Studies in the History of Religions, Supplements to Numen, 26. *Journal of the American Oriental Society* 96, pages 431–32.

"Tutankhamun and His World." In *Treasures of Tutankhamun*, edited by Katherine Stoddart Gilbert, Joan K. Holt, Sara Hudson, pages 19–31. New York: Metropolitan Museum of Art.

"A Chronology of the New Kingdom." With Charles C. Van Siclen III. In *Studies in Honor of George R. Hughes, January 12, 1977*, edited with Janet H. Johnson, pages 217–61. Studies in Ancient Oriental Civilization 39. Chicago: University of Chicago Press.

1977

"The Chronology of the New Kingdom." Ann Arbor: University of Michigan Television Publication.

"Individual Research." In *The Oriental Institute Annual Report 1976–77*, edited by John A. Brinkman, pages 55–56. Chicago: Oriental Institute.

"[Obituary notice of John A. Wilson]." *The Journal of Egyptian Archaeology* 63, page 4.

Review of *An Outline of the Egyptian Verbal System*, by Paul John Frandsen. *Journal of Near Eastern Studies* 36, pages 310–12.

1978

"Individual Research." In *The Oriental Institute Annual Report 1977/78*, edited by John A. Brinkman, page 56. Chicago: Oriental Institute.

"Mummy of the 'Elder Lady' in the Tomb of Amenhotep II: Egyptian Museum Catalogue No. 61070." With James E. Harris, Charles F. Cox, Ibrahim el-Nawaway, Charles J. Kowalski, Arthur T. Storey, William R. Russell, Paul V. Ponitz, Geoffrey F. Walker. *Science* 200, pages 1149–51.

1979

The Temple of Khonsu, Volume 1: *Scenes of King Herihor in the Court with Translations of Texts, Plates 1–110.* Epigraphic Survey. Participating co-author. Oriental Institute Publications 100. Chicago: Oriental Institute.

"The Identification of the Mummy of the 'Elder Lady' in the Tomb of Amenhotep II as Queen Tiye." With James E. Harris and others. *Delaware Medical Review* 2, pages 39–93.

"Individual Research." In *The Oriental Institute Annual Report 1978/79*, edited by John A. Brinkman, page 95. Chicago: Oriental Institute.

"Preface." In *The Temple of Khonsu,* Volume 1: *Scenes of King Herihor in the Court with Translations of Texts, Plates 1–110*, by the Epigraphic Survey, pages ix–xvii. Oriental Institute Publications 100. Chicago: Oriental Institute.

"Response to Robert A. Oden's 'The Contendings of Horus and Seth' (Chester Beatty Papyrus No. 1): A Structural Interpretation." *History of Religions* 18, pages 370–72.

"Translations of the Texts." In *The Temple of Khonsu,* Volume 1: *Scenes of King Herihor in the Court with Translations of Texts, Plates 1–110,* by the Epigraphic Survey, pages 1–55. Oriental Institute Publications 100. Chicago: Oriental Institute.

Review of *L'Épouse du dieu Ahmes Néfertary: Documents sur la vie et con culte posthume*, by Michel Gitton. *Journal of Near Eastern Studies* 38, pages 70–72.

1980

An X-Ray Atlas of the Royal Mummies. Edited with James E. Harris. Chicago: University of Chicago Press.

The Tomb of Kheruef: Theban Tomb 192. Participating co-author. Oriental Institute Publications 102. Chicago: Oriental Institute.

"Age at Death of Pharaohs of the New Kingdom, Determined from Historical Sources." In *An X-Ray Atlas of the Royal Mummies*, edited with James E. Harris, pages 234–85. Chicago: University of Chicago Press.

"Genealogy of the Royal Family." In *An X-Ray Atlas of the Royal Mummies*, edited with James E. Harris, pages 122–62. Chicago: University of Chicago Press.

"Individual Research." In *The Oriental Institute 1979–1980 Annual Report*, edited by John A. Brinkman, page 54. Chicago: Oriental Institute.

"Translations of the Texts." In *The Tomb of Kheruef: Theban Tomb 192*, by the Epigraphic Survey, pages 30–77. Oriental Institute Publications 102. Chicago: Oriental Institute.

1981

The Temple of Khonsu, Volume 2*: Scenes and Inscriptions in the Court and the First Hypostyle Hall with Translations of Texts and Glossary for Volumes 1 and 2, Plates 111–207.* Epigraphic Survey. Participating co-author. Oriental Institute Publications 103. Chicago: Oriental Institute.

"Individual Research." In *The Oriental Institute 1980–1981 Annual Report*, edited by John A. Brinkman, page 53. Chicago: Oriental Institute.

"Some Remarks on the *ḥr.f* Formation in Late Egyptian." In *Studies Presented to Hans Jakob Polotsky*, edited by Dwight W. Young, pages 528–45. East Gloucester, Massachusetts: Pirtle and Poulson.

1982

"Funerary Beliefs of the Ancient Egyptians: An Interpretation of the Burials and the Texts." *Expedition: The University Museum Magazine of Archaeology and Anthropology* 24, pages 17–26.

"The Gurob Letter to Amenhotep IV." *Serapis: The American Journal of Egyptology* 6, pages 209–15.

"Mysticism in Pharaonic Egypt?" *Journal of Near Eastern Studies* 41, pages 161–79.

"Research on Ancient Egyptian Religion and History." In *The Oriental Institute 1981–1982 Annual Report*, edited by Robert McC. Adams, pages 85–86. Chicago: Oriental Institute.

1983

"Individual Research Activities." In *The Oriental Institute 1982–1983 Annual Report*, edited by Robert McC. Adams, page 54. Chicago: Oriental Institute.

Review of *Der Gott Tatenen nach Texten und Bildern des Neuen Reiches*, by Hermann Alexander Schlogl. *Journal of Near Eastern Studies* 42, pages 155–56.

Review of *Das Ende der Amarnazeit: Beiträge zur Geschichte und Chronologie des Neuen Reiches*, by Rolf Krauss. *Journal of Near Eastern Studies* 42, pages 315–18.

Review of *Das Buch von den Pforten des Jenseits nach den Versionen des Neuen Rieches, Part 1: Text*, edited by Erik Hornung with the collaboration of Andreas Brodbeck and Elizabeth Staehelin. *Journal of Near Eastern Studies* 42, pages 318–19.

1984

"Gods in Ancient Egypt." Review of *Conceptions of God in Ancient Egypt: The One and the Many*, by Erik Hornung. *History of Religions* 24, pages 178–81.

"Individual Research Activities." In *The Oriental Institute 1983–1984 Annual Report*, edited by Janet H. Johnson, pages 52–53. Chicago: Oriental Institute.

"Some Graffiti from the Reign of Hatshepsut." *Journal of Near Eastern Studies* 43, pages 47–54.

1985

"The Royal Mummies: Biology and Egyptology in the Cairo Museum [Abstract]." With James E. Harris. In Program and Abstracts of the Annual Meeting of the American Research Center in Egypt, 1985.

"Individual Research Activities." In *The Oriental Institute 1984–1985 Annual Report*, edited by Janet H. Johnson, pages 71–72. Chicago: Oriental Institute.

"A New Look at the Viceroy Setau's Autobiographical Inscriptions." In *Mélanges Gamal Eddin Mokhtar,* Volume 2, edited by Paule Posener-Kriéger, pages 347–59. Cairo: Institut français d'archéologie orientale.

Review of *The Ancient Egyptians: Religious Beliefs and Practices*, by Rosalie David. *History of Religions* 25, pages 109–11.

1986

"Individual Research." In *The Oriental Institute 1985–1986 Annual Report*, edited by Janet H. Johnson, pages 55–56. Chicago: Oriental Institute.

Review of *The Pharaonic Inscriptions from Faras*, by Janusz Karkowski. *Journal of Egyptian Archaeology* 72, pages 213–14.

1987

"The Nineteenth Dynasty: A Family Profile from the Biologic Viewpoint [Abstract]." With James E. Harris. In Program and Abstracts of the Annual Meeting of the American Research Center in Egypt, Memphis, 24–26 April 1987, page 31.

"Klaus Baer, June 22, 1930–May 17, 1987 [in Memoriam]." *The Oriental Institute News & Notes* 110, pages 2–3.

"Individual Research." In *The Oriental Institute 1986–1987 Annual Report*, edited by Janet H. Johnson, page 80. Chicago: Oriental Institute.

1990

Letters from Ancient Egypt. Edited by Edmund S. Meltzer. Society of Biblical Literature, Writings from the Ancient World 1. Atlanta: Scholars Press.

"Individual Research." In *The Oriental Institute 1988–1989 Annual Report*, edited by William M. Sumner, page 61. Chicago: Oriental Institute.

1991

"Individual Research." In *The Oriental Institute 1989–1990 Annual Report*, edited by William M. Sumner, page 82. Chicago: Oriental Institute.

1992

"Egyptian Religion." In *The Anchor Bible Dictionary*, Volume 2: *D–G*, pages 408–12. New York: Doubleday.

"Individual Scholarship." In *The Oriental Institute 1990–1991 Annual Report*, edited by William M. Sumner, page 73. Chicago: Oriental Institute.

"Rameses (Place)." In *The Anchor Bible Dictionary*, Volume 5: *O–Sh*, pages 617–18. New York: Doubleday.

"Ramesses II." In *The Anchor Bible Dictionary*, Volume 5: *O–Sh*, pages 618–20. New York: Doubleday.

"Royal Mummies of the Eighteenth Dynasty: A Biologic and Egyptological Approach." With James E. Harris. In *After Tutʿankhamūn: Research and Excavation in the Royal Necropolis of Thebes*, edited by C. N. Reeves, pages 2–20. London: Kegan Paul.

"A Taxing Problem." *Bulletin of the Egyptological Seminar* 10, pages 169–74.

1993

"Individual Scholarship." In *The Oriental Institute 1991–1992 Annual Report*, edited by William M. Sumner, page 118. Chicago: Oriental Institute.

"Individual Scholarship." In *The Oriental Institute 1992–1993 Annual Report*, edited by William M. Sumner, pages 101–02. Chicago: Oriental Institute.

1994

"Individual Research." In *The Oriental Institute 1993–1994 Annual Report*, edited by William M. Sumner, page 94. Chicago: Oriental Institute.

1995

"Individual Research." In *The Oriental Institute 1994–1995 Annual Report*, edited by William M. Sumner, page 86. Chicago: Oriental Institute.

"The Scribes of Ancient Egypt." In *Civilizations of the Ancient Near East*, Volume 4, edited by Jack M. Sasson, pages 2211–21. New York: Charles Scribner's.

"Who Was Who Among the Royal Mummies." *The Oriental Institute News & Notes* 144, pages 1–6. Also published on the World-Wide Website of the Oriental Institute: http: //www-oi.uchicago.edu/OI/IS/WENTE/NN_Win95/NN_Win95.html.

1996

Review of *Egyptian Historical Inscriptions of the Twentieth Dynasty*, by A. J. Peden. *Journal of the American Oriental Society* 116, pages 764–65.

"A Goat for an Ailing Woman (Ostracon Wente)." In *Studies in Honor of William Kelly Simpson*, edited by Peter Der Manuelian, pages 855–67. Boston: Museum of Fine Arts.

"Individual Research." In *The Oriental Institute 1995–1996 Annual Report*, edited by William M. Sumner, pages 113–14. Chicago: Oriental Institute.

1998

Review of *Chronologie des ägyptischen Neuen Reiches*, by Jürgen von Beckerath. *Journal of Near Eastern Studies* 57, pages 309–11.

"Individual Research." In *The Oriental Institute 1997–1998 Annual Report*, edited by Gene Gragg, pages 121–22. Chicago: Oriental Institute.

1

A MONUMENT OF KHAEMWASET HONORING IMHOTEP

JAMES P. ALLEN

The Metropolitan Museum of Art, New York

The object published here was brought to my attention in 1993, at which point it was in private hands. The owner of the object generously allowed me to examine it at length for more than a year and to publish it. Since then, it has entered the collection of the Egyptian Culture Center of Waseda University, Tokyo; I am grateful to the Center's director, Dr. Jiro Kondo, for allowing it to be published here. No information regarding its original provenience, other than that provided by its texts, is available; it is said to have stood for many years in a garden somewhere in the northeastern United States.

The object (fig. 1.1) is a rectangular basin of granite, 14.5 cm high, 54.0 cm wide, and 36.0 cm deep. Projecting an additional 4.5 cm from its front face is a rectangular spout 5.5 cm high and 10.5 cm wide. The bottom surface of this projection curves concavely toward the basin's bottom edge. Its upper surface is level with the basin's rim and is marked in the center by a shallow trough with a curved bottom, 3.0 cm wide and 0.5 cm deep, from front to back. A rectangular "pool" with slightly sloping sides has been excavated to an originally uniform depth of 9.0 cm in the stone, leaving a rim 4.0 cm wide on all four sides of the upper surface. At some point in the basin's history, a circular depression some 10.0 cm in diameter was roughed out in the floor of the pool, slightly off center, and a small hole 1.3 cm wide was bored entirely through the stone at the depression's lowest point, evidently to prevent water from sitting in the pool.

The basin and its spout were originally polished smooth on their outer and upper surfaces. If the sides and floor of the pool were once smoothed to the same degree, that finish has completely disappeared, leaving a very rough surface overall. The exterior sides and rim of the basin itself bear incised scenes and texts (figs. 1.2–8);

Figure 1.1. Basin of Khaemwaset, Overview. Photograph by Bill Barrette

Gold of Praise: Studies on Ancient Egypt in Honor of Edward F. Wente
Edited by Emily Teeter and John A. Larson
Studies in Ancient Oriental Civilization 58
Chicago: Oriental Institute, 1999

the bottom was finished only to a roughly level surface. The stone has suffered considerable wear, particularly at its outer corners and on nearly the entire surface of the rim. The material is a generally dark gray granite, with white inclusions.

Although the pool now looks as if it were unfinished, the presence of texts around its rim indicates that it is probably an original feature (except for the later hole). Judging from the content of its other texts and scenes, the basin was clearly designed to serve as a receptacle for libations of water, which could overflow through the trough at its front. A search through the literature has revealed no exact parallels for this particular combination of features in a single object, but the basin clearly belongs to a genre of rectangular libation receptacles that extends from the Old Kingdom at least into the Ramesside period.[1]

The basin's significance, however, lies not in its physical features but in the texts that decorate its rim and sides. These are reproduced in facsimile in figures 1.2–8, some in "normalized" hieroglyphs, with transliteration and translation below.[2] The decorative scheme is symmetrical on the front and sides. The front face holds two nearly identical scenes and texts facing each other on either side of the central spout (A–B), and a second set adorns the two sides (C–D). Mirroring these, the rim seems to have had facing inscriptions running from the central spout along the front and sides (F). The back of the basin contains two separate texts: one, in three lines, on the back face (E), and another above it on the rim (G).

A. RIGHT FRONT (VIEWER'S LEFT)

Figure standing at left wears leopard skin and "sidelock of youth" (fig. 1.2). Left hand, at side, holds vase; right arm is upraised, gesturing toward four columns of hieroglyphs:

1. *ḏd-mdw i nṯrw rsw nṯrw imnti m(i)*
2. *m iwn m(i) m iʿb*
3. *ḥtp.ṯn ḥr ḫt nbt nfrt ir n.ṯn*
4. *ꜣI-m-ḥtp wr sꜣ-Ptḥ*
5. *iwn-mwt.f sm sꜣ-(n)sw Ḫʿ-m-wꜣst*

Recitation: "O gods of the south and gods of the west, come in unison, come assembled, and be content with every good thing that Imhotep the Great, son of Ptah, has made for you."

Pillar-of-his-mother and *sm*-priest, Prince Khaemwaset.

B. LEFT FRONT (VIEWER'S RIGHT)

Figure standing at right is similar to that in the scene opposite (A) but less well preserved; right arm gestures toward four columns of hieroglyphs (fig. 1.3):

1. *ḏd-mdw i nṯrw rsw nṯrw imnti m(i)*
2. *m iwn m(i) m*
3. *iʿb mꜣ.ṯn [ḫt nbt ir n.ṯn]* [a]
4. *ꜣI-m-ḥtp wr [sꜣ-Ptḥ]*
5. *iwn-mwt.f sm sꜣ-(n)sw Ḫʿ-[m-wꜣst]*

Recitation: "O gods of the south and gods of the west, come in unison, come assembled, and see [everything that] Imhotep the Great, [son of Ptah, has made for you]."

Pillar-of-his-mother and *sm*-priest, Prince Kha[emwaset].

Note

[a] There is not enough room for the full text of the parallel on the right side (*ḫt nbt nfrt ir n.ṯn*); the group containing the adjective may have been omitted.

1. See, for example, Habachi 1977, pp. 17–21 (Old Kingdom), pp. 54–55 (Eighteenth Dynasty), pp. 42–43 (Ramesside).
2. The facsimile drawings were produced using a modification of the "Chicago House" method. Several photographs of each surface were taken under various lighting conditions and then scanned into high-resolution computerized images at a scale of 1:1. These served as the background for line drawings using a vector-based drawing program (CorelDRAW). A full-scale printout of each drawing, without its background photograph, was compared with the original and corrections were made on the drawing stored on computer. The "normalized" hieroglyphic transcriptions were produced using CorelDRAW and a font developed by the Egyptian Department of the Metropolitan Museum of Art.

a

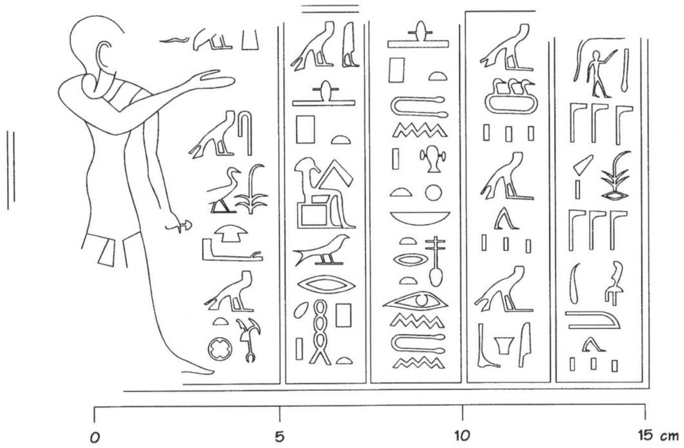

b

Figure 1.2. (*a*) Photograph and (*b*) Facsimile Drawing of Scenes and Inscriptions of Right Front Face of Basin of Khaemwaset. Photograph by Bill Barrette

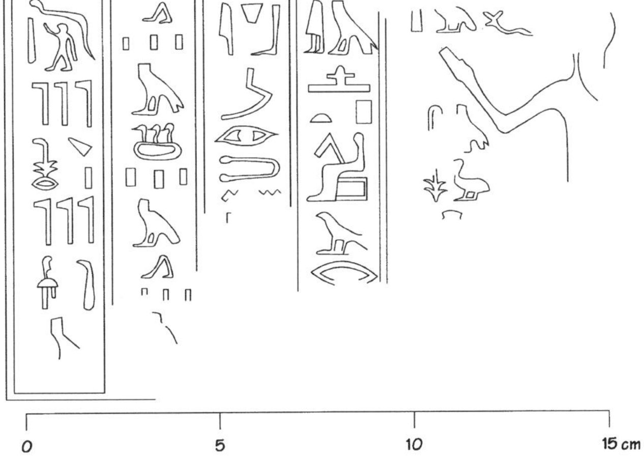

a

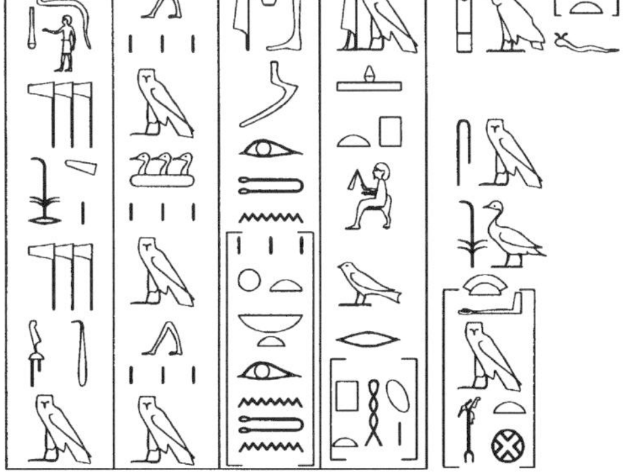

b

Figure 1.3. (*a*) Facsimile Drawing of Scenes and Inscriptions of Left Front Face of Basin of Khaemwaset and (*b*) Normalized Hieroglyphic Transcription

C. RIGHT SIDE

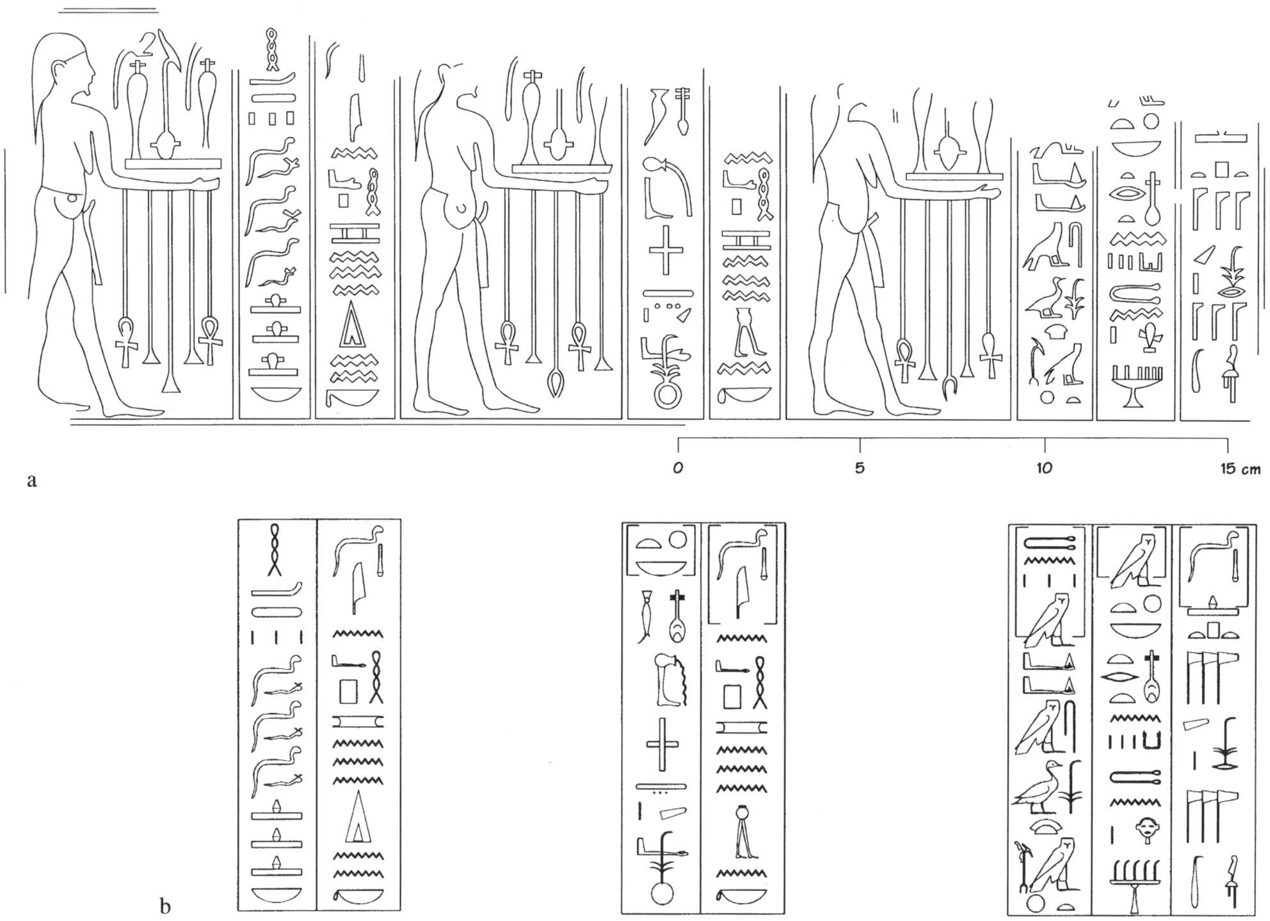

Figure 1.4. (*a*) Facsimile Drawing of Scenes and Inscription on Right Side of Basin of Khaemwaset and (*b*) Normalized Hieroglyphic Transcription

Three "Nile gods" bear trays and proceed from left (back) to right (front) (fig. 1.4); before each are columns of inscription, as follows:

a. Before the first (right/front) figure:

1. [*ḏd-mdw*] *ḥtp.t nṯrw rsw nṯrw ỉmntỉ*
2. *m ḫt nbt nfrt n kꜣw.ṯn ḥr ḫꜣyt.*
3. [*ṯn*][a] *m dd sm sꜣ-(n)sw Ḫ*ʿ*-m-wꜣst*

Recitation: Be content,[b] gods of the south and gods of the west, with every good thing for your *ka*s on [your] offering-table from the giving of the *sm*-priest, Prince Khaemwaset.

Notes

[a] Restoration is suggested by the available space and the context. The demonstrative *tn* ("this offering-table") is also possible, but the lacuna requires about half a group more than would have been occupied by *tn* alone.

[b] Translation is suggested by the context. Despite the singular form (for *ḥtp.twnỉ*), the lack of a determinative points to a form of the verb (here, second person singular stative) rather than the noun *ḥtpt* "offering." There is perhaps space enough in the lacuna for a low sign such as 𓈖 or 𓂋 before *ḥtpt*, or even for a tall sign if most of it were "tucked under" the *ḏd-mdw*, but I have no suggestions to offer.

b. Before the second figure:

1. [*ḏd-mdw ỉ*]*n Ḥ*ʿ*p ỉn.(n.ỉ) n.k*
2. [*ḫt nb*] *nfr bnr w*ʿ*b ỉmỉ Tꜣ šm*ʿ*w*

Recitation by the Inundation: I have gotten for you every good, sweet, and pure thing that is in the Nile Valley.

c. Before the third figure:

1. *ḏd-mdw ỉn Ḥʿp dỉ.n.(ỉ) n.k*
2. *ḥw ḏf(ꜣ)w ḥtpw nb*

   Recitation by the Inundation: I have given you all nourishment, sustenance, and offerings.

D. LEFT SIDE

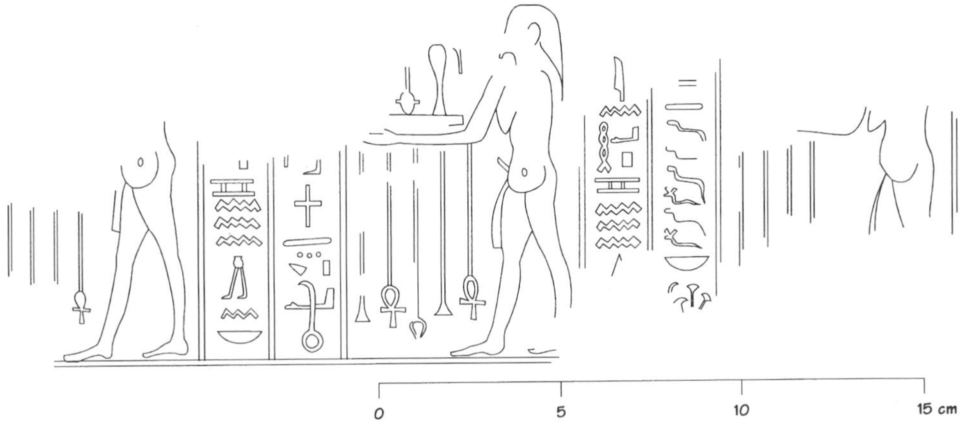

Figure 1.5. Facsimile Drawing of Scenes and Inscription on Left Side of Basin of Khaemwaset

Scene is equivalent to that on opposite side, but less well preserved (fig. 1.5; see fig. 1.4b for reconstruction).

a. Nothing remains of the initial three-column inscription.

b. Before the second figure:

1. [*ḏd-mdw ỉn Ḥʿ*]*p ỉn.*(*n.ỉ*) *n.k*
2. [*ḫt nb nfr bnr*] *wʿb ỉmỉ Tꜣ šmʿw*

   Recitation by the Inundation: I have gotten for you every good, sweet, and pure thing that is in the Nile Valley.

c. Before the third figure:

1. [*ḏd-mdw*] *ỉn Ḥʿp dỉ.*[*n.*(*ỉ*) *n.k*]
2. [*ḥw*][a] *ḏf*(*ꜣ*)*w nb rswỉ mḥwỉ* [b]

   Recitation by the Inundation: I have given you all nourishment and sustenance of the south and the north.

Notes

[a] The incision for is still visible, though abraded. The surface above is preserved to the same height and shows no similarly deep incisions: the three signs of *ḥtpw* are therefore unlikely. Despite the absence of plural strokes (as in the second column of the third inscription on the right side), *ḥw* is probably the best restoration and fits the available space.

[b] The tops of both signs are preserved. Compare Naville 1901, pl. 110, lower right.

E. BACK

Three lines of hieroglyphs across the entire expanse of the side face right and read from right to left (fig. 1.6).

The text is Episode 16 of the "Ritual of Amenhotep I," known elsewhere in three copies: P. C58030, from the reign of Ramesses II, where it is entitled *r n qbḥw 2nwt n nswt Ḏsr-kꜣ-Rʿ* "Spell of the second libation of King Djeser-ka-Ra";[3] a scene from the mortuary temple of Ramesses III at Medinet Habu;[4] and a scene from

3. Golénischeff 1927, pp. 138–39, pl. 14.

4. *MH* 4, pl. 241E.

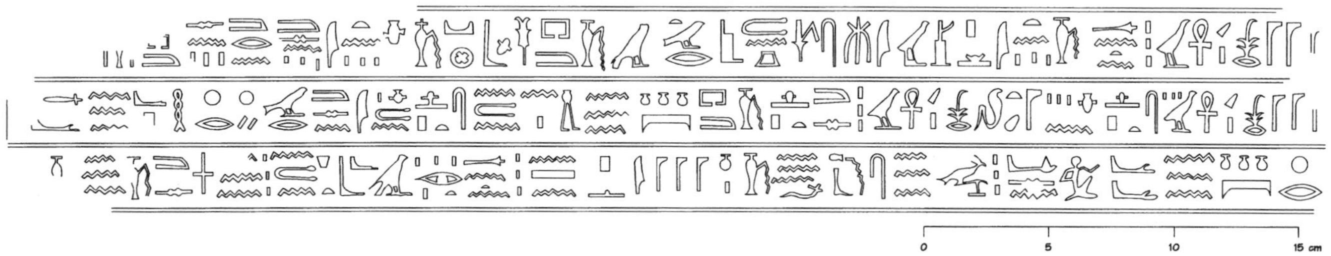

Figure 1.6. Facsimile Drawing of Scenes and Inscription on Back of Basin of Khaemwaset

the Ptolemaic temple of Edfu.[5] The copy on the basin is virtually identical to that from Edfu (E), while those from the Cairo papyrus (C) and Medinet Habu (MH) preserve a slightly different version.[6] On the basis of these parallels, the text can be transliterated and translated as follows:

1. *nṯrw rsw ꜥnḫw m-n.tn qbḥ.tn ỉp wṯsw ỉms.ṯn ḥr st wrt m qbḥ pr m ꜣbḏw qbḥ ỉb.tn ỉm.sn m rn.sn* [*n*] *pr m qbḥ s*[*qbḥ ỉbw n*]
2. *nṯrw rsw ꜥnḫw sḥtp ỉbw n nṯr*(*w*)*t rsw ꜥnḫw m sḥtp qbḥ pr m nw ỉn.ỉ n.ṯn sḥtp ỉb.ṯn ỉm.sn wr sp 2 ḥr Ḥꜥp ꜥꜣ* [*sp 2*]
3. *ḥr Nw ꜥwỉ.ỉ dỉ.sn bꜥḥ swꜥb.f qbḥ nw nṯrw ỉp n.sn m-n.tn ỉrt Ḥrw ꜥbt n.ṯn mw ỉmỉ.s qbḥ qbḥ* [*mr*]

Living gods of the south,[a] accept these[b] your cool waters, which your scepter elevates from beneath the Great Place,[c] being the cool waters that come from Abydos.[d] Let your heart(s) become cool through them, in their identity of what comes from the cool waters,[e] which cool the hearts of[f] the living gods of the south and content the hearts of the living goddesses of the south,[g] being the contentment of the libation that comes from the Inundation.[h] I have gotten for you those (waters) through which your heart(s) might be contented, very much from the Inundation and very greatly from Nu.[i] My arms are giving, and the flood is purifying, the libation of those gods for them.[j] Accept the Eye of Horus, the water in which has been collected for you.[k] Libation of the desired (amount of) cool water.[l]

Notes

[a] E has *nṯrw ỉmw ḏdw* "Gods who are in Busiris."

[b] *ỉp* here and in line 3 for *ỉpn*, as in C and MH; E has *ỉpw*.

[c] Probably with reference to the sanctuary (*st wrt*) within which the spell was recited; see Brovarski 1976, pp. 72–73; Spencer 1984, pp. 108–14.

[d] So also E, though clearly *ꜣbw* "Elephantine" is meant, as in C and MH.

[e] Perhaps designating the region of the First Cataract at Aswan (*Wb.* 5.29:5), but E has the spelling [hieroglyphs], indicating the homonymous designation of the celestial waters (*Wb.* 5.30); see Allen 1989, p. 8.

[f] Restored after E and MH (missing in C).

[g] E has *nṯrw ḥr*(*ỉ*) *ỉb Ḏdw* "the gods who are in the midst of Busiris" and *nṯrwt ỉm Ḏdw* "the goddesses who are in Busiris."

[h] So also E. C omits *s*[*qbḥ ỉbw n*] *nṯrw ꜥnḫw* and continues *sḥtp.tw pr m Nw*, apparently "Be contented, you who came from Nu." MH has *sqbb ỉb n ꜣImn-rꜥ nb nswt tꜣwỉ* [*ḥ*]*tpyt pr m Nw* "which cools the heart of Amun-Ra, Lord of the Thrones of the Two Lands, the offering that comes from Nu."

[i] C and MH omit the final clause (*ꜥꜣ sp 2 ḥr ḥꜥp*). *ḥr* here evidently designates the origin of the waters — compare *Wb.* 3.315:9; especially *prỉ ḥr* "come from": Pyr. 22a (of *qbḥw*), 905a; *Urk.* 4, p. 1198.6 — rather than their destination, though *ỉnỉ ḥr* normally denotes "bringing to" a person or place (*Wb.* 3.315:17).

[j] As Gardiner noted, the phraseology of this sentence derives from offering-formulae of the Middle Kingdom: Gardiner 1935, p. 81 n. 8; compare Barta 1968, pp. 65, 237, 312 (Bitte 82). After *wr ḥr Ḥꜥpỉ*, C has *ḥr ꜥwy rꜥ dỉ.f bꜥḥ ḥr swꜥb.f Ḏḥwtỉ ḥr wdn n.f qbḥ n nswt Ḏsr-kꜣ-rꜥ n.f*, evidently for "Ra is giving, the flood purifying, and Thoth offering the libation of King Djeser-ka-Ra to him"; compare Blackman 1915, p. 16, pls. 6–7. Similarly, MH has *wr.k ḥr Ḥꜥpỉ ꜥwỉ.f swꜥb n ꜣImn-rꜥ nb nswt tꜣwỉ*.

---

5. Rochemonteix 1892, pp. 212–13.

6. See Gardiner 1935, p. 81; Nelson 1949, pp. 214–16.

[k] This sentence is based on PT 108 (Pyr. 72a); compare also PT 144 (Pyr. 88a).

[l] E has *qbḥ qbḥ mry ḏỉ(t) snṯr ỉn nw-ꜣbd* "Libation of the desired (amount of) cool water. Giving incense by the monthly priest."

F. LEFT RIM

Figure 1.7. (*a*) Facsimile Drawing of Scenes and Inscription on Left Rim of Basin of Khaemwaset and (*b*) Normalized Hieroglyphic Transcription

A single line of hieroglyphs faces right and reads from right to left, beginning at the central trough (fig. 1.7). This is apparently the beginning of an invocation to the deceased Imhotep. A similar text probably occupied the right rim but is now completely lost. The inscription probably continued down the left rim; only its beginning is preserved, however, reading as follows:

1. *Skr-Wsỉr ʾI-m-ḥtp wr [sꜣ-P]t[ḥ ...]*

   Sokar-Osiris Imhotep the Great, son of Ptah ...

G. BACK RIM

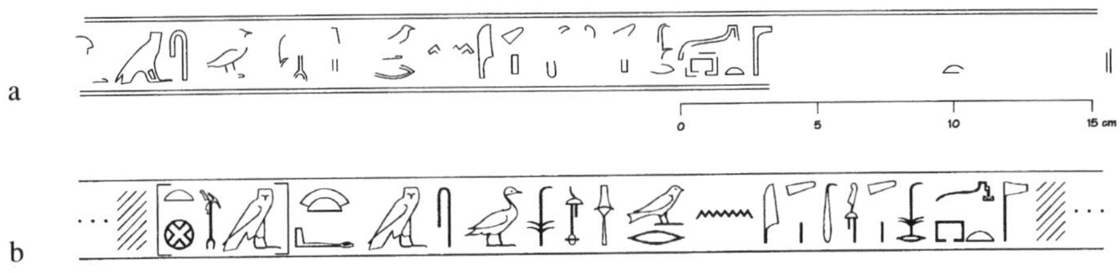

Figure 1.8. (*a*) Facsimile Drawing of Scenes and Inscription on Back Rim of Basin of Khaemwaset and (*b*) Normalized Hieroglyphic Transcription

A single line of hieroglyphs faces right and reads from right to left, beginning at the basin's right side (fig. 1.8). The relationship between this text and the others on the rim is uncertain, but it was probably independent and did not constitute an ending to one or both of them.

1. *... stpt* [a]*-nṯr rsw ỉmntỉ ỉn wr ḫrp ḥmwt sꜣ-(n)sw sm Ḫꜥ-[m-wꜣst]* [b]

   ... the southwestern Divine Temenos,[c] by the high priest of Memphis, prince and *sm*-priest, Khaemwaset.

Notes

[a] Probably some five or six groups lost at the beginning.

[b] Perhaps nothing more is after the name. About two and a half groups have been lost between the first group of the name (*Ḫꜥ*) and the inner margin of the left rim. The text of the latter, now lost, could have extended down to the outer margin of the back rim. If so, the text on the back rim would have extended only between the inner margins of both side rims. This would leave only the two and a half groups mentioned above for the end of the back rim text — hardly enough for more than the end of the name, with perhaps a final determinative.

[c] I am grateful to Geoffrey Martin for suggesting the reading of the *stp*-sign to me.

DISCUSSION

This offering basin is a unique addition to the extensive catalog of monuments dedicated by Khaemwaset, fourth son of Ramesses II, during his lifetime.[7] Like others, it bears representations of the prince with the

7. See Gomaà 1973, pp. 75–98. Despite numerous textual features that do not appear again until the Saite period or later (see below), the basin's orthography appears to be Ramesside, and there is no firm evidence for the creation of

sidelock and panther skin of the *ỉwn-mwt.f*-priest (A–B),[8] and attestations of his more common functional titles: *ỉwn-mwt.f* "Pillar-of-his-mother" (A 6, B 5); *sm s3-(n)sw* "*sm*-priest and prince" (A 6, B 5, C a 3, G); and *wr ḫrp ḥmwt* (G), the title denoting the high priest of Ptah of Memphis.[9]

The special interest of this monument, and its uniqueness, lies in its association with Imhotep, architect of the Third Dynasty pyramid complex of King Djoser at Saqqara, who was revered as a sage from the Middle Kingdom onward and was eventually elevated to divine status in the Saite period.[10] Imhotep's name appears on the basin as *ʾI-m-ḥtp wr s3-Ptḥ* "Imhotep the Great, son of Ptah" (A 4, B 4, F), a form hitherto attested with certainty first in the Late Period,[11] although Wildung has made a persuasive case — now confirmed by the present monument — for the mention of Imhotep as "son of Ptah" already in the reign of Ramesses II. In the inscription on the left rim (F), the name is preceded by *Skr-Wsỉr* "Sokar-Osiris." Since there is no evidence for the deification of Imhotep prior to the Saite period, this is probably a Memphite variation on the usual epithet *Wsỉr* "Osiris" denoting a deceased individual.[12]

As a libation receptacle commemorating Imhotep, the basin could be a concrete representation of the practice of offering *mw nw ps n sš nb n k3.k ʾI-m-ḥtp* "water of the libation-cup of every scribe for your ka, Imhotep."[13] Besides honoring Imhotep, the basin may also have been dedicated to him, as suggested by the apparent invocation on the left rim (F) and the second person masculine singular address in the speeches of the "Nile gods" on the sides (C b–c, D b–c). Its libation-text proper, however, invokes not Imhotep but the "living gods of the south" (E 1–2), and the first inscription on its sides (of which only the right is preserved) speaks of offerings given by Khaemwaset to the "gods of the south and gods of the west" (C a). This combination of features indicates that the basin was probably dedicated in honor of Imhotep but was meant to receive libations to the gods on his behalf rather than directly to his *ka* itself.

The deities invoked on the basin are identified in the texts on its front and sides as *nṯrw rsw nṯrw ỉmntỉ* "gods of the south and gods of the west"[14] (A 1, B 1, C a 1). Similar designations appear elsewhere in lists of gods associated with the cardinal points — for example, Pyr. 321a, 464a, 1522b; BD 141; KRI 2, 365.12; KRI 6, 384.6 — but the specific reference to "gods of the south and gods of the west" alone is apparently without parallel elsewhere. In the text on the back, the deities are called *nṯrw rsw ʿnḫw* "living gods of the south" (E 1–2) and *nṯr(w)t rsw ʿnḫw* "living goddesses of the south" (E 2). The phrase *nṯr ʿnḫ* "living god" can be applied to cosmic deities,[15] but it is also used with reference to the dead.[16] Since the latter are also *ỉmntỉw* "westerners" (*Wb.* 1.86:21), the two phrases *nṯrw/nṯr(w)t rsw ʿnḫw* "living gods/goddesses of the south" and *nṯrw rsw nṯrw ỉmntỉ* "gods of the south and gods of the west" may in fact refer to the same group of revered dead.

In the texts on the front (A–B), these deified ancestors are asked to "come in unison, come assembled, and be content with (var. "see") every good thing that Imhotep the Great, son of Ptah, has made for you." This can hardly be anything other than a reference to Imhotep's legendary accomplishment as architect of the pyramid complex of Djoser — hitherto attested by less specific evidence[17] — and it identifies the original provenience of

monuments in Khaemwaset's name after the Nineteenth Dynasty; see Gomaà 1973, pp. 72–74.

8. See *LÄ* 3 "Iunmutef," col. 212; Gomaà 1973, pp. 115, 133, pl. 2b.
9. See Gomaà 1973, pp. 20–26. For the sequence *s3-(n)sw sm* in G, see Gomaà 1973, pp. 108, 112, 118, 121, 127, 128, 136.
10. Wildung, *LÄ* 3 "Imhotep," cols. 145–48.
11. For the Ramesside evidence (Turin Canon), see Wildung 1977, pp. 30–32; Wildung 1980, col. 146. Apart from this papyrus and the basin texts, the form *ʾI-m-ḥtp wr s3 Ptḥ* first appears in the Twenty-seventh Dynasty, and perhaps as early as the Twenty-sixth Dynasty (Wildung 1977, pp. 33–34, 37–38). Apart from the basin, the first occurrence of *ʾI-m-ḥtp wr s3 Ptḥ* is less well dated to sometime between the Saite and Ptolemaic periods (Wildung 1977, pp. 47, 86–87, §55).
12. The designation of the deceased as Sokar-Osiris evidently first appears — outside this instance — in the Late Period (Bonnet 1953, p. 725; *LÄ* 5 "Sokar," col. 1058). The identification of the deceased with Sokar, however, is attested in both the Pyramid Texts and Coffin Texts (Pyr. 445b, 620c, 1824b, 1826b; *CT* 1, p. 178h; *CT* 3, p. 336a; *CT* 6, p. 272b). For the deification of Imhotep, see Wildung 1977, p. 300; Wildung, *LÄ* 3 "Imhotep," col. 146.
13. Text is from a Twenty-sixth or Twenty-seventh Dynasty statue (Louvre N. 4541; Wildung 1977, p. 37, pl. 3). Compare Wildung 1977, pp. 19–20, 33; also *qʿḥ n.k wʿbw ʿ.sn m mw ḥr s3tw mỉ ỉrrt n ʾI-m-ḥtp m pḥwy n psỉ* "May the *wab*-priests bend their arm(s) for you with water on the floor like that which is done for Imhotep from the bottom of the libation-cup" (text from TT C.1, cited by Wildung 1977, p. 19).
14. Probably so, rather than "southern gods and western gods," since *rsw* and *ỉmnty* are nowhere written with plural strokes. The consistent form *ỉmnty* may reflect the vocalized form of *ỉmntt* > Coptic (SA) ⲁⲙⲛ̄ⲧⲉ: Osing 1976, p. 312.
15. For example, Pyr. *1920c (N 720, Nt 740), with reference to Ra or Osiris. The Sphinx is also called *nṯr ʿnḫ* (Zivie 1976, p. 211, pl. 18); compare also *nb ʿnḫ* "lord of life" (*Wb.* 1.199:11–12).
16. Alliot 1937, pp. 128–43. Compare *CT* 5, p. 27e; also Leb. 142: *wnn ms nty ỉm m nṯr ʿnḫ* "Surely, he who is there will be a living god."
17. See Wildung 1977, p. 11.

the basin almost certainly as Saqqara. There is no direct indication that the basin was set up in the pyramid enclosure itself; but if not, the building with which it was associated should have been at least within sight of Djoser's complex. The structure for which it was dedicated may be the *stpt-nṯr rsw ỉmntỉ* "southwestern Divine Temenos" mentioned in the text on the back rim (G). The term *stpt* evidently denotes a temple enclosure of some sort: its most specific use is with reference to the open-air bay within which the statue of the Great Sphinx was carved (Zivie 1976, p. 286). If this parallel is any indication, the *stpt-nṯr* on the basin could refer to any of the enclosures within the Djoser complex, if not to the entire complex itself. The designation *rsw ỉmntỉ* "southwestern," however, would seem to point to the large open court south of the pyramid and west of the smaller enclosures of the *sed*-festival court and the "maison du sud" and "maison du nord." Significantly, it is in this court that Lauer found fragments of a restoration inscription of Khaemwaset that once stood on the casing blocks of the pyramid's south side.[18] It is not inconceivable that the basin was originally dedicated in conjunction with this inscription.

Whether or not the basin was in fact set up in the pyramid's south court, its orientation to the Djoser complex seems evident. In that light, the "gods of the south and gods of the west" invoked on it may well be the kings and queens whose pyramids were visible to the south of Djoser's: the deified dead (*nṯrw ỉmntỉ*, *nṯrw*/*nṯr*(*w*)*t* ... *ʿnḫw*) of South Saqqara (*nṯrw*/*nṯr*(*w*)*t rsw*).[19]

*****

Like its subject, this article is dedicated to a scholar whose accomplishments have served as an inspiration to all who study the texts and history of ancient Egypt, particularly those of the Ramesside period. I am privileged to have had the opportunity of studying under him, and like the ancient scribes *ỉw.ỉ ḥr qʿḥ n.f ʿwỉ.ỉ ỉm.*

*****

References

Allen, J. P.
1989 "The Cosmology of the Pyramid Texts." In *Religion and Philosophy in Ancient Egypt,* edited by J. P. Allen, J. Assmann, A. B. Lloyd, R. K. Ritner, and D. P. Silverman, pp. 1–28. Yale Egyptological Studies 3. New Haven: Yale University.

Alliot, M.
1937 "Un nouvel exemple de vizir divinisé dans l'Égypte ancienne." *Bulletin de l'Institut français d'archéologie orientale* 37: 93–161.

Barta, W.
1968 *Aufbau und Bedeutung der altägyptischen Opferformel.* Ägyptische Forschungen 24. Glückstadt: J. J. Augustin.

Blackman, A. M.
1915 *The Rock Tombs of Meir*, Part 2: *The Tomb-Chapel of Senbi's Son Ukh-Ḥotp (B, No. 2).* Archaeological Survey of Egypt 23. London: Egypt Exploration Fund.

Bonnet, H.
1953 *Reallexikon der ägyptischen Religionsgeschichte.* Berlin: Walter de Gruyter.

Brovarski, E. J.
1976 "Senenu, High Priest of Amun at Deir el-Baḥri." *Journal of Egyptian Archaeology* 62: 57–73.

Gardiner, A. H.
1935 *Hieratic Papyri in the British Museum,* Third Series: *Chester Beatty Gift* 1. London: British Museum.
1950 "The Baptism of Pharaoh." *Journal of Egyptian Archaeology* 36: 3–12.

Golénischeff, W.
1927 *Papyrus hiératiques.* Catalogue général des antiquités égyptiennes du Musée du Caire, nos. 58001–58036. Cairo: Musée du Caire.

Gomaà, F.
1973 *Chaemwese, Sohn Ramses' II. und Hoherpriester von Memphis.* Ägyptologische Abhandlungen 27. Wiesbaden: Otto Harrassowitz.

Habachi, L.
1977 *Tavole d'offerta, are e bacili da libagione, n. 22001–22067.* Catologo del Museo Egizio di Torino, serie seconda — collezioni, 2. Turin: Edizioni d'arte Fratelli Pozzo.

18. Lauer 1939a, p. 52; Lauer 1939b, p. 449; Gomaà 1973, p. 77 no. 8, p. 103 fig. 3a.
19. It is possible that the two cardinal directions stand for all four; compare Gardiner 1950, pp. 9–12 (I am grateful to Deborah Sweeney for this reference). But the consistent use of only *rsw* and *ỉmntỉ* throughout the texts on the basin suggests that only these two directions are meant.

Lauer, J. P.

1939a *La pyramide à degrés*, volume 3: *Compléments*. Cairo: Institut français d'archéologie orientale.

1939b "Fouilles du Service des antiquités à Saqqarah (secteur de la pyramide à degrés)." *Annales du Service des antiquités de l'Égypte*: 447–67.

Naville, E.

1901 *The Temple of Deir el Bahari*, Part 4. Egypt Exploration Fund Memoir 19. London: Egypt Exploration Fund.

Nelson, H. H.

1949 "Certain Reliefs at Karnak and Medinet Habu and the Ritual of Amenophis I." *Journal of Near Eastern Studies* 8: 201–29, 310–45.

Osing, J.

1976 *Die Nominalbildung des Ägyptischen*. Mainz: Philipp von Zabern.

Rochemonteix, M. de

1892 *Le temple d'Edfou*, volume 1. Mémoires publiés par les Membres de la mission archéologique française au Caire 10. Paris: Libraire de la Société asiatique.

Spencer, P.

1984 *The Egyptian Temple: A Lexicographical Study*. London: Kegan Paul.

Wildung, D.

1977 *Imhotep und Amenhotep — Gottwerdung im alten Ägypten*. Münchner ägyptologische Studien 36. Munich: Deutscher Kunstverlag.

Zivie, C.

1976 *Giza au deuxième millénaire*. Bibliothèque d'étude 70. Cairo: Institut français d'archéologie orientale.

2

FEUDS OR VENGEANCE? RHETORIC AND SOCIAL FORMS

JOHN BAINES

The University of Oxford, United Kingdom

In one of his important articles, "Mysticism in Pharaonic Egypt?" (1982), Edward F. Wente reinterprets crucial passages in well-known texts to show that they mobilized significant domains of experience and forms of social division in antiquity that Egyptologists had generally neglected or ignored. In homage to this and his many other achievements, I offer a discussion of a possible ancient social form that arises from thinking about a single sentence in a well-known inscription.[1]

Numerous social institutions familiar to ethnography and to literature from societies in the Mediterranean and elsewhere have not been identified for ancient Egypt. This sparsity of information about widely paralleled forms applies particularly to matters of general social organization, such as kinship,[2] and to violence and social control. "Criminal" law is known essentially from state-centered sources and relates mainly to matters in which the state had an evident interest. Among these are theft of state property, conspiracy against the king, and tomb robbery extending to royal burials (cf. Bedell 1973). Material from Deir el-Medina gives a rather more nuanced picture (McDowell 1990) but hardly extends to serious problems of social relations and social control. We do not know what happened in ancient Egypt after a homicide in a domestic or inter-familial context (cf. Eyre 1984, p. 93).

An example such as the Mesopotamian Laws of Hammurabi, which deal — realistically or otherwise — in severe penalties for often minor-seeming delicts but do not cover homicide, may suggest that matters of this sort were not fully within the purview of the Mesopotamian state, surprising though that might seem in modern terms.[3] Much later, Neo-Assyrian evidence supports such a reading since it appears to show the state participating in the process of homicide settlements, but in a supervisory role between the parties to legal processes that are conducted according to the same patterns as civil actions (Roth 1987). The state's interest is in a peaceful outcome, not in punishment or reparation through its own intervention. This possible parallel, together with the absence of evidence from Egypt — so far as absence can be a basis for argument — may then support a relatively modest reading of the role of central authority, in which many functions familiar in modern societies would not be centralized (cf. Cohen 1995, pp. 14–15, on pre–Meiji Japan).

David O'Connor (e.g., 1995, p. 320) proposes more broadly that the aspirations of Egyptian government to control the lives of citizens may have been relatively limited. James Hoch and Sarah Orel's study (1992) tends to point in the same direction; despite the authors' collection of much material, almost all of it from literary texts, they do not identify any case of reported homicide, as against intended or rumored killing or alleged acts (often plausible) in the distant past, that is not fictional or judicial. Homicide is not a topic of public or of extant private sources.[4] Such a distribution of material does not imply that homicide was a rarity; it is just completely

1. Despite the limited scope of this article, the matters discussed range widely, and I am very grateful to Jon Anderson, Alan Bowman, Michael Gilsenan, Norman Yoffee, Andrea McDowell, and Peter Machinist for pointing me to literature. The last two also kindly offered most valuable comments on a draft.

2. Kinship terminology has been successfully studied, especially for the Middle Kingdom (Robins 1979; Franke 1983; Willems 1983), but we do not have a real sense of the structure of kinship in Egyptian society.

3. The range of topics covered is not in itself strongly indicative because the work is not a real law code (see, e.g., Yoffee 1988). The restricted evidence I cite from later Mesopotamia agrees with the tenor of the Laws of Hammurabi.

4. Hoch and Orel do not include the Tale of Hay (Griffith 1898, pl. IV), which mentions a killing and concludes with a burial, or the longer Nagʿ-ed-Deir Letter to the Dead, which appears to have homicide as its theme (Fecht 1969). P. Mayer B, line 8 (Peet 1920; cited by Valbelle 1985, p. 305 with n.

Gold of Praise: Studies on Ancient Egypt in Honor of Edward F. Wente
Edited by Emily Teeter and John A. Larson
Studies in Ancient Oriental Civilization 58
Chicago: Oriental Institute, 1999

uninformative. The state employed homicide on its enemies (e.g., Ritner 1993, pp. 162–63), while Hoch and Orel's collection demonstrates at least considerable interest in the phenomenon. We have no access at all to evidence for rates of homicide, and little evidence of any kind for early periods. Non-textual evidence, of a different character from that collected by Hoch and Orel, can be found on skeletons, such as the bodies of soldiers killed in the reign of Nebhepetre Mentuhotep (Winlock 1945) or that of Seqenenre' Ta'o (Whitehouse 1980, p. 289). These probably all resulted from warfare and similar episodes rather than "everyday" homicide. An instance of a woman killed at the end of a life that had included several violent episodes was discovered at Abydos by Brenda Baker (1997). This may be suggestive of violence in a domestic context, but skeletal material cannot by itself provide evidence of a particular homicide within a social group.

Scholars have frequently painted a picture of ancient Egypt as a society with a low level of violence (e.g., Janssen 1975, col. 296). This view accords with the overall tenor of the available record. But cruelty is widely depicted in art so long as its victims are not Egyptians, and some is also celebrated in texts, strikingly so under Amenhotep II (e.g., the casual cruelty of his "letter" to the viceroy of Nubia Usersatet; see Helck 1955). Egyptians themselves are integrated into the basic subjection of people under royal authority, while enemies of the state are mentioned in violent terms in the execration texts and in curse formulas and oaths (Morschauser 1991). How much this type of violence in the service of the state occurred or how much it was a matter of gesture is almost impossible to say.

The best-known smaller group, the community of Deir el-Medina, also shows little evidence for violence.[5] The misdemeanors alleged of the chief workman Paneb are generally sexual (cf. Eyre 1984), although the papyrus detailing them mentions homicide (verso 2.4; Černý 1929, p. 246); nothing is said of consequential revenge, perhaps because Paneb was held to be in too powerful a position to be a target for it. A major source for the Saite and early Persian periods, the Petition of Peteese in P. Rylands 9 (Griffith 1909, pp. 60–102), paints a rather different picture in which hostilities between two groups of priests over a very long period involve physical and other violence. In the time of the papyrus, they stop short of homicide (2.12–3.3, pp. 68–69), but a case of it is reported from more than a century earlier (11.3–9, pp. 86–87). It is difficult to assess how much of what is described really happened. Moreover, the text itself may be either a document, as it superficially purports to be, or a work of literature comparable in dissimulation with Wenamun (cf. Wessetzky 1977; this issue is not discussed explicitly by Vittmann 1998, pp. 678–93). Since the provenience of the manuscript from el-Hibeh shows that the extant copy cannot have fulfilled the work's ostensible function as a petition to the central Persian administration, it may be more cautious to read it as a literary composition. As John Ray (1977, pp. 113–16) remarks, however, it is not the only text of its period from provincial Egypt that cites recourse to violence as endemic in society.

Material is also sparse among the far richer evidence from the Graeco-Roman period (Bagnall 1989). A basic pattern seems to have been that high local officials were addressed as mediators in disputes through receiving petitions — whether or not they responded to them — and on occasion forwarding them to central authorities. In a fictional context, such a pattern is attested as far back as the Tale of the Eloquent Peasant (Parkinson 1997, pp. 54–88), a text which surely implies that response to petitions was not necessarily to be expected. As Deborah Hobson (1993) emphasizes in her excellent discussion of related issues for the Roman period, disputes that enter the record are probably those in which complainants had exhausted other, less bureaucratic avenues of redress. In the petitions, moreover, people sometimes sought the identities of perpetrators of wrongs so that they could then pursue them with self-help, rather than expecting the authorities to punish them. Nonetheless, Hobson's material presents the crucial issue of whether recourse is taken to a higher authority that is backed up by coercive power and can impose a solution; that degree of authority seems to have been only partly realized in the Graeco-Roman period. If such a power comes to play a regular part in dispute settlement, more or less formal self-help responses to violence, such as feud, will lose their centrality, even if they retain ideological significance and motivating force between groups.

---

5), mentions the killing of two tomb robbers in seemingly clear fashion. This could have been in a dispute among the robbers, but it might also have been judicial execution or some other intervention by the authorities.

5. McDowell 1990, pp. 225–27; Valbelle 1985, pp. 308–09. O. Deir el-Medina 126, cited by Valbelle (Green 1976), contains one of very few clear references to a death, but the overall purport of the text is rather uncertain and may not relate to homicide. McDowell also cites evidence from Deir el-Medina for other forms of physical violence, but this too is exiguous and may not all be trustworthy.

In this article I suggest that indirect evidence is preserved in Egypt for some kind of institution of feud and hence for concomitant mechanisms of social control relating to homicide. But the single source known to me, which dates to the First Intermediate Period, presents itself in moralizing terms as transcending the institution and so is formulated in relation to centripetal values inherited from the Old Kingdom state, while it also implies that a well-ordered world would include neither homicide nor feuds. It may give a glimpse of possibilities among provincial groups in periods of weakened central control. But social institutions cannot survive in a vacuum; if they surface in "intermediate" periods, one should allow for their having had some existence also in centralized times, even if they were repudiated by the authorities and suppressed or pushed to the margins of society. I return to some of these issues after presenting the text.

TEXT 2 IN THE TOMB OF ANKHTIFY

The allusion to feuding that I propose is in the biographical inscription Jacques Vandier published as Text 2 in the tomb of Ankhtify at Moꜥalla, probably of the Ninth Dynasty (cf. Spanel 1984). The passage deals with Ankhtify's conquest of Edfu, which he portrays as a kind of rescue mission to restore order in a province or polity neglected by its ruling house — a presentation we should not necessarily take at face value. The text reads as follows, with the translation of the sentence (line 4) I wish to comment upon printed in italics:[6]

1. *⸢i̓w⸣-i̓ni̓.n-wi̓ Ḥrw r-wṯzt-Ḥrw* *n-ꜥnḫ wḏꜣ snb* *r-grg-s ⸢i̓ri̓.⸣n.i̓*	1. Horus brought me to the Horus Nome for the sake of life, prosperity, and health, in order to re-establish[a] it, and ⸢I did⸣ (so) (?).[b]
2. *wn-Ḥrw ḥr-mrt-grg.i̓-si̓* *ḥr-i̓ni̓.f-wi̓-r.s r-grg.s*	2. Horus wished that I re-establish it, and so he brought me to it in order to re-establish it.
3. *gmi̓.n.i̓ pr-Ḫww* *⸢ṯtfw⸣ mi̓-grgt* *mkḥꜣ.n-i̓ri̓.f m-st-ꜥi̓* *ẖnnw ẖr-sḫr n-ḥwrw*	3. I found the House of Khuu[c] ⸢flooded⸣ like a marsh (? *grgt*),[d] neglected by the one whose responsibility it was,[e] rendered chaotic (*ẖnnw*) under the charge of a wretch.
4. *i̓w-ḏi̓.n.i̓ qni̓-zi̓* *ḥnꜥ-smꜣ-i̓ti̓.f smꜣ-sn.f* *n-mri̓t-grg.i̓ wṯzt-Ḥrw*	4. *I caused a man to embrace* *the one who had killed his father and the one who had killed his "brother,"*[f] *in order that I might re-establish the Horus Nome.*
5. *nfr.wi̓ hrww* *ni̓-gmi̓.i̓ wḏꜣ m-spꜣt-tn*	5. How perfect was the day when I found prosperity in that nome!
6. *nn-šzpw-sḫm šmmt-⸢ꜣd⸣-i̓m.f* *m-sꜣ-sḥfꜣ.i̓ qd-nb-ḏw* *msḏḏw-rmṯw i̓rt.f*	6. No power will be accepted in which the heat of ⸢anger (*ꜣd*)⸣ is present[g] after my(?) driving out[h] of every evil character whose deeds people hate.[7]

Notes

[a] *grg* "to found" must refer in context to a refounding. Its use here may be hyperbole. I render consistently "re-establish." See also line 4, below.

[b] *i̓ri̓.n.i̓*(?). This reading is problematic; another possible rendering would be "and so that it re-establish my reputation" (*r grg.s ⸢rn⸣.i̓*) or "and so that my reputation re-establish it" (*r grg si̓ ⸢rn⸣.i̓*). The former gives a much less satisfactory sense; while the latter is possible, evidence is insufficient to establish a solution either way.

---

6. Vandier 1950, p. 163, pl. XV first column; Fecht 1968, pp. 50–51, with corrigenda sheet. Except in the last verse, my rendering follows Fecht's metrical analysis according to the rules he reconstructs for "Old Kingdom" meter (later meter gives a substantially different arrangement). I also keep close to Fecht's philological interpretation and therefore give few notes. Hans Goedicke (1995) gives a different interpretation of this passage and the reader may wish to compare our renderings; Goedicke does not discuss implications of the passage for social institutions.

7. The following passage of self-praise (Vandier 1950, Text 3, p. 171) could form a conclusion to this section, but it does not add to the understanding of the crucial sentence.

[c] *pr Ḫww* appears to be synonymous with "Horus Nome" in stanza 1. *pr* refers at once to a ruling house, that is, a family, and to the notion that the nome is the "estate" of its ruler.

[d] Following Fecht's reading. Much of the phrase's point must be *grgt,* whose meaning here is not clear; for the term, see Moreno García 1996.

[e] The sentence I present as a quatrain subdivides easily into two couplets but is nevertheless distinctively longer than those in the rest of the passage.

[f] *sn* here more probably signifies "lateral kin" than "brother" in a narrow sense. The nearest lateral relative of a man who has been killed may be obligated to seek vengeance for his death.

[g] My rendering of this rather problematic verse follows Fecht.

[h] I read *sḫfꜣ.i* because it seems most likely that there should be a first-person reference in this stanza as in all the others. This involves analyzing as a couplet a clause that Fecht took as a single verse. Either reading is possible.

It is tempting to see this final stanza as referring to exile, which is a widespread recourse for a person who commits homicide. The rendering of *sḫfꜣ* is, however, too uncertain for such an inference to be reliable (cf. Vandier 1950, p. 170, n. n; Fecht 1969, p. 53), even though it would fit other known patterns very well. Unlike stanza 4, this one does not focus explicitly on homicide.

The rhetoric of the passage is complex and the rendering of some elements is uncertain, but the general thrust is clear. Ankhtify asserts that his god commissioned him to conquer the Edfu Nome — I suggest in an oracle (Baines 1987, p. 89 with n. 59; Baines and Parkinson 1997) — and that he came in a spirit of peace and reconciliation to set it in order and to restore prosperity. As Gerhard Fecht (1968, pp. 55–56) notes, Ankhtify does not present himself exclusively as a man of violence but legitimizes his activities extensively in moral terms, very occasionally relating his position to higher authority.

The section at issue here comes after two introductory stanzas and consists of a quatrain, a triplet, a couplet, and a triplet, numbered 3–6 above (alternative reading of the last stanza as a couplet: n. h). These balance to form a negative-positive palindrome. The neglect Edfu suffered in 3 corresponds with the prosperity of 5, while the resolving of disputes in 4 matches the threat to disturbers of harmony in 6. Stanzas 4 and 6 also offer two possible resolutions of strife, the more positive form of reconciliation in 4 and the more adversarial one of driving out(?) in 6 (for possible significance, see n. h). The latter is presented more as something done in the past than as an achieved new state. Cross-culturally, "anger" as cited in stanza 6 is a typical prelude to homicide (e.g., Davis 1987, pp. 36–76) and hence must be avoided if killing is not to recur. A further refinement in presentation is the contrast between the abstract "prosperity (*wḏꜣ*)" of achieved harmony and the relatively concrete detail of stanzas 4 and especially 6. It is characteristically Egyptian to accord a higher value to abstract benefits than to concrete ones, as in the distinction between the "life and power" given by gods to the king, in comparison with his more concrete offerings to them (see Baines 1985, pp. 107–08, 209–10, 220–24, 346–52, with references).

The pattern of activity in the stanzas is violence — harmony — harmony — violence (implied), counterbalancing the alternation of themes. A third patterning feature is the slightly decreasing length of the stanzas, which produces a sense of progression that contrasts with the two thematic alternations and contributes to the overall forward thrust. It is typical of the general tenor of Ankhtify's inscriptions, several of which finish "I am a hero without equal" that the passage should conclude on a more aggressive assertion.

This tight organization throws great emphasis on the subject matter, which must be carefully considered. The woes of the Edfu Nome are attributed primarily to disorder, while order is characterized as bringing prosperity. Disorder is caused by the local ruler's neglect and is manifested by internal strife. Containment of the latter was a task shirked by "the one whose responsibility it was" — that is, the previous ruling house. Strife is summarized in terms of homicide; as we have seen, this is a rare overt theme in Egyptian texts. As a summary one might compare this with the widespread modern usage of the adjective "internecine" to characterize severely dysfunctional groupings. Although the passage's language is unusual, its sentiments have a proverbial air like so much in biographical texts, including the core statements that "I gave bread to the hungry" and so forth (see, in general, Perdu 1995). In view of this generality, the implications of this mention may go beyond Edfu or Moʿalla to suggest something broader about Egyptian society of its period and conceivably yet further afield.[8]

8. Compare the hierarchical conventions, according to which only the king may claim to have killed in battle, that can be read out of a comparison of the Second Intermediate Period stela of Emhab with Eighteenth Dynasty texts (Baines

Here, it is worth referring to narrative rhetorics of manhood widely reported for the Mediterranean and Middle East, within which individual biographies and the enacting, evocation, and mobilization of violence take their meaning.[9] Such a narrative quality pervades the inscriptions of Ankhtify and should be borne in mind as part of the overall context of specific assertions in them. While this tone is particularly characteristic of Ankhtify, the implications for biographies may be wider.

In context, the import of the sentence in Ankhtify appears to be his assertion that before he arrived, neglect by the Edfu rulers allowed a state of endemic conflict to develop in which people killed one another and the victim's kin responded with more violence. Since sons came to be protagonists for their victim fathers, the violence extended past a single generation; the same also applies to the "brothers," who would not necessarily belong to the same generation (see n. f, above). Ankhtify then persuaded the fighting parties to be reconciled. In so doing, he seems to present himself as performing a recognized role of a mediator who also had coercive force behind him. That is, he was a benevolent outsider who overcame what had been anarchy — or from another perspective a system of control appropriate to a different style of society (cf. the title of Black-Michaud 1975, *Cohesive Force*) — and replaced it with his own rule.

DISCUSSION

Should the institution that I suggest Ankhtify evoked be assigned to the category of feud, and is his statement that he caused the contending parties to "embrace" realistic?

Briefly, feud — a term that is much disputed — is a social situation in which violence, and especially homicide, is endemic between "structural" groupings in a society.[10] These groupings are normally of an intermediate level, such as secondary or tertiary sections in a tribe, and are articulated through the idiom of kinship. In feuds, a homicide or homicide equivalent requires that appropriate kin of the victim take vengeance in the form of a matching homicide against the perpetrator or his kin (men are almost always the protagonists of action and reaction). Feuds can be settled by payment of compensation ("blood wealth," "blood money," or "composition"), but this is generally seen as a last resort because it does not maintain the related notion of honor; feuds, thus, may last for decades or longer still. Indeed, the ultimate principle is held to be that feud is perpetual because it is intrinsic to the societal form. The societies for which feuds are reported are typically acephalous and lineage-based and may be nomadic, mixed transhumant, or small-scale agricultural. They are not organized in any meaningful sense as states. No single social form is categorized as feud in the literature, and there is argument about whether particular instances qualify for the term (for further examples, see, e.g., Boehm 1983; Peters 1990).

On this basis, ancient Egypt, as a state society with central coercive institutions — even its debris in the First Intermediate Period — may seem at first sight to be a quite inappropriate setting for the institution of feud, the more so since its (poorly known) kinship system does not appear to have been lineage-based. But in any simple form such a deduction would be hasty, for at least two reasons.

First, modern Mediterranean and Middle Eastern societies from which feud is typically reported are on the social and ecological margins of their areas. It seems at least as likely that feud might have been more widespread in the region but was generally suppressed or superseded in areas where the modern apparatus of government was imposed more thoroughly, as that there is a necessary connection between feud and harsh living conditions. While Jacob Black-Michaud (1975, pp. 160–76) in particular argues that there is an intrinsic link between "total scarcity" and the presence of feud, such that social groupings are defined by rigid adherence to rules of opposition and the upholding of honor, without which the actors believe that there would be complete anarchy, this approach seems too deterministic, even though it is formulated in "moral" as well as material terms. Moreover, comparable institutions, such as the duel, can survive in complex societies in which feuds

1986). A further implication of that comparison is that in centralized periods competitive activities could not be recorded for the elite, perhaps because they would create the possibility that royalty be found inadequate.

9. For example, Davis 1987; Gilsenan 1996; Herzfeld 1985; Meeker 1979; the same applies to the classical Greek orations discussed by Cohen (1995).

10. This outline broadly follows Black-Michaud (1975), but without implying that I subscribe to his conclusions. Evans-Pritchard (1940, pp. 152–62) is more nuanced. Almost all the large literature that has since developed around these questions is cited by Cohen (1995); Gilsenan (1996) treats similar themes.

have ceased to be defining features. The target of Ankhtify's claim is at least as likely to have been a form of elite behavior as a generalized phenomenon.

Second, there is no single way in which the "state" can be predicted to handle issues of social control, or of overall governmental intervention; the state may also in fact lack the coercive capability to override entrenched customs. For Egyptian possessions in Syria-Palestine, Mario Liverani (e.g., 1967; 1990, pp. 76–78) shows that it is best to see New Kingdom kings as allowing the endemic competition among small city-states to continue provided that it did not endanger Egyptian interests. For internal affairs, the suppression of violent patterns of self-help and response may again be limited to cases where the center deems it to be necessary, for example, when it becomes too disruptive; or suppression may simply be beyond the center's coercive capacity — as will often be the case in the marginal societies for which feud has typically been described. Again within Syria-Palestine, the Hebrew Bible preserves traces of institutions of vengeance, in the form of rules for asylum after homicide, that imply that attempts should be made to regulate the phenomenon, rather than that it could or should be eliminated entirely (Greenberg 1959). Classical Athens, by contrast, is a society in which institutions of competition analogous to feud appear to have been channeled into the familiar form of litigation while retaining many of their other characteristics and coming only very partially under state "control."

In addition to the variability of state involvement and control in different societies, there is widespread, largely anecdotal reporting of long-lasting family enmities and repeated patterns of family vengeance in complex societies up to the present; in current anecdote about Egypt these are typical particularly of Middle Egypt. Patterns of feud could range from the "pure" type of Black-Michaud (1975) and Peters (1990) to such less centrally structural phenomena, or to institutions that pervade only part of their societies (e.g., Gilsenan 1996). It is perfectly plausible that forms like these should have existed in ancient Egypt. An example of behavior that fits the relevant pattern and leaves archaeological traces is the frequent evidence of persecution of the memories of people through the defacement of their monuments; these show people's enemies (no doubt including state authority) pursuing them beyond this life into the next, and thus enacting one of the generally characteristic features of feud in a typically Egyptian arena. Another instance where such a focus seems apparent is in the longer Nagᶜ-ed-Deir Letter to the Dead, where a man who is haunted by someone who appears to have been killed writes to his father to enlist his support against the haunting (Wente 1990, pp. 212–13, with references; Fecht 1969). Yet neither the defacement of monuments nor this letter provides information about the siting of violent actions in kin groups or about the character of such groups;[11] consequently they too do not constitute evidence for a specific institution of feud. The same applies to a graffito next to a mutilated subsidiary figure in an Old Kingdom tomb at Saqqara that Etienne Drioton (1952)[12] interpreted somewhat adventurously as recording perpetually a son's avenging motivation for the mutilation that he perpetrated against the man who chained him and beat his father. Here, more than one generation may have been affected but apparently not by homicide. Cases like this are indicative of the presence and perhaps prevalence of violent behavior between enemies but not of particular social institutions. In comparison, Ankhtify's mention of the two essential kin categories of father and "brother" is much more informative.

It may be best to see the Ankhtify passage as showing a balancing of the two possibilities of endemic "feud" and of less constitutive forms of reciprocal violence that the center attempts to supervise and restrict. For his period, Ankhtify represents the centripetal force of "order" against the local interests of the oppressed and disorderly inhabitants of Edfu, who have resorted to self-help in the absence of a local authority that would properly regulate their disputes. It is immaterial here whether Ankhtify's assertion of control represents authority delegated to him from a theoretical central government — presumably the Heracleopolitan kings of the Ninth Dynasty[13] — or through his own standing as the most powerful local ruler. The body of his inscriptions could support either possibility. What is most significant for interpretation is that his claim is formulated in general, moralizing terms and thus exploits, no doubt deliberately, the ruler's ethical legitimation as the enactor of what is just, in a balance between the frequently self-assertive, militaristic tone of his texts as a whole on the one hand, and the more complex mediation and religious sanction he evokes elsewhere on the other (cf. Fecht 1968, pp. 55–56). It is noteworthy that the text does not describe the takeover of Edfu explicitly as a military conquest.

11. Compare Helck's (1957, pp. 542–43) comments on defacement.

12. For publication of the tomb, see Hassan 1975, pp. 7–9, pl. 3.

13. Such a reading would fit with the episode later in his inscriptions (Vandier Text 5, p. 186, IIβ3–IIγ1), in which he visits the Thinite Nome to meet an unnamed person who may be

The implication of the passage must be that feud would be nonexistent or outlawed in an ideal Egyptian society, but the reality may have been different. Imposed mechanisms of social control could have been quite weak in all but the central elite (and perhaps also there) and self-help the norm. If this was true of the far more pervasive state forms of the Roman period, as appears to have been the case (Hobson 1993), there is every reason to expect that it was so earlier. It is therefore reasonable to suggest that Ankhtify's claim to have suppressed feuding could have corresponded to a social reality of self-help that he encountered.

It is perhaps less reasonable to expect that he could have put an end to such behavior. Feuds will be suppressed by a powerful higher authority if they disturb the orderly life of society excessively, but in pre-modern times a relatively high level of violence and suffering has been widely tolerated and indeed expected;[14] from Egypt, the almost casual references to the use of killing as a political weapon in the Instruction for Merikare belong in this context (Helck 1977, e.g., §§2 end, 5, 18). The requisite background assumption of a pacific order may have been lacking. Someone who temporarily has greater access to coercion than do the disputing parties would hardly be able to suppress patterns of mutual revenge definitively; such practices tend to be too deeply entrenched for that to be possible. Moreover, the claim to make people embrace those who had previously been homicidally bent on each other seems exaggerated and implausible. It is likely to partake in the rhetoric of dispute settlement rather than the reality, in which it may be necessary to keep the parties apart during mediation. Ankhtify naturally did not say how he achieved his paradigmatic reconciliation; such successes might be in mediating between the parties to persuade them to accept compensation in lieu of continuing active hostility, as will be possible, if not easily achieved, in most such disputes (McDowell, personal communication; see also Roth 1987).

Thus, Ankhtify's claim is likely to be adopted from folk wisdom about the role of the good local ruler and dispute settler and to form part of his public rhetoric. Such wisdom could have been taken ready formulated from a stock of phraseology, but since Ankhtify's inscriptions show a high degree of originality, it could also have been newly composed in written form for him. An innovation of this sort, if innovation it was, demonstrates the motif's significance for Ankhtify, but it does not follow that the passage constitutes evidence for any specific events. Its rhetorical and generalizing character can hardly be related to any particular feuds or other lasting patterns of family vengeance that might have been among the population of Edfu during the time these are likely to have existed; the statement is not cast in a form that permits any inference about such patterns. But the fact that, in the quite brief passage describing his conquest, Ankhtify used the claim to have achieved this particular feat to summarize his successful imposition of peace and order emphasizes its ideological significance. More broadly and indirectly, the passage provides evidence for an ancient folk model according to which the absence of a strong ruler was accompanied by patterns of homicide between opposed kin groups in local society. That folk model can perhaps be seen in another form in the allusions to homicide as characterizing a state of disorder in the Admonitions of Ipuwer (Gardiner 1909, e.g., 5.10–11[?]; 8.9; 12.14; Parkinson 1997, pp. 176, 180, 186). Unlike Ankhtify, these are not so specific as to point to a particular social form according to which the violence would be patterned.

Since Ankhtify lived nearer to the ancient society than we do and we know so little about its configuration, we would do well to accept his vision, with due reserve as to whether it reports anything specific. The practices involved were surely more diverse than those described for the narrowly defined "feuding" societies of the Mediterranean evoked above, while the implications for an understanding of the role of government in society have a broad import. Here, an ancient source may also contribute something to the "ethnographic" range of what is known about the region.

Among Egyptian sources, Ankhtify's inscriptions provide evidence for many phenomena that are otherwise unknown. On this matter they also illustrate how effective a veil Egyptian materials draw over so much of ancient life. We cannot know whether the centripetal, hierarchical, and largely pacific values displayed in most Egyptian biographies mask other possibilities that may be more widespread in terms of general human conduct. Here too, Edward F. Wente (1984) makes a significant contribution in his analysis of the "erotic" graffiti in a grotto above the temple of Hatshepsut at Deir el-Bahri, which appear to constitute a political satire with overtones comparable to those of the male rhetoric of feuding and dispute settlement.

---

best understood as an agent of the central government. His way of mentioning this man is of course unflattering.

14. Compare the circumstances cited in Davis 1987 and for more recent "feuding" societies in Black-Michaud 1975.

References

Bagnall, R. S.
1989 "Official and Private Violence in Roman Egypt." *Bulletin of the American Society of Papyrologists* 26: 201–16.

Baines, J.
1985 *Fecundity Figures: Egyptian Personification and the Iconography of a Genre.* Warminster: Aris and Phillips; Chicago: Bolchazy Carducci.
1986 "The Stela of Emhab: Innovation, Tradition, Hierarchy." *Journal of Egyptian Archaeology* 72: 41–53.
1987 "Practical Religion and Piety." *Journal of Egyptian Archaeology* 73: 79–98.

Baines, J., and R. B. Parkinson
1997 "An Old Kingdom Record of an Oracle? Sinai Inscription 13." In *Essays on Ancient Egypt in Honour of Herman te Velde,* edited by T. van Dijk, pp. 9–27. Egyptological Memoirs 1. Groningen: Styx.

Baker, B. J.
1997 "Contributions of Biological Anthropology to the Understanding of Ancient Egyptian and Nubian Societies." In *Anthropology and Egyptology: A Developing Dialogue,* edited by J. Lustig, pp. 106–16. Monographs in Mediterranean Archaeology 8. Sheffield: Sheffield Academic Press.

Bedell, E.
1973 Criminal Law in the Egyptian Ramesside Period. Ph.D. dissertation, Brandeis University.

Black-Michaud, J.
1975 *Cohesive Force: Feud in the Mediterranean and the Middle East.* Oxford: Basil Blackwell.

Boehm, C.
1983 *Montenegrin Social Organization and Values: Political Ethnography of a Refuge Area Tribal Adaptation.* AMS Studies in Anthropology 1. New York: AMS Press.

Černý, J.
1929 "Papyrus Salt 824 (Brit. Mus. 10055)." *Journal of Egyptian Archaeology* 15: 243–58.

Cohen, D.
1995 *Law, Violence, and Community in Classical Athens.* Key Themes in Ancient History. Cambridge: Cambridge University Press.

Davis, N. Z.
1987 *Fiction in the Archives: Pardon Tales and Their Tellers in Sixteenth-Century France.* Stanford: Stanford University Press.

Drioton, É.
1952 "Une mutilation d'image avec motif." *Archiv orientalní* 20: 351–55.

Evans-Pritchard, E. E.
1940 *The Nuer: A Description of the Modes of Livelihood and Political Institutions of a Nilotic People.* Oxford: Clarendon Press.

Eyre, C. J.
1984 "Crime and Adultery in Ancient Egypt." *Journal of Egyptian Archaeology* 70: 92–106.

Fecht, G.
1968 "Zu den Inschriften des ersten Pfeilers im Grab des Ankhtifi (Moʿalla)." In *Festschrift für Siegfried Schott zu seinem 70. Geburtstag am 20. August 1967,* edited by W. Helck, pp. 50–60. Wiesbaden: Otto Harrassowitz.
1969 Der Totenbrief von Nagʿ ed-Deir. *Mitteilungen des Deutschen archäologischen Instituts, Abteilung Kairo* 24: 105–28.

Franke, D.
1983 *Altägyptische Verwandschaftsbezeichnungen im Mittleren Reich.* Hamburger ägyptologische Studien 3. Hamburg: Borg.

Gardiner, A. H.
1909 *The Admonitions of an Egyptian Sage, from a Hieratic Papyrus in Leiden (Pap. Leiden 344 recto).* Leipzig: J. C. Hinrichs.

Gilsenan, M.
1996 *Lords of the Lebanese Marches: Violence and Narrative in an Arab Society.* Society and Culture in the Modern Middle East. London and New York: I. B. Tauris.

Goedicke, H.
1995 "Administrative Notions in the First Intermediate Period." *Chronique d'Égypte* 70: 41–51.

Green, M. A.
1976 "The Passing of Harmose." *Orientalia* 45: 395–409.

Greenberg, M.
1959 "The Biblical Conception of Asylum." *Journal of Biblical Literature* 78: 125–32. Reprinted in *Studies in the Bible and Jewish Thought,* by M. Greenberg, pp. 43–50. Jewish Publication Society Scholar of Distinction Series. Philadelphia: Jewish Publication Society, 1995.

Griffith, F. Ll.
1898 *The Petrie Papyri: Hieratic Papyri from Kahun and Gurob.* 2 volumes. London: B. Quaritch.
1909 *Catalogue of the Demotic Papyri in the John Rylands Library Manchester,* Volume 3: *Key-List, Translations, Commentaries and Indices.* Manchester: University Press; London: B. Quaritch.

Hassan, S.
1975 *Excavations at Saqqara, 1937–1938,* Volume 3: *Mastabas of Princess Ḥemet-Rʿ and Others.* Re-edited by Zaky Iskander. Cairo: Arab Republic of Egypt, Antiquities Department.

Helck, W.
1955 "Eine Stele des Vizekönigs *Wśr-Śt.t.*" *Journal of Near Eastern Studies* 14: 22–31.
1957 *Zur Verwaltung des Mittleren und Neuen Reichs.* Probleme der Ägyptologie 3. Leiden: E. J. Brill.

1977 *Die Lehre für König Merikare*. Kleine ägyptische Texte. Wiesbaden: Otto Harrassowitz.

Herzfeld, M.
1985 *The Poetics of Manhood: Contest and Identity in a Cretan Mountain Village*. Princeton: Princeton University Press.

Hobson, D. W.
1993 "The Impact of Law on Village Life in Roman Egypt." In *Law, Politics and Society in the Ancient Mediterranean World*, edited by B. Halpern and D. W. Hobson, pp. 193–219. Sheffield: Sheffield Academic Press.

Hoch, J., and S. E. Orel
1992 "Murder in Ancient Egypt." In *Death and Taxes in the Ancient Near East*, edited by S. E. Orel, pp. 87–128. Lewiston: Edwin Mellen Press.

Janssen, J. J.
1975 "The Rules of Legal Proceeding in the Community of Necropolis Workmen at Deir el-Medina." *Bibliotheca Orientalis* 32: 290–97.

Liverani, M.
1967 "Contrasti e confluenze di concezioni politiche nell'età di el-Amarna." *Revue d'assyriologie* 61: 253–68.
1990 *Prestige and Interest: International Relations in the Near East ca. 1600–1100 B.C.* History of the Ancient Near East, Studies 1. Padua: Sargon.

McDowell, A. G.
1990 *Jurisdiction in the Workmen's Community at Deir el-Medina*. Egyptologische Uitgaven 5. Leiden: Nederlands Instituut voor het Nabije Oosten.

Moreno García, J. C.
1996 "Administration territoriale et organisation de l'espace en Égytpe au troisième millénaire avant J.-C.: *grgt* et le titre *ʿ(n)ḏ-mr grgt*." *Zeitschrift für ägyptische Sprache und Altertumskunde* 123: 116–38.

Meeker, M. E.
1979 *Literature and Violence in North Arabia*. Cambridge: Cambridge University Press.

Morschauser, S. N.
1991 *Threat-formulae in Ancient Egypt: A Study of the History, Structure, and Use of Threats and Curses in Ancient Egypt*. Baltimore: Halgo.

O'Connor, D.
1995 "The Social and Economic Organization of Ancient Egyptian Temples." In *Civilizations of the Ancient Near East*, Volume 1, edited by J. Sasson, pp. 319–29. New York: Scribner.

Parkinson, R. B.
1997 *The Tale of Sinuhe and Other Ancient Egyptian Poems*. Oxford: Clarendon Press.

Peet, T. E.
1920 *The Mayer Papyri A–B, Nos. M. 11162 and M. 11186 of the Free Public Museums, Liverpool*. London: Egypt Exploration Society.

Perdu, O.
1995 "Ancient Egyptian Autobiographies." In *Civilizations of the Ancient Near East*, Volume 4, edited by J. Sasson, pp. 2243–54. New York: Scribner.

Peters, E.
1990 *The Bedouin of Cyrenaica: Studies in Personal and Corporate Power*. Edited by J. Goody and E. Marx. Cambridge Studies in Social and Cultural Anthropology 72. Cambridge: Cambridge University Press.

Ray, J. D.
1977 "The Complaint of Herieu." *Revue d'égyptologie* 29: 97–116.

Ritner, R. K.
1993 *The Mechanics of Ancient Egyptian Magical Practice*. Studies in Ancient Oriental Civilization 54. Chicago: Oriental Institute.

Robins, G.
1979 "The Relationships Specified by Egyptian Kinship Terms of the Middle and New Kingdoms." *Chronique d'Égypte* 54: 197–217.

Roth, M. T.
1987 "Homicide in the Neo-Assyrian Period." In *Language, Literature, and History: Philological and Historical Studies Presented to Erica Reiner*, edited by F. Rochberg-Halton, pp. 351–65. American Oriental Series 67. New Haven: American Oriental Society.

Spanel, D. B.
1984 "The Date of Ankhtifi of Moʿalla." *Göttinger Miszellen* 78: 87–94.

Valbelle, D.
1985 *"Les ouvriers de la tombe": Deir el-Médineh à l'époque ramesside*. Bibliothèque d'étude 96. Cairo: Institut français d'archéologie orientale.

Vandier, J.
1950 *Moʿalla: La tombe d'Ankhtifi et la tombe de Sébekhotep*. Bibliothèque d'étude 18. Cairo: Institut français d'archéologie orientale.

Vittmann, G.
1998 *Der demotische Papyrus Rylands 9*. 2 volumes. Ägypten und Altes Testament 38. Wiesbaden: Otto Harrassowitz.

Wente, E. F.
1982 "Mysticism in Pharaonic Egypt?" *Journal of Near Eastern Studies* 41: 161–79.
1984 "Some Graffiti from the Reign of Hatshepsut." *Journal of Near Eastern Studies* 43: 47–54.
1990 *Letters from Ancient Egypt*. Society of Biblical Literature, Writings from the Ancient World 1. Atlanta: Scholars Press.

Wessetzky, V.
1977 "An der Grenze von Literatur und Geschichte." In *Fragen an die altägyptische Literatur: Studien zum Gedenken an Eberhard Otto*, edited by J. Assmann, E. Feucht, and R. Grieshammer, pp. 499–502. Wiesbaden: Ludwig Reichert Verlag.

Whitehouse, W. M.
1980 "Radiological Findings in the Royal Mummies." In *An X-ray Atlas of the Royal Mummies,* edited by J. E. Harris and E. F. Wente, pp. 286–99. Chicago: University of Chicago Press.

Willems, H.
1983 "A Description of Egyptian Kinship Terminology of the Middle Kingdom c. 2000–1650 B.C." *Bijdragen tot de Taal-, Land- en Volkenkunde* 139: 152–68.

Winlock, H. E.
1945 *The Slain Soldiers of Neb-ḥepet-Rēʿ Mentu-ḥotep.* Metropolitan Museum of Art, Egyptian Expedition 16. New York: Metropolitan Museum of Art.

Yoffee, N.
1988 "Context and Authority in Early Mesopotamian Law." In *State Formation and Political Legitimacy,* edited by R. Cohen and J. D. Toland, pp. 95–113. Political Anthropology 6. New Brunswick: Transaction Books.

3

THEBAN SEVENTEENTH DYNASTY

JÜRGEN VON BECKERATH

Schlehdorf, Germany

To begin with the definition of this group of kings we notice that, in the *Egyptian History* of Manetho (according to Africanus), the Seventeenth Dynasty is actually an addition of "shepherds" (local rulers in Lower and Middle Egypt, partly of Asiatic origin) and "Diospolites" (Theban kings of the same time), all of them being contemporaries and probably vassals — or at least tributaries — of the Hyksos of the Fifteenth Dynasty. Nevertheless, we are accustomed to call only the Theban rulers the "Seventeenth Dynasty" and all others the "Sixteenth Dynasty," although the latter do not form a homogeneous group. The kings of the Seventeenth Dynasty may have considered themselves as legitimate successors of the Thirteenth Dynasty. Both dynasties consist of rulers descended from various families. The reason for their distinction in Manetho and the Royal Canon of Turin is their difference of realms. The kings of the Thirteenth Dynasty ruled all Egypt as successors of the Twelfth Dynasty until the occupation of Memphis-Itjtowi by the Hyksos in the middle of the seventeenth century B.C. Only during the later part of the Thirteenth Dynasty were there independent local rulers in the Delta (Fourteenth Dynasty). We do not know whether the Seventeenth Dynasty began at the same time as the Hyksos rule — it may have been some years later — but at any rate, not before that event, because the Thirteenth Dynasty was certainly in possession of Upper Egypt to its very end. We may, therefore, describe the Seventeenth Dynasty as the group of kings reigning at Thebes during the period of the Hyksos, thus for about one hundred years.

Since the kings of the Thirteenth Dynasty were buried in the cemeteries of the Memphis area, the royal tombs of the Second Intermediate Period in the Theban necropolis must belong to the kings of the Seventeenth Dynasty as ascertained by Winlock (1924, pp. 217–77). The rulers attributed by him to that dynasty are:

Nubkheperreʿ Anyotef,
Sekhemreʿ-wepmaʿet Anyotef,
Sekhemreʿ-shedtowi Sebekemsaf,
Senakhtenreʿ Taʿo the Elder,[1]
Seqenenreʿ Taʿo (the Brave),
Wadjkheperreʿ Kamose (all mentioned in the Abbott Papyrus),

and further

Sekhemreʿ-herḥermaʿet Anyotef the Elder,
Sekhemreʿ-waḥkhaʿu Raʿḥotep,
Sekhemreʿ-wadjkhaʿu Sebekemsaf, and
Sekhemreʿ-sementowi Dḥuti.

Stock (1942, pp. 76–81) was able to identify these rulers in column XI (11.1–14) of the Turin Canon of Kings (here abbreviated T). While the arrangement of the last columns of T is not yet sure in detail, there is no doubt that column XI must be the last of the king list (verso of the papyrus), because there is a large empty space on the other side at the beginning of the text of the recto (tax list), which cannot have

1. It is true that, as pointed out by Vandersleyen (1983, pp. 67–70), there is no evidence for a King Senakhtenreʿ Taʿo. But it seems unlikely that the Abbott commission, having visited the tombs of Senakhtenreʿ and of Seqenenreʿ, should have made not only the mistake of confusing the similar words "nakht" and "qen" but over and above giving the name Taʿo the Elder without any reason to Senakhtenreʿ.

Gold of Praise: Studies on Ancient Egypt in Honor of Edward F. Wente
Edited by Emily Teeter and John A. Larson
Studies in Ancient Oriental Civilization 58
Chicago: Oriental Institute, 1999

been larger. There was little change in my reconstruction of the Seventeenth Dynasty against that of Stock (Beckerath 1964, pp. 165–93):

T X 30(?)	[Nubkheperreʿ] (Anyotef V)
XI 1	Sekhemreʿ-[waḥkhaʿu] (Raʿḥotep)
XI 2	Sekhemreʿ-[wadjkhaʿu] (Sebekemsaf I)
XI 3	Sekhemreʿ-se[mentowi] (Dḥuti)
XI 4	Seʿankh[en]reʿ (Mentuḥotep)
XI 5	Nebiriaw (I)
XI 6	Nebiriaw (II)
XI 7	Semenenreʿ
XI 8	Seweser[en]reʿ [2]
XI 9	Sekhemreʿ-shedwêset (Sekhemreʿ-shedtowi Sebekemsaf II)
XI 10	[Sekhemreʿ-wepmaʿet (Anyotef VI)]
XI 11	[Sekhemreʿ-herḥermaʿet (Anyotef VII)]
XI 12	[Senakhtenreʿ (Taʿo I)]
XI 13	[Seqenenreʿ (Taʿo II)]
XI 14	[Wadjkheperreʿ (Kamose)].

This reconstruction has since been challenged by Helck (1992, pp. 189–94), Vandersleyen (1993, pp. 189–91), and Bennett (1994, pp. 21–28). Of course, there are several uncertainties in this list.

The identification of these rulers in the Turin Canon, as first recognized by Stock, was based on the names of the indubitable Theban kings Nebiriaw (Sewadjenreʿ) in T XI 5 and Sekhemreʿ-shedwêset Sebekemsaf in XI 9.[3] Since the king list of T, in all probability, did not stop before the end of the Seventeenth Dynasty, we should expect at least the Taʿo kings (and presumably Kamose) in column XI 11.10–14. The other Theban kings of Winlock were inserted by Stock in XI 1–3 where two names beginning with "Sekhemreʿ" and another one with "Sekhemreʿ-se ..." are preserved.

While maintaining this reconstruction in general, Helck criticizes my putting Anyotef V on the top of the series of kings. Instead, Helck inserts him in T XI 12, omitting Kamose at the end. In line 15, the rest of a summary is preserved: "Sum 5 kings ... ." Summaries are rare in the king list and always designate the end of one or more dynasties. Examples are: I x+11 sqq. (Dynasty of the Gods), II 9–10 (the Followers of Horus), III 26–27 (First to Fifth Dynasties), IV 14–17 (Sixth to Eighth Dynasties and First to Eighth Dynasties), V 10 (Ninth/Tenth Dynasty), V 17 (Eleventh Dynasty), VI 3 (Twelfth Dynasty), IXb 7 or 8 (Fifteenth Dynasty). In Helck's opinion, we have in XI 15 only the sum of the last five Theban rulers whose names are lost in lines 10–14. It seems most improbable, however, that the scribe should have given here the sum only for the last five kings and left their predecessors without a summary. Furthermore, there is no *ỉr.n.f* formula in line 1 of the column.[4] Hence, here is not the beginning of a dynasty. We have to add, therefore, at least one further name at the end of the preceding column. Of course, there is no certainty that it must have been Anyotef V. However, I am still maintaining my suggestion (Beckerath 1964, p. 25) that the sum in XI 15 should be completed to "[1]5 kings."

Some of the kings could be dated either to the end of the Thirteenth Dynasty or to the Seventeenth Dynasty, and those whose prenomina begin with Sekhemreʿ or Sekhemreʿ-se ... may theoretically be inserted in T XI 1–3. These are:

Sekhemreʿ-neferkhaʿu Wepwawetemsaf,
Sekhemreʿ-wadjkhaʿu Sebekemsaf (I),
Sekhemreʿ-waḥkhaʿu Raʿḥotep,
Sekhemreʿ-sewesertowi Sebekḥotep (VIII),
Sekhemreʿ-seʿankhtowi Iykhernofret Neferḥotep (III), and
Sekhemreʿ-sementowi Dḥuti.

2. The full name of this king (Seweserenreʿ Bebʿankh) was found on a stela from Gebel ez-Zeit (Castel 1988, pp. 50–51).

3. There cannot be any doubt about the identity of this king with the Sekhemreʿ-shedtowi of P. Abbott and P. Leopold II + P. Amherst. The scribe of T. changed the name of this king (and possibly of other Theban rulers whose prenomina ended with -towi). Surely no king of that dynasty would have given up the claim to be a king of all Egypt in his name.

4. The restoration of an *ỉr.n.f* formula in line 10 by Farina (1938, p. 58) was gratuitous.

There must have been two kings named Sebekemsaf buried in the Theban necropolis. P. Leopold II + P. Amherst (2, lines 10–19; cf. P. Abbott 3, lines 1–7) reports that the thieves who entered the tomb of Sekhemreʿ-shedtowi Sebekemsaf and his wife Nubkhaʿes robbed it completely and set fire to the coffins. It is unlikely, therefore, that a heart scarab (Beckerath 1964, Belegliste XVII 2, no. 14) and a wooden canopic box (ibid., no. 13) could have survived that event. They are hence ascribed rightly by Winlock to Sebekemsaf I, in addition to other monuments that this king left behind at Thebes. He should be, therefore, among the rulers of the Seventeenth Dynasty, and most probably restored in T XI 2 where a reign of 16 years is noticed. The arguments given by Vandersleyen (1993, pp. 189–90) for putting him in the Thirteenth Dynasty are not compelling.

The three Anyotef kings (V–VII) certainly belong to the Seventeenth Dynasty. Nubkheperreʿ is discernible from the others by writing his name Anyotef with the reed-*ỉ* after *ỉn*. This may be true also with the apparently quite ephemeral Sekhemreʿ-herḥermaʿet, attested only by his poor coffin (Louvre E. 3020; Winlock 1924, pp. 235–36), although the *ỉ* was erroneously painted over by an *ʿꜣ* which is meaningless here. The coffin of Sekhemreʿ-wepmaʿet (Louvre E. 3019; Winlock 1924, pp. 234–37, pl. 14) was "given to him by his brother, the King Anyotef" (the last written with *ỉ* after *ỉn*; Pierret 1874, p. 86; Weill 1918, p. 358). The brother and successor of Sekhemreʿ-wepmaʿet could thus be either Nubkheperreʿ or Sekhemreʿ-herḥermaʿet. The two brothers were sons of a king, because on the pyramidion from the tomb of Anyotef VI he is designated as born by a king's wife.[5] Completing the vertical lines on the four sides of the pyramidion (1. Horus *Wp mꜣʿt* + serekh, 2. [*ny-sw*]*t*-[*bỉ*]*t Sḫm-Rʿ wp mꜣʿ*[*t*], 3. *Sꜣ*-[*Rʿ*] *ʾIn-ỉt.f* [*mry Ws*]*ỉr*,[6] 4. *ms n mwt-nsw ḥmt-nsw wr*(*t*) *ḥnmt-nfr-ḥḏt* [...]) we find that the name of the queen should be a very short one as, for example, Nubkhaʿes.

Some years ago, on the Luxor-Farshût road in the Western Desert, a team from the Oriental Institute of the University of Chicago found the remains of a small temple and inside the temple, among other blocks, was the fragment of a doorjamb preserving only a portion of a vertical inscription: [... *sꜣ-Rʿ ʾIn-ỉt.f* (with *ỉ* after *ỉn*) *ỉr.n sꜣ-Rʿ Sbk-m*-[*sꜣ.f*] (Darnell and Darnell 1993, pp. 50–51, fig. 4). The authors realized that a filiation "King X engendered by King Y" would be unique and in contradiction to the dogma of divine descent of the king, and therefore rightly completed the inscription as "Renewal of the monument for his father (or forefather), the Son of Ra, Inyotef, which the Son of Ra Sebekemsaf has made." In consequence there must have been a King Inyotef preceding King Sebekemsaf (I or II). This king should be, in all probability, the important Nebkheperreʿ rather than the ephemeral Sekhemreʿ-herḥermaʿet documented only by his poor coffin. Since there is no trace in T XI 1–8 fitting his name, he should be inserted before that series of rulers at the end of column X, as I suggested earlier.

In T XI 3, giving Sekhemreʿ-se ... , Stock inserts King Sekhemreʿ-sementowi Dḥuti. The connection of this king with the royal cemetery at Dra Abu el-Naga is based only on his canopic box in Berlin (no. 1175; Erman 1892, pp. 46–47), which was later dedicated to a Queen Mentuḥotep. The box was found at Thebes (Winlock 1924, pp. 269–70) and the queen was obviously buried there. But there is no proof that she and King Dḥuty should be dated to the Seventeenth Dynasty rather than to the later part of the Thirteenth Dynasty.

The king of T XI 4 is likewise uncertain, even the reading of his name being doubtful. It was read by Farina (1938, p. 58) as Seʿankh[en]reʿ whereas Gardiner (1959, pl. IV) read Sewadj ... . The king was identified first by Stock with a Mentuḥotep of whom two sphinxes have been unearthed at Edfu (Cairo JE 48874–5; Gauthier 1931, p. 2; Stock 1942, p. 80). A new proposal was made by Dautzenberg (1992, pp. 43–48) who reads the crucial sign as "nefer" and suggests the restoration of the name as Senefer[ib]reʿ. This is the prenomen of a King Sesostris (IV) whom I ascribed with doubt to the Thirteenth Dynasty (Beckerath 1964, Belegliste XIII F). There should be, however, a King Sesostris in the Seventeenth Dynasty after Sebekemsaf I (Drioton and Vandier 1962, p. 333). The name of this Sesostris could have stood in T XI 4 if the suggestion of Dautzenberg is correct. On the other hand, he identifies Seʿankhenreʿ Mentuḥotep with Seʿankhenreʿ Sewadjtu in T VII 5. This proposal seems to be corroborated by Vernus

5. British Museum 1913, pl. 29 (341), BM 478.

6. The restoration of *ỉr*[*.n* ...] suggested by Winlock (1924, p. 234), assuming apparently the name of the father here, would be in contradiction to the dogma of divine kingship.

(1989, pp. 145–61) who recognizes a close stylistic connection of this king with Sekhemreʿ-seʿankhtowi Neferḥotep III.

The following sequence of rulers of the Seventeenth Dynasty seems to me acceptable presently:

Nubkheperreʿ Anyotef V
Sekhemreʿ-waḥkhaʿu Raʿḥotep(??)
Sekhemreʿ-wadjkhaʿu Sebekemsaf I
Sekhemreʿ-se ...(?)
Seneferibreʿ Sesostris IV(?)
Sewadjenreʿ Nebiriaw I
Neferkareʿ(?) Nebiriaw II
Semenenreʿ
Seweserenreʿ Bebʿankh
Sekhemreʿ-shedtowi Sebekemsaf II
Sekhemreʿ-wepmaʿet Anyotef VI
Sekhemreʿ-herḥermaʿet Anyotef VII
Senakhtenreʿ Taʿo I
Seqenenreʿ Taʿo II
Wadjkheperreʿ Kamose

****

This contribution in honor of Edward F. Wente was written in autumn 1994. Consequently, later publications such as, for example, K. S. B. Ryholt, *The Political Situation in Egypt during the Second Intermediate Period, c. 1800–1550 B.C.* (CNI Publications 20; Copenhagen: Museum Tusculanum Press, 1997), are not considered.

****

References

Beckerath, J. von

1964 *Untersuchungen zur politischen Geschichte der Zweiten Zwischenzeit in Ägypten.* Ägyptologische Forschungen 23. Glückstadt: J. J. Augustin.

1992 "Zur Geschichte von Chonsemhab und dem Geist." *Zeitschrift für ägyptische Sprache und Altertumskunde* 119: 90–107.

Bennett, C.

1994 "The First Three Sekhemre Kings of the Seventeenth Dynasty." *Göttinger Miszellen* 143: 21–28.

Berlev, O.

1975/76 "Un don du roi Rahotep." *Orientalia Lovanensia Periodica* 6/7: 31–41.

Berlev , O., and S. Hodjash

1982 *The Egyptian Reliefs and Stelae in the Pushkin Museum of Fine Arts, Moscow.* Aurora: St. Petersburg.

Blumenthal, E.

1977 "Die Koptosstele des Königs Rahotep (London U.C. 14327)." In *Ägypten und Kusch*, edited by E. Endesfelder, pp. 63–80. Schriften zur Geschichte und Kultur des Alten Orients 13. Berlin: Akademie-Verlag.

British Museum

1913 *Hieroglyphic Texts from Egyptian Stelae, etc., in the British Museum*, Part 4. London: British Museum.

Castel, G.

1988 "Les mines de galène pharaoniques du Gebel el Zeit." *Bulletin de la Société française d'égyptologie* 112: 37–53.

Darnell, J. C., and D. Darnell

1993 "The Luxor-Farshût Desert Road Survey." In *Oriental Institute 1992/1993 Annual Report*, edited by W. M. Sumner, pp. 48–55. Chicago: Oriental Institute.

Dautzenberg, N.

1992 "Seneferibre Sesostris IV – ein König der 17. Dynastie?" *Göttinger Miszellen* 129: 43–48.

Drioton, É., and J. Vandier

1962 *L'Égypte: Des origines à la conquête d'Alexandre.* Clio, Les peuples de l'orient méditerranéen 2. Fourth edition. Paris: Presses Universitaires de France.

Erman, A.

1892 "Historische Nachlese: König Ḏḥwtj." *Zeitschrift für ägyptische Sprache und Altertumskunde* 30: 46–47.

Farina, G.

1938 *Il papiro dei re restaurato.* Roma: G. Bardi.

Gardiner, A. H.

1932 *Late-Egyptian Stories.* Bibliotheca Aegyptiaca 1. Brussels: Fondation Égyptologique Reine Élisabeth.

1959 *The Royal Canon of Turin*. Oxford: Oxford University Press.

Gauthier, H.
1931 "Deux sphinxes du Moyen Empire." *Annales du Service des antiquités de l'Égypte* 31: 2.

Helck, W.
1992 "Anmerkungen zum Turiner Königspapyrus." *Studien zur altägyptischen Kultur* 19: 151–216.

Petrie, W. M. F.
1896 *Koptos*. London: Quaritch.

Pierret, P.
1874 *Recueil d'inscriptions inédites du Musée du Louvre*, part 1: *Études égyptologiques*. Paris: A. Franck.

Stock, H.
1942 *Studien zur Geschichte und Archäologie der 13.–17.-Dynastie Ägyptens, unter besonderer Berücksichtigung der Skarabäen dieser Zwischenzeit*. Ägyptologische Forschungen 12. Glückstadt: J. J. Augustin.

Vandersleyen, C.
1983 "Un seul roi Taa sous la 17e dynastie." *Göttinger Miszellen* 63: 67–70.
1993 "Rahotep, Sebekemsaf Ier et Djehouti, rois de la 13e dynastie." *Revue d'égyptologie* 44:189–91.

Vernus, P.
1989 "La stèle du pharaon *Mntw-ḥtpi* à Karnak: Un nouveau temoignage sur la situation politique et militaire de la D.P.I." *Revue d'égyptologie* 40: 145–61.

Weill, R.
1918 *La fin du Moyen Empire égyptien: Étude sur les monuments et l'histoire de la période comprise entre la XIIe et la XVIIIe dynastie*. Paris: A. Picard.

Winlock, H. E.
1924 "The Tombs of the Kings of the Seventeenth Dynasty at Thebes." *Journal of Egyptian Archaeology* 10: 217–77.

4

INVENTORY OFFERING LISTS AND THE NOMENCLATURE FOR BOXES AND CHESTS IN THE OLD KINGDOM

EDWARD BROVARSKI

Museum of Fine Arts, Boston

For me, and I think for others who were privileged to study there in the 1960s and 1970s, the Oriental Institute was a special place whose abundant resources included teachers of the caliber of Klaus Baer, George Hughes, John A. Wilson, and, of course, Edward F. Wente. Since my earliest days in Egyptology, Professor Wente has been a source of inspiration. To me he is the quintessence of a scientific scholar and thinker — systematic and exact, impartial and unbiased. It was my privilege to take a number of courses in Late Period Egyptian hieroglyphic and hieratic with Professor Wente, an acknowledged master in those fields. As a teacher, he possesses an extraordinary ability to put a student at ease, to make him or her want to perform at their best, and to make the student feel that his or her suggestions or observations actually possess merit.*

One course in particular I remember with fondness, a seminar on architectural terms that Professor Wente agreed to teach. The class was small; in actual fact, it consisted of just the professor and the present writer. While not on architectural terms, the present article is likewise devoted to lexicography, and I hope it meets with his approbation.

The first part of this article appeared in the festschrift volume of an old friend and collaborator of Professor Wente.[1] Both parts utilize furniture lists that comprise one component of the inventory offering lists of Early Dynastic and Old Kingdom date as a source for the investigation of nomenclature for furniture in that period.[2]

*I express my thanks and appreciation to the following individuals: Dr. Rita E. Freed, Curator of Ancient Egyptian, Nubian, and Near Eastern Art, Museum of Fine Arts, Boston, permitted the reproduction of the photographs in fig. 4.10 taken during the Harvard University-Boston Museum of Fine Arts Expedition (all photographs from the expedition are hereafter referred to as Exp. Ph.). Dr. Anna Maria Donadoni Roveri, Soprintendente delle Antichità Egizie at the Museo Egizio, most kindly provided the photographs of the Turin objects reproduced as figs. 4.6, 4.9, and 4.15 in the present article, as well as information concerning them. Dr. James P. Allen and Professor Janet H. Johnson both shared their knowledge with me in a number of particulars, and the latter very agreeably looked up a number of words on my behalf in the files of the Chicago Demotic Dictionary Project. Thanks are also due Jordi Ensign for the drawing of the *ḥ3-ḫt-* and *ḏsr*-determinatives from the furniture list of Ny-hetep-khnum (15) reproduced in table 4.1. I am also indebted to my wife, Del Nord, and an old colleague and friend, Elizabeth Sherman, for editing and improving the manuscript. Finally, Dr. Peter Der Manuelian spent long hours scanning the numerous figures that accompany this article, formatting fig. 4.11 in particular, and compiling table 4.1.

1. Brovarski 1996. A third part, "CG 20506 and the Ancient Egyptian Word for 'Bed Canopy,'" is scheduled to appear in the volume for Abdel Aziz Sadek (part three) (Brovarski, forthcoming).

2. Several individuals provided access to unpublished lists, and their contributions are acknowledged below. The sources for both parts of the article are the same; see Brovarski 1996, pp. 127–29. The furniture lists are as follows: (1) Satba, niche stone, Helwan tomb no. 1241 H 9, end of the Second Dynasty (Saad 1947, p. 41, no. 20, pl. 24); (2) Ny-djefanesut, niche stone, in Hannover, No. 1935, 200, 46, first half of the Third Dynasty (Kestner Museum 1958, cat. no. 12); (3) Kha-bau-sokar, stone-lined niche from Saqqara, in Cairo, CG 1385, time of Djoser (Murray 1905, pl. 1); (4) Hathor-nefer-hetep, wife of Kha-bau-sokar, stone-lined niche from Saqqara, in Cairo, CG 1386–1388, time of Djoser (Murray 1905, pl. 2); (5) Sisi, niche stone, Helwan tomb no. D. H 6, late Third Dynasty (Saad 1947, pp. 46–48, no. 23, pl. 27); (6) Nedji, wooden panel of offering niche from Saqqara, early Fourth Dynasty (Badawi 1940, pp. 495–501, pl. 46); (7) Irensen, panel of offering niche or of false door from Saqqara, in Cairo, CG 1393, early Fourth Dynasty (Borchardt 1937, p. 52, pl. 13); (8) Metjen, panel of false door of stone-lined cruciform chapel from Saqqara, Berlin 1105 G, time of Khufu (Lepsius 1842–45, pl. 3; Königlichen Museen zu Berlin 1913, p. 81); (9) Rahotep, false door panel from Medum, in London, BM 1242, time of Khufu (Petrie 1892, pl. 13; James 1961, pl. 1 [2]); (10) Rahotep, left side of false door recess from Medum, in London, BM 1277, time of Khufu (Petrie 1892, pl. 13; James 1961, pl. 3 [3]); (11) Seshatsekhentiu, slab stela, Giza tomb G 2120, in

Gold of Praise: Studies on Ancient Egypt in Honor of Edward F. Wente
Edited by Emily Teeter and John A. Larson
Studies in Ancient Oriental Civilization 58
Chicago: Oriental Institute, 1999

It probably serves to reiterate that the investigation in this article of terms for furniture and their applications in periods later than the Old Kingdom is limited in scope and mainly included for purposes of comparison. See table 4.1, at the end of this article, for the determinatives of words for boxes and chests that occur in furniture lists referred to in the ensuing discussion.

Terms for furniture occur in furniture lists, sporadically in Old Kingdom tomb reliefs, in *frises d'objets* on sides of burial chambers or coffins from the Sixth to Eighth Dynasties, and in different kinds of documents, including the Pyramid Texts and the Abusir Papyri. In this article the terms for furniture are discussed first if they occur in furniture lists, second if in a tomb relief, third if in a burial chamber, and fourth if in papyri.

TERMS FOR FURNITURE TYPES DISCUSSED[3]

Furniture in Furniture Lists

aa.	*ꜥfḏt*	Small- or medium-sized rectangular box
bb.	*(m)ẖtm(t)*	Storage box or hamper
cc.	*hn(w)*	Box or chest
dd.	*ḥꜣ-ẖt*	Plain wooden box
ee.	*ẖr(t)-ꜥ*	Document case
ff.	*tnn*	Round-topped box
gg.	*ṯzt*	Chest-on-legs(?)
hh.	*dbn*	Round-topped box or coffret
ii.	*ḏsr(w)*	Coffret, ornamental casket

Furniture in Tomb Reliefs

jj.	*iṯnt*	Type of chest
kk.	*sṯpt*	Type of chest

Furniture in Burial Chambers

ll.	*pr-wꜥb*	Shrine-shaped box(?)
mm.	*sry*	Shrine-shaped chest(?)
nn.	*ḏḥꜣ*	Chest with vaulted lid(?)

Furniture in Abusir Papyri

oo.	*ḏbꜣw*	Type of box or chest
pp.	*šꜥt(?)*	Type of box or chest

Boston, MFA 06.1894, time of Khufu (Leprohon 1985, pp. 59–62); (12) Anonymous, slab stela, Giza, Junker Mastaba II n = G 4260, time of Khufu (Junker 1929, pp. 181–91, fig. 36, pl. 29a); (13) Anonymous, slab stela, Giza, Junker Mastaba VII nn = G 4770, time of Shepseskaf (Junker 1929, pp. 229–31, fig. 53, pl. 37b); (14) Izi, fragment of wall relief from Saqqara, in Copenhagen, AEIN 672, end Fourth Dynasty (Mogensen 1930, p. 90, pl. 93); (15) Ny-hetep-Khnum, right aperture of false door, Giza, Western Field, end Fourth Dynasty (Abu-Bakr 1953, fig. 10); (16) Merib, false door panel, Giza tomb G 2100-I-annexe, Berlin 1107 G, time of Shepseskaf-Userkaf (Lepsius 1842–45, pl. 19 = Königlichen Museen zu Berlin 1913, p. 99); (17) Setju, slab stela, intrusive in Giza tomb G 2353 B, in Boston, MFA 13.4341, end Fourth Dynasty or early Fifth Dynasty (Simpson 1980, p. 35, pl. 61a, fig. 47; Leprohon 1985, pp. 93–96); (18) Painted inventory list from "Covington's Tomb," Giza, South Field(?), end Fourth Dynasty or early Fifth Dynasty (Brovarski 1996, fig. 1); (19) Senenu, left aperture of false door, Giza, West Field, Abu Bakr excavation for University of Alexandria (1953), end Fourth Dynasty or early Fifth Dynasty (unpublished; see PM 3/1, p. 48); (20) Senenu, right aperture of false door, end Fourth Dynasty or early Fifth Dynasty (unpublished; see PM 3/1, p. 48); (21) Seshemnefer I, inventory list on east wall of chapel, Giza tomb G 4940, Userkaf-Neferirkare (Lepsius 1842–45, pl. 28); (22) Kapunesut Kai, inventory list on south wall of chapel, Giza, West Field, early to middle Fifth Dynasty (unpublished; discovered by Dr. Zahi Hawass in 1992; Dr. Hawass graciously permitted me to utilize the items herein); and (23) Kayemankh, Giza, West Field, G 4561; painted "Gerätekammer" on walls of burial chamber, Sixth Dynasty (Junker 1940, pp. 70–71, pl. 9). Henry G. Fischer very kindly called the lists of Senenu to my attention and placed his 1959 hand copies at my disposal.

3. In the ensuing discussion single, lowercase letters in parentheses are cross-references to items of furniture discussed in the first part of this article (Brovarski 1996): (a) *ꜣtt* "bed"; (b) *wrs* "headrest"; (c) *wṯz(t)* "carrying chair"; (d) *mꜥ* "footbath"; (e) *ḫꜣwt* "circular table"; (f) *ḫnd(w)* "bentwood chair, stool"; (g) *st-(n)-ẖt* "bed of wood"; (h) *st ḥms* "seat"; (i) *sꜣḥ* "table"; (j) *gs(ꜣw)t* "two-legged bed or backrest"; (k) *nḏrwt* "bedframe"; and (l) *ḥwdt* "palanquin." Double lowercase letters refer to the boxes and chests discussed herein.

FURNITURE IN FURNITURE LISTS

aa. *ꜥfḏt* "rectangular box": Murray 1905, p. 35; "tablette": Weill 1908, p. 253; "coffre": Montet 1925, p. 309; "Kasten": *Wb.* 1.183:15–17

In her furniture list (4), Hathor-nefer-hetep's *ꜥfḏt* is said to be made of *sꜣḏ*-wood. The word is determined by a rectangle bordered by double lines, which possibly represent the timber framework of the box or alternately a veneer or trim of a different kind of wood. The same sign serves as the determinative of *ḥꜣ-ḫt* (dd) in the list of Kapunesut Kai (22). Since certain of the determinatives in Hathor-nefer-hetep's list are drawn in elevation and others in plan,[4] it is not clear whether the determinative presents a top or a side view.

In the tomb of Ti, a carpenter is shown drilling a hole in the center of the lid of a small, plain, flat-lidded rectangular box supported on a pair of battens, presumably for the addition of a button handle (fig. 4.1a).[5] The legend above reads *hi͗t ꜥfḏt i͗n fnḫ* "drilling an *ꜥfḏt* by the carpenter" (Montet 1925, p. 304). Further along in the same register two carpenters are seen sanding a *h*[*nw*]-chest that differs from the *ꜥfḏt* only in that it is nearly three times as long (fig. 4.3a).

On the basis of the Ti scene, Montet (1925, p. 309) concludes that small boxes during the Old Kingdom were designated *ꜥfḏt* and large boxes *hn*(*w*). In the Abusir Papyri, both *ꜥfḏt*-boxes and *hn*(*w*)-boxes or chests contain incense or objects used in the daily cult, whereas only the latter were used for the storage of more bulky vases, papyrus, food, and especially cloth. Posener-Kriéger (1976, p. 185) thinks the discrepancy in usage confirms Montet's observation concerning the relative sizes of the two kinds of containers, at the same time noting that *hn*(*w*)-boxes may also be small in size. The definitive passage seems to be one in which three *ꜥfḏt*-boxes filled with incense are placed inside a *hn*(*w*)-box (Posener-Kriéger and de Cenival 1968, pl. 52A, 3c; Posener-Kriéger 1976, p. 374). In most cases the determinative of the *ꜥfḏt*-boxes in the Abusir Papyri is the same sign that serves to determine *hn*(*w*)-boxes or chests in these documents: a rectangular box supported on battens with or without a small handle in the center of the lid (Posener-Kriéger and de Cenival 1968, pls. 14A, 1; 49C, D; 52A, 3c). However, in one place (ibid., pl. 6A, d), *ꜥfḏt* is determined by a hieratic sign that seems to represent a box with taller legs. It is not entirely certain what value should be attached to the latter sign since no other determinative or depiction of an *ꜥfḏt*-box appears to share this feature.

Apart from the papyri, it is worthwhile calling attention to the *ꜥfḏt ḫry ꜥntyw ḫry mrḥt* "box containing myrrh and unguent," which was among the gifts presented to Sabni I of Aswan by the king upon his return from Wawat with the body of his deceased father Mekhu (*Urk.* 1, p. 139.12–13). Presumably, the unguent was contained in cosmetic jars (see Lepsius 1842–45, pl. 22b; Reisner-Smith 1955, p. 42, fig. 38, pl. 34a–c; Simpson 1978, fig.

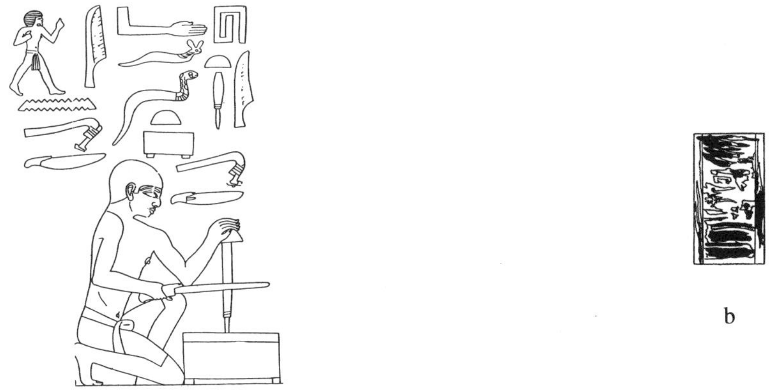

a

b

Figure 4.1. *ꜥfḏt*-boxes, after (*a*)Wild 1966, pl. 174, and (*b*) Jéquier 1922, fig. 47 = Maspero 1885, pl. 2

4. The determinatives of *hnw*, *tnn*, *dbn*, and *ḏsrw* are all clearly drawn in profile, and *ḫrt-ꜥ* probably in plan. As with *ꜥfḏt*, it is not certain which aspect of *ṯzt* is shown.

5. Killen (1994, p. 11) suggests that a small mushroom-shaped handle would have been inserted into the hole. All of the actual boxes of Old Kingdom date illustrated or referred to in the present article have a button handle in the middle of the lid. Killen (1994, p. 20, fig. 44D) mistakes the papyriform handle of an adjacent mirror for a mushroom-shaped handle at the front of a shrine-shaped box depicted in a burial chamber of the end of the Sixth Dynasty or later from South Saqqara (Jéquier 1929, fig. 50) and interprets this as the first occurrence of such a handle on a box. The "curtain box" of Queen Hetepheres I has been restored with a mushroom-

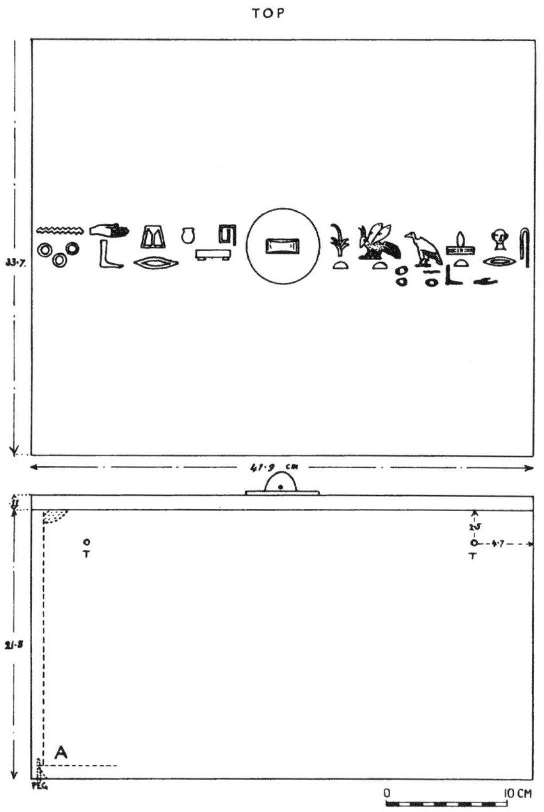

Figure 4.2. Bracelet Box of Queen Hetepheres I, after Reisner-Smith 1955, pp. 43–44, fig. 44

30, pl. 18). Once again it is likely that the box was a smallish one. The determinative in Sabni's inscription is a low, rectangular box with four battens or legs and a handle in the center of the lid. The box was made of *ssḏm*-wood.[6]

The evidence so far presented seems to suggest that *ʿfḏt* in the Old Kingdom was a term for a small, rectangular wooden box, wider than tall, and equipped with battens. In contrast to the examples cited above, the main dimension of the rectangular *ʿfḏt*-box depicted on one side of a stone-built burial chamber of late Old Kingdom date is vertical (fig. 4.1b). Though evidently made of imported ebony wood, this box is otherwise completely plain and lacks battens.

By the Middle Kingdom, *ʿfḏt* is often spelled *ʿfdt* (*CT* 1, p. 160a; *CT* 3, p. 76 l; *CT* 4, p. 54d; *CT* 6, pp. 408–09). From a series of Coffin Text spells it seems likely that *ʿfḏt* / *ʿfdt* designated the small rectangular chest seen on the forward deck of contemporaneous wooden model solar ships (Borghouts 1973/74, pp. 358–64). In Coffin Text Spell 695 an *ʿfdt ẖrt ʿ* contains a document, perhaps the credentials the deceased had to present to the great god in the next world (Wilson 1954, p. 254). The hieratic determinative of *ʿfdt* in all these instances is again a small, wide rectangular box with two pairs of battens or legs and a button handle in the center of the lid.

ʿfdt is the usual writing of the term in the ostraca of Ramesside date from Deir el-Medina (Janssen 1975, p. 197). In regard to the ostraca, Janssen (1975, p. 197) notes that thirty-one silver *ʿfdt* in P. Harris I, 13b, line 11, weigh only ca. 215 gr, so that they must have been very small. He also makes the observation that (the material of ?) the stone *ʿfdt* of P. Westcar 9, line 4, again points to smaller dimensions. The prices of the *ʿfdt*-boxes appear to confirm these suggestions as to size since they never exceed three *deben* (Janssen 1975, p. 197). In one ostracon an *ʿfdt* is said to contain papyri, which, as in the case of the *ʿfdt ẖrt ʿ* already referred to, probably points to a small- or medium-size container (Janssen 1975, p. 197).

The term survives into Ptolemaic and Roman period Demotic as *ʿft* (Erichsen 1954, p. 60).

---

shaped handle in the center of the lid, even though the original was almost completely decayed (Reisner and Smith 1955, p. 26, figs. 28–29, pls. 7, 11–13).

6. For this variety of wood, see, for example, Montet 1925, p. 307; Gardiner 1973, p. 483 (M29); Edel 1955, §60.

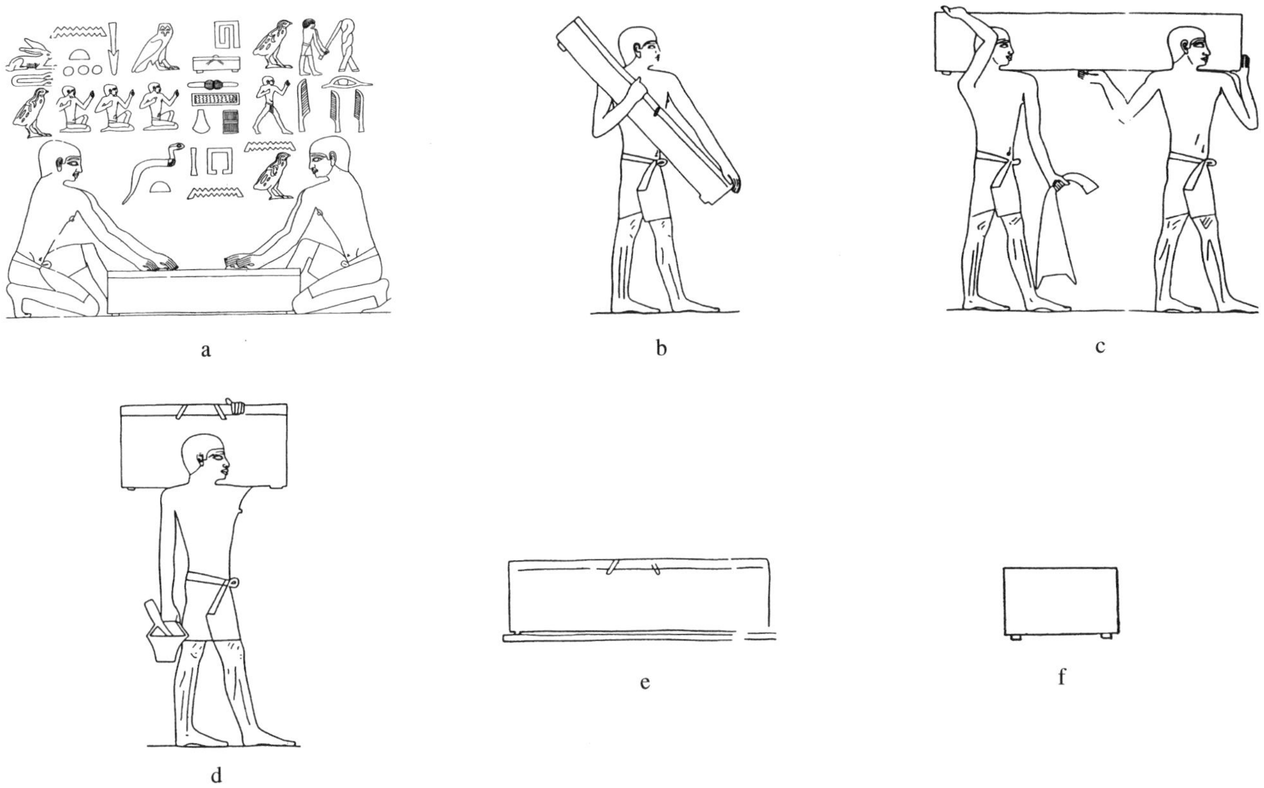

Figure 4.3. Plain *hn*(*w*)-boxes with Battens, after (*a*) Wild 1966, pl. 174; (*b*) Zeigler 1993, p. 119; (*c*) Zeigler 1993, p. 118; (*d*) Zeigler 1993, p. 168; (*e*) Zeigler 1993, p. 119; and (*f*) Jéquier 1921a, fig. 649 = Chassinat-Palanque 1911, pl. 20 (1)

bb. *mḫtm*(*t*) "Truhe": Junker 1940, p. 71; "closed" or "sealed receptacle": Gardiner 1955, p. 13

As Gardiner (1955, p. 13) observes, the word from its etymology clearly signifies a "closed" or "sealed receptacle." *Mḫtmt* is an example of a noun (*nomina instrumenti*) formed by a prefixed *m* from the triliteral verb *ḫtm*.[7] In the list in the burial chamber of Kayemankh (23), the determinative is the hieratic version of a rectangular box with a pair of battens and a small handle. In the furniture list of Seshemnefer [I] (21), on the other hand, the word is determined by a simple rectangle without detail. If any trust is to be placed in the relative size of the determinatives in the latter list, a *mḫtmt* was larger than a *ḥꜣ-ḫt*-box (dd). Seshemnefer's *mḫtmt* was made of ordinary wood (*ḫt*).

A variant *ḫtmt*, without the prefixed *m*, but presumably possessing the same meaning, occurs in the Abusir Papyri.[8] In one place a *ḫtmt* is mentioned together with a basin (*š*) and instruments utilized for the twice daily *qbḥw*-libation for the deceased king (Posener-Kriéger and de Cenival 1968, pl. 6A, f; Posener-Kriéger 1976, pp. 19–20, 185). In another fragment, what must have been a fairly good-sized *ḫtmt* apparently contained two jars and their contents, two baskets and a smaller *ḫtmt* of incense (*snṯr*), as well as thirty loaves of bread (Posener-Kriéger and de Cenival 1968, pl. 51, 2a; Posener-Kriéger 1976, p. 370). In two related accounts, two *ḫtmt* are confided to the laundrymen of Neferirkare's temple (Posener-Kriéger and de Cenival 1968, pl. 52A, 3a, c; Posener-Kriéger 1976, p. 372). In one of these, a large and a small *ḫtmt* are brought from the king's sun temple and turned over to a laundryman (Posener-Kriéger and de Cenival 1968, pl. 52A, 3a; Posener-Kriéger 1976, pp. 372–73). The determinative of *ḫtmt* in all these occurrences is once again the hieratic version of the rectangular box supported on a pair of battens and with or without a small handle. What was probably yet another example of a *ḫtmt*-box (a determinative is lacking), contained eight alabaster cylinder jars (of unguent?). It was of ebony (*Urk.* 1, p. 137.1).

7. Such formations are discussed by Grapow 1914; Jéquier 1921b, pp. 145–54; Gardiner 1973, p. 218, n. 1; Edel 1964, §§253–55.

8. Compare, for example, the words *ʿnḫt* and *mʿnḫt* (*Wb.* 1.206; 2.47:10–11); *ʿnḏt* and *mʿnḏt* (*Wb.* 2.48:1–8); and *ʿḥʿt* and *mʿḥʿt* (*Wb.* 1.221; 2.49:8–14).

a b

Figure 4.4. (*a*) *Hn*(*w*)-box, after Simpson 1978, fig. 30, and (*b*) Chest-on-legs, after Davies 1902a, pl. 14; compare Killen 1994, p. 13

In the Thirteenth Dynasty Ramesseum Dramatic Papyrus (Gardiner 1955, pl. 2 [35]), the determinative of *mḫtmt* bears a close resemblance to a type of wickerwork box or hamper that is very commonly represented in Old Kingdom wall reliefs .[9] As a hieroglyphic sign the hamper also serves as a determinative of Old Kingdom funerary feasts, in particular *Ḏḥwtt, Wꜣg,* and *Sꜣḏ*.[10] In the latter capacity, it appears to have functioned as a container for provisions (Jéquier 1910, pp. 89–94). It is possible that the determinative in the Ramesseum Dramatic Papyrus holds a clue to the sort of receptacle that was intended by that designation in the Old Kingdom. The only obstacle to the identification seems to be posed by the form of the determinatives in the furniture lists of Seshemnefer I and Kayemankh and, whereas the latter sign might be understood as a generic determinative as a result of the relatively late date of the list, it is not possible to discount entirely the form of the sign in Seshemnefer's list, which is that of a plain rectangular box.

From P. Westcar 12, line 5, it emerges that another *ḫtm*(*t*) was a container large enough to contain a grain sack.[11] It may have been of rather rough construction, since it was used for the storage of commodities (cf. Janssen 1975, p. 208). The *ḫtm*(*t*) in question was closed with leather straps (*i͗stnw m dḥrw*). Indeed, the passage suggests that the word refers to a type of container without a specific locking mechanism that had of necessity to be tied with straps or ropes. It is unclear if this definition should be applied to other (*m*)*ḫtm*(*t*).

Everything considered, it seems that (*m*)*ḫmt* was a term used for both good-sized wooden storage boxes of plain, utilitarian construction and for wicker work hampers, likewise utilized for storage.

cc. *hn*(*w*) "box": Griffith 1892, p. 38; "box": Murray 1905, p. 35; "coffre": Weill 1908, p. 253; "coffret": Jéquier 1921a, pp. 131, 247; "Kasten": *Wb.* 2.491:9–15

The gold-covered bracelet box of Queen Hetepheres I is inscribed on the lid (fig. 4.2): *hnw hr dbn* "box containing bracelets" (Reisner-Smith 1955, pp. 43–44, fig. 44, pls. 36a–b, 37–38). The box measures 41.9 cm long by 33.7 cm wide, and the height with the lid is 21.8 cm. It is covered inside and out with horizontally ribbed sheets of gold, bordered with a mat pattern (except for the bottom where there is only one plain sheet of gold). In the center of the lid is a small ivory button handle with a pierced semicircular projection for lifting it. In the inscription on the lid *hnw* is determined by a low rectangular box with a pair of battens, even though the box itself seemingly lacks battens.

The determinatives of *hn*(*w*) in the early lists show four forms:

i. Completely plain rectangular box (2[?], 5, 7, and 13)
ii. Rectangular box with button handle (10)
iii. Rectangular box with pair of battens, as on Queen Hetepheres' bracelet box (12)
iv. Rectangular box with small handle on lid and pair of battens (4 and 11)[12]

9. For example, Lepsius 1842–45, pl. 25; Mariette 1889, p. 93; Bissing 1905a, pl. 4 [11b]; Junker 1934, fig. 27; Hassan 1932, pl. 6B, CG 1558, 1566, 1696; Dunham and Simpson 1974, fig. 3a–b. A box of this shape is carried on the shoulder of a barber and was presumably used to store the tools of his trade; see Lepsius 1842–45, pl. 89c; for *ẖꜥḳw*, see *Wb.* 3.365:3–4; Montet 1931, pp. 178–89. The example reproduced here is from Jéquier 1910, fig. 21 (= CG 169b).

10. Jéquier 1910, pp. 91–92. Jéquier (1910, p. 90) notes that the sign also appears as a determinative of the word *ḥnkt* "offering, donation" in PT 150, 502.

11. Erman 1890. The word is determined by the house-sign, but is so translated by *Wb.* 3.352:5. For the disappearance of the final *t*, see Posener-Kriéger 1976, p. 20, n. 51; Edel 1955, §113.

12. The semicircular element in the center of the lid presumably represents the button handle preserved on actual boxes; see, for example, those illustrated in figs. 4.2 and 4.10. Compare the treatment of the pattern on the foot of the vase reproduced in Schäfer 1974, fig. 43e. The semicircular element in the center of the lid of the cavetto-corniced box in fig. 4.7d probably also represents a button handle. Alternatively, it might represent the type of button handle on Queen Hetepheres' box with the projecting vertical element.

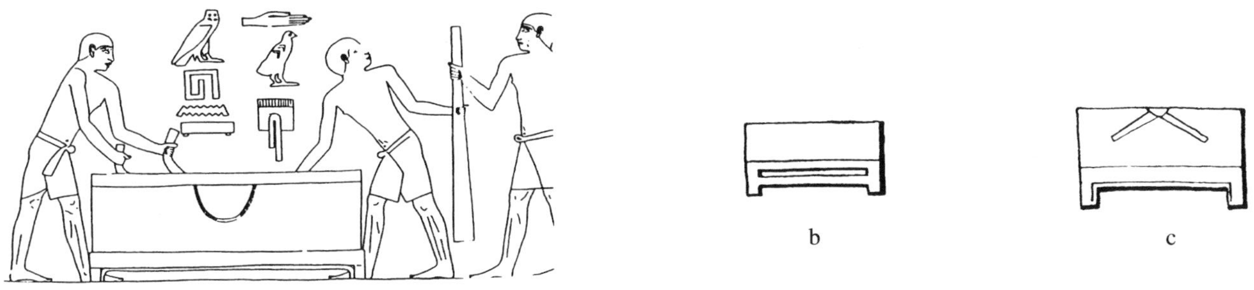

a

Figure 4.5. Flat-lidded *hn*(*w*)-boxes and Chests-on-frames, after (*a*) Zeigler 1993; (*b*) Bissing 1905a, pl. 5; and (*c*) Bissing 1905a, pl. 5

In the list of Hathor-nefer-hetep (4), form iv appears after *hnw* only, while the other boxes and chests have distinctive determinatives of their own. In the other early lists, although form i also functions as the determinatives of *ḥꜣ-ḫt* (hh) and *ḏsr*(*w*) (ii) boxes, forms ii–iv appear nearly exclusively as determinatives of *hn*(*w*).[13] Hence, the surviving evidence, slim as it may be, may indicate that forms ii–iv originally appertained to *hn*(*w*), only later becoming the generic determinative for all kinds of boxes and chests. By the end of the Fifth Dynasty, for example, in the Abusir Papyri, besides determining *hn*(*w*),[14] the hieratic equivalent of form iii and form iv accompanies *ꜥfḏt* (aa), (*m*)*ḫtmṯ* (bb), *šꜥt* (pp), and *ḏbꜣw* (oo) boxes. Similarly in the Pyramid Texts, in addition to *hn*(*w*), form iv determines the epithet *ṯzti͗* (see under gg, below) and a term for coffin, [*ḏr*]*wt*.[15] Whereas forms iii and iv seem perfectly suitable for *ꜥfḏt*-boxes (aa), which appear by and large to have been smaller versions of *hn*(*w*)-boxes, due to the limited nature of the evidence, it is not clear to what extent they functioned as generic, as opposed to specific, determinatives for (*m*)*ḫtm*(*t*) (bb), *šꜥt* (pp), *ṯzt* (gg), *ḏbꜣw* (oo), and [*ḏr*]*wt*. At any rate, in the discussions of boxes and chests in the present article, a more specific determinative is given greater weight than what appear to be more general signs.

Old Kingdom wall reliefs and paintings often depict *hn*(*w*)-boxes and chests on a larger scale than in the furniture lists and in greater detail. They show that the term *hn*(*w*) continued to denote rectangular boxes or chests of simple design and varying dimensions which were usually supported on battens (fig. 4.3a–e).[16]

In the tomb of Khufukhaf I, on the other hand, the word *hnw* designates a medium-size box (human figures provide the scale) of a different construction, that is, one with short legs that are evidently prolongations of the stiles or sideposts (fig. 4.4a).[17] The joints of the legs of this box are reinforced with bentwood braces, and in the center of the lid is a cord loop tie through which a short stick is passed. Similarly, a large chest labeled *hn*(*w*) in the Sixth Dynasty tomb of Ibi at Deir el-Gebrawi has relatively tall legs that also function as the stiles of the construction (fig. 4.4b).[18]

A *hn*(*w*)-box depicted in the Louvre mastaba of Akhethotep shows yet another form — a goodly sized clothing chest with a flat lid — which sits on a separately manufactured stand made to look like a low table (fig. 4.5a).[19] An actual chest-on-frame[20] of this type was found by Schiaparelli in the "Tomb of the Unknown Owners" at Gebelein (fig. 4.6).[21] The rectangular Gebelein chest (30.0 × 55.5 × 31.0 cm) also rests on a table-like framework with short legs, the joints at the front and back being reinforced with bentwood braces, while flush stretchers connect the side legs (Turin suppl. 13968: see Egyptian Museum of Turin 1987, pp. 199–200, 258;

13. The hieratic version of form iv also appears after *mḫtmt* in the latest of the furniture lists in the burial chamber of Kayemankh (23).
14. See Posener-Kriéger and de Cenival 1968, pls. 7A, h; 21, o; 22A, j; 22D; 25, e; 26f; 27C; 27D; 28G; 34, 1, c; 52A, 3c; 59C; 73E; 92A, a 2.
15. Sethe 1960a, Pyr. 184b; 491a; Sethe 1960b, Pyr. 2009a. On *ḏrwt*, see *Wb.* 5.601:3; Faulkner 1962, p. 324.
16. Captions at rear of file of porters on the left embrasure of entrance to the offering room of Akhethotep and at head of file on the south wall appear to identify boxes and chests alike as *hn*(*w*), even though term is written with ideogram of small, rectangular, flat-lidded box supported on two battens; see Zeigler 1993, pp. 118, 169; and fig. 4.3b–d herein. The former caption also seems to apply to a *dbn*-chest (fig. 4.14b). As Killen (1994, p. 11) notes, the box illustrated in fig. 4.3a is similar in its proportions to the curtain box of Queen Hetepheres I, for which see n. 5 above.
17. Simpson 1978, fig. 30 (*hnw ḫr snṯr*).
18. Compare Killen 1994, p. 13.
19. Zeigler 1993, p. 116 (*dw sšr m hn*(*w*)). The chest appears to have a top border of a different color, similar to the borders of the chest in Turin shown in fig. 4.6.
20. For the term chest-on-frame for an item of furniture set on a stand, see, for example, Fairbanks and Bates 1981, p. 52.
21. Turin suppl. 13968: see Egyptian Museum of Turin 1987, p. 137, wherein Schiaparelli dates the tomb to the second half of the Fifth Dynasty.

Figure 4.6. Chest-on-frame from Gebelein, Turin Suppl. 13968. Egyptian Museum of Turin 1987, p. 137

Donadoni Roveri et al. 1994, fig. 33). The top of the lid has a flat button handle in the center and two battens inside to hold the lid in place. The bottoms and borders of the chest are of a darker wood than the rest. When found, the chest contained various linen textiles and three lists of textiles in black ink were inscribed on the inside of the lid (Donadoni Roveri et al. 1994, p. 208). The table-like stand, reinforced by bentwood supports or simple stretchers, appears regularly in representations of *hn*(*w*)-boxes or chests hereafter (figs. 4.5a–c, 4.7b–f, 4.9, 4.11a–b, d).

From the end of the Fourth Dynasty and in the early Fifth Dynasty, the tops of many flat-lidded *hn*(*w*)-boxes and chests in relief show a cavetto cornice (only rarely ribbed) and torus molding (fig. 4.7a–f).[22] The cornice projects beyond the sides of the box. Although such boxes are generally set on low legs or on a table-like support, cavetto-corniced boxes without legs are sometimes represented (fig. 4.8a–c). Like the simple *hn*(*w*)-chests already examined, cavetto-corniced boxes or chests-on-frames occur in a variety of shapes and sizes (figs. 4.7a–f, 4.11a–b, d). Smaller boxes are sometimes more elaborate in design with superimposed pairs of bentwood stretchers (fig. 4.7e–f). Killen (1994, p. 19) points to an example in the mastaba of Khentika whose feet appear to have been shod with protective metal shoes (James 1953, pl. 34).

At least two types of cavetto-corniced chests are represented by actual examples. A small, square wooden box-on-frame (28.2 × 17.5 cm) in Turin comes once again from the "Tomb of the Unknown Owners" at Gebelein (fig. 4.9) (Turin suppl. 13985: see Donadoni Roveri et al. 1994, p. 137). Two pairs of legs are strengthened by curved braces, the others by straight rails or stretchers (not visible in the photograph).[23] The body and lid are painted white and the base red. The lid, recessed into the top of the box, is not visible when the

22. The earliest examples in relief are probably Dunham and Simpson 1974, fig. 5, pl. 5b; and Borchardt 1913, pls. 59–61 (= fig. 4.8b); see *LÄ* 4 "Möbel," col. 182; Killen 1994, p. 17. Only fig. 4.7d is expressly labeled (*hnw ẖr*(*y*) *snṯr*), but compare fig. 4.7c with Firth and Gunn 1926, 1, p. 97; 2, pl. 6D (*hn*(*w*) *n sštꜣ*).

23. One of the stretchers is missing, the other looks to be damaged by white ants.

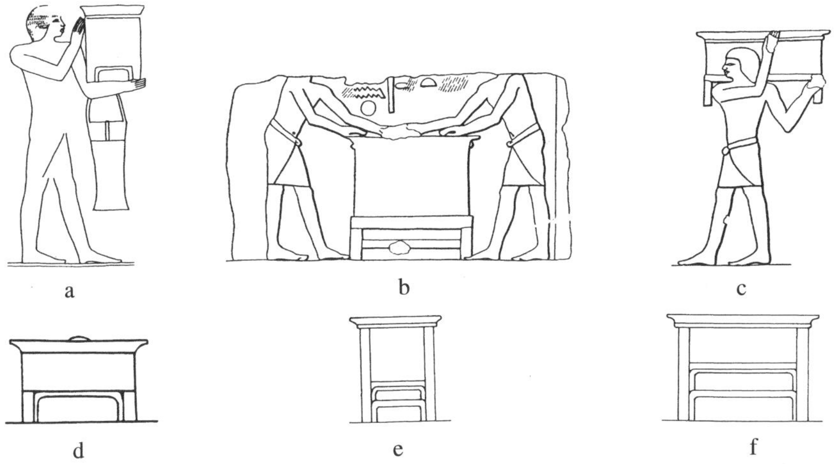

Figure 4.7. Cavetto-corniced *hn*(*w*)-boxes and chests, after (*a*) Badawy 1978, fig. 34; (*b*) Macramallah 1935, pl. 10 C; (*c*) Macramallah 1935, pl. 10 B; (*d*) Simpson 1976, fig. 24; (*e*) Baker 1966, fig. 55 = Sakkarah Expedition 1938a, pls. 94–95; and (*f*) Baker 1966, fig. 55

chest is viewed straight on. In the center of the lid is a flat button handle. Two essentially identical boxes from Nagʿ-ed-Deir tombs N 94[24] and N 4183[25] date to the end of the Sixth Dynasty or later.

A rectangular chest on a taller frame also derives from tomb N 4183 (fig. 4.10).[26] Like the two square boxes from Nagʿ-ed-Deir, it lacks the torus molding at the base of the cornice that appears in most Old Kingdom representations (see figs. 4.7a–f, 4.8a–c, 4.11a, b[?], d) and on the square box in Turin.[27] Stretchers hold the legs on the ends of the box in place, but the bentwood braces under the side legs appear to be more decorative than functional.

Sixth Dynasty cavetto-corniced chests sometimes have other than flat lids. A number of Mereruka's *hn*(*w*)-chests possess gable lids (fig. 4.11a),[28] while a chest in the tomb of his near contemporary, Ankhmahor Zezi, has a vaulted lid (fig. 4.11b). These large chests were fitted with retractable carrying-poles, as were plain, oblong chests (fig. 4.11c, e),[29] and flat-lidded cavetto-corniced *hn*(*w*)-chests (fig. 4.11d), the wood or metal(?) fittings of which are sometimes shown in considerable detail (fig. 4.11e).[30]

In the Abusir Papyri, the component members of one large *hn*(*w*)-chest are inventoried (Posener-Kriéger and de Cenival 1968, pl. 25e). They consisted of the body of the chest (*ḏs.f*), its lid (*ꜥꜣ*), its fastening (*ḏbꜣ*), and four carrying poles (? *ḫzꜣw*; see Posener-Kriéger 1976, pp. 191–94).

During the Old Kingdom, *hn*(*w*)-boxes or chests were utilized for the storage of a wide variety of commodities. Cloth was regularly kept in large *hn*(*w*)-chests.[31] Large- or medium-sized *hn*(*w*)-boxes or chests also

24. Reisner, *Naga-ed-Dêr Notebook* 1, p. 4; Exp. Ph. A 4478, 4481; C 4338–41, 8793–94. The contents consisted of a broken alabaster offering table and several small stone vessels suitable for unguents, including an alabaster jar (the cloth sealing tied around its mouth largely intact) similar to the two published in Jéquier 1929, fig. 95, left. Inside the coffin from this tomb were found twelve pleated dresses, on which see Riefstahl and Chapman 1970, pp. 244–58.

25. Reisner, *Naga-ed-Dêr Notebook* 3, pp. 92–93, 95; Exp. Ph. A 707; C 638. According to the Tomb Card for N 4183, reassembled by Caroline Nestmann Peck from the photographic record of the Harvard-Boston Expedition and now on deposit in the Museum of Fine Arts, the contents of the tomb, including this box, are now in the Phoebe Hearst Museum in Berkeley, California, LMA 6-2157/2164 and 2166(?). The present whereabouts of the box from N 94 (n. 27) and of the chest from N 4183 (n. 29) are unknown to the writer.

26. Exp. Ph. C 636, 8059–60. Among other objects, the chest contained a mirror, a cosmetic spoon, a small alabaster jar (like that described by Donadoni Roveri et al. 1994, p. 134, with cloth likewise intact), and four other stone vessels.

27. Note that the molding is also absent in the large cavetto-corniced chest from the late Sixth Dynasty tomb of Ibi at Deir el-Gebrâwi illustrated in fig. 4.17b.

28. For example, Sakkarah Expedition 1938a, pls. 70, 72, 74–76, 79, 98–99 (*hn*[*w*] *nw mnḫt*). The determinative in the label above the last example is a cavetto-corniced chest with flat lid. For what appear to be medium- and small-sized gable lid boxes, see James 1953, pl. 38.

29. Compare Borchardt 1913, pls. 59–60.

30. Compare Bissing 1911, pl. 36. See also the portable, gable-lidded chest from the tomb of Tutankhamun in Metropolitan Museum of Art 1976, cat. no. 7. For a discussion of the fittings in Old Kingdom portable chests, see Posener-Kriéger 1976, pp. 193–94.

31. For example, Firth and Gunn 1926, pl. 6; Borchardt 1913, pl. 59; Sakkarah Expedition 1938a, pls. 74–76, 98–99; Posener-Kriéger and de Cenival 1968, pl. 52A, 3c; Posener-Kriéger 1976, p. 373; Zeigler 1993, p. 116 (= fig. 4.5a).

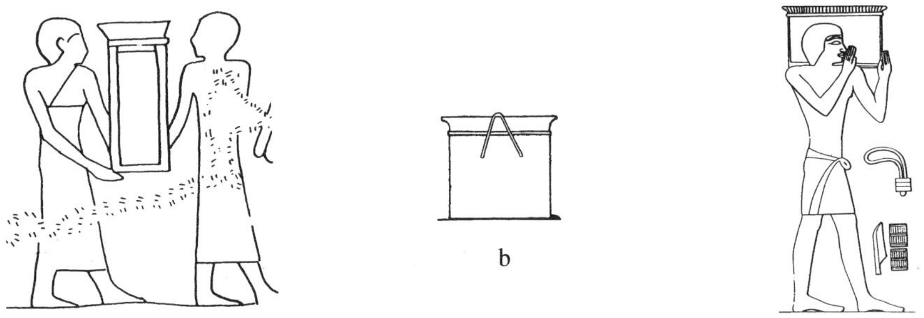

a b c

Figure 4.8. Cavetto-corniced Boxes without Legs, after (*a*) Dunham and Simpson 1974, fig. 8; (*b*) Borchardt 1913, pl. 60; and (*c*) Épron 1939, pl. 16

served for the storage of incense,[32] myrrh,[33] natron,[34] eyepaint,[35] perfumes and unguents,[36] *pḫrt*-medicaments,[37] sweets,[38] jewelry,[39] and, in at least one case, a scepter (Davies 1902a, pl. 14). Both the small square box and the rectangular chest from Nagᶜ-ed-Deir tomb N 4183 appear to have functioned as toilette boxes. In the pyramid temple of Neferirkare, a large *hn*(*w*)-chest held four smaller *hn*(*w*)-boxes that contained implements for the Opening of the Mouth ceremony (Posener-Kriéger and de Cenival 1968, pls. 20; 21, o; 22A, j, k; 22D; Posener-Kriéger 1976, p. 176). *Hn*(*w*)-chests also served for the safekeeping of documents (Sethe 1960a, Pyr. 491a; Posener-Kriéger and de Cenival 1968, pl. 73E, 92A, a 2; Posener-Kriéger 1976, pp. 176, 479), a usage well attested later on (*Wb.* 3.491:12).

On occasion, *hn*(*w*)-chests also appear to have served as measures of capacity. A medium-sized chest-on-frame in the tomb of Kagemni is thus labeled *hn*(*w*) *n ḫꜣt* "chest of measuring," and a much larger cavetto-corniced chest in the tomb of Mereruka (fig. 4.11d) is captioned *hn*(*w*) *n n* (sic) *ḫꜣt*.[40]

The Gebelein and Nagᶜ-ed-Deir chests-on-frames and the Gebelein box-on-frame, in addition to a flat button handle on the lid, have pairs of holes on opposite sides of the box for cords — a method of fastening known from Old Kingdom reliefs. On the clothing chest from the Louvre mastaba (fig. 4.5a), one of two loops of cord, which would probably have fitted around the button handle in the center of the lid and then been sealed with a lump of wet clay, hangs loose.[41] In a number of instances, what must be the sealing is shown (e.g., figs. 4.5c, 4.11e), although more commonly only the cord loop (fig. 4.8b) or its ends (fig. 4.3b, d–e) appear. The process of sealing the chests was shown in some detail in the pyramid temple of Sahure, but the scene is largely destroyed (Borchardt 1913, pl. 59). In the case of the determinative in one of Senenu's lists (19), two pairs of cord loops appear exceptionally to have been used to seal the box or chest, which is shown in plan.

The use of the term *hn*(*w*) for sarcophagi and coffins[42] suggests that *hn*(*w*)-chests could be very large indeed. Merenre sent Weni the Elder to fetch a sarcophagus — a *hn*(*w*) *n ʿnḫ* 'chest of life' — of black granite from the Ibhet granite quarry in Nubia (together with its lid) for his pyramid at Saqqara.[43] A short time later, the expedition leader Sabni I returned from Nubia with the body of his dead father enclosed in a wooden coffin (*hn*[*w*]) (*Urk.* 1, p. 137.1). Finally, two hieratic linen lists on the inside of the south end of a white-stuccoed

32. For example, Borchardt 1913, pl. 59; Sakkarah Expedition 1938b, pl. 118. The incense was probably in the form of bricks (*ḏbwt*); see Simpson 1978, fig. 30.
33. For example, Vandier 1964, pl. 13.
34. For example, Bissing 1905a, pl. 5 (= fig. 4.5c). Compare Posener-Kriéger 1976, pp. 196, 207; Posener-Kriéger and de Cenival 1968, pl. 22A j.
35. For example, Sakkarah Expedition 1938b, pl. 118.
36. For example, Macramallah 1935, pl. 10; Vandier 1964, pl. 13, fig. 160.
37. Martin 1979, pl. 29 (60). For *pḫrt*, see *Wb.* 1.549:10–11.
38. For example, Sakkarah Expedition 1938b, pl. 112 (*ḫt bnrt*). Compare Posener-Kriéger and de Cenival 1968, pl. 92A, a 2.
39. For example, Reisner-Smith 1955, pp. 43–44, fig. 44, pls. 36–38; Borchardt 1913, pl. 59; Kaplony 1976, no. 2, fig. on p. 22.
40. Bissing 1905a, pl. 5 (cf. fig. 4.5b, above); Sakkarah Expedition 1938b, pl. 112. The superfluous *n* in the latter caption presumably represents an instance of dittography. For *ḫꜣi* "measure (with a wooden bucket, etc.)," see *Wb.* 3.223:4–14; Montet 1925, pp. 229, 231, 321.
41. Compare James 1961, pl. 29 [2]. Killen (1994, p. 11) incorrectly, I believe, refers to these as "carrying ropes." However, elsewhere Killen (1994, p. 14) seems to realize that these "cord handles" could be pulled across the lid and tied in the center to hold it firmly in position.
42. See *Wb.* 2.491:16–17.
43. *Urk.* 1, p. 106.14–17. Merenre's sarcophagus is discussed by Donadoni Roveri 1969, p. 108 (A 14), and more recently by Wissa 1994.

Figure 4.9. Cavetto-corniced Box-on-frame, Turin Suppl. 13985. Courtesy of the Egyptian Museum, Turin

Figure 4.10. Rectangular Chest-on-frame from Nagʿ-ed-Deir Tomb N 4183. Harvard University-Boston Museum of Fine Arts Egyptian Expedition n.s. photograph C636. Courtesy, Museum of Fine Arts, Boston

wooden coffin of Old Kingdom date discovered by the Harvard-Boston Expedition in Nagʿ-ed-Deir tomb N 4183 are entitled *zš mḫw n hn(w) n ʿnḫ* "record of the contents(?) of the chest of life."[44]

Wooden coffins of Old to Middle Kingdom date regularly rest on two, three, or four battens,[45] and the coffin from tomb N 4183 also has four battens on its underside. The presence of battens at the bottom of coffins, which are essentially just very large plain *hn(w)*-chests, suggests that the small, square supports seen on the bottom of smaller, plain *hn(w)*-boxes or chests, like those in fig. 4.3a–f, are indeed battens rather than small legs.

At the end of the Sixth Dynasty, *hn(w)* is applied to several different kinds of boxes or chests in two separate burial chambers at South Saqqara (fig. 4.12a–d).[46] It is possible that by this time *hn(w)* had become associated with so many outwardly different types of boxes and chests that it had become the generic word for boxes or chests of every kind. The determinatives and in the captions above the boxes in fig. 4.12a, d clearly express only the general sense of the word and do not reflect the form of the specific type of box that they label. Indeed, in Middle Egyptian hieroglyphic, the latter sign serves regularly as the generic determinative for boxes (Gardiner 1973, p. 500, Q5), while the former sign also functions in that capacity, if only sporadically.[47]

Even if, by the end of the Old Kingdom, *hn(w)* had become the generic term for virtually any kind of box or chest, there is no question that it continued to be used to designate simple rectangular boxes and chests supported on battens. A *hn(w) n ḥsmn* "box of natron" is mentioned in funerary formulas in tombs and coffins of the end of the First Intermediate Period or early Middle Kingdom at Bersheh in Middle Egypt,[48] as in Spell 61 of the Coffin Texts which declares: "There is brought for you a box of natron by the *wʿb*-priest on his monthly duty" (*CT* 1, p. 259). The *hn(w) n ḥsmn* depicted beneath the offering table on the interior of a Tenth/Eleventh Dynasty coffin from Asyut is a small, flat-lidded rectangular box with two battens (fig. 4.3f).[49] A box of essentially identical form was found resting on the lower legs of a mummy in tomb N 4003 at Nagʿ-ed-Deir dated to the

44. Reisner, *Naga-ed-Dêr Notebook* 3, pp. 92–93, 95; Exp. Ph. C 8562–64. The determinative of *hn* is a simple rectangle without battens or handle. The coffin measured 128 × 54 × 51 inches and the body was wrapped in plain and "rucked" cloth, the former with a fringe.

45. For example, Junker 1944, pl. 12a; 8, fig. 40; Lacau 1904, pls. 1–7, 10, 12–13. One coffin from Akhmim exceptionally had six battens arranged in pairs (Lacau 1904, pl. 5 top).

46. In a burial chamber from the end of the Sixth Dynasty, a representation of a long coffer with a gabled lid set on a bed-like stand having the head of a lion at the two extremities, instead of one end like the example in fig. 4.12c, is termed *ḫsw-ḏdt*(?) (Daressy 1916, p. 202 [8]). Killen (1994, p. 20) points to a large flat-lidded cavetto-corniced box (in fact, a coffin or bier) equipped with carrying poles and bovine feet in the chapel of Tjefu at Saqqara (Hassan 1975, p. 108, fig. 56, pl. 84).

47. For example, Newberry 1893a, pl. 35.

48. For example, Griffith and Newberry 1894, p. 44, CG 28082, 28091, 28094.

49. Chassinat and Palanque 1911, p. 106, pls. 19–20. As is not infrequently the case, the line of the lid is omitted. The texts on the coffin include a *rꜣ n hn(w) n ḥsmn* "spell of a box of natron" (Chassinat and Palanque 1911, p. 107).

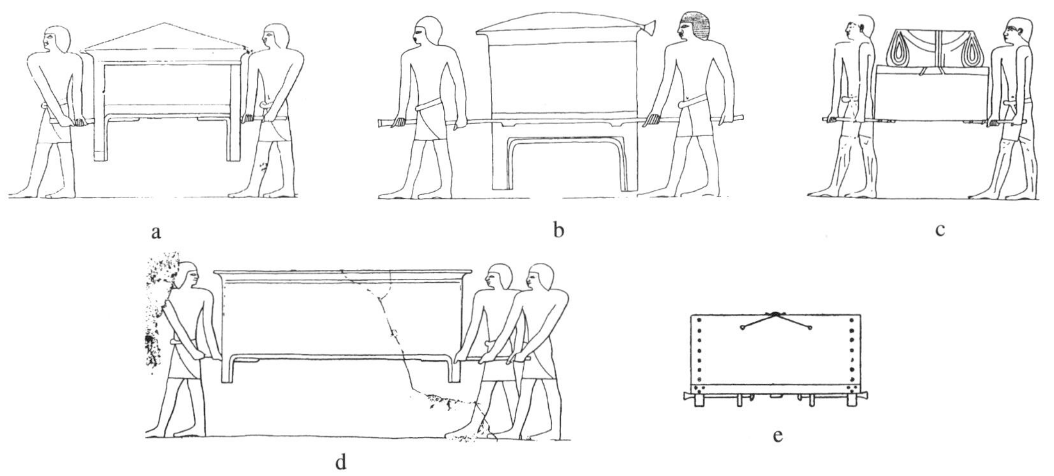

Figure 4.11. Large *hn*(*w*)-chests Equipped with Carrying Poles, after (*a*) Sakkara Expedition 1938a, pl. 79; (*b*) Badawy 1978, fig. 42; (*c*) Zeigler 1993, p. 118; (*d*) Sakkarah Expedition 1938b, pl. 112; and (*e*) Firth and Gunn 1926, p. 146, fig. 85

Ninth Dynasty. It is identified as *<hn*(*w*)> *pn n ḥsmn wʿb* "this box of pure natron" in the inscription on one of its sides.[50]

The same sort of simple box or chest (sometimes with knobs) appears in the Middle Kingdom title *zš n hn*(*w*) "scribe of the (document) chest."[51] From the Twelfth Dynasty on, however, the term is not infrequently also applied to a cavetto-corniced chest-on-legs with a shrine-shaped top.[52] In a scene of ceremonial purification in the tomb of Djehutyhotep at Bersheh (Newberry 1893b, p. 16, pl. 10), one shrine-shaped *hn*(*w*)-box contains natron and another clean clothes. The term *hn*(*w*) (*n*) *ʿnḫ* is also applied to wooden coffins in the Middle Kingdom (Lacau 1904, p. 82, CG 28031; Willems 1988, p. 46, n. 5).

During the New Kingdom *hn*(*w*) designates a variety of receptacles, including rectangular chests-on-frames and shrine-shaped boxes with and without legs.[53]

By analogy with *bnwt* > *bri͗*, Černý (1945, p. 39) thinks Late Period Egyptian *hr* might be the same as *hn*(*w*). Although this may be so, the radical *n* continues to appear in Graeco-Roman period hieroglyphic texts and in both Demotic *hn* and Coptic **ϩⲏⲛⲉ**.[54]

dd. *ḥꜣ-ḫt* "Dossier": Weill 1908, p. 253; "back(?) of wood": Murray 1905, p. 34; "Kasten aus Holz": *Wb.* 3.12:18

After *ḏsrw* (ii), *ḥꜣ-ḫt* is the most common box or chest in the furniture lists. Except for one questionable occurrence in a broken context in the Abusir archive (Posener-Kriéger and de Cenival 1968, pl. 71C; Posener-Kriéger 1976, p. 161), this term is apparently unknown outside of the furniture lists. We are therefore confined to the determinatives of the word in attempting to define the nature of the object in question. The sign that determines *ḥꜣ-ḫt* in the early lists of Kha-bau-sokar (3) and Hathor-nefer-hetep (4) is evidently a square box, albeit damaged in the former. The band around the margins of the box and across its center may represent a framework of timber with a central bar[55] or a veneer or inlays in a different colored wood. The material from

50. Brovarski 1989, pp. 665–67 with fig. 65. The box is now in the Phoebe Hearst Museum in Berkeley, California, where it bears the accession number LMA 6-2068; see Exp. Ph. C 639. Although the word *hn*(*w*) is written with the ideogram of a small, rectangular, flat-lidded box on two battens alone, given the parallels, there seems little question that it is to be so read. I would like to take this opportunity to thank Dr. Frank Norick, Principal Museum Anthropologist at the Hearst Museum, for permission to study and publish the inscribed material of First Intermediate Period date from Nagʿ-ed-Deir in Berkeley.

51. See, for example, Newberry 1893b, pls. 15, 18, 20, 27.

52. Newberry 1893b, pl. 10; *Urk.* 4, pp. 388.1, 427.6–7, 1015.17. In the Eighteenth Dynasty this type of box was not uncommonly utilized for the storage of scribal equipment; see, for example, Silverman 1982, cat. no. 389.

53. For example, *Urk.* 4, pp. 206.11–13, 388.1, 427.6–7, 1015.17, etc. For an actual frame-on-chest, essentially identical in construction to the chest illustrated in fig. 4.6, see Reeves 1990, p. 191, no. 585.

54. Reymond 1977, p. 70 (Pap. Vienna 6343, col. 3, line 1; reading is confirmed by Prof. Janet H. Johnson); Spiegelberg 1921, p. 376; Vycichl 1983, p. 304.

55. See, for example, Killen 1994, p. 35, pl. 24.

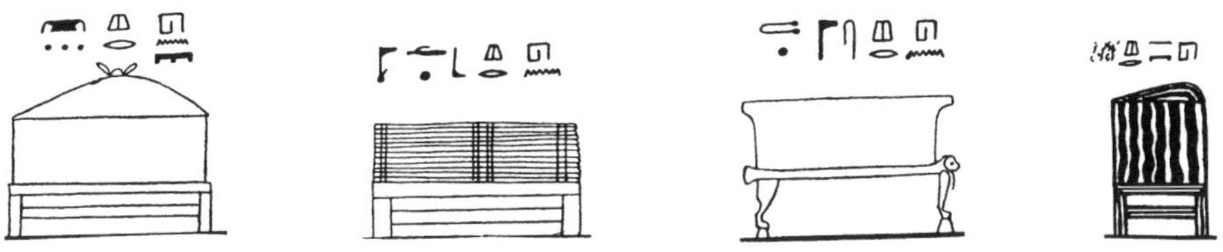

a b c d

Figure 4.12. *Hn*(*w*)-chests and Boxes from End of Sixth Dynasty, after (*a*) Jéquier 1929, pl. 16; (*b*) Jéquier 1929, pl. 16; (*c*) Jéquier 1929, pl. 16; and (*d*) Jéquier 1929, p. 124, fig. 140

which the box is made is stated in both cases to be *sꜣḏ*-wood. In the other lists, *ḥꜣ-ḫt* is determined by a squarish or rectangular box. In the furniture list of Kapunesut Kai (22), the determinative is a rectangle outlined by double lines, essentially the same sign that defines *ꜥfḏt* (aa) in Hathor-nefer-hetep's list (4), and which may once again represent a timber framework or a veneer or inlays in a different wood. The *ḥꜣ-ḫt*-box of Ny-hetep-Khnum (15) has an overall pattern of black and yellow streaks, the colors that generally denote ebony. Except for the box in the list of Seshemnefer I (21), there is no indication of a lid.

Thus, in contrast to *hn*(*w*) (cc), *ḥꜣ-ḫt* seemingly denotes a square or rectangular box without battens or legs of any sort. On occasion, it could be made of exotic woods or trimmed with wood of a contrasting color. If not for the appearance of a lid in the latest occurrence of the word in the tomb of Seshemnefer, it would be possible to suppose that the term *ḥꜣ-ḫt* characterized the type of box with a flat lid that could be slid in and out between grooves, and which would appear to be quite featureless when viewed head on.[56]

That *ḫt* is an integral part of the word seems to follow from the fact that it never stands in apposition to *ḥꜣ*, which is in clear contrast to *st*-(*n*)-*ḫt* (g), where *ḫt* is usually written in apposition, to indicate the material of which the object is made.[57] The scribe who laid out the list of Seshemnefer I may have experienced some confusion in this regard since he relegated the *ḫt*-branch to the compartment above, as if he understood it to represent the material from which the box was made, while the word is still spelled . A peculiar orthography in Kapunesut's list is perhaps to be explained by the stone carver's confusing an original simplified hieratic version of with a hieratic .[58]

ee. *ḫr*(*t*)-*ꜥ* "Scribe's Writing Tablet": Murray 1905, p. 35; "writing-case": Griffith 1892, p. 38; "ovaler Holzbehälter, hauptsächlich zum Aufbewharen von Akten bestimmt": Junker 1940, p. 71 (8); "porte-manuscrits," "valise à manuscrits": Montet 1925, pp. 146, 420; "nécessaire de scribe": Jéquier 1921a, pp. 264–65; "Behälter für Schreibzeug und Akten": *Wb.* 3.394:1 (aus Holz 2); "sacs ovales, paquets": Vandier 1964, p. 195; "Urkundenbehälter": Weber 1969, p. 57

The term *ḫr*(*t*)-*ꜥ* is composed of the *nisbe*-adjective *ḫr*(*y*)(*t*) used nominally and the noun *ꜥ* "piece of writing," "document"; and it literally means "that-which-bears-the-document," in other words, a "document case."[59] The word is written *ḫrt-ꜥ* in some furniture lists (4, 19, 21) and *ḫr-ꜥ* in others (5, 10).

Document cases depicted in Old Kingdom scenes of daily life provide considerably more detail than the small determinatives given in the furniture lists. On the other hand, the depictions are not labeled with their names. Still, they are so distinctive that there is little question they are identical with the *ḫr*(*t*)-*ꜥ* of the furniture lists. In most cases, the depictions are oval in form and fastened with cords (fig. 4.13a), but similarly bound rectangular examples do occur (fig. 4.13b). Document cases are, as shown in more detailed representations, usually supported on battens.

Vandier (1964, p. 195) evidently believed that these cases, which he refers to as "sacs ovales" and "paquets," were made from a pliable material (presumably cloth or leather) and were regularly seen as if set on edge.

Jéquier (1921a, pp. 264–65) remarks quite aptly that the specific form is difficult to ascertain because only one of its surfaces is regularly depicted. He also feels that it is the upper surface of the document case which is

56. See *LÄ* 4 "Möbel," cols. 182–83.

57. In the list of Kha-bau-sokar *ḫt* stands in an indirect genitival relation to *st;* only in the list of Hathor-nefer-hetep does *ḫt* follow on *st*.

58. Compare, for example, Goedicke 1988, p. 20a (M 3: Abusir 25, e; 31B.1; 65, 43) with Goedicke 1988, p. 26a–b (N 35).

59. See Weber 1969, p. 57.

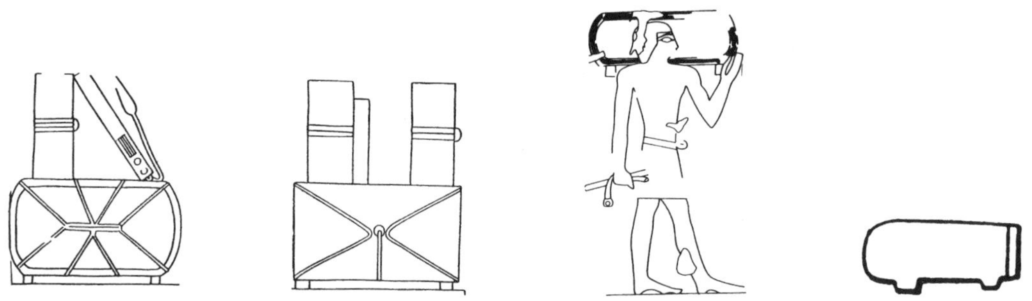

a b c d

Figure 4.13. Scribal Document Cases, after (*a*) Wild 1953, pl. 125; (*b*) Wild 1953, pl. 125; (*c*) Moussa and Junge 1975, p. 20, pl. 3 and frontispiece; and (*d*) Fakhry 1961, fig. 283

regularly depicted and that to a flat base, elongated and rounded at the two extremities, were attached sides made from basketwork or very thin wood that might be bent to the desired form. By way of a cover, four flaps of cloth or leather of triangular form were fixed at the top of the sides and closed the box by joining in the middle, where they were fastened by means of a clasp or some such device.

While agreeing with Jéquier in the main, I would differ in a few particulars. First, none of the depictions of document cases known to me show any pattern that might be interpreted as basketwork. Second, the lines that Jéquier presumably thought to represent the outline of the four cloth or leather flaps are almost certainly the cords used to secure the case when not in use. The individual strands of the cords are clearly indicated in the depiction of a document case in the tomb of Nesut-nefer at Giza (Junker 1938, fig. 27, pl. 5; cf. Simpson 1978, fig. 27). The thickening at the center of the cords in this example and others clearly represents a knot,[60] the loose ends of which are evident in at least one instance (Wild 1966, pl. 168).

The depiction of three document cases, which preserve extensive traces of color, seem to indicate that certain examples at least were made of wood. The first depiction is the *ẖr*(*t*)-*ʿ* determinative in the furniture list on the left side of the false door recess of Rahotep (10). The frame of the determinative is painted black, while the rest of the case is white, except for a black circle in the upper part of the case that presumably represents a button handle. The white color may indicate that the box was manufactured from a less costly or less attractive native wood, such as sycamore or acacia, and was covered with gesso to render its appearance more pleasing.[61] A second depiction of an oval document case in the tomb of Fetekta has a light brown body with a black colored border and round handle.[62] The third case, which belonged to the chief metalworker Sekhentiu (fig. 4.13c), is painted red, while the frame is black (outlined in yellow), red being the color usually spoken of as "cedar," and black or black streaked with yellow being utilized for "ebony" (Quibell 1913, p. 24; Williams 1932, p. 47). The battens in both cases are painted red-brown.

The Egyptians were skilled cabinet makers, and an oval-shaped box would undoubtedly have been within their capacity even at so early a date. In form and construction the document case was perhaps not very different from the cartouche-shaped box of Tutankhamun, except for the rectangular element at one end of the latter which represents the tied ends of the rope composing the name-ring (Metropolitan Museum of Art 1976, cat. no. 28). It may be no more than a coincidence that Tutankhamun's cartouche-shaped box, like Sekhentiu's document case, is made of a reddish brown wood (believed to be coniferous), while all the edges of the box and the cartouche on the lid are veneered with strips of ebony.[63]

One depiction of a document case is unlike all these others. This is the determinative of *ẖr*(*t*)-*ʿ* in the title *zš ẖr*(*t*)-*ʿ nswt* on a Fourth Dynasty stela belonging to a son of Snefru (fig. 4.13d) (Fakhry 1961, fig. 283, pls. 38–39). Only one end of the case is rounded, while the other is flat and provided with what is apparently a lid or cap. This case also is set on battens.

Oval *ẖr*(*t*)-*ʿ* with bindings appear in the object frieze on a number of Middle Kingdom coffins (*Wb*. 3.394:1; Jéquier 1921a, pp. 264–65, 282–83, figs. 694–95, 760–61). In one instance, the word is determined with the

60. See Junker 1938, p. 222. Unfortunately, Junker does not mention the colors of the document case, seal, or cords, even though the detail given in Junker 1938, pl. 5, appears to be from a color reconstruction.

61. See Baker 1966, p. 118.

62. Lepsius 1842–45, pl. 96.

63. See Edwards 1976, p. 139.

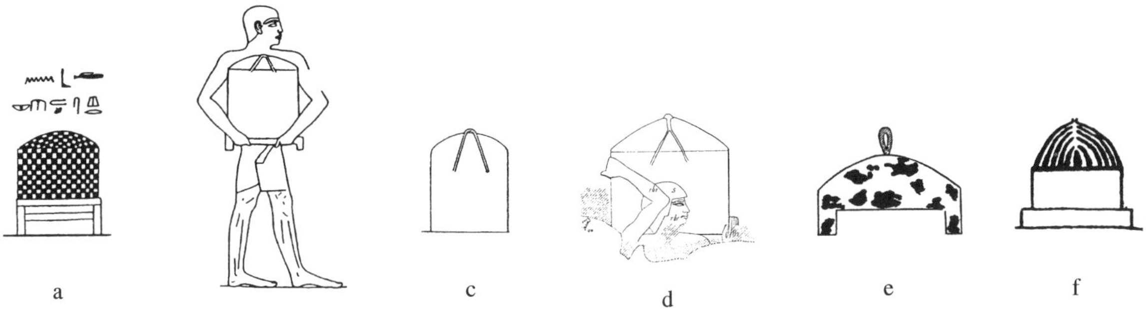

a b c d e f

Figure 4.14. Round-topped Boxes of the Old (*a–d*) and Middle (*e–f*) Kingdoms, after (*a*) Jéquier 1929, pl. 16; (*b*) Zeigler 1993, p. 118; (*c*) Borchardt 1913, fig. 59; (*d*) Borchardt 1907, fig. 58; (*e*) Jéquier 1921a, p. 249, fig. 656 = Birch 1886, pl. 25; and (*f*) Newberry 1893a, pl. 13

sign of the cow's skin, suggesting that this particular case might have been made from leather (Jéquier 1921a, pp. 282–83, fig. 761). *Wb.* 3.394:1–2, provides no references for *ḫrt-ʿ* later in date than the New Kingdom. Ramesses III donated a number of document cases, fabricated from persea wood and painted, to the temple of Ptah at Memphis, but the determinative indicates that these cases took a different form ( ) than the oval cases of earlier periods (Gaballa 1973, p. 113, fig. 3; Helck 1978, pp. 137–38).

Lastly, it might be mentioned that Fischer (1978, p. 54, n. 63) has assembled titles that contain the element *ḫr*(*t*)-*ʿ*.

ff. *tnn* "ein Mobel (aus Ebenholz)": *Wb.* 5.312:16

The word is a *hapax legomenon*, occurring in Hathor-nefer-hetep's list (4) between *gsꜣ* and *ḫrt-ʿ*. It was therefore in all probability an article of furniture. More specifically, from its determinative it appears to have been a round-topped box, taller and narrower than the *dbn*-chest named three compartments earlier. It is completely plain, but its material is given as ebony. In the absence of actual examples of either *tnn* or *dbn*, it is impossible to know what additional features may have distinguished these round-topped boxes.

gg. *ṯzt* "Bundle(?) or perhaps a cushion(?)": Murray 1905, p. 35; "tablette": Weill 1908, p. 253; "Kasten aus Holz": *Wb.* 5.404:14

As far as the furniture lists are concerned, *ṯzt* appears only in that of Hathor-nefer-hetep (4), where the determinative appears to be a rectangle (smaller than the rectangle determining the adjacent word for box, *ʿfḏt*) with narrow borders at either end, which may represent a timber framework or alternatively an inlay or trim of a darker wood. The determinative is so nondescript that Murray (1905, p. 35) was misled into thinking it might represent a bundle or cushion. Nevertheless, *ṯzt* is listed along with several other kinds of boxes — *ʿfḏt* (aa), *hn*(*w*) (cc), *ḥꜣ-ḫt* (dd), *dbn* (hh), *ḏsr*(*w*) (ii) — and like them was made of *sꜣḏ*-wood.

The term *ṯzt* evidently recurs in the biography of Washptah (Grdseloff 1951, pp. 127–40; Brovarski 1977, pp. 110–11). The equipment given to the elderly vizier by the king for the "booth of purification" (*ỉbw*) in which his body was to be ritually cleansed after his death included [*ṯ*]*zt*-chests. In contrast to the sign that determines *ṯzt* in Hathor-nefer-hetep's list, the determinatives of *ṯzwt* in Washptah's biography are three cavetto-corniced rectangular chests on two pair of low legs . The chests contained the *dbḥw* [*n ḥmt ḫry-ḥbt*] "requirements of the craft of the lector priest." [64]

In the Pyramid Texts (Sethe 1960a, Pyr. 184a–b; Faulkner 1962, p. 47), the king is identified as Osiris and addressed as "He-who-is-in-the-god's-booth, Who-is-in-the-censing(?), the *dbn*-coffer, the *ṯztỉ*-chest, and the *ỉnqtỉ*-sack." The determinative of *ṯztỉ* in the pyramid of Unis is a simple rectangular box with a pair of battens

64. Elsewhere the *dbḥw n ḥmt ḫry-ḥbt* are similarly contained in small rectangular chests with cavetto cornices and legs; see Sakkarah Expedition 1938b, pl. 130; Simpson 1976, fig. 24.

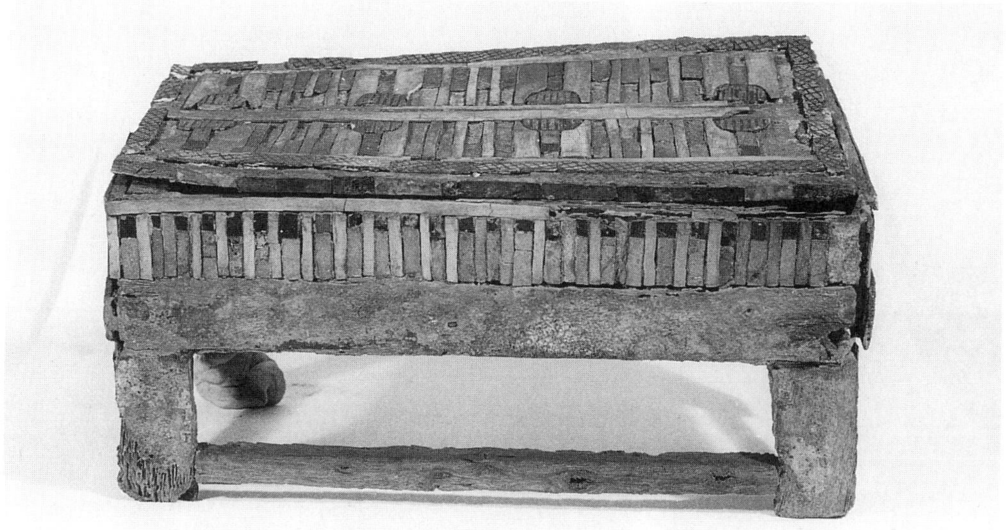

Figure 4.15. Chest-on-legs from Gebelein, Turin Suppl. 16735. Courtesy of the Egyptian Museum, Turin

and a handle, a sign which probably by this time had become the generic determinative for boxes and chests (above).[65]

Wb. 5.404:14 suggests a connection with *ṯzỉ* "to raise," "lift up" and it is possible that *ṯzt* represented a more specific term than *hn*(*w*) for a "chest raised on legs." Whereas this suggestion would suit the determinatives of *ṯzwt* in the biography of Washptah, it is difficult to reconcile with the determinative in Hathor-nefer-hetep's list.

hh. *dbn* "Circular Box": Murray 1905, p. 35; "coffre à couvercle bombé": Weill 1908, p. 253; "coffret bas, à petits pieds et à couvercle bombé": Jéquier 1921a, p. 248; "(runder) Kasten aus Holz": *Wb.* 5.437:16

Dbn appears to be derived from the verb *dbn* "to be round" (Osing 1976, p. 202). In the list of Nedji (6), the determinative of *dbn* is a plain box with a rounded or vaulted lid and a (button?) handle. The determinatives in the furniture lists of Hathor-nefer-hetep (4) and Rahotep (9) and in both lists of Senenu (19–20) exhibit a pattern of parallel vertical lines on the box itself, which may imply a slat construction. Except in one list (20), the vaulted lids are quite plain.[66] The determinative of *dbn* in the list of Irensen (7) is a plain box with a vaulted lid and (button?) handle set on short legs. Hathor-nefer-hetep's *dbn* was constructed of *sꜣḏ*-wood.

A *dbn*-box depicted on the walls of a stone-lined burial chamber of late Sixth Dynasty date at South Saqqara (fig. 4.14a) is a container for "festival perfume" (*sṯỉ-ḥb*). The box or coffret is set on a low table-like stand and has an overall checkered pattern. The actual coffret may have been inlaid with alternating ebony and ivory squares or been painted to imitate checkerboard marquetry.[67]

A different type of table-like stand supports a round-lidded box from an Old Kingdom mastaba (fig. 4.14b). A similar sign with a (button?) handle on the lid determines *dbn* in a First Intermediate Period temple inventory.[68] The latter box was made of copper.

Dbn-boxes were commonly sealed in the same manner as *hnw*-boxes and chests (fig. 4.14b–c). However, a fragmentary relief from the pyramid temple of Neuserre (fig. 4.14d) seems to suggest that some sort of a fastening or clasp may also have been utilized on occasion.[69] All three of these examples are useful for providing a relative scale for the *dbn*-boxes, which appear to be of medium size.

On the other hand, an epithet of Osiris in the Pyramid Texts (Sethe 1960a, Pyr. 184; cf. *Wb.* 5.437:12), *dbnỉ* "He-who-is-in-the-round-lidded-chest," seems to indicate that a *dbn* could on occasion be of quite substantial size. Given the context, *dbn* here probably alludes to the most common type of Old Kingdom coffin with rounded top and end bars (*LÄ* 5 "Sarkophag A," col. 471). The epithet is determined with .

65. In the parallel in Pepi II's pyramid *ṯztỉ* is determined by , the generic determinative of the verb *ṯzỉ* in the Pyramid Texts (e.g., Sethe 1960a, Pyr. 574d, 622a, 626a).

66. Compare Sakkarah Expedition 1938b, pl. 122.

67. For New Kingdom boxes so inlaid, see Freed 1982, cat. no. 234.

68. Goedicke 1994, p. 71, fig. 1, pl. 9. On the date, see now Fischer 1996.

69. None of the boxes in fig. 4.14b–d are specifically identified as *dbn*-boxes. In fact, the box illustrated in fig. 4.14b is apparently subsumed under the general heading *hn*.

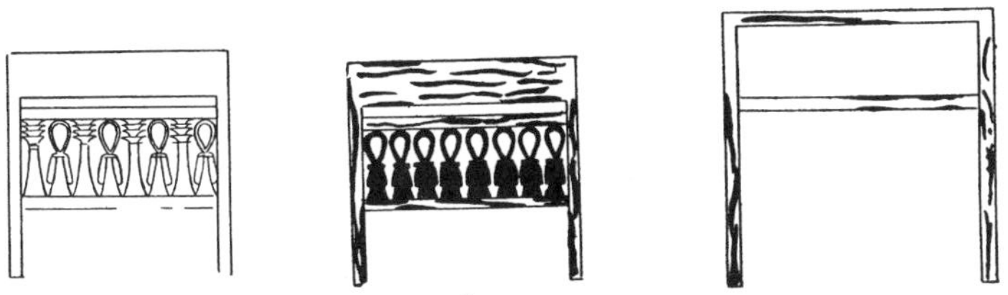

Figure 4.16. Chests- or Cabinets-on-legs from the Tomb of Hesyre, after (*a*) Quibell 1913, pl. 17 [25]; (*b*) Quibell 1913, pl. 18 [30]; and (*c*) Quibell 1913, pl. 18 [35]

Dbn is well attested in the Middle Kingdom, evidently with much the same meaning it had in the Old Kingdom (*Wb.* 5.437:16). *Dbn*, for example, is the term used to describe a low coffret with small feet and a rounded cover, fitted with a loop for lifting, on one side of the coffin of Amamu (fig. 4.14e). Amamu's coffret has an overall pattern of dappled cow hide. Since inlay simulating cow hide was apparently an innovation of the New Kingdom,[70] this gives rise to the possibility that the coffret was made of leather over a wooden frame. A small round-topped box on a rectangular base in the tomb of Amenemhat at Beni Hasan is captioned *dbn n ʿntyw* and thus evidently held myrrh (fig. 4.14f).[71] The pattern on its lid suggests wickerwork.

In the case of only two of the *dbn* referred to above are their contents mentioned with any surety; in one instance perfume is specified and in the other myrrh. If representative, this may indicate that smaller *dbn* at least served as coffrets for the storage of precious substances such as these.

Among the offerings made to the deceased in the funerary liturgy preserved in a papyrus from a tomb of the Thirteenth Dynasty discovered beneath the Ramesseum are "thirty cases of figs" (*dbn n dꜣb* 30) (Gardiner 1955, p. 11, pl. 2, col. 11). The determinative of *dbn* is damaged but does not appear to be round-topped. The *Wörterbuch* has no citations for *dbn* later than the end of the Middle Kingdom, and it is possible that the term was passing out of use or in some fashion being redefined.

It is therefore uncertain whether *dbn* "round-topped or vaulted box or coffret" is to be equated with a word *dbn* that occurs three times on a New Kingdom ostracon in Vienna as a container for toilet articles (Zonhoven 1979, fig. 1, lines 5, 8–9). In his commentary on the ostracon, Zonhoven expresses doubt over the identification and explains *dbn* in the ostracon as a corrupt spelling of *dbt*/*dbw*, a common word for "box" in the Deir el-Medina texts.[72] He then questions whether *dbw*/*dbt* goes back to Middle Egyptian *dbn* (Zonhoven 1979, p. 95, n. 47). The occurrence of *dbt* in a hieratic inscription on a wooden casket with vaulted lid from the tomb of Tutankhamun may, however, provide support for the latter derivation (Černý 1965, pp. 7 [46], 25).

Dbn has been identified with Coptic ⲧⲃⲏⲗ "Korb; Schutzdach" (*Wb.* 5.436:12–437:2; Spiegelberg 1921, p. 545; Meeks 1980, p. 434; Osing 1976, p. 202, n. 890), but this equation too has been called into question by Zonhoven (1979, p. 95, n. 43).

ii. *ḏsr*(*w*) "stool or table": Murray 1905, p. 35; "table ou siege": Weill 1908, p. 253; "Art Mobel": *Wb.* 5.617:10; "Kasten": Junker 1940, p. 71

In the furniture list in the niche of Kha-bau-sokar (3), a square chest inlaid with a *zꜣ*-sign between two *tit*-emblems determines the word *ḏsr*. In the niche stone of the Nubian Sisi (5) the determinative of *ḏsr* is a rectangular box with what may be a pattern of palace-facade paneling on its sides. On account of the small size of the determinatives in the niche of Hathor-nefer-hetep (4) and in the false door panels of Rahotep (9–10) and Metjen (8), it is not entirely certain whether a flat-lidded, rectangular chest-on-frame or a cabinet-on-legs is represented. The material from which Kha-bau-sokar's box was fashioned is unclear, but Hathor-nefer-hetep's is said to be made of *sꜣḏ*-wood.[73]

70. See, for example, the model folding stool with an imitation leopard-skin seat in Edwards 1976, cat. no. 11, color pls. 3–4.

71. Newberry 1893a, p. 38, reads *ḏwn*(?), but the reading is corrected by Montet 1911, p. 4.

72. Zonhoven 1979, pp. 94–95. On *dbt*, see Goedicke 1968, p. 128; Brunner 1974, p. 150; Janssen 1975, p. 203, §41.

73. The heading of *ḏsr* and *wrs* (b) is *ṯr*, determined by a scribal palette. Murray (1905, p. 34) suggests the meaning "colored" or "painted." Harris (1961, p. 155) notes that *ṯr* is a mineral substance, some form of which was used as a pigment, but that it also has the wider meaning of "red color." Possibly the two items were painted red or made from a red-

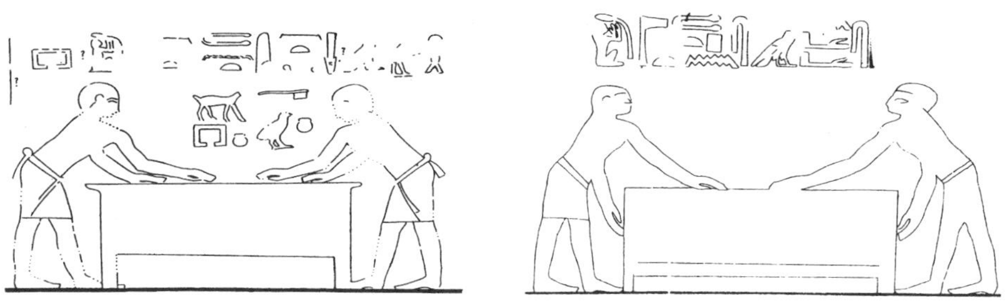

a b

Figure 4.17. Boxes of Old Kingdom Date, after (*a*) Davies 1902b, pl. 14, and (*b*) Davies 1902b, pl. 10

An actual Old Kingdom chest-on-frame from Gebelein, now in Turin, is supported on four legs connected by cross-rails or stretchers. The flat lid simply rests on the body and is secured by means of two tongues and grooves. This well-known chest, beautifully illustrated in color by Scamuzzi, is inlaid with ivory and black and blue faience.[74] The decoration on the lid consists of two sets of four stylized lotus columns alternating with vertical strips of blue and black rectangles, while the vertical fluting on the rectangular body reproduces the form of a reed prototype. The inside of the chest was stuccoed and painted red and contained a string of glazed beads.[75] The chest measures 37.5 cm long, 23.0 cm wide, and 19.0 cm high (Donadoni Roveri et al. 1994, pp. 137, 256, fig. 182). A less well-preserved chest-on-frame from Gebelein in Turin is illustrated here (fig. 4.15).[76] It has the same form as the first and a similar design on the lid. The lid of what may have been yet another chest-on-frame was found by Quibell (1898, pl. 8) in an Old Kingdom mastaba at Elkab. The pattern on the lid was likewise composed of small flat strips of ivory and pieces of blue and black faience. Unfortunately, the wood of the box was badly decayed, and its form could not be ascertained with any certainty. The box itself measured about 30.8 cm long, 20.5 cm wide, and 12.8 cm high (Quibell 1898, pp. 4, 19). The contents consisted of a small porphyry bowl, a shell, and some green paint; on this basis Quibell thought it to be a toilette box.

Similar looking articles of furniture in the paintings of Hesyre (fig. 4.16a–c), with frames of "Isis-knots" and *djed*-columns, are probably cabinets-on-legs rather than chests-on-frames. They resemble actual examples from the tomb of Tutankhamun, dating thirteen hundred years later.[77] The Tutankhamun cabinets open from the top and are divided internally by compartments to hold jewelry and toilet articles (Baker 1966, pp. 37, 91–92). They are taller and larger than the Gebelein chests, one of them, for example, measuring 67.94 × 43.80 × 40.00 cm (Baker 1966, p. 337, fig. 107).

In contrast to the preceding, the *ḏsrw*-chest in the offering list preserved in the copy in Boston (18) has a vaulted lid with circular inlays(?), while the design on the sides is a simplified "palace facade" motif. It rests on short legs. The determinatives of *ḏsr*(*w*) in the furniture lists of Nedji, Seshemnefer I, and Ka-pu-nesut Kai (6, 21, and 22) also have vaulted lids. That of Nedji is quite plain, while Seshemnefer I's has a simple frame. The sides of Ka-pu-nesut's chest, however, bear a design of *djed*-columns(?). Unlike these, the boxes from G 4770 and those in the lists of Ny-hetep-Khnum and Kayemankh (15 and 23), while also rectangular in form, have flat lids. The box from G 4770 is plain, but Ny-hetep-Khnum's box was seemingly made of ebony with two rows of ivory(?) inlays in the form of "Isis-knots." Kayemankh's box bears a pattern of three transverse lines that may just possibly represent a simplified palace facade design. Although the chests of Nedji and Seshemnefer lack

---

colored wood. Alternatively, *ṯr* may have been written in error for *ṯrt* "willow" (*Wb.* 5.385:15–386:3).

74. Turin Suppl. 15709: Scamuzzi 1965, pl. 11; see also Donadoni Roveri et al. 1994, pp. 137–38, fig. 182. The chest was discovered in the western pit of a great mastaba in the Old Kingdom necropolis at Gebelein, in which was also found a limestone basin with a hieroglyphic text giving the name of the owner, Perim; see Donadoni Roveri 1990, p. 24.

75. Turin Suppl. 15710. This information was kindly supplied by Dr. Anna Maria Donadoni Roveri (private communication, 10 July 1995), who also notes (1994, pp. 137–38) some confusion with the chest-on-frame from the "Tomb of the Unknown Owners" (fig. 4.6), which contained linen sheets.

76. Turin Suppl. 16735. Donadoni Roveri again supplies the information that the second, less well-preserved chest came from another great mastaba beside that of Perim, but that it is not possible from the preserved records to say if it contained anything. For a color photograph of Turin Suppl. 16735, see Donadoni Roveri et al. 1994, p. 30.

77. Baker (1966, p. 37) describes the last example (fig. 4.16c), which is plainer than the others, as a table with plain straight legs and stretchers, but as Quibell (1913, p. 27 [35]) observes, the panel represented by the solid area of the chest or cabinet is not blank but yellow with graining of horizontal red lines.

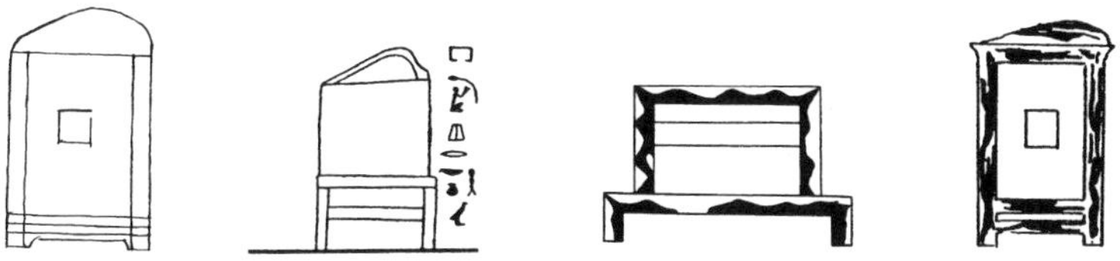

Figure 4.18. Miscellaneous Chests, after (*a*) Maspero 1885, pl. 2; (*b*) Jéquier 1929, pl. 16; (*c*) Newberry 1893a, pl. 13; and (*d*) Jéquier 1921a, fig. 653 = Maspero 1885, pl. 2

details, it is possible that these would have been added in paint, and hence these two chests might also have been made from exotic woods or ornamented with inlays. What is common to all five of these chests, and to the early chests of Kha-bau-Sokar and Sisi as well, is the lack of legs.[78]

Ember gives "raise," "support" as meanings of the verb *ḏsr* (Ember 1913, pp. 110–21; cf. *Wb.* 5.610, 613:14; Faulkner 1962, pp. 324–25). Such an etymology could perhaps explain the application of the term *ḏsr*(*w*) to a chest-on-frame or cabinet-on-legs. Hoffmeier (1985, pp. 30–58) believes these meanings to have been incorrectly applied to *ḏsr*, however. And, in point of fact, while suitable for chests supported on legs, *ḏsr*(*w*) in this sense could not be appropriately applied to the legless boxes in the furniture lists. Another meaning of *ḏsr* may therefore be pertinent in this context, that is, "costly" (*Wb.* 5.611:21; Faulkner 1962, p. 324). "Costly" might readily be applied to both types of chests, referring to their lavish ornamentation rather than their form. In other words, *ḏsr*(*w*) might refer to any elaborate box or chest, of whatever form, made from costly materials. Such a chest would be suitable for the storage of small objects such as jewelry, as in the case of the Turin chest-on-frame, or toilette articles, as in the case of the Elkab chest. It might thus be best to translate *ḏsr*(*w*) in English as "coffret" or "ornamental casket."

Due to their exceptional character, the determinatives of *ḏsr* in the two lists of Senenu (19–20) have been excluded from the preceding discussion. The determinatives are closely similar in form, but it is not easy to know exactly what they represent. Perhaps a rectangular chest on a sort of bentwood frame is intended.

Note should also be taken of the fact that in the list of Seshemnefer I *dšrwt* is written instead of *ḏsr*(*w*). It is possible that the scribe here confused *ḏsr*(*w*) with *ḏsr*(*w*)*t*, a well-attested word for a type of cult table.[79] However, the determinative in Seshemnefer's list has a slightly curved top, and it is hence more likely that a box with a vaulted lid rather than a table was intended.

FURNITURE IN TOMB RELIEFS

jj. *itnt* "Art Kasten": *Wb.* 1.151:11–12[80]

In a tomb relief of Ibi at Deir el-Gebrawi, two pairs of carpenters sand two large chests-on-legs. The first, identified as a *hn*, is flat lidded (fig. 4.4b). The second, captioned *itnt nt wꜥb*(*t*)-[*nṯr*](?) has a cavetto cornice (fig. 4.17a). In form, there is little to distinguish the latter from a large, cavetto-corniced *hn*(*w*)-chest-on-legs, for example, that illustrated in fig. 4.11. For that matter, the only point of difference between the two chests depicted in the tomb of Ibi is the cavetto cornice on the former.

Wb. 1.151:4 connects *itnt* with Late Period Egyptian *itynꜣ*, but Janssen (1975, pp. 374–75) doubts the association and instead identifies (*i*)*ṯyn* as part of a ship, perhaps a beam.

78. The determinative in the slab stela of Seshatsekhentiu is damaged. It is flat lidded and inlaid with *nfr*-signs(?), but it is unclear if a chest-on-frame, a cabinet-on-legs, or a legless chest was represented.

79. *Wb.* 5.617:11–12; Newberry 1893a, pl. 17; Jéquier 1938, pl. 85; see also Hoffmeier 1985, pp. 56–57.

80. Montet (1925, p. 306), I believe incorrectly, takes both *itnt* and *sṯpt* (kk) to be parts of a naos, in the case of the latter, the facade of a naos. It is clear from the remarks of Montet (1925, p. 310) that in the case of the caption containing *itnt* at least, he has mistakenly inverted the *wꜥb*- and *pr*-signs and read *pr-wꜥb* "naos," for which see the next entry (ll). Rightly or wrongly, I would prefer to restore *wꜥbt nṯr* "embalming house of the god" in both captions. There were two distinct *wꜥbts* or "workshops" in the Old Kingdom, one for the embalmers and the other for craftsmen; see Brovarski 1977, pp. 114–15.

kk. *sṯpt* "great chest": Davies 1902b, p. 11, pl. 10

In the workshop scene on the north wall of the tomb of Djau at Deir el-Gebrawi, two carpenters sand a large flat-lidded chest-on-legs (fig. 4.17b). As Davies (1902b) observes, the chest looks like the *hn*(*w*)-chest in the tomb of Ibi (fig. 4.4b) but is designated *sṯpt nt wˁb*(*t*)-*nṯr*.[81] In fact, Davies actually restores (*m*)*sṯpt,* apparently seeing some connection between the flat-lidded chest and *msṯpt*, which is in actuality the name of the lion-headed bier in the funeral procession on the east wall.[82] To the right of the *sṯpt*-chest in the tomb of Djau is a tall naos, while on its left stands a large scepter of electrum. Davies called attention to the parallels between this scene and the one on the north wall of the earlier tomb of Ibi, already discussed under *iṯnt* (jj). In Ibi's scene the flat-lidded box on legs is called *hn*(*w*) *n sḫm* "the box of the *sekhem*-scepter," and a carpenter squatting on the ground nearby holds the scepter in question. Alongside the two carpenters sanding the *hn*(*w*)-chest in Ibi's tomb are two others working on a cavetto-corniced chest-on-legs (fig. 4.17a). It is this box which is identified as an *iṯnt nt wˁb*(*t*)-[*nṯr*](?). Given the analogies between the scenes, it is not unlikely that one or the other of the artists who decorated the two tombs not only erred when he wrote out the word designating the term for one of the chests, but also applied the caption to the wrong-shaped chest (cf. also De Morgan 1903, fig. 6).

FURNITURE IN BURIAL CHAMBERS

ll. *pr-wˁb* "coffrets à couvercle bombé en talus": Jéquier 1921a, p. 248

In two separate burial chambers at South Saqqara, *pr-wˁb* is applied to chests that in form imitate the southern Egyptian sanctuary (fig. 4.18a–b). The first chest sits on a low table-like stand, the feet of which are reinforced by bentwood braces. The other chest rests on a higher stand, the legs of which are strengthened by stretchers. The contents of the latter chest are stipulated as *ḥknw*-perfume or oil, presumably stored in a stone jar within.[83]

At Beni Hasan early in the Twelfth Dynasty, the term *pr-wˁb* was assigned to a rectangular box of entirely different form (fig. 4.18c).[84] At about the same time, two shrine-shaped boxes with hunchbacked roofs on low table-like stands were denominated according to their contents: *pr-ˁntyw*, *pr-msdmt* (Lacau 1906, p. 45, nos. 67, 68 [CG 28091]). Then once again, around the end of the Thirteenth Dynasty, *pr-wˁb* was applied to a shrine-shaped box (Lacau 1904, p. 114, no. 11 [CG 28038]).

It is difficult to know what to make of the divergent example from Beni Hasan (fig. 4.18d). Perhaps it is relevant to recall that in the Old Kingdom the term *pr-wˁb* was also applied to an object of different shape, namely, a cavetto-corniced, straight-sided statue naos.[85] Given the different shapes the word encompasses, it is possible that, rather than being a technical term for a specific kind of box or chest, *pr-wˁb* represents an instance of periphrasis.[86] Still, there is no denying that the term is regularly associated with shrine-shaped chests.

In the Old Kingdom and again in the Middle Kingdom, these shrine-shaped chests appear to have been utilized especially for the storage of precious substances such as perfumes or unguents, myrrh, and eyepaint.

mm. *sry* "[coffret] à couvercle bombé en talus": Jéquier 1921a, p. 248

In a burial chamber unearthed by Maspero at South Saqqara, a tall cavetto-corniced chest-on-legs with a hunchbacked roof in imitation of the southern Egyptian shrine is labeled *sry* (fig. 4.18d). The frame of the chest consists of ebony, while the side panels are of a lighter wood inlaid(?) with a square panel at the center. The legs, which are prolongations of the sideposts, are reinforced with stretchers. Save for the cavetto-corniced top edge and the fact that it appears to be made of ebony, there is little to distinguish this chest from a neighboring chest that is labeled *pr-wˁb* (fig. 4.18a). Conceivably, this constituted sufficient reason for the ancients to designate the two chests by different names. On the other hand, if *pr-wˁb* does indeed represent an instance of pe-

81. Davies 1902b, p. 11. The house-sign does not follow *wˁb* here, as it does in the tomb of Ibi.
82. Davies 1902b, pl. 7; see Fischer 1968, p. 79 (4) and n. 337.
83. For *ḥknw*, see Murray 1905, p. 31; *Wb.* 3.180:5–7.
84. For *pr-wˁb n hbny*, see Newberry 1893a, pl. 13, p. 38.9.
85. See Brovarski 1977, p. 112.
86. See Montet 1925, p. 310, who makes the same assumption in regard to *iṯnt* (jj).

riphrasis, it is possible that *sry* is the technical term for a "shrine-shaped chest." The term evidently appears only in the present context.

nn. *ḏḥꜣ*

In the painted burial chamber of the vizier Ny-ankh-ba in the Unis cemetery at Saqqara, the word *ḏḥꜣ* survives in a badly damaged caption above five rectangular chests-on-legs (Hassan 1978, p. 46, pl. 28A). Two of the chests are plain and flat-lidded, while the others are also flat lidded but have cavetto-cornices. The former are essentially identical to the *hn*(*w*)-chests (cc) of fig. 4.4b and the latter to the *hn*(*w*)-chests of fig. 4.7d. However, the word *ḏḥꜣ* itself is determined by a square chest with a vaulted lid .

The term appears to be unattested elsewhere, although a silver ceremonial object designated *ḏḥꜣ* appears in the Abusir Papyri, where it is determined by the sign for basket.[87] In the Eleventh or early Twelfth Dynasty, a trunk with seemingly the same profile appears under a bed inside the cabin on one of the traveling boats of the vizier Meketre (Winlock 1955, fig. 38, p. 55; Arnold 1991).

FURNITURE IN ABUSIR PAPYRI

oo. *ḏbꜣw* "coffre": Posener-Kriéger 1976, p. 177

This object, made of imported wood (*ḫt ḫꜣst*), is listed in an inventory in the Abusir Papyri (Posener-Kriéger and de Cenival 1968, pl. 21p; Posener-Kriéger 1976, pp. 134, fig. 3; 135 (20); 177, inv. B 12; 179, n. 2). As Posener observes, the determinative of the object differs from that of the adjacent *hn*-boxes only in lacking a small handle. The sign may represent a generic determinative, however, and tell us little or nothing about the actual nature of the box. Unfortunately, the contents of the box, which might have provided a clue as to its nature, are not given.

The same or a related word *ḏbꜣ* occurs in Old Kingdom marsh scenes as a term for a wickerwork cage for captured birds (*Wb.* 5.561:14; cf. *Wb.* 5.360:12; Montet 1925, pp. 164–65 [*ṯb*]). The material of the object inventoried in the Abusir Papyri, which was presumably costly imported wood, seems to preclude the possibility that the term designates so crude an object as a cage or even a crate. If *ḏbꜣ*(*t*) is indeed a word used to designate a palace or part of a palace within a niched enclosure wall (Kees 1914, pp. 15–16; Roth 1994, p. 233), it is possible that *ḏbꜣw* in the Abusir Papyrus is a term for a wooden box with all-around decorative paneling.

A word for box, *ḏbꜣt* (also written *ḏbꜣwt* and *ḏbꜣw*), specifically a large box or coffin, is known in Middle and Late Period Egyptian (*Wb.* 5.561:9–12). According to Černý (1976, p. 180) this word is perhaps the same as Coptic **ⲧⲏⲏⲃⲉ**, rather than **ⲧⲁⲓⲃⲉ** as Steindorff thought (Crum 1939, Add. p. xxii).

pp. *šꜥt*(?) "coffret(?)": Posener-Kriéger 1976, p. 181 (B 18)

This term is known from the Abusir Papyri (Posener-Kriéger and de Cenival 1968, pl. 26A, B 18), where the object in question is fabricated from acacia wood (*šnḏ*). The reading remains uncertain, and in the original publication the group was transcribed as *mnṯ*. After examination of the original, however, Posener-Kriéger (1976, p. 181) felt confident that the first sign is and the last . The sign determining the word is the hieratic equivalent of the rectangular box with a pair of battens that may or may not tell us something about the nature of the box or chest in question.

87. Posener-Kriéger and de Cenival 1968, pl. 15A. Posener-Kriéger (1976, pp. 82–83) identifies the object as a winnowing basket or sieve.

CONCLUSION

Many of the terms for types of furniture discussed herein (and in Brovarski 1996) evidently fell into disuse at the end of the Old Kingdom:

mꜥ (d)	*st-(n)-ḫt* (g)	*st ḥms* (h)	*sꜣḥ* (i)	*gs(ꜣw)t* (j)	*nḏrwt* (k)	*ḥꜣ-ḫt* (dd)
tnn (ff)	*ṯzt* (gg)	*ḏsr(w)* (ii)	*sṯpt* (kk)	*sry* (mm)	*ḏḥꜣ* (nn)	*šꜥt* (pp)

Others continued in use as late as the Middle Kingdom:

ꜣṯt (a)	*wrs* (b)	*wṯz(t)* (c)	*ḫꜣwt* (e)	*ḫnd(w)* (f)	*ꜥfḏt* (aa)
(m)ḫtm(t) (bb)	*hn(w)* (cc)	*ḫr(t)-ꜥ* (ee)	*dbn* (hh)	*pr-wꜥb* (ll)	*ḏbꜣw* (oo)

Others continued to be used in the New Kingdom:

ꜣṯt (a)	*wrs* (b)	*wṯz(t)* (c)	*ḫꜣwt* (e)	*ḫnd(w)* (f)
ꜥfḏt (aa)	*hn(w)* (cc)	*ḫr(t)-ꜥ* (ee)	*dbn* (hh)(?)	

A few seem to have survived into Ptolemaic hieroglyphic:

ꜣṯt (a) *ḫꜣwt* (e) *ꜥfḏt* (aa)

A few survived into Demotic:

ḫꜣwt (e) *ꜥfḏt* (aa) *hn(w)* (cc)

And a few survived into Coptic:

ḫꜣwt (e) *hn(w)* (cc) *dbn* (hh)(?)

It is not always easy to ascertain why certain of the terms for furniture disappeared, while others survived, especially since Old Kingdom traditions of furniture manufacture and design persisted with little change into the Eighteenth Dynasty.[88] In the case of *mꜥ* (d), *gs(ꜣw)t* (j), and possibly *ḫwdt* (l), it is likely that the disappearance of the term corresponded with the actual abandonment of that particular article of furniture after the Old Kingdom. In the case of *ꜣṯt* (a) and *st-(n)-ḫt* (g), increased specialization seems to explain the replacement of one term by another within the course of the Old Kingdom.

Of course, to some extent, the picture that emerges is due to the nature of the later evidence which is heavily inscriptional rather than representational in character. Sufficient testimony does exist, however, to show that a number of terms were transformed in meaning with the passage of time. This is true of *ḫnd(w)* (f), which in the New Kingdom came to mean the steps of a throne rather than the throne itself. Similarly, whereas *ꜣṯt* (a) continued to be used of practical beds at least into the Second Intermediate Period, the term came increasingly to be applied to funerary beds formed by the heads, bodies, legs, and tails of two lions. Although King Pi(ankh)y uses *ꜣṯt* to refer to a practical bed, this usage may constitute an archaism since *ꜣṯt* had apparently come to designate a funerary lion-bed by the Ramesside period at the latest. If the change in signification came about earlier, it could explain why *ḥꜥtỉ* appears to have been applied to Tutankhamun's lion-legged beds which, except for a dipping in the center, are essentially identical with *ꜣṯt*-beds fabricated more than a thousand years before (Černý 1965, pp. 16, 28, no. 69; Baker 1966, pp. 102–04; Reeves 1990, pp. 180–82).

Fashion may be another reason why the nomenclature for furniture changed over time. Thus, the general enthusiasm for things foreign may help to explain how a foreign loanword, *krk(r)*, came to replace *ḥꜥtỉ* and the other words for beds in the period of empire and later.[89] The first mention of *krk(r)* is seemingly in the Annals of Thutmose III, who brought back to Egypt in the plunder from Lebanon and Megiddo a *ssnḏm bꜣk m nbw mꜥꜣt nb ḥꜥtỉ m sḫr n krkr n ḫrw pf* "bed of *ssnḏm*-wood, wrought with gold and all costly stones in the fashion of a *krkr* of this foe."[90]

The terms that remained in evidence till the end of the pharaonic period and beyond seem to be very common, to wit the terms for small and large boxes, *ꜥfḏt* (aa) and *hn(w)* (cc), and for altars of any kind, *ḫꜣwt* (e). It bears repeating, however, that our investigation of the nomenclature for furniture in periods after the Old Kingdom is limited in scope, and further research may prove even these observations to be overly simplistic.

---

88. See Baker 1966, p. 60.

89. *Krk(k)* is evidently Demotic *glg* (Erichsen 1954, p. 591) and Coptic **ϭⲗⲟϭ** (Sahidic), **ϭⲗⲟϫ** (Bohairic) (Vycichl 1983, p. 340); see Osing 1978, p. 188. References are courtesy of Janet H. Johnson and the Chicago Demotic Dictionary Project.

90. Compare Breasted 1962, §436; Janssen 1975, p. 185.

Table 4.1. Signs Determining Words for Furniture in Furniture Lists

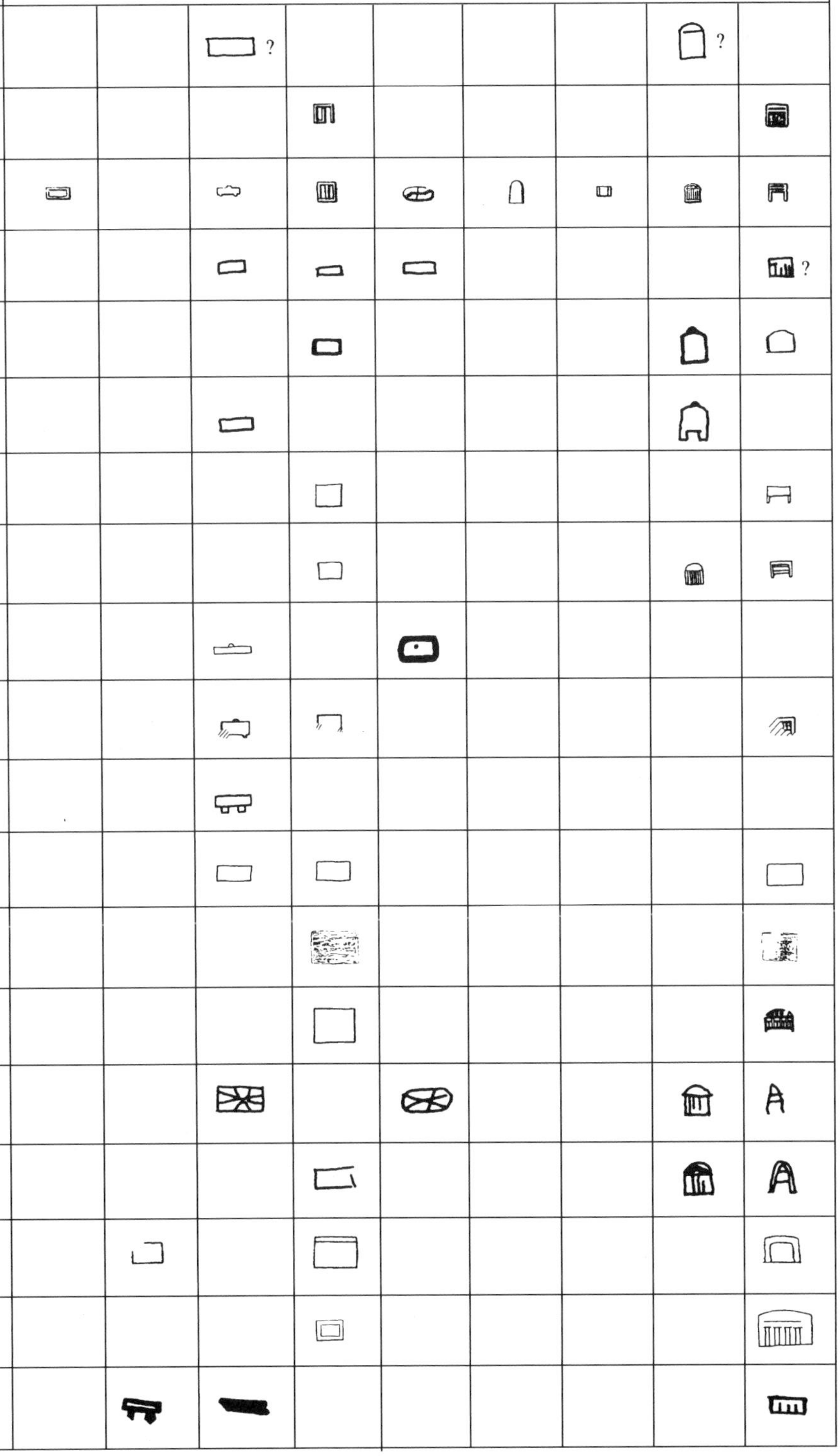

Furniture List*	Word for Furniture								
	ʿfḏt aa	(m)ḫtm(t) bb	ḥn(w) cc	ḥȝ-ḫt dd	ḥr(t)-ʿ ee	tnn ff	ṯzt gg	dbn hh	ḏsr(w) ii
2. Ny-djefa-nesut			[sign] ?					[sign] ?	
3. Kha-bau-sokar				[sign]					[sign]
4. Hathor-nefer-hetep	[sign]		[sign]	[sign]	[sign]	[sign]	[sign]	[sign]	[sign]
5. Sisi			[sign]	[sign]	[sign]				[sign] ?
6. Nedji				[sign]				[sign]	[sign]
7. Irensen			[sign]					[sign]	
8. Metjen				[sign]					[sign]
9. Rahotep				[sign]				[sign]	[sign]
10. Rahotep			[sign]		[sign]				
11. Seshatsekhentiu			[sign]	[sign]					[sign]
12. Anonymous (G 4260)			[sign]						
13. Anonymous (G 4770)			[sign]	[sign]					[sign]
15. Ny-hetep-Khnum				[sign]					[sign]
18. "Covington's Tomb"				[sign]					[sign]
19. Senenu			[sign]		[sign]			[sign]	[sign]
20. Senenu				[sign]				[sign]	[sign]
21. Seshemnefer I		[sign]		[sign]					[sign]
22. Kapunesut Kai				[sign]					[sign]
23. Kayemankh		[sign]	[sign]						[sign]

*Furniture Lists 1, 14, 16, and 17 do not have signs determining these words for furniture and are omitted from this table. See footnote 2, pages 27 f., above for information on the furniture lists.

Abbreviations

CG 1295–1808 — *Denkmäler des Alten Reiches (Ausser den Statuen) im Museum von Kairo*, 2 volumes. L. Borchardt. Catalogue général des antiquités égyptiennes du Musée du Caire 97, 100. Berlin: Reichsdruckerei, 1937; Cairo: Organisme général des imprimeries gouvernementales, 1964

CG 28001–28126 — *Sarcophages antérieurs au Nouvel Empire*, 2 volumes. P. Lacau. Catalogue général des antiquités égyptiennes du Musée du Caire 11, 14. Cairo: Institut français d'archéologie orientale, 1904–1906

References

Abu-Bakr, A.-M.
1953 *Excavations at Giza 1949–1950*. Cairo: Government Press.

Arnold, D.
1991 "Amenemhat I and the Early Twelfth Dynasty at Thebes." *Metropolitan Museum Journal* 26: 5–48.

Badawi, A. M.
1940 "Denkmäler aus Saḳḳarah, 1." *Annales du Service des antiquités de l'Égypte* 40: 495–501.

Badawy, A.
1978 *The Tomb Nyhetep-Ptah at Giza and the Tomb of ʿAnkhmʿahor at Saqqara*. Berkeley: University of California Press.

Baker, H. S.
1966 *Furniture in the Ancient World*. New York: Macmillan.

Birch, S.
1886 *Egyptian Texts of the Earliest Period from the Coffin of Amamu in the British Museum*. London: n.p.

Bissing, F. W. von
1905a *Die Mastaba des Gem-ni-kai*, Volume 1. Berlin: Alexander Duncker.
1905b *Das Re-Heiligtum des Königs Ne-Woser-Re (Rathures)*, Volume 2: *Der kleine Festdarstellung*. Berlin: Alexander Duncker.
1911 *Die Mastaba des Gem-ni-kai*, Volume 2. Leipzig: J. C. Hinrichs.

Borchardt, L.
1907 *Das Grabdenkmal des Königs Ne-User-Reʿ*. Wissenschaftliche Veröffentlichungen der Deutschen Orientgesellschaft 7. Leipzig: J. C. Hinrichs.
1913 *Das Grabdenkmal des Königs Sʿaꜣḥu-Re*, Band 2: *Die Wandbilder*. Wissenschaftliche Veröffentlichungen der Deutschen Orientgesellschaft 26. Leipzig: J. C. Hinrichs.
1937 *Denkmäler des Alten Reiches (ausser den Statuen) im Museum von Kairo*, Volume 1. Catalogue général des antiquités égyptiennes du Musée du Caire 97. Berlin: Reichsdruckerei.

Borghouts, J. F.
1973/74 "The Enigmatic Chests." *Jaarbericht van het Vooraziatisch-Egyptisch Genootschap "Ex Oriente Lux"* 23: 358–64.

Breasted, J. H.
1962 *Ancient Records of Egypt*, Volume 2. Reprint. New York: Scribner.

Brovarski, E.
1977 "The Doors of Heaven." *Orientalia* 46: 107–15.
1983 "A Stele of the First Intermediate Period from Naga-ed-Dêr. *Medelhavsmuseet Bulletin* 18: 3–11.
1989 The Inscribed Material of the First Intermediate Period from Naga-ed-Dêr. Ph.D. dissertation, University of Chicago.
1996 "An Inventory List from 'Covington's Tomb' and Nomenclature for Furniture in the Old Kingdom." In *Studies in Honor of William Kelly Simpson*, Volume 1, edited by P. D. Manuelian, pp. 117–55. Boston: Museum of Fine Arts.
NYP "CG 20506 and the Ancient Egyptian Word for 'Bed Canopy.'"

Brovarski, E.; S. K. Doll; and R. E. Freed, eds.
1982 *Egypt's Golden Age: The Art of Living in the New Kingdom 1558–1085 B.C.* Boston: Museum of Fine Arts.

Brunner, H.
1974 "*Dbt* 'Kasten.'" *Zeitschrift für ägyptische Sprache und Altertumskunde* 100: 150.

Chassinat, E., and Ch. Palanque
1911 *Une campagne de fouilles dans la nécropole d'Assiout*. Mémoires de l'Institut français d'archéologie orientale du Caire 14. Cairo: Institut français d'archéologie orientale.

Černý, J.
1945 "The Will of Naunakhte and the Related Documents." *Journal of Egyptian Archaeology* 31: 29–56.
1965 *Hieratic Inscriptions from the Tomb of Tutʿankhamun*. Tutʿankhamun's Tomb Series 2. Oxford: Griffith Institute.
1976 *Coptic Etymological Dictionary*. Cambridge: Cambridge University Press.

Crum, E. W.
1939 *A Coptic Dictionary*. Oxford: Clarendon Press.

Daressy, G.
1916 "La nécropole des grand prêtres de Héliopolis sous l'Ancien Empire." *Annales du Service des antiquités de l'Égypte* 16: 193–220.

Davies, N. de G.
1902a *The Rock Tombs of Deir el Gebrâwi*, Part 1: *Tomb of Aba and Smaller Tombs of the Southern Group*. Archaeological Survey of Egypt 11. London: Egypt Exploration Fund.
1902b *The Rock Tombs of Deir el Gebrâwi*, Part 2: *Tomb of Zau and Tombs of the Northern Group*. Archaeological Survey of Egypt 12. London: Egypt Exploration Fund.

de Morgan, J.
1903 *Fouilles à Dahchour*. Vienna: Adolphe Holzhausen.

Donadoni Roveri, A. M.
1969 *I sarcofagi egizi dalle origini alla fine dell'Antico Regno*. Università di Roma, serie archeologica 16. Rome: Istituto di Studi del Vicino Oriente.
1990 "Gebelein." In *Beyond the Pyramids: Egyptian Regional Art from the Museo Egizio, Turin*, edited by G. Robins, pp. 23–30. Atlanta: Emory University Museum of Art and Archaeology.

Donadoni Roveri, A. M.; E. d'Amicone; and E. Leospo
1994 *Gebelein: Il villagio e la necropoli*. Turin: Artema.

Dunham, D., and W. K. Simpson
1974 *The Mastaba of Queen Mersyankh III*. Boston: Museum of Fine Arts.

Edel, E.
1955 *Altägyptische Grammatik*, Volume 1. Analecta Orientalia 34. Rome: Pontificium Institutum Biblicum.
1964 *Altägyptische Grammatik*, Volume 2. Analecta Orientalia 39. Rome: Pontificium Institutum Biblicum.

Edwards, I. E. S.
1976 "Catalogue." In *Treasures of Tutankhamun*, pp. 97–173. New York: Metropolitan Museum of Art.

Egyptian Museum of Turin
1987 *Egyptian Civilization: Daily Life*. Edited by A. M. Donadoni Roveri. Milan: Electa.

Ember, A.
1913 "Kindred Semito-Egyptian Roots." *Zeitschrift für ägyptische Sprache und Altertumskunde* 51: 110–21.

Épron, L.
1939 *Le tombeau de Ti*, fascicle 1. Mémoires de l'Institut français d'archéologie orientale du Caire 65/1. Cairo: Institut français d'archéologie orientale.

Erichsen, W.
1954 *Demotisches Glossar*. Copenhagen: Einar Munksgaard.

Erman, A.
1890 *Die Märchen des Papyrus Westcar*. Königliche Museen zu Berlin, Mitteilungen aus den orientalischen Sammlungen 5/6. Berlin: W. Spemann.

Fairbanks, J. L., and E. B. Bates
1981 *American Furniture 1620 to the Present*. New York: Richard Marek.

Fakhry, A.
1961 *The Monuments of Sneferu at Dahshur*, Volume 2, Part 2. Cairo: General Organization for Government Printing Offices.

Faulkner, R. O.
1962 *A Concise Dictionary of Middle Egyptian*. Oxford: Oxford University Press.
1969 *The Ancient Egyptian Pyramid Texts*. 2 volumes. Oxford: Clarendon Press.
1973 *The Ancient Egyptian Coffin Texts*, Volume 1. Warminster: Aris and Phillips.
1977 *The Ancient Egyptian Coffin Texts*, Volume 2. Warminster: Aris and Phillips.
1978 *The Ancient Egyptian Coffin Texts*, Volume 3. Warminster: Aris and Phillips.

Fazzini, R.
1975 *Images for Eternity*. San Francisco: Fine Arts Museum of San Francisco; Brooklyn: Brooklyn Museum.

Firth, C. M., and B. Gunn
1926 *Teti Pyramid Cemeteries*. 2 volumes. Excavations at Saqqara 7. Cairo: Institut français d'archéologie orientale.

Fischer, H. G.
1968 *Dendera in the Third Millennium B.C. down to the Theban Domination of Upper Egypt*. Locust Valley: J. J. Augustin.
1978 "Five Inscriptions of the Old Kingdom." *Zeitschrift für ägyptische Sprache und Altertumskunde* 105: 47–59.
1996 "Notes on Some Texts of the Old Kingdom and Later." In *Studies in Honor of William Kelly Simpson*, Volume 1, edited by P. D. Manuelian, pp. 267–74. Boston: Museum of Fine Arts.

Freed, R. E.
1982 "Box with Sliding Lid." In *Egypt's Golden Age: The Art of Living in the New Kingdom 1558–1085 B.C.*, edited by E. Brovarski, S. K. Doll, and R. E. Freed, pp. 201–02, cat. no. 234. Boston: Museum of Fine Arts.

Gaballa, G. A.
1973 "Three Documents from the Reign of Ramesses III." *Journal of Egyptian Archaeology* 59: 109–13.

Gardiner, A. H.
1955 "A Unique Funerary Liturgy." *Journal of Egyptian Archaeology* 41: 9–17.
1973 *Egyptian Grammar*. Third edition revised. Oxford: Griffith Institute.

Goedicke, H.
1968 "*Dbt* 'work-bench.'" *Journal of the American Research Center in Egypt* 7: 128.
1988 *Old Hieratic Paleography*. Baltimore: Halgo.
1994 "A Cult Inventory of the Eighth Dynasty from Coptos (Cairo JE 43290)." *Mitteilungen des Deutschen archäologischen Instituts, Abteilung Kairo* 50: 71–84.

Grapow, H.
1914 *Über die Wortbildungen mit einem Präfix m- in Ägyptischen*. Abhandlungen der Königlich preussischen Akademie der Wissenschaften, philosophisch-historische Klasse 5. Berlin: Verlag der Königliche Akademie der Wissenschaften.

Grdseloff, B.
1951 "Nouvelles données concernant la tente de purification." *Annales du Service des antiquités de l'Égypte* 51: 127–40.

Griffith, F. Ll.
1892 "The Inscriptions." In *Medum*, edited by W. M. F. Petrie, p. 38. London: David Nutt.

Griffith, F. Ll., and P. E. Newberry
1894 *El Bersheh*, Part 2. Archaeological Survey of Egypt 4. London: Egypt Exploration Fund.

Harris, J. R.
1961 *Lexicographical Studies in Ancient Egyptian Minerals*. Deutsche Akademie der Wissenschaften zu Berlin, Institut für Orientforschung. Berlin: Akademie-Verlag.

Hassan, S.

1932 *Excavations at Giza*. Oxford: University Press.

1975 *Excavations at Saqqara 1937–1938*, Volume 2: *Mastabas of Ny-ʿankh-Pepy and Others*. Re-edited by Z. Iskander. Cairo: Arab Republic of Egypt, Antiquities Department.

1978 *Excavations at Saqqara 1937–1938*, Volume 3: *Mastabas of Princess Ḥemet-Rʿ and Others*. Re-edited by Z. Iskander. Cairo: Arab Republic of Egypt, Antiquities Department.

Helck, W.

1978 "200 Persea-Baüme im Ptātempel von Memphis?" *Journal of Egyptian Archaeology* 64: 137–38.

Hoffmeier, J. K.

1985 *Sacred in the Vocabulary of Ancient Egypt: The Term ḎSR, with Special Reference to Dynasties I–XX*. Orbis Biblicus et Orientalis 59. Freiburg: Universitätsverlag; Göttingen: Vandenhoeck and Ruprecht.

James, T. G. H.

1953 *The Mastaba of Khentika called Ikhekhi*. Archaeological Survey of Egypt 13. London: Egypt Exploration Society.

1961 *Hieroglyphic Texts from Egyptian Stelae, etc.*, Volume 1. Second edition. London: British Museum.

Janssen, J. J.

1975 *Commodity Prices from the Ramessid Period*. Leiden: E. J. Brill.

Jéquier, G.

1910 "Note sur deux hiéroglyphes." *Bulletin de l'Institut français d'archéologie orientale* 7: 89–94.

1921a *Les frises d'objets des sarcophages du Moyen Empire*. Mémoires publiés par les membres de l'Institut français d'archéologie orientale du Caire 47. Cairo: Institut français d'archéologie orientale.

1921b "Les préfixes dans les noms d'objets du Moyen Empire." *Recueil de travaux relatifs à la philologie et à l'archéologie égyptiennes et assyriennes* 39: 145–54.

1922 "Matériaux pour servir à l'établissement d'un dictionnaire d'archéologie égyptienne." *Bulletin de l'Institut français d'archéologie orientale* 19: 1–271.

1929 *Tombeaux de particuliers contemporains de Pepi II*. Excavations at Saqqara 11. Cairo: Institut français d'archéologie orientale.

1938 *Le monument funéraire de Pepi II*, volume 2: *Le temple*. Cairo: Institut français d'archéologie orientale.

Junker, H.

1929 *Giza* 1: *Die Mastabas der IV. Dynastie auf dem Westfriedhof*. Denkschriften der Akademie der Wissenschaften in Wien 69/1. Vienna and Leipzig: Hölder-Pichler-Tempsky.

1934 *Giza* 2: *Die Mastabas der beginnen den V. Dynastie auf dem Westfriedhof*. Akademie der Wissenschaften in Wien, philosophisch-historische Klasse. Vienna and Leipzig: Hölder-Pichler-Tempsky.

1938 *Giza* 3: *Die Mastabas der vorgeschriffenen V. Dynastie auf dem Westfriedhof*. Akademie der Wissenschaften in Wien, philosophisch-historische Klasse. Vienna: Hölder-Pichler-Tempsky.

1940 *Giza* 4: *Die Mastaba des* Kꜣjmʿnḫ (*Kai-em-anch*). Akademie der Wissenschaften in Wien, philosophisch-historische Klasse 72/3. Vienna: Hölder-Pichler-Tempsky.

1944 *Giza* 7: *Der Ostabschnitt des Westfriedhof*. Denkschriften der Akademie der Wissenschaften in Wien 69/1. Vienna and Leipzig: Hölder-Pichler-Tempsky.

Kaplony, P.

1976 *Studien zum Grab des Methethi*. Bern: Abegg-Stiftung.

Kees, H.

1914 "'Pr-dwꜣt' und 'Ḏbꜣt.'" *Recueil de travaux relatifs à la philologie et à l'archéologie égyptiennes et assyriennes* 36: 1–16.

Kestner Museum

1958 *Ausgewählte Werke der aegyptische Sammlung*. Edited by Irmgard Woldering. Hannover: Kestner Museum.

Killen, G.

1994 *Ancient Egyptian Furniture*, Volume 2: *Boxes, Chests and Footstools*. Warminster: Aris and Phillips.

Königlichen Museen zu Berlin

1913 *Aegyptische Inschriften aus den Königlichen Museen zu Berlin*, Volume 1. Leipzig: J. C. Hinrichs.

Lacau, P.

1904 *Sarcophages antérieurs au Nouvel Empire* 1. Catalogue général des antiquités égyptiennes du Musée du Caire 11. Cairo: Institut français d'archéologie orientale.

1906 *Sarcophages antérieurs au Nouvel Empire* 2. Catalogue général des antiquités égyptiennes du Musée du Caire 14. Cairo: Institut français d'archéologie orientale.

Leprohon, R. J.

1985 *Stelae* 1: *The Early Dynastic Period to the Late Middle Kingdom*. Museum of Fine Arts, Boston, Corpus Antiquitatem Aegyptiacarum. Mainz am Rhein: Philipp von Zabern.

Lepsius, C. R.

1842–45 *Denkmaeler aus Aegypten und Aethiopien*, Part 2: *Denkmaeler des Alten Reiches*. Berlin: Nicolaische.

Macramallah, R.

1935 *Le mastaba d'Idout*. Cairo: Institut français d'archéologie orientale.

Málek, J.

1982 "New Reliefs and Inscriptions from Five Old Tombs at Giza and Saqqara." *Bulletin de la Société d'égyptologie, Genève* 6: 47–67.

Mariette, A.

1889 *Les mastabas de l'Ancien Empire*. Edited by G. Maspero. Paris: F. Vieweg.

Martin, G. T.

1979 *The Tomb of Ḥetepka, and Other Reliefs and Inscriptions from the Sacred Animal Necropolis, North Saqqâra 1964–1973*. London: Egypt Exploration Society.

Maspero, G.
1885 *Trois années de fouille dans les tombeaux de Thèbes et de Memphis*. Mémoires publiées pars les membres de la Mission archéologique français au Caire 2. Paris: Ernest Leroux.

Meeks, D.
1980 *Année lexicographique* I (1977). Paris: Dimitri Meeks.

Metropolitan Museum of Art
1976 *Treasures of Tutankhamun*. New York: Metropolitan Museum of Art.

Mogensen, M.
1930 *La Glyptothèque Ny Carlsberg: La collection égyptienne*. Copenhagen: Levin and Munksgaard.

Montet, P.
1911 "Notes sur les tombeaux de Béni-Hassan." *Bulletin de l'Institut français d'archéologie orientale* 9: 1–36.
1925 *Scenes de la vie privée dans les tombeaux égyptiens de l'Ancien Empire*. Strasbourg: Librairie Istra.
1931 "Contributions à l'étude des mastabas de l'Ancien Empire." *Kêmi* 4: 161–89.

Moussa, A. M., and F. Junge
1975 *Two Tombs of Craftsmen*. Mainz am Rhein: Philipp von Zabern.

Murray, M. A.
1905 *Saqqara Mastabas*, Part 1. Publications of the Egyptian Research Account 10. London: B. Quaritch.

Newberry, P. E.
1893a *Beni Hasan*, Part 1. Archaeological Survey of Egypt 1. London: Egypt Exploration Fund.
1893b *El Bersheh*, Part 1. Archaeological Survey of Egypt 3. London: Egypt Exploration Fund.

Osing, J.
1976 *Die Nominalbildung des Ägyptischen*. 2 volumes. Mainz: Philipp von Zabern.
1978 Review of *Coptic Etymological Dictionary*, by J. Černý. *Journal of Egyptian Archaeology* 64: 186–89.

Petrie, W. M. F.
1892 *Medum*. London: David Nutt.
1898 *Deshasheh*. Memoirs of the Egypt Exploration Fund 15. London: Egypt Exploration Fund.

Posener-Kriéger, P.
1976 *Les archives du temple funéraire de Néferirkarê-Kakaï (Les papyrus d'Abousir)*. 2 volumes. Bibliothèque d'étude 65/1–2. Cairo: Institut français d'archéologie orientale.

Posener-Kriéger, P., and J. L. de Cenival
1968 *The Abu Sir Papyri*. Hieratic Papyri in the British Museum 5. London: British Museum.

Quibell, J. E.
1898 *El Kab*. Publications of the Egyptian Research Account 3. London: B. Quaritch.
1913 *Tomb of Hesy*. Excavations at Saqqara 5. Cairo: Institut français d'archéologie orientale.

Reeves, N.
1990 *The Complete Tutankhamun*. London: Thames and Hudson.

Reisner, G. A.
n.d. *Naga-ed-Dêr Notebook* 1. Department of Ancient Egyptian, Nubian, and Near Eastern Art, Museum of Fine Arts, Boston; Harvard University-Boston Museum of Fine Arts Expedition.
n.d. *Naga-ed-Dêr Notebook* 3. Department of Ancient Egyptian, Nubian, and Near Eastern Art, Museum of Fine Arts, Boston; Harvard University-Boston Museum of Fine Arts Expedition.
1955 *A History of the Giza Necropolis*, Volume 2. Completed and revised by W. S. Smith. Cambridge: Harvard University Press.

Reymond, E. A. E.
1977 *From the Contents of the Libraries of the Suchos Temples in the Fayyum*, Part 2: *From Ancient Egyptian Hermetic Writings*. Mitteilungen aus der Papyrussammlung der Österreichischen Nationalbibliothek, neue Serie, 11. Folge. Vienna: Brüder Hollinek.

Riefstahl, E., and S. E. Chapman
1970 "A Note on Ancient Fashions: Four Early Egyptian Dresses in the Museum of Fine Arts, Boston." *Bulletin of the Museum of Fine Arts, Boston* 68/354: 244–58.

Roth, A. M.
1994 "The Practical Economics of Tomb-building in the Old Kingdom: A Visit to the Necropolis in a Carrying Chair." In *For His Ka: Essays Offered in Memory of Klaus Baer*, edited by D. P. Silverman, pp. 227–40. Studies in Ancient Oriental Civilization 55. Chicago: Oriental Institute.

Saad, Z. Y.
1947 *Ceiling Stelae in Second Dynasty Tombs from the Excavations at Helwan*. Supplement to Annales du Service des antiquités de l'Égypte 21. Cairo: Institut français d'archéologie orientale.

Sakkarah Expedition
1938a *The Mastaba of Mereruka*, Part 1: Chambers A 1–10, Plates 1–103. Oriental Institute Publications 31. Chicago: University of Chicago Press.
1938b *The Mastaba of Mereruka*, Part 2: Chambers A 11–13, Doorjambs and Inscriptions of Chambers A 1–21, Tomb Chamber, Exterior, Plates 104–219. Oriental Institute Publications 39. Chicago: University of Chicago Press.

Scamuzzi, E.
1965 *Egyptian Art in the Egyptian Museum of Turin*. New York: Harry S. Abrams.

Schäfer, H.
1974 *Principles of Egyptian Art*. Oxford: Clarendon Press.

Sethe, K.
1960a *Die altägyptischen Pyramidentexte*, Volume 1: *Spruch 1–468 (Pyr. 1–905)*. Second edition. Hildesheim: Georg Olms.
1960b *Die altägyptischen Pyramidentexte*, Volume 2: *Spruch 469–714 (Pyr. 906–2217)*. Second edition. Hildesheim: Georg Olms.

Silverman, D. P.
1982 "Scribe's Equipment Box." In *Egypt's Golden Age: The Art of Living in the New Kingdom 1558–1085 B.C.*, edited by E. Brovarski, S. K. Doll, and R. E. Freed, pp. 283–84, cat. no. 389. Boston: Museum of Fine Arts.

Simpson, W. K.

1976 *The Mastabas of Qar and Idu*. Giza Mastabas 2. Boston: Museum of Fine Arts.

1978 *The Mastabas of Kawab, Khafkhufu I and II*. Giza Mastabas 3. Boston: Museum of Fine Arts.

1980 *Mastabas of the Western Cemetery*, Part 1. Giza Mastabas 4. Boston: Museum of Fine Arts.

Spiegelberg, W.

1921 *Koptisches Handwörterbuch*. Heidelberg: Carl Winter.

Vandier, J.

1964 *Manuel d'archéologie égyptienne*, volume 4. Paris: Picard.

Vycichl, W.

1983 *Dictionnaire étymologique de la langue copte*. Leuven: Peeters.

Weber, M.

1969 Beiträge zur Kenntnis des Schrift- und Buchwesens der alten Ägypter. Ph.D. dissertation, University of Cologne.

Weill, R.

1908 *La IIe et la IIIe dynasties: Les origines de l'Égypte pharaonique*, part 1. Paris: Ernest Leroux.

Wild, H.

1953 *Le tombeau de Ti*, fascicle 2: *La chapelle* (première partie). Mémoires de l'Institut français d'archéologie orientale du Cairo 65. Cairo: Institut français d'archéologie orientale.

1966 *Le tombeau de Ti*, fascicle 3: *La chapelle* (deuxième partie). Mémoires de l'Institut français d'archéologie orientale du Caire 65. Cairo: Institut français d'archéologie orientale.

Willems, H.

1988 *Chests of Life: A Study of the Typology and Conceptual Development of Middle Kingdom Standard Class Coffins*. Leiden: Ex Oriente Lux.

Williams, C. R.

1932 *The Decoration of the Tomb of Per-neb*. New York: Metropolitan Museum of Art.

Wilson, J. A.

1954 "A Group of Sixth Dynasty Inscriptions." *Journal of Near Eastern Studies* 13: 243–64.

Winlock, H. E.

1955 *Models of Daily Life in Ancient Egypt*. Cambridge: Harvard University Press.

Wissa, M.

1994 "Le sarcophage de Merenre et l'expédition à Ibhat (I)." In *Hommage à Jean Leclant*, volume 1: *Études pharaoniques*, edited by C. Berger, G. Clère, and N. Grimal, pp. 379–87. Bibliothèque d'étude 106/1. Cairo: Institut français d'archéologie orientale.

Zeigler, C.

1993 *Le mastaba d'Akhethetep: Une chapelle funéraire de l'Ancien Empire*. Paris: Réunion des Musées Nationaux.

Zonhoven, L. M. J.

1979 "The Inspection of a Tomb at Deir el-Medîna (O. Wien Aeg. 1)." *Journal of Egyptian Archaeology* 65: 89–98.

5

A CASE FOR NARRATIVITY: GILT STUCCO MUMMY COVER IN THE GRAECO-ROMAN MUSEUM, ALEXANDRIA, INV. 27808

LORELEI H. CORCORAN

The University of Memphis, Tennessee

Professor Wente generously shared his understanding of Egyptian religion, derived from his careful reading and analysis of religious texts, with the students in his classes. His classroom instruction and his insights, suggestions, and encouragement as a member of my dissertation advisory committee were invaluable to me. Although my own focus has always been on ancient Egyptian art, Professor Wente influenced and inspired me to "contextualize" and "translate" the visual images from ancient Egypt. This article is offered as a token of my appreciation for his gift to me, the great joy of discovery in visual and textual decipherment.[1]

BACKGROUND AND INTRODUCTION

One of the most intriguing and beautiful mummy cases preserved from Roman Egypt is in the collection of the Graeco-Roman Museum, Alexandria (Inv. 27808). It is the mummy of an adult, swathed in linen, which was then covered in a coat of stucco modeled with scenes from Egyptian mythology, gilded, painted, and inlaid with glass. The modern history of the object, dating to 1963/64, is the subject of a tale, related to me by Dr. Henri Riad, former director of the museum, that could be the source of a mystery novel. Samir Lama, a film producer working at the oasis of el-'Areg near Siwa, brought the mummy back to his home in Alexandria for display. Subsequently, his maid encountered the mummy case and became afraid. She went to the police with the story that Lama was keeping a dead body in his apartment! It was perhaps at this time that an inexpert attempt was made to extract from the mummy case its face cover, which was most probably made of the same gilt stucco as the body cover, perhaps inlaid with glass and semi-precious stones, although it might possibly have been a painted panel portrait. When the police arrived at Lama's apartment, they removed the "corpse" to the police station where it spent the night. The next morning, Dr. Riad escorted the mummy to the museum where it was cataloged into the collection and has since remained on exhibit.

The mummy case is 62.5 inches in length, 13.0 inches across its widest point (the shoulder area), and 11.0 inches in depth. The height of the footcase is 11.0 inches; the width is 8.0 inches. The body field is divided into six registers (fig. 5.1), the top register being decorated with a broad collar. A figure of a cobra winds its way along the length of each side of the body field. A floral wreath is modeled into the stucco surrounding the head and a grapevine, modeled in stucco, encircles the back of the head.

Both the construction and the iconography of the mummy case date it to the first quarter of the second century A.D. (cf. Bianchi 1983, p. 15). Parallels can be drawn between this gilt stucco case, modeled with scenes from Egyptian mythology that are arranged in horizontal registers, and the covers of portrait mummies unearthed by Sir Flinders Petrie at Hawara, such as CG 33.215 and CG 33.216 in the Egyptian Museum, Cairo.

1. I thank the members of the High Committee of the Supreme Council of Antiquities and am grateful to Mme Dorya el-Sayed, Director, and the members of the High Committee of the Graeco-Roman Museum, Alexandria, for permission to publish the mummy case here discussed. I also thank the American Research Center in Egypt and the University of Chicago (Ryerson Travel Fellowship) for support. The Institute of Egyptian Art and Archaeology, the University of Memphis, provided funding for the production of the drawings by William Schenck. Drawings in figs. 5.1–8 are by William Schenck. Photographs in figs. 5.2, 5.6, 5.8–10 are the author's, printed by permission of the Graeco-Roman Museum, Alexandria. Illustrations for figs. 5.11–12 in the Addendum are provided courtesy of James E. Harris.

Gold of Praise: Studies on Ancient Egypt in Honor of Edward F. Wente
Edited by Emily Teeter and John A. Larson
Studies in Ancient Oriental Civilization 58
Chicago: Oriental Institute, 1999

Figure 5.1. Drawing of Gilt Stucco Mummy Cover. Graeco-Roman Museum, Alexandria, Inv. 27808

Glass and stone inlays are used on the Egyptian Museum mummy cases, and glass inlays are also used on portrait mummies with body covers of rhombic-wrapped linen bandages also datable to the early second century (e.g., Egyptian Museum, Cairo, CG 33.222; Musées Royaux d'Art et d'Histoire, Brussels, Inv. E 4857). The same scene, "baptism of pharaoh" (Corcoran 1995, pp. 59–60), depicted in the register just above the feet (not, *contra* Bianchi 1983, pp. 15–16, "in the area of the thighs") on the Alexandria museum mummy case occurs on two portrait mummies (Egyptian Museum, Cairo, CG 33.219 and CG 33.220) dated to the first quarter of the second century and a third (Egyptian Museum, Cairo, Inv. prov. 17/10/16/1) dated approximately to the second or early third century A.D.

It was Professor Wente who first suggested to me that the decorative program of Roman portrait mummy cases might be gainfully analyzed from bottom to top, by comparing the disposition of the horizontal registers that depict the actors and actions of episodic events decorating the body fields of the mummy coverings to the arrangement of registers or zones of figures and scenes which occur on tomb and temple walls in pharaonic art. He cited a model with which he was closely familiar from his experiences working with the Epigraphic Survey (*RIK* 4, p. 1): the bottom to top disposition of the eastern registers of the Seti I battle reliefs on the north exterior wall of the hypostyle hall at Karnak temple, a sequence of scenes that follows the chronological order of the battles as they were waged during the reign of King Seti (Gaballa 1976, pp. 100–05).

In order to arrive at the focal meaning of any design, like the decorative program of a tomb or temple or of a mummy case, the decoration of the work must be scrutinized "as a semiological whole" (Davis 1993, pp. 21–22), iconographically complex but coherent. "It would be misleading to isolate individual figures, groups of figures, motifs, or signs and try to identify their meaning independent of their metaphorical and narrative context within a particular image" because "an image is a concatenation of passages of depiction functioning for a viewer as a referential whole; no detail in or compositional zone of the pictorial text can be ignored" (ibid., p. 25). These zones are "linked with one another as the episodes in the story of [a] narrative, or the poles of a metaphor, in particular top and bottom, left and right, side to side, or obverse to reverse relations" (ibid., p. 27). In the decorative program of a mummy case, all details of the decoration should then be semiotically and symbiotically related and contribute to the religious symbolism that manifests in visual terms the religious convictions of the deceased. Reading the imagery of the Roman portrait mummy cases from bottom to top worked successfully for me (Corcoran 1988, pp. 96–146) in reconstructing a narrative which embodied the main elements of those events which characterized the afterlife aspirations of individuals who elected the portrait mummy design as their funerary outfit.

Subsequently, Barbara Borg (Doxiadis 1995, p. 236, n. 5, to "The Religious Context") proposes that the body field registers of portrait mummies (e.g., Artemidoros, British Museum Inv. 21810, for color plate see ibid., p. 70, pl. 57) be read from top to bottom. Following that, if a viewer were to read the body field of Artemidoros from top to bottom in order to synthesize a focal meaning from the sequence of events, the order of its five horizontal registers would be:

1. A broad collar of gold, with Horus falcon terminals; two seated figures of Maat, positioned to fill the space left open by the upswept curve of the collar, to either side of a centrally positioned vessel; and a Greek text ("Artemidoros, farewell") in a band below;
2. Anubis libating a corpse on a lion-headed bier while two goddesses (Isis and Nephthys) look on;
3. Horus and Thoth adoring the Abydos fetish of Osiris;
4. The awakened Osiris, with his *ba*, resting on a lion-headed bier;
5. A winged sun disk; the foot cover depicts bare feet (where the mummy's actual feet would be) and an elongated *atef*-crown is positioned upside-down (i.e., facing the mummy's head) between the feet.

Identifying the mummy in the top register with Osiris and following the events of his embalmment and ultimate resurrection, this order of events (top to bottom) relies upon a linear progression of time. As initially suggested, the reading of these same scenes from bottom to top, on the other hand, would have incorporated a more timeless approach to the narrative; that is, it is only on account of the triumph of the resurrection of the gods Ra and Osiris in the first instance (respectively depicted at the bottom of the case as a winged sun disk and as the raised mummiform figure on the lion bier) and the celebration (cultic reenactment) of that event, that a mortal could aspire, through assimilation with the deity (the mummy on the lion bier being identified then as both the deceased and the god Osiris), to experience a similar resurrection after death. The potential for the resurrection of any mortal individual and its eternal guarantee would be predicated, therefore, on the miracle of resurrection that occurred once, yet which will also continue to occur in perpetuity, for the gods Ra and Osiris. Admittedly then, although "the viewer's experience of the story and text varies with the point of entry" (Davis 1993, p. 27), a re-ordering of the sequence of events does not change the intended point of the story.

It is perhaps best, then, for us not to be rigidly dogmatic concerning the direction of the narrative reading of visual images from ancient Egypt, but rather to concentrate on (1) an elucidation of the central concern of the image maker and patron and (2) a description of the mechanics of organization behind the selection and sequencing of the events depicted that reflect that concern. In a fresh approach to the reading of scenes on prehistoric palettes, Davis (1993, pp. 26–27) proposes that "the narrative experience as a whole would not be greatly compromised if a viewer begins with the 'bottom' ... rather than with the 'top' since the fabula can be reconstructed from the story sequence however it is ordered ... . It is only by 'reading through' all of the pictorial material that the viewer will discover that, in the logic of the fabula, the 'beginning' of the story on the 'obverse top' is actually the logical *end* of the fabula."

This point is made clear with reference to the eastern registers of the Seti I battle reliefs. Whereas the visual images appear to have been ordered from bottom to top, the accompanying texts relate events in reverse sequence (*RIK* 4, p. 3). The perceived discrepancy might be dismissed as a "scribal error," but in light of the complementarity of text and image in Egyptian art the Epigraphic Survey (*RIK* 4) suggests that "the co-existence of accounts" serves as an artistic device which binds the depiction of episodic battle reliefs into a "single tableau" that emphasizes the "rhetorical point" of the decorative program of the wall: "the king's role as defender of Egypt." The complementarity of text and image was therefore an *intentional* reference to the intrinsic similarity of the king's battles in terms of the predestined outcome, in every instance, of his victory.

As long as the initiated viewer is familiar with the intended meaning of the story, that capable viewer may then enter the story at any point, simultaneously reconstructing and/or re-ordering the sequence of events. This engagement of the viewer in the process is, in fact, a desirable effect, as it involves the viewer in the process of the narrative.[2] The experience of the patron/viewer is not then of "viewing" as a passive receptor of data but as an active participant in a drama. For liturgical narrative, this level of participation is equal to participation in the celebration of a cultic act.

As analyzed by Davis (1993, p. 27), the surfaces of prehistoric palettes are organized into decorated zones that "form the several episodes of the story from which the fabula can be projected." With the funerary art of the mummy cases, we are dealing with the pictorially represented fabulae of the myths of Ra and Osiris. The central concern of those mythic episodes, when linked as discrete acts in a progressive linear fashion or when endlessly reenacted as an epic within a temporal realm governed by time measured in cyclical terms, is the triumph and resurrection of the gods. The visual imagery is present then on one level for the gods, firstly to commemorate the occurrence of the archetypal triumphal act and secondly to invite and ensure the perpetual recurrence of that act. The attainment of this objective on the divine plane is then however only the starting point for another sequence: the dependent yet parallel chain of ritual events represented for the benefit of the initiated patron/deceased who has assimilated with Ra and/or Osiris. On that plane, the selected scenes of the narrative culminate in the triumph and resurrection of that initiated mortal for whom the myths are re-enacted in visual terms. This relationship is clearly set forth "in a mythical tale [The Contendings of Horus and Seth, wherein] the god Ptah says to Osiris, 'Now after the manner of gods, so also shall patricians and commoners go to rest in the place where you are'" (Wente 1982, pp. 23–24). It is, in part, because of the ancient Egyptians' belief in the potential of time to operate according to two separate but equal systems, both linear (*ḏt*) and cyclical (*nḥḥ*) (see ibid., pp. 22–23), and in equal part because of their ability to hold ideas which would logically appear to be self-contradictory[3] that any liturgical narrative as it was expressed in canonical (pharaonic and later) Egyptian art could be correctly interpreted by the initiated viewer without respect to the arrangement of the sequence of events which might be identified as a "logical" beginning, middle, or end and that the objectives of those narratives could apply equally to the "divine" or "mortal" realm.

2. Compare Davis's (1993, pp. 24–25) description of the responsibility of the viewer in completing the ellipses in the sequence of events portrayed on the Hunters' Palette or his description (1993, pp. 43–44) of the mechanics of representation by which the viewer is drawn into the vortex of events that culminates in the "striking blow" delivered by the victorious ruler depicted on the Narmer Palette.

3. See Hornung 1982, pp. 240–42. The "dual unity" of linear and cyclical time in fact gives rise to the "continuity of time" (Assmann 1995, p. 62).

DESCRIPTION OF GILT STUCCO MUMMY CASE

The mummy case consists of a 0.375 inch layer of white stucco, painted with a red undercoat for gilt. Figures are modeled in raised relief with impressed lines (see fig. 5.1). Some of the figures are painted, others are unpainted. The only paint colors used are black, orange-red, and white. The horizontal bands that separate the registers are inlaid with rectangular-shaped colored glass. The thin, rectangular glass inlays, laid vertically, are of solid colors in either light blue (simulating turquoise), orange-red (simulating carnelian), or dark blue (simulating lapis lazuli). Wide, rectangular glass inlays laid horizontally are white with stripes of blue and red.

Foot Cover

The footcase is 11.0 inches high and 8.0 inches wide (fig. 5.2). The underside of the footcase is decorated with a single motif: a falcon with profile head and outstretched downswept wings whose head is topped by a sun

a

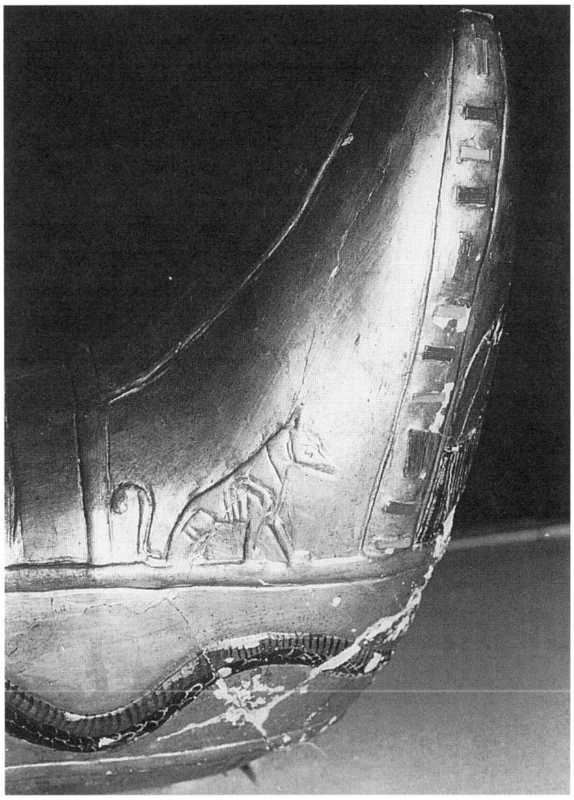

b

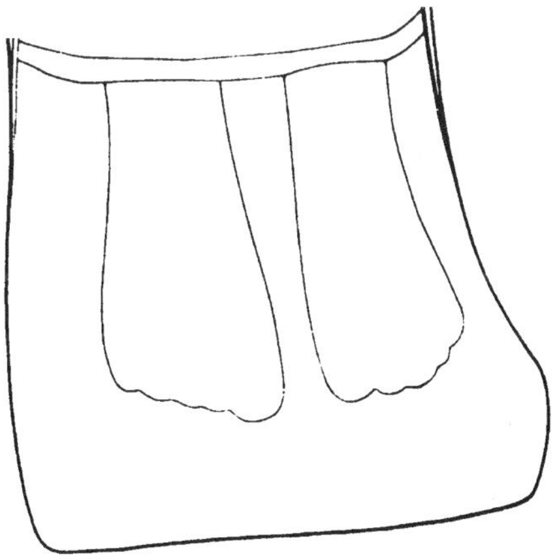

c

Figure 5.2. Photographs of (*a*) Falcon on Underside of Footcase and (*b*) Jackal on Side of Footcase and (*c*) Drawing of Foot Cover. Gilt Stucco Mummy Cover. Graeco-Roman Museum, Alexandria, Inv. 27808

disk with an upraised uraeus at each side (fig. 5.2a). The falcon probably represents the god Sokar-Ra (a solarized form of the underworld deity Sokar). The underside of the footcase is damaged, with some stucco loss below the body of the bird. Stucco fragments at the sides and one small fragment near the center bottom preserve the tail ends of the upraised uraei that decorate the sides of the mummy case.

An avian motif on the bottom of the footcase is rare in comparison with the numerous examples from Egyptian royal and funerary art where the outstretched wings of birds cradle the head. The earliest known representation of the motif of a falcon (representing the god Horus) at the back of a human head is that of Chephren as the Living Horus (Egyptian Museum, Cairo, CG 14), a concept repeatedly expressed for the benefit of royalty from the Old Kingdom (e.g., Neferefre, Egyptian Museum, Cairo, JE 98171) to the Late Period (e.g., relief from the Roman Birth House at Dendara). Falcons appear frequently on the back of the heads of late first century A.D. plaster head covers, for example, CG 33.131 (Edgar 1905, pp. 23–24, pl. 12) and CG 33.212 (Edgar 1905, p. 68, pl. 30). A falcon with outstretched wings, but that wears a double crown (Ra-Horakhty?), is depicted at the back of the head of a stucco portrait mummy (Egyptian Museum, Cairo, Inv. prov. 17/10/16/1). Other examples appear to represent the human-headed *ba* of the deceased: one, CG 33.135 (Edgar 1905, p. 30, pl. 16), is labeled "Ba-en-Hor."

On the upperside of the footcase, appended from a raised plaster line above where the mummy's actual feet would be, are depicted two human feet, 6.0 inches long and 2.5 inches wide, that are incised in the plaster. The toenails are indicated with incised lines. The feet are unshod.

At either side of the footcase (fig. 5.2b) is incised a muscular jackal, seated on its haunches but with its forelegs straight. Each jackal wears a collar. The tall ears of these jackals are erect. Their tails curl behind them in an upraised S-curve. These jackals probably represent the dual Wepwawets that serve as openers of the way for the sun god (Corcoran 1995, pp. 51–52).

The front edge of the footcase is inlaid with a row of alternately horizontal and vertical rectangles of colored glass in solid colors of red, light blue, or dark blue.

Register One

An undecorated band, 1.0 inch in width, separates the gilt strip at the top of the incised feet from the 1.0 inch wide strip inlaid with glass rectangles that forms the base of the first register (fig. 5.3). The colored glass rectangles in this strip are all inlaid horizontally.

Figure 5.3. Drawing of Register One. Gilt Stucco Mummy Cover. Graeco-Roman Museum, Alexandria, Inv. 27808

Register one is 6.25 inches in height. It is positioned just above the ankles. It depicts a scene that is quite common on Roman period mummies (*contra* Bianchi 1983, pp. 15–16, who states that the motif is "without precedent on monuments of this type"). It appears on three contemporary Roman portrait mummies in the Egyptian Museum, Cairo (CG 33.219, CG 33.220, and Inv. prov. 17/10/16/1; see Corcoran 1995, pls. 14–15, 22). This is the "baptism of pharaoh" motif that assimilates the deceased whether male or female with the purification and rebirth rituals originally associated with Egyptian royalty (ibid., pp. 59–60). All figures are incised and slightly modeled. Paint is added to detail the figures.

In the center of the register is a male figure dressed only in a pleated, knee-length kilt and broad collar. His torso is depicted frontally, but his head is turned in profile to the left. The figure, identified as a child by his diminutive size and characteristic hairdo (the sidelock of youth or "Horuslock"), stands between two larger anthropomorphic figures with avian heads. To his left stands the falcon-headed Horus, facing inward, wearing a shoulder-length wig, the red crown, and a pleated, knee-length kilt with a pleated fabric that is visible between his legs. In his raised hands, he holds a bowling-pin shaped vessel from which he pours a single stream of water over the body of the child. To the child's right stands the ibis-headed Thoth, facing inward, wearing a shoulder-length wig, *atef*-crown, and pleated, knee-length kilt like that of Horus. Thoth holds, in his upraised hands, a vessel similar to that held by Horus. No stream of water is indicated as emerging from the vessel. All figures are barefoot.

Register Two

A 1.125 inch strip inlaid with colored glass rectangles laid alternately vertically and horizontally (center horizontal with three vertical to each side, one horizontal, three vertical, one horizontal at each end) forms the base for register two (fig. 5.4).

Figure 5.4. Drawing of Register Two. Gilt Stucco Mummy Cover. Graeco-Roman Museum, Alexandria, Inv. 27808

Register two is 6.25 inches in height. It depicts a kneeling, winged goddess (Nut or Maat), facing left, who holds a *maat*-feather aloft in each upraised hand. A red sun disk tops her chin-length bob. Within each inner corner created by the curve of an upswept wing is a horned bull that lies atop a brick(?) structure resembling the Egyptian hieroglyph for gold (Gardiner's Sign List, S12).

The figure of the kneeling goddess is incised and slightly modeled. Details of the figure (the delicate features of her face, the feathers of her outstretched wings, her broad collar, and red dress spangled with black stars) are in paint. The figures of the horned bulls, each of which faces outward, are only incised.

The goddess Nut more often appears across the upper chest of decorated mummies with cartonnage covers, spreading her wings protectively over the wrapped body that has taken on the aspect of the reborn sun. Typical examples from contemporary portrait mummies are Egyptian Museum, Cairo, CG 33.215 and CG 33.216 (Corcoran 1995, pls. 18–19).

The bulls might represent the Apis bull of Memphis, a deity associated with Ptah, who, when identified with Osiris (but always in that form represented as an adult male), was known in the Late Period as Serapis. Alternatively, the bulls might represent the Mnevis (the bull at right has a sun disk between its horns, an attribute of the Mnevis of Heliopolis) or the Buchis (sacred to Montu at Hermonthis). All of these bulls had strong solar associations and were embodiments of creative force.

Register Three

A 1.0 inch strip inlaid with colored glass rectangles laid alternately vertically and horizontally (center horizontal with three vertical to each side, one horizontal, three vertical, one horizontal, two vertical at each end) forms the base for register three (fig. 5.5), which is 6.25 inches in height. It depicts the four sons of Horus, the gods who protected the deceased's internal organs, divided in two pairs facing inward. All four gods are depicted in mummiform with their idiosyncratic heads (baboon, human, hawk, and jackal), each topped by a sun disk. Each holds both of his hands before his chest and grasps a linen cloth (funerary bandage) before him. A fabric flap or sash, cut at a diagonal end, falls from below each of their hands to the top of their feet.

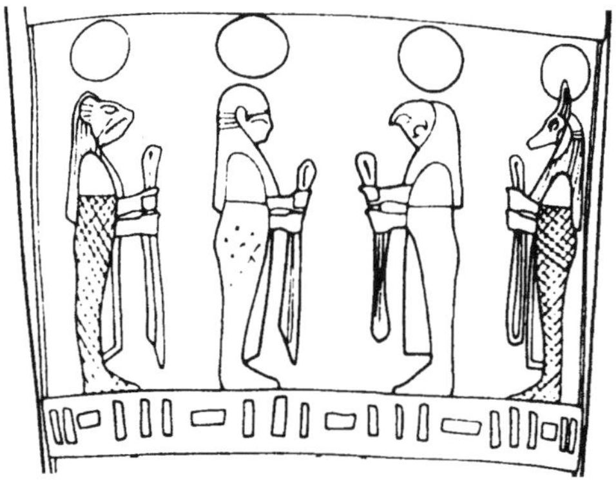

Figure 5.5. Drawing of Register Three. Gilt Stucco Mummy Cover. Graeco-Roman Museum, Alexandria, Inv. 27808

The left pair of figures includes the hawk-headed Qebehsenef and the jackal-headed Duamutef. The right pair of figures are the human-headed Imsety and the baboon-headed Hapy. The bodies of the gods at center (Qebehsenef and Imsety) are decorated in paint as if their shrouded bodies were covered with bead net covers. The bodies of the gods at the outer edges (Duamutef and Hapy) are only incised in a rhombic pattern simulating wrapped linen bandages.

Register Four

A 1.0 inch strip inlaid with colored glass rectangles laid alternately vertically and horizontally (center horizontal with three vertical to each side, one horizontal, three vertical at the right, two vertical at the left, one horizontal, one vertical at the right end, and four vertical at the left end) forms the base for register four (fig. 5.6), which is 6.0 inches in height. At the center is a cloaked and bearded Osiris, depicted frontally, wearing the *atef*-crown. On each of his sides is a standing female figure, facing inward, with near arm bending downward and crossing in front of her body while her far arm, crooked at the elbow, is raised toward the god's head. Each female, representing the goddesses Isis and Nephthys, is dressed in an ankle-length sheath (breasts in profile), has shoulder-length hair, and wears a sun disk between two cow's horns. At the right end is a striding male figure, facing inward, with a jackal head (or mask?) who wears an ankle-length garment visible beneath a cloak that covers his shoulders and neck and falls in heavy folds over his breast. A sun disk rests atop his head (between his erect ears). At the left end is a striding male figure, dressed as a *sm*-priest in a panther skin garment and double feather headdress attached to a fillet, the ends of which trail behind him. In his outstretched hands, this figure holds an unrolled papyrus that is inscribed in black paint with letters that simulate a Demotic text.

b

a

Figure 5.6. (*a*) Photograph and (*b*) Drawing of Register Four. Gilt Stucco Mummy Cover. Graeco-Roman Museum, Alexandria, Inv. 27808

This scene recreates a funerary ritual involving the active participation of priests and priestesses (or actors and actresses?; for the use of lay participants in the dramatic enactments of the burial of an Apis bull, see Thompson 1988, pp. 198–203).

The figures of the characters are depicted awkwardly: the smiling grimace on the cloaked jackal recalls the childhood fairy tale of Little Red Riding Hood with the wolf dressed up as grandma and the *sm*-priest (fig. 5.6a) in his animal pelt and feathers looks like a cartoon bunny from an Easter parade. But the scene is not unique and has a parallel in the top left panel of a child's portrait mummy in the British Museum (Inv. 21809; Dawson and Gray 1968, p. 32, pl. 16b), where a similarly garbed priest holding a text before him recites a spell for the Osiris he addresses.

Register Five

A 1.0 inch strip inlaid with colored glass rectangles laid alternately vertically and horizontally (center horizontal with three vertical to each side, one horizontal, three vertical, one horizontal, two vertical at the right end, and three vertical at the left end) forms the base for register five (fig. 5.7).

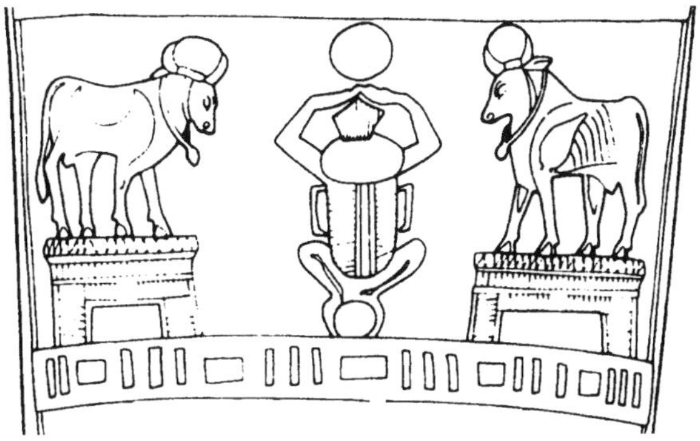

Figure 5.7. Drawing of Register Five. Gilt Stucco Mummy Cover. Graeco-Roman Museum, Alexandria, Inv. 27808

Register five is 5.375 inches in height. It depicts a scarab beetle, positioned vertically, that pushes a disk before it. The beetle is flanked by two bulls facing inward in profile that stand on brick(?) platforms resting on supports with chamfered sides.

The scarab pushing the disk is a depiction of the sun god Khepri who rolls the orb of the sun across the day-sky as a beetle rolls a ball of dung across the desert. The birth of young beetles from these dung balls was explained as a reference to the regenerative powers of the creator solar deity.

The two horned bulls, each with a sun disk between its horns and wearing a decorative collar, are related to the two bulls in register two. The bull at right is painted black with white coloring along its flank; the bull at left is totally black as was considered fitting for the Mnevis bull, symbol of the sun god Ra at Heliopolis. The red sun disks between the horns of the bulls associate both bulls with solar powers.

Register Six

A 0.875 inch strip inlaid with colored glass rectangles laid alternately vertically and horizontally (center horizontal with three vertical to each side, one horizontal, three vertical, one horizontal, two vertical at the right end, and four vertical at the left end) forms the base for register six (fig. 5.8).

The breast area of the body is covered, for a height of 8.5 inches with an elaborate broad collar. A human-headed *ba*-bird (a form of the soul of the deceased) standing and facing inward fills the outer corner at each end created by the curve of the collar.

The broad collar is composed of seven rows of bead elements of various shapes (teardrop, star, tube, and dot) in either a running pattern or a triangular design, each of which is separated by a narrow, plain spacer row. The beads are detailed in red, white, and black paint. The terminals of the collar are composed of falcon heads, with feather details rendered in paint, in profile facing outward, each topped by a red disk.

The human-headed *ba*-birds vary slightly in detail, especially in the rendering of the feathers at the breast (shown crosshatched on bird at left, plain on bird at right) and the tail (shown rounded at the bottom and folded into the wing feathers on the bird at left; squared at the bottom with wing tips separately delineated on the bird

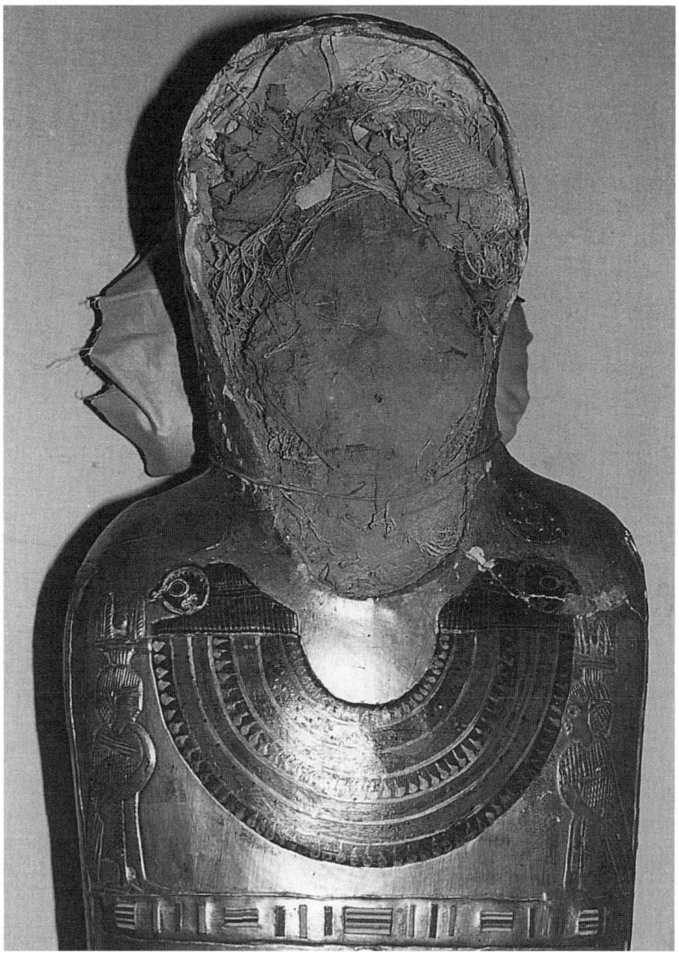

a

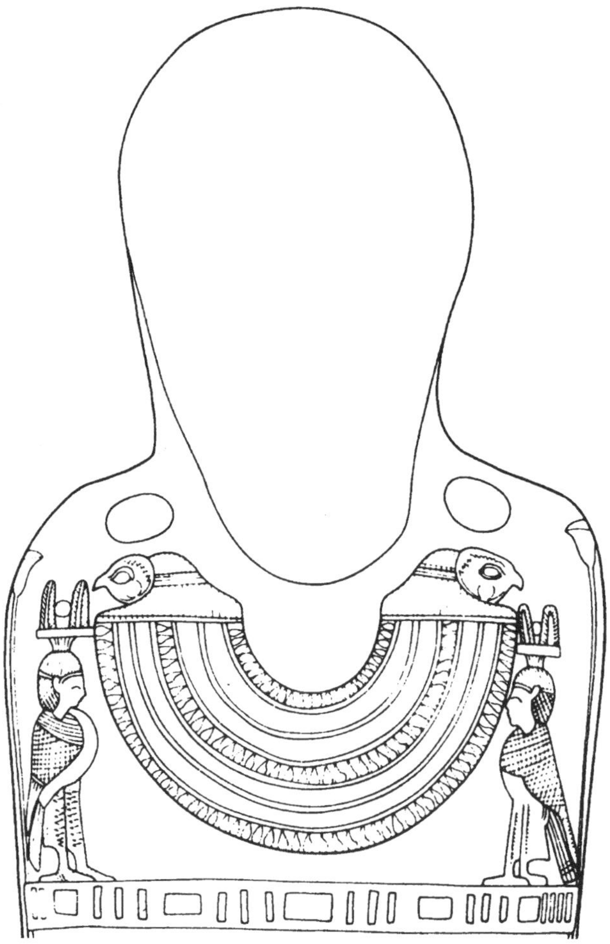

b

Figure 5.8. (*a*) Photograph and (*b*) Drawing of Register Six and Face Cover. Gilt Stucco Mummy Cover. Graeco-Roman Museum, Alexandria, Inv. 27808

at right). Each *ba* wears a short, crosshatched wig tied with a fillet, atop which is a modius that supports a horizontal base for a crown of two plumes that flank a sun disk.

The decorative face covering of the mummy case was intentionally removed at some point. Its loss mars an appreciation of the mummy case, a loss intensified by the impression that it must have been of exquisite workmanship and significant also because it prevents us from attributing with certainty the mummy case to a man or woman based on gender-specific stylistic criteria (but see *Addendum*, below, where Harris suggests that this individual is female). The area of loss is 11.5 inches in height and 6.5 inches in width. The loss of the face covering exposes the layers of scrap linen packing that were used to pad the surface of the face.

A wreath or garland, modeled in stucco, frames the head (fig. 5.9). The wreath, suffering from stucco loss, consists of two chains of three-petaled flowers (or three leaf clusters bound together), the tips of which face inward, that join at an oval-shaped disk in the center. The oval disk is, however, off-center of the nose of the mummy by two inches to the right. Behind the wreath and encircling the head is a grapevine modeled in stucco. The spray consists of five-petaled grape leaves and clusters of berries. The grapevine motif, popular within the Hellenistic milieu, is perhaps also one of many visual motifs that "migrated" from the walls or ceilings of tombs (especially common in New Kingdom tombs, for example, TT 96 of Sennefer) to the exterior and interior of coffins and mummy cases.

Left and Right Sides

Upright cobras with splayed hoods are depicted along the length of the mummy on either side (fig. 5.10). The cobras are flanked by scepters topped by lotus finials. The scepters terminate at the inlaid glass strip along the edge of the footcase, but the tails of the cobras curve around the base of the footcase. The details of the cobras are depicted in black, white, and red paint.

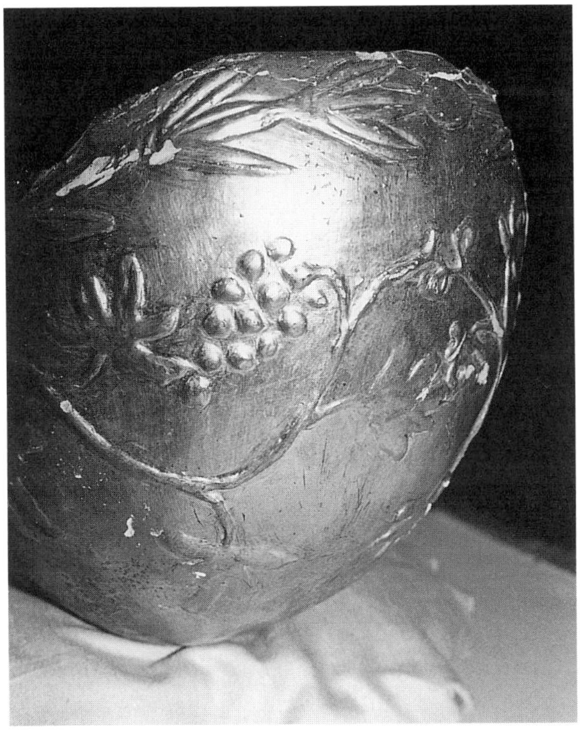

Figure 5.9. Photograph of Head Cover. Gilt Stucco Mummy Cover. Graeco-Roman Museum, Alexandria, Inv. 27808

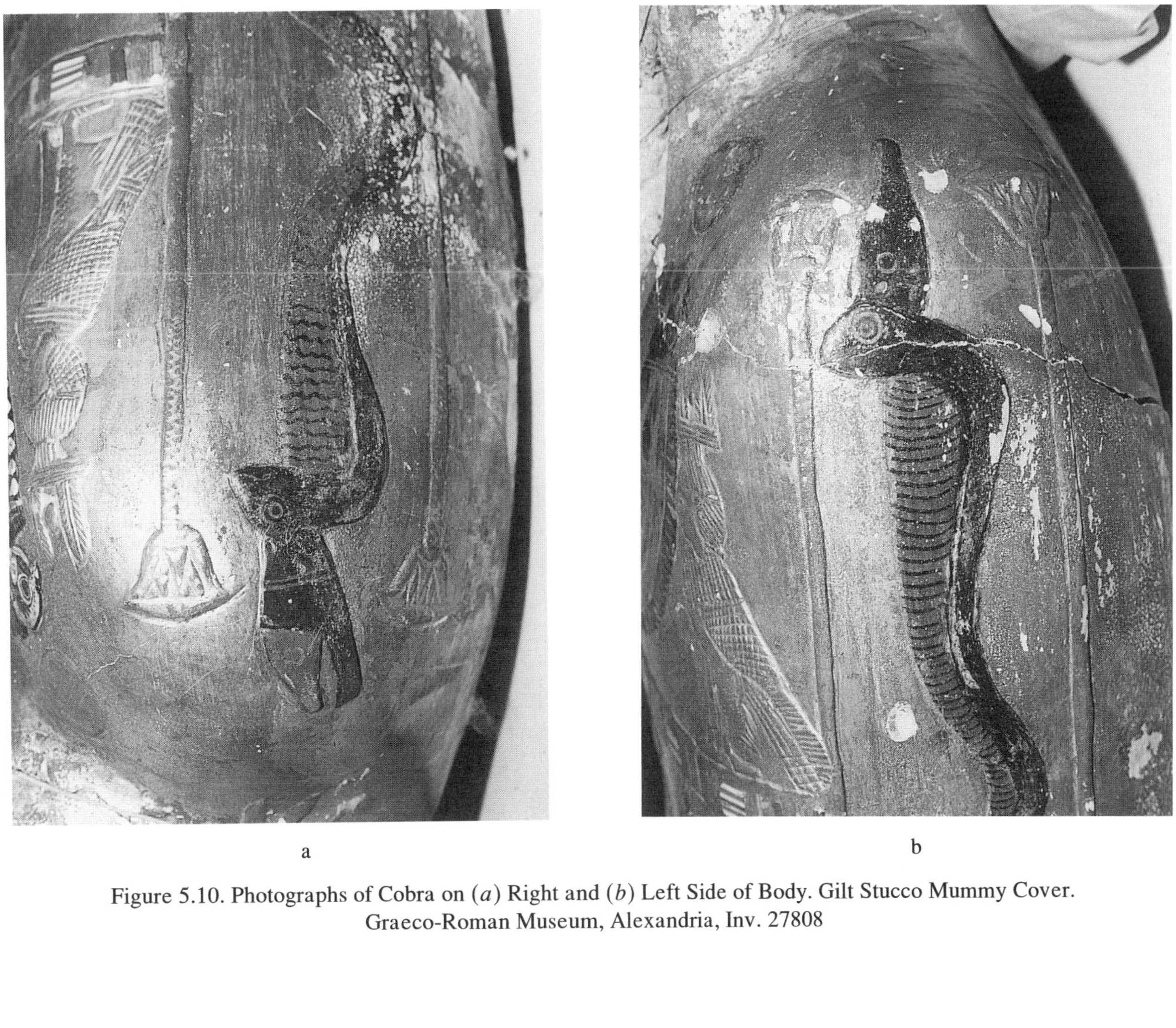

a b

Figure 5.10. Photographs of Cobra on (*a*) Right and (*b*) Left Side of Body. Gilt Stucco Mummy Cover. Graeco-Roman Museum, Alexandria, Inv. 27808

The cobra along the right side of the mummy (fig. 5.10a) wears the double crown of Upper and Lower Egypt. The cobra along the left side of the mummy (fig. 5.10b) wears only the white crown of Upper Egypt. Such cobras are often used as decorative devices at either side of a doorway in Ptolemaic and later temples and appear frequently on the sides of anthropoid wooden coffins of the Ptolemaic period, a motif perhaps traceable to royal antecedents such as the coffin lid of Ramesses III (Fitzwilliam Museum, Cambridge, Inv. E.1.1823).

CONCLUSION

The iconography of this stucco mummy case from Roman Egypt invokes the powerful mythology of the traditional gods of the Egyptian afterlife, Ra and Osiris. The lavish use of gilt on the case alludes to the glittering flesh of the sun god, Ra. The scenes modeled and painted on the body field and foot cover commemorate, celebrate, and perpetually renew the fabulae of the narratives that witness the creative and regenerative powers of the solar and chthonic forces inherent in the divine personae of Ra and Osiris. The representation of those events through visual imagery and through dramatic association recreated and effectively ensured a corresponding revitalization for the initiated patron and viewer.

The challenge in deciphering the focal meaning of the decorative program of mummy cases from Egypt of the Roman era is to relate each detail of the iconography to every other *and* to the fundamental religious belief (or beliefs) that each referenced, all of which would have been immediately apparent to the initiated viewer, no matter at which point of the narrative that viewer might have begun. It seems only fitting, therefore, that although these mummy cases date to the very end of pharaonic civilization in Egypt, the religious convictions they embody are those which can be traced to its very beginning.

ADDENDUM
COMMENTS ON AN X-RAY EXAMINATION OF MUMMY, GRAECO-ROMAN MUSEUM, ALEXANDRIA, INV. 27808

JAMES E. HARRIS

University of Michigan, Ann Arbor

I have studied the cranium detail. The dentition and supporting tissues indicate loss of dentition (the maxillary first molar), a generalized attrition, and loss of periodontal support (recession of the gums). Although dentition alone gives a crude index of aging, the long bones (femurs) confirm that this individual's age was probably in the fifties or older.

I compare the lateral x-ray cephalograms with standards we devised for modern Nubian people and an American sample from Ann Arbor (fig. 5.11).

Variable *	Nubian	American	27808
SNA	82/83	83	82
SNB	79	78	78
ANB	3.68	5/6#	4
Cranial base	133/135#	130	125
1/1	118/117#	134/128#	128
SN/Mand	36	30/33#	40
1/Mand	97	94/92#	96
Y-axis	92/90#	94	88

*Cephalometric angular measurements are commonly employed to measure craniofacial variation by the anthropologist and the orthodontic profession and tends to be independent of size factors.

#Male/female values are shown when different.

The cephalometric measurements indicate that this individual was within the range of the American Standards (European or Mediterranean), compared with that of the Nubian samples (see fig. 5.12a). Although my initial impression was that the dentition was somewhat prognathic, it was not confirmed by the cephalometric measurements. When the mandible (lower jaw) is adjusted by occlusion to the upper jar (maxillary dentition), the craniofacial complex is relatively retrognathic. The mandibular incisors are slightly more prognathic than the American samples, but the interincisal angle (the angle between the maxillary and mandibular incisor) is still closer to the American Caucasian population than the Nubian samples. The lower face is relatively short compared with that of the upper face. The lateral x-ray cephalometric view suggests a relatively delicate facial morphology. The frontal sinus is compressed to the point of non-existence, often associated with female growth pattern. My impression is that this individual is female; unfortunately I do not have a pelvic view to confirm this conclusion.

The postcranial skeleton is complete and the mummy appears to be relatively well preserved (compared with many mummies of this period that although beautifully packaged consist of loose bones). The cranium may

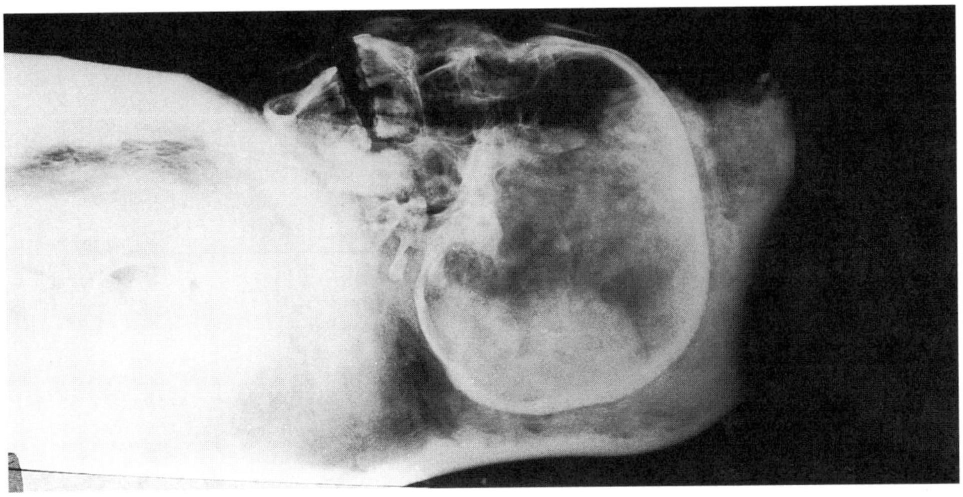

Figure 5.11. Lateral X-ray Cephalogram of Mummy 27808, Taken with GE 70 KV X-ray Machine, Blue Brand Film with Dupont High Contrast Cassettes

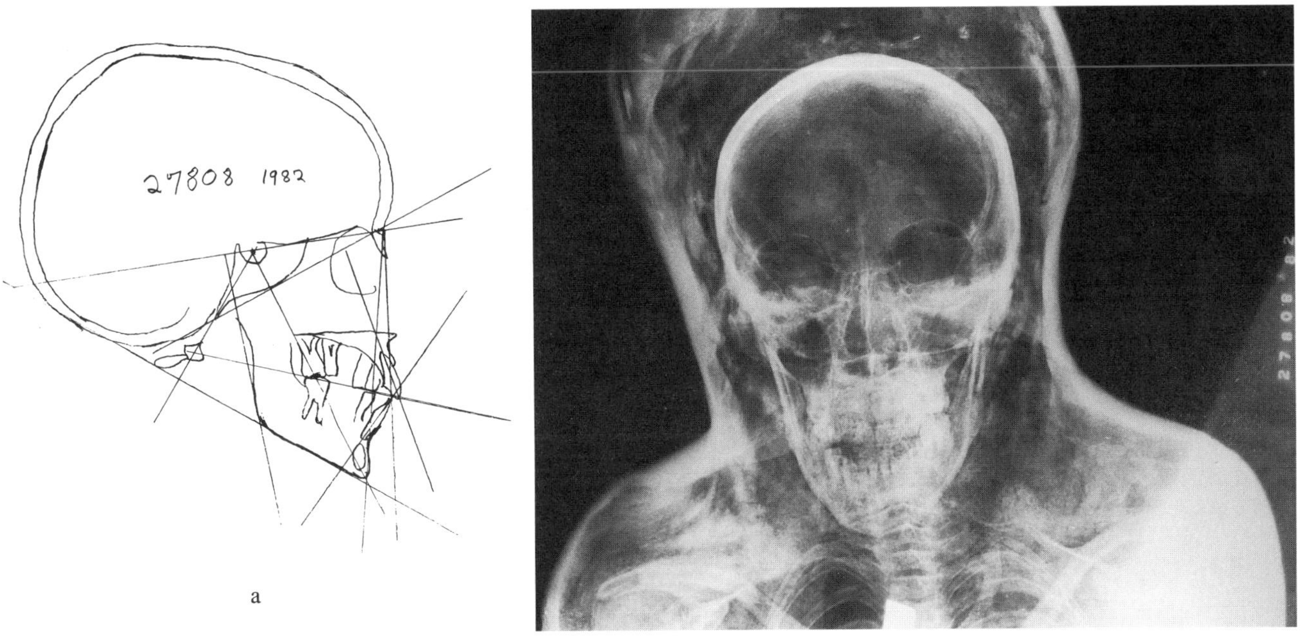

a

b

Figure 5.12. (*a*) Cephalometric X-ray Tracing of Mummy 27808, Taken in 1982 at the Graeco-Roman Museum, Alexandria, and (*b*) Posterior-anterior X-ray Cephalogram of Mummy 27808, Taken with GE 70 KV X-ray Machine, Blue Brand Film with Dupont High Contrast Cassettes

be dislocated from the cervical vertebrae. The arms are placed at the side. The centers of ossification are closed and the diathroidal or synovial joints that develop sharp margins with age may be observed here in the distal junction of the femur with the tibia. The overall appearance of the skeleton suggests an individual in middle age.

References

Assmann, J.
1995 *Egyptian Solar Religion in the New Kingdom: Re, Amun and the Crisis of Polytheism.* Translated by A. Alcock. London: Kegan Paul.

Bianchi, R. S.
1983 "Those Ubiquitous Glass Inlays, Part II." *Bulletin of the Egyptological Seminar* 5: 9–29.

Corcoran, L. H.
1988 Portrait Mummies from Roman Egypt. Ph.D. dissertation, University of Chicago.
1995 *Portrait Mummies from Roman Egypt (I–IV Centuries A.D.) with a Catalog of Portrait Mummies in Egyptian Museums.* Studies in Ancient Oriental Civilization 56. Chicago: Oriental Institute.

Davis, W.
1993 "Narrativity and the Narmer Palette." In *Narrative and Event in Ancient Art*, edited by P. J. Holliday, pp. 14–54. New York: Cambridge University Press.

Dawson, W. R., and P. H. K. Gray
1968 *Mummies and Human Remains.* Catalogue of Egyptian Antiquities in the British Museum 1. London: British Museum.

Doxiadis, E.
1995 *The Mysterious Fayum Portraits: Faces from Ancient Egypt.* New York: Harry N. Abrams.

Edgar, C. C.
1905 *Graeco-Egyptian Coffins, Masks, and Portraits.* Catalogue général des antiquités égyptiennes du Musée du Caire 26. Cairo: L'Institut français d'archéologie orientale.

Gaballa, G. A.
1976 *Narrative in Egyptian Art.* Mainz am Rhein: Philipp von Zabern.

Gardiner, A. H.
1973 *Egyptian Grammar.* Third edition revised. Oxford: Griffith Institute.

Hornung, E.
1982 *Conceptions of God in Ancient Egypt: The One and the Many.* Translated by J. Baines. Ithaca: Cornell University Press.

Thompson, D. J.
1988 *Memphis under the Ptolemies.* Princeton: Princeton University Press.

Wente, E. F.
1982 "Funerary Beliefs of the Ancient Egyptians." *Expedition* 24, no. 2: 17–26.

6

OPENING OF THE MOUTH AS TEMPLE RITUAL

EUGENE CRUZ-URIBE

Northern Arizona University, Flagstaff

The temple of Hibis in Kharga Oasis is a Late Period temple dedicated to the Theban god Amun-Ra, king of the gods who dwells in Hibis. The temple survives relatively intact and is the only temple surviving in such a state from the Saite-Persian period. The temple was erected by an earlier Saite king, Psammetichus II, upon the site of some earlier New Kingdom structure. During the reign of Darius the Great (519–486 B.C.), the temple was refurbished by the Persian ruler who added a rededication inscription and additional scenes (see Cruz-Uribe 1987, pp. 225–30). The temple then had an uninscribed hypostyle hall added during the reign of Achoris and, like many temples in Egypt, Nectanebo (I and II) added a portico (for drawing, views, and floor plan, see Winlock 1941).

While the temple itself was formally dedicated to Amun-Ra with Mut and Khonsu, it has been shown that the Theban triad are often identified with the triad Osiris, Isis, and Horus. This identification of Amun-Mut-Khonsu is consistent with similar events that took place in Thebes during the Late Period (see Cruz-Uribe 1994, pp. 169–89). Egberts (1995, pp. 6–7) argues that liturgical texts which deal with cult practices within temples are not to be viewed as having a direct relationship with the large corpus of texts that are frequently known as mortuary liturgies. In the discussion below I argue that the opposite is actually the case because there are many cases where the temple ritual and its associated liturgy are borrowed directly from the mortuary liturgy.[1]

Mark Smith (1993) published several Demotic texts entitled "The Opening of the Mouth for Breathing" and notes that these texts have numerous parallels to the New Kingdom versions of the Opening of the Mouth ritual scenes found in New Kingdom tombs (see Otto 1960). These Demotic texts are seen as Late Period variants of that ritual, which were ultimately derived from the earlier liturgies.

Smith argues that the text "Opening of the Mouth for Breathing" is to be seen as an example of mortuary liturgy, that is, used and recited in a ritual for the benefit of the deceased and used by the living (mortuary priest) performing rites at the tomb, but not to be read by the deceased in the hereafter (Smith 1993, pp. 6–7). Assmann (1990) is cited as the authority on this classification scheme. In addition, Assmann notes that in the Ptolemaic period the Theban clergy took rituals and liturgies of the temple cult into the tomb ritual and associated them with Book of the Dead spells.

Assmann (1990, p. 2) notes that the extra-textual criteria of redaction, transmission, and locational context are characteristic of the mortuary liturgy. It would appear that we must argue the same for temple liturgies and ask a further question: were temple liturgies and mortuary liturgies seen as the same? This might explain why the Theban priests used "temple liturgy" texts for "mortuary liturgy" and why the scenes at Hibis temple (a Saite-Persian period Theban temple transplanted to the oasis) have texts of a "mortuary liturgy" nature used as temple liturgy.

At Hibis temple, the evidence seems to be the opposite of what Egberts and Smith suggest. In one case, in hypostyle M on the lintel to the north door, we have a scene showing the king offering to Amun-Ra, Osiris, and Isis. Here we have a complete version of Book of the Dead chapter 15, a hymn to Ra-Horakhty. To this was added a separate portion of a hymn to the sun god. Daumas notes that these hymns are known to have been used in the daily temple ritual (Barucq and Daumas 1980, pp. 306–08; for the text, see Davies 1953, pl. 30; for translation and commentary, see Cruz-Uribe 1988, pp. 116–17).

---

1. This article is based on a presentation to the International International Congress of Egyptologists, Cambridge, United Kingdom, 1995.

Gold of Praise: Studies on Ancient Egypt in Honor of Edward F. Wente
Edited by Emily Teeter and John A. Larson
Studies in Ancient Oriental Civilization 58
Chicago: Oriental Institute, 1999

A second case at Hibis temple is found in the stairwell K1. There, the hymn by Horus invokes self-praise as he passes the various gates of the netherworld. This text is taken directly from a Book of the Dead manuscript for a woman (as indicated by the determinatives) of Spell 146w of the Book of the Dead (= CT Spell 1079; text: Davies 1953, pl. 23; translation and commentary: Cruz-Uribe 1988, pp. 100–02; see also Kákosy 1981, p. 118). Rooms K, K1, and K2 at Hibis temple are paralleled in a series of rooms found in several Theban mortuary temples from the New Kingdom (Hölscher 1934, pp. 23–25, pl. 2). All of these rooms involve the rebirth of the sun god, Ra-Horakhty. Here at Hibis the rooms involve the rebirth of Osiris (Amun).

On the east wall of room E on the roof of Hibis temple (fig. 6.1) is a scene of the king before a large offering list which is labeled: "The fashioning and opening of the mouth of the image in the House of Gold. Opening the mouth and eyes of Amun of Hibis, ... , which the king ... performed" (Davies 1953, pl. 16; Cruz-Uribe 1988, p. 77). The offering list itself was labeled by Barta (1963, p. 151) as an anomalous list and is paralleled by Pyramid Text Spells 73–78, 90–92, and miscellaneous others.

The beginning of our text, "the fashioning and opening of the mouth of the image in the House of Gold," is a variant of the standard title for the Opening of the Mouth ceremony. The reference to opening the eyes and mouth would refer to standard scene numbers 26, 27, 32, 33, 36, and 46, each dealing with the opening of the mouth and eyes by the *sm*-priest who officiates in a tomb ceremony (scene numbers follow Barta 1963).

On the west wall of room E1 at Hibis temple is an interesting scene showing the king censing the gods, presenting an offering table of gifts, and reciting a hymn to Ra-Horakhty (Davies 1953, pl. 17; Cruz-Uribe 1988, pp. 75–77). In this hymn the king is identified with Thoth. The hymn and censing are shown in front of Amun, Mut, Khonsu, Osiris, Horus, and Isis. First one should note that the scene itself is found in the Opening of the Mouth ritual as scene 71, in which the *sm*-priest censes the statue and presents an offering table of gifts along with a hymn to Ra-Horakhty, identifying himself with Thoth. Second, one should note that the hymn dedicated to Ra-Horakhty on this wall is the same as found in the New Kingdom tomb scenes. Otto (1960, p. 161) argues that this hymn was not originally part of the Opening of the Mouth ritual but was adapted in the New Kingdom from the daily temple ritual of Theban temples. Third, one should note that it is only rarely outside of Hibis temple that one finds scenes where Osiris and Amun-Ra are found combined in such a grouping.

On the north and south wall of room E at Hibis are two scenes depicting a large number of gods and goddesses. Elsewhere I have shown that they represent the decans of the dual year who serve as protective deities of the temple, and to whom the priests made offerings each year at the new year's festival in order to invoke their protective capacities (Cruz-Uribe 1988, pp. 185–91). The invoking of the gods in general to protect and assist the deceased is found as scene 59D in the Opening of the Mouth ceremony (Otto 1960, p. 137).

The broken pilasters at the entrance to room E at Hibis have representations of Horus and Thoth purifying those who enter the room with water while a pair of Iunmutef priests invoke Geb and Dewenawy (Davies 1953, pl. 15; Cruz-Uribe 1988, pp. 74–75). This representation is a parallel to scenes 2 and 3 in the Opening of the Mouth ceremony (Otto 1960, pp. 37–44).

It would appear that room E at Hibis temple and its inscriptions were drawn from New Kingdom mortuary literature and must be that part of the temple dealing with the Hibis temple version of the Opening of the Mouth ceremony as used in a cult temple. The descriptions and scenes represented there do not include many of the standard scenes associated with an Opening of the Mouth ritual as used in a mortuary context from the New Kingdom. For example, we do not have examples of the priest symbolically opening a mouth with an adze or representations of slaughtering scenes. In general the abbreviated representations provide good evidence that the Opening of the Mouth ritual at Hibis temple is clearly related to the New Kingdom funerary rite of the same name. This rite does not originate with New Kingdom examples but derives from earlier rituals (see Roth 1993).

These examples thus show that Hibis temple contains scenes which suggest that part of the daily temple ritual used scenes and texts that have been thought to pertain only to mortuary contexts and not to daily temple ritual. The appearance of several scenes in Hibis temple related directly to the Opening of the Mouth ritual is significant. This ritual is well known from New Kingdom sources (see Otto 1960 and Schulman 1984 for scenes found on stelae). A standard version (if one can exist) is found in the tomb of Rekhmire. The seventy-five episodes of the ritual detail a series of presentations, offerings, and ritual acts involved with revivifying the deceased (represented by a statue) so that the individual may become identified with the gods (especially the sun god). The ceremony concludes with the priest censing the deceased, presenting a table of offerings, and reciting a hymn to the sun god Ra.

Hibis temple is not the only temple where scenes from the ritual of the Opening of the Mouth are found. Blackman and Fairman (1946) note that the Opening of the Mouth ritual was used at Edfu temple and argue that the ritual caused the gods and goddesses depicted on the walls of the temple to become animate and to serve as the protector deities of the temple. They suggest that the ritual was performed during the time of the new year's festival and that it represented a consecration of the temple complex. Despite their comments, Blackman and Fairman do not emphasize the fact that the Opening of the Mouth ritual is found in parallel with the daily temple ritual scenes.

Reymond (1963, p. 68) recognizes the suggestion of Blackman and Fairman and notes that the Opening of the Mouth ritual animates the gods and goddesses of the temple who are worshiped as the ancestor gods of the temple. These gods also serve as the protective deities of the temple. Reymond suggests that the performance of these rituals meant that the temple was reconsecrated and renewed each year at the new year's festival.

In his volume on the Opening of the Mouth for Breathing, Smith (1993, pp. 6–21) distinguishes the use of that Demotic ritual from earlier rituals but notes that it has much in common with its earlier antecedents, including the invocation to deities, Thoth as actor/priest of the ritual, and presentations of various offerings. Smith argues that the texts were used in two different ways: first as mortuary liturgy recited by the living outside the tomb, and then as funerary literature used by the deceased in the afterlife where it continued its effective character.

The question to be resolved is what was the basic function of the Opening of the Mouth ritual and its post-New Kingdom variants? Was it simply used to reanimate the deceased, to bring them back to life in order to carry on life in the netherworld? Or was it to reanimate gods in their protective roles in a temple setting? The examples that have been presented suggest that these texts might have fulfilled both functions. Perhaps we should look at it from a different perspective.

Egyptian religion is a religion of ritual, the performance of ritual being that function of the king which is required of him in order to maintain Maat on earth. The king is then able to present it back to the gods as evidence of the proper and good milieux in which the Egyptians lived (see Morenz 1960, chapter 5). Over a cyclical se-

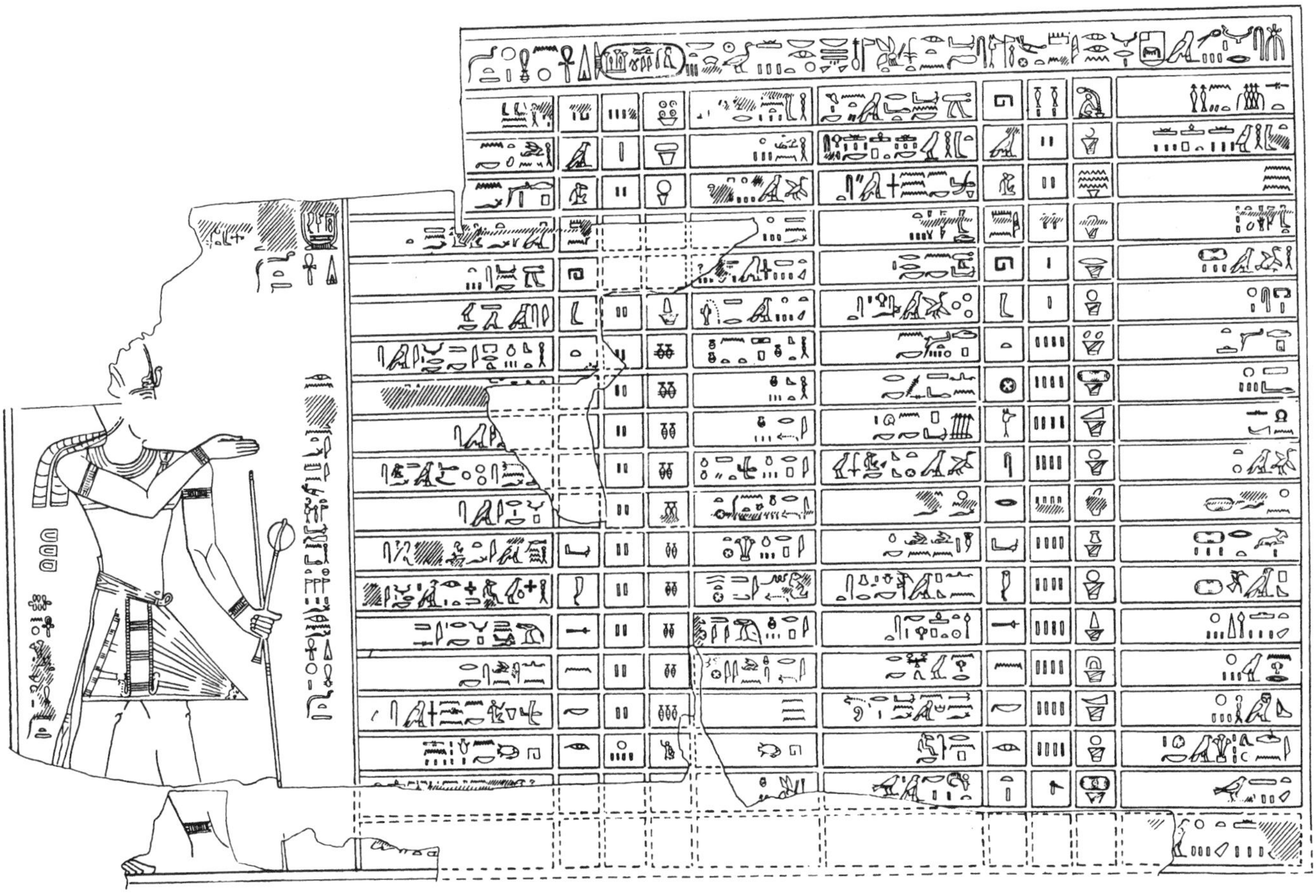

Figure 6.1. East Wall of Room E1 at Hibis Temple (Davies 1953, pl. 16).
Reproduced with Permission of the Metropolitan Museum of Art

quence of time, the rituals were repeated in order to confirm the proper nature of the king's reign. In every era of Egyptian history we find numerous examples of the king performing necessary rituals. Modern scholars have separated mortuary rituals from those which took place within a cult temple. Our evidence from the use of the Opening of the Mouth ritual at Hibis temple may force us to re-examine that notion. Here we have a ritual, with variants over time, that is found both in a purely mortuary context (as in the recitation of a ritual and performance of ritual acts outside the tomb) as well as in a temple context (as in the recitation of a ritual and performance of ritual acts in the temple). In both spheres, the ritual exhibits the same basic forms.

In mortuary texts there is the wish to re-animate a deceased person in order to survive or continue living in the netherworld amongst the gods. In the temple context, the king invokes the gods to be re-animated in order to serve as protective deities and to reconsecrate the temple. Each, however, is intended to have a continuing effect. In the mortuary context, the deceased continues to have an essential power to control his destiny in the afterlife. In the temple context, the temple becomes re-animated, is protected by the deities, and continues to symbolize Egyptian life. Perhaps these contexts are not as different as has been suggested and they are to be considered one and the same. The performance of the ritual of the Opening of the Mouth at the tomb before burial and during the new year's festival at the temple both provide a context for invoking reanimation and for the use of primordial power to continue life in the Egyptian sphere. The transition from death to life, or actually from life to the afterlife, is similar to the continued reconsecration of the temple and its symbolic use as a model for the Egyptian cosmos (Hornung 1992, pp. 115–29).

The variations in the Opening of the Mouth ritual seen in the New Kingdom examples, at Hibis temple, in the Ptolemaic temples such as Edfu, and on the Demotic papyri from the Roman period, each share in the basic ritual of re-animation of people and gods in order to carry on with the task of life. The performance of the ritual itself rather than its context was the important aspect leading to a common outcome.

As a final thought, the use of "mortuary" liturgy in temple contexts suggests that the king himself in many situations was both the giver of offerings to the "deceased" gods as well as the recipient of those offerings. Nelson (1942) and Haeny (1982) present arguments that the temples on the west bank at Thebes were not in actuality "mortuary" temples as often represented, but rather as temples dedicated to Amun as well as the living/dead king. The existence of texts that can serve in both a mortuary and temple context argues that distinction should be dropped, as well as the notion that the temples on the west bank were mortuary complexes.[2]

References

Assmann, J.

1990 "Egyptian Mortuary Liturgies." In *Studies in Egyptology Presented to Miriam Lichtheim*, Volume 1, edited by S. I. Groll, pp. 1–45. Jerusalem: Magnes Press.

Barta, W.

1963 *Die altägyptische Opferliste*. Münchner ägyptologische Studien 3. Berlin: Bruno Hessling.

Barucq, A., and F. Daumas

1980 *Hymnes et prières de l'Égypte ancienne*. Littératures anciennes du proche-orient 10. Paris: Éditions du Cerf.

Blackman, A., and H. Fairman

1946 "The Consecration of an Egyptian Temple according to the Use at Edfu." *Journal of Egyptian Archaeology* 32: 75–91.

Cruz-Uribe, E.

1987 "Hibis Temple Project: Preliminary Report, 1985–1986 and Summer 1986 Field Seasons." *Varia Aegyptiaca* 3: 215–30.

1988 *Hibis Temple Project*, Volume 1: *Translations, Commentary, Discussions and Sign List*. San Antonio: Van Siclen Books.

1994 "The Khonsu Cosmogony." *Journal of the American Research Center in Egypt* 31: 169–89.

Davies, N. de G.

1953 *The Temple of Hibis in el Khargeh Oasis*, Part 3: *The Decoration*. Edited by L. Bull and L. Hall. Metropolitan Museum of Art Egyptian Expedition 17. New York: Metropolitan Museum of Art.

Egberts, A.

1995 "Action, Speech, and Interpretations: Some Reflections on the Classification of Ancient Egyptian Liturgical Texts." In *Abstracts of Papers* (Seventh International Congress of Egyptologists, Cambridge, 3–9 September 1995), edited by C. Eyre, pp. 6–7. Oxford: Oxbow Books.

Haeny, G.

1982 "La fonction religieuse des 'chateaux de millions d'années.'" In *L'égyptologie en 1979: Axes prioritaires de recherches* 1, edited by J. Leclant, pp. 111–16.

2. I wish to thank Emily Teeter for the last two references.

Colloques internationaux du Centre national de la recherche scientifique 595. Paris: Éditions du Centre national de la recherche scientifique.

Hölscher, U.
1934 *The Excavation of Medinet Habu,* Volume 1: *General Plans and Views*. Oriental Institute Publications 21. Chicago: University of Chicago Press.

Hornung, E.
1992 *Idea into Image: Essays on Ancient Egyptian Thought*. New York: Timken.

Kákosy, L.
1981 "Temples and Funerary Beliefs in the Graeco-Roman Epoch." In *L'égyptologie en 1979: Axes prioritaires de recherches* 1, edited by J. Leclant, pp. 117–27. Colloques internationaux du Centre national de la recherche scientifique 595. Paris: Éditions du Centre national de la recherche scientifique.

Morenz, S.
1960 *Egyptian Religion*. Ithaca: Cornell University Press.

Nelson, H.
1942 "The Identity of Amon-Re of United-With-Eternity." *Journal of Near Eastern Studies* 1: 127–55.

Otto, E.
1960 *Das ägyptische Mundöffnungsritual*. Ägyptologische Abhandlungen 3. Wiesbaden: Otto Harrassowitz.

Reymond, E.
1963 "Worship of the Ancestor Gods at Edfu." *Chronique d'Égypte* 38: 49–70.

Roth, A. M.
1993 "Fingers, Stars, and the 'Opening of the Mouth': The Nature and Function of the *Nṯrwj*-Blades." *Journal of Egyptian Archaeology* 79: 57–79.

Schulman, A.
1984 "The Iconographic Theme: 'Opening of the Mouth' on Stelae." *Journal of the American Research Center in Egypt* 21: 169–96.

Smith, M.
1993 *The Liturgy of Opening the Mouth for Breathing*. Oxford: Griffith Institute.

Winlock, H.
1941 *The Temple of Hibis in El Khargeh Oasis,* Part 1: *The Excavations*. Metropolitan Museum of Art Egyptian Expedition 13. New York: Metropolitan Museum of Art.

7

A LETTER OF REPROACH

R. J. DEMARÉE

Leiden University, The Netherlands

The subject of this article is a mid-Eighteenth Dynasty hieratic letter written on a small papyrus that was acquired for a Dutch private collection many years ago.[1] I hope that Professor Edward Wente appreciates this article as an expression of our long-standing friendship and a contribution to mark his anniversary.

DESCRIPTION OF THE PAPYRUS

When acquired, the papyrus seemed to be in a bad state of preservation (figs. 7.1–2, alas of poor quality), although the nature of the document was readily discernible from the writing visible through the gaps. Fortunately, skilled hands were able to unfold the papyrus, which surprisingly turned out to be of better quality than expected (figs. 7.3–4). The document, in its present condition, is a rectangular sheet of papyrus, about 23.5 cm wide by 9.5 cm high — one piece cut off from a papyrus roll in the manner described by Černý (1939, pp. xvii–xviii) and Bakir (1970, pp. 21–22). The papyrus is light brown in color with some darker areas and rather coarse. Except for the missing parts, the state of preservation is good: one line of writing is nearly completely lacking and most other lines show some gaps but can be restored.

The main text, clearly a letter, begins and ends on the technical recto of the papyrus in lines running against the so-called horizontal fibers that on the recto lie uppermost. As usual, to write a letter the scribe turned (the section of) the papyrus roll sideways, so that the original horizontal direction of the fibers became vertical in relation to the direction of writing. On the verso he wrote the address, of which, owing to the big central gap, only a few signs are still visible. These practices being quite normal in New Kingdom letters or memoranda, our document confirms the well-known facts (Černý 1939, p. xviii; Bakir 1970, pp. 19–20; Caminos 1963, p. 29; Allam 1987, p. 25, for the terminology of recto and verso).

The recto bears six full lines of writing, while the verso shows only the address. The full lines are about 21–22 cm in length and stretch across the entire width of the page, the side margins on the left being extremely nar-

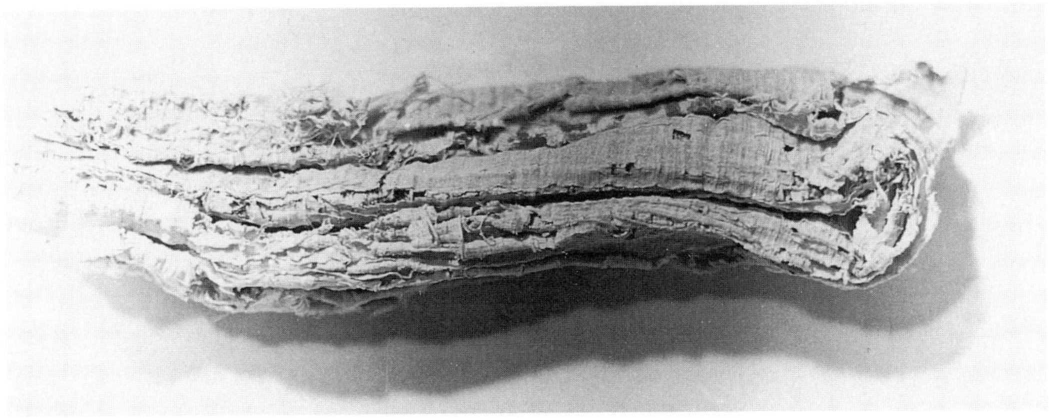

Figure 7.1. P. Leiden F 1996/1.1 Before Unrolling

1. Nothing unfortunately is known about the original provenience or find circumstances. Meanwhile this document has been presented to the National Museum of Antiquities, Leiden; it now bears the inventory number F 1996/1.1. I wish to thank my colleagues Dr. J. F. Borghouts and Dr. A. Egberts for their useful comments on earlier versions of this article.

Gold of Praise: Studies on Ancient Egypt in Honor of Edward F. Wente
Edited by Emily Teeter and John A. Larson
Studies in Ancient Oriental Civilization 58
Chicago: Oriental Institute, 1999

Figure 7.2. P. Leiden F 1996/1.1 Before Unrolling

row and on the right somewhat larger. Using black ink only, the scribe dipped his brush three times per line — a practice followed by other scribes as well (Caminos 1963, p. 29; see also the color photograph of P. Berlin 10463 in Eggebrecht 1987, p. 129, nr. 35).

When prepared for dispatch, the letter was folded into six narrow, elongated folds parallel to the lines of writing, and then it was bent twice with the creases in about one-third of the length,[2] addressed, possibly tied with a string, and sealed. The result was a flat oblong package, about 8.0 cm by 1.8 cm (figs. 7.1–2). Judging from the state in which the papyrus was found, one might conclude that this letter too had never been opened (or was it folded again, after being read?).[3]

This letter is yet another addition to the still small corpus of hieratic letters datable to the mid-Eighteenth Dynasty, the reigns of Thutmose III and Amenhotep II, approximately between 1450 and 1400 B.C. (see list by Buchberger 1991, p. 78). While palaeography and grammar already point to that period, the sender of this letter dates it almost beyond doubt (see notes to the translation below).

Nothing is known about the provenience of the papyrus — though Thebes is the most probable findspot — or the circumstances of its discovery. It is published here for the first time.

TRANSLITERATION

Recto (fig. 7.3a–b)

1. *ḥry mḏꜣy Ddw ḏd.n mḏꜣy Nb-sny n Tꜣ-ỉw.t r-nty ỉn.tw n=k sš pn*
2. *r-ḏd ḥr-m pꜣy=k tm spr r šd.t tꜣ šrỉ.t Ḥw-pꜣ-t ỉw=k rḫ.*
3. *tỉ r-ḏd šdỉ=ỉ śy rdỉ.n=ỉ(?) … n pr-ꜥꜣ … šdỉ*
4. *m(?) ṯꜣwt k(y)-ḏd my ꜣś.tỉ sp-2 ẖry nhy n rmṯ (ḥnꜥ) ḏd ỉr*
5. *sḏr=k ꜥꜣ n wḫꜣ m=k ỉw ỉnk ỉy r ỉnỉ.t=k ḏs-ỉ ḥnꜥ ḏd n Mḥw ḥr-m pꜣy=k thỉ*
6. *r tꜣ šrỉ.t ỉw šdỉ=ỉ śy ỉn ỉw tm nḥỉ.t r=ỉ ỉrf pꜣ ỉrỉ.n=k ỉw hꜣb=ỉ n=k*

Verso (fig. 7.4a–b)

ḥry mḏꜣ(y Ddw n) // (mḏꜣy Nb-sny n Tꜣ)-ỉw.(t)(?)

2. See Bakir 1970, p. 24 ff., fig. 7 on p. 26, for the manner of folding and the place of the address on the verso. The double crease seems to be unusual but can also be observed on letter MMA 27.3.560; compare Hayes 1957, p. 89.

3. Other examples include the letter of mayor Sennufe; see Caminos 1963, p. 37; Leiden Papyri I 360, 363, 364, 365, 366, 367; compare Janssen 1960, p. 33; two Coptic letters; compare Barns 1959, p. 81.

a

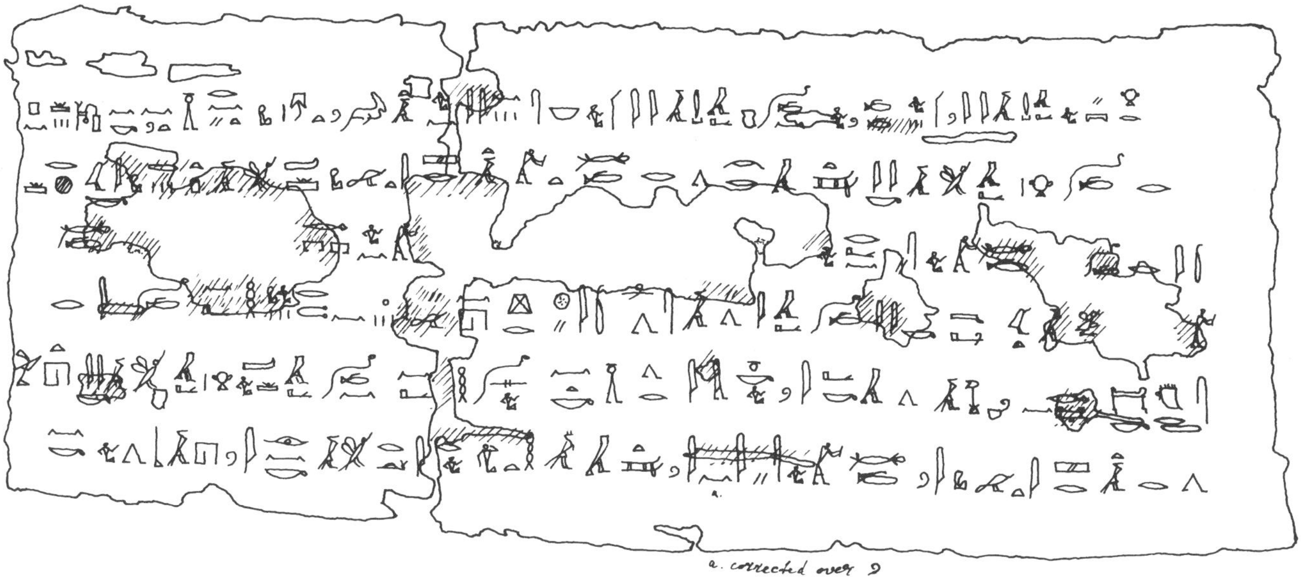

b

Figure 7.3. (*a*) P. Leiden F 1996/1.1 Recto and (*b*) Transcription

TRANSLATION

Recto

[1] The captain of police [a] Dedu [b] addresses [c] policeman Nebseny [d] of Ta-iwet: This letter is brought to you [2] to say: [e] What's the meaning of your not proceeding to take away [f] the girl [g] Hupat,[h] while[i] you know [3] that [j] I have taken her away,[k] after I have given(?) [l] ... of Pharaoh ...[m] take[n] [4] away secretly(?).[o] A further matter: [p] Come very quickly [q] with some men. And further: [r] If [5] you are idle there[s] in seeking,[t] lo, then I will come to fetch you myself.[u] And further [v] to Mahu: [w] What is the meaning of your interfering [x] with [6] the girl, after I had taken her away?[y] Was it failing to trust me what you did,[z] after I had written to you? [aa]

Verso

[Address] The captain of po(lice Dedu) to // (policeman Nebseny of) Ta-iw(et)(?).[ab]

a

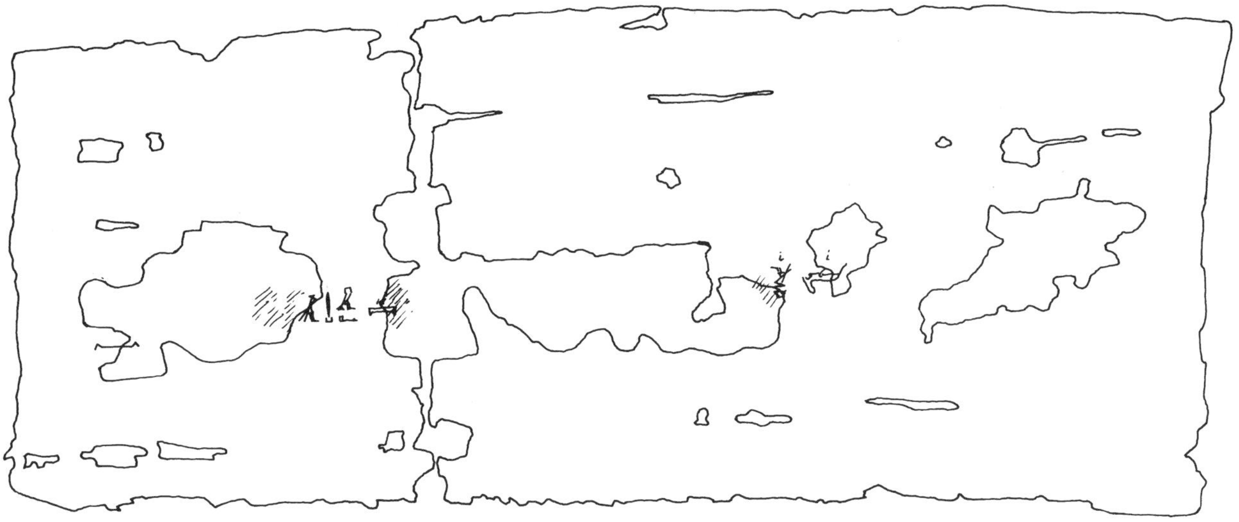

b

Figure 7.4. (*a*) P. Leiden F 1996/1.1 Verso and (*b*) Transcription

COMMENTARY

[a] For the title *ḥry mḏꜣy* "chief of police," see Černý 1973, p. 261.

[b] The sender of this letter most probably is the captain of police Dedu known from his tomb at Khôkha, TT 200; compare PM 1/1, pp. 303–04. His other titles include "Governor of the Deserts on the West of Thebes" and "Head of the Guard of the King." He held office under Thutmose III and Amenhotep II, as proven by the names of these kings. Some of the texts from his tomb are to be found in *Urk*. 4, pp. 994–95, 1515 ff. His name is written *Dydw*, *Dd,* or *Ddỉ* and is known for other persons as well; compare Ranke 1935, p. 401.14.

[c] The introductory formula *ḏd.n* is of the type IIIa in Bakir 1970, p. 48: "Sender says to Recipient" = S *ḏd.n* R.

[d] The policeman Nebseny is not known to me from any other source; his name is rather common during the New Kingdom; compare Ranke 1935, p. 186.14. The reading of the apposition to his name constitutes a problem. The hieratic hardly allows for anything else but the female name *Tꜣ-ỉw.t*, which is known from Ranke 1935, p. 353.15; idem 1952, p. 394 (albeit from the later New Kingdom). By comparison with the construction of the name of Ahmose of Peniaty (Glanville 1928, p. 300), this would make our policeman Nebseny acting in the service of or under the command of a woman Ta-iwet, a situation for which I cannot cite a parallel.

[e] The phrase *ỉn.tw n=k sš pn r-ḏd* is an example of what Bakir (1970, pp. 85–86) calls a "formula of transition" that always follows the introductory formula "S *ḏd.n* R." The use of *r-ḏd* in this formula is rare in real letters; compare Caminos 1963, p. 32 (add to his examples also P. Cairo 58055 recto 2).

[f] *ḥr-m pꜣy=k tm spr r …* "on account of what your not proceeding to/succeeding in …" (literally); for this interrogative construction, which is already Late Period Egyptian, see Groll 1970, section 55, pp. 178–82; Korostovtsev 1973, §§234, 251. Here we seem to have the earliest example on record. Its positive counterpart, also in an interrogative sentence, is to be found below in recto 5/6. For *ḥr-m* as an interrogative adverb at the head of a clause, see also Kroeber 1970, p. 189 Ex. 4 (= P. Cairo 58054 recto 2: "charakteristisch für die frühneuägyptische Syntax"); Allam 1987, p. 14, note (c).

spr r "to approach" (literally) as an auxiliary verb means "to proceed" or even "to succeed in"; compare Caminos 1954, p. 94; Wente 1967, p. 71, note p.

šdỉ (here *šd.t* infinitive) "to take away" of a person (*Wb.* 4.561:14). This verb occurs four times in this letter, almost certainly everywhere with the same meaning. In P. Louvre 3230b "taking away" a girl (a female servant) is expressed by the verbs *nḥm* and *iṯi* (Peet 1926, pl. 17); both verbs seem to be without a notion of force, which idea would be expressed by the verb *ỉṯ3* (Edwards 1982, p. 131, note w).

[g] *t3 šrỉ.t* "the girl." *t3* as a definite article is already common in the Eighteenth Dynasty; see Gardiner 1973, §112, and several instances in the Ahmose of Peniaty correspondence (cf. also Kroeber 1970, pp. 25–30). The same girl is referred to in line 6, where *t3* might still convey the notion of the (weak) demonstrative pronoun (cf. Buchberger 1991, pp. 64–65).

[h] *Ḥw-p3-t* "Hupat," the name of the girl, certainly a foreign name (Asiatic?), is not found in Ranke 1935; idem 1952; Schneider 1992.

[i] *ỉw=k rḫ.tỉ* is a subordinate clause with a "while" connotation; compare Černý and Groll 1975, p. 568. Recto line 3 is the most damaged line of this letter; only a few signs can be reconstructed with a reasonable certainty.

[j] *r-ḏd* introduces the contents of the foregoing statement; compare Erman 1933, §§428, 725. Here it is followed by a perfective *sḏm=f*. Gardiner (1973, §224, p. 174) notes that by the Eighteenth Dynasty it is used, though rarely, even after *rḫ*, meaning "that."

[k] *šdỉ=śy* "I have taken her away." The main characters of the verb are almost completely lost in the lacuna, yet *šdi* is probable in view of the remaining traces, the determinative, and the available space. For the *sḏm=f* replacing the earlier use of the *sḏm.n=f*, see Kroeber 1970, p. 100.

[l] In view of the following lacuna it cannot be ascertained whether we should read *rdỉ.n=i* or *rdỉ n=ỉ*, i.e., "after I had given/made" or "after X gave/made to/for me."

[m] In the middle of the central gap the few remaining signs seem to refer to an official of pharaoh. Similarly, *n3.n srw n pr-ʿ3* "officials of pharaoh" are mentioned, for example, in P. Cairo 58053 recto 5 (Allam 1987, pl. 1a).

[n] At the end of line 3 the traces almost certainly point to the very *šdỉ* with the determinative as the first sign of the next line.

[o] As indicated by the tentative reconstruction of the first part of line 4, between the determinative of the foregoing verb and what is to be read as *ṯ3wt* there is room for two or three signs or groups. Probably before *ṯ3wt* there was an *m*, together forming an expression that allows for three possible translations: (taken away) "through theft," "as forfeit/penalty," or "stealthily, furtively"; compare Caminos 1954, p. 95. The choice is difficult in view of the substantial damages in the preceding sentences.

[p] *k(y)-ḏd* "a further matter" according to Bakir (1970, pp. 82–83) is a formula of transition, especially when preceding instructions, as here.

[q] *3ś.tỉ sp-2* "quickly, quickly" is a stative used as an adverb with the repetition to express the superlative; compare Gardiner 1973, §§314, 207. For the stative as "eine adverbiale Verbalform," see also Schenkel 1989, p. 181. For *sp-2,* see Daumas 1975/76.

[r] (*ḥnʿ*) *ḏd* "and further" fits the surviving traces very well, which again according to Bakir (1970, p. 83) is a formula of transition, implying a continuation of the communication.

[s] *ỉr sḏr=k ʿ3 n wḫ3* "if you are inactive/inert there on account of seeking." The sense seems clear, especially in view of the meaning "to lie down, be inactive" for *sḏr*, suggested by Gunn (1924, p. 28 [6]); a similar use of this verb is found in P. Cairo 58053 verso 1 (Allam 1987, pp. 6, 12, note jj). The *n* before *wḫ3* might well stand for *m* "with, when, while." For the interchange between *n* and *m* already in the Eighteenth Dynasty, see Kroeber 1970, pp. 42–46.

ʿ3 "there" is characteristic for the Eighteenth Dynasty; compare Erman 1933, §594; for another example, see P. Cairo 58055 recto 3 (Allam 1987, pp. 20, 22, note [i]).

[t] *wḫ3* "to seek out," "to come and fetch someone" (*Wb.* 1.353:14–15); compare Wente 1967, p. 44, note b (on 22/14).

[u] *m=k ỉw ỉnk ỉy r ỉnỉ.t=k ḏs=ỉ* "See, it is I who will come to fetch you myself." For the particle *m=k* in letters, see Johnson 1984. The use of the futural *ỉw* before a participial statement would seem a Late Period Egyptian development; compare Korostovtsev 1973, §265; for an example of *m=k + ỉw=f r sḏm*, see Kroeber 1970, p. 137 Ex. 3 = P. Cairo 58053 recto 5 (Allam 1987, p. 8, note r).

[v] *ḥnʿ ḏd n* "next (I) say to" is the common formula of transition introducing a new message for another person; compare Bakir 1970, pp. 83–84.

[w] *Mḥw* "Mahu" is a very common personal name in the New Kingdom; compare Ranke 1935, p. 163.27. It seems impossible therefore to identify the person in question, probably a colleague of policeman Nebseny.

[x] *ḥr-m pꜣy=k thi͗ r tꜣ šri͗.t* "on account of what your interfering with the/this girl" is a fine example of the positive counterpart of the construction discussed above in the commentary to line 2. For *tꜣ* as a definite article or demonstrative pronoun, see also the commentary to line 2 above.

thi͗ r "to attack, to interfere, to mistreat" (*Wb.* 5.319:9); compare also P. Metropolitan Museum 27.3.560, line 2 (Hayes 1957, pp. 89–90); for the meaning, see Wente 1967, p. 19, note l ("doing wrong to"); see also the late Eighteenth/early Nineteenth Dynasty examples in P. Cairo 58053 recto, lines 2, 4 (Allam 1987, p. 7, note g, "transgresser, s'en prendre [une personne ou une chose]"); P. Cairo 58054 recto, line 5; verso, line 4 (Allam 1987, p. 13).

[y] *i͗w šdi=i͗ śy* "after I had taken her away." For the *i͗w sḏm=f* in Late Period Egyptian with a pluperfect meaning, see Groll 1969, pp. 184–91; Borghouts 1971, p. 98; see also Kroeber 1970, p. 119 ff.

[z] *i͗n i͗w tm nḥi͗.t r=i͗ i͗rf pꜣ i͗ri͗.n=k* "was it a not-trusting me what you did." For the "cleft sentence" in the interrogative sentence pattern, see Quack 1991, pp. 201–04. I cannot cite an exact parallel to the construction with *i͗n i͗w* (the scribe seems to have had some problems himself, writing *i͗n* over earlier *i͗w*). For the non-enclitic particle *i͗rf* reinforcing the interrogative meaning, see Gardiner 1973, §491.3.

nḥi͗ r "to believe, to trust (someone)." See Gilula 1977, pp. 295–96, and an example in P. Bankes I recto, line 12 (Edwards 1982, p. 131, note p).

[aa] *i͗w hꜣb=i͗ n=k* "after I had written to you" is another example of the *i͗w sḏm=f* similar to the one at the beginning of this line.

[ab] *ḥry mḏꜣ(y Ddw n) // (mḏꜣy Nb-sny n Tꜣ)-i͗w.(t)(?)* "The captain of po(lice Dedu) to // (policeman Nebseny of) Ta-iw(et)(?)." The title of the sender is still visible, but his name is lost in the lacuna, as is the greater part of the title and name of the recipient. For the position of the names of sender and recipient, see Bakir 1970, p. 24 ff., especially fig. 7 on p. 26; Allam 1987, p. 25.

Clearly, this document is a business letter written by a high-ranking functionary to some of his inferiors. The general tone, the epistolary formulae, and the lack of an opening greeting, a salutation of any kind, and a farewell all evoke the picture of an irritated, angry official going straight to the point and hauling his subordinates over the coals: "Why this, why not that, what have you done, etc.?"

It is a well-established fact that letters always presuppose a knowledge of the people described therein and the context of the action. The present letter however shares with most letters from ancient Egypt a sometimes frustrating lack of information — to the modern, curious reader, that is. Of course, the urgent, imposing questions and remarks of the captain of police Dedu provide us with a general understanding of the message as a whole, notably in view of the position of the sender. Yet the real heart of the matter seems to escape us because we have no information on the foregoing events — unfortunately just there where this letter might have furnished us with some data, we are faced with the unavoidable lacunae. Nevertheless, the following facts can be deduced:

1. Of the four persons involved, the captain of police Dedu and the girl Hupat are "here" since he writes to policeman Nebseny and Mahu who are "there" (somewhere else within the official territory of Dedu).

2. Dedu is the superior of Nebseny and probably also of Mahu; Dedu has a special relationship with the girl Hupat, who was possibly placed in his custody or was given to him by an official of pharaoh.

3. Despite an order to do so, Nebseny does not come to collect the girl.

4. Although being informed about this, Mahu behaves towards the girl in an "incorrect" manner.

Several important questions remain unanswered: What was the nature of the "incorrect" behavior towards Hupat by Mahu and why did he not trust Dedu? Why Nebseny had to collect Hupat and why he had to come with some men? Furthermore, in view of the fact that we do not know the exact nature of the relationship between Dedu and Hupat, it is difficult to decide whether the whole affair was private or official business — in other words, did Dedu act in the line of his duties or simply on his own behalf?

Although theoretically there are several possible reconstructions of the background and the context, a plausible history of events would seem as follows:

a. At a given moment the girl Hupat "arrives" at the place where the captain of police Dedu lives or holds office.
b. Dedu informs Mahu about Hupat's arrival.
c. Despite this, at a later stage Mahu "mistreats" the girl Hupat.
d. Dedu reproaches Mahu about his behavior towards Hupat.
e. Dedu reproaches his subordinate Nebseny for not having come to collect Hupat and urges him to come with some men to do so; Dedu threatens otherwise to come himself to fetch Nebseny.

Disputes over servant girls/maidservants apparently were a common theme, as shown by at least two other Eighteenth/Nineteenth Dynasty letters. In P. Louvre 3230b (Peet 1926, pp. 71–74) Ahmose of Peniaty asks his superior why a maidservant (*bꜣk.t, šrỉ.t*) placed in his charge has been taken away (*nḥm*) from him and given to someone else. And P. Bankes I (Edwards 1982, pp. 126–32; Satzinger 1994, pp. 233–35) vividly describes the problems concerning a servant girl (*ḥm.t, bꜣk.t*) who had been abducted (*iṯꜣ*) or even unlawfully sold as a slave. The text of our new letter however contains too many uncertainties to speculate about what really was the matter with the poor subject of the dispute, the girl Hupat.

Two more points deserve reconsideration. In the first place, this new letter poses once more the problem of the postal service in ancient Egypt (Wente 1990, pp. 8–11). Since the external address does not seem to indicate the place to which the letter was to be sent, it is more than likely that a messenger was entrusted with its delivery. Regular contact between the central police administration and the local stations is to be understood anyhow. Secondly, there is the problem of literacy (Baines and Eyre 1983, pp. 65–72; Janssen 1992, p. 81). We must assume that, as a high-ranking official, the captain of police Dedu could read and write; whereas it is to be doubted whether his subordinates were literate. The communication therefore most probably would have been read aloud to them by a professional scribe or other functionary. If indeed this letter was found unopened — for whatever reason, we can only guess — Nebseny and Mahu never read or heard the reproaches of their superior. Although we can only speculate, most probably the captain of police Dedu found other ways and means to communicate his anger.

[After completion of the text of the above contribution, the following article on the position of slave or servant girls appeared: B. G. Davies and J. Toivari, "Misuse of a Maidservant's Services at Deir el-Medina (O. CGC 25237 recto)." *Studien zur altägyptischen Kultur* 24 (1997): 69–80.]

References

Allam, S.
1985 "Trois lettres d'affaires." In *Mélanges Gamal Eddin Mokhtar*, volume 1, edited by P. Posener-Kriéger, pp. 19–30. Bibliothèque d'étude 97/1. Cairo: L'Institut français d'archéologie orientale.
1987 "Trois missives d'un commandant." *Annales du Service des antiquités de l'Égypte* 71: 5–25.

Baines, J., and C. Eyre
1983 "Four Notes on Literacy." *Göttinger Miszellen* 61: 65–96.

Bakir, A. M.
1970 *Egyptian Epistolography, from the Eighteenth to the Twenty-First Dynasty*. Bibliothèque d'étude 48. Cairo: Institut français d'archéologie orientale.

Barns, J. W. B.
1959 "Two Coptic Letters." *Journal of Egyptian Archaeology* 45: 81–84.

Borghouts, J. F.
1971 "The Magical Texts of Papyrus Leiden I 348." *Oudheidkundige mededelingen uit het Rijksmuseum van Oudheden te Leiden* 51.

Buchberger, H.
1991 "*Ḥtp an ꜣIpw-rs.tỉ* - Der Brief auf dem Gefäß München ÄS 4313." *Studien zur ägyptischen Kultur* 18: 49–87.

Caminos, R. A.
1954 *Late Egyptian Miscellanies*. Oxford: Oxford University Press.
1963 "Papyrus Berlin 10463." *Journal of Egyptian Archaeology* 49: 29–37.

Černý, J.
1939 *Late Ramesside Letters*. Bibliotheca Aegyptiaca 9. Brussels: Édition de la Fondation Reine Élisabeth.

1973 *A Community of Workmen at Thebes in the Ramesside Period*. Bibliothèque d'étude 50. Cairo: Institut français d'archéologie orientale.

Černý, J., and S. I. Groll
1975 *A Late Egyptian Grammar*. Rome: Biblical Institute Press.

Chevereau, P.-M.
1994 *Prosopographie des cadres militaires égyptiens du Nouvel Empire*. Antony, France: n.p.

Daumas, F.
1975/76 "Quelques aspects de l'expression du distributif, de l'itératif et de l'intensif en égyptien." *Orientalia Lovaniensia Periodica* 6/7: 109–23.

Edwards, I. E. S.
1982 "The Bankes Papyri I and II." *Journal of Egyptian Archaeology* 68: 126–33.

Eggebrecht, A., ed.
1987 *Ägyptens Aufstieg zur Weltmacht*. Mainz am Rhein: Philipp von Zabern.

Erman, A.
1933 *Neuaegyptische Grammatik*. Second edition. Leipzig: Verlag Wilhelm von Engelmann.

Gardiner, A. H.
1973 *Egyptian Grammar*. Third edition revised. Oxford: Griffith Institute.

Gilula, M.
1977 "Egyptian NHT = Coptic NAHTE 'to Believe.'" *Journal of Near Eastern Studies* 36: 295–96.

Glanville, S. R. K.
1928 "The Letters of Aahmose of Peniati." *Journal of Egyptian Archaeology* 14: 294–312.

Groll, S. I.
1969 "*iw sḏm.f* in Late Egyptian." *Journal of Near Eastern Studies* 28: 184–91.
1970 *The Negative Verbal System of Late Egyptian*. Oxford: Oxford University Press.

Gunn, B.
1924 *Studies in Egyptian Syntax*. Paris: Libraire Orientaliste Paul Geuthner.

Hayes, W. C.
1957 "Varia from the Time of Hatshepsut 5: An Administrative Letter to Thuty." *Mitteilungen des Deutschen archäologischen Instituts, Abteilung Kairo* 15: 89–90.

Janssen, J. J.
1960 "Nine Letters from the Time of Ramses II." *Oudheidkundige mededelingen uit het Rijksmuseum van Oudheden te Leiden* 41: 31–47.
1992 "Literacy and Letters at Deir el-Medîna." In *Village Voices* (Proceedings from the Symposium "Texts from Deir el-Medîna and Their Interpretation," Leiden, 31 May–1 June 1991), edited by R. J. Demarée and A. Egberts, pp. 81–94. Centre of Non-Western Studies Publication 13. Leiden: Leiden University.

Johnson, J. H.
1984 "The Use of the Particle *mk* in Middle Kingdom Letters." In *Studien zu Sprache und Religion Ägyptens* 1: *Sprache*, edited by F. Junge, pp. 71–85. Göttingen: Hubert.

Korostovtsev, M.
1973 *Grammaire du néo-égyptien*. Moscow: Edition Naouka.

Kroeber, B.
1970 Die Neuägyptizismen vor der Amarnazeit: Studien zur Entwicklung der ägyptischen Sprache vom Mittleren zum Neuen Reich. Diss., University of Tübingen.

Manuelian, P. D.
1987 *Studies in the Reign of Amenophis II*. Hildesheimer ägyptologische Beiträge 26. Hildesheim: Gerstenberg Verlag.

Murnane, W. J.
1977 *Ancient Egyptian Coregencies*. Studies in Ancient Oriental Civilization 40. Chicago: Oriental Institute.

Peet, T. E.
1926 "Two Eighteenth Dynasty Letters: Papyrus Louvre 3230." *Journal of Egyptian Archaeology* 12: 70–74.

Quack, J. F.
1991 "Die Konstruktion des Infinitivs in der Cleft Sentence." *Revue d'égyptologie* 42: 189–207.

Ranke, H.
1935 *Die ägyptischen Personennamen* 1. Glückstadt: J. J. Augustin.
1952 *Die ägyptischen Personennamen* 2. Glückstadt: J. J. Augustin.

Satzinger, H.
1994 "Übersetzungsvorschläge und Anmerkungen zu einigen neuägyptischen Texten." In *Essays in Egyptology in Honor of Hans Goedicke*, edited by B. Bryan and D. Lorton, pp. 233–42. San Antonio: Van Siclen Books.

Schenkel, W.
1989 *Einführung in die klassisch-ägyptische Sprache und Schrift*. Tübingen: n.p.

Schneider, T.
1992 *Asiatische Personennamen in ägyptischen Quellen des Neuen Reiches*. Orbis Biblicus et Orientalis 114. Freiburg: Universitätsverlag; Göttingen: Vandenhoek and Ruprecht.

Wente, E. F.
1967 *Late Ramesside Letters*. Studies in Ancient Oriental Civilization 33. Chicago: University of Chicago Press.
1990 *Letters from Ancient Egypt*. Society of Biblical Literature, Writings from the Ancient World 1. Atlanta: Scholars Press.

8

CREATION ON THE POTTER'S WHEEL AT THE EASTERN HORIZON OF HEAVEN

PETER F. DORMAN

The Oriental Institute, Chicago

Creativity often seemed to be an essential aspect of preparation for Professor Wente's language classes. Whether the text was a hymn from the tomb of Kheruef or an unpublished Ramesside ostracon, the student would soon discover the one passage where all memorized rules of grammar apparently broke down, leaving one with a sense of doom and a host of possible but implausible translations. As the deadline for class approached, heralded perhaps by the morning glow in the eastern horizon, creativity in trying to make sense out of the intransigent inscription would reach fever pitch — ultimately to be met in the classroom, after a reading of the passage in question, by a justifiably skeptical silence and raised eyebrows. Elucidation would then follow like the clarity of the morning sun. This paper discusses creativity of a different sort, represented in several of the underworld books of the Theban royal tombs, which have been of keen interest to Professor Wente for much of his scholarly life. It is dedicated to him with admiration and affection.*

The potter's wheel is a familiar sight in tomb scenes showing potters at work fashioning ceramic vessels of all sorts.[1] The earliest reference to a potter's wheel apparently occurs in an inventory of workshop equipment in the Abusir Papyri;[2] the word for the potter's instrument, *nḥp*, is otherwise found in numerous contexts, in literary documents and religious texts as well as tomb and temple scenes. The most common temple context for representations of the potter's wheel is the series of reliefs depicting the divine birth of the king, in which the divine potter Khnum is shown fashioning the child-figures of the pharaoh and his *ka* (Holthoer 1977, pp. 18 [NKA 1], 19 [NKA 4], 23–26 [LPA 1–12]; Nelson 1981, pl. 66). In particular, the temple of Khnum at Esna is full of textual references to his creation of the world and of all living things by means of modeling upon the wheel.[3] Six of the scenes in the extant portion of the temple portray the pharaoh offering a potter's wheel to Khnum, providing him with the means of regeneration.[4] One of the essential functions of Khnum of Esna is the setting up of the potter's instrument and thus separating heaven from earth, a re-enactment of the genesis of the created world, commemorated by one of the great annual festivals of the Latopolite region.

The association of the potter's wheel with the primordial event of the separation of heaven from earth stems from a corpus of inscriptions and representations dating at least to the New Kingdom that pertains neither to Khnum the potter nor to his participation in the miraculous birth of the pharaoh, but which has to do with the

---

*A version of this article was presented in Atlanta on April 30, 1995, at the annual meeting of the American Research Center in Egypt. For facilitating photography in the royal tombs, I express deep appreciation to Dr. Mohammed Saghir, Supervisor of Pharaonic Antiquities for Upper Egypt, Dr. Sabry Abd el-Aziz, Chief Inspector of Antiquities of the West Bank, and Mr. Ibrahim Suleiman, Inspector of Antiquities at Gurna. I am also most grateful to Dr. John Darnell for his thoughtful comments, contributed during several discussions on this topic.

1. The most complete compilation of such scenes, including evidence from painted tomb walls, temple reliefs, tomb models, and literary documents, is Holthoer 1977, pp. 6–26, to which can be added Nelson 1981, pl. 66. For the usual context of pottery ateliers in conjunction with bread- and beer-making workshops, see Drenkhahn 1976, pp. 86–87.

2. As mentioned by Arnold 1993, p. 42; the inventory itself is found in Posener-Kriéger and de Cenival 1968, pl. 11; Posener-Kriéger 1976, pp. 45, 512.

3. For example: "dieu du tour, qui tourna les dieux et modela tout le monde sur son tour" (Sauneron 1962, p. 89); "il modela au tour les dieux et les hommes; il façonna les animaux, petits et grands; il fit les oiseaux ainsi que les poissons" (Sauneron 1962, p. 95); "dieu sacro-saint, qui crée les forme(s) chaque jour, au coeur excellent, aux bras vigoureux, quand il désire organiser (le pays)" (Sauneron 1962, p. 199).

4. These scenes were carved by six different rulers: Ptolemy VI (Sauneron 1963, pp. 34–37, text 15); Domitian (Sauneron 1963, pp. 137–38, text 61); Trajan (Sauneron 1968, pp. 376–79, text 395); Hadrian (Sauneron 1968, pp. 141–44, text 254); Nerva (Sauneron 1968, pp. 226–29, text 311); and

Gold of Praise: Studies on Ancient Egypt in Honor of Edward F. Wente
Edited by Emily Teeter and John A. Larson
Studies in Ancient Oriental Civilization 58
Chicago: Oriental Institute, 1999

daily rejuvenation of the sun god in the eastern horizon, in which the potter's wheel seems to play a central role. One of the pertinent texts of this corpus, studied by Assmann (1970, pp. 3–39), is a hymn to the rising sun preserved in the Theban tombs of Tjaynefer and Pedamenope, in the funerary papyrus of Khay in the British Museum, and in four Theban temples: Luxor, Medinet Habu, Deir el-Bahri, and the edifice of Taharqa at Karnak. The opening lines of the hymn describe the sun god at his emergence at dawn.

> *ỉw nsw.t* N. *dwꜣ=f Rꜥ m nhp m pr.t=f*
> *wbꜣ=f nḥp=f ḥfd=f r p.t m Ḫprỉ*
> *ꜥḳ=f m rꜣ pr=f m ỉḥ.ty m msw.t=f n.t ỉꜣb.t n.t p.t*
> *wṯs sw ỉt=f Wsỉr šsp sw ꜥ.wy Ḥḥ Ḥḥ.t*
> *ḥtp=f m mꜥnḏ.t*

> König N, er betet Ra an in der Morgenfrühe, bei seinem Herauskommen, (wenn) er sein *nḥpw* öffnet, (wenn) er auffliegt zum Himmel als Chepri. Er tritt ein in den Mund, er kommt heraus aus den Schenkeln bei seiner Geburt des Ostens des Himmels. Sein Vater Osiris hebt ihn empor, die Arme von Huh und Hauhet empfangen ihn. Er läßt sich nieder in der Morgenbarke (Assmann 1970, p. 20).

The phrase of particular interest is *wbꜣ nḥp*, for which Assmann renders the word *wbꜣ* in its usual meaning of "to open," leaving *nḥp* untranslated but dismissing the term "dungball."[5] In his discussion of *nḥp*, Assmann suggests that the term should include both the potter's wheel and the lump of clay on top, so that the action *wbꜣ* would signify the opening up of the formless clay mass by the fingers of the potter:

> Der Sinn der Aussage würde sich dann in einer Richtung verlagern, die zum Kontext (auch der meisten anderen Belege) ganz vorzüglich paßt: vom "Einsetzen der Gestalten bildenden Schöpferkraft" (für die "Töpferscheibe" ein zentrales Symbol ist) auf die eigene spontane Gestaltwerdung des Gottes (für die die Verwandlung des Tonklumpens auf der Töpferscheibe aus formlosem Stoff in Form ein bildkräftiges und beziehungsreiches Symbol abgeben würde) (Assmann 1970, p. 25).

This lends some sense to the otherwise abstruse translation "opening the potter's wheel," but in other contexts the word *nḥp* is never combined or confused with the material modeled on top of it, despite a relatively sophisticated lexicography for ceramic manufacture that includes words for Nile silt, marl, groundmass, the processes of kneading and wedging, and perhaps smoothing and proofing pottery as well.[6] The usual expression for beginning to work the mound of clay at the beginning of the pot-shaping process is *spḫꜣ ꜣḫ.t* "opening the clay" (Arnold 1993, p. 49, fig. 43 on p. 42). The chief difficulty with accepting a broader definition of *nḥp*, one including both wheel and clay, is the temptation to render the word solely as "lump (ball) of clay," omitting the wheel itself altogether from the sense of the translation.[7]

Yet if *nḥp* denotes only the potter's wheel and not the malleable clay mass on top, a different understanding of *wbꜣ* must then be reached. The verb *wbꜣ* normally means "to open," "reveal," "dig," or "pierce," depending to a large extent on context, while in its figurative use in combination with other nouns of the body it can mean "clever," "clear-sighted," or "enlightened" (*Wb.* 1.290:21–291:6; Ward 1978, pp. 57–60). Where it occurs in the sun hymn, the verb *wbꜣ* is an action performed by the sun god, with *nḥp* as the direct object: "he *wbꜣ*s his potter's wheel." It is tempting to translate *wbꜣ* as "release," "loose," "activate," in the sense of setting it into operation, following Sauneron in his translations of the religious texts from Esna, *wbꜣ nḥp* signifying "mettre en œuvre le tour" (Sauneron 1962, p. 88, n. x on p. 92).

Some clarification of this question can be obtained from the text and representations of the last hour of the Book of the Night, which describes the liminal area of the east just before the rising sun appears in the horizon. Several versions exist: two complete depictions in the tomb of Ramesses VI (in Corridor C and in the Sarcopha-

---

Decius (Sauneron 1975, pp. 84–87, text 503). In the scenes left by Hadrian and Nerva, the potter's wheel is presented with a figure of a small child on top of it, seated in the former case, standing in the latter.

5. The hesitancy of Assmann (1970, p. 23) to accept the meaning of *nḥp* as "dungball" is well grounded: "Die Bedeutung von *nḥp(w)* ... als 'Mistkugel,' die *Wb.* 2.294:13 vorschlägt, ist aus dem bekannten, aber erst bei den klassischen Autoren bezeugten Vergleich der Sonne mit der Mistkugel des Scarabaeus sacer erschlossen, in der sich seine Larve ernährt."

6. See Harris 1961, pp. 199–210; Holthoer 1977, pp. 37–40; Arnold 1993, pp. 12–14, 49. For a large lump of clay being set in position on a wheel by a potter's assistant, see Arnold 1993, fig. 89 on p. 75.

7. As, for example, in Hornung 1990, p. 92, where *nḥp* appears as "Tonklumpen"; in Assmann's later translation of the sun hymn it is rendered as "Kugel" (Assmann 1983a, p. 65) or as "ball" (Assmann 1995, p. 45). In a more poetic sense, it has even been rendered "prison d'argile" (Sauneron 1988, p. 86). Roulin (1996/1, p. 349) opts for *nḥp* as "sphère modelée (sur le tour de potier)."

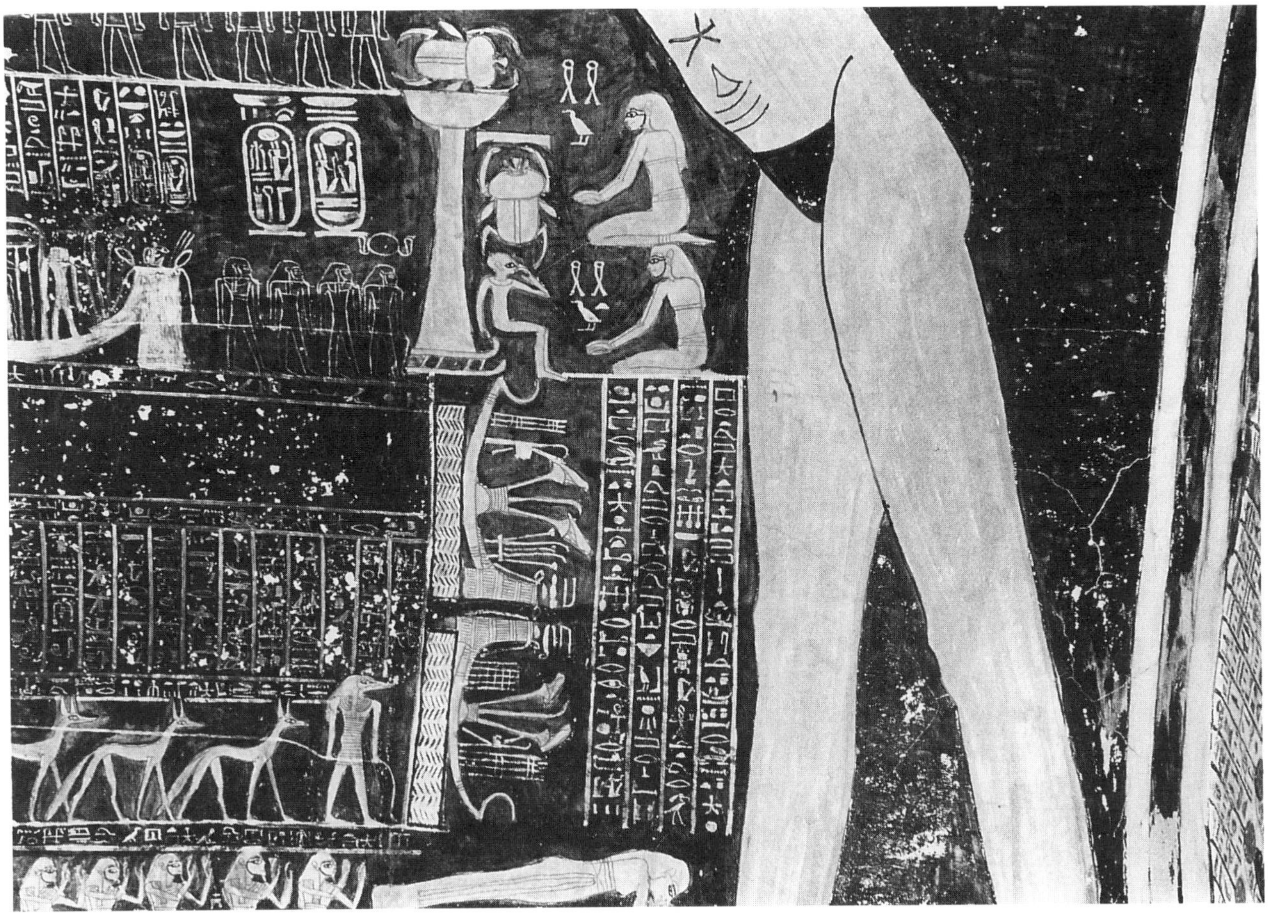

Figure 8.1. Book of the Night, Ceiling of Sarcophagus Hall, Tomb of Ramesses VI

gus Hall) and a third in the rear galleries of the tomb of Pedamenope at Thebes (TT 33).[8] The text in these three versions contains a more extensive variant of the initial portion of the sun hymn just cited.

Assmann sees the complementary images of entering into the mouth (*r͗*) of the sky goddess and emerging from the vulva as a reference to the complete cycle of solar death and rebirth summarized in a single passage:

> Hier wirkt die Abschweifung auf den Sonnenuntergang sogar noch befremdlicher als in der kosmographischen Beschreibung, die ja in den Zusammenhang eines "Buches" gehört, das den gesamten Zyklus abbildet. Als Hinweis auf den Zyklus hat die Bemerkung auch bei der Sonnenaufgangs-Beschreibung ihren Ort.[9]

The word *r͗,* however, is commonly used in the sense of "opening" in general, and in combination with *ỉd.t* "womb" it refers to the vulva (*Wb.* 2.391:7). If, in this passage that so clearly describes the emergence of the newborn sun from the body of Nut, the word *r͗* is understood not as "mouth" but as the constricted "opening" or entrance of the birth canal, there is no need to comment on thematic digression. The excerpt from the Book of the Night can be construed as describing what is pertinent only to the last hour of darkness — impending sunrise; in fact, the text is a clinically accurate description of natural childbirth on a cosmic scale.[10] Its caption is "going forth from the Duat (while) resting in the morning bark," and the text continues as follows:

8. For the Ramesses VI versions, see Piankoff 1954, pp. 409–28; for Pedamenope, see Dümichen 1894, pl. 24. Other representations of the Book of the Night exist, but they are incomplete: hours 1–9 are inscribed in the Abydene cenotaph of Seti I and hours 1–4 in the tomb of Ramesses IV, neither of which includes the last hour of night; abridged versions were carved on one of the walls in the tomb of Osorkon II (Montet 1947, pl. 25) and on the ceiling of the sarcophagus chamber of the tomb of Ramesses IX (Guilmant 1907, pl. 88). For other sources, and for a comparison of pertinent texts, see Roulin 1996/1, pp. 18–21, 23–25, 340–52; 1996/2, pp. 158–66.
9. Assmann 1970, pp. 26–27; similar remarks appear on p. 41 ff.
10. A passage from the last hour of Amduat cited by Assmann (1970, p. 42) describes solar birth in similar terms: "Geboren wird dieser Große Gott in seiner Erscheinungsform des Chepri bei dieser Höhle. Es entstehen Nun und Naunet, Huh und Hauhet bei dieser Höhle zur Geburt dieses Großen Gottes, daß er herausgehe aus der Dat, sich niederlasse in der Tagesbarke und hervortrete aus den Schenkeln der Nut"

sḳd.t Nnw r wnw.t n.t Rꜥ ptr<.t>-nfr.w-nb=s	Traversing Nun at the hour of Ra (called) "she who beholds the beauty of her lord" (the last hour of the night),
ḫpr m Ḫprỉ ḫfd r ꜣḫ.t ꜥḳ m rꜣ pr<.t> m kꜣ.t	coming into being as Khepri, rising toward the horizon, entering the (birth) opening, emerging from the vulva,
wbn m rꜣ-ꜥꜣ.wy ꜣḫ.t r wnw.t sḫꜥ-nfr.w-Rꜥ	appearing in the double-leaved door of the horizon at the hour (called) "she who causes the beauty of Ra to appear" (the first hour of the day)
r ỉr.t ꜥnḫ rmṯ ꜥw.wt ḥfꜣ.w nb ḳmꜣ.n=f	in order to revivify mankind and all walking and crawling creatures that he has created.

In these texts the term *wbꜣ nḥp*, which is present in the sun hymn, has been deleted and replaced by a roughly equivalent phrase, "coming into being as Khepri"; similarly, the "double-leaved door of the horizon" is a more decorous but nonetheless graphic circumlocution for the thighs of Nut (*ỉḥ.ty*) specified in the sun hymn. Next to the text there is a rebus or a trigram that serves as a visual reference to the wheel: a vertical stand resting on a sledge and supporting a scarab positioned horizontally (see fig. 8.1). Assmann recognizes the stand as the potter's wheel, correctly explaining that the sledge stands for Atum, the scarab for Khepri, and the wheel itself for the predawn transfiguration of the dying sun into the nascent solar disk, a symbol that clearly alludes to the purely textual description found in the sun hymn (Assmann 1970, p. 24).[11] In support of his interpretation of this unusual trigram, Assmann notes that in the tomb of Pedamenope the caption *wbꜣ nḥp* has been written out vertically next to the potter's wheel trigram (fig. 8.2).[12]

Beyond the phenomenon of daily solar rebirth, allusion is made in all versions of the Book of the Night to the initial creation of the world by the textual reference to Nun, the primeval waters, and by the kneeling figures of Heh and Hehet, the deities of pre-existence who, as we have seen, are also mentioned in the opening verses of the sun hymn.[13]

The meaning of the phrase *wbꜣ nḥp* "opening the potter's wheel" must now be considered in light of the related composition that often accompanies the last hour of the Book of the Night: the first hour of the Book of the Day. This composition appears in two complete versions, both in the tomb of Ramesses VI (again in Corridor C and in the Sarcophagus Hall), and in more abbreviated form in the tomb of Ramesses IX at Thebes and the tomb of Osorkon II at Tanis. Sunrise is depicted, of course, as the opening section of the Book of the Day but the representations contain a number of elements corresponding to those of the last hour of the Book of the Night. In both treatises, for example, the barks of the day and night are portrayed with their prows almost touching, as Isis and Nephthys lift up the solar disk, transferring it from the bark of the night to that of the day; often the goddesses stand on the prows of the barks to effect this passing of the disk.[14] Although Heh and Hehet are not named in the Book of the Day, in the tombs of Ramesses VI and Ramesses IX two goddesses are depicted beneath the winged scarab, kneeling opposite each other with their arms raised and witnessing the appearance of

(text in Hornung 1987, pp. 91–92; translation from Hornung 1963, p. 184).

11. Piankoff (1942, p. 80; 1954, p. 427) describes the stand as an altar.

12. As compared by Roulin (1996/2, p. 165), the word for "potter's wheel" presents a variety of orthographies in the Book of the Night, due to misunderstanding on the part of either ancient scribes or modern collators. In the phrase *wbꜣ=f nḥp=f* on the ceiling of the cenotaph of Seti I at Abydos (Frankfort 1933, pl. 81; Neugebauer and Parker 1960, pl. 44, text E), the *m*-owl has been written instead of the expected *nḥ*-bird.

13. For Nun and the other deities of the Ogdoad as representatives of the primordial cosmos and helpers at the creation and the daily rebirth of the sun, see Allen 1988, pp. 20–21; *LÄ* 1 "Achtheit," cols. 56–57; *LÄ* 2 "Heh," cols. 1082–84; Hornung 1982, pp. 161–62. *Ḥḥ* and *Ḥḥ.t* are to be carefully distinguished from the *ḥḥ*-gods who support the heavens, as Bickel 1994, pp. 27–29, notes.

14. Compare, for example, Piankoff 1954, pls. 149 and 150; pls. 187 and 196; Montet 1947, pl. 25. Transfer of the solar disk from the realm of the underworld to that of the living at daybreak is likewise expressed in the sun hymn as a transfer between divine entities, with Osiris as the representative of the Duat and Heh and Hehet as elements of the watery world within Nun: "As Osiris lifts him up, Heh and Hehet receive him." See also the remarks in Assmann 1970, pp. 43–44. For other portrayals of or references to Isis and Nephthys transferring or nurturing the solar disk, see, for example, the "Schlußbild" to the Book of Gates (e.g., Hornung 1981, fig. 1 on p. 218); Assmann 1969, p. 188, lines 38–40, n. 15 on pp. 197–98. See also Piankoff 1942, p. 1 and references in n. 1. At Esna, the word for "morning," *dwꜣ(w)*, is written as an ideogram portraying Isis and Nephthys passing the disk between them; see Sauneron 1982, p. 123, #53. The same ideogram is used at Edfu, for example, in descriptions of daybreak: "he flies up to heaven in the early morning (*tp dwꜣw*)" (Rochemonteix and Chassinat 1984, p. 22).

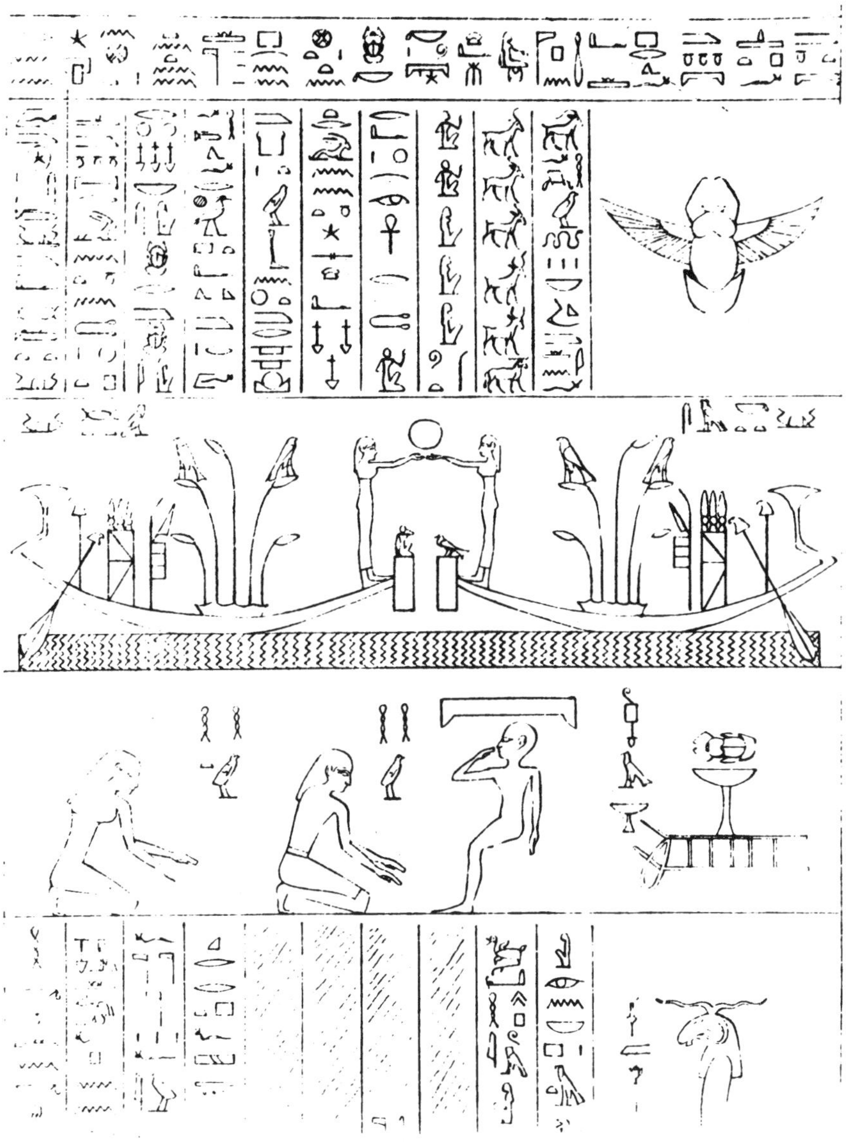

Figure 8.2. Book of the Night, Tomb of Pedamenope (after Dümichen 1894, pl. 24)

the sun between them (figs. 8.3–4);[15] in the tomb of Osorkon II they are shown as a pair of male deities (fig. 8.5). They are doubtless to be viewed as the two gods of pre-existence named in the Book of the Night since they are both supported from below by a figure of Shu with his hands raised, an obvious re-enactment of the primordial separation of heaven and earth.[16]

Between the kneeling deities in all versions sits a figure shown from a frontal perspective, which scholars have consistently identified as a second depiction of Nut, shown in smaller scale than the enormous arching figure above, about to give birth to the solar child depicted within her swollen womb.[17] In view of the elaborate textual description of childbirth provided by the Book of the Night, this would seem entirely logical. But the pregnant figure is cut off below the womb at the ground line, and the hands are held in a curious position, often

15. Piankoff (1954, p. 389) states that "the goddess of the sky is represented as a pregnant woman holding the disk, who kneels between two assisting goddesses, Isis and Nephthys." The goddesses, however, are not labeled, and Isis and Nephthys are otherwise depicted below this scene on the barks of the morning and evening.

16. For Shu's role at the creation and his association with (indeed, engendering of) the *ḥḥ*-gods as the supporters of heaven, see te Velde 1981/82, pp. 26–27; *LÄ* 5 "Schu," cols. 735–37; Bickel 1994, pp. 193–95.

17. For example, "[die Himmelsgöttin] wird, zwischen zwei helfenden Göttinnen, in ungewöhnlicher Vorderansicht gezeigt, ihr schwangerer Leib umschließt die Scheibe mit dem Sonnenkind" (Hornung 1984, p. 488); "une petite scène représentant Nout elle-même portant le jeune soleil dans son sein, assistée de deux déesses agenouillées ..." (Piankoff 1942, p. 2); and in similar terms, Piankoff 1961/62, p. 266.

Figure 8.3. Book of the Day, Ceiling of Sarcophagus Hall, Tomb of Ramesses IX

very low at either side of the body, rather atypical for the pose of pregnant women. And as Assmann notes, Nut herself is never described as a catalyst in the process of creation but serves only as a sort of passive backdrop against which the celestial drama is played out.[18]

The most prominent element missing from this scene — but present in the Book of the Night — is the trigram of the potter's wheel and the label *wbꜣ nḥp*; and this omission seems to be the clue to the identity of this central figure shown in frontal perspective. It is not the pregnant sky goddess who is portrayed in the first hour of the Book of the Day, but rather the creator god at work at his potter's wheel, modeling his lump of clay into the form of a child who — at least in the tomb of Ramesses VI — appears at the center. The position of the god's hands at the rim of the disk emphasizes the rotary motion of the wheelhead, and for *wbꜣ nḥp* one can propose the idiomatic translation "to spin the potter's wheel."[19] If the figure is seen as the strict equivalent of the potter's wheel trigram, one may suggest that the potter at work is the sun god in his aging aspect of Atum, spinning his wheel in order to rejuvenate himself in the hour before dawn.[20]

18. "Ihre aktive Mutterrolle wird nicht eigens betont, weil sie nur als kosmischer Raum — mit Osten und Westen, Schenkel und Mund — für den Zyklus des 'Ein- und Ausgehens' (*ʿq* und *prj* sind 'Leitworte') inrede steht, der ganz vor der Aktivität des Sonnengottes her dargestellt wird" (Assmann 1970, p. 43).

19. Given the determinative of the word — a boring drill, Gardiner Sign List U24 — it is not surprising that the word *wbꜣ* should signify, among its other meanings, rapid rotation around a central axis; the surprise is rather that this connotation apparently pertains in such a limited sense. For the argument that *msnḥ* does not mean to rotate upon an axis, as in the famous phrase from Amenemope 2.8, "the land turns as does a potter's wheel," see Federn 1966.

20. The potter figure in the extant versions of the Book of the Day is never labeled. While he is probably to be considered as Atum by virtue of the thematic correspondence of this scene to the trigram in the Book of the Night, his precise identity is less important than the (self-)regenerative aspect of the spinning wheel. In any case, Allen (1988, p. 36) notes in another context that Egyptian creation accounts "reflect a philosophy that is more developmental than causal. In this view, the question of an external agent is superfluous." The identity of the celestial potter on the ceilings of the royal tombs as Atum is further suggested through a series of sun hymns to be found in several private Theban tombs, in which the deceased says: "Hail to you, O Amun, when you spin the potter's wheel as Atum-Horakhty" (Assmann 1983b, Texts

Figure 8.4. Book of the Day, Ceiling of Corridor C, Tomb of Ramesses VI

It is possible that there was some ambiguity even in ancient times as to whether the central figure was to be represented as a potter or a pregnant goddess. On an ostracon in Cairo, for example, a sketch of this same figure shows that the torso has been broadened to bring it more clearly into line with the perimeter of the wheelhead. On the other hand, the ceiling of the sarcophagus chamber in the tomb of Ramesses IX shows a fairly large disk, protruding far beyond the outlines of the deity whose hands are placed on its rim (fig. 8.3). The ceiling of Osorkon II likewise shows a clear demarcation between the torso of the god and the disk, revealing the latter as a separate element (fig. 8.5). In several versions the potter is shown with heavy breasts and belly wrinkles;[21] these features need not be taken as indicative of the female gender, but may signify the aging solar god at the end of a prosperous life-span or alternatively the androgynous nature of the primeval creator of the cosmos.[22]

As for the phenomenon depicted on the potter's wheel, the sequence of events clearly indicates that the spinning of the wheel is not equivalent to parturition, but to conception, or at least the enlivening of the fetus within the celestial womb.[23] To offer a new translation of the sun hymn:

17.1–2, 186.1–2), obviously a conflation of the aging and rejuvenated aspects of the sun god at the eastern cusp of the world.

21. Daressy 1901, Cat. 25074, pp. 15–16, pl. 15; Piankoff 1934, p. 104; Bruyère 1930, p. 180; I am grateful to Emily Teeter for the last reference.

22. These pendulous breasts and wrinkles are most clearly seen on the Cairo ostracon (Daressy 1901, pl. 15); in the Sarcophagus Hall of Ramesses VI (Piankoff 1954, pl. 187); and in the tomb of Ramesses IX (fig. 8.4). For pendulous breasts as a sign of old age, see Baines 1985, pp. 125–26. For the androgynous characteristics of Atum, see Bickel 1994, pp. 37–38.

23. The moment at which Nut becomes pregnant with the solar fetus appears to be somewhat variable, and the spinning of the wheel in the last hour of night may not be strictly equivalent with conception. For celestial conception through Nut's swallowing the sun in the second hour of night, see Allen 1988, p. 66, n. 29; the notion of Nut being pregnant for much of the night would seem to be alluded to by a phrase in a sun hymn that addresses the solar deity as *sḏr ỉwr* "der du des Nachts in Schwangerschaft getragen wirst" (Assmann 1969, p. 169, n. 5 on p. 175). P. Carlsberg suggests that the movement of the nascent sun toward earth (the quickening of the child in the womb?) begins in the ninth hour: "It happens that he orders his withdrawal towards mankind from the Duat in the hour of *sḥtp.n.s*. It is the ninth hour of the night" (following the translation of Neugebauer and Parker 1960, pp. 50–51, lines 9–11).

> It is at his (Ra's) emergence that King N. adores Ra in the early morning. When he spins his potter's wheel, he rises toward heaven as Khepri, as he enters into the (birth) opening and emerges from the thighs at his birth in the east of heaven. As his father Osiris lifts him up, the arms of Heh and Hehet receive him.

After the moment of solar conception or quickening represented by the spinning wheel, the fully formed child drops into the birth passage, through the labia of Nut, and emerges as Khepri, the winged scarab, into the world of the living.

In the version of the Book of the Night on the ceiling of the Sarcophagus Hall of Ramesses VI, Assmann also notes the presence of what he describes as a second trigram next to the potter's wheel, consisting of a small child below a scarab, both positioned under a heaven sign. He describes this as the visual equivalent of the phrase that occurs in the sun hymn, *ḥfd≈f r p.t* "when he flies up to heaven," with the small child read as the determinative of *ḥfd* "to fly up" (Assmann 1970, p. 24). All other depictions from the Book of the Night, however, show these three elements as partially recombined: either the scarab and heaven sign appear together and the child is shown separately (as in Corridor C of Ramesses VI and Osorkon II), or the child and heaven sign are grouped together, with the winged scarab alone (as in Pedamenope, fig. 8.2). The scarab and child are rather to be regarded as different forms of the sun god beginning his ascent to heaven during the first hour of morning, with the former identified as Khepri, the winged scarab who flies up into the land of the living. The embryonic child is to be read not as the verb *ḥfd* but perhaps as the noun *sḏ.ty* "child" or equally "he of the flame," the morning glow visible in the eastern sky before sunrise.

Van Dijk (1979/80, pp. 12–13), in an article on the birth of Horus, comments on a vignette from the Creation of the Solar Disk in order to show the deliberate punning on the words *sḏ.ty* "child" and *sḏ.t* "flame." In the vignette from the tomb of Ramesses IX (Guilmant 1907, pl. 92), the central ithyphallic figure emits a stream of fiery semen connected to two signs: a child and a flame. The label reads: "This god is doing this (*m sḫr pn*): he procreates flame (*wtt≈f sḏ.t*)"; the appearance of the two images together, the child and the flaming brazier, can equally suggest the outwardly dual form *sḏ.ty* "child." The figure of a child is also shown as the product of the streams of flaming semen, indicated as a row of dots, that issue from the phalluses of bending shadow figures in Corridor C of the tomb of Ramesses IX; each is labeled in partially enigmatic script as *sḏ.ty*.[24] The same graphic interchange is occasionally to be seen on the prow of the morning bark. While a small figure of a child often appears squatting on the forestem of the bark above a hanging beaded net (as in fig. 8.3), in the burial chamber of the tomb of Ay the child is replaced by two small flames (fig. 8.6) — both devices are to be read as *sḏ.ty*.[25] Among the forms of the sun god depicted in the Litany of Ra, one is labeled *sḏ.ty*, suitable for a manifestation of the fiery disk; the deity is shown as a standing mummiform figure with a shaved head, indicative of youthfulness, and wearing a divine beard.[26] In the text of the litany itself, this youthful solar form is hailed as an elder god who has been transformed into a child, similar to the rejuvenating alteration that takes place by means of the potter's wheel (Hornung 1975, p. 70):

smsw ꜥꜣ m-ḫnt Dwꜣ.t Ḫpri ḫpr sḏ.ty	O great elder one within Duat, Khepri who has become a child,
twt is ḥꜣ.t sḏ.ty	Yours is indeed the body of a child.[27]

24. Guilmant 1907, pls. 80–81. These examples were pointed out to me by Dr. John Darnell, whom I thank for the reference. Note also that a rivulet appears to issue from the mouth of the scarab positioned on top of the potter's wheel trigram in Corridor C of Ramesses VI (Piankoff 1954, pl. 149). Though usually interpreted as water (e.g., Roulin 1996/1, p. 350, for whom it "évoque peut-être un thème supplémentaire, celui de la création par crachat attesté dès les *Textes des Pyramides*"), the rivulet is not a zigzag of ripples, but a connected chain of rounded shapes, similar to dots of flame, signifying the emission of a stream of light. The same rivulet of light can be seen in the Sarcophagus Hall of the same tomb (fig. 8.1), although it seems to have been painted over by the ancient painters of the ceiling.

25. The child often alternates on the prow of the morning bark with a sparrow; for the solar connotations of the sparrow and its relation to the morning glow, see Patch 1994, pp. 110–16. The seated child is frequently shown with what appears to be a tassle of hair falling down the back of its head (as in fig. 8.3), and this may represent a stream of light, similar to the glowing ray emitted from the mouth of the scarab atop the potter's wheel in fig. 8.1.

26. Illustrated, for example, in Piankoff 1964, fig. A on p. 14, register 3, no. 30; and p. 13, where the name is translated as "He of the Two Children." Hornung (1976, n. 170 on p. 117) notes that the representation of this form in the tomb of Ramesses IV is "mit Seitenlocke dargestellt, dazu rot bemalt."

27. See also the hymn to the morning sun in the edifice of Taharqa at Karnak, which ends, "... [and the *rḫyt* make for him the *hnw*-acclamation in his appearances of being rejuvenated (*nḥnw*), of Ra the child (*sḏ.ty*) com]ing out as

Figure 8.5. Book of the Day, Tomb of Osorkon II (after Montet 1947, pl. 25)

The difference between conception or quickening (the embryonic child) and the actual emergence of the newborn sun (the winged scarab), delineated in both text and illustration in the Books of the Day and Night, is reflected in the physical phenomenon of sunrise. Both child and flame refer to the morning glow in the hour before dawn: solar conception has already taken place on the spinning wheel of the creator god, heralded by the formation of the child (that is, the flame) that brightens and reddens the liminal east. Solar emergence (birth) occurs only later, as the rim of the disk — Khepri — rises over the eastern hills, at the "double-leafed door of the horizon," the thighs of Nut. The lightening of the horizon before dawn also signals the rekindling of the fire to which the enemies of Ra are condemned in the eastern place of destruction.[28] The cosmic triumph is thus consummated at the simultaneous quickening of the solar deity and the annihilation of his foes.

Khepri!" (following the translation of Parker et al. 1979, p. 40, parallels shown on pl. 33). As depicted on the ceilings of several Ptolemaic temples, the manifestation assumed by the sun god during the early hours of morning is that of a child; see Daressy 1917.

28. Numerous texts equate the appearance of the sun in the morning with the destruction of Ra's enemies, as, for example, in the hymn to the rising sun treated by Assmann 1969, p. 169, lines 13–14: "Re lebt, der Feind ist tot! Du bist bleibend, dein Widersacher ist gefallen!"; or in the hymn to

The imagery of the potter's wheel is not limited to the underworld books of the royal tombs. The earliest reference to the wheel in a religious text is a passage from the Coffin Texts, Spell 882 (*CT* 7, p. 93). The text is fragmentary and somewhat obscure in sections, but it can be recognized as an utterance of the creator sun god:

ink iḫḫ.w ḥr rmn.wy Wr	I am the morning glow on the shoulders of the great one;
ii.n=i šꜣs=i p.t nmi=i n iḫḫ.w Rꜥ sšd	it is traversing the heaven, crossing over to the twilight of Ra who glistens, that I have come.
ink ḥꜣ=f ipw [...] prr.wt tw ꜣd.t.n=i ḥr Šw ḫfd.n=i ḥr qnqn [...]	I am his protector [...] those who have come forth, whom I have attacked on behalf of Shu. I have risen up upon the *qnqn*[29] [... ,]
[mḥ].n=i rd=i r ns wpš m iꜣb.t	I have [hastened][30] toward the fire that gleams in the east,
sḏ.t nḥpw wbꜣ itn r[...]f tp.w-ꜥ.wy=i iry=i pr m nw pn	the flame of the potter's wheel when the disk is spun[31] [...] my predecessor, that I might create the one who has gone forth at this time of day ... .

It is likely that the spinning wheel of the potter is conflated with the sun's disk in this utterance, a conflation reflected in Corridor C of Ramesses VI, where the creator god spins a wheel that is shown from an overhead perspective, as an oval painted bright red, in the center of which is shown the yellow figure of a child (fig. 8.4).

The redness that appears as a consequence of the spinning potter's wheel and the progressive lightening of the morning sky in the hours before dawn are elaborated upon in the Book of Nut, in which a series of captions traces the unfolding events of sunrise with remarkable specificity.[32] It is clear from the representation of Nut's outstretched figure that the re-animation of the nascent disk begins not in the area of her womb, but — perhaps oddly — from the region of her feet, placed below the surface of the wavy ground line, where a large disk is depicted resting on her toes (fig. 8.7).[33] The ambiguity concerning the precise point at which the sun disappears in the evening and reappears in the morning sky is caused by a spatial discrepancy imposed by the representation of Nut: her mouth (the point of solar ingress) and vulva (the point of solar emergence) are both raised high above the ground line of the earthly horizon, the apparent human reference for both sunset and sunrise. On the eastern side of the Nut depiction, a curving line connects the wavy ground line, where the sun should physically appear, to the knees of Nut, the cosmological birthplace, and represents an artistic attempt to resolve this quandary. The signs for *ꜣḫ.t iꜣbt.t* "eastern horizon" are in fact written next to Nut's pubic triangle, rather than the end of the ground line where a small disk seems about to emerge from the earth (next to text G). It seems clear

Amen-Ra in the Berlin papyri translated by Sauneron 1953, p. 68: "car tu brilles, et brillant, flamboyant, tu triomphes de tes ennemis ... car tu as mutilé la puissance des Rebelles et l'ennemi de Rê est tombé dans le feu." See also Zandee 1960, p. 161, B.7.a; van Dijk 1979/80, p. 14.

29. The translation of the phrase is problematic since *qnqn* is an unknown word. Determined with the walking legs, *ḫfd* has usually been rendered as "climb" or "rise up" (Faulkner 1978, p. 47; Barguet 1986, p. 502), following *Wb.* 3.75:6–9, although the preposition *ḥr* lends to the verb the connotation "aufsteigen, emporklimmen mit Hilfe von ... ." A second meaning of *ḫfd ḥr* is markedly different: "(sich) setzen an/auf" (*Wb.* 3.75:12). This alternative meaning corresponds rather neatly to the gloss to the Book of Nut preserved in P. Carlsberg I of the passage containing the phrase *wbꜣ=f nḥp=f*, a gloss that may describe the potter-creator god sitting down to work before his wheel: "he sits on his cloth [*ḥms=f ḥr diꜣ*], that is to say, on his birth-brick [*ḥr tby n ms*] — that is to say, he is accustomed to do it ... he ... in the form of Khepre, and he assumes the form of the sun-disc ..." (Neugebauer and Parker 1960, p. 48).

30. Restoring *[mḥ.n]=i rd=i*, after Barguet 1986, p. 502, "j'ai (allongé?) le pas."

31. Taking *wbꜣ* as a passive circumstantial *sḏm=f*, which seems preferable to assuming an active form with the omission of the 1st person suffix-pronoun that is otherwise consistently written out. Other translations take *sḏ.t* as a writing of the verb *sḏ.t(w)* "to break" with *nḥpw* as the subject: "die den *nḥpw* zerbricht" (Assmann 1970, p. 23); "the potters' wheels are broken" (Faulkner 1978, p. 47); "la boule (du scarabée) est brisée" (Barguet 1986, p. 502).

32. Two monumental versions exist: the cenotaph of Seti I at Abydos (Frankfort 1933, pp. 72–75, pl. 81) and the tomb of Ramesses IV (Hornung 1990, pp. 90–96, pls. 68–71), which describe the movements of the sun and stars around a figure of Nut spread over the earth. P. Carlsberg I contains a later hieratic version of most of the texts, as well as glosses in Demotic to explain specific passages in relation to the representation of the sky goddess. For a comparative treatment of the texts, see Hornung 1990, pp. 92–96; Neugebauer and Parker 1960, pp. 43–94. For the solar associations of the color red, see Kees 1943, pp. 447–52.

33. The P. Carlsberg gloss of the overall caption to the picture of Nut states that "he caused the hind part [*pḥ.t*] to be the beginning that is to say, it is the place of birth," following the translation of Neugebauer and Parker 1960, p. 43.

Figure 8.6. Morning Bark, Tomb of Ay

that the lowermost captions tucked into the area below the curving line describe pre-dawn events that are beyond the visibility of mere mortals.[34]

The sequence of texts followed here is different from that outlined by Neugebauer and Parker.[35] On the basis of the sequence of events described in the solar hymn and in the Book of the Night, they should be read as follows, texts M and E-F-G initiating the solar transit from the regions of primeval non-creation near Nut's feet to the land of the living:

(M) The majesty of this god goes forth from her hindquarters.
(E) When he spins his potter's wheel, he swims in his redness.[36]

34. In a similar way, the signs for *ꜣḫ.t imnt.t* are located next to Nut's mouth. The text that describes the setting of the sun (Aa) refers to events that take place in the first hour of night in the underworld, as soon as the sun disk sinks from view but before darkness falls. The sun is said to "set in life in Duat" *ḥtp m ꜥnḫ m Dwꜣ.t*, a caption also written out on Nut's wrists (text Kk), where the sun's nightly journey apparently begins. The single vulture wing extending downward from the large disk at Nut's mouth has doubtless been depicted for the same reason as the curving line at her knees: to connect the cosmological and the visible points of the sun's disappearance, her mouth and the "physical" horizon below her arching body. The word for evening, *mšrw*, the onset of darkness, is written out next to Nut's ear (Neugebauer and Parker 1960, p. 81). For *mšrw* as a parallel concept to *knm.t* "darkness" rather than sunset, see Assmann 1969, p. 174.

35. Neugebauer and Parker base their sequence largely on the order of texts followed by P. Carlsberg I (which omits several of the monumental texts) and in part on what appears to be the logical progression of the sun's emergence from the body of Nut; for the papyrus, see Lange and Neugebauer 1940. In addition to the picture of Nut, the Seti I cenotaph records in tabular format the stations of the sun disk during its nightly journey through the goddess's body. In the ninth hour, the sun "begins in Nut's intestines and ends at her vulva [at the tenth hour] and may thus be considered 'born' or 'risen'" (Neugebauer and Parker 1960, p. 83); the disk then moves on toward her thighs, and in the eleventh and twelfth hours toward her feet. "All this time, although actually outside the body of Nut, the sun is not visible" (Neugebauer and Parker 1960, p. 83). In fact, it is apparently in the twelfth hour of night that the solar deity begins rising up toward the vulva from the feet of Nut, to be reborn in the first hour of day.

36. Neugebauer and Parker (1960, p. 48, n. 39) refer to both Seti I and Ramesses IV versions as corrupt, translating "he opens his <ball of clay>." For the emendation of Seti I, see note 12, above; the ceiling of Ramesses IV writes *ḥtp* in place of *nḥp* as noted by Allen (1988 [reprint 1995], pp. 3, 76). As noted earlier, the phrase *wbꜣ=f nḥp=f* as it occurs in

(F) He is purified in the arms of his father, Osiris; then his father lives and he becomes effective through him.[37]

(G) The redness after he is born.[38]

Text G, written below a small disk at the very point where it touches the intersection of the curved horizon and the wavy ground line of the scene, describes the redness of the morning glow. Two captions, slightly higher up along Nut's shin, yet still below the horizon, describe the increasing animation of the celestial bodies, signaling the revivification of the created world:

(N) Then he proceeds toward earth, having appeared (re)born.[39]

(D) The *knm.t*-decan lives, together with the *štꜣ*-decan;[40] it means that Horus is alive.[41]

The continuing journey within the body of Nut, described as "proceeding toward earth" after the red morning glow has been made manifest before daybreak, is reminiscent of the progress made by the solar child in the Book of the Night prior to parturition. Two additional texts, located along Nut's thigh and below her pubic triangle, which is labeled *ꜣḫ.t ỉꜣbt.t* "eastern horizon," at last describe the physical emergence of the solar child into the world, as full morning finally breaks over the land:

(O) Then he causes himself to ascend; then he opens the thighs of his mother, Nut; then he flies up toward heaven.

(H) Then he enters as this (winged scarab);[42] he has come into being like his manifestation at the first occasion.

(K) Then his mind and his strength develop; he sees Geb (the earth); he is a child when he shows himself on the day he goes forth.[43]

There is a distinction between the texts that are written upon the body of Nut (M-N-O) and those that are crowded in below her shins and thighs (D-E-F-G-H-K). In content, the former group refers to the process of solar childbirth through the body of the sky goddess. They appear along the line of her legs and most are written upside down in relation to the orientation of the ceiling itself. The latter group describes phenomena that are largely astral or celestial in nature and are sequentially oriented along the line of a 90-degree arc that curves from Nut's toes (D-E-F) to her vulva (K). Either group can be understood separately as a complete description of sunrise: M-N-O on the one hand and D-E-F-G-H-K on the other. It is only the latter texts that are copied out and glossed in P. Carlsberg I.[44]

Solar childbirth (on the body of Nut)		Astral phenomena (glossed in P. Carlsberg)
Text M	=	Texts D-E-F
Text N	=	Text G
Text O	=	Text H-K

the Book of the Night is replaced in the sun hymn by *ḫpr m Ḫprỉ* "coming into being as Khepri." In Pyramid Text §697a, the morning glow and Khepri are equated: *ỉỉ.n* N. *r P ḏsr r sḏ.t ꜥnḫ r Ḫprỉ* "it is redder than fire, more alive than Khepri, that N. has come to Pe"; see Sethe 1908, p. 378.

37. Purification in the arms of Osiris happens also in the first hour of night (texts Aa), a phenomenon associated with transiting the twilight cusps of morning and evening, in the region of the *ꜣḫ.t* "horizon," which Allen (1988, p. 6) renders literally as "place of becoming effective"; for an elaboration of his remarks, see Allen 1989, pp. 19–21.

38. The gloss in P. Carlsberg I reads, "The redness comes into being after birth; it is <in> the color which develops in the sun disk at dawn that he (that is to say, Ra) rises" (compare the slightly different translation of Neugebauer and Parker 1960, p. 49).

39. The phrase *ḫꜥ.w ms(.w)* signifies the regeneration of the youthful god within the womb, who is now infused with life but has not yet emerged (physically born) into the world. Correspondingly, text D seems to signal, through astral observation, the viability of the solar child still below the horizon.

40. For the reading of only two decan names here, see Neugebauer and Parker 1960, p. 47, notes to line 33.

41. See also text W (Neugebauer and Parker 1960, p. 87), which contains labels that reiterate text D. As used in texts N and P, "'life' means 'rising' and in the Nut picture we see the decan *štw* just above the horizon, the sun [disk of text G] in the horizon, and the decan *knmt* just below the horizon" (Neugebauer and Parker 1960, p. 87). The star decans are shown to the right of the curving line, within the visible world of mankind, and signal impending daybreak because they can be glimpsed in the lightening eastern sky before dawn.

42. The word is not written out. The lacuna in the text pointedly refers to the large representation of the scarab above, as noted by Lange and Neugebauer (1940, p. 20).

43. This translation of the last portion of text K largely follows that of van Dijk 1979/80, p. 17.

44. Text J, also glossed in P. Carlsberg, has its own distinct physical orientation and seems to be a summary of the sun's origins that is somewhat independent of the two parallel sequences, though surely closer to the theme of "astral" phenomena.

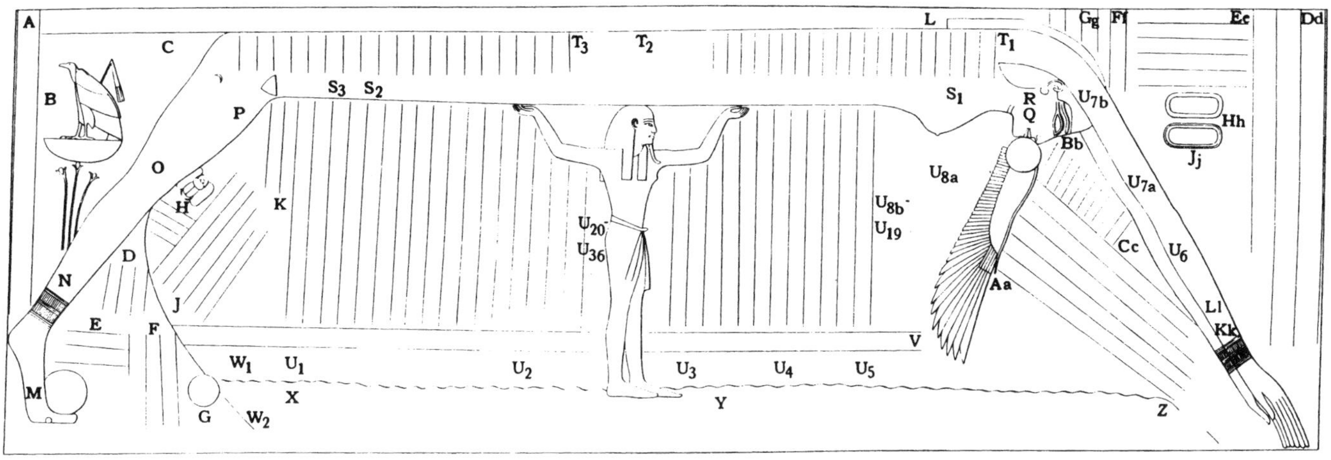

Figure 8.7. Diagram of Ceiling of Cenotaph of Seti I, Abydos (after Neugebauer and Parker 1960, p. 39)

The compositions reviewed thus far — the sun hymn, the Books of the Day and Night, and the Book of Nut — share a number of parallel elements in common, present either in text or in representation, referring to the appearance of the sun in the eastern horizon. The imagery includes cosmic childbirth, regeneration through the potter's wheel, and both visible and invisible astronomical phenomena.

The significance of the potter's wheel as a symbol of creative energy does not diminish with the eventual obsolescence of the underworld books discussed above. At the temple of Khnum at Esna the hieroglyphs of the wheel and small child commonly appear in cryptographic writings of the names of both the god and the city.[45] The festival that is most extensively recorded in the hypostyle hall is that of the installation of the potter's wheel, covering fourteen of the eighteen columns (Sauneron 1962, p. 71). But in the context of the New Kingdom compositions just discussed, it is clear that this festival is given prime importance not only because of Khnum's traditional activity at the potter's wheel — the god who fashions clay in the shape of gods, kings, mankind, and beasts — but in particular because Khnum appears at Esna in the role of the creator sun god, for whom the spinning wheel is an allegory of primordial creation and daily rebirth.[46]

Several passages from Esna may be cited to illuminate certain concepts already considered. On column 9, a circumlocution for "potter's wheel" is found, which reinforces the idea of its rapidly spinning motion (Sauneron 1968, p. 177, text 275, 9; Sauneron 1962, pp. 147–48). Instructions for pronouncing the rituals in connection with the setting up of the wheel are worded as follows:

nỉs tꜣ mḏ.t ꜥꜣ.t sḥr ꜥpp r mḥ-ỉb n ꜣḫty ḥnꜥ ḥm n nṯr pn	"Recite the great book (of) overthrowing Apophis in order to appease the Horizoner and the majesty of this great god;
šd tꜣ wp-r m rn n H̱nm pn mỉt.t=s ḏr-nty Ptḥ pw	pronounce the opening-of-the-mouth for this Khnum as well, for he is Ptah.[47]
swḏꜣ wbꜣ-mẖn ḥr ỉmn.t ỉꜣb.t m rw.t-dỉ-mꜣꜥ.t [...] *nb nẖp*	Install the circling spinner upon the west and east at the gate where justice is given [...] the lord of the potter's wheel."[48]

The compound noun *wbꜣ-mẖn* is determined by the sign of the potter's wheel and clearly refers to the instrument, the public installation of which is the culmination of the entire festival. The element *mẖn* not only empha-

45. The potter's wheel can stand for *n*, which appears in the spellings of Esna, *Sn.t*, and Khnum, *H̱nm*; the seated child has a wider variety of phonetic possibilities, among which are *ẖ*, *n*, *m*, and *s* (Sauneron 1982, pp. 115–16, #16–17, and 180, #341). For the abundant cryptographic orthography of the name of Khnum, see Sauneron 1982, pp. 197–202.

46. In the six scenes at Esna in which potter's wheels are presented to the local deity, listed above in note 4, Khnum is in every case conflated with Ra, reinforcing the solar association of the potter's wheel.

47. Following Sauneron's emendation of the orthography (1962, p. 148, n. c).

48. Assmann (1970, n. 6 on p. 24) seems to have taken *wbꜣ* as the word for "set up," that is, for Sauneron's "dresser (le tour)," whereas the verb *swḏꜣ* precedes the noun; the phrase is to be read *swḏꜣ wbꜣ-mẖn* "install the circling spinner." Another occurrence of this compound noun, in place of the usual word *nẖp* "potter's wheel," is found at Edfu: *H̱nm nẖp nṯr.w ḥr wbꜣ-mẖn=f* "Khnum, who models the gods upon his circling spinner"; see Chassinat 1910, p. 17, Tableau A s. 2 d. I.

sizes the rotating motion of the wheel, but alludes to the serpent that guards the solar deity in his journey through the sky and the underworld.[49]

The final ritual of the celebrations invokes Khnum to transfer his creative powers to women, in whom the mythic activity of the potter's wheel will ensure the perpetual conception of the human race. The following spell is found on column 12 at Esna:

rꜣ n smn nḥp m ẖ.t n ḥm.wt nb.w
ḏd-mdw ỉ nḥp qmꜣ swḥ.t ḥr nḥp=k
ṯs=k nḥp m-ẖn ỉd.wt ꜥpr štꜣy.t m tỉ=k

Utterance for setting up the potter's wheel in the bellies of all women: Words spoken: "O divine potter, who creates the egg upon your[50] wheel: may you set up the potter's wheel within the uterus, providing the womb with your (own) image."[51]

It is Khnum himself who actively takes a part in this fashioning within the womb. While his role can be expressed as that of a sexual consort,[52] the fertility of women is also described as the result of his celestial activity at the potter's wheel (Sauneron 1962, p. 210; Sauneron 1968, p. 349, text 377, 7):

nḥp=k r p.t nḥp r tꜣ sꜥnḫ nḫn.w m ẖ.t n mw.wt=sn m r-ꜥ.wy=k

May you model on the wheel in heaven, making potter's work on earth, so that children are brought to life within the wombs of their mothers by the action of your arms.

The image of the rotating wheel is extended to other deities not traditionally associated with the activity of potters. For example, within the local cosmogonies of other late temples, such as Dendara and Edfu, it is clear that Hathor and Horus likewise acted in the same capacity as Khnum — that is, as local creator gods in their own right. The symbol of the spinning wheel and the light it sheds was incorporated into litanies that appear in identical wording on the sanctuaries at Dendara and Edfu:

Dendara (Chassinat 1934, p. 5 ff.; addressed to Hathor):
twt rṯ wbꜣ nḥp m Nnw.t mḥ tꜣ m nkr ꜥnḫ m Bꜣḫw sḥr m Mꜣnw sḏr m ỉn.t rꜥ nb

Edfu (Rochemonteix and Chassinat 1984, p. 14 ff.; addressed to Horus):
twt rf wbꜣ nḥp m Nnw.t mḥ tꜣ m nkr ꜥnḫ m Bꜣḫw sḥr m Mꜣnw sḏr m Bḥd.t rꜥ nb

You are, moreover, the one who spins the potter's wheel in Naunet, who fills the earth with golden motes of sunlight, who comes alive in the liminal east and sets in the liminal west, who passes the night in Dendara/Edfu every day.[53]

While Nun is the primeval setting mentioned in the underworld books, in these Ptolemaic litanies it is his feminine counterpart, Naunet,[54] who appears as the topos for the conception of the solar deity, an idea in keeping with the potter's wheel as the creative force within the female procreative organs. The activation of the

49. For example, in the Book of the Day in the Sarcophagus Hall of Ramesses VI (Piankoff 1954, pl. 187), the nascent disk that is passed from the bark of the night to that of the day contains a standing child within it; on either side of the disk rears a serpent, both of which are labeled *mḥn*.

50. Within a vocative phrase, the 3rd person pronoun *=f* is to be expected. The translation above, however, is preferable to the imperative alternative: "create the egg upon your wheel; may you set up the potter's wheel … ."

51. Sauneron reads *ṯs=k ḫnm* for *ṯs=k nḥp*, translating, "O, dieu du tour, qui crées l'oeuf sur son tour, puisses-tu fixer l'activité-créatrice-du-tour à l'intérieur des organes féminins, et pourvoir cette matrice de ton image" (Sauneron 1962, p. 235; Sauneron 1968, p. 246, text 320, 21).

52. For example, "le mâle copulateur qui monte sur les femelles; pas de conception(?) d'où son oeuvre soit absente!" (Sauneron 1962, p. 164); "tu es Khnoum, le mâle copulateur qui rend les femmes enceintes" (Sauneron 1962, p. 209).

53. The translation in Blackman and Fairman 1941, p. 400, reads, "it is he who opens the ball of dung (?) in Naunet, who filleth the earth … ." Kurth (1994b, p. 82) paraphrases the sense of the passage perfectly: "denn du bist es ja, der mit der Schöpfung beginnt am (Morgen)himmel und das Land mit Goldstaub erfüllt … ."

54. Contra Alliot (1949, p. 152) who opts for interpreting the word as "Nut," noting the orthographic confusions between both names at Edfu.

potter's wheel at the cusp of the world is emphasized, too, in a hymn to Horus in the mammisi at Edfu (Chassinat 1933, p. 92, line 5), as the god appears at the eastern horizon:

> *twt rk wbꜣ nḥp m ḏ.t=k gs m ꜥq gs m pr.t*
>
> "You are, moreover, the one who spins the potter's wheel in your half-concealed and half-emerging form." [55]

The ceilings of Ptolemaic temples that depict the changing forms of the sun during the daytime hours show the early morning disk occupied by a small child.[56] The ceiling in the *wꜥb.t* at Edfu contains a caption that refers to the potter's wheel as the initiator of the solar sequence (Rochemonteix and Chassinat 1894, pl. 33c):

> *ḫpr.w wr.w n.ṯ ḥm n Rꜥ-Bḥd.ty nṯr ꜥꜣ sꜣb šw.t ḏr wbꜣ=f nḥp m dwꜣ.t tp.t r ꜥḳ m rꜣ*
>
> The great forms of the majesty Ra the Behdetite, the great god, dappled of feathers, from the time he spins his potter's wheel in the early morning until (re)entering the mouth.[57]

In summary, the potter's wheel is used as a symbol of regeneration in several contexts having to do with the rebirth of the solar disk in the eastern horizon of heaven: in the sun hymn studied by Assmann, in the Books of the Night and Day, in the Book of Nut, in a Coffin Texts spell, and in Ptolemaic cosmogonies pertaining to local creator gods within their own temples. The spinning of the wheel signals cosmic regeneration in the east, the promise of a new dawn heralded by the childlike flame of the red morning glow, the fiery destruction of Ra's enemies, and the creative energies latent in the womb. In the case of Khnum at Esna, the true significance of the potter's wheel stems not from his traditional associations with this instrument, but from the key role it plays in the regenerating hands of Khnum-Ra as the creator sun god. And finally, the mundane image of the potter working at his wheel, well known from a number of workshop scenes and birth temples, may now be recognized in one or two unexpected locations: the cosmological scenes in the royal tombs at Thebes and Tanis.[58]

References

Allen, J. P.

1988 *Genesis in Egypt: The Philosophy of Ancient Egyptian Creation Accounts.* Yale Egyptological Studies 2. New Haven: Yale University. Second printing 1995.

1989 "The Cosmology of the Pyramid Texts." In *Religion and Philosophy in Ancient Egypt,* edited by J. P. Allen, J. Assmann, A. B. Lloyd, R. K. Ritner, and D. P. Silverman, pp. 1–28. Yale Egyptological Studies 3. New Haven: Yale University.

Alliot, M.

1949 *Le culte d'Horus à Edfou au temps des ptolémées.* Bibliothèque d'étude 20/1. Cairo: Institut français d'archéologie orientale.

Arnold, Do.

1993 "Fascicle 1. Techniques and Traditions of Manufacture in the Pottery of Ancient Egypt." In *An Introduction to Ancient Egyptian Pottery*, edited by Do. Arnold and J. Bourriau, pp. 1–141. Deutsches archäologisches Institut Sonderschrift 17. Mainz: Philipp von Zabern.

Assmann, J.

1969 *Liturgische Lieder an den Sonnengott.* Münchner ägyptologische Studien 19. Berlin: Bruno Hessling.

1970 *Der König als Sonnenpriester.* Abhandlungen des Deutschen archäologischen Instituts, Abteilung Kairo, 7. Glückstadt: J. J. Augustin.

1983a *Re und Amun.* Orbis Biblicus et Orientalis 51. Göttingen: Vandenhoeck and Ruprecht.

1983b *Sonnenhymnen in thebanischen Gräbern.* Theben 1. Mainz: Philipp von Zabern.

1995 *Egyptian Solar Religion in the New Kingdom.* Translated by A. Alcock. London: Kegan Paul.

Baines, J.

1985 *Fecundity Figures.* Warminster: Aris and Phillips.

Barguet, P.

1986 *Les textes des sarcophages égyptiens du Moyen Empire.* Paris: Éditions du Cerf.

Bickel, S.

1994 *La cosmogonie égyptienne avant le Nouvel Empire.* Orbis Biblicus et Orientalis 134. Göttingen: Vandenhoeck and Ruprecht.

55. Kurth (1994a, p. 78) translates: "Du (Horus) bist doch der, der (die Arbeit) an der Töpferscheibe eröffnet, in deiner Gestalt halb im Eindringen, halb im Hervorkommen."

56. Brugsch 1883, pp. 57–58; Daressy 1917. In one case the child is labeled *nḥn*, in another *Rꜥ-Bḥd.ty*.

57. Similarly, in a text in the offering hall of Edfu (Rochemonteix and Chassinat 1984, 481, Tableau Ro. 4d.II), the potter's wheel serves to denote the end of the nighttime hours: *dwꜣ [Rꜥ] ḥtp=f m ꜥnḫt.t r wbꜣ=f nḥp m hn n Nw.t* "adoring [Ra] from the time he sets in the west until he spins the potter's wheel in the body of Nut."

58. Mr. Harold Hays has kindly pointed out to me the figure above the doorway to the tomb of Ramesses IX (Guilmant 1907, pl. 4), which is very suggestive of the celestial potter in the Book of the Day. Because of the condition of the scene, it is difficult to clarify the extant imagery and its relation to this underworld composition.

Blackman, A., and F. Herbert
1941 "A Group of Texts Inscribed on the Facade of the Sanctuary in the Temple of Horus at Edfu." In *Miscellanea Gregoriana*, pp. 397–428. Monumenti Vaticani di archeologia e d'arte 6. Rome: Max Bretschneider.

Brugsch, H.
1883 *Thesaurus inscriptionum aegyptiacarum*. Leipzig: J. C. Hinrichs.

Bruyère, B.
1930 *Mert Seger à Deir el Médineh*. Mémoires publiés par les Membres de l'Institut français d'archéologie orientale du Caire 58. Cairo: Institut français d'archéologie orientale.

Chassinat, É.
1910 *Le mammisi d'Edfou*. Mémoires publiés par les membres de l'Institut français d'archéologie orientale 16. Cairo: Institut français d'archéologie orientale.
1933 *Le temple d'Edfou* 8. Mémoires publiés par les membres de la Mission archéologique française 25. Cairo: Institut français d'archéologie orientale.
1934 *Le temple de Dendara* 1. Cairo: Institut français d'archéologie orientale.

Daressy, G.
1901 *Ostraca*. Catalogue général des antiquités égyptiennes du Musée du Caire. Cairo: Institut français d'archéologie orientale.
1917 "Les formes du soleil aux différentes heures de la journée." *Annales du Service des antiquités égyptiennes* 17: 197–208.

Drenkhahn, R.
1976 *Die Handwerker und ihre Tätigkeiten im alten Ägypten*. Ägyptologische Abhandlungen 31. Wiesbaden: Otto Harrassowitz.

Dümichen, J.
1894 *Der Grabpalast des Patuamenap in der thebanischen Nekropolis*, Volume 3. Leipzig: J. C. Hinrichs.

Faulkner, R. O.
1978 *The Ancient Egyptian Coffin Texts*, Volume 3. Warminster: Aris and Phillips.

Federn, W.
1966 "... As Does a Potter's Wheel." *Zeitschrift für ägyptische Sprache und Altertumskunde* 93: 55–56.

Frankfort, Henri
1933 *The Cenotaph of Seti I at Abydos*. Egyptian Expedition Memoirs 39. London: B. Quaritch.

Guilmant, Félix
1907 *Le tombeau de Ramsès IX*. Mémoires publiés par les membres de l'Institut français d'archéologie orientale 15. Cairo: Institut français d'archéologie orientale.

Harris, J. R.
1961 *Lexicographical Studies in Ancient Egyptian Minerals*. Berlin: Akademie-Verlag.

Holthoer, R.
1977 *New Kingdom Pharaonic Sites: The Pottery*. Scandinavian Joint Expedition to Sudanese Nubia 5:1. Lund: Berlings.

Hornung, E.
1963 *Das Amduat: Die Schrift des verborgenen Raumes*, Band 2. Ägyptologische Abhandlungen 7. Wiesbaden: Otto Harrassowitz.
1975 *Das Buch der Anbetung des Re im Westen (Sonnenlitanei)*, Teil I: *Text*. Aegyptiaca Helvetica 2. Geneva: Ägyptologisches Seminar der Universität Basel and Centre d'études orientales de l'Université de Genève.
1976 *Das Buch der Anbetung des Re im Westen (Sonnenlitanei)*, Teil II: *Übersetzung und Kommentar*. Aegyptiaca Helvetica 3. Geneva: Ägyptologisches Seminar der Universität Basel and Centre d'études orientales de l'Université de Genève.
1981 "Zu den Schlußszenen der Unterweltsbücher." *Mitteilungen des Deutschen archäologischen Instituts, Abteilung Kairo*, 37: 217–26.
1982 *Conceptions of God in Ancient Egypt: The One and the Many*. Translated by J. Baines. Ithaca: Cornell University Press.
1984 *Ägyptische Unterweltsbücher*. Second edition. Zurich and Munich: Artemis.
1990 *Zwei ramessidische Königsgräber: Ramses IV. und Ramses VII*. Theben 11. Mainz: Philipp von Zabern.

Kees, H.
1943 "Farbensymbolik in ägyptischen religiösen Texten." *Nachrichten von der Gesellschaft der Wissenschaften zu Göttingen phil.-historische Klasse Fachgruppe I (Altertumswissenschaft)* 8: 413–79.

Kurth, D.
1994a "Stylistik und Syntax." In *Edfu: Studien zu Vokabular, Ikonographie, und Grammatik*, edited by D. Kurth, pp. 72–102. Die Inschriften des Tempels von Edfu, Begleitheft 4. Wiesbaden: Otto Harrassowitz.
1994b *Treffpunkt der Götter: Inschriften aus dem Tempel des Horus von Edfu*. Zurich and Munich: Artemis.

Lange, H. O., and O. Neugebauer
1940 *Papyrus Carlsberg No. I: Ein hieratisch-demotischer kosmographischer Text*. Copenhagen: Munksgaard.

Montet, P.
1947 *Les constructions et le tombeau d'Osorkon II à Tanis*. Nécropole royale à Tanis 1. Paris: Jourde et Allard.

Nelson, H. H.
1981 *The Great Hypostyle Hall at Karnak*, Volume 1, Part 1: *The Wall Reliefs*. Edited by W. J. Murnane. Oriental Institute Publications 106. Chicago: Oriental Institute.

Neugebauer, O., and R. A. Parker
1960 *Egyptian Astronomical Texts*, Volume 1: *The Early Decans*. Brown Egyptological Studies 3. Providence: Brown University Press.

Parker, R. A.; J. Leclant; and J.-C. Goyon
1979 *The Edifice of Taharqa by the Sacred Lake of Karnak*. Brown Egyptological Studies 8. Providence: Brown University Press.

Patch, D.
1995 "A 'Lower Egyptian' Costume: Its Origin, Development, and Meaning." *Journal of the American Research Center in Egypt* 32: 93–116.

Piankoff, A.
1934 "La déesse Chenit." *Egyptian Religion* 2: 100–05.
1942 *Le livre du jour et de la nuit*. Bibliothèque d'étude 13. Cairo: Institut français d'archéologie orientale.
1954 *The Tomb of Ramesses VI*. Bollingen Series 40/1. New York: Pantheon Books.
1961/62 "La vierge 'Znamenie' et la déesse Nout." *Bulletin de la Société d'archéologie copte* 16: 261–69.

1964 *The Litany of Re*. Bollingen Series 40/4. New York: Pantheon Books.

Posener-Kriéger, P.
1976 *Les archives du temple funéraire de Néferirkarê-Kakaï (Les papyrus d'Abousir)*. Bibliothèque d'étude 65. Cairo: Institut français d'archéologie orientale.

Posener-Kriéger, P., and J.-L. de Cenival
1968 *Hieratic Papyri in the British Museum,* Fifth Series: *The Abusir Papyri*. London: British Museum.

Rochemonteix, M. de, and É. Chassinat
1894 *Le temple d'Edfou* 1: *Plates*. Mémoires publiés par les membres de la Mission archéologique française 10. Cairo: Institut français d'archéologie orientale.
1984 *Le temple d'Edfou* 1: *Text*. Mémoires publiés par les membres de la Mission archéologique française 10. Second edition. Cairo: Institut français d'archéologie orientale.

Roulin, G.
1996 *Le livre de la nuit: Une composition égyptienne de l'au-delà* 1–2. Orbis Biblicus et Orientalis 147/1–2. Göttingen: Vandenhoeck and Ruprecht.

Sauneron, S.
1953 "L'hymne au soleil levant du papyrus de Berlin 3050, 3056, et 3048." *Bulletin de l'Institut français d'archéologie orientale* 53: 65–90.
1962 *Les fêtes religieuses d'Esna aux derniers siècles du paganisme*. Esna 5. Cairo: Institut français d'archéologie orientale.
1963 *Le temple d'Esna*. Esna 2. Cairo: Institut français d'archéologie orientale.
1968 *Le temple d'Esna*. Esna 3. Cairo: Institut français d'archéologie orientale.
1975 *Le temple d'Esna*. Esna 6. Cairo: Institut français d'archéologie orientale.
1982 *L'écriture figurative dans les textes d'Esna*. Esna 8. Cairo: Institut français d'archéologie orientale.
1988 *Les prêtres de l'ancienne Égypte*. Second edition. Paris: Éditions Perséa.

Sethe, K.
1908 *Die altaegyptischen Pyramidentexte*. Leipzig: J. C. Hinrichs.

van Dijk, J.
1979/80 "The Birth of Horus According to the Ebers Papyrus." *Jaarbericht van het Vooraziatisch-Egyptisch Genootschap "Ex Oriente Lux"* 26: 10–25.

te Velde, H.
1981/82 "Some Aspects of the God Shu." *Jaarbericht van het Vooraziatisch-Egyptisch Genootschap "Ex Oriente Lux"* 27: 23–28.

Ward, W. A.
1978 *The Four Egyptian Homographic Roots B-ȝ*. Studia Pohl, Series Maior 6. Rome: Biblical Institute Press.

Zandee, J.
1960 *Death as an Enemy according to Ancient Egyptian Conceptions*. Leiden: E. J. Brill.

9

THE BORDER AND THE YONDER SIDE

GERTIE ENGLUND

Uppsala University, Sweden

The borders treated here are not the political borders between Egypt and its neighboring countries (except the symbolical use of the political borders), but the border between the well-known sublunar world of everyday life and the other world of the yonder side (the Duat) and of realms that are homologous to it.

According to the Egyptians, the created world was in fact tripartite, consisting of the sky, the earth, and the Duat. According to the monistic world view of the Egyptians the three parts were intimately connected and there was continuous interaction going on between them. It is therefore interesting to determine where the Egyptians located the border between the well-known earthly experience and the yonder more-or-less unknown side of the created world and what types of contact existed between the two sides of the border.

In the Egyptian way of thought, the yonder side is different but not completely unknown. The accumulated knowledge of it was considerable, and according to the Egyptian attitude of pushing the border further and further away, more and more was gradually disclosed of what was unknown.

THE BORDER IN MAN AND IN SOCIETY

The border that is most evident in the experience of man is the border between the world of the living and the world of the dead (fig. 9.1). Although belonging to one and the same creation, and being actually two complementary poles of life, life on this side differs very much from life on the yonder side. The two sides are so different that they are mysterious to one another, and that is why it might be possible to talk about two worlds for lack of a more appropriate expression. The Egyptians were of the opinion that man continued to live after death in his *ba*, his *ka*, and in all his different forms of existence. Of all the different forms of existence it is above all the *ba* that constitutes a means of communication between the two worlds and maintains the contact between the mummy in the tomb and the world outside. By crossing the border of the unknown world, the *ba* could manifest itself to the living.

The Man Who Was Tired of Life

In the story the Man Who Was Tired of Life, the *ba* manifests itself to the man as an aspect of himself unknown to him up to that moment. The man is in a crisis. The standards according to which he had formed his life are no longer valid. Everything that he valued in life is now disregarded by his fellow citizens. He considers life not worth living in a world that is so different from his ideal. At the peak of the crisis his *ba* appears and starts a dialogue with him. His *ba* is an aspect of himself, his inner voice as it were, that holds opinions on life as well as on the meaning of life and the way life is to be lived that do not correspond to his own opinions. His *ba* wants him to cling to life and to profit from life on earth (Faulkner 1956, p. 30, line 150), even though the experience is bitter; whereas he himself wants to leave his miserable life on earth and make an abode on the yonder side together with his *ba*.

The example of the Man Who Was Tired of Life shows that the border between the known and the unknown can manifest itself within man, and that man can thus himself constitute a bipolar world.

The Human Being and His Dreams

Dreams are another example of contact with the unknown. In his dreams, man crosses a border and enters another world. The memory of images and events met with in the dream world can accompany the dreamer across the border into the familiar world of everyday life. This border is interior to man himself.

Gold of Praise: Studies on Ancient Egypt in Honor of Edward F. Wente
Edited by Emily Teeter and John A. Larson
Studies in Ancient Oriental Civilization 58
Chicago: Oriental Institute, 1999

The dream world presents itself to the dreamer in fantastic visions. Dreams use an unknown language of symbolic images that need to be interpreted, but once interpreted, they can bring knowledge to the dreamer. "God created dreams to show the way to the dreamer whose eyes are obscured," as the Egyptians themselves put it (Lichtheim 1980, p. 211: P. Insinger 32.13; Lichtheim 1983, p. 230). The Egyptians were of the opinion that the dreams emanating from the unknown world of sleep could give warnings and guidance about everyday life and about how to conduct one's life on earth and to handle daily events.

Significant dreams containing guidance and warnings could come spontaneously. There was, however, another category of dreams — induced dreams — that were the result of special dream therapy in the temples. As the symbolic language of dreams had to be interpreted, specialists were available in the temples both for spontaneous and induced dreams.

Although there was, in general, a positive attitude towards dreams, there is evidence for fear of dreams. There is an example of a wish for sleep without dreams, as the sleeper fears bad dreams and says that they are like being attacked by demons (Westendorf 1966, p. 145).

Thus, the other side of the border that opens up during sleep could be considered either as something attractive and interesting, endowed with a positive potential that could be helpful to man, or as frightening and negative, something to be avoided.

Bipartition of Society

The polarization of the world into "I" and "you" or "we" and "they" is generally linked to moral evaluations resulting in ideas like "I am right" and "you are wrong" or "we are good" and "they are bad." In the wisdom literature, Egyptian society was divided into good and bad citizens according to this principle. The Good Ones were those who lived according to the rules of Maat set up by society and presented by the teachings of the sages; the Bad Ones were those who refused to heed and to follow the recommended rules of good behavior. These groups were labeled the Silent Ones and the Hotheaded Ones. There is a tendency to identify these as two completely separate groups, every individual belonging to one or the other category. That is the impression — and the probable intent — that most of the teachings give. Every one should make his choice, and the right choice is to obey and to follow the teaching:

> Useful is hearing to a son who hears;
> If hearing enters the hearer,
> The hearer becomes a listener,
> Hearing well is speaking well.
> Useful is hearing to one who hears,
> Hearing is better than all else,
> It creates good will.
> How good for a son to grasp his father's words,
> He will reach old age through them.
> He who hears is beloved of god,
> He whom god hates does not hear.
> The heart makes of its owner a hearer or non-hearer,
> Man's heart is his life-prosperity-health!
> The hearer is one who hears what is said,
> He who loves to hear is one who does what is said.
> How good for a son to listen to his father,
> How happy is he to whom it is said:
> "The son, he pleases as a master of hearing."
> The hearer of whom this is said,
> He is well endowed
> And honored by his father;
> His remembrance is in the mouth of the living,
> Those on earth and those who will be.
> (Lichtheim 1973, p. 74: Ptahhotep, lines 534–563)

Figure 9.1. Door, Although Looking Impassable, Can Be Opened on Initiative of This Side or of the Yonder Side. Vignettes from the Book of the Dead, after Hornung 1979, p. 50; Naville 1971, pl. 104

Listening to, repeating, and copying instructions like that over and over again must have influenced the pupils so that they identified themselves with the ideal even if they did not manage to live up to it entirely. The negative image of the non-hearer is most likely to have been projected onto others and not realized in oneself: "I am a hearer, you are a non-hearer." The strength of the projection is probably proportional to the strong focusing of the instructions regarding good.

Since the goal of the teachings was to educate loyal and obedient civil servants and citizens, it was in the interest of the sages to aim high and to present a perfect ideal. To refuse the ideal was unthinkable; hearing it meant adhering to it. "He who loves to hear is one who does what is said," as Ptahhotep puts it. No wonder then that the older teachings give the impression that the Silent Ones constitute the majority of the population and that the Hotheaded Ones are rare exceptions. This can, of course, be a pedagogical trick in order to emphasize even more the importance of right behavior. With elevated ideals like those of the wisdom literature, it seems most likely, however, that the Silent Ones must have been in the minority.

Wherever the border was situated, it is, however, clear that there was a border splitting the population into two parts, the Silent Ones and the Hotheaded Ones, and that the border was drawn according to moral, ethical, and psychological criteria.

Scribe Khonshotep in Instruction of Any

Despite the age-old tradition of projecting what is bad onto others, the scribe Khonshotep in the Instruction of Any manifests a surprising insight into his own psyche. He realizes that the border between the Silent One and the Hotheaded One is situated within himself:

> The scribe Khonshotep answered his father, the scribe Any:
> I wish I were like (you),
> As learned as you!
> Then I would carry out your teachings,
> And the son would be brought to his father's place.
> Each man is led by his nature,
> You are a man who is a master,
> Whose strivings are exalted,

Whose every word is chosen.
The son, he understands little
When he recites the words in the books.
But when your words please the heart,
The heart tends to accept them with joy.
Don't make your virtues too numerous,
That one may raise one's thoughts to you;
A boy does not follow the moral instructions
Though the writings are on his tongue!
(Lichtheim 1976, p. 144: Instruction of Any, Epilogue)

The scribe Khonshotep realizes that his innate character does not correspond to the ideal, and he is not willing to change in order to be able to follow the example of his teacher and father. He would rather select what pleases him and disregard the rest. Furthermore he realizes that the fact of repeating the instructions word by word does not mean that one is following them. He realizes that there is a difference between saying and acting, and that the two are not always in accordance. He is aware of the fact that man can be divided within himself and that there is thus a border between Good and Evil within man.

There are a few important passages in the epilogue that I would like to bring to the fore before leaving this interesting text. In his reply to his son, Any uses several metaphors that are worth noticing. In order to make his son understand that one should not only follow one's nature, he says:

The fighting bull who kills in the stable,
he forgets and abandons the arena;
He conquers his nature,
Remembers what he's learned,
And becomes the like of a fattened ox.
The savage lion abandons his wrath,
And comes to resemble the timid donkey.
The horse slips into its harness,
Obedient it goes outdoors.
The dog obeys the word,
and walks behind its master.
The monkey carries the stick,
Though its mother did not carry it.
The goose returns from the pond,
When one comes to shut it in the yard.
One teaches the Nubian to speak Egyptian,
The Syrian and other strangers too.
Say: "I shall do like all the beasts,
Listen and learn what they do."
(Lichtheim 1976, p. 144: Instruction of Any, Epilogue)

What Any wants to stress is that nature can be plied, instincts can be conquered, and those who are completely different — the symbols of otherness — like the Nubians and the Syrians, can be taught to speak Egyptian, i.e., be transformed into civilized beings.

The importance of these quotations from Any lies in the fact that they bring up psychological problems and that they refer to psychological borders within man. A further interesting thing about them is that the "otherness" that manifests itself in man, and which does not conform to the ideals established by society, can be tackled, influenced, and corrected.

Thus the Instruction of Any illustrate a psychological problem within man showing him as the battlefield of two opposite forces and the meeting place of the two worlds. When Any tries to make his son understand the conflict he is living and the way out of it he uses a few metaphors to explain that man can tame his aggressiveness; that man can conquer his innate nature; that he does not necessarily have to follow all his impulses; and that man can become the master of his own house and follow the standards set up by society in order to be a civilized and well-adapted, cultivated human being.

Any's metaphors are interesting, particularly those of the fighting bull, the lion, and the Syrians and Nubians, i.e., the wild animals that can be tamed and the foreigners who can be transformed into cultivated human beings who speak Egyptian. These four images — the bull, the lion, and the two eternal enemies *par excellence* — are particularly significant, as they are symbols from royal iconography. We are wont to interpret them as symbols of chaotic forces that the king has to conquer as part of his social and political task to watch over and secure the frontiers of Egypt so that the established cosmic order of Maat can be maintained.

It seems that these metaphors are employed quite naturally in Any's speech in order to explain the psychological problem he is discussing with his son. Were they used because they already had that psychological meaning? And if so, what does that imply for our understanding of royal iconography and kingship?

KINGSHIP AND THE BORDER

The inclusion of a psychological dimension into the ideology of kingship would not invalidate any of the most commonly cited characteristics of this ideology: the king as the representative of the gods on earth, the duty of the king to maintain the order of Maat, the king's task to secure the borders of Egypt and to prevent the intrusion of foreigners, the identification of Egypt with the cosmos and the foreign countries with chaos — all of which are part and parcel of the king's socio-political task on earth as the representative of sacral kingship, being the son of the creator, and a god incarnate. To include the psychological meaning only adds a further dimension to these images in a typical Egyptian additive manner.

This dimension of the iconographic motif does, however, have consequences for the role of the king. He would then be a symbol also in a psycho-spiritual meaning. Just as Any's son is asked to conquer hostile forces within himself, the king's combat could be inside himself, and he could be a symbol of the one who realizes man's victory over his own dark side. He would be the perfect human being realized on earth, which is an important aspect of the prototype of all human beings.

The interpretation of the victory over the foes as a psycho-religious theme would also well suit the location of such scenes on temple walls. Their location can, of course, also be explained by the fact that the temple is constructed as an image of the place of the creation of the world, and that the battle against the chaotic forces is part of that event. The destructive chaotic forces symbolized by the constant threat of Apophis always tend to obstruct the structuring process of creative forces. The destructive forces are omnipresent. They menace from the yonder side as well as from within creation. That is why it is appropriate to place the scenes of slaughter on the outside of the temple, so that the cultic activities that are regulating the course of events are not disrupted and endangered either from the yonder side or from this side. This is yet another example of the aspective way of thought; one interpretation does not exclude the other.

We are now wont to follow Hornung (1966) and consider the scenes representing events of the chronological history in the temples as ritual images, which means that the reliefs above all emphasize the non-historical aspects of the events described. They are part of the Egyptian myth. The myth never petrifies; it is never attached to a single past moment of chronological time, but rather there is a constant re-adaptation of myth to the circumstances of the moment. The myth is continually updated. This continuous reshaping of myth emphasizes that the struggle depicted on the temple walls is a process that is always ongoing. The re-adaptation of the myth stresses the importance of renewed fighting of destructive forces on all levels, metaphysical and physical, outer as well as inner.

Taking it as a hypothesis that there is a psychological dimension in the metaphors, and that the king as the prototype of humanity takes up the fight with evil and chaotic forces also within himself and conquers them, it would be interesting to see if this kind of interpretation can apply to other parts of the textual and iconographic material related to the king, in particular to the material connected with borders and the crossing of borders.

The royal tombs provide information on this point. Entering the tomb means crossing a border: the border between this world and the other. The tomb itself represents the other world. Through the fact that one from this world enters it, it becomes a meeting place of the two worlds: the known and the unknown world, the day world and the night world, a meeting place of "Diesseits" and "Jenseits."

The royal tombs of the New Kingdom describe how the sun goes down into the world from which it emerged. The sun entering the underworld is the son of yesterday's sun, and he is now himself in his turn old and exhausted tottering over the border. On the other side he meets his mother and transforms himself inside her body in order to appear again as her son, being at the same time his own son. He is a Kamutef, the bull of his mother. The king, in whose tomb it is described, is a homologue of the sun Ra, being himself a *sꜣ Rꜥ*, and enters an analogous process.

The decorations of the royal tombs present a cosmic process. As the old sun is considered to die in the west and as the dead king is included in the process, it is also presented as a postmortal process. What is actually happening during this process?

If one wants to characterize the events in an overall manner without too many details, one can say that it is a question of a meeting between the light traveling through the night hours and all that exists in the darkness and the immobility of the other world. The meeting between the light and the darkness involves communication, sustenance, and punishment.

The communication aspect of the meeting is important. The sun god Ra talks to the entities of the other world and his words enliven them and make them happy for the period of the passage. After the momentary awakening they fall back into their inert state when the sun has passed.

The meeting between alertness and light on the one side and inertia and darkness on the other, and their dialogue, is important. It brings life back to the entities of the other world for a while and it also makes the regeneration of Ra possible. The climax of the regeneration is made possible through the encounter with Osiris and the fusion between Osiris and Ra. So this communication is not a one-way affair, but it is a question of a reciprocal action where light and alertness revive what is inert and dark and are at the same time enlivened and regenerated by it. "Erleuchte die Urfinsternis, (damit) das 'Fleisch' lebe und sich erneuere!" (Hornung 1963/2, p. 55, Amduat second hour, final text).

The sustenance aspect is also important and can be considered as part of the communication. It is everywhere stressed that the sun Ra distributes nourishment (bread and beer, vegetables, and all the ordinary offerings of the Egyptian tradition) on his passage through the other world. These offerings as well as the verbal contact bring about the revival.

Another important aspect of the meeting of Osiris and Ra is the punishment of all hostile forces that might threaten the journey through the hours of the night and the destruction of all hostile actions of those entities, whether they originate in the hereafter (like the attack of Apophis) or are actions pertaining to the life on earth of these entities. Those who lived according to Maat have nothing to fear, but to those who passed a life disregarding the rules of Maat, terrible punishments are administered during the encounter with the sun god Ra.

The encounter of Ra and Osiris and the unification of the two is the synthesis of all that takes place in the Duat. Osiris is the symbol of all that is dark, reposing, static, and apparently dead, but nonetheless filled with potential life. Ra and Osiris represent the two sides of the same god. They are his day side and his night side. So it is in meeting the dark side of himself that Ra is regenerated. It is the fusion of the two sides that makes the regeneration possible, the merging of darkness and light, of inertia and alertness.

If we consider Ra as the diurnal consciousness, the diurnal consciousness is regenerated through the encounter with its own nocturnal unconscious. This suits the Kamutef aspect of the process well because it is a question of self-regeneration. New forces are brought to the diurnal consciousness through the encounter with the self, i.e., its own dark and so far unknown depths (Hornung 1989, p. 105).

This seems perhaps a too human interpretation of a cosmic process. It seems, however, that the Egyptians presented their ideas about the hereafter in relation to man; they created an anthropomorphous cosmos (Assmann 1990, p. 198). It was done in such a way that man recognizes himself in the structures of the cosmos. The cosmos and the cosmic processes are a projection of man's inner experiences, leading to the homology between the outer and inner worlds. The inner world is related to the outer world in the same way as the world of the hereafter is related to the visible world on earth. "Die menschliche Innenwelt bildet ein ähnliches 'Jenseits' der sichtbaren Wirklichkeit wie es das Reich des Osiris darstellt," as Assmann (1990, p. 119) puts it. The hereafter can be located in the depths of the created world, but also in the depths of our own soul (Hornung 1982, p. 65).

The Egyptians themselves pointed this out in saying that the knowledge of the other world was important also for man living on earth. This knowledge was stressed in the Book of the Dead as well as in the royal tombs "Es ist nützlich (*ꜣḫ*) für einen Mann auf Erden" (e.g., Amduat, second hour, upper register; Amduat, second hour, final text; for a survey of references to the importance of this text genre for man on earth, see Wente 1982, pp. 161–79). This knowledge means attaining insight, it means an epistemological breakthrough (*ꜣḫ*), and this insight is thus not only a postmortal possibility, nor is it reserved solely for the king. The fact that the Egyptians themselves so clearly stressed the idea of an anthropomorphous cosmos supports the suggestion that the king was considered to be the prototype of man.

AMBIVALENCE OF THE YONDER SIDE

The border is thus ubiquitous, dividing the universe into "chaos" and "cosmos" and fractioning the cosmos, the society, and the individual in two — this side and the yonder side. How did the Egyptians evaluate that which was situated on the other side of the border? The ambivalence of the other world stands out very clearly in many contexts. Both the positive and the negative aspects of the other world are obvious in the decorations of the royal tombs and in all the literature related to the hereafter.

The transformations that are possible in the Duat, thanks to the special conditions reigning there, constitute its positive side. The underworld is part of the cosmos. It is a border area between chaos and cosmos. It is an area where the cosmic forces work together in their creational processes. It is an area situated outside the known world of everyday life, yet part of creation and part of the cosmic process (e.g., the night journey of the sun is located there). It represents the half of the solar cycle that takes place out of sight of the human being. The night journey is compared with death and resurrection. The resurrection is possible through the fact that the sun descends in the border area where the dimensions of time and space do not work as on earth. Space has collapsed, the orientations are weary (Book of Gates, second hour, lower register), and with space the time dimension has also ceased. As in dreams, time exists but does not function as it does in our world. It exists, but has no extension (e.g., Book of Gates, fourth hour, middle register), and that is the main thing of the Duat and its positive aspect, because that means that time is reversible. Thus those who enter the Duat can move backwards through time, as all time is available, and find earlier and younger forms of themselves. Rejuvenation and regeneration are possible.

So the rejuvenation of Ra through the encounter with Osiris — the main theme of all the decorations of the royal tombs of the New Kingdom — is one of the best examples of the positive side of the other world.

Another example is the possibility offered in the other world of meeting the gods and entering into contact with them. It is possible to merge with the gods there just as Ra merges with Osiris and becomes one with him. The total identification between two entities that merge one into the other and thus become one is a possibility frequently stressed in the literature of the hereafter (Pyramid Texts, Coffin Texts, Book of the Dead, passim). This identification of the goal to be reached is expressed by exclamations like: "I am Ra," "I am Atum."

The other world is neutral, like the primordial state. It is neither good nor bad; it is a world in a state before the two things had as yet come into existence. Yet these identifications always concern what, from the point of view of the human being, are considered to be the positive powers. Apophis is never evoked in these exclamatory identifications. Because of his positive aspect as the killer of hostile forces, Seth is, however, sometimes evoked as an entity worth identifying with, but the contexts of the examples in the Coffin Texts are unfortunately obscure (*CT* 5, p. 267f, Spell 424; *CT* 6, p. 163g, Spell 564).

The yonder side is also an area where knowledge is available. The identifications such as "I am Ra" probably express that the "I" has come to understand what the god mentioned stands for, he has reached another epistemological level and a new insight into the meaning of that god, that is, of that concept. The identification means that otherness has been eliminated.

CONCLUSIONS

There exists thus a border: a border between good and evil (Instruction of Any), between traditional and non-traditional values about life experiences (The Man Who Was Tired of Life), between the familiar world and what is beyond it (Egypt and the Nine Bows, the world of the living and the world of the dead, the world of the day and the world of the night, the world of waken experiences and the world of dream experiences). All these different pairs of worlds, realms of experience, levels of consciousness, or whatever terms one wants to use to describe them, are homologous and function one toward the other according to the same rules.

The two sides function as contrasts, chaos versus the created world, or as a border area of chaos versus the created world. The Egyptians seem to have been of the opinion that the communication between the two sides was of prime importance. There must be an exchange, a free flow between them, to keep the created world in balance as shown in the cult. There must be a meeting of the two to solve life problems as shown in the experience of the man who was tired of life and in the dream examples and, as shown in the royal tombs of the New Kingdom, regeneration depended upon a fusion of chaos and the created world.

Man structures his world out of his experiences — his own frame of reference. Since his own body and mind are his reference, his physical and mental experiences are projected onto the world outside him where they become the structuring principles he lives by (cf. Lakoff and Johnson 1980).

The experience of a hidden unknown world within himself and of the interaction between his consciousness and that unconscious side of himself is likely to be the reference for his perception of the world. That is how the correspondences between all levels come about and that is the origin of the system of structuring in homologies.

The border and the yonder side are thus primarily experienced within the human being and then projected onto the outside world and that is why the metaphors used lend themselves so easily to a psychological interpretation. Thus the king protecting his borders against foreign intrusion can at the same time be the vigilant mind defending itself against the attacks of destructive forces and tendencies within itself. The physically impossible rebirth after the night journey in the Duat becomes a truth. It is an experience that is psychologically verifiable showing how contact with the hidden side of oneself brings new energy, new life, and new knowledge — the epistemological shock that the Egyptians called *ꜣḫ* which corresponded to an enlightened state.

As Professor Wente (1982, pp. 161–79), to whom I have the honor of offering this article, shows with a rich collection of examples from Egyptian texts, the Egyptians have clearly manifested their opinion that their texts and compositions were not intended for the dead exclusively but also for those living on earth. The same holds true for the enlightened state of *ꜣḫ* that is also said to occur on earth (Englund 1978, pp. 39, 101, 151, 189, 192). These assertions prove that the yonder side was thought to be accessible here on earth. With the usual Egyptian discretion, however, nothing was said about the means of crossing the border. In agreement with Federn (1960, p. 247) I can, however, see no reason why there should not have been initiatory ways available to men in their society as in most others. Professor Wente cautiously puts a question mark in the title of his article "Mysticism in Pharaonic Egypt?" But do we have to question this mysticism? Do we not have material enough in the Egyptian texts to talk of mysticism? Were there not possibilities for communication across the border of the yonder side? Do not features such as the participation of divine light and insight, the experience of identity with the divine, and the divinization of the individual — the very criteria of mysticism — conform exactly to what we find elsewhere in the world?

> *"I am Atum*
> *being alone in the Nun,*
> *I am Ra at his first appearings,*
> *I am the Great God, who came into being by himself."*

References

Assmann, J.
1990 *Maʿat: Gerechtigkeit und Unsterblichkeit im alten Ägypten.* Munich: C. H. Beck.

Englund, G.
1978 *Akh - une notion religieuse dans l'Égypte pharaonique.* Acta Universitatis Upsaliensis, Boreas 11. Uppsala: Almqvist and Wiksell.

Faulkner, R. O.
1956 "The Man Who Was Tired of Life." *Journal of Egyptian Archaeology* 42: 21–40.
1973 *The Ancient Egyptian Coffin Texts,* Volume 1. Warminster: Aris and Phillips.
1977 *The Ancient Egyptian Coffin Texts,* Volume 2. Warminster: Aris and Phillips.
1978 *The Ancient Egyptian Coffin Texts,* Volume 3. Warminster: Aris and Phillips.

Federn, W.
1960 "The 'Transformations' in the Coffin Texts: A New Approach." *Journal of Near Eastern Studies* 19: 241–57.

Hornung, E.
1963 *Das Amduat,* 1–2. Ägyptologische Abhandlungen 7. Wiesbaden: Otto Harrassowitz.
1966 *Geschichte als Fest.* Darmstadt: Wissenschaftliche Buchgesellschaft.
1979 *Das Totenbuch der Ägypter.* Zurich: Artemis Verlag.
1982 "Zur Sonne werden … ." *Neue Züricher Zeitung* 247: 65.
1989 *Geist der Pharaonenzeit.* Zurich: Artemis Verlag.

Lakoff, G., and M. Johnson
1980 *Metaphors We Live By.* Chicago: University of Chicago Press.

Lichtheim, M.
1973 *Ancient Egyptian Literature,* Volume 1: *The Old and Middle Kingdoms.* Berkeley: University of California Press.

1976 *Ancient Egyptian Literature*, Volume 2: *The New Kingdom*. Berkeley: University of California Press.
1980 *Ancient Egyptian Literature*, Volume 3: *The Late Period*. Berkeley: University of California Press.
1983 *Late Egyptian Wisdom Literature in the International Context: A Study of Demotic Instructions*. Orbis Biblicus et Orientalis 52. Freiburg: Universitätsverlag; Göttingen: Vandenhoeck and Ruprecht.

Naville, E.
1971 *Das ägyptische Totenbuch des XVIII. bis XX. Dynastie*. Graz: Akademische Druck.

Volten, A.
1937/38 *Studien zum Weisheitsbuch des Anii*. Copenhagen: Levin and Munksgaard.

Wente, E. F.
1982 "Mysticism in Pharaonic Egypt?" *Journal of Near Eastern Studies* 41: 161–79.

Westendorf, W.
1966 "Beiträge aus und zu den medizinischen Texten." *Zeitschrift für ägyptische Sprache und Altertumskunde* 92: 128–54.

Zába, Z.
1956 *Les maximes de Ptahhotep*. Prague: Editions de l'Académie Tchecoslovaque des Sciences.

10

ENJOYING THE PLEASURES OF SENSATION: REFLECTIONS ON A SIGNIFICANT FEATURE OF EGYPTIAN RELIGION

RAGNHILD BJERRE FINNESTAD

University of Bergen, Norway

In his "Egyptian 'Make Merry' Songs Reconsidered," Edward F. Wente (1962) traces a fascinating aspect of Egyptian mentality: its epicurean inclination. In this article I take his route and follow it into the heart of Egyptian religion.[1]

Enjoying the pleasures of life is a theme abundantly represented in the decoration of Egyptian tombs, both in words and in pictures: festive banquets, the pouring of beer and wine, music-making, singing, dancing, fragrant flowers, garlands around the neck, lotus in the hand or on the head — these are well-known motifs. In the harper's songs the theme is explicitly formulated:

> Put incense and fine oil together to thy nostrils
> And garlands of lotus and *rrmt*-flowers upon thy breast;
> While thy sister whom thou lovest sits at thy side.
> Put song and music before thee,
> Cast all evil behind thee;
> Bethink thee of joys ...
> (Lichtheim 1945, p. 178: Tomb of Neferhotep, Theban Tomb 50)

The songs are a popular object of study; they have received numerous translations, and their contents and motivations are hotly debated. My own interest in them lies in their pronounced admonitions to enjoy life. For the present, I leave aside the questions of whether they were sung in secular or sacral contexts of life, or whether they addressed the living or the dead, or whether they were impious, heretic protests against established traditions of assured blissful existence in the beyond. I return to these issues, after relating their hedonistic calls to a fundamental characteristic of Egyptian religion, most impressively expressed in situations of worship, namely, its strong appeal to the senses and the rich documentation that sensuous pleasure was involved. Adoring the sunshine, enjoying the sounds of music and the rhythms of dance, relishing the sweet scent of flowers and incense and the intoxication of wine — these well-known, almost emblematic forms of Egyptian cultic experience are the forms of a religion according to which the divine was perceived through the senses: the eyes, the ears, the nose, the mouth, the entire body.

This feature of Egyptian worship is often pointed out. Nevertheless — or perhaps because its expressions appear commonplace by their abundance — the scope and significance of sensory experiences in Egyptian religion have not been satisfactorily exposed. There is more to it than an idiosyncratic bias towards a full-bodied experience of the divine. The dominant role played by sense experiences is bound up with a particular conception of man, the cosmic world, and god, and of the relationship between the three. There is plenteous documentation that Egyptian religion perceived an essential connection between man, the cosmic world, and god, and also underlined its importance. This emphasis is of consequence for the ways in which we understand its epicurean expressions of sensuous pleasure — whether found in or outside tombs.

1. I acknowledge my deep gratitude to Paul John Frandsen and Anne Zeeberg at the Carsten Niebuhr Institute in Copenhagen for the librarian assistance rendered. This manuscript was completed in 1996.

Gold of Praise: Studies on Ancient Egypt in Honor of Edward F. Wente
Edited by Emily Teeter and John A. Larson
Studies in Ancient Oriental Civilization 58
Chicago: Oriental Institute, 1999

THE SENSUOUS ASPECT OF EGYPTIAN WORSHIP

The relationship between concepts of god and concepts of the world is a well-known theme in the historical study of religions; it has mustered a continuous fascination in cross-cultural research since the days of Max Müller. It has also been extensively dealt with in studies of Egyptian religion. Scholars have demonstrated the important place occupied by cosmological traditions in Egyptian theology. There has, however, been a tendency to "interpret away" the blatant references to concrete, physical reality. Whenever physical phenomena are given the names of gods, scholars have been inclined to understand them as symbols pointing to trans-physical reality, while their physical nature fades away to the point of insignificance. It seems as if the category of religion currently implied creates a strong disposition for such interpretation. Within both historical and anthropological studies religion is frequently defined as a system of traditions relating to a "belief in spiritual beings."[2] Another, rather popular definition, has as its core criterion "belief in supernatural powers," i.e., powers outside the regular processes of nature.[3] Thus when nature-immanent gods have been identified in the source material under consideration, these conceptual traditions are, as a matter of course, deciphered as a version of nature-transcendent gods revealing themselves in empirical reality, this being their medium, while their "true" being eludes sensory experience.[4]

There can also be seen a reticence in working out the implications of the noted feature of Egyptian worship with regard to Egyptian definitions of man. Any conception of god implies an appraisal of man. Inherent in these forms of religious worship is a valuation of human properties, a definition of what basically is man. We are confronted with a view of man as a sensing being. By stressing man's senses in the context of cultic communication with immanent gods, man's substantial relatedness to the empirical world is authorized as essential. The worshipping man is a sensing being and, as such, is a being who is intrinsically akin to the natural world.

The fact that our source material does not merely formulate sensory experiences of gods, but also exhibits an attitude of taking pleasure in sensation, should be considered in this perspective. The markedly sensuous character of Egyptian sensory experiences of nature-immanent gods has tended to be slighted in research. But the sensuality is a warning against interpreting these forms of worship (whether directed to gods or to ancestors) as examples of communication with a spiritual reality essentially separated from physical reality. Nor are there any indications to justify the view that Egyptian worship intended an extra-natural divine world.

A handful of well-known examples chosen at random from the overwhelming quantity of source material illustrates the fundamental position of sensory and sensuous experiences in Egyptian worship. Perhaps the most important sense organ was the eye; seeing god was used metonymically for worship. What does it mean "to see" in contexts of worship,[5] when regarded from the perspective just presented? Recent expositions of solar theology show an interest in deducing the theory of visual perception underlying the religious act of seeing. These attempts have in particular turned to documents of the worship of Aten. The hymns to Aten reveal, perhaps more clearly than earlier solar hymns, their implied suppositions: the luminous power immanent in the world effects an ongoing appearance of forms.[6] Further, there is a close affinity between sunlight, the eye, and that which is seen. Anything that is seen is seen because it is suffused with the light of the sun. The eye itself sees by having received the qualities of its nature through a metamorphosis caused by the light: seeing is partaking in the nature of the sunlight. Thus, an innate reciprocity connects all components of visible reality. Through the act of seeing, man is an integral part of an all-comprehensive cosmological communion.[7] According to these hymns, seeing was not merely observing, it was experiencing human life as being immersed in the life of a cosmos defined as a creation of light. In this nature philosophy the object-subject dichotomy so important in Western thought concerning sensing man is not given significance; seeing the world of light is not perceiving it as an external, physical object outside a spiritual subject. The inner world of the mind and the outer world of the cosmos, having appeared in the light, are not distinguished as two separate spheres of reality.

---

2. This is the key variable of E. B. Tylor's famous definition in his *Primitive Culture* (1871).

3. For example, "... religion assumes, and refers to, the existence of powers beyond human power and outside the regular processes of nature. These powers, often conceptualized as beings, are called supernaturals and superhuman" (de Waal Malefijt 1968, p. 6).

4. Behind such approaches Platonistic models of reality can be discerned.

5. See the discussion by van der Plas 1989, pp. 4–35.

6. The rich terminology of sunshine gives an indication of the course taken by Egyptian thought about the luminous quality of the sun; compare *LÄ* 3 "Licht," cols. 1033–34.

7. Compare Assmann 1992, p. 157. For discussion of examples in hymns to Amun-Ra, see, for example, Zandee 1992, p. 51 f.

In the hymns to Aten the (natural) act of seeing is expressly presented as a sacred act: the scene is the natural world of Egypt but the sun is perceived as a live god, a divine "eye" that sees all which is immersed in its light. Inherent lies an idea of a divine omnipresence; everything that is seen belongs to this god. Seeing the light of the sun is thus apprehended as a sacramental act. A life-giving god is taken in by the eyes: "The sight of your rays / is breath of life to their noses" (Assmann 1992, p. 148). The words are matched by pictorial representations of the rays of Aten holding the sign of *ankh* under the nose of the king or the royal couple. A particular conception of air appears to be involved: light is mingled in the air and is thus also inhaled.[8]

The representations of this sensory, sacramental act bear the marks of the sensuous. This is especially noticeable in representations of Amarna art. The worshippers[9] lift up their offerings and receive life from the sunlight represented in the form of rays shaped like hands stretching down to them — almost caressing them. Embraces and kisses allude to the affection evoked by this god. So do the bodies indulgently basking in the sunshine.[10] It is a highly sensuous style.

References to joy are a regular feature in the worship of the sun god. Again, the pictures and texts of Amarna provide material for a most rewarding study. When the king and the queen are depicted worshipping Aten, their daughters are shown rattling their sistra (Davies 1905, pls. 5, 7–8; Davies 1908, pls. 3, 26, 33). Exalted joy is ascribed to all living beings that see and are seen in his light:

> By the sight of your rays all flowers exist,
> What lives and sprouts from the soil grows when you shine.
> Drinking deep of your sight all flocks frisk,
> The birds in the nest fly up in joy;
> Their folded wings unfold in praise
> Of the living Aten, their maker.
> (Lichtheim 1976, p. 92)

A rejoicing world frequently occurs in hymns to other solar gods as well: "Every land rejoices at his rising, Every day gives praise to him"[11] are stock phrases.

The place occupied by sound in religious ceremonies and festivals is central. Recitals, songs, and playing on instruments like the sistrum, tambourine, drum, lyre, harp, clappers, and oboe are documented in texts and pictures. Hymns to Hathor evoke a vivid image of the shaking of sistra, the beating of tambourines, the strumming of harps, and the lively dance that accompanies the music. The goddess is called Mistress of Music and Mistress of Dance.[12] Pictorial sources sharpen the impression. In Hathor's temples at Dendara and on Philae, music playing is often represented in decoration, above all the playing of sistra but also other instruments, like the lyre. In the mammisis at Dendara, Edfu, and Philae, presided over by this goddess, tambourine players are notably represented.

The cosmic dimensions of sound find a rich variety of expressions. Sound travels far and has far-reaching consequences. Amenemhab, "singer of the noble harp of Amun," can claim: "I purify my mouth. I adore the gods. I exalt Horus who is in the sky. I adore him. The Ennead listens, the inhabitants of the Underworld rejoice. They appear at my voice" (Manniche 1991, p. 60). Sound is even attributed a cosmogonic capacity. The cry from The Great Honker sets the silent and inert chaos in motion (P. Leiden I 350, iv, lines 6–7), and the Shabaka-text gives a presentation of the twofold creation of the gods/the world, effected through the utterance of powerful words — the process explicitly comprising both mind and body.

The sacramental aspect of producing and listening to sound is easily recognized. Gods were in the music, in the song, in the recital of words; divine presence was taken in through the ear. By producing and by listening to sound the ancient Egyptians conversed with divine powers.

---

8. Assmann 1983, p. 164: "Licht und Luft sind die Lebenspendenden Elemente, die vom Sonnengott ausgehen." For examples from the theology of Amun as sun god, see Zandee 1992, pp. 460–70. Also the heat of the sun is mingled in the air, for example, "Dein Atem reicht zu den Nasen der Menschen, sie atmen vom warmen Hauch deines Mundes" (Zandee 1992: hymn to Amun as sun god, P. Leiden I 344, 12 v, 10).
9. In the representations the worshippers are the king together with the queen or the family. This is not the place to go into the discussion of how to interpret the iconographic conventions and functions of the motif of the royal family in Amarna art. It should be borne in mind, though, that even in the worship of Aten the king functioned as the priest *par excellence,* representing both the god and the Egyptian people.
10. Compare the numerous stelae representing the king and queen, together with their daughters.
11. Lichtheim 1976, p. 88: to Amun when he rises as Harakhti.
12. Examples in Junker 1906, p. 106. For the connection between Hathor and dance, see Brunner-Traut 1958.

The sensual aspect of sound and rhythm is indicated in both verbal and pictorial representations: music and dance are mates; man's responses to music come from the whole body. The borders between the sensual and the erotic are easily crossed in these sensations. Likewise, the erotic aspect has a sacramental aspect: Hathor is Mistress of Love (Manniche 1987, esp. pp. 31–51).

The element of joy and merriment cannot be missed; exhortations to exult, rejoice, and be merry are repeatedly uttered. The joy has a cosmic aspect; "heaven, sun and moon, and earth rejoice when they sense the goddess, the animals dance in exultation, Egypt and all the lands praise her, the whole world praises her."[13]

The scent of incense, ointments, and flowers pervaded Egyptian worship. The use of scents was extensive. The smoke of incense filled the halls of temples and wafted around processions and festivals. Statues of gods were anointed. Bouquets of flowers topped the offering table and adorned its bottles of drink.[14]

The lotus, in particular the blue lotus, and the papyrus are in a class apart. They occur in pictorial representations pertaining to a variety of situations — in temples, tombs, dwellings, and out-of-door places. Research focuses on the iconographical functions of these plants; they are signs that trigger rich symbolic meaning having to do with sacred cosmology and the regeneration of life. But somehow the religious meaning of the *fragrances* of these flowers vanish in the expositions, even though it is evidently hinted at in the scenes; the flowers are held under the nose,[15] or their sweet scents are expressly mentioned. One should not interpret these scenes in ways that disregard the religious experience of smelling; the ancient Egyptians attributed deep meaning to the nose as a sensory organ and had a rich tradition of sensing and reacting to fragrance. The nose clearly was significant in the Egyptian experience of a divine cosmos. Flowers were not merely visually articulated messages to be apprehended intellectually. Their fragrances involved body and soul in a relationship of communion with gods: they had the capacity of mediating an experience of divine presence.

The sacramental aspect of this communion is obvious. The fragrance that arose from the lotus held to the nose was mythologically conceived as a young god, Nefertem. Similarly, through inhaling the incense, the substance of life-giving gods was inhaled: the incense was the perspiration from their bodies. It was a vitalizing act, by which gods and men were "nourished" (e.g., Žabkar 1992, p. 240).

In representations, the revitalizing function attributed to the sensory experience of smelling could be underlined by combining the shape of the flower with the sign of the *ankh* (e.g., Schott 1953, pp. 49, 55, illus. 15). Inhaling the fragrance involves breathing: that which all beings need to be alive. The relationship between fragrance and air was just as close as that between light and air. The act of inhaling connects man with the air, and with the sunshine and scents that mingle with the air.[16] Solar gods and gods of the air and scent joined in this life-sustaining act, for example, Ra, Shu, Amun, Nefertem. The syncretizing of these gods in religious texts and images[17] corresponds to the cosmological conception of the close relationship between light, air, and scent.

As it was with the experience of light and sound, the experience of fragrance had erotic undertones. Hathor, Mistress of Myrrh and Mistress of Garlands, was also Mistress of Love. Perfume enveloped musicians and dancers who performed in her cult. Also the art of Amarna expresses the erotic appeal of floral scent.[18]

Smelling the scent was a sensory experience that obviously gave the ancient Egyptians much pleasure. Sweet smells and merry feasting belonged together. The importance that fragrance, aromatic ointments, and incense had on all festive occasions, whether in temples, tombs, or in private places, is amply documented. Thus the garlands and bouquets, the incense cones and the ointment cups, when occurring in situations of worship, are highly charged signs of a cultic mentality stressing joy and pleasure.

Food and drink loomed large in Egyptian worship. Again, the study of the religious meaning of food and drink is also a study of sensory experience. Whether the meals were consumed after having reverted from the offering tables dedicated to gods or in mortuary banquets, the menu is not without interest: the tables contained the ingredients of delicious meals.

---

13. For example, the processional song in the temple of Dendara (Junker 1906, pp. 125–27).
14. For the use of flowers in mortuary context, see Schott 1953, pp. 48–63.
15. Examples of this gesture are found all through the history of Egyptian religion.
16. Both as stationary and in the state of motion; the life-endowing capacity of wind is described in terms similar to those describing the smelling of fragrance: "North wind sweet to thy nostril, breath of what thy nose loveth" (Lichtheim 1945, p. 184).
17. For example, a young sun god sitting in a lotus as Nefertem; see examples in Morenz and Schubert 1954, esp. pp. 4 f., 52 ff.
18. For example, the lid of the chest found in Tutankhamun's tomb, depicting the queen holding big bouquets of lotus and papyrus and poppies to the king's nose; the two are completely surrounded by lotus, papyrus, and poppies — arranged in garlands, bouquets, and stems. Below them, a representation of attendants collecting the mandrake fruit underlines the erotic character of the scene (Cairo Museum no. 61477).

Eating and drinking were sacramental acts that not merely connected man corporeally with the *ka*-powers of cosmic life, but also with the gods who were the ultimate givers of this life.[19] Similarly, the references to the effects of wine and beer drunk in religious feasts are not to be taken as figurative allusions to that "spiritual" intoxication, inspiration. They meant physical drunkenness. Drunkenness had, evidently, sacramental functions; it admitted the presence of divinities. Thus Hathor was also Mistress of Drunkenness (*LÄ* 2 "Hathor," cols. 1024–33, nn. 37–38).

Pleasure was involved. The oxen and wild game, the fruits and vegetables, and the bread all belonged to "the good things" relished by ancient Egyptians. A gastronomic flair is unmistakably reflected. This appreciation of meals is easily associated with other pleasures; eating and drinking were accompanied by music, scents, and merry entertainment.

In all our examples of sensory experiences in Egyptian worship, sensuous pleasure and joy are companions. Through the delights of form and color, scent, music and rhythm, and eating and drinking, the ancient Egyptians entered into a communion with the gods. The gods who were thus worshipped were not primarily attributed with perfection, superiority, and eternity — those criteria that set them apart from human beings — but with regenerative life in its fullness. Physical enjoyment accompanied such gods.

These traditions outline the semantic landscape to which the make-merry songs belonged.

THE MAKE-MERRY SONGS EVALUATED AS EXPRESSIONS OF A RELIGIOUS MENTALITY

The sensory features of Egyptian worship discussed above have implications for how to approach the calls to make merry, to enjoy life, and to follow one's desires and indicate that the epicurean inclination of Egyptian religion was deep-rooted — it permeated both mortuary and divine cult and was found both in and outside situations of worship. Through enjoying their life, the ancient Egyptians kept close contact with the sacred powers of the world. Egyptian worship reflects a conception of man, world, and god, bringing these hedonistic calls in accord with a truly religious attitude.

When approaching the make-merry songs from this point of departure, the question of whether they were sung at mortuary or at secular banquets does not appear to be a decisive issue.[20] There is a noticeable lack of clear conceptual distinctions between sacral and secular spheres of life in Egyptian culture, and this makes the scholar's categorization of mortuary banquets as sacral and other banquets as secular appear too rigid; the more so, as it carries with it an unwarranted dichotomy with regard to ethical values.

"I was a lover of drink, a lord of the feast day" [21] — this is something on which the dead man prides himself; it belongs to the virtues that justify him. He embroiders his virtue in more detail:

> I fulfilled my life on earth in heart's content,
> By the grace of the gods;
> No worry entered the room I was in,
> No sorrow arose in my dwelling.
> Singers and maidens gathered together,
> Made acclaim like that of Meret,
> Braided, beauteous, tressed, high-bosomed,
> Priestesses richly adorned,
> Anointed with myrrh, perfumed with lotus,
> Their heads garlanded with wreaths,
> All together drunk with wine,
> Fragrant with the plants of Punt,
> They danced in beauty doing my heart's wish.
> Their rewards were on their limbs.
> I followed my heart inside the garden,
> I roamed the marshes as I wished.
> They know I am righteous — the prophets and priests (Lichtheim 1980, p. 56).

19. The relationship of reciprocity is generally recognized in the offering institution of the cult of gods.

20. For make-merry songs at mortuary banquets, see Lichtheim 1945; at secular banquets, see Wente 1962; Brunner 1966.

21. The biographical sarcophagus-lid inscription of Wennofer (Lichtheim 1980, p. 55).

The words of this Ptolemaic text,[22] written in classical language, take up our classical theme in Egyptian mortuary literature. Is the author talking about a temple feast or a private one? Daumas (1968, pp. 1–17) has problems in recognizing religious piety in a *bon vivant* and draws attention to the fact that the description contains "Hathorian elements," suggesting that, actually, a religious feast is being described — and that the lack of precise reference was designed to guard religious secrets.[23] From our point of view, it makes no great difference whether a religious feast is being described here or if the scene is representative of a life enjoyed; the one does not exclude the other. A life sensuously enjoyed was a life lived close to the gods. Hathor was, of course, important in temple feasts and mortuary feasts, but so was she also in many pleasures that are rubricized as "secular" according to modern Western classification of social activities.

On this background, the view that the hedonistic exhortations are impious seems oddly out of place.[24] Even the pessimism and doubt concerning life after death can be regarded as a component belonging to Egyptian piety, and not as an intruding parenthesis from the non-religious skeptic. Scholars have long had difficulty in combining the *carpe diem* theme of certain make-merry songs with their theme of assured life after death and have inclined towards seeing them as "heretic,"[25] even as a protest against conventional religion.[26] With the perspective applied by this article, the exhortations to enjoy life appear as expressions of a religious sentiment that was sanctioned by established conceptions of life and death, even when combined with complaints about the transitoriness of life and the bleak prospects after death.

Apart from this, the material we studied indicates that the afterlife is located in the natural world; when there is talk of life after death, it is a life that belongs to this world; it is this world that is the world of the gods. However, there are various concepts of person employed in Egyptian thought about life after death; they define the identity of the dead variously, and they imply various ways of being re-integrated into the world. There is the life of the individual person. And there is the life of the corporate person, comprising living and dead members of the social group in question, the family, or the people of Egypt — jointly owned and reproducing itself in the ongoing stream of generations. The corporate person is the object of the frequently occurring identifications with the gods;[27] its life extends beyond that of the individual person. The individual person, however, vanishes when he no longer is remembered. "A man is revived when his name is pronounced!"[28] is a saying that alludes to the aim of many mortuary rites, daily or festive — including banquets, and the dance and music accompanying them.[29]

Even when the boundary lines between these aspects of the identity of the dead man are not clear, it does not appear too venturesome to say that the *carpe diem* reminder is meant for the individual person (alive or "remembered"). Individual life is transitory and brief; assured eternity is for those aspects of man that transcend the individual person.

"Following the heart" succinctly expresses the ethos correlated with the make-merry exhortations, and Lichtheim's (1980, p. 24) interpretation of the expression seems apposite: "to make the best and fullest use of what life holds; it is being active, generous, and joyful." The request can be given the mold of the *carpe diem.* The brevity of life rouses fear and makes one sad. Thus, on the conceptual background sketched above, the *carpe diem* exhortations are parallel with the utterances of assured belief in a trans-individual, regenerative life.

The evanescent pleasures of the individual's life nevertheless acquire deeper meaning from the idea of human existence as a biological *factum* irretrievably imbedded in a divine, natural world. The idea of a continuum or "consubstantiality"[30] between the life of the individual and the life of the world can be traced in many mortuary traditions.

---

22. The biography of Wennofer, inscribed on the lid of his sarcophagus (Lichtheim 1980, pp. 54–57).
23. Daumas (1968, p. 17) interprets the allusions of the text from this point of view.
24. The view of the songs as impious was early represented in research; see the survey given in Lichtheim 1945, p. 178 ff. Lichtheim (1980, p. 52) holds a modified view: "It is worth emphasizing that the urge to enjoy life was an integral part of this piety. It was only when the 'make merry' motif was coupled with doubts about the reality of the afterlife, as in the Middle Kingdom *Harper's Song from the Tomb of King Intef,* that it became impious."
25. See Lichtheim 1945, p. 180; compare Assmann 1977, p. 65 ff.; Osing 1992, p. 13.
26. See Altenmüller 1978, p. 21, n. 47; Baines 1991, p. 148.
27. For example, through the name of Osiris, or through explicit declarations such as those of the Pyramid texts.
28. Biographical inscription of Petosiris (Lichtheim 1980, p. 46); compare also the Speech of Totrekh Son of Petosiris (Lichtheim 1980, p. 52 f.).
29. For example, Altenmüller 1978: dance and music bring the deceased back to the living for the purpose of a reunion during the banquet; compare Schott 1953.
30. Compare Žabkar's discussion (1963, pp. 57–63).

SOME ADDITIONAL IMPLICATIONS OF EGYPTIAN "EPICUREANISM"

In Egyptian worship, as in all religious worship, a conception of reality was intended that was deeper than "meets the eye." By equating the elements of light, sound, air, and fragrance with gods, these natural phenomena were given symbolic functions. But to all appearances this did not mean that the physical aspect of these phenomena was overlooked or depreciated. On the contrary, it was evaluated as belonging to divine reality. Egyptian gods did not transcend physical reality. Nor were they spirit incarnate in matter. In worship, the essential nature of the empirical world was defined as an indissoluble unit of spiritual[31] and material qualities. Thus Egyptian worship was not a frustrating communication with evasive gods difficult to grasp with the mind; it was a communion with tangible reality through both mind and body. This gives a very different meaning to sensory experiences from what is found in dualistic systems like Gnostic religions and Gnostically influenced Christianity.

One of the methodological implications of this stance should be mentioned: it precludes a description of theophanies as supernatural phenomena. Nor should we "find" miracles in Egyptian religion, which should be borne in mind when we ask such a question as: to what particular kind of experience does the Egyptian sensory communion with gods refer?

The miracle, as a category for cross-cultural description of religions, comprises events that are thought to suspend the laws of the natural world, through the interference of powers set above the laws of nature. Even as belief in supernatural beings "outside the regular processes of nature" has been an almost obligatory criterion of religion, so too has the occurrence of "miracles." But with the approach taken in this article, the miracle is not an apposite tool in the analysis of Egyptian religion. This religion presents the natural world as divine and as governed by the laws of Maat. Only when the natural world appears as an illusion or as secondary to a divine world in duration or perfection or power is there room for breakthroughs that go against the laws of nature. The closest synonyms to terms like *nṯr* and *nṯry* are "god" and "divine." These translations should not delude us into including those connotations of supernatural reality and of a god conventionally characterized as "das ganz Andere" that "god" and "divine" have in Western theology.[32] In Egyptian religion the sensorially experienced "gods" were perceived as natural events, such as the recurrent coming into being of the world, although some of these events were perceived as wonders. It might be profitable to differentiate between miracle and wonder. The categories partly coincide, but differ on this significant point. According to common usage, to be a miracle the criterion of "going against the laws of nature" is required. A miracle is a wonder, but a wonder need not be a miracle.

Of course, the ancient Egyptians did not live in perpetual awe and wonder at the world. Any functioning ontology belongs to the things that tend to go without saying. Nevertheless, Egyptian religion offered the possibility of experiencing the world as wondrously divine. Such experiences are most often documented in the context of worship, where the divine aspect of the world was expressly set forth. But they could also occur outside this context; unusual events, or events effected by powers of unknown places, could be experienced as wonders.[33]

Our reading of the texts and pictures should thus be done according to two levels of meaning. They have a literal meaning, dealing as they do with empirical reality, and they have a symbolic meaning because they refer to a perception of empirical reality as ultimate and absolute. This point is especially important when reading such hymns as those composed to Aten because it excludes the option of interpreting Akhenaten's iconoclasm as a negation of the sacral meaning of the world.[34] Rather, Akhenaten's "act of iconoclastic destruction" (Assmann 1992, p. 162) meant that he discarded mythological modes of expression. Through his demythologization, the world appears *qua* natural world, and not as a collection of acting beings. But as regards his evaluation of the natural world, this king — with great determination and consequence — treads on hallowed ground in the footsteps of his predecessors. Demythologization does not necessarily mean de-divinization.[35] That

31. "Spirit" and "spiritual" have a long history of usage and are common words both in the discipline of the history of religions and in Christian theology, variously defined in both contexts. Herein the spiritual quality is antithetical to material and corporeal, in accordance with current popular usage.
32. Rudolph Otto's famous *Das Heilige* (1917), drawing on material from the Christian and Jewish religions, has deeply influenced research on religion, even studies of other religions.
33. The difficulties involved in translating such words as *bi͗ꜣyt* are demonstrated in, for example, Shirun-Grumach 1993.
34. As Assmann (1992, p. 162) sees it, "Akhanyati was the first to find a way out of religion. Akhanyati's explanation of the world as nature is, above all, an act of iconoclastic destruction, of negating the world's religious significance."
35. As Assmann (1992, p. 163) suggests.

Akhenaten demonstrated the natural character of reality[36] is true enough. But he also, with unprecedented stringency, explicitly demonstrated the divine character of natural reality. To regard his religion as "a decisive move towards what Max Weber called the 'disenchantment of the world,' " as Assmann (1992, p. 144) proposes, is to overlook the implications of this momentous feature and presupposes not only Western conceptions of god but also Western conceptions of nature.[37] Reading his hymns as a first step towards a de-divinization of the world appears well-nigh to turn matters upside-down.

By approaching the make-merry calls from the central role played by sensory and sensuous experiences in Egyptian worship, I contend that the make-merry calls are deeply religious, without diminishing or circumscribing their unmistakably worldly hedonistic character.

References

Allen, J. P.
1989 "The Cosmology of the Pyramid Texts." In *Religion and Philosophy in Ancient Egypt,* edited by J. P. Allen, J. Assmann, A. B. Lloyd, R. K. Ritner, and D. P. Silverman, pp. 1–28. Yale Egyptological Studies 3. New Haven: Yale University.

Altenmüller, H.
1978 "Zur Bedeutung der Harfnerlieder des Alten Reiches." *Studien zur altägyptischen Kultur* 6: 1–24.

Assmann, J.
1977 "Fest des Augenblicks — Verheissung der Dauer: Die Kontroverse der ägyptischen Harfnerlieder." In *Fragen an die altägyptischen Literatur: Studien zum Gedenken an Eberhard Otto,* edited by J. Assmann, E. Feucht, and R. Grieshammer, pp. 55–84. Wiesbaden: Otto Harrassowitz.
1983 *Re und Amun.* Orbis Biblicus et Orientalis 51. Göttingen: Vandenhoeck and Ruprecht.
1992 "Akhanyati's Theology of Light and Time." *Proceedings of the Israel Academy of Sciences and Humanities* 7, no. 4: 143–76.

Baines, J.
1991 "Society, Morality, and Religious Practice." In *Religion in Ancient Egypt,* edited by Byron E. Shafer, pp. 123–200. New York: Cornell University Press.

Brunner, H.
1966 "Wiederum die ägyptischen 'Make Merry.'" *Journal of Near Eastern Studies* 25: 130–31.

Brunner-Traut, E.
1958 *Der Tanz im alten Ägypten.* Ägyptologische Forschungen 6. Glückstadt: J. J. Augustin.

Daumas, F.
1968 "Les propylées du temple d'Hathor à Philae et le culte de la déesse." *Zeitschrift für ägyptische Sprache und Altertumskunde* 95: 1–17.

Davies, N. de G.
1905 *The Rock Tombs of El Amarna* 2. Archaeological Survey of Egypt 14. London: Egypt Exploration Society.
1908 *The Rock Tombs of El Amarna* 5. Archaeological Survey of Egypt 17. London: Egypt Exploration Society.

de Waal Malefijt, A.
1968 *Religion and Culture: An Introduction to Anthropology of Religion.* London: Macmillan.

Gardiner, A. H.
1905 "Hymns to Amon from a Leiden Papyrus." *Zeitschrift für ägyptische Sprache und Altertumskunde* 42: 12–42.

Junker, H.
1906 "Poesie der Spätzeit." *Zeitschrift für ägyptische Sprache und Altertumskunde* 43: 101–27.

Lichtheim, M.
1945 "The Songs of the Harpers." *Journal of Near Eastern Studies* 4: 178–212.
1976 *Ancient Egyptian Literature,* Volume 2: *The New Kingdom.* Berkeley: University of California Press.
1980 *Ancient Egyptian Literature,* Volume 3: *The Late Period.* Berkeley: University of California Press.

Manniche, L.
1987 *Sexual Life in Ancient Egypt.* London and New York: Routledge and Kegan Paul.
1991 *Music and Musicians in Ancient Egypt.* London: British Museum Press.

Morenz, S., and J. Schubert
1954 *Der Gott auf der Blume.* Ascona: Verlag Artibus Asiae.

Osing, J.
1992 "Les chants du harpiste au Nouvel Empire." In *Aspects de la culture pharaonique: Quatre leçons au Collège de France (février–mars 1989),* by J. Osing, pp. 11–24. Mémoires de l'Académie des Inscriptions et Belles-Lettres, n.s., 12. Paris: Diffusion de Boccard.

Otto, R.
1917 *Das Heilige: Über das Irrationale in der Idee des Göttlichen und sein Verhältnis zum Rationalen.* Reprint, 1987. Munich: C. H. Beck.

Schott, S.
1953 *Das schöne Fest vom Wüstentale: Festbräuche einer Totenstadt.* Abhandlungen der Geistes- und Sozialwissenschaftlichen Klasse, 1952, no. 11. Wiesbaden: F. Steiner.

36. Assmann (1992, p. 161) concludes that to Akhenaten, "God is nothing else but the sun, and he is also nature."

37. My theoretical stance here is that even the concept of nature is a cultural construct and that viewing nature is not solely a matter of inborn perceptual capacities.

Shirun-Grumach, I.
1993 *Offenbarung, Orakel und Königsnovelle*. Ägypten und Altes Testament 24. Wiesbaden: Otto Harrassowitz.

Tylor, E. B.
1871 *Primitive Culture: Researches into the Development of Mythology, Philosophy, Religion, Language, Art, and Custom*. Seventh edition, 1924. New York: Brentano.

van der Plas, D.
1989 " 'VOIR' DIEU. Quelques observations au sujet de la fonction des sens dans le culte et la dévotion de l'Égypte ancienne." *Bulletin de la Société française d'égyptologie* 115: 4–35.

Wente, E. F.
1962 "Egyptian 'Make Merry' Songs Reconsidered." *Journal of Near Eastern Studies* 21: 118–28.

Žabkar, L. V.
1963 "Herodotus and the Egyptian Idea of Immortality." *Journal of Near Eastern Studies* 22: 57–63.
1992 "A Hymn to Incense in the Temple of Arensnuphis at Philae." In *Studies in Pharaonic Religion and Society in Honour of J. Gwyn Griffiths*, edited by A. B. Lloyd, pp. 236–45. Occasional Publications 8. London: Egypt Exploration Society.

Zandee, J.
1992 *Der Amunhymnus des Papyrus Leiden I 344, Verso*, Band 2. Leiden: Rijksmuseum van Oudheden.

11

SOME COMMENTS ON KHETY'S INSTRUCTION FOR LITTLE PEPI ON HIS WAY TO SCHOOL (SATIRE ON THE TRADES)

JOHN L. FOSTER

Chicago, Illinois

It is a pleasure to be able to contribute this small piece to a volume honoring my friend and colleague Edward F. Wente on his retirement from teaching. My acquaintance with Ed goes back to 1967 when I was a rather over-age student in his class on second-year Middle Egyptian texts. He has been for many years the resident expert on the hieratic ostraca in the collection of the Oriental Institute, and when over two decades ago I expressed my interest in ancient Egyptian literature and the literary ostraca, he very graciously relinquished his own claim on them and encouraged me to work with and catalog them. He has shared his transcriptions of the literary pieces with me and has always been ready with help in studying them. I offer this essay — which has so much to do with hieratic ostraca and their variations and permutations — in his honor.

SATIRE ON THE TRADES

The so-called Satire on the Trades, containing Khety's instruction to his son Pepi, is one of the most confusing, garbled, and unintelligible literary texts to survive from ancient Egypt. There is no primary copy that one can use to form an eclectic text from the many fragmentary copies which now exist. There is no source text one can confidently say harks back to the original. The only "complete" copy is on P. Sallier II, which (along with P. Anastasi VII) has quite possibly the most corrupt text of all and which often wanders off into arrant nonsense. The only use of Sallier II is to provide the structuring of the total poem — its sequence of verse lines and stanzas. Because of this "completeness," Sallier II appears first in parallel-text editions and obscures just how misleading is that copy (cf. Helck 1970).

Take as an example the well-known couplet in Stanza 2: "I have seen many beatings — / Set your heart on books!" (Lichtheim 1973, p. 185). Other current translations have similar phrasing (Helck 1970, p. 19; Simpson 1973, p. 330; Brunner 1988, p. 159; Hoch 1991/92, p. 89). Here, the connection seems to be between beatings and schooling. Only Simpson has "those who have been beaten," thus indicating that *qnqnw* refers to persons rather than acts. The point of this is that of the several copies for this passage, only DeM 1043 has a seated-man determinative with plural strokes to indicate persons; and only Simpson's translation makes use of this (see Helck 1970 for parallel-text edition). Of the nine copies showing the end of this phrase, only one suggests that the *qnqnw* are persons; all imply that student scribes are beaten (perhaps with canes and presumably for not studying).

The entire tone of the poem — the attitude the reader is expected to take toward the material — is misrepresented if the two lines are read this way. The tenor or thrust of the poem, as I hope to make clear, is the attractiveness of learning — Khety is attempting to persuade little Pepi that the scribe's ("scholar's") life is a fine one, where the love of learning comes to exceed the love of one's own mother, as Khety says in Stanza 3. It would be poor psychology for Khety to begin his dissertation on schooling (whatever might be the facts of the scribal schoolroom) with corporal punishment. At any rate, and building upon Simpson's translation, I think the connection between the two clauses of the sentence is better served by seeing the *qnqnw* as "those who have been beaten down" by life in general — the downtrodden. Khety has seen the misery of so many types of persons and the hardship involved in so many occupations that he begins his instruction of his son with the warning

Gold of Praise: Studies on Ancient Egypt in Honor of Edward F. Wente
Edited by Emily Teeter and John A. Larson
Studies in Ancient Oriental Civilization 58
Chicago: Oriental Institute, 1999

to succeed at the scribal school since life at the humbler levels of society is brutal. Read this way, the sentence not only makes smoother sense but also forms a more apt introduction to the succeedir.g portraits of the various servant-types and tradesmen. Don't fail in your chance at learning, Khety tells his son, or you may have to live like they do, in hard labor and misery.

The conclusion one reaches from consulting a parallel-text edition like Helck's is that all surviving copies of a passage must be scrutinized in order to make an educated guess as to its original meaning. There simply is no way, lacking a primary text (such as P. Millingen for the Instruction of Amenemhat), to rely on one copy over another. One *can* say that P. Sallier II and P. Anastasi VII should be consulted only when all else fails. Both scholarly deductions and leaps of the scholarly imagination are regularly required to make any sense at all of this interesting and confusing text. Because of these problems, a great deal of uncertainty surrounds anyone's recovery of the original text written by Khety (or its pseudonymous author).

Helck's edition and translation, as well as the translations of Simpson and Lichtheim, were produced in the 1970s. It was only later in the decade that fascicles of the third volume of Posener's (1978) comprehensive edition of the Deir el-Medina literary ostraca began to appear, the second fascicle of which has almost one hundred and fifty ostraca offering fragments of our text (DeM 1442–1590). Of the translations mentioned above, only those of Brunner and Hoch were able to utilize these additional fragments. For instance, the passage from Stanza 2 discussed above appears on DeM 1466, 1467, and 1472, and of these DeM 1467 has the seated man determinative and plural strokes. This does not make the reading correct, but it does indicate support for it. The additional Deir el-Medina ostraca do indeed correct many readings and solidify many others in Khety's instruction to Pepi.

Still another publication affects the text, though to a lesser extent. López (1978–82) published the Turin ostraca, several of which offer portions of Khety's instruction to Pepi, and one of which (57082) provides major help for a portion of the text that has not survived very well (Stanzas 25–28).

RECOVERY OF THE TEXT

The difficulty of recovering the text of Khety's instruction to Pepi certainly derives from the unreliability of the surviving copies, but it is compounded by disagreement over the tone of the poem. Opinion is divided over its seriousness. To some it is a thoughtful moral text in the tradition of the Instruction of Ptahhotep or Any; to others it is a satire — humorous, ridiculing, or smiling at the lives and situations of the tradesmen characterized by Khety. Both opinions are current right up to the most recent studies of the text by Brunner and Hoch.

In poetry, as the late American poet Robert Lowell (1961, p. xi, quoting Boris Pasternak) said over thirty years ago, "tone is of course everything." And the attitude one takes toward Khety's poem influences assessment of its seriousness. To me, there is no satire whatsoever: the poem is an earnest disquisition on schooling and education aimed at the young son of the author as they travel toward the boy's boarding school at the Residence. Indeed, the piece is a noble and at times moving defense of education that still has relevance today.

Satire is "a work or manner that blends a censorious attitude with humor and wit for improving human institutions or humanity" (Holman 1986, p. 423). It involves criticism, a making fun of through laughter, a judgment according to some standard, with often a belittling or ridicule of an object or person; and its intent is indeed to instruct or improve. Those who find Khety's instruction to Pepi a satire emphasize the portraits of the various tradesmen in the first two-thirds of the poem because Stanzas 4–21 present a succession of characterizations — vivid portraits — of persons in humble occupations. And, certainly, Khety portrays them in order to warn little Pepi, to instruct and improve him, so that he will make good use of his time at school.

But even through the difficulties of the text — our misreadings as well as miscopyings by the ancient scribes — we can see that there is no laughter and no belittling. What Khety reveals is a spectrum of human misery. Learning helps one avoid this misery, he tells his son; one need not be an underling (Helck's Stanza 2.b). And Khety later adds, in the famous couplet that sums up the pragmatic side of the instruction (Stanza 21.h–i): "All trades have their overseers except for the scribe; he *is* the overseer." There is, in fact, a distinct undercurrent of sympathy on Khety's part for the unfortunates whose lives he describes for his son. The gardener (Stanza 12) is old and worn out, able to do nothing but tend the vegetables and herbs — and (if the translation is correct) his mind is obsessively concerned with death and his good name. Or there is the washerman (Stanza 19) who becomes so exhausted cleaning filthy clothes that he despairs, and the washtub whispers to him to jump in and drown himself. The stoker (Stanza 17) smells like the dead; the mat-maker (Stanza 14) has to pay the door guard just to see the sun; the potter (Stanza 9) is covered with slime and shunned by other persons. These human beings are miserable; they are not laughable; they are not being belittled. They are used by Khety as examples — but not objects of satire — of what Pepi might become or have to endure if he does not pay attention to his studies. Learning helps one avoid such misery, Khety is pointing out. Far from displaying satire, I would suggest Khety's words show compassion for the downtrodden; they might have done better in life. He does not want little Pepi forced into such degrading and backbreaking kinds of work.

The quality that some scholars see as humor, satire, or irony (this last trait occurring fitfully in the text, as in calling the washerman's occupation a distinguished one) is rather the rhetorical wordplay normal to the ancient Egyptian thought couplet. It is the "Witz" mentioned by Helck (1970, p. 161) as he takes issue with Brunner's identification of wit with humor. Helck refers to this wordplay — which he argues is neither humorous nor satiric — as "das oft barocken Sprache jener Epoche." This kind of wit need not at all be humorous or inspire laughter; it can be very sober, as I suggest it occurs in Khety's instruction to Pepi, where the play of thought and the intellect is seen in a very serious context. The ancient Egyptian sage often used such word play — as in the punning upon the word *sḏm* in the Instruction of Ptahhotep or the permutations of Maat in the individual "complaints" of The Eloquent Peasant (cf. Foster 1989/90). Such rhetoric — replete with its parallel and contrasting phrases, sound repetitions, plays on vocabulary, and apt or elegant expressions — is a fundamental characteristic of Egyptian poems. A failure to distinguish between wit and humor, seriousness and laughter, is easy in a piece where the very words and phrases are so difficult to discover and disentangle.

Khety's instruction for his son Pepi is a serious treatise on education. It is aimed at a young boy who does not want to leave home and does not particularly want to have to study. In this context Khety warns him of the possible consequences of neglecting his studies, through a spectrum of both negative examples (the tradesmen) and positive injunctions (the more traditional maxims concerning correct public behavior that constitute the final third of the poem). But looming behind the specific examples and advice given the fledgling scholar are more general statements on the value of education: "Nothing is so valuable as education; / it is a bridge (*mi͗t*) over troubled waters" (Stanza 2); or the entirety of Stanza 3, where the "beauties" or "perfections" of learning distinguish it above all other occupations, professional or otherwise. "Love it more than your mother," Khety says. In Stanza 22 he adds, "Your days in school will be precious to you — / their benefit will last to the end of time!" And the wider implications of what Khety is telling his son are summed up in the climax of the work in its two final stanzas, 29–30. Stanza 29 is explored in detail below because it seems to me the clearest presentation of the seriousness of Khety's theme, as well as an exhibition of the problems faced in understanding and interpreting the poem as a whole.

STRUCTURE OF THE TEXT

Khety's advice for little Pepi is written as a piece of literature; his words are cast as a poem that utilizes the strategies of the ancient Egyptian genre of didactic verse. The nature of the text thus raises certain questions that are literary. For instance, what is the dramatic situation of the poem? To be sure, it is an instruction, an attempt to pass knowledge on from a father to a son, a situation that is quite standard in the Egyptian genre of wisdom literature. But in this case, there is a detailing of the situation that shapes the poem as literature. Khety and Pepi are on the Nile traveling upstream to reach the Residence, where Pepi is about to be enrolled as a student at the scribal school connected to the royal palace. Dramatically speaking, the entire instruction is given aboard ship. Little Pepi, whose age is not specified but who is perhaps under ten years old, is leaving his home and his mother (the fundamental place of the mother in Egyptian consciousness is proverbial) to attend boarding school. Khety is certainly aware of the advantages to be gained by his son through mingling with the sons of the noblest and best in the kingdom as they all undergo the educational process. And among Khety's first words are those warning Pepi against squandering this once-in-a-lifetime opportunity for advancement and success; the alternative to education is a life of drudgery and heavy labor. Khety then exhibits the gallery of miserable lives endured by the uneducated.

Little Pepi is not interested in school, he presumably does not want to leave home, and he seems to have no affection for learning (Stanza 22.g) — hence his father's many references to the love of learning, which Khety is sure the boy will develop once he enrolls and attends to his lessons. It is noteworthy, however, that Khety, despite the portrait gallery of the miserable, stresses the positive side of education — and teaching — in more than one passage (Stanzas 2–3, 22, 29–30). It is not a matter of beatings, as mistranslation has it, but of study that develops into satisfaction (Stanza 29.c, utilizing DeM 1529 and 1572). The whole tenor of Khety's remarks is to soothe and persuade the young boy that a new world is about to open up to him — both through the social advantage of living at the Residence city and through the mental enrichment of education.

In addition, what I see as the simplicity of the language and the clarity of the concepts presented by Khety (this point is open to question, certainly, in a text so garbled) is a further function of the dramatic situation. Because Pepi is young, the wisdom is presented at the level of understanding of a young boy, a neophyte, and a homesick prospective student. The entire poem is tailor made for the teaching staff at a scribal school like Deir el-Medina (of which more below).

As a piece of literature, the poem is written in verse, and this too has implications both for understanding and translating. Of the translations mentioned here, those of Lichtheim, Simpson, and Helck are in prose. Lichtheim, at times, does not even follow the stanza divisions. The more recent translations of Brunner and Hoch are set as verse.

Khety's instruction for Pepi is composed in thought couplets — those structural and clause units that usually constitute the sentences of ancient Egyptian verse. In the genre of the wisdom text, the couplets seem to be quite strict. That is, in some of the poems, particularly in the narrative genre, the patterning often makes use of triplets and even quatrains (e.g., Sinuhe, The Shipwrecked Sailor), but the instructions usually are limited to units of two. This phenomenon is particularly clear in Khety's instruction for Pepi, wherein all the verse lines are there (the poem amounts to 260 verses) and all are marked by red verse points so that their total number is sure.

Because of this stability in the couplet structuring, one can even determine places where structural garbling has occurred. For instance, in Stanza 28, if I read a difficult passage correctly, there are two triplets in the middle of a twelve-line stanza, which should not occur in a poem observing the couplet form so strictly. The reading is difficult no matter what, but I suggest there is a misunderstanding earlier in the tradition of transmitting the poem. The other example occurs in Stanza 25. Helck's 25.a has no partner ("Be serious and act with dignity"), while the remaining four verses of the stanza occur in pairs. It seems to me a verse-line has dropped out. Finally, the only clear triplet occurs in the final stanza's first three lines: "I have set you on the way of God; / but the good fortune of a scribe rests on his own two shoulders / from the day of his birth." The final adverbial phrase constitutes the third verse line of a triplet and is used to emphasize Khety's culminating bit of wisdom. The remainder of the poem is in couplets.

The couplet structure has certain further implications, because the clauses occur in pairs. Take Stanza 14 in literal translation:

> The mat-maker within [his] cubicle —
> he is worse off than a woman;
> With his knees [pressed] to his stomach
> he cannot breathe the air.
> If he diminishes [wastes] the day through not weaving,
> he is beaten with the leather [strap] fifty blows;
> And he must offer food to the doorkeeper
> to allow him to go out into the daylight.

One notes that the thought units of this passage progress in pairs of verse lines and that there seems to be a heavier pause after each second line (i.e., with the rhetorical weight of either a semicolon or a period): the mat-maker's situation is more miserable than even a woman's; his knees are so forced into his stomach that he can hardly breathe; if he does not weave, he is beaten; and he must bribe the guard in order to go outside. These are thoughts expressed in pairs of clauses. My point is that few of the translations of Khety's instruction for Pepi make use of this patterning, with the prose translations following the couplet form little or not at all and the two more recent translations catching the pattern better through their use of verse format. Couplet structuring has a good many ramifications that can lead to more accurate translations and products which vary less widely from translator to translator.[1]

In terms of the poem's larger structure, the division into thirty stanzas is clear from the rubrics that are present in many of the copies. In addition to its couplet and stanza divisions, the work as a whole has several sections. A number of scholars have already noted its division into two unequal parts, the first portraying the

1. See *Thought Couplets in The Tale of Sinuhe* (Foster 1993) for an attempt to identify the grammatical and clausal implications of the thought couplet, both within the individual line and between the two lines constituting the couplet.

various tradesmen (whence the name "satire") and the second comprising several stanzas of more general good advice for pursuing the scribal profession. One might note that of the thirty stanzas only six (one-fifth of the poem) are concerned with such maxims. Certainly the spectrum of portraits of the tradesmen is the most vivid as well as the largest section of the poem, thus giving rise to its traditional title. And there are other stanzas that place Khety's observations in a larger context.

One might divide the overall structure of the poem as follows:

Stanzas 1–3	The dramatic situation of the poem and the special calling of the scribal profession.
Stanzas 4–21	Vignettes (negative but not satiric) of various humble trades, ending with "the scribe is the overseer of all these."
Stanza 22	Coda praising the love of learning: a summary stanza.
Stanzas 23–28	Traditional maxims, primarily concerning the conduct of the scribe in public affairs and as serving eminent persons.
Stanzas 29–30	Conclusion: the nobility of learning and the path of the Everlasting.

It is in Stanzas 1–3, 22, and 29–30 that the seriousness of the poem is most obvious.

STANZA 29

Stanza 29 strikes me as the finest in the poem. With the aid of the Deir el-Medina and Turin ostraca, and utilizing the structures of verse and thought couplet, I hope to bring greater clarity and understanding to the passage. The eclectic text that I developed for the twelve-line stanza and a literal translation follow:

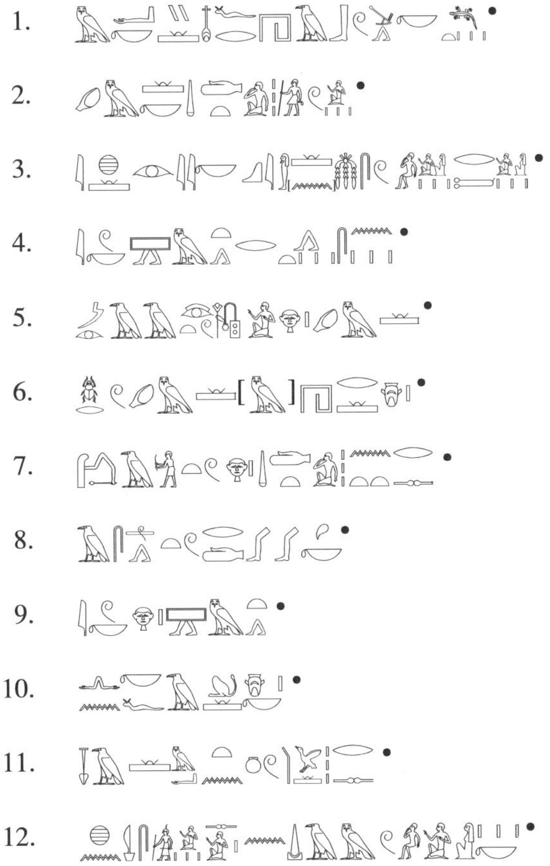

1. Now, it is good that you should cultivate many things
2. so that you may hear the words of great men;
3. Then, you can create a standard for the children of the People
4. while you are walking according to their going [way].
5. The scribe is seen as listening [and obeying],
6. and the listening develops into satisfaction.
7. Fight for the words of that which concerns these things,
8. hasten your footsteps —
9. And while you are on your way,
10. you shall never [need to] conceal your heart.
11. Cleave to the paths concerning it [learning] —
12. the friends of Man belong to your company.

One need only glance at other translations of this passage to see how widely they differ from this one. I repeat: no version of Khety's instruction for Pepi can claim to be definitive; and the translator simply must fall back upon what the poem as a whole seems to deal with and to what degree each line or each copy furthers that overall aim.

Thus the translation of Stanza 29 above is also tentative. I believe it has two advantages over the translations cited earlier: (1) the many, if fragmentary, readings provided by the Deir el-Medina and Turin ostraca; and (2) the constraints and structuring provided by the thought couplet. In general, the translations of the other scholars see this stanza as much more specific in its references than I do — expressing an additional set of maxims or good advice. But, this stanza is the culmination of everything Khety has attempted to pass on to his son; it is a climactic stanza that speaks in much more general or universal terms (as the Egyptians then knew them) about the value of learning. My more specific arguments and suggestions concerning this stanza follow.

Line 1: The word *hꜣb* creates a major problem and launches the stanza in the wrong direction from the start. The meaning seems perfectly clear: to "send," usually to "write letters" — that is what scribes do and what young boys are sent to scribal school to learn. The copies are almost unanimous in this reading. Nevertheless, I think the reading of DeM 1529 brings a greater clarity and unity to the beginning of this stanza: that is, with the plow determinative, *hꜣb* is a substitute spelling for *hbỉ* "to plow" or "to cultivate." With the *nfr* reinforced by more recently published copies, we have "it is good that you should cultivate many things (*ꜣšꜥw*)."

Line 2: This line is the second half of a couplet and so should be connected to the preceding line grammatically. *Sḏm.f*s in following position are usually dependent clauses of purpose or result; and the line would then read "so that you may" do such and such. A problem faced by all translators of Egyptian texts — especially poetry — is just how specific or general a meaning to assign a given word. In this verse line there are two such difficult words, *sḏm* and *mdwt*. Specifically, of course, they mean "to hear" and "words." But this is a case where a more generalized meaning is desirable. *Sḏm* means not only "to hear" but also "to listen and obey" — to have the words heard sink in. And in this passage the meaning of "to learn" is particularly apt. The same is true of *mdwt*, where the words that are learned amount to much more than mere words; and the meaning expands to something like "wisdom" — that is, the wisdom of the instruction tradition (not the kind of wisdom, *sỉꜣ*, that is limited to the king and is sometimes deified). Human wisdom in this context is *mdwt,* and indeed *mdwt nṯr* becomes not only "the words of the god" but also "divine wisdom" as it is revealed to humankind. In this poem we have the wisdom of "great men."

Line 3: The *ỉḫ sḏm.f* indicates that the results which follow from "learning the wisdom of the sages (i.e., great men)" in the first two lines of the stanza allow the student (calling him a "scribe" is once more to apply too narrow a meaning to the Egyptian word) to participate in the education (*qỉ* "shaping" or "patterning") of the children of the Egyptians (*rmṯ* here is used in contrast to what I see as a more general use of the word *z* in line 12). That is, the student will not only learn wisdom, he will pass it on as a teacher.

Line 4: The *ỉw.f* [*ḥr*] *sḏm* construction indicates an action concomitant with the preceding line; thus, the student can go about his job of educating at the same time as he is learning and following in the footsteps (or "according to the gait" — *nmtt*) of the *srw* of Line 2.

Line 5: The scribe is seen (a passive) in the act of (while) listening (*ḥr sḏm*) or learning. This is his characteristic attitude.

Line 6: This line is a second independent clause in the couplet and is therefore a compound sentence. The process of listening and learning becomes a source of satisfaction to the student later in life as he gains knowledge and competence. More recently published ostraca (DeM 1529 and 1572) provide the key to this line, *hr-ỉb* "pleasure," "contentment," or "satisfaction." The meaning seems fairly clear, but it requires the addition of *m* in order to read "develop into."

Line 7: In the second half of the stanza Khety turns from his statement of the purpose of learning and its pleasures to direct exhortation of little Pepi. He uses imperatives: *ꜥḥꜣ ḥr* "'fight for' or 'fight to protect' the words ('knowledge') of that which (*ntt*) pertains to it (*r.s*)." What concerns learning or wisdom is to be protected, defended, and disseminated.

Line 8: A second imperative is in the second line of the couplet: "Hasten (*ꜣs tw*) your feet!" The *tw* needs to be extracted from the spellings of the three copies available at this point, where the *t* wrongly precedes the determinative.

Line 9: *iw.f ḥr sḏm*, concomitant action. The clause is independent grammatically, thus beginning a new couplet, but it also links closely with the preceding couplet: "and while you are upon going" or "and while you are on your way."

Line 10: *nn* for *nn wn* "there shall be no" (hiding or masking of your heart). That is, if Pepi follows the path of wisdom, he will never need to dissimulate or act deviously; he can be straightforward and truthful in all he does. For once the reading of Sallier II seems most fruitful and is supported by the more recent DeM 1578.

Lines 11–12: If I read it correctly, the final couplet of this stanza is the finest of several fine passages in the poem. Here, more than anywhere else in the instruction, I would take issue with the available translations. This stanza as a whole is a generalizing stanza; it brings Khety's teaching to a close since the final stanza deals once more (as in Stanzas 1–2) with the sphere Pepi is about to enter and the final blessing bestowed by the father for the good fortune of his son. The last six lines of Stanza 29 are Khety's culminating invitation for Pepi to join the world of learning. In Line 11 he expresses another imperative, gentle but life-determining: *smꜣ* "cleave to" or "step forth on" or "land on." Since the word for pathways (*mtnw*) follows, Pepi is urged to set out on the path "concerning this," which is a reference, as in Line 7, to learning or wisdom (i.e., *mdwt*).

Line 12: This final line is an independent statement to parallel the first half of the couplet. The young scholar scribe who sets out on the paths of learning will find himself accompanied by the friends of Man as his companions. *Ḫnmsw* is clear, followed by *z*, which in its most specific meaning indicates "a man," and in an extended usage "a man of some prominence." Here I think it means "man" generically, or "Man." After the more general and philosophical statements and exhortations of this stanza, it would be incredible if Khety should be so specific as to say, "Pick out friends from your own age group." The *n* reads as "belong to," and the *ḏꜣmw*, while it can refer to "young men" or "troops" or "the young generation," certainly has the wider meaning of "company" or "companions." Thus, the couplet suggests that the great and wise men of past generations are already out on the pathways of learning, waiting for the beginners — the current generation — and that when Pepi and his fellow students set out on that road they will have such men as their companions. If this reading is correct, the couplet becomes one of the finest to survive from ancient Egypt (like Maat, in The Eloquent Peasant, accompanying a just man down to the very grave).

DIFFICULTIES THAT FACE THE TRANSLATOR

Certain particular difficulties face the translator of ancient Egyptian poems. First, with a text as garbled as Khety's instruction for Pepi, one simply accepts a high degree of uncertainty in one's own choices. There is no help for it barring discovery of new copies and better texts, which has occurred here, to a degree, through Posener's publication of the additional Deir el-Medina ostraca and López's similar publication of the Turin ostraca, which have enhanced the probabilities for a believable basic text — a situation that, for the last third of the poem particularly, was not possible earlier.

A second difficulty is the lack of understanding of the structure of ancient Egyptian verse, the thought couplet. Awareness of such strict patterning makes an enormous difference in how the translator reads the successive verse lines of a text.

A third difficulty pertains to the range of meaning of a given word, like *sḏm* or *mdwt* or *ḏꜣmw* above. It is sometimes difficult to determine whether a word should be translated according to (1) its concrete or its abstract meaning, (2) its literal or its symbolic meaning (the *rnnwtt* and *msḫnt* of Stanza 30), (3) its specific or general meaning (as with the three words just mentioned), or (4) its strictly denotative or its imaginative meaning. All translators are aware of the difficulty of such choices, but the tradition of literal translation for scholarly material can blind the scholar to the implications of the words and meanings: "imaginative" translations are wrong, unscholarly. But this simply is not true. An example from this poem is Helck's translation of *iryw pt* in Stanza 20 (1970, p. 114) as "birds." This translation is correct, literally, but it is absolutely ruinous to the imaginative aura with which Khety seems to be enfolding the stanza on fowling; the literal birds are seen as "guardians of heaven" or of "the sky," a part of God's realm. The imaginative meaning — in this case there in the text — affords the reader so much more in the way of both pleasure and understanding. This example shows the limitations of literal translations, necessary as they are. Used as a means for fellow scholars to understand as simply and rapidly as possible what the writer has in mind, they are an indispensable shorthand; yet they are nevertheless reductive; they demean and diminish the imaginative and emotional richness that can be discovered inhering in the text. Literal translations never convey with any fullness what the original text signifies. This is especially true of the poetry.

A fourth difficulty is the translator's too great concentration on the smaller units of a text — the words and individual clauses — to the detriment of the intermediate or larger units like paragraphs or stanzas. The reader often has difficulty in following the thread of meaning in a translation from beginning to end of a unit. One might cite as an example Helck's translation of this poem (prose in his version), which seems to me especially convoluted and wooden. Helck has done too much for the field of Egyptology to need any defense, but I think his translation errs in just this regard: there is too much emphasis upon the word, the individual phrase, and the grammatical relationships between individual words and not enough upon the larger units of thought and meaning.

CONCLUSION

Khety's instruction to Pepi is an invitation to learning, a kind of treatise on the joys and benefits of education using both negative examples and positive encouragement. As Helck (1970, pp. 161–62) well understood, it is a very serious piece of literature, neither a satire nor an instance of humor. It is aimed at a young boy who does not want to leave home and does not particularly want to have to study. Khety, the father, attempts to persuade his son that the initial strangeness, difficulty, and even loneliness of learning are succeeded by satisfaction, success, comfort, and prestige — that the goal is both a noble one and well worth any effort the young boy must expend. But Khety uses the devices of persuasion — gentleness, rationality, vivid examples, and even idealism — to assuage the fears and the opposition that little Pepi carries along on the trip upriver. Despite the vignettes of misery, there are no threats, no warnings of punishment by the father, nothing about shaming the family name through failure. And this is why that one word, *qnqnw*, when translated as "beatings," is so false to the spirit of the poem. It is not about schoolboys being beaten for laziness or ignorance; it is about the thrill of joining in the great tradition of the wise men of ancient Egypt as they walk the path to knowledge.

No wonder the teaching staff of the scribal school at Deir el-Medina were so attracted to this poem. Of course it is a piece of propaganda — as they used it. The text perfectly well expresses the aims of the education they were trying to pass on to their young pupils: "The good fortune of a scribe rests on his own two shoulders / from the day he enters school" (literally, "from the day of his birth"; Stanza 30). These two lines from the final stanza are certainly what the teachers tried to inculcate in their young charges. Perhaps, because the poem seems so apt and the dramatic situation of a father speaking to his young son on the way to school so relevant, the text was used as one of the first for the new students as they attempted to learn their hieroglyphs — not the first strokes, but their first connected passages. The lines and stanzas dictated or otherwise disseminated to them reminded the students both of the dangers of failure to apply oneself to one's studies and of the rewards that lay ahead for the industrious, which might explain why, on the surviving evidence, there are so many copies. It might also explain why there are so many patent errors in those copies since they were the result of initial attempts by hands that were not yet competent to spell.

Finally, if this Khety (or Dua-Khety, if we prefer) is the one identified by the New Kingdom scribe as "that best of them all," we can begin to see why he was held in such esteem by the elders of those in the classes at Deir el-Medina. The Instruction for Little Pepi on His Way to School has suffered more through the vagaries of its transmission and from the faults of our own misunderstanding than through the mediocrity of Khety's imagination:

It is good to study many things
    that you may learn the wisdom of great men;
Thus you can help to educate the children of the People
    while you walk according to the wise man's footsteps.
The scribe is seen as listening and obeying,
    and the listening develops into satisfaction.
Hold fast the words which hearken to these things
    as your own footsteps hurry;
And while you are on your journey,
    you need never hide your heart.
Step out on the path of learning —
    the friends of Man are your company.

Abbreviation

DeM Ostraca published in *Catalogue des ostraca hiératiques littéraire de Deir el Médineh, nos. 1410–1606*, tome 3. Georges Posener. Documents de fouilles. Cairo: Institut français d'archéologie orientale, 1978.

References

Brunner, H.
1988 *Altägyptische Weisheit: Lehren für das Leben.* Zurich: Artemis Verlag.

Foster, J. L.
1989/90 "Wordplay in *The Eloquent Peasant*: The Eighth Complaint." *Bulletin of the Egyptological Seminar* 10: 61–76.
1993 *Thought Couplets in the Tale of Sinuhe: Verse Text and Translation with an Outline of Grammatical Forms and Clause Sequences and an Essay on the Tale as Literature.* Münchner ägyptologische Untersuchungen 3. Frankfurt am Main: Peter Lang Verlag.

Helck, W.
1970 *Die Lehre des Dwꜣ-Ḫtjj.* 2 volumes. Kleine ägyptische Texte. Wiesbaden: Otto Harrassowitz.

Hoch, J.
1991/92 "The Teaching of Dua-Kheti: A New Look at the Satire of the Trades." *Society for the Study of Egyptian Antiquities Journal* 21/22: 88–100.

Holman, C. H., and W. Harmon
1992 *A Handbook to Literature.* Sixth edition. New York: Macmillan.

Lichtheim, M.
1973 *Ancient Egyptian Literature*, Volume 1: *The Old and Middle Kingdom.* Berkeley: University of California Press.

López, J.
1978–82 *Ostraca ieratici, 57001–57449*, volume 3. Catalogo del Museo Egizio di Torino. Milan: Istituto Editoriale Cisalpino.

Lowell, R.
1961 *Imitations.* New York: Farrar, Straus, and Giroux.

Posener, G.
1978 *Catalogue des ostraca hiératiques littéraire de Deir el Médineh, nos. 1410–1606*, tome 3. Documents de fouilles. Cairo: Institut français d'archéologie orientale.

Simpson, W. K.
1973 *The Literature of Ancient Egypt: An Anthology of Stories, Instructions, and Poetry.* New Edition. New Haven: Yale University Press.

12

ON FEAR OF DEATH AND THE THREE *BWTS* CONNECTED WITH HATHOR

PAUL JOHN FRANDSEN

Carsten Niebuhr Institute, Copenhagen

In many of the principal Graeco-Roman temples, shorter and longer versions of a well-known hymn to Hathor are attested.[1] The two longest and intact versions of the text, which formed part of a ritual aimed at the pacification or appeasement of Hathor,[2] are found in Dendara, located in the *salle des offrandes* (*Dendara* 7, pp. 39–43) and on the first gate of the temple of Ptah at Karnak (Legrain 1902, p. 52 ff.; Firchow 1957, pp. 134.1–135.18). In this hymn, which was recited on the twentieth day of the first month of inundation (Thoth) when the feast of drunkenness was celebrated, some very common epithets applied to the king are found as sort of a refrain: *ỉb⸗f ꜥqꜣ ẖt⸗f pw pẖꜣ⸗t(ỉ) n snk m ḥꜣty⸗f* "His heart is straight, his belly is open (i.e., free from evil), there is no darkness in his heart" (*Dendara* 7, p. 41.4–5, 7, 12).[3] In one stanza it is followed by the phrases

> *bwt⸗f pw snm n kꜣ⸗t bwt⸗f pw ḥqr ỉb bwt⸗f pw štꜣ n ʾItnt*
>
> What is *bwt* for him is the *snm* of your (i.e., Hathor) *ka*, what is *bwt* for him is (your) hunger and (your) thirst, what is *bwt* for him is the *štꜣ* of the sun goddess (*Dendara* 7, p. 41.7–8).[4]

The feast of drunkenness, with its joy, music, and dancing, apparently excluded the presence of *snm* and *štꜣ*, and the first question this paper addresses is what was meant by these two terms, including the extension *snm-ns*.[5] Subsequently, the reasons for the grouping together of these three *bwt*s are discussed.*

SNM

The meaning of *snm* must undoubtedly be found within the wider category of words meaning "mourning," "grief," and such. It is, however, a rather rare word that does not occur in any of the funerary or mortuary contexts, in which other words with the same general meaning, such as *ỉꜣkb*, are so common. It is difficult to say whether this might be due to a curious gap in our documentation. The word is known in texts earlier than the Late Period, although its distribution, so far, seems limited to two literary texts of the "Middle Kingdom." In the Admonitions of Ipuwer it is generally believed to be used four times, but none of the occurrences provide clear information as to the meaning of the term. In Admonitions of Ipuwer 1.5 the context is very fragmentary, but the

---

*This paper was written in 1995 prior to the publication of Penelope Wilson's *A Ptolemaic Lexikon: A Lexicographical Study of the Texts in the Temple of Edfu* (Orientalia Lovaniensia Analecta 78; Leuven: Peeters, 1997).

1. The texts have recently been studied and republished by Sternberg-El Hotabi 1992. To this material should be added the fragmentary version on an ostracon, O. Glasgow D.1925.91, for which see McDowell 1993, pl. 33.

2. The destructive forces could be unleashed against a "rebellion" (Yoyotte 1980/81, pp. 84–90), but the negative power was also a crucial part of the nature of that goddess; Yoyotte (1980, p. 59) in a different context says "Le propos des litanies d'Hathor-Sekhmet est donc clair: non point prier la divinité pour qu'elle écarte le mal, mais la conjurer de ne pas lâcher contre le roi et l'Égypte le mal qui est en elle."

3. For *ꜥqꜣ*, see *Wb.* 1.233:8; Otto 1964, pp. 113–14. For *pẖꜣ*, see *Wb.* 1.542:15 ff.; Otto 1964, pp. 125–26; in P. Hearst 213 *pẖꜣ ẖt* is interpreted as *rdỉ hꜣ ḏwt* "to let the evil go out" (see Deines and Westendorf 1961, p. 283); compare also Rochemonteix and Chassinat 1984, pp. 113–14, where *wꜥb* seems to substitute for *pẖꜣ*, as stated by Junker (1906, p. 111). For *ḥꜣty*, see *Wb.* 4.175; Otto 1964, pp. 148–49.

4. Compare Mariette 1870a, pl. 31; Firchow 1957, p. 134.28–29; see Junker 1906, pp. 103, 113. For the reading *ʾItnt* rather than *Rꜥt*, see Junker 1906, p. 113. Translations by Lichtheim 1980, pp. 107–08; Barucq and Daumas 1980, pp. 445–46; Sternberg-El Hotabi 1992, pp. 25–26.

5. For *snm*, see *Wb.* 4.165:4–9, "traurig sein," "trauern," "das Trauern." For *štꜣ*, see *Wb.* 4.556:1, "als etw. das verabscheut, vertrieben wird"; compare also *Wb.* 4.558:3 ff.; Vercoutter 1962, p. 41, n. (K). For *snm-ns*, see *Wb.* 1.320:17; *Wb.* 4.165:3; compare also Otto 1964, pp. 26, 148.

Gold of Praise: Studies on Ancient Egypt in Honor of Edward F. Wente
Edited by Emily Teeter and John A. Larson
Studies in Ancient Oriental Civilization 58
Chicago: Oriental Institute, 1999

meaning of the word could very well be something like to feel sorry, sad, or dejected about something. Admonitions 2.5 is usually rendered *ḥmw iry ib=sn snm.w* "the slaves of them (i.e., the former possessors of property) are sad," but surely it makes better sense to render "their hearts are filthy" or just possibly "greedy."[6] Despite a lacuna, the context of Admonitions of Ipuwer 3.4 is much less ambiguous: "Noble women roam the land and married women say 'O that we had something to eat.' Indeed, the noble women [...][7] their bodies are wretched (or squalid) in rags" (*ḥꜥw=sn snm.w m-ꜥ isyt*). P. Leiden I 344 recto 12, line 7, and the Instruction for a Man by His Son, the only other Middle Kingdom example known to me, are both transitive and less clear.[8]

The context and meaning of the late evidence is rather more precise, and the *bwt* on the behavior termed *snm* may therefore apply only to the Graeco-Roman period. In the Canopus Decree the term is used with reference to the rites of mourning performed after the death of a princess, and it is furthermore stated that this *snm* can be *swꜥb*. The Greek text is unambiguous in that for *snm* it has πένθος and the term for *swꜥb* is ἀπολύω "relieve from," "remove," "be delivered" or ἀπόλυσις.[9] That *snm* was something which must be removed or cleansed, in short, that it belonged to the category of the unclean, is supported by evidence from other sources. In the very same ritual scene at Dendara, where the king's presentation of the offering is accompanied by the hymn, his actions are, moreover, characterized as follows in the royal "Randzeile."[10]

> *ḥr yꜥ ꜥwy ḥr wꜥb ḏbꜥw ḥr bwt snm n irt Rꜥ sw mi Ḥr dr štꜣ n ꜣItnt rwi sḏb wḥꜥ ḫbnt*
>
> (The King of Upper and Lower Egypt is upon his throne ...) cleansing the hands and purifying the fingers, holding the *snm* of the Eye of Ra (Hathor) to be *bwt*. He is like Horus who drives away the *štꜣ* of the sun goddess, who removes impurities and expels crime (*Dendara* 7, p. 42.9–10).[11]

Other types of evidence are in harmony with this view. In Esna, people in the state of *snm*-misery were forbidden access to the temple in connection with the feast of taking the staff.[12] In Edfu, one of the Nile gods of the sanctuary carries the epithet *wꜥb st nb r snm* "who cleanses all places of *snm*" and Horus in the Ier chambre ouest is qualified as *wḏꜥ snm m tꜣ*.[13]

On Bab el-Abd, the gate in front of the temple of Monthu at Karnak, the king offers to Harendotes and Isis, who has the epithets:

> *mwt nṯr ... di ḥꜥw m pt wḏꜥ snm m tꜣ di sꜣ ḥr nst it=f*
>
> Mother of the god ... who puts joy in heaven and removes *snm* from the land, who puts the son on the throne of his father (Bab el-Abd 20c = Firchow 1957, p. 19.4–5).

And on the gate of Ptolemaios III Euergetes the king addresses Khonsu with the prayer:

---

6. As done, for example, by Lichtheim (1973, p. 151); compare *Wb.* 4.165:2; *pace* Helck 1995, p. 6, n. a.
7. Helck (1995, p. 12) restores a *t* and a fish after *bw* and interprets the whole as *bwt* ("Ekel [ist das Leben für (4) die Herzen] der Edelfrauen"), but neither the two published facsimiles (Hooiberg in Leemans 1846, pl. 106; Gardiner 1909, pl. 3 n. c) nor the facsimile that Maarten J. Raven kindly made for me seem to support Helck's reading. The typical *bwt*-fish is out of the question; if the "tick" above the two *n*s is read as a *t*, then what is left cannot even be read as the fish (Möller 1927, no. 253).
8. See Fecht 1972, p. 70; Fecht 1978, p. 17.
9. Canopus Decrees 26, 29 = Sethe 1904, pp. 144.11, 146.9.
10. For this literary form, see Winter 1968; Vassilika 1989, p. 8 ff.
11. For *sḏb*, see *Wb.* 4.381:7 ff.; Vernus 1979, pp. 179–80; Gunn 1927, p. 227. For the phrase, compare Mariette 1870a, pl. 31; there are many parallels to this phrase in other contexts in the material from Dendara and Edfu. In what follows, only those passages that also contain the *bwt*-element are cited:

    wnn nsw bity PN *ḥr nst=f ... ḥr yꜥ ꜥwy ḥr wꜥb ḏbꜥw ḥr bwt snm n irt Rꜥ sw m Ḥr dr štꜣ n ḥnwt=f ...* (*Dendara* 2, p. 69.12–13)

    wnn nsw bity PN *ḥr nst=f ... ḥr yꜥ ꜥwy ḥr wꜥb ḏbꜥw ḥr bwt snm n irt Rꜥ sw mi Ḥr* (*Dendara* 2, p. 78.12–14)

    wnn nsw bity PN *ḥr p=f ... ḥr yꜥ ꜥwy ḥr wꜥb ḏbꜥw ḥr bwt snm n irt Rꜥ sw mi Ḥr dr štꜣ n ꜣItnt rwi sḏb wḥꜥ ḫbnt* (*Dendara* 3, p. 82.3–5)

    wnn nsw bity PN *ḥr ḥmm=f ... ḥr yꜥ ꜥwy ḥr wꜥb ḏbꜥw ḥr bwt snm n irt Rꜥ sw mi ꜣIḥi nfr n ḥnwt.f ḥtp ib=s ḥr mꜣ ḥr=f* (*Dendara* 4, p. 246.9–11)

    wnn nsw bity PN *ḥr nst=f ... ḥr yꜥ ꜥwy ḥr wꜥb ḏbꜥw ḥr bwt snm n irt Rꜥ sw mi Ḥr* (*Dendara* 7, p. 161.9–10)

    wnn nsw bity Ptlmys ḥr nst=f ... ḥr yꜥ ꜥwy ḥr wꜥb ḏbꜥw ḥr bwt snm n irt Rꜥ sw mi Ḥr dr štꜣ n ꜣItnt rwi sḏb wḥꜥ ḫbnt (*Edfou* 4, p. 88.11–13)

    wnn nsw bity Ptlmys ḥr nst=f ... ḥr ꜥbw/wꜥb gbty ḥr twr ḥꜥw ḥr nmmty bwt gp n ḥnwt sw mi Ḥr (*Edfou* 4, p. 245.1–3). The odd *nmmty* must be a mysterious grapheme for *snm*, placed before *bwt*.
12. *nn ꜥq snm m-ḫnw ḥwt-nṯr tn* (Sauneron 1968, p. 197.18); compare Sauneron 1962, pp. 344–45.
13. Rochemonteix and Chassinat 1987a, p. 325.11–12, and idem 1984, p. 127.12, respectfully; compare also ibid., p. 320.15–16, where despite the determinative one should probably read *wꜥb=f st-wrt=k r sꜣmt*. For *sꜣmt* "mourning," see *Wb.* 4.18:10; Borghouts 1971, pp. 72–75; Janssen 1980, pp. 140–41.

> *wḏꜥ⸗k n⸗f ỉꜣt n ỉt⸗f Wsỉr ḥqꜣ⸗f nst n Wnn-nfr mꜣꜥ-ḫrw … wḏꜥ⸗k snm n mwt⸗f ꜣIst snḏm⸗k ỉb n wrḏ-ỉb*
>
> May you give judgment for the office of his father Osiris to him (Horus = the young sun god = the calf), that he may rule on the throne of Wennofre, the justified, … may you dispel the *snm* of his mother Isis, may you make glad the heart of the weary-hearted (Bab el-Amara 89c = Firchow 1957, pp. 74.24–75.1).[14]

The general picture should be clear enough. *Snm* is the wretchedness, misery, pollution, and squalor that is connected with behavior related to bereavement and death; it is incompatible with the feast of joy of Hathor and possibly also other feasts (Esna). *Snm* appears to be the opposite of rejoicing in general, and it would further seem to be on par with the state of the inert "weary-hearted" or death-bound husband of Isis (see further Firchow 1957, p. 71.12–14). When *snm* has been chased away, Horus is restored to the office of his dead father.[15]

ŠTꜣ

The third *bwt*, *štꜣ,* must be rather close in meaning to *snm*. The two terms occur in similar contexts and are often parallel, as in much of the evidence adduced above,[16] as well as in the next examples.

The king who carries the epithets already encountered in the hymn as a sort of refrain, *ꜥq ỉb ḫr mwt⸗f pẖꜣ ẖt ḫr ḥnwt⸗f n snk m ḥꜣty⸗f,* is offering to Hathor with the words:

> *sꜥr⸗ỉ n⸗t mnw m ỉryw⸗f … ḫn* [hieroglyphs] *pw ḫr ḥnwt(⸗ỉ) nḥm r snm n kꜣ⸗t bwt⸗ỉ pw štꜣ n ꜣItnt*
>
> I present to you the *mnw*-offering with its accessories … it is a dancing presentation[17] to my mistress, a deliverance from sorrow for your *ka*, the *štꜣ* of the sun goddess is my *bwt* (Bab el-Amara 85a, f = Firchow 1957, p. 71.2, 12–14).[18]

In some of the extremely concise Serapeum/Apis stelae in the Louvre, there occurs a formula in which the words under discussion are found together. In stela F, supplemented with stelae E and G, the dedicator says:

> *ỉnk bꜣk mꜣꜥt st-ỉb n nṯr ꜥꜣ štt⸗ỉ ḥꜥw⸗ỉ ḫft prt r pt ꜣb⸗ỉ*[19] *r t mw [r km hrw 4]*[20] *[wnn(⸗ỉ) ḥꜣw sd.kwỉ ḥr pḥwy⸗ỉ]*[21] *km.n(⸗ỉ) hrw 70 ḥr štꜣ* [hieroglyphs] *ḥr snm*[22] *r ḥbs(⸗ỉ) m ḫḫ⸗ỉ ỉw⸗ỉ m ỉhy rꜥ-nb*

---

14. See Clère 1961, pl. 60. See also the unpublished Philae <1622> = *Wb.* 4.165:7, where the gods make Horus the successor of his father, thus *dr⸗sn snm m tꜣ r-ḏr⸗f* "driving away the grief in the entire land"; compare Schott 1929, p. 115.13–16, where the "old" text of P. Louvre 3129 has *fdq.n⸗ỉ snm m tꜣ pn* "I gave heads to those who had no heads having brought the grief in this land to an end"; the Late Period Egyptian version of the same papyrus uses the words *šꜥd* and *ḏmꜥ*.

15. Given that "squalor," "filth," and "dirt" make up the basic semantic component of the meaning of *snm*, the extension *snm-ns* becomes perfectly intelligible (*Wb.* 2.320:17; *Wb.* 4.165:3; compare also Otto 1964, pp. 26, 148). For the collaborators of the *Wörterbuch*, the meaning of *snm-ns* was uncertain, and on the (few) *Wb-Zetteln* they rendered it "Trauer." However, while *snm* by itself does indeed seem to mean "to be sad" or "mourning," this translation does not suit the context of *snm-ns* very well, and the editors of the *Wörterbuch*, therefore, adopted the rendering "lügen, verleumden o.ä. (Gegs. Wahrheit)." Also the chronological distribution of the term is rather unusual in that, apart from one example from the late New Kingdom, the word is only known from Graeco-Roman sources and mainly from a single context, i.e., as an element of an epithet of *Maat* and gods receiving an offering of *maat*. As a typical instance, see *Edfou* 7, p. 255.9–10, where on the external side of the girdle wall at Edfu the king presents *maat* to Horus and Hathor, who are called *nbw mꜣꜥt ḥtp mꜣꜥt bwt kꜣ⸗sn snm-ns* "the lords of *maat*, who are satisfied with *maat*, and for whose *ka* it is *bwt* to malign." Similarly, see Rochemonteix and Chassinat 1987b, p. 521.5–6; *Edfou* 8, p. 122.8, (*maat*-scene on the pylon); Bab el-Amara 73d = Firchow 1957, p. 60.15 = Clère 1961, pl. 31; *Dendara* 3, p. 13.13–14 = Mariette 1870b, pl. 52 (room I, to the southeast behind sanctuary); *Dendara* 5, p. 58.8 = Mariette 1871, pl. 16a; *Dendara* 6, p. 37.10–11 = Mariette 1871, pl. 55b.

16. Compare the examples from the Hathor hymn above; see also *Dendara* 2, p. 69.12–13: *wnn nsw bỉty* PN *ḥr nst.f … ḥr yꜥ ꜥwy ḥr wꜥb ḏbꜥw ḥr* ***bwt snm n ỉrt Rꜥ*** *sw m Ḥr* ***dr štꜣ*** [hieroglyphs] *n ḥnwt.f …* ; *Dendara* 3, p. 82.3–5: *wnn nsw bỉty* PN *ḥr p.f … ḥr yꜥ ꜥwy ḥr wꜥb ḏbꜥw ḥr* ***bwt snm n ỉrt Rꜥ*** *sw m Ḥr* ***dr štꜣ*** [hieroglyphs] ***n ꜣItnt*** *rwỉ sḏb wḥꜥ ḫbnt*; *Edfou* 4, p. 88.11–13: *wnn nsw bỉty Ptlmys ḥr nst.f … ḥr yꜥ ꜥwy ḥr wꜥb ḏbꜥw ḥr* ***bwt snm n ỉrt Rꜥ*** *sw mỉ Ḥr* ***dr štꜣ*** [hieroglyphs] ***n ꜣItnt*** *rwỉ sḏb wḥꜥ ḫbnt.*

17. For *bwt⸗ỉ*, there can be little doubt that the extant sign should be replaced by the *bwt*-fish. For the *mnw*-offering, see Guglielmi 1991, p. 85. In the context of this rendering of the rite, *ḫn* may not be too farfetched; see Gutbub 1961, pp. 55–69; Wild 1963, p. 109, no. 100, *passim*.

18. See Clère 1961, pl. 68.

19. There are traces of *ꜣb*, but the verb is in any case preserved in the other versions of this text. For the transitive use of *ꜣb*, see Vercoutter 1962, p. 30, n. (H); Caminos 1977, p. 19, nn. 3–5.

20. Only in stelae E and G.

21. Only stela E. Stela F has nothing, and stela G has a different version. For the interpretation, see Jansen-Winkeln 1994, p. 36, n. h.

22. Stela E has *ḫpr.kwỉ mm šwꜣw ḥr šṯ ḥr sꜣmt*, and stela G has *ḫpr[.k]wỉ m-ꜥ ḥwrw ḥr šṯ ḥr sꜣmt.*

I am a true servant, a favorite of the great god (Apis), one who wrapped his body when (it, i.e., Apis) went to heaven; I deprived myself of bread and water [for four whole days. I was naked being dressed only on my behind] and completed the 70 days of grief and mourning until my throat was coated, as I was in cries of woe every day ... (Louvre IM. 4051 = Vercoutter 1962, doc. F, lines 3–5).[23]

As already indicated, the verb *sꜣm* "to mourn" seems to have replaced *snm* in the formulae found in Serapeum stelae E and G, while the writing of *štꜣ*  in the same two versions looks like the verb *št* used in the first of these mourning formulae.[24] One cannot help wondering, therefore, whether these writings represent the same word.[25] Among the six examples of the phrase "driving away the *štꜣ* of the sun goddess (or "his mistress") or holding it to be *bwt*," only *Edfou* 4 (p. 88.13) and *Dendara* 7 (p. 41.8) have the writing *št*. In the same phraseology we meet the word *snm*. But since *snm* and *sꜣm* are likely to be two different words one just might have two related, yet different sequences: *sꜣm* - *št* and *snm* - *štꜣ*.

On the basis of this evidence, however, it does not seem possible to determine a more precise sense of *štꜣ*. It occurs together with, and has the same determinative as, several words meaning "mourning" or the like. In connection with the goddess (*ꜣItnt* or *ḥnwt*), it is something that must be *bwt* or driven away, in the same way as the *snm* of the goddess (*ỉrt Rʿ*) must be forced away or held to be *bwt*.

Summing up the evidence, we may say that the behavior denoted by the terms *snm* and *štꜣ* was one of mourning. In the Graeco-Roman temples that behavior was *bwt* during certain religious feasts — notably those of Hathor and her hypostases — of which drinking and joy, music and dancing, and plenitude and abundance were an essential part. Whatever the specific character of the *snm*-behavior, it is of the "earth" as opposed to "heaven," and its element of pollution may be *swʿb, wʿb r, wḏʿ, fdq*, or *dr*, in short, separated and removed.

ḤQR ꜣIB

The *bwt* on "hunger" and "thirst" must also refer to Hathor because the king is said not to have cut short her loaves nor to have diminished her bread (*n ỉw.n⸗f m t⸗ṯ n nh.n⸗f m wḫꜣ⸗t*),[26] an act that in itself would be considered *bwt*. This interpretation may also be borne out by the fact that the text was intended for use during the joyful feast of drunkenness and, as far as Dendara is concerned, was found in the *salle des offrandes*.[27] It is, furthermore, not inconceivable that bread and beer, and thus hunger and thirst, may have yet another non-material connotation. The passage in question occurs in a text that deals with the offerings of food, and the dancing and singing of the king as a part of the presentation. Dancing and the performance of music can be said to be the nourishment of Hathor, the goddess of music and dancing, who in the cult would receive an offering consubstantial with the goddess herself (Frandsen 1989). This may be inferred from the dancing presentation itself but is explicitly stated to be so in a scene from the kiosk at Medamud, where the accompanying hymn opens with the words:

> *mỉ⸗t nwbty wnm m ḥsy gr t ỉb⸗s pw ỉbꜣ*
>
> Come, Golden One, who feeds on music making, because the bread of her heart is dancing (Drioton 1927, pp. 25–27, text no. 328).[28]

23. New edition of the texts by Jansen-Winkeln 1994.
24. For an important discussion of the word *sꜣm*, see Borghouts 1971, pp. 72–75; compare also Jansen-Winkeln 1994, p. 37, n. k. For the mourning formulae, see *Wb.* 4.558:3 ff.; Vercoutter 1962, p. 29, n. (E), who renders the formula "j'ai pris le deuil"; compare also the writings of *Wb.* 4.559:3 ff., "sanctuary."
25. See Borghouts 1971, pp. 60–61, for the opinion that several words written *štyw* and *štwꜣ* are simply derivatives of *štꜣ* "hidden" or "mysterious."
26. *Dendara* 7, p. 41.6–7 (sic!, *pace Wb.* 2.280:12, which reads *nh n⸗f*). Compare (I am one of your [Ptah's] servants) *šw ṯs sḫr bwt⸗k (s)šr mw n qbḥwt⸗k ḥtpw m ʿb[ꜣ⸗k] dꜣ rꜣ m šbt⸗k wʿb* "free of all fault, who has kept at a distance/kept away from your *bwt*s; to diminish the water from your cool water and the offerings from your offering table, as well as eating your pure food" (CG 807 = Borchardt 1930, p. 105 top, Twenty-sixth Dynasty). I owe this example, its reading, and its interpretation to the kindness of Herman de Meulenaere. Further, in the list of *bwt*s in P. Jumilhac XII, lines 16 ff.: *ḫbꜣ ḥtp-nṯr n pr⸗f* (XII, lines 18–19 = Vandier 1961, p. 123); similar to Chassinat 1990, p. 256, line 3: *bwt.sn pw ḫbỉ ḥt*. For the interdiction in general, see Maystre 1937, p. 38; Gutbub 1973, p. 149 ff.
27. For the position of the other versions, see Sternberg-El Hotabi 1992, pp. 9–18, 30, Abb. Compare also the Festival Calendar from Esna, where on Paophi 4 (2 *ꜣḫt* 4) it is said that *nṯrt m hrw pn nbtww bwt⸗s ḥqr ib* "the goddess of this day is *nbtww* for whom hunger and thirst is *bwt*" (Sauneron 1963, text no. 55.3; cf. Sauneron 1962, pp. 13–14).
28. For *wnm*, possibly read *qq*, here written with the two bags, which was apparently also the interpretation of Daumas (Barucq and Daumas 1980, p. 443). For *ỉb⸗s*, the emendation to *ṯ* suggested by Barucq and Daumas (1980, p. 443, n. a) is unnecessary. For the phrase, compare Firchow 1957, p. 71.12–14.

Be this as it may, the *bwt* on hunger and thirst with regard to the festive occasions of Hathor and the appeasement of other goddesses is well attested. On the southwestern door post of the Ptolemaic gate to the Mut enclosure at Karnak, a very fragmentary scene is accompanied by this two-line inscription:

> (Line 1) *wsḫt nbt wnm ḥnwt sꜥm wrt ꜥꜣbt ꜥšꜣt mrr nbt ỉꜣw ꜥšꜣt ꜣpdw kꜣw* [*ḥr*] *ḫt ꜣpdw ḥr ḏbꜥ qnt pḥ.n=s pt bwt=s ḥqr ỉb* ??? *pw dḫn* ///
>
> (Line 1) Court, the possessor of food, mistress of consumption, great of provisions, with numerous offerings, the lady of cows, with numerous fowl, oxen on flame and fowl on the fire, the smoke of the fat, it reached the sky, hunger and thirst are *bwt* for her(?), is it for making music(?) (Sauneron 1983, pl. 19).

For line 2, I can do no better than quote Sauneron's translation:

> (Line 2) Come, "jouons de la harpe ronde et droite pour elle, tambourinons pour elle, jouons de la harpe pour elle, [...], faisons pour elle les danses *nfr, ỉhb, ꜣb, ksks, ḫnt,* faisons pour elle la lutte au bâton et la danse des singes de Mout-Sekhmet pour [elle] sans qu'ait de cesse la figure chorégraphique que nous faisons pour elle" (Sauneron 1983, p. 21, text 29).

In the Festival Calendar from Esna, the entry on Paophi 4 (2 *ꜣḫt* 4) says that this day is the:

> *gm.n.tw ỉrt Ḥr m bꜣ=s m bꜣḫ nṯrt m hrw pn Nbt-ww bwt=s ḥqr ỉb*
>
> (Feast of *Gm-bꜣw=s* [Hathor]). Thanks to her power, the Eye of Horus was found on the eastern mountain. The goddess of this day is Nebetuu (Hathor), for whom hunger and thirst is *bwt* (Sauneron 1963, text no. 55.3).[29]

Hunger and thirst are obviously very concrete conditions, and as such they were associated with ideas and behavior connected with death. Lack of space precludes an in-depth discussion of all the relevant aspects of this problem, and we therefore confine ourselves first to a brief mention of the abstention from drinking and eating as parts of the ritual behavior of mourning, and second to discussing the fear of hunger and thirst as a real (threat of) punishment of the dead that is nothing but a vital component of the more comprehensive reversal theme, which in turn is closely connected with the fear of "true" death.

FASTING

In a general way, the connection between hunger and thirst and the observance of (rites of) mourning is well attested.[30] Thus in the Prophecies of Neferti, we have the well-known passage in which it is said that:

> One will make arrows of copper and request bread with blood; one will laugh loudly at a sick man and will not shed a tear for the dead; one will not participate in a wake fasting for a dead (*nn sḏr.tw ḥqr.w n mwt*), each man's heart is concerned with himself (Helck 1970, 9a–c).

And in a magical text from the New Kingdom against scorpion bites we find another reference to abstention from eating and drinking as a part of the mourning process:

> *nn dỉ=ỉ ḥw Ḥꜥpy ḥr mryt nn dỉ=ỉ wbn Šw ḥr sꜣtw nn dỉ=ỉ ḫpr prt nn ỉr=ỉ ỉr.tw bỉt nn dỉ=ỉ ꜥṯḥ dsw n tꜣ 365 n nṯrw nty sḏr ḥqr.w wrš* {*ḥqr*} *<ỉb> tw grḥ qrs Wsỉr*
>
> (As for the night when the wife of Horus bites you,) I will not let Hapy overflow the bank, I will not let Shu rise over the earth, I will not let the seed germinate, I will not let bread be made, I will not let jars be brewed for these 365 gods who spend the night fasting and the day being thirsty (i.e., who observe the requirements of mourning) on the night of burying Osiris (P. Turin 1993 verso 5, lines 1–4 = Pleyte and Rossi 1869–76, p. 137, lines 1–4).[31]

29. For the goddess Nebetuu, who is but one hypostasis of the pacified Eye of the Sun that has returned to Egypt, see *LÄ* 4 "Nebet-uu," cols. 363–64. For the phrase, see Sauneron 1962, pp. 13–14; compare also Grimm 1994, pp. 35, 243–44, where the *gm*-passage is rendered "Finden des Horusauges mit seinem Glanz im Ostgebirge."

30. Compare, for example, Desroches-Noblecourt 1947, pp. 216–18; Posener 1956, pp. 151–52, mentioning the texts to follow; Vercoutter 1962, texts C–G; Jansen-Winkeln 1994. See also the well-known passage in the Leiden letter to a dead wife, in which the husband says that after her death he spent "many, many months without eating and drinking as an ordinary human being" (P. Leiden I 371 verso, lines 30–31).

31. For this papyrus, see Borghouts 1987; idem 1978, no. 115. Compare also Gardiner 1935, p. 56, n. 1. For the wives of Horus, see Ritner 1998.

The co-text mentioning the prohibition on making bread and beer requires substituting *i͗b* for the second *ḥqr*, and for this emendation some confirmation may be found in the next example, even though it is of a much later date and despite the fact that there the association is "day-hunger" and "night-thirst." In this text, which was recently dubbed *Le livre de parcourir l'éternité* by its latest editor, the context of the relevant passages would seem to narrow down the range of pertinent mourning ceremonies to those related to the embalming process. The deceased is told:

> *nb n.k sꜥḥ šps m i͗rw.f hrw ẖw ꜥḥꜥw=f … sr.ti͗ n=k sr i͗n nṯrw sḥ-nṯr hrw pẖr sṯꜣt … mꜣꜣ=k ꜣIry-mḥ ḥr srq m tbn hrw pfy n sḏfꜣ wtṯw=f wrš ḥqr sḏr i͗b bwt kꜣ=k wꜣw r ḥm=k*
>
> A mummy, august of form, is fashioned for you on the day of protecting his body, … , the *sr*-tambourine is beaten for you by the gods of the god's booth on the day of traversing the necropolis … . You will see *ꜣIry-mḥ* beating the *tbn*-tambourine on the day of providing for his begetter; passing the day fasting and the night thirsty is the *bwt* of your *ka* — be it far from your person (P. Leiden T. 32, VI, lines 2–3, 5, 11–13 = Herbin 1994, pp. 465, 467, 64, 222).[32]

While the general avoidance of eating and drinking as a part of the funerary rites obviously has some bearing on the ban on behavior related to mourning during the Hathoric feasts of joy, it can hardly explain why the hunger and thirst of Hathor should be the *bwt* of the king, and we must therefore approach the problem from a different angle.

FEAR OF HUNGER AND THIRST

The demand for the vital offerings is well attested in all periods and thus one example suffices to illustrate the fear that the deceased shall have nobody making offerings for him and that he shall therefore suffer hunger and thirst. Having specified the details of his donation of land to a statue of Ramesses VI in Nubia, the Deputy of *Wawat, Pn-ni͗wt,* concludes the document with a threat to anyone who might want to dispute this arrangement:

> As for anyone who shall speak against it, Amun-Ra, king of the gods, shall be after him in order to destroy him, Mut shall be after his wife, Khonsu (shall) be after his child, so that he shall hunger and be thirsty, he shall become weak and he shall suffer want (*ḥqr=f i͗b=f gꜣb=f i͗ꜣd=f*) (KRI 6, 351.15–352.2).

In the Late Period, death is often described as a tantalizing state in which the dead is surrounded by water, yet suffers thirst. A precursor of this attitude may be seen in one of the inscriptions of the royal scribe Nebneteru (Twenty-second Dynasty), who, in the frequently quoted inscription from the left side of his Cairo statue says:

> I spent my lifetime in heart's delight, without worry, without illness. I made my days festive with wine and myrrh having banished inertness from my heart,[33] for I knew of the darkness in the valley. He who does his heart's wish is no fool. … How happy is he who spends his life in following his heart in the favor of Amun. … I had surpassed the lifetime of everyone in my time when I reached the valley (of death) in his favor. The land was in lamentation when I passed away, there was no difference between my surviving relatives and (the lamentation of) the people.[34] Do not worry lest something like it may happen (*m mḥ sꜣw ḫpr mi͗tt=f*). Mourning is for him who lives with head on the knee. Do not be tight-fisted (*m ḫns ꜥ*) with what you have. Do not act empty-handed (*m i͗r šw ꜥ*) with your property. Do not sit in the hall of worry foretelling the morrow before it has come (*m ḥms m sḥ n ḥꜣm-i͗b ḥr sr dwꜣ n i͗w<t>=f*). Do not deny the eye of its water lest it come back threefold.[35] Do not sleep when the sun is in the east (*m sḏr i͗w i͗tn m i͗ꜣbt*). Do not thirst next to the beer (*m i͗b r-gs ḥnkt*). … The heart is a god, his chapel the stomach, he rejoices when the limbs are in their feast (*nṯr pw i͗b kꜣr=f m rꜣ-i͗b msẖꜣ=f ḥꜥw m ḥb=sn*) (Cairo 42225, e, 4–11).[36]

The stela of Isenkhebe in Leiden, dated to the Saite period, has this description of the situation:

> *sḏr.ki͗ m i͗nt m ḥwnt i͗b.kwi͗ i͗w mw r-gs=i͗ ꜣrw=i͗(?) [or ꜣr wi͗(?)] m ẖt n nw ḫpr ꜥn.k(wi͗) r pr=i͗ m ktt n sꜣ=i͗ i͗m=f snkt bwt n nẖn ꜥr wy sy ḥr=i͗ mnd tp rꜣ=i͗ … i͗nk ẖt i͗wty wn=s*

32. For identification of the musical instruments, see Hickmann 1955, p. 596; Ziegler 1979, p. 71.

33. Despite the arguments adduced by Jansen-Winkeln (1985, p. 131, n. 54), I follow in the wake of Lorton (1968, p. 44).

34. For this rendering, see Jansen-Winkeln 1985, p. 132, n. 60.

35. I follow Jansen-Winkeln (1985, pp. 133–34, nn. 64–65).

36. See Jansen-Winkeln 1985, pp. 498, 117 ff., for translation and bibliography.

> I spent the night in the valley (of death) being (but) a small girl and suffered from thirst though there was water beside me. I was snatched away in childhood, before the (proper, i.e., "my") time had come, having turned my back to my house as a kid, before I had had my fill in it. Darkness — the *bwt* of a child — came upon me, while the breast was still in my mouth … . I am an innocent young girl (Leiden V, 55.2–6).[37]

And finally, in the famous stela of Taimhotep, dated to the very end of the Ptolemaic period, death is lamented in these terms:

> O my brother, my husband, friend, and high priest, may your heart not be tired of drinking and eating, of getting drunk and making love, have a wonderful day and follow your heart day and night … . The West, it is a land in sleep, darkness weighs on the dwelling place, those who are there are asleep in their mummy-form (*kkw dns [m] st-ḥms nꜣ nty ỉm qd m sm≈sn*),[38] they do not wake up to see their brothers, they see not their fathers nor their mothers, their hearts miss their wives and their children. The water of life in which there is fertile soil / nourishment for everyone, it is thirst for me (*mw ꜥnḫ nty tꜣ* [𓇾 or 𓇿] *r nb ỉm≈f ỉbt pw ḫr≈ỉ*), it comes to him who is upon earth, but for me there is thirst, although there is water at my side (*ỉy≈f r* [written *ỉw*] *nty ḥr-tp tꜣ ỉbt n≈ỉ mw r-gs≈ỉ*). I do not know where it is since I came to the entrance of this valley. O give me water that flows, say to me: "May your person not be far from water" (BM 147.15–18).[39]

The theme of fear of hunger and thirst is encountered already in the Pyramid Texts and the Coffin Texts, but there it is integrated in a wider theme of the world reversed. A few examples must suffice to give an idea of the content of this material.

> Hunger is what PN *bwt*s, he does not eat it. Thirst is what PN *bwt*s, he does not drink it. PN is indeed he who will give[40] bread to those who exist, and *ꜣIat* is his wet nurse. It is she who makes him live and it was she who bore PN. PN was conceived in the night and he was born in the night. He belongs to those who are in the suite of Ra before the morning star. PN was conceived in the primaeval waters (*nw*) and he was born in the primaeval waters. It is with the bread of those[41] that he found there that he has come to you (Sethe 1908, §§131a–132d = Pyramid Text Spell 211).[42]

---

37. See Boeser 1915, pl. 15, no. 13; Erman 1915; for new copy and translation of text, see Jansen-Winkeln 1993, pp. 44–46 (I owe this reference to Herman de Meulenaere). For further bibliography and translation, see Lichtheim 1980, pp. 58–59, to which should be added Meulenaere 1962, pp. 135–36.

38. Following Lichtheim 1980, p. 64, nn. 14–15. With Erman and Lichtheim, I would read 𓇋𓅓𓀁𓏥 as *ỉm*.

39. See Reymond 1981, p. 171. For further bibliography and translation, see Lichtheim 1980, pp. 62–63, to which should be added Bianchi 1988, cat. 122; Ockinga 1988.

40. *Pace* Schenkel 1987, p. 275 ff.; Schenkel adduces two arguments of which the first one concerns the structure of the sentence. In Schenkel's opinion *Wnỉs pỉ wnnt rdỉ≈f tꜣ n ntyw* cannot possibly be a cleft sentence because this would allegedly require the presence of an *ỉn*; otherwise we would have a "Neuägyptizismus, wenn nicht Koptizismus." This, however, is not absolutely necessary; see already Gunn 1924, p. 49; Polotsky 1976, pp. 16–17; Doret 1990, §§6.2, 6.3. Compare also Allen 1984, pp. 189–90. Compare also, for what it is worth, the *N* version of this passage *swt wnnt dỉ t n ntyw*. Schenkel's second argument is more interesting. According to his understanding of the passage, the king is supposed to be the recipient of the bread, and Schenkel therefore emends the text of Unas so that we get *Wnỉs pỉ wnnt rdỉ* <*n*>*≈f tꜣ n ntyw* "W. ist in der Tat einer, <dem> das Brot der Lebenden gegeben wird." Schenkel further substantiates this interpretation by referring to the *S* version, where the *n* is preserved (Hayes 1937, pl. 5, 308). But this interpretation is by no means without problems. First, the remaining Pyramid Texts must be emended into <*n≈f*>. Second, if *S* has the "correct" version it must derive from a source other than the extant Pyramid Texts and since *T*, *M*, and *N* cannot have the Unis version as their *Vorlage*, one may infer that the Unis version, the other "original" Pyramid Texts, and the Sesostris-ankh version are independent copies from a common source, in which case those who copied two of the three versions (Unis and the other Pyramid Texts) made similar mistakes when copying from the original. Third, and most importantly, the proposed emendation creates a very serious problem of overall interpretation, as Schenkel himself seems to have realized at the end of his discussion. Schenkel translates Pyramid Text 132d "… indem er [the king] euch (*d.i.* den Göttern […]) das Brot derer bringt … " and he then writes "Handelt es sich bei dem Brot, das der Verstorbene den Göttern mitbringt um das 131e [!, read c] genannte 'Brot der Seienden,' das Unas dort für sich selbst reklamiert, so sind 'die, die er im Nun antraf' eben diese Seienden: Das Brot ist das, das er von unten, aus dem Land der Seienden bzw., aus dem Nun, beim Aufstieg zum Himmel mitnehmen will und von dem er den Göttern im Gefolge des Re etwas abgibt, um diese bei guter Laune zu halten - wenn er selbst sich als Re an ihre Spitze setzt" (Schenkel 1987, p. 278). This interpretation is really the only one that makes sense and consequently the king must also be the "subject" of the action in 131c. For the relationship between the Unis and the *S* versions, see now Kahl 1995.

41. Literally "bringing to you the bread of [or perhaps "for," i.e., meant for?] those" … .

42. For *nw*, see Allen 1988, pp. 4 ff., 20. This spell was recently the subject of a somewhat inordinate amount of grammatical discussion; see, for example, Westendorf 1981; Frandsen 1986, especially p. 150 ff.; Depuydt 1986, especially p. 105; Schenkel 1987; Doret 1992, especially p. 66 ff. For further discussions of this sentence type, see Barta 1993.

HUNGER, THIRST, AND REVERSALS

In the Coffin Texts, this repertoire is expanded in a more systematic way so as to be inseparable from the idea of being or having to walk upside down (*sḫd*). After death the dead was in a quandary. The threshold of death is associated with many fears and temptations and the reversal texts lend themselves to the interpretation that one of the dangers is to be offered the possibility of living a life "merely" as an antipode[43] because this is what the invitations to accept un-normal food purports to imply. The link between being upside down and consuming faeces and other detestable things is clear, even though modern reflections as to the precise nature of this link have given rise to speculations not quite unlike those concerning the hen and the egg. The reversed position might, according to Kees, be derived "Aus der Analogie mit der gestirnhaften Wanderung des Verklärten, vor allem der Gleichsetzung mit den Sternen" in the Pyramid Texts,[44] so that one "wenn man eines dieser auf den Kopf gestellten Wesen ist, gezwungen sein könnte, mit dem Kopf auf der Erde schleifend den Kot in den Mund zu bekommen" (Kees 1956, p. 199).[45]

Zandee and Hornung, on the other hand, have argued that an upside-down position necessarily entails a reversed direction of the functioning of the bowels so that the mouth serves as the anus (Zandee 1960, pp. 73–77; Hornung 1968, p. 13). However, although the determinative normally accompanying the verb *sḫd* represents a man in an upside-down position, it is not quite certain that this simple image is always a true picture of what it really means to be reversed because the very idea of a "Gegenhimmel" also implies that a part of the universe is of necessity upside down. This comes out quite clearly in the so-called Schlussszenen (Hornung 1979 and 1981), the oldest of which are roughly contemporaneous with the oldest version of the Book of the Dead 101. In these images that try to grasp, and shape, the eternal and daily cycle of the sun, the components are made in such a way that the image can be read both ways. And thus, in the famous version from the Book of Gates, Nun and Osiris are depicted so that the latter is always shown upside down vis-à-vis the former.

In the Coffin Texts, we have descriptions like an "evil being ... who lives on his urine," whose "tongue is in his crotch," and whose "phallus is in his mouth" (*ns⸗k m ṯt⸗k ḥnn⸗k m r3⸗k*) (*CT* 6, p. 332g–i, Spell 698).[46] And in another spell, the dead is told that if he refuses, as he does, to eat faeces and walk upside down, then he will not be able to join Ra because this requires acceptance of a reversed world:

> (146) Excrement is *bwt* for me, I will not eat for you. Urine is *bwt* for me, I will not drink for you. Walking upside down is *bwt* for me, and I will not perform the offering recitation for you.
>
> What will you live on (147) at this place to which you have come? Can't you see[47] these seven transfigured spirits who lift up Ra, who show Ra,[48] who live on excrement (148) and quench their thirst with urine, and who walk upside down (*f33w Rꜥ ddw Rꜥ ꜥnḫw m ḥs ḥtm ỉbw⸗sn m wsst šmw sḫdw*)?
>
> Then this PN shall say that he rejects those seven transfigured spirits who lift up Ra ... (*ḏd.k3* PN *ny⸗f 3ḫw 7 f33w Rꜥ* ...) (*CT* 3, pp. 146–49b, Spell 205).

In short, the real danger expressed in these reversal texts, whether phrased in negative or, less often perhaps, positive formulae, was the attempt to talk the dead into believing that his salvation was dependent on his acceptance of the idea of life beyond death as being but a reversal of this-worldly life. The dead is constantly

43. Sethe (1922, p. 37) was probably the first to come up with the connection between *sḫd* and the "Antipodenvorstellung von der Unterwelt, über der sich ein Gegenhimmel [hieroglyph] wölbte."

44. Compare Sethe 1910, §1516b: *sỉꜥ⸗ṯ pt n* PN *sḫdḫd⸗ṯ n⸗f sb3w* "that you may present the sky to the king and hang up the stars for him."

45. Similarly, see van de Walle 1953, p. 178, n. 2; Ritner 1993, pp. 83, 168.

46. Compare also the description of the demon *sh3qq* found in P. BM 10731 verso, line 1, for which see Edwards 1968; O. Leipzig 42; O. Gardiner 300; Černý and Gardiner 1957, pls. 3.1, 91.1, respectively: "Turn back, *sh3qq*, who has come forth from heaven and earth, whose eyes are in his head, whose tongue is in his anus (*ꜥrt*) and who eats the bread of his buttocks." Compare also Borghouts 1978, no. 22.

47. Reading *n m3.n⸗k*; alternatively one might read *n(n) m3n⸗k*, as does Barguet 1986, p. 397. Faulkner (1973, p. 167) translates "There will not look at you those seven spirits ... ."

48. This rendering of *ddw rꜥ*, which is also that of Faulkner (1973, p. 167), is not totally clear to me. Barguet (1986, p. 397) translates: "qui offrent Rê." For *dỉ* with the sense "to show," see Caminos 1977, p. 57, n. 6. For the present writer it is extremely tempting to translate "seven spirits, who lift up Ra, whom Ra causes to live on excrement, to quench their thirst with urine, and to walk upside down." The objection to this interpretation is not so much the role that the passage would then attribute to Ra. Witness, for example, the beginning of Spell 214 (*CT* 3, p. 173a) where Khnum is said to be the purveyor of excrement ("not to walk upside down, to repel Khnum who brings excrement"). The real problem is one of grammar since this translation requires a reading such as *ddw rꜥ ꜥnḫ.w ... ḥtm.w ... šm.w ...* , which is hardly possible.

being enticed into accepting the reversals as the norm,[49] and he is even told that the food he is offered derives from none other than Horus and Seth: "Why will you not eat excrement and drink urine from the bottom of Horus and Seth?" goes the question in Spell 220. But it is precisely at this point that the dead must be able to distinguish. The world reversed must be rejected because it embodies chaos and evil, and the dead knows that the gods have no place in it. *ỉr ḏd=k wnm nn wnm.kꜣ Rʿ šṯw* "If you say 'Eat this,' then Ra would have to eat tortoises" (*CT* 5, p. 30e–f, Spell 368).[50] Or *nṯr nb ḏd wnm=ỉ bwt=ỉ wnm=f ḥnʿ=ỉ* "(Excrement are *bwt* for me and I will not drink its sister urine.) Each god who tells me to eat that which is *bwt* for me, may he eat with me" (*CT* 6, p.198n–p, Spell 581).

REVERSALS AND DEATH

In the world of the Coffin Texts, conception of the hereafter is infinitely more complex and differentiated than the cosmography and cosmology of the Pyramid Texts, which is undoubtedly due to the fact that the possibility of eternal participation in the cosmos was extended to people of non-royal status. The hereafter encountered in the Coffin Texts is in many ways a true reflection of the community from which the dead had recently departed. And just as the earlier part of his life on earth had been a process of socialization into the Egyptian society, he must now prove that he is in possession of the necessary qualifications, and thus identity, to be integrated into the otherworld. There is an enormous body of knowledge that he must master in order to attain his goal. It goes without saying that he must know the way to get there and the means to avoid or pacify dangers in the shape of demons or bird-catchers that will try to prevent him from reaching it. But nothing is as important as being able to partake of the nourishment of those who live in that realm because this more than anything else shows that the dead has become "one of them." Sharing food is a metonymic act in most societies. If food is offered and accepted, if one can eat together, the most important step in social acceptance will have been taken — as may be observed everyday in contemporary society where some people claim that they have nothing against immigrants and refugees, they just don't like their food and the way it smells. And the Egyptians were no exception.[51] The prominent role that interrogations concerning nourishment therefore seems to play in the reversal texts does not mean that this is what they "really" are about. Statements about the social importance of food abound in that material. The food of the dead is said to come from the offering table of Ra in Heliopolis, the dead eats together with the gods and so on. However, of all the phrases that deal with reception of food the most central are those referring to the "portions" reserved for the dead. In these formulae, there is an insistence on the equal relevance of food given on earth and in the otherworld. The distribution is nearly always in terms of an uneven number, and even though no one so far has been able to account for this phenomenon (cf. Cannuyer 1991) it does not affect the basic conception behind those formulae, that is, the insistence on the fundamental importance of a full integration into the ordered cosmos of the Egyptians, i.e., into this world as well as into the otherworld. But while the societal knowledge about the role of food is of crucial importance in itself, it is certainly not new. What is novel is the relevance of these social acts for the salvation of the individual and hence the necessity of gaining access to the knowledge relevant to this dimension of existence.

The dead is in a state of transition, and in that so-called liminal phase he is subjected to a number of trials and tribulations. Interrogations are one of the ordeals that the dead must go through in order to prove himself a god, and in the reversal texts he must show himself able to distinguish *mꜣʿt* from *ỉsft,* or between cosmic life and cosmic death. By virtue of its metonymic character food is one of the principal means of putting his ability to a test. He is in a state of want and, still in terms of a metonymy, hunger and is therefore encouraged to eat what purports to be the life-giving food of the otherworld. "Eat," they repeatedly say to him in Spell 173, whereby he

---

49. Compare also "... O, young man, who cries out: 'Excrement!,' do not bring <your> excrement to me" (*CT* 3, p. 99b–c, Spell 191) and "Keep away from me, bearer of excrement" (*CT* 3, p. 111c, Spell 193). See further "O excrement, your name is not excrement" (*CT* 3, p. 125b, Spell 200); spell with heading "Not to walk upside down, to repel Khnum who brings excrement" (*CT* 3, p. 173a, Spell 214); Spell for Not Walking Upside Down: *sẖdẖd=ỉ sẖsdẖd=f* "If I am upside down then he will be upside down," *šm=ỉ ʿḥʿ.kwỉ n šm=ỉ sẖd.kwỉ* "I will walk upright; I will not walk upside down" (*CT* 5, pp. 28d–30g, Spell 367).

50. For the tortoise as a representative of evil, see van de Walle 1953, p. 178 ff.; Säve-Söderbergh 1956.

51. This is thus the reason for the specific mention of a case to the contrary, dictated by the exigencies of politics, regarding a meal shared by the Hittites and Egyptians celebrating the marriage between Ramesses II and a daughter of the Hittite king; see KRI 2, 251.4: "They ate and drank together being as one heart and like brothers."

is being offered the possibility of integration into a new social community. That food stands for something much more far reaching is not an inference made on the basis of some comparative cross-cultural model. The metonymic character comes out quite clearly in the answers to the invitation to eat, in which the dead insists on his divine aspirations instead of talking about food. Without being properly equipped with knowledge — *ʿpr* is the technical term[52] — the dead would not be able to ensure his own salvation.

In one of the reversal spells, we have a passage in which all the essential elements would seem to be brought together. The text is Spell 1011, known so far, only from P. Gardiner II:

> (226d) O you two pillars (*ỉwnwy*) of Ra between whom I go out and enter (*prr=ỉ ʿq=ỉ*), my hair being put up, my braided lock hanging down (*šnw=ỉ ʿḥʿ[.w] ḥnskt=ỉ sḫdḫd[.w]*), because I am one whose mouth is pure and whose teeth are healthy (*rwd*) and what is *bwt* for me is that which is *ỉsft* to Atum (*bwt=ỉ pw ỉsft n Tm*), because I am one provisioned (*ỉmȝḫ*) and am a *tknw*,[53] the possessor of seven portions in Heliopolis. Three portions of mine are in the house of Horus; two portions of mine are in the house of Seth; two portions of mine are on earth with Geb. It is the day-bark that brings (them) to me from upon the altars of the gods.
>
> O you great gods who are on your (*sn*) standards, I will not eat excrement for you nor drink urine, I will not go upside down for you, because I am Ra, the possessor of his eyes, I will not eat what Geb lifts up,[54] I will have no contact (*ḫm*) with that on which those who are in Nun live.
>
> O you doorkeeper, Plunderer of the Two Lands, make me a path in it that I may pass. I am one of those who wash their mouths and chew myrrh, and who live on Maat. Make me a path in it that I may live on what they live on, (227) in that I am alive and flourishing forever, going and coming between the two pillars (*ỉwnwy*) of Ra and the two pillars (*ḏd*) of Geb,[55] my hair being put up, my braided lock hanging down. Efflux is *bwt* for me, I will not eat [...], I will live on the sweet things that are issued from the shrine. Awake, you early risers, you who are in Kenzet, before the Bittern who went up from the orchard and Wepwawet who emerged from Siut(!). Excrement stands in awe of me, urine stands at a respectful distance from me, just as Thoth stands in awe of the dead  (*CT* 7, pp. 226d–27j, Spell 1011).[56]

The last part of the quotation contains one of the later versions of the Pyramid Text Spell 210, but for the present purpose the principal interest lies in the parallelism between the two sets of phrases in which the deceased lays claim to unhindered passage between one or two sets of pillars marking the path between earth and sky. The demand is based on assertions of purity, explicitly or through the well-known *bwt*-phrases, and the comparison of the two phrases leaves no doubt that the essence of the protestations are to be found in the clause where the *ỉsft* of Atum is said to be *bwt* for the dead.

This opposition is the heart of these spells: the dead must be cognizant of this crucial set of opposites, that is, know as much — and probably no more — about the elements of *ỉsft* as to be able to reject them. This is the essential point of all these spells that otherwise come under the more comprehensive heading of "salvation

52. Compare this Coffin Text example: "Come (*ỉw*) as an equipped transfigured spirit!" says Orion to me, *ỉw ʿpr.n=k ȝḫw=sn nbw n smḫ=k ỉm m ṯw ỉy.t(ỉ) ȝḫ.t(ỉ) ʿpr.t(ỉ) smn ṯw r=k m st=k ... my ḏd n=k ỉrt nṯr ỉw ʿprw wp n=f tȝ m rḫt.n=f hrw mrrw=f ỉwt ỉm wʿb sʿḥ ṯw ḥms ḥr st=k* "You have acquired all their powers, you have forgotten nothing. You have come being spiritualized and equipped. Establish yourself on this throne of yours. ... Come and tell what the god does who comes equipped and who opens the earth for himself through what he knows on the day when he desires to come thence. Pure and noble are you, sit on your throne" (*CT* 7, pp. 236s–37c, 237t–v, Spell 1017).

53. For this entity, see Hornung 1983, pp. 462–64.

54. Compare Faulkner 1973, p. 160, n. 2 (Spell 194); *CT* 2, pp. 115 f., Spell 105; 117l–m, Spell 106; *CT* 7, p. 226s, Spell 1011.

55. (226y) *ỉr n=ỉ wȝt* (z) *ʿnḫ=ỉ m ʿnḫt=sn ỉm* (227a) *ʿnḫ.kỉ wȝs.kỉ ḏt r nḥḥ* (b) *šm.ỉ ỉw.ỉ ỉmyt(w)*. This passage is open to several additional interpretations. Thus *ʿnḫ.ỉ* may be a circumstantial form; the statives may be instances of the independent use of the first person; and *šm=ỉ* and *ỉw=ỉ* rendered as prospective forms or as the so-called indicative *sḏm=f*. Faulkner (1978, p. 111) translates "Prepare a path for me, for I live on what they live on, and I am alive and flourishing forever and ever. I come and go between ... ; my hair stands up ... ." Barguet (1986, p. 415) translates "Fais-mois un chemin, (car) je vis de ce dont ils vivent, étant vivant et prospère ... ! Je vais et viens ... mes cheveux étant dressés ... ."

56. For the tentative dating on paleographical criteria of P. Gardiner II to the Sixth Dynasty, see Gardiner 1933; Allen 1950, p. 31 (P. Gardiner II and III); Roccati 1982, p. 18. In the light of the recent finds of some very fragmentary Coffin Texts in Balat, this dating may not be as unlikely as hitherto believed; compare Valloggia 1986, pp. 74–78, 167 ff. For a more skeptical view — again on paleographical criteria — see Goedicke 1988, pp. XXI–XXII (though his remarks on the direction of the writing is due to a misunderstanding of the evidence); Lapp 1991. See further Bidoli 1976, p. 25; Jürgens 1988, p. 30, whose analysis of the sources for Coffin Text Spell 75 entails an early date for the editing of the oldest version.

through knowledge." In addition to the external criteria of transmission, Coffin Texts are usually classified in terms of their content (themes), form, and purpose, the outcome being referred to as offering texts, transformation spells, ferryman texts, and so forth. It might also, however, be meaningful to organize the spells in relation to their possible function within what is now considered to be the standard model for the analysis of a ritual process, the three-phase model originally developed to explain the "rites de passage" (see van Gennep 1909; idem 1960; Turner 1964). In a classification according to which of the three stages in this process they become relevant, the currently accepted division of the texts may result in a somewhat different categorization, not only of individual spells as such but also of the way we imagine many liturgies to have been. But whichever rites were performed in the first phase of the entire process in which the dead must be presumed to have been separated from his previous existence, the reversal texts and other "salvation through knowledge" texts were a part of the liminal phase.

In this phase, the dead is tried in a number of different ways. His previous conduct is scrutinized, and he is tested on his knowledge of what is required for him to be admitted to his new form of existence. The reversal texts, and all the other "salvation through knowledge" texts (ships parts, etc.) are relevant to this phase of the process. Having passed the judgment and obtained the verdict of being "true of voice" and having successfully proved himself in possession of the required insight and knowledge, the dead is finally incorporated or transposed into the sphere of the *ꜣḫw*, the transfigured spirits. And this is where the mortuary texts, texts bearing on the cult, come in, such as the *sꜣḫw*-liturgies (cf. Assmann, *LÄ* 6 "Verklärung," col. 1002).

Having given satisfactory evidence of his knowledge to the effect that the world beyond is not governed by a different principle, and that it is therefore not reversed, the dead has at the same time proved his ability to make the crucial distinction between existence and non-existence, and between latent existence and sheer non-existence, and in the final analysis one might therefore say that at a higher level of abstraction the theme of the reversal texts is the awareness of the possibility of the second death.[57]

The last example to be adduced from the Coffin Texts takes us back to the starting point:

> (112) Recitation for not eating excrement:[58] Ra is hungry, Hathor is thirsty,[59] and I will not eat what Geb lifts up (i.e., dust) and what those who roam the earth trample on (*ḫmmt ḥtyw-tꜣ im*).[60] Oh you doorkeeper of the soil of the Two Lands,[61] bring me(?) my ferry.[62] <Place me under your care in this ferry of yours, as I am pure among the pure ones near the Lords of Eternity, one who chews myrrh and lives on Maat, being strong and having attained the state of being provisioned (*imꜣḫ*)> (*CT* 3, p. 112, Spell 194).

In light of the preceding discussion this text becomes rather more intelligible, the meaning being quite clearly that even if one were to be confronted with the worst of all situations, the hunger and thirst of the supreme god and his female counterpart, one knows that this is a trap and that one must keep away from the attributes of the world reversed.[63]

57. As it happens, this view comes very close to that of Müller (1972, p. 121): "In a world where the normal order of things is reversed, the familiar corn-measurer or street vendor, from whom he [the dead] used to purchase his groceries, are in reality 'sanitary engineers' who empty the cesspools of the hereafter. Those who see through their disguise pass unharmed into the realm of the blessed; those deceived by their misleading external appearance lose their purity, 'die a second time,' and become the condemned."

58. Texts B9C, B1L, and T1C are three versions of Coffin Text Spell 194, of which only text T1C has this title (*CT* 3, p. 112, Spell 194).

59. Texts B1L and B9C have *ḥqr Rꜥ ib sp-sn Ḥwt-ḥr* and text T1C has *ḥqr Rꜥ sp-sn ibt Ḥwt-ḥr sp-sn* (*CT* 3, p. 112, Spell 194). It is tempting to assume that the "original version" would have had a balanced sentence similar to Pyramid Text 696c–d: *ḥqr* PN *ḥqr Rwty ibb* PN *ibb Nhbt*. For such sentences, see Allen 1984, pp. 126–32.

60. *ḫmmt im* (texts B1L and T1C) and *ḫmt* (text B9C) do not seem to be known elsewhere. The geminated form plus *im* shows that *ḫmt* in the latter text is not likely to be a mere variant of *ḫmw*, the well-known word for dust (*Wb.* 3.277:15), but the verb may be related to Bohairic ϩⲟⲙϩⲉⲙ "to crush." Bidoli (1976, pp. 52–53, following *Wb.* 3.343:8) thinks that the *ḥtyw tꜣ* are *Zugvögeln*, but in that case I would be even more at a loss as to the meaning of *ḫmmt*.

61. For this troublesome expression, see Barguet 1986, p. 390, n. 1, who translates "portier du dieu-Glèbe," written *ꜥq/ꜣḥ-t/ꜣwy*, literally, "glèbe du Double Pays"; Clère 1979, pp. 305–07.

62. All three texts appear to have *(i)in n=i*, but then the problems start. Text B1L has , text T1C has , and text B9C has . If *ḏꜣ* is taken as an imperative, we have no object for the imperative *in* (thus Barguet 1986, p. 390: "amène-(le) [what?] moi et traverse-moi"). And with Faulkner's translation, which I have followed, we have problems with both the pronoun and *ḏꜣ*(?), which in text T1C, moreover, seems to be confused with *ḏꜣi ḥr* (*Wb.* 5.514:9). This is the end of the long sequence preserved on text B1L. The two other texts add a few more — somewhat corrupt — sentences.

63. Thus Faulkner (1973, p. 160) translates "Even if Rēꜥ ... and Hatḥōr ... , I will not eat ..."; Barguet (1986, p. 390) renders the passage as "Rê aura faim, Hathor aura soif, mais je ne mangerai pas ce que soulève Geb."

CONCLUSION

Now, there is no denying that each of the groups of material so far considered has its proper "Sitz im Leben." What these instances have in common, however, is that they show the *bwt*s of Hathor during certain feasts (thirst, hunger, and phenomena related to a form of behavior connected with death and/or burial) and the acceptance of the idea of a world reversed to be two sides of the same coin because they both are expressive of the fear of the second death, i.e., the real death.

Despite the fact that death did not mean the termination of existence, there is no real reason to believe that the Egyptians were not afraid of death, especially perhaps, premature death (de Buck 1950).[64] Being the victim of slaying could likewise be fatal. Two words, *ẖdb* and *smꜣ,* clearly stand out from the Egyptian vocabulary for "killing" and "slaying." There would seem to be a chronological difference between their use, but as of the end of the Old Kingdom, at any rate, a semantic difference made itself felt: *ẖdb* was used with the neutral sense "to kill, to take the life of" and *smꜣ* was reserved for the more specialized use of slaughtering or killing as a part of a ritual (*Wb.* 3.403:3–13; 4.122:7 ff.). Not surprisingly, therefore, no instances of an association of *ẖdb* and *bwt* are known, whereas killing (*smꜣ*) somebody who was not an enemy or killing in an unlawful manner was always likely to have been regarded as *bwt*[65] because that type of killing had the character of a ritual putting to death, of a sacrifice.[66] Therefore, being killed (*smꜣ*) was in principle tantamount to the real death, the second death.[67] It was a catastrophe, the total annihilation of one's existence. This state of non-existence was thus the fate of enemies, of *maat*-antagonistic forces, or it was the outcome of (the fear of) being executed at the Place of Annihilation.[68]

The destruction brought about by the wild and angry Eye of the Sun belongs to the same category. Thus, in the famous "Ritual of repelling the aggressor" the seventh chapter begins with this passage:

> (28) O you fallen enemy, you rebel against the Foremost of the Westerners, (29) the Great One is in rage against you in order to annihilate (*sbỉ*) your body [The wrath of the Great One is against you in order to let you perish (*ꜣq*)] [this is referring to the *wedjat*-eye] (30) so that you are destroyed in the Place of Destruction (*nmt nt ḥtmyt*) [you are destroyed in the Place of Slaughtering Apophis (*nmt n ꜥpp*)], your body is in/as ashes (*m ssf*), your *ba* does no longer exist in the brazier of Mut-who-carries-her-brother, (32) who is in the nome of Heliopolis (*nn wn bꜣ⸗k m ꜥẖ n mwt-ẖry-sn⸗s ḥry-ỉb Ḥqꜣ-ꜥnḏ*) [and your flesh is reduced to ashes, while your *ba* does not escape the brazier of Mut-who-carries-her-brother, who is in Heliopolis (*ỉw bn pꜣy.k bꜣ pr n pꜣ ꜥẖ mwt-ẖry-sn.s nty m ꜣIwnw* [*Ḥbt*][69])], which encloses all the human cattle (*rmṯ-ꜥwt*)[70] [which has grasped all men who made rebellion], (33) so that they burn (*hꜣw*) in the flame of the Eye of Ra [in order to burn (*ḏꜣf*) them in the fire of the Eye of Ra] (Schott 1929, pp. 77.10–79.2).[71]

---

64. Add to this material the unique preliminary remark to Book of the Dead 101 in the Youiya version (*rꜣ bwt hn*); compare Naville 1908, pl. 13.
65. For example, MMA 98.4.3 = Petrie 1900, pls. 8c (bottom, right), 35b (*smꜣ rmṯw*); compare Schenkel 1965, pp. 129–30; Fischer 1968, pp. 138–41; Louvre no. 2, Ehepaar, Eighteenth Dynasty, known to me from a *Wb-Zettel* (*n smꜣ(⸗ỉ) mꜣr m ỉst⸗f bwt nb nṯrw*); KRI 6, 23.11 (*nn smꜣ⸗ỉ mꜣr*); Naville 1886, pls. 134.5 (*n smꜣ⸗ỉ rmṯ*), 133.12 (*n smꜣ⸗ỉ*) = Book of the Dead 125; compare Maystre 1937, pp. 37–38; Stèle de l'excommunication, 5–7 (= Schäfer 1905, pp. 111.12–112.3 = Grimal 1981, p. 38): *smꜣ s n wn btꜣ⸗f* "to kill an innocent man"; Chassinat 1910, p. 47.18–19: *bwt kꜣ⸗k pw msd.n ḥm⸗k smꜣ ỉrt nb ꜥnḫ* "to kill any living being."
66. Compare, for example, Sethe 1910, §1544b = Pyramid Text Spell 580; Leclant 1956, pp. 142–43; Yoyotte 1980/81, pp. 100–01; for *smꜣ,* see most recently Labrique 1993, p. 176.
67. It is conceivable that a proper funeral might counteract the effect of having been slain by the enemies, and this would then be the reason for retrieving the corpses of important officials, as reported in some of the famous Aswan inscriptions (Sethe 1933, pp. 134.13–16, 135.17 ff.). For dying after death and for the second death, see Zandee 1960, pp. 186–88; Grieshammer 1970, pp. 69–70; Schenkel 1977, p. 108.
68. See, for example, Coffin Text Spells 87 (*CT* 2, p. 53h, one should restore *nmt nṯr*), 114, 388, 389, 407, 535, 536, 553, 564, 640; Book of the Dead 17, 28, 50, 130, 149 (eighth mound). Compare Zandee 1960, pp. 166–67, 169–71; Hornung 1968, especially pp. 33–34; Yoyotte 1980/81, pp. 89–90.
69. Sauneron 1951; compare Donadoni 1954. I owe these references to H. de Meulenaere.
70. Compare Yoyotte 1980/81, p. 96.
71. Compare also Yoyotte 1980/81, p. 43: "Sekhmet ..., est, ... en tant qu'Oeil-de-Rê, le feu lui-même, agent de toute destruction totale, auxiliaire colérique et dévorant du dieu solaire, danger permanent dont il convient de calmer l'appétit féroce et les fureurs exterminatrices par des offrandes carnées et de boissons enivrantes, entité protectrice, aussi de l'ordre universel puisque cette déesse incommode se charge d'anéantir, car elle est le cobra-*uraeus* qui se dresse sur le front du soleil comme sur le front du roi, les perturbateurs ophidiens de l'ordre cosmique, les agresseurs d'Osiris et les rebelles égyptiens ou étrangers qui s'opposent à la monarchie." See further Yoyotte 1980/81, pp. 90, 95–101. For the various ways of being completely exterminated, see also Leahy 1984; Grimm 1988; Willems 1990; Labrique 1993; Quaegebeur 1993.

In the various myths about the rebellion against the sun god, Ra wished mankind to be exterminated, to be reduced to unchangeable non-existence. In the end Ra regretted his wish. The lioness-goddess (Hathor, Sekhmet, Eye of the Sun, the "Remote Goddess"), who had been charged with the murderous task, was pacified by means of beer camouflaged as blood and was eventually brought back to Egypt. The pacification (*sḥtp*) of that Remote Goddess,[72] or the transformation of the ferocious lion-goddess into Bastet, was therefore of, literally, vital importance and was the object of an extensive series of celebrations. And just as it had seemed to have been forbidden to hunt lions during the feast of Bastet,[73] the celebrations of Hathor obviously had no place for anything that might connect her with her other "nature" and former destructive activities. On the contrary, drinking and eating, music and dancing, and plenitude and abundance were the essential ingredients of her feast. And here, then, was the reason for the mentioning of the three *bwt*s because — as interdictions on activities and behavior connected with death, with total annihilation brought about by the destructive force of the angry Hathor as the Eye of Ra, or with accepting the idea, even if only inadvertently, of a world reversed — they were inadmissible during the joyous celebrations of the feast of drunkenness.

Abbreviations

Dendara 2 — *Le temple de Dendara* 2. É. Chassinat. Cairo: Institut français d'archéologie orientale, 1934

Dendara 3 — *Le temple de Dendara* 3. É. Chassinat. Cairo: Institut français d'archéologie orientale, 1935

Dendara 4 — *Le temple de Dendara* 4. É. Chassinat. Cairo: Institut français d'archéologie orientale, 1935

Dendara 5 — *Le temple de Dendara* 5. É. Chassinat. Cairo: Institut français d'archéologie orientale, 1952

Dendara 6 — *Le temple de Dendara* 6. É. Chassinat and F. Daumas. Cairo: Institut français d'archéologie orientale, 1965

Dendara 7 — *Le temple de Dendara* 7. É. Chassinat and F. Daumas. Cairo: Institut français d'archéologie orientale, 1972

Edfou 4 — *Le temple d'Edfou* 4. É. Chassinat. Mémoires publiés par les Membres de la Mission archéologique française au Caire 21. Cairo: Institut français d'archéologie orientale, 1929

Edfou 6 — *Le temple d'Edfou* 6. É. Chassinat. Mémoires publiés par les Membres de la Mission archéologique française au Caire 23. Cairo: Institut français d'archéologie orientale, 1931

Edfou 7 — *Le temple d'Edfou* 7. É. Chassinat. Mémoires publiés par les Membres de la Mission archéologique française au Caire 24. Cairo: Institut français d'archéologie orientale, 1932

Edfou 8 — *Le temple d'Edfou* 8. É. Chassinat. Mémoires publiés par les Membres de la Mission archéologique française au Caire 25. Cairo: Institut français d'archéologie orientale, 1933

References

Allen, J. P.

1984 *The Inflection of the Verb in the Pyramid Texts.* Bibliotheca Aegyptia 2. Malibu: Undena Publications.

1988 *Genesis in Egypt: The Philosophy of Ancient Egyptian Creation Accounts.* Yale Egyptological Studies 2. New Haven: Yale University.

Allen, T. G.

1950 *Occurrences of Pyramid Texts with Cross Indexes of These and Other Egyptian Mortuary Texts.* Studies in Ancient Oriental Civilization 27. Chicago: University of Chicago Press.

Barguet, P.

1986 *Textes des sarcophages égyptiens du Moyen Empire: Introduction et traduction.* Littératures anciennes du proche-orient 12. Paris: Éditions du Cerf.

Barta, W.

1993 "Zur Ambivalenz des ApwB-Satzes nach Parallelen der Pyramidentexte und der Sargtexte." *Zeitschrift für ägyptische Sprache und Altertumskunde* 120: 116–24.

Barucq, A., and F. Daumas

1980 *Hymnes et prières de l'Égypte ancienne.* Littératures anciennes du proche-orient 10. Paris: Éditions du Cerf.

72. For the web of myths related to the conception of the Remote Goddess, see Schenkel 1977, p. 99 ff.; Hornung 1982, p. 93.

73. Compare the "negative confessions" on the Great Stela of Ramesses IV at Abydos: *nn wnm=ỉ bwt=ỉ nn ʿwn.n=ỉ ỉ3d ḥr ḫt=f nn sm3=ỉ m3r* (...) *n sty=ỉ r m3ỉ-ḥs3 m ḥb n b3stt nn ʿrḳ=ỉ n b3-nb-ḏd m pr nṯrw nn dm=ỉ rn n t3 ṯnn* "I have not eaten what is *bwt* for me, I have not despoiled a pauper of his property, I have not killed the weak, (...) I have not shot a lion during the feast of Bastet, I have not sworn by Banebded in the house of gods, I have not pronounced the name of Tatenen" (KRI 6, 23.11–13).

Bianchi, R., ed.
1988 *Cleopatra's Egypt: Age of the Ptolemies*. Mainz: Philipp von Zabern.

Bidoli, D.
1976 *Die Sprüche der Fangnetze in den altägyptischen Sargtexten*. Abhandlungen des Deutschen archäologischen Instituts Kairo, Ägyptologische Reihe 9. Glückstadt: J. J. Augustin.

Boeser, P. A. A.
1915 *Beschrijving van de Egyptische Verzameling in het Rijksmuseum van Oudheden te Leiden*, Volume 7: *De Monumenten van den Saïtischen, Grieksch-Romeinschen, en Koptischen Tijd*. The Hague: Martinus Nijhoff.

Borchardt, L.
1930 *Statuen und Statuetten von Königen und Privatleuten im Museum von Kairo (= CGC no. 1–1294)*, Teil 3. Berlin: Reichsdruckerei.

Borghouts, J. F.
1971 "The Magical Texts of Papyrus Leiden I 348." *Oudheidkundige mededelingen uit het Rijksmuseum van Oudheden te Leiden* 51.
1978 *Ancient Egyptian Magical Texts*. Religious Texts Translation Series, Nisaba 9. Leiden: E. J. Brill.
1987 "The Edition of Magical Papyri in Turin: A Progress Report." In *La magia in Egitto ai tempi dei faraoni* (Atti convegno internazionale di studi Milano 29–31 ottobre 1985), edited by A. Roccati and A. Siliotti. Turin: Rassegna internazionale di cinematografia archeologica arte e natura libri.

de Buck, A.
1950 "The Fear of Premature Death in Ancient Egypt." In *Pro regno pro sanctuario: Een bundel studies en bijdragen van vrienden en vereerders bij de zestigste verjaardag van Prof. Dr. Gerardus van der Leeuw*, edited by W. J. Kooiman and J. M. van Veenpp. 79–88. Nijkerk: G. F. Callenbach.

Caminos, R. O.
1977 *A Tale of Woe*. Oxford: Griffith Institute.

Cannuyer, C.
1991 "Répartitions quinaire et septénaire des rations alimentaires du défunt dans les textes funéraires égyptiens: Évolution du thème et essai d'interpretation." In *Humana condicio: La condition humaine*, edited by A. Théodoridès, P. Naster, and A. van Tongerloo, pp. 321–30. Acta Orientalia Belgica 6. Brussels: Société belge d'études orientales.

Černý, J., and A. H. Gardiner
1957 *Hieratic Ostraca*, Volume 1. Oxford: Griffith Institute.

Chassinat, É.
1910 *Le mammisi d'Edfou*, fascicle 1. Mémoires publiés par les Membres de l'Institut français d'archéologie orientale 16/1. Cairo: Institut français d'archéologie orientale.
1987 *Le temple d'Edfou* II[1]. Deuxième édition revue et corrigée par S. Cauville et D. Devauchelle. Mémoires publiés par les Membres de la Mission archéologique française d'archéologie au Cairo 11/II[1]. Cairo: Institut français d'archéologie orientale.
1990 *Le temple d'Edfou* II[2]. Deuxième édition revue et corrigée par S. Cauville et D. Devauchelle. Mémoires publiés par les Membres de la Mission archéologique française d'archéologie au Cairo 11/II[2]. Cairo: Institut français d'archéologie orientale.

Clère, J. J.
1979 "Recherches sur le mot  des textes gréco-romains et sur d'autres mots apparentés." *Bulletin de l'Institut français d'archéologie orientale* 79: 285–310.

Clère, P.
1961 *La porte d'Évergète à Karnak*, 2e partie. Mémoires publiés par les Membres de l'Institut français d'archéologie orientale 84. Cairo: Institut français d'archéologie orientale.

von Deines, H., and W. Westendorf
1961/62 *Wörterbuch der medizinischen Texte*. Grundriss der Medizin der alten Ägypter 7/1–2. Berlin: Akademie-Verlag.

Depuydt, L.
1986 "The Emphatic Nominal Sentence in Egyptian and Coptic." In *Crossroad: Chaos or the Beginning of a New Paradigm* (Papers from the Conference on Egyptian Grammar, Helsingør 28–30 May 1986), edited by G. Englund and P. J. Frandsen, pp. 91–117. Carsten Niebuhr Institute Publications 1. Copenhagen: Museum Tusculanum Press.

Desroches-Noblecourt, Ch.
1947 "Une coutume égyptienne méconnue." *Bulletin de l'Institut français d'archéologie orientale* 45: 185–232.

Donadoni, S.
1954 "La città di ." *Annali della facoltà di filosofia e lettere dell'Università di Milano* 7: 303–05.

Doret, É.
1990 "Phrase nominale, identité et substitution dans les textes des sarcophages [deuxième partie]." *Revue d'égyptologie* 41: 39–56.
1992 "Phrase nominale, identité et substitution dans les textes des sarcophages [troisième partie]." *Revue d'égyptologie* 43: 49–74.

Drioton, É.
1927 *Rapport sur les fouilles de Médamoud (1926): Les inscriptions*. Fouilles de Institut français d'archéologie orientale 4/2. Cairo: Institut français d'archéologie orientale.

Edwards, I. E. S.
1968 "Kenhikhopshef's Prophylactic Charm." *Journal of Egyptian Archaeology* 54: 155–60.

Erman, A.
1915 "Zwei Grabsteine griechischer Zeit." In *Festschrift Eduard Sachau, zum siebzigsten Geburtstag gewidmet von Freunden und Schülern*, edited by G. Weil, pp. 103–12. Berlin: G. Reimer.

Faulkner, R. O.
1973 *The Ancient Egyptian Coffin Texts*, Volume 1: *Spells 1–354*. Warminster: Aris and Phillips.
1978 *The Ancient Egyptian Coffin Texts*, Volume 3: *Spells 788–1185 and Indexes*. Warminster: Aris and Phillips.

Fecht, G.
1972 *Der Vorwurf an Gott in den* Mahnworten des Ipu-wer (*Pap. Leiden I 344 recto, 11.11–13.8; 15.13–17.3*):

Zur geistigen Krise der ersten Zwischenzeit und ihrer Bewältigung. Abhandlungen der Heidelberger Akademie der Wissenschaften, philosophisch-historische Klasse, 1972, No. 1. Heidelberg: Carl Winter.

1978 "Schicksalsgöttin und König in der 'Lehre eines Mannes für sein Sohn.'" *Zeitschrift für ägyptische Sprache und Altertumskunde* 105: 14–42.

Firchow, O.

1957 *Thebanische Tempelinschriften aus griechisch-römischer Zeit*, Band 1. Urkunden des ägyptischen Altertums, Abteilung 8. Berlin: Akademie-Verlag.

Fischer, H.

1968 *Dendera in the Third Millennium B.C. down to the Theban Domination of Upper Egypt*. New York: J. J. Augustin.

Frandsen, P. J.

1986 "On the Relevance of Logical Analysis." In *Crossroad: Chaos or the Beginning of a New Paradigm* (Papers from the Conference on Egyptian Grammar, Helsingør 28–30 May 1986), edited by G. Englund and P. J. Frandsen, pp. 145–59. Carsten Niebuhr Institute Publications 1. Copenhagen: Museum Tusculanum Press.

1989 "Trade and Cult." In *The Religion of the Ancient Egyptians: Cognitive Structures and Popular Expressions* (Proceedings of Symposia in Uppsala and Bergen 1987 and 1988), edited by G. Englund, pp. 95–108. Acta Universitatis Upsaliensis, Boreas 20. Uppsala: Almqvist and Wiksell.

Gardiner, A. H.

1909 *The Admonitions of an Egyptian Sage from a Hieratic Papyrus in Leiden (Pap. Leiden 344 recto)*. Leipzig: J. C. Hinrichs.

1933 "A Hieratic Papyrus." *British Museum Quarterly* 8/2: 73–74.

1935 *Hieratic Papyri in the British Museum,* Third Series, *Chester Beatty Gift,* Volume 1: *Text*. London: British Museum.

Gennep, A. van

1909 *Les rites de passage*. Paris: E. Nourry.

1960 *The Rites of Passage*. Translated by M. B. Vizedom and G. L. Caffee. London: Routledge and Kegan Paul.

Goedicke, H.

1988 *Old Hieratic Paleography*. Baltimore: Halgo.

Grieshammer, R.

1970 *Das Jenseitsgericht in den Sargtexten*. Ägyptologische Abhandlungen 20. Wiesbaden: Otto Harrassowitz.

Grimal, N.-C.

1981 *Quatre stèles napatéennes au Musée du Caire, JE 48863–48866: Textes et indices*. Études sur la propagande royale égyptienne 2; Mémoires publiés par les Membres de l'Institut français d'archéologie orientale 106. Cairo: Institut français d'archéologie orientale.

Grimm, A.

1988 "Feind-Bilder und Bilderverbrennung: Ein Brandopfer zur rituellen Feindvernichtung in einer Festdarstellung der 'Chapelle Rouge.'" *Varia Aegyptiaca* 4: 207–13.

1994 *Die altägyptischen Festkalender in den Tempeln der griechisch-römischen Epoche*. Ägypten und Altes Testament 15. Wiesbaden: Otto Harrassowitz.

Guglielmi, W.

1991 *Die Göttin* Mr.t: *Entstehung und Verehrung einer Personifikation*. Probleme der Ägyptologie 7. Leiden: E. J. Brill.

Gunn, B.

1924 *Studies in Egyptian Syntax*. Paris: Librairie Orientaliste Paul Geuthner.

1927 "The Stela of Apries at Mîtrahîna." *Annales du Service des antiquités de l'Égypte* 27: 211–37.

Gutbub, A.

1961 "Un emprunt aux textes des pyramides dans l'hymne à Hathor, dame de l'ivresse." In *Mélanges Maspero* I/4: *Orient ancien*, pp. 31–72. Mémoires publiés par les membres de l'Institut français d'archéologie orientale du Caire 66/4. Cairo: Institut français d'archéologie orientale.

1973 *Textes fondamentaux de la théologie de Kom Ombo*. 2 volumes. Bibliothèque d'étude 47/1–2. Cairo: Institut français d'archéologie orientale.

Hayes, W. C.

1937 *The Texts in the Mastabeh of Se'n-wosret-Ankh at Lisht*. Publications of the Metropolitan Museum of Art Egyptian Expedition 12. New York: Metropolitan Museum of Art.

Helck, W.

1970 *Die Prophezeiung des* Nfr.tj. Kleine ägyptische Texte 11. Wiesbaden: Otto Harrassowitz.

1995 *Die "Admonitions": Pap. Leiden I 344 recto*. Kleine ägyptische Texte. Wiesbaden: Otto Harrassowitz.

Herbin, F.-R.

1994 *Le livre de parcourir l'éternité*. Orientalia Lovaniensia Analecta 58. Leuven: Peeters.

Hickmann, H.

1955 "Terminologie musicale de l'Égypte ancienne." *Bulletin de l'Institut d'Égypte* 36: 583–618.

Hornung, E.

1968 *Altägyptische Höllenvorstellungen*. Abhandlungen der sächsischen Akademie der Wissenschaften zu Leipzig, philologisch-historische Klasse, 59/3. Berlin: Akademie-Verlag.

1979 "Die Tragweite der Bilder altägyptische Bildaussagen." *Eranos Jahrbuch* 48: 183–237.

1981 "Zu den Schlussszenen der Unterweltsbücher." *Mitteilungen des Deutschen archäologischen Instituts, Abteilung Kairo* 37: 217–26.

1982 *Der ägyptische Mythos von der Himmelskuh: Eine Ätiologie des Unvollkommenen*. Orbis Biblicus et Orientalis 46. Freiburg: Universitätsverlag; Göttingen: Vandenhoeck and Ruprecht.

1983 "Fisch und Vogel: Zur altägyptischen Sicht des Menschen." *Eranos Jahrbuch* 52: 455–96.

Jansen-Winkeln, K.

1985 *Ägyptische Biographien der 22. und 23. Dynastie*. Ägypten und Altes Testament 8/1–2. Wiesbaden: Otto Harrassowitz.

1993 "Zwei Jenseitsklagen." *Bulletin de la Société d'égyptologie, Genève* 17: 41–47.

1994 "Zu den Trauerriten bei der Apisbestattung." *Bulletin de la Société d'égyptologie, Genève* 18: 33–39.

Janssen, J. J.
1980 "Absence from Work by the Necropolis Workmen of Thebes." *Studien zur altägyptischen Kultur* 8: 127–52.

Junker, H.
1906 "Poesie aus der Spätzeit." *Zeitschrift für ägyptische Sprache und Altertumskunde* 43: 101–27.

Jürgens, P.
1988 "Textkritische und Überlieferungsgeschichtliche Untersuchungen zu den Sargtexten." *Göttinger Miszellen* 105: 27–39.

Kahl, J.
1995 "Das überlieferungsgeschichtliche Verhältnis von Unas und Sesostrisanch am Beispiel von PT 302–312." *Studien zur altägyptischen Kultur* 22: 195–209.

Kees, H.
1956 *Totenglauben und Jenseitsvorstellungen der alten Ägypter: Grundlagen und Entwicklung bis zum Ende des Mittleren Reiches.* Berlin: Akademie-Verlag.

Labrique, F.
1993 "Transpercer l'âne à Edfou." In *Ritual and Sacrifice in the Ancient Near East* (Proceedings of the International Conference Organized by the Katholieke Universiteit Leuven from the 17th to the 20th of April 1991), edited by J. Quaegebeur, pp. 156–89. Orientalia Lovaniensia Analecta 55. Leuven: Peeters.

Lapp, G.
1991 Review of *Chests of Life. A Study of the Typology and Conceptual Development of Middle Kingdom Standard Class Coffins*, by H. Willems. *Bibliotheca Orientalis* 48: cols. 801–812.

Leahy, A.
1984 "Death by Fire in Ancient Egypt." *Journal of the Social and Economic History of the Orient* 27: 199–206.

Leclant, J.
1956 "La 'mascarade' des boeufs gras et le triomphe de l'Égypte." *Mitteilungen des Deutschen archäologischen Instituts, Abteilung Kairo* 14: 128–45.

Leemans, C.
1846 *Aegyptische Monumenten van het Nederlandsche Museum van Oudheden te Leyden* 2: *Monumenten behoorende tot het burgerlijk leven.* Leiden: E. J. Brill.

Legrain, M. G.
1902 "Le temple de Ptah Rîs-Anbou-F dans Thèbes." *Annales du Service des antiquités de l'Égypte* 3: 38–66.

Lichtheim, M.
1973 *Ancient Egyptian Literature*, Volume 1: *The Old and Middle Kingdom.* Berkeley: University of California Press.
1980 *Ancient Egyptian Literature*, Volume 3: *The Late Period.* Berkeley: University of California Press.

Lorton, D.
1968 "The Expression *Šms-ib*." *Journal of the American Research Center in Egypt* 7: 41–54.

Mariette, A.
1870a *Dendérah. Description générale du grand temple de cette ville*, tome 1. Paris: Librairie A. Franck.
1870b *Dendérah. Description générale du grand temple de cette ville*, tome 2. Paris: Librairie A. Franck.
1871 *Dendérah. Description générale du grand temple de cette ville*, tome 3. Paris: Librairie A. Franck.

Maystre, C.
1937 *Les déclarations d'innocence (livre des mortes, chapitre 125).* Recherches d'archéologie, de philologie et d'histoire, 8. Cairo: Institut français d'archéologie orientale.

McDowell, A. G.
1993 *Hieratic Ostraca in the Hunterian Museum Glasgow: The Colin Campbell Ostraca.* Oxford: Griffith Institute.

Meulenaere, H. de
1962 "De vrouw in de laat-egyptische autobiografie." *Phoenix* 8: 134–38.

Möller, G.
1927 *Hieratische Paläographie: Die aegyptische Buchschrift in ihrer Entwicklung von der fünften Dynastie bis zur römischen Kaiserzeit*, Volume 2/2: *Von der zeit Thutmosis' III bis zum Ende der Einundzwanzigsten Dynastie.* Leipzig: J. C. Hinrichs.

Müller, D.
1972 "An Early Egyptian Guide to the Hereafter." *Journal of Egyptian Archaeology* 58: 99–125.

Naville, E.
1886 *Das aegyptische Todtenbuch der XVIII. bis XX. Dynastie aus verschiedenen Urkunden zusammengestellt und herausgegeben,* Einleitung. 2 volumes. Berlin: Verlag A. Asher.
1908 *The Funeral Papyrus of Iouiya.* Theodore M. Davis' Excavations, Bibân el-Molûk 4. London: Archibald Constable.

Ockinga, B.
1988 "Grabstele des Taiemhotep." In *Texte aus der Umwelt des Alten Testaments* 2, edited by O. Kaiser, pp. 540–44. Gütersloh: Gütersloher Verlagshaus Gerd Mohn.

Otto, E.
1964 *Gott und Mensch nach den ägyptischen Tempelinschriften der griechisch-römischen Zeit: Eine Untersuchung zur Phraseologie der Tempelinschriften.* Abhandlungen der Heidelberger Akademie der Wissenschaften, philologisch-historische Klasse, 1964, No. 1. Heidelberg: Carl Winter.

Petrie, W. M. F.
1900 *Dendereh 1898.* Egypt Exploration Fund 17. London: Egypt Exploration Fund.

Pleyte, W., and F. Rossi
1869–76 *Papyrus de Turin.* 2 volumes. Leiden: E. J. Brill.

Polotsky, H. J.
1976 *Les transpositions du verbe en égyptien classique.* Israel Oriental Studies 6. Tel-Aviv: Tel-Aviv University.

Posener, G.
1956 *Littérature et politique dans l'Égypte de la XIIe dynastie.* Paris: Librairie ancienne Honoré Champion.

Quaegebeur, J.
1993 "L'Autel-à-feu et l'abattoir en Égypte tardive." In *Ritual and Sacrifice in the Ancient Near East* (Proceedings of the International Conference Organized by the Katholieke Universiteit Leuven, 17–20 April 1991), edited by J. Quaegebeur, pp. 329–53. Orientalia Lovaniensia Analecta 55. Leuven: Peeters.

Reymond, E. A. E.
1981 *From the Records of a Priestly Family from Memphis*, Volume 1. Ägyptologische Abhandlungen 38. Wiesbaden: Otto Harrassowitz.

Ritner, R. K.
1993 *The Mechanics of Ancient Egyptian Magical Practice*. Studies in Ancient Oriental Civilization 54. Chicago: Oriental Institute.
1998 "The Wives of Horus and the Philinna Papyrus (*PGM* XX)." In *Egyptian Religion: The Last Thousand Years. Studies Dedicated to the Memory of Jan Quaegebeur*, Volume 2, edited by W. Clarysse, A. Schoors, and H. Willems, pp. 1027–41. Orientalia Lovaniensia Analecta 84. Leuven: Peeters.

Roccati, A.
1982 *La littérature historique sous l'Ancien Empire égyptien*. Littératures anciennes du proche-orient 11. Paris: Éditions du Cerf.

Rochemonteix, M. de, and É. Chassinat
1984 *Le temple d'Edfou* I[1]. Deuxième édition revue et corrigée par S. Cauville et D. Devauchelle. Mémoires publiés par les Membres de la Mission archéologique française au Caire 10/I[1]. Cairo: Institut français d'archéologie orientale.
1987a *Le temple d'Edfou* I[3]. Deuxième édition revue et corrigée par S. Cauville et D. Devauchelle. Mémoires publiés par les Membres de la Mission archéologique française au Caire 10/I[3]. Cairo: Institut français d'archéologie orientale.
1987b *Le temple d'Edfou* I[4]. Deuxième édition revue et corrigée par S. Cauville et D. Devauchelle. Mémoires publiés par les Membres de la Mission archéologique française au Caire 10/I[4]. Cairo: Institut français d'archéologie orientale.

Säve-Söderbergh, T.
1956 "Eine ramessidische Darstellung vom Töten der Schildkröte." *Mitteilungen des Deutschen archäologischen Instituts, Abteilung Kairo* 14: 175–80.

Sauneron, S.
1951 "Le nom d'Héliopolis à la basse-époque." *Revue d'égyptologie* 8: 191–94.
1962 *Les fêtes religieuses d'Esna aux derniers siècles du paganisme*. Esna 5. Cairo: Institut français d'archéologie orientale.
1963 *Le temple d'Esna*, tome 2. Cairo: Institut français d'archéologie orientale.
1968 *Le temple d'Esna*, tome 3. Cairo: Institut français d'archéologie orientale.
1983 *La porte ptolémaïque de l'enceinte de Mout à Karnak*. Mémoires publiés par les Membres de l'Institut français d'archéologie orientale du Caire 107. Cairo: Institut français d'archéologie orientale.

Schäfer, H.
1905 *Urkunden der älteren Äthiopenkönige* 1. Urkunden des ägyptischen Altertums, Abteilung 3/1. Leipzig: J. C. Hinrichs.

Schenkel, W.
1965 *Memphis, Herakleopolis, Theben: Die epigraphischen Zeugnisse der 7.–11. Dynastie Ägyptens*. Ägyptologische Abhandlungen 12. Wiesbaden: Otto Harrassowitz.
1977 *Kultmythos und Märtyrerlegende: Zur Kontinuität des ägyptischen Denkens*. Göttinger Orientforschungen 4. Reihe, Band 5. Wiesbaden: Otto Harrassowitz.
1987 "Zur Struktur des Dreigliedrigen Nominalsatzes mit der Satzteilfolge Subjekt - Prädikat im Ägyptischen (mit disproportionalen Bemerkungen zu einigen Pyramidentext-Stellen, insbesondere zu Pyr. §131a–d)." *Studien zur altägyptischen Kultur* 14: 265–82.

Schott, S.
1929 *Urkunden mythologischen Inhalts*. Urkunden des ägyptischen Altertums, Abteilung 6. Leipzig: J. C. Hinrichs.

Sethe, K.
1904 *Hieroglyphische Urkunden der griechisch-römischen Zeit* 1: *Historisch-biographische Urkunden aus den Zeiten der Makedonischen Könige und der beiden ersten Ptolemäer*. Urkunden des ägyptischen Altertums, Abteilung 2. Leipzig: J. C. Hinrichs.
1908 *Die altägyptischen Pyramidentexte nach den Papierabdrücken und Photographien des Berliner Museums*. Leipzig: J. C. Hinrichs.
1910 *Die altägyptischen Pyramidentexte nach den Papierabdrucken und Photographien des Berliner Museums*. Leipzig: J. C. Hinrichs.
1922 "Die Sprüche für das Kennen der Seelen der heiligen Orte (Totb. Kap. 107–09, 111–16). Göttinger Totenbuchstudien von 1919." *Zeitschrift für ägyptische Sprache und Altertumskunde* 57: 1–50, 1*–13*.
1933 *Urkunden des Alten Reiches*. Second edition. Urkunden des ägyptischen Altertums, Abteilung 1. Leipzig: J. C. Hinrichs.

Sternberg-El Hotabi, H.
1992 *Ein Hymnus an die Göttin Hathor und das Ritual 'Hathor das Trankopfer darbringen' nach den Tempeltexten der griechisch-römischen Zeit*. Rites égyptiens 7. Brussels: Fondation Égyptologique Reine Élisabeth.

Turner, V. W.
1964 "Betwixt and Between: The Liminal Period." In *The Rites of Passage* (Proceedings of the American Ethnological Society, Symposium on New Approaches to the Study of Religion, 1964), pp. 4–20. St. Paul: American Ethnological Society. Reprinted in *Reader in Comparative Religion: An Anthropological Approach*, edited by W. A. Lessa and E. Z. Vogt, pp. 234–43. New York: Harper and Row, 1979.

Valloggia, M.
1986 *Le mastaba de Medou-Nefer*. Balat 1; Fouilles de l'Institut français d'archéologie orientale 31/1–2. Cairo: Institut français d'archéologie orientale.

Vandier, J.
1961 *Le papyrus Jumilac*. Paris: Centre national de la recherche scientifique.

Vassilika, E.
1989 *Ptolemaic Philae*. Orientalia Lovaniensia Analecta 3. Leuven: Peeters.

Vercoutter, J.
1962 *Textes biographiques du sérapéum de Memphis: Contribution à l'étude des stèles votives du sérapéum*. Bibliothèque de l'École des hautes études, IVe section, tome 316. Paris: Librairie ancienne Honoré Champion.

Vernus, P.
1979 "Un décret de Thoutmosis III relatif à la santé publique (P. Berlin 3049, v[0] XVIII–XIX)." *Orientalia* 48: 176–84.

Walle, B. van de
1953 "La tortue dans la religion et la magie égyptiennes." *La nouvelle clio* 5: 173–89.

Westendorf, W.
1981 *Beiträge zum altägyptischen Nominalsatz*. Nachrichten von der Akademie der Wissenschaften in Göttingen, philologisch-historische Klasse, No. 3. Göttingen: Akademie der Wissenschaften.

Wild, H.
1963 "Les danses sacrées de l'Égypte ancienne." In *Les danses sacrées*, pp. 33–117. Sources orientales 6. Paris: Aux Éditions du Seuil.

Willems, H.
1990 "Crime, Cult and Capital Punishment (Moʿalla Inscription 8)." *Journal of Egyptian Archaeology* 76: 27–54.

Winter, E.
1968 *Untersuchungen zu den ägyptischen Tempelreliefs der griechisch-römischen Zeit*. Österreichische Akademie der Wissenschaften, philosophisch-historische Klasse, Denkschriften 98. Vienna: Böhlau Verlag.

Yoyotte, J.
1980 "Une monumentale litanie de granit: Les Sekhmet d'Aménophis III et la conjuration permanente de la déesse dangereuse." *Bulletin de la Société française d'égyptologie* 87/88: 47–75.
1980/81 "Héra d'Héliopolis et le sacrifice humain." *Annuaire de l'École pratique des hautes études, Ve section - sciences religieuses* 89: 29–102.

Zandee, J.
1960 *Death as an Enemy according to Ancient Egyptian Conceptions*. Studies in the History of Religions (Supplements to *Numen*) 5. Leiden: E. J. Brill.

Ziegler, C.
1979 *Catalogue des instruments de musique égyptiens*. Musée du Louvre Départment des Antiquités Égyptiennes. Paris: Éditions de la Réunion des musées nationaux.

13

TWO INLAID INSCRIPTIONS OF THE EARLIEST MIDDLE KINGDOM

HANS GOEDICKE

The Johns Hopkins University, Baltimore

It was a reminder of how time flies when I received the invitation to contribute to a festschrift dedicated to Edward F. Wente. There are so many memories of days spent in Cairo in 1957/58. For both of us, it was early in our acquaintance with Egypt. We were confronted with opportunities of all kinds, and the array of ancient Egypt seemed to have no end. Later we drifted apart, and many notes taken with the idea of possible later joint study were tucked away in notebooks. What happened to some of the objects we had an opportunity to see, I do not know. It is all the more appropriate to go back to old notes and make some of them generally available.

WOODEN COFFIN OF ONURIS-NAKHT

We had been asked to "look" at some antiquity, as the customary term used to be. Our destination turned out to be a rather disreputable-looking house in Bulaq, where we were shown a substantial cedar beam. It was 2.2 m long, 11.0 cm thick, and 16.5 cm wide. There was no doubt that it was the top section of a wooden coffin. It was inscribed in a long horizontal line that was complete, except for its very beginning, which was restored without problem:

> "The king graciously gives and Anubis who is on his mountain, the *ʾImywt*, the lord of the holy land his proper burial in his tomb of the god's land of the Western Desert (and) a funerary offering for the *pʿt*-speaker, the count, honored one with the great god lord of heaven *ʾIn-ḥrt-nḫt,* the Middle, right-of-voice."

Nothing is known about the origin of the piece. Nevertheless, the identity of the man can be established to a considerable degree.

First, the man apparently belonged to a family of consequence, which insisted on using one specific name almost like a family name.[1] Second, it is certain that the man held an elevated social position, as it is reflected in the designation *rꜣ-pʿt*. The latter is commonly rendered "prince,"[2] without necessarily considering the consequences. *ʾIn-ḥrt-nḫt* (Onuris is strong) was neither vizier, nor was he in any way connected with the royal

---

1. A similar case is *Ppy-ʿnḫ* of Meir (Blackman 1924, pls. IV–IVA) though of earlier date; compare also Ranke 1952/2, p. 11.
2. Gardiner (1947, 14*–19*) renders it "hereditary prince," "crown-prince" and by doing so injects notions into ancient Egypt that do not seem applicable. This applies to the rendering "crown-prince," as there is no cause for attributing legitimism to ancient Egypt, especially not for the times prior to the Twenty-sixth Dynasty. It also concerns the interpretation "hereditary prince" because in no case can it be demonstrated that the holder of the designation had it from his early youth onwards, nor did the descendants continue to hold it. Helck (1950, p. 416 ff.) considers that "ursprünglich war *rpʿt* der Titel des neuen Weltkönigs," while considering the philological meaning of "des Titels *rpʿt* als 'Leiter der Menschen.'" Subsequently, he sees the significance of the designation as reflecting a play in which it denoted the representative of the king at the *sed*-festival, until at the beginning of the Third Dynasty it became applied to a specific son of the king who represented him. At the end of the Fifth Dynasty *rpʿt* became a court rank (Hofrang) which, however, retained its original significance in denoting the representative of the king. For Strudwick (1985, p. 307) it is an honorific title born especially by the viziers.

Gold of Praise: Studies on Ancient Egypt in Honor of Edward F. Wente
Edited by Emily Teeter and John A. Larson
Studies in Ancient Oriental Civilization 58
Chicago: Oriental Institute, 1999

house. He was, as is discussed shortly, a provincial administrator whose background might very well have been in the military establishment. There is nothing that would identify him as "regent," as "hereditary prince," or similar rank. When the designation is read *rꜣ-pʿt* "speaker of the *pʿt*" ("nobility"), his role would seem to become transparent. The bearer of this designation, who occasionally can also be a woman, is a representative of the upper stratum of Egyptian society, who for lack of a better term can be called "nobility." There is no indication that this role as "speaker of the nobility" was a permanent one, but it appears more likely that it was particular to a specific occasion, when the opinion of the *pʿt* was being pronounced. The occasion was, without going here into a detailed discussion of the question, that of royal succession. To have participated in such a process would have, indeed, been a great distinction, and it would make good sense that such "speakers of the nobility" made reference to it. It would seem important to realize that this role was a specific, i.e., temporary one, the distinction of which was indicated even after the actual performance had long passed. As "speaker of the nobility" the designated one is not directly linked with the family of the king, although its members are not necessarily excluded from it either.

While the provenience of the object concerns us later, a preliminary date can be proposed on the basis of the epithet *mꜣʿ ḫrw* following the name, which clearly excludes an attribution to the Old Kingdom and the First Intermediate Period (Polotsky 1929, §81). Its principal meaning, "right-of-voice," becomes a central tenet of eschatological concepts, especially in connection with Osiris as lord of the physical hereafter. However, in its primary usage, *mꜣʿ ḫrw* "right-of-voice" is not necessarily funeral oriented, but appears to have, first of all, a moral significance.[3] It appears, although it has not been sufficiently investigated under these auspices, that *mꜣʿ ḫrw* "right-of-voice" possesses a political aspect rooted in the turmoil Egypt experienced during the Eleventh Dynasty and at the very beginning of the Twelfth Dynasty. The possibility to be considered is whether the epithet *mꜣʿ ḫrw* might not reflect political behavior in support of the king. This could concern people taken over from the Heracleopolitan to the Theban rule, or what appears more likely, alludes to the exercise of loyalty during the tensions in the early part of Amenemhat I's reign.

What made this section of a wooden coffin particularly impressive was the artistic quality of the decoration. The overall background was painted blue, with the hieroglyphs colored, though partly faded. The most unusual aspect, however, was the fact that a number of the signs were not merely inscribed on the surface but were actually inlaid. The signs so treated were the following: all  in hard blue faience;  and 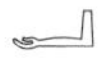 in carnelian;  and  also in carnelian; and  in black stone.  was also inlaid, but the information is lost. The technique of inlays in wood is indeed old and has its earliest and most stunning example in the furniture of Queen Hetepheres I (Reisner 1955, p. 36 ff., figs. 28–30). I am not aware of other instances of private coffins decorated in this fashion.

What enabled Onuris-nakht to have such an unusual artistic display remains obscure. It was, however, not the only piece to which this technique was applied. In my possession also is a copy of another inscription of this same man, this one, however, made by Wente. If my recollection is correct, we split forces to cope with the unexpected epigraphic find. There is no indication about the nature of the object on which the inscription was placed, but I am fairly certain that it was another head beam of the same wooden coffin.

This second inscription reads in the opposite direction to the other, i.e., it faces right. Especially for historical concerns it is even more important than its counterpart:

It can be rendered as follows:

> "The king graciously allows and Osiris, lord of *Ḏdw* and Khenty-imentyw, lord of Abydos, an invocation offering for the *rꜣ-pʿt*, count, nobleman, Unique's associate, lector priest, overseer of Upper Egypt, chief administrator of the eighth and tenth Upper Egyptian districts, as he crosses the firmament, *ʾIn-ḥrt-nḫt*, the Middle one."

3. When the epithet *mꜣʿ ḫrw* appears in the very early Middle Kingdom, especially in conjunction with *ỉqr*, it is more likely to be of mundane, i.e., political significance, just as the term in the Old Kingdom reflects a "righteous claim" ("guten Ruf") in the social setting, rather than an eschatological moral evaluation. See also the important study by Anthes 1954, pp. 21–51.

Of particular interest are the various designations indicated for Onuris-nakht. In addition to *rꜣ-pꜥt* and *ḥꜣt-ꜥ*, which are the only designations given in the other text, there are also five others provided. 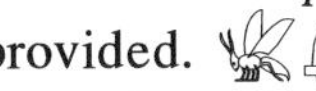 is commonly read *sḏꜣwty-bỉt* and rendered "seal-bearer of the King of Lower Egypt" and is translated here as "nobleman," without substantiation of this interpretation.[4] The usual rendering of *smr-wꜥty* as "unique friend" flies in the face of any logic by its frequent occurrence. As long as one is willing to grant the ancient Egyptians the ability to think with basic logic, it is inadmissible to have them speak of a multitude of "unique friends."[5] The designation appears to have some military significance, which, however, should not necessarily be seen within a tightly structured organization. "Lector priest" might be less a professional than an intellectual indication, i.e., the ability to hold, and possibly also direct, religious ritual.[6]

The remaining designations are those with administrative significance. According to the copy the first is written , constituting something of a quandary. Basically there are three feasible interpretations for these signs: first as *ỉmy-r nswt(yw)* "overseer of royalists"; second, *ỉmy-r Šmꜥ* "overseer of Upper Egypt"; and third, *ỉmy-r rsy* "overseer of the South." Of the three theoretical possibilities, the last one is the least likely in view of the lack of any parallels. As for *ỉmy-r nswtyw,*[7] it would seem improbable that the *nisbe* plural and the determinative are omitted. Despite the epigraphic discrepancy, the reading *ỉmy-r Šmꜥ* "overseer of Upper Egypt" would seem the most likely. This designation, however, does not concern all of Upper Egypt, nor is it "honorific," as has been assumed due to the number of office holders (Kees 1932, p. 85 ff.; Helck 1954, p. 117 ff.). As I have pointed out before (Goedicke 1956, pp. 1–10), the administration of the drawn-out Upper Egypt was subdivided into three more or less equally sized parts, each headed by an "overseer of Upper Egypt" (*ỉmy-r Šmꜥ*), above whom was one other holder of the same designation. The occurrence in the text under discussion indicates that the administrative structure for Upper Egypt was still in force at the very beginning of the Middle Kingdom. It is, however, uncertain whether it is a direct continuation of the Old Kingdom or if it is a revival following the Eleventh Dynasty. There is not enough evidence for the latter to make an evaluation possible. Unquestionably the most important position held by Onuris-nakht the Middle is that of *ḥry-tp-ꜥꜣ-n-Tꜣ-wr n Wꜣḏt* "head administrator of the eighth and the tenth districts of Upper Egypt." *Ḥry-tp-ꜥꜣ* is frequently rendered "nomarch" (Meyer 1921, p. 24, §§262 ff.; Kees 1932, p. 90 ff.) or "Great Overlord" (Fischer 1964, p. 44; Fischer 1968, pp. 74 ff., 224 ff.).[8] These renderings might suggest a degree of independent authority that does not seem inherent in the designation. It rather seems that the position denoted as *ḥry-tp-ꜥꜣ* is the result of a continued effort to make the provincial administration more efficient by local concentration. The progression appears to be in three steps: first, the administration of Upper Egypt becomes a separate entity in the Fifth Dynasty. In the Sixth Dynasty, as a second step, the administration of Upper Egypt is subdivided into three regions. Third, in the late Sixth Dynasty, the local representatives of the central administration are placed under one "head administrator" (*ḥry-tp-ꜥꜣ*) responsible for one administrative district. Although the position encompassed a wide range of administrative duties, these were ultimately carried out on behalf of the central administration. The "head administrator" held no independent administrative authority, so that it would be inappropriate to call him "nomarch." At the same time, it should be noted that some provincial administrators were *de facto* in a position to do as they pleased; however, such virtual autonomy is not implicit in the designation but is rather the consequence of political circumstance.

Onuris-nakht the Middle was "head administrator" in two districts, presumably at the same time. The combination of the affairs of the eighth and tenth Upper Egyptian districts occurred already in the Fifth Dynasty.[9] It is also attested in Hemamiyeh for two *Kꜣ ḫnt* dating to the late Sixth Dynasty (Mackay, Harding, and Petrie 1929, pls. 17 ff., p. 25).[10] All these people seem to have had a military career. There is no indication that Onuris-nakht the Middle followed the same profession, although it cannot be excluded that in his younger years

4. For the moment, it has to suffice that there is no reason to see in it a reference to the Lower Egyptian king, especially as all designations reflecting an association with the institution of kingship are formed with *nswt*. Furthermore, it should be noted that the bearer of this designation was unquestionably living in Upper Egypt and that there is no indication that this part of the country had any link with Lower Egypt.
5. It is only an achievement of modern intellectual imprecision that formulations such as "very unique" or "most unique" have become common idioms.
6. The degree to which it reflects an ability to read is uncertain. The main feature seems to be the ability to conduct religious services, which might be by memory or tradition.
7. For this designation, see Martin-Pardey 1976, p. 80.
8. *Wb.* 3.140B gives "grosses Oberhaupt," which is also used by Helck 1958, p. 199 ff.; see Martin-Pardey 1976, p. 111 ff.
9. *Nswt-nfr*: Junker 1938, fig. 28; compare Helck 1974, p. 95; Martin-Pardey 1976, cit. 75.
10. British Museum 1911, pl. 15 = James 1961, p. 12, pl. 8.

he was in the military. At the time his coffin was made he indicates only his role as administrator, and that in the eighth and tenth districts. Why the two, which have no common border, had a history of association escapes me.[11] If there is anything in common, it might be the presence of military installations in them.

Preceding the name, but following the listing of titles, stands . This kind of arrangement occurs in a limited number of instances following the very end of the Old Kingdom (Graefe 1971, p. 44 ff.). In view of the fact that the *nswt-ḥtp-di͗* formula is connected with two deities,[12] the singular suffix *f* cannot refer to them but only to the beneficiary of the funerary grant mentioned next. Formulated as a verbal clause with a *sḏm.f* as predicate, the statement requires taking it as circumstantial or as a temporal clause, specifying the time when the granted favor of an invocation offering (*prt-ḫrw*) is to be performed.[13] When seen this way, *ḏꜣ.f bi͗ꜣ* "when he crosses the *bi͗ꜣ*," which occurs parallel with *smꜣ tꜣ* "to join the earth," the two statements together encompass the funerary process by combining the physical joining of the ground with the desired attainment of a hereafter. It is at this crucial point, when the deceased passes from one sphere to the other, that the invocation offering is to be performed, as stipulated by the grant.

As in the inscription discussed previously, this one too has some inlaid hieroglyphs. They are principally the same, with the addition of  that in both its occurrences is made of carnelian and  which is black stone.

In order to make suggestions for a possible provenience of the stray object, it would help if the time of its removal from the tomb were known. Nothing in this line was available and objects have an uncanny tendency to move in clandestine channels. The two geographical indications the inscription contains point clearly to southern Middle Egypt. Considering the extent of exploration in the Abydos region, the latter would seem improbable. Although the combination of the two Upper Egyptian districts occurs three times at Hemamiyeh, it would seem unlikely that the coffin concerning us here came from there. The name *ꜣIn-ḥrt-nḫt* occurs several times at Nagꜥ-ed-Deir, although none with the addition *ḥry-i͗b* (Dunham 1937, nos. 38, 43, 61, 66, 71, pp. 50 ff., 73 ff., 66 ff., 83 ff.; Schenkel 1965, §§231–33).[14] However, it should be noted that in at least two cases the title *rꜣ-pꜥt* is borne by *ꜣIn-ḥrt-nḫt*. None of the stelae give the epithet *mꜣꜥ ḫrw,* which would point to a date later than that of the other uses of the name. A relation between the different bearers of the name Onuris-nakht is likely, but an identity is nevertheless improbable. While it is ultimately impossible to decide from where the coffin parts were taken, it seems likely that *ꜣIn-ḥrt-nḫt* was a recurrent name in a distinguished family in southern Middle Egypt that was important from the First Intermediate Period into the (early) Middle Kingdom.

STELA OF *Ṯꜣwti͗*

In 1957, Wente and I saw a brightly painted stela in Cairo. What became of the object, then in private hands, I do not know, but it seems more than justified to make it properly known to Egyptologists because it has been previously cited only in excerpts (Vandier 1950, p. 172 ff.). For reasons I no longer recall, I have a photograph of the piece (fig. 13.1), which does not give full credit to the liveliness of its rendering.

The stela is made of a very hard fine-grained limestone. Except for its lower right corner, it is complete. The measurements are approximately 110 × 70 cm. Surrounded by a band in alternating blocks of red, blue, and yellow, the actual stela is precisely delineated in red. The upright rectangular space is divided into inscribed and largely pictographic sections.

The inscription part consists of six horizontal lines; in each one the hieroglyphs are painted in a different color, namely blue, red, and yellow, with the separating lines in yellow, blue, and red. In addition to the six hori-

11. It would seem feasible that both areas were home for military installations, which could be assumed from the grandeur of the tombs at Qaw el-Kebir and Nagꜥ-ed-Deir. However, Akhmim, located in the ninth district, appears to have been another center of military personnel.

12. Although Khenty-imentyw becomes eventually absorbed by Osiris, the different geographical association suggests that the two deities were at this time still considered to be separate.

13. The distinction between the two types of clauses is principally a modern one and would seem doubtful as far as ancient Egypt is concerned. For this use of the *sḏm.f,* see Gardiner 1973, §454.4. The present formulation can be compared with cases where the *nswt-ḥtp-di͗* formula includes a specification *m i͗n.f sꜣ.f* (Cairo 20027, b,3; 20048; 20117; 20225; 20235; 20372). Different from Gardiner, who considers such statements as relatively past, it would seem more appropriate to consider them as relative present, i.e., defining the time when the granted favor is to be performed.

14. The sign  after the name is clearly a substitute for ; for this practice, see Fischer 1964, p. 124 ff.

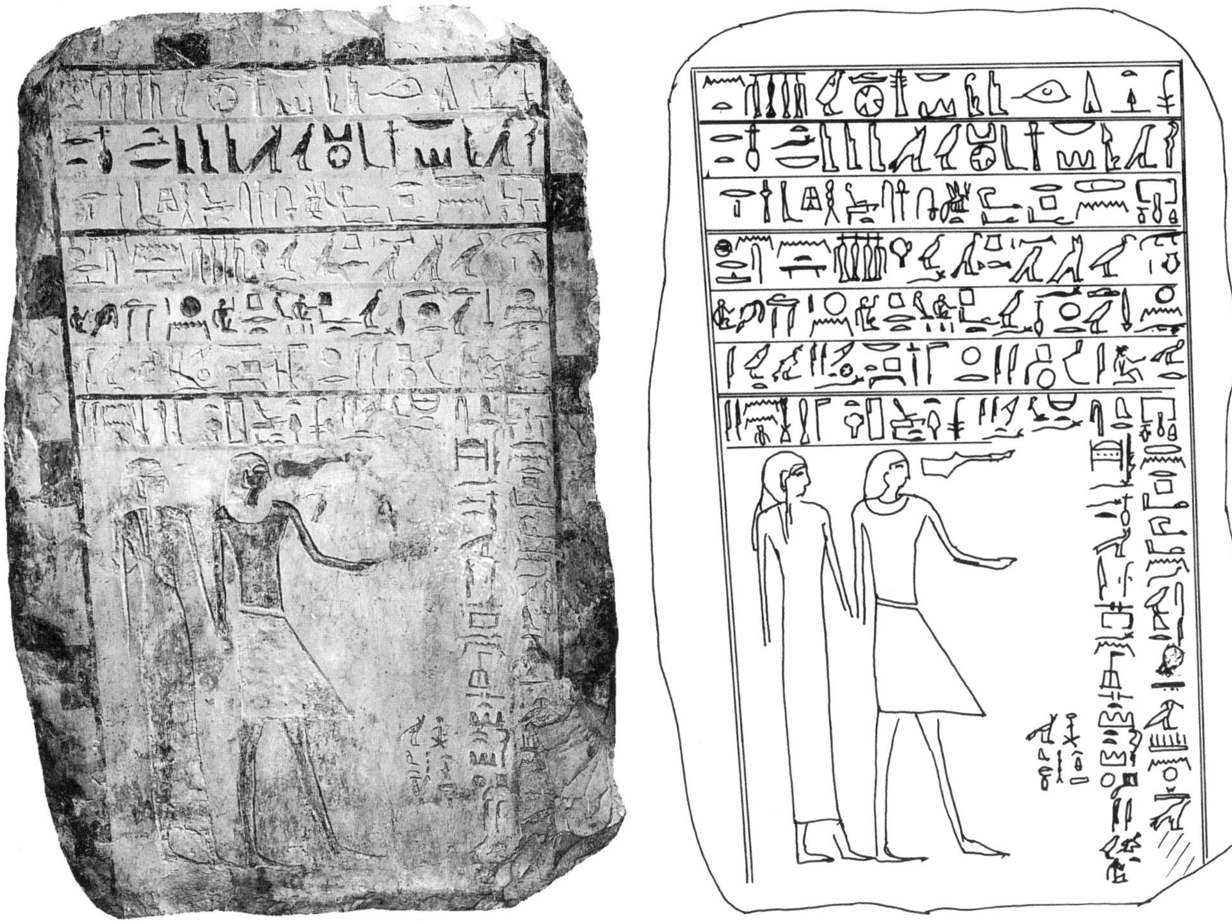

Figure 13.1. Stela of *Ṯꜣwtỉ*

zontal lines, there are also two vertical columns to the right of the picture of a standing couple, as well as a horizontal line of inscription above them that concerns only the woman.

The main text reads:

> "The King graciously grants and Osiris, lord of the desert of *Ḏdw* and the Khenty-imentyw, lord of the desert of Abydos, in all his proper places,[a] an invocation offering for the *rꜣ-pꜥt,* count, nobleman, Unique's associate, lector priest,[b] skillful of mouth, collected of mind,[c] who found a solution when it was lacking about the beginning of the land belonging to the governance of the rebel,[d] who spoke according to his voice, while the nobility was silent, on the day of placing the feared one,[e] the "general," the honored one with the Great god, lord of heaven, the beloved one of his town *Ṯꜣwtỉ*." [f]

The text contains a number of idiosyncrasies, in addition to some indications of a political nature, which require discussion.

[a] As in the texts discussed earlier, Osiris and Khenty-imentyw are not fully identified, but separated geographically. What is unusual is that the two deities are not merely associated with a place name, Osiris with *Ḏdw* and Khenty-imentyw with Abydos, but that in either case their link with the place specifically concerns the area indicated as 𓈉. While a reading *ḫꜣst* might be tempting, *smỉt* "desert" would seem equally, if not even more, appropriate.[15] What makes the present formulation so interesting is the fact that Osiris and Khenty-imentyw are associated only with the desert tract and not with the entire settlement, as is usual.[16]

The attachment *m swt.f nb(t) nfrt* can concern either deity. It appears to extend the realm where ritually proper burials can be performed for the deceased beyond the limits of the two cemeteries listed before. It re-

15. *Ppy-ꜥnḫ ḥry-ỉb* at Meir (*Urk.* 1, p. 222.8) boasts that he was the one who "opened this area (*wꜥrt*)" to become a formal burial ground (*ẖrt-nṯr*). Neither the orthography nor the specific administrative connotation would support the reading *wꜥrt* in the text concerning us.

16. The emphasis on the "desert" makes it clear that the two deities originally had an exclusively funerary role, which only secondarily expanded to include the settlement of the living from which the cemetery was reached.

quires that the two deities were acknowledged not only there, but that either branches of the cult or associated places of worship could exist elsewhere as well.[17]

[b]The grant, a *prt-ḫrw,* is the same as listed in the inscription discussed earlier and can be considered "standard." It is the topic of the vertical text that lists specifics for its performance. See note i, below.

The designations for the man are the same as those given for Onuris-nakht the Middle and can be considered typical for the kind of man represented by provincial stelae of the period.

[c]The specification of the social position is followed by a description of the personal qualities. It should be noted that they concern mental and not physical qualities. For the pair *ʿbꜣ rꜣ - sꜣq ib* "skillful of mouth," "collected of mind," see Polotsky 1929, §64c; Janssen 1946/2, p. 9 f.; Vandier 1950, p. 175; and Cairo 1666, which has principally the same text as occurs here (Borchardt 1964, p. 124, pl. 88 = Petrie 1900, pl. 8, bottom).[18]

[d]The passage has an exact parallel in the Ankhtify inscriptions, where it was rendered "j'etais un homme qui trouvait la solution quand elle faisait defaut dans le pays grâce à des plans avises."[19] The ability "to find a sentence, when it is needed" is a repeatedly emphasized quality (cf. Janssen 1946/2, Gb). The statement becomes a dubious generality when neither the topic nor the occasion is specified. As for the problem for which *Ṯꜣwtỉ* claims to have found a "sentence," i.e., "solution," it has to be seen in the adjoined *ḥr* *n sḫr ḫn.* The previous renderings[20] were based on the notion that the words contain a compound preposition *ḥr-ḫnt.*[21] The latter is attested only once in a variant of Chapter 7 of the Book of the Dead, where it appears to be an error.[22] Thus, *ḥr* has to be recognized as introducing the topic "about" which a solution had been found.

Because of the separation of *ḥr* and its recognition as a single preposition, *ḫnt* has to be seen as an independent entity. The writings and in the variants make it clear that *tꜣ* is the word for "land." This leaves for *ḫnt* only two possibilities: it could be either a *nisbe*, i.e., "One who is foremost in" or a noun closely associated with *tꜣ*. As *ḫnt* is well attested for denoting the "beginning" of a land with the connotation of "southern,"[23] "the beginning of the land" would make sense only if the meaning of *tꜣ* "land" were defined. This I see in the attached *n sḫr ḫn,* which I understand as qualifying *ḫnt-tꜣ,* either as an indirect genitive or as a possessive, "belonging to."

There are no problems as far as *sḫr* "plan," "governance," "design" is concerned.[24] The situation is different for . *Wb.* 3.286:19 ff., lists it as a verb, which among others means "(den Arm) rühren." Vandier envisaged it to be "un mot exprimant une qualité," leading him to render *n sḫr ḫn* as "grace à un plan avisé."[25] However, there is no attested cognate. Furthermore, the crocodile, presumably serving here as a determinative, is for the Egyptians not a metaphor for intelligence, but rather one for greed; in *Urk.* 4, p. 968.11 ff., the Count of Thinis, Antef, claims *wꜥf bṯnw spr ḫn* "who subdues the rebel and expels the *ḫn.*"[26]

The same derogatory meaning applies also in Louvre C 1 (Sethe 1928, p. 82, 2), *n zp ỉry.ỉ tp-ḫn* "never shall I commit an act of rebellion."[27] A political meaning such as "to rebel," "to grab" would suit the given context provided that *ḫn* is a nominally used participle. This is indeed possible considering the negative connotation, and also the fact that subsequently the word *snḏ* has as its determinative, while in Moʿalla it is lacking. The result of these deliberations is the rendering "who found a solution when it was lacking about the southern end of the land belonging to the governance of the rebel." When understood in this way, the statement by *Ṯꜣwtỉ*

17. The question of the distribution of cults is still a basically untouched field. For example, it is not clear how the worship of Ptah at Karnak was related to the cult of Amun and how it was linked with the Ptah cult at Memphis.

18. Schenkel (1965, p. 46) apparently reads it *sḫm-rꜣ* in view of his translation "der seiner Worte mächtig ist."

19. Vandier 1950, p. 171 ff.; Schenkel (1965, p. 46) translates "einer, der die Entscheidung findet, wenn sie nottut, als einziger im Land, auf Grund klugen Planens"; Fischer (1968, p. 141) gives as translation of the Dendara parallel "one who is a director of speech, who collects (his) understanding (lit. "heart"), who finds a statement when it is wanting, who speaks up ... when the people are silent on the day when fear is aroused."

20. Schenkel (1965, p. 46, note e) gives as a literal meaning "der die Entscheidung findet ... an der Spitze des Landes; d.h. wohl: als an der Spitze des Landes Stehender, als isoliert an allerhöchster Stelle Stehender."

21. Vandier (1950, p. 174) refers to *Wb.* 3.303:8, a compound *ḥr-ḫnt* meaning "in."

22. Naville 1886/2, p. 18, Ca. The variant Ai has *ḥr wʿ* "unique face(d)" as a reference to Raʿ as the sun.

23. See *Wb.* 3.306:6 ff.; Schlott-Schwab 1981, p. 11 ff.

24. Faulkner 1962, p. 242 ff.; Ptahhotep 85: "If you are a leader while commanding the governance of commoners."

25. W. Schenkel renders "auf Grund klugen Planens."

26. Compare Burkhardt 1984, p. 358, "der den Frevler niederzwingt und den Rebellen beruhigt."

27. Unclear is the occurrence in *CT* 2, pp. 280–81e = Book of the Dead, Chapter 115 = Sethe 1922, p. 23, p. 4.

as well as those of Ankhtify of Moꜥalla and Mereri of Dendara directly concern the political developments in southern Upper Egypt that culminated under Theban leadership in the secession of the "Head of Upper Egypt" from the united country, i.e., the schism between the Tenth and the Eleventh Dynasty.

[e] The claim to have found a solution in the face of the political emergency is coupled with one about efforts on a specific occasion, which, however, were made in vain because of lack of support. It has a number of parallels, which Vandier has already assembled.[28] There is, however, a feature of major significance in the *Ṯꜣwtỉ* version which Vandier did not indicate. This is the use of as a determinative after . As a result, *snḏ* has to be recognized as denoting a person, either "feared one" or "fearful one."

The traditional rendering of *mdw r ḫrw.f* "one who spoke according to his voice," i.e., to speak freely, is maintained here.[29] The statement appears to reflect a specific historical event, presumably associated with the opening rift between the "Head of Upper Egypt" and the rest of the country, which was under Heracleopolitan rule. While *Ṯꜣwtỉ* and a few others, such as Ankhtify and Mereri, had taken a stand, the others participating in the occasion were silent. Those people are specified as *pꜥt* and should thus be seen as members of the nobility, i.e., the upper stratum of Egypt's society. To find the *pꜥt* in a decisive role agrees with *Ṯꜣwtỉ*'s holding the designation *rꜣ-pꜥt* "speaker of the *pꜥt*."[30]

The occasion when *Ṯꜣwty* and others claim to have voiced their opinion is described as *hrw n dy snḏw*.[31] Fischer[32] quotes a suggestion by Anthes that be understood as a passive *sḏm.f*, which is followed here. *Snḏ*, in view of the determinative, clearly refers to a person, which, as already pointed out, could be taken as a nominally used active or passive participle. Because the majority of cases omits the determinative, I see this as conveying a derogatory aspect and thus would opt for a rendering "feared one." Who is denoted in this circumlocutious fashion cannot be determined with certainty.[33]

[f] After the string of laudable statements, the designation *ỉmy-r mšꜥ* is given, which was not among those listed earlier.[34] It is followed by *ỉmꜣḫy ḫr nṯr-ꜥꜣ nb pt* and the epithet *mry nỉwt.f*. For *mry nỉwt.f*, see Janssen 1946/2, Aw 25, 28, 30, 34, 38.

Inscriptions accompanying the depiction of the couple are two vertical columns concerning *Ṯꜣwtỉ* and a horizontal line for his wife. The former might best be understood as a repetition of the granted invocation offering, followed however by religious rather than political statements as provided in the upper section. The two columns read:

> "An invocation offering for the *rꜣ-pꜥt*, foremost of the excellent commoners on earth,[g] efficacious spirit [in the necropolis][h] when he is buried properly in his necropolis tomb [in] the Western Desert,[i] the honored one *Ṯꜣwtỉ*.

[g] The line of social designations of *Ṯꜣwtỉ* would seem considerably shorter than in line 3. Fischer felt uneasy about the conjunction of *ḥꜣty-ꜥ* and *nḏ-ỉqr tp-tꜣ*, considering it necessary to think of *ḥꜣty-ꜥ* as meaningless (Fischer 1968, pp. 87–88). The frequent suggestion of honorific titles or ephemeral uses of designation is, however, less due to the ancient Egyptians than to an unwillingness to consider them literally and in their context. As I point out in another paper, the literal meaning of *ḥꜣty-ꜥ* is "the foremost of the document/register/list," thus

28. Vandier (1950, p. 177 ff.) renders it "(Je fus un homme) qui sut parler librement, à un moment où les gens se taisaient, le jour où il fallut semer la crainte"; Schenkel (1965, p. 46) gives for it "Ich bin der Held ohne Gleichen, der das zu Sagende sagt, wenn das Volk nicht zu sprechen wagt, in bangen Tagen (lit. "am Tag des Legens der Furcht")"; and Fischer (1968, p. 141 ff.) translates "who speaks up (lit. according to his voice) when the people are silent on the day when fear is aroused."

29. The use of as a determinative in Griffith and Newberry n.d., pl. 13, line 26, would support this rendering, as long as the particular hieroglyph is not . All other instances are without a determinative, which would also allow a rendering "one who speaks against his enemy," but epigraphic uncertainties prevent a final decision.

30. It should be noted that *rḫyt* could also exert influence as results from Griffith and Newberry n.d., pl. 13, p. 26, which lists them parallel to *pꜥt gr.tỉ* and also *rḫyt m sgr*, which would seem to correspond to *šmꜥ m sgr* "Upper Egypt was made silent" in the Ankhtify formulation.

31. On the stela of Zennakht is instead *hrw n sḥꜥ* "day of the great council."

32. Fischer 1968, p. 142; compare Edel 1955, §565.

33. It is tempting to think of Akhtoes, the first king of the Ninth Dynasty, who according to Manetho's epitomes was "behaving more cruelly than his predecessors, wrought woes for the people of all Egypt, but afterwards he was smitten with madness, and was killed by a crocodile" (Waddell 1948, p. 61).

34. For the epigraphic shape of , see Fischer 1968, p. 133, fig. 23.

making it possible to apply it over a wide range.[35] In the present occurrence concerning *Ṯ3wtỉ's* outstanding role during his earthly existence, the position juxtaposed is between his role vis-à-vis the two strata making up Egypt's population. While he is "speaker" in regard to the nobility (*pꜥt*), he is "the foremost of the document list of the excellent commoners." This does not necessarily make him a "commoner" (*nḏs*) himself, but it is an appropriate definition of his exalted social standing.

[h]For *3ḫ mnḫ m ḫrt-nṯ*, see Clère 1941, p. 460 ff. It matches *Ṯ3wtỉ's* distinguished role in life with the appropriate spiritual state once he is in the necropolis.

[i] The invocation offering is to be performed during the funeral. I understand *qrs.f* as a passive *sḏm.f* used in a circumstantial statement. *Nfr* is an adverb (*Wb.* 2.256:12; Gardiner 1973, §205.4). The tomb is carefully specified in regard to its status and location. Accordingly, *ỉs.f n ḫrt-nṯr* "his tomb of the necropolis" indicates that *Ṯ3wtỉ's* burial place had the status of being in a sanctified cemetery, literally, "of god's property." The indication reflects the awarding of the kind of ritual burial that came to be considered prerequisite for a meaningful afterlife. While the tomb has necropolite status, it is nevertheless located in "the Western Desert," which means that only the tomb but not its surrounding was necessarily considered *terra sacra*.

The annotation for his wife reads "his wife, his beloved one, *ḫqrt-nswt wꜥtt*, priestess of Hathor, *Snnwy*." While "sole ornament of the king" is a philological rendering of the lady's designation, I am at a loss as to what it actually means.

The provenience of the stela offers problems. The name *Ṯ3wtỉ* is well attested at Qasr es-Sayyad, Dendara, and at Khozzam (PM 5, p. 121 ff.; Fischer 1968, p. 103 ff.; Fischer 1964, p. 47 ff.), but none are associated with *Snnwy*, whose name I am unable to trace. Much would speak for a Nagꜥ-ed-Deir provenience, but the extreme colorfulness as well as the phraseology of the text make it doubtful. Chronologically, the stela would seem close to Ankhtify's tomb at Moꜥalla and that of Mereri at Dendara. What makes it particularly significant is its reflection of events determining the First Intermediate Period.

References

Anthes, R.
1954 "The Original Meaning of *m3ꜥ ḫrw*." *Journal of Near Eastern Studies* 13: 21–51.

Baer, K.
1960 *Rank and Title in the Old Kingdom*. Chicago: University of Chicago Press.

Blackman, A.
1924 *The Rock Tombs of Meir*, Volume 4. Archaeological Survey of Egypt 25. London: Egypt Exploration Society.

Borchardt, L.
1964 *Denkmäler des Alten Reiches (ausser den Statuen)*. Catalogue général des antiquités égyptiennes du Musée du Caire, nos. 1295–1808. Cairo: Government Press.

British Museum
1911 *Hieroglyphic Texts from Egyptian Stelae, etc., in the British Museum*, Volume 1. London: British Museum.

Burkhardt, A., ed.
1984 *Urkunden der 18. Dynastie: Übersetzung zu den Heften 5–16*. Berlin: Akademie-Verlag.

Clère, J. J.
1941 "Une stèle de la Ire periode intermédiaire comportant un hiéroglyphe nouveau." In *Miscellanea Gregoriana, raccolta di scritti pubblicati nel I centenario dalla fundazione del Pont. Museo Egizio (1839–1939)*, pp. 455–66. Vatican City: Topografia Poliglotta Vaticana.

Dunham, D.
1937 *Naga-ed-Dêr Stelae of the First Intermediate Period*. Oxford: Oxford University Press.

Edel, E.
1955 *Altägyptische Grammatik*. Analecta Orientalia 34/39. Rome: Pontificium Institutum Biblicum.

Faulkner, R. O.
1962 *A Concise Dictionary of Middle Egyptian*. Oxford: Griffith Institute.

Fischer, H. G.
1964 *Inscriptions from the Coptite Nome Dynasties VI–XI*. Analecta Orientalia 40. Rome: Pontificium Institutum Biblicum.
1968 *Dendera in the Third Millennium B.C.* Locust Valley: J. J. Augustin.

35. For example, "the foremost of the register" in regard to an incorporated community is its "mayor," while for a population living on open land in unincorporated communities it denotes a "count."

Gardiner, A. H.
1947 *Ancient Egyptian Onomastica*. 3 volumes. Oxford: Oxford University Press.
1973 *Egyptian Grammar*. Third edition revised. Oxford: Griffith Institute.

Goedicke, H.
1956 "Zu *imj-rꜣ* und *tp-Šmꜣ* im Alten Reich." *Mitteilungen des Instituts für Orientforschung* 4: 1–10.

Graefe, E.
1971 Untersuchungen zur Wortfamilie *bjꜣ*. Ph.D. dissertation, University of Cologne.

Griffith, F. Ll., and P. E. Newberry
n.d. *El Bersheh*, Volume 2. Archaeological Survey of Egypt 4. London: Egypt Exploration Fund.

Helck, W.
1950 "*Rpꜥt* auf dem Thron des Gb." *Orientalia* 19: 416–34.
1954 *Untersuchungen zu den Beamtentiteln des ägyptischen Alten Reiches*. Ägyptologische Forschungen 18. Glückstadt: J. J. Augustin.
1958 *Zur Verwaltung des Mittleren und Neuen Reichs*. Probleme der Ägyptologie 3. Leiden: E. J. Brill.
1974 *Die altägyptischen Gaue*. Beihefte zum Tübinger Atlas des vorderen Orients, Reihe B, Nr. 5. Wiesbaden: Ludwig Reichert Verlag.

James, T. G. H.
1961 *Hieroglyphic Texts from Egyptian Stelae, etc.*, Volume 1. Second edition. London: British Museum.

Janssen, J.
1946 *De traditioneele egyptische autobiografie voor het Nieuwe Rijk*. 2 volumes. Leiden: E. J. Brill.

Junker, H.
1938 *Gîza* 3. Vienna and Leipzig: Hölder-Pinchler-Tempsky.

Kees, H.
1932 "Beiträge zur altägyptischen Provinzialverwaltung und der Geschichte des Feudalismus." *Nachrichten von der Gesellschaft der Wissenschaften zu Göttingen*: 85–119.

Mackay, E.; L. Harding; and W. F. Petrie
1929 *Bahrein and Hemamieh*. Egyptian Research Account Memoire 47. London: British School of Archaeology in Egypt.

Meyer, E.
1921 *Geschichte des Altertums*, Band 1, Teil 2. Fourth edition. Stuttgart: Cotta.

Martin-Pardey, E.
1976 *Untersuchungen zur ägyptischen Provinzialverwaltung bis zum Ende des Alten Reiches*. Hildesheimer ägyptologische Beiträge 1. Hildesheim: Gerstenberg Verlag.

Naville, E.
1886 *Das ägyptische Totenbuch*. 3 volumes. Berlin: Verlag von A. Asher.

Petrie, W. M. F.
1900 *Dendereh*. Memoirs of the Egypt Exploration Society 17. London: Egypt Exploration Fund.

Polotsky, J.
1929 *Zu den Inschriften der 11. Dynastie*. Untersuchungen zur Geschichte und Altertumskunde Aegyptens 11. Leipzig: J. C. Hinrichs.

Ranke, H.
1952 *Die ägyptischen Personennamen*, Volume 2. Glückstadt: J. J. Augustin.

Reisner, G. A.
1955 *A History of the Giza Necropolis*, Volume 2: *The Tomb of Hetep-Heres the Mother of Cheops*. Cambridge: Harvard University Press.

Strudwick, N.
1985 *The Administration of Egypt in the Old Kingdom*. London: Kegan Paul.

Schenkel, W.
1965 *Memphis, Herakleopolis, Theben: Die epigraphischen Zeugnisse der 7.–11. Dynastie Ägyptens*. Ägyptologische Abhandlungen 12. Wiesbaden: Otto Harrassowitz.

Schlott-Schwab, A.
1981 *Die Ausmasse Ägyptens nach altägyptischen Texten*. Ägypten und Altes Testament 3. Wiesbaden: Otto Harrassowitz.

Sethe, K.
1922 "Die Sprüche für das Kennen der Seelen der heiligen Orte." *Zeitschrift für ägyptische Sprache und Altertumskunde* 57: 85–119.
1928 *Ägyptische Lesestücke*. Leipzig: J. C. Hinrichs.
1933 *Urkunden des Alten Reiches*. Leipzig: J. C. Hinrichs.

Vandier, J.
1950 *Moꜥalla: La tombe d'Ankhtifi et la tombe du Sébekhotep*. Bibliothèque d'étude 18. Cairo: Institut français d'archéologie orientale.

Waddell, W. G.
1948 *Manetho with an English Translation*. Cambridge: Harvard University Press.

14

HISTORICAL BACKGROUND TO THE EXODUS: PAPYRUS ANASTASI VIII

S. I. GROLL

The Hebrew University of Jerusalem

It is with great pleasure and honor that I dedicate this study of a Late Egyptian Letter to Professor Wente, whose erudition in the field is well known to every Egyptologist.

P. Anastasi VIII, a letter from the scribe *Rʿ-msw* to the scribe *Ḏḥwty-m-ḥb*, exhibits a number of motifs that are also present in the story of the Exodus. No one single motif provides indisputable "proof" of the Exodus — there is no mention of an Egyptian prince of Hebrew origin whose brother turns staffs into serpents. Yet, the sum of these motifs cannot be considered casual or insignificant. Many of these motifs are also present in the literary text the Prophecies of Neferti. The importance of P. Anastasi VIII is that it is an authentic letter dealing with immediate historical events.[1]

The similarities between P. Anastasi VIII and the story of Exodus are apparent through a comparison of the following motifs.

1. SEMITES IN EGYPT

> Exodus 1:7: "But the Israelites were fertile and prolific; they multiplied and increased very greatly, so that the land was filled with them."

The presence of numerous Semites during this period in Egypt in general, and in the Delta in particular, is a well-known and undisputed fact, and P. Anastasi VIII gives its share of examples. The most obvious Semite is *ꜣny* (Heb. *ʾly* "Eli"), son of *Pyꜣy* (cf. Heb. *plʾ* "wonder"), who is, moreover, specifically mentioned as being from the Delta (see below). *Srdy* (cf. Heb. *śryd* "remnant") is a fisherman of unknown provenience.[2] *ʾIꜣ*, who is certainly of non-Egyptian ancestry and may be a Semite, had managed to advance to the important office of personal scribe of the powerful *Ḏḥwty-m-ḥb* (P. Anastasi VIII verso, lines 7–9): "Write (me) ... with the assistance of the servant *ʾIꜣ*, after you (*Ḏḥwty-m-ḥb*) write a letter of protocol with his (*ʾIꜣ*'s) assistance ... ."

2. EASTERN DELTA AND REED SEA

> Exodus 9:26: "Only in the region of Goshen, where the Israelites were ..."

Although the precise location may be disputed, there is scholarly consensus that the land of Goshen is to be located in the Eastern Delta: "The evidence at hand suggests that the biblical 'land of Goshen' was located in the [Eastern] Egyptian Delta in the general region of modern Fâqûs, Saft el-Hinna, and Tell ed-Dabʿa / Qantîr" (Freedman 1992, p. 1077).

1. For a translation of the entire text and philological notes, see Groll 1997b; eadem 1998, pp. 173–88. Compare Wente 1990, pp. 120–22. The present article is a slightly updated version of my study, "The Historical Background to the Exodus: Papyrus Anastasi VIII" (Groll 1997a, pp. 109–14).
2. *Srdy* works from a *kꜣ-rꜣ*-boat. The *kꜣ-rꜣ*-boats were small boats of Semitic origin, the name equivalent to Hebrew *kly* (e.g., Isa. 18:2: *kly gmʾ* "reed boats"), as opposed to the native Egyptian *mnš*-boats and the *ʿḥʿ.w*-boats. Antipathy towards Semitic culture may be reflected in P. Anastasi VIII recto III, lines 13–14: "Furthermore, as for the *kꜣ-rꜣ*-boats of the fishermen, what's their size anyway? As for the *ʿḥʿ.w*-boats of [the] fishermen, you can depend on them." *Ḏḥwty-m-ḥb* had issued an order that the Egyptians not use the *kꜣ-rꜣ*-boats, as, in his opinion, only the native Egyptian boats could be trusted.

Gold of Praise: Studies on Ancient Egypt in Honor of Edward F. Wente
Edited by Emily Teeter and John A. Larson
Studies in Ancient Oriental Civilization 58
Chicago: Oriental Institute, 1999

Much of P. Anastasi VIII revolves around people who are associated with the Eastern Delta. *Rʿ-msw* is known to have lived in Thebes, but he was also responsible for royal lands in the Delta and in the letter he expresses his intention to undertake a (military) journey to Pi-ramesses (biblical Ramesses; P. Anastasi VIII recto II, lines 5–10; see Eyre 1980, p. 137, nos. 20–21).

The Semite *ꜣny* was from a town called "*ʿpr-ꜣl* of the great statue of Ramesses, l.p.h., the sun of the rulers."[3] It would seem that *ʿpr-ꜣl* is to be located at or near Qantîr because of the colossi that were found there (Eyre 1980, pp. 76–80).

Dḥwty-m-ḥb was, among other things, responsible for the salaries of sailors in the Eastern Delta (P. Anastasi VIII recto I, lines 1–6) and the supply of oats to Pi-ramesses (P. Anastasi VIII recto III, lines 11–12).

Rʿ-msw suspects that the high-ranking official *Pꜣ-sr* embezzled supplies that were meant for the cenotaph of Ramesses II at Pi-ramesses (P. Anastasi VIII recto I, lines 9–11): "As for the oats of the god who is in (the) tomb of Ramesses-Meri-Amon (Ramesses II), l.p.h., which is on the bank of the river *Pꜣ-rʿ*, to whom were they given as a shipment? Did not the scribe [*Pꜣ-sr*] go in order to cause that they be sold as [his] (private) shipment?"[4]

Rʿ-msw speaks of the produce of a region called *Pꜣ-ṯwf* (P. Anastasi VIII recto III, lines 4, 12, without the definite article *pꜣ*). The word has the determinative "plant," *ṯwf* in effect being an Egyptian word for "reed." The same place name occurs in the Onomasticon of Amenope (418) where it is given the determinatives "Delta," "plant," and "town." In P. Anastasi III recto II, lines 11–12, *Pꜣ-ṯwf* is praised in parallel with *Shi-Ḥor*, the eastern offshoot of the *Pꜣ-rʿ* branch of the Nile, as the place from which Pi-ramesses receives its reeds. It must have been a very well-watered region. Bietak (1975, Abb. 23) locates *Pꜣ-ṯwf* south of Shi-Ḥor. The location and the phonetic and semantic similarity indicate that *Pꜣ-ṯwf* is, in effect, the Yam Suf "Reed Sea" of the Exodus (Bietak 1975, p. 136; cf. Groll 1998, pp. 189–92; Dayan 1998).

3. TROUBLED CONDITIONS

> Exodus 6:6: "Say, therefore, to the Israelite people: I am the LORD. I will free you from the labors of the Egyptians and deliver you from their bondage. I will redeem you with an outstretched arm and through extraordinary chastisements."

While I would be the last to claim that they died for not having sprinkled blood on their doorposts and lintels, I know of no other non-literary Egyptian text that reports the (non-judicial) deaths of so many people. The Semite sailor *ꜣny* and his children have all died in apparently suspicious circumstances.[5] The crewmen of another *mnš*-boat have also died.[6]

The conditions are so unsettled that *Rʿ-msw* has decided to depart on a (military) journey (*mšʿ*) to Piramesses to rectify the situation by force (P. Anastasi VIII recto II, lines 5–10): "We are about to go on a (military) journey. ... I will spend from the 8th to the 10th of the second month of the Inundation there (Memphis) and then we will depart for Pi-Ramesses-Meri-Amon, l.p.h., if we are alive." The statement "if we are alive" does not seem to be hyperbole, for it is not at all a common expression.

3. The word *ʿpr-ꜣl* is composed of two Semitic words: *ʿpr* (*ʿbd* "servant," "worshipper"; see Hoch 1994, pp. 63–65) and *ꜣl* (*ʾl*, the Semitic deity El) and literally means "the servant, worshipper of El." It contains two determinatives: "reversed legs" and "town." "Reversed legs," a very peculiar determinative for a place name, perhaps indicates that the city and the temple of the same name had to do with fugitives, perhaps Semitic nomads who came through *Pꜣ-ṯwf* (see below). The temple would have been their first station in Egypt for worshipping the deity El. That this entry into Egypt was authorized by Ramesses II is shown, I believe, by the fact that the temple contained a colossal statue of him.

4. The river *Pꜣ-rʿ* is the easternmost branch of the Nile. See Bietak 1975, p. 120, Abb. 23.

5. P. Anastasi VIII recto I, lines 6–9: "Furthermore, I (*Rʿ-msw*) heard as follows: The crewman of the *mnš*-boat *ꜣny*, son of *Pyꜣy*, of the town 'Servant of El of the great statue of Ramesses, l.p.h., the sun of the rulers' has died together with his children. Is it true? [Is it] false? What did the Commander of the Gate of the Fortress do with the shipment for the temple (that was entrusted to *ꜣny*)?" I believe that the question "What did the Commander ... do with the shipment for the temple?" indicates that *Rʿ-msw* suspects that this official was in some way involved in *ꜣny*'s death.

6. P. Anastasi VIII recto I, lines 13–16: "Look, his *mnš*-boat captain [...] to go to have [these] two men of ours loaded with cargo, because they have this huge quantity of silver as cargo because their crewmen have died."

4. DROUGHT

> Exodus 14:21: "Then Moses held out his arm over the sea and the LORD drove back the sea with a strong east wind all that night, and turned the sea into dry ground."

P. Anastasi VIII recto I, lines 2–6: "[The] Commander of the Gate of the Fortress sent me a letter saying that you were to bring three bars of silver in the form of a load of fish and oats … , but 600 *šn*-stones and 700 [+ X] *deben* of silver [in the form of] fish is the total that you have this year, which is fitting that you ship in a single day."

P. Anastasi VIII recto III, lines 3–5: "(If) there are no tamarisks in the *P3-ṯwf* region and if there is no (agricultural) tax produce which is supposed to be ready for me, under no circumstances is the barge to be manned and sent empty … ."

P. Anastasi VIII recto III, lines 11–12: "As for the barge which sails to the city Ramesses II, [l.]p.h., loaded with oats each year, it will not come to you loaded with (agricultural) tax produce of (the) *ṯwf* (region)."

As noted above, *P3-ṯwf* was a well-watered region renowned as the source of papyrus for Pi-ramesses. Nevertheless, in the year that *Rʿ-msw* wrote P. Anastasi VIII, there was a shortage of fish, oats, tamarisk, and other agricultural tax products from *P3-ṯwf*, which indicates severe drought conditions. These conditions provided the background to the tradition of the crossing of the Reed Sea.

5. MIDDLE YEARS OF THE REIGN OF RAMESSES II

The main characters in the letter are all very well known. They represent an elite group that managed Egyptian economic and political affairs during the middle years of the reign of Ramesses II. The author of P. Anastasi VIII, *Rʿ-msw*, is, in my opinion, the dominant figure of the period (see Černý 1973, pp. 316–27). I believe *Dḥwty-m-ḥb* to be the same *Dḥwty-m-ḥb* who, as a specialist in medical herbs, was sent to the land of the Hittites in order to heal the daughter of the Hittite king. We know that *Dḥwty-m-ḥb* made this journey in year 35 of Ramesses II (Edel 1976, pp. 59–63). The letter would seem to be later than this date because *Rʿ-msw* makes an allusion to *Dḥwty-m-ḥb*'s knowledge of medicine and to the fact that he has now become a very important person (P. Anastasi VIII recto II, line 15–III, line 3):

> Had you tru[ly] anointed yourself with *3s*-ointment (play on the word *3s* "quickness") and had you tru[ly] anointed yourself with the best of the *dr*-ointment (play on the word *dr* "entirety"), is it all the way to Heliopolis, empty, with a crew of six aboard that you would have sent the cattle barge which used to carry oats under the supervision of the (single) sailor *Stw*? (That's) right! You're (quite) a man now. (But) is it appropriate to be silent (in deference) to you concerning this act of negligence which you have committed?

Rʿ-msw, on the other hand, died (or disappeared from the extant documentation) in year 39 of Ramesses II (Černý 1973, p. 321). We can therefore date P. Anastasi VIII to years 36–39 of Ramesses II, which accords well with the period to which many scholars date the Exodus (Bright 1972, pp. 121–22).

CONCLUSION

P. Anastasi VIII is written in the non-literary language of the Nineteenth Dynasty. It can therefore not be likened to the Prophecies of Neferti that were written in the literary language of its time. There is indeed much similarity between the two texts. Yet the Prophecy of Neferti is a political-socio-theological treatise on the general state of affairs in Egypt during several hundred years, whereas P. Anastasi VIII is an authentic letter dealing with the practical, everyday life of administrating a region of the Eastern Delta at a known date with historical personages.

The place, time, drought, troubled conditions, and Semite presence are authentic historical motifs that relate P. Anastasi VIII to the story of the Exodus and the story of the Exodus to the middle years of Ramesses II. On the other hand, it should be noted that the inauthentic (literary) chariot motif of the story of the Exodus which, as Couroyer (1990, pp. 321–58) points out, was borrowed from the reliefs in the temple of Ramesses II at Piramesses, is not present in P. Anastasi VIII.

References

Bietak, M.
1975 *Tell El-Dabʿa* 2. Denkschrift der Gesamtakademie 4. Vienna: Verlag der Österreichischen Akademie der Wissenschaften.

Bright, J.
1972 *A History of Israel*. Second edition. Philadelphia: Westminster Press.

Černý, J.
1973 *A Community of Workmen at Thebes in the Ramesside Period*. Bibliothèque d'étude 50. Cairo: Institut français d'archéologie orientale.

Couroyer, L. B.
1990 "L'exode et la bataille de Qadesh." *Revue biblique* 97: 321–58.

Dayan, G.
1998 "The Term *ʿpꜣ-ṯwf* in the Spiegelberg Papyrus." In *Jerusalem Studies in Egyptology*, edited by I. Shirun-Grumach, pp. 133–35. Ägypten und das Altes Testament 40. Wiesbaden: Otto Harrassowitz.

Edel, E.
1976 *Ägyptische Ärzte und ägyptische Medizin am hethitischen Königshof: Neue Funde von Keilschriftbriefen Ramses' II. aus Bogazköy*. Opladen: Westdeutscher Verlag.

Eyre, C. J.
1980 Employment and Labour Relations in the Theban Necropolis. Ph.D. dissertation, Oxford University.

Freedman, D. N., ed.
1992 *The Anchor Bible Dictionary*, Volume 2. New York: Doubleday.

Groll, S. I.
1997a "The Historical Background to the Exodus: Papyrus Anastasi VIII." In *Études égyptologiques et bibliques à la mémoire du Père B. Couroyer*, edited by M. Sigrist, pp. 109–14. Cahiers de la Revue biblique 36. Paris: J. Gabalda.
1997b "Unconventional Use of the System of Shifters as a Means of Signaling the Use of Different Sources: Papyrus Anastasi VIII in the Light of the 'Standard Theory.'" *Lingua aegyptia* 5: 43–56.
1998 "The Egyptian Background of the Exodus and the Crossing of the Reed Sea: A New Reading of Papyrus Anastasi VIII." In *Jerusalem Studies in Egyptology*, edited by I. Shirun-Grumach, pp. 173–92. Ägypten und Altes Testament 40. Wiesbaden: Otto Harrassowitz.

Hoch, J.
1994 *Semitic Words in Egyptian Texts of the New Kingdom and Third Intermediate Period*. Princeton: Princeton University Press.

Wente, E. F.
1990 *Letters from Ancient Egypt*. Society of Biblical Literature, Writings from the Ancient World 1. Atlanta: Scholars Press.

15
THE MUMMY OF AMENHOTEP III

JAMES E. HARRIS
University of Michigan, Ann Arbor

The mummy of Amenhotep III (CG 61074) was discovered by Victor Loret in a cache in the tomb of Amenhotep II in the Valley of the Kings in 1898 (fig. 15.1). The much-damaged mummy had been rewrapped by the priests of the Twenty-first Dynasty. "Upon the shroud ... there is a long hieratic inscription in ink written vertically," according to the anatomist G. Elliot Smith (1912, p. 46) who removed the wrappings on September 23, 1905. Wente (1992, p. 10) states "As for Amenophis III (CG 61074), an inscription on the outer wrappings of the mummy refers to the renewing of the burial of King Nebmaʿrēʿ (i.e., Amenophis III) by the Twenty-first Dynasty high priest of Amūn Pinūdjem I ... ." The lid of the coffin "was intended for the reburial of Sethos II, but was secondarily inscribed in hieratic with the prenomen of Amenophis III," while the coffin itself "bore the names of Ramesses III." Wente (1992, p. 10) states "Here the evidence is by no means unequivocal" in reference to the identity of this mummy! The mummy was badly damaged in ancient times with the body held together through the use of bandages. In fact, its horrendous condition has led Wente (1992, p. 6) to speculate whether the damage was not from random grave robbers but by "willful desecration."

Smith (1912, p. 49) further describes the mummification as very different from any other mummy of the Eighteenth Dynasty in which an "attempt had been made to restore the limbs and body of the dead Pharaoh [to] some semblance of the form these parts had possessed in life, but had lost during the earliest stages of the process of mummification." This mummification technique consisted of placing resin mixed with inorganic matter under the skin. It should be noted that this technique was quite different from the Late Period of the New Kingdom when the mummies were packed with resin, linen, and mud, as observed in Queen Henuttowy, Makare, and Nodjme.

Interestingly Smith (1912, p. 50) notes the great difference between the mummy of Amenhotep III (CG 61074) and the mummy of Smenkhkare (CG 61075) found in tomb KV 55 in the Valley of the Kings. This tomb, believed

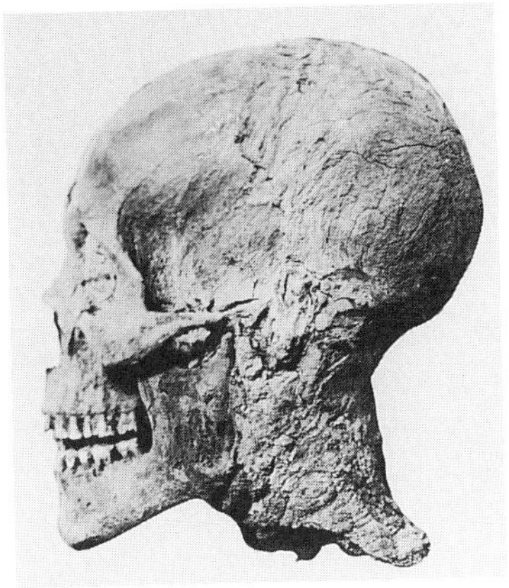

b

a

Figure 15.1. (*a*) Mummy and (*b*) Skull of Amenhotep III (from Smith 1912)

Gold of Praise: Studies on Ancient Egypt in Honor of Edward F. Wente
Edited by Emily Teeter and John A. Larson
Studies in Ancient Oriental Civilization 58
Chicago: Oriental Institute, 1999

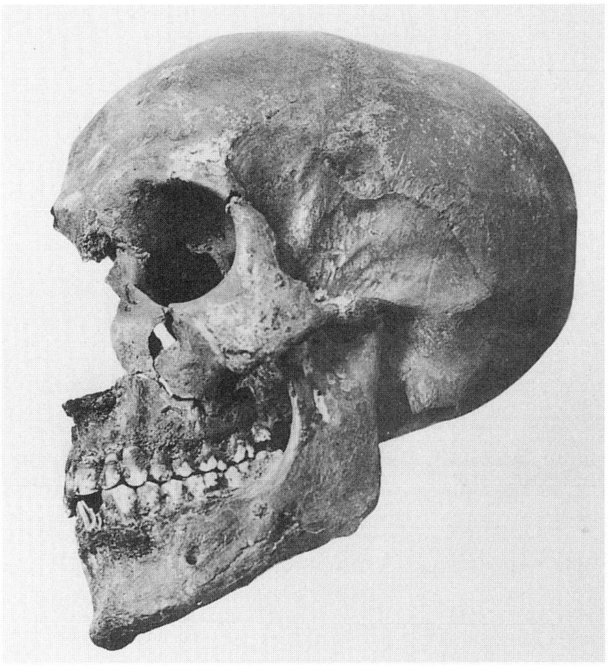

Figure 15.2. Broken Skull of Amenothes IV (Smenkhkare) from Tomb 55 (Smith 1912)

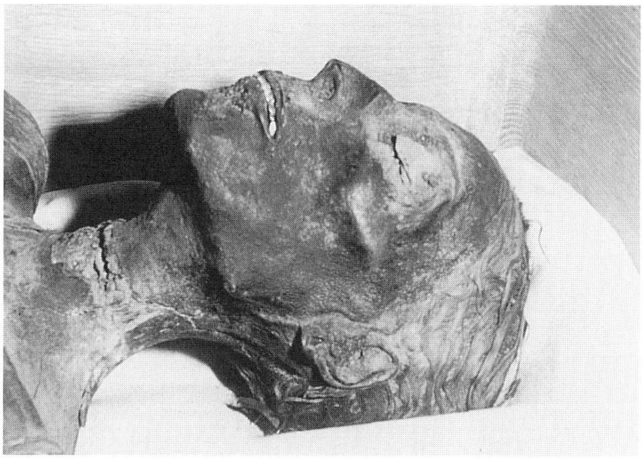

a

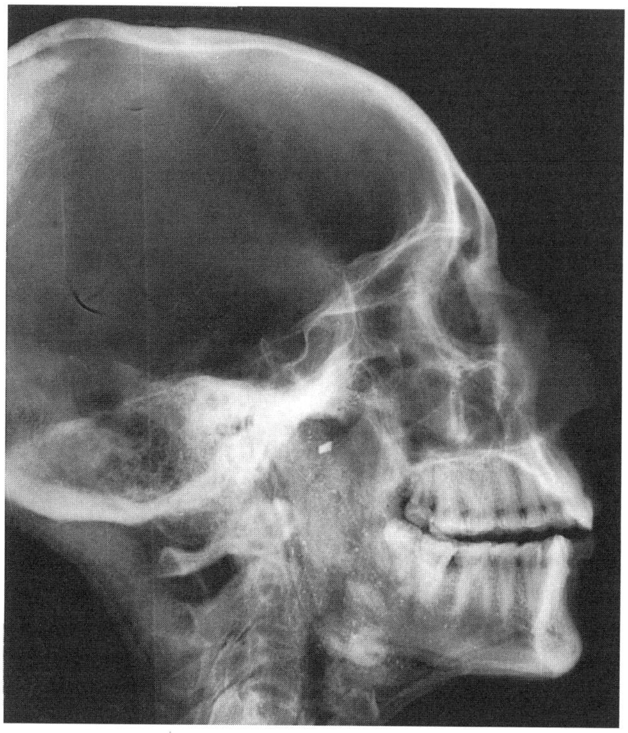

b

Figure 15.3. (*a*) Head and (*b*) Cephalometric X-ray of Thutmose IV

to have been built originally for Tiye, the Great Queen of Amenhotep III, was ultimately usurped for the burial chamber of Amenhotep IV (Akhenaten) or his co-regent Smenkhkare (fig. 15.2). Smith (1912, p. 50) comments about the mummy of Amenhotep III (CG 61074): "The chin is narrow and pointed; the mandible low and slightly built: its typically Egyptian form is in marked contrast to the equally definitely alien shape seen in the next skeleton to be discussed [mummy in Tomb 55]." Strangely, Smith did not comment on how different the craniofacial complex of the mummy of Amenhotep III (CG 61074) was from his father Thutmose IV (CG 61073; fig. 15.3). The latter is much more similar both to the occupant of Tomb 55 (CG 61075) and to the mummy of Tutankhamun (fig. 15.4).

Recently, the mummy of Amenhotep III (CG 61074) was completely reviewed, as was the mummy-skeleton (CG 61075) from KV 55 (Harris and Hussein 1991, pp. 237–39); see figs. 15.5–6. Although the present investigation continues to focus on craniofacial variation as revealed by x-ray cephalometrics, the anatomy of the postcranial skeleton and full anthropometric evaluations were repeated, and the work of Smith re-examined. It should be indicated here that after extensive investigation of the skeletal remains from KV 55 (CG 61075) and the reconstruction of the previously crushed skull utilizing an x-ray cephalometric template, Harris and Hussein (1991, p. 238) determined this individual to be a male in his thirties with a very delicate build; he is referred to as Smenkhkare in this discussion (fig. 15.7).

Although Smith (1912, p. 50) found the mummy of Amenhotep III (CG 61074) to be "typically Egyptian," present studies suggest that the skull of Amenhotep III is singularly different from that of any other royal mummy from the New Kingdom period (Wente and Harris 1992, p. 6; Harris and Hussein 1987, pp. 1–10). The cranium (length of 194 mm) is two standard deviations larger than would be expected for his body size or height (149.6 cm or less than five feet); see table 15.1. This reconstruction of stature or height from the cranium and postcranial skeleton was conducted by the physical anthropologist Fawzia Hussein at the Egyptian Museum. Since this mummy was found in terrible condition with the head and limbs disarticulated, the height of the mummy was re-evaluated by Hussein (1987, p. 2), utilizing the full-body x-rays as a template, who determined

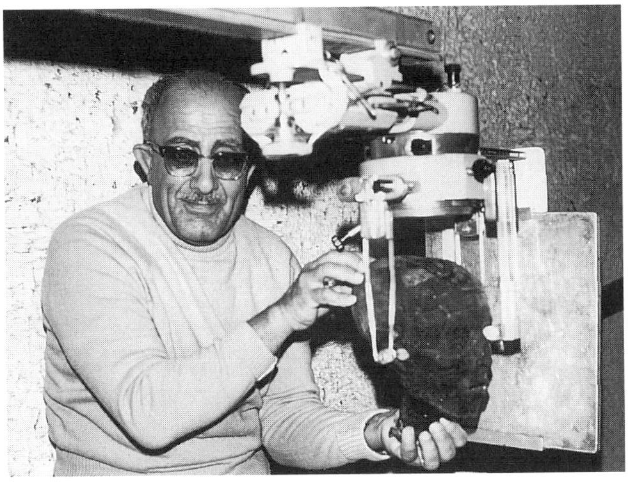

a

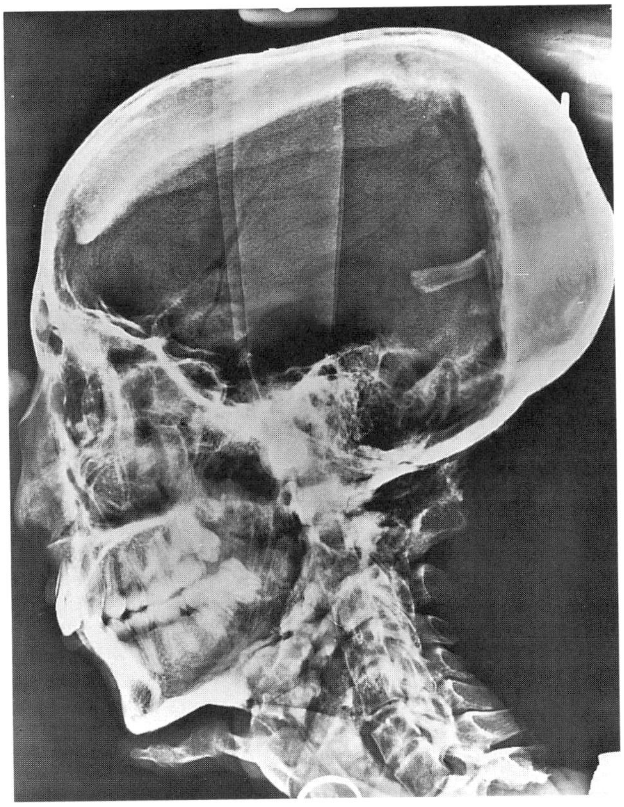

b

Figure 15.4. (*a*) Head and (*b*) Cephalometric X-ray of Tutankhamun

Amenhotep III to be 149.64 cm in height compared with the 156.1 cm measurement of Smith (1912, p. 50); see fig. 15.8. Even without examining the measurable variables derived from the digitized computerized tracings of the craniofacial skeleton, the great differences in size and shape between the skulls of the mummies of Amenhotep III (CG 61074) and his father Thutmose IV (CG 61073) and his grandsons (sons) Tutankhamun and Smenkhkare (CG 61075) are apparent (fig. 15.9).

The mandible of the mummy of Amenhotep III (CG 61074) has a more divergent growth pattern with an anti-gonial notch not seen in the other Eighteenth Dynasty mummies (fig. 15.10). By contrast, Thutmose IV (CG 61073), Smenkhkare (CG 61075) from Tomb 55, and Tutankhamun all represent similar craniofacial patterns much more typical of the Eighteenth Dynasty. Their craniofacial skeletons are characterized by delicate features observed by the noted physical anthropologist Wilton Krogman (1979). In fact, most of the articulated (intact) mummies of the kings of the Eighteenth Dynasty do not have the obvious skeletal robustness and muscle mass evident in the Ramesside periods. Bryan (1992, p. 128) notes "The mouth of Thutmosis IV was broad and unrimmed, but showed the family's trait of an *overbite* in his pursing upper lip." Undoubtedly Bryan is referring to the retrognathic face of the Eighteenth Dynasty kings compared with the Nineteenth or Twentieth Dynasty kings, i.e., the Ramessides. From the viewpoint of the clinical field of orthodontics, the Eighteenth Dynasty represents a dentally heterogeneous sample ranging from Thutmose I and II with those craniofacial features characteristic of the Nubian people (dental and alveolar protrusion) to the straight profiles of Thutmose IV, Amenhotep II, Smenkhkare, and Tutankhamun.

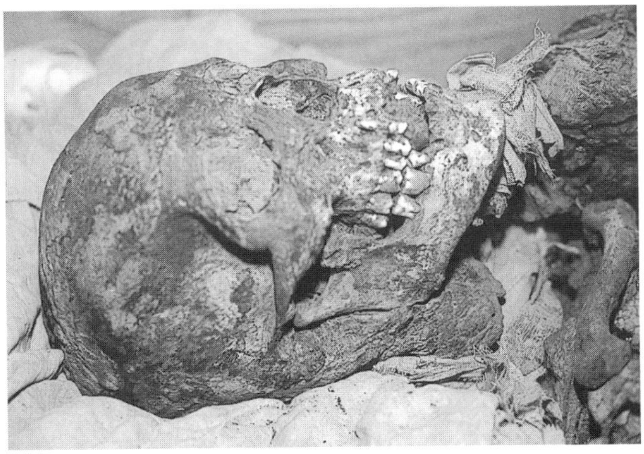

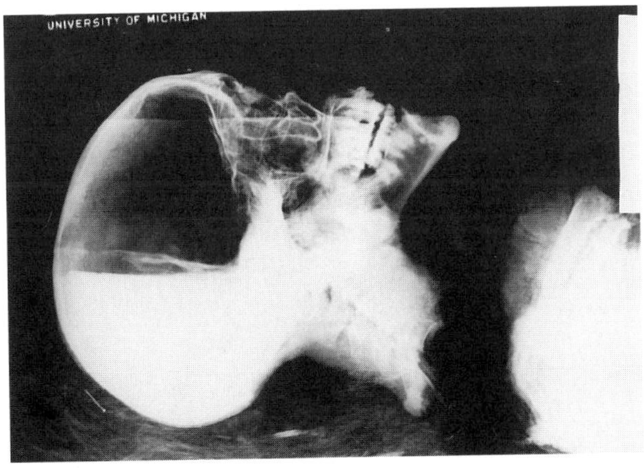

a b

Figure 15.5. (*a*) Head and (*b*) Cephalometric X-ray of Amenhotep III

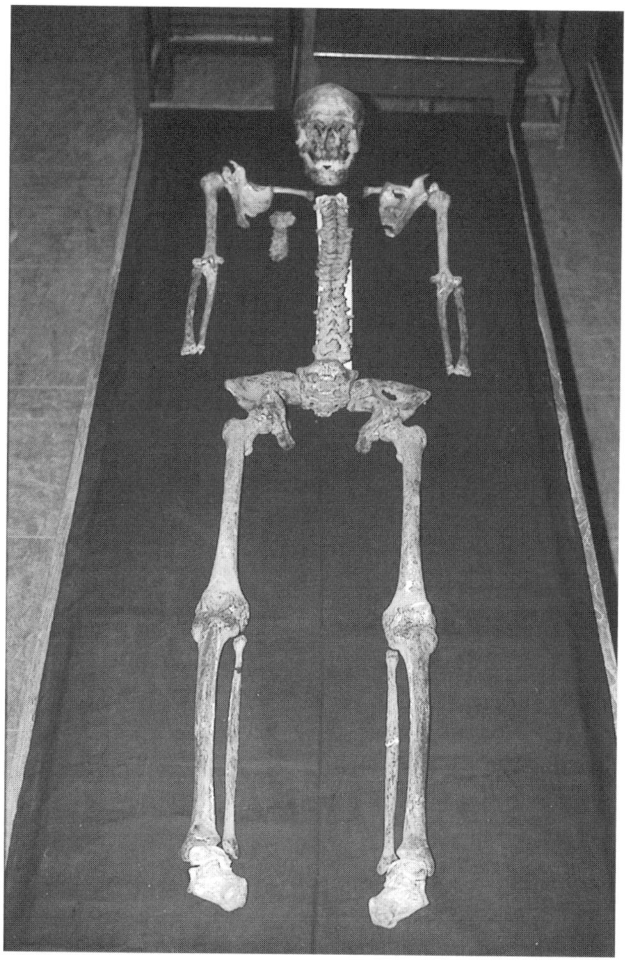

Figure 15.6. Skeletal Remains of Mummy Found in Tomb 55 (Smenkhkare)

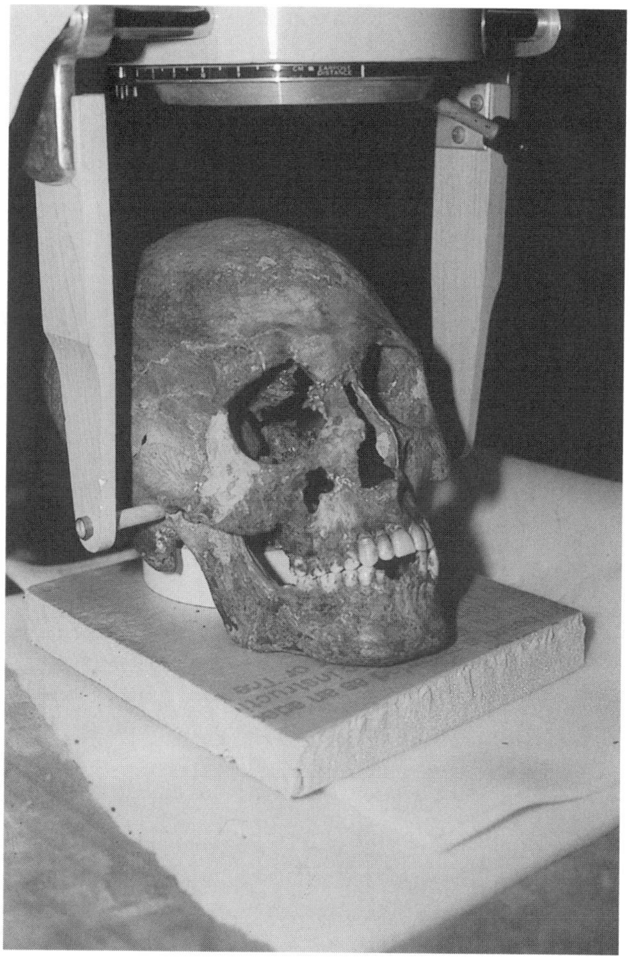

a

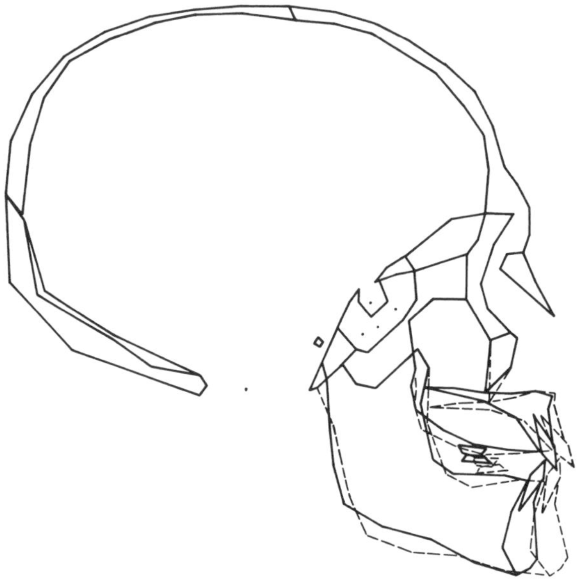

b

Figure 15.7. (*a*) Reconstructed Skull and (*b*) Cephalometric Tracing of Skull Found in Tomb 55 (Smenkhkare) where broken lines represent original positions of the mandible and maxilla

If the other royal mummies of the Eighteenth Dynasty are considered as a base line, the mummy of Amenhotep III (CG 61074) represents an atypical or aberrant growth pattern similar to that represented by the temple art and statuary of his son, the heretic king Amenhotep IV (Akhenaten). The cranium is ovoid or short in the anterior-posterior dimension while the other Eighteenth Dynasty kings tend to be elliptical or dolichocephalic, much exaggerated in the portraits of Tutankhamun during the Amarna period (fig. 15.11).

Aldred (1968, pp. 134–35) suggests that Fröhlich's Syndrome may represent a medical diagnosis of the artistic portraits of Amenhotep IV (Akhenaten). This disorder exhibits infantile genitalia, corpulence, and a feminine distribution of fat in the breasts and abdomen. It is unfortunate that Aldred is not with us today because he would have been intrigued with the great advances in chromosomal abnormalities and the location and position of deleterious gene loci. For example, Klinefelter's Syndrome (or XXY sex chromosomes) is associated with sterility and there is substantial evidence for a genetic etiology in pseudohermaphroditism, or hermaphroditism. In either condition, feminization and sterility are a frequent clinical finding. Aldred (1968, pp. 136–38) argues that from the historical record, it is unlikely that Akhenaten was the father of the daughters of Nefertiti.

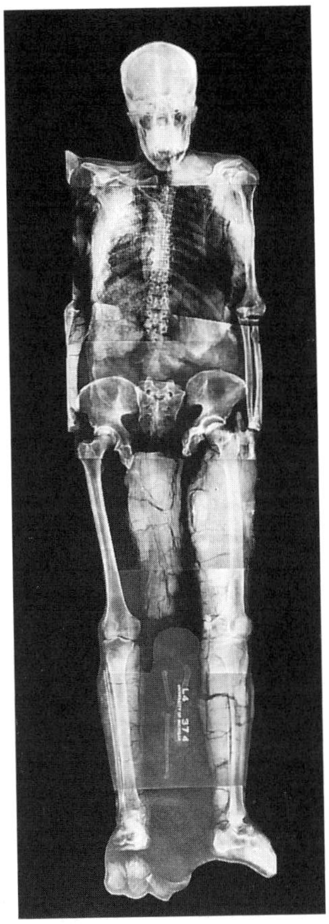

Figure 15.8. Full Body X-rays of Mummy of Amenhotep III

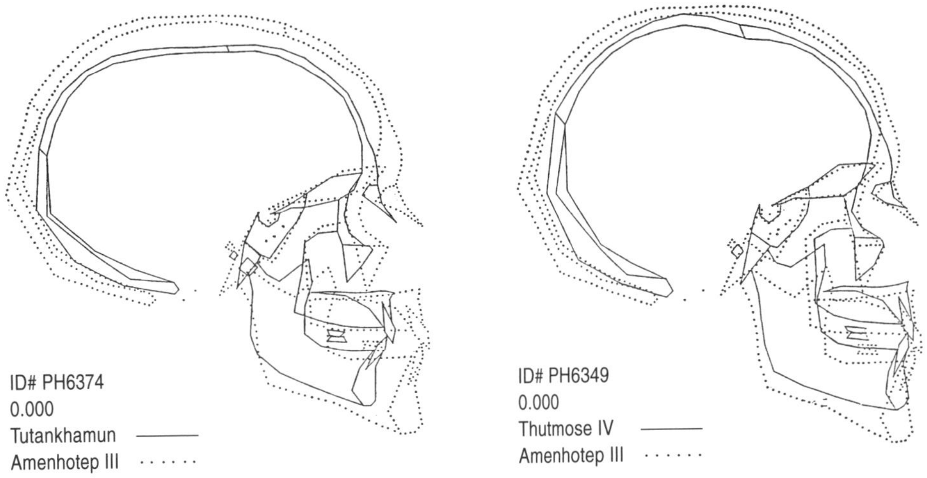

Figure 15.9. Cephalometric Tracings of Skull of Amenhotep III Compared with that of (left) Tutankhamun and (right) Thutmose IV

How do we account for this biologic discontinuity in the biologic record of the late Eighteenth Dynasty? If the mummy of Amenhotep III (CG 61074) has been correctly identified, then Amenhotep IV may not be uniquely biologically aberrant as assumed by Aldred and others, but explained simply by the fact that he was his father's son. However, assuming that Thutmose IV was the biologic father of Amenhotep III and that Queen Mutemwia was foreign to the Nile Valley, it is still difficult to accept the mummy of Amenhotep III (CG 61074) as their normal biologic son. Further, neither the mummy of Tutankhamun nor that of Smenkhkare (CG 61075) represent acceptable candidates to be the offspring of Akhenaten (as portrayed in temple and tomb art), or obviously of the mummy of Amenhotep III (CG 61074).

Who then was Amenhotep III? Did he come from Thebes or elsewhere? Scholars do not dispute that he was the son of Thutmose IV, but the background of his mother remains an interesting question. Both Wente and Aldred may give us a clue to this dilemma. Aldred (1968, p. 88) suggests that the mother of Amenhotep III was Mutemwia, and he suggests that she should have been a sister or half-sister of Thutmose IV. Wente states (1980, p. 134) that "Although Queen Mutemwia, like Queen Tiaa, bore the title of Great King's Wife, none of her titles indicate that she was of royal origin. According to some scholars she may have been the daughter of a God's Father and Master of Horses Yey, who probably hailed from Akhmim." Wente continues: "If Yey's unknown father was also the father of Queen Tiaa, the mother of Thutmose IV, the marriage between Thutmose IV and Mutemwia may have been one between first cousins, but this is admittedly pure speculation."

Amenhotep III married Tiye, daughter of commoners Yuya and Thuya, also from the region of Akhmim. Wente (1980, p. 134) speculates that "If the similarly titled Yey was the father of Yuya as well as of Queen Mutemwia, then Amenhotep III's marriage to Tiye was a marriage to his first cousin (similar to Thutmose IV and Mutemwia)."

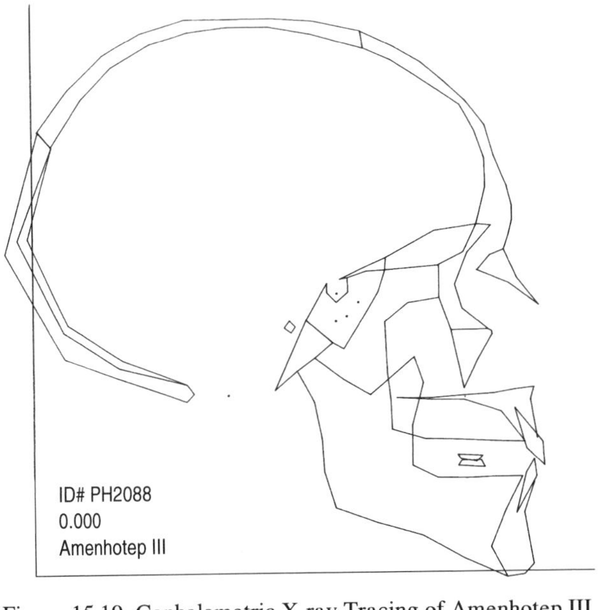

Figure 15.10. Cephalometric X-ray Tracing of Amenhotep III

If we assume the mummy of Amenhotep III (CG 61074) to be correctly identified by the priests of the Twenty-first Dynasty and the identification by Harris et al. (1978, pp. 1149–51) of the mummy of his wife Tiye

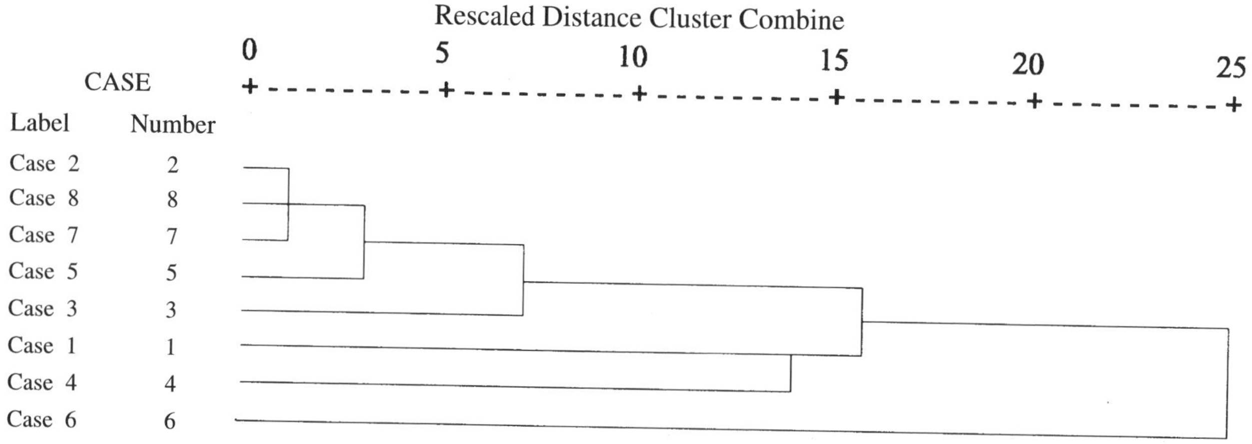

Figure 15.11. Cluster Analysis Illustrating Difference Between Amenhotep III and Other Kings of Eighteenth Dynasty (Amenhotep is depicted by No. 6)

(CG 61070) in the tomb of Amenhotep II to be valid, then their son Akhenaten could easily have had the biologic features depicted on the heretic king, assuming artistic liberties and exaggeration. Even without Tiye, and substituting the mummies of Yuya and Thuya whose identities seem certain, the same conclusions would be acceptable. To the casual observer, the face (soft tissue mask) and long neck of the mummy of the elder lady (Queen Tiye, CG 61070) found in the tomb of Amenhotep II is more similar to the statue of Nefertiti than that of the famous head of Queen Tiye in the Berlin Museum (fig. 15.12).

However, it would take a greater leap of faith to accept the mummies of Tutankhamun or Smenkhkare (CG 61075) as the sons or first degree relatives of either Akhenaten or Amenhotep III (CG 61074). The former are both very similar from the viewpoint of craniofacial variability to each other as well as to the mummies of Thutmose IV (CG 61073) or even earlier Eighteenth Dynasty kings. Tutankhamun and Smenkhkare (CG 61075), particularly after the reconstruction of the skull of the latter, demonstrate very similar craniofacial skeletons (Harris and Wente 1980, p. 3; Harrison and Abdalla 1972, p. 10; Derry 1972) and it would be difficult not to accept them as first degree relatives, probably half brothers as supposed by many scholars.

The human morphologic variation observed in the craniofacial skeleton, consisting of the cranium, maxilla, mandible, and dentition, is highly complex and variable. The Department of Orthodontics at the University of Michigan has a long history of support from the National Institutes of Health to examine the inheritance of the craniofacial complex in families with patients in the graduate clinic. These studies confirm the polygenetic mul-

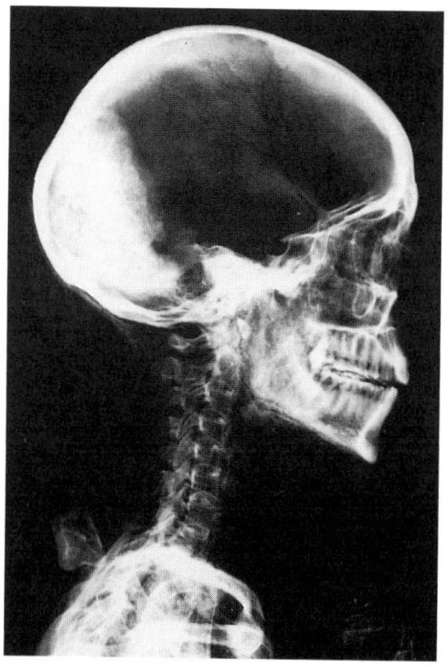

Figure 15.12. Cephalometric X-ray of Elder Lady (Queen Tiye) from Tomb of Amenhotep II

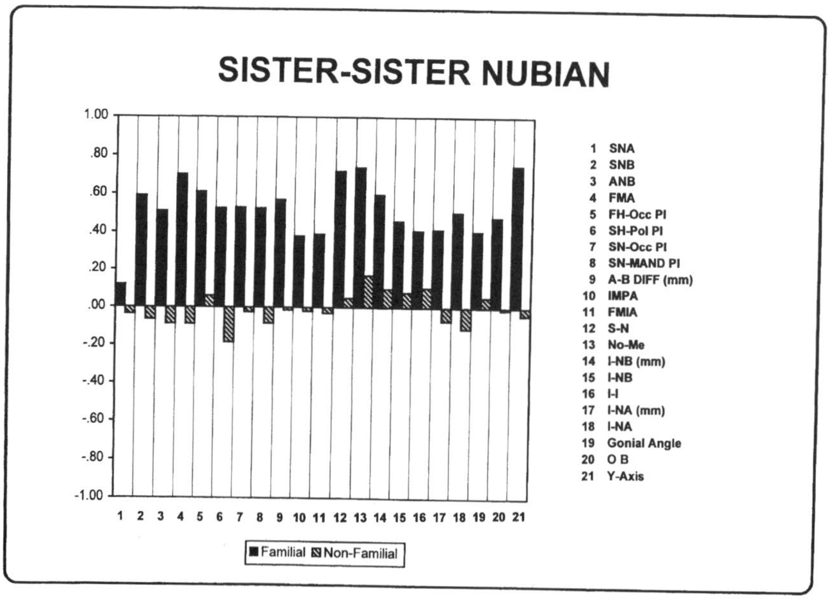

Figure 15.13. Correlation Coefficients between Nubian Sibling Pairs and Non-related Nubian Pairs Derived from Traditional Clinical Cephalometric Measurement

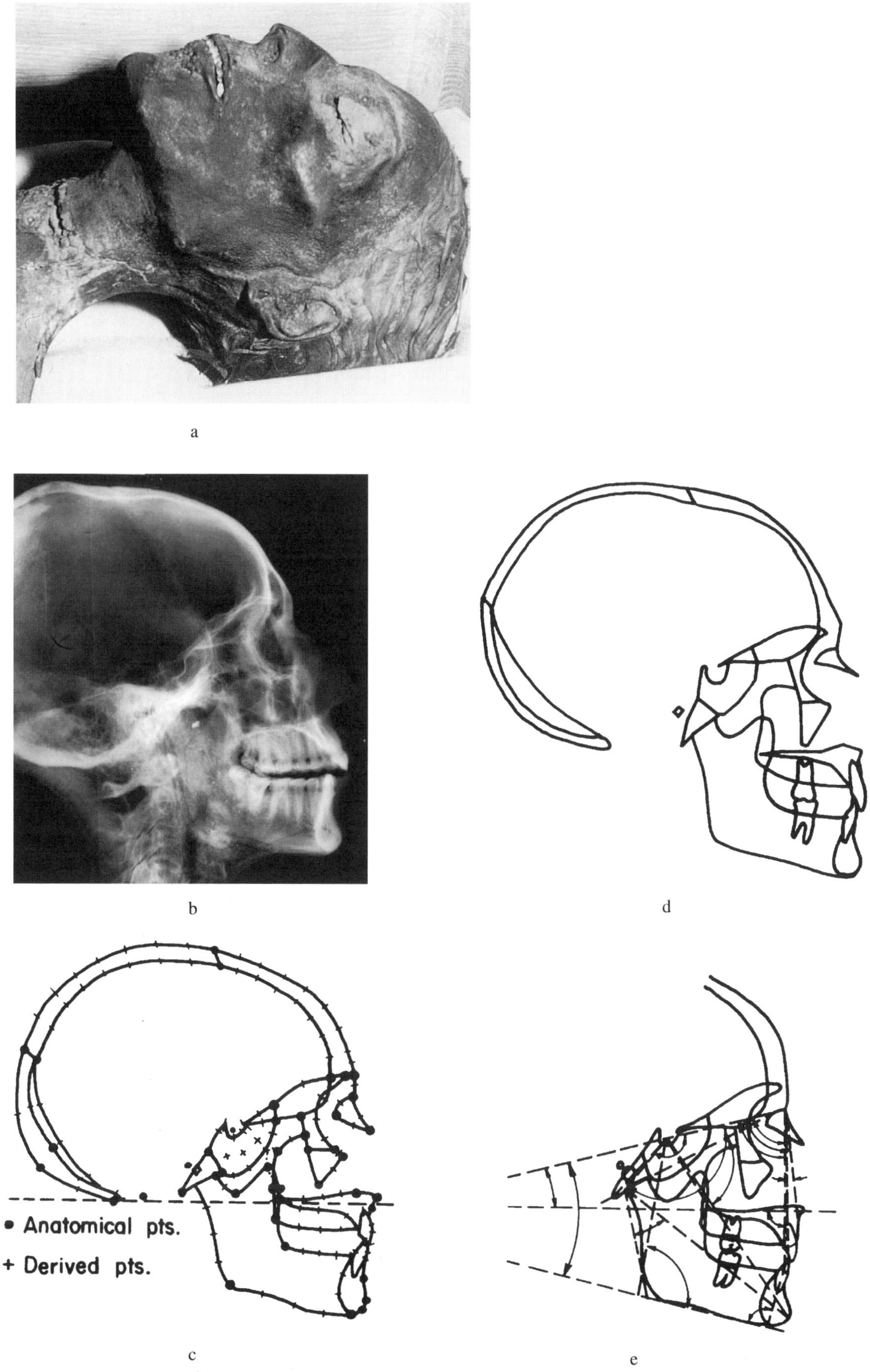

Figure 15.14. Method for Deriving Measurable Variables from Cephalometric X-rays: (*a*) Head of Thutmose IV, (*b*) Cephalometric X-ray of Head, (*c*) Cephalometric Tracing, (*d*) Computerized Digitization, and (*e*) Computer-derived Angular Measurements

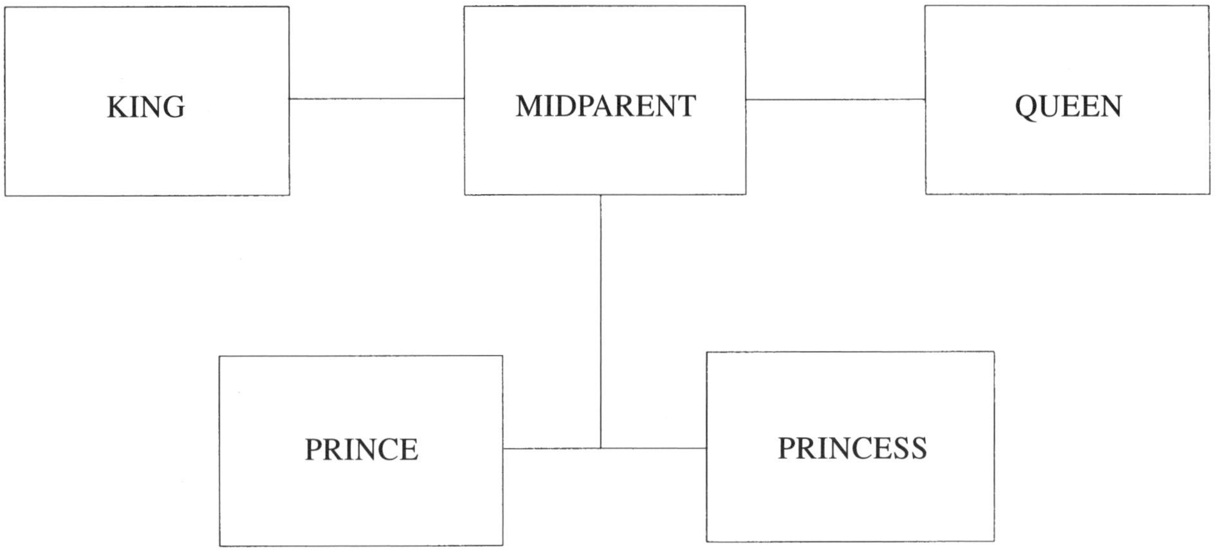

Figure 15.15. Nuclear Family with Midparent Construct

tifactorial heritability of the craniofacial skeleton. The point is that the morphology of the skull is highly variable and there is much more similarity between family members than between individuals drawn randomly from the population at large.

Diagnostic measurements, taken from x-ray cephalograms of the craniofacial skeleton utilized routinely in the orthodontic clinic, indicate that on average there is a .5 correlation between sibling pairs and between offspring and their parents, while the correlation between measurements of non-family members approximates 0. Even the relatively homogeneous samples from Nubian villages of Abu Simbel supported this hypothesis (fig. 15.13). Hence, craniofacial measurements represent a powerful tool to detect familial relations in the general population. This argument assumes continuously variable (measurable) traits and hence assumes that neither Mendelian dominance nor recessive traits or characters are applicable to this model (observed in soft tissue features, i.e., nose, lips, and eyes). First cousin marriages could affect genetic equilibrium in this model if it were assumed that the royal family was homogeneous or marriage was only within families of the Nile Valley.

The standardized cephalometric x-ray studies of the royal mummies provide the opportunity to measure and compare craniofacial variables of each mummy without disturbing the mummy and permit comparison of each individual in the collection. Cephalometric x-ray plates are traced and digitized by computer, and the plots may be used to inspect visually craniofacial variation, or the coordinate points may be used to generate an infinite number of linear and angular measurements (fig. 15.14). Those variables selected to examine the royal mummies were the same clinical variables utilized in the clinical and family studies at the University of Michigan. After all, families are families! Angular measurements were chosen in order to compare shape and position of bones rather than linear measurements, which tend to be sensitive to size differences.

Inspecting overlays of the x-ray cephalograms, Harris, Kowalski, and Walker (1980, p. 349) noted the great differences between members of the Eighteenth Dynasty such as between Thutmose III and Thutmose IV, Amenhotep II and Thutmose I, and Thutmose IV and Amenhotep III. Cluster analysis is a multivariate or statistical approach to examining similarities or dissimilarities between individuals and one may note the considerable biologic separation between Amenhotep III and the other Eighteenth Dynasty kings included in this analysis (ibid., table 3).

There are two major problems in the study of the mummies of the Eighteenth Dynasty. The first is the question of the correct identification of each royal mummy by the priests of the Twenty-first Dynasty. All mummies, except those of Tutankhamun, Yuya, and Thuya, were rewrapped and their identification must be to some extent inferential. The second problem is that each king is assumed to be the biologic father of the succeeding king.

In the study of inheritance, the polygenetic model is based on the availability of the two parents; in the collection of New Kingdom royal mummies at the Egyptian Museum there are no known queens from the late Eighteenth Dynasty. Only Tetisheri (tentative), Ahmes-Nefertari, and Merytamun, all queens of the Seventeenth and the very beginning of the Eighteenth Dynasty, were found in the royal caches. The polygenetic model assumes that the offspring shares one-half of his or her genes with either a fellow sibling or each of his

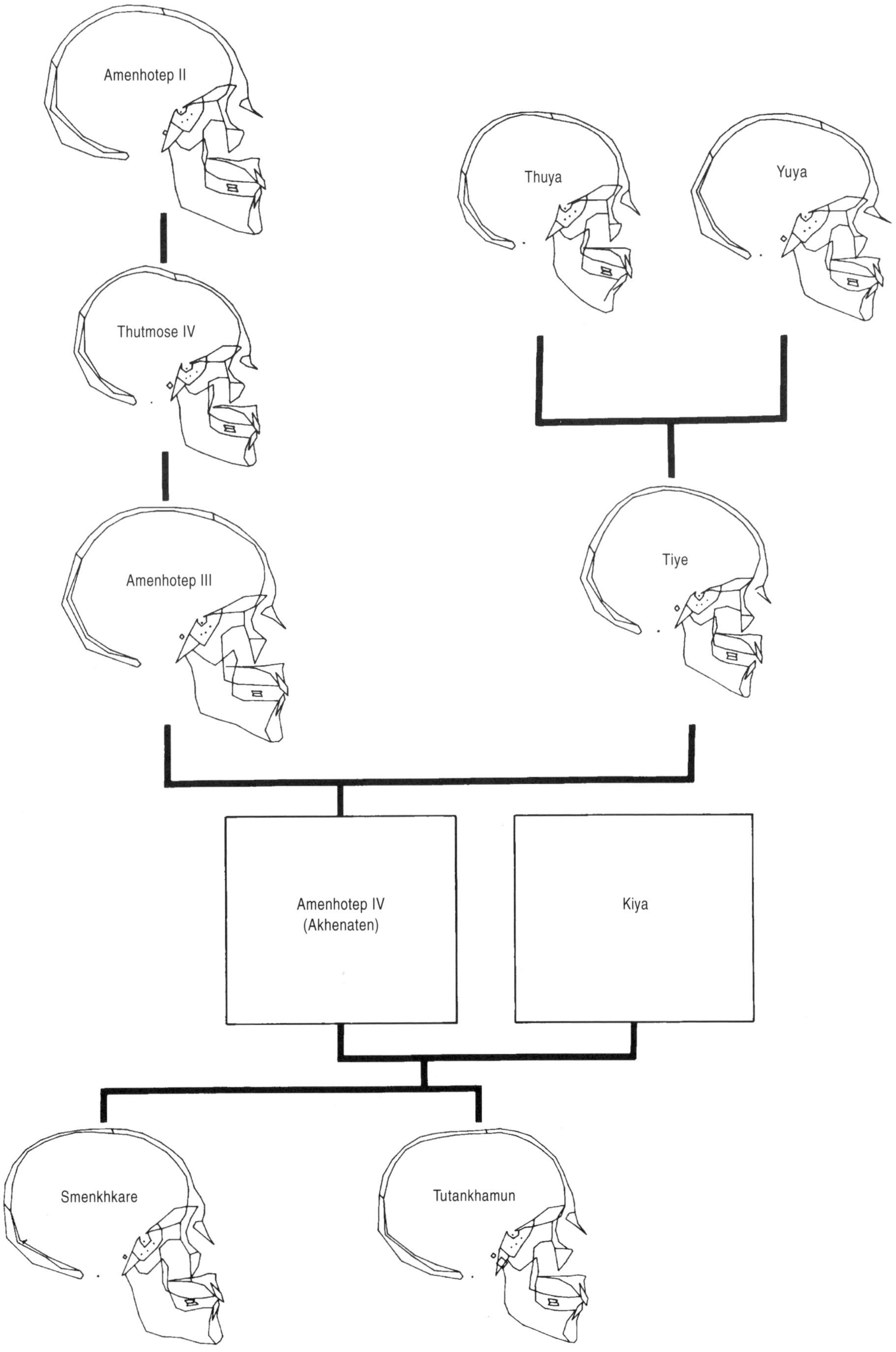

Figure 15.16. X-ray Cephalograms of Family of Amenhotep III

Table 15.1. Measurements of Stature and Cranium of Eighteenth Dynasty Royal Mummies

Mummy	*Anatomic Measurement*[1] *Body Height*	*Cranial Length*	*Face Height*	*Cephalometric*[2] *Cranial Length*	*Face Height*	*Anatomic*[3] *Face Height*
Thutmose I	154.5 cm	180.0 mm	114.0 mm	188.0 mm	119.0 mm	114.0 mm
Thutmose II	168.4 cm	191.0 mm	122.0 mm	200.0 mm	128.0 mm	119.0 mm
Thutmose III	161.5 cm	196.0 mm	125.0 mm	210.0 mm	135.0 mm	119.5 mm
Amenhotep II	167.3 cm	177.0 mm	107.0 mm	214.0 mm	146.0 mm	117.0 mm
Thutmose IV	164.6 cm	184.0 mm	121.0 mm	212.0 mm	130.0 mm	109.0 mm
Amenhotep III	156.1 cm 149.6 cm[3]	194.0 mm	122.0 mm	216.0 mm	141.0 mm	124.0 mm
Smenkhkare	164.4 cm	189.0 mm	—	210.0 mm	129.0 mm	116.0 mm
Tutankhamun	167.6 cm[4]	188.0 mm[4]	118.0 mm[4]	213.0 mm	131.0 mm	—

[1]Smith 1912. [2]Harris and Wente 1980, pp. 347–65. [3]Harris and Hussein 1992. [4]Derry and Hamdi 1972.

parents. The similarity or dissimilarity of a king to his father or his son would depend to some extent on the biologic difference between a given queen (the mother) and the respective kings (father).

A convenient way to visualize the relationship between members of a nuclear family such as the Eighteenth Dynasty royal family is the utilization of a midparent concept (fig. 15.15). The midparent represents a mathematical mean or average of those measurements utilized to characterize the two parents. Since siblings or offspring in a polygenetic model share one-half of their parents' genes they too could be represented by this midparent value. If the parents (king and queen) are biologically similar, then it is reasonable to assume that the midparent value would be close to both parents. If the parents are quite dissimilar, the midparent value will be substantially more distant from each parent. The problem here is that in most cases the mummies of the queens are not identified and only the king and the son are known. For example, in the case of the parents of Amenhotep III, how different genetically and biologically would Queen Mutemwia have to be from Thutmose IV to have produced a son who is so different from other Eighteenth Dynasty kings?

This discussion would not be complete without at least mentioning other tools utilized in the examination of the pedigree of the Egyptian royal families. Harrison (1969, pp. 325–26) utilized the antigens present on red blood cells or other tissue cells to examine ABO and MN systems in several of the royal mummies, including Smenkhkare, Tutankhamun, Yuya, and Thuya. He finds similar blood groups in Smenkhkare and Tutankhamun, but not Yuya and Thuya. Unfortunately, subsequent studies by Frederick Rossing revealed serological blood group antigens such as ABO to be unstable through time. DNA, or genetic, fingerprinting has recently been cited in the literature; however, there have been no published successes in the scientific literature other than that of the often-reported work of Paabo (1985, pp. 644–45). It is possible that the artificial mummification process itself is the culprit. There has been reported success with mitochondrial DNA in the cytoplasm; however, this genetic material is only useful in tracing maternity. There appears to be far greater success in the study of genetic fingerprinting in naturally mummified tissue in other parts of the world.

It is apparent that there is disagreement in the scientific community in regard to the interpretation of the biologic record of ancient Egypt, in much the same way that Egyptologists have differing interpretations of the historical record. Forensic, medical, and molecular science have advanced exponentially in the past few years, and their application to the study of ancient man has really just begun. Ultimately, it is up to the Egyptologists to determine the weight that is to be placed upon the relevance of biologic research in the understanding and interpretation of life in the ancient Nile Valley, including the royal families of Egypt.

SUMMARY AND CONCLUSIONS

Recent examination revealed the mummy of Amenhotep III (CG 61074) to be an individual who was morphologically dissimilar to the mummies of his predecessor Thutmose IV (CG 61073) and his heirs Tutankhamun and Smenkhkare (CG 61075). His facial features and stature reflect the stylized body and face often associated with the Amarna period. There is considerable evidence that Amenhotep III's mother Mutemwia (whose body has yet to be identified) was not from the Egyptian royal family or Thebes. If her face and skull were very different from those of Thutmose IV, then the midparent distance from either parent (king or queen) may have resulted in their son Amenhotep III's craniofacial skeleton (face and skull) not being similar to his father. Nevertheless, the degree of morphologic difference between the mummies of Thutmose IV (CG 61073) and Amenhotep III (CG 61074) stretches the imagination to accept this hypothesis.

If the mummy of Amenhotep III (CG 61074) was *correctly* identified 3,000 years ago by the priests of the Twenty-first Dynasty, then his son Amenhotep IV was not uniquely biologically aberrant but a biologic sum or normal variant of his father Amenhotep III and his mother Tiye. Akhenaten was his father's son!

There is substantial evidence from both the historical and biologic viewpoint that if the mummy of Amenhotep III (CG 61074) was incorrectly identified by the priests of the Twenty-first Dynasty, then this mummy is an excellent candidate to be Amenhotep IV, the heretic King Akhenaten. In time, with patience, caution, and a better understanding of the application and interpretation of biological techniques in the study of mummified tissues, the mummy of Amenhotep III may reveal its own true identity (fig. 15.16).

A list of the kings and queens of the Eighteenth Dynasty is provided below.

KINGS AND QUEENS OF EIGHTEENTH DYNASTY (after Wente 1980)

King Thutmose I Father: Unknown Mother: Senisoneb	Wife: Queen Ahmes Father: King Ahmose Mother: Queen Ahmes-Nefertari Wife: Queen Mutnofret Father: Unknown Mother: Unknown
King Thutmose II Father: King Thutmose I Mother: Queen Mutnofret	Wife: Queen Hatshepsut Father: King Thutmose I Mother: Queen Ahmes
King Thutmose III Father: King Thutmose II Mother: Queen Isis	Wife: Queen Meryetre-Hatshepsut Father: Unknown Mother: Unknown
King Amenhotep II Father: King Thutmose III Mother: Queen Meryetre-Hatshepsut	Wife: Queen Tiaa Father: Unknown Mother: Unknown
King Thutmose IV Father: King Amenhotep II Mother: Queen Tiye	Wife: Queen Mutemwia Father: Yey Mother: Unknown
King Amenhotep III Father: King Thutmose IV Mother: Queen Mutemwia	Wife: Queen Tiye Father: Yuya Mother: Thuya
King Amenhotep IV (Akhenaten) Father: King Amenhotep III Mother: Queen Tiye	Wife: Queen Nefertiti Father: Aye Mother: Unknown Wife: Queen Kiya Father: Unknown Mother: Unknown
King Smenkhkare Father: King Akhenaten or Amenhotep III Mother: Unknown	Wife: Queen Meritaten Father: King Akhenaten Mother: Queen Nefertiti
King Tutankhamun Father: King Akhenaten or Amenhotep III Mother: Unknown	Wife: Queen Ankhesenamun Father: King Akhenaten Mother: Queen Nefertiti

References

Aldred, C.
1968 *Akhenaten: Pharaoh of Egypt: A New Study*. London: Thames and Hudson.

Bryan, B. M.
1992 "Royal and Divine Statuary." In *Egypt's Dazzling Sun: Amenhotep and His World*, edited by A. P. Kozloff and B. M. Bryan, pp. 128–84. Cleveland: Cleveland Museum of Art.

Derry, D. E., and S. B. Hamdi
1972 "Anatomical Report on the Mummy of King Tutankhamon." In *The Human Remains from the Tomb of Tutankhamun*, edited by F. F. Leek, pp. 11–19. Tutankhamun Tomb Series 5. Oxford: Griffith Institute.

Harris, J. E.
1981 "The Heritability of Malocclusion: Implications for the Orthodontic Practitioner." In *Orthodontics: The State of the Art*, edited by H. Barrer, pp. 257–68. Philadelphia: University of Pennsylvania Press.

Harris, J. E., and F. Hussein
1987 "The Mummy of Amenhotep III: End of Season Report to the Organization of Antiquities." *Cairo*: 1–10.
1991 "The Identification of the Eighteenth Dynasty Royal Mummies: A Biologic Perspective." *Journal of Osteoarchaeology* 1: 235–39.
1992 Anatomic Measurements Obtained during the 1992 Radiographic Survey of the Royal Mummies, Egyptian Museum. Unpublished.

Harris, J. E., and C. J. Kowalski
1976 "All in the Family: Use of Familial Information in Orthodontic Diagnosis, Case Assessment and Treatment Planning." *American Journal of Orthodontics* 69: 493–510.

Harris, J. E.; C. J. Kowalski; and G. Walker
1980 "Craniofacial Variation in the Royal Mummies." In *An X-ray Atlas of the Royal Mummies*, edited by J. E. Harris and E. F. Wente, pp. 346–79. Chicago: University of Chicago Press.

Harris, J. E., and E. F. Wente, eds.
1980 *An X-ray Atlas of the Royal Mummies*. Chicago: University of Chicago Press.

Harris, J. E.; E. F. Wente; C. F. Cox; I. el-Nawawy; C. J. Kowalski; A. T. Storey; W. R. Russell; P. V. Ponitz; and G. F. Walker
1978 "Mummy of the Elder Lady in the Tomb of Amenhotep II: Egyptian Museum Catalogue Number 61070." *Science* 200: 1149–51.

Harrison, R. G., and A. B. Abdalla
1972 "The Remains of Tutankhamun." *Antiquity* 46: 8–14.

Harrison, R. G.; R. C. Connolly; and A. B. Abdalla
1969 "Kinship of Smenkhare and Tutankhamun Affirmed by Serological Micromethod." *Nature* 224: 325–26.

Krogman, W. M.
1979 Personal communication during his investigation of age at death ascertained from cranial and postcranial x-rays of the royal mummies. Ann Arbor.

Paabo, S.
1985 "Molecular Cloning of Ancient Egyptian Mummy DNA." *Nature* 314: 644–46.

Reeves, N.
1990 *The Complete Tutankhamun*. London: Thames and Hudson.

Romer, J.
1981 *Valley of the Kings*. New York: William Morrow.

Smith, G. E.
1912 *The Royal Mummies*. Catalogue général des antiquités égyptiennes du Musée du Caire, nos. 61051–61100. Cairo: Institut français d'archéologie orientale.

Wente, E. F.
1980 "Genealogy of the Royal Family." In *An X-ray Atlas of the Royal Mummies*, edited by J. E. Harris and E. F. Wente, pp. 122–62. Chicago: University of Chicago Press.

Wente, E. F., and J. E. Harris
1992 "Royal Mummies of the Eighteenth Dynasty: A Biologic and Egyptological Approach." In *After Tutʿankhamun: Research and Excavation in the Royal Necropolis at Thebes*, edited by N. Reeves, pp. 2–17. London: Kegan Paul.

16

FRAGMENTARY QUARTZITE FEMALE HAND FOUND IN ABOU-RAWASH

ZAHI HAWASS

Giza, Egypt

I met Professor Wente in the United States for the first time when we cooperated on the revision of a script for a pyramid film produced by Unicorn Projects and also during a visit to Chicago. I also had the honor of meeting him in Giza. I always respect his opinions and his ideas. It is to Ed Wente that I dedicate this article.

****

On January 9, 1996, Nabil Swelim visited the site of the pyramid of King Djedefre, son of Khufu, at Abou-Rawash. During his visit he found a large fragment of a quartzite statue (fig. 16.1) at ground level on the east side, just in front of the large indentation in the rock nucleus of the pyramid, where a large granite block is situated.[1]

This site was excavated during the 1993/94 season. When the area of the upper temple was cleared, we found a large mudbrick structure, identified as an ancient church on the basis of the architectural style of the building as well as the pottery found there. The location of this newly found structure is near the valley temple of Djedefre.[2]

Description of Fragment (fig. 16.1):	Material: Quartzite	Length: ca. 18.0 cm	Width: ca. 16.0 cm
Dimensions of Hand (fig. 16.1b):		Length: 10. 5 cm	Width: 5.0 cm

a

b

Figure 16.1. (*a–b*) Two Views of Quartzite Statue Fragment from Abou-Rawash. Photograph Courtesy Peter Windszuz, German Archaeological Institute, Cairo

1. When Nabil Swelim found this quartzite statue, he gave it to the guard at the site. Swelim called me that evening to inform me of the discovery. The next day I advised the chief inspector of Imbaba to go to Abou-Rawash and bring back the fragment. It is registered in the Imbaba Register and stored in the magazine of the Giza plateau under number 1320.

2. The site was first excavated by É. Chassinat; see Chassinat 1921/22; Vyse 1842, pp. 8–9; Lepsius 1849,

Gold of Praise: Studies on Ancient Egypt in Honor of Edward F. Wente
Edited by Emily Teeter and John A. Larson
Studies in Ancient Oriental Civilization 58
Chicago: Oriental Institute, 1999

Figure 16.2. Group Statue of Djedefre and His Wife (Louvre 12627).
Photograph Courtesy Musée du Louvre, Paris

Surface of block is very smooth and has no inscription on it. A female hand is carved in relief on far right of block; small finger is missing and part of thumb is destroyed. Block is curved in front on right side, as if bent knee were depicted.

REMARKS ON THE FRAGMENT

Block appears to portray subject in seated position with legs flexed at knee. A hand is superimposed upon a thigh. It is hard to say whether it is the left or the right hand, but most probably it is the left.

The block is highly worked, polished and burnished. The craftsman was not only skilled in working stone, but also accomplished as an artist in that he conveyed the movement of the body through visual reference and imparted a fluidity of movement that is quite lifelike.

The workmanship of the hand was delicately executed. The finely modeled fingers would originally have included detailed fingertips, which although now damaged by time, were, in their original state, beautifully executed. The fine modeling of the hand identifies it as that of a woman. The fragment was probably originally part of a pair statue, with one of the woman's hands placed on a knee and the other arm most likely wrapped around her companion.

The block is made of quartzite, a red sandstone. The quarry for that stone was at el-Gebel el-Ahmar ("Red Mountain") located near Heliopolis, center of the sun god. The stone was considered sacred and divine by the Egyptians because of the proximity of the quarry to the center of the sun god Ra. The same material was used in sculpting statues of Djedefre. Significance is attached to Djedefre's use of quartzite because he was the first king to bear the title *sꜣ Rʿ*, "Son of Ra." Akhenaten also used sandstone and also bore the title "Son of Aten" (Vandier 1954, p. 16).

Chassinat found hundreds of small blocks of statues scattered everywhere in the area of the pyramid complex of Djedefre (PM 3/1, pp. 2–3). None of these blocks was whole. However, Chassinat also found approxi-

---

pls. 11–12; PM 3/1, pp. 1–3. For the archaic area found to the west of the church, see Hawass 1987a. The recent excavation was directed by the author. Since 1995, French (Nicolas Grimal), Swiss (M. Valloggia), and Egyptian (Z. Hawass) expeditions have pursued the excavation.

mately twenty-one statues at the site, all of which were missing many parts, and he divided these statues, as well as the fragments, into five groups (Wilkinson 1994, p. 87).

There were six large statues, as high as 168 cm. Two others would have reached 120 cm if complete. Seven statues could have been about 80 cm. Four small statues could have been 60 cm. Two, smaller still, could have been no more than 30 cm. All of these statues represent the king, either standing or sitting. After the death of Djedefre, the statues were broken and a great number of the blocks destroyed. The damage was motivated by revenge; it was not incidental to theft. It has been suggested that the younger brother Khafre sought to avenge Kawab, the eldest son of Khufu, who was supposed to have inherited the throne but was assassinated by Djedefre.[3]

I propose that Khufu modified his developing cult and appointed himself the sun god during his own lifetime. Therefore he accommodated his pyramid complex to the new cult (Hawass 1987b, pp. 83–85; Hawass 1993). Djedefre did not follow his father's new cult. Rather, he left Giza and built his pyramid complex at Abou-Rawash. Khafre destroyed his brother Djedefre's pyramid complex and may have been responsible for the assassination of Djedefre. Khafre returned to Giza and made provisions in his pyramid complex for the worship of his father Khufu within the temples. The Sphinx and its temple were designed to represent Khafre worshipping his father Khufu as the sun god who rises and sets within the Sphinx temple (Hawass 1993).

The statues of Djedefre are in a very realistic style, especially the one in the Louvre (E. 12626; Vandier 1958, pl. I.2), which may be the first statue in the shape of a sphinx.

Djedefre's statues impress one with their similarity to the statue of his grandfather Sneferu in the Brooklyn Museum (Brooklyn 46.167; Vandier 1958, pl. I.6; Aldred 1949, p. 29, pl. 13), and to another statue that was found by A. Fakhry at Dashur, which is now in the magazine of the Inspectorate (Fakhry 1959, 1961), as well as to the ivory statue of Khufu at the Cairo Museum (Cairo 36143; Vandier 1958, p. 15, pl. I.4).

The lower part of a group statue of Djedefre at the Louvre (E. 12627) represents the king sitting on a chair with his wife, the queen, sitting on his left (fig. 16.2; Vandier 1958, p. 17, pl. II.1).[4] On the right of the chair the name of the king is written in a cartouche. Above it are the *serekh* and Horus with the double crown. The queen is represented wearing a wig that reaches the eyebrows. Her face is done in a beautiful feminine style. Her eyes are narrow and her mouth is well modeled. She wears the traditional tight dress of the Fourth Dynasty. With her right hand she holds the left leg of the king. This statue is thought to be the earliest royal group statue (Smith 1958, p. 113). The left hand and a part of the arm are missing. One might surmise that our fragment is the missing part, but that statue is too small for our block. We have considered other fragments that are kept in Munich, but they are also too small to fit our block.

Further excavations by the French, Swiss, and Egyptian expeditions may reveal the missing pieces.

References

Aldred, C.
1949 *Old Kingdom Art in Ancient Egypt*. London: Alec Tiranti.

Chassinat, É.
1921/22 *À propos d'une tête en grès rouge du roi Didoufri (IVe dynastie) conservée au Musée du Louvre*. Monuments et mémoires publiés par l'Académie des inscriptions et belles-lettres 25. Paris: E. Leroux.

Fakhry, A.
1959 *The Monuments of Sneferu at Dashur*, Volume 1: *The Bent Pyramid*. Cairo: General Organization for Government Printing Offices.
1961 *The Monuments of Sneferu at Dashur*, Volume 2: *The Valley Temple*. Two parts. Cairo: General Organization for Government Printing Offices.

Hawass, Z.
1987a "Archaic Graves Recently Found at North Abou-Rawash." *Mitteilungen des Deutschen archäologischen Instituts, Abteilung Kairo* 36: 229–44.
1987b The Funerary Establishments of Khufu, Khafre and Menkaure during the Old Kingdom. Ph.D. dissertation. Philadelphia: University of Pennsylvania.
1993 "The Great Sphinx at Giza: Date and Function." In *Atti del sesto congresso internazionale di egittologia*, volume 2, edited by G. M. Zaccone and T. R. di Netro, pp. 177–95. Turin: n.p.

3. Vandier 1954, p. 86; Reisner and Smith 1955, p. 7. Junker (1944, p. 26) believes that Djedefhor's tomb was destroyed during the First Intermediate Period, which could also apply in Djedefre's case.

4. I would like to thank Madame C. Ziegler for providing me with a photograph of the lower part of the statue of Djedefre (E12627) from the Louvre.

Junker, H.
1944 *Giza 7: Grabungen auf dem Friedhof des Alten Reiches: Der Ostabschnitt des Westfriedhofs*. Vienna and Leipzig: Hölder-Pichler-Tempsky.

Lepsius, R.
1849 *Denkmäler aus Aegypten und Aethiopien,* Volume 1. Reprint. Geneva: Éditions des Belles-Lettres.

Reisner, G. A., and W. S. Smith
1955 *A History of the Giza Necropolis 2: The Tomb of Hetep-heres, the Mother of Cheops*. Cambridge: Harvard University Press.

Smith, W. S.
1958 *The Art and Architecture of Ancient Egypt*. London: Pelican.

Vandier, J.
1954 *Manuel d'archéologie égyptienne,* tome 2: *Les grandes époques: Architecture funéraire*. 2 volumes. Paris: J. Picard.
1958 *Manuel d'archéologie égyptienne,* tome 3: *Les grandes époques: La statuaire*. 2 volumes. Paris: J. Picard.

Vyse, R. W. H.
1842 *Operations Carried Out on the Pyramids of Gizeh in 1837,* Volume 3. London: J. Fraser.

Wilkinson, R. H.
1994 *Symbol and Magic in Egyptian Art*. New York: Thames and Hudson.

17

TWO STELAE OF KING SEQENENREʿ DJEHUTY-AA OF THE SEVENTEENTH DYNASTY

HELEN JACQUET-GORDON

Institut français d'archéologie orientale, Cairo

It is with great pleasure that I look back almost exactly forty years to a trip on the night train to Luxor where I first met Ed Wente, and to the delightful breakfast that we had, together with our fellow-travelers Henri Wild and Jean and Michelle Yoyotte in the Luxor Hotel gardens, still at that time a wilderness of trees and shrubs. It is with equal pleasure that I contribute this small article concerning Seqenenreʿ's stelae to Ed's *Studies*.

It was in 1975, during the excavation of the treasury of Thutmose I at Karnak North carried out on behalf of the French Institute of Archaeology in Cairo (cf. J. Jacquet 1983 and 1994; H. Jacquet-Gordon 1988), that a fragmentary limestone stela (Karnak North inv. no. A3507+A3518) bearing the cartouche of King Seqenenreʿ Djehuty-aa[1] was discovered (fig. 17.1; cf. H. Jacquet-Gordon 1999, pp. 153–54). It formed part of a stratum of fill with which the early Eighteenth Dynasty bakeries (situated to the south of the treasury between the outer stone wall of that building and its mudbrick enclosure wall) had been covered prior to the laying of a new stone pavement at a higher level than the original floor and connected with the more carefully organized bakeries dating to the Ramesside period.

Only the upper part of the stela is preserved. The lower section, with the legs of the two figures represented and whatever there may have been of inscription added at the bottom, is lost. Its present dimensions are: height 35.0 cm; width 31.8 cm; thickness 10.5 cm. The scene is carved in a shallow sunk relief and in certain areas has been completely worn off. Occupying the curved upper portion of the stela is a sun disk with pendant uraei (of which one has been broken away) and with wings drooping down on either side. Below, on the left, the king is represented wearing the white crown, a wide necklace, and a skirt with tail attached at the waist. He offers three bolts of material on a tray to Amun who faces him on the right. The god, sporting the usual crown with two high feathers, a wide necklace, and a tight-fitting robe supported by shoulder straps and with tail attached at the waist, grasps a *was*-scepter in his outstretched right hand. The left hand, hanging at his side, no doubt held an *ankh* that has now disappeared. Above the king, a cartouche containing his name "Djehuty-aa" preceded by *sꜣ Rʿ* "son of Ra" (of which only the top of the sun disk and the feet of the bird are still discernible) and followed by the words *di ʿnḫ* "given life" is clearly preserved. The god has fared less well. Chisel marks in front of him make it evident that his name has been intentionally hacked out except for parts of two vertical hieroglyphs at the bottom of the inscription, possibly the remains of the epithet *nṯr ʿꜣ* "the great god." No traces of color can be detected.

The stratum of fill in which this stela was found contained a certain number of objects that appear to have belonged to the treasury furnishings. For example, a statue of Renenutet (Karnak North inv. no. A3894) protectress of the granaries, discovered in the same stratum as the stela, had no doubt been dedicated in the treasury, and a small headless serpent (Karnak North inv. no. A4044) probably representing the same goddess, and likewise found in this stratum, seems to have been left for repairs in the workshops to the east of the treasury build-

1. It is now more than thirty years since Beckerath (1964, p. 186, n. 3) first proposed this reading of Seqenenreʿ's personal name. Since then the suggestion has been repeated several times without any decisive step being taken towards its definite adoption (Parlebas 1975, p. 41; *LÄ* 5 "Seqenenre," col. 864; Vandersleyen 1995, p. 189, n. 4). The reading of the name as Djehuty-aa, which Parlebas so convincingly demonstrates as plausible, has two advantages over the current reading Taa. First, it is meaningful in contrast to the meaningless Taa, and second, that meaning is in harmony with the preference for lunar-oriented names so noticeable in the nomenclature of the royal family at the end of the Seventeenth and beginning of the Eighteenth Dynasty. I see no reason why we should not adopt it definitively.

Gold of Praise: Studies on Ancient Egypt in Honor of Edward F. Wente
Edited by Emily Teeter and John A. Larson
Studies in Ancient Oriental Civilization 58
Chicago: Oriental Institute, 1999

Figure 17.1. Stela of King Seqenenreʿ Djehuty-aa (Karnak North inv. no. A3507+A3518).
Photograph by A. Lecler, Institut français d'archéologie orientale

ing together with other broken and unfinished objects discovered there.[2] It is more than probable that the monument of Seqenenreʿ likewise was on display somewhere within the walls of the treasury. But, we may well ask, under what circumstances could a stela of Seqenenreʿ dating from the end of the Seventeenth Dynasty have been preserved in the Eighteenth Dynasty treasury of Thutmose I? That it was so preserved and was still visible in the time of Akhenaten appears to be indicated by the intentional erasure of the god's name, although it must be admitted that the divine figure has not been mutilated.

In order to answer this question, it is necessary to visualize the position of the treasury in relation to the surrounding stratification. The treasury is, in fact, situated on the northern slope of the mound of Karnak which already at the beginning of the Eighteenth Dynasty was of considerable extent, spreading, as we discovered during the excavations, over earlier strata of both the Second Intermediate Period and the Middle Kingdom. In order to prepare a level area on which to build the treasury, Thutmose's architect[3] cut into the slope of the mound for a distance of about fifty meters from north to south and a similar distance from east to west thus removing a considerable portion of the earlier strata at that point. Many objects must have come to light during this work, several of which appear to have been carefully preserved in the treasury once that building was completed. Besides Seqenenreʿ's stela, there can be mentioned a statue of Senusret III (Karnak North inv. no. A474), now broken at the waist, which lay on the floor of one of the treasury storerooms, a fragment of a large stone mortar on whose rim can be read the name of King Senusret's Queen Khnemetneferhedjet (Karnak North inv. no. A2661), and fragments of a scene in sunk relief dating to the time of King Ahmose[4] which, judging by its beveled edges, had later been inserted into one of the walls of the treasury (see Jacquet-Gordon 1988, pp. 90–92,

2. All of these objects as well as those mentioned further on in this article are published in Jacquet-Gordon 1999.

3. The architect is unknown, as the treasury is not mentioned by Ineny in his tomb among the constructions he supervised.

4. The moon sign in his name presents the form characteristic of the early part of his reign (form 2); see Vandersleyen 1971, p. 205.

Figure 17.2. Stela of King Seqenenre' Djehuty-aa (Karnak, Sheikh Labib Magazine, inv. no. 87CL358). Photograph by Labib Habachi, Chicago House, University of Chicago

pls. 22–23). Thutmose I appears to have been meticulous in preserving the memory of his royal predecessors and their monuments.

In 1975, at the time when Seqenenre''s stela came to light, it was, as far as I could ascertain, the only stela of that king as yet known. Some years later, however, while working on the archives of Labib Habachi, now

Figure 17.3. Stela Depicting Royal Daughter Ahmes (Karnak North inv. no. A2923). Photograph by A. Lecler, Institut français d'archéologie orientale

housed in the Chicago House library at Luxor, I came upon a photograph recording a second stela of King Seqenenreᶜ (fig. 17.2).[5] Labib was notoriously careless about marking proveniences or references on his photographs, and there was nothing on this particular one to indicate where and when the stela had been found or its present whereabouts. Nevertheless I prepared to publish it in the hope that someone might recognize it and come forward with information on its place of origin. Meanwhile, by chance, I showed Labib's photograph one afternoon to Luc Gabolde of the Franco-Egyptian Centre who was immediately able to identify it as an object now housed in the magazine called "Sheikh Labib" at Karnak. It is registered there under the inventory number 87CL358 as a limestone stela whose dimensions are: height 65 cm; width 40 cm; depth 10 cm.[6] Unfortunately its provenience remains a mystery, but its presence in the Karnak magazine gives credence to the presumption that it was found somewhere within the precincts of the temple or its near environs.

This second stela is even more fragmentary than the one found at Karnak North. Its lower part has been almost entirely eaten away by moisture and only a small area constituting the upper left-hand corner of the scene engraved on its surface in sunk relief has survived. The sun disk with uraei and pendant wings that occupied the curved upper portion of the stela has all but disappeared with the exception of the tips of three feathers still visible on the left. Below, the king, wearing a tight-fitting cap with uraeus and a wide collar, raises his right hand in adoration while with his left hand he proffers incense to the divinity standing opposite him. The god is unfortunately completely destroyed except for the rounded back of his head from which hangs a ribbon. Possibly we have here the figure of Amun represented as on the Hanover stela of King Ahmose (Vandersleyen 1977, p. 226), the two high feathers of his headdress being attached directly to his skull without an intervening crown. However, no trace of the feathers themselves has survived and it can be objected that the line projecting from the back of the god's head is placed too low on the skull to represent the ribbon of his headdress; it should be higher up, just below the feathers.[7] If the divinity depicted here is not Amun, a possible alternative identification may be Ptah. In that case the object in back of his head would be the ribbon attached to the clasp of his *menat*-necklace that is occasionally depicted extending rather high up behind the god's head. An examination of the stela itself rather than of a photograph might reveal further identifiable traces but access to the objects in the Sheikh Labib magazine is not possible at present.[8]

Behind the king stands a female figure of somewhat smaller dimensions represented with her left hand resting on the king's shoulder. She wears a tripartite wig with vulture headdress and a wide collar. Nothing more of

5. I present it here with the kind permission of Dr. Peter Dorman, whom I thank most heartily.

6. I am much obliged to Luc Gabolde for his prompt help in locating the stela and to François Larché, Director of the Franco-Egyptian Centre of Karnak, for permission to continue with the publication of it.

7. See also a fragment of a Seventeenth Dynasty stela found by Petrie (1909, pl. 30, no. 4) at Gurna where the ribbon holding the feathers is likewise placed high on the skull.

8. The magazine is closed at present for inventory because of recently discovered thefts.

her is visible. The names of these two personages are written above their heads: over the king *s3 [Rꜥ] Ḏḥwty-ꜥ3 di ꜥnḫ* "The son of [Ra] Djehuty-aa, given life" and above the lady *s3t nswt ḥnwt t3wy ꜣIꜥḥ-ms ꜥnḫ.ti* (with the name Ahmes written in a cartouche)[9] "the royal daughter, the mistress of the Two Lands, Ahmes, living." Is this latter personage one of the known royal ladies named Ahmes or is she still another of that name to be added to the family tree? From her vulture headdress and the fact that her name is written in a cartouche, we can presume that she held queenly rank, but she is not specifically designated as a royal wife. If she were one of Djehuty-aa's numerous daughters, all called Ahmes, her name would not be written in a cartouche during the lifetime of her father even if we consider her the wife or destined wife of his heir. An alternative is to see in her a sister of the king and perhaps one of his secondary queens. There is some evidence for the existence of such a person. Hayes (1959, p. 11) mentions a limestone stela of the Eighteenth Dynasty belonging to a man named Thuty, one of whose relatives was a priest of the temple of "Aꜥḥ-mosĕ (written in a cartouche with the later form of the moon hieroglyph[10]) daughter of Tetisheri, the justified." He proposes to identify this lady with Queen Ahmes-Nefertari, giving to the word "daughter" the extended meaning of "granddaughter." However, the text of this stela seems perfectly straightforward and, I believe, should be taken literally. Moreover it seems most unlikely that a temple dedicated posthumously to Ahmes-Nefertari should have referred to her simply as "Queen Ahmes," omitting all her usual epithets. I propose then to identify the Queen Ahmes of the Sheikh Labib stela with Queen Ahmes the daughter of Tetisheri, and to consider her a secondary wife of her brother Seqenenreꜥ, who possibly died at an early age.[11] It is to be noted however that she is not here given the title "royal sister."

We may add to these two documents concerning Seqenenreꜥ a further fragmentary stela found in the treasury (Karnak North inv. no. A2923), on which his name does not figure, but where we see depicted a small personage who appears to be one of his daughters (fig. 17.3). The fragment belongs to the left-hand edge of a limestone stela depicting a man of whom only the shoulder and hanging arm are visible; he wears a wide collar. Behind the man stands a very small female figure wearing a long fitting robe and a tripartite wig; she is *s3t nswt ꜣIꜥḥ-ms* "the royal daughter Ahmes," whose name is not enclosed in a cartouche but is written as on the Sheikh Labib stela with the earlier form of the moon sign (form 2 of Vandersleyen 1971). In all probability, the king depicted here was Seqenenreꜥ himself accompanied by one of his daughters named Ahmes.

The fragmentary state of these stelae is of course to be deplored, but it is improbable that they ever contained texts of any great historical value apart from possible dates. Their principal *raison d'être* appears to be to assert the presence of Seqenenreꜥ as the legitimate master of Thebes, showing him together with various members of his family, sacrificing to the local gods. The presence of several of these documents at Karnak North can be linked to the existence of extensive remains dating to the late Second Intermediate Period below and around the treasury of Thutmose I.[12]

References

Beckerath, J. von
1964 *Untersuchungen zur politischen Geschichte der zweiten Zwischenzeit in Ägypten.* Ägyptologische Forschungen 23. Glückstadt: J. J. Augustin.

Gitton, M.
1975 *L'épouse du dieu Ahmes Nefertary.* Centre de recherches d'histoire ancienne 15. Annales littéraires de l'Université de Besançon 172. Les belles lettres 15. Paris: n.p.

Hayes, W. C.
1959 *The Scepter of Egypt,* Volume 2. New York: Metropolitan Museum of Art.

Jacquet, J.
1983 *Karnak Nord 5: Le trésor de Thoutmosis Ier. Étude architecturale.* Fouilles de l'Institut français d'archéologie orientale 30/1–2. Cairo: Institut français d'archéologie orientale.
1994 *Karnak Nord 7: Le trésor de Thoutmosis Ier. Installations antérieures et postérieurs au monument.* Fouilles

9. The horizontal line between the queen's two epithets is, I suppose, merely an indicator of change of line.

10. Vandersleyen's (1971) form 4 or 5 if Gitton's hand copy is exact; compare Gitton 1975, p. 34, n. 54.

11. See *LÄ* 6 "Tetischeri," col. 458, on the family of Tetisheri.

12. Compare also the fragmentary inscription mentioning Ahmes Sapaïr, the eldest son of Seqenenreꜥ (according to Vandersleyen 1983, pp. 311–24), found at Karnak North by Varille and published by Zivie 1972, pp. 77–78, no. 8.

de l'Institut français d'archéologie orientale 36/1–2. Cairo: Institut français d'archéologie orientale.

Jacquet-Gordon, H.

1988 *Karnak-Nord* 6: *Le trésor de Thoutmosis Ier. La décoration.* Fouilles de l'Institut français d'archéologie orientale 32/1–2. Cairo: Institut français d'archéologie orientale.

1999 *Karnak Nord* 8: *Le trésor de Thoutmosis Ier. Statues, stèles et blocs réutilisés.* Fouilles de l'Institut français d'archéologie orientale. Cairo: Institut français d'archéologie orientale.

Parlebas, J.

1975 "Sur l'origine de la valeur *Ḏḥwty* de  et le groupe  dans les noms de personnes." *Göttinger Miszellen* 15: 39–43.

Petrie, W. M. F.

1909 *Qurneh.* Egyptian Research Account 16. London: British School of Archaeology in Egypt.

Vandersleyen, C.

1971 *Les guerres d'Amosis fondateur de la XVIIIe dynastie.* Monographies Reine Élisabeth 1. Brussels: Fondation Égyptologique Reine Élisabeth.

1977 "Une stèle de l'an 18 d'Amosis à Hanovre." *Chronique d'Égypte* 52/104: 223–44.

1983 "L'identité du prince Ahmes-Sapair." *Studien zur altägyptischen Kultur* 10: 311–24.

1984 "Seqenenre." In *Lexikon der Ägyptologie* 5, edited by W. Helck, E. Otto, and W. Westendorf, cols. 864–66. Wiesbaden: Otto Harrassowitz.

1995 *L'Égypte et la vallée du Nil*, volume 2. Paris: Les Presses Universitaires de France.

Zivie, A.-P.

1972 "Fragments inscrits conservés à Karnak-Nord." *Bulletin de l'Institut français d'archéologie orientale* 72: 71–98.

18

A MARITAL TITLE FROM THE NEW KINGDOM

JAC. J. JANSSEN

Leiden University, The Netherlands

The scholar to whom the following pages are dedicated has indicated by several of his publications his interest in the simple daily life of the ancient Egyptians. So it may be hoped that a study like this interests him. That it has a rather trendy flavor, dealing with the history of women, may be regretted by some of our colleagues, but not, I expect, by him.

Several years ago, Oleg Berlev published an epoch-making article on the Middle Kingdom title *ʿnḫw-n-niwt* (Berlev 1971), a designation of soldiers. In that period it was, he states, exclusively used for men,[1] whereas during the New Kingdom and later it occurs merely as a feminine title. Therefore, the two should be studied separately. Until now, that seems not to have been undertaken with the feminine form, the following pages being an initial attempt.

The phrase *ʿnḫ(t)-n(t)-niwt* (for the spelling, see below) is usually translated as "citizeness."[2] Although inspired by the word *niwt* "city," this translation is rather misleading. The English word, and even more so its French equivalent "citoyenne," reminds us of the French Revolution and the slogan "liberté, egalité, fraternité," but of course such concepts were alien to an ancient Egyptian. The Berlin *Wörterbuch* renders it as "Städterin," or even "Bürgerin" (*Wb.* 1.201). As shown below, the title occurs frequently with women from the workmen's community of Deir el-Medina, and that was just not a "city." In the language of these people *niwt* is Thebes, but it was not there that these *ʿnḫw-nw-niwt* lived.

Gardiner seems to have realized how false the usual translation was, and in his commentary on the Wilbour Papyrus he simply renders the title as "lady" (Gardiner 1948a, II, p. 76). Even that could suggest nobility, which is of course not meant. His example has, moreover, not been followed by the next generation of Egyptologists. They seem to have been mainly influenced by Černý's ideas brought forward in his discussion of the Will of Naunakhte (Černý 1945, p. 44). Here he states that the title *ʿnḫw-n-niwt* was "at this time [i.e., in the Twentieth Dynasty] given to all free women who were not in service and were consequently not *ḥmt*, 'slaves.'" In the footnote connected with these words he adds categorically: "Wives of workmen of the King's Tomb are called *ʿnḫ-n-niwt* in" [several documents].

This seems to have been generally accepted, although some particular aspects of the use of the title have been observed. Gay Robins (1993, p. 115), for instance, notes that it occurs only in hieratic sources and seems to indicate a married woman. That goes back to a note in the dissertation of Pestman (1961, p. 11, note 2), which, however, is formulated cautiously: "One gets a strong impression that a woman who bears this title is either married or a widow"; at least, the author states that he knows of no example to the contrary.

Barbara Lesko (1994, pp. 35–36), discussing women in Deir el-Medina, adds another detail. Acknowledging that she does not know how widely the title was used, she specifies that "women are generally so referred to in administrative and juridical texts, with the further addition 'of the necropolis' (*ḫr*)." She does not quote any example of the latter, and I do not remember ever having seen it. If it occurs anywhere, it is extremely rare. Neither she, nor Gay Robins, says anything about the frequency of *ʿnḫ-n-niwt* as compared with that of other identifications of women in documents concerning the workmen's community or outside of it.

In order to gain an insight into the use of the title it is necessary to study its distribution. We will do that mainly on account of ostraca and papyri from Deir el-Medina since these are numerous and, because so much of the background is known, they are the most easy to evaluate. Later on we will discuss a few occurrences in texts from elsewhere, in order to obtain an overall picture from the Ramesside period.

1. This is not quite correct; see Ward 1986, pp. 61–65.

2. Černý (1945), in his publication of the Will of Naunakhte, rendered "citoyenne."

Gold of Praise: Studies on Ancient Egypt in Honor of Edward F. Wente
Edited by Emily Teeter and John A. Larson
Studies in Ancient Oriental Civilization 58
Chicago: Oriental Institute, 1999

The first point to note is that, so far as I know, not a single stela contains the words *ꜥnḫ-n-niwt*. I have checked several major publications such as that of the British Museum stelae (Hieroglyphic Texts 1914–82, Parts 5–10), those in the Turin Museum (Tosi and Roccati 1971), Černý's publication of the Bankes collection (Černý 1958), that by Demarée of the *ꜣḫ iḳr n Rꜥ* stelae (Demarée 1983), and nowhere does the title occur. Neither have I found *ꜥnḫ-n-niwt* on any other monument, for instance, on an offering table, nor in one of the workmen's tombs in the Valley of Deir el-Medina. Everywhere women are either called *nbt-pr,* "mistress of the house," or identified as a member of the family: his/her daughter, sister, mother, etc. In some cases the specific title of women, "chantress (*šmꜥyt*) of Amun," is used. There is no feminine counterpart of the men's title on the monuments: *sḏm-ꜥš m st Mꜣꜥt* (Černý 1973, p. 43), which is the official designation for what in ostraca and papyri is *rmṯ-ist* "man of the gang," "workman." The absence of *ꜥnḫ-n-niwt* from monuments is, of course, not due to the hieroglyphic script, but to their religious and funerary purpose. In that sphere the title was clearly not used; it belongs to daily life.

From ostraca and papyri from Deir el-Medina I have collected approximately 175 names of women, some belonging to more than one individual. In total, a woman is mentioned about 425 times. No more than thirty-five of them are ever called *ꜥnḫ-n-niwt*.[3] The spelling varies, a conspicuous and rather frequent variant being plural strokes after *niwt* as if the inhabitants of the City were designated. A common abbreviation is *ꜥnḫ-niwt*, or even simply *ꜥnḫ*.[4] Nowhere in Deir el-Medina, however, and seldom in texts from elsewhere, do we find an instance of **ꜥnḫt-nt-niwt*.[5] This form, used by Gay Robins and Barbara Lesko in their studies quoted above, shows the hyper-correctness of modern Egyptologists.

Let us now look at the categories of texts in which the title occurs. Firstly, the letters. Only in one instance is it found in the address, and that in a letter on papyrus, which tends to be slightly more formal than one written on an ostracon (Pap. DeM XV; Černý 1978, pl. 30). Twice it is used in the body of a letter.[6] In most instances, the female author or addressee is identified by her name alone, or by a term of relationship, rarely by her occupation, "chantress of Amun."

A class of texts in which *ꜥnḫ-n-niwt* is common, as Barbara Lesko has noticed, is that on legal affairs, charges,[7] and others.[8] However, this custom was not always consistently followed. Pap. Turin 167+$\frac{2087}{219}$ 198 verso 5 ff. (= Allam 1973, pl. 107), from year 13 of Ramesses IX, records a legal conflict between a scribe of the necropolis and a woman called Tkharu. Even in the court's verdict (verso 8) no title is mentioned.

A third type we should discuss are texts with economic contents — not "administrative" texts as Barbara Lesko has it, for these texts deal with the work in the Royal Tomb and with deliveries to the workmen, that is, their wages; these are the matter of men. It is rather the records of sales transactions and other private economic activities which frequently contain the title. A clear example is O. BM 5633 (*HO,* pl. 86, 1), enumerating objects which were sold to the *ꜥnḫ-n-niwt* Ubekht. In verso II, 4, a *qbw*-vessel is mentioned of another *ꜥnḫ-n-niwt* called Mantuḥata,[9] whereas in the preceding line an amount of copper is recorded of a certain *Tnt-niwt*.[10] Why the latter does not bear a title is obscure.

In O. DeM 195 a woman is said to have bought a chair (*qni*) and to have paid for it. She is called an *ꜥnḫ-n-niwt,* but her name is mostly lost. From the traces it seems possible that it was Naunakhte, but whether she was

3. In a few cases, the same lady bears the title in two texts, for example, Ēse in O. DeM 235 and 239, and Ḥunero in O. UC 19614 and Pap. Salt 124, but that happens seldom. In those instances in which we can be certain that the same person is meant, she appears one or more times with her name only, and only once as *ꜥnḫt-n-niwt*.

4. For example, O. Cairo 25572, 10, in a later addition above the line. Also in Pap. Salt 124, 2, 2–3, and in Pap. DeM XV.

5. For this reason the transcription in O. Gardiner 123 (= *HO*, pl. 54, 1), 1, seems doubtful. The only certain instance I came across is Pap. Cairo 65739 (Gardiner 1935, pls. 13–16).

6. O. Petrie 61 (= *HO*, pl. 23, 4), 2; O. DeM 335, 5. O. Berlin 12630 (= Allam 1973, pl. 11) is no letter but rather a statement, although Wente (1990, Nr. 256) included it in his publication.

7. For example, O. DeM 225, 235, 239; O. Nash 1 (= *HO*, pl. 46, 2); Pap. Turin 1966 verso III (unpublished, transcribed by Černý, MSS 3.651); perhaps also O. Petrie 18 (= *HO*, pl. 70, 1). Once two women called *ꜥnḫ-n-niwt* seem to be mentioned as members of the local court: O. Gardiner 150 (= *HO*, pl. 71, 3); compare Allam 1992, p. 143, note 9. The role of the six *ꜥnḫw-n-niwt* — if the restoration is correct — in Pap. DeM XXVI A, 3 (= Allam 1973, pl. 92 = Černý 1986, pl. 12), is obscure.

8. For example, O. Petrie 16 (= *HO*, pl. 21, 1) and Pap. Bulaq X = Pap. Cairo 58092 (= Janssen and Pestman 1968, pls. 1–2). Other related documents are O. UC 19614 (= Allam 1973, pls. 74–75), mentioning a divorce (note that the lady here is neither married nor a widow). The subject of O. AG 24 (unpublished) is obscure since only the three bottom lines have survived.

9. *Mꜥnṯwḥwti* (= *manuššḫata*); see Hoch 1994, 130 f., nr. 169.

10. In O. Petrie 64 (= *HO*, pl. 21, 2) a *Tnt-niwt* occurs who is indeed indicated as *ꜥnḫ-n-niwt,* but it is uncertain whether that is the same person.

the famous lady of the Will, or one of her granddaughters, is not certain. According to O. Gardiner 123 an *ʿnḫ-n-nỉwt,* whose name is lost, sold the workdays of a slave (*HO*, pl. 54, 1). O. Gardiner 133 records various sales (KRI 7, pp. 182–83). In verso 4 a sarcophagus, covered with paint, is stated to be for the *ʿnḫ-n-nỉwt*[11] Taysen, a woman who is also mentioned, with the title, in verso, line 16.

One further example may suffice. O. Cairo 25677 contains a long list, both on the recto and the verso, of all kinds of goods; perhaps it is an inventory of the contents of a house.[12] The first seven lines, however, record gifts to an *ʿnḫ-n-nỉwt*, mostly bundles of papyrus.[13] What the relation could be between this text and the rest is a mystery.

Other lists of gifts of a similar kind (e.g., O. Cairo 25598) do not mention the title, nor does any *ʿnḫ-n-nỉwt* occur in what I think are records of gifts brought to a party.[14] It appears clear, therefore, that O. Cairo 25677 was an exception. By far not all texts with an economic content contain the women's titles. It seems that it is not their economic, but their official, perhaps legal nature that determines whether the women are formally indicated.

Related to the preceding types are documents on the division of property and suchlike that show such a legal aspect.[15] Accordingly, these documents are apt to mention women as *ʿnḫ-n-nỉwt*. As an example, I can refer to O. Gardiner 90 (*HO*, pl. 51, 2), although it is presented in the form of a speech by a sculptor to his son. The father bequeaths him the days of service of some slaves, which formerly belonged to his mother, the *ʿnḫ-n-nỉwt* Maatnofre.[16] In O. Louvre E. 2425[17] the division of a storeroom between two daughters of a certain Nebamente is recorded. The women bear no title, "his daughter" clearly being conceived sufficient. In lines 5–6, however, we read that a cellar (*štꜣt*) was divided between the workman (*rmṯ-ỉst*) Neferḥotpe and the *ʿnḫ-n-nỉwt Ḥwt-ỉyt,* who in line 9 is simply called his (Neferḥotpe's) sister. Hence, only in contrast to *rmṯ-ỉst* is the title used. Elsewhere in similar testaments all women remain without any closer identification than their name (e.g., O. DeM 108 and 112). Evidently, despite the legal character of these texts, mention of the title was not obligatory.

In texts which, in my opinion, record credit and debts (Janssen 1994) women are also sometimes called *ʿnḫ-n-nỉwt*, but by no means invariably. Examples are O. Cairo 25572, 10–11,[18] and O. Varille 24 (= KRI 7, p. 341; Janssen 1994, p. 134). Other instances are unpublished, for example, O. Černý 8 and O. BM 29555. In O. Petrie 51 (= *HO*, pl. 28, 1) verso 5 (Janssen 1994, pp. 129–30), however, a woman appears without a title but is identified by the name of her mother, while the lady who, according to O. Gardiner 204 (= *HO*, pl. 50, 1), received extensive credit is referred to by her main title "chantress of Amun."[19]

These are all texts which in our terms deal with economic matters. Quite a different category are the questions put to the oracle of Pharaoh Amenhotep I, the local patron.[20] They seldom contain names of women, but where they do, no title is used. The only exception is a more extensive record of a consultation of the god, namely O. Cairo 25555 verso, where in line 3 a woman is called *ʿnḫ-n-nỉwt*. Were the shorter appeals to the deity not official enough to require more than names only?

The majority of the papyri from Deir el-Medina, being administrative, do not mention women, but a few refer to them for a specific reason. One of these is Pap. Salt 124 (Černý 1929) from the late Nineteenth Dynasty, an enumeration of the deeds of misbehavior of the chief workman Paneb. In recto 2, 2–4, he is accused of intercourse with three ladies, all three called *ʿnḫ*[*-n-nỉwt*], as well as with the daughter of one of them who bears no

11. The *n* (𓈖) is written as an afterthought above the line. In verso 16 the correction was not made. Does this mean that the *n* was not anymore heard in the pronunciation? Examples of *ʿnḫ-n-nỉwt* without the *n* are rather common.

12. Similar texts are O. Cairo 25678 and 25679 (only the recto) and O. Varille 19 (unpublished).

13. For *wꜣḏ*, see the article by Susan Johnson 1996.

14. See Janssen 1982. Instances in which women are listed are O. DeM 134; O. DeM 643; O. IFAO 1322 + O. Varille 8 + O. Cairo 25705 (only the last fragment has been published); O. Petrie 31 (= *HO*, pl. 35, 1). See now my *Village Varia: Ten Studies on the History and Administration of Deir el-Medîna* (Leiden, 1997), chapter IV.

15. For example, Pap. Turin 2070/154 verso II (= Allam 1973, p. 121; discussed bv Muszynski 1977, pp. 186–87); also Pap. DeM XXX (Černý 1986, pl. 21), a division of landed properties (*swt*) of a certain Praʿḥotpe between a Twerḥotpe, an *ʿnḫ-n-nỉwt* called Mut, and a Nesamun.

16. The text is related to O. Colin Campbell 17 (= O. Hunterian Museum, Glasgow, D.1925.83); published by McDowell 1993, pl. 25, pp. 22–25.

17. Also numbered O. Louvre E. 13156 (originally O. Anastasi; published by Allam 1973, pls. 60–61).

18. Janssen 1994, p. 131. For the use of *ʿnḫ* as abbreviation, see note 4, above.

19. Janssen 1994, pp. 130–31. The use of this title makes that of *ʿnḫ-n-nỉwt* superfluous. See, for example, Pap. BM 10417, 9 (= Blackman 1926, pl. 38), where the same Shedemdwae is also called "chantress of Amun, King of the Gods."

20. Černý 1935a; idem 1942; idem 1972; also O. DeM 572–76 and 600.

title. Whether this is because she was still a young girl, or because the addition "her daughter" was sufficient identification, is hard to know. All three older women were living with a man. The first one is said to be his "wife" (*ḥmt*), the other two simply to be "with" (*m-dỉ*) him. This seems to express a different kind of marital status, but it clearly did not influence the use of *ʿnḫ-n-nỉwt*.

A similar affair is encountered in the Turin Strike Papyrus, recto 4, 8–9 (Gardiner 1948b, p. 57, 14–16). Here, the three women, all said to be *ʿnḫ-n-nỉwt*, are explicitly recorded as being married (*ḥmt-ṯꜣy*). Both the documents are more or less official. Pap. Salt 124 was sent to the authorities, as the postscript (verso 2) demonstrates; the Turin Strike Papyrus, although used for various memoranda, shows, at least on the recto, the stylistic signs of an official report.

Equally formal are the documents collectively known as the Will of Naunakhte (Černý 1945), particularly Document I (= Pap. Ashmolean Museum 1945.97) with its introduction presenting the date and the composition of the court. In the following lines four daughters of Naunakhte are mentioned, all called *ʿnḫ-n-nỉwt*, while the sons are called *rmṯ-ỉst*. In Documents II and III (= Pap. DeM XXIII, XXV; Černý 1986, pls. 7–8 and 10–11), however, the same two daughters who inherited are listed without a title. These texts, with roughly the same contents (Document III is more extensive), are clearly less formal. Naunakhte herself is also called *ʿnḫ-n-nỉwt* (e.g., in 1, 5), but she declares herself to be a *nmḥy n pꜣ tꜣ n pr-ʿꜣ*, whatever the juridical meaning of this expression. These words are nowhere in any text used as a title.

We now pass on to texts not wholly dealing with the community of necropolis workmen. The Tomb Robbery Papyri mention, apart from the artisans, inhabitants of other settlements on the Theban West bank, and even some from the other side of the Nile. Yet, the people of Deir el-Medina were sufficiently involved in the thefts to have them recorded in the journals of the necropolis, especially in the so-called Giornale dell'anno 17 (Botti and Peet 1928). In these affairs, several women played a role, either as witnesses or as suspects. They are usually indicated as *ʿnḫ-n-nỉwt*, for instance, in Giornale 17 recto 5, 3 ff. (pls. 21–22)[21] and in 17A verso 4, 9, and verso 7, 10. The title is also common in the Tomb Robbery Papyri proper, for example, in Pap. BM 10054 verso 2 and 3,[22] 10053,[23] 10052,[24] and Pap. Mayer A.[25] One detail is worthy of attention. In Pap. BM 10052, 1, 8–9, a certain Nesmut is called *ʿnḫ-n-nỉwt*,[26] but another Nesmut, the wife of a Paynehsy (2, 29), remains without a title. Both were married, so that cannot be the reason for the difference. Moreover, the first Nesmut is called the sister of Mutemwia (3, 9), without a title, although the latter occurs in 6, 15 as a married lady and an *ʿnḫ-n-nỉwt*. The writing of the title was evidently not conceived to be throughout necessary.

One point regarding women's titles should be briefly mentioned. Some of the ladies of Deir el-Medina held a real function, although it is not clear to what extent it was merely a part-time occupation, namely that of "chantress of Amun." Whether they all belonged to the élite of the community, as Barbara Lesko suggests (1994, p. 154, note 35), should be the subject of another study. As with *ʿnḫ-n-nỉwt*, it was not absolutely necessary to use the title of "chantress."[27] In a few instances, a woman is once mentioned with one, in another case with the other title,[28] but never with both in one text. Since "chantress" was a real occupation, it made the vague *ʿnḫ-n-nỉwt* superfluous.

With the Tomb Robbery Papyri we have already crossed the border of the Deir el-Medina documents. In texts from elsewhere — always papyri because there are hardly any New Kingdom ostraca from other sites — women with the title rarely occur. The earliest example known to me is Pap. Gurob II, 1, 3 and II, 2, 2, dated to year 33 of Amenhotep III (Gardiner 1906, pp. 35 and 37). In both cases a woman named *Py-ỉḥy* is called *ʿnḫ-n-nỉwt* (written ). The people indicated as *ʿnḫ*[*w*]-*nw-nỉwt* in Pap. Berlin 9785, which belongs to the same

21. The same text as Pap. BM 10053, 5, 4 ff.

22. Peet 1930, pp. 64–65, pl. VII (all women called *ʿnḫ*). This is not a list of thieves, but of persons who received emmer in order to bake it into bread.

23. Peet 1930, p. 104 ff. (pls. XVII ff.).

24. Peet 1930, p. 142 ff. (pls. XXV ff.).

25. Peet 1920; see especially p. 13C, a list of eleven women, all called *ʿnḫ-n-nỉwt*.

26. Although the name is omitted, it is evident from 3, 8 that it should be Nesmut, the wife of Perpatjēw; see Peet 1930, p. 158, note 3 and p. 160, note 20.

27. There is little doubt that the chantress of Amun Bakenseti of O. Turin 57150, 3, is the same woman who occurs without a title in O. Gardiner 136 (= *HO*, pl. 60, 5), 3 and 4, and in O. Berlin 12343 (= *Hier. Pap. Berlin* III, pl. 34), 6. Very probably the chantress *Ḥentwaʿty* of O. DeM 679 is the same individual as the wife of Mose in O. DeM 643, 8, without a title.

28. For example, Khaʿtnub in the Will of Naunakhte, Document I, 4, 7 and in O. BM 50737, 2–3 (unpublished); Merut in O. DeM 671, 2 (chantress) and in Pap. Turin 2070, II verso 2 (= Allam 1973, pl. 121); also, without title, in O. IFAO 1322+, 3 (see note 14).

dossier, are men. This seems to be a survival of the Middle Kingdom title, although perhaps not anymore designating soldiers.

From the Nineteenth Dynasty dates Pap. Cairo 65739, published by Gardiner under the title "A Lawsuit Arising from the Purchase of Two Slaves" (Gardiner 1935). All women in this text, including some of the witnesses, are called *ʿnḫt-nt-nỉwt* (the only document in which the *t*s are written), once abbreviated to *ʿnḫ* (line 14). Another instance is Pap. Berlin 3047 (Helck 1963) of year 46 of Ramesses II, dealing with a lawsuit concerning the inheritance of fields before a court of priests. In lines 25–31 several women are recorded, all called *ʿnḫ-n-nỉwt*.

All these papyri are of a juridical nature. So, too, is the fourth one, which is called the Turin Indictment Papyrus, from the reign of Ramesses V (= Pap. Turin 1887 = Gardiner 1948b, pp. 73–82). In recto 1, 5–6, we find a similar case as in Pap. Salt 124 and in the Turin Strike Papyrus: a man is charged with having had intercourse with two married women. Both are identified by their father's name ("daughter of" PN), but, although their status seems to be equal,[29] only the first one is also called *ʿnḫ-n-nỉwt*.

An unexpected detail occurs on a stela with an "abnormal hieratic" inscription, now in the Cairo Museum.[30] Although this is a stela, the script as well as the way in which the text is formulated strongly suggests that it is a copy of a document on papyrus, and, therefore, not really an exception to the rule that the title does not occur on monuments. The text begins with a statement by a sandal-maker: "As for me, the *ʿnḫ-n-nỉwt* Shedēse, a slave (*ḥmt*) of mine, came to me saying: 'Look after me while I am alive, and you will find the arable land of mine. Do not let me give it to another man, a stranger.'" Apart from the fact that we encounter here a woman who possesses a field[31] which she is clearly free to sell to whom she wants, although she is a slave, it is conspicuous for our study that a slave is here called *ʿnḫ-n-nỉwt*.[32] One may suggest that Shedēse is a widow and had inherited the field from her husband, but that is nowhere stated.

Ownership of land by women is in itself not rare. In Pap. Brooklyn 16.205 (Parker 1962, Appendix I, p. 49 ff. and pls. 17–19), the second memorandum records a dispute concerning some sections of a field, which was the property of an *ʿnḫ-n-nỉwt* and had been sold by her kinsman. Although the lady lost her case before the oracle of Hemen of Hefat, it is clear that she conceived herself to be the owner of the field. Another instance of fields that belonged to women occurs in the famous stela of Iuwelot, also known as the Stèle d'Apanage.[33] The young high priest of Amun Iuwelot buys land from several persons, among whom are two women, both called *ʿnḫ-n-nỉwt* (lines 12–13 and 18). The men are called *mnḫ* or bear titles indicating their occupation, such as priest, rower, or shield-bearer. Once again, although written on stone, the text evidently copies a papyrus document.

These are a few examples of the use of *ʿnḫ-n-nỉwt* outside Deir el-Medina, during the New Kingdom and later.[34] The pattern is the same: the title was used in a legal context, including some on the sale of fields, that is, with an economic purpose.

The title sometimes occurs, however, in a general description. The most revealing case may be the Pap. Abbott 4, 1–2 (Peet 1930, p. 39 and pl. II), where are mentioned "the tombs and burial chambers in which are resting the blessed ones of old, the *ʿnḫ-n-nỉwt* and the *rmṯ n pꜣ tꜣ*, on the West of Thebes." The two expressions together comprise all people. In the list of Pap. BM 10054 verso 2–3, all persons who received emmer, including the women, are called *rmṯ n pꜣ tꜣ* (Peet 1930, p. 64, pl. VII). A less formal variant occurs on a Twentieth Dynasty statue in Turin,[35] in an appeal to future generations: *ỉ rmṯ nb, ʿnḫ-nỉwt nb, nty ỉw ḥr-sꜣ.n* "Oh all you men and women who shall come after us … ." *Rmṯ* stands here for *rmṯ n pꜣ tꜣ*, of which *ʿnḫ-nỉwt* is the female counterpart. In this case it means no more than "women" in general.

---

29. There is a subtle distinction. Of the first one is said: *ỉw.s m ḥmt m-dỉ* D.; of the other: *ỉw.s m ḥmt* A.; but I fail to see how this could cause the lack of a title of the latter.

30. Stela Cairo 11867 (formerly $\frac{27|6}{24|3}$), published by Bakir 1952, pls. II–IV.

31. In Pap. Wilbour male slaves occur as possessors; see Gardiner 1948a, II, p. 84.

32. Černý's (1945) statement, quoted above, is clearly not wholly correct.

33. Published by Legrain (1897), with comments by Erman. It is regrettable that this important document has not been the subject of a more up-to-date study.

34. See, for example, the division of an inheritance from Miwer; Pap. BM 10568 (= KRI 7, 100–01). In line 6, two women appear, one called *ʿnḫ-nỉwt* the other *ʿnḫ-nt*[sic]*-nỉwt*.

35. Maspero 1883, p. 149, nr. XXXV, quoted by Gardiner 1930, p. 225, nr. 26. The statue of a *rwḏw* called Amenemope-men seems never to have been adequately published. I have failed to discover its inventory number (according to Ranke, *Personennamen*, it is C 10).

Finally, it is worth noting that the feminine title here discussed, *ʿnḫ-n-nỉwt,* does not occur in the New Kingdom onomastica. *Rmṯ* is mentioned (Gardiner 1947, I, 98* ff.), but as the first in a series of ancient names for mankind: *rmṯ, pʿt, rḫyt,* and *hmmt*, not as an abbreviation of *rmṯ n pꜣ tꜣ*. Is that because the title, except for the example from Pap. Abbott, does not occur without a name? In many Deir el-Medina ostraca and papyri we come across a group of, or even a single, *rmṯ-ỉst*, but never one or a group of *ʿnḫ-n-nỉwt*.

Let us try to reach a conclusion. Although the European languages possess similar expressions for women, they exhibit minor differences. In Britain an elderly unmarried lady can be and is still called "Miss." Every Egyptologist knows at least one example, namely the late Miss Moss. In German, there is a strong tendency to call a lady after the age of adolescence "Frau," whether married or not. Fräulein sounds too much a diminutive, only suitable for girls. Nobody would ever call the former Vienna Professor "Fräulein" Thausing.

Of course, the Egyptian *ʿnḫ-n-nỉwt* does not in itself indicate a specific age. It seems that it could be used, at least during the New Kingdom, for every female who was not anymore a child. In most instances that will have meant that she was or had been married; so far as we know there were few unmarried adult women. Yet, it seems not *per se* to have designated a "married woman," even though ladies so called almost always have or have had that status. The specific Egyptian aspect was not age, nor, in theory, the marital status, but its use in a formal context of a hieratic document. On monuments it does not occur. An exact translation in our languages is hardly possible. In most instances Mrs. (Frau) may be the best.

Abbreviations

Hier. Pap. Berlin III	Gardiner 1911
HO	Černý and Gardiner 1957
O. AG	Ostracon Alan Gardiner (fragmentary). Mostly unpublished
O. BM	Ostracon British Museum
O. DeM	Černý 1935–70 and Sauneron 1959
O. Cairo	Černý 1935a
O. IFAO	Ostracon de l'Institut français d'archéologie orientale du Cairo
O. Turin	López 1978–84
O. UC	Ostracon University College London
Pap. Salt 124	Černý 1929

References

Allam, S.

1973 *Hieratische Ostraka und Papyri*, Band 1, Tafelteil. Transkriptionen aus dem Nachlass von J. Černý. Tübingen: n.p.

1992 "Legal Aspects in the 'Contendings of Horus and Seth.'" In *Studies in Pharaonic Religion and Society in Honour of J. Gwyn Griffiths*, edited by A. B. Lloyd, pp. 137–45. London: Egypt Exploration Society.

Bakir, A. M.

1952 *Slavery in Pharaonic Egypt*. Supplément aux Annales du Service des antiquités de l'Égypte 18. Cairo: Institut français d'archéologie orientale.

Berlev, O.

1971 "Les prétendus 'citadins' au Moyen Empire." *Revue d'égyptologie* 23: 23–48.

Blackman, A. M.

1926 "Oracles in Ancient Egypt." *Journal of Egyptian Archaeology* 12: 176–85.

Botti, G., and T. E. Peet

1928 *Il giornale della necropoli di Tebe*. Turin: Fratelli Bocca Editori.

Černý, J.

1929 "Papyrus Salt 124 (Brit. Mus. 10055)." *Journal of Egyptian Archaeology* 15: 243–58.

1935a *Ostraca hiératiques*. Catalogue général des antiquités égyptiennes du Musée du Caire, nos. 25501–25832. Cairo: Institut français d'archéologie orientale.

1935b "Questions adressées aux oracles." *Bulletin de l'Institut français d'archéologie orientale* 35: 41–58.

1935–70 *Catalogue des ostraca hiératiques non littéraires de Deir el Médineh* (*nos. 1–705*). Documents de fouilles 3–7 and 14. Cairo: Institut français d'archéologie orientale.

1942 "Nouvelle série de questions addressées aux oracles." *Bulletin de l'Institut français d'archéologie orientale* 41: 13–24.

1945 "The Will of Naunakhte and the Related Documents." *Journal of Egyptian Archaeology* 31: 29–53.

1958 *Egyptian Stelae in the Bankes Collection*. Oxford: Griffith Institute.

1972 "Troisième série de questions adressées aux oracles." *Bulletin de l'Institut français d'archéologie orientale* 72: 49–69.

1973 *A Community of Workmen at Thebes in the Ramesside Period*. Bibliothèque d'étude 50. Cairo: Institut français d'archéologie orientale.

1978 *Papyrus hiératiques de Deir el-Médineh*, tome 1 (*nos. I–XVII*). Catalogue complété et édité par Georges Posener. Documents de fouilles 8. Cairo: Institut français d'archéologie orientale.

1986 *Papyrus hiératiques de Deir el-Médineh*, tome 2 (*nos. XVIII–XXXIV*). Catalogue complété et édité par Yvan Koenig. Documents de fouilles 22. Cairo: Institut français d'archéologie orientale.

Černý, J., and A. H. Gardiner

1957 *Hieratic Ostraca*, Volume I. Oxford: Griffith Institute.

Demarée, R. J.

1983 *The* ꜣḫ iḳr n Rꜥ *Stelae: On Ancestor Worship in Ancient Egypt*. Egyptologische Uitgaven 3. Leiden: Nederlands Instituut voor het Nabije Oosten.

Gardiner, A. H.

1906 "Four Papyri of the 18th Dynasty from Kahun." *Zeitschrift für ägyptische Sprache und Altertumskunde* 43: 27–47.

1911 *Hieratische Papyrus aus den Königlichen Museen zu Berlin*, Band 3 (Ostraka = pl. 26–42). Leipzig: J. C. Hinrichs.

1930 "The Origin of Certain Coptic Grammatical Elements." *Journal of Egyptian Archaeology* 16: 220–34.

1935 "A Lawsuit Arising from the Purchase of Two Slaves." *Journal of Egyptian Archaeology* 21: 140–46.

1947 *Ancient Egyptian Onomastica*. 3 volumes. Oxford: Oxford University Press.

1948a *The Wilbour Papyrus*. 3 volumes. Oxford: Oxford University Press.

1948b *Ramesside Administrative Documents*. London: Oxford University Press.

Helck, W.

1963 "Der Papyrus Berlin P 3047." *Journal of the American Research Center in Egypt* 2: 65–73.

Hieroglyphic Texts

1914–82 *Hieroglyphic Texts from Egyptian Stelae, etc.*, Parts 5–10. London: British Museum.

Hoch, J. E.

1994 *Semitic Words in Egyptian Texts of the New Kingdom and Third Intermediate Period*. Princeton: Princeton University Press.

Janssen, J. J.

1982 "Gift-giving in Ancient Egypt as an Economic Feature." *Journal of Egyptian Archaeology* 68: 253–58.

1994 "Debts and Credits in the New Kingdom." *Journal of Egyptian Archaeology* 80: 129–36.

Janssen, J. J., and P. W. Pestman

1968 "Burial and Inheritance in the Community of the Necropolis Workmen at Thebes." *Journal of the Social and Economic History of the Orient* 11: 137–70.

Johnson, S.

1996 "A New View on Some Old Vegetables: A Study of the Generic Words *wꜣḏ* and *smw*." *Göttinger Miszellen* 150: 75–80.

Kitchen, K. A.

1975–89 *Ramesside Inscriptions: Historical and Biographical*. 7 Volumes. Oxford: B. H. Blackwell.

Legrain, G.

1897 "Deux stèles trouvées à Karnak en février 1897." *Zeitschrift für ägyptische Sprache und Altertumskunde* 35: 12–19.

Lesko, B. S.

1994 "Rank, Roles, and Rights." In *Pharaoh's Workers: The Villagers of Deir el-Medina*, edited by L. H. Lesko, pp. 15–39. Ithaca: Cornell University Press.

López, J.

1978–84 *Ostraca ieratici*. Catalogo del Museo Egizio di Torino, serie seconda - collezioni, volume 3. Milano: Istituto Editoriale Cisalpino.

McDowell, A. G.

1993 *Hieratic Ostraca in the Hunterian Museum Glasgow* (*The Colin Campbell Ostraca*). Oxford: Griffith Institute.

Maspero, G.

1883 "Rapport à M. Jules Ferry, ministre de l'instruction publique, sur une mission en Italie." *Recueil de travaux, relatifs à la philologie et à l'archéologie égyptiennes et assyriennes* 4: 125–51.

Muszynski, M.

1977 "P. Turin Cat. 2070/154." *Oriens Antiquus* 16: 183–200.

Parker, R. A.

1962 *A Saite Oracle Papyrus from Thebes in the Brooklyn Museum*. Providence: Brown University Press.

Peet, T. E.

1920 *The Mayer Papyri A and B. Nos. M. 11162 and M. 11186 of the Free Public Museums, Liverpool*. London: Egypt Exploration Society.

1930 *The Great Tomb-Robberies of the Twentieth Egyptian Dynasty*. Oxford: Clarendon Press.

Pestman, P. W.

1961 *Marriage and Matrimonial Property in Ancient Egypt: A Contribution to Establishing the Legal Position of the Woman*. Leiden: E. J. Brill.

Robins, G.

1993 *Women in Ancient Egypt*. London: British Museum Press.

Sauneron, S.

1959 *Catalogue des ostraca hiératiques non littéraires de Deir el-Médineh* (*nos. 550–623*). Documents de fouilles 13. Cairo: Institut français d'archéologie orientale.

Tosi, M., and A. Roccati
1971 *Stele a altri epigrafi di Deir el Medina.* Catalogo del Museo Egizio di Torino, serie seconda - collezioni 1. Turin: Edizione d'Arte Fratelli Pozzo.

Ward, W. A.
1986 *Essays on Feminine Titles of the Middle Kingdom and Related Subjects.* Beirut: American University of Beirut.

Wente, E. F.
1990 *Letters from Ancient Egypt.* Society of Biblical Literature, Writings from the Ancient World 1. Atlanta: Scholars Press.

19

REMARKS ON CONTINUITY IN EGYPTIAN LITERARY TRADITION

RICHARD JASNOW

The Johns Hopkins University, Baltimore

Egyptian literature is not the least important among the many fields in which Professor Wente has distinguished himself. It is a pleasure to contribute the following comments on that subject to a volume in his honor.

In recent years, new texts and studies have enriched our knowledge of Late Period Egyptian literature.[1] P. Vandier (Posener 1985) and the Brooklyn Wisdom Text (P. Brooklyn 47.218.135; Jasnow 1992) have appeared. There are, moreover, strong indications that these are not isolated examples of late hieratic literary compositions.[2] The specialty of Demotic has also been very productive in texts and insights.[3] Certainly one of the challenging questions for those interested in Egyptian literature is the relationship between this Late Period material and the earlier works of the Old, Middle, and New Kingdoms. How many classical[4] works survived, and what was the nature of their influence on the later compositions? The state of the evidence precludes a definitive answer, but I believe such important questions should still be asked. A few scholars have already profitably occupied themselves with this subject. Lichtheim (1983) and Tait (1992, 1994, 1995), for example, have contributed significant remarks on the problem. I would like here to collect and comment on the evidence, being fully aware of the speculative nature of the discussion.[5]

There are obvious differences between the corpus of classical texts and that of the Late Period. We have no direct Late Period evidence for such typically New Kingdom creations as love poetry, satiric letters, or the Late Period Egyptian Miscellanies.[6] The Demotic scribes in their turn certainly developed new genres and structures. Perhaps in part as a response to the troubled history of the first millennium, these scribes composed lengthy military narrative tales with more enthusiasm than their ancestors.[7] The Demotic Satire of the Harper is unique enough that Thissen can plausibly argue for its owing more to the Greek than the Egyptian tradition (Thissen 1992, pp. 13–15). So, too, the predominantly single-line structure of the wisdom texts is a Late Period characteristic that is much less common in older works (Lichtheim 1983, pp. 1–12). The absence of earlier genres, the appearance of new ones, and the structural differences between the classical and Late Period compositions have

1. For the purposes of this discussion, Late Period designates the span of time from the Twenty-fifth Dynasty through the Roman period. I have also included a few quotations and texts that may date to the Twenty-second Dynasty. I have excluded Wenamun, preserved on a Twenty-second Dynasty papyrus (see *LÄ* 6 "Wenamun," col. 1215), and the "Tale of Woe," inscribed on a papyrus possibly of the same date (see Caminos 1977, p. 3). I would like to thank Dr. Emily Teeter for her comments on an earlier version of this paper.
2. Burkard and Fischer-Elfert 1994, p. 10 (numbers 178, 179, 181, 182, 183).
3. In recent years there has been a welcome increase in the number of scholars interested in Demotic literature, a trend amply documented in the "Demotische Literaturübersicht," published annually in *Enchoria* since 1971. Among the important new literary texts or re-editions are Bresciani, Pernigotti, and Betrò 1983; H. Smith and Tait 1983; Zauzich 1983; Thissen 1984; de Cenival 1985; de Cenival 1988; de Cenival 1990; Chauveau 1991; Frandsen 1991; Thissen 1992; Hoffmann 1995.
4. "Classical" in this essay means that the text derives from the Old, Middle, or New Kingdoms and does not denote possible status within the literary tradition.
5. The problem of the literary tradition is one aspect of the larger question of cultural and linguistic continuity in the Late Period. Of recent works or remarks relevant to questions of continuity, I may mention M. Smith 1979 (religion and language); Derchain-Urtel 1990, p. 115 (monumental inscriptions); Ritner 1993 (magic); Jansen-Winkeln 1994 (language); Manuelian 1994 (archaizing Saite reliefs and inscriptions); Corcoran 1995 (art). Significant, too, is the discussion of linguistic continuity from Late Period Egyptian through Demotic to Coptic in the conclusions of Johnson 1976, pp. 298–302.
6. For a preliminary statistical survey of the various genres attested in Demotic, see Mertens 1992, p. 234.
7. Chauveau (1991) comments on the remarkable popularity of the narrative military epic in Demotic literature in contrast to the pharaonic tradition.

Gold of Praise: Studies on Ancient Egypt in Honor of Edward F. Wente
Edited by Emily Teeter and John A. Larson
Studies in Ancient Oriental Civilization 58
Chicago: Oriental Institute, 1999

naturally tended to underscore the apparent break in literary tradition between the end of the New Kingdom and about the middle of the first millennium, when we once more begin to have abundant literary material.

In considering this question of literary continuity, it is well to keep in mind the rarity of "literary" works in general. While of course the situation may have varied from library to library, it is probable that "literary" tales, wisdom texts, or the like would have been quite few in comparison to holdings of religious, magical, or medical works.[8] Moreover, even if a Late Period library possessed a hieratic copy of Westcar or Sinuhe, this does not mean that scribes would have thought it necessary or useful to have translated such texts into Demotic. While examples exist of "translations" of a literary work from one stage of Egyptian to another, it does not appear to have been a very common practice, even in the New Kingdom.[9] Moreover, certain famous texts, for example, the Dialogue of a Man with his *Ba*,[10] The Eloquent Peasant,[11] or The Tales of P. Westcar[12] may not in fact have been widely known, having already fallen into relative obscurity during the New Kingdom. We should not expect to find much Late Period evidence for texts that may not have been widely read by New Kingdom times.[13]

Evidence that Late Period scribes knew the classical texts is chiefly of two kinds: copies[14] and quotations. In the following, I present Late Period copies of classical compositions; Late Period hieratic literary narratives and wisdom texts that may reflect an awareness or knowledge of an earlier text but lack obvious classical antecedents; a representative selection of Late Period quotations[15] from or allusions[16] to classical compositions that various scholars regard as "modeled" on classical texts, some of which are more convincing than others; and Demotic references to, or paraphrases of, The Tale of Sinuhe, a classic of Egyptian literature.

LATE PERIOD COPIES OF CLASSICAL COMPOSITIONS

Instruction of Hordjedef

Writing Tablet Brooklyn 37.1394 E

Date: Twenty-fifth/Twenty-sixth Dynasty

Reference: Posener 1966, pp. 62–65; Quack 1992, p. 13

Instruction of Khety

Writing Tablet Louvre E. 8424

Date: Twenty-fifth/Twenty-sixth Dynasty or later

Reference: Sauneron 1950; Posener 1966, pp. 51, 65; Seibert 1967, pp. 100–02; *LÄ* 3 "Lehre des Cheti," cols. 977–78; Quack 1992, p. 13

8. I formed this impression when examining the papyri in the Brooklyn Museum, including the many boxes of fragments. Sauneron (1970, pp. viii–ix) tentatively proposes that these hieratic papyri came from the libraries of the temples at Heliopolis.
9. Quack 1992/93, p. 128. See also Vernus 1990; Fischer-Elfert 1992a, pp. 44–47; Manuelian 1994, p. 58.
10. Preserved on a single papyrus of the Twelfth Dynasty; see *LÄ* 2 "Gespräch des Lebensmüden," cols. 571–73.
11. Parkinson (1991, p. xxix) remarks that while it is often thought that the Eloquent Peasant had fallen out of fashion by the end of the Thirteenth Dynasty, the quotation in Menna from Deir el-Medina may indicate that this was not entirely the case. The comments of Fecht (*LÄ* 1 "Bauerngeschichte," col. 642) are apt: "Ostraka fehlen, und damit jeder Hinweis auf Schulbenutzung der B<auerngeschichte>. Das sehr ungenaue Zitat nach B 1, 28–29 (offenbar nach Erinnerung) auf Ostr. Orient. Inst. Univ. Chicago 12073 verso 6–7 ... zeigt nur, dass die B<auerngeschichte> in der Ramessidenzeit (Zeit Ramses III.) nicht ganz unbekannt war. Dass dieses Ostr. mit dem Zitat aus dem Schiffbrüchigen beginnt, lässt vermuten, dass sein Verfasser auf seine Kenntnis sonst wenig bekannter älterer Literaturwerke stolz war." For a skeptical attitude to these quotations, see Goedicke 1987, p. 78.
12. Preserved on a single papyrus of the Hyksos period; see *LÄ* 4 "Pap. Westcar," col. 744.
13. It is difficult to determine how widely known were those compositions that did not become "school texts." Blumenthal (1972, p. 16) observes that the Late Egyptian stories never seem to have attained the status of school texts. On the question of Egyptian "classics," see Assmann 1985.
14. I refer to "copies," although in most cases it is a matter of "extracts," and not complete copies of the texts in question.
15. Several scholars have done important work on quotations; see Brunner 1979; *LÄ* 6 "Zitate," cols. 1415–20; Fischer-Elfert 1992b; Grimal 1980; Guglielmi 1984; *LÄ* 5 "Sprichwort," cols. 1219–22; Lichtheim 1984; Quack 1992, p. 13; idem 1994, pp. 194–205. See also my remarks on possible allusions to classical literature, for example, in Mythus and the Book of Thoth, at the end of this article.
16. In some cases the Late Period passages are perhaps better understood as "indirect, but pointed or meaningful" references to earlier passages, i.e., "allusions" (Morris 1981, p. 36) rather than "quotations."

Writing tablet from Thebes
Date: Twenty-fifth Dynasty
Reference: Bietak 1972, pl. 17; Posener 1973, p. 251, n. 1; Quack 1993, p. 10

Instruction of Amenemhat
P. Berlin 23045
Date: Thirtieth Dynasty(?)
Reference: Burkard 1977, pp. 7–8; Quack 1992, p. 13; Burkard and Fischer-Elfert 1994, p. 119 (number 177)

Instruction of Any
Egypt Exploration Society Saqqara Papyrus of Any
Date: Twenty-sixth Dynasty(?)[17]
Reference: Unpublished

Berlin Wooden Tablet 13592 (8934)
Date: Twenty-fifth/Twenty-sixth Dynasty
Reference: Erman 1894; Quack 1994, p. 11

Instruction of Amenemope
P. BM 10474
Date: Twenty-fifth/Twenty-sixth Dynasty
Reference: Posener 1966, pp. 59–62[18]

Louvre E. 17173
Date: Twenty-fifth/Twenty-sixth Dynasty(?)
Reference: Posener 1966, pp. 46–50

Turin 6237
Date: Twenty-fifth/Twenty-sixth Dynasty
Reference: Posener 1966, pp. 54–62

Turin Supplement 4661
Date: Twenty-fifth/Twenty-sixth Dynasty
Reference: Posener 1973

Moscow 1 ı δ 324
Date: Twenty-fifth/Twenty-sixth Dynasty(?)
Reference: Posener 1966, pp. 50–54

LATE PERIOD HIERATIC LITERARY NARRATIVES AND WISDOM TEXTS

Tale of Neferkare and General Sisene[19]
P. Chassinat I = P. Louvre E. 25351
Date: Twenty-fifth Dynasty
Reference: Posener 1957; Quack 1992, p. 13; Kamerzell 1995b, p. 966

Fragmentary Ghost Story
P. Chassinat II = P. Louvre E. 25352
Date: Tenth–seventh centuries B.C.
Reference: Posener 1958

17. "Für die Datierung muss man einen Zeitraum mindestens von der 22. bis zur 26. Dynastie in Betracht ziehen, wobei ich den späteren Zeitpunkt für wahrscheinlicher halte, u.a. wegen des im gleichen Kontext gefundenen frühdemotischen Papyrus" (Quack 1994, p. 11).

18. Quack (1994, p. 211) proposes to date Amenemope to the Third Intermediate Period and not to the Twentieth Dynasty, as does Grumach-Shirun (*LÄ* 3 "Lehre des Amenemope," col. 971). Amenemope is possibly mentioned in a list of book titles from the Twentieth or Twenty-first Dynasty (Burkard and Fischer-Elfert 1994, p. 121, number 180).

19. In P. Brooklyn 47.218.148 and 47.218.85, which date to the Thirtieth Dynasty or early Ptolemaic period, the papyrus is said to have been "discovered in the time of the King of Upper and Lower Egypt Neferkare, justified of voice" (Sauneron 1989, p. 60).

P. Vandier

P. Vandier

Date: Twenty-fifth/Twenty-sixth Dynasty(?)

Reference: Posener 1985; Fischer-Elfert 1987; Kamerzell 1995c

Brooklyn Wisdom Text

P. Brooklyn 47.218.135

Date: Twenty-sixth Dynasty(?)

Reference: Jasnow 1992; Quack 1993; Burkard 1994b

SELECTED LATE PERIOD QUOTATIONS OF CLASSICAL COMPOSITIONS

Quotation 1. Statue of Hor CG 42230, d, lines 8–9 = Merikare E, lines 117–118

ḫm mn n mkḥꜣ tw ỉn.t ỉw wꜥ ky rwỉ=f ỉn wꜥ sẖꜣ n=f ky ỉnk wꜣḥ ḫt n tpy.w-ꜥ sn.w šm ẖr-ḥꜣ.t (Statue of Hor CG 42230, d, lines 8–9)

"One should not forget the tomb, one does not neglect the western valley! One comes, the other goes. The one should think of the other! I was one who offered to the ancestors, my brothers, who had gone before" (Jansen-Winkeln 1985, pp. 173, 533)

ỉn wꜥ smnḫ ky ỉr s n nty ẖr ḥꜣ.t=f m mry.t smnḫ ỉr.n=ỉ (read: *ỉr.n=f*) *ỉn ky ỉy ḥr-sꜣ=f* (Merikare E, lines 117–118)

"It is one who benefits another, as a man acts for the one who is before him, so that another, who comes after him, restores what he has done"

Date: Twenty-second Dynasty

Reference: Guglielmi 1984, p. 357; Jansen-Winkeln 1985, pp. 173, 533

Quotation 2. Cairo Statue JE 37512, line 4 = Loyalist Instruction 14, line 11

ỉw šfd ḥr ḏd ꜣḫ n ỉr=f ṯꜣw n rꜣ ꜣḫ n sꜥḥ mỉ ntt r ỉsy.w (Cairo Statue JE 37512, line 4)

"A papyrus roll says: 'It is beneficial for the one who does it: a breath of the mouth for the mummy,' in accordance with the old books" (Jansen-Winkeln 1985, pp. 218, 220–21, 562)

... *ỉr r ỉrw n=f* (Loyalist Instruction 14, line 11)

" ... for the one who does (it) than for the one for whom it is done" (Posener 1976, p. 139)

Date: Twenty-second/Twenty-third Dynasty

Reference: Posener 1976, p. 139; Brunner 1979, pp. 160–61;[20] Guglielmi 1984, pp. 350–51 (with doubts); *LÄ* 6 "Zitate," col. 1420

Quotation 3. Piye Victory Stela, line 3 = Sinuhe B, lines 222–223

ḥꜣty.w-ꜥ ḥqꜣ.w ḥ.wt m ṯsm.w m ỉry rd.wy=f (Piye Victory Stela, line 3)

"the counts and rulers of domains are as dogs at his feet"

nn sẖꜣ <R>tnw n=k ỉm=s mỉtt ṯsmw=k (Sinuhe B, lines 222–223)

"I do not mention <Ra>tenu: it belongs to you like your dogs"[21]

Date: ca. 724 B.C.

Reference: Brunner 1979, p. 146; Grimal 1980, p. 42; Grimal 1981, pp. 16, 284

20. Brunner suggests that quotations from the Loyalist Instruction may still be found in Ptolemaic tomb inscriptions; see Vernus 1976. Brunner (1979, p. 151) also cites a quote from Loyalist Instruction 7, lines 1–3, in the tomb of Ibi (Saite period), probably copied from another tomb.

21. All Sinuhe citations are from Gardiner 1909. Two other quotations are worth mentioning here: compare *ỉrr ḥm=f mrr=f* "what his majesty does is as he wishes" (Piye Victory Stela, line 80) and *ỉrr ḥm=k m mr.t=f* "Your majesty does as he wishes" (Sinuhe B, line 236); *dḥr m qs=ỉ* "illness is in my bones" (Piye Victory Stela, line 135) and *qs mn.n=f ỉꜣwy* "The bones ache through old age" (Ptahhotep; Prisse 5, line 1 = Žába 1956, p. 16, line 17). For a discussion of these quotations, see Grimal 1980, pp. 42–43.

Quotation 4. Piye Victory Stela, line 12 = Sinuhe B, line 274

šrm pḏ.t sfḫ ˁḥ3 (Piye Victory Stela, line 12)

"Rest the bow; loosen the arrow"

nft ˁb=k sfḫ ssr=k (Sinuhe B, line 274)

"Slacken your bow; loosen your arrow"

Date: ca. 724 B.C.
Reference: Grimal 1980, p. 41; Grimal 1981, p. 284; Guglielmi 1984, p. 353

Quotation 5. Piye Victory Stela, line 27 = Merikare E, line 73[22]

iṯ=sn sw mi gp n mw (Piye Victory Stela, line 27)

"so that they took it like a cloudburst"

iṯ.n=i s mi gp n mw (Merikare E, line 73)

"I took it like a cloudburst"

Date: ca. 724 B.C.
Reference: Grimal 1980, p. 43; Grimal 1981, p. 285; Quack 1992, p. 13 (with doubts)

Quotation 6. Piye Victory Stela, lines 51–52 = Shipwrecked Sailor, lines 69–70

nm sšm tw sp-2 nm ir sšm tw sšm tw [...] ... *n=k w3.t n ˁnḫ* (Piye Victory Stela, lines 51–52)

"Who has led you? Who has led you? Who has led you then? Who has led you, that you [...] the path of life?"

nm in tw sp-2 nḏs nm in tw (Shipwrecked Sailor, lines 69–70)

"Who has brought you, who has brought you, little one? Who has then brought you?" (Blackman 1972, p. 43)

Date: ca. 724 B.C.
Reference: Blackman 1972, p. 43; Grimal 1980, p. 42; Grimal 1981, pp. 64, 285; Guglielmi 1984, p. 361 (accepts this quote); Baines 1990, p. 56 (doubts this quote)

Quotation 7. Piye Victory Stela, line 73 = Amenemhat IIIb

n gm.n=i mri n hrw qsn (Piye Victory Stela, line 73)

"I did not find a comrade on the day of woe"

ḥr ntt nn wnn mr.w n s hrw n qsn.t (Amenemhat IIIb; Helck 1969, p. 22)

"For no man has adherents on the day of woe"

Date: ca. 724 B.C.
Reference: Caminos 1958, p. 121;[23] Helck 1969, p. 22; Brunner 1979, p. 147; Grimal 1980, p. 41; Grimal 1981, pp. 78–79; Guglielmi 1984, p. 353

Quotation 8. Kawa Taharqa temple T, first court, east wall, south half = Amenemhat XIIc

[ptpt].n=f ḫ3s.wt bšd.w di=f ir=sn šm ṯsm.w (Kawa Taharqa temple T, first court, east wall, south half)

"He [crush]ed the foreign countries that revolted. He caused them to make the walk of dogs" (Macadam 1955, pl. 11)

iw di.n=i (sic) *iry=i Sttyw ḥr šm.t ṯsm.w* (Instruction of Amenemhat XIIc)

"I made the Setiu to walk as dogs" (Helck 1969, p. 78)

Date: Reign of Taharqa (690–664 B.C.)
Reference: Macadam 1955, pp. 64–65, pl. 11; Helck 1969, p. 78; Brunner 1979, p. 145

22. Citations of the Instruction to Merikare are from Quack 1992.

23. Caminos (1958, p. 121) detects a possible allusion to Amenemhat in the Chronicle of Osorkon: "He caused those amongst them who did not possess to become equal to those who did by his giving to them"; Caminos compares Instruction for Amenemhat IIId: *iw di.n=i pḥ iwty n=f mi nty wn* "I caused him who did not possess to attain success even as the man of consequence" (Helck 1969, p. 24).

Quotation 9. Dream Stela of Tanutamun, line 33 = Ptahhotep, line 116

wḏ.t n nṯr pw ḫpr⸗s (Dream Stela of Tanutamun, line 33)

"Its happening is what the god has commanded" (Schäfer 1905, p. 72)

wḏ.t nṯr pw ḫpr.t (Ptahhotep, line 116)

"What happens is what the god commands" (Žába 1956, p. 25)[24]

Date: 664 B.C.

Reference: Schäfer 1905, p. 72; Žába 1956, p. 25; Seibert 1967, p. 68, n. 79 (with doubts); Brunner 1979, p. 135

Quotation 10. P. Brooklyn 47.218.135, lines 4/8 = Djedefhor VII, line 1

mr pꜣy⸗k pr stp n⸗k ḫnì ꜥšꜣ (P. Brooklyn 47.218.135, lines 4/8)

"Love your household; choose for yourself a multitude of harem-women"

stp n⸗k ḫnì.wt m rmṯ (Djedefhor VII, line 1)

"Choose for yourself harem-women(?) from the people" (Helck 1984, p. 19)

Date: Saite period (664–525 B.C.)(?)

Reference: Helck 1984, p. 19; Jasnow 1992, pp. 81–82; Quack 1993, p. 14

Quotation 11. Biography of *Wḏꜣ-Ḥr-rsn.t*, line 44 = Sinuhe B, lines 28–29

fꜣy.n wì ḫꜣs.tyw m ḫꜣs.t r ḫꜣs.t (Biography of *Wḏꜣ-Ḥr-rsn.t*, line 44)

"The foreigners brought me from land to land" (Posener 1936, p. 21)[25]

rdì.n wì ḫꜣs.t n ḫꜣs.t (Sinuhe B, lines 28–29)

"Foreign land gave me to foreign land"

Date: 519 B.C.

Reference: Posener 1936, p. 21; Guglielmi 1984, p. 357

Quotation 12. Onkhsheshonqy 6, line 10 = Any B 19, lines 4–6

m-ìr ḫꜣꜥ ḥꜣṯ⸗k r pꜣ nkt n ky ḏ ìw⸗y ꜥnḫ n-ìm⸗f my ḫpr n⸗k ḥꜥ⸗k (Onkhsheshonqy 6, line 10)

"Do not rely on the property of another, saying, 'I will live on it'; acquire your own"[26]

m-ìr mḥ ìb⸗k ꜣḫ.t kꜣy sꜣw tw ìry⸗k n⸗k m ìr ḥꜣn⸗k nk.t kꜣy bw-ìry⸗f ṯsì m pr⸗k (Any B 19, lines 4–6)

"Do not rely on another's goods; guard what you acquire yourself; do not depend on another's wealth, lest he become master in your house"

Date: Ptolemaic

Reference: Quack 1994, pp. 203–04

24. Brunner (1979, pp. 130–31) also cites Dream Stela of Tanutamun, line 7 (Schäfer 1905, p. 63): *ꜣḫ pw n tì s m ìb⸗f s*[...] ... *n ḫm s* "It is beneficial for the one who places it in his heart ... to the one who ignores it" and compares to it Ptahhotep, line 50: *m ꜣḫ.t n sḏm.ty.fy st m wgg.t n nty r th.t st* "being useful for the one who will hear it, being injurious to the one who will transgress it" (Žába 1956, p. 20). Brunner points out, however, that it may be based on Amenemope 3, lines 10–11, and observes that such a "quote" may not indicate that the author of the Dream Stela actually knew the earlier compositions.

25. Lefebvre (1923/24, vol. 1, p. 90) suggests that another quote from Sinuhe may be in Petosiris, inscription 58, lines 32–33: *ìr.t-ḥr wꜣḏ.ty m-ḫn pr⸗k n dnw⸗s mì mw*, which he renders "Le vin est frais(?) dans ta demeure, et abondant comme l'eau" (Lefebvre 1923/24, vol. 2, p. 31). Lefebvre compares Sinuhe B, line 82: *wr n⸗f ìrp r mw* "It had wine more (abundant) than water."

26. Citations of Onkhsheshonqy are from Glanville 1955.

Quotation 13. Onkhsheshonqy 11, line 7 = Any B 16, lines 1–2

i͗-i͗ry n=k ḥm.t i͗w=k ʿḥʿ rnp.t 20.t ḫpr n=k šr i͗w=k ẖl (Onkhsheshonqy 11, line 7)

"Make for yourself a wife, when you are 20 years old, that a son may be yours when you are old"

i͗r n=k ḥm.t i͗w=k ʿḏdi͗w i͗ry=s n=k s3=k i͗r=k msi͗.tw n=k i͗w=k m rnn (Any B 16, lines 1–2)

"Make for yourself a wife when you are young, that she may make for you your son, born to you while you are young"

Date: Ptolemaic
Reference: Quack 1994, p. 204

Quotation 14. Onkhsheshonqy 22, line 15 = Merikare E, lines 97–98[27]

bw-i͗r msḥ ṯ rmt tmy (Onkhsheshonqy 22, line 15)

"A crocodile does not take a townsman"

ʿm pw msḥ ḥr mry.t=f ḫnp=f r w3.t wʿ.t n i͗ṯ.n=f r dmi͗ nw.t ʿš3.t (Merikare E, lines 97–98)

"The Asiatic is a crocodile on its shore, it snatches from a deserted road. It does not seize from the quay of a populous town"

Date: Ptolemaic
Reference: *LÄ* 3 "Krokodil," cols. 794–95

Quotation 15. Onkhsheshonqy 7, line 13 = Amenemope 25, line 17

m-i͗r wsṯn p3 ʿ3 i͗-i͗r=k (Onkhsheshonqy 7, line 13)

"Do not be presumptuous to the one who is greater than you"

m-i͗r sḥwr ʿ3 i͗-r=k (Amenemope 25, line 17)

"Do not curse the one greater than you" (Lange 1925, p. 127)

Date: Ptolemaic
Reference: Lange 1925, p. 127; Quack 1994, p. 204

Quotation 16. Onkhsheshonqy 12, line 5 = Any B 17, line 11–Any B 18, line 4; especially 17, line 14, and 18, line 2

m-i͗r ḥrr r ti͗.t ḫpr n=k ḥ.t ḥr p3 tw bw-i͗r rḫ=k ʿ p3y=k ʿḥʿ (Onkhsheshonqy 12, line 5)

"Do not delay to acquire for yourself a tomb on the mountain; you do not know the extent of your lifetime"

smnḫ s.t=k nt m t3 i͗n.t (Any B 17, line 14)

"Embellish your tomb which is in the valley"

i͗w bw rḫ=k p3y=k mwt (Any B 18, line 2)

"whereas you do not know your death"

Date: Ptolemaic
Reference: Quack 1994, p. 204

Quotation 17. Onkhsheshonqy 17, lines 23–24 = Djedefhor III, lines 1–3

my sb3 p3y=k šr r sẖ r sk3 r ḥm r grg r-ḏb3 wʿ.t rnp.t sṯ3 Ḥʿpy mtw=f gm p3 ḥw n3.w i͗r=f (Onkhsheshonqy 17, lines 23–24)

"Let your son learn to write, to plow, to fish, to hunt on account of a year when Hapy withdraws, and he may (yet) find the profit of that which he has done"

... r sẖ r sk3 r ḥ3m grg m-s3 ḫpr rnp.t n.t š3ww [wn]m.n=f i͗r=f (sic) *m ʿ.wy=fy* (Djedefhor III, lines 1–3)

"... to write, to plow, to fish, to hunt, after a year of need has happened, that he may [ea]t (from) what he has done with his own two hands"

Date: Ptolemaic
Reference: Posener 1966, p. 65, n. 3

27. Quack (1992, p. 13) points out similarity between the ideas expressed in Merikare E, lines 130–138, and the twenty-fourth chapter of Insinger, without asserting that it is necessarily proof of knowledge of Merikare during the Late Period.

Quotation 18. Mendes Stela, line 17 = Khety Nile Hymn, II, lines 7–8

ỉr ḫbꜣ ṯ pꜣ.t.⸗f ḫr ḥḥ ꜣq m rmṯ.w (Mendes Stela, line 17)

"If his offerings are reduced, myriads of people perish" (Sethe 1904, p. 44)

ỉr ḫbꜣ.tw m pꜣw.ty nṯr.w ḫr ḥḥ ꜣq m rmṯ (Khety Nile Hymn, II, lines 7–8; van der Plas 1986, p. 25)

"If the divine offerings are reduced, myriads of people perish"

Date: 264 B.C.

Reference: Sethe 1904, p. 44; van der Plas 1986, p. 25; *LÄ* 3 "Lehre des Cheti," col. 978; *LÄ* 4 "Nilhymnus," col. 495, note 55;[28] see also Guglielmi 1984, p. 350

Quotation 19. P. Insinger 3, line 13 = Any B 19, lines 10–12

tm ṯ n⸗k ḥms ẖr-ḥꜣ.t n pꜣ ỉ-ỉr sq-ḥr (P. Insinger 3, line 13)

"Do not take for yourself a seat before the one who is a dignitary" (so Lichtheim 1983, p. 198; Lexa 1926, p. 8)

ỉm⸗k ḥmsỉ ỉw ky ꜥḥꜥ ỉw⸗f (m) ỉꜣw.t ỉr⸗k m-r-pw ỉw⸗f sꜥꜣy ỉr⸗k m ỉꜣw.t⸗f (Any B 19, lines 10–12)

"You should not sit while another is standing, he being older than you or he being more important than you in his office"

Date: Ptolemaic

Reference: Lexa 1926, p. 8; Lichtheim 1983, p. 198; Quack 1994, p. 204[29]

Quotation 20. Krugtext A, lines 14–15 = Amenemope 20, lines 4–6

m-ỉr tỉ.t ỉr n⸗k ḥꜣṯ⸗k ḥny nꜣ-bỉn pꜣ ls rmt pꜣ nt ỉr ḥnmy n-ỉm⸗f m-qty pꜣ ḥny pꜣ ḏy (Krugtext A, lines 14–15)

"Do not let your heart be for you a steering oar; bad is the tongue of a man; the one which steers him, the like of one who steers the ship" (Spiegelberg 1912, p. 50)

m-ỉr ỉr ḥm n ns⸗k ỉr ns n rmt ḥm n ỉmw nb r ḏr pꜣy⸗f ỉry-ḥꜣ.t (Amenemope 20, lines 4–6)

"Do not make for yourself a steering-oar of your tongue. If a man's tongue is the steering-oar of a boat, the lord of all is his pilot" (Lange 1925, p. 98)

Date: Roman

Reference: Spiegelberg 1912, p. 50; Lange 1925, p. 98; Brunner 1979, p. 165; Brunner-Traut 1979, p. 40

Quotation 21. Rituel de l'Embaumement 7, lines 3–4 = Djedefhor VIII, line 3

smnḫ ꜥḥꜥ.t⸗k nty ỉmnt.t s(ỉ)qr⸗f sḫr.w⸗k nw ẖr.t-ntr (Rituel de l'Embaumement 7, lines 3–4)

"Your tomb of the west has been excellently furnished, so that it makes effective your plans of the necropolis" (Sauneron 1952, p. 23)

smnḫ[⸗k pr⸗k] sỉ[qr⸗k s.t⸗k] (Djedefhor VIII, line 3)

"[You] should furnish [your house! You should] make ex[cellent your place!]" (Helck 1984, p. 23)

Date: Second century A.D.

Reference: Sauneron 1952, p. 23; Brunner 1979, p. 116; compare Guglielmi 1984, p. 352; Helck 1984, p. 23

DISCUSSION

The extant late copies or extracts of Djedefhor, Khety, Amenemhat, Any, and Amenemope cited above bear witness to the strong continuity of the wisdom tradition. It is certainly no accident that the spiritual outlook of Petosiris and the Late Period tomb biographies in general is quite similar to that of Amenemope and the other classical texts.[30] The individual fate of several wisdom compositions is nevertheless problematic. The ideas of Ptahhotep, for example, may be present in later works such as Onkhsheshonqy,[31] but there are scarcely any

28. Brunner accepts this as a quote of the Nile Hymn; Assmann believes that both texts are merely repeating a saying.

29. Quack further compares Onkhsheshonqy 13, line 23: *m-ỉr ḥms ḥr twn ꜥꜣ r-r⸗k* "Do not sit by one greater than you!"

30. See, for example, Altenmüller 1983, pp. 8, 14; Derchain-Urtel 1989, pp. 214–22, references in index on p. 266.

31. See the remarks of Thissen in *LÄ* 3 "Lehre des Anch-Scheschonqi," col. 975, n. 4. The date of composition for

manifest quotations (Quotation 9?), and this wisdom text has also not yet appeared in a Late Period manuscript. The same may be said for the Loyalist Instruction (Quotation 2?).[32] There is, moreover, not a single Late Period copy of the great narratives; Sinuhe and The Shipwrecked Sailor are only found in possible quotations or allusions (Quotations 3, 4, 6, 11).[33] So, too, the important prophetic tradition certainly continues into the Late Period (e.g., Zauzich 1983), but none of the earlier prophecies and lamentations such as the Admonitions of Ipuwer and the Prophecies of Neferti have surfaced in later manuscripts or quotations.

The copying of classical texts seems to continue fairly strongly into the Twenty-sixth Dynasty; the latest is a papyrus fragment of the Instruction of Amenemhat, if one accepts the Thirtieth Dynasty date. The available evidence therefore ceases just when Demotic begins to come into its own as a vehicle for literature, about the fifth or fourth century B.C.[34] Published Ptolemaic- or Roman-period hieratic copies of classical texts are lacking; for that later age our knowledge of possible literary continuity derives chiefly from the indirect evidence of quotations or even onomastica.[35]

The two main Late Period hieratic "original" compositions are P. Vandier and the Brooklyn Wisdom Text. Posener (1985, p. 13) dates the tale of the former to the Twenty-fifth/Twenty-sixth Dynasty. The language and style of P. Vandier are extremely similar to those of the Demotic narratives (ibid., pp. 12–15). Shisha-Halevy (1989), in particular, emphasizes the Demotic nature of the language in contrast to Late Egyptian. While P. Vandier is a Late Period text with strong New Kingdom antecedents (Posener 1985, pp. 17–18),[36] Kamerzell (1992) also points out a possible Demotic version of this tale.[37]

The Brooklyn Wisdom Text was, I think, composed when the classical texts were still actively studied and read, perhaps during the Saite period. See column six, for example, with its detailed description of the farmer, concluding: "The farmer is the chief of every occupation. For him do they work. His hands are their breath of life in [...]," may be understood within the tradition of the Satire of the Trades (Jasnow 1992, p. 128). The suggestion that the author of the Brooklyn Wisdom Text should have known this composition encounters no difficulties since Late Period extracts of the Satire are preserved.[38] In my edition, I quote sayings and passages in the Brooklyn Wisdom Text that also display a close relationship with the Demotic compositions (Jasnow 1992, pp. 34, 41). This combination of Late Period and classical features or connections distinguishes both the Brooklyn Wisdom Text and P. Vandier.

Such compositions as P. Vandier and the Brooklyn Wisdom Text represent, in my opinion, a true intermediary stage in Egyptian literature. In the period immediately preceding the widespread use of Demotic for literary purposes, presumably the sixth through fourth centuries B.C., the scribes would still resort to hieratic but use an

---

such wisdom texts as Onkhsheshonqy is still disputed. Thus, Leahy (1992, p. 161, n. 37) suggests that the Saite period is not impossible, while Thissen (ibid., col. 974) prefers a late Ptolemaic date for the compilation. Lefebvre (1923/24, vol. 1, p. 37) remarks on the influence of Ptahhotep and the Instruction of Amenemhat on Petosiris (fourth century B.C.) and suggests (p. 36) that the author of the inscriptions was familiar with Sinuhe.

32. The few mooted quotations are very uncertain.

33. Such quotations persuade specialists in Sinuhe that the tale was still known in the first millennium; see, for example, Blumenthal 1995, p. 884. Manuelian (1994, pp. 6–7) discusses another quotation of Sinuhe, "He flew up to heaven, joined with the sun-disk, the god's limbs being merged with the one who made him," in the Saite Adoption Stela of Ankhnesneferibre.

34. Compare Kaplony-Heckel 1974, p. 228: "Es ist unklar, wann die Spätzeit im schriftgeschichtlichen Sinn beginnt. Literarische Texte der älteren Kursive, in Hieratisch, gibt es noch im V. und IV. vorchristlichen Jahrhundert, also noch zu einem Zeitpunkt, als das Demotische längst in voller Blüte steht. Schulkinder müssen Teile dieser hieratisch geschriebenen literarischen Texte auch in der Spätzeit kopieren."

35. The name Hordedef, for example, was still venerated in Roman Tebtunis; see Tait 1977, pp. 33–35. For the name *Ḥr-ḏd=f*, see also Vittmann 1990, p. 108.

36. When we have a clear New Kingdom antecedent of a Demotic narrative, the Demotic version seems to be a reworking of the same story, and not a parallel. As H. Smith (1975, p. 258) remarks, the Horus and Seth episodes found in the Saqqara and Berlin papyri are "the only example of a Demotic text of a literary work already known to be extant in the New Kingdom." The text published by Zauzich (1984) displays strong connections with the Late Period Egyptian story "Horus and Seth," but it is not identical. Derchain (1974, pp. 13–15) identifies a passage in the Edfu texts that is very similar to the conclusion of the New Kingdom version of Horus and Seth. De Cenival (1988, p. ix) reports that Bresciani discovered in Florence a New Kingdom hieratic fragment with a text closely related to Mythus, but this has not yet been published.

37. This identification is apparently not accepted by Quack; see Kamerzell 1995c, p. 975.

38. This fits in well, of course, with the view that the Satire on the Trades also influenced Ben Sira; see Quack 1994, p. 210. Seibert (1967, p. 100) maintains that Ben Sira 38, 24–39, is dependent on the Satire but denies that it sheds any light on the history of that text because the dating of Ben Sira itself is not certain. More complicated would be the mechanism of influence on the Song of Songs by the Egyptian love songs since no Late Period copies of the latter are extant; see Fox 1985, pp. 191–93.

idiom more closely approximating that of Demotic. The quite elaborate fourth century B.C. Saqqara Demotic compositions surely presuppose a vigorous tradition of narrative literature (H. Smith and Tait 1983),[39] which suggests in turn that the scarcity of literary material from the period preceding the fifth century B.C., be it in hieratic or Demotic, may be the result of mere chance.

Kaplony in fact suggests that some of the best-known Demotic compositions could be translations from the hieratic.[40] While the possibility exists that at least portions of Demotic works ultimately derive from hieratic manuscripts such as the Brooklyn Wisdom Text, I nevertheless am still inclined to think that the Demotic literary texts such as Onkhsheshonqy or Insinger in their present form were probably composed in that script, and not "translated" from hieratic versions written in somewhat more archaic stages of the language.[41] To my knowledge, there do not exist any certain examples of writings which would clearly indicate that these Demotic literary texts were transcribed from the hieratic, in contrast, perhaps, to some mortuary or theological compositions.[42]

With regard to the classical quotations, I believe that those of the Ethiopian period (Quotations 3–9) are the most convincing. As Grimal has made very evident, the Ethiopian texts are significant for our understanding of the Late Period literary tradition. Even if one does not accept every allusion discussed by Grimal, he does present a persuasive case that the author of the Victory Stela inscription was intimately familiar with the classical works.[43] Indeed, it is difficult to imagine so magnificent a composition being produced within a literary vacuum. The erudite author apparently quotes still unknown wisdom texts, judging from such didactic statements as "The heart is a rudder which capsizes its owner through that which is the wrath of god" (line 54).[44] Sections of the Brooklyn Wisdom Text may have been composed not long after the Victory Stela inscription. There are similarities between the two works. The description of the weakness of a leaderless army (Victory Stela, line 15), for example, is reminiscent of the passage extolling the king as a champion commanding an army helpless without him (P. Brooklyn 47.218.135, 2, lines 9–14). The later popular Demotic narratives, which

39. It should be emphasized that P. Rylands 9 (dated to 513 B.C.) certainly has impressive literary characteristics. As Vittmann (1994, p. 301) well states "Fast ist man versucht, die harte Wirklichkeit, die hinter diesem Dokument steht, zu vergessen und es für einen literarischen Text ähnlich wie Wenamun oder die "Tale of Woe" zu halten (alle diese Handschriften wurden in Hibeh entdeckt!)." See also Tait 1992, p. 303, n. 1.

So too, Kamerzell (1995a, p. 955) describes the Bentresh Stela as a text displaying "literary" characteristics: "Obwohl das folgende Dockument (scil., the Bentresh Stela) sich seiner äusseren Gestalt nach als offizielles Denkmal historisch-religiösen Inhalts präsentiert, besitzt es genügend Charakteristika, die seine Klassifizierung als literarischer Text im engeren Sinne rechtfertigen," which he regards as "fiktionalität, Intertextualität und Rezeption." He believes that the Bentresh Stela text, which he dates to the sixth–fourth centuries B.C., is basically Middle Egyptian, although it also contains elements of Late Period Egyptian and early Demotic. In his study of this document, Morschauser (1988, p. 206) comments that "it is apparent that the writer of the Bentresh Stela was acquainted with historical/literary works of the Ramesside Period."

40. "Texte der demotischen Schönen Literatur, welche Könige der 23., 24. und 26. Dynastie erwähnen, können alle aus einer neuägyptisch-hieratischen Vorlage übersetzt sein" (Kaplony 1977, p. 298). See also Betrò 1982, pp. 27–28.

41. Admittedly, recent research makes it increasingly clear that Late Period scribes could quite effectively translate Middle Egyptian texts into Demotic; see Quack 1992/93. Evidence for the abilities of Late Period scribes to deal with Middle Egyptian has been steadily growing. Very valuable in this respect is the first century A.D. Tebtunis onomasticon that Osing is preparing for publication, which is composed in Middle Egyptian and has Demotic translations; see Osing 1992, p. 42. M. Smith (e.g., 1993, pp. 18–19) studies the Middle Egyptian of Demotic scribes in his various publications. See also Sternberg 1985, p. xvi.

42. Occasionally, a Demotic literary text may contain "archaizing" features. Loprieno (1995, p. 1066), for example, describes a section of Mythus thus: "Diese hymnische Passage ist in einem archaisierenden Demotisch voller Anlehnungen an die klassische Sprache geschrieben." On the re-copying of hieratic texts into Demotic, Devauchelle (1984, p. 59) remarks: "Les prêtres, peut-être sous l'impulsion de savants grecs — ou du moins du milieu intellectuel bilingue — ont recopié de nombreux documents hiératiques en démotique. Ainsi, s'ils devaient écrire un mot égyptien qui n'était plus usité en démotique, ils l'écrivaient alphabétiquement — comme les mots d'origine étrangère — et quand un signe ou un groupe de signes n'existait pas en démotique, ils recopiaient l'original hiératique. On peut supposer que les mêmes milieux d'astrologues et de magiciens, qui ont favorisé la naissance de l'écriture copte, ont poussé les milieux sacerdotaux à transcrire leurs écrits hiératiques en démotique." Vleeming (1990) published a very strange Demotic "transliteration" of a sun hymn from Chapter 15a of the Book of the Dead. See Vos 1993, pp. 10–30, for remarks on the complex hieratic / Demotic manuscript tradition of the Apis Embalming Ritual.

43. Compare "Mehr oder weniger vage Anspielungen an die MR-Literatur finden sich vor allem in Spätzeit-Biographien und Königsinschriften der Äthiopienzeit" (Guglielmi 1984, p. 357). See also Manuelian 1994, p. 2.

44. Or, as Grimal (1981, pp. 58, 65) renders, "Le coeur est un gouvernail quit fait chavirer son possesseur, puisqu'il est aux mains de la divinité."

feature warrior heroes, such as the Inaros Cycle, can perhaps also be understood in light of the vivid military drama, dialogue, and narrative of the Victory Stela.[45]

The quotations in the Demotic corpus are more difficult. Many of these are so aphoristic that they can hardly prove the ancient author's knowledge of an earlier text (e.g., Quotations 13, 14), or so vague as to be scarcely compelling (Quotation 16).[46] This may be due in part to the Egyptian tendency not to cite literally (Guglielmi 1984, p. 352), but the relatively small number of certain classical quotations is nevertheless striking, particularly in view of the length of Onkhsheshonqy and Insinger. Within the Demotic wisdom texts themselves one can readily identify several connections, comparing, for example, Onkhsheshonqy with P. Louvre 2414 (Hughes 1982) and P. Ashmolean 1984.77 (Jasnow 1991). The most that can be safely asserted, in my opinion, is that while the classical texts were perhaps still known to some in the Graeco-Roman period, they had only an indirect influence on the authors or compilers of the Demotic wisdom texts.[47]

The Demotic narratives do not reveal any indisputable references to classical compositions. Of course, a high percentage of the former are Inaros Cycle texts, and thus represent a genre hardly found in the earlier periods. Possible quotations or allusions to The Shipwrecked Sailor and The Instruction of Amenemhat in the recently re-edited *Ägypter und Amazonen* texts are uncertain.[48] Within the Demotic corpus, too, the few parallels observed between the literary narratives and the wisdom literature are of a proverbial character (Lichtheim 1984, p. 133; Hoffmann 1995, p. 98).

A combination of factors probably contributed to the scarcity, indeed absence, of Late Period copies of classical texts and to the paucity of direct quotations within Demotic literature.[49] The troubled history of the Late Period possibly resulted in disruption of the manuscript tradition. Burkard (1994a, p. 104) describes well the nature and consequences of the Persian conquest, which might have led to the destruction of libraries and scriptoria.[50] In a similar way, Posener (1963, pp. 28–29) suggests that copies of Ptahhotep were lost in the First Intermediate Period, but this has been denied by other scholars (e.g., Quack 1994, pp. 20–21). Still, the undoubted and repeated disturbances in the first millennium may have been a factor in the preservation and dissemination of classical works, even if it is not the only, or most significant, factor.

Changing methods of scribal education also influenced the general knowledge of classical literature in the Late Period (Tassier 1992; Devauchelle 1984). Most of the New Kingdom literary texts are, of course, school copies; they were used in the education of young scribes. In the Graeco-Roman period students were no longer usually required to copy out edifying literature.[51] Most of our Late Period literary compositions are therefore preserved in unique copies on papyri; scholars have often remarked on the rarity of literary ostraca,[52] the sort of material that might have been used and produced by apprentice scribes. It is not surprising that the author of Onkhsheshonqy considers it significant that the sage is required to write his wisdom text on potsherds, ostraca; he evidently thought it a somewhat irregular procedure.[53] In any case, it is clear that the classics did not form the basis of scribal training in the Graeco-Roman period.

45. A king *Pyꜣ* seems to play a role in one of the narratives preserved on a fragment in Copenhagen; see Zauzich's description in Frandsen 1991, p. 6. Hoffmann (1995, p. 63) discusses a turn of phrase found in both the Piye inscription and the Inaros text re-edited by him.

46. See the comments of Quack 1994, p. 205; Guglielmi 1984, pp. 348–49.

47. Though I would not exclude the possibility that at least the author of Insinger may have been directly familiar with the classical works.

48. As stated quite rightly by Hoffmann 1995, pp. 65, 82–83. The sentence is 4/8: *bw-ỉr⸗w qnqn* [*n*] *pꜣ kky ꜥn* "One does not fight in the darkness ever" and Amenemhat VIIe: *nn swt qn m grḥ* "But no one is strong at night" (Helck 1969, p. 50). One might also compare Onkhsheshonqy 19/7: *mn šr pr-ꜥꜣ* (*n*) *grḥ* "There is no son of pharaoh at night." The supposedly similar phrase to Shipwrecked Sailor 69–70 (compare Quotation 6) in the Inaros text is 6.x +29: [*nm pꜣ*] *ỉ-ỉr ỉn.ṯ⸗k n⸗n r m-bw-nꜣy ꜥn r tm ỉr n⸗n tḥỉ r tm ỉr sḥn bn n pꜣy⸗n tmy* "[Who is the] one who has brought you to us here so as not to do hurt to us, and so as not to do wrong to our town?" (Hoffmann 1995, p. 82). As Hoffmann says, this is not a very compelling parallel.

49. One need hardly emphasize that the lack of material from the Delta has perhaps distorted our understanding of Late Period literature.

50. For an excellent overview of ancient Egyptian libraries, see Burkard 1980. On the damage to houses of life, see also Sternberg-el Hotabi 1994, p. 251, n. 110; Morschauser 1988, pp. 216–19; Lloyd 1982, pp. 173–74; H. Smith 1974, p. 56 (loss of cult objects). Manuelian (1994, pp. 54–55) comments on the possible destruction of *Musterbücher* by the Assyrians. The Chronicle of Osorkon may also describe destruction in the temple scriptoria, but the wording is obscure; see Caminos 1958, p. 42.

51. Note, however, that Kaplony-Heckel (1974, p. 228) maintains that scribal students would have still copied the hieratic literary texts in the fifth and fourth centuries B.C.

52. See, for example, the remarks of Devauchelle 1984, p. 56.

53. Of course, the irregularity is underscored by Onkhsheshonqy's having to use the broken potsherds of the wine jars brought to him in prison.

While this cannot be proved, one wonders whether the Ptolemaic- and Roman-period scribes most familiar with the classics may have been chiefly employed in composing religious, mortuary, or monumental texts, be they in the hieratic, Demotic, or hieroglyphic scripts. In such genres there is little opportunity for making obvious classical literary allusions (but compare Quotations 11, 18, and 21). It would be only an exceptional Demotic work, a Mythus or Book of Thoth,[54] written by particularly erudite scholars of the "House of Life," that might contain classical allusions.

Given the present lack of known Graeco-Roman copies of classical texts and the rarity of indisputable classical quotations, it may seem foolhardy to theorize that much survived at this late date of Egyptian history. Nevertheless, if one accepts that the classical literary tradition, at least in part, continued well into the Saite period, as the evidence of the copies and the hieratic compositions suggests, is there sufficient reason to assume that this tradition should have been totally broken between the sixth and fourth centuries? I think not. So, to the question "Did works such as Sinuhe, Amenemope, Amenemhat, and Khety fall into complete obscurity after the Saite period?" I would answer again "I think not." The causes for the absence of extant Graeco-Roman hieratic copies of the classics and the rarity of exact quotations are to be sought rather in the scarcity of such manuscripts in general, in the transition to Demotic for literature, a reluctance to translate hieratic literary texts into that script, and the lack of emphasis on literature in both the Demotic and hieratic Graeco-Roman period scribal curriculum. Knowledge of these classical texts did not vanish entirely, but it did become increasingly restricted; consequently, their influence on the popular Demotic literature became indirect and rare. Most Demotic literary texts were written by scribes with little firsthand knowledge of the classical works but who may nevertheless have been indirectly influenced by them. Such indirect influence may have come through contact or association with scholars, perhaps "hieratic specialists," more familiar with the ancient classical tradition.

While I cannot prove the point, I do think it quite possible, then, that at least some classics of Egyptian literature survived well into the Roman period.[55] I conclude by offering two possible instances of Demotic references to, or paraphrases of, the Tale of Sinuhe.

SAQQARA DEMOTIC PAPYRUS 23: A PARAPHRASE OF SINUHE'S FLIGHT?

1. […] … […]	1. […] … […]
2. *n pꜣ dmy bn-pw=y mt* … […]	2. in the town. I did not speak … […]
3. *n-ỉm=w ḫpr twy* […]	3. there. Then came the morning of … […]
4. *ẖt* … […]	4. northwards … […]
5. *pḥ=y pꜣ sbṯ* … […]	5. I reached the wall … […]
6. *=y nꜣ mt.w nt ḫpr n-ỉm*[…]	6. I […] the things that had happened in the […]
7. *nꜣ mt.w nt ḫpr n-ỉm=w* […]	7. the things which had happened there […]
8. *stby ỉr=y* […]	8. prepare(?). I made […]
9. … *rsty* … […]	9. … next day … […]

H. Smith and Tait (1983, pp. 190–91) publish this small fragment, dated to the fourth or third century B.C., under the title "A Narrative Mentioning a Journey." They are quite rightly non-committal regarding the nature of the fragment, which may be a letter and not literary at all. Nevertheless, I would like to point out the similarities to the passages describing the flight of Sinuhe.

54. The Book of Thoth may make an allusion to the search of Chufu for the *ỉpt.w* of Thoth described in P. Westcar. For the Book of Thoth, see Jasnow and Zauzich 1998. De Cenival (1987, p. 7), observing that Ptolemaic monumental writings are very rare in Mythus, asserts that it was the hieratic texts that such scribes were reading in the scriptoria.

55. This is, of course, no unparalleled conclusion. Posener (1966, p. 65) himself maintains that the Satire, Sinuhe, and Instruction of Amenemhat had not been forgotten in the Late Period. Brunner (1988, p. 55) emphasizes the familiarity of Late Period Egyptian scribes with the wisdom text of Djedefhor. After a careful survey of the evidence, Quack (1992, p. 13) states "Insgesamt deutet die Anzahl der Belege aber darauf hin, dass die Lehre für Merikare auch in der Spätzeit noch in Umlauf war." Very significant too are the remarks of P. Derchain (1974, p. 15) concerning the Saqqara Demotic copy of Horus and Seth, "Le fait de la traduction prouve l'existence de l'original et, d'autre part, nous savons que les prêtres et *a fortiori* les hiérogrammates qui composaient les textes sacrés devaient, à l'époque gréco-romaine, savoir l'hiératique, donc le néo-égyptien, dans lequel ils rédigeaient encore partiellement certains textes."

Line 2: Sinuhe reaches the *dmỉ ngꜣw* "town of Negau" (= Sinuhe B, lines 12–13).

Line 2: Sinuhe is fearful (and silent?) "He saluted me while I was afraid of him" (= Sinuhe B, line 11).

Line 3: "Departing at dawn I encountered a man who stood on the road" (= Sinuhe B, lines 10–11).

Line 4: "Then I made my way northward" (= Sinuhe B, lines 15–16).

Line 5: "I reached the walls of the ruler" (= Sinuhe B, lines 16–17).

Lines 6–7: Two references to "the things which had happened." No explicit parallel in Sinuhe, though this could refer to the death of the ruler, comparing the question of Ammunenshi in Sinuhe B, lines 35–36, "Has something happened in the Residence?"

Line 9: "At dawn I reached Peten" (= Sinuhe B, line 20).

Despite the differences in sequence and phrasing, the number of points of agreement in this tiny fragment of text with Sinuhe B, lines 1–36, is intriguing. Is this a paraphrase of a version of Sinuhe?

MYTHUS 5, LINES 29–32: AN ALLUSION TO SINUHE?

In the Myth of the Sun's Eye, dating to about the second century A.D., there is a long section extolling the importance of one's home. In good Egyptian fashion a passage deals with the desire to be buried in one's native town (Mythus 5, lines 29–32):

> *hꜣy=k ḥr tꜣy=k ḏꜣry.t gm=k / tꜣy=k nhy.t pꜣy ḏ pꜣ šꜥy n pꜣy=f mrwṱ mwt=k [n] pꜣy=k tmy / r-ms=k n-ỉm=f gm=k tꜣy=k qsy.t qsy=w ṱk mtw=k ḥtp n pꜣy=k ḥnw nt ỉw tꜣy=k nhy.t r=ḏ=f tꜣy*
>
> "You will descend to your coffin. You will find your sycamore," said *Pshai* to his beloved one, "You will die in your town in which you were born. You will find your burial. They will bury you and you will rest in your coffin, of which he said, this is your sycamore" (Spiegelberg 1917, pp. 20–21).

Sinuhe exclaims: "What can be more important than joining my dead body to the land where I was born" (Sinuhe B, line 159). The king reassures the unhappy exile that "you shall not die in a foreign land, and Asiatics will not escort you. You will not be placed in the skin of a ram, (but rather) your coffin will be made" (Sinuhe B, lines 197–198). I need not emphasize here the obvious play on Sinuhe's name (literally, "Son of the Sycamore") in the "sycamore" of the Mythus passage. The superficially obscure designation of the king as *Pshai*, "Fate," is in fact quite a plausible one since in the Late Period the king is identified with *Shai* (Quaegebeur 1975, pp. 109–18). The passage in Sinuhe even clarifies a puzzling word in Mythus. The term used in Sinuhe B, line 198, for "coffin" is *ḏrw.t* "Sarg" (*Wb.* 5.598:12; 5.601:3), which is also spelled *ḏry.t*. I suggest, therefore, that the word in Mythus 5, line 29, *ḏꜣry.t*, hitherto translated "threshing-floor" (Erichsen 1954, p. 683) is actually identical with the *ḏrw.t* "coffin" in Sinuhe, a rendering that yields much more satisfactory sense in the Mythus passage.

****

The references for this article are complete through 1996. I have not added references to works appearing after that date. I do wish to cite here the very important *Ancient Egyptian Literature: History and Forms*, edited by A. Loprieno (Probleme der Ägyptologie 10; Leiden: E. J. Brill, 1996), and note that several contributors to that volume offer observations on the subject of this article, of which I may especially mention that of J. Baines, "Classicism and Modernism in the New Kingdom," p. 158.

****

References

Altenmüller, H.
1983 "Bemerkungen zu Kapitel 13 der Lehre des Amenemope (Am. 15, 19–16.14)." In *Fontes atque Pontes: Eine Festgabe für Hellmut Brunner*, edited by M. Görg, pp. 1–17. Ägypten und Altes Testament 5. Wiesbaden: Otto Harrassowitz.

Assmann, J.
1985 "Gibt es eine "Klassik" in der ägyptischen Literaturgeschichte? Ein Beitrag zur Geistesgeschichte der Ramessidenzeit." *Zeitschrift der Deutschen morgenländischen Gesellschaft, Supplement* 6 (22. Deutscher Orientalistentag vom 21. bis 25. März 1983 in Tübingen: Ausgewählte Vorträge, edited by W. Röllig), pp. 35–52.

Baines, J.
1990 "Interpreting the Story of the Shipwrecked Sailor." *Journal of Egyptian Archaeology* 76: 55–72.

Betrò, M. C.
1982 "Considerazioni in margine ad un testo: Anchscescionqi e il suo mondo." *Egitto e Vicino Oriente* 5: 25–33.

Bietak, M.
1972 *Theben-West (Luqsor): Vorbericht über die ersten vier Grabungskampagnen (1969–1971)*. Akademie der Wissenschaften in Wien, philosophisch-historische Klasse, Sitzungsberichte 278/4. Vienna: Böhlau Verlag.

Blackman, A. M.
1972 *Middle-Egyptian Stories*. Bibliotheca Aegyptiaca 2. Brussels: Édition de la Fondation Égyptologique Reine Élisabeth.

Blumenthal, E.
1972 "Die Erzählung des Papyrus D'Orbiney als Literaturwerk." *Zeitschrift für ägyptische Sprache und Altertumskunde* 99: 1–17.
1995 "Die Erzählung des Sinuhe." In *Mythen und Epen* 3, edited by E. Blumenthal, pp. 884–911. Texte aus der Umwelt des Alten Testaments 3/5. Gütersloh: Gütersloher Verlagshaus.

Bresciani, E.; S. Pernigotti; and M. C. Betrò
1983 *Ostraka demotici da Narmuti* I (nn. 1–33). Quaderni di Medinet Madi 1. Pisa: Giardini Editori e Stampatori.

Brunner, H.
1979 "Zitate aus Lebenslehren." In *Studien zu altägyptischen Lebenslehren*, edited by E. Hornung and O. Keel, pp. 105–71. Orbis Biblicus et Orientalis 28. Freiburg: Universitätsverlag; Göttingen: Vandenhoeck and Ruprecht.
1988 "Djedefhor in der römischen Kaiserzeit." In *Das hörende Herz: Kleine Schriften zur Religions- und Geistesgeschichte Ägyptens*, edited by W. Röllig, pp. 49–58. Orbis Biblicus et Orientalis 80. Freiburg: Universitätsverlag; Göttingen: Vandenhoeck and Ruprecht.

Brunner-Traut, E.
1979 "Wechselbeziehungen zwischen schriftlicher und mündlicher Überlieferung im alten Ägypten." *Fabula* 20: 34–46.

Burkard, G.
1977 *Textkritische Untersuchungen zu ägyptischen Weisheitslehren des Alten und Mittleren Reiches*. Ägyptologische Abhandlungen 34. Wiesbaden: Otto Harrassowitz.
1980 "Bibliotheken im alten Ägypten." *Bibliothek: Forschung und Praxis* 4: 79–115.
1994a "Literarische Tradition und historische Realität. Die persische Eroberung Ägyptens am Beispiel Elephantine." *Zeitschrift für ägyptische Sprache und Altertumskunde* 121: 93–106.
1994b Review of *A Late Period Wisdom Text*, by Richard Jasnow. *Enchoria* 21: 156–59.

Burkard, G., and H.-W. Fischer-Elfert
1994 *Ägyptische Handschriften*, Teil 4. Verzeichnis der orientalischen Handschriften in Deutschland 19/4. Stuttgart: Franz Steiner Verlag.

Caminos, R.
1958 *The Chronicle of Prince Osorkon*. Analecta Orientalia 37. Rome: Pontificium Institutum Biblicum.
1977 *A Tale of Woe*. Oxford: Griffith Institute.

de Cenival, F.
1985 "Les nouveaux fragments du mythe de l'œil du soleil de l'Institut de papyrologie et égyptologie de Lille." *Cahier de recherches de l'Institut de papyrologie et d'égyptologie de Lille* 7: 95–115.
1987 "Remarques sur le vocabulaire du 'mythe de l'œil du soleil.'" In *Aspects of Demotic Lexicography*, edited by S. Vleeming, pp. 3–8. Studia Demotica 1. Leuven: Peeters.
1988 *Le mythe de l'œil du soleil*. Demotische Studien 9. Sommerhausen: Gisela Zauzich Verlag.
1990 "Fragment de sagesse apparentée au papyrus Insinger (P. Université de Lille III Inv. P. dem Lille 34)." *Cahier de recherches de l'Institut de papyrologie et d'égyptologie de Lille* 12: 93–96.

Chauveau, M.
1991 "Montouhotep et les babyloniens." *Bulletin de l'Institut français d'archéologie orientale* 91: 147–53.

Corcoran, L.
1995 *Portrait Mummies from Roman Egypt (I–IV Centuries A.D.) with a Catalog of Portrait Mummies in Egyptian Museums*. Studies in Ancient Oriental Civilization 56. Chicago: Oriental Institute.

Derchain, P.
1974 "Miettes." *Revue d'égyptologie* 26: 7–20.

Derchain-Urtel, M.-T.
1989 *Priester im Tempel: Die Rezeption der Theologie der Tempel von Edfu und Dendera in den Privatdokumenten aus ptolemäischer Zeit*. Göttinger Orientforschungen 4/19. Wiesbaden: Otto Harrassowitz.

1990 "Ägypten in griechisch-römischer Zeit." *Zeitschrift für ägyptische Sprache und Altertumskunde* 117: 111–19.

Devauchelle, D.
1984 "Remarques sur les méthodes d'enseignement du démotique (À propos d'ostraca du Centre franco-égyptien d'étude des temples de Karnak)." In *Grammata Demotika: Festschrift für Erich Lüddeckens zum 15. Juni 1983*, edited by H.-J. Thissen and K.-Th. Zauzich, pp. 47–59. Würzburg: Gisela Zauzich Verlag.

Erichsen, W.
1954 *Demotisches Glossar*. Copenhagen: Ejnar Munksgaard.

Erman, A.
1894 "Eine ägyptische Schulübersetzung." *Zeitschrift für ägyptische Sprache und Altertumskunde* 32: 127–28.

Fischer-Elfert, H.-W.
1987 "Der Pharaoh, die Magier und der General — Die Erzählung des Papyrus Vandier." *Bibliotheca Orientalis* 44: 5–21.
1992a "Vermischtes." *Göttinger Miszellen* 127: 33–47.
1992b "Synchrone und diachrone Interferenzen in literarischen Werken des Mittleren und Neuen Reiches." *Orientalia* 61: 354–72.

Fox, M.
1985 *The Song of Songs and the Ancient Egyptian Love Songs*. Madison: University of Wisconsin Press.

Frandsen, P. J., ed.
1991 *Demotic Texts from the Collection*. Carlsberg Papyri 1; Carsten Niebuhr Institute Publications 15. Copenhagen: Museum Tusculanum Press.

Gardiner, A. H.
1909 *Die Erzählung des Sinuhe und die Hirtengeschichte*. Hieratische Papyrus aus den Königlichen Museen zu Berlin 5. Leipzig: J. C. Hinrichs.

Glanville, S. R. K.
1955 *The Instructions of ʿOnchsheshonqy (British Museum Papyrus 10508)*. Catalogue of Demotic Papyri in the British Museum 2. London: British Museum.

Goedicke, H.
1987 "Menna's Lament." *Revue d'égyptologie* 38: 63–80.

Grimal, N.-C.
1980 "Bibliothèques et propagande royale à l'époque éthiopienne." In *Livre du centenaire 1880–1980*, pp. 37–48. Mémoires publiés par les Membres de l'Institut français d'archéologie orientale du Caire 104. Cairo: Institut français d'archéologie orientale.
1981 *La stèle triomphale de Pi(ʿankh)y au Musée du Caire JE 48862 et 47086–47089*. Études sur la propagande royale égyptienne 1; Mémoires publiés par les Membres de l'Institut français d'archéologie orientale du Caire 105. Cairo: Institut français d'archéologie orientale.

Guglielmi, W.
1984 "Zur Adaption und Funktion von Zitaten." *Studien zur altägyptischen Kultur* 11: 347–64.

Helck, W.
1969 *Der Text der "Lehre Amenemhets I. für seinen Sohn."* Wiesbaden: Otto Harrassowitz.
1984 *Die Lehre des Djedefhor und die Lehre eines Vaters an seinen Sohn*. Wiesbaden: Otto Harrassowitz.

Hoffmann, F.
1995 *Ägypter und Amazonen: Neubearbeitung zweier demotischer Papyri P. Vindob. D 6165 und P. Vindob. D 6165 A*. Mitteilungen aus der Papyrussammlung der Österreichischen Nationalbibliothek, neue Serie, 24. Folge. Vienna: Verlag Brüder Hollinek.

Hughes, G.
1982 "The Blunders of an Inept Scribe (Demotic Papyrus Louvre 2414)." In *Studies in Philology in Honour of Ronald James Williams: A Festschrift*, edited by G. E. Kadish and G. Freeman, pp. 51–67. Toronto: Benben Publications.

Jansen-Winkeln, K.
1985 *Ägyptische Biographien der 22. und 23. Dynastie*. Ägypten und Altes Testament 8. Wiesbaden: Otto Harrassowitz.
1994 *Texte und Sprache in der 3. Zwischenzeit: Vorarbeiten zu einer spätmittelägyptischen Grammatik*. Ägypten und Altes Testament 26. Wiesbaden: Otto Harrassowitz.

Jasnow, R.
1991 "A Demotic Wisdom Papyrus in the Ashmolean Museum (P. Ashm. 1984.77 Verso)." *Enchoria* 18: 43–54.
1992 *A Late Period Hieratic Wisdom Text (P. Brooklyn 47.218.135)*. Studies in Ancient Oriental Civilization 52. Chicago: Oriental Institute.

Jasnow, R., and K.-Th. Zauzich
1998 "A Book of Thoth?" In *Proceedings of the Seventh International Congress of Egyptologists, Cambridge, 3–9 September 1995*, edited by C. J. Eyre, pp. 607–18. Orientalia Lovaniensia Analecta 82. Leuven: Peeters.

Johnson, J. H.
1976 *The Demotic Verbal System*. Studies in Ancient Oriental Civilization 38. Chicago: Oriental Institute.

Kamerzell, F.
1992 "Ein demotisches Fragment der Merire-Erzählung? pTebtunis Tait Nr. 9 und pLille 139." *Göttinger Miszellen* 127: 53–61.
1995a "Ein ägyptischer Gott reist nach Bachatna, um die von einem Dämonen besessene Prinzessin Bintrischji zu heilen (Bentresch-Stele)." In *Mythen und Epen* 3, edited by E. Blumenthal, pp. 955–64. Texte aus der Umwelt des Alten Testaments 3/5. Gütersloh: Gütersloher Verlagshaus.
1995b "Von der Affäre um König Nafirku'ri'a und seinen General." In *Mythen und Epen* 3, edited by E. Blumenthal, pp. 965–69. Texte aus der Umwelt des Alten Testaments 3/5. Gütersloh: Gütersloher Verlagshaus.
1995c "Mi'jare' in der Unterwelt (Papyrus Vandier)." In *Mythen und Epen* 3, edited by E. Blumenthal, pp. 973–90. Texte aus der Umwelt des Alten Testaments 3/5. Gütersloh: Gütersloher Verlagshaus.

Kaplony, P.
1977 "Die Definition der schönen Literatur im alten Ägypten." In *Fragen an die altägyptische Literatur: Studien zum Gedenken an Eberhard Otto*, edited by J. Assmann, E. Feucht, and R. Grieshammer, pp. 289–314. Wiesbaden: Otto Harrassowitz.

Kaplony-Heckel, U.
1974 "Schüler und Schulwesen in der ägyptischen Spätzeit." *Studien zur altägyptischen Kultur* 1: 227–46.

Lange, H. O.
1925 *Das Weisheitsbuch des Amenemope aus dem Papyrus 10,474 des British Museum.* Det Kgl. Danske Videnskabernes Selskab, historisk-filologiske Meddelelser 11/2. Copenhagen: Bianco Lunos Bogtrykkeri.

Leahy, A.
1992 "'May the King Live': The Libyan Rulers in the Onomastic Record." In *Studies in Pharaonic Religion and Society in Honour of J. Gwyn Griffiths*, edited by A. Lloyd, pp. 146–63. Occasional Publications 8. London: Egypt Exploration Society.

Lefebvre, G.
1923/24 *Le tombeau de Petosiris.* 3 volumes. Cairo: Institut français d'archéologie orientale.

Lexa, F.
1926 *Papyrus Insinger: Les enseignements moraux d'un scribe égyptien du premier siècle après J.-C.* Paris: Librairie Orientaliste Paul Geuthner.

Lichtheim, M.
1983 *Late Egyptian Wisdom Literature in the International Context: A Study of Demotic Instructions.* Orbis Biblicus et Orientalis 52. Freiburg: Universitätsverlag; Göttingen: Vandenhoeck and Ruprecht.
1984 "Demotic Proverbs." In *Grammata Demotika: Festschrift für Erich Lüddeckens zum 15. Juni 1983*, edited by H.-J. Thissen and K.-Th. Zauzich, pp. 125–40. Würzburg: Gisela Zauzich Verlag.

Lloyd, A.
1982 "The Inscription of Udjaḥorresnet: A Collaborator's Testament." *Journal of Egyptian Archaeology* 68: 166–80.

Loprieno, A.
1995 "Der demotische 'Mythos vom Sonnenauge.'" In *Mythen und Epen* 3, edited by E. Blumenthal, pp. 1038–77. Texte aus der Umwelt des Alten Testaments 3/5. Gütersloh: Gütersloher Verlagshaus.

Macadam, M. F. L.
1955 *The Temples of Kawa* 2: *History and Archaeology of the Site.* London: Oxford University Press.

Manuelian, P. D.
1994 *Living in the Past: Studies in Archaism of the Egyptian Twenty-sixth Dynasty.* London: Kegan Paul.

Mertens, J.
1992 "Bibliography and Description of Demotic Literary Texts: A Progress Report." In *Life in a Multi-Cultural Society: Egypt from Cambyses to Constantine and Beyond*, edited by J. H. Johnson, pp. 233–35. Studies in Ancient Oriental Civilization 51. Chicago: Oriental Institute.

Morris, W., ed.
1981 *The American Heritage Dictionary of the English Language.* Boston: Houghton Mifflin.

Morschauser, S.
1988 "Using History: Reflections on the Bentresh Stela." *Studien zur altägyptischen Kultur* 15: 203–23.

Osing, J.
1992 *Aspects de la culture pharaonique.* Mémoires de l'Académie des inscriptions et belles-lettres, Nouvelle série 12. Paris: Boccard.

Parkinson, R.
1991 *The Tale of the Eloquent Peasant.* Oxford: Griffith Institute.

van der Plas, D.
1986 *L'hymne à la crue du Nil.* Egyptologische Uitgaven 4/1–2. Leiden: Nederlands Instituut voor het Nabije Oosten te Leiden.

Posener, G.
1936 *La première domination perse en Égypte.* Bibliothèque d'étude 11. Cairo: Institut français d'archéologie orientale.
1957 "Le conte de Néferkaré et du général Siséné (recherches littéraires, VI)." *Revue d'égyptologie* 11: 119–37.
1958 "Une nouvelle histoire de revenant (recherches littéraires, VII)." *Revue d'égyptologie* 12: 75–82.
1963 "L'apport des textes littéraires à la connaissance de l'histoire égyptienne." In *Le fonti indirette della storia egiziana*, edited by S. Donadoni, pp. 11–30. Studi Semitici 7. Rome: Centro di studi semitici.
1966 "Quatre tablettes scolaires de basse époque (Aménémopé et Hardjédef)." *Revue d'égyptologie* 18: 45–65.
1973 "Une nouvelle tablette d'Aménémopé." *Revue d'égyptologie* 25: 251–52.
1976 *L'enseignement loyaliste.* Hautes études orientales 5. Geneva: Librairie Droz.
1985 *Le papyrus Vandier.* Bibliothèque générale 7. Cairo: Institut français d'archéologie orientale.

Quack, J. F.
1992 *Studien zur Lehre für Merikare.* Göttinger Orientforschungen 4/23. Wiesbaden: Otto Harrassowitz.
1992/93 "pWien D 6319: Eine demotische Übersetzung aus dem Mittelägyptischen." *Enchoria* 19/20: 125–29.
1993 "Ein neuer ägyptischer Weisheitstext." *Die Welt des Orients* 24: 5–19.
1994 *Die Lehren des Ani.* Orbis Biblicus et Orientalis 141. Freiburg: Universitätsverlag; Göttingen: Vandenhoeck and Ruprecht.

Quaegebeur, J.
1975 *Le dieu égyptien Shaï dans la religion et l'onomastique.* Orientalia Lovaniensia Analecta 2. Leuven: Peeters.

Ritner, R. K.

1993 *The Mechanics of Ancient Egyptian Magical Practice*. Studies in Ancient Oriental Civilization 54. Chicago: Oriental Institute.

Sauneron, S.

1950 "Le titre de l'enseignement de Kheti sur une tablette du Louvre." *Revue d'égyptologie* 7: 186–88.

1952 *Rituel de l'embaumement*. Cairo: Imprimerie nationale.

1970 *Le papyrus magique illustré de Brooklyn (Brooklyn Museum 47.218.156)*. Wilbour Monographs 3. Oxford: Brooklyn Museum.

1989 *Un traité égyptien d'ophiologie*. Bibliothèque générale 11. Cairo: Institut français d'archéologie orientale.

Schäfer, H.

1905 *Urkunden der älteren Äthiopenkönige I*. Urkunden des ägyptischen Altertums 3/1. Leipzig: J. C. Hinrichs.

Seibert, P.

1967 *Die Charakteristik: Untersuchungen zu einer altägyptischen Sprechsitte und ihren Ausprägungen in Folklore und Literatur*. Ägyptologische Abhandlungen 17. Wiesbaden: Otto Harrassowitz.

Sethe, K.

1904 *Hieroglyphische Urkunden der griechisch-römischen Zeit*. Urkunden des ägyptischen Altertums 2/1. Leipzig: J. C. Hinrichs.

Shisha-Halevy, A.

1989 "Papyrus Vandier *Recto*: An Early Demotic Literary Text?" *Journal of the American Oriental Society* 109: 421–35.

Smith, H. S.

1974 *A Visit to Ancient Egypt: Life at Memphis and Saqqara (c. 500–30 B.C.)*. Warminster: Aris and Phillips.

1975 "Demotic Literary Papyri and Letters." In *Proceedings of the 14th International Congress of Papyrologists, Oxford, 24–31 July 1974*, pp. 257–59. Graeco-Roman Memoirs 61. London: Egypt Exploration Society.

Smith, H. S., and W. J. Tait

1983 *Saqqâra Demotic Papyri I*. Texts from Excavations 7. London: Egypt Exploration Society.

Smith, M.

1979 The Demotic Mortuary Papyrus Louvre E. 3452. Ph.D. dissertation, University of Chicago.

1993 *The Liturgy of Opening the Mouth for Breathing*. Oxford: Griffith Institute.

Spiegelberg, W.

1912 *Demotische Texte auf Krügen*. Demotische Studien 5. Leipzig: J. C. Hinrichs.

1917 *Der ägyptische Mythus vom Sonnenauge (Der Papyrus der Tierfabeln-"Kufi") nach dem Leidener demotischen Papyrus I 384*. Strasbourg: Strassburger Druckerei und Verlagsanstalt.

Sternberg, H.

1985 *Mythische Motive und Mythenbildung in den ägyptischen Tempeln und Papyri der griechisch-römischen Zeit*. Göttinger Orientforschungen 4/14. Wiesbaden: Otto Harrassowitz.

Sternberg-el Hotabi, H.

1994 "Die 'Götterliste' des Sanktuars im Hibis-Tempel von El-Chargeh." In *Aspekte spätägyptischer Kultur: Festschrift für Erich Winter zum 65. Geburtstag*, edited by M. Minas and J. Zeidler, pp. 239–54. Aegyptiaca Treverensia 7. Mainz am Rhein: Philipp von Zabern.

Tait, W. J.

1977 *Papyri from Tebtunis in Egyptian and in Greek (P. Tebt. Tait)*. Texts from Excavations 3. London: Egypt Exploration Society.

1992 "Demotic Literature and Egyptian Society." In *Life in a Multi-Cultural Society: Egypt from Cambyses to Constantine and Beyond*, edited by J. H. Johnson, pp. 303–10. Studies in Ancient Oriental Civilization 51. Chicago: Oriental Institute.

1994 "Egyptian Fiction in Demotic and Greek." In *Greek Fiction: The Greek Novel in Context*, edited by J. R. Morgan and R. Stoneman, pp. 203–22. London: Routledge.

1995 "Change and Development in Ancient Egyptian Literature." In *Abstracts of Papers* (Proceedings of the Seventh International Congress of Egyptologists, Cambridge, 3–9 September 1995), edited by C. Eyre, p. 182. Oxford: Oxbow Books.

Tassier, E.

1992 "Greek and Demotic School-Exercises." In *Life in a Multi-Cultural Society: Egypt from Cambyses to Constantine and Beyond*, edited by J. H. Johnson, pp. 311–15. Studies in Ancient Oriental Civilization 51. Chicago: Oriental Institute.

Thissen, H.-J.

1984 *Die Lehre des Anchscheschonqi (P. BM 10508)*. Papyrologische Texte und Abhandlungen 32. Bonn: Dr. Rudolf Habelt.

1992 *Der verkommene Harfenspieler*. Demotische Studien 11. Sommerhausen: Gisela Zauzich Verlag.

Vernus, P.

1976 "La formule 'Le souffle de la bouche' au Moyen Empire." *Revue d'égyptologie* 28: 139–45.

1990 "Entre néo-égyptien et démotique: La langue utilisée dans la traduction du rituel de repousser l'agressif (étude sur la diglossie 1)." *Revue d'égyptologie* 41: 153–208.

Vittmann, G.

1990 "Bemerkungen zu einem frühdemotischen Papyrusfragment in Kairo (CG 31241)." *Göttinger Miszellen* 115: 107–11.

1994 "Eine misslungene Dokumentenfälschung: Die 'Stelen' des Peteese I (P. Ryl. 9, XXI–XXIII)." In *Acta Demotica: Acts of the Fifth International Conference for Demotists, Pisa, 4th–8th September 1993*, edited by E. Bresciani, pp. 301–15. Egitto e Vicino Oriente 17. Pisa: Giardini Editori e Stampatori.

Vleeming, S.

1990 "Transliterating Old Egyptian in Demotic." *Göttinger Miszellen* 117/118: 219–23.

Vos, R. L.

1993 *The Apis Embalming Ritual: P. Vindob. 3873.* Orientalia Lovaniensia Analecta 50. Leuven: Peeters.

Žába, Z.

1956 *Les maximes de Ptaḥḥotep.* Prague: Éditions de l'Académie tchécoslovaque des sciences.

Zauzich, K.-Th.

1983 "Das Lamm des Bokchoris." In *Festschrift zum 100-jährigen Bestehen der Papyrussammlung der österreichischen Nationalbibliothek: Papyrus Erzherzog Rainer* (*P. Rainer Cent.*), pp. 165–74. Vienna: Verlag Brüder Hollinek.

1984 "Der Streit zwischen Horus und Seth in einer demotischen Fassung (Pap. Berlin P 15549 +15551 +23727)." In *Grammata Demotika: Festschrift für Erich Lüddeckens zum 15. Juni 1983*, edited by H.-J. Thissen and K.-Th. Zauzich, pp. 275–81. Würzburg: Gisela Zauzich Verlag.

20

ETHNIC CONSIDERATIONS IN PERSIAN PERIOD EGYPT

JANET H. JOHNSON

The Oriental Institute, Chicago

It is a pleasure for me to dedicate these comments[1] as a small token of esteem and appreciation to a man who as teacher, colleague, and friend has set the highest standards of scholarship, inspired interest in the widest variety of topics concerning ancient Egypt, and always generously shared his thoughts and his incomparable files.

****

Modern scholars, faced with a world full of "ethnic" identifications and distinctions frequently used for less than humanitarian purposes, wonder whether and how people in earlier times made such distinctions. Many ancient peoples distinguished between themselves and "others" in terms corresponding to the Greek "people" versus "barbarians." But how much can we learn about ancient societies, and the individuals of which they were composed, by focusing on the question of ethnicity? That the evidence preserved from a given ancient culture helps direct and define the discussion remains obvious; what we must do is try to avoid applying inappropriate modern distinctions to the ancient situation.[2]

We must start by distinguishing between ethnicity as a definition of self vis-à-vis other(s), that is, a social distinction which is made and accepted by people themselves, and the formal official use of ethnicity as a category by which to make distinctions among "citizens" or "subjects." The former may have slippery boundaries because the differences that are considered important may change through time or when an individual or group deals with more than one "other"; the latter must have a carefully defined, somewhat inflexible list of "character traits" by which to make or impose distinctions. Some governments made formal use of ethnicity as a category; some did not. Some used ethnicity to identify individuals; others used ethnicity as one basis for granting privileges.[3] Therefore, one question that needs to be asked, but one to which a definitive answer can not be given here, is whether or not the Achaemenid administration of Egypt made *formal* use of ethnicity (for judicial, political, or other purposes).

But first we must consider the informal or social concept of ethnicity. Goudriaan (1988, p. 10), discussing ethnicity in Ptolemaic Egypt, argues:

> Ethnicity can be defined as a type of social organization based on self-ascription and ascription by others; this categorical ascription "is (quoting Fr. Barth) an ethnic ascription when it classifies a person in terms of his basic, most general identification, presumptively determined by his origin and background. To the extent that actors use ethnic identities to categorize themselves and others for purposes of interaction, they form ethnic groups in this organizational sense."

Such ethnicity does not involve objective, innate qualities; rather, it consists of categories applied in social interaction by actors wishing to divide participants in the interaction into an "in-group" and an "out-group" (for

1. An earlier version of this paper was presented during my participation in a panel discussion on "Ethnicity and Community in the Persian Period" at the SBL meetings held in Chicago during November 1994. I would like to thank the organizers of that panel, Tamara C. Eskenazi and Kenneth G. Hoglund, for prompting me to look at this question, and my fellow panelists, Matthew W. Stolper, Pamela Gordon, Ben C. Ollenburger, and Harold C. Washington, and Charles E. Jones, for stimulating discussions of the ethnic situation in other parts of the Achaemenid world. I would also like to thank Pierre Briant, Csaba La'da, Bezalel Porten, and Richard Steiner for reading earlier drafts of this manuscript and making useful and interesting suggestions and providing several important bibliographic references; it must be noted, however, that responsibility for the suggestions made here remains solely that of the author.
2. For a useful discussion of the influence of the contemporary on historical perceptions and questions, see Samuel 1989.
3. For example, Ptolemaic versus Roman Egypt. The use of ethnic designations in Ptolemaic Egypt has been summa-

Gold of Praise: Studies on Ancient Egypt in Honor of Edward F. Wente
Edited by Emily Teeter and John A. Larson
Studies in Ancient Oriental Civilization 58
Chicago: Oriental Institute, 1999

purposes of the cohesiveness of the in-group or divisiveness against the out-group). It is not identical with class (an economic category), "nationality" or "citizens' rights" (a juridical category), or religion, although it more closely converges with religion than other categories. It is frequently bound up with place of origin and (native) language.

For a group to maintain an ethnic identity, its members must continually use and validate "inclusion" rules. Here, cultural features play a part, but there is no simple, rigid one-to-one relationship between ethnic units and cultural similarities and differences. Features taken into account are not the sum of "objective" differences but only those which the actors themselves regard as significant. Traits used to define a given "ethnic" might also differ depending on to which (of two or more contemporary) "others" the group or individual is relating: What made an Aramaean different from a Jew in Persian-period Egypt might not be identical with what made an Aramaean different from an Egyptian or a Persian.

But ethnicity, and the maintenance of ethnic groups, proceeds not so much by cultural content as by social boundaries within which the groups are enclosed (and social boundaries may or may not coincide with geographical boundaries). Since not all cultural traits are relevant, those traits which are, and how significant a given trait is, may also change with time. Thus, the cultural characteristics of members of an ethnic group could change through time, but if some sort of ethnic boundaries were maintained throughout, the group could retain ethnic identity. As long as ethnic boundaries exist, there is a tendency for new forms of behavior to be dichotomized, reinforcing the separateness of groups. If ethnic boundaries are lost — through the reduction of important social differences, the congruence of codes and values, etc. — ethnic identity is lost.

In order to look at the role of ethnicity in an ancient situation, several questions need to be asked: In which circumstances did inhabitants of, say, Egypt, label themselves? What labels were used? What criteria determined the use of the label? Are there indications of ethnic mobility (synchronic or diachronic)? Did the government or administrative body use these (or other) ethnic identifications to categorize (or extend privileges to) individuals or groups?

By the Persian period, Egypt, and urban Egyptians, had a long history of exposure to individual foreigners living in Egypt,[4] a fair amount of exposure to groups of foreigners in Egypt,[5] but little previous exposure to incorporation in a foreign empire and the imposition of a foreign administrative scheme on Egypt and Egyptian bureaucrats. Egyptians distinguished themselves from people living to their north, south, east, and west; people with whom the Egyptians had a military conflict were frequently referred to derogatorily.[6] Descriptions and depictions of non-Egyptians were often quite detailed, indicating differences in hair, skin color, facial features, dress, accoutrements, etc. The Egyptians could, when appropriate, also distinguish themselves as Upper versus Lower Egyptians. But the important distinctions depended heavily on language.[7] Several New Kingdom ostraca credit the god Thoth with having *wp* "divided" the languages of different countries.[8] Non-Egyptians *ỉꜥꜣw* "babbled," the same word used of the braying of a donkey, and communicated through interpreters who learned to babble.[9]

---

rized by Csaba La'da as follows (personal communication; see also his forthcoming Ph.D. dissertation): "Ethnic designations did serve official purposes in Ptolemaic Egypt but these purposes did not include ethnic discrimination. These purposes were individual identification (real ethnic designations) and (fiscal/social) status differentiation on the basis of occupation (fictitious ethnic designations)." As summarized by La'da, "The Romans introduced an entirely new system of social privilege which was based on a mixture of interrelated ethnic-cultural and legal criteria." See also La'da 1994.

4. For example, Asiatic and Nubian prisoners of war. Some Egyptian names reflect foreign origin (e.g., *Pꜣ-Nḥsy* "the Nubian" and *Pꜣ-Ḫꜣrw* "the Syrian," both of which are attested in hieroglyphs and Demotic), but it is not clear that all the people who had such names were foreign born (or even second- or third-generation foreign born). Some foreign born slaves (prisoners of war?) kept their original names (which Egyptian scribes tried to write in Egyptian), others took or were given Egyptian names which might or might not indicate their foreign birth.

5. For example, the Greek- and Semitic-speaking traders and mercenaries who had been residing in the Delta and Memphis for several generations.

6. For a good discussion and summary of ethnicity, and especially of Egyptian representations of Libyans from late predynastic times until the middle of the first millennium, see Baines 1996, especially pp. 360–84.

7. As did the Upper versus Lower Egyptian distinction, as shown, for example, by the oft-quoted jibe from the New Kingdom scribe Hori to his fellow scribe Amenemope: "Your discourses are collected on my tongue and remain fixed on my lips, for they are so confused when heard that no interpreter can unravel them. They are like a Delta man's conversation with a man of Elephantine" (P. Anastasi I, translated by Wente 1990, p. 109).

8. For *wp*, see Černý 1948, p. 120; another New Kingdom text used *stnw* (< *sṯnỉ*) "to distinguish."

9. For *ỉꜥꜣw*, see Bell 1976.

The Egyptian norm seems to have been for the foreigner to learn Egyptian,[10] not vice versa, and there are numerous examples of non-Egyptians living in Egypt who Egyptianized, adopting Egyptian customs and sometimes Egyptian names. Examples from the Persian period include a group of foreigners settled in the Memphite area who left grave stelae reflecting greater or lesser degrees of Egyptianization. Stelae carved on behalf of Carians range from Egyptian(izing), although with both Carian and Egyptian hieroglyphic inscriptions, to purely East Greek (but with a winged sun disk across the top), where many incorporate both Egyptian and East Greek iconography (Martin and Nicholls 1978; Gallo and Masson 1993, p. 271, n. 19).[11] One recently published example has, in the upper register, a slightly Egyptianized Greek mourning scene with a Greek inscription and, in the lower register, a scene of offering before Osiris (Gallo and Masson 1993). Other examples combining mourning scenes with typically Egyptian offering scenes have inscriptions in Aramaic;[12] a frequently studied example is the Carpentras Stela, which has a hymn to Osiris written in Aramaic at the bottom of the stela (Fitzmyer and Kaufman 1992, B.3.f.18, p. 141). There are also a number of typically Egyptian funerary stelae[13] or sarcophagi[14] to which a personal name has been added in Aramaic. Aramaic prayers were also added, as graffiti, to Egyptian religious scenes.[15]

A well-known example of Persian officials living in Egypt who adopted an Egyptian name and began to honor Egyptian deities involves two brothers who served in the area of Coptos and left graffiti in the quarries in the Wadi Hammamat. Of these graffiti, Posener (1936, p. 178) says,

> Les graffiti de ces deux Perses s'échelonnent sur 37 ans et permettent de suivre l'influence croissante du pays conquis sur les étrangers. Les premières inscriptions d'Atiyawahi [fils d'Artamès et de la dame Qandjou] ne contiennent que la date et les noms propres. Le titre[16] du fonctionnaire est transcrit de l'araméen. En l'an 10 de Xerxès Atiyawahi ajoute l'image de Min, en l'an 12 on lit une brève invocation au même dieu. Les textes d'Ariyawrata, plus récents, sont toujours accompagnés de la représentation d'un dieu. Ariyawrata traduit son titre en égyptien et adopte le surnom égyptien , *Djého*. Il invoque Min; Min, Horus et Isis; et Amonrasonter.

It has recently been suggested by Lemaire (1991, pp. 199–201) that the temple at Aswan built by the Persian chief of the garrison there was dedicated to an Egyptian deity (Osiris the strong).[17] Both this dedication, if Lemaire's re-reading and reinterpretation are correct, and the invocations of Egyptian deities by Ariyawrata/Djeho need not be interpreted as Persians converting and accepting Egyptian deities but rather as examples of the well-attested Persian respect for local deities and local culture.[18]

10. The Instruction of Any, a New Kingdom didactic text, includes a passage (10/6) that states, "One teaches the Nubian Egyptian (*mdt rmṯ n Kmt*), and the Syrian and all foreigners likewise." There certainly are examples of Egyptians, especially Egyptian scribes stationed in or sent to western Asia, who learned foreign languages (e.g., the scribe who wrote the Amarna Letters of Abimilki, prince of Tyre, if Albright [1937, pp. 196–203] is correct), although they didn't always learn it very well (see the sarcastic comments by Hori directed at Amenemope in P. Anastasi I [translated by Wente 1990, especially pp. 106–09]). For an analysis of Semitic vocabulary that occurs in New Kingdom and Third Intermediate Period Egyptian texts, see Hoch 1994.
11. One stela shows the traditional Greek scene of the deceased on a bier with mourners around, but the deceased is portrayed by beard and costume as Persian (Stela Berlin 23721; see Martin and Nicholls 1978, p. 66, #C1). One should also note the earlier, Saite, bronze statue base for a statue of the goddess Neith found in Susa. The statue was made in Egypt by a man named Padineith, who added a marginal inscription in Carian to the traditional Egyptian hieroglyphic inscription (for the reference, see Yoyotte and Masson 1988, p. 177).
12. For example, Stela Vatican 287 (Fitzmyer and Kaufman 1992, B.3.f.28, p. 144); Stela Wadi el-Saba Rigala (Fitzmyer and Kaufman 1992, B.3.e.22, pp. 129–30, from the Memphite area).
13. For example, Stela Ptah (Fitzmyer and Kaufman 1992, B.3.e.9, p. 127, from Saqqara).
14. For example, Fitzmyer and Kaufman 1992, B.3.f.4, p. 137, from Aswan; B.3.e.27, p. 135, from Saqqara.
15. For example, Graffito Wadi el-Hudi, added to a cippus of Horus (Fitzmyer and Kaufman 1992, B.3.f.20), and G. Abydos, added to the temple of Osiris (Fitzmyer and Kaufman 1992, B.3.f.23, p. 142).
16. For a discussion of the meaning of this title (*saris*), see Briant 1996b, p. 288.
17. If Stela Aswan (Fitzmyer and Kaufman 1992, B.3.f.3, p. 136) dates from year 7 of Artaxerxes II (as Lemaire 1991), rather than Artaxerxes I, then this stela belongs to the small group of Aramaic documents from Aswan recording dates in the reign of Artaxerxes II several years after the successful revolt by Amyrtaeus in the Delta. If this dating is correct, then the Persian chief of the garrison could even be seen as playing to Aswan's incorporation into the newly independent Egypt (Briant 1996b, p. 1008).
18. See Briant 1988, pp. 166–67, who also notes (pp. 160–61) other possible examples of Persians who adopted a second, Egyptian, name.

A recently discovered and published stela from Saqqara can "be considered as constituting the first certain evidence of a union between a Persian and an Egyptian" (Mathieson et al. 1995). The top register of this funerary stela shows the traditional Egyptian scene of the mummified deceased on a lion-bier being attended by Isis, Nephthys, and Anubis, with the four canopic jars under the bier. Inscriptions in both hieroglyphic and Demotic Egyptian invoke Osiris on behalf of a man named DjedHorBes, whose mother's name was Tanofreher (both Egyptian names) but whose father had the Persian name Artames (*ꜣrṯm*). The lower register shows an offering scene, but the recipient of the offerings is not a deity, such as Osiris, but a "seated, bearded official whose throne and dress proclaim him as a Persian dignitary of very high rank" (Mathieson et al. 1995, p. 29). This dignitary wears a circlet with rosettes around his head[19] and holds a cup to his mouth in one hand and a flower in the other.[20] Before the official stand two offering tables (one typically Egyptian, one perhaps more Achaemenid) and two people in typical Late Period Egyptian costume making offerings. The exact identity of the recipient of the offerings and of the offering bearers is uncertain (perhaps the principal offerer is DjedHorBes, the recipient his father Artames) and the absence of titles for either father or son has been the point of some discussion (Mathieson et al. 1995, p. 38).

There is a good deal of evidence of foreigners living in Egypt during the Saite and Persian periods, especially mercenaries[21] and merchants, located in the Delta in the Memphite/Saqqara area and at Elephantine.[22] Among the people attested in written records found at Saqqara are people with names that can be classified as Carian, Aramaean (non-Jewish), Babylonian, Sidonian, Moabite, Ionian, Cretan(?), Hyrcanian, Lydian, and Arab (Segal 1983). The presence of Greeks is attested archaeologically as well as textually.[23] Nesuhor,[24] the Overseer of Doors of/to Southern Foreign Lands, i.e., the chief of the garrison at Elephantine, under the Saite King Apries, refers in a hieroglyphic inscription to *s.t qsn.t m-ꜥ pḏtyw ꜥꜣmw ḥꜣw-nbw sttyw kyw* "difficulty from soldiers (literally, bowmen), *ꜥꜣmw*-Asiatics, Greeks, *sttyw*-Asiatics, and others." Presumably he is referring to a rebellion by the garrison stationed at Elephantine. In any case, this inscription seems to imply that the soldiers in this garrison included people from two different Asiatic groups.[25]

This same distinction between two Asiatic groups of mercenaries is found in a Demotic document from Elephantine dated to year 41 of the following Saite ruler Amasis (529 B.C.).[26] This text lists individuals participating in an expedition to Nubia under Amasis. These individuals are divided into groupings defined by the term *rmṯ* "man (of)."[27] The groups mentioned include *rmṯ Ḫ(ꜣ)rw* "man of Khor/Syria," using an old term for Syria, and *rmṯ ꜣIšwr* using the new term frequently translated "Assyria." The basis for differentiation could have been geographical place of origin, as suggested by Erichsen (1941, p. 59, n. v), who identifies the two groups as Palestinians and Syrians. However, since in Demotic *sẖ ꜣIšwr* means Aramaic writing,[28] it seems possible that *rmṯ*

19. This is the earliest attestation of this circlet or ringlet; see Briant 1996c, p. 20.

20. Briant (1996c, p. 20) finds a parallel for the man raising the cup to his mouth and holding the flower in a sealing from the Murashu archive from Babylonia (Legrain 1925, pl. 59, sealing #984).

21. Thus, the graffiti left by troops of Psammetichus II at Abu Simbel during the war of Psammetichus with the Ethiopians show the Egyptian forces to have included Carians, Ionians, Rhodians, and Phoenicians. Leaders of the troops, Psammetichus, the son of Theokles, and Ebedptah, the son of Jagureshmun, have been suggested to be, respectively, a Greek and a Phoenician born in Egypt (so Porten 1968, p. 9, with references in footnotes 29–30). Recently a small Egyptian cube statue dedicated in Greek by a man named Pedon, the son of Amphinneus, who served as a mercenary under King Psammetichus, was found near Priene, Turkey (Şahin 1987). The statue itself can be dated stylistically to the time of Psammetichus I (Ampolo and Bresciani 1988; Yoyotte and Masson 1988); Yoyotte argues that the inscription is contemporary and Pedon served Psammetichus I; Bresciani leaves open the possibility that the inscription is secondary and that the king served by Pedon was Psammetichus II.

22. For example, the Egyptianizing stela, sarcophagi, and graffiti mentioned above as well as the extensive Aramaic documentation of both Jewish and non-Jewish "detachments," especially those located in the Aswan area (discussed, e.g., in Porten 1968).

23. See, for example, Boardman 1980; Coulson and Leonard 1981; and the list of Greek names, with city-ethnic designations, dating from the middle of the fourth century (SB V 8306).

24. Otto 1954, p. 163, #25a, and bibliography mentioned by Porten 1968, p. 15, n. 55.

25. Porten (1968, p. 15) assumes the reference to refer to Jews and Aramaeans.

26. P. Berlin 13615, originally published by Erichsen (1941); more fragments are discussed by Zauzich (1992).

27. A term regularly used in descriptions of military men where "man of" may indicate, among other things, the place of origin of foreign mercenaries or the place where native Egyptian soldiers were stationed. One of the terms for Egyptian soldiers rather frequently attested during the Saite and Persian periods is *rmṯ ḏ(ꜣ)m* "man of the generation (eligible for conscription)," which seems to have been the source for Herodotus's much-discussed Ἑρμοτύβιες (Thissen 1994, pp. 89–91).

28. See, for example, the record of Darius's call for the compilation of the laws of Egypt, of which copies were to be made

ʾIšwr indicates not so much a man from *ʾIšwr* "Assyria" as a speaker of Aramaic. If this is so, such a categorization would fit with the Egyptian use of language as a major criterion of ethnics.[29] In any case, it is clear that there were recognized groups of foreigners, with what may be ethnic identifications, in place in Egypt at the time of the Persian invasion. Whatever modifications the Persians made, they made them within an ongoing system.

Egyptians writing documents in Egyptian, both Demotic and hieroglyphic, continued to identify themselves by their name, patronymic (and occasionally matronymic), and less consistently, profession. Even in documents dealing with Persian officials, Egyptians normally identified themselves by their name only or by their name and title, although they might indicate the foreign origin of the Persian official by including at the end of his name the determinative that indicated a foreign name.[30] Examples of ethnics in Egyptian documents of the Persian period are quite rare. In the Demotic record there is one reference to a Blemmye, one to a *mty* "Mede," one broken reference to Medes, one reference to a Libyan, one to an Ethiopian, two to Assyrian/Aramaeans, one possible reference to a Greek, and a likely ethnic that is broken and uncertain.[31] An execration text from Saqqara (dated palaeographically to the early Ptolemaic period, although the contents may, perhaps, date earlier) mentions both Egyptian and foreign rulers, including *pꜣ wr n pꜣ tꜣ Ḫr* "the ruler of the country of Khor/Syria" and *pꜣ ṯs n nꜣ Yhytw* "the (military) commander of the Jews" (Ray 1978, p. 29). Other Egyptian documents from Saqqara mention both Medes (i.e., Persians) and Greeks (including the Quarter of the Greeks) as well as people with Persian names (Smith 1992). A fragmentary literary text[32] found at Saqqara contains two references to *Ḫry* "Syria/Syrians."

The use of possible ethnics was more common in some Aramaic documents, both private documents (Elephantine) and administrative records such as the Aramaic document from Saqqara, probably from the dockyards, mentioning Greeks and Carians (Segal 1983, pp. 41–43).[33] Similarly, the customs account from 475 B.C.

---

in *sẖ ỉšr sẖ šʿṯ* "Aramaic and Demotic (Egyptian) (literally, document-writing)" (P. Bibliothèque Nationale 215 verso, c/14, published in Spiegelberg 1914); for a recent discussion of the term, see Steiner 1993.

29. A third ethnic term in P. Berlin 13615 is not *rmṯ Tꜣ Nḥsy*, an otherwise unattested circumlocution for *Nḥsy* "Nubian," but *rmṯ Stm-mnṯ*, perhaps to be understood as "man of 'Asia'" combining two very old terms, *Sṯt* and *Mntyw* (as Zauzich 1992). If so, this term could correspond to *sttyw*-Asiatics in Nesuhor's inscription, leaving his *ʿꜣmw*-Asiatics to correspond to *rmt Ḫ(ꜣ)rw*, the new term *rmṯ ʾIšwr*, or the two together.

30. For example, in P. Loeb 1, dated to year 36 of Darius I (as Hughes 1984, pp. 76–77). In this text a person with a Persian name had overridden an instruction given to a person with an Egyptian name by another person with an Egyptian name; the Egyptian to whom the instruction had been given originally is complaining to the local Persian official before whom the original instruction had been given. In the text, Egyptian names are written normally, without any ethnic identification since the assumption was that they were Egyptians, but the Persian names consistently include the foreigner determinative.

31. P. Rylands 9 (Griffith 1909) is a long petition to a high official with an unreadable title (perhaps to be read *ṯꜣty* "vizier" or *sḏꜣw.ty* / *ḫtm.ty* "sealbearer"; for discussion, see Tait 1977, pp. 30–32, n. m) from the reign of Darius I by a priest of Amun of (GN) Teudjoy. The priest recounts how his ancestor's prebend in the temple of Amun of Teudjoy had been stolen by other priests and asks for its return. At one point, the high Persian official told a man with an Egyptian name and priestly title to go with the complainant to investigate. This man stalled for some time and finally told another man to go and investigate, which he did. The second man is identified as *Wꜣḥ-ib-Rʿ-mry-Rʿ* (?) (a perfectly good Egyptian name, based on the royal name *Wꜣḥ-ib-Rʿ* "Apries"), the Blemmye (*pꜣ Blhm*); for the reading, see Černý 1958, pp. 203–04. Blemmyes are also noted in Ptolemaic documents (especially the so-called Hauswaldt papyri from the Edfu area). The same P. Rylands 9 also seems to contain the last reference to the old Libyan military title Chief of the Me(shwesh); see Ritner 1990. The supposed Greek mentioned in a loan of year 16 of Nectanebo II (i.e., just before the re-incorporation of Egypt into the Persian Empire) has a good Egyptian name and patronymic, and the reading *wy*[*nn*] "Gr[eek]" has been questioned (Vleeming 1984, p. 354). A badly broken contract dated to year 3 of Achoris (Twenty-ninth Dynasty; P. Cairo 50099, line 1) seems to have been made by a *mty* "Mede" whose name began *Ps* (since the name was written alphabetically, it was probably foreign and could easily have been Persian). Two unpublished letters from Elephantine now in Berlin are said to contain references to an Ethiopian (P. Berlin 23639) and an Assyrian (*rmṯ ʾIšwr*?; P. Berlin 15808). A document from Saqqara dated (palaeographically) to the Persian period includes the statement by a man named *Ḥr-ḥb*: *hwn-nꜣw ỉnk pꜣ bꜣk wʿ Pyt* "I was the servant of a Libyan" (P. Cairo 50072, line 6). Another document from Saqqara mentions *rmṯ.rm.* (with foreigner determinative) *Ḏd-ḥr* (*sꜣ*) *Gre*, but how the broken word should be restored is unclear (Smith 1992, p. 396).

32. P. Saqqara 27, lines 1, 21 (Smith and Tait 1983, pp. 199–200, with n. d).

33. However, as remarked by Bezalel Porten (personal communication, December 1995), the ethnic designations in Aramaic documents are limited to foreigners: "The two true Egyptians who appear are civilians. They are not called 'Egyptian,' as the Jews and Aramaeans and Khwarezmians, etc., are called by their ethnics, but simply 'architect of Syene' or 'architect of the king' (TAD B2.6:2, 2.8:2)." A native is a native and doesn't have to be so designated. Although it is far beyond the reach or concern of

(Porten and Yardeni 1993; Yardeni 1994), recording customs duties levied on incoming or outgoing ships, regularly provided an ethnic identification of all captains.[34] Since customs rates were 1/10 on the smaller "Phoenician" ships but 1/5 on Greek ships, I wonder whether this reflects an attempt by the Persians to redirect Egyptian trade away from Greece and back within the Persian Empire, as suggested by Harrison (n.d.) on the basis of published archaeological materials in Egypt.

Both Demotic and Aramaic materials from Saqqara show mixed names (Semitic/Egyptian, Iranian/Egyptian) and people with different types of names interacting in the same document. Smith (1992, p. 299) summarizes:

> ... the well-known fact that the population of Memphis in the 5th–4th centuries was of very mixed [racial] origin, and that it was a truly cosmopolitan city. Aside from the onomastic interest of the names, what is impressive is how foreigners and people of foreign parentage appear in almost every class of Egyptian document, however ephemeral, mixed with pure Egyptians, taking part in Egyptian religious practices, Egyptian legal cases, Egyptian official, social, and domestic life. The value of finds like the Saqqara papyri, containing many very fragmentary documents, almost worthless in themselves, is that they tend to illustrate this sort of intercommunal penetration more fully than smaller collections of documents of much greater individual worth.

One extremely interesting small document found at Saqqara was a question directed to an oracle that asks whether *Gyg*, the Syrian or Aramaean (*ʾIšwr*), the wife of *Brq* (*Baraq*), will go to the land of *Ḫr* in a certain month. It is uncertain to which deity the question was directed; what is most interesting is that an Aramaean woman asking a deity whether she should travel to Aram posed the question not in Aramaic but in Demotic (Smith 1992, p. 298).[35]

There is an "us (Jews) against them (Egyptians)" feeling found repeatedly in documents from the Jewish garrison at Elephantine. For example, when they were petitioning for permission to rebuild their Temple in Elephantine, they claimed special (or at least fair) treatment because they, the Jews, had not rebelled when Egyptian detachments did (Porten 1968, p. 279).[36] When describing the destruction of their Temple, the Jews state that Nefayan, the son of Vidranga, "led out Egyptians with other forces," but they blame the destruction totally on the priests of the god Khnum and the corruptness of Vidranga, whom they claim must have been bribed by them.[37] No parallel anti-Jewish attitude is found in Egyptian documents. There is nothing in Egyptian documents to substantiate Porten's (1968) repeated suggestion that the Egyptians, who after all had been defeated by Persians, perceived the Jews who were working in their employ as members of a hated ruling class. One must conclude with Briant (1996a, p. 130) "La destruction du temple de Yahweh n'est pas d'abord le résultat ou la manifestation exacerbée d'une haine ethnique et religieuse relayée par de hauts administrateurs perses tout acquis à la foi de Khnûm ('égyptophilie') et/ou désireux de calmer la 'flambée nationaliste,' y compris en portant gravement tort à des garnisaires fidèles à la cause impériale."

There are several comments, hardly conclusions, that one can note with regard to the questions asked and the material surveyed here. Individuals could have two or more ethnic identities (either within one phase of their life or during the course of their life) depending on the "others" to whom they were relating, and on what

---

this paper, it is worth noting (as did Porten) that in Biblical material "natives" do sometimes get labeled (e.g., in the story of Joseph in Egypt, with its Egyptian setting, Potiphar, identified as a high official of the king of Egypt, is still labeled an "Egyptian") and in many of the Biblical passages where Jews are labeled they are in a foreign context (Moses and the Jews in exile in Egypt, Joseph in service to Potiphar, Mordecai serving the Persian king).

34. Of those for which the information is preserved, larger ships, carrying Ionian wine, among other things, all had Ionian captains; smaller ships carried Sidonian wine, among other things, leading the editors to suggest that the captains were Phoenicians.

35. There is no way to ascertain from this small text whether the deity being questioned was an Egyptian deity or whether Demotic was used because there was no scribe or priest available to write or present the question in Aramaic. It should be noted that Demotic script was used to write Aramaic by the scribe of P. Amherst 63 (see the bibliography in Fitzmyer and Kaufman 1992, B.3.f.27, pp. 143–44, to which can be added Steiner 1995; Steiner and Moshavi 1995).

36. This passage contains the only reference to *diglīn* of Egyptians (Cowley 1923, #27, lines 1 ff.; Porten and Yardeni 1986, A4.5).

37. For the plausible reconstruction that Vidranga's decision in favor of the Egyptian temple of Khnum was a legal decision (not a social, cultural, religious, or ethnic decision) based on the application of local Egyptian law and the possible inability of the Jews to document ownership rights to the property on which the Jewish temple stood, see Briant 1996a, especially pp. 122–28. There he also notes (p. 123) that it was common in the Persian Empire for a son to serve under and follow his father in office and so it would have been quite natural that Vidranga, when he was promoted from chief of the garrison to governor, would appoint his son chief of the garrison in his place. It was in his role as chief of the garrison, not as son of a compromised Vidranga, that Nefayan was carrying out the judicial order of the governor.

terms. A Carian soldier living in Memphis might see himself and be seen as Carian vis-à-vis his Egyptian neighbors and see himself and be seen as Egyptian vis-à-vis Carians back home. Similarly, the man with a Babylonian name who was head of a detachment in Elephantine might have thought of himself and been thought of as a Babylonian by himself and by the Persians for and with whom he worked, but at least in some situations he might have been thought of as a Persian by members of his detachment and various Egyptians, Jews, and Aramaeans with whom he came in contact.

One situation where we have people who are clearly identified by two different ethnics are individuals mentioned in the Aramaic documents from Elephantine, sometimes called "Jew of Elephantine," other times "Aramaean" and/or "of Syene" in others.[38] Based on secondary sources, I wonder whether Aramaean as used in Persian-period documents from Egypt is a general ethnic term, perhaps even recognized by the Persian government to categorize or describe all (Jewish and pagan) Aramaic-speaking people. The term Jew would be an informal or social "self-ascriptive" ethnic used by and about Jews to distinguish Jewish Aramaeans from "other" Aramaeans. Jews always had the option to use the generic Aramaic; perhaps they made a point of using the term "Jew" rather than "Aramaean" when making contracts with non-Jews or when writing a letter to Jewish officials of the Persian administration,[39] where use of the "in-group" term might help bring about the desired response. One might also consider whether different scribes (Jewish and non-Jewish) were more likely to use the more specific and less formal ethnic "Jew" rather than the more general "Aramaean."[40] Similarly, since the main administration for Aswan was at Syene, all stationed in Aswan could be called "of Syene," but those on Elephantine could also be classified more specifically as "of Elephantine." Such a theory would explain why Jews and Aramaeans served in the same detachment (*dgl*) — administratively and officially they were all the same ethnic; the subdivision was social, not formal or official.[41]

The hypothesis that the term "Jew" was a more specific social ethnic differentiating Jews from other Aramaeans would not, however, explain why a man with an Egyptian name and patronymic Pa-Khnum (the man belonging to the god Khnum), son of Besa, was called an Aramaean of Syene (Kraeling 1953, #11). In non-Elephantine Aramaic documents from Egypt, there is frequent intermixing of Egyptian and Aramaean names among father, son, and grandson.[42] In the Saqqara documents, one of four people labeled Aramaean has an Egyptian name; there are father-son and sibling pairs with mixed Egyptian/Semitic names.[43] In the Elephantine Demotic papyrus with lists of people participating in the expedition to Nubia under the Saite King Amasis, lists of Assyrians (who are suggested here to be Aramaic speakers) include people whose name and patronymic are both Semitic, whose name is Egyptian but patronymic is Semitic, and whose name and patronymic are both Egyptian. The easiest explanation involves the tendency of (some) immigrant mercenaries to give their children Egyptian names as they began to assimilate or at least began identifying themselves with or as Egyptians.[44] Following such a scenario, Pa-Khnum could easily be a third (or later) generation Aramaean born in Egypt and given an Egyptian name. The ethnic term Aramaean might or might not say much about such a man's "culture," religious affiliation, or mother tongue, but it continued to serve the useful administrative function of identifying his place in the Elephantine bureaucracy.

38. Porten (1968) suggests that references to Jews as Aramaeans probably were based on language.

39. For example, Jedaniah and his colleagues to Bagohi, the governor of Judah, asking permission to rebuild the Temple.

40. See the notes and discussion in Porten 1996.

41. I now turn from speculation to wild speculation. In a fifth-century deed of gift or exchange between a woman named Mibtahiah and Asori, the two women are called sisters, daughters of Gemariah (Cowley 1923, #43; Porten and Yardeni 1986, B5.5, a "mutual quitclaim"; Fitzmyer and Kaufman 1992, B.3.c.10). Mibtahiah is described, following Porten's (1989, pp. 174–76) reconstruction, as "[a Jewess] of Elephantine the fortress (and) an Aramean according to her detachment (*dgl*)" and Asori is described as "a Jewess of the same [detachment]." Since both sisters are members of the same detachment, and since both Jews and Aramaeans could serve in the same detachment, the meaning of the phrase "Aramean according to her detachment" is far from clear. Porten notes that the reconstructed double designation "[Jew(ess)] of Elephantine, Aramean according to detachment" is unique to Mibtahiah and that Asori's name appears to be Egyptian. If my hypothesis is correct that all Jews could be called Aramaeans, then stressing the "Aramaeanness" of Mibtahiah in contrast to Asori might have indicated that Mibtahiah had abandoned her Jewish faith and reverted to being only an Aramaean. Indeed, Cowley suggested that Mibtahiah's identification as an Aramaean may have resulted from marriage or something similar.

42. See especially the so-called Hermopolis papyri (Fitzmyer and Kaufman 1992, B.3.b.1, pp. 55–56).

43. In the Aramaic texts from Saqqara, 46% of the personal names are Egyptian, 12% are Iranian, and 30% are Semitic (Segal 1983, pp. 8–9).

44. There would be no need to assume any intermarriage with Egyptians; the tendency to name a child after a grandparent would lead to some "unexpected" Egyptian fathers with Semitic sons.

Especially at Elephantine, we see a foreign group, Jews, working as a community (e.g., the Jewish leaders write on behalf of the Jewish community when trying to get permission to rebuild their Temple). At Saqqara, too, evidence can be interpreted (without forcing it) to see foreign groups acting in concert as communities. But clearly these communities were not a geographical term.[45] Rather, from an Egyptological point of view, these terms seem to reflect an organizational scheme imposed by the Persians (or their predecessors?), providing an administrative structure within which they could structure and control a (large) group of "out-of-place" people in a way benefiting the Persian officials (i.e., it gives the Persian officials a chain of command for dealing with foreigners in Persian service).[46] It was secondarily useful, or made useful, by foreign communities as well.

But these formal organizational structures were not needed in Egypt of the Persian period. Egypt already had a well-organized, long-tested formal chain of command. Egyptians had interest groups (based especially on profession, family, and religious affiliation) that took care of them. Some Egyptians, and especially high Egyptian officials who owed their position, power, and wealth to the Saite dynasty, must have resented the Persian takeover and the appointment of Persian officials at the top levels of the existing administrative (not the social or religious) structure in Memphis and the provinces. But it is precisely for the early years of Persian rule in Egypt that there exists the strongest evidence for high-level Egyptian participation in the administration. Statues of such high Egyptian officials occasionally show them wearing lion torques or other "Persian" items, honoring their Persian masters, and/or showing off the rewards they received from the king.[47] Most of what had been identified as Persian innovation[48] has now been shown actually to develop during the Saite period and thus has no political or ethnic overtones at all (Johnson 1994, pp. 158–59, n. 43). In addition, these so-called collaborators[49] can be understood as working not merely for their own gain (as always with Egyptian bureaucrats) but to preserve Egyptian culture and enhance Egyptian input into the foreign administration (Holm-Rasmussen 1988; see also Briant 1988, pp. 158–59; Briant 1996b, p. 499).

Demotic documents provide examples of incompetent Persian officials, unwilling or unable to adjust to the peculiarities of the Egyptian situation. That seems to be the situation in P. Loeb 1, dated to year 36 of Darius I, in which a Persian countermanded the orders of an Egyptian concerning the storage of grain. The writer of the text, an Egyptian, complains to the Persian official in whose presence the original order had been given that the revised orders left the grain unprotected from local brigands. As Hughes (1984, pp. 85–86) notes, "The Egyptian knew this but the Persian official did not and would not listen. ... The letter thus deals with a purely local situation, which was no doubt a very normal one, without implications beyond an Egyptian's impatience and frustration with the ignorance of local conditions and intractability on the part of a Persian functionary whom he could not dissuade except by resorting to a superior Persian official." However, ethnicity was not a significant factor[50] in Egypt's anti-Persian rebellions — led by descendants of the Libyans who had ruled in and from the Delta, an area from which we have few records. The Persians seem to have given special attention to the Memphite and Theban areas, and there is no evidence of popular support in those areas for the Delta chieftains.[51] Rather, the rebellions in the Delta reflect a power struggle between the "ins" and "outs," just as, during the rest of pharaonic history, if an "outgroup" was strong enough, had good-enough leaders, and enough money, they might fight the current regime, and they might win.

45. Wherever we have sufficient information from Persian-period Egypt to be able to identify (or guess) the ethnic identity of people living in proximity, neighborhoods are clearly not exclusive; using only names as the criterion, both Saqqara and Elephantine show a mix of Egyptians, Semites (Jews, Aramaeans, Babylonians), Greeks, Persians, and others (including Caspians, Khorazmians). This is true not just on a general level but, clearly at Elephantine, on a house-by-house level.

46. Bezalel Porten (personal communication, 1995), too, suggests that the continued use of the ethnic terminology might be the result of community: "It's the immigrant who requires special designation and as long as immigrants remain in organized communities their descendants will continue to bear the original designation."

47. For the king to reward dutiful officials and valorous military service with golden jewelry and other tokens or emblems of extraordinary service was typical of both Egyptian and Persian kings (Yoyotte and Masson 1988, p. 177; Sancisi-Weerdenburg 1988; Briant 1996b, p. 499).

48. It was never clear whether such items were supposed to have been formally introduced by the Persians or were just co-terminus with their appearance and used by Egyptians and Persians to define themselves as Egyptians serving a good, albeit Persian, king.

49. The use of this term in the Egyptian context was influenced by Egyptologists who lived and wrote during the Second World War (e.g., Klasens 1946).

50. For a recent discussion of the causes of Egyptian rebellions against the Persians, see, for example, Briant 1988.

51. The Egyptian documents cited as containing references to rebellion do not contain such references; see, for example, Hughes 1984, pp. 85–86, on P. Loeb 1. The clear anti-Persian (literally, anti-Mede) statements in the so-called Demotic Chronicle (P. Bibliothèque Nationale 215) are framed within a statement outlining proper kingship. The

The Persians may well have undertaken some systematizing or organizing;[52] for example, Darius had the Egyptian laws translated, presumably so Persian officials could know what they were and apply them generally and broadly. Similarly, the convergence in form (whether the underlying system was identical or not) of such Demotic and Aramaic economic documents as loans, sales, and transfers of property (Porten 1968, Appendix 6; Porten 1992) perhaps reflects the need for all these to be registered with one central administration.[53] But it is hard to see ethnicity as a factor in changes that the Persians made in order to integrate Egypt into the empire, changes such as the establishment of Aramaic as the official administrative language, the replacement of the old Egyptian (grain) measure with the Persian *artaba* (*LÄ* 3 "Masse und Gewichte," col. 1210),[54] or the introduction of a Persian, or royal, silver standard.[55] The imposition of the *artaba* remained in use into the Coptic period, but even though Aramaic was the official language, correspondence between Egyptians and Persians, even the highest ranking Persians, could be carried out in Demotic.[56] Here it is important to note that Demotic and Aramaic social documents (e.g., marriage contracts; see Porten 1968, pp. 340–43), unlike economic documents, reflect major distinctions between the two groups. These distinctions presumably result from the lack of interest, and lack of interference, on the part of the Persian administration in the social and cultural concerns of the population, i.e., those concerns that could serve as the basis for social ethnics as discussed above.[57]

Thus, from the Egyptian point of view, study of ethnicity in Persian-period Egypt is the study of foreigners, especially foreign communities, and their relations with one another and with the administration.

References

Albright, W. F.
1937 "The Egyptian Correspondence of Abimilki, Prince of Tyre. Addendum: Egyptianisms in the Abimilki Correspondence." *Journal of Egyptian Archaeology* 23: 196–203.

Ampolo, C., and E. Bresciani
1988 "Psammetico Re d'Egitto e il mercenario Pedon." *Egitto e Vicino Oriente* 11: 237–53.

Baines, J.
1996 "Contextualizing Egyptian Representations of Society and Ethnicity." In *The Study of the Ancient Near East in the 21st Century: The William Foxwell Albright Centennial Conference,* edited by J. S. Cooper and G. M. Schwartz, pp. 339–84. Winona Lake: Eisenbrauns.

Bell, L. D.
1976 Interpreters and Egyptianized Nubians in Ancient Egypt Foreign Policy: Aspects of the History of Egypt and Nubia. Ph.D. dissertation, University of Pennsylvania.

Boardman, J.
1980 *The Greeks Overseas.* Revised Edition. London: Thames and Hudson.

---

name calling may reflect the real attitude of (some) high-level Egyptians; however, since the text we have was written during the early Ptolemaic period, the anti-Persian sentiments of the Greeks may have influenced the Egyptian text (Johnson 1983, 1984).

52. Various documents reflect the hierarchic nature of the Egyptian bureaucracy under the Persians (e.g., P. Rylands 9) and the detailed records and accounting that were required, but there is nothing "un-Egyptian" or inherently Persian in either the nature or mechanics of this bureaucracy. For example, one of the Aramaic Arsames letters records correspondence between the satrap and high-ranking Persian and Egyptian officials in Elephantine concerning the repairs to a boat belonging to the government and used by Egyptian boatmen employed by the government. But, as noted by Briant (1996b, p. 464), the concern that the old wooden planks removed from the boat during repairs be returned to the government is a very Egyptian concern, reflecting the scarcity of wood there.

53. Egyptian land-transfer documents were, from at least the Middle Kingdom on, registered with the central administration; frequently it is stated that they are registered in the office of the vizier. See Johnson 1996, p. 215, n. 22.

54. The Persians also introduced the *artaba* in Babylonia; see Briant (1996b, p. 426) for a discussion of possible implications of the introduction of this new measure.

55. The Persian silver standard appears in Aramaic documents although Demotic documents continued to use the Egyptian silver standards of Ptah or Amun.

56. For example, P. Loeb 1 and the correspondence between the priests of Khnum, of Elephantine, and the satrap Pharendates concerning the appointment of the new lesonis for the temple. P. Berlin 13539, from the priests to Pharendates, is written in "strictly idiomatic Demotic"; P. Berlin 13540, from Pharendates to the priests, "contains the unmistakable marks of a literal translation from an Aramaic original draft" (Hughes 1984, pp. 84, 77). The Demotic documents include occasional Persian technical or administrative terms, usually bureaucratic titles, but the extent to which these and Persian titles and orders of hierarchy found in Aramaic documents reflect significant changes in the administration is not altogether clear.

57. I have argued elsewhere that one of the major contributions of the Persians to the development of Egyptian culture during this period was the Persians' laissez-faire attitude, allowing the continuing development of local culture without imposition from the Persians (Johnson 1994, especially p. 159).

Briant, P.

1988 "Ethno-classe dominante et populations soumises dans l'empire achéménide: Le cas de l'Égypte." In *Achaemenid History* 3: *Method and Theory* (Proceedings of the London 1985 Achaemenid History Workshop), edited by A. Kuhrt and H. Sancisi-Weerdenburg, pp. 137–73. Leiden: Nederlands Instituut voor het Nabije Oosten.

1996a "Une curieuse affaire à Élephantine en 410 av. n.è.: Widranga, le sanctuaire de Khnûm et le temple de Yahwey." *Méditerranées* 6/7: 115–35.

1996b *Histoire de l'empire perse, de Cyrus à Alexandre.* Paris: Fayard.

1996c "Images perses de Babylonie et d'Égypte: Un rapprochement." *La lettre de Pallas* 4: 20.

Černý, J.

1948 "Thoth as Creator of Languages." *Journal of Egyptian Archaeology* 34: 121–22.

1958 "Some Coptic Etymologies III." *Bulletin de l'Institut français d'archéologie orientale* 57: 203–13.

Coulson, W. D. E., and A. Leonard, Jr.

1981 *Cities of the Delta* 1: *Naukratis.* American Research Center in Egypt, Reports 4. Malibu: Undena.

Cowley, A. E.

1923 *Aramaic Papyri of the Fifth Century B.C.* Oxford: Clarendon Press.

Erichsen, W.

1941 "Erwähnung eines Zuges nach Nubien unter Amasis in einem demotischen Text." *Klio* 34: 56–61.

Fitzmyer, J. A., and S. A. Kaufman

1992 *An Aramaic Bibliography,* Part 1: *Old, Official, and Biblical Aramaic.* Baltimore: Johns Hopkins University Press.

Gallo, P., and O. Masson

1993 "Une stèle 'hellénomemphite' de l'ex-collection Nahman." *Bulletin de l'Institut français d'archéologie orientale* 93: 265–76.

Goudriaan, K.

1988 *Ethnicity in Ptolemaic Egypt.* Amsterdam: Gieben.

Griffith, F. Ll.

1909 *Catalogue of the Demotic Papyri in the Rylands Library at Manchester.* 3 volumes. Manchester: University Press.

Harrison, T.

n.d. The Nature and Impact of the Persian Occupation of Egypt, 525–404 B.C. Unpublished class paper.

Hoch, J. E.

1994 *Semitic Words in Egyptian Texts of the New Kingdom and Third Intermediate Period.* Princeton: Princeton University Press.

Holm-Rasmussen, T.

1988 "Collaboration in Early Achaemenid Egypt: A New Approach." In *Studies in Ancient History and Numismatics Presented to Rudi Thomsen*, pp. 29–38. Aarhus: Aarhus University Press.

Hughes, G. R.

1984 "The So-called Pherendates Correspondence." In *Grammata Demotika: Festschrift für Erich Lüddeckens zum 15. Juni 1983*, edited by H.-J. Thissen and K.-Th. Zauzich, pp. 75–86. Würzburg: Gisela Zauzich Verlag.

Johnson, J. H.

1983 "The Demotic Chronicle as a Statement of a Theory of Kingship." *Journal of the Society for the Study of Egyptian Antiquities* 13: 61–72.

1984 "Is the Demotic Chronicle an Anti-Greek Tract?" In *Grammata Demotika: Festschrift für Erich Lüddeckens zum 15. Juni 1983*, edited by H.-J. Thissen and K.-Th. Zauzich, pp. 107–24. Würzburg: Gisela Zauzich Verlag.

1994 "The Persians and the Continuity of Egyptian Culture." In *Achaemenid History* 8: *Continuity and Change* (Proceedings of the Last Achaemenid History Workshop Held in Ann Arbor, Spring 1990), edited by H. Sancisi-Weerdenburg, A. Kuhrt, and M. C. Root, pp. 149–59. Leiden: Nederlands Instituut voor het Nabije Oosten.

1996 "The Legal Status of Women in Ancient Egypt." In *Mistress of the House, Mistress of Heaven: Women in Ancient Egypt*, edited by A. E. Capel and G. E. Markoe, pp. 175–86, 215–17. New York: Hudson Hills Press in association with Cincinnati Art Museum.

Klasens, A.

1946 "Egypte onder Perzen en Grieken-Romeinen, Cambyses en Egypte." *Jaarbericht van het Vooraziatisch-Egyptisch Genootschap "Ex Oriente Lux"* 3: 339–49.

Kraeling, E. G.

1953 *The Brooklyn Museum Aramaic Papyri.* New Haven: Yale University Press.

La'da, C. A.

1994 "Ethnicity, Occupation and Tax-status in Ptolemaic Egypt." *Egitto e Vicino Oriente* 17: 183–89.

Legrain, L.

1925 *The Culture of the Babylonians from Their Seals in the Collections of the Museum.* Publications of the Babylonian Section 14. Philadelphia: University Museum, University of Pennsylvania.

Lemaire, A.

1991 "Recherches d'épigraphie araméenne en Asie Mineure et en Égypte et le problème de l'acculturation." In *Achaemenid History* 6: *Asia Minor and Egypt: Old Cultures in a New Empire* (Proceedings of the Groningen 1988 Achaemenid History Workshop), edited by H. Sancisi-Weerdenburg and A. Kuhrt, pp. 199–206. Leiden: Nederlands Instituut voor het Nabije Oosten.

Martin, G. T., and R. V. Nicholls

1978 "Hieroglyphic Stelae with Carian Texts and Carian Stelae with Egyptianizing or Hellenizing Motifs." Part 2 of *Carian Inscriptions from North Saqqâra and Buhen,* by O. Masson, edited by T. G. H. James. Texts from Excavations 5. London: Egypt Exploration Society.

Mathieson, I.; E. Bettles; S. Davis; and H. S. Smith
1995 "A Stela of the Persian Period from Saqqara." *Journal of Egyptian Archaeology* 81: 23–41.

Otto, E.
1954 *Die biographischen Inschriften der ägyptischen Spätzeit, ihre geistesgeschichtliche und literarische Bedeutung*. Probleme der Ägyptologie 2. Leiden: E. J. Brill.

Porten, B.
1968 *Archives from Elephantine: The Life of an Ancient Jewish Military Colony*. Berkeley: University of California Press.
1989 "Fragmentary Aramaic Deeds of Obligation and Conveyance: New Collations and Restorations." *Journal of Near Eastern Studies* 48:161–83.
1992 "Aramaic-Demotic Equivalents: Who Is the Borrower and Who the Lender?" In *Life in a Multi-Cultural Society: Egypt from Cambyses to Constantine and Beyond*, edited by J. H. Johnson, pp. 259–64. Studies in Ancient Oriental Civilization 51. Chicago: Oriental Institute.
1996 *The Elephantine Papyri in English: Three Millennia of Cross-cultural Continuity and Change*. Documenta et Monumenta Orientis Antiqui 22. Leiden: E. J. Brill.

Porten, B., and A. Yardeni
1986 *Textbook of Aramaic Documents from Ancient Egypt*, Volume 1: *Letters, Texts and Studies for Students*. Jerusalem: Hebrew University.
1989 *Textbook of Aramaic Documents from Ancient Egypt*, Volume 2: *Contracts*. Jerusalem: Hebrew University.
1993 *Textbook of Aramaic Documents from Ancient Egypt*, Volume 3: *Literature, Accounts, Lists, Texts and Studies for Students*. Jerusalem: Hebrew University.

Posener, G.
1936 *La première domination perse en Égypte: Recueil d'inscriptions hiéroglyphiques*. Bibliothèque d'étude 11. Cairo: Institut français d'archéologie orientale.

Ray, J. D.
1978 "The Non-literary Material from North Saqqâra: A Short Progress Report." *Enchoria* 8, Sonderband: 29–30.

Ritner, R. K.
1990 "The End of the Libyan Anarchy in Egypt: P. Rylands IX, cols. 11–12." *Enchoria* 17: 101–08.

Şahin, M. Ç.
1987 "Zwei Inschriften aus dem südwestlichen Kleinasien. 1. Archaische Inschrift aus Priene, aus der Zeit des Psammetichos." *Epigraphica Anatolica* 10: 1–2.

Samuel, A. E.
1989 "Modern Views of the Period after Alexander." Chapter 1 of *The Shifting Sands of History: Interpretations of Ptolemaic Egypt*. Publications of the Association of Ancient Historians 2. Lanham: University Press of America.

Sancisi-Weerdenburg, H.
1988 "Gifts in the Persian Empire." In *Achaemenid History 3: Method and Theory* (Proceedings of the Achaemenid History Workshop Held in 1985 in London), edited by A. Kuhrt and H. Sancisi-Weerdenburg, pp. 129–46. Leiden: Nederlands Instituut voor het Nabije Oosten.

Segal, J. B.
1983 *Aramaic Texts from North Saqqara with Some Fragments in Phoenician*. Texts from Excavations 6. Documentary Series 4. London: Egypt Exploration Society.

Smith, H. S.
1992 "Foreigners in the Documents from the Sacred Animal Necropolis, Saqqara." In *Life in a Multi-Cultural Society: Egypt from Cambyses to Constantine and Beyond*, edited by J. H. Johnson, pp. 295–301. Studies in Ancient Oriental Civilization 51. Chicago: Oriental Institute.

Smith, H. S., and W. J. Tait
1983 *Saqqâra Demotic Papyri* I. Texts from Excavations 7. London: Egypt Exploration Society.

Spiegelberg, W.
1914 *Die sogenannte Demotische Chronik des Pap. 215 der Bibliothèque National zu Paris nebst den auf der Rückseite des Papyrus stehenden Textes*. Demotische Studien 7. Leipzig: J. C. Hinrichs.

Steiner, R. C.
1993 "Why the Aramaic Script Was Called 'Assyrian' in Hebrew, Greek, and Demotic." *Orientalia* 62: 80–82.
1995 "Papyrus Amherst 63: A New Source for the Language, Literature, Religion, and History of the Aramaeans." In *Studia Aramaica: New Sources and New Approaches* (Papers Delivered at the London Conference of the Institute of Jewish Studies, University College London, 26th–28th June 1991), edited by M. J. Geller, J. C. Greenfield, and M. P. Weitzman, pp. 199–207. Oxford: Oxford University Press.

Steiner, R. C., and A. M. Moshavi
1995 "A Selective Glossary of Northwest Semitic Texts in Egyptian Script." In *Dictionary of the North-West Semitic Inscriptions*, edited by J. Hoftijzer and K. Jongeling, pp. 1249–66. Leiden; E. J. Brill.

Tait, W. J.
1977 *Papyri from Tebtunis in Egyptian and in Greek* (*P. Tebt. Tait*). Texts from Excavations 3. London: Egypt Exploration Society.

Thissen, H.-J.
1994 "Varia Onomastica." *Göttinger Miszellen* 141: 89–91.

Vleeming, S.
1984 Review of *Choix de textes juridiques en hiératique anormal et en démotique, deuxième partie*, by M. Malinine. *Bibliotheca Orientalis* 41: 353–56.

Wente, E. F.
1990 *Letters from Ancient Egypt*. Society of Biblical Literature, Writings from the Ancient World 1. Atlanta: Scholars Press.

Yardeni, A.
1994 "Maritime Trade and Royal Accountancy in an Erased Customs Account from 475 B.C.E. on the

Aḥiqar Scroll from Elephantine." *Bulletin of the American Schools of Oriental Research* 293: 67–78.

Yoyotte, J., and O. Masson
1988 "Une inscription ionienne mentionnant Psammatique I[er]." *Epigraphica Anatolica* 11: 171–80.

Zauzich, K.-Th.
1992 "Ein Zug nach Nubien under Amasis." In *Life in a Multi-Cultural Society: Egypt from Cambyses to Constantine and Beyond*, edited by J. H. Johnson, pp. 361–64. Studies in Ancient Oriental Civilization 51. Chicago: Oriental Institute.

21

THE *NFRW*-COLLAR RECONSIDERED

W. RAYMOND JOHNSON

The Oriental Institute, Chicago

I consider it one of the great fortunes of my professional life that Ed Wente was teaching at the Oriental Institute when I began my graduate studies there. His enthusiasm, seemingly endless patience (the bounds of which we constantly tested), and inquiring mind made for lively and stimulating years spent in study with him. I am particularly happy to have participated in Ed's thought-provoking classes on Egyptian religion, where his innovative approach to the fundamentals of the ancient Egyptian world view laid the groundwork for much of my present work in the field. It is in the spirit of his great generosity to us, his former students, that this study is dedicated to him.

During the last decade I have undertaken a program of field research and documentation focusing on fragmentary monuments of Nebmaatre Amenhotep III scattered throughout Egypt, with an emphasis on those which shed light on the nature of his deification while alive.[1] My research indicates that this theological event stimulated significant modifications in the artistic style and iconography of Amenhotep III's royal monument decoration and launched the unparalleled artistic "revolution" of the Amarna period. I suggest elsewhere that the primary mechanism by which Amenhotep III attained his exalted state was his first jubilee celebration in year 30, a jubilee noteworthy for exceptional rites depicted in the Theban tomb of his minister Kheruef.[2] Professor Wente helped document this tomb for publication during his years with the Epigraphic Survey.

DISMANTLING AND REUSE OF AMENHOTEP III'S MONUMENTS

Although the monument-building activities and sculpture programs of Amenhotep III were probably unparalleled in Egyptian history, even during the reign of Ramesses II, most of these monuments were dismantled and dispersed by Amenhotep's successors for reuse in their own building programs after his death. His statuary, from life-size to colossal, was moved, appropriated, and reused; the incredible extent of this appropriation is only now being realized. The Theban area preserves the bulk of this material, but fragments of Amenhotep III's great complexes and sculptures can be found in all the major cult centers of the New Kingdom, from the Delta to the Fourth Cataract in Nubia.[3]

My long-standing association with the Epigraphic Survey in Luxor has allowed me to concentrate my field research in the Theban area, home of the best preserved of Amenhotep III's constructions at Luxor and Karnak temples on the east bank of the Nile. On the west bank, Amenhotep's once-sprawling mortuary complex, the largest ever built, and in its day larger than Karnak, now lies stripped of its sculpture-filled gateways, promenades, open courts, and sanctuaries. All that remains standing are the two sixty-five foot quartzite seated colossi of Amenhotep III that graced the front pylons. Eroded pieces of similar toppled colossi in quartzite and alabaster lie at the sites of other sets of pylon gateways, while the stumps of column bases exposed by Swiss Institute excavations in the 1960s, and a giant quartzite stela re-erected by the Egyptian Antiquities Organization

1. I would like to take this opportunity to thank the Oriental Institute and the Samuel H. Kress Foundation for their invaluable support of this documentation project over the last two years, and former Field Director of the Epigraphic Survey, Peter F. Dorman, for permitting me to discuss some of the reused material from Medinet Habu in this study. Special thanks must go to Yahya Salah Sabr Al-Masri, Director of Antiquities in Sohag, for the photograph of the Akhmim colossal queen. All other photographs and drawings are by the author.

2. Johnson 1993, pp. 231–36; 1996; 1998. For the tomb of Kheruef, see *Kheruef*, p. 43, pl. 24.

3. For the best compendium of Amenhotep III's monuments and sculpture to date, see Kozloff and Bryan 1992.

Gold of Praise: Studies on Ancient Egypt in Honor of Edward F. Wente
Edited by Emily Teeter and John A. Larson
Studies in Ancient Oriental Civilization 58
Chicago: Oriental Institute, 1999

are all that can be seen of the great solar court, three times the size of Amenhotep III's Luxor temple solar court.[4]

The cult of Amenhotep III lapsed after the reign of Horemheb. The mortuary temple, which extended far into the floodplain (where it was exposed to the annual Nile flood, purposefully, it seems), might have started to fall into ruin by the beginning of the Nineteenth Dynasty. Although Ramesses II emulated Amenhotep III's artistic and construction programs, it was this king who nonetheless was responsible for initiating the wholesale quarrying and reuse of Amenhotep III's temple complexes throughout Egypt, including the mortuary complex in Thebes. Ramesses II began by appropriating statuary from Amenhotep's mortuary temple for his own mortuary temple nearby, fragments of which can still be viewed in the ruins of the Ramesseum. Amenhotep's sandstone mortuary temple proper was left untouched, but Ramesses might have quarried one of the limestone satellite shrines in the complex, a program that his son and successor Merneptah continued. Excavations by Petrie (1897, pp. 9–11) in the mortuary temple of Merneptah, and more recently by the Swiss Institute, have exposed great limestone blocks from the north gate of Amenhotep's mortuary complex that might have led to a separate temple of Ptah-Sokar-Osiris.[5] These excavations have also revealed small reused papyrus bundle columns in sandstone, recumbent sandstone jackals on pedestals (also a colossal example in indurated limestone), and limestone androsphinxes of varying sizes reused in Merneptah's foundations. Several colossal statue groups in indurated limestone of Amenhotep III in the company of Queen Tiye and various deities, appropriated by Merneptah and re-inscribed for him, might also have come from this northern precinct.[6]

Ramesses III continued the quarrying of Amenhotep III's mortuary complex for reuse in his own mortuary temple at Medinet Habu. It is interesting to note that while this king appears to have inaugurated the demolition and reuse of Amenhotep's sandstone mortuary temple proper, Amenhotep III's mortuary cult was revived at this time.[7] The rear of Ramesses III's own mortuary temple was constructed at least partly of reused sandstone blocks, although no original decoration survives, and their origins are hence uncertain.[8] The outer mudbrick enclosure wall on the east, however, from a later phase of Ramesses III's construction, was pierced by a small doorway constructed of reused blocks of Amenhotep III, one inscribed with his Horus and *Nebty* names. Since blocks from Amenhotep's great mortuary temple solar court are known to have been reused by Ramesses III in his Khonsu temple at Karnak,[9] it is likely that the reused enclosure-wall door blocks are from Amenhotep III's mortuary temple as well. It is possible that Ramesses III quarried only Amenhotep III's solar court, leaving the rear sanctuary area for the revived cult. Additional remains of the solar court and rear sanctuary area were later demolished and reused in Ptolemaic and Roman additions to the small Amun temple of Hatshepsut and Thutmose III at Medinet Habu.

The likelihood that some of the undecorated blocks might have come from the Amenhotep III temple is bolstered by the fact that many sculptural fragments dating to Amenhotep III were recovered from Medinet Habu. These sculptures were appropriated by Ramesses III for reuse in his own sculpture program and were exposed during the excavations of both Georges Daressy at the turn of the century and the Oriental Institute in the 1920s and 1930s. The sculptures consist of life-size to colossal single-figure statues and statue groups in quartzite, granodiorite, indurated limestone, and various granites. They are now stored in magazines, blockyards, or scattered around the precinct, while a few pieces can be seen in the Egyptian Museum, Cairo, where they were taken by Daressy.[10] In the post-pharaonic period when the temple was the center of the Coptic town of Djeme, much of this sculpture was broken up for reuse in building construction, and almost nothing survives intact. But the isolated fragments can often tell us much about the sculpture programs of both Amenhotep III and Ramesses III. It is such a group of indurated limestone fragments that is the focus of this study.

4. For a preliminary report of the excavations and sculptural remains, see Haeny 1981.

5. The site of the north gate is marked by two fallen striding colossi of Amenhotep in quartzite visible in the cultivation. For a report on the Amenhotep III material, see Bickel 1997.

6. The reused Amenhotep III statuary is being prepared for publication by Dr. Hourig Sourouzian for the Swiss Institute.

7. See Graindorge-Héreil 1994, pp. 66–71, for a list of individuals from this time associated with the mortuary cult and the Ptah-Sokar cult.

8. I thank James B. Heidel for this observation. Dovetail cramp emplacements visible on the top surfaces of exposed wall blocks often do not line up or correspond to Ramesses III's walls, indicating an earlier date for the blocks.

9. These were reused along with blocks from the mortuary temples of Horemheb and Amenhotep Son of Hapu, among other structures. The Amenhotep III mortuary temple solar-court blocks feature detailed, small-scale jubilee scenes; see Borchardt 1926, pp. 37–51.

10. See, for example, Bryan 1994, pp. 25–30. Ramesses III's workmen re-inscribed the pieces and in many cases even modified the facial features.

INDURATED LIMESTONE COLOSSI OF AMENHOTEP III REUSED AT MEDINET HABU

The second court of Ramesses III's mortuary temple preserves two large statue emplacements made of sandstone blocks that are located on either side of the low, central ramp leading up to the back portico and main sanctuary area. The southern emplacement on the left is empty, but the northern emplacement on the right still preserves fragments of the indurated limestone pedestal of a colossal seated king. Broken outlines of the feet and throne are visible on the upper surface. Based on the elements that survive, Hölscher (1941, p. 9, pl. 38B) calculates that the northern colossus was ten to eleven meters in height, with a similar statue pendant to it on the south side of the ramp. The sides of the pedestal are inscribed with rows of kneeling nome gods and goddesses bearing food offerings. The style of the nome gods, which is paralleled by other relief work of Amenhotep III,[11] indicates that the sculpture belongs to the time of Amenhotep III and not Ramesses III. Amenhotep III favored this particular type of hard, glassy limestone, which was popular in the late Eighteenth Dynasty but was rarely utilized for sculpture later. I have documented two additional fragments from this statue elsewhere in the administrative area north and outside of the court: the very top of a colossal white crown (probably part of a double crown)[12] and part of the throne front with erased original inscription and broken outline of the stone that connected the left leg to the throne.[13] Because the sculpture's height was even by conservative estimates at least as high as the court and substantially larger than the portal to that court, it is likely that Ramesses III first moved the statue and its mate into place and then constructed his court around them, which indicates that the appropriation of Amenhotep III's sculpture was part of the earliest stages of Ramesses III's mortuary temple program.

I have documented two other fragments of a second colossal statue in indurated limestone in the same area which suggest that the southern mate to the seated king was a seated queen. One fragment is a colossal ankle and back heel, proportionally somewhat smaller than the seated king.[14] The second fragment is part of a female torso that preserves six rows of an elaborate beaded necklace or collar from the area of the chest between the breasts (figs. 21.1–2).[15] The material, scale, fine carving, and finish of the two fragments is stylistically in keeping with other indurated limestone sculptures of Amenhotep III, and the original statue was undoubtedly a colossus of Queen Tiye. The source for the two colossal statues was in all probability the great southern gateway of Amenhotep III's mortuary complex located near Medinet Habu. At that site Daressy found a similar seated dyad of Amenhotep III and Tiye in pieces at the turn of the century (fig. 21.3); it was over seven meters in height and accompanied by smaller standing figures of three daughters (the closest parallel to our fragments).[16] It is likely that Ramesses III was following the program of his predecessor Ramesses II, whose first court was dominated by two similar colossi in granite of the seated king and his mother.[17] It is probable that our statue was re-inscribed for the mother of Ramesses III.

NFRW-COLLAR

The fragment of the chest with necklace must have belonged to a colossal statue of a queen, which is indicated by a slight concavity from the space between the breasts and also by the form of an unusual necklace that is found only on the statuary of women (figs. 21.1–2). The necklace is reminiscent of the *wsḫ*-collar that features multiple rows of vertical cylindrical beads terminating in an outer row of drop beads, except that here the cylindrical beads have been replaced with vertical paddle- or spoon-shaped hieroglyphs that traditionally have been interpreted as rows of *nfr*-hieroglyphs ("beautiful") despite the absence of a crossbar at the top, an interpretation reinforced by its presence on statues of females. The spacer elements between each row of spoon-shaped beads in our fragment consist of two horizontal lines sandwiching a single row of small disks.[18]

11. See, for example, the Nile gods decorating the sides of Amenhotep III's "Memnon" colossi, "Nebmaatre Ruler of the Rulers"; also the nome gods on the base of the Karnak tenth pylon colossus of Amenhotep III, "Nebmaatre Montu of the Rulers" (Clère, Ménassa, and Deleuze 1975, pp. 159–66).
12. Height: 35.5 cm; width: 38.5 cm; depth: ca. 20.0 cm.
13. Height: 68.25 cm; width: 64.0 cm; depth: ca. 27.0 cm.
14. Height: 58.0 cm; width: 30.0 cm; depth: ca. 30.0 cm.
15. Height: 49.0 cm; width: 15.0 cm at the top, 12.0 cm at the bottom; depth: ca. 49.0 cm.
16. The seated dyad has been restored in the central atrium of the Cairo Museum; see Trad and Mahmoud 1995, pp. 40–45.
17. For a recent analysis of the colossal sculpture program of Ramesses II in the first court of the Ramesseum, see Leblanc 1994, pp. 71–101.
18. Dimensions, from the bottom: bottom (double line and disks) spacer element: 2.00 cm; terminal row drop beads: 6.25 cm;

Figure 21.1. Fragment of Colossal Queen Sculpture from Time of Amenhotep III, Reused by Ramesses III at Medinet Habu; Indurated Limestone

Figure 21.2. Necklace Detail of Colossal Queen Statue Fragment Showing Spoon-shaped and Drop Beads; Indurated Limestone

Sculptures bearing this particular necklace are few, and by far the majority of them date from the reign of Amenhotep III. The colossal Tiye figure of the great dyad in the Cairo Museum atrium is wearing exactly the same collar as our fragment (fig. 21.3),[19] as are the royal couple's three smaller-scaled daughters, Henuttaneb, Nebta, and one other (name destroyed), who stand against the throne. Fragments of a similar, although somewhat smaller, indurated limestone colossus of Queen Tiye wearing the collar were found in the mortuary temple of Merneptah where the figure was appropriated for reuse by that king.[20] Another daughter of Amenhotep III, Princess Isis, is depicted wearing a version of the collar (without the terminal row of drop beads) on a serpentine statuette that was part of a standing group statue of the princess, Amenhotep III (whose right foot is preserved), and perhaps Queen Tiye.[21] The so-called "white queen" (JE 31413/CG 600), found in 1896 by Petrie in the ruins of a mudbrick chapel north of the Ramesseum and dated to the reign of Ramesses II, also has the collar, carved in a style almost identical to that found on the statuary of Amenhotep III's family.[22] It is probable that the statue is a reworked Eighteenth Dynasty piece (with face extensively recarved). If it is original to the reign of Ramesses II, it is the only royal Ramesside parallel for the necklace of spoon-shaped beads.

The colossal statue inscribed for Ramesses II's daughter Merit-Amun (fig. 21.4), which was found at Akhmim in 1982 and has a variation of the necklace, is a usurped piece dating to the late Eighteenth Dynasty,

spacer element: 2.00 cm; bead row: 5.00 cm; spacer element: 2.00 cm; bead row: 4.75 cm; spacer element: 2.00 cm; bead row: 4.60 cm; spacer element: 2.00 cm; bead row: 4.75 cm; spacer element: 2.00 cm; bead row: 4.75 cm.

19. In fact so close is the pattern of the necklace that I checked to make sure that our fragment did not come from the Cairo Museum dyad; it does not; see Trad and Mahmoud 1995, p. 44, line drawing by Khaled Amin.

20. Personal communication, Hourig Sourouzian.

21. The George Ortiz Collection; Bryan 1992, pp. 206–08.

22. Saleh and Sourouzian 1987, catalog no. 208.

Figure 21.3. Family Group of Amenhotep III, Tiye, and Three Daughters Found by Daressy in Vicinity of Medinet Habu, Nos. 610 and JE 33906; Indurated Limestone. Courtesy Egyptian Museum, Cairo

Figure 21.4. Colossal Eighteenth Dynasty Queen Usurped by Ramesses II for His Daughter Merit-Amun, Akhmim; Indurated Limestone. Courtesy Yahya Salah Sabr Al-Masri, Director of Antiquities in Sohag

based on its style and shaved-down back support, and cannot be used as evidence that Ramesses II revived the use of the collar device in colossal sculpture.[23] The form of the collar on the Akhmim colossus gives us a valuable clue about its true nature. From the bottom, the collar is made up of a terminal row of pendant lotus petals, then a row of spoon-shaped beads, then another row of pendant lotus petals, then a row of disks or *išd*-fruit (fig. 21.5). The curving handle of the queen's lily scepter obscures two rows, but the top row appears to be more lotus petals. The rows are separated by a raised double border line, which is also found beneath the terminal row of lotus petals.

The Akhmim colossus links the paddle-shaped beads with the floral *w3ḥ n(y) m3ʿ-ḫrw*-collar, the collar of "justification," or "true of voice," associated with Osiris and the funerary cult.[24] It is directly related to a similar necklace on the anthropoid coffins and funerary mask of Thuya, mother of Queen Tiye, the only instance that I know where the spoon-shaped beads are found on a coffin.[25] Thuya's mummy mask (JE 95254/CG 51009) features a splendid gilded collar inlaid with polychrome glass, topped by a row of spoon-shaped beads, beneath which follow a row of pendant palmettes, three rows of pendant lotus petals, and a drop-bead terminus.[26] Her second coffin (CG 51006) features a similar elaborate collar with the third row down from the top made up of spoon-shaped beads and the rest consisting of pendant lotus petals, palmettes, and a row of drop beads (fig. 21.6). The third coffin (CG 51007) features two rows of the spoon-shaped beads at the top, followed by a row of

23. Al-Masri 1983, pp. 4–13, pls. 1–9; for the stylistic analysis linking the Akhmim colossus to the late Eighteenth Dynasty, see Johnson 1995, p. 148.
24. See *LÄ* 3 "Ma'a-cheru," cols. 1107–10; also *LÄ* 3 "Kranz der Rechtfertigung," col. 764.
25. The floral *w3ḥ*-collar becomes a standard feature of anthropoid coffins from the Nineteenth Dynasty onward, but without the spoon-shaped bead elements.
26. For the best photograph (in color, and after cleaning), see Saleh and Sourouzian 1987, catalog no. 145.

Figure 21.5. Schematic Rendering of Akhmim Colossus Collar, Bottom Three Rows of Beads

Figure 21.6. Detail of Necklace/Collar from Second Coffin of Thuya, Mother of Queen Tiye, CG 51006; Gilded and Inlaid Wood. Courtesy Egyptian Museum, Cairo

pendant palmettes, cornflowers, and lotus petals.[27] I know of one earlier example of the device that appears in the collar decoration of a female mummy mask in the Metropolitan Museum of Art, MMA 30.8.68 (found with male mummy mask 30.8.68, Theodore M. Davis 1915 bequest, Thutmoside in date). The elaborate collar is made up of four rows of spoon-shaped beads with a terminus row of drop beads, all painted gold against bands of green, blue, and red (see Hayes 1959, p. 223, fig. 132).

The device appears on the collars of at least two other statues. On the first, BM 484, the upper part of a granodiorite statue of a noble lady holding a *menat*-necklace, her floral collar consists of five rows of beads topped by an upper row of the spoon-shaped beads.[28] The second piece, a life-size indurated limestone bust of a noblewoman, Cincinnati Art Museum 1966.266, sports a similar floral collar, this time featuring six rows of beads, but again with the uppermost row made up of the spoon- or paddle-shaped beads (fig. 21.7; see Capel and Markoe 1996, pp. 169–72, cat. no. 92).

The spoon-shaped beads depicted on the statuary, masks, and Thuya's coffins represent real bead necklaces, a few examples of which have survived. A gold collar from the Tomb of the Three Princesses (Metropolitan Museum of Art 26.28.135A, 1982.137.3), inscribed on the shoulder pieces with the prenomen of Thutmose III, is of the type of which all but one row are made up of the spoon-shaped hieroglyphs (Aldred 1971, pl. 66). In 1966 the Egyptian Museum of Turin x-rayed the two mummies found in the intact burial of the architect Kha and his wife Merit (TT 8, time of Amenhotep III), discovered at Deir el-Medina by Ernesto Schiaparelli in 1906. The x-rays showed that both mummies were bedecked with fine jewelry, Kha with a single strand *shebyu*-collar of large gold disk beads, plus assorted earrings, armbands, bracelets, and amulets. Merit's jewelry included an elaborate floral collar of faience and precious stones arranged in seven rows. The top row consists of the paddle-shaped beads.[29] A collar of gold and electrum with some glass inlay (CG 52674), found on the body

27. Quibell 1908, pls. 11–12; compare with Yuya's coffin collars that do not feature the device (ibid., pls. 4–5).

28. Preserved height is 17.5 inches. Note that the face has been completely recarved, possibly in the late Ramesside period, with resultant wear to the inner edges of the great wig which frames her face (author's observation).

29. For x-ray photographs, see Forbes 1998, p. 247. For a detailed drawing of Merit's necklace based on the x-rays, see Egyptian Museum of Turin 1987, p. 229, fig. 321.

Figure 21.7. Schematic Rendering of Collar on Indurated Limestone Bust of Noblewoman. Cincinnati Art Museum 1966.266

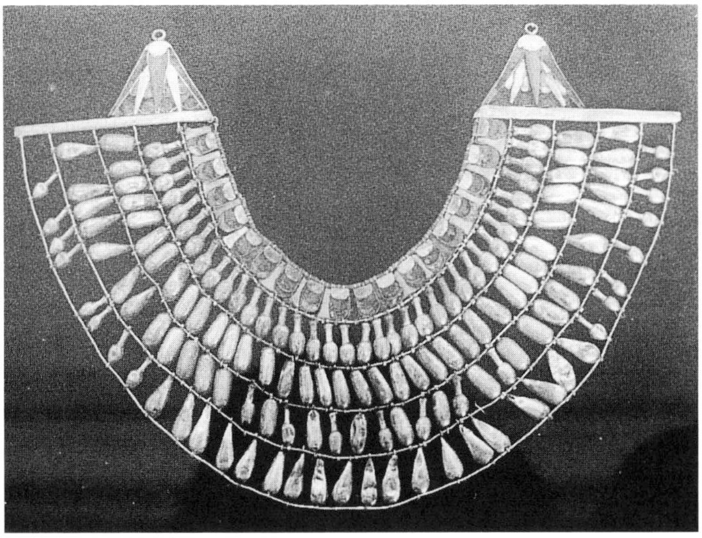

Figure 21.8. Gold, Electrum, and Glass Inlay Collar Found on Mummy in KV 55, CG 52674. Courtesy Egyptian Museum, Cairo

of the mummy in KV 55, features at least one row of spoon-shaped beads, as well as tubular and drop beads (fig. 21.8; see Aldred 1971, pl. 71).

While examining eight polychrome faience-bead *wꜣḫ*-collars from the tomb of Tutankhamun on display in the Egyptian Museum, Cairo, I discovered two faience necklaces that contained these beads. On one (#948) the upper row is made of red spoon-shaped beads, and the other rows are made up of cartouche-shaped, grape-cluster, and lotus-petal beads. The other (#945), however, features a row of green *nfr*-signs with distinct crossbars at the top, and a bottom row made up of identical green *nfr*-signs next to yellow spoon-shaped beads (fig. 21.9). In this necklace, the ancient artisans made a clear distinction between the spoon-shaped sign and the *nfr*-sign, and their differentiation here suggests that the two signs were not meant to be interpreted as the same device.

A unique, painted representation of the true *nfr*-sign in a collar appears in the tomb of Ramesses II's chief queen Nefertari (QV 66). Two figures of the queen on either side of the burial-chamber stairwell wear elaborate, painted *wꜣḫ*-collars that contain a single row of true *nfr*-signs, carefully drawn with crossbars (fig. 21.10).[30] This is the only instance in which the device occurs in any royal form firmly dated to the Ramesside period and is a further indication that the spoon-shaped sign was not utilized after the late Eighteenth Dynasty.

Although others might have existed, I have found only one statue where the true *nfr*-sign has been worked into a collar, and it is from the early Ramesside period. The limestone pair statue of Yuni and Renenutet (MMA 15.2.1), from the time of Seti I, depicts Yuni's wife Renenutet wearing an elaborate floral collar arranged in five rows, beneath two strands of small beads. The upper row of the collar is made up of true, unmistakable *nfr*-signs carved in high raised relief (fig. 21.11).[31]

30. The queen offers to two sets of goddesses in these scenes, to Isis and Nephthys on the left, and to Hathor and Selkit on the right; see PM 1/2, 764 (22, 23); Goedicke 1971, figs. 46, 53, 145. For an excellent color photograph of the queen's figure on the left, with collar, see Forbes 1996, p. 23.

31. MMA, Rogers Fund, 1915, 15.2.1; height: 84.5 cm (Capel and Markoe 1996, pp. 172–74, cat. no. 93).

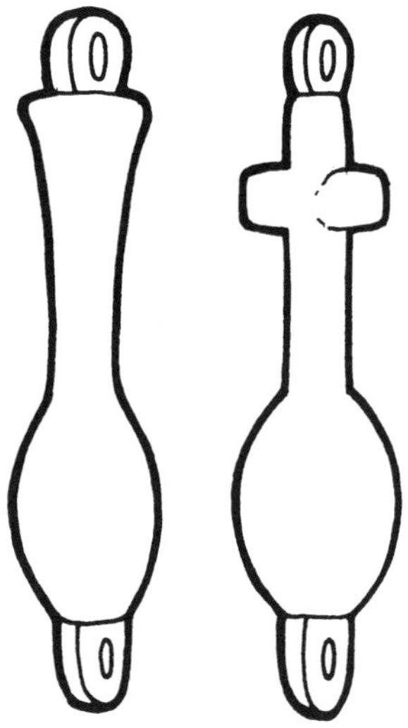

Figure 21.9. Schematic Rendering of Two Types of Faience Beads Found in Faience Collar Tut 945 from Tomb of Tutankhamun. Egyptian Museum, Cairo

Figure 21.10. Figure of Queen Wearing Necklace with Real *Nfr*-signs (second row from top). Nefertari's Tomb, West Wall, Descending Corridor

THE *WꜣḤ*-COLLAR

The association of the spoon-shaped sign with the *wꜣḥ*-collar in the necklaces, sculptures, and coffins mentioned above suggests that the proper reading of the element is not *nfr*, but *ḫrw*, and the sign is the *ḫrw*-oar meaning "voice," as in "true of voice" (Gardiner 1973, p. 499, P8). That the device is found almost exclusively on mid- to late-Eighteenth Dynasty sculptures of queens, the coffin of the mother of a queen, and in queenly and high-status burials suggests that the *ḫrw*-collar was a rare form of the floral *wꜣḥ* or *wꜣḥ n*(*y*) *mꜣꜥ-ḫrw*-collar.

The floral *wꜣḥ*-collar was studied at great length by Martha Bell, who wrote that it is first mentioned in the Pyramid Texts as being placed around the head as a headband, or the neck as a collar. In the New Kingdom it could be spelled *mꜣḥ* and is found in the expression *wꜣḥ n*(*y*) *mꜣꜥ-ḫrw*, the "collar of justification," associated with Osiris and the vindicated dead. An elaborate example made of real lotus petals and leaves sewn on papyrus was found in the burial of Tutankhamun around the neck of his innermost, anthropoid coffin, and additional real floral collars were found in an embalming cache from a pit outside of the tomb; perhaps these collars were worn by the participants of a funerary repast in honor of the deceased king (Hepper 1990, pp. 9–10). Bell (1987, p. 57; 1988, p. 20) cites a text from the portable chest of Tutankhamun that explains the function of the floral collar as a symbol of regeneration and rebirth:

> May you take the *wꜣḥ*-collar of justification which was at the neck of Wennefer (that is Osiris) (so that) your limbs may become young and your heart may become strong (again) when you are examined/assessed by the Ennead.

While the lotus-petal *wꜣ*ḥ-collar without the *ḫrw*-signs was depicted on figures of Amenhotep III in his royal monument decoration, among other iconographic innovations, to express his own rejuvenation and timeless divinity after his deification in year 30,[32] the *ḫrw*-collar was utilized for the female members of his family who

32. Prior to Amenhotep III's last decade, the *wꜣḥ nỉ mꜣʾ-ḫrw*-collar is never utilized in royal, non-funerary monument decoration because of its Osiride and funerary associations. It is, however, found on royal figures depicted in private

played an essential part in that deification program and also shared in its benefits.[33] During this time Queen Tiye and the royal daughters took on the aspect of Egypt's goddesses and the iconographic accoutrement associated with those goddesses, such as the horned, plumed crown with sun disk associated with Hathor that Tiye, in her role as consort of the sun god, especially favored. The *ḫrw*-collar was utilized at this time to show the divine status of the living royal women, stressing their role as the source of all life, and their special relationship to the sun god. The *ḫrw*-collar with its Osirian connection to rebirth and rejuvenation goes back at least to the reign of Thutmose III when it was associated with royal wives and their role in the continuation and perpetuation of life, even after death. The gold *ḫrw*-collar found among the burial goods of these wives might even have been, at that time, specifically funerary in nature.[34] One cannot help but wonder if another phonetic association of the oar hieroglyph, *wsrw*, which means "oars," may have been utilized as an intentional pun on the name of Osiris, *Wsỉr*, further emphasizing the Osiris connection. Osiris as the horizon can be a female counterpart to the male sun, and it may be that this particular sexual association is being stressed in the *ḫrw*-variation of the *wꜣḫ*-collar (Darnell 1995, p. 594, n. 145). Should we perhaps be referring to the collar as the *wsrw*-collar?

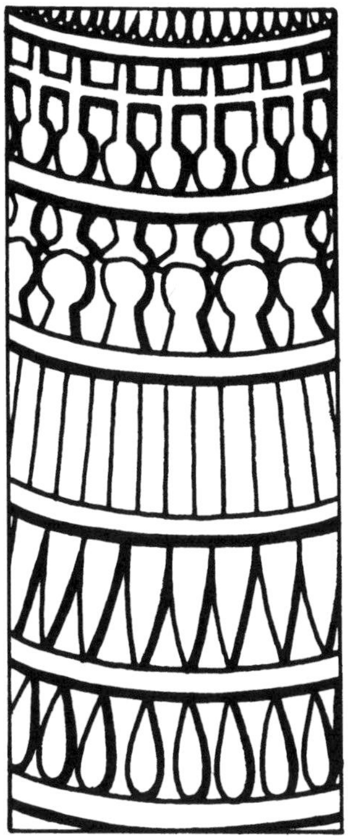

Figure 21.11. Schematic Rendering of Renenutet (MMA 15.2.1) Collar with *Nfr*-signs (Top)

Outside of the two faience collars found in Tutankhamun's tomb, there is only one other documented instance of the *ḫrw*-collar associated with a presumed male, on the mummy found in KV 55, CG 52674 (fig. 21.8; see Aldred 1971, pl. 71), made of gold and electrum inlaid with polychrome glass. One possibility is that the collar (and the vulture pectoral found on the mummy's head) was part of Queen Tiye's burial equipment and was placed on the KV 55 mummy by a sympathetic soul at the time Queen Tiye's body was removed from KV 55. Or its presence could indicate that the mummy was thought to be female at the time of burial. It may be that, like the faience *ḫrw*-beaded collars in Tutankhamun's tomb, both burials contained a mishmash of unwanted objects associated with an episode in Egyptian history best forgotten, and whose original significance had become irrelevant.[35]

---

tombs from the time of Amenhotep II onward in scenes showing the king enshrined in a timeless state of being where he is merged with the creator/sun god and is wearing a specific costume which underscores that association: *shebyu*- and *wꜣḫ*-collars, falcon-tail sporrans, looped and hanging sashes on either side of his sporran, sun-disk-crowned sporran uraei, etc.

33. After his jubilee/deification rites Amenhotep III ruled as a new kind of king, a living manifestation of all of Egypt's gods, including Osiris, with a strong emphasis on the creator/sun god Atum-Re, while his son Amenhotep IV/Akhenaten took on the aspect of Shu, firstborn of the creator god, male and female combined. The art style and iconography of both kings changed radically in a conscious effort to reflect this theological event. These parallel changes supported the long joint rule of both kings, a seeming requirement of Amenhotep III's deification program based on the mythological model that Atum cannot exist without Shu, whose "birth" or separation from his father caused both deities to come into existence; see *LÄ* 5 "Schu," col. 735.

34. Many of the other iconographic devices later adapted by Amenhotep III for his deification iconography derived from funerary contexts.

35. Another small set of gold *ḫrw*-beads was recently found in the Memphite tomb of the vizier Aper-El. They were part of a beaded faience and glass headband found preserved in a mass of bitumen at the bottom of what may have been Aper-El's own wooden sarcophagus, among other bits of gold foil and jewelry. The burial chamber was in great disarray from ancient looting when excavated, so it is uncertain whether the owner of the headband was Aper-El or his wife Taweret; see Zivie 1993, p. 11; Looten-Lacoudre 1993, pp. 17–23.

CONCLUSIONS

Amenhotep III's deification was a theological event shared by his entire family, including the royal women, and was deemed significant enough to require a new artistic and iconographic vocabulary to express it. This vocabulary, which was based on earlier or traditional solar/funerary iconography, continued to change and evolve in what seems a very un-Egyptian fashion, culminating in what we generally refer to as Akhenaten's artistic "revolution."

One of the chief iconographic devices that was utilized to indicate Amenhotep III's deified status while alive was the *shebyu*-collar of gold-disk beads, traditionally awarded to deserving male members of the court who had served their king exceptionally well. The symbolism is clear; when a private individual received the "collar of gold" from the king, his status in the court was raised several notches. When the king was depicted wearing the device, the intention was to show the king's uplifted status as a god. Hence, the device was used to show the king in private tombs of high officials in eternal, *djet*-time in his potential, postmortem, deified state, with the favored tomb owner serving him for eternity. Thutmose IV, who would probably have gone through the rites of deification-while-alive himself had he lived long enough, is the first king depicted wearing the *shebyu*-collar and arm bands in a non-funerary monument, on a relief from Giza where he is shown worshipping the Great Sphinx/Horemakhet. The intention here was to show his identification with that god.[36] At least thirty years were to pass before the device was used again in a non-funerary monument, by the deified Amenhotep III. What then of the *ḫrw*-collar worn by the female members of Amenhotep III's family that proclaimed their own special divinity?

The evidence suggests that in the Eighteenth Dynasty the *ḫrw*-collar represented the same uplifted court status for honored women that the *shebyu*-collar represented for favored men. It is found at least as far back as the *shebyu*-collar, the time of Thutmose III, in the form of real necklaces associated with Thutmose's wives' burials, and is represented prominently on the mummy mask of at least one noblewoman of that time. Both Yuya and Thuya's mummies were found despoiled of their jewelry, but the opened bandages at the head and neck areas of both individuals indicate that both were wearing necklaces which were robbed. The presence of the *ḫrw*-collar on Thuya's coffins suggests that she probably was wearing a real *ḫrw*-collar, just as Yuya was undoubtedly wearing a gold *shebyu*-collar, both reflecting their exceptional status as the parents of the principal queen.

The intact mummies of Kha and Merit in Turin give us our strongest evidence of the association of the two sets of necklaces, since the x-rays reveal that Kha is wearing a *shebyu*-collar and that Merit is wearing the *ḫrw*-necklace. It is logical that Amenhotep III would utilize the female equivalent of the *shebyu*-collar to indicate the uplifted state of his wife and daughters.

But in this mercurial period even the boundaries between male and female iconography could blur. By the time of Amenhotep III's third jubilee in year 37, Queen Tiye is depicted at least once enthroned beside her husband wearing a double *shebyu*-necklace similar to that of the deified king.[37] To this author's knowledge it is the only instance where a queen is ever shown wearing the *shebyu*-necklace, and it underscores the extraordinary nature of Tiye's own divinity and identification with her husband.[38]

The ongoing documentation and analysis of Nebmaatre Amenhotep III's sculpture reused at Medinet Habu is allowing a clearer understanding of the mortuary-temple sculpture programs of both Amenhotep III and Ramesses III, as well as the thought behind those programs. The *ḫrw*-collar problem is only a tiny piece of a very large puzzle, but even the smallest pieces add to the whole. It is with heartfelt gratitude that I dedicate this study to the man who will always be an inspiration, and who taught me to always ask "why?"

36. According to Hassan (1953, fig. 17), the relief, which shows back-to-back figures of the god being worshipped by Thutmose IV, was probably the upper part of a limestone stela.

37. *Kheruef*, pl. 51. Only Nefertiti ever shared in the divine nature of her husband quite to this extreme.

38. Only two noblewomen are so far known to have been depicted wearing the *shebyu*-necklace, and not coincidentally, both were royal nurses: Ay's wife Tiye, the nurse of Nefertiti, shown wearing the necklace in the couple's private tomb at Amarna; and the nurse of Tutankhamun, Maya(t), in her recently discovered tomb at Saqqara. Thanks to Maya(t)'s discoverer, Alain Zivie, for this observation.

References

Aldred, C.

1971 *Jewels of the Pharaohs: Egyptian Jewelry of the Dynastic Period.* London: Thames and Hudson.

Bell, M.

1987 "Regional Variations in Polychrome Pottery of the Nineteenth Dynasty." *Cahiers de la céramique égyptienne* 1: 49–76.

1988 "Floral Collars, *Wꜣḥ ny Mꜣꜥ Ḫrw* in the Eighteenth Dynasty." In *Abstracts of Papers* (Fifth International Congress of Egyptology), edited by A. Cherif, p. 20. Cairo: International Association of Egyptologists.

Bickel, S.

1997 *Untersuchungen im Totentempel des Merenptah in Theben,* 3: *Tore und andere wiederverwendete Bauteile Amenophis' III.* Beiträge zur ägyptischen Bauforschung und Altertumskunde 16. Stuttgart: Franz Steiner Verlag.

Borchardt, L.

1926 "Jubiläumsbilder, 2: Verbaute Blöcke aus dem Chons-Tempel in Karnak." *Zeitschrift für ägyptische Sprache und Altertumskunde* 61: 37–51.

Bryan, B. M.

1992 "Princess Isis." In *Egypt's Dazzling Sun: Amenhotep III and His World,* edited by A. P. Kozloff and B. M. Bryan, pp. 206–08. Cleveland: Cleveland Museum of Art.

1994 "Amenhotep III United in Eternity: A Join for Two Statue Parts from Medinet Habu." In *Essays in Egyptology in Honor of Hans Goedicke,* edited by B. M. Bryan and D. Lorton, pp. 25–30. San Antonio: Van Siclen Books.

Capel, A. K., and G. E. Markoe, eds.

1996 *Mistress of the House, Mistress of Heaven: Women in Ancient Egypt.* New York: Hudson Hills Press in association with Cincinnati Art Museum.

Clère, P.; L. Ménassa; and P. Deleuze

1975 "Le socle du colosse oriental dressé devant le Xe pylône de Karnak." *Karnak* 5 (1970–1972): 159–68.

Darnell, J. C.

1995 The Enigmatic Netherworld Books of the Solar-Osirian Unity: Cryptographic Compositions in the Tombs of Tutankhamun, Ramesses VI, and Ramesses IX. Ph.D. dissertation, University of Chicago.

Egyptian Museum of Turin

1987 *Egyptian Civilization: Daily Life.* Edited by A. M. Donadoni Roveri. Milan: Electa.

Forbes, D. C.

1996 "Editor's Special Report." *KMT: A Modern Journal of Ancient Egypt* 7, no. 1: 15–29, 74–79.

1998 *Tombs. Treasures. Mummies. Seven Great Discoveries of Egyptian Archaeology.* Sebastopol: KMT Communications.

Gardiner, A. H.

1973 *Egyptian Grammar.* Third edition revised. Oxford: Griffith Institute.

Goedicke, H.

1971 *Nofretari: A Documentation of Her Tomb and Its Decoration.* Graz: Akademische Druck.

Graindorge-Héreil, C.

1994 *Le dieu Sokar à Thèbes au Nouvel Empire.* Göttinger Orientforschungen 28. Wiesbaden: Otto Harrassowitz.

Haeny, G., ed.

1981 *Untersuchungen im Totentempel Amenophis' III.* Beiträge zur ägyptischen Bauforschung und Altertumskunde 11. Wiesbaden: Franz Steiner Verlag.

Hassan, S.

1953 *Excavations at Giza, 1936–1937,* Volume 8: *The Great Sphinx and Its Secrets.* Cairo: Government Press.

Hayes, W. C.

1959 *Scepter of Egypt* 2: *The Hyksos Period and the New Kingdom.* New York: Metropolitan Museum of Art.

Hepper, F. N.

1990 *Pharaoh's Flowers: The Botanical Treasures of Tutankhamun.* London: Her Majesty's Stationary Office.

Hölscher, U.

1941 *The Excavation of Medinet Habu,* Volume 3: *The Mortuary Temple of Ramses III,* Part 1. Oriental Institute Publications 54. Chicago: University of Chicago Press.

Jaritz, H.

1994 "What Petrie Missed." *Egyptian Archaeology: Bulletin of the Egypt Exploration Society* 5: 14–16.

Jaritz, H., and S. Bickel

1994 "Une porte monumentale d'Amenhotep III: Second rapport préliminaire sur les blocs réemployés dans le temple de Merenptah à Gourna." *Bulletin de l'Institut français d'archéologie orientale* 94: 277–85.

Johnson, W. R.

1993 "The Deified Amenhotep III as the Living Re-Horakhty: Stylistic and Iconographic Considerations." In *Atti del sesto congresso internazionale di egittologia,* volume 2, edited by G. M. Zaccone and T. R. di Netro, pp. 231–36. Turin: n.p.

1995 "Hidden Kings and Queens in the Luxor Temple Cachette." *KMT Communications: Amarna Letters* 3: 129–49.

1996 "Amenhotep III and Amarna: Some New Considerations." *Journal of Egyptian Archaeology* 82: 65–82.

1998 "Monuments and Monumental Art Under Amenhotep III: Evolution and Meaning." In *Amenhotep III: Perspectives on His Reign,* edited by D. O'Connor and E. H. Cline, pp. 63–94. Ann Arbor: University of Michigan Press.

Kozloff, A. P., and B. M. Bryan

1992 *Egypt's Dazzling Sun: Amenhotep III and His World.* Cleveland: Cleveland Museum of Art.

Leblanc, C.

1993/94 "Les sources grecques et les colosses de Ramses Rê-en-Hekaou et de Touy, au ramesseum." *Memnonia: Bulletin édité par l'Association pour la sauvegarde du ramesseum* 4/5: 71–101.

Looten-Lacoudre, V.
1993 "Fouille et restauration de bijoux nouvellement découverts dans le matériel de la chambre funéraire d'ʿAper-El." *Bulletin de la Société française d'égyptologie* 126: 17–23.

al-Masri, Y. S. S.
1983 "Preliminary Report on the Excavations in Akhmim by the Egyptian Antiquities Organization." *Annales du Service des antiquités de l'Égypte* 69: 4–13.

Petrie, W. F.
1897 *Six Temples at Thebes*. London: B. Quaritch.

Quibell, M. J. E.
1908 *The Tomb of Yuaa and Thuiu*. Catalogue général des antiquités égyptiennes du Musée du Caire, nos. 51001–51191. Cairo: Institut français d'archéologie orientale.

Russmann, E. R.
1995 "A Second Style in Egyptian Art of the Old Kingdom." *Mitteilungen des Deutschen archäologischen Instituts, Abteilung Kairo* 51: 269–79.

Saleh, M., and H. Sourouzian
1987 *The Egyptian Museum, Cairo: Official Catalogue*. Mainz: Philipp von Zabern.

Trad, M., and A. Mahmoud
1995 "Amenhotep III in the Egyptian Museum, Cairo." *KMT: A Modern Journal of Ancient Egypt* 6, no. 3: 40–50.

Zivie, A.
1993 "ʿAper-El, Taouret et Houy: La Fouille et l'enquête continuent." *Bulletin de la Société française d'égyptologie* 126: 5–16.

22

THE WEALTH OF AMUN OF THEBES UNDER RAMESSES II

K. A. KITCHEN

The University of Liverpool, United Kingdom

The wealth and opulence of imperial Thebes, and especially of Amun-Ra, during the New Kingdom is a commonplace of Egyptology. The monumental stelae and dedicatory inscriptions of the Eighteenth Dynasty and Ramesside kings speak of vast and noble temples incorporating choice stone and valuable timbers, of handsome endowments, of magnificent shrines and statuary, and of sacred barques glittering with gold and gems. But the details of real estate, agricultural wealth, and personnel that sustained all this pomp are mostly veiled from our gaze, visible only in part and at intervals, in such documents as the great P. Harris I (Ramesses III/IV), P. Wilbour (Ramesses V), and the often fragmentary contents of Alan Gardiner's *Ramesside Administrative Documents* (Ramesses II–XI, passim). When compared in detail with some of these documents, the little-studied text of Ostracon Gardiner 86 yields results that may be worthy of notice in gaining some idea of the wealth of the god Amun during the long reign of Ramesses II.

OSTRACON GARDINER 86

Translation

Recto

[1] The Royal Scribe and Chief of the Treasury [...], Panehsy, who is in the northern region, [speaks to the prophet ...] [2] of Amun in the southern city, Hori:

> "Greetings! This is a communication to inform you of the [state of the possessions of] [3] the domain of Amun, which are here under my authority, in the northern region, beginning from the door [of ... , down to] [4] the (northern) extremiti(es) of the Delta, (and) by the three streams, on the great river, [the western river], [5] and the water(s) of Avaris, namely the occupations(?) of every man of the domain of Amun, i.e., [the cultivators] [6] and herdsmen of every (class of) livestock that is in the pasture, which belong to the domain of Amun in the southern city, namely:
>
> > [Cultivators], [7] cowherds, goatherds, shepherds, swineherds, donkey- [8] drov[ers], mule(?)-drovers, fowl-keepers, fishermen, [9] fowlers, vintagers, salt-collectors, natron-gatherers, foragers(?), [10] who are in the papyrus beds, cutting reeds-for-matting, and rope-makers."

[11] [I] hereby forward the list of them, every man of them according to [his occupa]tion(?), [with their wives] [12] and their offspring. The list of them is [in the possession of the steward?] [13] of the house of (Queen) Tiyi, may she live, in the estate of Amun (of?) Bak-puy, I having [...]. [14] I have assessed what is due in taxes, and I have fo[und (the amount of) their produce? ...]. [15] [...] people [...].

Verso

[1] [...] in regnal year 24, 1st month of summer, day 21, under the majesty of the king of Upper and Lower Egypt, [Usimare Setepenre, l.p.h., son of Ra, Ramesses II Miamun, l.p.h., given life for ever and ever.]

[2] [In]forming the Prophet Hori of them, (of) each man according to his occupation(?). The summary [of the property of the domain of Amun in the northern region?]:

> [3] [Cultiva]tors, 8,760 men, each of them producing 200 sacks of barley; cowherds, [...] men, [4] [in charge of ca]ttle, namely a drove for each man of them, (each) in charge of 500 animals;

Gold of Praise: Studies on Ancient Egypt in Honor of Edward F. Wente
Edited by Emily Teeter and John A. Larson
Studies in Ancient Oriental Civilization 58
Chicago: Oriental Institute, 1999

goatherds, 13,080 men, [each of them in charge of ... goats]; [5] fowl-[keepers], 22,530 men, each of them in charge of 34,230 birds; fishermen, [... men], their [product [6] (reckoned)] at 3 *deben* of silver annually; the donkey-drovers, 3,920 [+ *x*] men, [each of them [7] in charge of] 870 (beasts); the mule(?)-drovers, 13,227 men, each of them in charge of 551 (beasts).

(As for) men [under my authority?, [8] this is] how I have dealt with them:

Now, I have taken men from among them, (and) I have caused [them] to buil[d] [9] a large granary for the guard(?) of Memphis, (and) to which belong 10 *arourae* (of land). [I have made?] [10] [grain] bins in it on (all) its four sides, total, 160 grain bins, being [40 on each side?].

[11] [I have collected?] the goods (due to) the treasury, abounding in silver and gold, copper, clothing" [... (remainder lost)].

The date of the document is determined by the conjunction of the date of "year 24" of verso line 1 with the mention of the Chief Treasurer Panehsy in recto line 1. Among the Ramesside kings, only Ramesses II, III, and XI reigned for over 24 years, and a Chief Treasurer Panehsy is securely attested under Ramesses II by a statue (BM 1377) bearing that sovereign's cartouches. Hence the dateline in this ostracon (and the report on Amun's northern wealth) can be identified as year 24 of Ramesses II, or about 1256 B.C. on a minimal computation (accession, in 1279 B.C.).

Within an overall letter format, this document takes the form of a summary report (*sehwy*, verso line 2) by the chief treasurer to Hori as representative of Amun of Thebes, a man who presumably had some responsibility for Amun's estates and the income therefrom. This Hori cannot yet be identified with any certainty. It is remotely possible that he was "the deputy of the estate of Amun, Hori," owner of Tomb 28 in the Asâsîf sector of western Thebes. Our document purports to assess the wealth of Amun in terms of grain and livestock in the "northern region" of Egypt as then understood. In brief parenthesis, construction of a new granary at Memphis is dealt with, drawing on the personnel already listed.

The geography of the document is (or was) precise, in defining the limits of the "northern region" from south to north, from "door [of ...]" to the northern shores of the Delta. Unfortunately, a lacuna spoils that precision for the south boundary. But a reasonably close approximation can be suggested. In his year 54, grain for a cult statue of Ramesses II was drawn "from the southern region, from the township of Mound-of-Nahiho in Nefrusi" (P. BM 10447; Gardiner 1941, pp. 58–59; Gardiner 1948, p. 59, 4–5), which datum sets Nefrusi of the 15th Upper Egyptian Nome securely within the southern region. So our "door [of ...]" must be north of Nefrusi and probably of the 15th Nome. On the other hand, Hardai in the 17th Upper Egyptian Nome would seem in late Ramesside times to have been situated in the northern region, if one grants the identity of Viceroy Panehsy's destruction of Hardai with the "hostilities in the northern region" when Thebans were killed, mentioned with others "whom Panehsy slew."[1] This is not irrefutable proof, but it is feasible. If accepted, then not only Hardai, but presumably the 17th Upper Egyptian Nome *in toto,* also belonged to this northern region. If, as Helck (1974, pp. 110, 111, 115) suggests, the 16th Nome had already become an annex of the 15th Nome in the New Kingdom, then perhaps the boundary between the south and north (administrative) regions in effect coincided with the boundary between the 16th and 17th Nomes, and the "door [of ...]" is to be located somewhere there, between modern Tehneh and Samalut.

Thus, in Ramesside times, Egypt's administrative northern region may have comprised not only the Delta itself but also the northernmost section of the Nile Valley proper, from Memphis upstream to at least the environs of modern Samalut, thus including the six northernmost Upper Egyptian Nomes of tradition (16th to 22nd) with their relatively broad arable plain along the west bank of the Nile, as well as the Fayum district. Hence this northern region was a very substantial economic entity (greater than the rest of Upper Egypt, the "southern region"), a matter of some importance in what follows.

Leaving the more minute details of O. Gardiner 86 for treatment elsewhere,[2] we may compare some of its data with other sources from Ramesside and New Kingdom Egypt. Amun's northern cultivators are given as 8,760 men producing 200 sacks of barley each, for a gross revenue of 1,752,000 sacks in all. So considerable a figure is not out of scale in the light of our other sources. About a century later, in P. Harris I, 12b, line 3, the gross annual revenue in grain payable by the dependents of Ramesses III's great memorial temple at Medinet

1. See Helck 1964, p. 15 n. 1; Kees 1936, pp. 8–9; Peet 1930, p. 152 (p. 10, line 18), pl. 31; Peet 1920, p. 18, pl. 13, B: 2–3.

2. Kitchen, forthcoming 1, section 87, item 3. The translation given above was prepared (with a first draft of this paper)

Habu, plus his four minor Theban temples, is set at 309,950 sacks, but these were contributed from both the northern and southern regions. Thus, from all Egypt, just this *one* royal temple plus four very minor eastern Theban shrines together enjoyed a grain revenue of between one-fifth and one-sixth of the entire figure for Amun under Ramesses II. If we consider that the entire figure covers revenue not only for the Ramesseum (Ramesses II's equivalent of Medinet Habu) and minor foundations at Thebes (in his case, e.g., chapels for Queens Thuya and Nefertari at the Ramesseum), but also for the huge temple of Karnak proper, the great hypostyle hall as an economic unit, the great temple of Luxor (with its new forecourt), the temples of Mut, Khons, Maat, and Montu, the other royal memorial temples in western Thebes, and the whole range of other foundations and temples belonging to Amun's estate the length of Egypt and Nubia from Pi-Ramesses to Napata, then the 1.75 million sacks is not so vast proportionally. In that same document (p. 16b: 13–15), Ramesses III donated 2,981,674 sacks of grain to the permanent Theban cults of Amun, Mut, Khons, and their fellows during his 31 years, i.e., averaging 96,183 sacks per year. This was not their total income in grain but merely what he *added* to their basic annual revenue. If Amun's overall annual income in grain was comparable with that under Ramesses II, then the new gifts by Ramesses III probably did not exceed about 1/10th of the whole.

It is instructive to look at the revenue of just *one* part of Karnak in the supposedly impoverished days of the mid-Twentieth Dynasty, in contrast with the prosperous epoch of Ramesses II. In P. Amiens 5, line 5, under Amun's aegis, the great hypostyle hall at Karnak features as an economic entity, deriving an income of 5,653 1/8 sacks of grain from the 10th Upper Egyptian Nome alone (Gardiner 1941, p. 41, cf. pp. 44–45; Gardiner 1948, p. 7, 14–15). This was by no means its sole income, as is shown, for example, by P. Wilbour §117, covering areas north of Tehneh. The full annual grain income of the hypostyle hall at Karnak must have reached five figures (10,000/15,000 sacks?), while the grain income of the main Karnak temple of Amun would have been correspondingly much greater still. If Amun fared so well in an age of famine, he doubtless did even better in the prosperous times of Ramesses II. Between these two periods, the Bilgai stela under Siptah and Twosret has an official boasting of producing double the annual revenue in grain for Siptah's memorial temple — 140,000 sacks per annum instead of the stipulated 70,000 sacks (Helck 1963, p. 472 [276], §2).

The figure of 200 sacks of barley due per cultivator is well attested from other sources and is even modest. Precisely that figure is assessed two years running for a royal cult statue in years 54–55 of Ramesses II (Gardiner 1941, pp. 59–60, esp. 62; Gardiner 1948, p. 59), as well as in P. Bologna 1086 (cf. Helck 1961, p. 288 [1070]). Clearly larger assessments are to be found; for example, a putative 300 sacks are mentioned in a sarcastic page of Gardiner's *Late-Egyptian Miscellanies* (Gardiner 1937, pp. 122–23; Caminos 1954, p. 453), and a real 1,421 sacks in P. Louvre 3171, 3, line 1, of the Eighteenth Dynasty (Gardiner 1941, pp. 21, 57). Similarly, the figure of 8,760 cultivators may itself be regarded as realistic, even modest. If one adds up the entire work force for Amun in the northern region in O. Gardiner 86, it totals some 61,517 workers, plus two figures wholly lost, and some units from a third figure. This figure of over 61,000 people only just compares with the 62,626 people (P. Harris I, 10, line 3) with whom Ramesses III endowed his Medinet Habu temple alone (excluding any other). Thus, the figure here for all of Amun's northern possessions for all his temple revenues would not be excessive.

Regrettably, the number of Amun's northern cowherds is lost in O. Gardiner 86; we know only that each cared for 500 animals. The figures for donkeys and mules (870 and 551 per drover) are comparable. But on these our external sources fail, and it is not yet possible to know whether 3,920 drovers × 870 = 3,410,440 donkeys and 13,227 drovers × 551 = 7,228,071 mules(?) is fact or fantasy. Certainly, 23,530 fowl-keepers in charge of a remarkably precise 34,230 birds each would give a staggering total of 771,201,900 birds (as Helck 1963, p. 503 [307] notes). Pigeons, at least, proliferate on a grand scale throughout Egypt to this day, but he would be a brave man who could count some 700 million of them or so! The number of goats in our ostracon is lost, preventing true comparisons.

Returning to cattle proper, P. Harris I, 10, lines 7–11, merely gives us a total of 3,264 drovers to care for 5 new herds of Ramesses III — but no figure for the animals. From his second Libyan war in year 11, Ramesses III brought back 3,609 cattle (besides over 28,000 other animals), of which 1,309 are counted separately.[3] Helck (1963, p. 475 [279]) suggests that the smaller figure constituted the "Striking the Meshwesh" herd of this king, cared for by 971 Meshwesh Libyans. If so, these were slave-herders in the fields, with 1 herdsman per every 1 or 2 beasts. If the whole 3,609 came under this heading, it would be 3 or 4 beasts per herdsman. They would,

some 21 years ago and then revised in 1985 for Kitchen, forthcoming 2. Previous translations include those by Helck 1963, pp. 467–68 [271–72]; Wente 1990, pp. 118–19, 227, no. 141; Kitchen 1982, pp. 131–12 (incomplete).

3. See, conveniently, Edgerton and Wilson 1936, pp. 67–68 with notes.

perhaps, come in groups under chief herders, which (at 500 beasts each) is probably what the O. Gardiner 86 herdsmen were. This would reflect in part the hierarchy of people in charge of royal and temple herds, visible in P. Harris I, 7, line 9 (as previously noted by Helck 1963, p. 474 [278] end). Probably none of the foregoing should be confused with the "assorted livestock, 421,362 (head)" of P. Harris I, 11, line 5, although it may have included the 28,000 various animals from the second Libyan war.

Sheep and goats often formed considerable booty (cf. Helck 1963, pp. 488–89 [292–93]) but cannot be compared here because the figure for goats is lost and the number of sheep is not mentioned. The last substantial matter mentioned in our ostracon is the building of a quite large quadrangular granary, with 40 grain bins on each side (hence 160 total). Granaries often appear in Egyptian tomb scenes and as models, but usually with bins along 1 side, or 2 or perhaps 3 sides so far, not yet 4.[4] If our state granary had bins only a meter or a yard wide, the whole structure could not have been less than about 50 meters or some 170 feet long and wide. If the bins were wider, it would, of course, have been proportionately larger. Official granaries might well have matched or exceeded such a scale.

We must hope that fresh comparable material may emerge in the future to show whether this ostracon was indeed a copy of a real report, or a school adaptation of such a report, or even simply an imaginary "school" composition, taking its cue (and some statistics) from real reports. May it at least amuse a long-treasured colleague, first met in sunny Luxor in 1962/63, now so long ago!

References

Caminos, R.

1954 *Late-Egyptian Miscellanies.* Brown Egyptological Studies 1. London: Oxford University Press.

Edgerton, W., and J. Wilson

1936 *Historical Records of Ramses III: The Texts in Medinet Habu,* Volumes 1 and 2. Studies in Ancient Oriental Civilization 12. Chicago: University of Chicago Press.

Gardiner, A. H.

1937 *Late-Egyptian Miscellanies.* Bibliotheca Aegyptiaca 7. Brussels: Fondation Égyptologique Reine Élisabeth.

1941 "Ramesside Texts Relating to the Taxation and Transport of Corn." *Journal of Egyptian Archaeology* 27: 19–73.

1948 *Ramesside Administrative Documents.* Oxford: Oxford University Press.

Helck, W.

1961 *Materialien zur Wirtschaftsgeschichte des Neuen Reiches,* 2: 1. *Die Eigentümer - b) die Provinztempel und säkulare Institutionen;* 2. *Eigentum und Besitz von Grund und Boden.* Akademie der Wissenschaften und der Literatur, Mainz, Abhandlungen der geistes- und sozialwissenschaftlichen Klasse, Jahrgang 1960, 11. Wiesbaden: Franz Steiner Verlag.

1963 *Materialien zur Wirtschaftsgeschichte des Neuen Reiches,* 3: 3. *Eigentum und Besitz an verschiedenen Dingen des täglichen Lebens, Kapitel A–O.* Akademie der Wissenschaften und der Literatur, Mainz, Abhandlungen der geistes- und sozialwissenschaftlichen Klasse, Jahrgang 1963, 2. Wiesbaden: Franz Steiner Verlag.

1964 *Materialien zur Wirtschaftsgeschichte des Neuen Reiches,* 5: *Einzelbetrachtung von Lebensmitteln und Materialien.* Akademie der Wissenschaften und der Literatur, Mainz, Abhandlungen der geistes- und sozialwissenschaftlichen Klasse, Jahrgang 1964, 4. Wiesbaden: Franz Steiner Verlag.

1974 *Die altägyptische Gaue.* Tübinger Atlas des Vorderen Orients, Beihefte B/5. Wiesbaden: Ludwig Reichert Verlag.

Kees, H.

1936 *Herihor und die Aufrichtung des thebanischen Gottesstaates.* Nachrichten von der Gesellschaft der Wissenschaften zu Göttingen, philologisch-historische Klasse, Fachgruppe 1, n.F., 2/1. Göttingen: Vandenhoeck and Ruprecht.

Kitchen, K. A.

1982 *Pharaoh Triumphant: The Life and Times of Ramesses II, King of Egypt.* Warminster: Aris and Phillips.

NYP/1 *Ramesside Inscriptions, Translated and Annotated: Notes and Comments,* 3.

NYP/2 *Ramesside Inscriptions, Translated and Annotated: Translations,* 3.

Peet, T. E.

1920 *The Mayer Papyri A and B.* London: Egypt Exploration Society.

1930 *The Great Egyptian Tomb-Robberies of the Twentieth Egyptian Dynasty,* Part 1: *Text.* Oxford: Oxford University Press.

Vandier, J.

1978 *Bas-reliefs et peintures: Scènes de la vie agricole à l'Ancien et au Moyen Empire.* Manuel d'archéologie égyptienne 6. Paris: Éditions A. et J. Picard.

Wente, E. F.

1990 *Letters from Ancient Egypt.* Society of Biblical Literature, Writings from the Ancient World 1. Atlanta: Scholars Press.

4. For a list of early models, see Vandier 1978, pp. 223–25; for scenes, see ibid., p. 238, fig. 103, p. 276, fig. 118, respectively).

23

WIE JUNG IST DIE MEMPHITISCHE PHILOSOPHIE AUF DEM SHABAQO-STEIN?

ROLF KRAUSS

Ägyptisches Museum und Papyrussammlung, Berlin

Edward F. Wente habe ich in einer mir unvergesslichen Weise im Sommer 1985 in einem Restaurant auf dem Campus der Chicagoer Universität kennengelernt. Gut gelaunt sprach er über die Probleme, die sich der Identifizierung der Königsmumien in den Weg stellen und erhoffte eine Lösung durch ein "juggling with the mummies and their labels." Im Gegenzug offeriere ich meinem hochgeschätzten älteren Kollegen ein juggling mit der Steinplatte BM 498 und ihrem Label "Shabaqo." [1]

Der Shabaqo-Stein kam im Jahre 1805 als Geschenk eines Earl of Spencer ins Britische Museum (Erman 1911, 916 Anm. 1) wo er zunächst die Inventarnummer 135* erhielt, später 498 (Sethe 1928, 1). Es scheint nicht bekannt zu sein, woher Spencer das Objekt hatte. Im Anschluss an J. H. Breasted wird das Gestein in der Literatur als schwarzer Granit bezeichnet (Breasted 1901, 40). Aber nach einer vom Research Laboratory des BM durchgeführten Untersuchung handelt es sich um ein Konglomeratgestein, wie es im Wadi Hammamat vorkommt.[2]

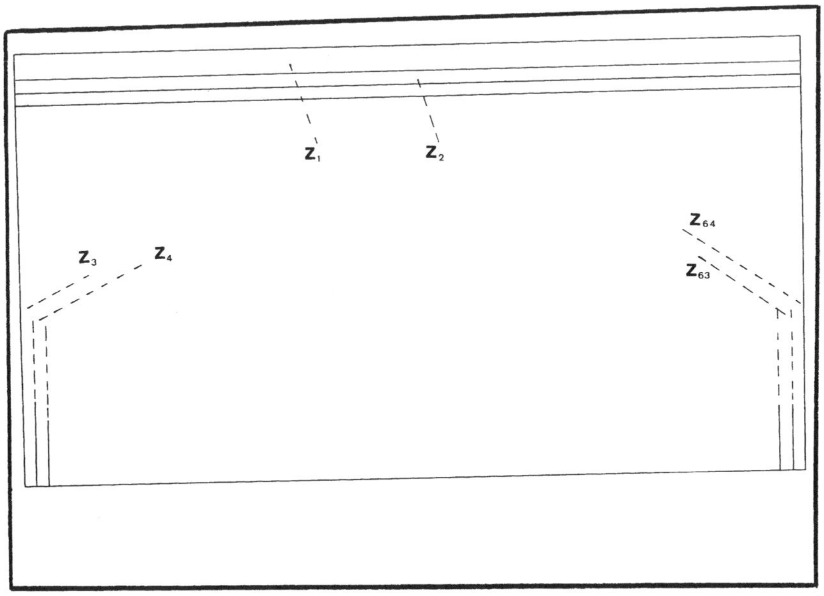

Figure 23.1. Layout-Schema des Shabaqo-Textes

Die Steinplatte selbst ist ca. 137 cm breit, die Höhe beträgt links ca. 91 cm, rechts ca. 95 cm (fig. 23.1).[3] Das Textfeld ist (oben) ca. 132 cm breit und (links) ca. 68.8 cm hoch. Bei Umrechnung in altägyptische Fingerbreiten = 1.875 cm, gilt 132 cm = 70.4 Fingerbreiten und 68.8 cm = 36.7 Fingerbreiten. Aufgrund meiner zugegebenermassen geringen Kenntnisse über das Layout altägyptischer Texte vermute ich,[4] dass als Breite des Textfeldes (70 + 1/3) Fingerbreiten geplant war und als Höhe (36 + 2/3) Fingerbreiten. Der Text ist in zwei

1. Zum meroitischen Suffix *-qo*, s. Hintze 1979, 194 f.
2. A. J. Spencer, mündlich.
3. Ich danke B. Fay, die diese Masse für mich mit Digital Calipers gemessen hat.
4. Vgl. beispielsweise Krauss 1994, 50 f.

Gold of Praise: Studies on Ancient Egypt in Honor of Edward F. Wente
Edited by Emily Teeter and John A. Larson
Studies in Ancient Oriental Civilization 58
Chicago: Oriental Institute, 1999

horizontalen Zeilen Z_1 und Z_2 sowie 61 (sic) vertikalen Zeilen Z_3 - Z_{64} ausgelegt; dazu kommt die kurze waagrechte Zeile Z_{48}, die mit den vertikalen Zeilen Z_{49a} bis Z_{51a} kombiniert ist.[5] Die rechts gemessenen Höhen betragen 3.9 cm bei Z_1, 2.10 cm bei Z_2 und bei der darauf folgenden Leerzeile 2.18 cm; vermutlich waren diese Höhen als (2 + 1/12) Fingerbreiten und (1 + 1/8) Fingerbreiten bzw. ihre Summe als (4 + 1/3) Fingerbreiten geplant. Die Breiten jeweils der beiden äusseren Vertikalzeilen betragen (links unten) ca. 2.29 cm (Z_3) bzw. ca. 2.08 cm (Z_4) sowie (rechts unten) ca. 2.10 cm (Z_{63}) bzw. ca. 2.22 cm (Z_{64}). Wenn eine konstante Zeilenbreite beabsichtigt war, dann vermutlich eine Breite von (1 + 1/11 + 1/16) f. Ob dieses Layout für die Datierung des Shabaqo-Steins nutzbringend herangezogen werden kann, lässt sich angesichts der rudimentären ägyptologischen Kenntnisse über altägyptisches Layout nicht sagen.[6]

Z_1 enthält die Widmungsinschrift von König Shabaqo, bestehend aus einer fünfteiligen Königstitulatur und konventionellen Epitheta. Z_2 gibt als Kolophon Auskunft über Alter und Zustand der Vorlage des vertikal geschriebenen Textes sowie über die Aufstellung der Platte selbst im memphitischen Ptahtempel. Laut Z_2 war es Shabaqo, der die Vorlage gefunden hat als "ein Werk der Vorfahren, indem es von Würmern zerfressen war."

Massgeblich ist die Textkopie, die Breasted für das 1897 angelaufene Projekt des Berliner Wörterbuchs gemacht hat (Breasted 1901, 40; Breasted 1950, 47). Im Archiv des Berliner Wörterbuches steht den Ägyptologen überdies ein aus Sethes Zeiten stammender Papier-Abklatsch zur Verfügung.[7] Nach meinen Feststellungen ist dieser Abklatsch noch immer brauchbar, wenn auch infolge einer Schrumpfung des Papiers die Masse gegenüber dem Original um ca. 3–4% kleiner geworden sind.

Mit dem Textinhalt haben sich zuerst J. H. Breasted (1901) dann vor allem A. Erman (1911), K. Sethe (1928), sowie H. Junker (1939, 1941), und in letzter Zeit J. Allen (1988, 42–47) und E. Iversen (1990, 485 ff.) interpretierend beschäftigt.[8] Nach übereinstimmender Auffassung der bisherigen Bearbeiter besteht der in senkrechten Zeilen geschriebene Text formal aus drei Einheiten A, B und C, über deren Feineinteilung die Meinungen jedoch auseinandergehen. Abschnitt A bietet in dramatischer Form Auszüge aus der Horus- und Osirissage. Der teilweise zerstörte Abschnitt C1 bietet den gleichen Mythos und zwar in erzählender Form, während C2 das Thema von C1 nochmals aufnimmt. Der dazwischen stehende Teil B enthält einen Traktat über Wesen und Bedeutung des Gottes Ptah. Der Inhalt von A und C lässt sich nach Junker so umreissen (Junker 1941, 7 f.): Ägypten war durch den Streit zwischen Horus und Seth zerrissen. Geb setzte dem Streit ein Ende und teilte das Land unter die beiden Götter auf, wobei Seth den Süden erhielt und Horus den Norden. Dann bereute Geb seinen Entschluss und wies das gesamte Land dem Horus zu. Horus ist aber in Wirklichkeit Ptah-Tatenen, der das Land in Memphis vereinigt hat. In Memphis steht auch die Königsburg als Wahrzeichen der Reichseinheit, ferner liegt in Memphis das Grab des Osiris. Im altägyptischen Rahmen läuft dies auf die Vorrangstellung des Gottes Ptah-Tatenen und seiner Stadt Memphis hinaus.

Die Bearbeitungen von Breasted, Erman, Sethe und Junker haben den Abschnitt B des Shabaqo-Textes als die aus Sicht der Ägyptologen älteste philosophische Lehre der Ägypter etabliert, die mindestens aus dem AR stammen soll, wenn nicht gar aus der Thinitenzeit. Immerhin gab es die Dissidentenmeinung von F. v. Bissing,[9] die aber ungehört verhallte.[10] 1912 bezeichnete v. Bissing (1912, 89) unseren Text als eine zur Zeit von Shabaqo produzierte Fälschung, wenn er auch Textabschnitt A als alt akzeptierte: "Orthographie wie Inhalt, die Angabe einer Anzahl von Lücken, die in Wirklichkeit im Text gar nicht vorhanden sind, scheinen mir auf eine Fälschung äthiopischer Zeit hinzuweisen, bei der wohl freilich ein alter mythologischer Text, der den Tod des Osiris erzählte, benutzt worden ist."

In den 70er Jahren kam F. Junge zu einem ähnlichen Ergebnis wie v. Bissing, und zwar ohne die Meinung seines Vorgängers zu kennen (Junge 1973, 195 ff.). Junge sichtete die orthographischen und sprachlichen Indizien, die im Sinne der meisten früheren Bearbeiter des Textes für ein hohes Alter sprechen sollten, und kam zu dem Schluss, dass diese Details besser als Archaismen der Spätzeit zu erklären sind. Zu Recht machte Junge den früheren Bearbeitern den Vorwurf, dass sie die Behauptung des Kolophons über die Auffindung des

5. Lichtheim 1973, 51; Clagett 1989, 595, zählen irrtümlich 62 vertikale Zeilen; Allen 1988, 42 zählt 63 "vertical columns."

6. Zur Planung von Tempeldekorationen, s. Vassilika 1989, 1 ff., 199 ff.

7. Sethe 1928, 1 f. Zur Zeit ist nur einer von zwei für Sethe gemachten Abklatsche vorhanden.

8. Die Literatur zum Thema ist ausufernd. Zur älteren Literatur s. Sethe1928, 1 f.; zur neuer Literatur s. *LÄ* 1 "Denkmäler memphitischer Theologie," 1065–69; Clagett 1989.

9. von Bissing 1912, 89 ff.

10. Dieser Artikel ist mir nur dadurch bekannt geworden, dass ich in einer im Giftschrank des Berliner Ägyptischen Museums stehenden obskuren Publikation über einen Hinweis stolperte: Frenkian 1946, 47.

Haupttexts durch Shabaqo nicht in Frage gestellt und auf eine Prüfung von Inhalt und Sprache des Haupttextes auf Anachronismen verzichtet haben (Junge 1973, 195).

Später hat H. Schlögl (1980, 110 ff.) als Altersindiz gefunden, dass die aus Ptah und Tatenen zusammengesetzte Gottesform Ptah-Tatenen, die für den Shabaqo-Text charakteristisch ist, erst seit der Ramessidenzeit vorkommt. Schliesslich konnte U. Luft zeigen (1978, 146 ff.), dass bestimmte Textkolumnen auf dem Shabaqo-Stein viel zu lang sind, als dass sie–wie doch im Text impliziert — in der Shabaqo-Zeit von einer sehr alten Papyrusrolle übertragen worden sein könnten.

Während Allen (1988, 43) das Schlöglsche Altersindiz halbherzig akzeptierte, hat sich Iversen (1990, 485, 490) zwar zugunsten von Junkers originaler Datierung des Shabaqo-Textes in die 5. Dynastie ausgesprochen, dem Text in anachronistischer Weise aber auch einen "essentially Hermetic character" bescheinigt.

Für eine altertümliche Abfassungszeit des Shabaqo-Textes bzw. seiner angeblichen Vorlage spricht in erster Linie sein eigenes Kolophon, wogegen der Text selbst nach Junges Urteil evident in die Spätzeit gehört. Wer die Aussage des Kolophons ernst nimmt, die Majestät des Shabaqo selbst habe die Vorlage zur Steininschrift gefunden, läuft Gefahr sich an der Nase herumführen zu lassen. Die Tatsache, dass der Topos von der "gefundenen alten Schrift" sowohl aus Altägypten bekannt ist (*LÄ* 1 "Alte Schriften," 149 ff.), als auch sonst aus den antiken Literaturen (Speyer 1970), sollte eine Warnung sein. Unter dieser Voraussetzung wage ich es, einen Schritt über Junge und auch v. Bissing hinauszugehen und zu fragen, ob die Memphitische Theologie vielleicht später als Shabaqo abgefasst und die Zuschreibung lediglich fingiert sein kann, um dem neuverfassten Text durch einen wohlklingenden alten Namen Geltung zu verschaffen? Die historischen Möglichkeiten dafür wären eingeengt, weil Psammetich II. das Andenken aller kuschitischen Könige, mithin auch von Shabaqo, verfolgen liess. Nach Yoyottes Beweisführung war der Anlass zu dieser Aktion der Krieg den Psammetich II. in seinem dritten Regierungsjahr (591 v. Chr.) gegen das Reich von Kusch führte (Yoyotte 1951, 215 ff.). Für den Rest der auf Psammetich II. folgenden Saitenzeit, dann für die persischen Herrschaften und die letzten ägyptischen Dynastien scheinen die Chancen für einen auf Shabaqos Namen fingierten und im memphitischen Ptahtempel präsentierten Text gering zu sein.

Immerhin bewirkte die Tilgung der kuschitischen Herrschernamen unter Psammetich II. keine Auslöschung ihres Andenkens, wie die Erwähnungen Shabaqos bei Herodot, Diodor und in der manethonischen Tradition zeigen. Aber nicht nur im literarischen Bereich lebte Shabaqos Name weiter, wie der aus dem Jahr 256 v.Chr. stammende demotische P. Leiden I 379 zeigt (*LÄ* 4 "Papyri, Demotische," 835). Laut diesem Papyrus gab es in der memphitischen Nekropole eine nach Shabaqo benannte Strasse (*LÄ* 5 "Schabaka," 504, Anm. 114). Die einzige publizierte Übersetzung der Textstelle hat E. Revillout (1880, 126), vor über hundert Jahren vorgelegt. Auf meine Bitte hin hat sich S. P. Vleeming die Zeilen mit dem Königsnamen angesehen:[11] "Revillout is generally considered untrustworthy … but for once I can not exclude that he has read the passage correctly, as I should also read (from a photograph): '*jꜣbt tꜣ mj.t* [—] - *Šbkꜣ* ꜥ.[*w.*]*s*.; east: the avenue [—] - Shabaka l.[p.]h.' - In the published facsimile, there are some traces preceding Shabaka's name, which have now virtually disappeared, so the exact relation between the Avenue and Shabaka may be marked as uncertain, but the reading of the two words themselves seems in little doubt."

Zunächst könnte man vermuten, dass ein Strassenname vorliegt, der bis in die Zeit von Shabaqo selbst zurückgeht und sich trotz der "damnatio memoriae" unter Psammetich II. über die Jahrhunderte gehalten hat. Gegen eine solche Vermutung spricht, dass aus dem genuin altägyptischen Milieu bisher keine mit Personennamen gebildeten Strassenbezeichnungen belegt sind. Nach mündlicher Mitteilung von S. Grunert, kennt man aus den thebanischen demotischen Papyri beispielsweise "den Weg des Königs," nicht aber Bezeichnungen wie "Weg des Königs NN." Strassennamen von letzterem Typ benutzten aber die Griechen in Ägypten (Rink 1924, 17–25), und vielleicht liegt beim "Weg des *Šbkꜣ*" eine durch griechischen Brauch angeregte ägyptische Neubildung vor. Wie auch immer, so scheint der Leidener Papyrus für das 3. Jh. v. Chr. die Existenz eines mit dem Namen von Shabaqo gebildeten Toponyms zu bezeugen.

Günstig für meine Annahme einer sehr späten Fingierung des Shabaqo-Textes ist die ptolemäerzeitliche Rehabilitierung der kuschitischen Könige, die sich in der Wiederherstellung ihrer von Psammetich II. getilgten Namen zeigt. Leclant (1951b, 115 ff.) hat einige thebanische Fälle von Restaurierungen der Namen Shabaqos und Taharqos bekannt gemacht. Nach seinen detaillierten Untersuchungen kam es zu solchen Restaurierungen in Karnak sowie im Kleinen Tempel von Medinet Habu. In Karnak existiert möglicherweise eine Darstellung

11. Brief vom 1. 10. 1992.

Taharqos aus ptolemäischer Zeit (Russmann 1997, 54). Nach meiner Meinung darf man die Restaurierungen als nachträgliche Anerkennung der rechtmässigen Herrschaft der Kuschiten über Ägypten interpretieren. Eine solche Anerkennung hätte im politischen Interesse der Ptolemäer gelegen, da auch sie Fremdherrscher waren. Weil man mithin in der Ptolemäerzeit die Namen kuschitischer Herrscher und insbesondere von Shabaqo wieder offiziell in Stein schrieb, wäre damals auch eine auf den Namen dieses Königs fingierte Inschrift möglich gewesen — möglich, nicht mehr und nicht weniger.

Dagegen kann die Art, in der auf dem Shabaqo-Stein die Königsnamen getilgt sind, in positiver Weise für eine posthume Fälschung auf den Namen Shabaqos sprechen. 1951 hat Yoyotte bei den damals bekannten achtzehn Denkmälern Shabaqos die auf Psammetich II. zurückgehenden Namenstilgungen untersucht und festgestellt, dass Horusname, Nebtiname und Goldhorusname im allgemeinen nicht angetastet wurden. Aber der persönliche Name Shabaqo wurde in praktisch allen Belegen getilgt,[12] insbesondere auch in den drei Fällen, in denen der Name auf dem Shabaqo-Stein erscheint.[13]

Im Fall des Thronnamens Neferkare sind bei Yoyottes (1951, No. 33) Belegen alle drei Zeichen nur in einem einzigen Fall getilgt. Von dieser Ausnahme abgesehen blieb "Ra" sonst verschont, während "nefer" zusammen mit "Ra" in drei Fällen verschont blieb.[14] Allein im Fall des Shabaqo-Steins blieben alle drei Zeichen des in Z_1 zweimal vorhandenen Thronnamens unangetastet.

Seit Yoyottes Bearbeitung sind zum Shabaqo-Dossier noch einige Dokumente aus Memphis hinzugekommen,[15] die zum Teil keine Tilgungen aufweisen. Bei den Elementen von einer Kapelle rechnet Leclant mit der Möglichkeit, dass sie früh verbaut wurden und den Tilgungen zur Zeit Psammetichs II. daher entgangen sind (Leclant 1981, 289-94; *LÄ* 5 "Schabaka," 501, Anm. 56). Dabei ist in einem Fall (Berlin 39/66) "Shabaqo" nicht getilgt, im andern Fall (Kairo 13/1/21/12) ist Neferkare nicht angetastet. Leclant erinnert in diesem Zusammenhang an Yoyottes Vorschlag, die Verschonung des Namens Neferkare auf dem Shabaqo-Stein aus memphitischer Pietät gegenüber dem auch noch im spätzeitlichen Memphis verehrten Neferkare-Pepi II. zu erklären. Diese Erklärung lässt sich zwar nicht von der Hand weisen, aber aus dem Nebeneinander von unversehrtem Thronnamen Neferkare und getilgtem Geburtsnamen Shabaqo folgt als Möglichkeit, dass der Shabaqo-Text aus der Ptolemäerzeit stammen kann. Der Name Shabaqo könnte von der gleichen Hand zuerst geschrieben und dann getilgt worden sein, um die Inschrift möglichst authentisch scheinen zu lassen. Die Tilgung der kuschitischen Namen war insbesondere in der Ptolemäerzeit eine bekannte Tatsache, wie aus der damals erfolgten Restaurierung von Kuschiten-Namen folgt. Die auf dem Shabaqo-Stein vorliegende und von den Tilgungen unter Psammetich II. sonst nicht bekannte Verschonung aller drei Hieroglyphen des Thronnamens Neferkare wäre dann überlegter Weise geschehen, um den König in dieser Inschrift mit seinem bekannten Thronnamen identifizieren zu können, wofür sich die anderen Teile seines Protokolls schlecht eignen.

Schwerer als die von der Regel abweichende Art in der Shabaqos Thronname getilgt ist, wiegen inhaltliche Anachronismen im Shabaqo-Text zugunsten einer ptolemäischen Abfassungszeit. Hinsichtlich inhaltlicher Anachronismen erinnere ich an Breasteds Urteil, demzufolge der Shabaqo-Text historische Vorgriffe auf Konzepte der griechischen Philosophie enthält. Herz und Zunge des Ptah erkannte Breasted als "the later notion of λόγος and νοῦς, hitherto supposed to have been introduced into Egypt from abroad at a much later date. Thus the Greek tradition of the origin of their philosophy in Egypt undoubtedly contains more truth than has in recent years been conceded."[16]

Wenn die von Breasted vermutete ideengeschichtliche Verwandtschaft tatsächlich besteht, dann wäre es angesichts der im altägyptischen Rahmen gegebenen Isoliertheit des Shabaqo-Textes historisch sinnvoll, eine Ableitung der philosophischen Aussagen des Shabaqo-Textes aus der griechischen Philosophie zu versuchen, statt ohne weiteres auf die umgekehrte Abhängigkeit zu schliessen. Dabei sehe ich durchaus, dass das aus der griechischen Philosophie und nach Breasted aus dem Shabaqo-Text bekannte Thema des schöpferischen Logos mit einigem interpretatorischem Geschick auch in sehr alten ägyptischen Texten wiedergefunden werden kann. Beispielsweise sind nach Allen (1988, 46–47) in den Sargtexten die Mittel beschrieben

> through which Atum effected his own development, by "surveying in his heart" ... and realizing the concept through "the speech of that august self-developing god ... ." The "Memphite Theology" reflects the same no-

12. Das *Ba*-Zeichen blieb lediglich in Yoyotte 1951, No. 40 verschont.
13. Am Original meine ich, in den zwei links stehenden Kartuschen, jeweils Spuren des *kꜣ* von *Šꜣ -bꜣ -kꜣ* zu erkennen.
14. Yoyotte 1951, No. 30, 31, 38. Siehe auch Leclant 1951a, 457.
15. Die Amun-Statue Kairo CG 38020 könnte statt Shabaqos Namen den von Shebitqo tragen, vgl. *LÄ* 5 "Schabaka," 501, Anm. 58.
16. Breasted 1901, 54; s. auch Breasted 1950, 53.

tion when it describes how "Atum's image" developed "through the heart and the tongue" … . Here, however, the principle is viewed as operating upon Atum from a higher source: "So were all the gods born, Atum and his Ennead as well." …

It is easy to conclude that this higher power is Ptah. The text clearly refers to "his making everything and every divine speech as well." … The earlier description in the Coffin Texts, however, just as clearly subordinates Ptah to a creator, to whom he functions as "Annunciation in his mouth and Perception in his belly." … Though separated by perhaps 800 years, the two texts are not necessarily incompatible.

Wie sich Allen die Kompatibilität der zitierten Aussagen und damit implizit die innerägyptische ideengeschichtliche Verbindung zwischen der Memphitischen Theologie und älteren Texten in diesem besonderen Punkt vorstellt, mag man bei ihm selbst nachlesen. Ich möchte für meine Zwecke sehr eng umschriebene und gegenüber anderen altägyptischen Texten isolierte Aussagen des Shabaqo-Textes heranziehen und gehe dabei von Junkers Einsicht aus (1939, 69 f.), dass in Textabschnitt B Sätze einer "Naturlehre" eingefügt sind: "Es wechseln … Abschnitte mit religiösem Inhalt mit anderen ab, die Naturbeobachtungen mitteilen. … (Als dritter Abschnitt) folgt die Lehre über die Bedeutung von Herz und Zunge in allen Lebewesen; die beiden Organe beherrschen alle übrigen Glieder. Die Aussagen werden beziehungslos gemacht, ohne Verbindung mit der vorhergehenden religiösen Lehre.[17] … die der Reihe nach herausgenommenen Abschnitte der Naturlehre ergeben ohne irgendeine Umstellung eine zusammenhängende Abhandlung über die Bedeutung von Herz und Zunge bei den Lebewesen." Die erste dieser Lehren lautet in der Übersetzung Junkers:[18] "Es ist so, dass Herz und Zunge Macht über alle Glieder haben, auf Grund der Lehre (Erwägung), dass es (das Herz) in jedem Leibe ist, und dass sie (die Zunge) in jedem Munde ist, von allen Göttern, allen Menschen, von allem Vieh, allem Gewürm und (allem) was lebt; indem es (das Herz) denkt alles, was es will, und sie (die Zunge) befiehlt alles, was sie will."

Laut dieser Lehre sind Vernunft und Sprache nicht nur bei Göttern und Menschen, sondern uneingeschränkt bei allen tierischen Lebewesen vorhanden. Sprechende Tiere, wie die Rinder des Bata, sind aus altägyptischen Texten bekannt, doch scheint mir dieser erzählerische Kunstgriff im Zwei-Brüder-Märchen etwas anderes zu sein als die Aussage des Shabaqo-Textes über das Denk-und Sprachvermögen aller lebenden, nicht-pflanzlichen Wesen. Eine gleichwertige Aussage lässt sich in anderen altägyptischen Texten nicht nachweisen. Aber eine entsprechende Lehrmeinung ist mindestens seit dem 4. Jh. v. Chr. aus der griechischen Philosophie bekannt. Es war bekanntlich diese Lehrmeinung von der Vernunft-und Sprachbegabtheit aller Lebewesen, die dann im 2. Jh. v. Chr. einen Streitpunkt in der Auseinandersetzung zwischen den Stoikern und den in der Nachfolge von Platon stehenden Akademikern ausmachte. Der Akademiker Karneades stellte sich damals entschieden gegen die anthropozentrischen Stoiker, die die Gabe des Logos auf Götter und Menschen beschränken, und zusätzlich bei den Menschen alters- und reifebedingte Einschränkungen machen wollten (Pohlenz 1978, 177). Diese Lehre hat mithin in der griechischen Philosophie eine Tradition und wird aus tiefliegenden Ansätzen gespeist, wie etwa der aristotelischen Auffassung, "dass es vom Bereich des Leblosen bis zum Menschen nirgendwo eine scharfe Grenze gibt, sondern alles ein Kontinuum mit gleitenden Übergängen bildet" (Flashar 1983, 415).

Eine weitere in altägyptischen Texten isolierte Aussage bietet die im Shabaqo-Text enthaltene Lehre über die Sinne: "Das Sehen der Augen, das Hören der Ohren, das Luftatmen der Nase, sie bringen dem Herzen Meldung. Es (das Herz) ist es, das jede Erkenntnis hervorkommen lässt." Bereits Junker (1939, 71) hat diese Passage als kurze Lehre darüber aufgefasst, wie das im Herzen wirkende Denkvermögen die Sinneseindrücke aufnimmt und umsetzt. Als geistiges Zentralorgan ist das Herz dem Ägyptologen gut bekannt, und sei es auch nur aus Brunners "Hörendem Herzen" von 1965. Eine ähnliche Rolle haben auch die Griechen und sogar Aristoteles selbst dem Herzen zugeschrieben. Allerdings gab es schon vor Aristoteles die von Alkmaion, Hippokrates und Platon vertretene Ansicht, das Gehirn sei das die Sinneswahrnehmungen verarbeitende Zentralorgan. In der allgemeinen Auffassung vom Herzen als Zentralorgan kongruieren die altägyptische Auffassung und zumindest ein Teil der griechischen Philosophie.

Allerdings macht die Lehre des Shabaqo-Steins einen Unterschied zwischen dem, was die Sinne an das im Herzen wirkende Denkvermögen melden und dem, was dort im Herzen aufgrund dieser Meldung als Erkenntnis entsteht. In prinzipiell gleicher Weise hat Aristoteles zwei Dinge unterschieden: Zum einen die sinnliche

17. Die von Junker (1939) gesehene Beziehungslosigkeit ist wohl nicht gegeben, s. Junge 1973, 203.

18. Junker 1939, 71. Die neuere Übersetzung von Lichtheim 1973, 51f., weicht hier von Junker nicht ab.

Wahrnehmung und zum andern das davon verschiedene Anschauungsbild, welches in der im Herzen sitzenden Seele nach der Übermittlung der sinnlichen Wahrnehmung entsteht (Zeller 1921, 533 ff.). Wie Aristoteles, so scheint auch der Shabaqo-Text zu sagen, dass das Auge zunächst sieht, worauf das Auge das Gesehene an das Herz meldet und darauf im Herzen eine Erkenntis des vom Auge Gesehenen entsteht.

Meines Wissens ist aus anderen altägyptischen Texten keine vergleichbare Sinneslehre bekannt. Klassisch ist die Formulierung von Grapow (1954, 31): "Dass die Ohren hören, wurde ebenso wie das Sehvermögen der Augen als etwas Naturgegebenes und Selbstverständliches hingenommen." In gleicher Weise bezeichnet Grapow (1954, 38) auch "Riechen und Luft einatmen als etwas für die Nase Selbstverständliches." Mithin spricht der Shabaqo-Text eine Sinnes-Lehre aus, welche die Ägyptologen auch nicht ansatzweise aus Altägypten nachweisen können und die philosophiegeschichtlich zuerst aus einer Formulierung von Aristoteles bekannt ist.

In diesem Zusammenhang will ich noch auf einen begleitenden Umstand hinweisen, dass nämlich der Shabaqo-Text von den uns sprichwörtlich bekannten fünf Sinnen nur drei nennt, nämlich Sehen, Hören und Riechen als Funktionen der Augen, der Ohren und der Nase. Auch für diese Beschränkung lässt sich eine Entsprechung bei Aristoteles finden, der die drei höheren Sinne — Sehen, Hören und Riechen — von den zwei niederen Sinnen — Tast- und Geschmackssinn — unterschieden hat (Flashar 1983, 406, 414). Die drei in Augen, Ohren und Nase sitzenden Sinne kommen nach Aristoteles nur den höher organisierten Lebewesen zu, insbesondere den Menschen, während die niederen Lebewesen lediglich am Tast- und Geschmackssinn teilhaben. Impliziert diese Nichterwähnung der niederen Sinne im Shabaqo-Text, dass sie ohne "Erkenntnis im Herzen" funktionieren?

Wie die Grapow-Zitate zeigen, sind die entsprechenden Lehren des Shabaqo-Textes weder sinngemäss noch vom Ansatz her in der den Ägyptologen bekannten altägyptischen Ideenwelt nachweisbar. Auch ist es nicht wahrscheinlich, dass diese Lehren in verlorenen genuin altägyptischen Schriften enthalten gewesen sein können, die ihrerseits nicht unter dem Einfluss griechischer Philosophie entstanden wären. Doch hat mich K.-Th. Zauzich in einer kritischen Bemerkung darauf hingewiesen, dass sich allein unter den Carlsberg Papyri schätzungsweise tausend Fragmente von quasi-literarischen Texten befinden. Daran ist zu ermessen, wieviele verschiedene Manuskripte in einer Tempelbibliothek vorhanden gewesen sein können. Einerseits ist damit zu rechnen, dass in den verlorenen Texten auch Dinge standen, die sonst nirgendwo erhalten sind und über die wir daher nichts mehr erfahren können. Andererseits versteht es sich von selbst, dass in den verlorenen altägyptischen Texten nicht jede beliebige denkbare Aussage gestanden haben kann. Beispielsweise würde man nicht erwarten im verlorenen Teil der altägyptischen Literatur ein Äquivalent zur Lehre des Demokritos zu finden, dass die Materie aus unteilbaren Atomen aufgebaut ist. Man erwartet auch nicht in einer genuin altägyptischen Schrift eine Erörterung der Gründe zu finden, die gegen eine geozentrische Welt und stattdessen im Sinne von Aristarchos für eine heliozentrische Welt sprechen.

Unter dieser Voraussetzung geht es nicht darum, ob den Ägyptologen — zugespitzt formuliert — ein bestimmtes altägyptisches Manuskript fehlt, in dem ein Äquivalent der aristotelischen Sinneslehre formuliert war. Wesentlich scheint mir zu sein, dass ganz allgemein altägyptische Texte naturkundlich-philosophischen Inhalts fehlen, die auch nur auf dem Niveau der ionischen Naturphilosophie des 6. Jahrhunderts v. Chr. stünden. Solange solche altägyptischen Texte nicht auftauchen, darf man in den entsprechenden Aussagen des Shabaqo-Textes ägyptische Adaptionen griechischer Philosophie vermuten. Weil sinngemäss gleiche Aussagen ihren historischen und systematischen Platz in der griechischen Philosophie seit dem 4. Jh. v. Chr. haben, halte ich eine ptolemäische Abfassungszeit des Shabaqo-Textes für möglich. Ich erinnere an den Fall der Hungersnotstele, welche Inschrift vorgibt aus der Zeit von Djoser zu stammen, aber in der Tat unter Ptolemaios V. verfasst wurde.[19] Eine solche Abfassungszeit ist auch für den Shabaqo-Text mit all seinen Archaismen denkbar, ohne dass die historischen Umstände, die ich im folgenden nenne, für eine solche Datierung beweisende Kraft hätten. Die im Shabaqo-Text dick aufgetragene Propaganda für Memphis dient memphitischen Interessen im allgemeinen und den Interessen des Ptah-Tempels im besonderen. Die Adressaten dieser Propaganda könnten ein in Alexandria herrschender König und seine griechischen Ratgeber gewesen sein, denen Ptah und seine Interessensphäre um so sympathischer hätte erscheinen sollen, wenn die mit diesem Gott verbundene Lehre an Lehren der griechischen Philosophie erinnerte. Ptolemaios V. scheint ein offenes Ohr gehabt zu haben für zugunsten von Memphis werbende Stimmen. Er war der erste Ptolemäer,

19. Barguet 1953, 33 ff.; s. auch *LÄ* 3 "Hungersnotstele," 84.

dessen Krönung in Memphis sicher bezeugt ist;[20] auch die unter diesem König gehäuft abgehaltenen Priestersynoden können als Aufwertung der alten Hauptstadt gegenüber Alexandria verstanden werden, soweit sie in Memphis stattfanden.[21] Durch die Verbindung mit einem kuschitischen Namen können die memphitischen Autoren des Textes versucht haben den Sympathien der ptolemäischen Fremdherrscher für die kuschitischen Fremdherrscher entgegenzukommen. Ein denkbarer *terminus post quem* für die Abfassung des Textes ist beispielsweise die endgültige Niederlage des oberägyptischen Gegenkönigs Anchonnofris im Jahre 186 v.Chr. (*LÄ* 4 "Ptolemaios," 1186). Die erneute Angliederung Oberägyptens liesse sich mit der im Shabaqo-Text beschriebenen urzeitlichen Einigung des Landes vergleichen, als der in Unterägypten herrschende Horus durch Gebs Entscheidung auch den oberägyptischen Landesteil des Seth zur Beherrschung erhielt.

References

Allen, J.
1988 *Genesis in Egypt.* Yale Egyptological Studies 2. New Haven: Yale University.

Barguet, P.
1953 *La stèle de la famine, à Séhel.* Bibliothèque d'étude 24. Cairo: Institut français d'archéologie orientale.

Breasted, J. H.
1901 "The Philosophy of a Memphite Priest." *Zeitschrift für ägyptische Sprache und Altertumskunde* 39: 39–54.
1950 *Die Geburt des Gewissens.* Zurich: Morgarten Verlag.

Clagett, M.
1989 *Ancient Egyptian Science: A Source Book,* Volume 1: *On Knowledge and Order.* Philadelphia: American Philosophical Society.

Erman, A.
1911 "Ein Denkmal memphitischer Theologie." *Sitzungsberichte der Königlich preussischen Akademie der Wissenschaften* 42: 916–50.

Flashar, H.
1983 *Ältere Akademie - Aristoteles - Peripatos: Grundriss der Geschichte der Philosophie.* Die Philosophie der Antike 3. Basel: Schwabe.

Frenkian, A. M.
1946 *L'orient et les origines de l'idéalisme subjectif dans la pensée européenne* 1: *La doctrine théologique de Memphis (l'inscription du roi Shabaka).* Paris: Librairie Orientaliste Paul Geuthner.

Grapow, H.
1954 *Anatomie und Physiologie: Grundriss der Medizin der alten Ägypter* 1. Berlin: AkademieVerlag.

Hintze, F.
1979 *Beiträge zur Meroitischen Grammatik.* Meroitica 3. Berlin: Akademie-Verlag.

Iversen, E. I.
1990 "The Cosmogony of the Shabaka Text." In *Studies in Egyptology Presented to Miriam Lichtheim,* Volume 1, edited by S. I. Groll, pp. 485–93. Jerusalem: Magnes Press.

Junge, F.
1973 "Zur Fehldatierung des sog. Denkmals memphitischer Theologie, oder der Beitrag der ägyptischen Theologie zur Geistesgeschichte der Spätzeit." *Mitteilungen des Deutschen archäologischen Instituts, Abteilung Kairo* 29: 195–204.

Junker, H.
1939 *Die Götterlehre von Memphis (Schabaka-Inschrift).* Abhandlungen de Preussischen Akademie der Wissenschaften, philosophisch-historische Klasse, 23. Berlin: Verlag der Akademie der Wissenschaften.
1941 *Die politische Lehre von Memphis.* Abhandlungen der Preussischen Akademie der Wissenschaften, philosophisch-historische Klasse, 6. Berlin: Verlag der Akademie der Wissenschaften.

Krauss, R.
1994 "Tilgungen und Korrekturen auf Senenmuts Denkmälern Berlin 2066 und 2096." *Journal of the American Research Center in Egypt* 31: 49–53.

Leclant, J.
1951a "Fouilles et travaux en Égypte, 1950–1951, I." *Orientalia* 20: 453–75.
1951b "Les inscriptions "éthiopiennes" sur la porte du IVe pylône du grand temple d'Amon à Karnak." *Revue d'égyptologie* 8: 101–20.
1981 "Varia Aethiopica." *Mitteilungen des Deutschen archäologischen Instituts, Abteilung Kairo* 37: 289–97.

Lichtheim, M.
1973 *Ancient Egyptian Literature,* Volume 1: *The Old and Middle Kingdoms.* Berkeley: University of California Press.

Luft, U.
1978 *Beiträge zur Historisierung der Götterwelt und der Mythenschreibung.* Studia Aegyptiaca 4. Budapest: Université Eötvös Loránd.

20. Otto 1908, 301, vermutete, dass es schon vor Ptolemaios V. Krönungen in Memphis gab, aber dafür sind auch heute keine Belege bekannt; s. Thompson 1988, 118.

21. Zu den Synoden, s. Thompson 1988, 119 ff.

Otto, W.
1908 *Priester und Tempel im hellenistischen Ägypten: Ein Beitrag zur Kulturgeschichte des Hellenismus,* Volume 2. Leipzig and Berlin: B. G. Teubner.

Pohlenz, M.
1978 *Die Stoa. 5. Aufl. 177.* Göttingen: Vandenhoeck and Ruprecht.

Revillout, E.
1880 "Hypothèque légale de la femme et donations entre époux." *Revue égyptologique* 1: 122–36.

Rink, H.
1924 Strassen und Viertelnamen von Oxyrhynchus. Dissertation, Giessen.

Russmann, E.
1997 "Two Bracelets with Anachronistic Cartouches, with Remarks on Kushite Royal Jewelry and on the Commemoration of Kushite Kings in Egypt." *Bulletin of the Egyptological Seminar* 13: 47–58.

Schlögl, H. A.
1980 *Der Gott Tatenen: Nach Texten und Bildern des Neuen Reiches.* Orbis Biblicus et Orientalis 29. Freiburg: Universitätsverlag; Göttingen: Vandenhoeck and Ruprecht.

Sethe, K.
1928 *Dramatische Texte zu altägyptischen Mysterienspielen.* Untersuchungen zur Geschichte und Altertumskunde Ägyptens 10. Leipzig: J. C. Hinrichs.

Speyer, W.
1970 *Bücherfunde in der Glaubenswerbung der Antike.* Göttingen: Vandenhoeck and Ruprecht.

Thompson, D.
1988 *Memphis under the Ptolemies.* Princeton: Princeton University Press.

Vassilika, E.
1989 *Ptolemaic Philae.* Orientalia Lovaniensia Analecta 34. Leuven: Peeters.

von Bissing, F.
1912 *Neue Jahrbücher für das klassische Altertum, Geschichte und deutsche Literatur und für Pädagogik.* 1. Abteilung, 29. Band, 2. Heft. Leipzig and Berlin: B. G. Teubner.

Yoyotte, J.
1951 "Le martelage des noms royaux éthiopiens par Psammétique II." *Revue d'égyptologie* 8: 215–39.

Zeller, E.
1921 *Die Philosophie der Griechen.* 2. Teil, 2. Abteilung, 4. Auflage. Leipzig: Reisland.

24

"LISTENING" TO THE ANCIENT EGYPTIAN WOMAN: LETTERS, TESTIMONIALS, AND OTHER EXPRESSIONS OF SELF

BARBARA S. LESKO

Brown University, Providence

Few have done more to facilitate the study of the ancient Egyptian woman than Edward F. Wente, whom I am proud to call friend and former professor. Wente's translations and publications of letters, first *Late Ramesside Letters* (1967), and more recently *Letters from Ancient Egypt* (1990), have made available to a wide research community the very words of ancient women, something rarely heard from antiquity.

Egyptologists sometimes forget how fortunate we are to be able to talk about specific, actual people of the past, to know names not only of priests, scribes, and officials, but also those of their families, and to have some details of the careers they pursued, the responsibilities they handled, and the places they frequented. We have many more texts available than do our colleagues in most other areas of ancient studies, and texts are the most essential building blocks for constructing social history. The letters Wente has published provide insights into true-life situations of ordinary people.

Reading the anguished Letters to the Dead, the worried letters to absent relatives, the demands of harried administrators intensifies ancient Egyptian reality. In particular though, we welcome the publication of letters to and from women, as these Egyptian letters offer rare opportunities to listen to ancient women and to learn about their expectations and concerns. The letters Wente selected were produced over a wide span of centuries and offer to Egyptology and Women's Studies rare material the like of which is seldom available to historians of any time before the modern age. Too much ancient documentation used to reconstruct ancient women's lives has been the product of men — the work of artists or of professional writers of the elite scribal class, an urban group, an educated minority who cannot be trusted to portray accurately or sufficiently what ancient women were like. For this we must turn to documents generated by women themselves. Besides private letters, there is at least one other body of texts that preserves women's speech: the papyri recording testimony in a legal context. Like the letters from women, this testimony was spoken and taken down by a professional scribe. In neither case does the dependence on dictation preclude the genuineness of such spoken words, as even today courtroom testimony is recorded and regarded as an accurate and vital rendition of the testifier's intentions.

Rhetoric is often defined as the "art of persuasion," and the surviving letters and court testimonies of women from ancient Egypt do usually try to persuade a listener or reader to believe, to agree, or to act on the advice or command of the "speaker." Thus, the documentation I discuss here is among the world's earliest evidence for the rhetoric of women.

In his article "Ancient Egyptian Rhetoric," Michael Fox (1983) overlooks both letters and legal testimony as sources and concentrates on only the didactic texts and their teachings about the efficacy of speech when he argues for the ancient Egyptians' "rightful place in the history of rhetoric" by bringing the Instruction of Ptahhotep and the later writers to the attention of the larger scholarly community. Fox discerns five basic canons of rhetoric in the didactic texts. All five are emphasized in the earliest of such texts attributed (surely as an argument from authority) to the Old Kingdom vizier. The other texts, ranging from 1900 B.C. to perhaps as late as 100 B.C., contain some, but not all, of his five points. Perhaps this more limited range of possibilities may be attributed to the changing fortunes of Egyptian society and the oppressive growth of the political and theological forces that resulted in the weakening of individual freedom and the increase of pietistic "resignation" as pointed out by John A. Wilson (1951, pp. 303–05). The latest texts, from a period of political reversals for the country, are so cautious that silence seems to have been the safest course: "Muteness is better than a hasty tongue" (Lichtheim 1980, p. 171).

Gold of Praise: Studies on Ancient Egypt in Honor of Edward F. Wente
Edited by Emily Teeter and John A. Larson
Studies in Ancient Oriental Civilization 58
Chicago: Oriental Institute, 1999

According to Fox (1983, pp. 12–15), the five tenets of effective speech originally recognized by the Egyptians include:

1. Keeping silent; allowing the opponent his say
2. Finding the right moment to speak up
3. Restraining passionate words
4. Demonstrating command of the facts and avoiding exaggerations and evasions
5. Truth; belief that truth will win out in the end, and false words will eventually bear witness against their speaker

Fox (1983, p. 16) believes that, for the Egyptians, these five tenets originally constituted an ethos that was "itself a form of proof. The didactic literature gives no thought to argumentation, as such, and shows no awareness of the possibility that argumentation could operate independently of ethos. Ethos stands on its own."

Assuming that the continual reaffirmation of the official guidelines might have been taught by the state and temple schools for generations, might one compare this with the actual speech of people? The sage Ptahhotep, of course, tells us that, in his opinion, "fine speech" may be found among maid servants, probably the most humble group he could imagine. So the ancient wise man did not rule out the possibility of uneducated eloquence. It is difficult to imagine a society in which every office holder was the model of decorum, able "constantly to practice the virtues of silence and self-control" as Fox (1983, p. 17) believes. The state publications themselves, the official inscriptions on the walls of temples and on monumental stelae, have long been recognized as being true forms of propaganda in their claims of divine support, their demeaning of adversaries, covering up of political reversals, and finding victories where none existed (Wilson 1951, p. 246; Säve-Söderbergh 1951, p. 64). Thus surely it is naive to think that Egyptians could not have "conceived of an instrumental rhetoric of deceit" (Fox 1983, p. 19, n. 7). Indeed, the use of "fine words and choice phrases" to divert a hearer is mentioned in the Prophecies of Neferti (Redford 1995a, p. 2233), and although not necessarily related to deceit, is seemingly used to disarm.

Even in official records of ordinary people one finds examples of outlandish claims, as in a woman's legal document manumitting slaves wherein she takes an oath that includes an obscene curse:

> ... I make the people whom I have recorded freemen of the land of Pharaoh. Should a son or a daughter or a brother or a sister of their mother or of their father contest with them — except for this son of mine, Pen-diu — for they are no longer slaves to him, but are brothers and sisters to him, being freemen of the land — may a donkey copulate with him and a female donkey copulate with his wife, he who shall call one of them a slave ... (Wilson 1948, p. 148).

Not surprisingly, one finds plenty of evidence in the letters and testimonies of both men and women that hyperbole and dishonesty came naturally to people on the defensive or under duress. The most famous example of extreme rhetorical declarations is surely the literary piece the Eloquent Peasant (or Oasis Dweller as some prefer). Fox is aware of this but attributes the popularity of the story to its providing the official class with a nice contrast to their own carefully controlled daily behavior. However, the official in the story is the one who appears in the most negative light and suffers throughout the berating of the peasant and the humiliation of not being supported by his king. As Donald B. Redford has pointed out recently, the First Intermediate Period produced a literature of expression for the non-official, those at odds with, and critical of, the ruling class (Redford 1995a, p. 2233). Thus the Eloquent Peasant may not have been intended to delight the bureaucrats, but instead any and all who had suffered "the law's delay" and "the insolence of office," as Shakespeare put it.

The Egyptian ruling elite clearly appreciated the power of speech and even feared it. In the Instruction to Merikare, the king advises his son that "a talker is a mischief-maker; suppress him, kill [him], erase his name" (Lichtheim 1973, p. 99; Redford 1995a, p. 2224). Obviously the government schools would have aimed at discouraging those who would question authority openly. Thus they ridiculed and indeed declared irreligious the speech of the "heated man," the protester.

It is possible that the teachings did have some effect among officials, as the "moral personality" was elaborated upon in the "autobiographical" texts of the Middle Kingdom (Lichtheim 1988, p. 6), but too much unbiased documentation has been lost, and too much of the surviving source material was government- and temple-generated to allow us much insight into the opinions and actions of the majority. There are the rare exceptions, of course, such as the accusations in several Deir el-Medina letters and complaints: the Salt Papyrus and the texts regarding the protesting hungry workers of that community reflected in the Strike Papyri come instantly to mind.

LETTERS

It is in the dictations and testimonies of private people, concerned with life's trials and tribulations, that one hears the unbridled emotions of the ancient people. The letters and testimonies of women read as genuine outpourings from the heart even when the subject is their public responsibilities.

The earliest female letter published by Wente is one written about a family matter by a wife to her deceased husband during the Sixth Dynasty (ca. 2250 B.C.). This is Cairo Linen CG 25975 (Wente 1990, p. 211, no. 340). Clearly the inheritance of an estate is at stake because the rightful heir is being turned out of his father's house, perhaps because the father had been married previously and engendered children by an earlier wife. The widow hopes not only to encourage her son's father to protect his claim, but also to involve other deceased relatives in persecuting the other claimants who have already entered the property and carried off its furnishings. The widow's approach is an appeal to fatherly feeling and loyalty, and she emphasizes her consternation by declaring she would rather be dead than to have to witness the ruination of her son by these envious parties.

Remarkably, two letters survive from about 800 years apart, in which a woman directly addresses her king. Reflecting a primary occupation of women, both letters concern weaving and reveal the sender to be in charge of a weaving studio. Surprisingly, these women with authority over others in the workplace seem to exhibit little trepidation about communicating with the all-powerful god-king of Egypt, even though in the case of the earlier letter the sender uses no professional title that would distinguish herself (P. Kahun III, 3, from the Twelfth Dynasty; Wente 1990, p. 82, no. 101). The woman supervisor apparently has a problem that she must explain and she is excusing herself by implying that the problem would not exist if the king had supplied ration-pay to her workers on time. She stresses the difficulty of her situation by asking the king to step in and solve it himself. This surely is an odd letter because even if the sender *were* in charge of royal weaving studios, one would not expect her to trouble her *sovereign* with the news that the quota is not being met, and it is surprising to find her scolding the king about his neglectfulness. However, our correspondent is presumably having difficulty getting her staff of largely foreign laborers to work due to the lack of ration deliveries, which come from the royal storehouses. Instead of appealing to an officer of the treasury or even the vizier, the lady Irer, in her desperation, writes for help directly to her king!

The second letter, from P. Gurob III recto, also concerns foreign workers but in a royal weaving studio of the Nineteenth Dynasty, and I quote it because the strong personality of the writer is well conveyed.

> I shall have myself boasted about because of them and not let fault be found with me. It is advantageous that my Lord, l.p.h., has had people sent to *me* to be taught and instructed how to perform this important occupation (of weaving). It is fortunate that my Lord has found someone fit to do that the like of which had not been done for Pre, because those who are here are senior apprentices. It is only such people as are like those people whom my Lord, l.p.h., sent who are *capable* of functioning and who are *capable* of receiving my personal instruction, since they are foreigners like those who used to be brought to us in the time of Usermare-setepenre, l.p.h., (Ramesses II), the Great God, your good (grand)father, and who would tell us, "We were quite a number in the households of the officials," and who would receive instruction and so be able to perform whatever was told them (Wente 1990, p. 36, no. 34; italics mine).

In this letter our unfortunately unidentified but elderly correspondent expresses pride in her accomplishments. Apparently she has met quotas and deadlines and wants the king to know that the products of her harem palace workshops are fit for the gods. She also boldly tells her royal boss that he is fortunate to have *her* in charge. She appreciates having "senior apprentices" who are capable of being trained by her and she reminds the king that she has been training expert weavers since the reign of his grandfather.

While these women may have been speaking truthfully, there is nothing of the carefully restrained speech in their letters to their sovereign. They complain, boast, and offer excuses. The first woman had the ready justification of being obliged to serve her one month of temple duty which, legitimately it would seem, took her away from her workshop responsibilities.

Women also occupied positions of authority in temples in ancient Egypt. If not always as chief celebrants of the cult, they could, as some letters from the late Ramesside period indicate, have responsibility for looking after the storehouses from which offerings for the resident deity of the temple would be taken, and for distributing the regular rations for those offerings on a daily basis. It has been suggested that such authority came to a woman only through marriage (Robins 1993, p. 124), but nepotism was rife for men as well — allowing sons to prosper — so benefiting from family connections was not unique to women and there is no way to know that women would have handled responsibilities for a husband only in his absence from the job and only while he lived. The above-mentioned women administrators in the palace factories could well have been single, just as were some of the highly placed women involved with major temples. The Twentieth Dynasty's Tomb Robbery Papyri indicate that there were at least four group tombs in the Theban necropolis for female singers associated with the divine votaresses of the Ramesside period (Peet 1930, p. 39), which suggests that unmarried women with temple careers existed and were so consecrated to the temples that they merited special arrangements upon death. The careers of these female singers could well have been full-time careers, and we should not assume that celibacy was unknown among ancient Egyptian women.

Among Wente's collected letters are three that demonstrate the active involvement of women in the receiving and dispensing of temple grain, one of which is from Henuttowy, Chantress of Amun-Ra, to Nesamenope, her (presumed) husband and a necropolis scribe, dated to the Twentieth Dynasty. Henuttowy's letter provides insight into the problems she faced in his absence:

> You wrote me saying, "Receive the 80 *khar*-measures of grain from this transport boat of the fisherman Iotnefer," so you said [in] writing. I went [to] receive them and found only 72.5 *khar*-measures with him. I asked him, "What's the meaning of only 72.5 *khar*-measures of grain," so I asked him, "whereas it is 80 *khar*-measures that are stated in his letter?" The men replied, "It is three completely full withdrawals that we have measured out for ourselves, each having 2.5 *khar*-measures, thus netting 72.5 *khar*-measures of grain," so they replied. I maintained my silence thinking that until you return, Amon, United with Eternity, will have done every sort of bad thing to me. ...
>
> Now Amon, United with Eternity, has caused the grain to be put in a chest and has caused a seal to be affixed to it. See, you shall join up with Paseny and you two shall consult with the overseer of granaries concerning the grain for Amon, United with Eternity, because he (Amon) hasn't got even one *oipe*-measure's worth for his divine offerings today. You mustn't abandon him, either of you two (Wente 1990, p. 174, no. 290).

Clearly the woman administrator is beside herself facing an arrears in deliveries she had expected for her temple stores. Henuttowy fears the wrath of her god and is intent on impressing her correspondent with the fact that she is hard pressed to come up with any grain for the divine offerings and has had to find it from elsewhere, possibly her own home stores. So Henuttowy beseeches the men she trusts to take up the matter with the overseer of granaries and not to abandon the god to whom she is responsible. It is interesting to note that Henuttowy says she "maintained my silence" before the displeasing explanations of the delivery men, and only poured out her indignation to her intimate correspondent. Whether Henuttowy held her tongue rather than make accusations about being cheated because it was the proper way for educated people to behave or because she was timid is problematic. Deborah Sweeney (1995, pp. 180–81) points out that Henuttowy was quite free in insisting that Nesamenope take action. It surely is also significant that Henuttowy mentions, at the end of her long letter, that she feels pressured because of the letter the vizier had written *to her*.

Again from the Twentieth Dynasty comes a letter from a more highly placed female temple cult leader, and probably the wife of a high priest. This letter not only shows female authority over temple supplies, but is also noteworthy for the self-confident, if not arrogant, manner in which this principal of the temple's *ḫnr* addresses a troop commander:

> The principal of the harem of Amon-[Re, King of] the Gods, Herere, to the troop captain Peseg. Quote:
>
> What's this about the personnel of the [great] and noble necropolis [concerning whom] I wrote to you, saying, "Give them rations," that you haven't yet given them any? [As soon as my let]ter reaches you, you shall look for the grain which [I wrote you] about and give them rations from it. Don't make [...] complain to me again. Have them prepared [for] people [...] commission them (Wente 1990, p. 200, no. 324).

Clearly not all women administrators felt they had to use carefully moderated speech when addressing men and did not hesitate to issue commands and make demands. The Late Ramesside Letters give incontrovertible proof that women could have authority over others — even men — in the workplace and some highly placed women could issue orders even to military officers on matters of public importance.

LEGAL TESTIMONY

Naunakhte's is the most famous testimony of a woman to survive from ancient Egypt and is thus well known to the reader, but a number of women were brought to testify before the important tribunal investigating the robberies of royal tombs in the late Twentieth Dynasty.

What follows is a woman's testimony, the beginning unfortunately lost, recorded on papyrus (BM P. 10052):

> Now when some days had elapsed this brother of mine came together with the foreigner Userhetnakht and the incense-roaster Shedsukhons and the incense-roaster Nesamūn and Perpethew, total 4 men. They went to this workshop(?). And I went after them. They reviled (?) me. And I said to them, What am I to [split] with you? This brother of mine said to me, Go, bring me five pieces of wood. I brought them to them. And they divided a mass of treasure and made it into four (*sic*) parts, ten *deben* of silver and 2 *deben* of gold and 2 seals falling to each man among them. I took the share of my husband and put it aside in my store-room and I took one *deben* of silver thereof and bought *shesh*-grain with it. Now when some days had passed Amenkhau the son of Mutemheb came with the scribe of the divine records Nesamūn. They said to me, Give up this treasure. He was with Amenkhau my own brother! They said to me, Give up this treasure. But I said to them with an air of boldness, My brother will not let me be interfered with. So said I, and Amenkhau gave me a blow with a spear on one of my arms, and <I> fell [down](?). I got up and entered the store-room, and I brought this silver and I handed it over to him together with the 2 *deben* of gold and the two seals, one of real lapis lazuli and one of turquoise: there was a weight of 6 *kite* of fine gold in them in mounting and setting. She said, I saw nothing else (Peet 1930, pp. 148–49; underline mine).

Another woman was questioned by the high tribunal:

> The citizeness Ēse was brought, the wife of the gardener Ker of the funerary chapel of Ramōse. There was given to her the oath by the Ruler to the effect that if she spoke falsehood she should be mutilated and placed on the stake. The vizier said to her, What is the story of this silver which your husband brought away from the Great Tombs? She said, I did not see it. The scribe Dhutmōse said to her, How did you buy the servants which you bought? She said, I bought them in exchange for crops (?) from my garden. The vizier said, Let Painekh her servant be brought that he may accuse her (Peet 1930, p. 152).

For the record, the servant was examined, but his testimony was inconclusive. Other women were brought who likewise claimed their recently increased buying power was due to their selling of crops. One woman claimed to have earned a considerable amount of silver "in exchange for barley in the year of the hyenas when there was a famine" (Peet 1930, p. 153).

The testimonies are fascinating, and while we can suspect evasion and dishonesty in some, it must be remembered that they were delivered under threat of a horrible penalty and that some were extracted under torture. The first woman recounted, with some pride, the boldness of her confrontation with men, first the tomb robbers from whom she asked for a portion from their take, even though they had reviled her for following them, and then with another group of men who eventually do persuade her — by brute force — to fetch and hand over to them her husband's portion of the stolen property.

The alibi as defense is demonstrated next by the woman who claimed that she knew nothing about any stolen property and then claimed that her increased buying power was the result of her own clever marketing of homegrown produce. This alibi in the face of severest punishment might not have been convincing, but it testifies to one of the economic roles open to women and the possible independence or self-reliance this could avail her. A similar claim was made by another woman in testimony before this court.

Just before this citizeness Ese was brought in to testify, a man in the "witness box" recalled the exasperated words of his mother to a man of her family involved in tomb robbing: "Silly old man that you are, what you have done is committing a theft" (Peet 1930, p. 152). This retort to a man is similar to another instance, found among Late Ramesside Letters (Wente 1967, p. 80; 1990, p. 173, no. 289). In a letter referring to the telling of jokes to a chief tax master (at the suggestion of the letter writer's wife), the scribe Dhutmose recalls the case of a "wife blind in one eye who had been living in the house of a man for twenty years; and when he found another woman, he said to her, 'I shall divorce you because you are blind in one eye,' and she answered him, 'Is this what you have just discovered during these twenty years that I've spent in your house?'" [1]

---

1. I thank Joris Borghouts for reminding me of this small but telling example of the lack of temerity in the rhetoric of ancient Egyptian women.

ROYAL RHETORIC

Bold speech on the part of a queen was credited by the ancient Egyptians themselves for turning the course of the uprising against the Hyksos in favor of the Thebans. It is unfortunate that we have nothing specific on how Queen Ahhotep rallied the troops (*Urk.* 4, p. 21.25). From the monuments of Hatshepsut come references to the female king speaking directly to her people "who listened, falling down in awe" (*Urk.* 4, p. 245.1).

It may be asked whether Hatshepsut's "speeches" as recorded truly reflect female rhetoric, or whether they are actually typically royal, i.e., male in tone and theme? Examination of her Deir el-Bahri and Speos Artemidos inscriptions reveals metaphors and citations that specifically reflect upon Hatshepsut's place in history and her gender. For example, when Hatshepsut states at Speos Artemidos that she "raised up what had been ruined formerly, when the Asiatics were in the fold of the Delta at Avaris," the text appears written for her time and reflects her interest in reconstructing major buildings in her realm. The same text uses the female pronoun when Hatshepsut claims that she was "foretold"; "she will become a conqueror" it was said. However, the prediction that a young royal person will become a conqueror is traditional royal rhetoric found at least as early as the reign of Senwosret I, who claimed to have been "mighty even in the egg ... I was hailed as a born conqueror" (Redford 1995b, p. 166).

At Deir el-Bahri, however, the gender of Hatshepsut and the texts written specifically for her are obvious, as in the description of the successful completion of the Punt expedition:

> I will act as the Great One for the Lord of Eternity. I will do more than what was formerly done. I will cause it to be said in the future: "How beautiful is she, through whom this happens."

This possible allusion to Hatshepsut's comely appearance (goodness is also another possible translation, of course) would seem more appropriately placed in the mouth of a female ruler and could well be original to Hatshepsut's proclamation. The word for beauty appears more clearly again on her obelisk base inscription where she is proclaimed the female Horus, "daughter of Amun-Ra, his favorite, his only one, who exists with him, the splendid image of the All-Lord, whose beauty the souls of Heliopolis created" (*Urk.* 4, p. 361.2).

Hatshepsut's claims of divine birth and being the favorite of her father and of Amun-Ra were protestations of one who was attempting the almost unprecedented, reminding one of her colossal and her leonine sculpted images. Hatshepsut's speeches are strong — full of bombast and divine metaphor. One can feel the queen's pride but still sense her insecurity with her daring undertaking. The Speos Artemidos and obelisk texts were presented as genuine oratory and may actually reflect remarks the queen made to her court. Indeed, such a situation is described in the recounting of the Punt expedition, where it is specifically stated that in year 9 the ruler appeared, wearing the Atef crown, seated on the great throne of electrum in the seclusion of the palace, and the officials and friends of the court hastened in to hear the nature of (her) command (*Urk.* 4, p. 349.1). Hatshepsut may act as king, but her texts often reveal her femininity and would seem to represent in essence her own oratory, similar to today's speeches professionally written for political leaders that are credited to them but represent their own personalities and ideas.

It is obvious that ancient Egyptian royalty did not abide by the strictures to be honest, cautious, and humble, but then they were judged divine and not truly part of the human community. The schools taught moderation, fairness, and honesty to those who would serve royalty and the state.

Similarly, the outbursts of the frustrated, frightened, or exasperated common-born women cannot be expected to compare favorably (by ancient Egyptian standards) with the teachings about rhetoric or proper speech that survive in the didactic texts, the context of which is entirely different. On the other hand, the teachers were presenting a theoretical situation that may confront a bureaucrat. Letting subordinates have their say, or defending oneself before an agitated complainer, is not similar to the situation of the women in our examples.

Of course these female rhetorical texts constitute but a minority of the few texts to survive from ancient Egypt that are rhetorical in nature. Other texts, such as those on statues and tomb walls, are customarily placed in the mouth of the male head of the family and preserve only the names and titles of women and their family members, little else — as illustrated by Lichtheim's (1988, p. 38) survey of autobiographies. The paucity of female rhetorical texts is probably due to several causes, including the bias of their portrayers: the male draftsmen and artists who also do not show women playing an active role in society or even the home. It is indeed difficult to fathom why, when universally women cook, sew, raise crops, tend animals, weave baskets, and create ceramics, Egyptian women are not depicted doing so in the tomb paintings. Obviously, these must not be reliable glimpses into a real world but rather into some other sphere. Even when, as on public monuments, a queen takes "decisive" action — like Nefertiti assuming a kingly pose and smiting a captive — she smites a female, not a male. Robins (1993, pp. 169, 172) suggests that it would have been a breach of decorum for a woman to be shown in tomb paintings as mourned by her husband or in a superior role or honorific positioning on a monument vis à vis a man. Queens appear alone in their tombs perhaps for this reason. There are innumerable examples of such gender biases in the art of Egypt and in the literature as well, with its differentiation of good and bad women and the honoring of motherhood. The Instruction of Any, with its appreciation of the efficiency of house mistresses and its cautions against marital quarrels, comes as a welcome relief in the realm of literature. The letters to dead wives prove that Egyptian men did, in actual fact, mourn their spouses (Wente 1990, pp. 216–19, nos. 352–53). Although I have argued for the genuineness of a few of the female-sung love songs, the majority of the "women's songs" are too contrived and literary to be anything but the work of professional writers (Lesko 1986, pp. 523–29). With so much "artificiality" and bias in the representation of women in the ancient source material, the letters Wente has published loom all the more important as major documents in the actual history of women.

References

Breasted, J. H.
1906 *Ancient Records of Egypt*, Volume 2. Reprint 1962. New York: Russell and Russell.

Černý, J.
1945 "The Will of Naunakhte and the Related Documents." *Journal of Egyptian Archaeology* 31: 29–53.

Fox, M. V.
1983 "Ancient Egyptian Rhetoric." *Rhetorica* 1: 9–22.

Gardiner, A. H.
1946 "Davies's Copy of the Great Speos Artemidos Inscription." *Journal of Egyptian Archaeology* 32: 43–56.

Lesko, B. S.
1986 "True Art in Ancient Egypt." In *Studies in Honor of Richard A. Parker,* edited by L. H. Lesko, pp. 85–97. Hanover: University Press of New England.
1997 "Women's Rhetoric from Ancient Egypt." In *Listening to Their Voices: The Rhetorical Activities of Historical Women,* edited by M. M. Wertheimer. Columbia: University of South Carolina Press.

Lichtheim, M.
1973 *Ancient Egyptian Literature*, Volume 1: *The Old and Middle Kingdoms.* Berkeley: University of California Press.
1976 *Ancient Egyptian Literature*, Volume 2: *The New Kingdom.* Berkeley: University of California Press.
1980 *Ancient Egyptian Literature*, Volume 3: *The Late Period.* Berkeley: University of California Press.
1988 *Ancient Egyptian Autobiographies Chiefly of the Middle Kingdom.* Orbis Biblicus et Orientalis 84. Freiburg: Universitätsverlag.

O'Connor, D., and D. P. Silverman, eds.
1995 *Ancient Egyptian Kingship.* Probleme der Ägyptologie 9. Leiden: E. J. Brill.

Peet, T. E.
1930 *The Great Egyptian Tomb-Robberies of the Twentieth Egyptian Dynasty,* Part 1: *Text.* Oxford: Oxford University Press.

Redford, D. B.
1995a "Ancient Egyptian Literature: An Overview." In *Civilizations of the Ancient Near East,* Volume 4, edited by J. M. Sasson, pp. 2223–41. New York: Scribner.
1995b "The Concept of Kingship during the Eighteenth Dynasty." In *Ancient Egyptian Kingship*, edited by D. O'Connor and D. P. Silverman, pp. 157–84. Probleme der Ägyptologie 9. Leiden: E. J. Brill.

Robins, G.
1993 *Women in Ancient Egypt.* Cambridge: Harvard University Press.

Säve-Söderbergh, T.
1951 "The Hyksos Rule in Egypt." *Journal of Egyptian Archaeology* 37: 53–71.

Sweeney, D.
1994 "Henuuttawy's Guilty Conscience (Gods and Grain in Late Ramesside Letter No. 37)." *Journal of Egyptian Archaeology* 80: 208–12.
1995 "Women and Language in the Ramesside Period." In *Abstracts of Papers* (Seventh International Congress of Egyptologists, Cambridge, 3–9 September 1995), edited by C. Eyre, pp. 180–81. Oxford: Oxbow Books.
1998 "Women and Language in the Ramesside Period or, Why Women Don't Say Please." In *Proceedings of the Seventh International Congress of Egyptologists, Cambridge, 3–9 September 1995*, edited by C. Eyre. Orientalia Lovaniensia Analecta 82. Leuven: Peeters.

Wente, E. F.
1967 *Late Ramesside Letters.* Studies in Ancient Oriental Civilization 33. Chicago: University of Chicago Press.

1990 *Letters from Ancient Egypt*. Society of Biblical Literature, Writings from the Ancient World 1. Atlanta: Scholars Press.

Wilson, J. A.

1948 "The Oath in Ancient Egypt." *Journal of Near Eastern Studies* 7: 129–56.

1951 *The Culture of Ancient Egypt*. Chicago: University of Chicago Press.

25

SOME FURTHER THOUGHTS ON CHAPTER 162 OF THE BOOK OF THE DEAD

LEONARD H. LESKO

Brown University, Providence

As one of Professor Wente's first student-colleagues on the Oriental Institute's Epigraphic Survey in Luxor and also as one of his first students in Late Egyptian language courses at the University of Chicago, I have long had the highest regard for both his scholarship and his mentoring. Epigraphy and careful collation were second nature to Ed and he really made the Late Ramesside Letters practically come alive in class. This little tribute may not be totally suited to his main interests as evidenced by his publications, but his personal interest in everything Egyptological should lead him to read and critique it anyway. Because he himself has accepted the fact that some women of ancient Egypt were literate, it should come as no surprise that some of his students would try to explore the possibilities (Wente 1990, p. 9).

In studying the one, almost complete Book of the Dead manuscript in the John Hay Library at Brown University, which I am now preparing for publication with the assistance of Stephen E. Thompson, I was struck immediately by the vignette and the final spell (162) in this Late Period (actually Ptolemaic) text. The imagery in this concluding text is rather remarkable both because of and despite the fact that this is a fairly common ending for late Books of the Dead following the sequence Spells 163, 164, 165, and 162, which is also the sequence of the Hay Papyrus. This group of spells as a whole also occurs in numerical order occasionally and can be followed by one or even a few other spells, but it is almost always near the end of a manuscript.

The spells do not seem to have a great deal in common with one another, but if we can believe the note preceding Spell 163 found in the Turin Papyrus of the Ptolemaic period, at that time they were apparently considered spells that had been taken from another papyrus to serve as additions to the book of Going Forth by Day, which, of course, is known today as the Book of the Dead. In this case, the note added to the end of Spell 162 on another Late Period papyrus would likely indicate the end of this group of additions and also identify the papyrus roll from which the group came as Mistress of the Hidden Seat/Temple, but not everyone would agree with this (see below). Even if this identification of a separate book in the Ptolemaic period is correct, however, it apparently marks neither the beginning nor the end of the story of this particular composition.

Spell 162, of course, also survived independently in abbreviated form on many Late Period hypocephali since it is a spell for providing heat under the head of a spirit. Spell 162 in its earliest full form, which was independent of the other three spells, included a rubric with the instruction that it was "to be said over a figure of the heavenly cow made of fine gold and placed at the neck of the corpse," or "put in writing on a new sheet of papyrus placed under (the deceased's) head." There is no way of knowing how many heavenly cow amulets of fine gold were used for this purpose, but because an option was provided, many people obviously would have chosen the less expensive hypocephali as we know them, and lacking intrinsic value, many of these roundels have survived.

What seemed remarkable to me at first is the fact that the Hay Papyrus belonged to a "god's father," perhaps a "prophet," named Hor, and yet he resorted to the imagery of a cow, even a heavenly cow, to attract his polymorphic god, in one way or another. It is not clear until more than halfway through the spell that the deceased god's father is not actually identified with the cow. Quite the contrary, the otherwise unidentified speaker who addresses the mighty lion, who adores his name and asks him to "hear my voice today" seems to be identifying himself with the cow, even saying twice that "I am the Ihet-cow," until she (the cow) eventually says, "Come to the god's father Osiris Hor, that you may place heat under his head."

Gold of Praise: Studies on Ancient Egypt in Honor of Edward F. Wente
Edited by Emily Teeter and John A. Larson
Studies in Ancient Oriental Civilization 58
Chicago: Oriental Institute, 1999

Spell 162 is a carefully crafted prayer to an unnamed mighty god, whose epithets probably describe Amun-Ra. The speaker in this spell, i.e., the "heavenly cow," addresses the "mighty lion," "lord of the phallus," "the great god to whom the crier has come," in an interesting combination of animal, sexual, and religious imagery, clearly designed to attract the god's attention and make him responsive. The lion, the bull of heaven, and the sun god would all have to respond to this heavenly cow's plea. But what the cow-goddess is asking is not something for herself, but for the sun god to provide heat under the head of the deceased because "he/she is you and vice versa." "O father, most hidden of the hidden ones, father, who art in heaven, give your attention to the corpse of your son, Osiris N. that you may keep him safe in the necropolis." While I was relieved to learn that the priest Hor was not identifying himself with the cow-goddess, I was also impressed by this intercession on his behalf by a goddess considered so knowledgeable, caring, and effective.

Of the history of Spell 162 much more will be learned if and when all the variants are collected and compared. For now, however, I can make only a few observations. We now know that there are more than seventy-two Book of the Dead documents that include some portion of Spell 162. The dates presently assigned to these manuscripts range between the Twenty-first Dynasty and the Roman period, with the majority dating between the Twenty-sixth Dynasty and the Ptolemaic period. The manuscripts were produced originally for both men and women with an approximately equal distribution, except that a majority of the manuscripts known to date prior to the Twenty-fifth Dynasty belonged to women.

A woman named *Tꜣ-wgš*, daughter of *Tꜣ-miw*, an *iḥyt* (sistrum player) of Amun from the Twenty-second or Twenty-third Dynasty, had one of these manuscripts with Spell 162 as its last spell, but without the group Spells 163–165 preceding it (P. Louvre 3252; cf. Bellion 1987, p. 214). A man's text concluded with the sequence Spells 161–165 (P. Amherst 34 belonged to *Ns-pꜣwty-tꜣwy* of the Twenty-second Dynasty; cf. Bellion 1987, p. 8), but a woman named *Pꜣ-šbt-Mwt-wbḫt* owned perhaps the earliest document (P. Berlin 3031) containing Spell 162, dated to the Twenty-first Dynasty. This dating was based on palaeography since the manuscript has a handwriting comparable to that of the Book of the Dead of Neskhons, the wife of the high priest of Amun Pinedjem II (Möller 1905, p. [2]). The usefulness of palaeography for dating Book of the Dead manuscripts has recently been questioned (cf. Mosher 1992, p. 169), but unfortunately there is no better tool. It just has to be improved by the inclusion of more accurately dated handwritings. *Pꜣ-šbt-Mwt-wbḫt*'s long narrow manuscript (2.86 m × 11.00 cm) is generally well written in fourteen short columns (one of which is on the reverse) with each containing six to nine horizontal lines of hieratic text lacking any accompanying vignettes.

What is especially interesting is the fact that Spell 162 was the first rather than the last spell in *Pꜣ-šbt-Mwt-wbḫt*'s book, and it was also so clearly written there — even though the whole work was in the same hand, its later spells appeared more hurried (Möller 1905, p. [2]). The name *Pꜣ-šbt-Mwt-wbḫt* was repeated many times in the fourteen short columns of text in P. Berlin 3031, and although it may raise a few questions, it is still certain that this was a woman's name. The problem is that at first glance the owner's name appears masculine, beginning as it does with a masculine definite article, but it also has the regular abbreviated seated-woman determinative for a feminine name, with a single dot to differentiate it from a seated-man determinative. We can also be reasonably sure that *Pꜣ-šbt-Mwt-wbḫt* was female because almost all of the pronouns used to refer to her within the text of Spell 162 are feminine. The woman is described as *ir n Tꜣ-šd-Ḫnsw*, and to complicate matters, the editor took this parent as her father (perhaps because it had *ir* rather than *ms* or even better *mst*) despite the fact that the determinatives for both names are identical. The parent named was almost certainly *Pꜣ-šbt-Mwt-wbḫt*'s mother, and at least two women who had the name *Tꜣ-šd-Ḫnsw* are known to us.

Although *Pꜣ-šbt-Mwt-wbḫt* is not otherwise known, her mother could have been the *Tꜣ-šd(t)-Ḫnsw* of the Twenty-first Dynasty who was "a songstress of Amun, a prophetess of Amun, a prophetess of Mut of the Birth House, and a prophetess of Nekhbet, the white one of Hierakonpolis." It should be pointed out that while this manuscript might have had an Upper Egyptian origin, we learn from another manuscript (P. Marseilles 91) that Spell 162, if it concludes the group beginning with Spell 163, might have come from Tanis (Yoyotte 1977, pp. 198–99). Spell 162 does refer to the Lion of Might as the "Lord of the Upper Egyptian Crown," however, and a large percentage of the eighty-six or so known hypocephali can also be traced to Thebes (Varga 1961, p. 241). Since many women of the priestly families of this period often held at least one or more religious office or title, it is possible that *Pꜣ-šbt-Mwt-wbḫt*, who lacked even the "songstress" title, died young, and perhaps one could even speculate that her mother composed or dictated the selection of spells on this book. A by-product of our Late Egyptian "names" project might be an explanation of the large number of individuals' names recorded with maternal parent alone.

Spell 162 is also found without the other three spells of this group on three British Museum papyri, as the final spell on two of them and the penultimate spell on the other. Niwinski (1989, pp. 333, 336, 339–40) dates each of these to the Twenty-second Dynasty; two of them belonged to chantresses of Amun (BM 10044, 10329) and one to a priest of Amun and draftsman (BM 10207). All are complete in seven or eight spells and the last is not illustrated. "Opening of the mouth" and "heart" spells (23–26, 28, 27) precede 162 on these, and Spell 180 completes BM 10044.

Clearly, modern scholars are in considerable disagreement about where to end the Book of the Dead proper. While Erik Hornung omits Spells 162–165 from his translation of *Das Totenbuch* (1979, p. 339) saying that they do not belong to the New Kingdom, Jean Yoyotte (1977, p. 197) apparently wants to see the whole additional group of Spells 162–165, which he labels "Todtenbuch," as well as Spells 166–167 labeled "Pleyte," as being of Ramesside origin based on the notes accompanying these spells on some manuscripts. The note beginning Spell 166 on P. Leiden 25 (of the songstress *Ns-Ḫns* of the late Twenty-first Dynasty) says that "the book was found at the neck of Usermaat-Ra in the Necropolis" and Yoyotte is probably correct in arguing that this was a reference to Ramesses II rather than to Ramesses III as Pleyte had thought (Pleyte 1881/2, p. 52). There are other interesting variants on this note as well. The note attached to the beginning of Spell 166 on P. Leiden T. 30 (which had been made for another late Twenty-first Dynasty songstress *Mwt-m-ỉpt*) said that "the book had been found at the neck of the Osiris songstress of Amun, Isis," and according to P. Leiden T. 31 it was "found in the necropolis in the time of *User-ma-Ra*."

Incidentally, the note evidently applies only to the version of Spell 166 that appears for the first time in the Twenty-first Dynasty. The Pleyte version of Spell 166 indeed was already attested in P. Berlin 3031 (mistakenly referred to as 3081 in Yoyotte 1977, p. 197, n. 20), and as stated above, this papyrus is one of the earliest manuscripts that has Spell 162. While Allen (1974, p. 162), Faulkner (1985, p. 161), and Hornung (1979, pp. 339–40) include in their translations only the Eighteenth Dynasty version of Spell 166, i.e., the spell for the headrest from Nebseny's Papyrus, this was not at all the same text as the later version of Spell 166; only Barguet (1967, p. 239) includes a translation of both versions of this interesting spell.

Pleyte's Spell 167 is clearly and closely connected with 162 and 166. Because it has a note saying that it was found west of Memphis under the head of a radiant one by Prince Khaemwaset, it should have been some form of hypocephalus, also supposed to be Ramesside, and this spell does include similar magical names.

Based on the association of Spells 162 and 166 on the same early document, P. Berlin 3031, their similar use of magical phrases or loanwords, and the use of Late Egyptianisms, I suspected at first that the origin of these spells would not have been much earlier than the document on which they were found, especially since notes attributing discoveries of such texts are notoriously suspect. The secret names occurring on Spells 162 and 166 might have been either Semitic borrowings, as is frequently suggested, or magical invocations, as seems more likely. The note in Spell 166 of P. Berlin 3031 that "this book was found at the neck of King User-ma-Ra in the Necropolis," indeed, no longer seems impossible, especially since this spell has several references to "Your Majesty" including one that refers to the "ushabtis which belong to Your Majesty, Osiris *Pꜣ-šbt-Mwt-wbḫt*"! Since the Theban royal tombs had recently been plundered and the high priests of Karnak in the Twenty-first Dynasty were involved with the reburial of the mummies, they could have discovered texts in the process, with which they would not have been familiar, especially if the Ramesside royal mummies had been prepared in the north. This might also help explain the unusual magical phrases or loanwords. The tomb robberies and reburial of the royal mummies obviously provided some impetus to improve on the mortuary literature generally available to non-royals, as seen also in the spread of Amduat papyri, and it is noteworthy that these particular additions to the Book of the Dead persisted throughout the later periods.

It would still be possible to argue for the borrowing of the properly labeled Spell 166 and at the same time for the originality of Spell 162 on P. Berlin 3031, but I cannot do it now with any great confidence. If one argues that Spell 162 originated in P. Berlin 3031, which is the earliest known version, there is generally no problem until the end of the text where the word "son" apparently refers to the deceased. Indeed, Barguet translates "He is your soul" earlier perhaps to avoid this problem, and there is an inconsistency in the writing of the two signs (*sꜣ* and *bꜣ*) in this spell, but he could not use "soul" in the final line. The final line says, "Give your attention to the corpse of your *son*, Osiris *Pꜣ-šbt-Mwt-wbḫt* … , that you may keep *him* safe in the necropolis." If this *sꜣ* were *bꜣ*, the "him" could be translated "it," but would "your soul" make any sense here? There is, of course, also the masculine article beginning *Pꜣ-šbt-Mwt-wbḫt*'s name that could have confused the scribe who would have copied the text for her, but it is still probably more likely that the text from which our earliest known examples of this spell were taken was written originally for a man. I think that it is enough here to show that priestly women were involved, perhaps in the discovery and probably in the selection of these additions to the Book of the Dead for their own and some of their relatives' funerary papyri. It does seem that the entrance of these spells, especially Spell 162 and the new version of Spell 166, into the corpus of the Book of the Dead spells is likely to have been due to one or the other of these Twenty-first Dynasty priestesses.

As stated above, Hornung omits Spells 162–165, but Barguet on the other hand considers Spell 162 to be the concluding spell of the Book of the Dead and takes Spells 163–192 as additional chapters. This assumes that the colophon after Spell 162 on some papyri was original and that the order of the spells was 162–165 originally. Of course, the colophon is also found after Spell 161 (cf. Yoyotte 1977, p. 198) and elsewhere as well. After "spells added from another book as a supplement to Going Forth by Day," P. Marseilles 91 adds that they were found in the temple of Amun-Ra, Lord of the Thrones of the Two Lands in Tanis." This unique prefatory title even without the addition certainly did not "always" precede Spell 163 as stated by Mosher (1992, p. 155). Yoyotte considers the third of his six stages in the development of Spell 162 as the canonical version of the Saite period, proceeding from Spell 162 to Spell 164, while his next stage was called the "deutero-canonical" Spells 163, 164, 165, and 162. Mosher (1992, p. 155) takes the former arrangement as his not very well-attested Memphite tradition and the latter as his Theban tradition, but he also argues that the colophon after Spell 162 marks the end of the Book of the Dead. It would seem to me that the canonical order ("vulgate" as Yoyotte elsewhere terms it) should be Spells 163, 164, 165, and 162 and a secondary, actually much less frequent, version sometimes had Spells 162–165. It would also seem that the colophon could originally have marked the end of this particular group of additional spells (perhaps called Mistress of the Hidden Seat/Temple) rather than the whole book.

At any rate, it is interesting to see how little agreement there is among modern scholars about where the Book of the Dead ends. Even when there may be chronological and geographical clues, they are not always credible enough to convince. The deutero-canonical group may be labeled as found at Tanis, but the textual evidence of Spells 163–165 points to a Nubian connection as I shall demonstrate elsewhere. If we accept that the origin of Spell 162 considerably predates the group, there is another link between Spells 162 and 163. The goddess Neith is mentioned several times in Spell 163 and as Yoyotte (1977, p. 202) has shown she can be linked to the heavenly cow at this time and she can also be described as the mother of Ra. If the intercession of the goddess in Spell 162 is also maternal, it would be even more significant. *Ad Jesum per Mariam* comes to mind. The cow goddess of Spell 162 is not named but has generally been taken to be Hathor. Mosher even points to a parallel with Spell 186, a clear Hathor spell, that concluded a number of Nineteenth Dynasty Books of the Dead. The celestial cow of Spell 162 could have represented either or both goddesses originally, but perhaps the importance of the spell in Saite and later times was the emphasis on Neith, or at least the ambiguity would have permitted either interpretation.

Although each of these additional texts apparently had a separate origin, the connections between the spells are of various interesting types. Clearly, the amulet aspect was or became an important link as indicated by the vignettes and rubrics of the canonical version. But the spells also had links with regard to the body parts (head, eye, mouth, heart) and they were linked in language, strange names, time, and perhaps even place.

What is especially interesting in the case of Spell 162 is the fact that this spell attained the status of the final or concluding spell in so many extant Books of the Dead from later periods and continued an independent existence on the hypocephali. The imagery of the heavenly cow with a solar disk between her horns both in the vignette to Spell 162 and prominently on the hypocephali provides another logical connection since a sun disk on the head would certainly accomplish the task of providing heat under the head. One final thought concerns the significance of providing heat under the head. If the heart had been deemed so all-important earlier, was not this emphasis on the head a significant change in thinking?

Again, the source of the earliest known version of Spell 162 (P. Berlin 3031) might have been written for a man, but the inclusion of this and several other new spells in the Book of the Dead of the Twenty-first Dynasty points to the involvement of women in the transmission process. It probably is significant as well that this papyrus roll comes from the same period during which we have so many Books of the Dead written for women. And we even have an example of a new spell (41a) for a woman that was added to the corpus of texts chosen for inclusion in some subsequent manuscripts including the Book of the Dead of the high priest Pinudjem II (Lesko 1994, pp. 183–84).

References

Allen, T. G.
1974 *The Book of the Dead or Going Forth by Day: Ideas of the Ancient Egyptians Concerning the Hereafter as Expressed in Their Own Terms.* Studies in Ancient Oriental Civilization 37. Chicago: University of Chicago Press.

Barguet, P.
1967 *Le livre des morts des anciens égyptiens.* Paris: Éditions du Cerf.

Bellion, M.
1987 *Égypte ancienne: Catalogue des manuscrits hiéroglyphiques et hiératiques et des dessins, sur papyrus, cuir ou tissu, publiés ou signalés.* Paris: Epsilon.

de Cenival, J.-L.
1992 *Le livre pour sortir le jour: Le livre des morts des anciens égyptiens.* Paris: Pujol.

Faulkner, R. O.
1985 *The Ancient Egyptian Book of the Dead.* Edited by Carol Andrews. London: British Museum.

Hornung, E.
1979 *Das Totenbuch der Ägypter.* Zurich and Munich: Artemis Verlag.

Kitchen, K. A.
1973 *The Third Intermediate Period in Egypt (1100–650 B.C.).* Warminster: Aris and Phillips.

Lesko, L. H.
1994 "Some Remarks on the Books of the Dead Composed for the High Priests Pinedjem I and II." In *For His Ka: Essays Offered in Memory of Klaus Baer*, edited by D. P. Silverman, pp. 179–86. Studies in Ancient Oriental Civilization 55. Chicago: Oriental Institute.

Möller, G.
1905 *Hieratische Papyrus aus den Königlichen Museen zu Berlin*, Volume 2. Leipzig: J. C. Hinrichs.

Mosher, M., Jr.
1992 "Theban and Memphite Book of the Dead Traditions in the Late Period." *Journal of the American Research Center in Egypt* 29: 143–72.

Naguib, S.-A.
1990 *Le clergé féminin d'Amon thébain à la 21e dynastie.* Orientalia Lovaniensia Analecta 38. Leuven: Peeters.

Niwinski, A.
1989 *Studies on the Illustrated Theban Funerary Papyri of the 11th and 10th Centuries B.C.* Orbis Biblicus et Orientalis 86. Freiburg: Universitätsverlag; Göttingen: Vandenhoeck and Ruprecht.

Pleyte, W.
1881 *Chapitres supplémentaires du livre des morts, 162, 162*, 163 [164 à 174].* 3 volumes. Leiden: E. J. Brill.

Varga, E.
1961 "Les travaux préliminaires de la monographie sur les hypocéphales." *Acta Orientalia* 12: 235–47.

Wente, E. F.
1990 *Letters from Ancient Egypt.* Society of Biblical Literature, Writings from the Ancient World 1. Atlanta: Scholars Press.

Yoyotte, J.
1977 "Contribution à l'histoire du chapitre 162 du livre des morts." *Revue d'égyptologie* 29: 194–202.

26

ROYAL ICONOGRAPHY OF DYNASTY 0

THOMAS J. LOGAN

Monterey Peninsula College, California

I am delighted to contribute to this volume honoring Edward Wente who taught us all what a great teacher should be by his personal example: to share your knowledge unselfishly with your students.

This study focuses on the art history and iconography of royal representations during late Dynasty 0 (Nagada IIIa–b).[1] As Kemp (1989, pp. 46–47) says, the "basic iconography of kingship and rule" was an essential element of Egyptian society and Dynasty 0 was a time "of great codifying of traditions." According to Baines (1995, p. 95), "the oldest potential evidence for kingship is iconographic." The essential elements of kingship that set the ruler apart from his subjects and elevated him to the status of a divine ruler were ritualized during Dynasty 0.[2] This process was certainly not complete, but the distinctive type of kingship unique to Egypt was then established. Fortunately there are representations of the king participating in ceremonies, rituals, and possible historical events in the reliefs from Dynasty 0. The nature of the king's role can be determined by ana-

1. On Dynasty 0 in general, see Kaiser and Dreyer 1982, pp. 211–69; Beckerath 1984, pp. 45–46; Williams and Logan 1987, p. 245 ff., Appendix A; Helck 1990, p. 90 ff.; Brink 1996, especially table 5, p. 191.

   Breasted (1931, pp. 709–24) realized that there was a predynastic line of kings. Kaiser (1964, p. 108 ff., fig. 5) shows that Tura was already under the domination of Nagada III/Dynasty 0 kings some 100–150 years before the First Dynasty, further evidence of which is seen in the German excavations at Minshat Abu Omar that show a clear Nagada II presence in the Eastern Delta (Kroeper and Wildung 1985, p. 67) as well as serekhs from Kaiser's Horizon A on Nagada III pottery (ibid., figs. 84, 213), the serekh of King Scorpion at the same site (Wildung 1981, p. 37), and two serekhs of Narmer (Kroeper and Wildung 1985, fig. 213). This evidence shows that the Eastern Delta was part of the Nagada II/III culture as Fischer already suggested in 1958 (pp. 64–88). By the beginning of Nagada III, Egypt was unified by a single culture from Nubia to the Eastern Delta, and by Nagada IIIc the same area was politically unified. The King's Mace-head (see table 26.1, below) depicts a scene from the "wars of consolidation" with a pre-Narmer ruler wearing a red crown. In fact, a Horizon A serekh has been found at Gaza (Gophna 1970, p. 53 ff.), another dating to Horizon A–C was found in Rafiah (Amiran 1970, p. 89 ff.), a serekh containing an amorphous shape that dates to Horizon B was found at ʿEn Besor (Schulman 1976, pp. 25–26), and it is well known that the serekh of Narmer appears in Arad in southern Israel (Amiran 1974, p. 4 ff.) and in Tell Gath (Yeivin 1960, p. 196 ff.), possibly along with that of Scorpion (Yeivin 1963; 1968). For a discussion of the Egyptian presence in Israel/Palestine and for references, see Schulman 1991/92, pp. 88–89, with nn. 43–49. For Egyptian pottery in Israel, see Dreyer 1993a, p. 55, n. 46. To the south, a Dynasty 0 king carved a relief in Lower Nubia (see Murnane 1987, pp. 282–84, fig. 1A–B, the so-called Djer rock inscription).

   The necropolis for the kings of the Thinite Dynasty was Abydos, which began before the First Dynasty with the tombs of at least three of his predecessors: Iry-Hor/Ro (Kaiser and Dreyer 1982, p. 236; *LÄ* 6 "Thinitenzeit," col. 486, B1/2; for a different point of view, see Wilkinson 1993, pp. 241–43); Ka/Sekhen (Kaiser and Dreyer 1982, p. 236; *LÄ* 5 "Sechen," cols. 777–78; *LÄ* 6 "Thinitenzeit," col. 487, B7/9); and Narmer (Kaiser and Dreyer 1982, p. 236; *LÄ* 4 "Narmer," cols. 348–49; *LÄ* 6 "Thinitenzeit," col. 487, B17/19), all of whom should be placed in Dynasty 0. (See now Brink 1996, table 5, p. 151). Note that the development of the cemetery is in an unbroken horizontal sequence showing no break at the modern interval that divides Dynasty 0 and the First Dynasty. And the German excavations have shown that the early U Cemetery at Abydos had begun already in Nagada IId (Dreyer 1993a, p. 26 ff., fig. 9, U127/5; Dreyer 1993b, pp. 10–12).

   The presence of a pre-Thinite Dynasty is implied by the absence of a tomb for Scorpion at Abydos and the presence of the very large Tombs 1 and 2 in the Nagada II/III cemetery in the Fort Wadi at Hierakonpolis and at Nagada itself.

   From an art-historical standpoint Smith (1946, pp. 130–31) shows that there are two art-style periods after the predynastic: the Formative Dynasty 0/1, and the Archaic Dynasty 2/3 prior to the reign of Huni. Williams and Logan (1987, p. 272) conclude that representations from Nagada II to Dynasty 0 show that much of the ritualistic and ceremonial nature of pharaonic kingship was already present (both in Egypt and Nubia) and conclude that Dynasty 0 was not "predynastic."

   The concordance used here is Dynasty 0 equals Nagada IIIa and Nagada IIIb, or Kaiser's Horizons A and B; see Brink 1996, table 5, p. 151. But note that because of recent discoveries at Abydos by Dreyer et al., Dynasty 0 may "have to be stretched more and more" (Brink 1996, p. 154).

   I wish to thank Drs. Peter Dorman and Emily Teeter for valuable suggestions.

2. Or "commemorated" (Redford 1986, p. 133).

Gold of Praise: Studies on Ancient Egypt in Honor of Edward F. Wente
Edited by Emily Teeter and John A. Larson
Studies in Ancient Oriental Civilization 58
Chicago: Oriental Institute, 1999

lyzing his place in ritual, the iconography of the king, and his dress, accouterments, retainers, and activities on these documents. By establishing what existed during that period, the original ritualistic basis of kingship can be looked at and perhaps we can gain a more reliable idea of the aspects of royal ritual during the course of Dynasty 0. This study is limited, as far as possible, to contemporary source documents.[3]

ROYAL REPRESENTATIONS IN RELIEF

The starting point is a trio of ceremonial or memorial "documents"[4] from Hierakonpolis — the Narmer Mace-head, Cylinder Seal, and Palette — followed by a brief look at the Scorpion Mace-head.

Narmer Mace-head

The Narmer Mace-head is the subject of many interpretations:

- Records conquest of the north (Schott 1951, pp. 23–24)
- Records wedding to the heiress of the northern kingdom (Emery 1961, p. 47; Hoffman 1979, pp. 322–23)
- Records year date of the "appearance of the king of Lower Egypt" or viewing the prisoners and booty captured in battle (Kemp 1989, p. 60; Millet 1990, p. 56)
- Records *sed*-festival (Vandier 1952, p. 602 ff.; Clayton 1994, p. 19)

The Narmer Mace-head depicts a ceremony centered on the king. To determine the nature of the ceremony, nine items on the Narmer Mace-head and Niuserra *sed*-festival reliefs are compared (figs. 26.1–8, 10).

Standards (fig. 26.1): Four standards include a jackal, cushion/placenta, and two falcons,[5] which are four elements also present on the Narmer Palette. Note that the jackal dominates on both the Narmer and Niuserra *sed*-festival reliefs.

a b

Figure 26.1. Comparison of Standards on the (*a*) Narmer Mace-head and (*b*) Niuserra *Sed*-festival Reliefs (after Kaiser 1971, fold-out pls. 4–5)

3. It is tempting to use later, more complete material for reconstructions, but this results in viewing one phenomenon through many later layers. As Birkstam (1977, p. 279) states, "Although there are already in the Early Dynastic Period several allusions to some of the rituals which were connected with kingship, our knowledge of their details and of their course and extent is for these early times with few exceptions very limited and has many gaps. Consequently the author's account of the early rituals is to a large extent a reconstruction based on materials of a much later date. This, of course, gives to the account of the early rituals a very hypothetical character." Or, as Kemp (1989, p. 59) says, "It is tempting with Egyptian religion to combine sources from all periods in order to create a comprehensive explanation. ... But continuity of forms masked changes in meaning and practice. ... For each period the sources should be interpreted within the spirit and for the illumination of that age alone."

4. See Baines 1989, p. 475; Williams and Logan 1987, p. 245 ff. The presumption is that these reliefs are as valid as historical documents as reliefs from dynastic times because some depict a specific event, some a wish, some a ceremony, and some propaganda.

5. The standards are probably the *šmsw-ḥrw* standards; see Kaiser 1959, pp. 119–32; Beckerath, *LÄ* 3 "Horusgeleit," cols. 51–52. The Khons/placenta/*nḫn*-sign has been interpreted as originally a skin (ibid., col. 51) or a "cushion-like object" equated with *Nḫn* and Hierakonpolis (Baines 1995, p. 120). The jackal is probably to be equated with Wepwawet (Emery 1961, p. 126) or Khenty-imentyw of Abydos, later Anubis (Baines 1995, p. 120).

Retainers (fig. 26.2): Narmer is followed by retainers. The major figure is labeled *ṯ* (on the Narmer Palette the same official is labeled *ṯt*) and wears a distinctive robe.[6] It is difficult to be sure who this might be among the multitude of officials in the Niuserra *sed*-festival reliefs, but the *sm*-priest wears a similar garment with a tail.

a b

Figure 26.2. Comparison of Retainers on the (*a*) Narmer Mace-head and (*b*) Niuserra *Sed*-festival Reliefs (after Kaiser 1971, fold-out pls. 4–5)

Sandal bearer (fig. 26.3): The other major attendant is a sandal bearer,[7] who is present on the Niuserra *sed*-festival reliefs and labeled *smr* "retainer." On the Narmer Mace-head, and on the Narmer Palette, the attendant wears a loincloth with a large frontal tie.

a b

Figure 26.3. Comparison of Sandal Bearers on the (*a*) Narmer Mace-head and (*b*) Niuserra *Sed*-festival Reliefs (after Kaiser 1971, fold-out pls. 4–5)

Fan bearers (fig. 26.4): Other retainers include fan bearers. Baines (1995) equates these with the formula "all protection and life." The fans protect the king from harm and the Egyptians from the king.

a b

Figure 26.4. Comparison of Fan Bearers on the (*a*) Narmer Mace-head and (*b*) Niuserra *Sed*-festival Reliefs (after Kaiser 1971, fold-out pls. 4–5)

6. Beckerath (1962, p. 5) sees *ṯ* here and *ṯt* on the Narmer Palette as related to *wṯt* and translates this as "prince"; *ṯꜣty* is also possible (Helck 1987, pp. 140–41).

7. *ḥm-nswt*(?) or *wdpw-Ḥr* "cup bearer" (Helck 1987, p. 141). For the rosette as palm tree, see Williams 1988, p. 31 ff.

Running men (fig. 26.5): Instead of the king running the boundaries (i.e., the circuit of the field), as we would expect, there are three men with hands clasped to their chest.[8] Unless these running men are the king, they might be the three Great Ones with hands clasped. If, however, the men running actually do have their hands bound, the meaning is clear. The evidence for earlier Dynasty 0 and late Nagada II shows that the ceremony which was antecedent to the *sed*-festival might have included defeated enemies or human sacrifice.[9]

a b

Figure 26.5. Comparison of Running Men on the (*a*) Narmer Mace-head and (*b*) Niuserra *Sed*-festival Reliefs (after Kaiser 1971, fold-out pls. 4–5)

Royal children (fig. 26.6): The royal children (*msw-nswt*) who are depicted seated in a carrying chair with hooped canopy are usually depicted in the plural (Gohary 1992, p. 211, n. 174), but not so here. The children as depicted on the Scorpion Mace-head are bound and being ushered to the right by someone with a mace.[10]

a b

Figure 26.6. Comparison of Royal Children on the (*a*) Narmer Mace-head and (*b*) Niuserra *Sed*-festival Reliefs (after Kaiser 1971, fold-out pls. 4–5)

List of cattle (fig. 26.7): Millet (1990, p. 57) feels that the enumeration of cattle and prisoners negates a *sed*-festival interpretation of the Narmer Mace-head. However, a good parallel is the "enumeration of bovine," which is part of the festivities surrounding the *sed*-festival in the Niuserra *sed*-festival reliefs.

a b

Figure 26.7. Comparison of Lists of Cattle on the (*a*) Narmer Mace-head and (*b*) Niuserra *Sed*-festival Reliefs (after Kaiser 1971, fold-out pls. 4–5)

8. Millet (1990, p. 55, n. 5), who examined the mace-head, says the men are not fettered.
9. Williams and Logan 1987, p. 271. Human sacrifice is first depicted in the Painted Tomb 100 at Hierakonpolis (Nagada II) and continues to be depicted until the time of the Scorpion Mace-head. Human sacrifice seems clear on the labels of Hor-aha (Petrie 1902, pl. 3, no. 6; Helck 1987, p. 149) and Djer (Emery 1961, p. 59, fig. 21, upper register; see Clayton 1994, p. 22, who identifies the scene in question as human sacrifice). For *sed*-festival elements in Tomb 100, see Kemp 1989, p. 38.
10. For the Scorpion Mace-head, see Vandier 1952, p. 600 ff.; for good photographs, see Kantor 1974, pl. 215; Málek 1986, p. 29; Millet 1990, p. 55; idem 1991, fig. 2. Bound prisoners (the predecessor of the *msw-nswt*?) are part of the ceremonies depicted on the Turin Linen, Painted Tomb 100, and Scorpion Mace-head.

King and royal canopy (fig. 26.8): The king holds a flail, is swathed in a long robe, and sits on a single throne. This scene is closely paralleled on the Den label a with single throne-box (fig. 26.9) and Niuserra *sed*-festival reliefs where he sits on a double throne (fig. 26.8b). The royal canopy with two poles is also present on the University College King's Mace-head (Adams 1974, p. 3, pls. 1–2; Kantor 1974, fig. 28).

a b

Figure 26.8. Comparison of King and Royal Canopy on the (*a*) Narmer Mace-head and (*b*) Niuserra *Sed*-festival Reliefs (after Kaiser 1971, fold-out pls. 4–5)

Figure 26.9. Single Throne-box on the Den Label (after Kaiser 1971, fold-out pls. 4–5)

Boundary stones (fig. 26.10): The running of the boundary stones[11] is a very typical part of the *sed*-festival. Here we just have the stones, but as Spencer (1978, p. 52) points out, the stones always occur in *sed*-scenes in triplicate on either side of the king.

a b

Figure 26.10. Comparison of Boundary Stones on the (*a*) Narmer Mace-head and (*b*) Niuserra *Sed*-festival Reliefs (after Kaiser 1971, fold-out pls. 4–5)

Many of these features (figs. 26.1–8, 10) are not diagnostic by themselves, but in context with each other (especially figs. 26.2–3, 5–8) they do seem conclusive: the Narmer Mace-head depicts a *sed*-festival. This is not to say that during Dynasty 0 the *sed*-festival could not be combined with other activities, such as the presentation of booty in the context of a *sed*-ceremony (Baines 1995, p. 118), or that the meaning did not change. But this was a formative period when many of the distinctively Egyptian rituals were defined.

The next two documents, the Narmer Palette and Narmer Cylinder Seal, both depict conquest (real, desired, or a re-enactment of the accomplishments of Horus) and the king's role as protector. The seal refers to Tjhenu (Libya or the Western Delta; Gardiner 1947, pp. 116*–19*) and the palette to *Tꜣ-mḥw* (the Delta).[12]

11. The running between the *ḏnbw*; see Naville 1892, pl. 16; Spencer 1978, pp. 52–55.

12. Millet (1990, p. 59) suggests "Year of the Smiting of the Northland" as a year-dated temple gift.

Narmer Cylinder Seal

A cylinder seal was found at Hierakonpolis (Quibell 1900, pl. 15:7). Narmer is depicted as a raging catfish with human arms smiting fettered Libyans (fig. 26.11).[13]

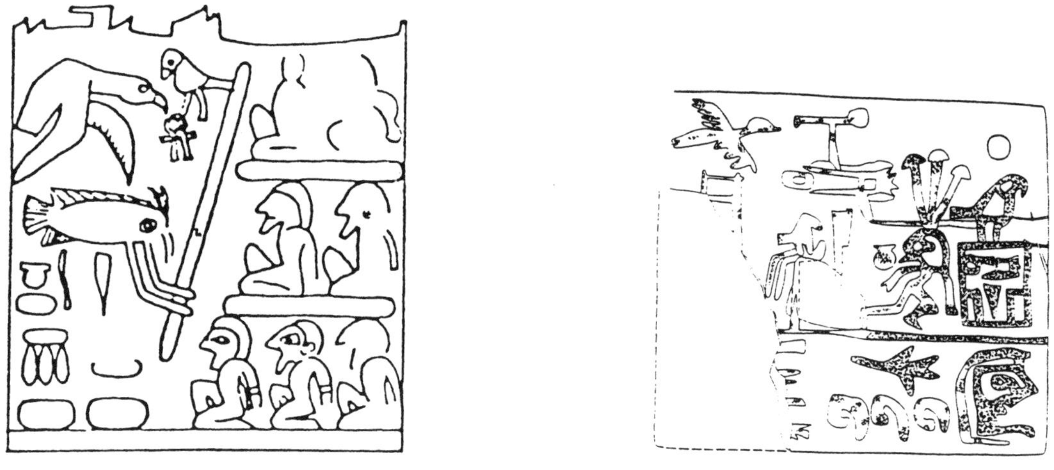

a b

Figure 26.11. (*a*) Narmer Cylinder Seal, Drawing by Michelle Germon Riley (after Baines 1989, p. 475), and (*b*) Narmer Ivory Label from Abydos (after Dreyer et al. 1998, fig. 29)

A protective vulture hovers over Narmer (as on the Narmer Mace-head) while Horus offers Narmer *ankh*-signs. The vulture is probably Nekhbet, who is associated with the ruler as a protective force. Here the context is military conquest as seen on the Khasekhem vases from Hierakonpolis depicting his conquest(?) of the north.[14] There Nekhbet stands upon the *šnw*-signet encircling two hieroglyphic signs (*b, š*) next to a mace smiting a foe sporting papyrus plants from his head. This scene is reminiscent of the vignette on the Narmer Palette.[15]

Later, of course, Nekhbet, in conjunction with Horus, or the cobra Wadjet grasping a *šnw*-sign are commonly associated with the king as protective elements.[16]

The conquest of Tjhenu depicted on the Narmer Cylinder Seal and Narmer Ivory Label are stylistically and thematically reminiscent of the scene on the Libyan Tribute Palette. To determine whether these two documents are chronologically contemporary and thus describe the same event, it is necessary to try to date the palette. The Libyan Tribute Palette contains a scene of military conquest, which Vandier (1952, p. 590, fig. 388) groups chronologically with the Narmer Palette.[17] While the dating of the palettes is difficult, it is obvious that there are different artistic styles involved, but are the differences chronological or regional?

Table 26.1 reflects an artistic development on seventeen documents (ten palettes, three mace-heads, two knife-handles, and two fragments) from drilled eyes to lenticular to plastic eyelids; from etched to modeled ribs; from fleshy to thinner nose; from lion's mane extending to hindquarters to extending to middle of back; from simple knee to more elaborate detailed knees; from no attenuation to attenuation; and from the absence of a groundline to a groundline. The order of the documents in table 26.1 generally agrees with Vandier (1952, pp. 573–99) that ceremonial documents can be placed in a chronological development. An alternative interpretation is regional variation, but the documents from Hierakonpolis do not stand apart from the rest; indeed they fit

13. On this type of anthropomorphism and this document in particular, see Baines 1989, p. 475.
14. Emery 1961, p. 100, fig. 63; Quibell 1900, pls. 36–38.
15. Barta (1975, p. 101) published it as part of his preservation/slaying the enemies ritual. Is this to be equated with the *bꜣš*-Bakhu of the Sahura Libyan scene? For the Sahura reliefs, see Borchardt 1910, pl. 1.
16. For other early representations of Nekhbet as protective royal element, see the Djoser niche relief from his south tomb at Saqqara depicting Djoser as he runs the boundary markers (Spencer 1993, p. 100); for an example from the reign of Pepi II, see Gardiner and Peet 1952, pl. 8; idem 1955, p. 62 f. For a wonderful Old Kingdom example of Nekhbet and Wadjet as protective forces, see the Djedkara Isesi stone vessel in the British Museum (Quirke 1992, p. 62, fig. 35, or PT 1451: "You have protected me, O Nekhbet"). The fans depicted in the Narmer Mace-head above also act as protective elements.
17. Vandier's (1952, pp. 590–99) second (later) group includes the Libyan Tribute, Bull, Metropolitan Museum of Art Fragment, and Narmer Palettes; the first (earlier) group of palettes includes scenes of hunting or animals (ibid., pp. 573–89). Vandier bases his division of the groups on Bénédite 1916, pp. 18–25, and Ranke 1924/25, pp. 3–12, emended by Fischer 1958, pp. 64–65.

into the development seen in the table. The sequence of the documents as listed in table 26.1 seems to be the relative chronological order. Two fixed dates are Narmer at the end of the sequence and the end of Dynasty 0, and the U-127 Knife-handle fragments that are datable to Nagada IId from associated pottery found in the tomb (Dreyer 1993a, pp. 26–27).

The stylistic criteria developed in table 26.1 suggest that the Libyan Tribute Palette and the Narmer Palette are either stylistically contemporary or temporally very close to each other; therefore, the Narmer Cylinder Seal depicting victory over Tjhenu and the Libyan Tribute Palette are likewise stylistically contemporary or temporally close to each other. These two documents — depicting the conquest of Tjhenu and the bringing of tribute (prisoners on the Narmer Cylinder Seal and livestock consisting of oxen, donkeys, and small bovine on the Libyan Tribute Palette) — could be the precedent for such reliefs as the Sahura Libyan reliefs (and later copies), wherein we see similar tribute from Tjhenu: living prisoners, cattle, and two kinds of bovine.[18]

There also seems to be a development of the royal propaganda from the earlier documents to the Narmer Cylinder Seal. In the earlier tradition seen on the Libyan Tribute[19] and Bull Palettes, standards bring the prisoners. On the King's Mace-head, Horus is responsible for the military victory and the ruler is passive, but on the Narmer Cylinder Seal the king, as the Nar-catfish, is the active vanquisher, which is identical to the rampaging bull or lion as king. An important iconographic change has occurred and perhaps we can see the conclusion on the next document.

Narmer Palette

The other document from the reign of Narmer is the much discussed Narmer Palette with its depiction of the conquest of Lower Egypt.[20] Whether this document records a specific historical event (Redford 1986, p. 133) or a "token of royal achievement" (Baines 1989, pp. 478–79) — a non-specific celebration of the triumph of order — is not important for this discussion. Nor is it important to describe this well-known document. The discussion is limited to a few points.

The rendering of the kneecaps (see table 26.1) is unique, but it is part of the development seen on the other documents (see especially the slightly[?] earlier form on the Vulture Palette as well as fuller treatment on the Scorpion and Narmer Mace-heads; for a similar depiction of a kneecap, see the Min statues from Coptos[21]). The depiction of the detailed leg musculature is unique and is not seen in the earlier documents; the closest parallel is a similar treatment of Djoser's leg on the central stela from his pyramid complex at Saqqara (Firth and Quibell 1935, pl. 16; Kemp 1989, p. 60, fig. 20).

The rendering of large ears is typical for this period for both relief work and statuary (see the fairly contemporary ivory statuette BM 37996 found by Petrie at Abydos, discussed under *Royal Statuary*, below).[22]

The detailed plastic bull's eye has a close parallel in the Bull Palette (see table 26.1). The bull's foreleg and shoulders with their appliqué look, similar human eyes, and groundline also have parallels on the Bull Palette. In fact, the whole rendition of the bull is so similar on both objects it appears that the two are contemporary, which has also been suggested by Baines (1985, p. 45).

The *ṯt*-retainer on the reverse of the Narmer Palette wears a robe with shoulder  -ties or ornaments similar to the robe worn in the Sahura reliefs.[23] This distinctive robe is also worn by a retainer holding a sheaf of grain on the Scorpion Mace-head. There we see one shoulder strap and the tie with a  -tassel in front.

The standards accompanying the victory scene are two falcons, a jackal, and a cushion/placenta. These are the same four standards depicted on the Narmer Mace-head although in a different order. Kaiser (followed by Beckerath; see fn. 5, above) concludes that these standards were the later *šmsw ḥrw,* which had three functions: to accompany the king, to indicate government or cult activity, or to indicate an ancient group of kings.

18. Note Pyramid Text 455: the taking of the Great Crown from the Great Ones(?) of the Thenu.

19. There is debate whether the animals on the Libyan Tribute Palette are hacking the cities (Baines 1985, p. 45) or founding the cities (Bietak 1986, pp. 29–35), or whether the animals represent the "coalition" or royal numina (Kaplony 1965, p. 137, n. 2).

20. See Vandier 1952, pp. 595–99. For a very good photograph of the upper portion, see Málek 1986, pp. 14–15. For a recent discussion of the palette with bibliography, see Trigger 1979, pp. 409–10; Kemp 1989, p. 42.

21. See especially Kemp 1989, pp. 80–81; for a good photograph, see Málek 1986, p. 25.

22. Ivory statuette found by Petrie in the tomb of Djer at Abydos (Spencer 1980, no. 483, p. 67, pl. 55; Smith 1946, pl. 1a).

23. Borchardt 1910, pl. 1. Here the tie is shaped  . For this glyph, see Smith 1946, p. 129.

Table 26.1. Two Dimensional Reliefs: Palettes, Mace-heads, and Knife-handles

Document	*Human / Bovine Eye*	*Ribs / Body*	*Horn*	*Human Nose*	*Lion Mane*	*Human Knee*	*Standards / Deities*	*Attenuation of Body*	*Ground-line*	*Miscella-neous*
1. Manchester Palette[1]	Drilled	—	—	Beak-like	—	—	—	No	No	—
2. Hierakonpolis Palette[2]	Drilled	Etched	Etched	—	To hind-quarters	—	—	No	No	—
3. Louvre Fragment 3[3]	Drilled	Etched	Etched	—	—	—	—	—	—	—
4. Dog Palette[4]	Drilled	Etched	Etched on neck	—	To hind-quarters	—	—	No	No	—
5. Hunters' Palette[5]	Drilled	Etched	Etched	Pointed	To hind-quarters			No, stocky build	No	Double bull (*pr-nw*)
6. Metropolitan Museum of Art Palette A[6]	Drilled	Etched	Etched slightly on tails	—	—	—	Horus on serekh	No	No	—
7. Metropolitan Museum of Art Palette B[7]	Lenticular	No, tradition ends	Etching ends		—	—	—	No	No(?)	—
8. University College King's Mace-head[8]	Lenticular	Modeling begins	—	Yes	—	—	Horus	No	No(?)	Red crown
9. Louvre Fragment 1[9]	Lenticular	Modeled	—	—	—	Fleshy	—	No	No	—

1. Vandier 1952, p. 572, fig. 379. Drilled eyes for shell insets are common in Nagada I palettes; for example, see Spencer 1993, p. 28, fig. 12.

2. Vandier 1952, p. 579 ff., figs. 381–82. For a fragment of a similar palette, see Asselberghs 1961, pl. 91, Afb. 162.

3. Vandier 1952, p. 589, fig. 387 lower right (fragment in upper right is not predynastic, perhaps Roman). For a fragment of a similar palette, see Asselberghs 1961, pl. 91, Afb. 162.

4. Vandier 1952, p. 583, fig. 383.

5. Vandier 1952, p. 573, fig. 380. The hunters wear feathers in their hair and tails in their belts. Tails are later restricted to rulers and gods. Feather decoration can be seen in Nagada II painted-ware (D-ware) depictions of hunting scenes; for example, see Spencer 1993, p. 39, fig. 22. Baines (1995, p. 112) identifies the double bull as a "royal symbol."

6. Fischer 1958, figs. 19–20; Hayes 1955, p. 29. The depiction is of a series of dogs and pups and one serpopard (leopard with serpent neck) flanking Horus and serekh with, apparently, no indication of a royal name.

7. Hayes 1955, p. 29; Vandier 1952, p. 588, fig. 386 lower right. A fragment containing a single, bearded individual pierced by an arrow. The treatment of the eye and nose as well as the modeled body without etched ribs suggests that this piece is temporally very close to the Vulture Palette and Scorpion Mace-head.

8. Adams 1974, p. 3, pls. 1–2. Depiction is of Horus bringing a pigtailed captive tied with a rope and presenting the captive to a king who sits under a royal canopy with two poles. Adams (1974, p. 3, pls. 1–2, esp. pl. 1c) considers whether a scorpion is depicted in front of the king. The rendition of the eye and nose and the lack of attenuation or groundline place this document in the tradition of the Bull Palette, Libyan Tribute Palette, and the Metropolitan Museum of Art Knife-handle, but the style is slightly different (note the weak chin).

9. Vandier 1952, fig. 387 left. The scene of men with crooks leading prisoners is stylistically similar on both this document and the U-127 Knife-handle, which are here assumed to be contemporary. Dreyer (1993b, p. 12) dates Abydos cemetery U to Nagada II–III and the U-127 Knife-handle (below) to the Nagada IId period; accordingly, a date for the beginning of Dynasty 0 would predate this.

Table 26.1. Two Dimensional Reliefs: Palettes, Mace-heads, and Knife-handles (*cont.*)

Document	*Human / Bovine Eye*	*Ribs / Body*	*Horn*	*Human Nose*	*Lion Mane*	*Human Knee*	*Standards / Deities*	*Attenuation of Body*	*Ground-line*	*Miscella-neous*
10. U-127 Knife-handle[10]	Lenticular	Modeled	—	—	—	Fleshy	—	No	No	—
11. Metropolitan Museum of Art Knife-handle[11]	—	—	—	No	—	Not delin-eated	—	—	—	Rosette, white crown
12. Vulture Palette[12]	Plastic / applied lids	Modeled 	—		To middle of back			No	No	—
13. Libyan Tribute Palette[13]	Plastic / applied lids	Modeled	—	—	To middle of back			No	Yes	—
14. Bull Palette[14]		Modeled	—		—	Fleshy		No	Yes	—
15. Scorpion Mace-head[15]	Plastic eye line	Modeled	—	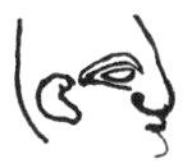	—			Slight	Yes	—
16. Narmer Mace-head[16]	—	Modeled	—	—	—			Slight	Yes	—
17. Narmer Palette[17]	Plastic eye line 	Modeled	—	Early nose ends 	—			Yes	Yes	—

10. A fragment of an ivory knife-handle(?) found at Abydos in tomb U-127 dating to Nagada IId (Dreyer 1993a, pl. 6d–f).

11. Williams and Logan 1987, pp. 273–74, figs. 1–2. The scene includes a boat procession; a file of men, some with crooks; a ruler wearing the white crown; and a tent shrine; and a palace facade or shrine matting.

12. Vandier 1952, p. 584 ff.; for good photographs, see Málek 1986, pp. 22–23; Spencer 1993, pp. 54–55. From the Libyan Tribute Palette, King's Mace-head, Bull Palette, and Narmer Cylinder Seal parallels, the figure leading away the prisoner should be a standard, god, or ruler. The robe with lozenge patterning, however, is hard to identify. In comparison with the ivory statue found by Petrie at Abydos (BM 37996; Glanville 1931, p. 65 ff.; Spencer 1993, cover), it is tempting to see this robe as a Dynasty 0 royal dress. The broken glyph is usually read as *Tȝ-mḥw*, but a reading of *ṯḥnw* in this formative period for writing may not be entirely impossible.

13. Vandier 1952, p. 590, fig. 388; Kantor 1974, pls. 214–15. The totems/standards attacking the walled towns include Horus, lion, scorpion, falcon pair, and three standards lost in a lacuna. Baines (1995, p. 112) reconstructs a bull, catfish, vulture, cobra, or elephant in the lacuna and sees all of these as "symbolic of royal power." Baines (ibid., p. 112) and Dreyer (1992, pp. 259–63) both interpret these "dangerous" animals (as well as Seth and the crocodile) as royal symbols.

14. Vandier 1952, p. 593, figs. 389–90; for a good photograph, see Saleh 1986, pl. 29; Berman 1996, p. 35; for a drawing, see Baines 1985, p. 43, fig. 12. Four standards, two jackals (Wepwawet and Khenty-imentyw?), an ibis (Thoth?), Horus, and Min emblem hold a rope attached to a prisoner as part of the wars of consolidation. Note the walled towns.

15. Vandier 1952, p. 600 ff.; for good photographs, see Kantor 1974, pl. 215; Málek 1986, p. 29; Millet 1990, p. 55; idem 1991, fig. 2. The best point of comparison with the Narmer Palette is the musculature and kneecap renderings. In the latter, the knee is very detailed as are the muscles in the lower leg. Standards include Seth, Min, Horus, and the desert(?).

16. Vandier 1952, fig. 394; Millet 1990, p. 53 ff.

17. Vandier 1952, fig. 391–92; for a good photograph of the upper portion, see Málek 1986, pp. 14–15.

As Frankfort (1948, p. 92) determined, the standards accompanying the king here are "standards of kingship." The idea that there was a Dynasty 0 confederation or alliance of principalities is seen on the series of palettes depicting the warfare concomitant with the unification of Egypt. How the Dynasty 0 kings as well as Horus of Nekhen ultimately triumphed over the alliance and diminished their power is not certain.

The smiting-of-enemies scene — dispatching a foreign enemy of Egypt — depicts, of course, an important royal function. This scene appears first in the Nagada II period (Painted Tomb 100 at Hierakonpolis) and continues to be represented until Roman times.[24] But here it is "codified." The main scene on the obverse of the Narmer Palette occurs without standards (but with Horus); the standards on the reverse of the Narmer Palette, as in the battlefield scene of the Vulture Palette, review the dead *after* the battle is over.

Later the smiting of enemies is frequently associated with a Wepwawet standard. In the reign of Den we see a clear association. On a recently discovered ebony piece the Wepwawet standard "bears" a mace (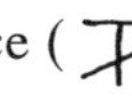).[25] The famous Den label in the British Museum shows Den smiting a dweller of the Eastern Desert (Spencer 1993, p. 87, fig. 17). As on the Narmer Palette, King Den holds the enemy by the hair in one hand and a raised mace in the other. Here the king wears a ureaus (for the first time) and is accompanied by the Wepwawet standard with full *šdšd*-protuberance.[26] This warlike aspect of Wepwawet is still to be seen in the Old Kingdom and has led scholars to interpret Wepwawet as originally being a war god.[27]

But this interpretation does not explain other depictions of Wepwawet or his standard. Wepwawet also frequently occurs with the *Jmy-wt*-fetish[28] (this association with embalming indicates that Wepwawet also had a funerary aspect); with the fashioning of statues;[29] in association with the *sed*-festival;[30] in association with the Khons/skin/*nḫn*-standard in a foundation ceremony (reign of Khasekhem);[31] and in a foundation ceremony (Sa-nakht).[32]

Of course, other standards/gods are associated with the smiting of enemies.[33]

The Narmer Cylinder Seal, Narmer Ivory Label, and Narmer Palette all depict the same event.

Scorpion Mace-head

There are controversies over the chronological placement of King Scorpion, over his very existence as a king, or whether "scorpion" is simply a numen for other kings. Two important sealings found by Dreyer, however, clearly list the rulers of the late predynastic and early dynastic periods as Narmer, Aha, Djer, Djet, Den, Adjib, Semerkhet, and Qaʿa (one includes Meritneith as "King's [Kings'?] Mother"; see Spencer 1993, p. 64; Dreyer et al. 1996, p. 72). These sealings come from Abydos and clearly omit a King Scorpion as a valid Thinite king after Narmer, which leaves us with three alternatives:

Scorpion predated Narmer
Scorpion was an ephemeral (Hierakonpolite?) ruler
Scorpion was a royal numen

Serekhs enclosing the name of King Scorpion, which come from Minshat Abu Omar and Tarkhan,[34] suggest that Scorpion was indeed a ruler. Since there is no tomb at Abydos associated with Scorpion in the B cemetery,

24. See Clayton 1994, p. 18; Kemp (1989, pp. 46–50) refers to this as the "icon of majesty."
25. Dreyer 1993a, pl. 13. For the tradition of anthropomorphic standards, see Baines 1989, pp. 474–75. A similar Wepwawet standard is found in PT 455a (note with reference to Libya).
26. Spencer 1980, p. 87, fig. 67; Smith 1946, p. 121:1; Vandier 1952, p. 859. I include this tablet because it is widely accepted as authentic, but certain stylistic elements could be questioned.
27. On Wepwawet with "smiting of the *Jwntjw*," see Gardiner and Peet 1952, pl. 2:7. For the warlike interpretation, see Emery 1961, pp. 126–27.
28. Djer sealings: see Logan 1990, p. 62; Kaplony 1963, pl. 47, fig. 175A–B.
29. A statue of Den: see Petrie 1900, pl. 14; Smith 1946, p. 120, fig. 36.
30. Helck 1987, p. 7; a possible example is a Djer sealing (Petrie 1902, pl. 15, no. 108; Vandier 1952, p. 862 lower right; Kaplony 1963, fig. 237, pl. 67), on which Wepwawet occurs with depictions of Djer wearing the red crown, then a white crown, and wearing a long robe like the *sed*-festival garment; Den label (the top of the standard is destroyed, but the mace bisecting the standard pole suggests Wepwawet; Vikentiev 1951, p. 204, fig. 11).
31. Cairo relief perhaps from Gebelein; see Smith 1946, pl. 30/d.
32. Cairo relief originally from Sinai; see Gardiner and Peet 1952, pl. 4; idem 1955, p. 55; Smith 1946, pl. 30c.
33. On an unusual lion-god(?), see a Djer document (Emery 1961, p. 60, fig. 23). There are numerous examples with Horus; see Snefru relief at Magharah (Gardiner and Peet 1952, pl. 2:5; idem 1955, p. 56).
34. For Minshat Abu Omar, see Kroeper and Wildung 1985, fig. 213. For Tarkhan, see Kaplony 1963, pl. 2; Kaiser 1964, p.

we must look elsewhere for his burial.[35] At Hierakonpolis, Stone Tomb 1 is very close to and, perhaps, associated with a wall of graffiti that begins with a possible Dynasty 0 serekh (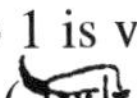), which Michael Hoffman, Bruce Williams, and I have long felt was a serekh of Scorpion. Though not conclusive, the Scorpion Mace-head, a possible tomb, and the many depictions of scorpions[36] found at Hierakonpolis suggest that King Scorpion was a Hierakonpolite ruler and that he was buried there.

From an art-historical perspective, Scorpion can be dated to near the end of Dynasty 0, before Narmer (see table 26.1, above). Scorpion is not identical to Narmer. Specifically, the groundline, slight attenuation, and form of the standards on the Scorpion Mace-head indicate a late Dynasty 0 date, while the pug nose is the end of a tradition that is altered by Narmer's artist, as is the older "rosette"-sign for kingship; the larger "coalition" of standards is "abbreviated" by Narmer to the followers of Horus. For the plastic or applied look of the eyes, the best parallel is the treatment of the eyes on the stone figurine in the Ashmolean Museum at Oxford, the so-called MacGregor Man dated by Kantor as late Nagada II.[37]

The ceremony depicted on the Scorpion Mace-head has been interpreted as one of submission, the opening of the first canal of the planting season, or the foundation of a temple.

Kaiser's (1964, p. 95) original chronology with Scorpion predating the Thinite kings (Ka, Narmer, Aha, etc.) seems correct.[38]

ROYAL STATUARY

There is a paucity of dated royal, or divine, statues from this period.[39] The few statues that do survive come from temple deposits (Hierakonpolis, Abydos, Elephantine, etc.); they have a wide chronological range, are hard to date precisely, or have no firm provenience, and thus they present many problems.

For example, the MacGregor Man, of unknown provenience, mentioned above, can be compared with the Scorpion Mace-head (cf. the treatment of the eyes) and the Min statues' knees; the treatment of the ears (exaggerated) is clearly archaic. If the MacGregor Man had an archaeological context, it would be more valuable.

A clearly archaic ivory statuette (BM 37996), excavated by Petrie at Abydos,[40] was found in the Osiris temple. The statue was in a mixed deposit that only suggests an archaic date, but from an art-historical view it has obvious parallels to the two-dimensional reliefs of Narmer.

This small statue represents a king wearing the white crown and swathed in a tight-fitting garment or cloak. The garment is completely decorated with diamond-shaped lozenges. The lower legs are missing, but Glanville (1931, pp. 65–66) determined from the broken stubs of the legs that the king was striding forward. The arms of the king are under the garment, but their forms are sculpted as in later representations of kings in *sed*-festival garments. Although the hands are almost completely worn away, Glanville is able to determine that they emerged from the robe and held the flail and archaic crook. The head droops forward, the chin down, and there

103, who reads this as King *Snd*-goose; Helck 1987, pp. 92–93. For a possible Scorpion Palette, see Kaplony 1965, pp. 132–67. See Wilkinson 1993, p. 241, n. 5.

35. A large (9.10 × 7.30 m or 66.43 m^2) twelve-room tomb in the U cemetery (U-j) has several inscriptions of a scorpion; Dreyer (1993b, p. 12) concludes that Scorpion was "in all probability the name of the tomb owner." Because of the date of the tomb — Nagada IIIa2 — the excavators do not equate this tomb with the Scorpion of Hierakonpolis. It is obvious that this is a very important tomb because it is by far the largest in the U cemetery and is comparable in size to B1, 7, and 17, which are royal. In addition, the *ḥḳꜣ*-scepter found in tomb U-j seems conclusive: U-j is a royal Nagada IIIa2 tomb. Are there two King Scorpions? The answer must rely upon chronology. While Kaiser's predynastic chronology based upon the Nagada tombs is a quantum leap forward, it is a relative, not an absolute chronology, and there are regional variations. For instance, while black-top ware ends in Nagada at the end of Nagada II, it continues into Nagada IIIa1 at Hierakonpolis. Pottery types do overlap (Brink 1996, p. 149). And while most of the contents from the latter Dynasty 0 kings' tombs, Iry-Hor (B1/2), Ka/Sekhen (B7/9), and Narmer (B17/18), date to Nagada IIIb, there are items that in isolation would be dated to Nagada IIIa2 (a W51 jug and a fish palette). A carbon-14 date suggests an absolute date of 3150 B.C. for Nagada IIIa2 (Boehmer, Dreyer, and Kromer 1993, pp. 63–68). We still need more material in order to determine the absolute dates for the rulers of the various branches of Dynasty 0.

36. See Quibell 1900, pls. 12, 17–19, passim.

37. Smith 1946, pl. 1b; Kantor 1974, pls. 218–19; for a good photograph of the face and "plastic" eyes, see Málek 1986, p. 24.

38. His conclusions then were based upon the ceramic sequence that still seems to be the most reliable; see Wilkinson 1993, p. 242, n. 14; Brink 1996, p. 149 ff.

39. From a stylistic comparison, the Min statues can be dated to Narmer's reign. There is a depiction of a divine statue in Painted Tomb 100; see Williams and Logan 1987, p. 278, fig. 13.

40. Glanville 1931, p. 65 ff. For a good photograph, see Spencer 1993, p. 75.

is no indication of a beard; as in the early ivories there is little indication of a neck, and the ears are exaggerated and stick out from the face. The treatment of the ears seems typical for late Dynasty 0 to the Second Dynasty: compare the archaic seated figure in Cairo (Smith and Simpson 1981, p. 47, fig. 29), the naked ivory figure from Hierakonpolis in Philadelphia (Smith and Simpson 1981, p. 30, fig. 8), the naked ivory female figure in the Louvre (Smith 1946, pl. 1c), and the MacGregor Man (Kantor 1974, pls. 218–19). Good comparative pieces that are seated include the University College King's Mace-head from Hierakonpolis (Adams 1974, pls. 1–2) and the figure of Den in the Den label (fig. 26.9, wherein Den is also depicted running the *sed*-festival course; Petrie 1900, pl. 11:14; Emery 1961, p. 76, fig. 37; Spencer 1993, p. 66, fig. 45).

Altogether this small masterpiece is very naturalistic. The question is the function of the piece. This statue has been interpreted as dressed in *sed*-festival apparel. Is there any connection with the figure on the obverse of the Vulture Palette who also wears a robe decorated with lozenges?

CONCLUSIONS

The Vulture, Libyan Tribute, and Bull Palettes date to the very end of Dynasty 0 and are probably contemporary with King Scorpion or Narmer.[41]

The predynastic wars of conquest left the ruler in a powerful political position. His status was further elevated by ritualizing his role in society. We see this in the documents that commemorate the conquest and consolidation of Egypt. This codification of victory made the ruler much more than just a political leader. He became a uniquely Egyptian king. This process can also be seen in the king's association with the standards or totems originally representing allies in the wars of conquest.[42] Specifically, the king alone becomes the vanquisher of enemies. The standards, once full participants in the battles, become observers.

The alliance is transformed during Dynasty 0 or the early Archaic period into a generic protective source restricted to the king (in the Archaic/Old Kingdom periods standards and gods are never found in association with a non-royal figure). The impression is that the Dynasty 0 "coalition" represented by the standards was no longer needed once Egypt was unified; indeed, they then represented a powerful decentralizing force. The coalition/standards are thus transferred by rulers like Narmer into his entourage. On his palette the standards are seen only after the battle. They then appear in the *sed*-festival scene on the Narmer Mace-head and Niuserra *sed*-festival reliefs, where they become the "followers of Horus" (those in his retinue). We are reminded of Louis XIVth who transformed the nobles into court butterflies. (This comparison is even more apt on the Niuserra *sed*-festival reliefs where the standards now watch as the king is dressed, carried, etc.). Even the totem of the powerful site of Nagada (Seth) is denigrated into the enemy of the royal house.[43]

In the same fashion, the bearded foes depicted on the ceremonial palettes are later ritualized as the bearded captive prisoners depicted on the base of royal statues upon whom the king alone triumphantly stands.[44] This can also be seen in the icon of the conquered *rḫyt* seen hanging in defeat from the standards on the Scorpion Mace-head as the later analogous Nine Bows and *rḫyt* found under the feet of the king on royal statuary.[45]

Similarly, the niched-brick architecture as well as the gateway seen at Hierakonpolis becomes the early emblem for the royal name, the serekh,[46] and Horus of Hierakonpolis becomes the symbol of kingship itself. The impression that the king almost alone conquered and unified Egypt is strengthened by the bellicose names

41. Davis (1989, pp. 149–52) concludes that the Libyan Tribute and Vulture Palettes are just slightly earlier in date than Narmer's reign.

42. Nekhbet, for instance, is seen both on the Narmer Cylinder Seal and Narmer Mace-head. Her association with Narmer's gifts to the temple at Hierakonpolis was originally as goddess of nearby Elkab. She is transformed from military partner to royal protector. This coalition must have included the very large predynastic settlements like Nagada. Indeed we see its totem Seth present on the Scorpion Mace-head in the series of standards vanquishing the *rḫyt*. But given the size of Nagada, Seth is surprisingly absent from the records of Narmer and Hor-aha (except in the perhaps old title for a queen "she who sees Horus and Seth"). The elite/royal tomb of Neithotep at Nagada attests to its early importance.

43. Menu (1996, pp. 339–42) comes to a similar conclusion. Menu divides the standards into "enseignes" (= my coalition) and "étendards" (*šmsw-Ḥrw*) and notes that the former disappear by the reign of Narmer; only the standards are left.

44. For example, see the Djoser statue base from Tanis (illustrated in Málek 1986, p. 95).

45. From a Djoser statue base found in the colonnade of the Step Pyramid complex at Saqqara (see Smith 1946, p. 14; Málek 1986, p. 89).

46. Weeks 1971/72, with Kemp 1989, pp. 40–41, fig. 11.

from Dynasty 0 and the First Dynasty: Scorpion, Raging Catfish, Ensnarer, Cobra-like, Decapitator, and With-Uplifted-Arm.[47] This is re-inforced by the royal numina developed in Dynasty 0: Bull, Lion, and Falcon.

Even the dress of the king becomes distinctive and exclusive in Dynasty 0. The red and white crowns are fully developed, as is the distinctive *sed*-festival tunic (crossing one shoulder only; deities in Fifth Dynasty reliefs wear this, too; thus the separation of royal and divine is blurred).[48] The short beard, the tail (earlier all the hunters on the Hunters' Palette wear a tail), the exclusivity of the standards and of divine representations (I know of no deities represented in private tombs or reliefs until the Eleventh Dynasty), the holding of a flail, the receiving of *ankh*-signs, and so forth, are all royal prerogatives already in evidence.

But clearly the ritual that was critical in this evolution of pharaonic power was the *sed*-festival. References to it are seen in many of the Dynasty 0 documents. However, until more Dynasty 0 documents are found, the precise ceremony will remain wrapped in mystery.

Although these conclusions are based upon the few documents that have survived and our picture is very incomplete, I agree with Millet (1990, p. 58) that a real "codification of ritual" and "many features of the pharaonic system ... had already become well established by Narmer's reign."

From the discussion above we can summarize those items of the distinctive Egyptian royal system that were already present at the end of Dynasty 0:

Vanquishing Egypt's external enemies (and thus establishing rule and order): Narmer and Vulture Palettes and the "smiting of enemies" in Painted Tomb 100, Hierakonpolis (Nagada II)

Vanquishing chaotic internal natural forces (Kemp's "Containment of Unrule in the Universe"): Hunters' Palette, Hippo Hunt,[49] and predynastic "Files of Animals"

Royal Festivals (like the *sed*-festival, an exclusive ceremony restricted to the king, with royal dress and stately trappings, including crowns, *sed*-robe, flail, throne, palace, serekh, and warlike name): Narmer Mace-head

Exclusive association with Horus and divinities: Narmer Palette and Cylinder Seal

Following of Horus: Narmer Palette, Narmer Mace-head, and perhaps already on the Scorpion Mace-head[50]

Foundation of temples: Scorpion Mace-head(?)

This list can be supplemented by documents from the subsequent reign of Hor-aha:

Burial ritual: Hor-aha/Menes label[51]

Foundation or erecting of a temple: Hor-aha label B (Emery 1961, p. 52); Djer label B (Emery 1961, p. 59, fig. 20); and *wꜣdj*-label A (Vikentiev 1959, p. 6, fig. 1; Helck 1987, p. 155)

Fashioning of divine statue or standard: *Jmy-wt* on Hor-aha label B; and Khenty-imentyw on the "Conquest of Nubia" label (Emery 1961, p. 51; Helck 1987, p. 145; Logan 1990, p. 64, fig. 2)

Royal rituals (like receiving the [*šsp*] of Upper and/or Lower Egypt): Hor-aha label C; Djer label A (Petrie 1902, pl. 3, no. 4)

When Dynasty 0 ended, Egypt was under the authority of a ruler who already had the distinctive ceremonial trappings that made him an Egyptian king.

47. See Redford 1986, p. 130, n. 10; Godron 1990, p. 19; Baines 1989, p. 476. Note that this type of bellicose name ends in the Second Dynasty.

48. Smith (1946, p. 129) notes that the robe or tunic that crosses one shoulder only is restricted to the *sed*-festival robe or clothing for the gods.

49. Kemp 1989, p. 46 ff. On the hippopotamus hunt, see Säve-Söderbergh 1953. For a representation of King Den hunting hippopotami, see Petrie 1902, pl. 7a.

50. For First Dynasty examples, see Semerkhet Label A (Petrie 1900, pl. 12, no. 1; Emery 1961, p. 86, fig. 49); Ka'a Label C (Petrie 1900, pl. 12, no. 2).

51. The label perhaps depicts Hor-aha burying Menes (Emery 1961, p. 50). We can add one point to this much discussed label: it is very early in Hor-aha's reign. The Horus falcon is still depicted rather horizontal with tail not touching the top of the serekh, so characteristic of the Dynasty 0 style. His stance becomes more upright in those labels that are later in the reign (Emery 1961, pp. 52–53).

References

Adams, B.

1974 *Ancient Hierakonpolis*. Warminster: Aris and Phillips.

1996 "Elite Tombs at Hierakonpolis." In *Aspects of Early Egypt*, edited by A. J. Spencer, pp. 1–15. London: British Museum.

Amiran, R.

1970 "A New Acquisition: An Egyptian First Dynasty Jar." *Israel Museum News* 8: 89–94.

1974 "An Egyptian Jar Fragment with the Name of Narmer from Arad." *Israel Exploration Journal* 24: 4–12.

Asselberghs, H.

1961 *Chaos en Beheersing: Documenten uit aneolithisch Egypte*. Documenta et Monumenta Orientis Antiqui 8. Leiden: E. J. Brill.

Baines, J.

1985 *Fecundity Figures*. London: Aris and Phillips.

1989 "Communication and Display: The Integration of Early Egyptian Art and Writing." *Antiquity* 63: 471–82.

1995 "Origins of Egyptian Kingship." In *Ancient Egyptian Kingship*, edited by D. O'Connor and D. P. Silverman, pp. 95–156. Probleme der Ägyptologie 9. Leiden: E. J. Brill.

Barta, W.

1975 *Untersuchungen zur Göttlichkeit der regierenden Königs: Ritus und Sakralkönigtum in altägypten nach Zeugnissen der Frühzeit und des Alten Reiches*. Münchner ägyptologische Studien 32. Munich: Deutscher Kunstverlag.

Beckerath, J. von

1962 "Ein Torso des Mentemḥet in München." *Zeitschrift für ägyptische Sprache und Altertumskunde* 87: 1–8.

1984 *Handbuch der ägyptischen Königsnamen*. Münchner ägyptologische Studien 20. Munich: Deutscher Kunstverlag.

Bénédite, G.

1916 "Le couteau de Gebel el-ʿArak: Étude sur un nouvel objet préhistorique acquis par le Musée du Louvre." In *Monuments et mémoires*, tome 22, by Académie des inscriptions et belles-lettres, pp. 11–34. Fondation Eugène Piot. Paris: Ernest Leroux.

Berman, L.

1996 *Pharaohs: Treasures of Egyptian Art from the Louvre*. Cleveland: Cleveland Museum of Art.

Bietak, M.

1986 "Naissance de la notion de ville dans l'Égypte ancienne." *Cahier de recherches de l'Institut de papyrologie et d'égyptologie de Lille* 8: 29–35.

Birkstam, B.

1977 Review of *Untersuchungen zur Göttlichkeit des regierenden Königs*, by W. Barta. *Chronique d'Égypte* 52: 279–84.

Boehmer, R. M.; G. Dreyer; and B. Kromer

1993 "Einige frühzeitliche ^{14}C-Datierungen aus Abydos und Uruk." *Mitteilungen des Deutschen archäologischen Instituts, Abteilung Kairo* 49: 63–68.

Borchardt, L.

1907 *Das Grabdenkmal des Königs Ne-User-Reʿ*. Ausgrabungen der Deutschen Orient-Gesellschaft in Abusir 1902–04, 1. Wissenschaftliche Veröffentlichung der Deutschen Orient-Gesellschaft 7. Leipzig: J. C. Hinrichs.

1910 *Das Grabdenkmal des Königs Sꜣḥ-Re*, Band 1: *Der Bau*. Leipzig: J. C. Hinrichs.

Breasted, J. H.

1931 "The Predynastic Union of Egypt." *Bulletin de l'Institut français d'archéologie orientale* 30: 709–24.

Brink, E. van den

1996 "The Incised Serekh-Signs of Dynasties 0–1, Part 1: Complete Vessels." In *Aspects of Early Egypt*, edited by A. J. Spencer, pp. 140–58. London: British Museum.

Cialowicz, K.

1982–85 "Predynastic Graves with Weapons Found in Egypt and Nubia." *Fontes archaeologici Posnanienses, Annales Musei Archaeologici Posnaniensis* 34: 157–80.

Clayton, P.

1994 *Chronicles of the Pharaohs*. London: Thames and Hudson.

Davis, W.

1989 *The Canonical Tradition in Ancient Egyptian Art*. Cambridge: Cambridge University Press.

Dreyer, G.

1992 "Recent Discoveries at Abydos Cemetery U." In *The Nile Delta in Transition: 4th–3rd Millennium B.C.*, edited by E. van den Brink, pp. 293–99. Jerusalem: Israel Exploration Society.

1993a "Umm el-Qaab: Nachuntersuchungen im frühzeitlichen Königsfriedhof, 5./6. Vorbericht." *Mitteilungen des Deutschen archäologischen Instituts, Abteilung Kairo* 49: 23–62.

1993b "A Hundred Years at Abydos." *Egyptian Archaeology* 3: 10–12.

Dreyer, G.; E.-M. Engel; U. Hartung; T. Hikade; E. C. Köhler; and F. Pumpenmeier

1996 "Umm el-Qaab: Nachuntersuchungen im frühzeitlichen Königsfriedhof, 7./8. Vorbericht." *Mitteilungen des Deutschen archäologischen Instituts, Abteilung Kairo* 52: 11–82.

Dreyer, G.; U. Hartung; T. Hikade; E. C. Köhler; V. Müller; and F. Pumpenmeier

1998 "Umm el-Qaab: Nachuntersuchungen im frühzeitlichen Königsfriedhof, 9./10. Vorbericht." *Mitteilungen des Deutschen archäologischen Instituts, Abteilung Kairo* 54: 77–167.

Emery, W.
1961 *Archaic Egypt*. Harmondsworth: Penguin Books.

Firth, C. M., and J. E. Quibell
1935 *The Step Pyramid* 2: *Plates*. Excavations at Saqqara 14. Cairo: Service des antiquités de l'Égypte.

Fischer, H.
1958 "A Fragment of a Late Predynastic Egyptian Relief from the Eastern Delta." *Artibus Asiae* 21: 64–88.

Frankfort, H.
1948 *Kingship and the Gods: A Study of Ancient Near Eastern Religion as the Integration of Society and Nature*. Chicago: University of Chicago Press.

Gardiner, A. H.
1947 *Ancient Egyptian Onomastica*. 3 volumes. Oxford: Oxford University Press.

Gardiner, A. H., and T. E. Peet
1952 *The Inscriptions of Sinai*, Part 1: *Introduction and Plates*. Egypt Exploration Society, Memoir 45/1. Second edition revised and augmented by J. Černý. London: Egypt Exploration Society.
1955 *The Inscriptions of Sinai*, Part 2: *Translations and Commentary*. Edited and completed by J. Černý. Egypt Exploration Society, Memoir 45/2. London: Egypt Exploration Society.

Glanville, S.
1931 "An Archaic Statuette from Abydos." *Journal of Egyptian Archaeology* 17: 65–67.

Godron, G.
1990 *Études sur l'Horus Den et quelques problèmes de l'Égypte archaïque*. Cahiers d'orientalism 19. Geneva: Patrick Cramer Éditeur.

Gohary, J.
1992 *Akhenaten's Sed-festival at Karnak*. London: Kegan Paul.

Gophna, R.
1970 "A Protodynastic Egyptian Jar from Rafiah." *Museum Haaretz Bulletin* 12: 53–54.

Hayes, W.
1955 *The Scepter of Egypt*, 1: *From the Earliest Times to the End of the Middle Kingdom*. New York: Metropolitan Museum of Art.

Helck, W.
1987 *Untersuchungen zur Thinitenzeit*. Ägyptologische Abhandlungen 45. Wiesbaden: Otto Harrassowitz.

Hoffman, M.
1979 *Egypt before the Pharaohs*. New York: Alfred A. Knopf.

Kaiser, W.
1959 "Einige Bemerkungen zur ägyptischen Frühzeit, 1: Zu den *šmsw-Ḥr*." *Zeitschrift für ägyptische Sprache und Altertumskunde* 84: 119–32.
1964 "Einige Bemerkungen zur ägyptischen Fruhzeit, 3: Die Reichseinigung." *Zeitschrift für ägyptische Sprache und Altertumskunde* 91: 86–125.
1971 "Die kleine Hebseddarstellung im Sonnenheiligtum des Neuserre." In *Zum 70. Geburtstag von Herbert Ricke*, edited by Gerhard Haeny, pp. 87–105. Beiträge zur ägyptischen Bauforschung und Altertumskunde 12. Wiesbaden: Franz Steiner.
1983 "Zu den  der älteren Bilderdarstellungen und der Bedeutung von *rpw.t*." *Mitteilungen des Deutschen archäologischen Instituts, Abteilung Kairo* 39: 261–96.

Kaiser, W., and G. Dreyer
1982 "Umm el-Qaab: Nachuntersuchungen im frühzeitlichen Königsfriedhof, 2. Vorbericht." *Mitteilungen des Deutschen archäologischen Instituts, Abteilung Kairo* 38: 211–70.

Kantor, H.
1974 "Ägypten." In *Frühe Stufen der Kunst*, edited by M. J. Mellink and J. Filip, pp. 227–56. Propyläen Kunstgeschichte 13. Berlin: Propyläen Verlag.

Kaplony, P.
1963 *Die Inschriften der ägyptischen Frühzeit*. 3 volumes. Ägyptologische Abhandlungen 8. Wiesbaden: Otto Harrassowitz.
1965 "Eine Schminkpalette von König Skorpion aus Abu Umuri." *Orientalia* 34: 132–67.

Kemp, B.
1989 *Ancient Egypt: Anatomy of a Civilization*. London: Routledge.

Kroeper, K., and D. Wildung
1985 *Minshat Abu Omar: Münchner Ostdelta-Expedition, Vorbericht 1974–1984*. Schriften aus der ägyptischen Sammlung 3. Munich: Karl M. Lipp.

Logan, T. J.
1990 "The Origins of the *Jmy-wt* Fetish." *Journal of the American Research Center in Egypt* 27: 61–69.

Málek, J.
1986 *In the Shadow of the Pyramids: Egypt during the Old Kingdom*. Norman: University of Oklahoma Press.

Menu, B.
1996 "Enseignes et porte-étendards." *Bulletin de l'Institut français d'archéologie orientale* 96: 339–42.

Millet, N. B.
1990 "The Narmer Macehead and Related Objects." *Journal of the American Research Center in Egypt* 27: 53–59.
1991 "The Narmer Macehead and Related Objects." *Journal of the American Research Center in Egypt* 28: 223–25.

Murnane, W.
1987 "The Gebel Sheikh Suleiman Monument: Epigraphic Remarks." In "The Metropolitan Museum Knife Handle and Aspects of Pharaonic Imagery Before Narmer," by T. J. Logan and B. B. Williams. *Journal of Near Eastern Studies* 46: 282–85.

Naville, E.
1892 *The Festival Hall of Osorkhon II*. Egypt Exploration Fund, Memoir 10. London: Kegan Paul.

Petrie, W. M. F.
1900 *Royal Tombs of the First Dynasty* 1. Egypt Exploration Fund, Memoir 18. London: Egypt Exploration Fund.
1902 *Royal Tombs of the First Dynasty* 2. Egypt Exploration Fund, Memoir 21. London: Egypt Exploration Fund.

Quibell, J. E.
1900 *Hierakonpolis* 1. Egypt Research Account, Memoir 4. London: Egypt Exploration Society.

Quirke, S.
1992 *Ancient Egyptian Religion*. London: British Museum Press.

Ranke, H.
1924/25 "Altertum und Herkunft der ägyptischen 'Löwenjagd-Palette.'" *Sitzungsberichte der Heidelberger Akademie der Wissenschaften in Heidelberg* 5: 3–12.

Redford, D.
1986 *Pharaonic King-lists, Annals and Daybooks*. Society for the Study of Egyptian Antiquities, Publications 4. Ontario: Benben.

Säve-Söderbergh, T.
1953 *On Representations of Hippopotamus Hunting as a Religious Motive*. Uppsala: Appelbergs Boktryckeri.

Saleh, J. M.
1986 "Interprétation globale des documents concernant l'unification de l'Égypte." *Bulletin de l'Institut français d'archéologie orientale* 86: 227–38.

Schott, S.
1951 *Hieroglyphen: Untersuchungen zum Ursprung der Schrift*. Akademie der Wissenschaften und der Literatur, Abhandlungen der geistes- und sozialwissenschaftlichen Klasse, Jahrgang 1950, Nr. 24. Wiesbaden: Franz Steiner.

Schulman, A.
1976 "The Seal Impressions from ʿEn Besor." *Atiqot* 11: 16–26.
1991/92 "Narmer and the Unification: A Revisionist View." *Bulletin of the Egyptological Seminar* 11: 79–105.

Smith, W. S.
1946 *A History of Egyptian Sculpture and Painting in the Old Kingdom*. Boston: Museum of Fine Arts.

Smith, W. S., and W. K. Simpson
1981 *The Art and Architecture of Ancient Egypt*. New York: Penguin Books.

Spencer, A. J.
1978 "Two Enigmatic Hieroglyphs and their Relation to the Sed-Festival." *Journal of Egyptian Archaeology* 64: 52–55.
1980 *Catalogue of Egyptian Antiquities in the British Museum* 5: *Early Dynastic Objects*. London: British Museum Press.
1993 *Early Egypt*. London: British Museum Press.

Trigger, B.
1979 "The Narmer Palette in Cross-Cultural Perspective." In *Festschrift Elmar Edel, 12. März 1979*, edited by M. Görg and E. Pusch, pp. 409–19. Ägypten und Altes Testament 1. Bamberg: n.p.

Vandier, J.
1952 *Les époques de formation: La préhistoire*. Manuel d'archéologie égyptienne 1/1. Paris: A. and J. Picard.

Vikentiev, V.
1951 "Les monuments archaïques, 4–5: Deux rites du jubilé royal à l'époque protodynastique." *Bulletin de l'Institut d'Égypte* 32: 171–228.
1959 "Études d'épigraphie protodynastique, 2." *Annales du Service des antiquités de l'Égypte* 56: 1–31.

Weeks, K. R.
1971/72 "Preliminary Report on the First Two Seasons at Hierakonpolis, Part 2: The Early Dynastic Palace." *Journal of the American Research Center in Egypt* 9: 29–34.

Wildung, D.
1981 *Ägypten vor den Pyramiden*. Mainz: Philipp von Zabern.

Wilkinson, T. A. H.
1993 "The Identification of Tomb B1 at Abydos: Refuting the Existence of a King *Ro/*Iry-Hor." *Journal of Egyptian Archaeology* 79: 241–43.

Williams, B. B.
1988 *Decorated Pottery and the Art of Naqada III*. Münchner ägyptologische Studien 45. Munich: Deutscher Kunstverlag.

Williams, B. B., and T. J. Logan
1987 "The Metropolitan Museum Knife Handle and Aspects of Pharaonic Imagery before Narmer." *Journal of Near Eastern Studies* 46: 245–86.

Yeivin, S.
1960 "Early Contacts between Canaan and Egypt." *Israel Exploration Journal* 10: 193–203.
1963 "Further Evidence for Narmer at 'Gat.'" *Oriens Antiquus* 2: 205–13.
1968 "Additional Notes on the Early Relations between Canaan and Egypt." *Journal of Near Eastern Studies* 27: 37–50.

27

THE AUCTION OF PHARAOH

J. G. MANNING

Stanford University, California

It is a great pleasure to dedicate this paper to Professor Wente on the occasion of his retirement. His inspirational seminars on Late Egyptian texts will always be fondly remembered by me and I wish him well in his retirement.*

Sometime (the exact date is not stated) in the year 221/220 B.C., in the shadow of the newly begun temple dedicated to the falcon god Horus at Edfu, a herdsman (*ꜥꜣm*) named *Pa-tꜣ.wy* son of *Pa-bḥt* and ten of his colleagues made an agreement with five other people to purchase forty-five arouras of land and its *ꜥw n ẖy* "excess of measure." The type of land is not specified, but it is designated as "the southern *ḏrꜥ* in the tamarisk island" and, later in the text, *tꜣ mꜣy.t* "the island."[1] The agreement, known as P. Hauswaldt 16, was made before Mnesarchos (*Msrqws*) the Thebarch (*ḥry Nỉw.t*)[2] and other royal officials (*nꜣ rṱ.w n pr-ꜥꜣ* "the agents of pharaoh"). It is interesting to note that although the Thebarch was an official in charge of the general finances of the Thebaid, he is found in contexts even where relatively small fines were collected. The Thebarch's presence in the Hauswaldt agreement suggests relatively firm Ptolemaic control of the Nile Valley in the third century B.C. In a group of texts from Thebes, the official nominally in charge of auctions of derelict property was the vice-Thebarch who communicated with the *komogrammateus* as well as the *topogrammateus*, the local scribe in charge of translating Demotic texts into Greek for the benefit of the vice-Thebarch (Wilcken 1935, pp. 266–95; Criscuolo 1979).

P. Hauswaldt 16 forms part of a family archive consisting of several marriage agreements as well as private conveyances of both royal and temple land within the divine endowment of Horus of Edfu (*ḥtp-nṯr Ḥr bḥtt*). The agreement itself, recording payment for the land in cash as well as grain,[3] is the only known occurrence in a Demotic text of an arrangement to acquire land at public auction;[4] other examples listed in the tables occur in sale documents which mention that the property being conveyed had been initially acquired through public auction. Source material is far more abundant in the Greek papyri from Hellenistic Egypt no doubt because the institution was a Greek invention introduced into Egypt by the Ptolemies and administered in Greek through the institution of the *sḥn n pr-ꜥꜣ* "royal bank."

*This paper was completed in December 1995.

1. The context of the family archive in which this agreement was a part suggests that land involved in the transaction was located in the southern part of the Edfu Nome, described as the so-called "Hauswaldt zone" (Meeks 1972, pp. 123 n. 254, 146). The term *mꜣy.t* may also be used in the sense of cultivable land. The term *ḏr/lꜥ* ϫωωλε (Erichsen 1954, 685; Vycichl 1983, 325) is a Semitic loan word and has as its root meaning "to gather, collect." See Meeks 1972, pp. 113–14, for a discussion of the term and Greek occurrences as a place name πετλαρης, πεσλα; Ritner 1984, p. 179, n. 16. Is *ḏlꜥ* a technical term used of land "collected together" for the purpose of auction? Its use in P. Cairo 30753, line 5 (Sethe 1920, text 6), if an auction is involved, implies so.

2. The title was previously read as *mr*(?) *ỉp* "overseer of accounts" (Spiegelberg 1913, p. 52) and subsequently *ḥry ỉp*. Compare the translation of the title as "Oberrechnungsrat" (Peremans and Van 't Dack 1950, no. 924). For the suggested reading *ḥry* rather than *mr*, see Thissen 1979, p. 65. The Demotic writing here may be compared with similar writing in P. Berlin Elephantine 15522:

P. Hauswaldt 16, line 4

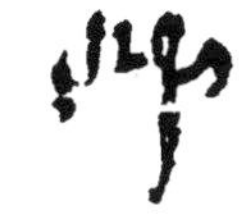

P. Berlin Elephantine 15522, line 3

The official Mnesarchos also occurs in P. Dem. Elephantine 18 and 28, P. Dem. Berlin 13537 (Zauzich 1993), and P. Bon. to be republished by Lucia Criscuolo and Willy Clarysse. I owe the suggested new reading of the Demotic title to both Professor Karl-Theodor Zauzich and Sven Vleeming. For the office of Thebarch, which was based in Ptolemais, see Thomas 1975, pp. 69–70; Van 't Dack 1975, pp. 646–55.

3. Perhaps because arrears were due in grain. For a similar arrangement, see PSB 5865 (cited by Pringsheim 1949, p. 303).

4. I leave out of the present discussion the problematic papyri published by Sethe (1920, texts 1–6). Some of the wording

Gold of Praise: Studies on Ancient Egypt in Honor of Edward F. Wente
Edited by Emily Teeter and John A. Larson
Studies in Ancient Oriental Civilization 58
Chicago: Oriental Institute, 1999

The various stages of the process of the auction are well known. The procedure was as follows:

1. Public announcement of auction to be held
2. Auction is held
   a. Introduction is proclaimed by herald
   b. Bidding begins, lasting several days
   c. Highest bid is posted for several more days
   d. New overbidding is accepted
   e. Knocking down to the highest bidder
   f. Transfer of goods auctioned to highest bidder is made upon receipt of taxes and payment of first installment of price[5]
   g. At transfer of goods (f, above), an order (διαγραφή) is given to royal bank to accept price in several installments
   h. New overbidding is still accepted until first installment is received
3. Within specified time limit, original owner of auctioned property has right to re-acquire goods by paying auction price to purchaser

The Hauswaldt papyrus records the payment of the first installment and a private agreement over the remaining installments. P. Greek Elephantine 14, dated ca. 223 B.C., records the first stage in the auction process (announcing the auction itself) and may well be part of the same event that our papyrus records. In any case, the event publicized in P. Greek Elephantine 14 is connected to the sale of derelict property belonging to a family of priests in Edfu.[6]

The amount of the land purchased in P. Hauswaldt 16 is striking (forty-five arouras; one aroura = 0.66 acre) and is probably a function of the number of people taking part in the agreement (sixteen).[7] All of the parties bear the title *ꜥꜣm bꜣk Ḥr bḥtt* "herdsman, servant of Horus of Edfu."[8]

Table 27.1. Purchase of Land at Auction in Demotic Papyri

Text	*Location*	*Date*	*Size of Plot*	*Description*
P. Hauswaldt 16[a]	Edfu south	221/220 B.C.	45 arouras	"The island"; the southern *ḏrꜥ* in the tamarisk island
P. Mainz ε + δ[b]	Thebes	184 B.C.	35 arouras	High land + excess of measure in divine endowment of Hathor
P. Strassburg 21[c]	Krocodilopolis	176 B.C.[d]	1 ground cubit	Empty plot (*wrḥ*)
P. BMFA 38.2063b[e]	Deir el-Ballas (Dendara)	175 B.C.	22 + 14 + 41 1/2 arouras[f]	Island + high land + excess of measure in divine endowments of Hathor and Isis
P. BM 10591[g]	Asyut	160s B.C.	1 1/2 arouras	An increase in measure (*ꜥw n ḫy*)

[a] Manning 1997, pp. 130–34.
[b] Zauzich 1968, pp. 37–40, 85–87.
[c] Spiegelberg 1902, pp. 21–22.
[d] The actual date of this papyrus is 145 B.C., but it mentions that the plot of land being transferred was originally acquired through the public auction thirty-one years previously.
[e] Parker 1964.
[f] Several plots of land were purchased at auction that were subsequently signed over from a father (a *pastophoros*-priest of Hathor) to his son. Plot 4: 22 arouras; plot 7: 14 arouras; plot 9: 41 1/2 arouras. In these instances, the land was purchased jointly with one, or in the case of plot 9, two other persons.
[g] Thompson 1934.

in these texts may suggest that auction was the mode of acquisition of the fodder (*sm*) land. In one text, number 6 (P. Cairo 30753), Sethe restored the word *ꜥš* in a lacuna, a term used of public auctions, but it is far from certain that the word in fact occurs. Interestingly, the land in this text is said to be *ḏlꜥ* "collected" in order to be registered. On the term *ḏlꜥ*, see note 1, above.

5. There was at times a lengthy delay between the end of the auction and the payment of the first installment. See the remarks of Pestman 1995, p. 117.
6. For an English translation of P. Greek Elephantine 14, see Hunt and Edgar 1934, p. 233.
7. Two other examples of land initially acquired at auction record transfers of thirty-six (Plots 4 + 7; P. BMFA 38.2063b; Parker 1964) and thirty-five arouras (P. Mainz ε + δ; Zauzich 1968, pp. 37–40, 85–87).
8. The text gives the title and name of the first person in the group; others named as parties in the first group have the Demotic *mỉ-nn* "likewise" instead of the specific title. *Mỉ-nn* is even written before a woman's name which implies, surprisingly, that she too bore the title *ꜥꜣm bꜣk Ḥr bḥtt*.

While it cannot be proven that all parties to the agreement were related, nevertheless it seems likely that they were at least part of an extended family or status group associated with herding in the Edfu area.

Although some scholars have assumed that the text records a lease of land ("Pachtvertrag"), there is no direct evidence that the document records a lease.[9] Whether the acquisition of land at auction was by lease or real sale, there was little to distinguish the two in the auction process itself (Pringsheim 1949, p. 284, n. 3). It would be helpful if we knew whether crown or temple land was involved in the Hauswaldt example. Whatever the exact legal arrangements or status of the land, property acquired at auction was the subject of subsequent sale by private legal instrument. Second, the language of the Demotic regarding the transaction (*ỉn r-ḏbꜣ ḥḏ ḥr pꜣ ʿyš n pr-ʿꜣ*) is in some cases that of a sale not a lease. The notion that land was not freely bought and sold in Hellenistic Egypt but, rather, was let on long-term leases, goes back to Rostovtzeff's rigid view of land tenure which has now been abandoned in favor of a system with much more variety in land-holding patterns.[10] As P. Greek Elephantine 14, lines 22–23, also makes clear, the variety of landholding patterns was sanctioned by the Ptolemies:

> κυριεύσουσιν δὲ καθὰ καὶ οἱ πρῶτον κύριοι ἐκέκτηντο
>
> They will own the property in the same manner as those who held it formerly

In the Hauswaldt agreement, the first group, eleven "herdsman, servant of Horus of Edfu" declare to the second group, led by *Pa-bḫt* son of *Pa-lhw*, the principal figure in the Hauswaldt dossier, and four *ỉry.w* "colleagues,"[11] that they are responsible for the payment schedule of a certain plot of land termed "the southern 'collection' in the tamarisk island," which the second group of people had "received," or "accepted" (*šp*), at the auction of pharaoh.[12] Lüddeckens (1960, p. 234) assumed that the forty-five arouras would have been divided among the five men forming party B to the transaction, but there is no mention in the agreement of the way in which the land was to be divided or used.[13] Payment was to be made both in cash and in in-kind installments (*tš.w*) to the royal bank. Payment by installment was a normal method of payment for auctioned property and is mentioned in P. Greek Elephantine 14, lines 19–20:

> [τῆς] δ[ὲ τίμ]ης τάξονται παραχρῆμα τὸ δ̄' μέρος τὸ δὲ λοιπὸν ἐν (ἔτεσι) γ ...
>
> They (the buyers) shall pay one fourth of the price immediately, and the remainder in three years ...

If either group of people defaulted on the purchase agreement, they were liable for the payment on which they agreed and the fine stated in the penalty clause.

PUBLIC PURCHASE OF PROPERTY BY ROYAL AUCTION

The auction of pharaoh (*ʿyš n pr-ʿꜣ*, lit. "proclamation of pharaoh")[14] is an institution that first appears in the Hellenistic period and its application as a method of disposing of derelict property is closely parallel to its use at Athens and elsewhere in the Hellenistic world.[15] It is "certainly a Greek institution" (Pringsheim 1949, p. 288). The published Demotic evidence is at present limited to Upper Egypt and, except for two examples, to the second century B.C. (Zauzich 1971a, p. 80; P. BM 10828). The term derives from Egyptian *ʿš* meaning "to cry out, proclaim."[16] According to Pestman (1978, p. 64, n. 4), "au moyen de *ʿyš* 'la criée' le démotique désigne la vente publique dont l'annonce était en effet faite par un héraut: προκήρυξις."

9. Delekat 1964, p. 104. Lüddeckens (*LÄ* 4 "Papyri, Demotische, Berlin," col. 770), in a list of Berlin papyri, also places the text under "Pacht."
10. See the discussion in Keenan and Shelton 1976, p. 7.
11. Compare P. Berlin 3146A, 6 (Grunert 1981), in which the holder of the plot to the west of the plot being sold is *Pa-ḫnm* son of *Pa-ws.t* and "his colleagues."
12. I wonder whether the Demotic is translating a form of the Greek verb ἔχω as in the phrase ὁμολογῶ ἔχειν παρὰ ... . On *šp* "to lease, buy," see Sethe 1920, p. 9. On the Greek phraseology, see, for example, P. Gen. inv. no. 1 in Pestman 1978, p. 60, text 7.
13. "Da treten elf Personen einen Acker von 45 Aruren an fünf Personen ab, so daß nach Abschluß des Handels 9 Aruren auf eine Person, oder — wohl richtiger — auf die Familie des einzelnen Bebauers entfielen." The agreement is clearly between two groups totaling sixteen people and is not a cession by eleven people to the other five, as Lüddeckens summarized the text.
14. Zauzich (1971a, pp. 79–82; 1990, pp. 161–62) gathers all known occurrences of the term. To this list must be added the Asyut archive examples discussed below, as well as the recently published P. BM 10828 (212 B.C., Thebes; Andrews 1990, text 17) and P. BM 10721 (182 B.C., Thebes; Andrews 1990, text 9).
15. See, in general, Pringsheim 1949; Oates 1969.
16. *Wb.* 1.227:14; ⲟⲉⲓϣ (Crum 1939, 257b). This special use of *ʿš* as "auction" is not listed in Erichsen 1954, 71. The Greek

As in the Greek examples, a wide range of property was auctioned, from temple land to days of service in a temple (liturgy days), graves, and houses.

Table 27.2. Purchase of Property Other Than Land at Auction in Demotic Papyri

Text	*Location*	*Date*	*Item*	*Description*
P. BM 10828	Thebes	212 B.C.	House	1/2 share, "built and roofed"
P. BM 10721	Thebes	182 B.C.	House	"Destroyed, and everything pertaining to it"
P. Turin 6080 [a]	Thebes west	171 B.C.	Liturgy days	—
P. Turin 6081	Thebes west	159 B.C.	Chapel + appurtenances[b]	—

[a] There are two occurrences of the auction of liturgy days in this text.

[b] The context does not make clear whether all of the listed property was purchased at auction or only the last one, the ground itself. The text lists: *tꜣ s.t-mnṱ.t ỉrm nꜣ nt m-sꜣ.s ḥnʿ tꜣ ʿb n ꜣs.t nꜣ sʿnḫ.w nꜣ ꜣḥ.w nt wn ḥry r-tỉ.y n.k nꜣ mꜣʿ.w nt ḥry ḫn.w r-ỉn.y r-ḏbꜣ ḥḏ ỉwt.y ỉrm.k ḥr pꜣ ʿyš n pr-ʿꜣ ỉw.w ỉr n.n tygrphꜣ r-r.w* "the dovecote and those things attached to it and the chapel of Isis, the emoluments, the land which is listed above from which I gave to you the places listed above which I purchased between me and you at the auction of pharaoh, they making for us a *diagraphe* for them."

The Greek evidence pertaining to auctions of property in Ptolemaic Egypt suggests that proceeds from the sale of the auction went into the ἴδιος λόγος (Swarney 1970, pp. 38–40). The Greek evidence also suggests that this was the standard method of disposing of property of many kinds — property either confiscated because of tax arrears or declared to be "without owner" (ἀδέσποτος).[17] Although the evidence for the institution of the *idios logos* exists only from the reign of Ptolemy VI Philometor, public auctions of derelict property extends back to the end of the third century both in the Greek and in the Demotic papyri.[18]

Evidence for the confiscation and subsequent auction of derelict or ownerless property occurs in Greek texts from both Upper Egypt and the Memphis region.[19] In both cases, the property in question was ἀναλαμβάνειν εἰς τὸ βασιλικόν "taken back to the crown" (Swarney 1970, pp. 23–26). A hitherto obscure Demotic phrase might reflect land that was so reclaimed by the crown:

> [*ꜣḥ*] *nt* (or *wn-nꜣw*) *sẖ r pr-ʿꜣ*
>
> "[land] which is [or 'used to be'] assigned to pharaoh"[20]

I have suggested above that the auction mentioned in P. Hauswaldt 16 might have been the one announced in P. Greek Elephantine 14, written some two years before. Whether the Hauswaldt document and the announcement of auction found at Elephantine record one or two separate auctions, both took place at Edfu. P. Greek Elephantine 14 is part of the archive of the official Milon, the *praktor* at Edfu, who had fled to Elephantine to escape personal harm. Within his papers is preserved the record of the financial troubles of a priestly family at Edfu. The sons of Estphenis acquired thirty arouras of land and made the *tš mḥ 1* "first installment."[21] They were, however, unable to make further payments and ceded their claim on the land to Zenon son of Dionysius. Although the brothers did not own the land outright since complete payment had not yet been made, nonetheless their claim to the land could apparently be transferred legitimately to a third party who would continue to make the remaining payments due to the royal bank (Pringsheim 1949, p. 302).

Land falling into disuse is the most likely explanation for the seizure and sale by public auction of large tracts of land at Pathyris beginning on 8 November 187 B.C., at the time when the northern Thebaid was regained from the rebellion that had caused widespread unrest in southern Upper Egypt (between 207 and 186

equivalent uses a form of the verb ὠνέομαι + ἐκ βασιλικοῦ. See Pestman 1978, p. 60.

17. For Theban sales of property, see Wilcken 1935, pp. 266–95.
18. Concerning the absolute date for the government account of receipts received from such sales, Swarney (1970, p. 40) states that "a date for the establishment of the *idios logos* cannot be exactly determined. Presumably it came at a time when the turnover of private property during the chaos of the mid-second century B.C. necessitated a separate account for recording payments from confiscated and abandoned property."
19. As in the case of the seizure of the priests' property at Edfu documented in the Milon archive, the Memphite texts, known as the Zois Papyri, document the default on a tax farming agreement. See further Wilcken 1927, pp. 523–36.
20. P. BMFA 38.2063b, B I, line 37; B II, line 4. See the note by Parker 1964, p. 98, who did not explain the phrase. For the phrase *sẖ r* "établir par écrit qqch. en faveur de qqn.," see Malinine 1961, p. 159 n. (c); Betrò 1984, p. 57 n. 17.
21. P. Dem. Elephantine 2.

B.C.).[22] This upheaval probably resulted in many persons temporarily abandoning their land, which would have been sufficient grounds for the government to declare the land ἀδέσποτος, to seize the land, and to auction it to the highest bidder.[23]

A bank *diagraphe* (Demotic *tygrpw*,[24] *tyꜣgrphꜣ* [25]) was issued ordering the royal bank, to which payment was made, to accept the price in several installments. This receipt, or "deposit slip" (Swarney 1970, p. 10), was the means by which a party could prove legal title to a plot of land purchased at auction (Pestman 1978, p. 64, n. k). As a proof of legal purchase, it was transferred at the time of sale along with any other important legal documents.[26]

Outside of the Hauswaldt example, the Demotic evidence is clustered around the years just after the cessation of the Theban uprising. From Dendara we learn of an auction of two large plots acquired by a priest and conveyed to his son in the form of a will. One plot was located in the *ḥtp-ntr* of Hathor consisting of *ꜣḥ mꜣy* "island land" and *ꜣḥ qꜣy* "high land," along with an empty plot (*wrḥ*),[27] and another plot of forty-one and one-half arouras was divided into two parcels, one of twenty-eight and one-half, the other of thirteen, also within the *ḥtp-ntr* of Hathor. P. Mainz ε + δ is a record of the sale and cession of thirty-five arouras of high land and its "excess of measure" in the *ḥtp-ntr* of Hathor, originally purchased at auction. Plots immediately adjacent to the south and north were also purchased at the public auction at the same time. At the other end of the spectrum, P. Strassburg 21 is the sale agreement for an empty plot (*wrḥ*) consisting of just one ground cubit (*mḥ ỉtn 1*) purchased thirty-one years previously at auction. The agreement over the installment payments contained in P. Hauswaldt 16 and the other texts discussed here proves that the public auction had a wider scope than the domain of Hathor, despite Grunert's proposal to the contrary (1979, p. 65, n. 33).

Further evidence that the public auction extended to other temple estates has recently been brought to bear by Zauzich's (1990, pp. 161–62) new reading in P. BM 10591 recto, vi, lines 16–17, the court record from the Asyut family dispute over ten arouras of land in the temple estate of the local god Wepwawet. At first sight the situation revolving around the public auction in the Asyut case appears to be unique. At the conclusion of the main part of the legal proceedings, after both parties had stated the evidence that they thought relevant to the ownership of the ten arouras, the judges asked Chratianch if there was a man who made her plea. The woman responded that in fact there was and he, a certain Oertes,[28] proclaimed that:

> there is a *diagraphe* that was made to Tuot son of Petetum, the husband of Chratianch on account of [the auction][29] of pharaoh in year eleven, Pharmuthi, for one and one-half arouras of land as an increase of measure which was found in relation to them.

Two things deserve comment here. The first is that there does not appear to be any relationship between the assertion that a *diagraphe* was found for one and one-half arouras of extra land and the dispute over the ownership of the ten arouras which was the subject of the legal dispute within the family. Could such a *diagraphe*-receipt over an excess amount of land act as at least partial proof of ownership for the entire plot? Secondly, what did the public auction have to do with an increase in the plot under dispute? There is evidence that in cases when family property came up for public auction, other family members assumed a privileged position at the

22. See Vandorpe 1986, p. 297. The land involved in the so-called "Erbstreit" archive mentioned in the sale and cession documents P. Mainz ε + δ, was originally acquired during this government seizure and sale. The Erbstreit archive is to be republished by Sven Vleeming and Katelijn Vandorpe. The most recent summary of the evidence for the Theban revolt is that of Pestman 1995.

23. For another example of this procedure, see Swarney 1970, pp. 28–29. Clarysse (1979, pp. 101–06) published a text from Trinity College, Dublin (P. Gr. Dublin ined.; cf. Pestman 1995, p. 121, text ww), that reports some of the negative effects of the Thebaid revolt (the text is dated by the author to post-187 B.C.): "The land has gone dry. When therefore, as is regular practice, the land which did not have owners was registered among the γῆ ἀδέσποτος, some of the survivors encroached upon the land bordering their own and got hold of more than was allowed. Their names are unknown since nobody pays for this (land) to the treasury … . But of the uncultivated area, nothing has been overlooked, because the land-measurement of what is sown happens every year, and the taxes are being exacted." On this text, see also the comments of Pestman 1995, pp. 121–22.

24. P. BM 10591 recto, vi, line 13; Thompson 1934, p. 24.

25. P. Turin 6081, line 21; Botti 1967, text 4. The reading was corrected from the editio princeps by Zauzich (1971b, p. 49). For a listing of Demotic occurrences, see Clarysse 1987, pp. 22–23.

26. P. Mainz ε, line 5; Zauzich 1968, p. 38.

27. P. BMFA 38.2063b, line A10; Parker 1964.

28. On the foreign name *Wrts*, see Thompson 1934, p. 24, n. 106, wherein it is suggested that this name is Armenian; Lüddeckens (1981, p. 122) also equates the name with Βάρτας.

29. The scribe omitted *ʿyš*.

bidding, but there is no evidence that land had been seized by the government in the Asyut case. Rather, it is apparent that government officials discovered that the plot in question was larger than previously recorded, and therefore a price was paid into the royal bank. The situation described here has many similarities to P. Amherst 31, in which a woman was found to have enclosed extra land to plant palm trees.[30] Although there is no mention of an auction, royal officials intervened, resurveyed the land, and found that the woman had a small excess (two cubits) of waste land (χέρσος) that was liable to a "fine" (πρόστιμον), which became the purchase price of the land. Thus the Demotic term "auction of pharaoh," like its Greek counterpart, has a wider scope than "auction," incorporating also financial payments to the crown for land that was technically in excess of the booked amount. The transaction was a government sale "without the formality of purchase" (Swarney 1970, pp. 15–16). As in the P. Amherst case, the extra land in the Asyut archive may have been "simply waste land which may not even have been recorded in the local scribe's office, but which nevertheless might not be arbitrarily added to any nearby property" (Swarney 1970, p. 17).

A different interpretation of the Asyut case has recently been suggested by Bogaert (1988), although it must be stressed that the author was presumably unaware of Zauzich's new reading. In his new interpretation, Bogaert claims that the one and one-half arouras of extra land was "terre royale concédée par bail emphytéotique au plaignant" (1988, p. 214). There is, however, absolutely no reason to assume that this extra land was royal land since the land involved in the case is elsewhere described as being in the divine endowment of Wepwawet. Payment of the price along with the taxes in kind (*swt.w*) was paid to the royal bank, but this was the standard procedure in purchase at auction, whether tenure was acquired through lease or sale.[31]

Rowlandson (1996, pp. 48–53) has outlined the evidence for public auctions of land in Roman Egypt, most of which accords well with the Ptolemaic material. The auctions were publicly advertised and were of two types. The first involved land that was unproductive (ὑπόλογος). In this case, the price was fixed at a very low rate and came with the added benefit of being tax-free for the first three years as an added incentive to bring the land under cultivation. The second type of auction, when land had been returned to the state either because its owners did not have an heir or because the land was in tax arrears, required the submission of tender offers and the price could go as high as the market would bear. The successful bidder acquired full ownership of the land. Rowlandson (1996, p. 53) concludes that:

> We should expect land available for sale at auction to have been most abundant at times of demographic or economic stress, when more people died without heirs or were unable to meet their tax obligations. But the evidence is so sparse that it provides no scope for determining fluctuations in the availability of the land.

Although it is, of course, dangerous to make sweeping conclusions from a handful of texts, the clustering of the Demotic evidence, such as it is, for the auctioning of property in the second century is concordant with the economic stress well known during this period throughout Egypt.[32] All but the Hauswaldt example and P. BM 10828 date to the post-Theban revolt era when the Ptolemies made a special effort to reassert control of the Thebaid. It is generally argued that the origins of the Ptolemaic *idios logos*, the "privy purse" of the crown into which was paid the proceeds of sales of derelict or ownerless land, lay in the second century B.C. (Rathbone 1993, pp. 105–06). The basis for this institution was in the royal claim to administering all land in Egypt. The Hauswaldt example provides valuable confirmation of the operation of this theory in the far south of Egypt and suggests, furthermore, that the origins for the *idios logos* may lie in the third rather than the second century B.C.

There is a growing consensus that, in contradiction to Karl Polanyi and Moses Finley's views, markets were a feature of ancient economic life.[33] One place where markets existed was in the public auction during Ptolemaic Egypt. More work needs to be done on just how extensive was this market and on how prices were determined. This paper has addressed the issue of the Demotic evidence for such public auctions of property. I have suggested that government intervention is an indication of firm Ptolemaic control of the countryside, even in Upper Egypt on temple estates.

This paper cannot be the last word on the subject. Integration with the much more abundant Greek material is necessary and will no doubt show that the Demotic examples reflect the pragmatic adaptation by the Ptolemies to Egypt. No doubt other examples will come to light; the paucity of the Demotic evidence published

30. See the remarks by Swarney 1970, pp. 14–18.
31. "The government sale was a true sale, not a lease ..." (Swarney 1970, p. 34).
32. Reekmans 1949. On the development of the Ptolemaic *idios logos*, see Swarney 1970, pp. 33–40.
33. See, for example, Silver 1995, pp. 95–152.

so far, however, is consistent with the view that the institution of public auction was a Greek innovation and was administered directly by the crown.

References

Andrews, C.
1990 *Catalogue of Demotic Papyri in the British Museum*, Volume 4: *Ptolemaic Legal Texts from the Theban Area*. London: British Museum.

Betrò, M. C.
1984 "Due tavolette demotiche e il P. Gr. Amherst II 31." *Egitto e Vicino Oriente* 7: 41–60.

Bogaert, R.
1988 "Les opérations en nature des banques en Égypte gréco-romaine." *Ancient Society* 19: 213–24.

Botti, G.
1967 *L'archivio demotico da Deir el-Medineh*. Firenze: Felice Le Monnier.

Clarysse, W.
1979 "Ptolemaic Papyri from Lycopolis." In *Actes du 15e Congrès international de papyrologie*, volume 4: *Papyrologie documentaire*, pp. 101–06. Papyrologica Bruxellensia 19. Brussels: Fondation Égyptologique Reine Élisabeth.
1987 "Greek Loan-Words in Demotic." In *Aspects of Demotic Lexicography* (Acts of the Second International Conference for Demotic Studies, Leiden, 19–21 September 1984), edited by S. P. Vleeming, pp. 9–33. Studia Demotica 1. Leuven: Peeters.

Criscuolo, L.
1979 "UPZ II 218–221 e l'amministrazione del territorio Tebano." In *Actes du 15e Congrès international de papyrologie*, volume 4: *Papyrologie documentaire*, pp. 95–100. Papyrologica Bruxellensia 19. Brussels: Fondation Égyptologique Reine Élisabeth.

Crum, W. E.
1939 *A Coptic Dictionary*. Oxford: Clarendon Press.

Delekat, L.
1964 *Katoche, Hierodulie und Adoptionsfreilassung*. Münchner Beiträge zur Papyrusforschung und antiken Rechtsgeschichte 47. Munich: C. H. Beck.

Erichsen, W.
1954 *Demotisches Glossar*. Copenhagen: Ejnar Munksgaard.

Grunert, S.
1979 "Ägyptische Erscheinungsformen des Privateigentums zur Zeit der Ptolemäer: Liturgietage." *Zeitschrift für ägyptische Sprache und Altertumskunde* 106: 60–79.
1981 *Thebanische Kaufverträge des 3. und 2. Jahrhunderts v. u. Z.* Berlin: Akademie-Verlag.

Hunt, A. S., and C. C. Edgar
1934 *Select Papyri*, Volume 2: *Public Documents*. Loeb Classical Library. Cambridge: Harvard University Press.

Keenan, J. G., and J. C. Shelton
1976 *The Tebtunis Papyri*, Volume 4. Graeco-Roman Memoirs 64. London: Egypt Exploration Society.

Lüddeckens, E.
1960 *Ägyptische Eheverträge*. Ägyptologische Abhandlungen 1. Wiesbaden: Otto Harrassowitz.
1981 *Demotisches Namenbuch*, Band 1, Lieferung 2: *iʿḥ-i.ir-tj-s – br*. Wiesbaden: Ludwig Reichert Verlag.

Malinine, M.
1961 "Taxes funéraires égyptiennes à l'époque gréco-romaine." In *Mélanges Mariette*, pp. 137–68. Bibliothèque d'étude 32. Cairo: Institut français d'archéologie orientale.

Manning, J. G.
1997 *The Hauswaldt Papyri: A Third Century B.C. Family Dossier from Edfu*. Demotische Studien 12. Sommerhausen: Gisela Zauzich Verlag.

Meeks, D.
1972 *Le grand texte des donations au temple d'Edfou*. Bibliothèque d'étude 59. Cairo: Institut français d'archéologie orientale.

Oates, J. F.
1969 "A Rhodian Auction of a Slave Girl." *Journal of Egyptian Archaeology* 55: 191–210.

Parker, R. A.
1964 "A Demotic Property Settlement from Deir el-Ballas." *Journal of the American Research Center in Egypt* 3: 89–103.

Peremans, W., and E. Van 't Dack
1950 *Prosopographia ptolemaica* 1: *L'administration civile et financière, no. 1 à no. 1824*. Studia Hellenistica 6. Leuven: Catholic University of Leuven.

Pestman, P. W.
1978 *Textes grecs, démotiques et bilingues*. Papyrologica Lugduno-Batava 19. Leiden: E. J. Brill.
1995 "Haronnophris and Chaonnophris: Two Indigenous Pharaohs in Ptolemaic Egypt (205–186 B.C.)." In *Hundred-Gated Thebes* (Acts of a Colloquium on Thebes and the Theban Area in the Graeco-Roman Period), edited by S. P. Vleeming, pp. 101–37. Papyrologica Lugduno-Batava 27. Leiden: E. J. Brill.

Pringsheim, F.
1949 "The Greek Sale by Auction." In *Scritti in onore di Contardo Ferrini pubblicati in occasione della sua beatificazione*, volume 4, pp. 283–303. Università Cattolica del Sacro Cuore, pubblicazioni, n.s., 28. Milan: Società Editrice "Vita e Pensiero."

Rathbone, D.
1993 "Egypt, Augustus and Roman Taxation." *Cahiers du Centre Gustave Glotz* 4: 81–112.

Reekmans, T.
1949 "Economic and Social Repercussions of the Ptolemaic Copper Inflation." *Chronique d'Égypte* 24: 324–42.

Ritner, R. K.
1984 "A Property Transfer from the Erbstreit Archives." In *Grammata Demotika: Festschrift für Erich Lüddeckens zum 15. Juni 1983*, edited by H.-J. Thissen and K.-Th. Zauzich, pp. 171–87. Würzburg: Gisela Zauzich Verlag.

Rowlandson, J.
1996 *Landowners and Tenants in Roman Egypt: The Social Relations of Agriculture in the Oxyrhynchite Nome*. Oxford: Clarendon Press.

Sethe, K.
1920 *Demotische Urkunden zum ägyptischen Bürgschaftsrechte, vorzüglich der Ptolemäerzeit*. Abhandlungen der philologisch-historischen Klasse der sächsischen Akademie der Wissenschaften 32. Leipzig: B. G. Teubner.

Silver, M.
1995 *Economic Structures of Antiquity*. Westport: Greenwood Press.

Spiegelberg, W.
1902 *Die demotischen Papyrus der Strassburger Bibliothek*. Leipzig: J. C. Hinrichs.
1913 *Die demotischen Papyri Hauswaldt: Verträge der ersten Hälfte der Ptolemäerzeit (Ptolemaios II–IV) aus Apollinopolis (Edfu)*. Leipzig: J. C. Hinrichs.

Swarney, P. R.
1970 *The Ptolemaic and Roman* Idios Logos. American Studies in Papyrology 8. Toronto: A. M. Hakkert.

Thissen, H.-J.
1979 "Demotische Graffiti des Paneions im Wadi Hammamat." *Enchoria* 9: 63–92.

Thomas, J. D.
1975 *The Epistrategos in Ptolemaic and Roman Egypt,* Part 1: *The Ptolemaic Epistrategos*. Abhandlungen der rheinisch-westfälischen Akademie der Wissenschaften, Papyrologica Coloniensia 6. Opladen: Westdeutscher Verlag.

Thompson, H.
1934 *A Family Archive from Siut from Papyri in the British Museum Including an Account of a Trial before the Laocritae in the Year B.C. 170*. Oxford: Oxford University Press.

Vandorpe, K.
1986 "The Chronology of the Reigns of Hurgonaphor and Chaonnophris." *Chronique d'Égypte* 61: 294–302.

Van 't Dack, E.
1975 "Le thébarque Stratôn." In *Le monde grecque: Hommages à Claire Préaux*, pp. 646–55. Brussels: n.p. Reprinted in *Ptolemaica selecta: Études sur l'armée et l'administration lagides*, pp. 272–87. Studia Hellenistica 29. Leuven: Catholic University of Leuven, 1988.

Vycichl, W.
1983 *Dictionnaire étymologique de la langue copte*. Leuven: Peeters.

Wilcken, U.
1927 *Urkunden der Ptolemäerzeit* 1: *Papyri aus Unterägypten*. Berlin: Walter de Gruyter.
1935 *Urkunden der Ptolemäerzeit* 2: *Papyri aus Oberägypten*. Berlin: Walter de Gruyter.

Zauzich, K.-Th.
1968 *Die ägyptische Schreibertradition in Aufbau, Sprache und Schrift der demotischen Kaufverträge aus ptolemäischer Zeit*. Ägyptologische Abhandlungen 19. Wiesbaden: Otto Harrassowitz.
1971a "ʿyš n pr-ʿꜣ." *Enchoria* 1: 79–82.
1971b "Korrekturvorschläge zur Publikation des demotischen Archivs von Deir el-Medina." *Enchoria* 1: 43–56.
1990 "Noch eine Versteigerung." *Enchoria* 17: 161–62.
1993 *Papyri von der Insel Elephantine*. Demotische Papyri aus der staatlichen Museen zu Berlin, Preussischer Kulturbesitz, 3. Berlin: Akademie-Verlag.

28

SEMI-LITERACY IN EGYPT: SOME ERASURES FROM THE AMARNA PERIOD

PETER DER MANUELIAN

Museum of Fine Arts, Boston

Few Egyptologists have done as much to unlock the writings and thought processes of the ancient Egyptians as the scholar honored in this volume. His many contributions include years devoted to the Epigraphic Survey's distinguished projects, grammatical essays, and unsurpassed translations. Less tangible, yet equally impressive, is the number of students he has enlightened on all stages of the Egyptian language. They bear testimony to his unique combination of academic astuteness and kind encouragement. May this note on a topic and era he knows far better than I be of some interest and amusement to him.[1]

In a recent article on texts and images in Egyptian art, Betsy M. Bryan (1995, pp. 28–29; 1996) explored how discrete portions of a scene or image might speak to different audiences or segments of the ancient Egyptian population. This raises in a new form the question of literacy in ancient Egypt and, more specifically, levels or degrees of literacy. For example, the impression conveyed to an ancient viewer by the image alone of a seated-pair statue might differ significantly from that conveyed by the image combined with all of its identifying inscriptions and prayers. The key variable is the perception of the viewer in question, and whether the viewer could appreciate the two human figures by themselves, the figures and the simple *ḥtp di̓ nsw* formula provided for the viewer, or both of these plus a long and perhaps complicated text with administrative titles, family genealogy, and biographical narrative. In each of these instances, the viewer would walk away with a different perception of the object in question. In the case of monumental works of art, such as propagandistic battle reliefs on temple walls, the state could reach a multitude of individuals on a multitude of levels (Bryan 1996; Simpson 1982; idem 1996). In short, not all Egyptian monuments spoke to their audiences with the same voice; the varying potential meanings were in the "mind's eye" of the ancient beholder.

Assessing the literacy rate of an ancient people is a formidable task. In the Egyptian case, estimates currently run at less than five percent of the population (Baines 1983, pp. 584–86; Baines and Eyre 1983, pp. 65–96; Lesko 1990, pp. 656–67; Bryan 1996, n. 14). How much more difficult must it be to assess the various levels of ancient literacy?[2] John Baines summarized several possible levels, which I have condensed and portrayed in the chart in fig. 28.1.

Modern text-critical analyses of Egyptian inscriptions have long been contributing to our understanding of the competence of the literate Egyptian, noting dependence on tradition, both oral and written, and examples of scribal errors, such as dittographies, auditory mistakes, etc. Most of these analyses focus on an elite class of Egyptians already so well schooled as to be able to compose texts and in some cases even research and reproduce earlier stages of the language (Manuelian 1994). But what about further "down" the literacy ladder? It may be possible to gain a brief glimpse into some of these levels with a look, not at what the Egyptians inscribed on a wall, but, ironically, what they scratched out. In other words, erasures of portions of an Egyptian inscription might tell us more about Egyptian literacy levels than the writings themselves.

Usurpations, recarvings, and willful destruction of inscribed materials have long histories and multiple causes (*LÄ* 6 "Usurpator" and "Usurpierung," cols. 904–06). Redirecting the mortuary benefits of another, alter-

1. For their helpful comments on earlier versions of this paper I am indebted to John Baines and Christian E. Loeben.

2. The subject receives relatively little attention in *LÄ* 1 "Ausbildung," esp. cols. 572–74; compare also Brunner 1957 (new edition in preparation by H.-W. Fischer-Elfert); E. Otto 1956, pp. 41–48. On schoolboy education, see now Janssen and Janssen 1990, pp. 67–89 (for this reference I thank Christian E. Loeben).

Gold of Praise: Studies on Ancient Egypt in Honor of Edward F. Wente
Edited by Emily Teeter and John A. Larson
Studies in Ancient Oriental Civilization 58
Chicago: Oriental Institute, 1999

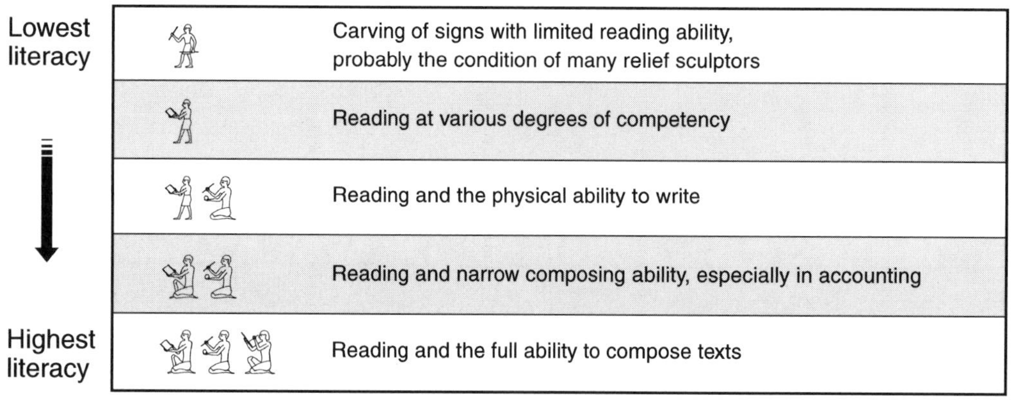

Figure 28.1. Chart of Potential Egyptian Literacy Levels (after Baines 1983, p. 584)

ing the historical record, attacking personal enemies, censuring a religious element, all of these are potential motives for the "mark of the second hand" on Egyptian inscriptions (Fischer 1977, pp. 113–42, esp. p. 119). As far as ancient literacy is concerned, an erasure primarily represents a directed and highly focused attack on some aspect of the scene, which in turn presupposes a certain amount of knowledge on the part of the attacker, or at least of his superior. That level of knowledge is economical, practical, and even necessary; otherwise entire texts, statues, or tomb or temple walls would have to be destroyed to achieve the desired effect of *damnatio memoriae*.

The following paragraphs touch on a few erasures, primarily from the Amarna period at Thebes, as a glimpse at part of the semi-literate classes during the Egyptian New Kingdom. It is no secret that Akhenaten went on the offensive against certain texts and scenes in the traditional artistic repertoire. Almost every scholarly treatise on the king's reign mentions the iconoclastic program, but few seem to delve into the subject in any systematic detail.[3] What is not so clear is how his commands were given, and exactly who carried out his iconoclastic orders on the monuments themselves.[4] One author has even suggested that the haphazard nature of some erasures implies Akhenaten's absence from the decision-making process:

> ... la mission de martelage semble avoir été assez imprécise, et les ouvriers chargés de ce travail ont, pour le moins, fait preuve de beaucoup de négligence. On peut dès lors se demander si cette mission était formellement ordonnée par Akhenaton, ou si l'on n'a pas là le témoignage d'excès (sans doute tolérés par le pouvoir royal), attribuables à des thuriféraires fanatiques, couverte par l'autorité de quelque haut fonctionnaire de la cour (Hari 1984, p. 1040).

We examine below three discrete categories of textual erasures attributed to the Atenists: the treatment of the name of the god Amun (*ʾImn*), the various forms of the word for deity (*nṯr*), and various meanings of *mwt*. The caveat should be noted that much trust is placed in the facsimile drawings of a number of tomb publications. Additional collation of individual drawings with their monuments might do much to confirm or revise some of the examples discussed below.

DESTRUCTION OF AMUN

The name of the chief state deity of the Eighteenth Dynasty probably ranked first on Akhenaten's list of "expugnables," to judge by the overwhelming number of erasures of *ʾImn* throughout Egypt and Nubia. Only when we consider the mutually threatening nature, as Jan Assmann describes it, of an iconic versus aniconic cultic perspective can we begin to understand the dimensions of Akhenaten's campaign of defacement.[5] Perhaps internal chronologies for the Amarna period could be aided by analysis of the erasure of Amun

3. Hornung 1971, pp. 43, 249; Saad 1972; Hari 1984, pp. 1039–41; Hornung 1995, pp. 97–99.

4. There are no indexed entries for erasure in either Redford 1984 or Aldred 1988, nor have I been able to locate entries in the *Lexikon der Ägyptologie* specifically devoted to the subject of erasures. For the situation in the Twenty-sixth Dynasty, see Yoyotte 1951, pp. 215–39. Schulman (1964, p. 67) argues that Akhenaten's "campaign" could not have taken place without the full support of the military (for bringing this reference to my attention, I thank John Baines). See Norman Davies 1923a, pp. 132–52, in general on Akhenaten's activity in the Theban area. For Amarna period bibliography, see Martin 1991. Discussions of Amarna texts and grammar include Behnk 1930; Silverman 1991; Murnane 1995; Silverman 1999.

5. Personal communication. I am grateful to Professor Assmann for sharing his unpublished work on this topic (concerning Moses in particular) with me in manuscript form.

occurring within the cartouches of Amenhotep III, because with royal names Akhenaten's agents seem on occasion to have shown restraint. Such restraint is not evident in fig. 28.2, a peridotite standing statue of Amenhotep III from Gebel Barkal (originally from Soleb?), now in Boston (MFA 23.734),[6] on which Akhenaten erased his father's prenomen as well as every other occurrence of Amun's name on the statue. Whether the causes of this censorship campaign lay in a political attack by the monarchy against a growing theocracy, a cult-inspired desire to eliminate everything "hidden" (*ỉmn*), beyond visible nature, or some other (combination of) factors, is not our focus here. Rather, the name of the deity as the subject of erasure reveals some interesting evidence for the (il)literacy of the agents who carried out the king's orders.

Many Theban tombs bear the "standard" erasures of Amun's name.[7] We may mention instead a few cases where Akhenaten's adherents have apparently misread the texts. Countless Egyptian words are, of course, composed with the same biliteral 𓏠 and phonetic complement 𓈖 used in the writing of Amun; these were ap-

Figure 28.2. Peridotite Standing Statue of Amenhotep III from Gebel Barkal (MFA 23.734); Courtesy Museum of Fine Arts, Boston

6. See Dunham 1970, pp. 17 (with bibliography), 19, fig. 5, pl. 5; Müller 1988, pp. iv–6, pl. 1a–d; Kozloff and Bryan 1992, p. 465. It is interesting to note the post-Amarna history of this piece because the cartouches once containing the nomen of Amenhotep III have been partially restored with the king's prenomen *Nb-mꜣʿt-Rʿ*. For other monuments treated similarly, see Griffith 1926, p. 2; and the pedestal of the granite falcon statue of Amenhotep III (originally from Soleb?), also found at Gebel Barkal (MFA 23.1470), Dunham 1970, pp. 25, 27, fig. 20, pl. 25d.
7. Among them Ramose (TT 55), Userhat (TT 56), Djehuty (TT 110), Puyemre (TT 39), Amenemhat (TT 82), Rekh-

parently mistaken for the god's name on several occasions (Hari 1984, p. 1041). In the tomb of Amenemhat (TT 82), which bears many examples of the "correctly" erased group ʾ*Imn*, the following excerpted text occurs on the south wall of the passage (see fig. 28.3).[8]

> (1) *ỉrt qrst nfrt n sš ḥsb ỉt* [ʾ*Imn*]*-m-ḥꜣt* (2) *m-ḫt* [*mnỉ*] *wḏꜣ r ḫrt-nṯr šms* (3) *sš* [ʾ*Imn*]*-m-ḥꜣt mꜣʿ ḫrw r ỉmnt*(*t*) *nfrt šms* (4) *ḥry mrwt n* [ʾ*Imn* ʾ*Imn*]*-m-ḥꜣt r wỉꜣ* ...
>
> (1) Performing a good burial for the scribe who counts the grain [Amen]emhat, (2) after [passing away]. Proceeding to the necropolis, accompanying (3) the scribe [Amen]emhet, justified, to the beautiful west. Accompanying (4) the chief of the weavers of [Amun, Am]enemhat, to the barque ...

If we can trust the drawing reproduced in the tomb publication, the verb erased in line 2 must be *mnỉ*, erased for the *mn*- and *n*-signs by the same agents charged with erasing ʾ*Imn* in the rest of the text. Even the ceiling texts contain erasures in this tomb, but in one instance, the Atenists have chiseled out the verb *mn* "be established":[9]

> *ḏd mdw ỉmy-r ḥsb wnnwt sš* [ʾ*Imn*]*-m-ḥꜣt mꜣʿ-ḫrw*
> *ḏd rn=k m ḫnw ḥwt=k twtw=k m ỉtrwt.sn bꜣ=k ʿnḫ ḫꜣt=k* [*mn.tỉ*] *m ỉs=k n ḫrt-nṯr*
> [*rn=k mn*] *wꜣḥ m rꜣ msw=k ḏt*
>
> Recitation: O steward who counts that which exists, scribe [Amen]emhet, justified. May your name endure inside your mansion, may your images be in their chapels; may your *ba* be living, your corpse [established] in your tomb of the necropolis, [your name being established] and lasting in the mouth(s) of your children forever.

Two examples here of misreading the *mn* of ʾ*Imn* combination, occurring in the same text beside actual erasures of ʾ*Imn*, would seem to confirm a logographic approach to the work of defacement on behalf of Akhenaten. A more competent reading knowledge of Egyptian would not have confused ʾ*Imn* "Amun" with *mnỉ* "to perish" or with *mn* "be established."

The tomb of Puyemre (TT 39) shows erasure of the word *mnʿt* "nurse." In Puyemre's biographical text stela on the tomb's facade, the deceased is identified as "... born of the judge Puya," *ms n mnʿt wrt Nfr-ỉʿḥ mꜣʿt-ḫrw* "born of the chief nurse Nofret-yoh, justified." (The text was restored after the Amarna period.) In an

Figure 28.3. Scene from Tomb of Amenemhat (TT 82) (after Norman Davies and Gardiner 1915, pl. 7)

mire (TT 100), Kheruef (TT 192), User (TT 21), Amenhotep(?) (TT 73), Nebamun (TT 17), Amenemhat Surer (TT 48), Amenhotep-sa-se (TT 75), Kenamun (TT 93), Kenamun (TT 162), Djeserkareseneb (TT 38), Hepu (TT 66), Nakht (TT 52), and Nebamun and Ipuky (TT 181). References may be found in PM 1/1, passim.

8. Norman Davies and Gardiner 1915, p. 53, nos. 1–2, pl. 10.
9. Norman Davies and Gardiner 1915, p. 101, nos. 5–6, pl. 27.

example of post-Amarna semi-literacy (or perhaps merely scribal error or confusion resulting from hieratic?), the name of Amun has been incorrectly restored in line 47 to read . The *mn* and *n* combination have been erased in a number of words in this tomb (Norman Davies 1923b, pp. 21, 94, n. 2).

An interesting erasure occurs in the tomb of Userhat (TT 56). The wall to the right of the entrance bears the inscription reproduced in fig. 28.4, with erasures of both the name of *ʾImn nb tȝwy* "Amun, Lord of the Two Lands" (fig. 28.4, line 2) and *ḫnty ỉmntyw* "foremost of the westerners" (fig. 28.4, line 4).[10] Why would the phrase *ḫnty ỉmntyw* attract the attention of Akhenaten's adherents? The epithet's relation to Osiris is no explanation because in the preceding line the god's name remains intact.[11] One of two possibilities seems likely: the word *ỉmntyw* was spelled with one of its rare variants employing the group . According to the *Wörterbuch*, this is primarily an Old Kingdom spelling of the word;[12] its usage here is perhaps made even more unlikely owing to the complementary scene to the left of the entrance, which uses the standard (Beinlich-Seeber and Shedid 1987, p. 43, text 4, line 2, p. 44, fig. 9, pls. 3, 30d). The second possibility involves an auditory error, but it is dubious that one of the iconoclasts read the text aloud and confused the pronunciation of *ỉmn* of *ỉmntyw* with the god *ʾImn* since the vocalization of the two words was not all that similar.[13] Perhaps this is an example of the agents' preference for overkill to an error of omission. Others have noted this practice as well:

> An einigen Stellen ist die Zeichengruppe Amun-Ra stehengeblieben, an anderen Stellen dagegen sind so unsystematisch Zeilen mit unverfänglich scheinenden Worten bzw. Wortreste zerstört, daß man den Eindruck gewinnt, die Tilgungen seien de facto von jemandem ausgeführt worden, der nicht lesen konnte und daher benachbarte Zeilen "sicherheitshalber" gleich mitausgehackt hat (Beinlich-Seeber and Shedid 1987, p. 18).

Whatever the correct explanation is here, we can at least eliminate mere sloppiness, that is, the erasure of *ḫnty ỉmntyw* due to its proximity to *ʾImn* since the fully intact text of column 3 separates the two erasures.

The final example may appear to betray a higher level of literacy at hand, in this case taking the form of caution. The female "form" of the god Amun, *ʾImn.t,* is left intact two or three times in the small texts on the side wall of the passage of the tomb of Kenamun (TT 162; Nina Davies 1963, pl. 19).[14] Either the agents failed to read the name correctly and realize Amunet's association with her male counterpart, or they actually could distinguish between the male and female forms, the one (*ʾImn*) on the proscribed list, the other (*ʾImn.t*) to be left untouched.

MONOTHEISM VERSUS POLYTHEISM: ERASURE OF *NṮRW*

Apart from selected deities, there was never an attempt to efface from memory the names of every god other than the Aten. Should one refrain from labeling Akhenaten's religion truly monotheist in the modern sense of the term? And yet, some element of "the many," the concept of deific plurality, versus "the one," certainly conflicted with his religious and political agenda (Hornung 1971, pp. 42–43, 248–49; Hornung 1995, esp. pp.

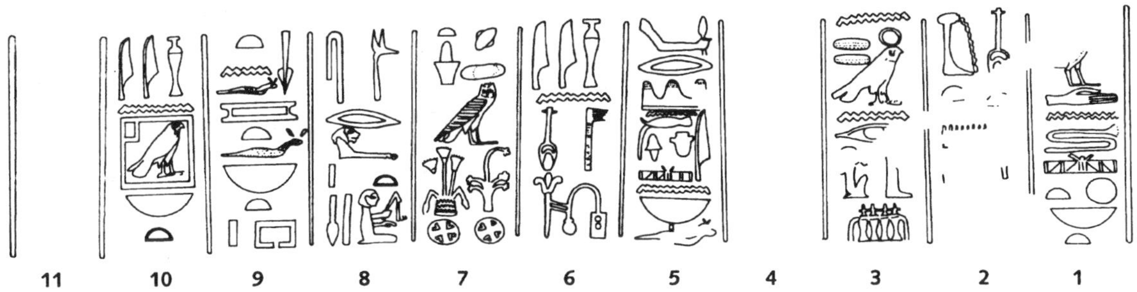

Figure 28.4. Text from Tomb of Userhat (TT 56) (after Beinlich-Seeber and Shedid 1987, p. 50, fig. 17)

10. Beinlich-Seeber and Shedid 1987, p. 50, fig. 17, text 10, line 4, pl. 2, and, for a summary of the erasures in this tomb, see pp. 17–18.

11. Osiris's name was apparently, however, the occasional object of erasure by the Atenists; compare the tomb of Hepu (TT 66; Nina Davies 1963, p. 12 [pl. 13]).

12. *Wb.* 1.86:20; Faulkner (1962, p. 21) cites a New Kingdom spelling with the group from Naville 1901, pl. 115.

13. On the likelihood that the Egyptians read most, if not all, of their texts by reciting them aloud, see Baines 1983, pp. 581 with esp. n. 21, and 595, n. 27.

14. On this deity, see *LÄ* 1 "Amaunet," col. 183.

97–104). Fischer's comment (1977, p. 119, n. 32), echoed by Hari (1984, p. 1041), that *nṯrw* suffered attack because of its relation to Amun's frequent epithet *nswt nṯrw*, "king of the gods," does not seem to go far enough in explaining the situation.[15] *Nṯrw* was hacked in numerous contexts where Amun's name and epithets are absent, leading us to return to the polytheistic nature of the term as the reason for its removal. Eventually, if not right from the start of the censorship campaign, Akhenaten placed the hieroglyphs for "gods," *nṯrw*, on the list of words to be expunged (Aldred 1975a, p. 62).

Examples abound for the erasure of the 𓊹-sign throughout the Theban necropolis and, of course, elsewhere along the Nile as well.[16] What is important for this study is how these examples reflect the level of reading competence of the king's agents. How difficult was it to handle singulars and plurals in ancient Egypt and, to go one step further, to handle their potential variant spellings? Akhenaten's agents were instructed to deface a plural; in the form of three *nṯr*-signs, this would have been easy enough to recognize, assuming a modicum of scribal education on their part.[17] For convenience, we call the writing of 𓊹𓊹𓊹 the "long form" of the plural *nṯrw*. Apparently, the "short form," written 𓏪𓊹, caused the agents some difficulties. Could the three strokes replacing three *nṯr*-signs have proven a challenge to the agents' reading skills? Or was it simply easier for the eye to gloss over the short form of *nṯrw*, with its single, less conspicuous tall sign? One could imagine that the agents were skimming the wall texts quickly, looking for three 𓊹-signs, and simply missed the variants with three strokes. But so many examples of the survival of 𓏪𓊹 — on so many different monuments — are preserved as to suggest a more fundamental cause for this oversight. I would suggest difficulty with reading plurals not spelled out clearly.

In the tomb of the vizier Rekhmire (TT 100), on the upper section of the east half of the north wall in the passage, the tomb owner returns from successful confirmation in office to be greeted by his son, Menkheperraseneb (see fig. 28.5). The son's text reads *n kꜣ.k sty šꜣw prt m-bꜣḥ nb* [*nṯrw ꜣImn*] *pꜣwty-tꜣwy* ... "For your *ka*, the scent of flowers which came forth from the presence of the lord of the [gods, Amun], the primeval one of the Two Lands ... ." Here the long form of *nṯrw*, 𓊹𓊹𓊹, has been hacked out (and, according to Norman Davies [1943, p. 65, n. 65], subsequently clumsily restored after the Amarna period). Further to the left, however, in (Davies's) columns 16–17, Rekhmire's vigilance is praised concerning *mnw nb m pr-*[*ꜣImn*] *r.w-prw nw nṯrw Šmꜥw Mḥw* ... "all (kinds of) monuments in the temple of [Amun] and the chapels of the gods of Upper and Lower Egypt ... ." Here, the name of Amun is erased — certifying Atenist attention paid to this part of the tomb — but in the very next column the plural *nṯrw*, written 𓏪𓊹, is left untouched.

In the tomb of the vizier Ramose (TT 55), the word for the ennead 𓏪𓊹 has escaped destruction (Norman Davies 1941, p. 4, n. 1, pls. 28, 40). Either the single 𓊹 sign masked the concept of plurality, or Akhenaten's agents were actually reading the word *psḏt*, against which they had no quarrel. One text shows the very rare erasure of both the long 𓊹𓊹𓊹 and short 𓏪𓊹 forms of *nṯrw* (ibid., pl. 6), but the Atenist who noted both plural variants here was perhaps not so skilled in discerning the various usages of the *mwt*-vulture (see below).

In the tomb of Djehuty (TT 110), evidence of Atenist activity is present in the erasures of the name of Amun and the long form of *nṯrw* (Norman Davies 1932, pp. 279–90). But *nṯrw*, written in the short form, survives intact in several instances. The most notable example occurs on the north-wall stela (fig. 28.6), where *ꜣImn* is hacked out at least six times, but the phrase *nswt nṯrw* survives twice in the short form 𓏪𓊹, right next to [*ꜣImn*] (ibid., pl. 42). In the lunettes of the north- and south-wall stelae, *nswt nṯrw* survives two more times in the same phrase with [*Amun*]-*Ra*.[18] To remind us that the word for "gods" definitely was on Akhenaten's list here, the long form of *nṯrw* 𓊹𓊹𓊹 is erased in the main texts on both of these stelae (ibid., pls. 36, 39, 37, 40), and on the west wall (ibid., pl. 41).

Another example of the survival of the short form of *nṯrw* in close proximity to an erased *ꜣImn* occurs on the above-mentioned statue of Amenhotep III from Gebel Barkal (fig. 28.2). The Amun of Amenhotep's cartouche is expunged in all four of its occurrences, including the tiny belt inscription. On the back pillar, the second half

15. On this emblem in general, see Newberry 1947, p. 90; Hornung 1971, chapter 2, pp. 33–65.

16. Examples include the tombs of Kheruef (TT 192), User (TT 21), Amenemhat (TT 82), Ramose (TT 55), Kenamun (TT 93), Nakht (TT 52), Puyemre (TT 39), Nebamun and Ipuky (TT 181), and Senenmut (TT 71; Dorman 1991, p. 47, text 13, note f; fig. 10, pls. 12a, 25d); additional references in PM 1/1.

17. Note the curious detail in the tomb of Puyemre (TT 39), wherein Norman Davies (1923b, pp. 68–69, pls. 23, 25a) suggests that the Atenists erased a leatherworker's products shown above his figure due to their resemblance to the *nṯr*-sign. The erasures, however, to judge from pl. 25a, seem too slight and fail to bear any traces to support his interpretation.

18. Norman Davies 1932, pl. 38b–c. Note that, curiously, the name of *ꜣImn* in the nomen of Hatshepsut survives; Norman Davies 1932, p. 288, n. 3.

Figure 28.5. Text from Tomb of Rekhmire (TT 100) (after Norman Davies 1943, pl. 70)

of the titulary reads ... *Nb-mꜣʿt-Rʿ sꜣ Rʿ n ẖt.f mr.f [Nb-mꜣʿt-Rʿ] mry [ʾImn]-Rʿ nswt nṯrw dỉ ʿnḫ ḏt* ... "Nebmaatre, bodily son of Ra, whom he loves, [Nebmaatre (restored)] beloved of [Amun]-Ra, king of the gods, given life forever." While Amun's name was carefully removed — with only minimal damage to the name of Ra immediately below — the following *nṯr*-sign, with its three plural strokes, was left untouched (Dunham 1970, p. 19, fig. 5).

A similar situation may be found in shrine 14 at Gebel es-Silsila (Caminos and James 1963, p. 40, pl. 32). The lintel shows the erasure of Amun *nṯr.t nfr[t] Mꜣʿt-kꜣ-Rʿ [mr]y.t [ʾImn-Rʿ nb nswt tꜣwy]* on one side of the mirror-imaged text centered on an *ʿnḫ*-sign, but the survival in the very same line of the short form of *ʿnḫ nṯr nfr Mn-ḫpr-Rʿ mry Nwn ỉt nṯrw*.

MOTHERS, GODDESSES, AND VULTURES: THE VULTURE HIEROGLYPH

As the consort of Amun, the goddess Mut also came under frequent attack during the Amarna period. In this case, we are dealing not with a word composed of three signs (*ʾImn*), nor with the Egyptians' reading of plural groups, but with a single hieroglyph, the *mwt*-vulture . Consequently, the Atenist erasures take on different characteristics. In addition to the erasure of the goddess' name, we find attacks on the vulture hieroglyph in a multitude of contexts unrelated to the Theban triad. We should hardly be surprised at the erasure of personal names containing the vulture hieroglyph because to the Atenist mind the goddess's name was just as potent or heretical in a personal name such as Senenmut (Dorman 1991, p. 67) as it was standing alone and referring to the goddess herself directly. Hence, in the tomb of Userhat (TT 56), there are several erasures of the deceased wife's name, *Mwt-nfrt,* and *Mwt-twy*'s(?) name is erased in the tomb of Kenamun (TT 162).[19]

Additionally, however, the vulture hieroglyph has not always escaped destruction in those cases where it bears little or no direct relation to the goddess Mut. In the tomb of Amenemhat (TT 82), Gardiner noted on the upper half of the south wall, "The sign for 'mother' has everywhere on this wall been erased by the Akhenaton-worshippers, the same hieroglyph (the vulture) being employed to write the name of the Theban goddess Mut ..." (Norman Davies and Gardiner 1915, p. 35, n. 6, pl. 7). Similarly, the mother of Senenmut suffered the era-

19. On Userhat (TT 56), see Beinlich-Seeber and Shedid 1987, p. 49, fig. 15, text 8; p. 50, fig. 17, text 10, line 11; p. 73, fig. 30, text 18, line 13); on Kenamun (TT 162), see Nina Davies 1963, p. 15, pl. 16.

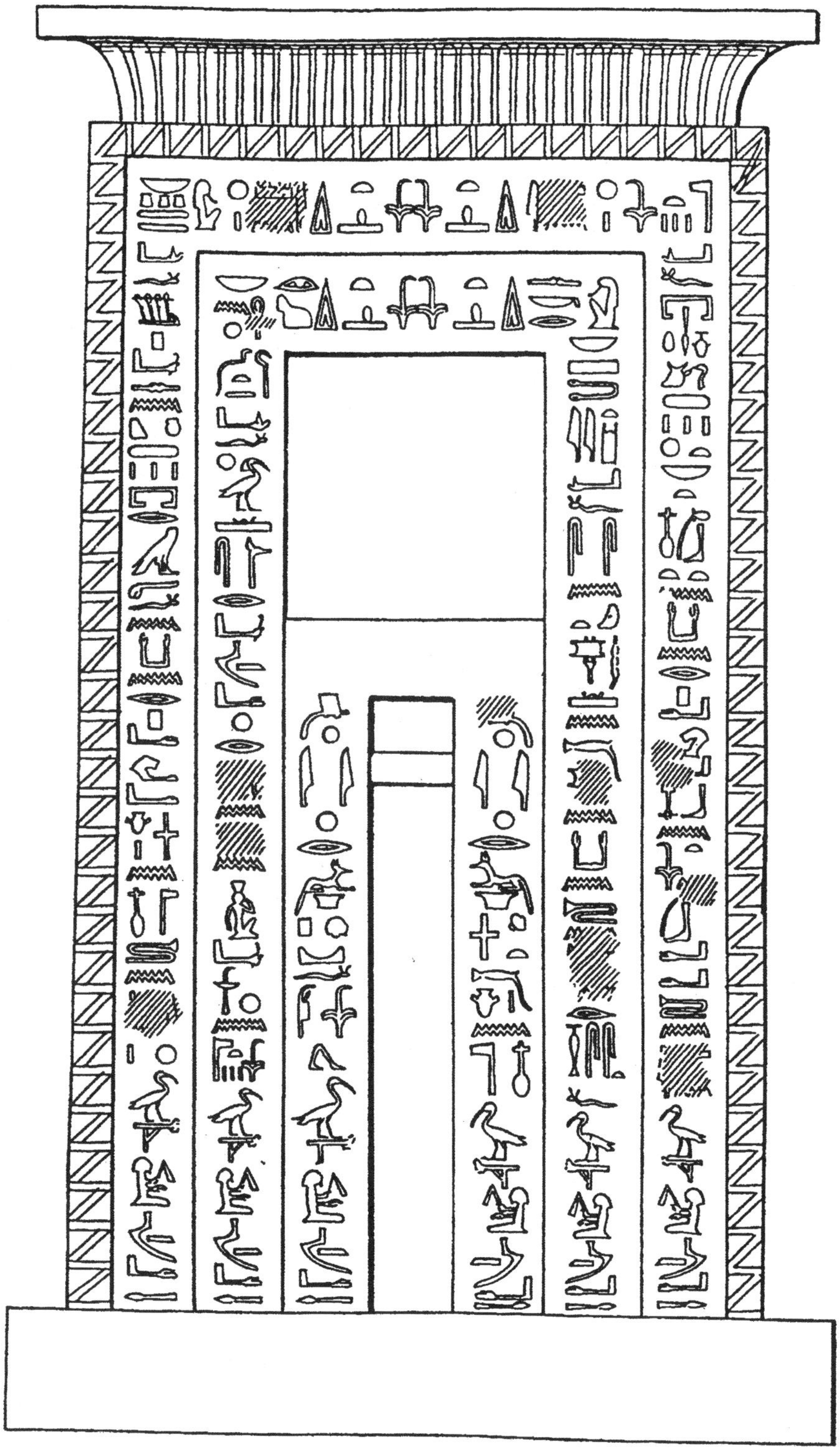

Figure 28.6. North Wall Stela Text from Tomb of Djehuty (TT 110) (after Norman Davies 1932, pl. 42)

sure of her identifying caption in the upper portion of her son's tomb (TT 71): *[mwt].f mr* … "his beloved [mother] …" (Dorman 1991, p. 44, text 11, line 5, pl. 11b, fig. 9).

Even further afield from the goddess Mut than the word for "mother" are examples of erasures in purely secular words. In the tomb of Ramose (TT 55; see fig. 28.7), several words have come under attack on the south half of the east wall, above the seated couple May and Werel. We find Amun's name erased in lines 1 (… *prrt m-bꜣḥ [ʾImn]* … "which come forth from the presence of [Amun] …") and 12–13 (… *ỉmy-r nw n [ʾImn]* … "… the overseer of hunters of [Amun] …"), but the words *mnḫ* (line 5) and *mn* (line 6) survive, indicating a certain discriminatory literacy on the part of Akhenaten's agents. (They missed an opportunity to deface the long form of the plural *nṯrw*, however, in column 12.) In column 9, the goddess Mut's name is erased (*[Mwt] nbt*

Figure 28.7. East Wall Detail from Tomb of Ramose (TT 55) (after Norman Davies 1941, pl. 8)

ʾIšrw ...), but in column 2, the vulture hieroglyph is also effaced in the title  *i̓my-r ss*[*mwt*] *n nb tꜣwy* "overseer of horses of the lord of the Two Lands" (on the title, see Faulkner 1953, p. 43). Thus, in one case the agents distinguished the name of Amun from words spelled similarly, but erased the vulture sign in all instances, either out of an inability to recognize the word *ssmwt,* or a desire to eliminate the vulture sign in any context whatsoever. In another scene on the east wall (north half), the caption accompanying the figure of a *i̓wn-mwt.f*-priest also shows a damaged *mwt*-vulture (Norman Davies 1941, pl. 21). And in the tomb of Nebamun and Ipuky (TT 181), we find a vulture sign erased in the name of one of the four sons of Horus, *Dwꜣ-mwt.f* (Norman Davies 1925, pl. 15). Needless to say, none of the other sons of Horus suffered any damage.

We have seen the *mwt*-vulture erased in the name of the goddess Mut, in compound personal names employing *mwt*, in the word for mother, and in words requiring the phonetic combination *m* + *w* + *t* but otherwise bearing no cultic significance whatsoever. Were Akhenaten's agents simply handed an ostracon with a vulture on it and told to erase its every occurrence? The evidence might suggest so, but illiterate "picture-matching" seems less likely when taken in context with the erasures of *ʾImn* and *nṯrw* outlined above. Were then, on the other hand, more discerning eyes involved? And for the Atenists was the word "mother" more "directly related" to the cult of Mut than the secular word *ssmwt* "horses"?[20]

CONCLUSIONS

Many of the above examples raise interesting questions about the literacy level of the Atenist iconoclasts, as well as the symbolic and representative nature of individual hieroglyphs. Was a hieroglyphic sign, once deemed threatening and blasphemous to a particular cult, always deemed so regardless of context or usage? I have hardly scratched the surface of the corpus of erasures available for study, both in terms of their numbers and their widespread locations all over Egypt and Nubia. I might also mention here a category completely ignored above, namely, non-textual erasures such as the defacement of Amun's sacred *smn*-goose[21] and his ram-headed measuring cords,[22] or the chiseling out of countless figures of *s(t)m*-priests wearing their animal skins.[23] A catalog of the various aspects of defacement, from the types of chisels used to the subjects attacked, would help untangle the often complex history of Egyptian monuments subsequent to their construction. An "erasure catalog" would also shed further light on such topics as diverse literacy levels among the Egyptian population.

Erasures — and in some cases restorations and even modern graffiti — can tell us much about the subsequent history of a tomb, contributing to the reconstruction of its "internal chronology." Beyond providing the obvious *terminus ante quem* for monuments whose precise dating may be difficult, the diagnostic usefulness of erasures becomes most clear at a site like Gebel Barkal, where statuary fragments predating Akhenaten's reign bear Amarna period erasures, while those heaped together with them in the same findspots but dating later, of course, do not (Dunham 1970, pp. 17–37).

A range of literacy levels may be represented by the small corpus above, from misreadings, through difficulties in recognizing plurals, to examples of overkill and "erasure by association." Some of the examples focus our attention on the conditions under which the agents were working (see below). We might need to imagine different literacy levels for Akhenaten's many agents. One scenario involves completely illiterate individuals "armed" with ostraca bearing the names and words, to them merely the "graphic forms," to be expunged. In this case, a *mwt*-vulture or a *nṯr*-sign would perhaps differ little from the image of a *smn*-goose. They did their best in the matching of signs but were often misled by combinations, such as *mn* , similar to those they were ordered to destroy. Another scenario grants them limited reading ability, but not enough experience as to avoid mistaking *ʾImn* for *mnỉ*, *mn*, or *mnʿt*, etc. Rather than attempting pictorial matches of signs and words on the walls to the types provided on their ostraca, they — or their supervisor(s) — would actually have read, or at least sounded out, the texts on the walls. If auditory errors were the cause of some erasures, such as *ỉmntyw* for *ʾImn*, then we are indeed perhaps dealing with a more literate group reading and comprehending the texts on some level. What is difficult to determine is in what cases the adherents were accompanied by more literate supervisors, whether different levels of literacy can be established in different tombs, and if and when the list of words or images to be destroyed evolved and changed over the course of Akhenaten's reign. But it can at least be concluded with certainty from the corpus above, and perhaps not surprisingly, that the king's best-educated administrators were hardly directly involved in the defacement process.

Another issue that must have affected the nature and results of the Atenists' handiwork was the conditions under which they labored. What were the socio-religious aspects of defacing the monuments of the prevailing cults of the time? Did the Atenists have to show any sensitivity to the reactions of Theban citizens to the defacement of their ancestors' sepulchres? Were the attacks carried out under cover of darkness, "no one seeing, no one hearing," or did the agents march into the necropolis in broad daylight, perhaps even with the support of the military? If the agents had to work without adequate time, light, or equipment (e.g., ladders), this might explain

20. For the potentially separate origins of the cult of the goddess Mut and the word *mwt* "mother," see *LÄ* 4 "Mut," col. 246 with nos. 9–10; and more generally, te Velde 1989, pp. 395–403.

21. Examples of the erasure of the *smn*-goose may be found in the tombs of Kenamun (TT 93), Kenamun (TT 162), Nakht (TT 52), and Rekhmire (TT 100), among others.

22. See, for example, the tomb of Djeserkareseneb (TT 38) in the east wall of the hall, top register (Nina Davies 1963, pl. 2).

23. Examples occur in the tombs of Userhat (TT 56; Beinlich-Seeber and Shedid 1987, p. 18 with n. 60), Ramose (TT 55; Norman Davies 1941, pls. 23, 25), User (TT 21), Amenemhat Surer (TT 48), Amenhotep-sa-se (TT 75), Djeserkareseneb (TT 38), Puyemre (TT 39), and Nebamun and Ipuky (TT 181), among others.

some of the missed examples and inconsistencies.[24] Additional study might establish a correlation between a given word or name's location within the tomb's chambers, and its chances for surviving intact.

In determining internal chronology and later history, erasures can tell us when a particular tomb was accessible and for how long, and whether additional elements, such as niche statues, were still in place at the time of attack. I mention here, for example, the stelophorous statue of Nakht, whose textual erasures demonstrate that it was still in situ in a niche above the tomb's entrance forty or fifty years after its emplacement, when Akhenaten's adherents were active.[25]

Even the internal chronology of Akhenaten's iconoclastic program itself needs clarification because there is evidence to suggest that not all items were "blacklisted" simultaneously.[26] Perhaps at the time the agents damaged the statue of Amenhotep III from Gebel Barkal (discussed above; see fig. 28.2), the order had not yet been given to deface the word 𓊹𓊹𓊹 "gods." If Akhenaten had added *nṯrw* to his list sometime after *ʾImn*, that could explain the pattern found on many monuments where 𓊹𓊹𓊹 *nṯrw* survives in immediate proximity to an erased 𓇋𓏠𓈖 *ʾImn*. Similarly, there is inconsistency in the erasure of the nomen of Amenhotep III; this might be mapped out better chronologically. While *ʾImn-ḥtp* is defaced on the Gebel Barkal statue mentioned above and at Thebes (for example, in portions of the throne scene in the tomb of Amenemhat Surer [TT 48]; Säve-Söderbergh 1957, pl. 30), it remains untouched in the tomb of Kheruef (TT 192: *Kheruef*, pls. 8, 9, 24, 26).

I conclude by citing one final example that indicates the difficult nature of the subject in question in all of its religious, chronological, economical, and practical aspects. Figure 28.8 shows an offering scene from the

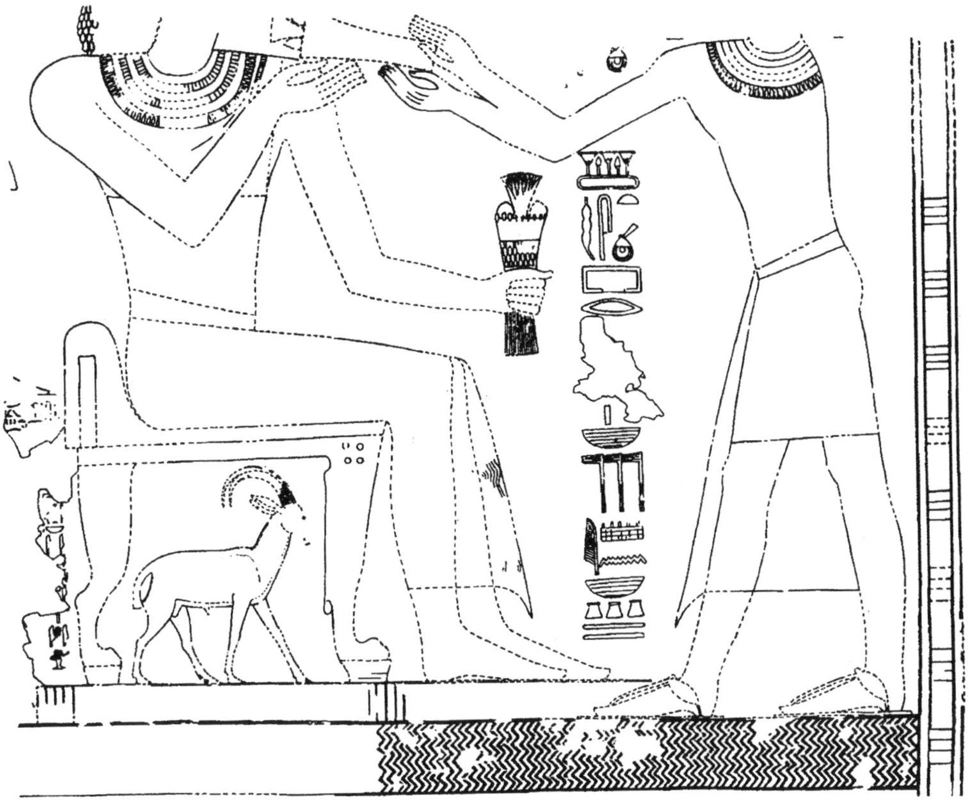

Figure 28.8. Northeast Wall Detail from Theban Tomb 73 (after Säve-Söderbergh 1957, pl. 8)

24. In the tomb of Ramose (TT 55), Amun's name, erased otherwise so many times, survives as the last word in the text *sšp ꜣw m ḫrt-hrw prrt m-bꜣḥ ʾImn* (Norman Davies 1941, pl. 11). In the same tomb, the agents also missed the god's name in a small inscription (ibid., pl. 15): *ḏd.f wꜥb n kꜣ n ʾImn nswt tꜣwy m-ḏrt ṯꜣty Rꜥ-ms mꜣꜥ-ḫrw*. Additionally, a single inscription (ibid., pl. 40) shows *nṯrw* in the long form both erased (line 9) and intact (line 11), the erasure of *ʾImn* (line 12), and the survival of *psḏt* (line 12). In the tomb of Kheruef (TT 192; *Kheruef*, pl. 78), the wooden door into the first columned hall opened to the north, hiding a text bearing the long form of *nṯrw*, which thus escaped erasure by the Atenists.

25. The statue was discovered by Davies in the debris of the burial shaft; Norman Davies 1917, pp. 36–39, fig. 6, pl. 28; Shedid and Seidel 1991, pp. 18–19, figs. 7–8. It was subsequently lost at sea in 1915.

26. *Kheruef*, p. 14, citing Aldred's claim that the erasures occurred in the last third of Akhenaten's reign, primarily since Queen Tiye was still alive: Aldred 1975a, p. 62; Aldred 1975b, text accompanying pls. 103–05.

northeast wall of the anonymous tomb TT 73 (perhaps Amenhotep?). The text reads *šꜣw nḏm sty pr [m-bꜣḥ] nb nṯrw ʾImn nb nswt tꜣwy* "flowers, sweet of scent which came forth [from the presence] of the lord of the gods, Amun, lord of the thrones of the Two Lands." Regarding the erasure of *m-bꜣḥ*, the editor of the tomb publication suggested it was due to the agents' expectation of the word Amun preceding the epithet *nb nṯrw*.[27] But this interpretation presents an interesting image of the Amarna period agents carefully reading the text and, based on their knowledge of parallel inscriptions, erasing the phrase *m-bꜣḥ,* ignoring the rest of the sentence, and moving on. There are several problems with this interpretation. First of all, any Amarna adherent capable of reading the text, even to the point of calling parallel inscriptions to mind, would hardly have confused the writing of *m-bꜣḥ* with *ʾImn*. Secondly, such a literate individual would probably not have failed to notice the two very prominent candidates for erasure directly following: (Amun's name) and (the long form of the plural for *nṯrw*). We are forced to wonder if Atentist agents were ever in the tomb in the first place; unfortunately, there is only a single half-decorated chamber to be studied. Amun's name survives in three fairly large-scale inscriptions (Säve-Söderbergh 1957, pls. 1, 5, 8), and also in a smaller one (Säve-Söderbergh 1957, pl. 1). There is thus reason to argue that the tomb escaped Amarna period erasures altogether, perhaps by virtue of its damaged nature or incomplete decoration. Returning then to our fig. 28.8 and the erasure of *m-bꜣḥ,* one wonders if this example might not be better explained by a much later Coptic desire to censor the scene and eliminate the phallus hieroglyph (or perhaps the full-faced owl, that is, the evil eye?) from the wall.[28] A Coptic erasure would represent a very different aspect of the literacy issue, and an unpharaonic approach to defacement by a group concerned not with Akhenaten's long-gone monotheistic agenda, but with an entirely new one of their own.

References

Aldred, C.

1975a "Egypt: The Amarna Period and End of the Eighteenth Dynasty." In *The Cambridge Ancient History* 2/2, pp. 49–97. Third edition. Cambridge: Cambridge University Press.

1975b *Akhenaten, Pharaoh of Egypt: A New Study.* London: Thames and Hudson.

1988 *Akhenaten, King of Egypt.* London: Thames and Hudson.

Assmann, J.

1995 *Egyptian Solar Religion in the New Kingdom: Re, Amun and the Crisis of Polytheism.* Translated by A. Alcock. London: Kegan Paul.

1996 "Preservation and Presentation of Self in Ancient Egyptian Portraiture." In *Studies in Honor of William Kelly Simpson,* edited by P. D. Manuelian, pp. 55–81. Boston: Museum of Fine Arts.

Baines, J.

1983 "Literacy and Ancient Egyptian Society." *Man*, n.s., 18: 584–86.

Baines, J., and C. Eyre

1983 "Four Notes on Literacy." *Göttinger Miszellen* 61: 65–96.

Behnk, F.

1930 *Grammatik der Texte aus El Amarna.* Paris: Geuthner.

Beinlich-Seeber, C., and A. G. Shedid

1987 *Das Grab des Userhat (TT 56).* Archäologische Veröffentlichungen 50. Mainz am Rhein: Philipp von Zabern.

Brunner, H.

1957 *Altägyptische Erziehung.* Wiesbaden: Otto Harrassowitz.

Bryan, B. M.

1995 "The Disjunction of Text and Image in Egyptian Art." In *Abstracts of Papers* (Seventh International Congress of Egyptologists, Cambridge, 3–9 September 1995), edited by C. Eyre, pp. 28–29. Oxford: Oxbow Books.

1996 "The Disjunction of Text and Image in Egyptian Art." In *Studies in Honor of William Kelly Simpson,* Volume 1, edited by P. D. Manuelian, pp. 161–68. Boston: Museum of Fine Arts.

Caminos, R. A., and T. G. H. James

1963 *Gebel es-Silsilah* 1: *The Shrines.* London: Egypt Exploration Society.

27. "This word has been erased, because the agent of the Atenists expected 'Amun' before 'Lord of the Gods,' and for once missed the actual occurrence of the name. The reading *prt* of the parallel text in the tomb of Rekhmire is out of the question here" (Säve-Söderbergh 1957, p. 9, n. 5). In the case of tomb of Rekhmire, the author is probably referring to the text cited above in our fig. 28.5; see Norman Davies 1943, pl. 70.

28. See Fischer 1974, p. 119, citing Petrie 1896, pls. 6 (6), 9, 22.

Davies, Nina de G.

1963 *Private Tombs at Thebes* 4. Oxford: Griffith Institute.

Davies, Norman de G.

1913 *Five Theban Tombs*. London: Egypt Exploration Society.

1917 *The Tomb of Nakht at Thebes*. New York: Metropolitan Museum of Art.

1923a "Akhenaten at Thebes." *Journal of Egyptian Archaeology* 9: 132–52.

1923b *The Tomb of Puyemrê at Thebes*. 2 volumes. New York: Metropolitan Museum of Art.

1925 *The Tomb of Two Sculptors at Thebes*. New York: Metropolitan Museum of Art.

1932 Tēuti: Owner of Tomb 110 at Thebes." In *Studies Presented to F. Ll. Griffith*, edited by S. R. K. Glanville, pp. 279–90. London: Egypt Exploration Society.

1941 *The Tomb of the Vizier Ramose*. Mond Excavations at Thebes 1. London: Egypt Exploration Society.

1943 *The Tomb of Rekh-mi-reᶜ at Thebes*. Publications of Metropolitan Museum of Art 11. New York: Plantin Press.

Davies, Norman de G., and A. H. Gardiner, eds.

1915 *The Tomb of Amenemhet (no. 82)*. Theban Tombs Series 1. London: Egypt Exploration Fund.

Dorman, P. F.

1991 *The Tombs of Senenmut: The Architecture and Decoration of Tombs 71 and 353*. Publications of Metropolitan Museum of Art Egyptian Expedition 24. New York: Metropolitan Museum of Art.

Dunham, D.

1970 *The Barkal Temples*. Boston: Museum of Fine Arts.

Dziobek, E.

1994 *Die Gräber des Vezirs User-Amun: Theben Nr. 61 und 131*. Archäologische Veröffentlichungen 84. Mainz am Rhein: Philipp von Zabern.

Faulkner, R. O.

1953 "Egyptian Military Organization." *Journal of Egyptian Archaeology* 39: 43.

1962 *A Concise Dictionary of Middle Egyptian*. Oxford: Griffith Institute.

Fischer, H. G.

1977 "The Mark of the Second Hand on Egyptian Antiquities." In *Ancient Egypt in the Metropolitan Museum Journal*, pp. 113–42 (= *Metropolitan Museum Journal* 9, pp. 5–34). New York: Metropolitan Museum of Art.

Griffith, F. Ll.

1926 "Stela in Honour of Amenophis III and Taya, from Tell el-ᶜAmarnah." *Journal of Egyptian Archaeology* 12: 1–2.

Hari, R.

1984 "La religion amarnienne et la tradition polythéiste." In *Studien zu Sprache und Religion Ägyptens zu Ehren von Wolfhart Westendorf* 2: *Religion*, edited by F. Junge, pp. 1039–55. Göttingen: Hubert.

Hornung, E.

1971 *Conceptions of God in Ancient Egypt: The One and the Many*. Translated by J. Baines. Ithaca: Cornell University Press.

1995 *Echnaton: Die Religion des Lichtes*. Zurich: Artemis and Winkler.

Janssen, R. M., and J. J. Janssen

1990 *Growing Up in Ancient Egypt*. London: Rubicon Press.

Kozloff, A. P., and B. M. Bryan

1992 *Egypt's Dazzling Sun: Amenhotep III and His World*. Cleveland: Cleveland Museum of Art.

Lesko, L. H.

1990 "Some Comments on Ancient Egyptian Literacy and Literati." In *Studies in Egyptology Presented to Miriam Lichtheim*, Volume 2, edited by S. I. Groll, pp. 656–67. Jerusalem: Magnes Press.

Manuelian, P. D.

1994 *Living in the Past: Studies in Archaism of the Egyptian Twenty-sixth Dynasty*. London: Kegan Paul.

Martin, G. T.

1991 *A Bibliography of the Amarna Period and Its Aftermath*. London: Kegan Paul.

Müller, M.

1988 *Die Kunst Amenophis' III. und Echnatons*. Basel: Verlag für Ägyptologie.

Murnane, W. M.

1995 *Texts from the Amarna Period in Egypt*. Writings from the Ancient World 5. Atlanta: Scholars Press.

Naville, E.

1901 *The Temple of Deir el Bahari* 4. London: Egypt Exploration Fund.

Newberry, P. E.

1947 "The Cult of the ┐-Pole." *Journal of Egyptian Archaeology* 33: 90–91.

Otto, E.

1956 "Bildung und Ausbildung im alten Ägypten." *Zeitschrift für ägyptische Sprache und Altertumskunde* 81: 41–48.

Petrie, W. M. F.

1896 *Koptos*. London: B. Quaritch.

Redford, D. B.

1984 *Akhenaten: The Heretic King*. Princeton: Princeton University Press.

Saad, R.

1972 Les martelages de la xviii.e dynastie dans le temple d'Amon-Ré à Karnak. Ph.D. dissertation, Lyon.

Säve-Söderbergh, T.

1957 *Four Eighteenth Dynasty Tombs*. Private Tombs at Thebes 1. Oxford: Griffith Institute.

Schulman, A. R.

1964 "Some Observations on the Military Background of the Amarna Period." *Journal of the American Research Center in Egypt* 3: 51–69.

Shedid, A. G., and M. Seidel

1991 *Das Grab des Nakht: Kunst und Geschichte eines Beamtengrabes der 18. Dynastie in Theben-West.* Mainz am Rhein: Philipp von Zabern.

Silverman, D. P.

1991 "Texts from the Amarna Period and Their Position in the Development of Ancient Egyptian." *Lingua Aegyptia* 1: 301–14.

1999 "The Spoken and Written Word." In *Pharaohs of the Sun: Akhenaten, Nefertiti, Tutankhamen*, edited by R. E. Freed, Y. J. Markowitz, and S. H. d'Auria, pp. 151–55. Boston: Museum of Fine Arts.

Simpson, W. K.

1982 "Egyptian Sculpture and Two-Dimensional Representation as Propaganda." *Journal of Egyptian Archaeology* 68: 266–72.

1996 "*Belles Lettres* and Propaganda." In *Ancient Egyptian Literature: History and Forms*, edited by A. Loprieno, pp. 435–43. Probleme der Ägyptologie 10. Leiden: E. J. Brill.

te Velde, H.

1989 "Mut, the Eye of Re." In *Akten des vierten Internationalen Ägyptologen Kongresses München 1985*, edited by S. Schoske, pp. 395–403. Hamburg: Helmut Buske Verlag.

Yoyotte, J.

1951 "Le martelage des noms royaux éthiopiens par Psammétique II." *Revue d'égyptologie* 8: 215–39.

29

VINEGAR AT DEIR EL-MEDINA

N. B. MILLET

Royal Ontario Museum, Toronto

The following is offered as a small tribute to an old friend and colleague, who has long interested himself in the affairs of the ancient Thebans of the west bank.

An area of ancient Egyptian life about which we are poorly informed is that of food preparation; no cookbooks have survived (if there ever were any) to cast light upon the arts of the kitchen as practiced in pharaonic times, and the ambitious but somewhat disappointing two-volume work by Darby, Ghalioungui, and Grivetti (1977) has been unable to add much to our knowledge in this area.

One suggestive word, however, for "vinegar" (*ḥmḏ*) was known to us earlier only as a *hapax legomenon* (Gardiner 1947, *256); it occurs several times in an ostracon from Deir el-Medina in the collection of the Royal Ontario Museum, in a context that may shed some light upon one aspect of Egyptian dietary habits in the New Kingdom.

ROYAL ONTARIO MUSEUM OSTRACON 906.20.6

White limestone 20 × 15 cm

Recto (fig. 29.1)

1. Regnal year 3, third month of the Inundation season, day 8:[1]
2. Basa: vinegar, *mnt*-jars 10, as payment for the door;
3. the village magician, Amunmose: vinegar, *mnt*-jars 10;
4. a door 1; a box 1; Ḳenymin: vinegar, *mnt*-jars 11(?);
5. Kaḥa: vinegar, *mnt*-jars 15; a mat ...;
6. the *wʿrtw*-official Ramose: vinegar ...;
7. (traces only)

Verso (fig. 29.2)

The verso is in a different and obviously later hand (during the time of Ramesses IV?)

1. ...] 14;
2. ...] *šꜣšꜣ*,[2] sack 1;
3. ...]-amun: hay,[3] donkey-load 1;
4. ...]: hay, donkey-loads 2;
6. ...], *nšw*-vessels 3?

Although the exact size of the *mnt*-measure is still in doubt,[4] quite large quantities of vinegar are clearly being distributed to certain members of the Deir el-Medina community at the same time. Now, although vinegar can be, and has been, used for the softening of limestone prior to digging it out,[5] the fact that it is individuals

1. The second part of the day numeral is written on the edge of the flake.
2. For *šꜣšꜣ*-fruit, see Grapow 1959, p. 479; Germer 1979, p. 321.
3. Helck (1964, p. 808), in his masterly work, believes that *dḥꜣ* is straw, but as he himself points out, it is fed to horses so that hay (meaning dried grasses) as opposed to the stalks of cereals is probably to be preferred.
4. See Janssen 1975, p. 340, for a discussion of this question.
5. Most notably perhaps in the mining that preceded the battle for Vimy Ridge; for which, see Berton 1986.

Gold of Praise: Studies on Ancient Egypt in Honor of Edward F. Wente
Edited by Emily Teeter and John A. Larson
Studies in Ancient Oriental Civilization 58
Chicago: Oriental Institute, 1999

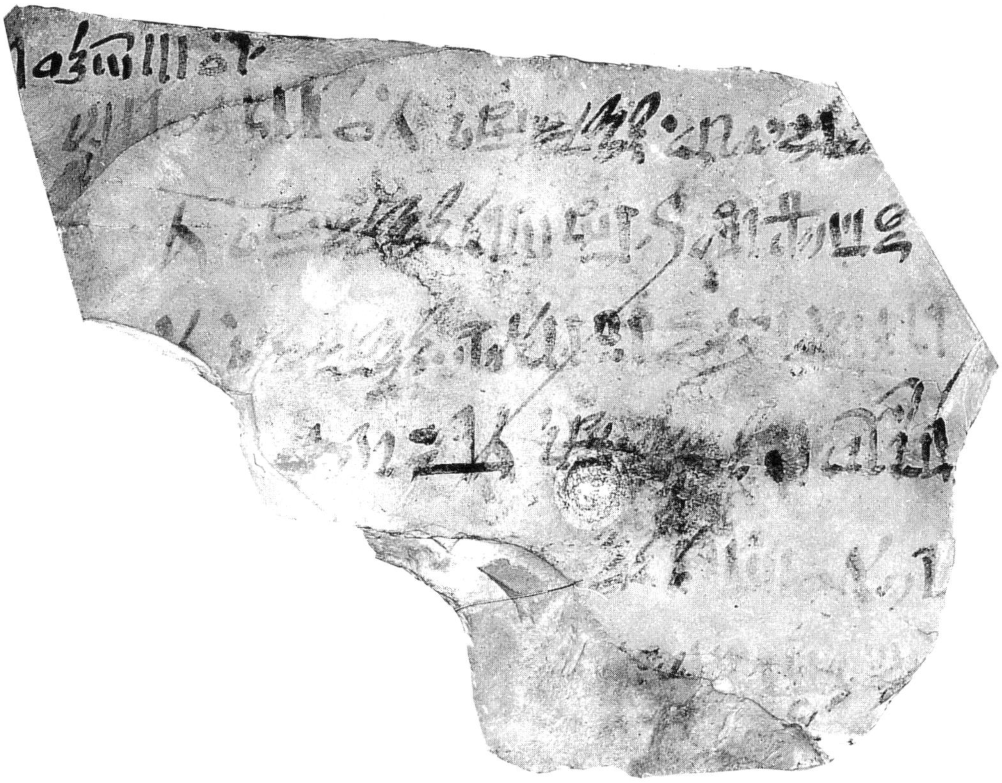

a

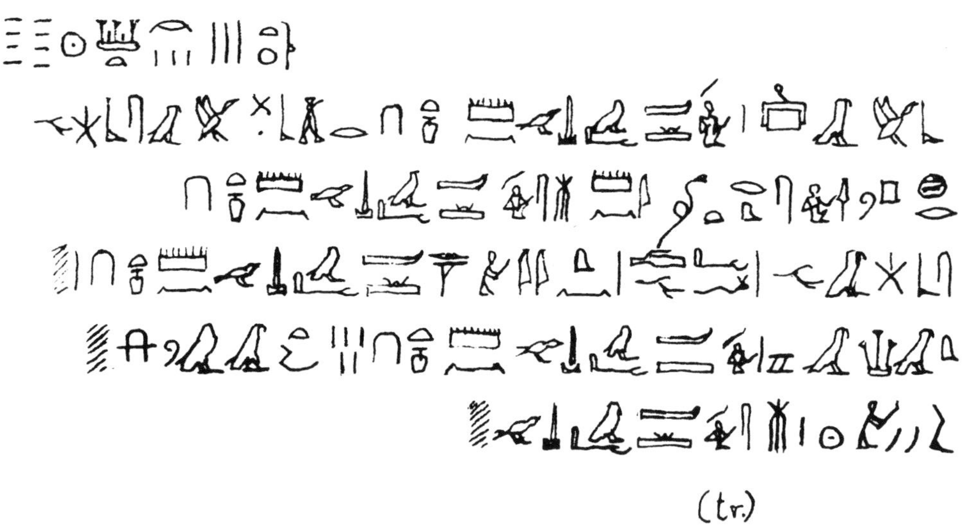

b

Figure 29.1. Hieratic Ostracon 906.20.6 Recto: (*a*) Photograph and (*b*) Transcription. Courtesy of the Royal Ontario Museum

rather than gangs as a whole who are here the recipients militates against our concluding that the vinegar was to be employed in the excavation of the royal tomb and suggests rather some domestic purpose. Since the date — in the third regnal year, presumably (from the known individuals named) of Ramesses II — works out to about the middle of September, there seems to be little doubt that the vinegar was to be used in a seasonal pickling operation undertaken by some of the households of Deir el-Medina, presumably of vegetables at the end of the summer growing season. At the end of a hot Egyptian summer there would certainly have been a great deal of soured wine available for such an operation. There is unfortunately no indication in the text as to who was making the disbursements.

a

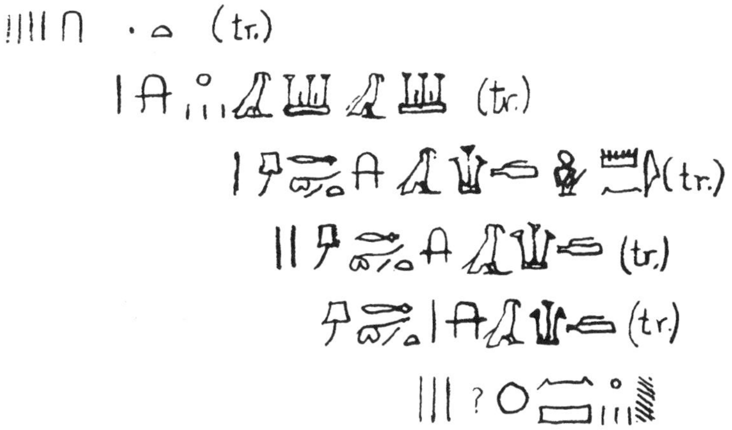

b

Figure 29.2. Hieratic Ostracon 906.20.6 Verso: (*a*) Photograph and (*b*) Transcription. Courtesy of the Royal Ontario Museum

As pointed out to me by my colleague Dr. James Hoch of Toronto, it is possible that the Deir el-Medina people were in fact drinking the vinegar as an inexpensive substitute for wine, as did the Roman legionaries; but if this were in fact their custom, I think that the word, apparently a *hapax legomenon* until now, would have appeared more often than it does in the voluminous records that have come down to us from that community. In support, however, of his suggestion is the fact that the only other occurrence of the word (in the Onomasticon of Amenemope) is at the end of a list of various kinds of wine. But this may of course simply be due to its origin as soured wine.

References

Berton, P.
1986 *Vimy*. Toronto: McLelland and Stewart.

Darby, W. J.; P. Ghalioungui; and L. Grivetti
1977 *Food: The Gift of Osiris*. 2 volumes. London: Academic Press.

Gardiner, A. H.
1947 *Ancient Egyptian Onomastica*. London: Oxford University Press.

Germer, R.
1979 *Untersuchungen über Arzneimittelpflanzen im alten Ägypten*. Hamburg: Universität Hamburg.

Grapow, E.
1959 *Wörterbuch der altägyptischen Drogennamen*. Berlin: Akademie-Verlag.

Helck, W.
1964 *Materialien zur Wirtschaftsgeschichte des Neuen Reiches, 5: Einzelbetrachtung von Lebensmitteln und Materialien*. Akademie der Wissenschaften und der Literatur, Mainz, Abhandlungen der geistes- und sozialwissenschaftlichen Klasse, Jahrgang 1964, 4. Wiesbaden: Franz Steiner Verlag.

Janssen, J. J.
1975 *Commodity Prices from the Ramessid Period*. Leiden: E. J. Brill.

30

OBSERVATIONS ON PRE-AMARNA THEOLOGY DURING THE EARLIEST REIGN OF AMENHOTEP IV

WILLIAM J. MURNANE

The University of Memphis, Tennessee

It was my good fortune to be a graduate student when Edward F. Wente returned from the Epigraphic Survey in Luxor to full-time teaching at the University of Chicago. His would be the paramount influence, not only throughout my student years, but also at every important turn in my professional development thereafter. I have much for which to thank him, beginning with the superb training he gave, with its blend of imagination and field experience, both grounded in philological rigor; the ongoing stimulus of his published research and informal advice; and — not the least in my case — the many opportunities he has made available for me to practice my craft. For all these things I am in his debt beyond any hope to repay. I hope he will accept this tribute, on a subject which interests us both, as a modest gesture of appreciation, along with my best wishes for many more productive years during his retirement.

However one may characterize the fully developed religion of Akhenaten — whether as monotheism,[1] reformed henotheism,[2] or some sort of masked atheism[3] — scholars at least have the luxury of being able to study it in detail: an extensive dossier can be compiled from royal documents and, especially, the private mortuary monuments of elite individuals at the "heretic capital" of Akhet-Aten, providing food for thought (if not comprehensive coverage) on a wide range of theological and ritual matters. Comparatively little attention, however, has been paid to the development of the heresy in its earliest years, when its founder was still known as Amenhotep IV. Detailed study has focused on iconographic details[4] and their implication for the history of the period,[5] or on the ongoing examination of monuments from the early years of Amenhotep IV's reign that have been recovered from later buildings at Karnak.[6] Valuable attention has also been paid to certain antecedents of the new cult's theology,[7] especially the attempt to rationalize Egypt's many gods into a single matrix — this being a process, already under way at least two centuries before the Amarna revolution, which would continue unimpeded after Akhenaten's initiative had failed (Assmann 1995, especially pp. 102–89). So far, however, no one has attempted to chart the evolution of "Atenist" theology in its formative period, during the few years of Amenhotep IV's reign when the new religion coexisted most conspicuously with the orthodox cults it would later seek to replace. This article, while it makes no claim to completeness, attempts to start discussion of this topic by calling attention to certain features that seem to point toward a solution.

1. See, among others, Hornung 1995, pp. 103–04; Aldred 1988, pp. 237–48; Hornung 1982, pp. 244–50. However, to the extent that the king and queen are viewed as forming a divine triad with the Aten, their father (substituting for Atum, Shu, and Tefnut: see Assmann 1984, pp. 251–52), this must be a "monotheism" of three persons, as advocates such as Aldred tacitly admit.
2. For example, N. de G. Davies 1923, pp. 149–50; Stock 1950, p. 631.
3. Thus Redford (1984, p. 176), although he speaks of Akhenaten's religion as "a monotheism that would brook no divine manifestations," also speaks of the Aten as the "hypostasis of divine kingship, a pale reflection of his (= Akhenaten's) own, projected heavenwards" (p. 178) and concludes that "what Akhenaten championed was in the truest sense of the word, atheism" (p. 234). Halfway between this position and monotheism is Johnson (1990, pp. 36–46), who sees the "living Aten" as a divine, solarized Amenhotep III associated with his children Shu/Akhenaten and Tefnut/Nefertiti. Entirely different is the view of Allen (1989, pp. 89–101), for whom the Aten is but a natural principle and Atenism became a religion only in the subjects' worship of the king.
4. For example, Bianchi 1990, pp. 35–40 with fig. 1; compare Cruz-Uribe 1992, pp. 29–32.
5. See, for example, Aldred 1959, pp. 19–33.
6. Aldred 1988, pp. 52–68; Redford 1984, pp. 57–136; Chappaz 1983, pp. 13–44.
7. See Doresse 1941/42, pp. 181–99; Anthes 1963, pp. 1–10; Fecht 1967, pp. 25–50; Tawfik 1973, pp. 77–82.

Gold of Praise: Studies on Ancient Egypt in Honor of Edward F. Wente
Edited by Emily Teeter and John A. Larson
Studies in Ancient Oriental Civilization 58
Chicago: Oriental Institute, 1999

EARLIEST "HORIZON OF ATEN" AT THEBES

In the foundation decree for his god's new city (the "Earlier Proclamation") Akhenaten repeatedly emphasizes that this foundation (Akhet-Aten, the "Horizon of Aten") shall be located at el-Amarna and nowhere else:

> I *have made* Akhet-Aten for the Aten, my father, in this place. I shall not make Akhet-Aten for him south of it, north of it, west of it, (or) east of it. I shall not go past the southern stela of Akhet-Aten toward the south, nor shall I go past the northern stela of Akhet-Aten downstream, in order to make Akhet-Aten for him there.[8] Nor shall I make <it> for him on the western side of Akhet-Aten; but I *have made* Akhet-Aten for the Aten, my father, on the orient (side) of Akhet-Aten — the place which he himself made to be enclosed for him by the mountain, on which he may achieve happiness and on which I shall offer to him. This is it! (Murnane and Van Siclen 1993, pp. 23–24 [K 11–12]; cf. Murnane 1995, pp. 76–77 [no. 37])

The apparent sense of this passage receives further emphasis, it appears, from the suffix conjugations employed in its opening and closing statements (italicized in the translation above): the text is preserved in two versions (on stelae K and X), and in both of these the verb *ỉrỉ* "to do, make" is written with a terminal *r* as a phonetic complement.[9] In Amarna period texts, which are heavily contaminated with Late Egyptianisms, such spellings admittedly do not define different verb forms as consistently as they did earlier in classic Middle Egyptian compositions. Even so, the spelling used in these highlighted passages, *ỉr*(*r*), can be read as a geminating second-tense form (*ỉrr*), a construction that might be expected in sentences which already have semantically emphasized adverbial phrases.[10] It thus seems permissible not only to understand these statements as "emphatic" — as stressing through the verb *where* the action will take place — but also to infer the same sense for the string of similarly constructed sentences, all beginning with *ỉr*(*r*)*.ỉ*, which follow somewhat later and declare the king's intention of constructing a number of buildings specifically "at Akhet-Aten in this place" (Murnane and Van Siclen 1993, pp. 24–25 [K 14–16]; cf. Murnane 1995, p. 77).

These repeated asseverations, stressing the identity of "Akhet-Aten" uniquely with "this place," are especially striking because, already by the beginning of Amenhotep IV's fifth regnal year, the term "Horizon of Aten" was a known quantity, with roots that lay far from el-Amarna. From Thebes, "The City" par excellence of the Aten's chief rival Amun-Ra King of the Gods, come a small number of objects that refer to a "Horizon of Aten" (consistently written *ȝḫt n ʾItn*, thus expressing with an indirect genitive[11] the connection which will regularly be conveyed at Amarna by a simple direct genitive, *ȝḫt-ỉtn*). Few though these examples are, they are sufficiently informative to be reviewed here in some detail.

"Akhet-en-Aten" is mentioned most prominently in texts carved on a number of granite offering stands[12] from Karnak.[13] These inscriptions, which specify the daily offerings to be presented to the Aten,[14] are arranged in two complementary variants that deserve to be quoted in extenso:

8. This does not mean, as has often been said, that the king would never leave Akhet-Aten, but only that he would not shift the boundaries to any significant degree; see Murnane and Van Siclen 1993, pp. 169–71.
9. Compare the forms in "I shall not make" (with the fully written prospective form *ỉry.ỉ*) or the relative "which he made" (especially in X, the earlier of the two texts, where it is written correctly as a perfective form *ỉr.f*). Further on, compare the clearly prospective sentences, each beginning "Let there be made" (and spelled *ỉr.tw* with no phonetic complement); see Murnane and Van Siclen 1993, p. 25, at K 16–17.
10. See Hartman 1967, p. 10, table 1 on pp. 13–16; Kroeber 1970, p. 98 (§32.31); Černý and Groll 1984, pp. lviii–lx, on Middle Egyptian equivalents of Late Egyptian emphatic forms, including the geminated emphatic *mrr.f* form and also the non-geminated emphatic *mrỉ.f* (which, though anomalous, must be a second tense).
11. It seems likely that the later "Akhet-Aten" is simply a contraction of the original term which had employed the indirect genitive *n* consistently; see Lefebvre 1955, §§144–47, who points to the wide semantic range of the indirect genitive and to its increasing currency in later stages of the language.
12. See Habachi 1965, pp. 73–79. Of the five pieces published there, the pertinent inscriptions are found on "altars" A, B, and E; the other two stands, C and D, are inscribed only with stereotyped divine and royal names.
13. As Habachi (1965, pp. 73–74) notes, "altars" A through C were found reused in the mudbrick ramp built against the northeast face of the first pylon; altar D was found in a magazine inside Karnak temple, but its exact provenience is unknown. The findspot of altar E was the modern settlement called Malkata that lies northwest of Karnak temple, not the Malkat el-Bairat (most commonly called "Malkata") on the west bank of Thebes; see Legrain 1901, p. 62; Hayes 1951, pp. 180–81, on the origins of the confusion between the two sites.
14. See, for convenience, the translation in Murnane 1995, pp. 99–100, no. 53.1.

Variant 1

A: HOR-ATEN[15] residing in "Rejoicing in Horizon of Aten" (*ꜣḫt n ꜥItn*) in Upper Egyptian Heliopolis (*ꜥIwnw Šmꜥw*), the great and primeval (place) of the Disk (*itn*).

B: Hor-Aten[16] residing in "Rejoicing in Horizon [of Aten"[17] in Upper Egyptian Heliopolis] ...

E: ... in "Horizon of Aten" in Upper Egyptian Heliopolis: [Dual King NEFERKHEPRURE-WAENRE, etc.

Variant 2

A: HOR-ATEN residing in "Rejoicing in Horizon of Ra" (*ꜣḫt n Rꜥ*) in his house in Upper Egyptian Heliopolis, the great and primeval (place) of Ra: what is offered to him at his rising in the eastern horizon of [heaven].

B: Hor-Aten, residing in "Rejoicing in Horizon of Ra": what is offered to him ...

E: [... residing in "Rejoicing in Horizon] of Ra" in his house in Upper Egyptian Heliopolis: what is offered to him in ...

At least one of these internal variations may reflect no more than an expedient to adapt the different elements in each variant to the same space. Since the expression "in his house" (Variant 2) is otiose — because who would interpret *Ḥꜥy m ꜣḫt n Rꜥ* as anything other than the foundation's name? — it seems likely that this phrase was inserted to even out the difference in space between *ꜣḫt n Rꜥ* and the longer *ꜣḫt n ꜥItn*. On the other hand, the juxtaposition of "Horizon of Ra" with "Horizon of Aten" on these pieces is too regular to be considered meaningless; some difference must have been defined thereby. In this connection, it is worth noting that the form "Horizon of Aten" (Variant 1) occupies what Habachi — in my opinion correctly — takes to be front and back sides of these pieces, where the king's name is most conspicuously juxtaposed with that of his god.[18] Variant 2, however, is scarcely less prominent for being mentioned only on the sides because it is to "Ra" at "Horizon of Ra" that offerings are made. The pattern, once again, is too regular to be fortuitous. By coordinating "Ra" (apparently subordinate on the sides) with the receipt of offerings, the primary purpose of these stands, a balance appears to be struck here between the two forms of the sun god. That Ra can be a virtual synonym for the Aten in texts throughout this reign should not, in itself, surprise students of the period;[19] but it would have seemed odd to contemporary worshippers. Until then, in the solar theology that had been evolving since the early Eighteenth Dynasty, a distinction had been drawn between the sun god himself and the "globe" which was merely his physical manifestation in the sky.[20] The "phrasing" found on these offering stands from Karnak — in which Ra, not Aten, is the receiver of offerings — suggests that this distinction was still sensed, at least, early in Amenhotep IV's reign when most of these offering stands were inscribed.[21] On the other hand, it seems clear that "Aten" was already the god's primary identity on these pieces. We return to the process by which the solar orb became more closely identified with the sun god himself in the discussion of Ra, Amun, and the Aten under Amenhotep IV, below.

What sort of foundation was "Rejoicing in Horizon of Ra/Aten"? It is barely mentioned in recent studies devoted to Amenhotep IV's "rediscovered" temples at Karnak,[22] even though its name, later to be adapted for the

15. Thus abbreviating the early didactic name of the Aten; capitalization here indicates that this name is written, as is normal, in cartouches.

16. Here, too, the early didactic name is used, but it is not enclosed in cartouches (something which is also true for "altars" C and D); see the text copies in Habachi 1965, pp. 73–79.

17. Restored by analogy with "altar" A, on which "Horizon of Aten" occurs on the sides adjoining "Horizon of Ra" on the front; see Habachi 1965, pp. 75–76, figs. 4–5.

18. Thus on "altars" A and B (as shown in the drawings referred to in the preceding note) and (by analogy) also on E.

19. This point has been made at length by, among others, Tawfik (1976a, pp. 217–26), although without citing the juxtaposition of "Aten" and "Ra" on these altars, even though he had noted them without further comment in another article published in the same year; see Tawfik 1976b, p. 60, n. 38.

20. For Aten, see *LÄ* 1 "Aton," col. 528, with references in n. 34. For solar religion, see Assmann 1995, p. 69; Redford 1980, pp. 21–34; Redford 1976, pp. 46–71.

21. Altars B, C, and D all preserve at least part of the Aten's didactic name written without cartouches, as was normal in the earliest part of Amenhotep IV's reign. The top of altar E, where the god's name would have been inscribed, is missing; so it is only on altar A that the didactic name can be shown to be enclosed within the two cartouches which became the norm in the talatat buildings at Karnak. Habachi (1965, pp. 74, 77) does not indicate that the king's nomen, "Akhenaten," was recarved from an erased "Amenhotep" here, so the piece should be located and examined afresh. Assuming that the later nomen *is* original here, we may hazard that this piece — which is demonstrably later than the others of its type — was prepared (perhaps as a replacement for a damaged prototype?) after the change in the king's nomen in year 5, but that its texts were laid out in the same form as the earlier "altars" among which it was to stand.

22. For example, it is not included among the buildings named in the talatat from Karnak (see Tawfik 1976b, pp. 61–63), and it is also ignored in Gohary 1992, pp. 26–39, as well as in the catalog that forms the bulk of this book, wherein she discusses Amenhotep IV's jubilee reliefs from Thebes.

more famous "House of Rejoicing" at el-Amarna, suggests a substantial building.[23] This neglect, unfortunately, owes more to the scandalously slow publication of materials excavated at Karnak than to any poverty in the materials themselves. A number of blocks from this very building were found re-used in the second and ninth pylons,[24] while still others, formally of unknown provenience, have made their way to museums in England and France (PM 2, p. 296). Among the latter is the famed "Gayer-Anderson relief" that shows Amenhotep IV (his name later changed to "Akhenaten") performing jubilee rites.[25] The block itself is made of limestone, which is the material of the blocks from this very building found in the second pylon at Karnak,[26] and its provenience from Upper Egypt would seem to be clinched by the reference to the Aten's being "in Upper Egyptian Heliopolis" below the god's cartouches.[27] These blocks, along with the offering stands discussed above, suffice to show that "Rejoicing in Akhet-en-Aten in Upper Egyptian Heliopolis" was an independent temple, substantially built of limestone (unlike the sandstone buildings that were the settings for most of the cultic activities on behalf of the Aten at Thebes). Its location at Karnak remains uncertain, and a more comprehensive understanding of the building's function will have to wait on a full publication of its surviving fragments.

What, then, of "Akhet-en-Aten" itself? It is described as being in "Upper Egyptian Heliopolis" (*m ʾIwnw Šmʿw*), a term that refers broadly to the area of Thebes;[28] it is further qualified as "the great and primeval (place) of Ra/Aten."[29] All this may suggest that we are dealing here not with another building, but with a larger territory that was the setting for Atenist Theban temples like "Rejoicing in Horizon of Aten." A few years later, in the foundation decree for his new city at el-Amarna, the king would describe this site as "Akhet-Aten, his place of the primeval occurrence" (*st.f nt sp tpy*).[30] Both name and concept are strikingly close to their antecedents at Thebes, and the supposition which follows — namely, that the Theban "Horizon of Ra/Aten" covered a similarly extensive area — seems to be borne out by our only other unambiguous reference to *ꜣḫt n ʾItn* in the Theban area.

Among several residents of the necropolis workmen's village at Deir el-Medina who can be dated to Amenhotep IV's reign or slightly later is a man named Nakhy, who was a "servant in the Place of Truth on the west of Akhet-en-Aten."[31] Since the only possible venue for this man's activity is the west bank of Thebes, it seems permissible to infer that "the west of Akhet-en-Aten" was located there. Now that it is clear that the Theban "Horizon of Aten" encompassed both sides of the river,[32] it seems logical to correlate it with the only other foundation at Thebes which did the same — namely, the "estate of Amun" (*pr-ʾImn*), which is so often described as the setting for the royal mortuary temples "on the west of Thebes" during the New Kingdom.[33] If so (and the data appears to admit no other interpretation),[34] what was the relationship between "the Horizon of Ra/Aten in Upper Egyptian Heliopolis" and the "House of Aten in Upper Egyptian Heliopolis" (*pr-ʾItn m ʾIwnw Šmʿw*)?[35] Since the Aten's "house" was his temple, one might infer from these terms a distinction between the

23. As noted by Tawfik 1976b, p. 60.

24. References in PM 2, 39, 182.

25. Most fully published by Aldred 1973, p. 97, no. 11; text in Sandman 1938, p. 152 (clx).

26. As are other blocks from this temple; see PM 2, 39; compare Doresse 1981, pp. 67–68, n. 14; Doresse 1955, pp. 121–22.

27. See the translation in Murnane 1995, p. 40, no. 11. Since such locative qualifiers regularly refer to the Aten's monuments in the neighborhood (cf. the numerous texts at Thebes and el-Amarna) the provenience from the Memphite area suggested by Aldred (reference in n. 31) seems untenable; the fact that Major Gayer-Anderson bought most of his collection from dealers in Cairo is hardly a serious argument against a provenience for this block in Upper Egypt.

28. See *LÄ* 1 "Armant," cols 435, 440, n. 4 (references), demonstrating that this term was associated with Armant only secondarily (contra Otto 1952, p. 86).

29. Since *ʿꜣt tpt* is feminine, it can refer to no antecedent in this text other than *ꜣḫt n ʾItn*.

30. Murnane and Van Siclen 1993, pp. 19 (K, col. x), 36. As the passage quoted above (K, cols. x–xi) makes clear, Akhet-Aten at this time was coterminous with the "bay" on the east side of the river at el-Amarna. The expansion of the city limits to include the adjacent lands on the west bank was only formalized in the following year, in the "Later Proclamation" (see Murnane and Van Siclen 1993, pp. 156–57).

31. Valbelle 1985, p. 12; Brugsch 1857, p. 274, pl. 50, no. 1345; also mentioned in Černý 1973, p. 51; translated in Murnane 1995, pp. 66–67, no. 34-A.

32. Another possible reference to it (though as "Akhet-Aten") is on the coffin of the lady Taʿo from Deir el-Medina; see Bruyère 1937, p. 104 with pls. x.1, xii. Compare Černý 1973, p. 51; Murnane 1995, p. 67, no. 34-C.

33. For convenience, see the list of foundation names in Otto 1952, pp. 107–18, especially nos. 1, 4, 5, 7, 8, 12, 15.

34. That *ꜣḫt n ʾItn* denoted a temple at Thebes (later writ large in the open air at el-Amarna) is maintained by Cannuyer (1985, pp. 7–9), though without considering the contrary implications of the inscription on Nakhy's chair. While references to the temple as an *ꜣḫt* are legion (see Brunner 1979, pp. 30–33), such buildings can be described by extension as a deity's "city" (see Gutbub 1973, p. 299 [b]) and the term *ꜣḫt* itself can be extended to cover towns and wider regions (*LÄ* 3 "Horizont," cols. 3–7).

35. For which, see Tawfik 1976b, p. 63.

god's cult buildings taken as a whole (his *pr*) and the wider territory (his "horizon") in which they stood.[36] By analogy with *Pr-ʾImn* (which was broadly the "estate of Amun"), however, it is also possible that *ꜣḫt-n-ʾItn* was a fancier alternative to the more prosaic *Pr-ʾItn*, and that both could refer to the whole of Aten's Theban domain. The uncertainty will be resolved only with further evidence.

The very existence of an earlier "Horizon of Aten" at Thebes would have challenged the uniqueness that the king would later claim for his new capital at el-Amarna. It is in this light, surely, that we should regard Akhenaten's repeated assertions that any other site was unthinkable — all the more so since that earlier rival, described as "the great and primeval (place) of Aten," was so closely identified with the new order's most conspicuous opponents. To identify the place from which the sun's orb rose with one spot in Egypt, to the exclusion of all others, might also have seemed odd. In religious literature the term *ꜣḫt* was primarily associated with the eastern edge of the firmament, where the sun appeared at dawn. By the time of the New Kingdom, however, Egyptians had come to distinguish between several of these *ꜣḫ.wt* at the main cardinal points, and some of the terms used for these subsidiary "horizons" could imply that each particular *ꜣḫt* was associated with a fixed rising — or setting — point of the sun. Traditionally, however, the *ꜣḫt* was not regarded as a single point on the horizon, but as a region lying on the border between the underworld and the lands in this world on which the sun shone. Such a concept would obviously be consistent with the seasonal movements of the sun at the eastern and western edges of the horizon.[37] Given this conceptual framework, one can easily see how a claim to being the sun's "horizon" might be appropriated, now by one locality, then by others. From the vantage point of each place the phenomenon seemed to be uniquely *there*, but it also occurred everywhere, just as the unique and sovereign attributes of the creator god could belong not merely to Ra or Amun but to the chief gods of other localities as well (cf. Assmann 1995, p. 103). One wonders, were other great centers such as Memphis[38] and Heliopolis (see Habachi 1971, pp. 35–45; Bakry 1972, pp. 55–67), also termed "horizons of Aten" in the first years of Amenhotep IV's reign? There is no evidence that they were, and since contemporary monuments from these northern cities survive in much fewer numbers than from Thebes, we may never know whether the Theban "Akhet-en-Aten" was defined as being "in Upper Egyptian Heliopolis" to distinguish it from other such domains elsewhere in Egypt. Similarly, it is impossible to be sure that Thebes was literally and uniquely "the great and primeval place of Ra/Aten" if other places were called "Horizon of Aten" at the same time. Thus, until evidence to the contrary comes to light, it may be best to take the evidence as it stands and assume that Amenhotep IV intended to remake Thebes in the image of his god, allowing it to keep under these new auspices the primacy of place which had hitherto come to it as the home of Amun. In any case, the special status of Thebes in the Atenist scheme of things leads to the question of how this new order still accommodated the nome's old lord, the quondam "king of the gods."

RA, AMUN, AND THE ATEN UNDER AMENHOTEP IV

Not the smallest paradox of Amenhotep IV's "pre-Amarna" period is the inconsistency of his relationship with Amun-Ra. Right at the beginning of his reign, when an expedition was sent to the quarry at Gebel es-Silsila, a commemorative stela was left there, showing the king before his divine father, the god of Thebes. Yet the text of this monument, far from glorifying Amun or vaunting the benefactions to be performed for him by his son, studiously ignores Amun and speaks instead of "a great forced-labor duty of quarrying sandstone in order to fashion the great *benben* of Horakhty in his name 'Light which is in the Orb' in Karnak."[39] This pattern of co-existence coupled with neglect would continue down to the king's departure for el-Amarna. Thus, in the fourth year of the reign, "a charge was given to the high priest of Amun May to bring *bekhen*-stone [for] the statue of the lord — may he live, prosper and be healthy!"[40] This undertaking, which obliged at least one important mem-

36. Hardly just the site of Karnak in the reign of Amenhotep IV, as suggested by Doresse 1955, p. 126.

37. See, in general, Kuentz 1920, pp. 121–90.

38. See Löhr 1975, pp. 139–87. A granary scribe named Hatiay belonged to the staff of the "House of Aten in Memphis": see A. Hassan 1976, p. 235 (4) with pl. vi.3; translation in Murnane 1995, p. 68, no. 34-D.2.

39. Legrain 1902, pp. 260–66; text in *Urk.* 4, p. 1962; translation from Murnane 1995, p. 30 (with improvements on earlier copies made available through the kindness of the late Ricardo A. Caminos, who also made it possible for me to examine Amenhotep IV's stela on site).

40. Goyon 1957, pp. 106–07 with pl. 25 (90); translation in Murnane 1995, p. 68, no. 35-A.1; compare Redford 1963, pp. 240–41.

ber of the high priest's staff to journey with the expedition into the Wadi Hammamat,[41] is interesting for several reasons: not only does it show that the Amun cult had not been suppressed by this point, but it also demonstrates that Amenhotep IV still included Amun's highest functionary in the country's religious hierarchy, to the extent of finding useful work for him to do,[42] and that this personage was in sufficiently good odor to be charged with the production of the king's own statue.[43] And yet the same king's benefactions within the temple of Amun were paltry indeed; the only addition that Amenhotep IV made to the fabric of the temple of Amun was a relief, which showed the king smiting prisoners-of-war[44] on the porch that his father had built in front of the third pylon[45] — a relief which, significantly, was never fully carved[46] even while the numerous temples to the Aten were rising nearby. Clearly, Amun played a role in the new Atenist order, but what was it and how are we to understand the Theban god's co-existence with the Aten alongside such conspicuous marks of disregard?

The beginnings of an answer may come from the west bank of Thebes — in particular the tomb of Kheruef (TT 192), the publication of which so signally involved the scholar we are honoring in this volume. On the facade and in the entrance passage of this tomb we find what are probably the earliest reliefs from the heretic's reign (*Kheruef*, p. 13). Amenhotep IV's all but invariable companion in other reliefs, Queen Nefertiti, makes no appearance here: the king officiates alone (on the south wall of the passage; *Kheruef*, pls. 12–13) or is followed by his mother, Queen Tiye (facade; *Kheruef*, pl. 9) — no doubt because the tomb owner owed his place in the royal entourage to the fact that he was the queen mother's steward.[47] Nor is Amenhotep IV's new god represented in these reliefs. The facade shows the king before Atum, Hathor, Ra-Horakhty, and Hathor (lintel), with Amun-Ra, Thoth, Anubis, Osiris, and Isis also being mentioned in the prayers carved on the doorjambs (*Kheruef*, pl. 8). Most of the other inscriptions in this part of the tomb — whether addressed to Osiris and his circle[48] or to the sun god[49] — are also cast in conventional molds and are paralleled in earlier or near-contemporary compositions. The only exception occurs on the south wall of the passage, at one side of a curious double scene in which two figures of Amenhotep IV are shown back-to-back; on the right he offers incense(?) and libation to his parents, Amenhotep III and Tiye, while on the left he is "causing a great hecatomb to be presented to Ra-Horakhty."[50] The offerings themselves are shown, but not the god; instead, there is a text addressed to the rising sun, whose presence would have been manifest in the rays that streamed through the passage at daybreak. This, of course, is common in private tombs, where the deceased appears at the outer door and greets the sun with an appropriate hymn,[51] but that this rite should be performed here by a king — and especially a king who later devoted himself so peculiarly to the sun god — is hardly commonplace in this environment, and it invites closer inspection of what the king has to say in his "adoration of Ra in the morning."

This composition,[52] unlike the other hymns nearby, is distinctly "un-standard" in form and (as I hope to show presently) in content also. In the first place, it is the earliest example of a rare genre of religious texts that are written in the fashion of a "crossword": the signs (words and/or groups of words, or determinatives) are ar-

41. Goyon 1957, p. 107, pl. 31 (91); translated in Murnane 1995, p. 68, no. 35-A.2.

42. The charge of organizing a quarrying expedition was by no means a servile one. Similar duties were undertaken by other members of the upper clergy, most notably the high priest of Amun Ramessesnakht during the reign of Ramesses IV; see Gardiner 1961, p. 295; texts in KRI 6, 1–3, 9–16.

43. Although the text has no determinatives that define the *twt n nb* "statue of the lord" as royal, this conclusion seems to be required by the formula "live, prosper, be healthy" attached to this term, which regularly applies to the king, members of the royal family, or royal institutions (*Wb.* 1.196:10–17). For the semantic range of *twt*, which can refer both to images on stelae and statues, see Kaplony 1966, pp. 403–12; Barta 1974, pp. 51–54.

44. Barely mentioned in PM 2, 59 (177); for a photograph, see Haeny 1970, pl. 2. Once covered by one of the walls with which Seti I masked the earlier structures on the eastern side of his Great Hypostyle Hall, it was dismantled and its blocks lay in this condition for many years (during which time they were examined by this writer). The relief was rebuilt by the Centre franco-égyptien pour l'étude des temples de Karnak during spring 1995 in the "musée en plein air" at the northeast corner of the precinct of Amun.

45. As demonstrated by W. Raymond Johnson (1992, pp. 104–05).

46. Paint traces indicate that it may have been finished in that medium, but this needs to be studied in detail.

47. See, in general, Habachi's discussion of Kheruef's career (*Kheruef*, pp. 17–26). Nefertiti's absence from the reliefs in this tomb, of course, does not necessarily mean that she became the king's wife only after they were carved.

48. *Kheruef*, pls. 19, 21, with translations by Wente in the text volume, pp. 37–40.

49. *Kheruef*, pls. 7, 22, with translations by Wente on pp. 30–32, 40; compare Murnane 1995, pp. 59–61, no. 30-C, D.

50. *Kheruef*, pls. 11–13, with translations by Wente on pp. 34–35; compare Murnane 1995, pp. 57–58, no. 30-B.

51. See the examples listed in Assmann 1983, xx–xxi, xxiv–xxv, xxxix.

52. *Kheruef*, pls. 14–15, with translation by Wente on pp. 35–37 (including references to other known "crossword" texts). Compare the transcription and translation in Assmann 1983, §181, pp. 251–53; translation in Murnane 1995, pp. 58–59, no. 35-B.

ranged in boxes on a grid, and they form two entirely different compositions depending on whether they are read horizontally or vertically. Amenhotep IV[53] addresses Ra-Horakhty in the vertical text, while in its horizontal analog he tenders an "adoration of Amun-[Ra]." Once past their unusual arrangement on the wall, however, these texts seem to fall into a recognizable pattern. Each hymn is constructed out of a series of epithets and divine names that define, not only his nature, but complementary "forms of being" (*ḫprw*) in the shape of other gods (see Appendix 30.1). Thus Horakhty is also Amun, Amun-Ra, Kamutef, Khepri, and Atum; while Amun-Ra enjoys subsidiary identities as Ra, Horus-the-Elder, Ra-Khepri, Atum, and Kamutef. Finding all these deities combined in this fashion is not surprising because similarly constructed eulogies occur earlier, during (and even before) the Eighteenth Dynasty — most notably the universalist hymn to Amun-Ra in P. Boulaq 17 (Grébaut 1875), as well as the shorter hymns in private tombs at Thebes. In all these compositions different aspects of the sun god's nature are expressed in terms of the gods who best personify them. Thus, for example, sovereignty and rule are the special attributes of Amun-Ra, while Ra-Horakhty embodies creativity, as it was in the beginning and continues to operate in the world.[54] Even some of the more unusual epithets can be paralleled in earlier texts — for example, "mother of mothers, father of fathers" (10M-N),[55] "soulful one" (2I),[56] "who traverses the sky" (*nmỉ pt* in 7D),[57] or references to the god as "Dual King" (7M).[58] Both in structure and ideas, then, the Kheruef crossword hymns seem to fall into the tradition of these earlier compositions.

Despite all these superficial similarities, however, there are notable differences that define the Kheruef crossword texts as "individual hymns," inhabiting a conceptual world somewhat different from what is found in the "standard texts" discussed above.[59] To begin with, even though the Kheruef texts employ many of the standard phrases found in earlier hymns, these are not assembled here in a way that reproduces earlier models. As compositions, the Kheruef crossword hymns seem to be unique.[60] Many specific epithets seem to be completely unparalleled, even by similar constructions,[61] in the standard texts — for example, [*ꜥꜣ*]-*sḫm.f* (7B),[62] *wr ḥkꜣw* (masculine, in 13L), *nb ỉmyw.f* (6D), *nswt* [*rḫ*]*yt* (13I),[63] *rs ḥꜣwt* (5C),[64] *ḥtpy*(?) *sꜣḫw* (N5-6), and *smsw sꜣḫw* (6M-N). Moreover, a number of the concepts evoked in these hymns seem to be new — or at least they are not presented by earlier compositions in quite the same sense as they occur here. The most striking of these are as follows:

53. Only in the horizontal text is the king's name fully written out as "Neferkheprure, Son of Ra, Amenhotep Ruler-of-Thebes" (see *Kheruef*, pl. 15:1 H-L). The nomen is also written with the epithet *ḥqꜣ Wꜣst* instead of Amenhotep IV's more usual *nṯr ḥqꜣ Wꜣst* "God who rules Thebes" in line 10:A-C and col. J:2-5; and the same spelling can be inferred from the traces in column A:10-12; but the next column (B:10-11) has a variant, "Amenhotep, Ra for E[gypt](?)" or similar. Since *ḥqꜣ Wꜣst* is normally used as an epithet inside cartouches of Amenhotep III, it has been suggested that the latter was the speaker in the address to Ra-Horakhty (= vertical text), while the (horizontal) hymn to Amun-Ra was uttered by his son; see Valentín 1991, pp. 216–17. But, since Valentín follows Wente in recognizing "Neferkheprure" as a speaker in the vertical text (G:1-3), and since Amenhotep IV is also *ḥqꜣ Wꜣst* in line 1, it seems preferable to assume that this was the sort of alternative form found early in a reign, before the writings of the new king's name had settled down into their most usual forms; see Murnane 1977, pp. 79–80; compare the anomalous writing of Amenhotep IV's nomen in the scenes on the front lintel of Kheruef's tomb (*Kheruef*, pl. 9), which includes both the "normal" *nṯr ḥqꜣ Wꜣst* and, more unusually, the epithet *ꜥꜣ m ꜥḥꜥw.f* "great in his duration" inside this cartouche instead of following it.
54. See, in general, Assmann 1995, pp. 102–32.
55. Compare Assmann 1983, §108b (*ỉt ỉtw.sn, mwt mwwt.sn*) and P. Leiden I 344 verso II, pl. 2:1 (*ʾImn ỉt mwt nṯr nṯrt*); see Zandee 1992, pp. 67–70.
56. An exact parallel is found only as of the Ramesside period (Assmann 1983, §156:28–29), but approximations are found earlier (e.g., Assmann 1983, §§5:10, 143:3).
57. Assmann 1983, §70:5; P. Leiden I 344 verso V, pl. 5:8 (Zandee 1992, pp. 444–48).
58. Compare Zandee 1992, pls. 6:9–8:4 (= strophes 14–16, pp. 581–707), where Amun-Ra is provided with an extended royal "titulary"; compare also P. Boulaq 17 ii, line 2, in Grébaut 1875, p. 6, §iv.
59. These terms are discussed in Assmann 1995, p. 8.
60. Unlike the other hymns from the tomb of Kheruef in Assmann 1983, neither antecedents nor parallels are cited for the crossword texts (no. 181 = pp. 251–53); and in Assmann 1995, the reference to them in the index (p. 232) sheds no further light on these compositions.
61. For example, *ỉrỉ nprỉ* is anticipated by *nb nprỉ* (P. Boulaq 17, 8:2 = Grébaut 1875, p. 21 [xviii]) and *ỉrỉ ỉt, btỉ* (P. Leiden I 344 verso IX, pl. 9:1 = Zandee 1992, pp. 768–76), both of which can be seen as close variants of this idea.
62. The closest parallels seem to be *sḫm nṯrw* (Assmann 1983, §110 [p. 149, variant], 77:2) and *sḫm špss* (Assmann 1983, §164:17).
63. Most references to a god as *nswt* in standard texts are post-Amarna, although Amun is occasionally cited as *nswt-tꜣwy* (Assmann 1983, §108b:2) or *nswt pt, ḥqꜣ tꜣ* (Assmann 1983, §127:3). The only approximately close parallel for this phrase is *Wrt-ḥkꜣw* [*sšm*(?) *rḫ*]*yt* (Assmann 1983, §75:12, in a passage referring to crowns).
64. Phrases constructed with *rs* tend to evoke the awakening of the sun god or the deceased at dawn in more extended phrases (e.g., Assmann 1983, §§102:15–16, 178:5).

Unknowability

The god is one *ỉwty rḫ.f* "whom no one can know" (H12), a concept that is not found in the "standard" corpus of hymns until after the Amarna period.[65] In earlier comparanda it is the number of the gods' names (*ʿš3 rnw, nn rḫ ṯnw.w*)[66] or the place where he is (*nn rḫ nṯr bw ẖr.f*)[67] that are unknown. It is precisely on this score that Akhenaten (who alone "knows" his god) is set apart from the mass of humanity, who merely experience the Aten as sunlight (Assmann 1992, pp. 159–60).

Identity of Ra with Nun

"His body is Nun" (13F), characterizing Amun-Ra (in the vertical text) and probably the sun god (horizontal), is a striking extension of the usual role of Nun vis-à-vis the sun. In most "standard" texts Ra merely *prỉ m* "emerges from" (cf. 10G) or *wbn m* "rises from" Nun, and sometimes he is called an "aged man who is in Nun" (Assmann 1983, §34:11). In a number of sun hymns[68] Nun is described as the sun god's father, but even this concept falls short of the virtual identity between the god and the underworld "Urozean" that is implied here.[69] The idea of the sun being within Nun continues to be expressed in the Ramesside period, notably in a "non-standard" passage that describes how the sun god "[o]pens Nun with the rays of his solar orb (*ỉṯn*)."[70] The closest identification between Nun and Ra in the Theban tombs is in a hymn dating to the reign of Ramesses IX, in which the sun god's orb is described as a *ḫpr Nnw* "manifestation of Nun."[71]

Expanded Role of the Solar Orb

Finally, we should call attention to the expanded role of the solar orb ("Aten") in these crossword hymns. In each text it is mentioned twice — possibly three times, if the tentative restoration at box 12N is accepted, although this latter reference does little to enhance understanding since too much of the surrounding text in both directions is gone. The same applies to the horizontal text at 3H-L, in which the solar beetle Khepri does something (lost) "as (*or* in) Aten."[72] The complementary passage in the vertical hymn — where the sun god is "satisfied when he sets in (*or* as) the solar orb" (L1-3) — is also conventional, in that it seems to maintain the traditional separation between the god and his celestial "body." Given the damage in the squares that come after this, it is not even certain whether the *wr* which follows *ỉtn* here qualifies it as an adjective or begins another phrase, balancing *ḥtp ḥtp.f m ỉtn*, as an adjective verb. Fortunately, the two remaining references to the solar orb are straightforward:

> (Amun) who made [every]thing, who has no equal, appearing on earth, his limbs being the solar orb (*ỉtn*) ... who knots together ... with his ... (11E-L)
>
> (Ra) who made grain, dazzling of forms, elder orb (= Aten), king of the [subj]ects, etc. (I8–13)

Both these passages, distributed as they are between the two divinities who traditionally dominate sun hymns, are quite unprecedented in the earlier "standard texts." While in these the sun god is universally conceived as being "in his orb" (*ỉmy ỉtn.f*),[73] here the solar orb is more closely associated with the god himself, forming part of his body; he also assumes the dignity of an elder god, like the primeval Horus in 3A-B.[74] The manner in

65. See Assmann 1983, §§156:47, 158:53, 223:4, 253:33, 254:19. None of these parallels is exact, but all convey the unknowability of the god's name, his nature, or the god himself. Compare Assmann 1995, pp. 136–39.
66. P. Boulaq 17, 9:3, in Grébaut 1875, pp. 23–24 (§xx).
67. P. Leiden I 344 verso IX, pl. 9:1, in Zandee 1992, pp. 764–65.
68. Including two from the tomb of Kheruef; see Assmann 1983, §§52:36, 165a:6, 180:11, 183:11.
69. For the identification of Nun with Amun in the Late Period, see Sethe 1929, §§140 (pp. 70–71).
70. Assmann 1983, §149.13 (TT 157 = tomb of Nebwenenef, during the time of Ramesses II).
71. Assmann 1983, §91:22–23.
72. However, compare *Ḫprỉ ... sḥḏ t3wy m ỉtn.f* "Khepri ... who illuminates the Two Lands with his solar orb" (in the second hymn of Suty and Hor; Fecht 1967, pp. 27, 42–43).
73. Compare P. Leiden I 344 verso III, pl. 3:3–4: [*ḏ3ỉ*(?) *p*]*t m b3.f pwy ỉmy ỉtn.f* (Zandee 1992, pp. 186–96), with many other examples in Assmann 1983, §§22:10, 28c:6, 228.XI:1–2, 242:8.
74. The flow of bimembral epithets that make up the rest of this passage (*ỉrỉ nrpỉ, ṯḥn ḫprw, nswt* [*rḫ*]*yt*) do not suggest that *ỉtn* and *smsw* are to be read as separate items here. Earlier in the Eighteenth Dynasty only Amun-Ra is referred to as *smsw n pt t3* "eldest one of heaven and earth" (Assmann 1983, §75:27), and *smsw* is used later to qualify Ra and Horakhty (Assmann 1983, §§165:22, 216:5, 236:3) but not the solar orb.

which the Aten is evoked independently in this latter passage is paralleled, of course, at the beginning of Suty and Hor's second hymn (Fecht 1967, pp. 26, 35–37; cf. Assmann 1983, §§18:7, 29:16, 88:13, all post-Amarna), but it is attested in "standard" texts only after the Amarna period (Assmann 1983, §§54:31–2, 160:5, 233c:1–5). The concept of the sun god's rays as "arms" might have been grounded in imagery that was used initially for Amun-Ra, "the one alone, with many arms," earlier in the Eighteenth Dynasty (P. Boulaq 17, 6:7 = Grébaut 1875, p. 18, §xvi; cf. Assmann 1995, p. 123; S. Hassan 1938, pp. 53–61); but it is first in the Kheruef crossword hymns that we begin to see the sun god and "his orb" becoming as one, on their way to the complete fusion which would be achieved in the mature Aten cult only a few years later (see Assmann 1995, pp. 67–70; cf. Assmann 1992, pp. 147–52).

CONCLUSION

The conceptual world of the Kheruef crossword hymns — in which many gods mingle their attributes to express, in the end, their underlying oneness — is still closer to that of the universalist hymn to Amun in P. Boulaq 17 than it is to the "new order" of el-Amarna. Even so, the several departures from orthodox theology in Amenhotep IV's "adoration of Ra in the morning" are all the more notable in that they occur in a pioneering statement of the king's religious beliefs — a record which his enemies later took such pains to obliterate.[75] The innovations seen in this text, coupled with its eminently orthodox henotheism, suggest the beginnings of an answer to the question posed earlier on the place of Amun (and other traditional gods) in Amenhotep IV's new religion. As a reading of both hymns will show (see Appendix 30.1), Amun-Ra plays a central role not only in promoting life on earth (F12-13) but as an alter ego of Ra-Horakhty in the sky (7A-I) who is also manifest as sunlight (5E-H). Both of these gods are facets of one another, an idea which already had a long history. What is new here is that each one is equated with the solar orb, eventually the king's preferred deity, which is becoming in this text more than merely the physical shell which contains the supreme creator; in other words, that which links Amun and Ra-Horakhty here is their identity with the solar orb. Further, it is Ra-Horakhty (who will embody the new god in the cult's earliest monuments) who is represented on the lintel of the tomb's facade, and he is accompanied not by Amun (although he is evoked in the texts on the jambs) but Atum, the primeval creator (who is not only the Aten's closest equivalent in the theology of Amarna but an important figure in the cult's Heliopolitan antecedents).[76] Cumulatively, then, what we are seeing in this part of Kheruef's tomb is not merely the Aten's "debut" as the underlying unity in the divine world, but the first cautious step toward his replacing of Amun-Ra as the "one" who contained "the many" in the form of Egyptian religion that had been developing since the earlier Eighteenth Dynasty.

Bolder steps would soon follow. Even before the king's break with Thebes and his departure for el-Amarna, he would requisition manpower and material to support his new cult from all over Egypt.[77] How heavily the new order weighed upon the temples and towns that were obliged to pay for it may become clearer once work on these fragmentary inscriptions is finished, but the neglect of orthodox cults, noted above, lends tangible support to the king's cupbearer Parennefer, who observes in his Theban tomb that "the revenues of every god are measured in *oipe*, but for the Aten one measures in heaps!" (Davies 1923, pp. 41–42, with pl. 25; cf. Murnane 1995, p. 66, no. 33.5). In this environment, neither the high priest of Amun's commission to convey stone from the Wadi Hammamat nor the bare support given to Amun's temple is out of place. What would be surprising is if no one found the screws to be too tight. Early in year 5, in the "Earlier Proclamation" on the founding of the new city, Akhenaten alludes obliquely to something (mostly lost in a break) "in Akhet-Aten" and goes on to declare it worse than anything heard in the first four years of his reign, worse than anything that his predecessors had heard, "worse [than] those things heard by any kings who had (ever) assumed the White Crown" (Murnane and Van Siclen 1993, p. 26, K:20-21; cf. Murnane 1995, p. 78, no. 37.4). While some have assumed an unseemly scramble among the king's officials for privileged places in the new royal cemetery, or even the overweening arrogance of the other gods' clergies, as the cause of the king's ire,[78] it seems likelier that something more concrete was at issue. Wealth and prestige have always ranked highest among the "fighting issues" that have di-

75. For an account of the damage inflicted on the tomb after its abandonment, see comments of Nims in *Kheruef*, pp. 13–16.

76. See, in particular, Myśliwiec 1982, pp. 285–89.

77. See Traunecker 1987, pp. 62–69.

78. Discussed with necessary skepticism in Murnane and Van Siclen 1993, pp. 166–69 with notes (pp. 211–14).

vided the human community. The one was clearly being directed away from the orthodox foundations even while the king continued to call himself "Amenhotep." Loss of the other, while more difficult to chart, is implicit in Akhenaten's abandonment and eventual persecution of the traditional gods — a course which we see beginning in Amenhotep IV's hymn to the sun in the tomb of Kheruef.

APPENDIX 30.1: DIVINITIES IN KHERUEF WORD SQUARE

The following translation, based on that of Professor Wente in the Oriental Institute's *Tomb of Kheruef* publication (*Kheruef*), is not a substantially improved rendering, although I have occasionally hazarded a suggestion to complete the text. It is subdivided to call attention to the assorted deities evoked in each hymn.

Vertical

(A1–12) Adoration of Ra-Horakhty, goodly spokesman(?) [of the] go[ds](?) by the Good God, Son of Ra, [Amenhotep] Rul[er-of-Thebes].

(A13–E5) [Hail to you] Amun, eldest one, perfect ... , [great]-of-his-power, lord of heaven. [It is][a] King(?) Amenhotep, Ra of E[gypt](?) [*who acts for*] the great god, lord of the two concl[aves], king of the gods, watchful of countenance, greatest(?) who (ever) came into being; who illuminates the land; rich in manifestations, pure lord who is at the forefront of what he makes; ... , [great of] terror, godly of appearances, who is in the bark and promotes the dawn, lord of those who are in (*or* with) him, who traverses the sky ... . May you be adored(?), ... , lord [of ... when(?)] he [*does something*]; beloved one, ... , repeating appearances and beginning[b] his ... .

(E6–9) Amun-Ra Kamutef, master of joy <at> the entrance of Manu every ... .

(E10–F6) Ra who made [every]thing [and ...] all the [...]s of the gods(?), ... , whose ... [pros]pers (*or* [pro]ceeds).[c]

(F7–H2) Amun-[Ra], lord of the thrones of the Two Lands, ... , image without its duplicate, who created what exists, whose body(?) is Nun — so says the Good God Neferkheprure, [great of] valor, ... lord of [...]s: (O) god Amun, great of kingship, who issued from Nun and appeared on earth; who advances everyone and causes the Two Lands to live; beautiful of manifestations, foremost one of his sanctuary.

(H3–12) Khepri, effective as sunlight (*or* glorious as Shu), sole unique one whose form is sunlight (= Shu), who fashions his (own) flesh, whom no one can know.

(H13–I8) Hail to your [face], Ra, soulful one(?) ... , beside whom there is none, who has no equal; who made grain.

(I9–J13) Dazzling of forms, solar orb (= Aten), elder one, king of the [subj]ects (of the) Son of Ra, Amenhotep Ruler-of-Thebes, ... , whose [... are] lasting, ... , master of ruler[s], ... , who ... himself.[d]

(K1–M3) Most hidden of those who are hidden, ... in ... , foremost of ... , [great] of streng[th], lord of everlastingness: Amun-Ra, Theban, who knots together ... when he has made ... ; satisfied when he sets as (*or* in) the solar orb, great of ... , ... when he makes provision[e] [on behalf] of continuity; [who ...] and causes everyone to live with[f] his ... . Grand of appearances,[g] great of magic, ruler of Thebes, mighty of countenance!

(M4–N13) Atum when he [enters *or similar*] Manu; elder one, Dual King, great one in front of[h] the Two Lands; mother of mothers ... (god): hail to you, who made everything, who is above his mother,[i] most peaceful(?) of the glorified ones. It is[j] the father of fathers [who ...] Aten[k](?) everlastingly.

Horizontal

(1A-M) Adoration of Amun-[Ra], the godliest of gods, the most beloved of [the gods(?)] by Neferkheprure, Son of Ra, Amenhotep Ruler-of-Thebes:

(1N–2N) Hail to you, Ra, great of appearances, ... , beautiful of manifestations, foremost one of his sanctuary, soulful one(?), most hidden of those who are hidden when he sets, mighty of countenance, who made everything.

(3A-F) Horus the elder, lord of the two concl[aves], king of the gods, who is in the bark and repeats appearances, ...

(3G-L) Ra-Khepri ... as (*or* in) the solar orb (Aten).

(3M–5D) Atum who is above the double horizon; perfect one, king of the gods; foremost one, who begins(?) his ... , [great of] valor, effective (*or* glorious) ... , satisfied with ... , great [of ... when] he ... his mother; good spokesman [of ...], watchful of countenance when the land brightens.

(5E–6D) Amun-Ra, [who issue]s forth(?) [gloriously *or similar*(?)] as Shu (*or* sunlight), ... , ruler of Thebes, foremost [of those who are in] Manu, most gracious(?) [of the gods(?)], ... , the greatest(?) who (ever) came into being, lord of those who are in (*or* with) him.

(6E-N) Kamutef, whose [... are great(?) *or similar*], lord of [...]s, unique one, beside whom there is none, ... , eldest of those who are glorified.

(7A–9M) It is [the one great]-of-his-power who illuminates the land and traverses the sky, the lord of rejoicing, Amun-[Ra] — the unique god without his equal, lasting(?), great of strength when he makes provision; Dual King, the god, lord of heaven, rich in manifestations ... (at) the [entra]nce of Manu; lord of the thrones of the Two Lands, whose form is hidden (but) who has made grain [when] he ... ; lord of everlastingness and chief of continuity; great and good one [for] the king; lord of purity, ... every ... , great of kingship, dazzling sunlight (Shu), ... , Amun-Ra, [glorious *or similar*] in front of the Two Lands.

(9M–11N) So says(?) the Son of Ra, Amenhotep Ruler-of-Thebes: May you be adored(?), Ra, perfect one who issued from Nun, who fashions what comes into being; lord of rulers, Theban, who causes everyone to live; mother of mothers, father of fathers; [Amun-at-peace], [i] Ra for Eg[ypt](?) who advances what he made; ... who made [every]thing; without his equal, his limbs (being) the solar orb ... , who knots together ... with his ... , ...

(12A–13N) Ruler [of Thebes], ... , lord [of ...], ... who created what exists and advances everything, whom no one can know; eldest one, ... , great of appearances(?), ... Aten(?): [Hail to you, ... , great of] terror, when he ... all the ... ; whose body(?) is Nun, who causes the Two Lands to live! Hail to your [face], king of the [subj]ects, ... himself when he had made ... , Great-of-Magic everlastingly!

Notes

[a] Restoring Lower Egyptian crown *n* (Gardiner Sign List S3), with the value *ỉn* in the vertical text (see *Wb.* 2.194:3), assuming a verb in B12. Dative *n* "on behalf of" seems less likely in this context.

[b] Assuming that *šsp* is arranged for graphic reasons beside the substantive which follows grammatically.

[c] Assuming [*w*]*ḏꜣ* [...].*f*.

[d] There does not seem to be enough room to restore *ḫpr* in the space at the top of this box.

[e] Restoring *ỉrỉ.f ḥn* (see *Wb.* 3.102:8–9).

[f] The traces suggest flat *m* here.

[g] Restoring *ꜥꜣ ḫꜥw* or similar.

[h] The traces strongly suggest *m-ḥꜣt* here.

[i] Perhaps visualized in terms of the sun being lifted up by or resting upon the head of the sky goddess (see *LÄ* 4 "Nut," col. 536, with nn. 18–19) or rising from upon her back (Assmann 1983, §71:H3).

[j] Tentatively restoring *ỉn*, as in 7A.

[k] Assuming that a verb stood in 11N; the only objection to restoring *ỉtn* in the following box (12N) is the off-center position of the disk; perhaps restore an otiose stroke to the right?

[l] Applying the literal meaning of the king's name to the god.

References

Aldred, C.

1959 "The Beginning of the el-ʿAmarna Period." *Journal of Egyptian Archaeology* 45: 19–33.

1973 *Akhenaten and Nefertiti*. New York: Brooklyn Museum.

1988 *Akhenaten, King of Egypt*. London: Thames and Hudson.

Allen, J. P.

1989 "The Natural Philosophy of Akhenaten." In *Religion and Philosophy in Ancient Egypt*, edited by W. K. Simpson, pp. 89–102. Yale Egyptological Studies 3. New Haven: Yale Egyptological Seminar.

Anthes, R.

1963 "... in seinem Namen und im Sonnenlicht ... ." *Zeitschrift für ägyptische Sprache und Altertumskunde* 90: 1–10.

Assmann, J.

1983 *Sonnenhymnen in thebanischen Gräbern*. Theben 1. Mainz: Philipp von Zabern.

1984 *Ägypten. Theologie und Frömmigkeit einer frühen Hochkultur*. Urban-Taschenbuch 366. Stuttgart: W. Kohlhammer.

1992 "Akhanyati's Theology of Light and Time." *Proceedings of the Israel Academy of Sciences and Humanities* 7/4: 143–76.

1995 *Egyptian Solar Religion in the New Kingdom: Re, Amun and the Crisis of Polytheism*. Translated by A. Alcock. London: Kegan Paul.

Bakry, H. S. K.

1972 "Akhenaten at Heliopolis." *Chronique d'Égypte* 47: 55–67.

Barta, W.

1974 "Der Terminus *twt* auf den Grenzstelen Sesostris' III. in Nubien." In *Festschrift zum 150-jährigen Bestehen des Berliner ägyptischen Museums*, pp. 51–54. Mitteilungen aus der ägyptischen Sammlung 8. Berlin: Akademie-Verlag.

Bianchi, R. S.

1990 "New Light on the Aton." *Göttinger Miszellen* 114: 35–40.

Brugsch, H.

1857 *Geographischer Inschriften altägyptischer Denkmäler* 1. Leipzig: J. C. Hinrichs.

Brunner, H.

1970 "Die Sonnenbahn in ägyptischen Tempeln." In *Archäologie und Altes Testament: Festschrift für Kurt Galling zum 8. Januar 1970*, edited by A. Kuschke and E. Kutsch, pp. 27–34. Tübingen: J. C. B. Mohr.

Bruyère, B.

1937 *Rapport sur les fouilles de Deir el-Médineh, 1933–1934*, 1: *La nécropole de l'Ouest*. Cairo: Institut français d'archéologie orientale.

Cannuyer, C.

1985 "Akkhet-Aton: Anti-Thèbes ou sanctuaire du globe?" *Göttinger Miszellen* 86: 7–9.

Černý, J.

1973 *A Community of Workmen at Thebes in the Ramesside Period*. Bibliothèque d'étude 50. Cairo: Institut français d'archéologie orientale.

Černý, J., and S. I. Groll

1984 *A Late Egyptian Grammar*. Studia Pohl, Series maior, 4. Third updated edition. Rome: Biblical Institute Press.

Chappaz, J.-L.

1983 "Le premier édifice d'Amenophis IV à Karnak." *Bulletin de la Société d'égyptologie, Genève* 8: 13–44.

Cruz-Uribe, E.

1992 "Another Look at an Aton Statue." *Göttinger Miszellen* 126: 29–32.

Davies, N. de G.

1923 "Akhenaten at Thebes." *Journal of Egyptian Archaeology* 9: 132–52.

Doresse, M.

1941/42 "Le culte d'Aton sous la XVIIIe dynastie avant le schisme amarnien." *Journal asiatique* 233: 181–99.

1955 "Les temples atoniens de la région thébaine." *Orientalia* 24: 113–35.

1981 "Observations sur la publication des blocs des temples atoniens de Karnak: The Akhenaten Temple Project." *Göttinger Miszellen* 46: 45–79.

Fecht, G.

1967 "Zur Frühform der Amarna-Theologie." *Zeitschrift für ägyptische Sprache und Altertumskunde* 94: 25–50.

Gardiner, A. H.

1961 *Egypt of the Pharaohs*. Oxford: Clarendon Press.

Gohary, J.

1992 *Akhenaten's Sed-Festival at Karnak*. Studies in Egyptology. London: Kegan Paul.

Goyon, G.

1957 *Nouvelles inscriptions rupestres du Wadi Hammamat*. Paris: Imprimerie nationale.

Grébaut, E.

1875 *Hymne à Ammon-Ra des papyrus égyptiens du Musée de Boulaq*. Bibliothèque de l'École des hautes études 21. Paris: A. Franck.

Gutbub, A.
1973 *Textes fondamentaux de la théologie de Kom Ombo*. Bibliothèque d'étude 47. Cairo: Institut français d'archéologie orientale.

Habachi, L.
1965 "Varia from the Reign of King Akhenaten." *Mitteilungen des Deutschen archäologischen Instituts, Abteilung Kairo* 20: 70–92.
1971 "Akenaton at Heliopolis." In *Zum 70. Geburtstag von Herbert Ricke*, edited by G. Haeny, pp. 35–45. Beiträge zur ägyptischen Bauforschung und Altertumskunde 12. Wiesbaden: Franz Steiner.

Haeny, G.
1970 *Basilikale Anlagen in der ägyptischen Baukunst des Neuen Reiches*. Beiträge zur ägyptischen Bauforschung und Altertumskunde 9. Wiesbaden: Franz Steiner.

Hartman, T. C.
1967 The Kadesh Inscriptions of Ramesses II: An Analysis of the Verbal Patterns of a Ramesside Royal Inscription. Ph.D. dissertation, Brandeis University.

Hassan, A.
1976 *Stocke und Stäbe im pharaonischen Ägypten bis zum Ende des Neuen Reiches*. Münchner ägyptologische Studien 33. Berlin: Deutscher Kunstverlag.

Hassan, S.
1938 "A Representation of the Solar Disk with Human Hands and Arms and the Form of Horus of Behdet, as Seen on the Stela of Amenhotep IInd in the Mud-Brick Temple at Giza." *Annales du Service des antiquités de l'Égypte* 38: 53–61.

Hayes, W. C.
1951 "Inscriptions from the Palace of Amenhotep III." *Journal of Near Eastern Studies* 10: 35–56, 82–111, 156–83, 231–42.

Hornung, E.
1982 *Conceptions of God in Ancient Egypt*. Translated by J. Baines. Ithaca: Cornell University Press.
1995 *Akhenaton: Die Religion des Lichtes*. Zurich: Artemis Verlag.

Johnson, W. R.
1990 "Images of Amenhotep III in Thebes: Styles and Intentions." In *The Art of Amenhotep III: Art Historical Analysis*, edited by L. M. Berman, pp. 26–46. Cleveland: Cleveland Museum of Art.
1992 An Asiatic Battle Scene of Tutankhamun from Thebes: A Late Amarna Antecedent of the Ramesside Battle-Narrative Tradition. Ph.D. dissertation, University of Chicago.

Kaplony, P.
1966 "Das Vorbild des Königs unter Sesostris III." *Orientalia* 35: 403–12.

Kroeber, B.
1970 Die Neuägyptizismen vor der Amarnazeit. Ph.D. dissertation, Tübingen.

Kuentz, C.
1920 "Autour d'une conception égyptien méconnue: L'*Akhit* ou soi-disant horizon." *Bulletin de l'Institut français d'archéologie orientale* 17: 121–90.

Lefebvre, G.
1955 *Grammaire de l'égyptien classique*. Bibliothèque d'étude 12. Second edition. Cairo: Institut français d'archéologie orientale.

Legrain, G.
1901 "Notes prises à Karnak." *Recueil de travaux relatifs à la philologie et à l'archéologie égyptiennes et assyriennes* 23: 61–65.
1902 "Notes d'inspection, 1: Les stèles d'Amenothes IV à Zernik et à Gebel Silsileh." *Annales du Service des antiquités de l'Égypte* 3: 259–66.

Löhr, B.
1975 "Ahanjati in Memphis." *Studien zur altägyptischen Kultur* 2: 139–87.

Murnane, W. J.
1977 *Ancient Egyptian Coregencies*. Studies in Ancient Oriental Civilization 40. Chicago: Oriental Institute.
1995 *Texts from the Amarna Period in Egypt*. Writings from the Ancient World 5. Atlanta: Scholars Press.

Murnane, W. J., and C. C. Van Siclen III
1993 *The Boundary Stelae of Akhenaten*. Studies in Egyptology. London: Kegan Paul.

Myśliwiec, K.
1982 "Amon, Atum and Aton: The Evolution of Heliopolitan Influences in Thebes." In *L'égyptologie en 1979: Axes prioritaires de recherche*, volume 2, pp. 285–89. Colloques internationaux du Centre national de la recherche scientifique 595. Paris: Éditions du Centre national de la recherche scientifique.

Otto, E.
1952 *Topographie des thebanischen Gaues*. Untersuchungen zur Geschichte und Altertumskunde Ägyptens 16. Berlin: Akademie-Verlag.

Redford, D. B.
1963 "The Identity of the High Priest of Amun at the Beginning of Akhenaten's Reign." *Journal of the American Oriental Society* 82: 240–41.
1976 "The Sun-Disc in Akhenaten's Program: Its Worship and Antecedents, I." *Journal of the American Research Center in Egypt* 13: 47–61.
1980 "The Sun-Disc in Akhenaten's Program: Its Worship and Antecedents, II." *Journal of the American Research Center in Egypt* 17: 21–34.
1984 *Akhenaten, the Heretic King*. Princeton: Princeton University Press.

Sandman, M.
1938 *Texts from the Time of Akhenaten*. Bibliotheca Aegyptiaca 8. Brussels: Fondation Égyptologique Reine Élisabeth.

Sethe, K.
1929 *Amun und die acht Urgötter von Hermopolis: Eine Untersuchung über Ursprung und Wesen des ägypti-*

schen Götterkönigs. Deutsche Akademie der Wissenschaften zu Berlin, philosophisch-historische Klasse, Abhandlungen, Jahrgang 1929, Nr. 4. Berlin: Verlag der Akademie der Wissenschaften.

Smith, R. W., and D. B. Redford
1976 *The Akhenaten Temple Project*, Volume 1: *Initial Discoveries*. Warminster: Aris and Phillips.

Stock, H.
1950 "Ägyptische Religionsgeschichte." *Saeculum* 1: 613–36.

Tawfik, S.
1973 "Aton Studies, 1: Aton before the Reign of Akhenaten." *Mitteilungen des Deutschen archäologischen Instituts, Abteilung Kairo* 29: 77–82.
1976a "Aton Studies, 4: Was Aton — the God of Akhenaten — Only a Manifestation of the God Re?" *Mitteilungen des Deutschen archäologischen Instituts, Abteilung Kairo* 32: 217–26.
1976b "Chapter 3: Aten and the Names of His Temple(s) at Thebes." In *The Akhenaten Temple Project*, Volume 1: *Initial Discoveries*, by R. W. Smith and D. B. Redford, pp. 58–63. Warminster: Aris and Phillips.

Traunecker, C.
1987 "Données nouvelles sur le début du règne d'Aménophis IV et son œuvre à Karnak." *Society for the Study of Egyptian Antiquities Journal* 14: 60–69.

Valbelle, D.
1985 *"Les ouvriers de la tombe": Deir el-Médineh à l'époque ramesside*. Bibliothèque d'étude 96. Cairo: Institut français d'archéologie orientale.

Valentín, F. J. M.
1991 "La tumba de Kheruef (TT 192): Indicios de una corregencía." *Boletín de la Asociación española de egiptologia* 3: 213–40.

Zandee, J.
1992 *Der Amunhymnus des Papyrus Leiden I 344, Verso*. 3 volumes. Leiden: Rijksmuseum van Outheden.

31

ZUM KULTBILDRITUAL IN ABYDOS

JÜRGEN OSING

Freie Universität Berlin, Germany

Im Tempel Sethos' I. in Abydos sind für die Osiristriade (Osiris, Isis, Horus), die Reichstriade (Amun-Ra, Ra, Ptah) und Sethos I. selbst sieben Kultkapellen nebeneinander angelegt.[1] Die Kapelle des Amun-Ra nimmt dabei die zentrale Position ein.[2]

Die Kapellen haben alle die gleiche Form, und von den sechs Götterkapellen sind vier (Isis, Horus, Ra, Ptah) auch alle in der gleichen Weise in zwei Registern mit insgesamt 36 Szenen aus dem täglichen Kultbildritual dekoriert. In der Kapelle des Amun-Ra haben zwei übergrosse, um die Barken von Mut und Chons erweiterte Barkenszenen zwei benachbarte kleine Ritualszenen verdrängt,[3] in der Kapelle des Osiris, die im Unterschied zu allen übrigen nur ein Durchgangsraum (zu dem dahinter liegenden Osiris-Trakt) ist, ist der Szenenbestand stärker reduziert und abgeändert. Die Szenen in der Kapelle Sethos' I. sind dagegen nicht die des Kultbildrituals, sondern betreffen die Krönung und die Versorgung mit Totenopfern.[4]

Die Abfolge der Szenen aus dem Kultbildritual ist Gegenstand schon mehrerer Rekonstruktionsversuche gewesen, doch haben diese ganz unterschiedliche Ergebnisse erbracht.[5] Gemeinsam ist ihnen allen nur, dass sie unmittelbar rechts vom Eingang der Kapelle einsetzen. Die weitere Szenenfolge wird meist in Form umlaufender Ketten gesehen: als ein Doppelstrang der übereinander stehenden Szenen (David 1973, 114–19; David 1981, 58–71) oder in zwei Strängen, das obere Register zuerst (Blackman 1920, 27–53; Barta 1966, 116–22) oder das untere (Mariette 1869, 17 f.; Alliot 1949, 76, n. 1). In Form von zwei Strängen, die nicht den ganzen Raum umlaufen, sondern zunächst die nördliche und dann die südliche Hälfte einnehmen, erscheint die Abfolge in den Ansätzen von Roeder (1960, 72–141), Altenmüller-Kesting (1968, 176–84) und Altenmüller (1969, 16–25), bei Roeder dabei noch unterteilt in die vordere und die rückwärtige Raumhälfte.

Bei aller Einfachheit sind diese Rekonstruktionsmuster doch so unterschiedlich, dass ohne zusätzliche, externe Indizien eine Lösung nicht möglich ist. In den grossen Papyri Berlin 3055 und 3014+3053 zum Kultbildritual des Amun (A) und der Mut (M) aus der 22. Dyn. stehen solche auch zur Verfügung.

Die Handschrift A ist vollständig erhalten, in M fehlen einige Seiten ganz oder teilweise. Die beiden Rituale, für die insgesamt 70 Sprüche gezählt werden, stimmen in Bestand und Abfolge ihrer Handlungen und Sprüche weitgehend überein, die Unterschiede halten sich in engen Grenzen.[6] In dem Abschnitt zwischen den Sprüchen 25 und 45 entfallen in M die Sprüche A 26 und 41 ("Öffnen des Gesichts" und "Darbringen der Maat") sowie die Wiederholung der Sprüche 10–17 (= A 27–34), und die langen Hymnen an die Gottheit gehen hier einer Weihräucherung voraus (M 43–44), während sie dieser bei Amun folgen (A 35–40, 42). Die beiden Sprüche für den Eintritt in das Allerheiligste (A 23–24) sind in M in ihrer Abfolge vertauscht, und es fehlen hier ausserdem die Sprüche 18–19, zwei Lobpreisungen. In A fehlt Spruch 70.

Gegen einen Vergleich der Szenen im Tempel Sethos' I. in Abydos und der beiden thebanischen Ritual-Papyri für Amun und Mut aus der 22. Dyn. könnte der örtliche und zeitliche Abstand ins Feld geführt werden. Beides ist jedoch m.E. unerheblich, da die Versionen in den Götterkapellen von Abydos ja in so weitgehend übereinstimmender Form erscheinen, auch und gerade in der zentralen Kapelle des Amun-Ra, und da in den

1. Calverley und Gardiner 1933, 1935. Die Dekoration der Kapellen ist ausführlich behandelt bei David 1973, 87–144, bes. 92–126 (mit weiterer Lit.); etwas weniger ausführlich in dies. 1981, 57–82, bes. 60–74.
2. Vgl. Barguet 1962a, 25 f.
3. Diese beiden Szenen (Nr. 11 u. 28) sind ihrerseits dann an die Stelle von zwei anderen getreten, und zwar von Nr. 7 und 32 (unter Verdrängung von Nr. 3 und 33).
4. Vgl. David 1973, 146–66; dies. 1981, 83–97.
5. Zusammengestellt in David 1973, 104–19. Vgl. auch Arnold 1962, 22–24; de Wit 1968, 145.
6. Vgl. Königliche Museen 1901, Einleitung; Altenmüller 1969, 17.

Gold of Praise: Studies on Ancient Egypt in Honor of Edward F. Wente
Edited by Emily Teeter and John A. Larson
Studies in Ancient Oriental Civilization 58
Chicago: Oriental Institute, 1999

beiden Ritualpapyri die Abfolge der Kulthandlungen, auf die es bei einem Vergleich vor allem ankommt, ja nicht nur so weitgehend übereinstimmt, sondern auch durchaus sinnvoll ist.

Wie ein Vergleich zeigt, finden sich die meisten von den 36 Abydos-Szenen in den beiden Ritualpapyri wieder. 14 Szenen sind dort nicht vertreten, doch lässt sich die Position der meisten hiervon durch Handlungsinhalt oder Kontext sicher oder als wahrscheinlich bestimmen. Für das zugrundeliegende Ritual wird man annehmen dürfen, dass die beiden thebanischen Ritual-Papyri aus der 22. Dyn. ebenso wie die Abfolge der Abydos-Szenen aus längeren Versionen verkürzt sind.[7]

Von den obengenannten Rekonstruktionen der Szenenfolge in den Abydos-Kapellen ist die von Roeder (1960, 72–141) die einzige, die sich durchgängig auf die beiden Ritualpapyri stützt und die dort nicht vertretenen Szenen nach Handlungsinhalt und Kontext plausibel einordnet. Dabei ist es allerdings sicherlich erforderlich, die jeweils zwei kongruenten, übergrossen Barkenszenen ausser Betracht zu lassen, bei denen als Kulthandlung immer die für Barkenszenen übliche Weihräucherung (auf Räucherarm) dargestellt ist (Altenmüller-Kesting 1968, 181 f.). Der Szene der Südwand sind zudem zwei unterschiedliche Sprüche beigeschrieben, die ihrerseits nur Dubletten zu den Sprüchen der Szenen 11 (so bei Amun-Ra, Ra [und einst Ptah?]) bzw. 33 oder 18 (so bei Horus und Isis und entsprechend bei Osiris) sind. In der Szene der Nordwand erscheint ein Spruch mit der Überschrift *ỉrt sntr ḫft wn ḥr m sḥtpy* "Weihräucherung mit dem Räucherarm beim Öffnen des Gesichts", der in den Ritual-Papyri fehlt, aber eng mit dem "Öffnen der beiden Türflügel" von Szene 5 verbunden sein dürfte.

Mit der Ausklammerung dieser beiden Barkenszenen ergäbe sich als Szenenfolge:

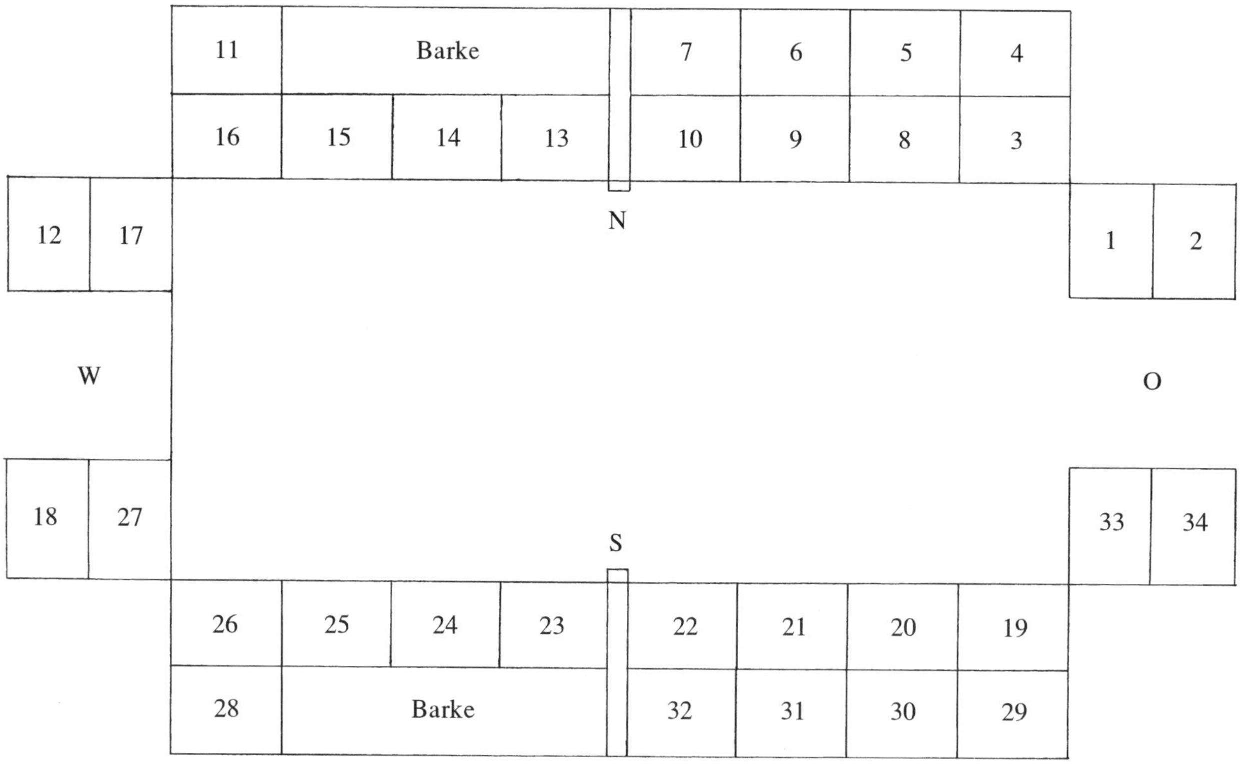

1: *ʿq r wn ḥr m ḫnw n ḥwt ʿ3t ḥnʿ pr.w nṯr.w nty r gs pr wr* eintreten, um das Gesicht zu öffnen in dem Tempel (*ḥwt ʿ3t*) und den Götterkapellen, die neben dem Sanktuar (*pr wr*) sind;

2: *sd sỉn* den Ton brechen;[8]

3: *sfḫt ḏbʿyt* das Siegel lösen;

4: *sṯ3 s* den Riegel fortziehen;

5: *wn ʿ3.wy* die beiden Türflügel öffnen;

6: *m33 nṯr* den Gott sehen;

7: *sn t3 rdt ḥr ḫt r sn t3 m ḏbʿ.w.f* die Erde küssen, sich auf den Bauch geben, um die Erde zu küssen mit seinen Fingern;

8: *ỉrt sntr n ʿrʿt* dem Uräus weihräuchern;

9: *ʿq r sḫm* in das Allerheiligste eintreten;

10: *ʿq r st wrt* (*n pr wr n nṯr pn*) in den Schrein (des Sanktuars dieses Gottes) eintreten;

11: *dw3 nṯr sp 4 ỉrt sntr ḫft ʿq r stp-s3* den Gott verehren viermal, weihräuchern beim Eintreten in den Schrein;

7. Vgl. Roeder 1960, 84; Barta 1966, 120–22.

8. Vgl. Graefe 1971, 147–55; ders. 1993, 155.

12: *dwꜣ nṯrt sp 4* die Göttin verehren viermal;

13: *ḏfw pr wr* das Sanktuar auswischen;

14: *rdt ꜥ.wy ḥr nṯr* die Arme auf den Gott legen;

15: *sfḫ(t) mḏt* die Salbe lösen;

16: *sfḫ mnḫt* die Kleidung lösen;

17: *smꜥr ḥꜥw m nms* den Körper mit dem *nms*-Tuch bekleiden;

18: *ỉrt ꜥbw m snṯr ḥr sḏt pḫr ḥꜣ sp 4* Reinigung vollziehen mit Weihrauch auf Feuer, herumgehen viermal;

19: *ḏbꜣ mnḫt ḥḏt* weisse Kleidung anlegen;

20: *ḏbꜣ mnḫt wꜣḏt* grüne Kleidung anlegen;

21: *ḏbꜣ mnḫt ỉnsy* rote Kleidung anlegen;

22: *rdt wsḫ* den Halskragen geben;

23: *rdt šspt mꜥnḫt* Halsbinde und -troddel geben;

24: *smnt šw.ty m tp* die Doppelfeder am Kopf befestigen;

25: *rdt wꜣs ḥqꜣ nḫꜣḫꜣ* das *wꜣs*-Szepter, Krummstab und Geissel geben;

26: *rdt (ḥnk) mḏt* Salbe geben (schenken);

27: *ḥbs m mnḫt ꜥꜣt ḥr sꜣ nn* danach mit dem 'grossen Gewand' bekleiden;

28: *ỉrt wšꜣ šꜥy* das Sandschütten machen;

29: *ỉrt ꜥbw m ṯꜣ.w 4 n bd* Reinigung vollziehen mit 4 Kugeln von *bd*-Natron;

30: *ỉrt ꜥbw m ṯꜣ.w 4 šmꜥwy nw Nḫb* Reinigung vollziehen mit 4 Kugeln von oberägypt. Natron aus Elkab;

31: *ỉrt ꜥbw m ṯꜣ.w 4 mḥwy nw Šrpt* Reinigung vollziehen mit 4 Kugeln von unterägypt. Natron vom Wadi Natrun;

32: *ỉrt ꜥbw m ỉꜥb n qbḥw m 4 ṯꜣ.w nw snṯr* Reinigung vollziehen aus dem Libationsgefäss mit 4 Kugeln von Weihrauch;

33: *ỉrt ꜥbw m snṯr ḥr sḏt pḫr ḥꜣ sp 4* Reinigung vollziehen mit Weihrauch auf Feuer, herumgehen viermal;

34: *ỉnt rd m hdn* 'den Fuss zurückholen' mit der *hdn*-Pflanze.

Entsprechungen zwischen den Kulthandlungen in Abydos (1. Spalte) und in den Ritualpapyri (2. Spalte):

1 = —	10 = (23)	19 = 52	28 = 60
2 = 8	11 = 35–40, 42	20 = 53	29 = 62
3 = 9	12 = —	21 = 54	30 = 63
4 = 9a	13 = —	22 = —	31 = 64
5 = 10	14 = 46	23 = —	32 = 66
6 = 11	15 = —	24 = —	33 = 67
7 = 12	16 = —	25 = —	34 = —
8 = —	17 = —	26 = 56	
9 = 23	18 = 50	27 = —	

Einige problematische Zuordnungen und die in den Papyri nicht vertretenen Szenen bedürfen dabei noch der Erläuterung:

1: Die Einordnung von *ꜥq r wn ḥr* "eintreten, um das Gesicht zu öffnen" ganz zu Anfang ist bisher von fast allen Bearbeitern (ausser Barta) als evident angenommen worden.

2–5: Die Abfolge 2–3 (so auch David) ist durch p3055 gesichert (in umgekehrter Folge bei Roeder, Altenmüller-Kesting, und Altenmüller). In p3053 ist der Spruch zum *sfḫ ḏbꜥ* (Sz. 3) durch den zum *sṯꜣ s* (Sz. 4) ersetzt. In dem späten Ritualpapyrus *PSI* I 70–2, 21–22 (Rosati 1998, 110, tav. 15) geht das *sfḫ ḏbꜥt*, mit *sḏ ỉdr* kombiniert, allerdings dem *sḏ sỉn* voraus.

Im Schrein des Horus ist Sz. 2 durch eine Begrüssungsszene ersetzt.

Mehrere von den Handlungen beim Öffnen des Schreins -mit Darstellung des Schreins- finden sich auch sonst zu Szenenfolgen zusammengestellt: Sz. 2-4-5 auf der Ostwand der grossen Säulenhalle von Karnak (Zeit Sethos' I.)[9]; (8-)2-4 im Totentempel Ramses' III. in Medinet Habu (*MH* 4, pl. 241; Nelson 1949a); 4-5 in dem von Sethos I. in Gurna (Anhang 14).

In den Szenen 1–5 zum Betreten und Öffnen des Sanktuars ist der Gott in dessen Innerem dargestellt.[10]

9: Die Übereinstimmung beschränkt sich auf den Spruchtitel. Spr. 23 selbst erscheint unter einem anderen Titel erst in Sz. 10.

11: In der Kombination von "Verehren" und "Weihräuchern" entspricht die Szene sicherlich den aufeinander folgenden Sprüchen 35–36 ("Weihräuchern") und 37–40, 42 ("Verehren") im p3055. Ohne eine solche Verbindung erscheint im p3055 ein "Verehren" des Gottes auch in Spruch 18–19.

---

9. Vgl. Nelson 1949a, 202–06; Nelson 1981, pls. 227, 264; Bakry 1968, pl. 15 nach S. 14.

10. So auch sonst (vgl. die genannten Szenen in Karnak und Medinet Habu sowie unten Anhang Nr. 14, 15A–B, 16A [*sfḫ ḏbꜥt*]).

12: Wohl noch eng mit Sz. 11 verbunden.

13: Beim "Auswischen, Putzen des Sanktuars" (*ḏfw pr-wr*), das mir sonst nur noch aus dem Totentempel Sethos' I. in Gurna und(?) dem Horus-Tempel in Buhen bekannt (Caminos 1974, 98 f., pls. 81 f.) ist (s.u. Anhang 14 und 9), werden in der Darstellung die Beine des Götterbildes gereinigt. Eine Einordnung vor die Szenen 14–16 ist daher sinnvoll.

14–16: Das "Lösen der Salbe" (15) und das "Lösen der Kleidung" (16) sollten in umgekehrter Reihenfolge zum "Anlegen der (weissen, grünen, roten) Kleidung" (20–22) und zum "Geben von Salbe" (27) stehen. Vgl. auch die Parallele auf dem Alexander-Sanktuar (s.u. Anhang 16).

In der 18. Dyn. sind die Handlungen von Sz. 14 u. 16 sowie von 16 u. 19–21 gelegentlich kombiniert (s. Anhang 3, 7, 10, 11).

Die gleichartigen Szenen 18 (bei Isis unter dem gleichen Titel allerdings ein anderer Spruch) und 33 liessen sich in ihrer Position austauschen.

17: Das "Bekleiden des Körpers mit dem *nms*-Tuch" (*smʿr ḥʿw m nms*), das erst nach dem "Lösen der Kleidung" (16) erfolgen kann, ist nach einer Parallele im Luxor-Tempel (Anhang 13) sicher vor die Reinigung mit *nmst*- und *dšrt*-Gefässen (— = 48–49) und mit Weihrauch (18 = 50) zu setzen. Vgl. auch die Parallelen in Anhang 16 und 14.

22–25: Das Anlegen von Halskragen (vgl. Handoussa 1981, 143–50), Halsbinde und -troddel (*šspt mʿnḫt*), Doppelfeder sowie *wꜣs*-Szepter, Krummstab und Geissel ist plausibel zwischen die genannten Szenen 19–21 und 26 gesetzt. In einer Luxor-Parallele steht das Anlegen von Armbändern und Halstroddel allerdings vor dem "Anlegen der Kleidung" (*ḏbꜣ mnḫt*) (s. Anhang 13).

ḥbs m mnḫt ʿꜣt ḥr sꜣ nn "danach mit dem grossen Gewand bekleiden" müsste sich bei der vorgeschlagenen Einordnung als Sz. 27 auf das Einhüllen des schon bekleideten, mit allen Insignien versehenen und gesalbten Götterbildes beziehen. Man könnte allerdings auch erwägen, es zwischen das "Anlegen der (weissen, grünen, roten) Kleidung" (19–21) und das Anlegen der übrigen Kleidungsstücke und der Insignien (22–25) einzuordnen.

31: Vom Titel des Spruches ist in p3053+3014, XXX 2 nur das abschliessende  [*Šr*]*pt* erhalten.

34: Das "Zurückholen des Fusses" ist als abschliessende Ritualhandlung gut bekannt.[11]

Wenngleich in beschränktem Rahmen einige Unsicherheiten verbleiben, ist die Rekonstruktion von Roeder insgesamt doch so schlüssig, dass sich nur noch die Frage stellt, nach welchen Gesichtspunkten die vorliegende Verteilung der Szenen geordnet ist. Es ist ein bestimmendes Prinzip zu erkennen, doch ist dieses durch mehrere interne Ausgleichungen abgeschwächt. Grundsätzlich folgen sich die Szenen vom Eingang an entgegen dem Uhrzeigersinn von einer Wandhälfte zur nächsten und mit den Szenen des oberen Registers vor denen des unteren. Auf den Längswänden beginnt die Abfolge dabei stets im Osten. In vier Punkten ist diese Anordnung abgeändert:

1. In der rückwärtigen Raumhälfte sind die Szenen der Nord- und der Südwand um die anschliessenden Szenen in der Nord- bzw. Südhälfte der Westwand erweitert, auf der Südseite allerdings nur im unteren Register.
2. Auf der Südwand ist das untere Register durchlaufend und nicht nach Wandhälften unterteilt dekoriert. Hierdurch ist hier das ganze obere Register mit Reinigungsszenen und das untere mit Szenen zur Bekleidung und Salbung des Götterbildes dekoriert.
3. Auf der Südwand geht in der Abfolge der Szenen ausserdem das untere Register dem oberen voran. Hierdurch sind die Reinigungsszenen hier im selben Register mit den beiden Reinigungsszenen in der Südhälfte der Ost- und der Westwand verbunden.

11. Vgl. *Wb.* 1.91:7; Davies und Gardiner 1915, 93 f.; Clère 1939, 215 f.; Nelson 1949a, 310–13; Nelson 1949b, 82–86; Altenmüller 1971, 146–53 (die dort vorgeschlagene Interpretation von *rd* "Fuss" als Schreibung von *rḏw* "Sekret, Ausfluss" ist nicht überzeugend); Lacau und Chevrier 1977, 293 u. 362; Lacau und Chevrier 1979, pls. 15 (156), 21 (257); Goyon 1984, 241–50.

4. Zu Anfang der Nordseite sind Sz. 1 u. 3 unter Sz. 2 u. 4 gesetzt. Hierdurch stehen die drei Szenen 2–4, die das Öffnen der Tür des Götterschreins behandeln und -zusammen mit Sz. 5- diese Tür auch darstellen, so nahe wie nur möglich an der Tür des Raumes, und die Szenen 5–7 schliessen unmittelbar an Sz. 4 an.

Ähnlich ist dies im Sanktuar des Amun-Ra von Karnak im Totentempel Sethos' I. in Gurna geschehen. Auch hier sind eben die drei Szenen, die das Öffnen der Tür des Götterschreins (3, 5) und dessen Auswischen (13) zum Gegenstand haben und den Schrein mit seiner Tür auch darstellen, direkt neben die Eingangstür gesetzt (als vierte Szene dazu das "Zurückholen des Fusses":[12] s. Anhang 14.

Es sei zum Schluss noch erwähnt, dass die einzelnen Kulthandlungen, wie ein Vergleich zwischen den Kapellen zeigt, nicht fest mit einem bestimmten Ornat des Königs verbunden sind.[13] Die Formen des Gewandes und der Kopftracht (verschiedene Hauben und die "Blaue Krone", aber keine eigentlichen Kronen) zeigen in den Versionen der verschiedenen Kapellen eine grosse Variation.

ANHANG: SZENENFOLGEN AUS DEM KULTBILDRITUAL IN ANDEREN TEMPELN

Ausschnitte aus dem Kultbildritual sind häufig in die Dekoration von Wänden, Säulen und Pfeilern von Tempeln aufgenommen. Meist erscheinen sie hier zwar nur isoliert neben den noch viel häufigeren Szenen aus dem Opferritual, mehrfach aber auch in längeren Sequenzen. Diese finden sich vor allem bei den Kultbildkammern, sonst nur vereinzelt (s.u. Nr. 1). Im folgenden sind solche längeren Sequenzen aus Tempeln des Neuen Reiches (vgl. hierzu grundlegend Arnold 1962, 7–24) und der griech.-röm. Zeit zusammengestellt. In denen aus Theben ist dabei fast immer Amun-Ra als Kultempfänger dargestellt, und zwar, wie in Theben bei Szenenfolgen dieser Art üblich, alternierend in normal menschengestaltiger und in ithyphallischer Form.

Es verdient Erwähnung, dass auf den inneren Längswänden einiger Sanktuare die Szenen retrograd angeordnet sind[14], d.h. von hinten nach vorn zum Eingang hin, umgekehrt zur Blickrichtung des Königs. In der thematischen Auswahl fällt der hohe Anteil an Reinigungsszenen auf.[15]

Den einzelnen Szenen ist im folgenden die Zählung der Abydos-Kapellen (1. Spalte) und der Ritualpapyri (2. Spalte) zugeordnet. Die hieroglyphischen Beischriften zu den Szenenfolgen 1–3, teilweise auch zu 5, verdanke ich J. Karkowski (1–2, 5) und M. G. Witkowski (3), die hierfür jeweils die Publikation vorbereiten. Die Angaben zu anderen Beischriften beruhen teilweise (Nr. 5–8) oder ganz (Nr. 14, 18) auf eigenen Unterlagen (1979).[16]

————————→ = Abfolge von Szenen

———— K ————→ = Blickrichtung des Königs

1. Totentempel der Hatschepsut in Deir el-Bahri, Südwand des oberen Hofes, unteres Register (PM 2, 358 (85), Abb. 35; Karkowski 1978, 399; Karkowski 1979, 217 f.)

Reinigung durch Seth und Horus	*dwꜣ nṯr sp 4* 11 = 37–40, 42	*sfḫt dbꜣ mnḫt* 16 = — und 19–21 = 52–55	*mw m nmst 4* — = 48	[*d*]*w mḏt* 26 = 56	*rdt wsḫ* 22 = —	großes Opfer

———————— K ————————→

12. In Zeichnung in Nelson 1949b, 83. Die Szene des *int rd* findet sich auch im Raum IX dieses Totentempels, aber auch sonst innen unmittelbar an der Tür eines Tempelraums (vgl. die Belege in Nelson 1949b, 82 f.; Brunner 1977, Tf. 22, 119).
13. Beim *int rd* (Sz. 34) ist der König allerdings, wie auch in den sonstigen Belegen aus der 19. und 20. Dyn. (Nelson 1949b, 83 f.), immer im langen Gewand dargestellt, ebenso in Sz. 14 und 32, beim *smnt šw.ty* immer mit der enganliegenden Haube.
14. Nr. 2A (a–c, d–e), 2B (a–b, d–e), 3 (e–i), 5 (XXIII), 7 (b–d), 10 (a–b, f–g), 17, 18B.
Bei hieroglyphischen Texten, die in Kolumnen geschrieben sind, kann sich, vor allem in engen Gängen oder Räumen, in ähnlicher Weise retrograde Anordnung finden: Lacau und Chevrier 1977, 92–94; Naville 1901, pl. 57–62 (Blöcke einer älteren Version aus der Zeit Amenemhats III. in Staatliche Museen zu Berlin 1913, 138 f., 268); *LD* 3, 12; die Inschriften Thutmoses III. und Sesostris' I. in Karnak (PM 2, 106 f., Nr. 328 u. 330; Habachi 1985, 349 ff.; Redford 1987, 46); *MH* 1, pls. 27–28.
15. Vgl. Altenmüller-Kesting 1968, 184 f., 189–91.
16. Aufgenommen im Rahmen eines Forschungsprojekts "Ritualszenen in ägyptischen Tempeln des Neuen Reiches", für das ich 1978/79 ein Stipendium der Deutschen Forschungsgemeinschaft erhalten hatte.

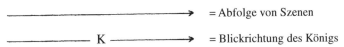

2A–B. Totentempel der Hatschepsut in Deir el-Bahri, (A) Barkenraum (Rückwände der 6 seitlichen Nischen) und (B) Kultbildkammer des Amun-Ra (PM 2, 366 f.; Arnold 1962, 11; Van Siclen 1987, 21–24; Karkowski 1983, 94–101; Karkowski 1990, 350; Wysocki 1986, 214 [Plan], 222 f.)

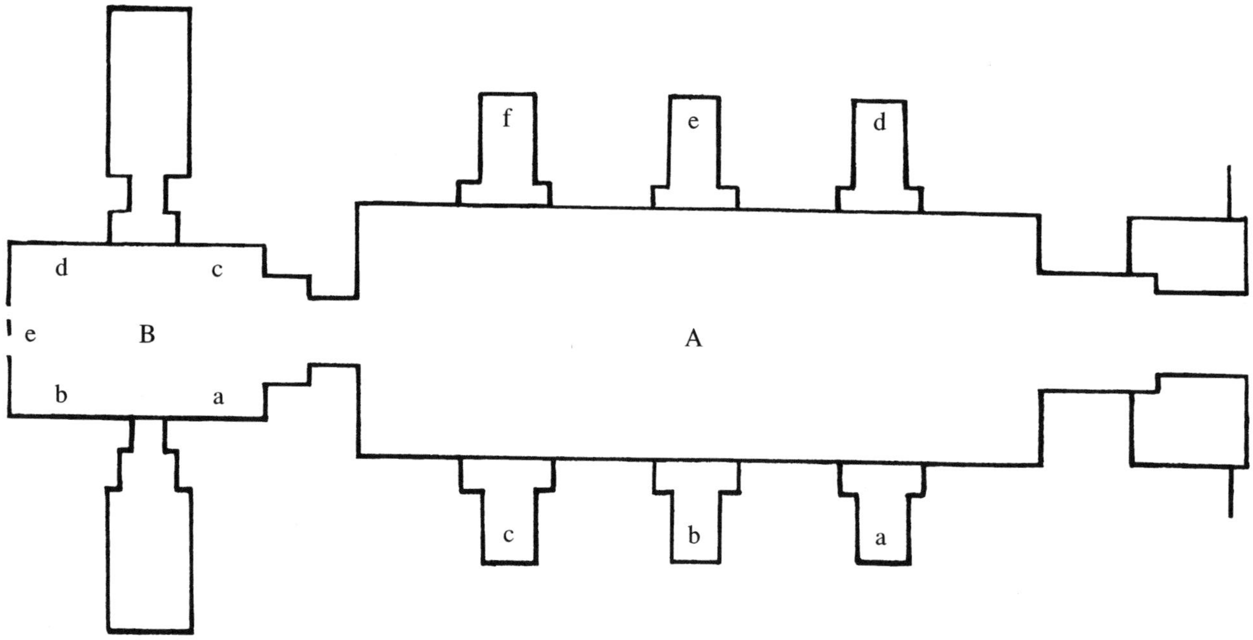

A. a: *snṯr tꜣ 1 iṯ r rʿ pẖr ḥꜣ sp 4* (32 = 66)
b: *nṯrỉ tꜣ 5 ỉṯ r rʿ pẖr ḥꜣ sp 4* (30–31 = 63–64)
c: *mw nmst 4 pẖr ḥꜣ sp 4* (— = 48)
d: *snṯr tꜣ 5 iṯ r rʿ pẖr ḥꜣ sp 4* (32 = 66)
e: *bd tꜣ 5 ỉṯ r rʿ pẖr ḥꜣ sp 4* (29 = 62)
f: *mw dšrt 4 pẖr ḥꜣ sp 4* (— = 49)

B. a: *snṯr tꜣ 1 pẖr ḥꜣ sp 4* (32 = 66)
b: *mw nmst 4 pẖr ḥꜣ sp 4* (— = 48)
c: *bd tꜣ (1) šmʿ ỉṯ r rʿ pẖr ḥꜣ sp 4* (29 = 62)
nṯrỉ tꜣ 5 mḥw ỉṯ r rʿ pẖr ḥꜣ sp 4 (30–31 = 63–64)
d: *[mw] dšrt 4 pẖr ḥꜣ sp 4* (— = 49)
e: nicht erhalten

3A–B. Totentempel der Hatschepsut in Deir el-Bahri, Kultbildkammern des Anubis im 2. und im oberen Hof (in Anlage und Dekoration übereinstimmend) (PM 2, 355, 362 f., Abb. 35 f.; Naville 1901, pl. 10–11 u. 44–45; Arnold 1962, 11–13 [2 und 4]; Witkowski 1989, 431–40; Witkowski 1990, 369–92)

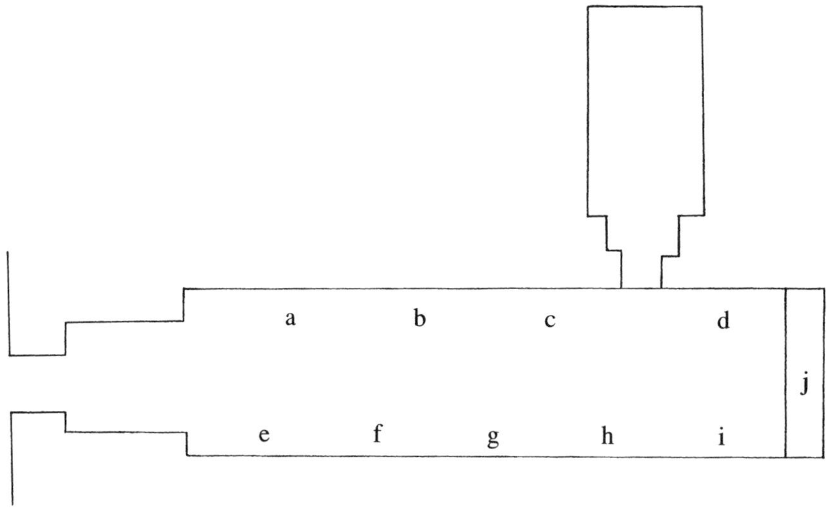

a: *dw mḏt* (26 = 56)
b: *wšꜣ šʿ* (28 = 60)
c: *swʿb m snṯr* (18 = 50 oder 33 = 67)
d: Empfangen von "Leben"
e: *nṯrỉ tꜣ 5 nṯrỉ tꜣ 1 ỉt r rʿ* <*pẖr*> *ḥꜣ sp 4* (30–31 = 63–64)
f: *bd tꜣ 5 bd tꜣ 1 ỉṯ r rʿ pẖr ḥꜣ sp 4* (29 = 62)
g: *mw dšrt 4 pẖr ḥꜣ sp 4* (— = 49)
h: *mw nmst 4 pẖr ḥꜣ sp 4* (— = 48)
i: *sfḫt ḏbꜣ mnḫt* (16 = — und 19–21 = 52–55)
j: *dwꜣ nṯr sp 4* (11 = 37–40, 42)

Die vier bzw. fünf Szenen aus dem Kultbildritual auf den Längswänden bilden zwei separate, kontinuierliche Abfolgen, auf der linken Wand (vom Eingang aus gesehen) nach innen hin fortschreitend, auf der rechten in retrograder Anordnung.

4. Quarzit-Sanktuar der Hatschepsut in Karnak: Drei zusammenhängende Blöcke mit Reinigung (Lacau und Chevrier 1977, 335–37; Lacau und Chevrier 1979, pl. 19)

[*mw nmst 4 pẖr ḥꜣ sp 4*] (— = 48)
mw dšrt 4 pẖr ḥꜣ sp 4 (— = 49)
ꜥ n snṯr pẖr ḥꜣ sp 4 (32 = 66)

5. Karnak, Kultbildkammern XX–XXIII in dem Trakt südlich vom Sanktuar des Philipp Arrhidäus, unteres Reg. (Zeit der Hatschepsut) (PM 2, 105 f., Abb. 12; Arnold 1962, 14 f. [6–9; Raum XXII und XXIII vertauscht], 48 f., 117 f. und Plan Abb. 6 [vgl. auch 73 f.]; Barguet 1962b, 146–48)[17]

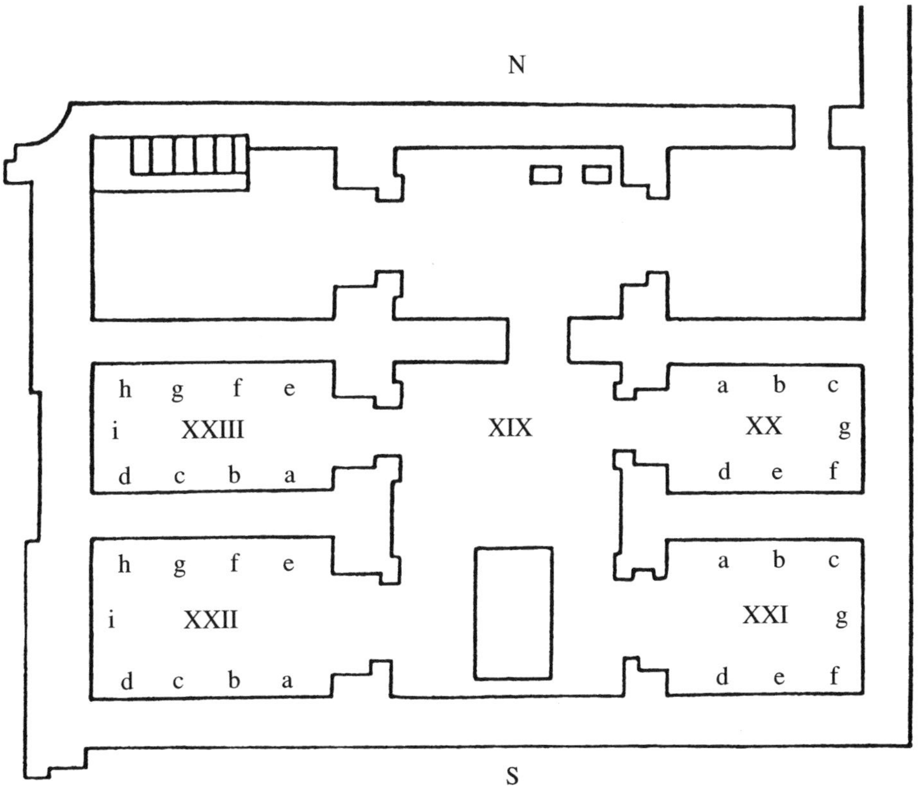

XX (alle Szenen vor dem ithyphallischen Amun-Ra):
- a: *rdt ỉrt ꜥ.wy ỉrt rd.wy* (4 Arm- und Fussbänder)[18]
- b: Verehrung
- c: Aufsetzen der Federkrone
- d: zerstört
- e: Hände an den Körper des Gottes gelegt
- f: zerstört
- g: 2 antithetische Szenen (Nord: Umarmung; Süd: zerstört)

XXI:
- a: Libation auf zwei Opferständer (Beischrift zerstört)
- b: *rdt ỉrp*
- c: zerstört
- d: weitgehend zerstört (Darbringen von Opfergaben)
- e: [*swꜥb*] *m nmst* (— = 48)
- f: [*rdt*] *qbḥ*
- g: [*rdt*] *mḏt* (26 = 56)

XXII:
- a: *bd ṯꜣ 1 ỉṯ r rꜥ ỉṯ r ꜥ pẖr ḥꜣ sp 4* (29 = 62)
- b: *bd ṯꜣ 5 ỉṯ r rꜥ ỉṯ rꜥ pẖr ḥꜣ sp 4* (29 = 62)
- c: *nṯrỉ ṯꜣ 1 ỉṯ r rꜥ ỉṯ rꜥ pẖr ḥꜣ sp 4* (30–31 = 63–64)
- d: *nṯrỉ ṯꜣ 5 ỉṯ r rꜥ ỉṯ rꜥ pẖr ḥꜣ sp 4* (30–31 = 63–64)
- e: zerstört
- f: *rdt wsḫ* (22 = —)
- g: *wšꜣ šꜥ* (28 = 60)
- h: *ỉrt snṯr*
- i: zerstört

17. Die Angaben zu den Szenen XXI d.f und XXIII a verdanke ich J. Karkowski.

18. Zu einer Parallele vgl. Lacau und Chevrier 1977, 362; Lacau und Chevrier 1979, pl. 21 (210).

XXIII:

a: weitgehend zerstört (Übergiessen mit Wasser [aus *dšrt*-Krug?]; — = 49?)

b: *mw nmst 4 pḫr ḥȝ sp 4* (Übergiessen mit Wasser aus *nmst*-Krug; — = 48)

c: *smʿ[r] m nms* "mit dem *nms*-Tuch bekleiden" (Hände auf die Schulter des Gottes gelegt; 17 = —)

d: Bekleidung[19] (Hände auf die Schulter des Gottes gelegt; 19–21 = 52–55)

e: [...] *pḫr ḥȝ sp 4* (wohl eine von den Szenen 29–31 = 62–64)

f: *snṯr tȝ 5 ỉṯ r rʿ ỉṯ rʿ pḫr ḥȝ sp 4* (32 = 66)

g: *dw mḏ* (4 Salbgefässe; 26 = 56)

h: zerstört

i: *wdn ḥtp nṯr*

Die meisten Szenen entstammen dem Kultbildritual, nur wenige dem Opferritual. Da in jeder Kapelle zwei Szenen zerstört sind, lassen sich keine Aussagen über die Szenenfolge in den einzelnen Kapellen treffen.

In den Szenen von Raum XX–XXIII ist als Gott ausschliesslich Amun-Ra dargestellt, alternierend in normal menschengestaltiger und in ithyphallischer Form. Inwieweit ein Zusammenhang mit den vier Göttern (Dedun, Sopd, Sobek, Horus) besteht, die mit dem auf der Rückwand von Raum XIX dargestellten *ḥts*-Fest verbunden waren, ist unklar.[20]

6. Medinet Habu, Tempel der 18. Dynastie (Thutmose III.)
(Nelson 1941, pl. 27; PM 2, 471 (67–70); Arnold 1962, 15)

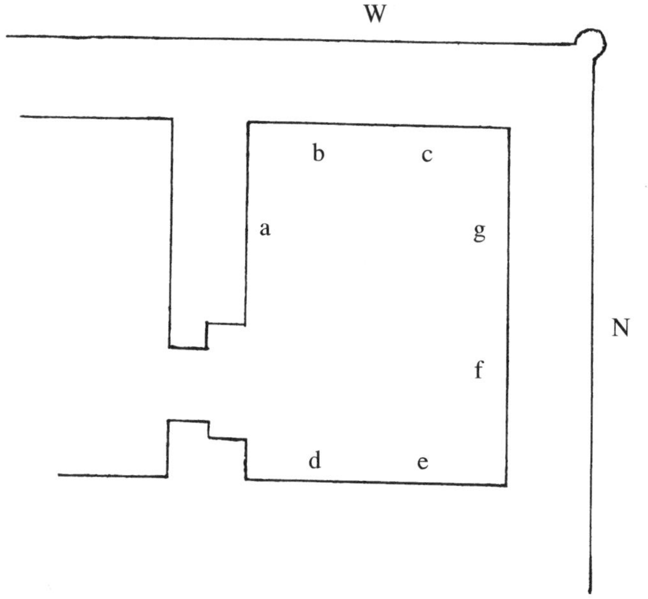

a: *rdt ỉrtt*

b: *ỉrt snṯr*

c: [*wšȝ*] *šʿ* (28 = 60)

d: *ḏbȝ mnḫt* (19–21 = 52–55)

e: zerstört

f: *mw* [*nmst*(?) (*dšrt*?) *4 ỉṯ r r ỉṯ r* ʿ] *pḫr ḥȝ* [*sp 4*] (— = 48/49)

g: *mw nmst 4 ỉṯ r r ỉṯ r ʿ pḫr ḥȝ sp 4* (— = 48)

In Szene f und g ist eine ursprüngliche Darstellung des Königs (Hatschepsut), von der darüber noch Kartuschen und ein fliegender Geier erhalten sind, getilgt und durch aufgehäufte Opfergaben und darüber ein *ʿnḫ*-Zeichen mit Armen, welches Amun ein (gelbes) Gefäss darreicht, ersetzt worden.

19. Von der Beischrift ist nur das abschliessende [𓏥] erhalten (vgl. Barguet 1962b, 146).

20. Vgl. Barguet 1962b, 145 f.; Parker, Leclant und Goyon 1979, 65–69 mit n. 1 auf 65 sowie pl. 26.

7A–B. Karnak, Sanktuare des Ptah und der Hathor im Ptah-Tempel (Thutmose III.)
(PM 2, 201, Abb. 16; Legrain 1902, 106 f.; Arnold 1962, 16 f. [vgl. auch 49])

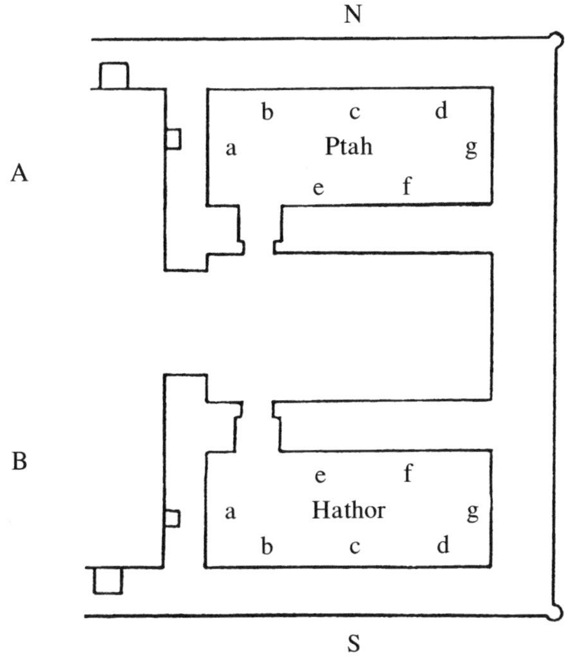

a: *wšꜣ šꜥ* (28 = 60)
b: (*bd*) *ṯꜣw 5 nṯrỉ ṯꜣw 5 ỉṯ r r ỉṯ r ꜥ pẖr ḥꜣ sp 4* (29 = 62 und 30–31 = 63–64)
c: *mw nmst* [*4*] *mw dšrt 4 ỉṯ r r ỉṯ r ꜥ pẖr ḥꜣ sp 4* (— = 48–49)
d: *sfḫt mnḫt ḏbꜣ mnḫt* (16 = — und 19–21 = 52–55)
e: *rdt qbḥw* (-)
f: König von der Gottheit umfangen (-)
g: *wrḥ ꜥntw* (Ptah) bzw. *dỉt mḏt* (Hathor; 26 = 56)

8. Karnak, Festtempel Thutmoses III., Raum XXX (PM 2, 120, Abb. 12 f.; Arnold 1962, 17)

Alle Kulthandlungen vor dem ithyphallischen Amun-Ra.

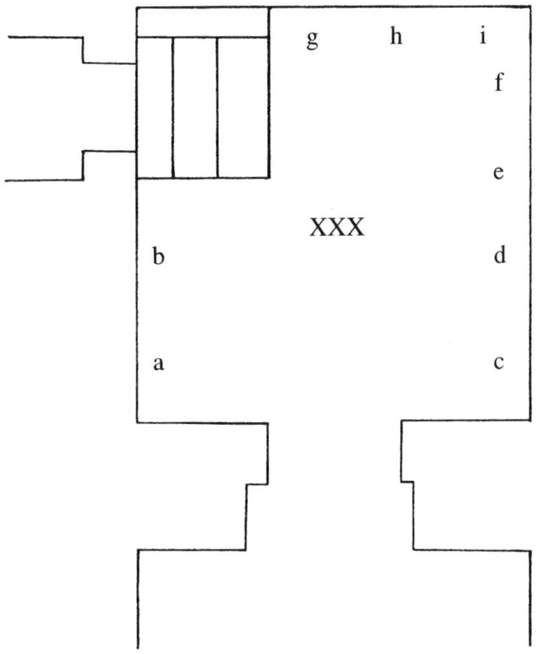

a: [*ꜥbw m nmst*] *4* (— = 48)
b: [*ꜥbw m*] *dšrt 4* (— = 49)
c–f: nicht erhaltene Kulthandlungen
g–i: weitgehend zerstörte Reinigungsszenen (Beischrift jeweils: ... *ỉṯ r r*] *ꜥ pẖr ḥꜣ sp 4* (wohl 29–32 = 62–64, 66)

9. Buhen, Sanktuar des Horus-Tempels (Thutmose III.) (Caminos 1974, 83–99, pl. 1 u. 72–82)

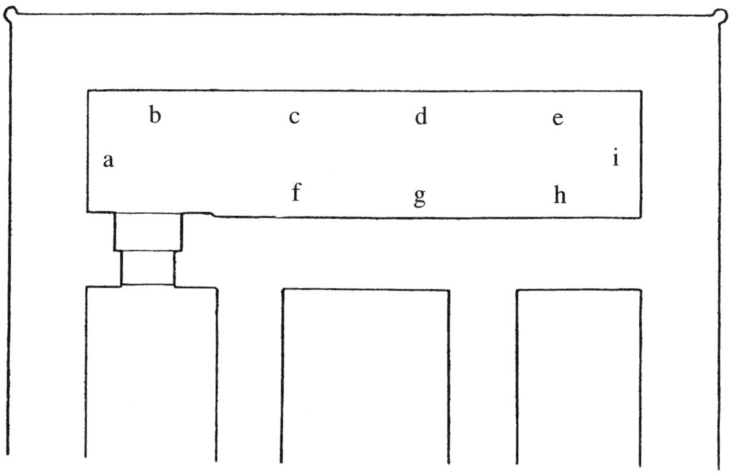

a: Auswischen des Sanktuars[21] (13 = —)

b:] *m ḫnw pr* (Verehrung oder "Schauen des Gottes"[22]; 11 = 37–40, 42 oder 6 = 11)

c: *bd* (*ṯꜣ*) *4 ỉṯ r r rmn pḫr ḥꜣ.f sp 4* (Reinigung; 29 = 62)

d:] *sp 4* (Reinigung; wohl eine von den Szenen 30–31 = 63–64)

e: *sntr ỉṯ r r rmn pḫr ḥꜣ.f sp 4* (Reinigung; 32 = 66)

f: Reinigung mit Wasser (— = 48–49?)

g:] *ṯꜣ ỉṯ r r rmn pḫr* [*ḥꜣ*]*.f sp 4* (Reinigung mit Natron; wohl eine von den Szenen 29–31 = 62–64)

h:] *qbḥ* [*sntr*] *ỉṯ r r rmn pḫr ḥꜣ.f sp 4* (32 = 66)

i: *ḥtp dỉ nswt*-Opfer

10. Amada, Sanktuare des Amun-Ra und des Reharachte (Thutmose III./Amenophis II.) (Barguet und Dewachter 1967, pl. 93–99, 109; Barguet, Youssef und Dewachter 1967, 49–51, 54–56, pl. 1; Aly, Abdel-Hamid, und Dewachter 1967, P 1–13 und R 1–13; Arnold 1962, 18 f.)

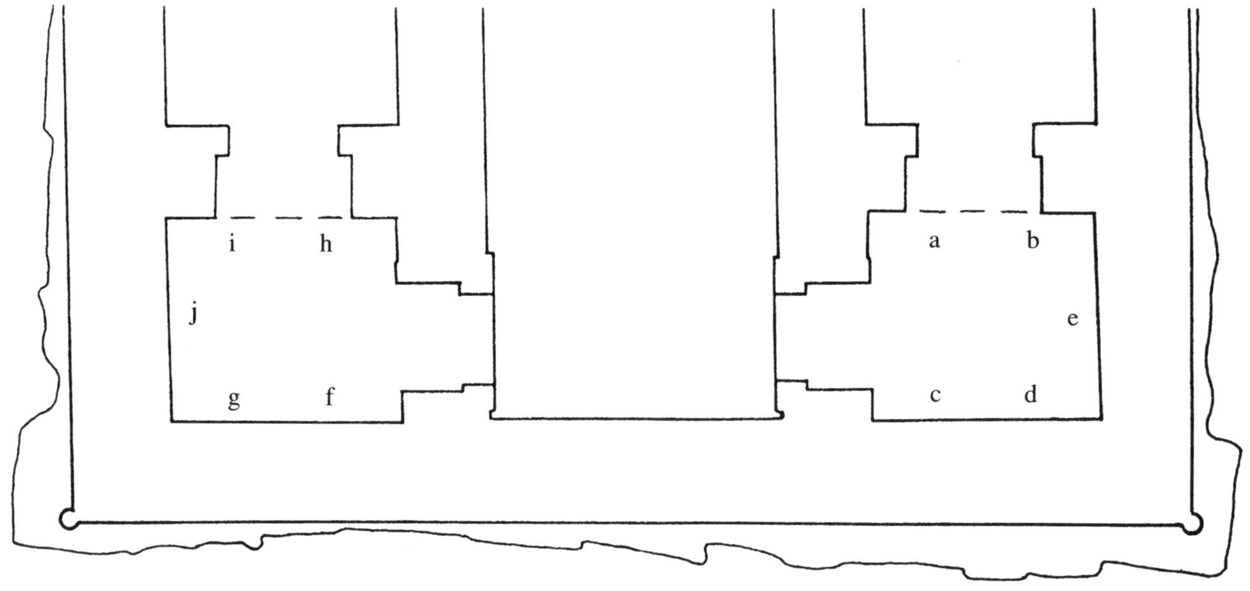

Die Wände der beiden Sanktuare sind in zwei Registern dekoriert, und zwar mit Szenen aus dem Kultbildritual (oberes Reg. der beiden Seitenwände, eine Szene im unteren) und dem Opferritual (unteres Reg., eine Szene im oberen sowie die Rückwand) sowie mit dem "Empfangen von Leben".

21. Eine identifizierende Beischrift fehlt. Ikonographisch entspricht die Szene am ehesten dem *ḏfw pr* im Totentempel Sethos' I. in Gurna (vgl. oben zu Sz. 13).

22. Nach der Ikonographie. Eine identifizierende Beischrift fehlt.

a oben: *ḏbꜣ mnḫt* (19–21 = 52–55)
b oben: *ỉrt ˁbw m nmst 4 nt mw [pḫr ḥꜣ sp 4]* (— = 48)
a–b unten: weitgehend zerstört
c oben: *rdt ˁ.wy ḥr nṯr sfḫt mnḫt* (14 = 46 und 15 = —)
d oben: *ˁb ḥtp-nṯr ṯs ḫt ḥr ḫꜣwt* (Opfer)
c unten: *rdt šˁt*, d unten: *ỉrt snṯr*
e oben: *rdt ḥḏw*, unten: *rdt ˁbw*
f oben: *rdt wꜣḏw msdmt* (— = 58–59)

g oben: *ḥnk m mḏt* (26 = 56)
f unten: *nḏ ḥr m nmst*
g unten: *rdt ˁntw* (— = 68)
h oben: Empfangen von Leben
i oben: *ỉrt ˁbw m dšrt 4 [nt mw] pḫr ḥꜣ sp 4* (— = 49)
h–i unten: weitgehend zerstört (h wohl wie die Szene darüber)
j oben: *rdt ỉrtt*, unten: *swˁb ḥtp-nṯr*

11. Kumma, Doppelsanktuar des Chnum *ỉtnw-pḏwt* und *ḥw ššꜣw* (Raum H und J; Amenophis II.) (PM 7, 146, 154; *LD* 3, 66c; *LD* Text 5, 216; Dunham und Janssen 1960, pl. 76–80; Caminos 1998, 82–88, pls. 65–73)

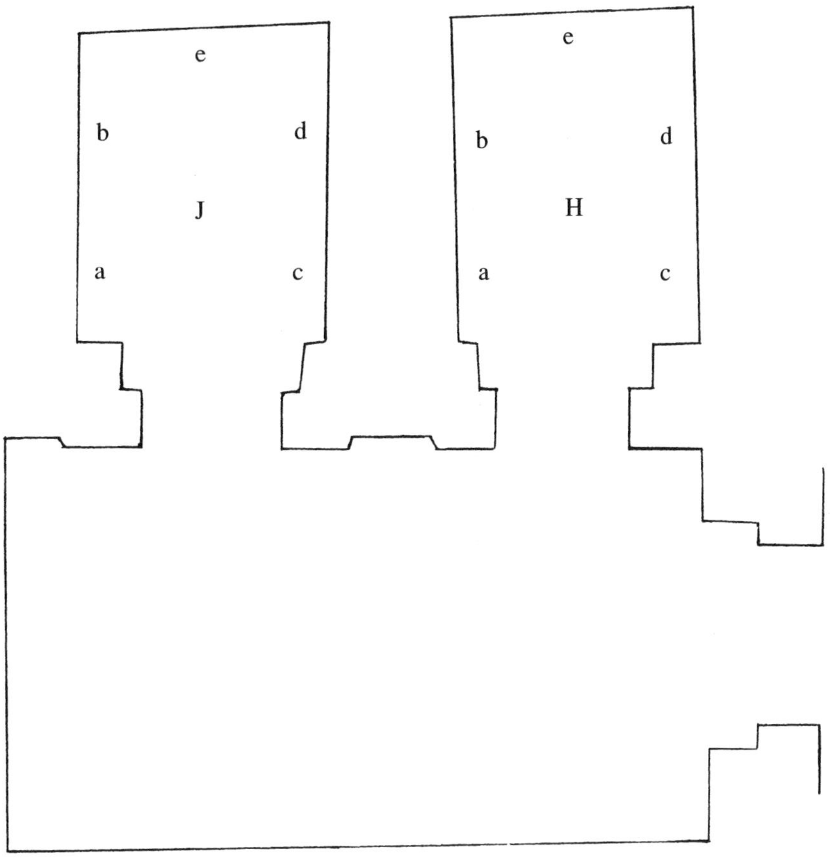

Die Szenen hier stimmen weitgehend mit denen aus dem Kultbildritual in den beiden Sanktuaren von Amada überein.

a: *rdt ˁ.wy ḥr nṯr sfḫt mnḫt* (14 = 46 und 15 = —)
b: *ḏbꜣ mnḫt* (19–21 = 52–55)
c: *ỉrt ˁbw m dšrt 4 nt mw pḫr ḥꜣ sp 4* (— = 49)
d: *ỉrt ˁbw m nmst 4 nt mw pḫr ḥꜣ sp 4* (— = 48)
e: *ỉrt qbḥ snṯr wdn ḥtp-nṯr* (Libation und Weihräucherung beim Opfer)

12A–B. Luxor, Sanktuar des Amun-Ra (Raum XIX), (A) Westwand und westl. Hälfte der Nordwand (neben der Tür), unteres Reg. und (B) Ostwand, mittleres Reg. (Amenophis III.) (Brunner 1977, Tf. 22–23, 25, 121–22, 124–28, 131–35)

A

4 Natrongefäße (29–31) = (62–64)	Salbe 26 = 56	Kleidung 19–21 = 52–55	Halstroddel 23 = —	5 Armbänder —	*wsḫ*-Halskragen 22 = —	Vasenlauf

← K — Westwand; ← K Nordwand

B

djt ʿ.wj ḥr nṯr 14 = 46	*r(d)t wḏ3w* —	*r(d)t ʿntw [ḥr] ḫ[t]*	*ḥnk mḏt* 26 = 56	Aufsetzen der Doppelfederkrone(?) 24 = —

Ostwand — K →

Der Spruchtitel *r(d)t ʿntw [ḥr] ḫ[t]* ist allein aus dem Opferritual bekannt (vgl. Nelson 1949a, 230 [Nr. 24] u. 225). Im Kultbildritual findet sich nur *k3p ʿntw* "Myrrhe räuchern" (— = 68).

13. Luxor, Sanktuar des Amun-Ra, Raum östl. des Sanktuars (XVIII), Westwand (= östl. Aussenwand des Sanktuars, unteres und mittleres Reg.; Amenophis III.) (Brunner 1977, Tf. 19 und 150–57)[23]

ḏb3 mnḫt 19–21 = 52–55	*swʿb m snṯr* 18 = 50	4 *dšrt*-Gefäße — = 49	4 *nmst*-Gefäße — = 48	*w3ḥ nms ḥr mḏ* —
smʿr nms ḥr mḏt —	*smʿr m nms* 17 = —	Hände auf den Gott legen 14 = 46(?)	Verehrung (*dw3 nṯr*?) 11(?) = 37–40, 42(?)	*ḫʿt nswt* Erscheinen des Königs —

← K —

Die Szene "die beiden Hände auf den Gott legen(?)" ist nicht sicher zu bestimmen, da eine Beischrift fehlt und das *dit ʿ.wy ḥr nṯr* auf der Ostwand des Sanktuars ikonograpisch anders dargestellt ist (Brunner 1977, Tf. 25, 135). Ikonographisch stimmt sie mit den drei folgenden Szenen zum Anlegen des *nms*-Tuches (*smʿr m nms, smʿr nms ḥr mḏt, w3ḥ nms ḥr mḏ*) überein.

23. Die beiden Zahlenreihen 150–54 und 155–59 sind hier vertauscht.

14. Totentempel Sethos' I. in Gurna, Sanktuar des Amun-Ra von Karnak (Raum XVI)
(PM 2, 414 f., Abb. 40; Arnold 1962, 21 f., Tf. 14)

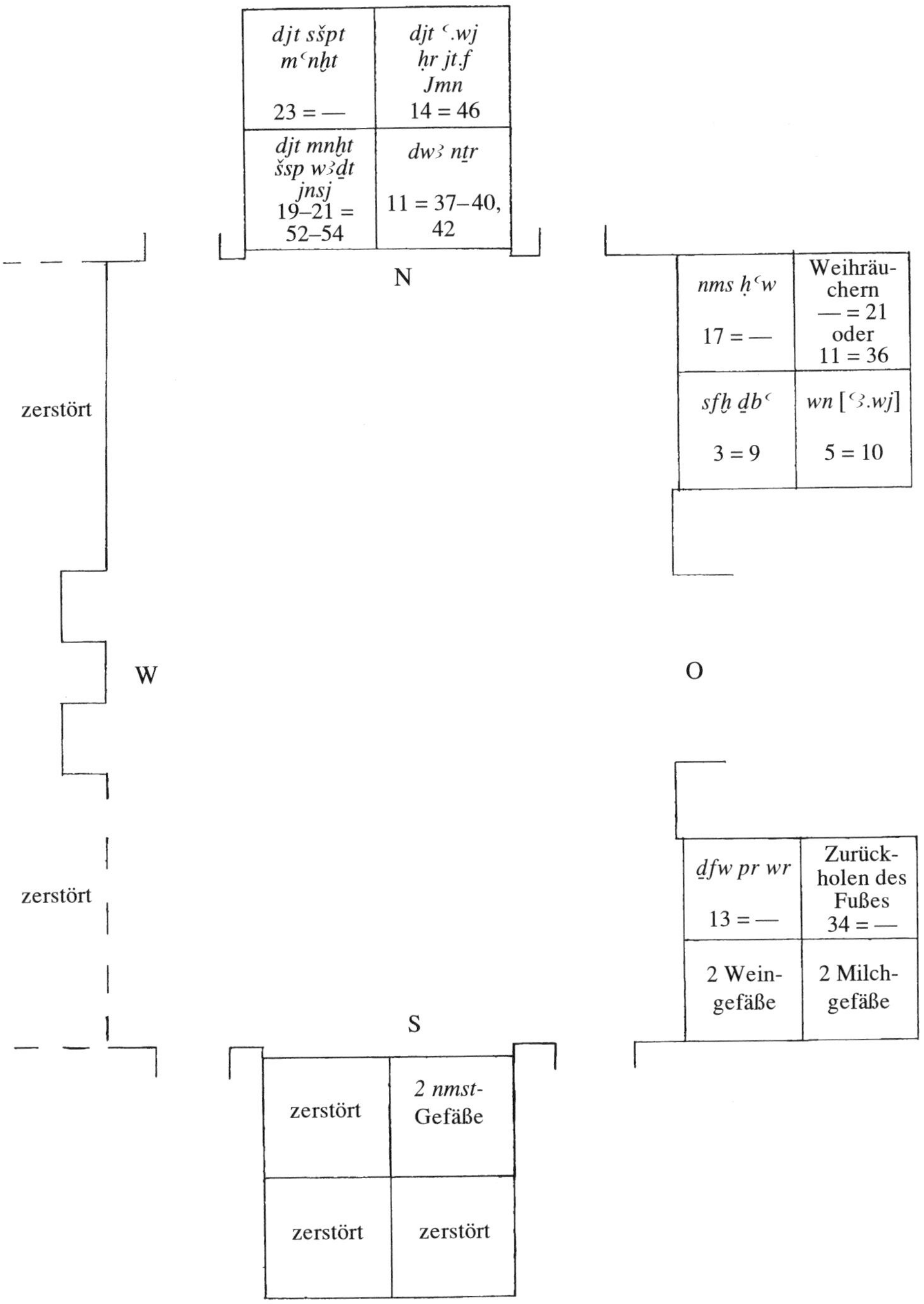

15A–B. Innere Längswände des Sanktuars im Horus-Tempel von Edfu (Ptolemäus IV.) und -nach diesem Vorbild- im Hathor-Tempel von Dendara (ca. 50–20 v.Chr.) (de Rochemonteix und Chassinat 1892, pl. 11–12; idem 1984, 24–51; Chassinat 1934, 40–51, 58–70 und pl. 51–70)[24]

Nach der überzeugenden Rekonstruktion von H. W. Fairman[25] folgen sich die Szenen, zum Inneren des Sanktuars hin ausgerichtet und unter Verschränkung der einander gegenüberstehenden Szenen auf den beiden Wänden, vom unteren Register aus nach oben. Anders als in Abydos steht das "Heraufgehen auf die Treppe (des Schreins)", bei dem auch der Schrein selbst dargestellt ist, hier ganz am Anfang und das Darbringen von

24. Zur Datierung der Dekoration des Sanktuars in Dendara vgl. Amer und Morardet 1983, 255–58; Devauchelle 1985, 172–74; Winter 1989, 75–85.

25. Bei David 1973, 128–32 (vgl. 305, Anm. 6 zu 126–32).

Salbe und Myrrhe vor dem Bekleiden mit verschiedenen Stoffen, die Reinigung mit 4 *nmst*- und *4 dšrt*-Gefässen hingegen danach. Das letztere hat seinen Grund vielleicht darin, dass die Reinigungsszenen hier wie in Abydos alle in einem einzigen, dem oberen Register zusammengefasst sind.

In Dendara sind auf den beiden Wänden des Sanktuars jeweils drei von den Szenen in Edfu durch andere ersetzt, die aus dem Kultbildritual sonst nicht bekannt und offenbar eng mit Hathor verbunden sind. Auch für diese Ersetzung ist eine kongruente Verteilung auf die beiden Wände gewählt (zwei Szenen im mittleren, eine im oberen Register).

pẖr ḥꜣ sp 4 m sntr ḥr sḏt 18 = 50	*pẖr ḥꜣ sp 4 m 5 ṯꜣw nw sntr* 32 = 66	*pẖr ḥꜣ sp 4 m 5 ṯꜣw šmʿj nw Nḫb* 30 = 63	*swʿb m 4 dšrt nt mw* — = 49		*swʿb m 4 nmst nt mw* — = 48	*pẖr ḥꜣ sp 4 m 5 ṯꜣw mḥwj nw Šrp* 31 = 64	*pẖr ḥꜣ sp 4 m 5 ṯꜣw nw bd* 29 = 62
	ḥnk mḏ 26 = 56	*ḏbꜣ mnḫt wꜣḏt* 20 = 53	*ḏbꜣ mnḫt ḥḏt* 19 = 52		*šms ʿntw* — = 68(?)	*ḏbꜣ mnḫt jrtw* —	*ḏbꜣ mnḫt jdmj* 21 = 55
	dwꜣ nṯr sp 4 11 = 37–40, 42	*wn ḥr ḥr nṯr* 5 = 10	*stꜣ jdr* — = 7	A	*pr r rt* — = 25	*sfḫ ḏbʿ* 3 = 9	*mꜣꜣ nṯr* 6 = 11

← K —————— —————— K →

ḥnk bb —	*jrt ʿbw m 5 ṯꜣw mḥwj nw Šrp* 31 = 64	*swʿb m 4 dšrt* — = 49		*swʿb m 4 nmst* — = 48	*jrt ʿbw m 5 ṯꜣw šmʿj nw Nḫb* 30 = 63	*ḥnk mnjt* —
ḥnk wnḫr.wj —	*ḥnk wḏꜣt* —	*ḥnk mnḫt* 19–21 = 52–55		*ḥnk mḏ* 26 = 56	*ḥnk wnšb* —	*jrt sššt* —
dwꜣ nṯr 11 = 37–40, 42	*wn ḥr* 5 = 10	*stꜣ jdr* — = 7	B	*pr r rd* — = 25	*sfḫ ḏbʿ* 3 = 9	*mꜣꜣ nṯr* 6 = 11

← K —————— —————— K →

16A–B. Alexander-Sanktuar in Luxor, Längswände aussen (jeweils drei Register mit Ausschnitten aus dem Opfer- und dem Kultbildritual), Ost (A) und West (B) (Abd el-Raziq 1984, 10 [unteres und mittleres Reg.] und 24 [alle drei Reg.] sowie Tf. 4, 5, 7–9)

	ḥnk mꜣʿt — = 41(?)	*mꜣ nṯr* 6 = 11	*dwꜣ nṯr sp 4*	*jrt [sntr] n jt.f*	
sn tꜣ n jt.f ← 7 = 12	*wn ʿꜣ.wj ḥr nṯr* —— 5 = 10	*sfḫ dbʿt* —— 3 = 9	*ʿq r st wrt* —— 10 = —	*pr r rdw* → — = 25	*bs nswt r ḥwt nṯr*

Ostwand

← K ——————

dj šw.tj → 24 = —	*r(d)t wꜣḏw msdm* → — = 58–59	*ḥnk mḏt* → 26 = 56			
jrt ʿbw m 4 nmst nt mw ← — = 48	*sfḫ mḏ[t]* → 15 = —	*sfḫ mnḫt* → 16 = —	*[sm]ʿr m nms{t}* → 17 = —	*ḏbꜣ mnḫt* → 19–21 = 52–55	
bs nswt r ḥwt nṯr	*swʿb m snṯr qbḥw* ← 33 = 67	*jrt ʿbw m 5 tꜣw n bd* ← 29 = 62	*jrt ʿbw m 5 tꜣw nw šmʿ* ← 30 = 63	*jrt ʿbw m 4 dšrt* ← — = 49	

——— K ———→ Westwand

17. Alexander-Sanktuar in Luxor, Innenwand West (ein Register mit drei Szenen) (Abd el-Raziq 1984, 43 f. [dort auch zur retrograden Anordnung], 46–48, Tf. 14b–15)

ḥnk mꜣʿt → — = 41	*rdt mnḫt* → 19–21 = 52–55	*ḥnk mḏt* → 26 = 56

←——— K ———

18A–B. Karnak, Sanktuar des Philipp Arrhidäus, innere Seitenwände Süd (3. Reg. v.o.; A) und Nord (2. und 3. Reg. v.o.; B) des Vorraums (PM 2, 101 [Raum IX, 293–94], Abb. 12)

		dwꜣ nṯr	*jrt ʿbw m 5 tꜣ n Nḫb* 30 = 63	*jrt ʿbw m 5 tꜣ n Mḥw* 31 = 64	*rdt mnḫt* 19–21 = 52–55	*rdt mḏt* 26 = 56	*rdt wsḫ* —	zerstört

←——— K ——— Südwand

			rdt mnḫt 19–21 = 52–55	*rdt wsḫ* —	*rdt mḏt* 26 = 56				
(*jrt ʿbw m 5 tꜣ n Nḫb*?) (30 = 63)	*jrt ʿbw m 5 tꜣ [n Mḥw?]* (31 = 64)	*jrt ʿbw m 4 dšrt* — = 49	*jrt ʿbw m 4 nmst* — = 48	*dwꜣ nṯr* 11 = 37–40, 42(?)	*jrt snṯr* 8 = —(?)	*sn tꜣ* 6 = 11	Verehrung	zerstört	zerstört

——— K ———→ Nordwand

References

Abd el-Raziq, M.

1984 *Die Darstellungen und Texte des Sanktuars Alexanders des Großen im Tempel von Luxor*. Deutsches archäologisches Institut, Abteilung Kairo, archäologische Veröffentlichungen 16. Mainz am Rhein: Philipp von Zabern.

Alliot, M.

1949 *Le culte d'Horus à Edfou au temps des ptolémées*, fascicule 1. Bibliothèque d'étude 20/1. Cairo: Institut français d'archéologie orientale.

Altenmüller, H.

1969 "Die abydenische Version des Kultbildrituals." *Mitteilungen des Deutschen archäologischen Instituts, Abteilung Kairo* 24: 16–25.

1971 "Eine neue Deutung der Zeremonie des *ỉnỉt rd*." *Journal of Egyptian Archaeology* 57: 146–53.

Altenmüller-Kesting, B.

1968 Reinigungsriten im ägyptischen Kult. Dissertation, Hamburg.

Aly, M; F. Abdel-Hamid; and M. Dewachter

1967 *Le temple d'Amada* 4. Collection scientifique 54. Cairo: Centre de documentation et d'études sur l'ancienne Égypte.

Amer, H. I., and B. Morardet

1983 "Les dates de la construction du temple majeur d'Hathor à Dendara à l'époque gréco-romaine." *Annales du Service des antiquités de l'Égypte* 69: 255–58.

Arnold, Di.

1962 *Wandrelief und Raumfunktion in ägyptischen Tempeln des Neuen Reiches*. Münchner ägyptologische Studien 2. Berlin: Verlag Bruno Hessling.

Bakry, H. S. K.

1968 "Reconstruction of the Third Pylon at Karnak." *Annales du Service des antiquités de l'Égypte* 60: 7–14.

Barguet, P.

1962a "Note sur le complexe architectural de Séti 1er à Abydos." *Kêmi* 16: 21–27.

1962b *Le temple d'Amon-Re à Karnak*. Recherches d'archéologie, de philologie et d'histoire 21. Cairo: Institut français d'archéologie orientale.

Barguet, P., and M. Dewachter

1967 *Le temple d'Amada II*. Collection scientifique 52. Cairo: Centre d'études et de documentation sur l'ancienne Égypte.

Barguet, P.; A. Abdel Hamid Youssef; and M. Dewachter

1967 *Le temple d'Amada III*. Collection scientifique 53. Cairo: Centre d'études et de documentation sur l'ancienne Égypte.

Barta, W.

1966 "Die Anordung der Wandreliefs in den Götterkapellen des Sethos-Tempels von Abydos." *Mitteilungen des Deutschen archäologischen Instituts, Abteilung Kairo* 21: 116–22.

Blackman, A.

1920 "The Sequence of the Episodes in the Egyptian Daily Temple Liturgy." *Journal of the Manchester Egyptian and Oriental Society* 1918/19: 27–53.

Brunner, H.

1977 *Die südlichen Räume des Tempels von Luxor*. Deutsches archäologisches Institut, Abteilung Kairo, archäologische Veröffentlichungen 18. Mainz am Rhein: Philipp von Zabern.

Calverley, A. M., and A. H. Gardiner

1933 *The Temple of King Sethos I at Abydos*, Volume 1: *The Chapels of Osiris, Isis, and Horus*. London: Egypt Exploration Society; Chicago: University of Chicago Press.

1935 *The Temple of King Sethos I at Abydos*, Volume 2: *The Chapels of Amen-Rēʿ, Rēʿ-Ḥarakhti, Ptaḥ, and King Sethos*. London: Egypt Exploration Society; Chicago: University of Chicago Press.

Caminos, R. A.

1974 *The New-Kingdom Temples of Buhen*, Volume 2. Archaeological Survey of Egypt 34. London: Egypt Exploration Society.

1998 *The New-Kingdom Temples of Semna-Kumma*, Volume 2. Archaeological Survey of Egypt 38. London: Egypt Exploration Society.

Chassinat, É.

1934 *Le temple de Dendara* 1. Cairo: Institut français d'archéologie orientale.

Clère, J. J.

1939 "La lecture des Termes ,  'virement (d'offrandes).'" *Journal of Egyptian Archaeology* 25: 215–16.

David, A. R.

1973 *Religious Ritual at Abydos (c. 1300 BC)*. Warminster: Aris and Phillips.

1981 *A Guide to Religious Ritual at Abydos*. Warminster: Aris and Phillips.

Davies, N. de G., and A. H. Gardiner

1915 *The Tomb of Amenemhēt*. Theban Tomb Series 1. London: Egypt Exploration Fund.

Devauchelle, D.

1985 "De nouveau la construction du temple d'Hathor à Dendara." *Revue d'égyptologie* 36: 172–74.

Dunham, D., and J. M. A. Janssen

1960 *Semna-Kumma*. Second Cataract Forts 1. Boston: Museum of Fine Arts.

Goyon, J.-C.

1984 "Une identification possible de la plante *hdn* des anciens Égyptiens." In *Studien zu Sprache und Religion Ägyptens*, Band 1: *Sprache. Zu Ehren von Wolfhart Westendorf überreicht von seinen Freunden und Schülern*, edited by F. Junge, pp. 241–50. Göttingen: n.p.

Graefe, E.
1971 "Die Versiegelung der Naostür." *Mitteilungen des Deutschen archäologischen Instituts, Abteilung Kairo* 27: 147–55.
1993 "Die Deutung der sogenannten 'Opfergaben' der Ritualszenen ägyptischer Tempel als 'Schriftzeichen.'" In *Ritual and Sacrifice in the Ancient Near East* (Proceedings of the International Conference organized by the Katholieke Universiteit Leuven from the 17th to the 20th of April 1991), edited by J. Quaegebeur, pp. 143–56. Orientalia Lovaniensia Analecta 55. Leuven: Peeters.

Habachi, L.
1985 "Devotion of Tuthmosis III to his Predecessors: Apropos a Meeting of Sesostris I with his Courtiers." In *Mélanges Gamal Eddin Mokhtar*, volume 1, edited by P. Posener-Kriéger, pp. 349–59. Bibliothèque d'étude 97/1. Cairo: Institut français d'archéologie orientale.

Handoussa, T.
1981 "Le collier ousekh." *Studien zur altägyptischen Kultur* 9: 143–50.

Karkowski, J.
1978 "Deir el-Bahari 1973–1974." *Études et travaux* 10: 397–406.
1979 "Deir el-Bahari 1974–1975 (travaux égyptologiques)." *Études et travaux* 11: 217–20.
1983 "Amenhotep, Son of Hapu and Imhotep at Deir el-Bahari: Some Reconsiderations." *Mitteilungen des Deutschen archäologischen Instituts, Abteilung Kairo* 39: 93–101.
1990 "Deir el Bahari: Temple of Hatshepsut: Egyptological Studies 1977–1980." *Études et travaux* 14: 349–63.

Königliche Museen zu Berlin
1901 *Hieratische Papyrus aus den Königlichen Museen zu Berlin,* Band 1: *Rituale für den Kultus des Amon und für den Kultus der Mut.* Leipzig: J. C. Hinrichs.

Lacau, P., and H. Chevrier
1977 *Une chapelle d'Hatshepsout à Karnak,* fascicle 1: *Texte.* Cairo: Institut français d'archéologie orientale.
1979 *Une chapelle d'Hatshepsout à Karnak,* fascicle 2: *Planches.* Cairo: Institut français d'archéologie orientale.

Legrain, G.
1902 "Le temple de Ptah Rîs-anbou-f dans Thèbes." *Annales du Service des antiquités de l'Égypte* 3: 38–66; 97–115.

Mariette, A.
1869 *Abydos: Description des fouilles exécutées sur l'emplacement de cette ville* 1. Paris: A. Franck.

Naville, E.
1901 *The Temple of Deir el-Bahari,* Part 4: *The Shrine of Hathor and the Southern Hall of Offerings.* Publication of the Egypt Exploration Fund 19. London: Egypt Exploration Fund.

Nelson, H. H.
1941 *Key Plans Showing Locations of Theban Temple Decorations.* Oriental Institute Publications 56. Chicago: University of Chicago Press.
1949a "Certain Reliefs at Karnak and Medinet Habu and the Ritual of Amenophis I." *Journal of Near Eastern Studies* 8: 201–35, 310–45.
1949b "The Rite of 'Bringing the Foot' as Portrayed in Temple Reliefs." *Journal of Egyptian Archaeology* 35: 82–86.
1981 *The Great Hypostyle Hall at Karnak*, Volume 1, Part 1: *The Wall Reliefs*. Edited by W. J. Murnane. Oriental Institute Publications 106. Chicago: Oriental Institute.

Parker, R. A.; J. Leclant; and J.-C. Goyon
1979 *The Edifice of Taharqa by the Sacred Lake of Karnak.* Brown Egyptological Studies 8. Providence: Brown University Press.

Redford, D. B.
1987 "The Tod Inscription of Senwosret I and Early 12th Dynasty Involvement in Nubia and the South." *Society of the Study of Egyptian Antiquities Journal* 17: 36–55.

de Rochemonteix, M., and É. Chassinat
1892 *Le temple d'Edfou* 1: *Planches.* Mémoires publiés par les Membres de la Mission archéologique française au Caire 10. Cairo: Institut français d'archéologie orientale.
1984 *Le temple d'Edfou* 1: *Texte.* Mémoires publiés par les membres de la Mission archéologique française 10. Second edition. Cairo: Institut français d'archéologie orientale.

Roeder, G.
1960 *Kulte, Orakel und Naturverehrung im alten Ägypten.* Zurich: Artemis Verlag.

Rosati, G.
1998 *Papiri geroglifici e ieratici da Tebtynis.* Edited by J. Osing and G. Rosati. Firenze: Istituto Papirologico "G. Vitelli."

Staatliche Museen zu Berlin
1913 *Aegyptische Inschriften aus den Königlichen Museen zu Berlin,* Band 1: *Inschriften von der ältesten Zeit bis zum Ende der Hyksoszeit.* Leipzig: J. C. Hinrichs.

Van Siclen, C. C.
1987 "Queen Ahmose Receives Offerings." *Göttinger Miszellen* 97: 21–24.

Winter, E.
1989 "A Reconsideration of the Newly Discovered Building Inscription on the Temple of Denderah." *Göttinger Miszellen* 108: 75–85.

de Wit, C.
1968 *Les inscriptions du temple d'Opet à Karnak,* 3. Bibliotheca Aegyptiaca 13. Brussels: Fondation Égyptologique Reine Élisabeth.

Witkowski, M. G.
1989 "Le rôle et les fonctions des chapelles d'Anubis dans le complexe funéraire de la reine Hatshepsout à Deir el Bahari." *Studien zur altägyptischen Kultur, Beihefte* 3: 431–40.
1990 "Quatre saisons de travaux de documentation dans les chapelles d'Anubis au temple de la reine Hatchepsout à Deir el-Bahari." *Études et travaux* 14: 369–92.

Wysocki, Z.
1986 "The Temple of Queen Hatshepsut at Deir el Bahari: Its Original Form." *Mitteilungen des Deutschen archäologischen Instituts, Abteilung Kairo* 42: 213–28.

32

SPORTIVE FENCING AS A RITUAL FOR DESTROYING THE ENEMIES OF HORUS

PETER A. PICCIONE

University of Charleston, South Carolina

The purpose of this study is to provide some meaning and context for the occurrences of sportive fencing in Egyptian religious texts and depictions of that sport in temples and tombs. At the heart of this study lies the essential relationship between religious ritual and athletic endeavor in ancient Egypt. I am pleased to dedicate this paper to Professor Edward Wente. As a teacher and researcher, he opened my eyes to the wondrous complexities of Egyptian religion, and he helped me to develop the tools to study this subject and its many incongruities. The first and most enduring lesson he taught me was that Aristotle's *Law of Noncontradiction* does not apply to Egyptian religious thought.

My interest in this topic arises from my general concern with the religious meanings attached to human body movement in ancient Egypt, especially in the areas of sporting, gaming, and medical practice (Piccione, in press), as well as from the fact that I have also been a competitive fencer.

Ritual is normally conceived as ceremonial activity, often the formalization of originally spontaneous action or the re-enactment of a past mythical event, performed in order to achieve some spiritual purpose. In many cases, re-creation of a past event or associating the activity with some myth is an important aspect of a ritual. Technically, speech must combine with the activity to formulate an effective ritual. Usually, a ritual is fully planned from beginning to end and with a predetermined conclusion.

Sport, on the other hand, is an activity of recreation and enjoyment, usually requiring some vigorous bodily exertion, and is performed according to pre-defined rules or procedures that may — or may not, depending on the skill of the participant — result in some desired consequence. An important element of sport is competition, either with oneself or others. With sport the outcome is always, to some extent, in doubt.

How do we reconcile these two seemingly disparate notions with each other? Understanding how sportive fencing coheres with ritualistic fencing will aid us in identifying the essential commonality between ritual and athletics in ancient Egypt.

PHYSICAL CONTEXT FOR SPORTIVE FENCING

The *Oxford English Dictionary* defines fencing as "the action or art of using the sword scientifically as a weapon of offense or defense; the practice of this art with a blunted sword, foil or stick." Despite the fact that stick fighting occurs in Egyptian art and literature, the term "fencing" is almost never applied to it in studies of these contexts or of Egyptian sports. Rather, these studies employ the terms "stick fighting," "single stick," or rarely, "stick fencing" to refer to this activity.[1]

Although it is usually stated that modern fencing appeared first in Spain in A.D. 1471 (e.g., Alaux 1975, pp. 3–4), by applying the definition above to Egyptian contexts it is clear that some kind of formalized sportive fencing did exist in ancient Egypt, certainly by the New Kingdom and perhaps as early as the Old Kingdom. However, unlike European-based fencing and Japanese *kendo*, both of which derived from the use of the sword and sword-fighting, Egyptian sportive fencing apparently originated in the use of the fighting club and mace warfare. The earliest references to fencing-like activity in the Pyramid Texts and rituals of the Middle Kingdom

1. See Wilson 1931, pp. 211–13, 219–20; Vandier d'Abbadie 1941; Touny and Wenig 1969, pp. 25–29, pls. 14–18; Decker 1992, pp. 82–87; Decker and Herb 1994, pp. 564–71. See also Piccione, in press.

Gold of Praise: Studies on Ancient Egypt in Honor of Edward F. Wente
Edited by Emily Teeter and John A. Larson
Studies in Ancient Oriental Civilization 58
Chicago: Oriental Institute, 1999

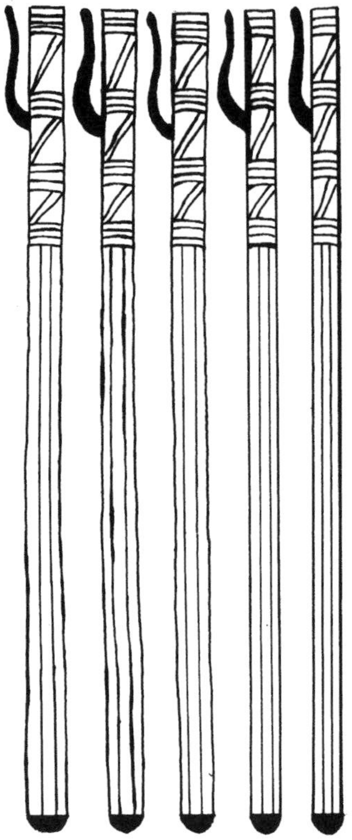

Figure 32.1. Military Fighting Sticks or Clubs of the New Kingdom (Tomb of Ramesses III; after Decker 1992, p. 83, fig. 52)

refer not to the sword, but to activities with fighting sticks, clubs, and even plant stalks. Indeed, the straight sword and the sickle-shaped *ḫpš*-scimitar were not adopted for use in Egypt until the New Kingdom — long after the first references to fencing appear in the religious texts.[2]

Like modern fencing, it is reasonable to assume that Egyptian sportive fencing began as a conventionalization of the exercises and drills used to train military personnel in the use of the club and mace and later also the scimitar and straight sword. By the New Kingdom, the traditional Egyptian fighting club apparently evolved into a highly maneuverable beating weapon often brandished by Egyptian soldiers (see, e.g., Wise and McBride 1981, p. 10). According to depictions and surviving examples in the archaeological record, this fighting stick or club was a long single rod, often banded with lashings or heavy metal foil, and sometimes with a weight or mace-head at the tip (Wise and McBride 1981, p. 18, illustration, center). Frequently, it was wider at the tip than at the handle, with a curved wooden prong attached to the hilt (see fig. 32.1). Since soldiers are always shown gripping the stick above this prong (see fig. 32.2), perhaps it functioned as a support in the grip for the heel of the hand. Several examples of such fighting sticks or clubs were found in the tomb of Tutankhamun (e.g., Carter and Mace 1923, pl. 71 [A]; Reeves 1990, p. 91 [top photograph, shown on box no. 370]). In the Kadesh battle reliefs, where the stick is depicted in use, it is often carried as a secondary weapon by the archers (Wreszinski 1923–38/2, pls. 92–92a). This stick or club was a true weapon, despite the fact that soldiers are sometimes depicted training or fencing with it (so fig. 32.2). However, it was probably from this particular weapon that the light and narrow sportive fencing stick evolved in the New Kingdom.[3] Thus, the techniques that developed for these fencing sticks would have been based upon the use of the real fighting stick or club, although probably influenced in some fashion by the newly adopted sword weapons.[4] Certainly by the New King-

2. Hayes 1959, p. 68; Wise and McBride 1981, p. 23; Shaw 1991, p. 43. Similarly, Carter (1933, p. 136) suggests that Tutankhamun's fencing sticks evolved from a club since they are wide at the tip and narrower at the handle.
3. See below for the descriptions of the fencing sticks in the fencing scenes represented in Theban tombs and temples; see Decker 1992, p. 84, fig. 53, for the various types of fencing sticks.
4. The earliest *ḫpš*-scimitars known in Egypt date to the Second Intermediate Period as a Hyksos or Canaanite import (Shaw 1991, 43). Two well-preserved examples were found in the tomb of Tutankhamun (Carter 1933, p. 137, pl. 45 [B–C]; Reeves 1990, 177); their short, curving, and pointed blades indicate that they were primarily slashing weapons designed to hack off limbs or to leave wide gashes in the flesh. The short straight swords also first appeared with the Hyksos (Hayes 1959, p. 68). By their design, they were primarily thrusting and piercing weapons. Also appearing by the New Kingdom (although probably of Egyptian origin) was the poleax, which was a bladed mace that combined the tradi-

Figure 32.2. Two Soldiers Fence or Train with Fighting Sticks or Clubs
(Louvre Ostracon E.25.309; after Peck 1978, p. 156 [87])

dom, fencing was depicted as an activity almost exclusively of soldiers (e.g., Decker and Herb 1994, pp. 564–71 [M1–M11]). Probably, it is such fencing exercises that are depicted among the Kadesh battle reliefs, conducted by young recruits or donkey-boys within the Egyptian camp (e.g., Decker and Herb 1994, pp. 568–69 [M7–M8]). In one of these scenes, the boys are being trained or commanded by an archery officer (Wreszinski 1923–38/2, pls. 92–92a).

Judging by Ramesside depictions, Egyptian sportive fencing was a highly stylized activity, as indicated by the conventionalized depictions of the fencers' parrying and attacking movements, their arched backs and bent legs, and the positions of their arms (see fig. 32.3). That methods of fencing might have been influenced by techniques associated with the scimitar and sword is suggested by one of the wooden fencing sticks found in the tomb of Tutankhamun. This stick appears to be based on a combination of fighting stick and scimitar;[5] it is long and thick with a handgrip at one end and a long curving sickle edge on the other. Hence, its sportive usage might have combined the techniques of both weapons.

While Egyptian fencing and its modern counterpart evolved from different weapons, they show remarkable coincidence and similarity in the movement and stances of the fencers and the manner in which they manipulate their weapons (cf. figs. 32.3 and 32.4). Interestingly, the *fellahin* of Upper Egypt still play a fencing game today, called in Arabic *el-taḥteeb* (or *liᶜb el-shuba/nabbut*), in which pairs of players use long sticks to attack each other and parry blows (cf. Vandier d'Abbadie 1941, pp. 479–81; Decker 1992, p. 189, n. 58).

RITUALIZED CONTEXT FOR SPORTIVE FENCING

Fighting with sticks and clubs as part of religious observance was prevalent through most of Egyptian history. While the New Kingdom evidence indicates that fencing was a formalized and regulated activity at that

tional mace-head with a pointed ax blade (e.g., Wise and McBride 1981, p. 18). Each of these weapons and the fighting stick or club would have utilized distinctive parrying and attacking techniques for which soldiers had to train and practice. These techniques were probably compatible with each other only on a rudimentary level. However, given the example of the origins of modern foil-fencing as a training technique for several different weapons, it is possible that Egyptian fencing could also have been used to enhance training for a variety of close combat weapons.

5. It has a grip of gold inlaid with glass and gold ferrules; Cairo Museum Tutankhamun object no. 122 (Carter catalog number uncertain); seen by the author in the Cairo Museum.

Figure 32.3. Two Soldiers Fence with Each Other (Medinet Habu, Temple of Ramesses III, First Court, South Wall, East of Window of Appearances; Photograph by P. Piccione)

time, descriptions of stick fighting in texts of the Late Period and Ptolemaic era suggest that in these later times combat might have been conducted in the manner of a melee or a free-for-all with hundreds of people taking part and beating each other with sticks.[6] How formalized and regulated this activity was in these later times is difficult to ascertain.

In ancient Egypt, fencing was a sport that ultimately came to be associated with the ideology of kingship. However, while kings are never depicted fencing with others in Egyptian art and iconography, it is certain that they actually did engage in the practice. In addition to the true fighting sticks or clubs, many different fencing sticks were found in the tomb of Tutankhamun.[7] That these were his personal property used in his lifetime is indicated by his names inscribed on the detachable knuckle guards and the fact that the guards show wear and usage. Also, fighting sticks or clubs, as described above, are portrayed among the military panoply of King Ramesses III on a wall in his tomb in the Kings' Valley (Decker 1992, p. 83, fig. 52; Decker and Herb 1994, p. 571 [M12], pl. 322 [M12]). The implication is that if Ramesses III himself did not actually with fence others, he was, at least, expected to do so in the hereafter.

A number of texts contain information about the ritual context of fencing activity in Egypt. One of the earliest references occurs in PT Spell 324, where it appears as a recitation of a medical incantation to heal the god Horus of disorders related to his scalp. The deceased king, who recites the spell, addresses two malevolent female entities:

6. See, for example, Herodotus' description of the festival of Aries at Papremis (Book II, 63) or the festival of "Seizing the Club," celebrated at Esna. For a recent discussion of the elements of these festivals, as well as a general analysis of the stick-fighting rituals of the Ptolemaic era, see Borghouts 1995, pp. 43–50, passim.

7. For example, Carter and Mace 1923, pp. 115, 121, pls. 71–72; Carter 1933, p. 136, pl. 45a; however, the long narrow stick carved with a spiral of "knots" and having a grip overlaid with gold foil and a gold tip (Carter and Mace 1923, pl. 72 [far right] = Cairo Museum Tutankhamun no. 663) could actually be a bat for the "Ritual of Striking the Ball" (see Naville 1901, pl. 100; cf. Borghouts 1973, pp. 122–23).

Figure 32.4. Fencer (near) Attacks Fencer (far) Who Parries Blow. Behind Each Fencer Stand Two Judges (Modern Sabre Tournament; Photograph by P. Piccione)

> Hail to you, O eternal hippo. Have you come against Teti as the eternal hippo?
> It is so that [he might strike] you with (it), that he has pulled away[8] from you one of the two *ꜣms*-sticks of Horus.
> Hail to you, O monstrous she-ass. Have you come against Teti as a monstrous she-ass?[9]
> It is with the *sd*-plant that grows in the Lake of Osiris that he has struck you (Sethe 1908, p. 267, §§522–23c).

The hippopotamus and the ass are Sethian animals. That the king attacks them with weapons connected with Horus and Osiris places this struggle within the context of the mythological conflict of Horus and Seth, which is consistent with the spell's theme of treating Horus's ailment (alluding to the disfigurement of Horus's eye in that struggle).

Generally, the *ꜣms*-stick was conceptualized as a fighting stick or baton with a bulbous handle, attached to which was a ribbon or streamer (Gardiner Sign List S44).[10] The *ꜣms* (var. *ms*) is regularly portrayed as a cult item in the frieze of objects painted inside Middle Kingdom coffins (Jéquier 1921, pp. 160–62). It also occurs as a fencing cudgel or club in the Ramesseum Dramatic Papyrus (see below).

The *sd* is an unidentified "tail"-like plant, probably not related to the *sd-ḫꜣsyt* ("tail of white bryony") or *sd-pnw* ("mouse-tail plant," i.e., the mallow) that are attested in the medical papyri (von Deines 1959, pp. 469–70). Rather, Faulkner appears correct in suggesting that *sd*, literally "tail," is a metaphor for a plant similar to a bulrush or some other tufted reed growing in water (Faulkner 1969, p. 104, n. 16). Because it grows in the Lake of Osiris (and he is a deity of new vegetation and growth), it embodies Osiris's positive creative power, and hence would be effective against evil.

PT Spell 469 refers to stick fighting by the leaders of the city of Letopolis who employ *mꜥꜣwt*-sticks in their activity:

> It is with his *ka* that this Pepi lives.
> Just as it (i.e., the *ka*) dispels the evil which is before Pepi,
> so it expels the evil which is behind Pepi,
> just like the *mꜥꜣwt*-(beating) of the foremost of Letopolis,
> which expels the evil which is before him
> and which dispels the evil which is behind him (Sethe 1910, p. 2, §908b–g).

---

8. So Faulkner 1969, p. 103, §522.
9. Faulkner 1969, p. 103, §522.
10. Gardiner 1973, p. 510, inaccurately identifies it as a "walking stick with flagellum."

The meaning of the text is that the king's *ka* removes evil and wickedness from around him in a manner similar to the *mꜥꜣwt*-stick fighting of Letopolis. Altenmüller (1964, pp. 271–79) made a compelling study in which he compared this text to two other examples of the stick-fighting genre, including the fighting ritual of Horus of Letopolis, as recorded in the Ramesseum Dramatic Papyrus, and the stick-fighting ritual of Papremis, mentioned in Herodotus II, 63, and which Altenmüller would locate at Letopolis.[11] Based upon the rituals of Letopolis and Papremis, he makes it clear that in the context of PT Spell 469, the *mꜥꜣwt*-sticks are not "throwsticks" (as they are usually identified), but fencing cudgels or ceremonial fighting clubs.

PT Spell 482 contains a veiled reference to ritualized fencing. Here it occurs as a funerary dance performed by the souls of Pe who dance and fence while singing during the funeral of Osiris (cf. Brovarski 1975, p. 8). Part of the spell reads:

> The gods of Pe have sympathy.
> They come to Osiris at the sound of the cries of Isis and Nephthys.
> The souls of Pe dance with sticks (*rwỉ*) for you;
> they beat their flesh for you;
> they strike their arms for you;
> they pull their hair for you (Sethe 1910, p. 64, §§1004–05).

The dancing occurs as part of the resurrection of Osiris, and in the spell the lyrics of the dancers' song (§§1006–08) equate their beating and striking with Horus's smiting and binding the enemies of Osiris. Given the aggressive activity associated with the "dancing with sticks" (i.e., the beating, striking, and pulling) and its associations with Pe and Osiris, the activity of the souls of Pe is construed as a combination of both dance and fencing.[12]

The Ramesseum Dramatic Papyrus dates to the Middle Kingdom, and among the various liturgies and cultic activities it describes is the liturgy of the cult of Horus at Letopolis.[13] During the festival of Horus, according to the text, *sḫnw-ꜣḫ*-priests portray the "children of Horus" who take up *mꜥꜣwt*-sticks in order to seek Osiris and to combat the "followers of Seth" who are armed with (*ꜣ*)*ms*-sticks (cf. Altenmüller 1964, pp. 273–77, passim). In this context, the (*ꜣ*)*ms* can only be a fencing stick or club. The illustrative vignette associated with the episode depicts two combatants, each wielding in one hand a stick tied with a ribbon, while holding in the other hand a long object such as a bow or scepter (see fig. 32.5). The text reads:

> (117) It happens that the *sḫnw-ꜣḫ*-priests act with the *mꜥꜣwt*-stick (*ỉrỉ m-ꜥ mꜥꜣwy*).
> (118 upper) Horus speaks words <to> the children of Horus "May you seek this my father."
> (119 upper) The children of Horus speak words to the followers of Seth "Raise your (*ꜣ*)*ms*-sticks up to heaven, your arses being for goats twisting around."[14]
> (118–19 lower) The children of Horus; *sḫnw-ꜣḫ*-priests; raising up the (*ꜣ*)*ms*-sticks of the followers of Seth. Acting with the *mꜥꜣwt*-stick; Ibis-Nome, Letopolis (Sethe 1928, pl. 21, cols. 117–19).

The final phrase, "acting with the *mꜥꜣwt*-stick" (*ỉrỉ m-ꜥ mꜥꜣwy*), appears both in the text and as the title of the accompanying vignette.[15] As noted above, Altenmüller has proposed that the festival of Letopolis and its fencing ritual were probably so long-lived that they were witnessed and described by Herodotus at the festival of Papremis as late as the fifth century B.C., although with some alteration (Herodotus II, 63; Altenmüller 1964, pp. 276–78). However, Lloyd more cautiously noted that "in the present state of our knowledge, the evidence is nowhere near being conclusive" that the two rituals were related other than thematically (Lloyd 1976, p. 285), a sentiment recently seconded by Borghouts (1995, pp. 43–45, passim).

Whether Altenmüller is right or wrong in identifying this ritual specifically with that of Papremis, it is clear that fencing rituals similar to that of Letopolis did continue into the Late Period, as witnessed by Herodotus. In-

11. See now Borghouts 1995 regarding this ritual, including a brief listing of other locations previously suggested for the town of Papremis.
12. Similarly, stick dancing is an activity still common in Upper Egypt today.
13. Columns 117–19, scene 38 [24], so in Sethe 1928, pp. 223–25, pls. 10, 21.
14. *Ṯnỉ* (*ꜣ*)*ms.ṯ*<*n*> *r pt ḫpdw.ṯ*<*n*> *n ꜥwt pḫrw* [⌈*ḥꜣ.f*⌉]. This line appears to be an invective as a challenge to fight.
15. In column 117 the phrase is fully written as *ỉrỉ m-ꜥ mꜥꜣwy*, whereas in column 119 the group *m-ꜥ* is written only once, *ỉrỉ* <*m-ꜥ*> *mꜥꜣw*<*y*>, causing Altenmüller 1964, p. 275, to translate the phrase as "Ein 'Prügel-(Schwingen)' machen."

Figure 32.5. Vignette of Fencing Ritual of Letopolis; Text reads: *sḫnw-ꜣḫ* "*sḫnw-ꜣḫ*-priest"; *iri* <*m-ʿ*> *mʿꜣwy* "Acting with the *mʿꜣwt*-stick"; *sḫnw-ꜣḫ* "*sḫnw-ꜣḫ*-priest" (Ramesseum Dramatic Papyrus; Sethe 1928, pl. 21 [24])

deed, Borghouts (1995, pp. 49–50) recounts an argument for another stick-fighting ritual, dating to the Ptolemaic period, called the festival of "Seizing the Club," documented at Esna temple.[16]

In the texts of the Old and Middle Kingdoms (and their successors in the Late Period), the fencing ritual generally conforms to a pattern in which the fencing ritualists represent a deity, such as Horus or Osiris, or are in the following of Horus, while their opponents are evil enemies to be defeated.

SPORTIVE FENCING IN THE NEW KINGDOM

From the New Kingdom onward, formalized fencing tournaments are occasionally represented on the walls of private tombs and temples in connection with the *sed*-festival, the feasts of certain deities and deceased kings, and other royal celebrations (see Decker and Herb 1994, pp. 564–74, pls. 315–22). Here the fencers are usually portrayed as Egyptian soldiers or marines. Depictions of fencing are also rendered on ostraca and in satirical papyri, where they occur in non-cultic contexts.[17] What follows is a discussion of the New Kingdom fencing scenes that occur in religious contexts, omitting the secular scenes on papyri and ostraca.

Tomb of Kheruef

In the Eighteenth Dynasty tomb of Kheruef (Theban tomb 192), fencing is represented as one of the communal activities of the *sed*-festival of Amenhotep III.[18] The fencing scenes are associated specifically with the ritual of erecting the *ḏd*-pillar, a rite which enacted the resurrection of Ptah-Sokar-Osiris (Wente 1969, pp. 90–91). Here the fencing occurs with scenes of boxing, dancing, and singing.

16. According to Borghouts 1995, although the inscriptions of the festival of "Seizing the Club" do not describe stick fighting specifically, they do share many themes in common with the Papremis festival. Also, a mythical battle occurs, and Apophis is slain.
17. See Vandier d'Abbadie 1941, pp. 468–76, fig. 53; Touny and Wenig 1969, p. 26, fig. 7; Omlin 1971, p. 31 [x+12], pls. 11, 13–14; Peck 1978, p. 156 [87]; Decker 1992, p. 85, fig. 55; Decker and Herb 1994, pp. 570–71 [M10, M11], pls. 321–22.
18. De Vries 1960, pp. 223–30, passim; Touny and Wenig 1969, pl. 14; *Kheruef*, p. 64, pls. 61–63; Decker 1992, pp. 84, 86, fig. 56; Decker and Herb 1994, pp. 565–66 [M2], pls. 315–16, 323.

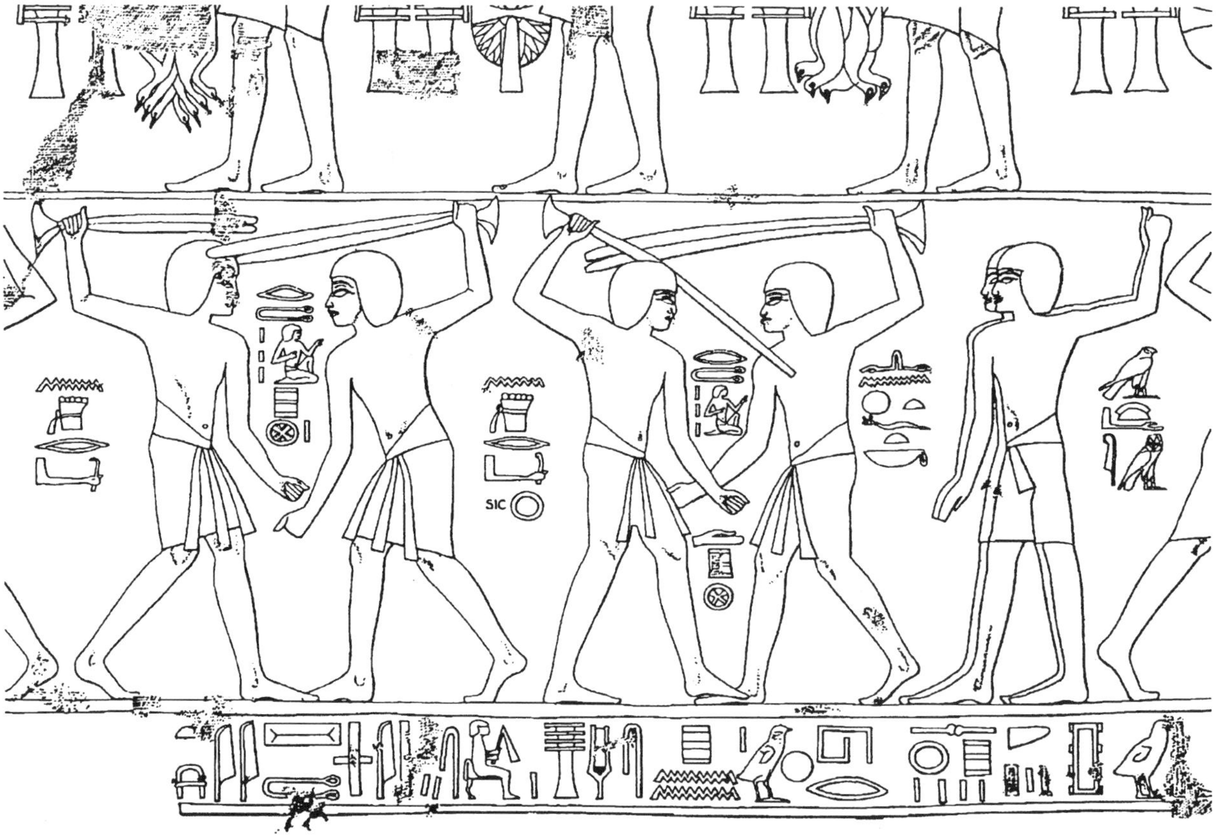

Figure 32.6. Four Fencers Depicted in Two Bouts; On Right Judges Render Judgment Call Against Fencer (left) Who Stands on Foot of Fencer (right) (Tomb of Kheruef; after *Kheruef*, pls. 61, 63)

A total of seven fencers are depicted engaged in three bouts (figs. 32.6–7). In two bouts, shown adjacent to each other, one pair of fencers fights in each (fig. 32.6). One pair is named "the men of Pe," the other "the men of Dep" (alternatively, both bouts might be understood as depicting men of Pe fencing with men of Dep). In the third bout, three fencers are depicted fighting each other, as though in a melee (fig. 32.7). As weapons, the fencers use a papyrus reed or bundled stalks of papyrus.

The captions that accompany the bouts record the speeches of each scoring player, utilizing a precise terminology (*Kheruef*, pls. 61–63):

> *nḏr* "hit!"
> *nḏr sp-sn* "hit 2 times!"[19]

The captions suggest that the combatants accumulated a number of scoring hits, just as in modern fencing. I propose that one of the bouts is refereed by two judges (see fig. 32.6).[20] John Wilson has already shown that Egyptian wrestling matches were often refereed by an official (Wilson 1931, pp. 213, 217); hence, it is not surprising that fencing bouts, likewise, could be judged. The two judges are depicted in overlapping profile with left arms upraised, standing behind the fencer on the right side. The representation and position of the judges suggest that they are probably to be understood as standing behind and beside that fencer, or more probably as flanking him on both sides. In this manner, they could observe both fencers simultaneously. The appearance of these judges bears an uncanny resemblance to the method of judging in modern non-electric fencing, where two judges likewise stand behind and beside each fencer (fig. 32.4).

19. Similarly, Decker and Herb 1994, p. 566 [M2]: "Treffer(?)," "Treffer zweimal(?)."

20. In the translations of *Kheruef*, p. 64, the judges are identified as a "pair of ritualists." Complicating their identification is that in the publication of the drawing, these persons are physically separated from the fencing scene by the join of pls. 61 and 63.

Figure 32.7. Three Fencers Fight Each Other in a Single Bout (Tomb of Kheruef; after *Kheruef*, pl. 63)

In the tomb of Kheruef, the judges raise their arms (as do modern judges), reacting specifically to the double hit of the fencer on the left (*nḏr sp-sn*). They declare:

nn <wn> ḫfty{t}.k
You have no opponent![21]

This statement is probably a judgment call and the officials' admonishment to the fencer on the left side, who is depicted scoring his two hits while stepping on his opponent's foot! No other figure in the tomb is shown standing in this manner.[22] Apparently, due to an unfair advantage (and violation of rules?), the judges are nullifying the hits of the attacking player.[23]

Importantly, the judges' activity also has an underlying symbolic meaning that is revealed in several factors:

(1) The judges' statement, *nn <wn> ḫfty{t}.k*, is also uttered in a nearby scene by a lector priest at the singing and dancing related to erecting the *ḏd*-pillar (*Kheruef*, pls. 49, 59, p. 63). In that context, the statement is addressed to the king as a triumphant being.[24]

(2) Standing behind that lector priest are two persons who are depicted in a pose that is identical to that of the fencing judges. They are identified as *ḥs*(*w*) "singers" (cf. "minstrels," *Kheruef*, pls. 49, 59, p. 63), and they also observe the singing and dancing associated with erecting the *ḏd*-pillar.

Because of the fencing judges' associations with the priest's speech and the singers' poses, they probably are also ritualists like those with the lector priest, and their judgment call would also have an ulterior religious meaning related to the victory of the king in erecting the *ḏd*-pillar.

Kheruef states explicitly in his tomb that Amenhotep III revived ancient ceremonies and rites for his *sed*-festival that had not been practiced in Egypt for a long period. He says:

It was His Majesty who did this in accordance with writings of old.
(Past) generations [of] people since the time of ancestors had never celebrated (such) rites of the jubilee (*Kheruef*, p. 43, pl. 28, cols. 9–10).

21. So *Kheruef*, p. 64; *Wb*. 3.277; Decker and Herb 1994, p. 566 [M2]: "nicht gibt es deinem gegner." The redundant *-t* in *ḫfty{t}.k* suggests a lesser alternative: *n <wn> ḫfty tk<kw>* "there is no opponent attacking." For the spelling of *tkk* "attack" with the single *k*, see *Wb*. 5.336; Lesko 1989, p. 100.

22. All of the other fencers and boxers have their feet on the groundline. However, while the dancers in the register above are sometimes shown with one foot elevated, they never step on any others' feet.

23. Similarly, we see a warning by a referee to a cheating wrestler among the wrestling scenes at Medinet Habu: *ỉmy-ḥr.k tw.k m-bꜣḥ pr-ꜥꜣ ꜥnḫ wḏꜣ snb pꜣy.k* [*nb*] "Beware, you are in the presence of Pharaoh, l.p.h., your lord!" (*MH* 2, pl. 111, col. 17; cf. Edgerton and Wilson 1936, p. 139).

24. So in the adjacent boxing scenes, each victory is also associated directly with the triumph of the king; each victorious boxer declaims, "Horus 'Appearing in Truth' (i.e., Amenhotep III) has prevailed" (*Kheruef*, p. 64).

Kheruef's statement is an indicator that fencing, as ritual combat, was a rite of the *sed*-festival in earlier times, probably as early as the Old Kingdom, and that this scene could have been copied from a source of such early date.

The fencing motif in Kheruef also contains clear parallels with the Pyramid Texts. Whereas Kheruef's fencers employ papyrus stalks as weapons, in PT 324 the king uses a *sd*-plant evocative of Osiris to strike the Sethian entities. Similarly, in Kheruef "men of Pe" fence within a context of erecting the *ḏd*-pillar that symbolizes the resurrection of Ptah-Sokar-Osiris, while in PT 482 the fencing dance is performed by the souls of Pe in the context of the funeral and resurrection of Osiris. Therefore, the fencing motif in Kheruef functions in an Osirian context that is consistent with the earlier fencing genre of the Old and Middle Kingdoms which stressed the resurrection of Osiris and the triumph of Horus over their enemies.

In the New Kingdom, this meaning was extended in logical fashion to royal theology, whereby fencing and wrestling by Egyptian soldiers in the presence of the king symbolized the destruction of Egypt's enemies, the triumph of the king as the living Horus, and the primacy of the Egyptian state.

Tomb of Meryre II at Amarna

At Amarna in the tomb of Meryre II, as part of the *durbar* of Akhenaten in year 12, Egyptian soldiers fence and wrestle before the dais of the king, while the foreign nations bow in submission to Akhenaten enthroned (Davies 1905, pls. 37–38; Touny and Wenig 1969, pp. 22–23, fig. 6; Decker and Herb 1994, p. 566 [M3], pl. 39). Clearly the fencing and wrestling occur within the general context of the triumphant nature of Egyptian kingship. Their presence here functions as a cosmological statement of royal supremacy.

Tomb of Amunmose

An important fencing scene occurs in the tomb of Amunmose (TT 19; reign of Ramesses II). One pair of fencers and two pairs of wrestlers are shown competing in the second court of the mortuary temple of Thutmose III, i.e., in the open area between the second pylon and the temple proper (Decker and Herb 1994, p. 567 [M5], pl. 39; Decker 1992, pp. 81–82, fig. 51; Touny and Wenig 1969, p. 15 [lower]; Vandier d'Abbadie 1941, p. 470, fig. 52, p. 477, fig. 55; Wilson 1931, pp. 211, 213–15, passim).[25] Observing the fighting rituals is the statue of Thutmose III standing in the bark shrine of the temple. These games take place during the festival of Amenhotep I.[26] The speech of the victorious wrestler asserts the king's divinely ordained dominance over every foreign land:

> Amun is the god who decreed the protection against every land to the ruler. Alas for you, O miserable soldier, who boasted with his mouth! ... (Wilson 1931, pp. 213 [text 8], 212 [text 1], pl. 38)

Tomb of Khonsu

In the tomb of Khonsu, First Prophet of Menkheperre (Theban tomb 31), two fencing scenes are portrayed as part of the festival of Montu at Armant.[27] The statue of Montu is towed across the river from the temple of Armant to the temple of Tôd, and thereafter back to Armant. In the two scenes that depict the towing of the god's bark in each direction, a pair of marines fence on the roof of the cabin of the tow ships. Above one pair is the text:

> *kḏn Rʿiꜣ n iḥ n Wsr-mꜣʿt-rʿ stp-n-rʿ*
> *ꜣImn di.f pꜣ ḳn*[*t*]
>
> The charioteer of the stable of Usermaatre-setepenre, Raia, (he says):
> "Amun, he has granted the victory" (Davies and Gardiner 1948, pl. 12).[28]

25. The combatants are depicted between the two pylons and directly before the structure of the sanctuary. Comparison with Ricke's (1939, pl. 5) archaeological plan of the temple suggests that the fighting occurs on the broad terrace before the doorway of the main temple.

26. PM 1/1, p. 33 (4). Decker (1992, p. 82) suggests that these scenes of combat represent funerary games held at the funeral or as part "of a periodic ceremony in memory of the deceased" individual.

27. Decker and Herb 1994, pp. 567–68 [M6], pls. 317–18; Decker 1992, p. 87, fig. 57; Davies and Gardiner 1948, pp. 14–15, pls. 11–12.

28. Similarly, Decker and Herb 1994, p. 568, "Amun (ist es) der den Sieg schenkt."

Figure 32.8. Egyptian and Nubian Soldiers Fence with Each Other (left); Victorious Fencer Makes Victory Address (right) (Medinet Habu, Temple of Ramesses III, First Court, South Wall, West of Window of Appearances; Photograph by P. Piccione)

While the character of the fencing scenes is similar to that of Meryre II and Amunmose, no king attends the ritual combat. Rather, since the fencers fight before the bark of Montu, Montu is witness to these events.

Temple of Medinet Habu

Among the most informative of all the fencing representations in the New Kingdom are those in the temple of Ramesses III at Medinet Habu (see figs. 32.3, 8). On the south wall of the first court below the window of appearances, three pairs of fencers and seven pairs of wrestlers are depicted before an assembly of the king's sons and the royal court.[29] Wilson, followed later by Nims, indicates that these fighting scenes were copied nearly exactly from the mortuary temple of Ramesses II at the Ramesseum, ultimately incorporating a decorated block from the Ramesseum in the wall at Medinet Habu (Wilson 1931, p. 212, n. 1; Nims 1976, pp. 169–70; *MH* 2, pl. 127B). Hence, the fighting scenes at Medinet Habu testify to the existence of fencing scenes (now lost) at the Ramesseum. From the accompanying texts and the portrayal of the contestants at Medinet Habu, it is clear that the tournaments were staged among the different ethnic elements within the Egyptian army, i.e., Egyptian soldiers versus Nubians, Libyans, and Syrians (see fig. 32.3). While one wrestling scene depicts a Libyan opponent, the accompanying text, mindlessly copied from the Ramesseum, refers to a Syrian (*MH* 2, pl. 111, col. 27; Edgerton and Wilson 1936, p. 140, n. 27a).

The entire scene at Medinet Habu is dominated by the king's window of appearances (see fig. 32.9). The spectators and the combatants are situated in relation to the now-empty window, in such a way that many directly face toward it. Clearly, they were meant to face the actual person of the king as he stood in the window observing the real tournaments. The architectonic relationship of the window to the representations indicates

29. Decker and Herb 1994, pp. 569–70, pls. 311, 319–21, Falttafel G; Decker 1992, pp. 78–81; *MH* 2, pls. 111–12; Touny and Wenig 1969, pls. 16–18.

that the fencing and wrestling activities were actually staged in the first court of the temple, and that they were overseen by the king himself. These tournaments would have been conducted during religious festivals since, with certain exceptions, these were the occasions when the public was permitted to enter the courtyards of the great temples to celebrate and petition the gods.

Unlike the earlier fencing scenes, each fencer at Medinet Habu wears protective clothing, including a head cloth and face strap. In addition, the tip of each fencing stick is bated with a small oval cap to prevent injury to the fencers. Characteristic of Ramesside fencing scenes, the fencer attacks with the weapon in his right hand and parries blows with his left arm, which is strapped from elbow to fingertip with a protective guard (see fig. 32.3). The fencers' stylized poses are nearly identical to the conventional stances depicted in the tombs of Amunmose and Khonsu, noted above. In one scene, an Egyptian fencer says to his Nubian opponent:

> *smn tw n.ỉ dỉ.ỉ ptr.k ḏrt ꜥḥꜣwty*
>
> Establish yourself for me (i.e., "on guard!"), for I shall cause you to see the hand of a warrior (*MH* 2, pl. 111, col. 30; cf. Edgerton and Wilson 1936, p. 140).

The depictions record only the Egyptians' victories; thus, a victorious fencer exclaims to the assembled:

> *ꜣImn pꜣ nṯr r wḏ sw pꜣ nḫ<t> n pꜣ ḥḳꜣ r tꜣ nb pꜣ sꜣ ꜥꜣ n Wsr-mꜣꜥt-rꜥ mry ꜣImn ꜥnḫ wḏꜣ snb pꜣ ḥꜣwty*
>
> Amun is the god who decrees the victory to the ruler over every land, O great company of Usermaatre-meriamun, Ruler, l.p.h., O captain! (*MH* 2, pl. 111, cols. 31–33; cf. Edgerton and Wilson 1936, p. 140)

This text is similar to the victory speeches in the tombs of Amunmose and Khonsu. As Wilson has shown, this address is typical of the triumphal refrains of victorious fencers and wrestlers competing before the king (Wilson 1931, pp. 211–20, passim). These refrains indicate that each Egyptian victory symbolized Amun's grant to the king of triumph over all foreign lands. Therefore, these games were a venue for enacting cosmological truths for the Egyptians, confirming Amun as the tutelary deity of the nation, while symbolically destroying the enemies of Egypt (perhaps even functioning in the manner of an execration), and maintaining the dominance of the Egyptian state.

FENCING AS SPORT AND RITUAL

According to Pyramid Text Spells 324, 469, and 482, fencing occurs within a physical context of ceremony and dance, and the outcome of the activity was pre-ordained. In the Ramesseum Dramatic Papyrus, fencing similarly functions as part of ritual with a predetermined end. At the same time, the scenes of fencing in Kheruef (which have antecedents in the Pyramid Texts) and those at Medinet Habu reflect the immediacy of a true sporting activity in which the contestants actually engaged to win and to cheat, if necessary.[30] Thus, in these latter instances of ritualized combat, an element of uncertainty seems to exist. On the other hand, the symbolic meaning that we have adduced for the judgment call in Kheruef would seem to nullify the fencing as real competition. Therefore, we are left to determine whether ritualized fencing in Egypt was actually mock fighting and dance or a true athletic endeavor.

The immediacy of the latter depictions and the admonishments against cheating indicate that the fencing bouts were real and not regularly fixed in the Egyptians' favor. Hence, the outcomes would always remain in doubt until the end of the bouts. This situation would not, otherwise, seem consistent with standard notions of ritual. However, whether Egyptians or Nubians actually won or lost their specific bouts was irrelevant to the cosmology and absolute meaning of the game. Two realities are involved here: the practical, ephemeral truth of playing, winning and losing, and the higher reality of religion that is eternal and which overshadows the former. The fencing occurs simultaneously on two planes, the temporal-sportive and the cosmic-ritualistic. On the cosmic-ritualistic plane, the religious significance of the fencing games does not depend on how the contestants actually performed, but on the fact that they are *depicted and recorded* on the walls as timeless Egyptian victories. These atemporal victories reflect the religious and political ethos of the Egyptian state, regardless of how the real fencers actually performed. In this manner, a Nubian could actually win his particular contest, while on a

30. At Medinet Habu, it is a wrestler who is warned by the referee against cheating.

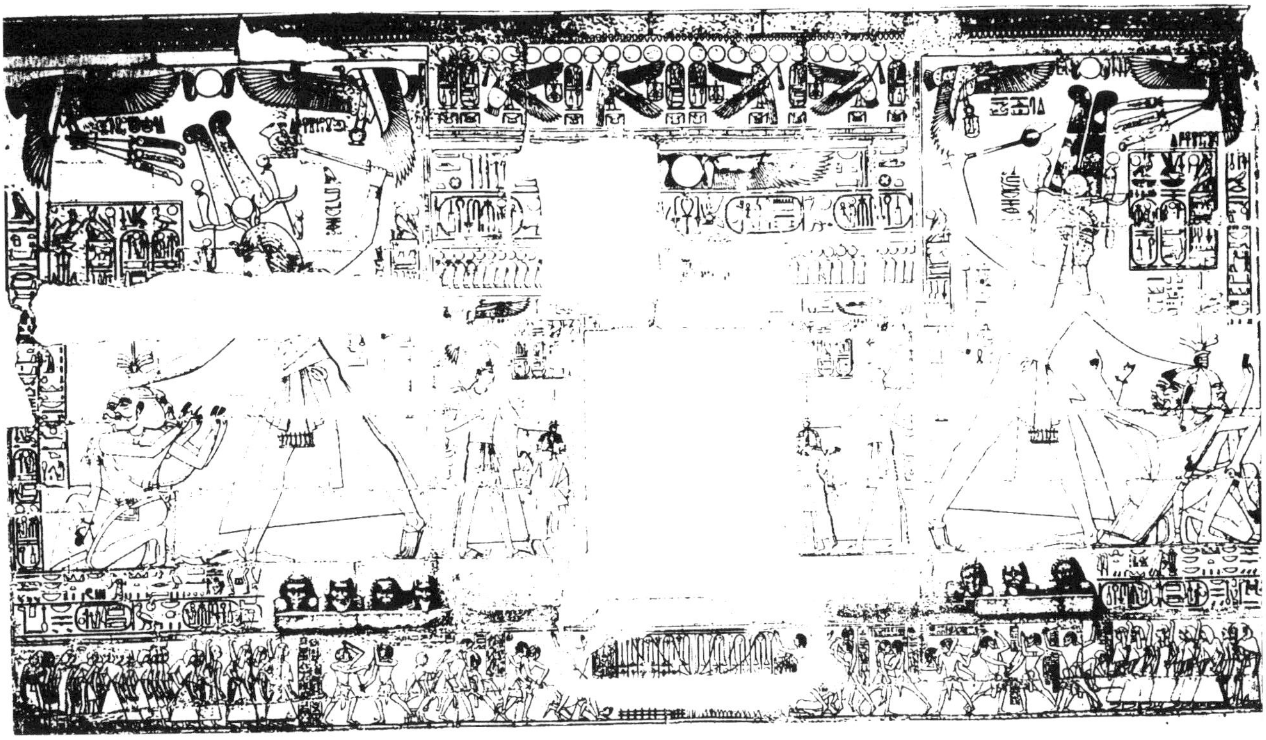

Figure 32.9. Window of Appearances Surmounts Scenes of Fencing and Wrestling (Medinet Habu, Temple of Ramesses III, First Court, South Wall; after Nelson and Hölscher 1931, p. 35, fig. 22)

cosmic level, all victories were still deemed as Egyptian.[31] Similarly, the judges in Kheruef's fencing scenes function on two planes: temporally, making judgment calls; cosmically, as ritualists, declaring cosmological statements about the victorious king. Likewise, the many fencing sticks that were placed into the tomb of Tutankhamun and which are depicted in the tomb of Ramesses III also have a symbolic meaning in addition to any practical significance. Their presence facilitates the cosmological victory for the dead king that is inherent in the fencing ritual (whether or not the king actually won or lost his bouts during his lifetime with those sticks). Religion and sport combine in the fencing contexts, and they do not contravene each other since they function on separate planes.

On another level, the Egyptians did not distinguish athletic and recreational activities from religious practices and rituals. Gaming and athletic tournaments formed a significant element of religious festivals, with such events being staged at the temples or festival sites in conjunction with religious ceremonies. During these feasts, the public entered the great temples to see and petition their deities and to watch athletes compete in combative sports. A courtyard full of contestants, perhaps all competing at once, would have excited worshippers and onlookers and elevated their emotional states to a high level. Norman Davies (1928, p. 62) interprets the performance of athletics at Egyptian festivals as a means to heighten the feelings of the spectators for religious purposes:

> Cruder religions regard it as a merit to reach a physical rhapsody, a throbbing emotion, which ... must be induced by the sight of rapid and violent physical action and the sound of strong monotonous rhythm. ... For this reason, perhaps, it was on solemn occasions in Egypt that the wildest physical displays were given that professional skill could provide. ... The emotion called up by strong pulsation and whirling motion added to processional rites is conceived as a proper response to the superhuman, and is repaid by an extraordinary pleasure, so that amusement and worship are confusedly mingled.

Davies is certainly correct in his assessment, although we also note his personal antipathy to this phenomenon.[32] The Egyptians would have perceived the emotional excitement of a sporting event performed in a religious set-

31. In a similar manner, the Egyptians could record high Nile levels in years of *sed*-festivals for religious purposes, when the river did not actually rise so high (Helck 1966).

32. Apparently, for Davies (1928, p. 62) this melding of athleticism and ritual signified a coarseness in religious thought, with dull-minded adherents who could only be swept up by dazzling physical images and breathtaking physical activity; so, for example, he states, "if the acrobat is given a place in religious ceremony ... [it] is the means of providing the proper quantity of emotion in the duller onlooker."

ting as conducive to religious experience. Thus, worshippers became spectators and fans in this situation. However, to this concept we add the notion of community. The strong emotions evoked among the spectators would have been shared communally, strengthening social bonds among them.

The final dimension of ritualistic fencing was a didactic one. In this study, we have seen that fencing — otherwise an act of public recreation and military training — occurred in religious contexts where it was a medium through which important mythological events were recreated on a communal scale. From the Old Kingdom through the Ptolemaic period, the fencers assumed the roles of gods or their followers, dramatizing myth and promulgating significant sacred principles through the fighting spectacle. Thus, the public orchestration of ritualistic fencing was one method by which cosmological beliefs and mythology were made incarnate and accessible to the general population of Egypt.

References

Alaux, M.
1975 *Modern Fencing.* New York: Scribner.

Altenmüller, H.
1964 "Letopolis und der Bericht des Herodot über Papremis." *Jaarbericht van het Vooraziatisch-Egyptisch Genootschap "Ex Oriente Lux"* 18: 271–79.

Borghouts, J. F.
1973 "The Evil Eye of Apophis." *Journal of Egyptian Archaeology* 59: 114–50.
1995 "Rethinking the Papremis Ritual (Herodotus II.63)." In *Hermes Aegyptiacus: Egyptological Studies for B. H. Stricker on His 85th Birthday,* edited by T. Du Quesne, pp. 43–52. Discussions in Egyptology, Special No. 2. Oxford: DE Publications.

Brovarski, E.
1975 "Varia." *Serapis* 3: 1–8.

Carter, H.
1933 *The Tomb of Tut-Ankh-Amen Discovered by the Late Earl of Carnarvon and Howard Carter*, Volume 3. London: Cassel.

Carter, H., and A. C. Mace
1923 *The Tomb of Tut-Ankh-Amen Discovered by the Late Earl of Carnarvon and Howard Carter*, Volume 1. London: Cassel.

Davies, N. de G.
1905 *The Rock Tombs of El-Amarna*, Part 2: *The Tombs of Panehesy and Meryra II.* Archaeological Survey of Egypt 14. London: Egypt Exploration Society.
1928 "The Graphic Work of the Egyptian Expedition 1925–1927." *Bulletin of the Metropolitan Museum of Art* 23 (February): 59–72.

Davies, N. de G., and A. H. Gardiner
1948 *Seven Private Tombs at Kurnah.* Edited by A. H. Gardiner. Mond Excavations at Thebes 2. London: Egypt Exploration Society.

De Vries, C. E.
1960 Attitudes of the Ancient Egyptians toward Physical Recreative Activities. Ph.D. dissertation, University of Chicago.

Decker, W.
1992 *Sports and Games of Ancient Egypt.* Translated by A. Guttmann. New Haven: Yale University Press.

Decker, W., and M. Herb
1994 *Bildatlas zum Sport im alten Ägypten: Corpus der bildlichen Quellen zu Leibesübungen, Spiel, Jagd, Tanz und verwandten Themen*, Two Volumes. Handbuch der Orientalistik, Abteilung 1, Der Nahe und der Mittlere Osten 14. Leiden: E. J. Brill.

von Deines, H.
1959 *Wörterbuch der ägyptischen Drogennamen.* Grundriss der Medizin der alten Ägypter 6. Berlin: Akademie-Verlag.

Edgerton, W. F., and J. A. Wilson
1936 *Historical Records of Ramses III: The Texts in Medinet Habu, Volumes I and II.* Studies in Ancient Oriental Civilization 12. Chicago: University of Chicago Press.

Faulkner, R. O.
1969 *The Ancient Egyptian Pyramid Texts.* Oxford: Clarendon Press.

Gardiner, A. H.
1973 *Egyptian Grammar.* Third edition revised. Oxford: Griffith Institute.

Hayes, W. C.
1959 *Scepter of Egypt: A Background for the Study of Egyptian Antiquities in the Metropolitan Museum of Art,* Part 2: *The Hyksos Period and the New Kingdom (1675–1080 B.C.).* New York: Metropolitan Museum of Art.

Helck, W.
1966 "Nilhöhe und Jubiläumsfest." *Zeitschrift für ägyptische Sprache und Altertumskunde* 93: 74–79.

Jéquier, G.
1921 *Les frises d'objets des sarcophages du Moyen Empire.* Mémoires publiés par les Membres de l'Institut français d'archéologie orientale du Caire 47. Cairo: Institut français d'archéologie orientale.

Lesko, L.
1989 *A Dictionary of Late Egyptian*, Volume 4. Providence: B. C. Scribe Publications.

Lloyd, A.
1976 *Herodotus Book II*, Volume 1: *Commentary 1–98*. Études préliminaires aux religions orientales dans l'Empire Romain 43. Leiden: E. J. Brill.

Naville, E.
1901 *The Temple of Deir el Bahari*, Volume 4. London: Egypt Exploration Fund.

Nelson, H. H., and U. Hölscher
1931 *Medinet Habu Reports: 1. The Epigraphic Survey, 1928–31; 2. The Architectural Survey, 1929/30: Third Preliminary Report*. Oriental Institute Communications 10. Chicago: University of Chicago Press.

Nims, C. F.
1976 "Ramesseum Sources of Medinet Habu Reliefs." In *Studies in Honor of George R. Hughes, January 12, 1977*, edited by J. H. Johnson and E. F. Wente, pp. 169–75. Studies in Ancient Oriental Civilization 39. Chicago: Oriental Institute.

Omlin, J. A.
1971 *Der Papyrus 55001 und seine satirisch-erotischen Zeichnungen und Inschriften*. Museo Egizio di Torino, catalogo, serie 1, monumenti e testi 3. Turin: Edizione d'Arte Fratelli Pozzo.

Peck, W. H.
1978 *Egyptian Drawings*. New York: E. P. Dutton.

Piccione, P. A.
NYP "Body-Related Games and Sports in Ancient Egypt." In *Materials for the History of the Human Body in the Ancient Near East*. Groningen: Styx Publications.

Reeves, N.
1990 *The Complete Tutankhamum: The King, the Tomb, the Royal Treasure*. London: Thames and Hudson.

Ricke, H.
1939 *Der Totentempel Tuthmoses' III.: Baugeschichtliche Untersuchung*. Beiträge zur ägyptischen Bauforschung und Altertumskunde 3/1. Cairo: n.p.

Sethe, K.
1908 *Die altägyptischen Pyramidentexten*, Volume 1. Leipzig: J. C. Hinrichs.
1910 *Die altägyptischen Pyramidentexten*, Volume 2. Leipzig: J. C. Hinrichs.
1928 *Der dramatische Ramesseumpapyrus*. Untersuchungen zur Geschichte und Altertumskunde Ägyptens 10. Leipzig: J. C. Hinrichs.

Shaw, I.
1991 *Egyptian Warfare and Weapons*. Shire Egyptology 16. Princes Risborough: Shire Publications.

Touny, A. D., and S. Wenig
1969 *Der Sport im alten Ägypten*. Leipzig: Edition Leipzig.

Vandier d'Abbadie, J.
1941 "Deux nouveau ostraca figurés." *Annales du Service des antiquités de l'Égypte* 40: 467–88.

Wente, E. F.
1969 "Hathor at the Jubilee." In *Studies in Honor of John A. Wilson, September 12, 1969*, edited by E. B. Hauser, pp. 83–91. Studies in Ancient Oriental Civilization 35. Chicago: University of Chicago Press.

Wilson, J. A.
1931 "Ceremonial Games of the New Kingdom." *Journal of Egyptian Archaeology* 17: 211–20.

Wise, T., and A. McBride
1981 *Ancient Armies of the Middle East*. Men-at-Arms Series 109. London: Osprey Publishing.

Wreszinski, W.
1923–38 *Atlas zur altaegyptischen Kulturgeschichte*. 3 volumes. Leipzig: J. C. Hinrichs.

33

AN OBLIQUE REFERENCE TO THE EXPELLED HIGH PRIEST OSORKON?

ROBERT K. RITNER

The Oriental Institute, Chicago

It is a pleasure to offer this small tribute to Edward Wente, whose contributions to the field of Third Intermediate Period studies are well known, and who was kind enough to discuss the preliminary findings here given formal presentation.[1]

In 1885, Maspero published selected inscriptions from a Third Intermediate Period sarcophagus, said to be excavated from the Theban Asâsîf, that detailed the genealogy of one Meresamenet, a female descendant of a King Takelot.[2] Although unstated by Maspero, the piece derived from the collective burials of the priesthood of Montu (Twenty-second to Twenty-sixth Dynasties), discovered by Mariette in 1858 within subterranean chambers at Deir el-Bahri.[3] As CGC 41035, the sarcophagus was fully published in 1913 by Moret,[4] yet its genealogical texts have received problematic treatment in general studies of dynastic history, with the royal Takelot variously identified as the first, second, or third of that name. The genealogy of Meresamenet is unmentioned in Kitchen's fundamental treatment of the period,[5] but its prominence within a series of subsequent studies[6] justifies a detailed re-examination.

The seven relevant texts of the sarcophagus, replete with orthographic peculiarities, are as follows:

1. Central Text on the Cover

... n kꜣ n Wsỉr ḥs (n) ḫnw (n) ʾImn Mr-s-ʾImn.t sꜣ.t Wsrkn pꜣ-Tꜣ-wḏꜣy nb ỉmꜣḫ

"... for the spirit of the Osiris, chantress (of) the residence[7] (of) Amun, Meresamenet, daughter of Osorkon, He of Teudjoy, possessor of reverence" [8]

2. Chest Exterior: Side 3 (= Maspero "Right Side"). A

... n kꜣ n Wsỉr ḥs n ḫnw n ʾImn Mr-s-ʾImn.t sꜣ.t Wsrkn mꜣʿ-ḫrw pꜣ-(Tꜣ)-wḏꜣy

"... for the spirit of the Osiris, chantress of the residence of Amun, Meresamenet, daughter of Osorkon, the justified, He of (Te)udjoy" [9]

3. Chest Exterior: Side 3 (= Maspero "Right Side"). B (lines 1–3)

Ḏd-mdw ỉn Wsỉr ḥs (n) ḫnw (n) ʾImn Mr-(s)-ʾImn.t mw.t=s ḥs (n) ḫnw (n) ʾImn Šꜣ-ʾImn-(ỉ)m=s

"Words said by the Osiris, chantress (of) the residence (of) Amun, Mere(s)amenet, whose mother is the chantress (of) the residence (of) Amun, She(m)amen(i)mes." [10]

---

1. I would like to thank John Sanders for assistance in reproducing the hieroglyphic texts, all scanned by computer from the original publications.
2. Maspero 1885, p. 11
3. For bibliography of the find, see PM 1/2, p. 643.
4. Moret 1913, pp. 290–98, pl. 36.
5. Kitchen 1986.
6. Most recently, Elias 1995, pp. 57–67.
7. Literally, "interior"; see Yoyotte 1962, p. 45.
8. Moret 1913, p. 291 = Maspero 1885, p. 11.
9. Moret 1913, p. 294 = Maspero 1885, p. 11.
10. Moret 1913, p. 295 = Maspero 1885, p. 11. Found only in this inscription, the intrusive ʿꜣ appearing in both ladies' titles (in varying order) seems a copying error for *n*; see note 23, below.

Gold of Praise: Studies on Ancient Egypt in Honor of Edward F. Wente
Edited by Emily Teeter and John A. Larson
Studies in Ancient Oriental Civilization 58
Chicago: Oriental Institute, 1999

4. Chest Exterior: Side 4 (= Maspero "Left Side"). A

… (n) *kꜣ* (n) *Wsỉr ḥs n ḫnw n ʾImn Mr-s-ʾImn.t mw.t⸗s Šm-ʾImn-*(*ỉ*)*m⸗s mꜣꜥ*(*.t*)*-ḫrw*

"… (for) the spirit (of) the Osiris, chantress of the residence of Amun, Meresamenet, whose mother is Shemamen(i)mes, the justified" [11]

5. Chest Exterior: Side 4 (= Maspero "Left Side"). B (lines 6–10)

… *n kꜣ n Wsỉr ḥs* (*n*) *ḫnw n ʾImn Mr-s-ʾImn*(*.t*) *mw.t⸗s nb*(*.t*)*-pr Šm-ʾImn-ỉwm*(*⸗s*)

"… for the spirit of the Osiris, chantress (of) the residence of Amun, Meresamene(t), whose mother is the housewife, Shemamenime(s)" [12]

6. Chest Exterior: Side 4 (= Maspero "Left Side"). B (lines 14–20)

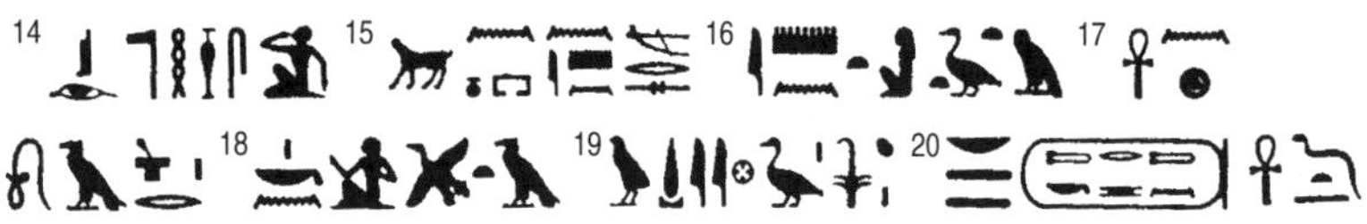

Wsỉr ḥs (*n*) *ḫnw n ʾImn Mr-s-ʾImn.t sꜣ.t m ꜥnḫ* (*n*) *Wsrkn pꜣ-Tꜣ-wḏꜣy sꜣ sꜣ*(?) *ny-sw.t nb tꜣ.wy Ṯkrỉṯ*{*n*} *ꜥnḫ ḏ.t*

"Osiris, chantress (of) the residence of Amun, Meresamenet, daughter in life[13] (of) Osorkon, He of Teudjoy, son of(?) the Royal Prince, Lord of the Two Lands, Takelot{en}, living forever" [14]

7. Chest Exterior: Side 4. B-Side 1 (= Maspero "Head End") (lines 24–28)

Wsỉr ḥs (*n*) *ḫnw n ʾImn Mr-s-ʾImn.t mw.t⸗s Šm-ʾImn-ỉm⸗s*

"Osiris, chantress (of) the residence of Amun, Meresamenet, whose mother is Shemamenimes" [15]

From these texts, it is clear that Meresamenet's parents are the royal scion Osorkon "He of Teudjoy" and the chantress and housewife Shemamenimes ("Sheamenimes" in contemporary pronunciation, as indicated by the phonetic spelling in text 3, above).[16] Regarding the role of the mother, this straightforward textual evidence is in opposition to the long repeated — but never substantiated — assertion that "chantresses of the interior" were sworn virgins, perpetuating their office exclusively by adoption.[17] Nothing in the inscriptions of CGC 41035 suggests that the chantress Shemamenimes is the *adoptive*,[18] rather than the *biological*, mother of chantress

11. Moret 1913, p. 296.
12. Moret 1913, p. 297 = Maspero 1885, p. 11.
13. The phraseology is odd but has drawn little comment beyond the obvious (Elias 1995, p. 64, n. 8). If it were translated "daughter by oath" (*Wb.* 1.202–03), it could constitute an expression of paternal adoption, in contrast to the dubious proposal for an adoptive relationship between mother and daughter, discussed below.
14. Moret 1913, p. 297 = Maspero 1885, p. 11.
15. Moret 1913, p. 297 = Maspero 1885, p. 11.
16. An early reflection of the phonology evident in the Coptic ϣⲉ; see *Wb.* 4.462; Černý 1976, p. 235. Elias' (1995, p. 65, n. 15) suggestion of elision should be disregarded.
17. First proposed in Yoyotte 1962. This brief lecture abstract does not contain footnoted references or any supporting documentation, yet its conclusions (based on a still unpresented dossier) have been accepted purely on faith and, for lack of critical assessment, have come to dominate discussion over thirty years later. Thus while Kitchen cites Yoyotte's analysis "provisionally" in 1973 (p. 329, n. 474), he presents the same article as established fact in 1990 (pp. 147, 149, n. 10).
18. No credence should be accorded the suggestion by Elias (1995, pp. 61–62) that the common expression *mw.t⸗s* "may well be adoptive" and thus "it is most prudent to view their relationship as adoptive as far as it can be known from the available evidence." In the so-called "blood genealogy" of Tafabart adduced as a parallel (p. 62), Elias follows Yoyotte (1962, p. 46) in confusing the father's mother with the daughter's. Yoyotte's "translation" of this, his only piece of evidence, suppresses the father's name to yield two mothers: "*la chanteuse de l'intérieur d'Amon Tafabart dont la mère est la chanteuse de l'intérieur d'Amon Tentmin et qu'a enfantée la maîtress de Maison Ditaouâouinêsé*" (ibid., p. 46). Using standard convention implying a direct translation, Yoyotte places his rendition of the text in italics. Since he does not cite his source, readers have assumed that the text reads precisely as he "quotes" it. On the contrary, Yoyotte has excised and inverted sections of the text for reasons that are nowhere explained. The Abydos stela actually reads: *ḥs* (*n*) *ḫnw* (*n*)

Meresamenet. On the contrary, the mother's secondary title of "housewife" (*nb.t-pr*) is completely inappropriate for a restricted, unmarried virgin.[19]

Less clear is the precise relation of Osorkon to King Takelot, as the seemingly redundant *sꜣ sꜣ ny-sw.t* of text 6 could indicate that Osorkon was the son of an *unnamed* prince of Takelot: *sꜣ* (*n*) *sꜣ ny-sw.t* (*n*) *nb tꜣ.wy Ṯkrỉṯ*{*n*} "son (of) the Royal Prince (of) the Lord of the Two Lands, Takelot{en}." Such an ellipsis would seem unlikely, however, and editors have preferred instead to understand *sꜣ ny-sw.t* as a highly unusual epithet of a ruling monarch: "Royal Prince and Lord of the Two Lands."[20] Most recently, Aston and Taylor have suggested that *sꜣ ny-sw.t* may be "a mere slip for *nsw-bỉty*."[21] Indeed, graphic irregularities are in no short supply within these texts, with the loss of *n*, *ỉ*, *s*, *t*, and *tꜣ*, and the intrusive presence of *w* (in *Šm-ꜣImn-ỉwm*(*=s*)) and *n* (in a unique spelling of Takelot[22]). Sign reversals, omissions, conflations, and redundancies are common.[23] The fluctuating presence of a final *-t* makes even the generally accepted name of the owner uncertain, as this could be only a visual marker for a feminine individual (yielding the more common name Meresamen[24]). Given the scribe's propensity for carelessness, and the vertical arrangement of the passage in question (), it would seem easiest to assume that *sꜣ sꜣ ny-sw.t* is but a conflation for *sꜣ ny-sw.t*,[25] applicable not to Pharaoh Takelot but to Osorkon, who — as the son of Lord of the Two Lands, Takelot — must have borne this title in any case. The relevant passage of text 6 should then read: "Meresamenet, daughter in life of Osorkon, He of Teudjoy, Royal Prince (of) the Lord of the Two Lands, Takelot." The question remains: which Takelot?

Despite an early suggestion by Budge,[26] scholars have not followed his identification of this king with Takelot I, the least known of all the Libyan pharaohs.[27] As recognized by Gauthier, there seems little reason to equate the prominent Osorkon II of Tanis, crown prince of this first Takelot, with the obscure Osorkon "He of Teudjoy." [28] Gauthier himself, however, was quite unsure of the identity of the Takelot on CGC 41035, and his suggestion of Takelot III is based only on the hesitant assumption that "Osorkon-Pa-Taouzaï" might be the "futur roi Osorkon

ꜣImn Tꜣfꜣbrṯ mꜣꜥ-ḫrw sꜣ.t Ptḥ-ỉ.ỉr-dỉ-sw mꜣꜥ-ḫrw ms nb(*.t*)*-pr Tỉ-ṯꜣw-ꜥ.wy-ꜣs.t mꜣꜥ-ḫrw mw.t=s ḥs* (*n*) *ḫnw* (*n*) *ꜣImn T*(*n*)*.t-Min mꜣꜥ-ḫrw* "the chantress of the interior of Amun, Tafabart, the justified, daughter of Ptahirdies, the justified, born of the housewife Titchauawyese, the justified, while her mother is the chantress of the interior of Amun, Tamin, the justified." The housewife Titchauawyese is most logically understood as the mother of Ptahirdies, whose spouse Tamin is the named mother of Tafabart (*mw.t=s*). The elimination of a named generation produces an artificial redundancy of mothers that is not merely "economical" but easily misleading for the uninformed reader. For the proper text, see Mariette 1982, p. 483, no. 1281. Yoyotte's translation and interpretation recur in Saphinaz-Amal Naguib 1990, pp. 206–07, 224–25, and 235.

19. *Wb.* 1.512:9–13: "Ehefrau." The incompatibility of the title for the notion of virginal chantresses was similarly evident to Kitchen (1990, p. 149, n. 17), who suggests that the Shemamenimes of text 5 might be "Meresamun's real mother?" Note also the existence of *marriage contracts* for chantresses of the interior, signalled by Yoyotte 1962, p. 48! Given the absence of any compelling, published evidence for virginal adoption, and the certain existence of cases (Shemamenimes, Tafabart) most likely contradictory to such a practice, it is now incumbent upon defenders of this old assertion to present any withheld dossiers for critical examination. As the *only* probative evidence to which Yoyotte alludes was inaccurately represented and need hardly support his conclusions, the notion of virginal chantresses should be discarded pending detailed investigation.

20. See Moret 1913, p. 322, index under Osorkon Patouzai: "fils du prince royal Takeloten." Maspero (1885) also associated the princely title with the enthroned Takelot: "fils du roi maître des deux pays *Tiklat*(*en*)." See likewise Aston and Taylor 1990, p. 132, who assume Osorkon to be "son of the 'King's Son, Lord of the Two Lands, Takeloth' (in cartouche)." A supposed parallel offered by Elias (1995, p. 64, n. 9) is readily dismissed, as the Ankh-Takelot under discussion was neither a king nor a "chief living son"; see Leahy 1992, p. 151.

21. Aston and Taylor 1990, p. 132.

22. For the variant orthographies of the name Takelot, see Berlandini 1979, pp. 95–97. The example from CGC 41035 is no. 32, p. 97.

23. Moret 1913, pp. 291 (reversal of *nṯr* and *b*, reversal of *nṯr* and *ꜥnḫ*, redundant *n ꜣImn*), 292 (loss of dative and genitive), 295 (*ꜥꜣ* wrongly for *n*), etc.

24. So understood by Maspero (1885). Examples without the final *-t* are just as common as those with the termination (six examples each). For spellings lacking the termination, see Moret 1913, p. 291, Cover, right side B, §I, line 5; p. 292, Cover, left side B', §I right, lines 4–5; p. 293, Cover, left side B', §I left, line 5, §II, lines 1–2, and §III, lines 1–2; p. 297, Chest, side 4 B, lines 8–9 (text 5, above). Compare also the otiose *-t* terminating the mother's name in text 7, above.

25. The scribe used two different, and thus redundant, writings for "son": the goose and the egg. Alternatively, the supposed "egg" may be only a garbled "*-t*" for *ny-sw.t*. Compare the writing of *sꜣ.t ny-sw.t* without honorific transposition on CGC 41036 in Moret 1913, pp. 300–01. Budge (1908) simply eliminates the "egg" from his copy; see the following note. The phrase "King's Son/Prince of the Lord of the Two Lands" is a fixed expression, termed "the style of the age" in Kitchen 1986, p. 119, §94. Thus a genitive should be restored between "Prince" and "Lord of the Two Lands."

26. Budge 1908, p. 45: "Uasarken, son of Thekeleth I" (without reference). In the same section, Budge conflates texts of High Priest and Prince Osorkon, the well-known son of Takelot II.

27. Kitchen 1986, pp. 310–12.

28. Budge's unsupported suggestion is cited, but not adopted, in Gauthier 1914, p. 391, n. 4.

IV?"[29] Such reasoning is no longer tenable, as Osorkon IV is now known to be the son of Sheshonq V, with a sphere of influence far removed from Thebes.[30] Gauthier's suggestion had found little support, and scholarly consensus instead favored Takelot II.[31]

Orthographic considerations would seem to confirm the identification with Takelot II because writings of the royal name with 𓈘 (Gardiner Sign List N36) are quite restricted in usage. As noted by Bonhême, "On remarque que le signe 𓈘 n'est jamais employé dans les graphies du nom propre de Takélot III, alors qu'il est très fréquent dans le nom de Takélot II."[32]

More recently, however, Leahy has revived the identification with Takelot III on the basis of the late orthography of "Osiris" on the Cairo coffin. As surveyed by Leahy, the few securely datable (post-Eighteenth Dynasty) examples of Osiris determined with the pennant (𓊹) appear first during the Twenty-fifth Dynasty in Thebes, with the earliest suggested example on a block from the Medinet Habu tomb of a daughter of King Rudamen, dating to about 740–730 B.C.[33] On the basis of this *terminus a quo*, Leahy thus re-attributes several supposed children of Takelot II to Takelot III:

> A generation after the death of Takeloth II would be ca. 800 B.C., a full 60–70 years before the earliest known example of this form. She must therefore be a daughter of Takeloth III. ... For the same reason, the *Di-ist-nsyt* and Osorkon mentioned on a coffin from Deir el-Bahari and CG 41035 respectively must have been offspring of Takeloth III and not an earlier king of that name.[34]

In this mention of Cairo 41035, however, Leahy fails to note that the coffin is contemporary *not with Osorkon* but with his daughter Meresamenet, necessarily *two generations* after the ancestral King Takelot. Were he Takelot II, as generally accepted, the coffin would still date to the period of Twenty-fifth Dynasty activity in Thebes (Alara, ca. 770 B.C.)[35] and precede the supposed earliest example by only thirty years — well within a reasonable margin of error for a stylistic dating criterion acknowledged by its author as "imprecise."[36] As there is no inherent reason for associating this minor spelling variation with the reign or policy of Piye,[37] the "Twenty-fifth Dynasty" practice could easily have begun a generation earlier. Some substantiation of this may be indicated by the presence of the same late spelling of Osiris on various objects dedicated by Piye's sister, Amenardis I, who had been installed as god's wife of Amun in Thebes early in the period of Kushite rule.[38]

Leahy's re-attribution of the king of Meresamenet's sarcophagus has now been acknowledged in a study of the family of Takelot III by Aston and Taylor, who, however, provide a different rationale for assigning Prince Osorkon to the sons of that Twenty-third Dynasty monarch.

> Meresamenet is otherwise unknown but her father Osorkon is probably to be identified with the Prophet of Amun-Re, King of the Gods, Osorkon, justified, son of the Lord of the Two Lands Takeloth, living for ever, born

29. Gauthier 1914, p. 391, §VII.2, n. 1 (for the entire section on the royal family): "Tous les monuments que je groupe sous cette rubrique ne sont pas clairs, et il est possible que certains d'entre eux aient une valeur autre que celle que je leur attribue."
30. Kitchen 1986, pp. 355, 372–76.
31. Gauthier's identification is questioned by Kees (1964, p. 149). For the standard identification with Takelot II, see Moret 1913, "Tableau généalogique" and p. 324; PM 1/2, p. 645.
32. Bonhême 1987, p. 192: "On pourrait peut-être postuler que les graphies nommant un roi Takélot et utilisant le signe 𓈘 désignent le roi Takélot II: critère vraisemblable d'identification."
33. Leahy 1979, pp. 141–53.
34. Leahy 1979, p. 148. It should be noted that CGC 41035 uses both the "later" spelling and the earlier writing with a seated god determinative; see Moret 1913, p. 297, side 4 B, line 24 (text 7, above).
35. See Priese 1970, pp. 16–32, and the suggested dates of ca. 780–760 in Kitchen 1986, p. 468. A recently proposed "minimal chronology" rests on weak suppositions and the mere possibility of disregarding more cogent evidence, as acknowledged by the author; see Depuydt 1993, p. 272.
36. Leahy 1979, p. 148 and compare p. 142: "a 'first' occurrence is, of course, only the first that we know of, and may, in fact, be considerably later than the actual first instance"; note also the small number of relevant, dated documents on ibid., p. 143. If, as suggested below, Prince Osorkon is to be identified with the octogenarian Osorkon "B," heir of Takelot II, then the generational gap could be much greater than the usual 25–30 years, and the coffin's date much later. The suggestion of an average generation of 25 years is at best an approximation, not a dictum; Bierbrier 1975, pp. xvi, 112–13, 116.
37. Note that Leahy's earliest example is on a private monument of the daughter of a local Theban ruler, not on a formal Twenty-fifth Dynasty work.
38. See Leahy 1979, pp. 143–44. The significance of this evidence would be greater if the objects could be dated to the early reign of Amenardis, particularly if she were installed by her father Kashta, as strongly indicated by his presence on her monuments (despite a curt dismissal by Kitchen 1986, p. 151, n. 289). As noted by Klaus Baer, "in every case where the evidence is clear, the Votaress was a (young) princess appointed by her father" (unpublished notes, Oriental Institute Archives File 1243). See further the arguments advanced in Wente 1976, p. 276.

> of the King's Daughter, King's Wife Irty-Bast. This filiation appeared on the fragments of a mummiform coffin found in 'Grab 27', north-west of the Ramesseum. The fragments, formerly in the Berlin Museum, are presumed to have been lost during the Second World War.[39]

By virtue of this "probable" identification, the authors are then able to restrict the king of 'Grab 27' — and CGC 41035 — to Takelot III.

> The name of the prince's mother eliminates the possibility of his being identified with Osorkon B, son of Takeloth II. Takeloth I is also unlikely to be the king in question, since his son Osorkon succeeded to the kingship as Osorkon II and was buried at Tanis.[40]

Unfortunately, however, there is no compelling reason for assuming that the Osorkons of the two coffins are identical. Anthes, the authors' source and publisher of the lost Berlin coffin, noted specifically that its Prince Osorkon "is otherwise unknown," and while one "might wish" to equate him with Osorkon *Pꜣ-tꜣ-wḏꜣjt,* in the absence of the epithet "that is not justified."[41]

Thus, the reference to the royal mother Irty-Bast in the Berlin text in no way excludes the possibility that the unnamed mother of the Cairo text might be Karomama "D," mother of the famous Prince Osorkon "B."[42] Moreover, *contra* Aston and Taylor, the texts of CGC 41035 *never* characterize the prince Osorkon as "merely an ordinary prophet" of Amun.[43] As is evident from the complete texts collected above, the only earthly titles accorded Osorkon are "He of Teudjoy" and "Royal Prince." It should be stressed that the personality of CGC 41035 is largely incidental to the authors' case for the existence of an Osorkon, son of Takelot III, best represented by the lost Berlin fragments.[44] Inadvertently, however, Aston and Taylor do raise several issues pertinent to an alternate identification of Osorkon *Pꜣ-tꜣ-wḏꜣy*: (1) the possible existence of other mentions of the family; (2) the significance of the epithet *Pꜣ-tꜣ-wḏꜣy*; and (3) the rare recognition in print that if this Osorkon be recognized as a son of Takelot II, then he would be the latter's crown prince, High Priest Osorkon ("B").[45]

Unnoted by Aston and Taylor, the family of Meresamenet may well be represented on yet another Cairo coffin, partially published by Maspero in 1883, two years prior to the first mention of CGC 41035. Described as "la plus jolie momie de femme que j'ai vue jusqu'à présent," the mummy case now bears the "temporary number" 21.11.16.5[46] and the inscription:

> *ḥs n ḫnw n ʾImn Šꜣwy-ʾImn-n-ỉm=s mꜣꜥ.t-ḫrw sꜣ.t n Ms n Mšwš Ṯkriwṯ mꜣꜥ-ḫrw*
>
> "Chantress of the residence of Amun, Sheamenimes, the justified, daughter of the Chief of the Meshwesh, Takelot, the justified"[47]

As recognized by Porter and Moss, both the title and name of Sheamenimes accord with those of the mother of Meresamenet.[48] In particular, the phonetic spelling of *šm* recalls that of text 3 from CGC 41035, copied above. Further paralleling CGC 41035, the orthography of Takelot utilizes , already noted as specific to the period

39. Aston and Taylor 1990, pp. 132–34, table p. 140 (quote on p. 132).
40. Aston and Taylor 1990, p. 133.
41. Anthes 1943, pp. 33–34, esp. 34: "Dieser Prinz Osorkon ist sonst nicht bekannt; allenfalls könnte man ihn mit dem Osorkon *Pꜣ-tꜣ-wḏꜣjt*, nach Gauthier einem Sohne Takelothis' III., gleichsetzen wollen, aber da der Beiname hier fehlt, ist das nicht berechtigt. ... So ist auch der König Takelothis nicht näher feststellbar." The identification that Anthes mentions only to reject would be hypothetically "desirable" simply as an expedient to associate the discovery with a known personage.
42. See Aston and Taylor 1990, pp. 133, 150, n. 6.
43. See Aston and Taylor 1990, pp. 133 (bottom), 150, n. 6.
44. The existence of a (different?) Osorkon "F," son of Takelot III, had already been postulated by Meulenaere; see discussions in Aston and Taylor 1990, pp. 133–34; Kitchen 1986, pp. 564–65 §485, 581 §521.
45. Compare Berlandini 1978, pp. 159–60.
46. Further given "no. 4937" according to Yoyotte 1961, p. 127.
47. Maspero 1883, p. 69.
48. For the temporary Cairo number and the identification with the family of Meresamenet and Takelot II, see PM 1/2, p. 823. Ranke (1935/1, p. 324, no. 19; 1935/2, p. 390) records no other Theban examples of the rare name. An alternative candidate for the mother of Meresamenet may be the chantress Sheamenimes, owner of an inner coffin now in Rio de Janeiro (inv. 532); for the coffin and suggested identification, see Kitchen 1990, pp. 145–49, pls. 136–38. This coffin, however, contains no genealogical information, and Kitchen's brief analysis of CGC 41035 explicitly follows the theories of Leahy and Aston and Taylor. Like these authors, he does not note the existence of Cairo 21.11.16.5.

of Takelot II. The title here accorded Takelot is extremely significant, and this inscription has been cited repeatedly as evidence for the retention of the Berber title *mas* "chief/lord" among the early Libyan rulers.[49] If this chantress Sheamenimes is accepted as the mother of the owner of CGC 41035, then the presence of the Berber title would favor an association with the era, and perhaps the person, of Takelot II, whom Porter and Moss state unequivocally is her father. Such an association would further imply that *both* of Meresamenet's parents were children (half brother and sister?) of a prominent Takelot, one or both of whom was Takelot II.[50] As noted above, this would make her father the crown prince Osorkon "B," local ruler in el-Hibeh and sometime high priest of Amun in Thebes.

Despite the statement of Aston and Taylor to the contrary,[51] the significance of the epithet *Pꜣ-tꜣ-wḏꜣy* has long been known, at least in so far as its literal meaning. In a 1917 study of Twenty-first Dynasty correspondence from el-Hibeh, Spiegelberg recognized that the epithet of Osorkon was to be translated "He of Teudjoy" with *Pꜣ* as a writing of the possessive prefix (Coptic ⲡⲁ < *Pꜣ* [*n*] "he of") and Teudjoy (ⲧⲉⲩϫⲟ / ⲧⲟⲩϫⲟⲓ < *Tꜣy=w-ḏꜣy.t* "Their wall") a typical spelling of the name of the garrison town of el-Hibeh.[52] Spiegelberg's interpretation was never subject to doubt, and his readings are easily found in the standard geographic dictionary of Gauthier[53] as well as recent scholarly treatments.[54] Almost eighty years after the fact, Elias now claims to have recognized the component "Teudjoy."[55] Unfortunately, he failed to rediscover the possessive prefix and was forced to invent a neologism: "Osorkon-the-Teudjoian."[56] Nonetheless, such a use of the possessive prefix to indicate geographic origin or attachment is in itself quite unexceptional.[57] The question, then, is not what does the epithet mean but why is it applied to the Prince Osorkon of CGC 41035?

Should this Osorkon be equated with the crown prince of Takelot II, a logical answer is readily forthcoming. Thanks largely to the efforts of the Oriental Institute's Epigraphic Survey, the vicissitudes of Prince Osorkon's sacerdotal career are well known.[58] Unlike other pontiffs of Amun, Osorkon's primary "headquarters"[59] was at el-

49. First recognized by Erman (1883, p. 69, n. 1) in a note to Maspero's publication of this coffin. See further *Wb.* 2.142:9: "libysch *mas*," termed Twenty-second Dynasty, with reference to the Dakhleh Stela (reign of Sheshonq I); compare Spiegelberg 1899, p. 16, n. 1; Gardiner 1933, p. 23; Bates 1970, p. 83. A full survey of the examples is found in Yoyotte 1961, pp. 123–24. As noted by Yoyotte, there is a marked tendency to suppress mention of Meshwesh affiliation in the later Twenty-second and Twenty-third Dynasties, though the Berber title recurs once for an "upstart" Libu in the reign of Sheshonq V; see Yoyotte 1961, pp. 144–45 §34. Disregarding all previous discussion, Elias (1995, pp. 61, 65, n. 15) translates the Berber title as "worthy."

50. For sibling or half sibling marriage in this period, see Kitchen 1986, p. 193, n. 23; Bierbrier 1984, p. 84. In the absence of a cartouche, it is perhaps more probable that the father of Sheamenimes is a recognized tribal leader other than Pharaoh Takelot II. A possible candidate for the Meshwesh chief is the Memphite pontiff Takelot "B," as suggested by Gardiner (1933, p. 23). The identification was followed by Yoyotte, to whom Elias (1995, p. 62) mistakenly credits the suggestion. Takelot "B" is a grandson of Osorkon II, like his contemporary and relative Takelot II; see Kitchen 1986, p. 101 §81 ("eldest son" of Sheshonq "D" but contrast "(younger?) son" of Sheshonq "D" in ibid., table 18, p. 487; see ibid., p. 193 §155, for the arbitrary position of Takelot in table 18). Sheamenimes and Prince Osorkon would then be cousins, a common marital relationship. In either case, if the two examples of the like-titled Sheamenimes are equated, then her husband Osorkon could not be a son of Takelot III, some six generations younger than his wife.

51. Aston and Taylor 1990, p. 132: "Each instance of his (*scil.* Osorkon's) name is followed by the phrase  var. 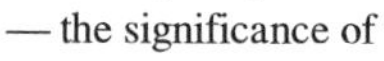 — the significance of which is not clear."

52. Spiegelberg 1917, p. 2: "der aus Teu-djo." Spiegelberg also notes that a comparable epithet was applied to another Twenty-second Dynasty individual, a "[Royal son of Ram]ses, Amenrud *Pn-Tꜣ-ḏꜣy*," whose father was the high priest of Amun Ankh-Takelot. See Spiegelberg 1917, p. 2, with reference to Chassinat 1912, p. 161. The text, engraved on an ebony box(?) fragment, was seen in the shop of a Cairo antiquity dealer in 1908 and was subsequently acquired as Leningrad 5528. The high priest is unrecorded by Kees (1964) or Kitchen (1986). For potential evidence of this pontiff, see Berlandini 1978, pp. 158–60, contra the skepticism of Meulenaere 1966, p. 113; idem 1982, p. 222. For examples of the name Ankh-Takelot, see the references gathered in Meulenaere 1982, p. 218, n. 4, and now the thorough study by Leahy 1992, pp. 151–53.

53. Gauthier 1929, p. 7 (bottom), s.v. "taiouzi(t)."

54. Berlandini 1978, pp. 159–60.

55. Elias 1995, pp. 58–61.

56. Elias 1995, p. 60, takes the possessive prefix as a simple definite article.

57. Compare Grapow 1937, pp. 44–53, esp. 49–50; Yoyotte 1961, p. 126, n. 1; Vernus 1981, pp. 435–37.

58. *RIK* 3 (the corresponding volume of translation and commentary, produced by a staff epigrapher, was subsequently published as Caminos 1958). Additional notes are now found in Jansen-Winkeln 1985, pp. 290–94. The following sketch of Osorkon's career is abstracted from these traditional studies. New and highly controversial attempts to reposition Takelot II as a contemporary of Sheshonq III would not invalidate the present study, as they cannot challenge the recorded facts of Osorkon's expulsions from Thebes, merely their length. For these revisionist studies, see Aston 1989; von Beckerath 1995, esp. pp. 9–10; Dautzenberg 1995, esp. pp. 25–26.

59. The apt term is used by Caminos 1958, p. 174; compare Kitchen 1986, p. 330 §292. Osorkon terms el-Hibeh his "residence" even on Theban monuments; see Caminos 1958, p. 17.

Hibeh, not Thebes. Having been appointed Theban high priest perhaps as early as year 10 of Takelot II,[60] the approximately twenty-year-old Osorkon[61] was forced to fight his way into Thebes on his first official visit in year 11.[62] From year 12, Osorkon made only "thrice-yearly visits to Thebes from el-Hibeh for the great festivals," and these brief visits were curtailed for a decade following year 15, when a local rebellion placed a rival claimant Harsiese ("B") upon the pontifical throne.[63] Reconciliation in year 24 lasted only until the death of Takelot in year 25 or 26,[64] with Osorkon next attested in years 22–29 of Takelot's usurping royal successor Sheshonq III.[65] Even these years were insecure for Osorkon, as Harsiese resumed local control in years 25–26.[66] Thereafter, Osorkon is again absent for a decade, re-appearing for a final time on two Theban monuments in year 39 of Sheshonq III, "still incurably forceful" and approximately 80 years old.[67] With the final expulsion of Osorkon after an intermittent career of some 55 years, the office of high priest remained securely in rival Theban hands.[68]

Were Meresamenet a daughter of Prince Osorkon (attached to the Theban choir of Amun in a period of calm), her death during one of his many expulsions — or after his final exit — would have presented the scribes of her coffin with a delicate situation. Her repudiated father could hardly be styled high priest when the office was held by hostile rivals, the superiors of the scribes themselves. A convenient alternative would be to acknowledge his rank as royal prince, but stigmatize him as "He of Teudjoy" — a singularly appropriate designation for the oft absentee pontiff. Such a solution accords with all of the evidence surveyed above and offers the only cogent explanation yet advanced for the presence of Osorkon's geographic epithet.

While Osorkon's parentage is certain, the matter of his own marriage and children is considerably less so. Caminos devotes not a word to the subject. Yet as early as 1889, Maspero had associated Turin stela 27 (now 1632) with the High Priest, declaring its dedicant "the housewife Shepenwepet" as his daughter and her mother Tent[...] as his wife.[69] In 1906, Legrain used this association in a misguided attempt to conflate the identities of High Priest Osorkon and Pharaoh Osorkon III.[70] Legrain's error was maintained in Gauthier's *Livre des rois*,[71] and subsequently corrected by Kees, who yet confirmed the affiliation of the housewife Shepenwepet with High Priest Osorkon.[72] In Kitchen's *Third Intermediate Period,* these putative relatives are included in the basic genealogical table of the Twenty-second and Twenty-third Dynasties, but the evidence for their relationship is neither discussed nor cited.[73] As multiple unions are the rule, not the exception, within the royal family, the marriage suggested by CGC 41035 need not exclude this Turin evidence.[74]

Since 1973, the date and family relationships of Turin stela 1632 have been called into question. Curiously, all recent analyses seem to have been conducted in apparent ignorance of the copious discussion the piece once gen-

60. Kitchen 1986, p. 199 §162.
61. Kitchen 1986, p. 330 §291, n. 481.
62. Caminos 1958, pp. 26–33, 152–55, 175; compare Kitchen 1986, pp. 330–31 §292. By revised chronology, Osorkon may have been the "usurper" from his opponent Harsiese; see Dautzenberg 1995, pp. 25–26.
63. Caminos 1958, pp. 88 §129, 161, 177; compare Kitchen 1986, p. 331 §§292–93, quote on p. 331 §292.
64. Kitchen 1986, pp. 107 §86, 331–33 §§293–94.
65. Caminos 1958, pp. 128 §199, 168–71 (text). As crown prince, Osorkon should have inherited the throne and clearly expected to do so; see Caminos 1958, pp. 15, 71 §102 n. c, 80 §117 n. d, 178 §289; compare Kitchen 1986, p. 332, n. 495. For recent suggestions that Sheshonq III was a ruler contemporary with Takelot II, see the bibliography in note 58, above.
66. See Kitchen 1986, pp. 338–39 §299.
67. In year 39, Osorkon is attested in both the Karnak Priestly Annals, fragment 7, and the Nile Level Records on the west face of the Karnak quay, text number 22. For the former, see Legrain 1900, pp. 55–56; idem 1909, p. 6; Kitchen 1986, p. 340 §300; Kruchten 1989, pp. 59–85. For the latter, see Legrain 1896a, pp. 111–18; idem 1896b, pp. 119–21; von Beckerath 1966, pp. 43–55 (photographs cited by von Beckerath on p. 43, n. 8, are Chicago Oriental Institute Photographs 8744–45). The Nile level text 22 is erroneously cited as dating to year 29 of Sheshonq III in Kitchen 1986, p. 339, n. 531, though this evidence is surveyed correctly on p. 107, n. 113. Recent attempts to collapse the reigns of Takelot II and Sheshonq III would lower Osorkon's age.
68. Kitchen 1986, pp. 196, 339 §299, table 13, p. 480: Takelot "E/F," youngest(?) son of Nimlot "C."
69. Maspero 1889, p. 741.
70. The equation was based on the supposed identity of the housewife Shepenwepet and the similarly-named god's wife of Amun, daughter of Osorkon III. See Legrain 1906a, pp. 156–58; idem 1906b, pp. 46–47 (on p. 46, n. 1, correct the page reference to Maspero 1889 from p. 471 to p. 741).
71. Gauthier 1914, pp. 386–87.
72. Kees 1964, p. 144. Recent attempts to revive the association fail to consider the matter of Shepenwepet; compare Aston 1989, p. 150. The discovery that Osorkon III also styled himself high priest of Amun does not prove his equation with Osorkon "B," but even if the equation were accepted it would not invalidate the thesis here advanced, as Meresamenet could have died prior to his accession; see Paleological Association of Japan, Egyptian Committee 1995, pp. 301–06, pl. 116.
73. Kitchen 1986, table 10, p. 477.
74. Contra Aston and Taylor 1990, p. 150, n. 8. See Kitchen 1986, p. 352 §312, for the contemporary "principal queen" and "lesser wife" of Osorkon III. Multiple marriages by chief dignitaries are common throughout the period; see ibid., pp. 115–16 §91.

erated as inventory number 27. Renewed interest in the text began with Munro's comprehensive study of late funerary stelae. In synopsizing the Turin stela of "Shepenwepet, daughter of the First Prophet of Amun, Osorkon, whose mother is *Ṯt-n-*[...]," Munro immediately acknowledges the similarity of Osorkon's name and title to those of the famous high priest attested as late as year 39 of Sheshonq III.[75] Because, however, the artistic style of the stela suggests to Munro a date ca. 720–700 B.C., he cautions that such an identification would require a late birth for the daughter and a lengthy lifetime. Given the obvious vitality of her proposed father, this would hardly be impossible. With caution, Munro declines to confirm the identification.[76] Munro's ambivalence is echoed in a 1978 survey of Theban priests and officials by Vittmann, who concedes the distinct possibility that Shepenwepet's father is the ill-fated Osorkon, son of Takelot II.[77] Vittmann then offers an alternate possibility, that the Turin Osorkon is a like-named descendant of the famous pontiff, occupying the primacy of Amun during the "half-century interval" placed by Kitchen between 754 and 704 B.C. A similar solution was proposed in the same year by Meulenaere. Rather strengthening Munro's argument, Meulenaere states that the Turin stela "could not be earlier than the end of the eighth century B.C."[78] The Turin Osorkon is thus cited as potential further evidence of a later like-named high priest attested on a Cairo statuette published by the author.

As synthesized by Kitchen in his revised volume, the suggestions of Vittmann and Meulenaere are embodied in a proposed Osorkon "F," son of Takelot III and object of the study by Aston and Taylor, discussed above.[79] Two small ironies derive from this creation of Osorkon "F." While Kitchen is careful to emend his table of Theban high priests to include the newcomer of Turin 1632, he fails to realize that this removes the unreferenced wife and daughter accorded Crown Prince Osorkon "B" in table 10. Moreover, as noted by Aston and Taylor, the various documents now put forth as evidence of Ororkon "F" are contradictory and produce a plethora of Osorkon "F"s.[80] Eliminating from this dossier the Osorkon of CGC 41035, and perhaps of Turin 1632, would simplify the situation.

In his extensive chronicle, High Priest Osorkon is not reticent in castigating his opponents as villains, enemies, and rebels against the gods. If correctly analyzed, the texts of Cairo 41035 would provide a unique counterperspective, preserving the Theban view of *Osorkon the outsider*.[81]

****

Subsequent to the completion of this study in 1995, the author expanded footnotes 17–19 as an article, "Fictive Adoptions or Celibate Priestesses?" (*Göttinger Miszellen* 164 [1998]: 85–90), which elicited a response by Erhart Graefe, "Die Adoption ins Amt der *ḥzwt njwt ḫnw nj jmnw* und der *šmsw.t dwꜣt-nṯr* (zu Ritners Artikel in GM 164, 1998, 85 ff)" (*Göttinger Miszellen* 166 [1998]: 109–12). Graefe attempts to defend Yoyotte's analysis of the Tafabart genealogy by claiming that such filiations normally mention the individual's mother directly after the father, so that the two mothers must belong to Tafabart (p. 109). On the contrary, late genealogies regularly interpolate ascendants of the father *prior* to mention of the mother. For an extreme case, see Ritner, "Denderite Temple Hierarchy and the Family of the Theban High Priest Nebwenenef: Block Statue Oriental Institute Museum 10729," in *For His Ka: Essays Offered in Memory of Klaus Baer*, edited by D. Silverman, pp. 205–26 (Studies in Ancient Oriental Civilization 55; Chicago: Oriental Institute, 1994). Such usage becomes standard, as in the Demotic Harkness Papyrus (MMA 31.9.7), written for "Tanaweruow, daughter of Hor the son of Tefnakht, whose mother is Tatita," where the third ascendant Tefnakht is clearly the father of Hor, not a second "adoptive father" of the deceased woman. Graefe acknowledges that the Tafabart stela provides no "clear proof" for supposed adoption (pp. 109–10), and that, if true, such practice ultimately had no implication for — and thus no basis in — celibacy ("eventuell ohne Implikation von Zölibat" [p. 110]). Graefe's suggestion that the certain example of *nb.t-pr* "housewife" in CGC 41035 may be "an error" because it contradicts his theory is, as the author notes, "ein schwaches Argument" (p. 111). Response to his dismissal of P. Louvre E. 10935 on the basis of an unpublished and unexplained re-reading by Vittmann must await the article of the latter author, who has defended the traditional reading in print (G. Vittmann, "Eine demotische Erwähnung des Pabasa," *Enchoria* 8/2 [1978]: 29, n. 7).

75. Said to derive from Abydos on the basis of style; see Munro 1973, pp. 261–62, pl. 27, fig. 98.

76. Munro 1973, p. 261: "Auf eine Identifikation wird darum hier verzichtet."

77. Vittmann 1978, pp. 61–62.

78. Meulenaere 1978, p. 68, n. 11.

79. Kitchen 1986, pp. 564–65 §485, 581 §521.

80. Aston and Taylor 1990, pp. 133–34; followed by Leahy 1990, p. 172.

81. Few traits are so characteristic of Late Period Egypt as regional chauvinism and factionalism, culminating in the xenophobia against even neighboring villages reflected in the Greco-Roman Instructions of ʿOnkhsheshonqy and the parodies of Juvenal.

More worrisome is Graefe's insistence that substandard original publication ("schlechten Publikationsstand" [pp. 110–11]) of primary evidence justifies the continued suppression of the priestess' dossier, said to contain 95 entries. Scholarly discussions typically confront the problem of publication quality, and advancement is hardly served by withholding evidence critical for standard theories. Thus Graefe's note 15, based only on the unpublished dossier, has no verifiable scholarly validity.

References

Anthes, R.

1943 "Die deutschen Grabungen auf der Westseite von Theben in den Jahren 1911 und 1913." *Mitteilungen des Deutschen archäologischen Instituts, Abteilung Kairo* 12: 1–68.

Aston, D. A.

1989 "Takeloth II — A King of the 'Theban Twenty-Third Dynasty'?" *Journal of Egyptian Archaeology* 75: 139–54.

Aston, D. A., and J. H. Taylor

1990 "The Family of Takelot III." In *Libya and Egypt c. 1300–750 BC*, edited by Anthony Leahy, pp. 131–54. London: Centre of Near and Middle Eastern Studies and the Society for Libyan Studies.

Bates, O.

1970 *The Eastern Libyans: An Essay*. Reprint of 1914 edition. London: Frank Cass.

Beckerath, J. von

1966 "The Nile Record Levels at Karnak and Their Importance for the History of the Libyan Period (Dynasties XXII and XXIII)." *Journal of the American Research Center in Egypt* 5: 43–55.

1995 "Beiträge zur Geschichte der Libyerzeit." *Göttinger Miszellen* 144: 7–13.

Berlandini, J.

1978 "Une stèle de donation du dynastie libyen Roudamon." *Bulletin de l'Institut français d'archéologie orientale* 78: 147–63.

1979 "Petits monuments royaux de la XXIe à la XXVe dynastie." In *Hommages à la mémoire de Serge Sauneron, 1927–1976* 1: *Égypte pharaonique*, pp. 89–114. Bibliothèque d'étude 81. Cairo: Institut français d'archéologie orientale.

Bierbrier, M. L.

1975 *The Late New Kingdom in Egypt (c. 1300–664 B.C.)*. Warminster: Aris and Phillips.

1984 "Two Confusing Coffins." *Journal of Egyptian Archaeology* 70: 82–86.

Bonhême, M.-A.

1987 *Les noms royaux dans l'Égypte de la troisième période intermédiaire*. Bibliothèque d'étude 98. Cairo: Institut français d'archéologie orientale.

Budge, E. A. W.

1908 *The Book of Kings*, Volume 2. Books on Egypt and Chaldea 24. London: Kegan Paul.

Caminos, R.

1958 *The Chronicle of Prince Osorkon*. Analecta Orientalia 37. Rome: Pontifical Biblical Institute.

Černý, J.

1976 *Coptic Etymological Dictionary*. Cambridge: Cambridge University Press.

Chassinat, É.

1912 "Petits monuments et petites remarques." *Bulletin de l'Institut français d'archéologie orientale* 10: 161–64.

Dautzenberg, N.

1995 "Bemerkungen zu Schoschenq II., Takeloth II. und Pedubastis II." *Göttinger Miszellen* 144: 21–29.

Depuydt, L.

1993 "The Date of Piye's Egyptian Campaign and the Chronology of the Twenty-fifth Dynasty." *Journal of Egyptian Archaeology* 79: 269–74.

Elias, J. P.

1995 "A Northern Member of the 'Theban' Twenty-third Dynasty." *Discussions in Egyptology* 31: 57–67.

Gardiner, A. H.

1933 "The Dakhleh Stela." *Journal of Egyptian Archaeology* 19: 19–30.

Gauthier, H.

1914 *Livre des rois*, volume 3. Mémoires publiés par les Membres de l'Institut français d'archéologie orientale du Caire 19. Cairo: Institut français d'archéologie orientale.

1929 *Dictionnaire des noms géographiques*, volume 6. Cairo: Société royale de géographie d'Égypte.

Grapow, H.

1937 "Ägyptische Personenbezeichnungen zur Angabe der Herkunft aus einem Ort." *Zeitschrift für ägyptische Sprache und Altertumskunde* 73: 44–53.

Jansen-Winkeln, K.

1985 *Ägyptische Biographien der 22. und 23. Dynastie*. 2 volumes. Ägypten und Altes Testament 8. Wiesbaden: Otto Harrassowitz.

Kees, H.

1964 *Die Hohenpriester des Amun von Karnak von Herihor bis zum Ende der Äthiopenzeit*. Probleme der Ägyptologie 4. Leiden: E. J. Brill.

Kitchen, K. A.

1973 *The Third Intermediate Period in Egypt (1100–650 B.C.)*. Warminster: Aris and Phillips.

1986 *The Third Intermediate Period in Egypt (1100–650 B.C.)*. Second edition with supplement. Warminster: Aris and Phillips.

1990 *Catalogue of the Egyptian Collection in the National Museum, Rio de Janeiro*. Warminster: Aris and Phillips.

Kruchten, J.-M.

1989 *Les annales des prêtres de Karnak (XXI–XXIIImes dynasties) et autres textes contemporains relatifs à l'initiation des prêtres d'Amon*. Orientalia Lovaniensia Analecta 32. Leuven: Peeters.

Leahy, A.

1979 "The Name of Osiris Written ." *Studien zur altägyptischen Kultur* 7: 141–53.

1990 "Abydos in the Libyan Period." In *Libya and Egypt c. 1300–750 BC*, edited by Anthony Leahy, pp. 155–200. London: Centre of Near and Middle Eastern Studies and the Society for Libyan Studies.

1992 "'May the King Live': The Libyan Rulers in the Onomastic Record." In *Studies in Pharaonic Religion and Society in Honour of J. Gwyn Griffiths*, edited by A. Lloyd, pp. 146–63. London: Egypt Exploration Society.

Legrain, G.

1896a "Textes gravés sur le quai de Karnak." *Zeitschrift für ägyptische Sprache und Altertumskunde* 34: 111–18.

1896b "Les crues du Nil depuis Sheshonq Ier jusqu'à Psametik." *Zeitschrift für ägyptische Sprache und Altertumskunde* 34: 119–21.

1900 "Notes prises à Karnak 1: Fragments des annales des prêtres d'Amon." *Recueil de travaux relatifs à la philologie et à l'archéologie égyptiennes et assyriennes* 22: 51–63.

1906a "Nouveaux renseignements sur les dernières découvertes faites à Karnak." *Recueil de travaux relatifs à la philologie et à l'archéologie égyptiennes et assyriennes* 28: 137–61.

1906b "Notes d'inspection." *Annales du Service des antiquités de l'Égypte* 7: 33–57.

1909 "Recherches généalogiques." *Recueil de travaux relatifs à la philologie et à l'archéologie égyptiennes et assyriennes* 31: 1–10.

Mariette, A.

1982 *Catalogue général des monuments d'Abydos découverts pendant les fouilles de cette ville*. Reprint of 1880, Paris, edition. Wiesbaden: LTR Verlag.

Maspero, G.

1883 "Notes sur quelques points de grammaire et d'histoire (suite), §XXXIX." *Zeitschrift für ägyptische Sprache und Altertumskunde* 21: 62–79.

1885 "Notes sur quelques points de grammaire et d'histoire (suite), §LXXIII." *Zeitschrift für ägyptische Sprache und Altertumskunde* 23: 3–13.

1889 "Les momies royales de Déir el-Baharî." *Mémoires publiés par les Membres de la Mission archéologique français au Caire*, tome 1, pp. 511–787. Paris: E. Leroux.

Meulenaere, H. de

1966 Review of *Die Hohenpriester des Amun von Karnak von Herihor bis zum Ende der Äthiopenzeit*, by H. Kees. *Chronique d'Égypte* 41, no. 81: 111–13.

1978 "La statuette JE 37163 du Musée du Caire." *Studien zur altägyptischen Kultur* 6: 63–68.

1982 "Une princesse libyenne ignorée." *Chronique d'Égypte* 57, no. 113: 218–22.

Moret, A.

1913 *Sarcophages de l'époque bubastite à l'époque saïte, CGC nos. 41001–41041*. Cairo: Institut français d'archéologie orientale.

Munro, P.

1973 *Die spätägyptischen Totenstelen*. 2 volumes. Ägyptologische Forschungen 25. Glückstadt: J. J. Augustin.

Naguib, S.-A.

1990 *Le clergé féminin d'Amon thébain à la 21e dynastie*. Orientalia Lovaniensia Analecta 38. Leuven: Peeters.

Paleological Association of Japan, Egyptian Committee

1995 *Akoris: Report of the Excavations at Akoris in Middle Egypt, 1981–1992*. Kyoto: Koyo Shobo.

Priese, K.-H.

1970 "Der Beginn der kuschitischen Herrschaft in Ägypten." *Zeitschrift für ägyptische Sprache und Altertumskunde* 98: 16–32.

Ranke, H.

1935 *Die ägyptischen Personennamen*. 2 volumes. Glückstadt: J. J. Augustin.

Spiegelberg, W.

1899 "Eine Stele aus der Oase Dachel." *Recueil de travaux relatifs à la philologie et à l'archéologie égyptiennes et assyriennes* 21: 12–21.

1917 "Briefe aus der 21. Dynastie aus El-Hibe." *Zeitschrift für ägyptische Sprache und Altertumskunde* 53:1–30.

Vernus, P.

1981 "Une grammaire du néo-égyptien." *Orientalia* 50: 429–42.

Vittmann, G.

1978 *Priester und Beamte im Theben der Spätzeit*. Beiträge zur Ägyptologie 1. Vienna: Institut für Afrikanistik und Ägyptologie der Universität Wien.

Wente, E. F.

1976 Review of *The Third Intermediate Period in Egypt*, by K. Kitchen. *Journal of Near Eastern Studies* 35: 275–78.

Yoyotte, J.

1961 "Les principautés du delta au temps de l'anarchie libyenne (études d'histoire politique)." In *Mélanges Maspero* I/4: *Orient ancien*, pp. 121–79. Mémoires publiés par les Membres de l'Institut français d'archéologie orientale du Caire 66/4. Cairo: Institut français d'archéologie orientale.

1962 "Les vierges consacrées d'Amon thébain." *Académie des inscriptions et belles-lettres, Comptes rendus* 1961: 43–52.

34

THE AHHOTEP COFFINS: THE ARCHAEOLOGY OF AN EGYPTOLOGICAL RECONSTRUCTION

ANN MACY ROTH

Howard University, Washington, D.C.

One of Professor Wente's many important achievements in the field of Egyptology has been his evaluation of the historical evidence for the genealogy and ages at death of various members of the New Kingdom royal family, undertaken as a control on the new scientific investigations of their physical remains (Harris and Wente 1980). It was my privilege to take part in Professor Wente's seminar on these questions in the spring of 1976 and, as a result, to write my first published article under his guidance. I am grateful for the opportunity to present to him some further work on the same questions,* along with my best wishes for a happy retirement.

TWO QUEENS?

According to a consensus formed in the late nineteenth century, there were two New Kingdom queens named Ahhotep.[1] Queen Ahhotep I was thought to be the wife of Seqenenreᶜ-Taᶜo II and the mother of two kings, Kamose and Ahmose, who bridged the Seventeenth and the Eighteenth Dynasties. In his 1912 survey of the royal family of this era, Gauthier attributed to her two coffins. The first was a gilded coffin (CG 28501; fig. 34.1a), found at Dra Abu el-Naga by Mariette, which contained her mummy along with considerable quantities of gold and silver grave goods. The second was a huge wood and cartonnage coffin (CG 61006; fig. 34.1b) from the Deir el-Bahri cache, which bore the same name, but held the body of Pinedjem I (Gauthier 1912, pp. 163, 182). This Queen Ahhotep was also said to be attested on an early funerary statue that honored a dead son named Ahmose,[2] on a stela at Karnak (CG 34001) dedicated by King Ahmose, and in several later texts where she was identified as a king's mother or the mother of Ahmose.

Queen Ahhotep II, according to this reconstruction, was the principal wife of Amenhotep I. As evidence for her existence, Gauthier again cited the coffin found in the Deir el-Bahri cache (CG 61006).[3] This queen was also thought to be the Ahhotep depicted on coffins and stelae of the Ramesside period, where she was shown in a role parallel to that of Amenhotep I's mother, Ahmes-Nefertari.[4]

When, in the middle 1970s, a number of scholars began to re-evaluate this material, the chimerical nature of Gauthier's Ahhotep II became obvious.[5] The Deir el-Bahri coffin, the only one of the two coffins that bore

*I would like to express my gratitude to those who have discussed these problems with me in recent years, notably Stephen P. Harvey and Catharine H. Roehrig. I am also grateful to Dorothea Arnold and the Department of Egyptian Art at the Metropolitan Museum of Art for providing the photographs used in figs. 34.1a and 34.2b. The remaining photographs were very kindly provided by the Oriental Institute.

1. According to Gitton (1984, p. 9, n. 2), this prevailing belief originated with Wiedemann (1884, pp. 316–17, for Ahhotep, alleged wife of Amenhotep I, and p. 302 for the earlier Ahhotep, whom Wiedemann took to be the wife of Kamose rather than Taᶜo II) and Maspero (1897, p. 104).
2. Louvre E. 15682, published by Winlock 1924, pp. 255–56, pls. 12, 18–20.
3. Gauthier (1912) gives different references for the publication of this coffin in his entries under Ahhotep I and Ahhotep II; he apparently thought that there were three coffins.
4. To add some minimal clarity to the discussion of the many early Eighteenth Dynasty royal family members who bore the name *ʾIᶜḥ-ms*, I have used the spelling Ahmose for male holders of the name and Ahmes for the female. Both names were, of course, written identically.
5. Gitton 1975, p. 37, n. 105; Vandersleyen 1977, p. 237; Roth 1977/78; Schmitz 1978; Troy 1979; Vandersleyen 1980, to name only the earliest articles on the subject. Gitton (1984, p. 9, n. 2) notes that the traditional interpretation had already been challenged by Sethe and a revision was first proposed in the middle 1960s by Yoyotte.

Gold of Praise: Studies on Ancient Egypt in Honor of Edward F. Wente
Edited by Emily Teeter and John A. Larson
Studies in Ancient Oriental Civilization 58
Chicago: Oriental Institute, 1999

the title *mwt-nswt*, could hardly have belonged to a queen of Amenhotep I, none of whose sons lived to be king.[6] There was, in fact, no evidence that Amenhotep I had a queen named Ahhotep, and the most reasonable conclusion was that this coffin was made for the mother of Ahmose, who clearly lived at least until year 10 of Amenhotep I, when she was mentioned in the Kares stela (CG 34003). She probably lived into the reign of Thutmose I since the stela of her steward Iuf (CG 34009), which specifically calls her the mother of King Ahmose, records that he also served Queen Ahmes, wife of Thutmose I, who was thus presumably already a queen when he transferred his service to her at his first patron's death.[7]

If the mother of Ahmose lived into the reign of Thutmose I and was buried in the Deir el-Bahri coffin, the ownership of the Dra Abu el-Naga coffin becomes a problem. This coffin was said to have contained a body (now lost), silver and gold jewelry, and other objects. Most surviving artifacts are inscribed with the name of Ahmose, but a few give the name of his predecessor Kamose. The burial can be dated prior to year 22 of Ahmose because sometime between his years 18 and 22 the moon hieroglyph, *jꜣḥ*, that occurs in the names Ahhotep and Ahmose changed from  to .[8] The sign takes this earlier form not only in the name Ahhotep on the smaller coffin, but in all the writings of the name of King Ahmose on the accompanying jewelry.[9] Since the title *mwt-nswt* "king's mother" is not given on this coffin, one solution to the problem it posed was to assume that it belonged to a principal wife of King Kamose, also named Ahhotep, who outlived him briefly.[10] According to the prevailing reconstruction, Kamose and Ahmose were sons of Taʿo II, who reigned successively because Kamose had no son.[11] Kamose's coffin had been discovered in the same area by Mariette's workmen the year before the discovery of Ahhotep's and contained similar grave goods; these circumstances are cited in support of this argument.

ONE QUEEN?

Another explanation for the Dra Abu el-Naga coffin was proposed by Schmitz (1978, pp. 207–15) and a variant of the same idea was argued more recently by Eaton-Krauss (1990). Both authors see the two coffins as the property of a single Queen Ahhotep. Such a reconstruction would greatly simplify the interpretation of the evidence: if both coffins belonged to the wife of Taʿo II and the mother of Ahmose, all the evidence could be assigned to the same woman, and there would be no evidence for a second Queen Ahhotep at all.

Schmitz proposes that the Dra Abu el-Naga coffin was an inner coffin and the larger Deir el-Bahri cache coffin was an outer coffin. Schmitz cites as a parallel the inner and outer coffins of another early Eighteenth Dynasty queen, Merytamun.[12] The Deir el-Bahri coffin and the outer coffin of Merytamun, she argues, are of similar dimensions and type.

The problem with this interpretation is the width and depth of the Dra Abu el-Naga coffin, which could never have fit inside the coffin from Deir el-Bahri. As both Troy (1981, p. 92, n. 36) and Blankenberg-van Delden (1982, p. 39, n. 1) point out, Maspero (1889, p. 545) states that the coffins would not nest. Examination of the measurements confirms his judgment. According to the measurements Schmitz cites,[13] the lid of the Dra Abu el-Naga coffin and Merytamun's smaller inner coffin are approximately the same length; however,

6. The argument of Hayes (1959, p. 52) that a small child who was reburied as "king lord of two lands, Amememhet" explains the *mwt-nswt* on the Ahhotep coffin from Deir el-Bahri has been dismissed by most recent writers on the subject. See, for example, Robins 1978.
7. If Ahmes was not yet queen at the time of the death of Ahhotep and the transfer of Iuf's services, it is hard to understand why the steward of so eminent a woman would have become the steward of a minor princess. Ahmes was never called a king's daughter, only a king's wife and king's sister. If the title king's daughter was not simply omitted, she was perhaps a half sister of Amenhotep I, born to Ahmes-Nefertari by a later husband.
8. See Vandersleyen 1971, p. 209, who also notes (1977, p. 227) that a year 18 stela with an earlier form of the sign reduces the period of this shift by an additional year.
9. A cartouche-shaped ivory jewelry box has been attributed to the burial that bears the post-year-22 form of the name Ahhotep and the title *ḥmt-nswt* (Müller-Feldman 1959, pp. 143–44, pl. vi [1]). It was not found with the rest of the burial, however, and might equally have come from the original burial of the Deir el-Bahri coffin or that of yet another Queen Ahhotep (see p. 370, below).
10. This solution was proposed by Gitton (1975, p. 35, n. 58); I argue the proposition further in Roth 1977/78, pp. 35–36. It is also adopted by Troy (1979, p. 82) and argued by Vandersleyen (1980, pp. 239–40).
11. Note, however, that the supposition that Kamose and Ahmose were brothers owes its origin to the fact that jewelry bearing both names was found in the Dra Abu el-Naga coffin of Ahhotep, who was assumed to be the mother of both on that (insufficient) evidence.
12. Winlock 1932, pls. 22–26; the measurements cited below and in table 34.1 are also from his report, pp. 16, 19, 71.
13. Schmitz (1978, p. 208) gives the measurements of CG 28501 (the Dra Abu el-Naga coffin) as 1.8 m × (no more than) 0.6 m.

Corteggiani and Eaton-Krauss describe the Dra Abu el-Naga lid as over 30 cm longer and 6 cm wider,[14] measurements that are proportionate with those of the published photograph. These more accurate measurements are compared with the Merytamun coffins in table 34.1.

Table 34.1. Measurements of the Ahhotep and Merytamun Coffins

	Length (in m)	*Maximum Width (in m)*	*Depth (Chest) (in m)*
Ahhotep (Dra Abu el-Naga)	2.12	0.66	0.60 [15]
Ahhotep (Deir el-Bahri) [16]	3.12	0.98	0.48
Merytamun (inner)	1.85	0.53	0.52
Merytamun (outer)	3.13	0.87	0.67

The two sets of coffins are clearly different in depth and width. The outer coffin of Merytamun is 19 cm deeper, and the inner coffin is 8 cm shallower than the two coffins of Ahhotep; even with this greater depth, it was necessary to cut a notch on the inner face of the outer coffin to allow clearance for the nose of the inner one (Winlock 1932, p. 19). The smaller of the Ahhotep coffins, in contrast, is probably about 12 cm deeper than the larger one. Although the difference in maximum widths is much less (34 cm for the Merytamun coffins and 32 cm for the Ahhotep coffins), the inner Merytamun coffin is much more tapered than the Dra Abu el-Naga coffin, and the outer coffin of Merytamun tapers less than the Deir el-Bahri coffin.

It may be argued, however, that only the lid of the Dra Abu el-Naga coffin was nested inside the Deir el-Bahri coffin. But while the Dra Abu el-Naga coffin is almost rectangular, the Deir el-Bahri coffin is much more anthropoid in shape. Although it is 98 cm wide at the elbows, it is greater than 67 cm wide for only about 150 cm of its length.[17] Assuming there is at least a 6 cm difference between the outer and inner width of the larger coffin[18] and another 1 cm for minimal clearance, these measurements imply that only 150 cm of the length of the Dra Abu el-Naga coffin could be more than 60 cm wide and still fit inside the Deir el-Bahri coffin. In fact, the smaller Ahhotep coffin is 60 cm wide at its foot, and though it tapers to 50 cm at the ankles, it widens again and does not finally become narrower than 60 cm until 194 cm above its base. Since there are not two points 194 cm apart at which the Deir el-Bahri coffin is 67 cm wide, even the lid of the smaller coffin will not fit inside the larger. Eaton-Krauss (1990, p. 200) surmises that the thickness of the lid, which is only 18 cm less than the maximum depth of the "outer" coffin, would prevent its insertion, but it is clear from the lack of tapering of the "inner" coffin that the width is equally limiting.[19]

Although Eaton-Krauss does not believe that the coffins could have nested, she maintains that both coffins were made at different times in the life of a single queen named Ahhotep, who was both the wife of Taʿo II and the mother of Ahmose. She convincingly argues that the smaller coffin found at Dra Abu el-Naga was made to

14. Eaton-Krauss 1990, p. 197 (length and width); Corteggiani 1986, p. 83 (length).
15. The lid alone is 30 cm deep. The total depth was estimated by Eaton-Krauss (1990, p. 200), based on the parallel with the very similar coffin of Seqenenreʿ Taʿo II. Puzzlingly, Corteggiani (1986, p. 84) notes that the lower portion of the coffin is painted blue and is not on display in the museum. Since it was said to be black by its discoverers, it is presumably extant.
16. The measurements are based on the Catalogue général des antiquités égyptiennes du Musée du Caire (Daressy 1909, p. 8). Two measurements of the width are given that are consistent with the proportions of the photograph; however, if the scale is taken from these measurements, the height of the coffin in the photograph appears to be 3.59 m, that is, 47 cm taller than the published measurement. The published measurement, however, must be correct, as this Ahhotep coffin is clearly almost exactly the same height as the coffin of Ahmes-Nefertari (CG 61003; published height: 3.08 m without headdress), as they are displayed in the Cairo Museum. The extra height must be due to parallax distortion in the photograph.
17. These and the following measurements are taken from the photographs. I have used the horizontal measurements to determine scale since the vertical scale of the photograph is distorted by the height of the coffin. The 150 cm vertical measurement discussed here is probably only slightly distorted since it is around the center of the coffin. I have rounded the number up to account for any distortion.
18. Although I can find no references to the thickness of the walls of the larger Ahhotep coffin, the walls of the similarly constructed Ahmes-Nefertari coffin average only 3 cm thick (Daressy 1909, p. 3). The coffin of Merytamun is constructed of solid wood, unlike that of Ahhotep, which is constructed of cartonnage ("successive layers of linen glued together") on a wooden frame (Winlock 1932, p. 59). Merytamun's coffin varies in thickness from roughly 3 to 6 cm, and the total outside dimension of the larger Merytamun coffin is between 12 and 22 cm greater than the inner coffin (ibid., p. 21).
19. Although it is difficult to quantify, the larger Ahhotep coffin also appears to be considerably more rounded in cross-section at the hips and legs than the lid of the smaller coffin, which is flatter and more box-like. This would render the insertion of the lid even more impossible.

match that of Taᶜo II.[20] She then argues that this earlier coffin could not have been used for the burial of any royal woman other than Taᶜo II's wife Ahhotep because the inscriptions were not altered to reflect the name and titles of a new owner, and it is "improbable" that Taᶜo II had two principal royal wives named Ahhotep.[21] Against the argument that the smaller coffin belonged to a queen of Kamose with the same name as Ahmose's mother, she sets the parallel with Taᶜo II's coffin and the fact that the Dra Abu el-Naga coffin was far richer than the ungilded, modified non-royal coffin in which Kamose was buried (Eaton-Krauss 1990, pp. 202–04).

Eaton-Krauss explains the similarity of the larger coffin to that of Amenhotep I's wife Merytamun with the suggestion that Amenhotep I ordered a new coffin to honor his grandmother at her death and had it made in the same style as his wife's. She argues that both Ahhotep coffins were originally buried together in Dra Abu el-Naga during the reign of Amenhotep I. There was, she believes, an abortive attempt to maneuver the older, smaller coffin (or its lid) inside the new, larger one at the funeral by removing the upper back of the larger coffin.[22] When this failed, she argues, the two coffins were buried side by side, with the queen's body in the smaller one. They became separated only in the late Twentieth Dynasty, when the older coffin was reburied to forestall tomb robbers, and the empty larger coffin was set aside and ultimately re-used for the burial of Pinedjem I in the Deir el-Bahri cache.

In justifying this reconstruction, Eaton-Krauss makes a number of assumptions that may not hold true. Although the parallels she draws between the Dra Abu el-Naga coffin and the coffin of Seqenenreᶜ Taᶜo II are convincing, they need not imply that the two owners were married. The Egyptians did not necessarily give the marriage bond the same primacy that modern western culture does. A king's mother seems to have been more important than his wife in most periods of Egyptian history.[23] While the paired coffins of Taᶜo II and Ahhotep cannot have been made for the king and his mother (because Ahhotep's coffin lacks the title *mwt-nswt*), the importance of the maternal relationship suggests the possibility that other blood relationships were also as important as the marital relationship in the ancient Egyptian kinship system. King's daughter and king's sister were both important titles during this period, and the Ahhotep who was named with Taᶜo on the statue of Prince Ahmose bore the former title. It is, of course, most likely that the matched coffins were made for a married couple, but this is by no means the only possibility.

In arguing against an attribution of the Dra Abu el-Naga coffin to the wife of Kamose, Eaton-Krauss also assumes that a queen's coffin must necessarily be less rich and elaborate than her husband's. However, since Kamose was buried before the final expulsion of the Hyksos, while the early Ahhotep coffin and its contents clearly date to the reign of Ahmose, the difference might simply be a result of the greater economic resources of the royal family during this later period. There was clearly no rule that a wife's coffin had to be inferior in quality to her husband's.[24]

Eaton-Krauss's hypothesis also overlooks the possibility that Taᶜo II may not have been the father of King Ahmose, an assumption based entirely upon his hypothesized marriage to a Queen Ahhotep. As Robins (1982, pp. 73–74) has already pointed out, the most likely king to have fathered Ahmose is in fact his predecessor, Kamose. The first part of Eaton-Krauss's conclusions may thus be correct (that is, that Taᶜo II had only one wife named Ahhotep, for whom he had a coffin made that was the mate to his own, and that his wife was buried in

20. This was already noted by Winlock (1924, p. 251), but Eaton-Krauss (1990, pp. 200–02) adds further correspondences to those noted by Winlock and makes a very convincing case for the simultaneous manufacture of the two coffins. The argument made by Blankenberg-van Delden (1982, p. 35) that the coffins of Sekhemre-Wepmaᶜat Intef and Nubkheperre Intef (pictured in Winlock 1924, pl. 14) are "identical in style" to the coffins of Taᶜo II and Ahhotep is simply not correct. Both are considerably cruder and more angular in appearance, and the faces, bodies, and headdresses are narrower than those of the later coffins.

21. That King Ahmose seems to have had at least two wives named Ahmes would tend to cast doubt upon her argument.

22. The lid of the larger Ahhotep coffin extends only from the top of the head to beneath the arms (unlike the Merytamun coffin, which has a full lid and can thus be opened for its full length). Eaton-Krauss (1990, p. 197) adopts the suggestion of Thomas (1980, p. 175, n. 37) that the removal of the upper part of the back of the Ahhotep coffin was the result of the funeral workers' attempt to fit the smaller coffin inside; she differs from Thomas, however, in that she believes that the coffins did not, in fact, nest together.

23. Seipel (*LÄ* 3 "Königin," col. 465) notes that only in the late Eighteenth Dynasty did the king's wife begin to outrank her mother-in-law. Mothers of kings seem to be buried with their royal sons rather than their royal spouses. For example, Ahmes-Nefertari was buried (and closely associated) with her son Amenhotep I rather than with her husband Ahmose.

24. A good parallel would be the burial of the parents of Senenmut a few reigns later. Dorman (1988, pp. 168–69) suggests that Senenmut's father was buried before Senenmut's rise to power, whereas Senenmut's mother died later and the quality of her grave goods benefited from her son's greater financial resources.

a b

Figure 34.1. (*a*) Coffin of Ahhotep from Dra Abu el-Naga (CG 28501; Photography by the Egyptian Expedition, The Metropolitan Museum of Art) and (*b*) Coffin of Ahhotep from Deir el-Bahri Cache (CG 61006; after Daressy 1909, pl. 9 center). Approximately Same Scale

that coffin), without precluding the possibility that Ahhotep, the mother of Ahmose, was a different woman, married to a different king, who was buried in a coffin of her own.

The coffins themselves raise other problems with Eaton-Krauss's reconstruction. They do not look like the same woman. Although renderings of Egyptian faces were rarely true portraits, and although there was always a tendency to depict people with features similar to those of the reigning king, the artist normally attempted to incorporate some aspects of the facial shapes and proportions of the person depicted.

The face on the Ahhotep coffin from Dra Abu el-Naga (fig. 34.1a) is marked by a long narrow nose with rather pinched nostrils, a short protuberant chin, and broad full cheeks. All of these characteristics are shared to some degree by its companion coffin, that of Seqenenreʿ Taʿo II (CG 61001), and to a lesser extent by some of the coffins of later generations, such as that of Ahmes-Nefertari (CG 61003; fig. 34.2a) and even Merytamun (fig. 34.2b). Ahhotep's face differs from Tao's in the sharp upward angle of her eyes toward their outer corners and the opposite angle of her eyebrows, which are raised high above the inner corners of her eye and angle down in almost a straight line, curving only slightly at the outer corners. Neither of these features appear in the coffins of later generations, although examples of the angled eyes and the unusual distance between their inner corner and the eyebrows may be seen in the statue of the young Prince Ahmose and the coffin of Kamose (Winlock 1924, pls. 12, 21 right). The rather crude coffins of two earlier Seventeenth Dynasty kings (Sekhemre-Horherma῾at Intef and Sekhemre-Wepma῾at Intef) also share these eyes and brows to a lesser extent (Winlock 1924, pls. 21 left, 14 right).

The coffin of the Deir el-Bahri Ahhotep (fig. 34.1b) shows a face that is quite different. Her eyes are level, not tilted, and her eyebrows curve down towards the inner corners of her eyes, following the contours of her upper eyelids. Her nose is broader, and her chin is longer and narrower. Her cheeks are flat, almost hollow, rendering the lower part of her face almost triangular. Her face is quite similar to that of Ahmose on his coffin (CG 61002), although his chin is squarer, and her eyes and brows are very like those on the coffin of Ahmes-Nefertari (CG 61003). While such similarities and differences are not dependable in arguing family relationships,[25] particularly when all the people represented are probably related to some degree, they do suggest that several different shapes of noses, chins, cheeks, eyebrows, and eyes occurred and were represented in this family. It is unlikely that the two Ahhotep coffins would have displayed such different selections of these features had they been meant to represent the same woman.

Eaton-Krauss's hypothetical reconstruction of the creation of the later Ahhotep coffin and its joining with and separation from the earlier coffin is equally doubtful. The style of the Deir el-Bahri coffin does not support her conclusion that it was made to match the coffin of Merytamun (Amenhotep I's wife and Ahhotep's granddaughter). Far closer in style to the large Ahhotep coffin is the coffin of Ahmes-Nefertari, the wife of Ahmose (CG 61003). These two coffins resemble each other more closely than either resembles Merytamun's coffin; however, several details shared by Merytamun and Ahmes-Nefertari's coffins, but lacking in Ahhotep's, suggest a chronological sequence of stylistic development.[26]

The Ahhotep coffin (fig. 34.1b) is clearly the earliest of the three. Its *rishi*-design is the least interrupted, flowing up over the crossed arms and onto the chest without a break. Only the hands are distinct, marked off from the body by a thin line at the wrists. The breasts are indicated only by a central depression above the wrists, which extends up to the throat. Similarly, the *rishi*-pattern seems to run smoothly from the wig onto the shoulders, with no line or sharp angle at the junction. The center parting on the wig is marked only by a break in the *rishi*-pattern; there is no depression. The front lappets fall straight and cylindrical from the sides of the forehead. The low modius on the head presumably carried two plumes like those preserved on the modius of Ahmes-Nefertari. Below the crossed arms, the body tapers to the knees almost in a straight line, and the lower part of the coffin is covered with a faint pattern of diagonally crossed wings.

Ahmes-Nefertari's coffin (fig. 34.2a) is very similar. However, the arms are defined by wide wristlets that break the *rishi*-pattern, so that the arms are marked off from the torso at least halfway to the elbow. The breasts are slightly more rounded, but the depression between them is shallower, though it is still marked by a gap between two straps of the dress. The borders of the *rishi*-pattern where the wig meets the shoulders are clearly indicated with a sharp angle. There is a slight depression along the lappets of the wig beside the temple and the upper part of the cheek, which suggests the shape of the Hathoric wig in which the lappets are pulled back behind the ears (although the ears are covered here); a slight depression marks the central parting of the hair. The modius is taller and covered with a *rishi*-pattern, and the plumed headdress is preserved. The body tapers smoothly to the knees, but there is more rounding to indicate the hips and thighs than in Ahhotep's coffin. Again, the lower torso and legs are wrapped in crossed wings.

25. It is doubtless meaningless, for example, that the face on the coffin of Ahmes-Nefertari bears some resemblance to the only known portrait of Jane Austen.

26. It was, in fact, this stylistic progression that first suggested to me that the traditional identification of the owner of the Ahhotep coffin was unlikely. Although the argument was the centerpiece of my presentation of the evidence at the 1977 meeting of the American Research Center in Egypt, this point was not included in my initial article on the subject (Roth 1977/78). Blankenberg-van Delden (1982, p. 35) notes differences in construction between the coffin of Merytamun and those of Ahhotep and Ahmes-Nefertari but does not discuss the stylistic differences or the differences between Ahhotep and Ahmes-Nefertari's coffins.

a b

Figure 34.2. (*a*) Coffin of Ahmes-Nefertari (CG 61003; after Daressy 1909, pl. 3 right; headdress cut off) and (*b*) Outer Coffin of Merytamun (after Winlock 1932, pl. 23 right; Photography by the Egyptian Expedition, The Metropolitan Museum of Art). Approximately Same Scale

The final stage in development is seen in the coffin of Merytamun (fig. 34.2b), in which the changes made in the Ahmes-Nefertari coffin were exaggerated, and more important differences were introduced. The arms, like those of Ahmes-Nefertari's coffin, have wristlets and are differentiated from the body above them almost to the elbow. Gaps between the body and the upper arms (not indicated at all in the other coffins) are marked by depressions. The breasts are modeled and rounded, but the depression between them is very slight and there is no central break in the *rishi*-pattern. The *rishi*-cells along the parting of the hair are extended, the center line is more markedly indented, and the depressions of the lappets by the temple and upper cheek are more prominent. The headdress has disappeared, however, and Merytamun holds papyrus stalks in her hands, rather than the ankhs held by her predecessors. Below her crossed arms, the sides of the coffin swell out slightly and do not begin to taper until just above the knees (probably to allow more space for the inner coffin). The *rishi*-pattern on this lower part of the coffin is entirely vertical, contrasting with the diagonally wrapped wings on the other coffins. The front of the foot extension revives the square, broad shape of many Seventeenth Dynasty coffins[27] rather than the more naturalistic rounding used for the coffins of the other two queens. Merytamun's coffin also opens along its entire length, rather than being accessible only by a removable upper panel extending to the base of the crossed arms, and it was constructed of cedar, rather than the cartonnage-covered wood-frame construction of the other two coffins.

The coffins of Merytamun and Ahhotep do not share a single characteristic that is not also found in the coffin of Ahmes-Nefertari, which is clearly the middle element of the sequence. The coffin of Ahhotep was thus clearly a prototype, rather than a copy of the coffin of Merytamun. Such progressive stylistic development could only have occurred if the coffins were made over a period of time, in the same order as the queens' historical and generational sequence. There was presumably a short lapse of time between the making of the coffins of Ahhotep and Ahmes-Nefertari and a somewhat longer period before the carving of Merytamun's. Merytamun seems to have been buried before the construction of Hatshepsut's temple at Deir el-Bahri,[28] so her coffin must have been manufactured between the accession of Amenhotep I and the end of the reign of Thutmose II. This range can be narrowed still further since her coffin must be later than Ahmes-Nefertari's coffin, which itself cannot be earlier than the early reign of Amenhotep I (since it bears the title king's mother). Moreover, according to Thomas's investigations (1980, p. 172), the location of Merytamun's tomb must have been completely lost to memory by the time Hatshepsut's temple at Deir el-Bahri was planned. The late reign of Amenhotep I through the early reign of Thutmose I seems the most likely time for the manufacture of Merytamun's coffin and her death. This limits the construction of Ahmes-Nefertari's coffin to the early reign of Amenhotep I, and the coffin of her mother Ahhotep to the period between year 18 of Ahmose (from the later form of the moon hieroglyph) and the early reign of Amenhotep I. Ahhotep's coffin was then presumably stored until her death, perhaps early in the reign of Thutmose I.

By Eaton-Krauss's reconstruction, the Dra Abu el-Naga coffin was made for this same Ahhotep, so both coffins must have been stored throughout most of the reign of Amenhotep I. Why, then, during this lengthy period, was the earlier coffin not passed on to another member of the royal family and re-inscribed? Unless they were meant to be nested (which Eaton-Krauss admits was not the case), it would be unparalleled for two coffins to be used for the burial of a single person.[29] And, indeed, why would the older coffin not have been re-inscribed during the first eighteen years of Ahmose's reign to add *mwt-nswt*, the highest female title in the country, since Eaton-Krauss's hypothesis implies that Ahhotep planned to be buried in it throughout that period? Given the ease with which inscriptions were altered, these questions throw considerable doubt on the scenario Eaton-Krauss proposes.

By Eaton-Krauss's hypothesis, however, the older coffin was still available and unaltered when, perhaps at Ahhotep's death, it was decided to nest them. Here, however, her reconstruction becomes even more problematic. If, for some reason, it was decided to bury Ahhotep in the older coffin and to place this coffin inside the more recently made one, it would have been obvious when they lay side by side that this was impossible. Her assumption that the Egyptians believed that they could fit a coffin that was (by her own estimate) about 60 cm deep into one that was 48 cm deep by cutting off part of the back of the shallower coffin supposes that the Egyptians were more ignorant of spatial relationships than our evidence allows. Eaton-Krauss (1990, p. 200, n. 2) argues that an "error in calculations" was "understandable" since the coffins were not made to fit together; however, the impossibility of nesting them would have been apparent visually, without the necessity of any calculations.

Eaton-Krauss's scenario also implies that the body would have been placed in the smaller older coffin with out-of-date titles, along with grave goods carefully selected so that none postdated the time, twenty-five years before her death, when the moon hieroglyph began to be written differently. (While this change is important to us because of its chronological usefulness, there is no reason that the Egyptians should have favored the earlier shape of the sign or even noticed the difference.) Eaton-Krauss gives no explanation for such a selection; instead, she argues that the grave goods found in the smaller coffin give only a *terminus post quem* for the burial. This is correct, in that a single object of early date does not in itself rule out a later burial. However, Ahhotep

27. See, for example, the Dra Abu el-Naga coffin shown in fig. 34.1a.

28. See a summary of the arguments in Thomas 1980.

29. The multiple sarcophagi of kings such as Thutmose I and Hatshepsut were used in sequence and re-inscribed for other owners after their abandonment; they did not form part of a single burial.

apparently lived through the latter part of her son's, all of her grandson's, and into the early part of Thutmose I's reign, presumably becoming increasingly powerful as she became more venerable and increasingly wealthy as Egypt grew more stable. If she were buried in the Dra Abu el-Naga coffin, as Eaton-Krauss argues, why should *none* of the objects buried with her have been manufactured during the last, most glorious, third of her life? Why should *all* the gifts from her son have dated from the earlier part of his reign? Why should there be no gifts from her grandson Amenhotep I or his successor?

The reported area of the burial also argues against the identification of the Dra Abu el-Naga mummy as the mother of Ahmose. Eaton-Krauss suggests that the original site of the burials was above its findspot in the Seventeenth Dynasty cemetery at Dra Abu el-Naga. This cemetery was not used for royal burials in the reign of Thutmose I. A more likely location for the burial of Ahmose's mother is an isolated tomb in one of the remote valleys behind the cliffs, like the cliff-tomb that was built for Hatshepsut as a queen. A tomb located in the Dra Abu el-Naga cemetery near the burial of Kamose suggests, like the coffin and the burial equipment found in it, a date early in the reign of Ahmose.

Moreover, the mechanism Eaton-Krauss suggests for the separation of the coffins is inconsistent with what we know about the activities of "pious" necropolis officials in the early Third Intermediate Period. Both Wente and Reeves suggest that the reburials of the early Third Intermediate Period were not a last-ditch attempt to salvage the poor remains of royal burials after they had been robbed, but rather a methodical government-sponsored stripping of intact tombs of some of their valuables.[30] This idea has been corroborated by the objects from several different royal tombs and the myriad fragments of gold leaf found in the fill of the tomb of Ramesses XI, which has led Romer to suggest that this tomb might have served as a place for collecting the grave goods and removing the gold that made them so desirable to thieves (Romer, personal communication, 1979). The spectacular gold and silver grave goods buried with Pseusennes I at Tanis (some inscribed with the names of earlier kings) may represent some of the profits of this venture (e.g., Stierlin and Ziegler 1987, pls. 42–43). If the tomb containing the smaller Ahhotep coffin had been examined at any time by officials who reburied the larger coffin, it is unlikely that they would have left the gold on its outer surface intact, much less the numerous gold and silver objects found with it.[31]

The most likely hypothesis to explain the find spot of the Dra Abu el-Naga coffin, its intact state, the apparent date of its contents, and its lack of a *mwt-nswt* title is that it was buried during the early part of the reign of Ahmose, containing the body of a royal woman, who was closely related to Taʿo II, but not the mother of a king, and that it remained hidden until the workmen of Mariette came across it. If the burial was intact and of this date, however, the coffin that eventually appeared in the Deir el-Bahri cache could not have been deposited at the same time since its owner, the mother of Ahmose, lived many years after that date. Instead, the larger coffin was presumably buried in one of the cliff tombs, with this later Queen Ahhotep inside it. When it was moved to the Deir el-Bahri cache, her body was taken out and was presumably among the unidentified rewrapped female mummies in the cache. The cutting of the back of the coffin might have been done in order to remove the body easily without damaging it or it might have been to facilitate the insertion of the (probably larger) mummy of Pinedjem I.

Thus, there must have been two burials and at least two queens named Ahhotep, one who was closely related to Taʿo II, based on Eaton-Krauss's stylistic comparison of the two coffins, and another who was the mother of Ahmose, based on the Karnak stela (CG 34001), the Iuf stela (CG 34009), and the title *mwt-nswt* on her coffin.

30. Wente suggested this interpretation in class lectures on the basis of Late Ramesside Letter #28, in which the high priest of Amun ordered several workmen to "uncover a tomb among the ancient tombs and preserve its seal until I return" (Wente 1990, p. 195). The same conclusion is reached on archaeological grounds by Reeves (1990, pp. 276–78, 281, n. 94).

31. The corresponding gold surface was apparently stripped from the coffin of Taʿo II, whose tomb was recorded as intact in Papyrus Abbott; see Winlock 1924, p. 248, who suggests that Tao's coffin "escaped the pillaging of the Necropolis thieves … , but at some period suffered from the more insidious attentions of its own lawful guardians."

THREE QUEENS?

Robins (1982, pp. 71–77) attempts to distinguish three queens named Ahhotep,[32] assigning the evidence as follows:

Ahhotep I	Queen of the gilded coffin found in Dra Abu el-Naga with gold and silver jewelry of Ahmose and Kamose, called *ḥmt-nswt wrt, ḫnmt nfr ḥḏt*
Ahhotep II	Queen of the Deir el-Bahri coffin, the Karnak stela (CG 34001), the Kares stela (CG 34003), and the Iuf stela (CG 34009); the mother of Ahmose, called *sꜣt-nswt, snt-nswt, ḥmt-nswt wrt, ḫnmt nfr ḥḏt, mwt-nswt*
Ahhotep III	Called *sꜣt-nswt wrt, ḫnmt nfr ḥḏt,* her name is placed parallel to King Taʿo's on a statue of a young Prince Ahmose, probably their son[33]

Robins's efforts are devoted to proving that Ahhotep III cannot be equated with Ahhotep II, an equation that underlies many of the assumptions made about the genealogy of the period. Robins argues that on the Karnak stela where Ahmose honored his mother,[34] Ahhotep is given only the title *ḥmt-nswt* and is called neither *ḥmt-nswt wrt* nor *ḫnmt nfr ḥḏt*, although both these titles occur on the Deir el-Bahri coffin. From this Robins concludes that these titles were only granted to Ahhotep II long after the death of her husband. Since the statue that pairs the names of an Ahhotep and a King Taʿo gives Ahhotep the *ḫnmt nfr ḥḏt* title, the queen on the statue must be a third Queen Ahhotep.

This conclusion does not necessarily follow. It could be argued that Ahhotep's wifely role was de-emphasized on the Karnak stela in order to stress her role as a woman of royal blood and (especially) her role as the royal mother who had served as a regent for the king during his minority. The distinction of being the "chief" royal wife might also have been less important after the death of the king and perhaps also of most of his secondary wives; the king's wife who was the mother of her husband's successor had no need to distinguish herself further from other royal wives. That the mother of Ahmose is called *ḥmt-nswt wrt* on the personal stela of her steward Iuf (CG 34009) also implies that this was a real title rather than a false one bestowed for the purpose of legitimizing her son's rule (especially since the stela dates to the reign of Thutmose II).

That said, however, it is odd that so many scarabs and other small objects have the simpler title *ḥmt-nswt*. Troy (1979, p. 88, category III B, C) cites fourteen small objects (#10 is the same object as #7) that were inscribed with Ahhotep's name and the title *ḥmt-nswt*. Troy could not date these objects, but all five of the pieces from the Metropolitan Museum of Art exhibit the post-year-18 form of the moon hieroglyph.[35] A sixth post-year-18 example is the hinged cartouche box (not cited by Troy) bearing the same simple title on the base of the cartouche (Müller-Feldman 1959, pl. vi [1]; also discussed in note 9, above). These objects cannot have belonged to Robin's Ahhotep I, who was buried before the change in the moon sign, or to Ahhotep III, who was a *ḫnmt nfr ḥḏt* and hence by implication a *ḥmt-nswt wrt*; if they belonged to Ahhotep II, it is strange that they omit her principal title in year 18 and later, *mwt-nswt*. These objects may belong to yet another Queen Ahhotep who was an obscure secondary wife of one of these kings during the post-year-18 period; but if so, it is odd that so many more of her small belongings survived than those of her more important namesakes.

TWO QUEENS

In her attempt to separate Ahhotep II (owner of the Deir el-Bahri coffin) and Ahhotep III (paired with Taʿo on the Prince Ahmose statue), Robins does not discuss a far more likely equation between Ahhotep III and Ahhotep I (owner of the Dra Abu el-Naga coffin). If one accepts Robins's argument that neither of these women was the mother of Ahmose, there is no reason why they should have been different queens. Both lived in the late Seventeenth Dynasty and are not attested after the change in the moon hieroglyph. Both were closely

32. Vandersleyen (1977, pp. 243–44) also suggests the possibility of three royal women named Ahhotep; however, he assumes Robins's Ahhotep II and Ahhotep III to be the same person. His third Ahhotep is depicted on the statue of a princess, Louvre N. 446, and it is unclear why he believes she cannot be the same woman as one of the other two queens.

33. Louvre E. 15682; Winlock 1924, pp. 255–56, pls. 12, 18–20.

34. CG 34001. The stela is undated, but the form of the moon sign dates it to before Ahmose's year 22.

35. Troy 1979, p. 88, III B #5–#9. I am grateful to Dr. Dorothea Arnold for allowing me access to the records and to Dr. Catharine Roehrig for helping me locate these pieces.

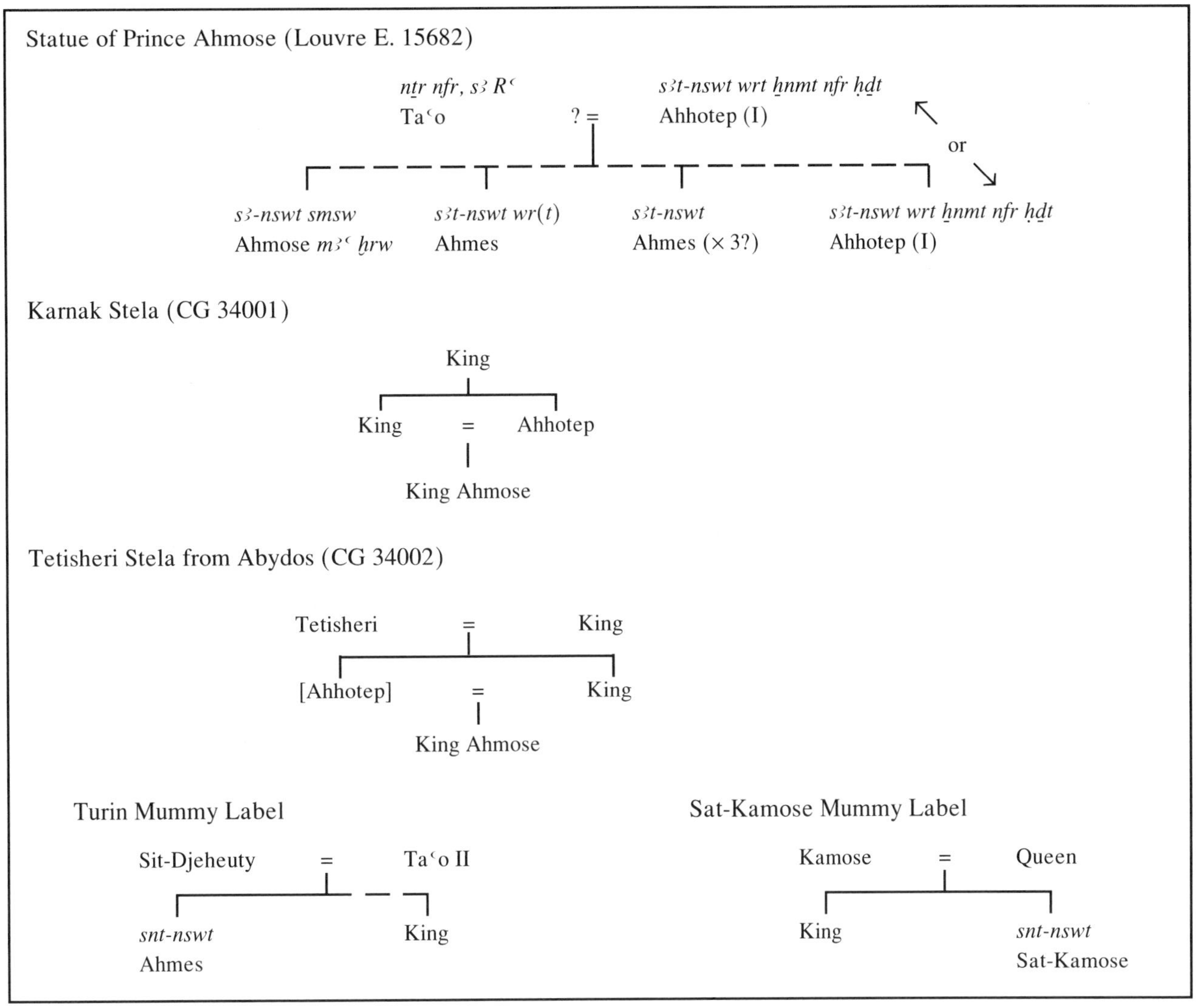

Figure 34.3. Genealogical Data from Textual Sources
(Stated Relationships Are in Solid Line; Implied Relationships Are in Dashed Line)

connected with King Taʿo. Both bore the title *ḫnmt nfr ḥḏt* preceded by one other title. On the coffin, this other title was *ḥmt-nswt wrt*, while on the statue it was *sꜣt-nswt wrt*. The former is generally implied by the title *ḫnmt nfr ḥḏt* and might have been omitted from the statue for that reason; the latter might have become less important with time, especially if the queen's royal father belonged to the earlier, otherwise unrelated, part of the dynasty. Alternatively, since there is only one sign's difference between the two titles, the discrepancy may be the result of a mistake in one of the inscriptions. An erroneous *sꜣt-nswt wrt* on the statue might have been inspired by the four other women named on the statue who bore the title *sꜣt-nswt*, and its position on the back pillar might have kept the error from notice and correction. If, on the other hand, this Ahhotep held the more unusual title of *sꜣt-nswt wrt*, it might have been mistakenly transformed into the more common title on her coffin. Moreover, as noted above, the angled eyes and high brow of the Dra Abu el-Naga coffin of Ahhotep I are echoed in the face of the little prince of the Louvre statue, who would by this reconstruction have been her son or brother.

It still seems most probable, then, that there were two great royal wives named Ahhotep. One, "Ahhotep I" (in which Robin's Ahhotep III is subsumed), was buried in the Dra Abu el-Naga coffin and had no son who had become king at the time of her death; the other, "Ahhotep II," was the owner of the Deir el-Bahri coffin and the mother of Ahmose.[36] An important point demonstrated in Robins's article is that we do not know to which kings these women were married. The principal genealogical evidence comes from their titles and from the inscrip-

36. I am adopting the numbers assigned to the two queens by Robins here to avoid endless repetition of the provenience of their coffins. Although the order implied may not be the order of their births, it is clearly the order of their deaths. It is also the order in which their coffins were discovered, which is not entirely irrelevant to the evolution of the reconstruction, as is discussed below.

tions on the Louvre statue (E. 15682), the Karnak stela (CG 34001), and the Tetisheri stela from Abydos (CG 34002). Texts naming two king's sisters are also significant. The genealogical information from these textual sources is summarized in fig. 34.3.

As argued above, Ahhotep I was the royal woman represented in parallel with King Taʿo on the statue of a king's son Ahmose. Since Taʿo was given no throne name on the statue, he could be either Taʿo I or Taʿo II.[37] It is unlikely that the owner of the Dra Abu el-Naga coffin was married to Taʿo I,[38] however, since she cannot have been the mother of Taʿo II and it would be odd for a king to make a matched set of coffins for himself and his stepmother or his sister-in-law. The most probable reconstruction, then, is that Ahhotep I was the wife of Taʿo II.

It is also possible that Ahhotep I was actually the daughter of the King Taʿo with whom she is represented, as her title "great royal daughter" suggests. The other title, *ẖnmt nfr ḥḏt*, represents a role normally filled by the chief royal wife; however, in this case it may have been filled by a daughter because of the death of the principal queen (perhaps while giving birth to the Prince Ahmose memorialized on the statue). This royal daughter might have later married her father's successor, Taʿo II (if the Taʿo on the statue was Taʿo I) or Kamose (if the Taʿo was Taʿo II). In the latter case the Dra Abu el-Naga coffin would have been made for her during Taʿo II's reign in her capacity as *ẖnmt nfr ḥḏt*. If the title *ḥmt-nswt wrt* on her coffin was a mistake for the less common *sꜣt-nswt wrt*, as suggested above, it is also possible that she never married at all.[39]

Ahhotep I thus might have been married to Taʿo II, Kamose, or no king at all; however, the simplest interpretation, as suggested both by the style of her coffin and the Louvre statue, is that she was the wife of Taʿo II. In all of these cases, the poverty of her tomb and wealth of her grave goods are easily explained. Her tomb will have been a modest one built during the struggle with the Hyksos, during the lifetime of her royal patron and perhaps near his own. By the time of her death, in the reign of Ahmose, however, the Hyksos were being successfully driven from Egypt and the royal family had greater wealth to contribute to her burial equipment (although the gilded coffin of Taʿo II was hardly plebeian). It might have been felt that she deserved some of the spoils of battle since Taʿo II (either her husband or her father) had been the initiator of the resistance[40] and almost certainly died in battle during its early stages (Harris and Wente 1980, p. 289).

There are also several possibilities for the spouse of Ahhotep II, who would also have been the father of Ahmose. Ahmose left monuments to his mother Ahhotep and his grandmother Tetisheri that tell us that he was the son and grandson of ruling kings since his grandmother Tetisheri was both a king's wife and a king's mother and his mother Ahhotep was a king's daughter, a king's sister, and a king's great wife. Tetisheri was called a king's great wife only after her death (CG 34002) and, unlike both queens named Ahhotep, she was never called *ẖnmt nfr ḥḏt*; she was perhaps a secondary wife brought into prominence by the accession of her son. (This circumstance is not surprising, given the fact that her father and mother bore only the very low titles *sꜣb*

37. I use the names Taʿo I and Taʿo II for Kamose's two predecessors, Kings Senakhtenre and Seqenenreʿ Taʿo, largely because of their brevity and clarity, despite the doubt that has been cast on the former's association with the name Taʿo (cf. also von Beckerath 1999, pp. 21–25, esp. note 1). Vandersleyen (1983) has questioned Winlock's (1924) assumption that the "Seqenenreʿ Taʿo the elder," listed after another "Seqenenreʿ Taʿo" in Papyrus Abbott (which notes "making a second Taʿo" after the second name), is actually a garbled reference to a Seventeenth Dynasty king named Senakhtenre. Vandersleyen feels the reference to a second Taʿo reflects the scribe's confusion and notes that the listing of the elder Taʿo in the second position contradicts Winlock's assumption that the tombs and the inspection were arranged in chronological order. Vandersleyen argues that, since Senakhtenre is never attested with the nomen Taʿo, we should not use it. While this is a useful caveat, it seems most probable to me that Winlock was correct in identifying two Taos (since the scribe, after all, says there were two), but perhaps misinterpreted *ʿꜣ*, which may mean "the great" rather than "the elder." Senakhtenre was probably relatively unknown at the time of the inspection; his successor, however, was the hero of a popular Ramesside story. Whoever made up the list might have mistakenly associated the hero's reputation with the tomb of the first and eldest Taʿo and applied the name Seqenenreʿ to it. When he came to the second tomb, he realized his error and marked the second name as the name of the "great" king, adding, however, that there were two kings named Taʿo. (Anyone who has visited sealed ancient tombs in modern times will understand how difficult it would probably have been to go back and check.) By this hypothesis, the tombs and the kings would come in the correct order, with the eldest first.

38. As has been argued by Bennett (1995, pp. 43–44), largely based on the assumption that the royal family of this period tended to give all their children the same names.

39. The body found in the Dra Abu el-Naga coffin has been lost, so it is impossible to estimate her age at death by physical means. Despite her survival into a later reign, she still might have died as a young, unmarried woman early in the reign of Ahmose if the reigns of Taʿo II and Kamose were at the shorter ends of their possible ranges.

40. In the beginning of a fragmentary Ramesside story, Seqenenreʿ Taʿo was clearly the initiator of the war.

and *nbt-pr*; see Daressy 1908, p. 137.) Ahmose's father and Ahhotep's husband must thus have been one of Ahmose's predecessors, Kamose, Taʿo II, or Taʿo I. All of these equations are possible, although the last two are much less likely than the first.

The simplest explanation, as Robins (1982, pp. 73–74) points out, would be to assume that Ahmose was the son of his predecessor Kamose. Tetisheri would then have been a secondary wife of Taʿo II (or Taʿo I, if Taʿo II were the brother of Kamose or Taʿo I), and Ahhotep II would have been the sister and a wife (possibly also secondary) of Kamose. This reconstruction would eliminate the problem of why Kamose was succeeded by someone who was not his son and it would also allow Ahhotep I to have filled the role of principal wife to either Taʿo II, Kamose, or neither of them. Furthermore, viewing these kings as closely spaced successive generations fits well with the very young age of Ahmose at his accession and also with the appearance of his grandmother Tetisheri at a temple dedication with him (Winlock 1924, p. 246). If Ahhotep II was herself quite young, Tetisheri might have served as regent in the very beginning of his reign.

A rather convincing piece of evidence for Kamose as the father of Ahmose is the existence of a "king's daughter and king's sister Sat-Kamose," who is known from a later label on her mummy,[41] but also seems to be depicted in the contemporary tomb of Tetiki.[42] Wente (Harris and Wente 1980, p. 125) argues that unless the title "king's sister" could be given to a cousin, this lady, despite her name ("daughter of Kamose"), must have been the daughter of Taʿo II and the sister of Kamose. However, as Wente himself points out a few pages later (ibid., p. 127), if Ahmose is assumed to be Kamose's son rather than his brother, Sat-Kamose was probably Ahmose's sister.

If Ahmose's father was not Kamose, Kamose must have had no son; otherwise the son of a predecessor would not have succeeded him. The traditional interpretation, that Taʿo II was the father of both Ahmose and Kamose, is still possible. One difficulty it raises, however, is that Taʿo II would then have been outlived by two queens bearing the titles of principal wife, Ahhotep I and Ahhotep II. It is generally thought that although secondary marriages were possible, only one queen at a time held the title of principal wife, *ḥmt-nswt wrt*, but both these women outlived Taʿo II and bear this title on their coffins. A reconstruction in which Taʿo II was the husband of Ahhotep II would imply that Robins is correct in supposing that Ahhotep, mother of Ahmose, did not hold the title *ḥmt nswt wrt*.

Vandersleyen (1977, p. 237) concludes that Kamose and Ahmose could not have been brothers because Kamose cannot be the son of Taʿo II. Vandersleyen argues that the Prince Ahmose statue shows him to have been the father of four daughters as well as an eldest son who died young and, since the mummy of Taʿo II was only 30 years old at death, that his second son could not have been old enough to fight a war only three years after his father's death. But this ignores several possibilities. The Taʿo on the statue may be Taʿo I rather than Taʿo II, and he is not said explicitly to be the father of any of the children named. If he was the father of these children, they may have had different mothers, which would considerably shorten the time needed to produce them, and Kamose could be the second (rather than the sixth) of the king's children since a living king's sons are rarely represented on monuments. Moreover, as Robins points out (1982, p. 74), more recent estimates have raised the age of Taʿo II to the 35–40 year range. Nonetheless, the existence of the king's sister Sat-Kamose and two principal wives make this solution unlikely.

The most complex reconstruction would be to suggest that Ahmose was the son of Taʿo I,[43] the first king of this branch of the Seventeenth Dynasty. Taʿo II, Kamose, and Ahmose would then all have been brothers or half-brothers, a succession that would not be improbable in time of war. By this hypothesis, Ahhotep II would have been Taʿo I's principal wife, and Tetisheri must have been a secondary wife of his predecessor and mother of Taʿo I.

This reconstruction, however, creates such a number of problems that it is barely tenable. Based on the Tetisheri stela, it would imply that both Taʿo I and Ahhotep II were children of a king from the earlier part of the Seventeenth Dynasty. Although it has been generally assumed that Taʿo I was not related to the earlier

41. Vandersleyen 1977, p. 241. The inscription on her mummy wrappings calls her *sꜣt-nswt, snt-nswt, ḥmt-nswt wrt* (*Sꜣt-Kꜣ-ms*).

42. The traces of the name are a bird-like diagonal over a short horizontal, a longer horizontal (part of *kꜣ*?), and two vertical lines that could be part of a *ms*-sign (Davies 1925, p. 14, n. 2, referring to fig. 34.2). She would be shown in parallel with Ahmes-Nefertari, who would be her sister by this reconstruction.

43. This genealogy has been advocated by Blankenberg-van Delden (most recently 1982, pp. 35–38), who makes several of the points that I cite but also makes several dubious assumptions, for example, that several kings had only one wife (thereby ruling out these kings as husbands for other queens), that kings with similar names must necessarily be related, and the converse.

kings of the dynasty (Robins 1982, p. 75, n. 5; Redford 1967, p. 31), this assumption seems to be based largely on differences in naming and the non-royal origin of Tetisheri; there is no clear evidence for a break. Tenuous support for some sort of connection can be seen in the account of Ahhotep II's steward Iuf (CG 34009), who records that, early in her career, Ahhotep II set up a memorial to Sobekemsaf, a queen from the early part of the Seventeenth Dynasty, which might suggest a family connection.[44]

A second problem with this reconstruction is the age of Ahhotep II. If she is assumed to have been the mother of Taʿo I's heir Taʿo II, she must have been a minimum of 99 years old by the time of her death (15 [45] + 35 [46] + 3 [47] + 46 [48] = 99), and equally problematically, must have given birth to her youngest child after the age of 50. If Taʿo II was the son of another wife of Taʿo I, however, this difficulty vanishes; Ahhotep might have been as young as 66 at her death (15 + 5 [49] + 46). But this reconstruction requires very short reigns for both Taʿo II and Kamose. Both the historical evidence and the analysis of Ahmose's mummy suggest that he began his 25 year reign when he was no more than 5 years old,[50] so that even if Ahmose were a posthumous son of Taʿo I, the reigns of Taʿo II and Kamose could not total more than six years. Kamose would have reigned only the three years required by his highest year date, and Taʿo even fewer, only long enough to have started the war and to have been killed in it. This is not impossible in time of war, but the gilded coffins of Taʿo II and Ahhotep I suggest a somewhat longer, more stable reign for him than for Kamose.

A final argument against Taʿo I as the father of Ahmose is the existence of a daughter of Taʿo II and Sit-Djehuty, the king's daughter and king's sister Ahmes.[51] As in the case of Sat-Kamose discussed above, this suggests that Taʿo II had a son who became king, presumably either Kamose or Ahmose, ruling out the possibility that all three kings were sons of Taʿo I. The only other explanation would be that the title was honorary or a mistake, or that Sit-Djehuty was the mother of one of these kings (though presumably not Taʿo II himself) by an earlier royal marriage.

The least problematic reconstruction identifies Ahhotep I as the wife of Taʿo II and Ahhotep II as the wife of Kamose and makes Kamose and Ahmose the sons of their predecessors on the throne. A tentative family tree based on these assumptions is given in fig. 34.4. However, the relationships depicted here are by no means the only possibilities, as the above arguments have shown. I have argued the various alternative relationships simply to demonstrate the great variety of possibilities allowed by the evidence. The chart gives the simplest reconstruction, but history, like life, does not always happen in the most straightforward way.[52]

THE ARCHAEOLOGY OF EGYPTOLOGICAL SCHOLARSHIP

Given the lack of information about the interrelationships between these people and the wide range of possible reconstructions that can be argued on the existing evidence, it is curious that the traditional sequence is so firmly established in the literature and in the minds of Egyptologists. Even those of us who have tried to argue

44. Robins (1982, p. 75, n. 5) argues that the "moon names" compounded with *iʿḥ*, Ahmose and Ahhotep, are attested in the latter half of the Seventeenth Dynasty but not in the allegedly unrelated earlier half. However, regardless of her antecedents, Ahhotep seems to have been the first member of the family to bear such a name.

45. Estimated minimum age for motherhood.

46. As noted above, the mummy traditionally identified as Taʿo II was approximately 35 to 40 years of age at his death (Harris and Wente 1980, p. 206). If Ahhotep were his mother, as well as the mother of Kamose and Ahmose, his entire lifespan must be added to hers.

47. The minimum reign of Kamose is three years; however, most recent reconstructions assign him six years.

48. Combined reigns of Ahmose and Amenhotep I, from Wente and Van Siclen 1976, p. 218.

49. Combined minimal reigns for Taʿo II and Kamose after the birth of Ahmose.

50. Vandersleyen (1971, pp. 197–200) argues that Ahmose did not go to war until year 11 of his reign, from which he concludes that he came to the throne as a child. The medical evidence (Harris and Wente 1980, p. 210) puts his age at death at 25 to 30 years of age, after a 25 year reign.

51. The names, relationships, and titles come from mummy wrappings from the Valley of the Queens, now in the Turin Museum (Schiaparelli 1924, p. 15, pls. 6–7). Winlock (1924, p. 257) is dubious about this evidence, but more recent writers accept it without question (e.g., Vandersleyen 1977, p. 238; Robins 1982, p. 74; Gitton 1984, p. 18, n. 42). It looks very clear to me.

52. The elegant genealogy constructed by Bennett (1995, p. 44), in which everyone who has the same name also has the same parents, for example, seems to me improbably tidy, despite the impressive number of parallels he has collected for the phenomenon (ibid., p. 43, n. 40). The fact that the eldest son of Ahmose and Ahmes-Nefertari was also named Ahmose, according to the Donation stela (Chevrier 1936, p. 137, pl. IIa), casts some doubt on the efficacy of this pattern as a genealogical tool. Moreover, his reconstruction does not account for the closeness of the coffins of Ahhotep I and Taʿo II and would imply that Ahhotep I was a king's mother, a title she did not bear.

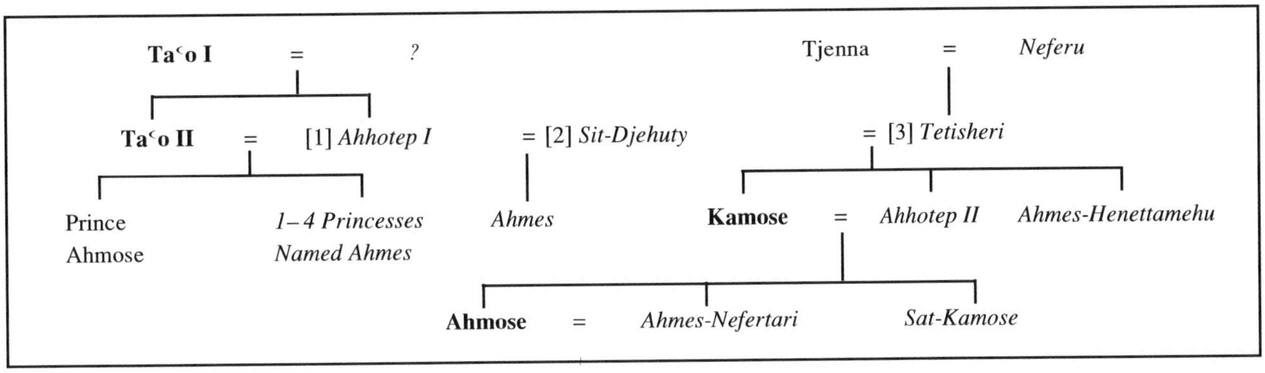

Figure 34.4. Simplest Possible Genealogy of Ahmosid Family (Kings' Names in Boldface, Women's Names in Italics)

alternate versions unquestioningly assume the truth of other elements of the traditional reconstruction, a reconstruction that is surprisingly flawed.

The main reason for the current state of the question seems to be the sequence in which information was discovered. As in an archaeological excavation, evidence from more recent times is usually more accessible than evidence from more remote periods. It is thus the first to come to the attention of scholars, and because it appears in a vacuum it tends to be given more weight than evidence discovered later.

Nineteenth-century scholars based their reconstructions on the evidence known to them, attempting to construct a coherent narrative that tied all the pieces of evidence together as compactly as their nature allowed. These reconstructions were often based upon unexamined assumptions: a man and a woman occurring together on a monument or otherwise linked were assumed to be husband and wife unless a different relationship was specifically stated, and the wife of a king was assumed to be more important than his mother, sisters, or daughters.

When new evidence appears, often more contemporary with the events and people it relates to, the scholars who deal with it have these earlier reconstructions already set in their heads; only rarely do they abandon these reconstructions entirely and rework the evidence from the ground up. Instead, in the conservative tradition of scholarship, they tend to keep the changes in the accepted reconstruction to a minimum, adjusting the details to accommodate any new evidence to what we already "know." Only the part of the reconstruction that is definitively contradicted by the new evidence is altered. As a result, an unnecessarily elaborate edifice is constructed that incorporates in its explanatory structure not only the available evidence, but also the effects of the sequence in which that evidence appeared. Had the evidence become available in a different order, the edifice might have had an entirely different shape.

Just as archaeologists must periodically rethink their interpretations so that the actions of people whose activities are reflected in the lower levels of their excavations are not analyzed in terms of the activities of people who lived long after them, so must historians periodically look skeptically at the entire edifice of historical reconstruction that has accumulated over the decades to eliminate the inconsistencies, unnecessary complexities, and unjustified assumptions that have crept into it over the decades.

In the case of the two queens named Ahhotep, the earliest published materials were Ramesside coffins and tombs linking a Queen Ahhotep with Amenhotep I, some of which were already published by Champollion (1845, pl. 153) and Lepsius (1849, pls. 2a, 2d). When the coffin of Ahhotep at Dra Abu el-Naga was discovered in 1859, associated with jewelry inscribed with the names of Ahmose and Kamose, it was assumed that Queen Ahhotep was the wife of the earlier king and the mother of the later one. The texts from the statue of Prince Ahmose were first published in 1889 (though the statue was already in Paris in private hands and was presumably known earlier) and suggested that the husband of this early Eighteenth Dynasty queen was not Kamose but Ta'o, whose name was adjacent to hers there. The fact that the dead prince and all his sisters were named Ahmose probably helped to secure the identification of the woman named on the statue with the mother of King Ahmose and implied that his father was Ta'o II. These assumptions were apparently confirmed by the discovery in 1902 of the Karnak stela of Ahmose honoring her as his mother.

By the time the Deir el-Bahri coffin was excavated in 1881, the identity of the earlier Ahhotep, owner of the coffin found at Dra Abu el-Naga was already well established. The owner of the coffin found in the cache could then be identified with the long-known Queen Ahhotep associated with Amenhotep I. No principal wife of

Amenhotep was known at that time,[53] and since the coffin bore that title Ahhotep II was assumed to have filled that role. When Merytamun was identified as a principal wife of Amenhotep I, the spurious Ahhotep was retained in the family tree, while the newly discovered queen took a secondary place to her in the discussions of Amenhotep's reign.[54] Had the Ramesside evidence appeared later and the Deir el-Bahri coffin earlier, it seems likely that the current state of the problem would have been reached long ago.

Perhaps the best example of the way the early conclusions about the relationships between these people has affected later reconstructions is the consistent assumption that Taʿo II must belong to the generation directly before Ahmose's and that Tetisheri was married to Taʿo I. Both of these conclusions are dependent upon the identification of the Ahhotep shown on the Louvre statue of Prince Ahmose with the Ahhotep who is described on the Karnak stela as the mother of Ahmose. Despite the evidence that these were two different women, the conclusions based upon their identity tend to be retained in the literature. Now that the Dra Abu el-Naga coffin can be seen to belong to an Ahhotep who was not the mother of King Ahmose, her equation with the Ahhotep of the Louvre statue seems obvious, based on titles, date, and the ties of both contexts with Taʿo II (the statue's juxtaposition of names and the coffin's similarities in style). The resulting reconstruction, in which the identity of King Ahmose's father is still somewhat uncertain, is markedly less clear and tidy than the old reconstruction, but it is more firmly grounded in all the available evidence.

The favoring of tidy reconstructions is not the only way in which aesthetics may have influenced this reconstruction. A final consideration that may subconsciously reinforce the conservatism of scholars working on this particular question is the beauty and richness of the grave goods found with the Dra Abu el-Naga coffin. The historical narrative we construct would be much more satisfying if we could view this treasure as a proper tribute to the mother of a conqueror, the great queen lauded by Ahmose on his Karnak stela, who helped guide Egypt out of the humiliation of the Hyksos domination and into the glories of the Eighteenth Dynasty. It is less agreeable to admit that this golden coffin and its impressive collection of gold, silver, and jewelry probably belonged to a queen about whom we know very little, the identity of whose royal husband is not known with any certainty, and who never had a son that became king. Despite our ignorance of her life history, however, this other Ahhotep may nonetheless have played a major role in the wars against the Hyksos.[55] New evidence may someday be discovered that will allow us to appreciate her role, that will enable us to incorporate her into our historical narrative in a more satisfying way, and that will reconcile us to her ownership of such very nice jewelry.

References

Beckerath, J. von

1999 "Theban Seventeenth Dynasty." In *Gold of Praise: Studies in Honor of Edward F. Wente*, edited by E. Teeter and J. A. Larson, pp. 21–25. Studies in Ancient Oriental Civilization 58. Chicago: Oriental Institute.

Bennett, C.

1995 "King Senakhtenre." *Göttinger Miszellen* 145: 37–44.

Blankenberg-van Delden, C.

1982 "A Genealogical Reconstruction of the Kings and Queens of the Late 17th and Early 18th Dynasties." *Göttinger Miszellen* 54: 31–45.

Champollion, J.-F.

1845 *Monuments de l'Égypte et de la Nubie*, volume 2. Paris: Firmin Didot Frères.

Chevrier, H.

1936 "Rapport sur les travaux de Karnak." *Annales du Service des antiquités de l'Égypte* 36: 131–57.

Corteggiani, J.-P.

1986 *The Egypt of the Pharaohs*. Paris: Hachette.

Daressy, G.

1908 "Les parents de la reine Teta-chera." *Annales du Service des antiquités de l'Égypte* 9: 137–38.

1909 *Cercueils des cachettes royales*. Catalogue général des antiquités égyptiennes du Musée du Caire, nos.

53. The burial of Merytamun, now assumed to be Amenhotep I's queen, was initially attributed to a Thutmoside Merytamun; see Thomas 1980, pp. 171–76, for a history of the attribution.

54. See, for example, Hayes 1959, pp. 52–53.

55. Such a role is suggested by the necklace of golden flies and bracelet with lions found in her coffin, jewelry that is elsewhere associated with military valor (Corteggiani 1986, p. 86).

61001–61044. Cairo: Institut français d'archéologie orientale.

Davies, N. de G.
1925 "The Tomb of Tetaky at Thebes (No. 15)." *Journal of Egyptian Archaeology* 11: 10–18.

Dorman, P.
1988 *The Monuments of Senenmut: Problems in Historical Methodology*. London: Kegan Paul.

Eaton-Krauss, M.
1990 "The Coffins of Queen Ahhotep, Consort of Seqeni-en-Re and Mother of Ahmose." *Chronique d'Égypte* 65: 195–205.

Gauthier, H.
1912 *Le livre des rois d'Égypte*, volume 2. Mémoires publiés par les Membres de l'Institut français d'archéologie orientale du Caire 18. Cairo: Institut français d'archéologie orientale.

Gitton, M.
1975 *L'épouse du dieu Ahmes Néfertary: Documents sur sa vie et son culte posthume*. Annales littéraires de l'Université de Besançon 172. Centre de recherches d'histoire ancienne 15. Paris: Belles-Lettres.
1984 *Les divines épouses de la 18e dynastie*. Annales littéraires de l'Université de Besançon 306; Centre de recherches d'histoire ancienne 61. Paris: Belles-Lettres.

Harris, J. E., and E. F. Wente
1980 *An X-ray Atlas of the Royal Mummies*. Chicago: University of Chicago Press.

Hayes, W. C.
1959 *Scepter of Egypt: A Background for the Study of Egyptian Antiquities in the Metropolitan Museum of Art*, Part 2: *The Hyksos Period and the New Kingdom (1675–1080 B.C.)*. New York: Metropolitan Museum of Art.

Lepsius, K. R.
1849 *Denkmäler aus Aegypten und Aethiopien*, Volume 3. Berlin: Nicholaische Buchhandlung.

Maspero, G.
1889 "Les momies royales de Déir el-Baharî." *Mémoires publiés par les Membres de la Mission archéologique français au Caire*, tome 1, pp. 511–787. Paris: E. Leroux.
1897 *Histoire ancienne des peuples de l'orient classique*, volume 2. Paris: Hachette.

Müller-Feldman, H.
1959 "Ein Toilettenkästchen der Königin Ahhotep." *Zeitschrift für ägyptische Sprache und Altertumskunde* 84: 143–45.

Redford, D. B.
1967 *The History and Chronology of the 18th Dynasty*. Toronto: University of Toronto.

Reeves, N.
1990 *The Valley of the Kings: The Decline of a Royal Necropolis*. London: Kegan Paul.

Robins, G.
1978 "Amenhotpe I and the Child Amenemhat." *Göttinger Miszellen* 30: 71–75.
1982 "Ahhotep I, II, and III." *Göttinger Miszellen* 56: 71–75.

Roth, A. M.
1977/78 "Ahhotep I and Ahhotep II." *Serapis* 4: 31–40.

Schiaparelli, E.
1924 *Relazione sui lavori della Missione archeologica italiana in Egitto* 1: *Esplorazione della valle delle regine*. Turin: G. Chiantore.

Schmitz, B.
1978 "Untersuchungen zu zwei Königinnen der frühen 18. Dynastie, Ahhotep und Ahmose." *Chronique d'Égypte* 53: 207–21.

Stierlin, H., and C. Ziegler
1987 *Tanis: Trésors des pharaons*. Fribourg: Seuil.

Thomas, E.
1980 "The Tomb of Ahmose(?) Merytamen, Theban Tomb 320." *Serapis* 6: 171–81.

Troy, L.
1979 "Ahhotep: A Source Evaluation." *Göttinger Miszellen* 35: 81–91.
1981 "One Merytamun Too Many: An Exercise in Critical Method." *Göttinger Miszellen* 50: 81–96.

Vandersleyen, C.
1971 *Les guerres d'Ahmosis*. Brussels: Fondation Égyptologique Reine Élisabeth.
1977 "Une stèle de l'an 18 d'Ahmosis à Hanovre." *Chronique d'Égypte* 52, no. 104: 223–44.
1980 "Les deux Ahhotep." *Studien zur altägyptischen Kultur* 8: 237–41.
1983 "Un seul roi Taa sous la 17e dynastie." *Göttinger Miszellen* 63: 67–69.

Wente, E. F.
1990 *Letters from Ancient Egypt*. Society of Biblical Literature, Writings from the Ancient World 1. Atlanta: Scholars Press.

Wente, E. F., and C. C. Van Siclen III
1976 "A Chronology of the New Kingdom." In *Studies in Honor of George R. Hughes, January 12, 1977*, edited by J. H. Johnson and E. F. Wente, pp. 217–61. Studies in Ancient Oriental Civilization 39. Chicago: Oriental Institute.

Wiedemann, A.
1884 *Ägyptische Geschichte*, Volume 1. Gotha: F. A. Perthes.

Winlock, H. E.
1924 "The Tombs of Kings of the Seventeenth Dynasty at Thebes." *Journal of Egyptian Archaeology* 10: 217–77.
1932 *The Tomb of Queen Meryet-Amūn at Thebes*. Publications of the Metropolitan Museum of Art Egyptian Expedition 6. New York: Metropolitan Museum of Art.

35

A LITANY FROM THE EIGHTEENTH DYNASTY TOMB OF MERNEITH

DAVID P. SILVERMAN

University of Pennsylvania, Philadelphia

Professor Edward F. Wente is the consummate scholar and teacher, and I consider myself privileged to have been one of his students. His classes, whether in philology, history, or religion, were designed not only to instruct in every possible aspect of the subject but also to inspire future scholars to use the courses as an impetus for their own research. Because of his interest in language and religion, I offer this modest study to him in gratitude for the many years I had the good fortune of studying with and learning from him.

Several years ago, while I was working for the Oriental Institute Museum and preparing for exhibition a case on the Amarna period, I came across a small limestone fragment (OIM 10595; 30 cm × 19 cm) that had been purchased from E. A. Abemayor in 1920. Preserved on it were three lines of well-formed hieroglyphs carved in raised relief, hereafter referred to as Inscription I (fig. 35.1a–b).[1] At the head of each of the lines is

a b

Figure 35.1. Inscription I. (*a*) Photograph and (*b*) Drawing of Relief Fragment of Merneith (OIM 10595). Photograph Courtesy of the Oriental Institute, University of Chicago. Drawing by J. R. Wegner

1. I would like to thank Dr. William Sumner, the director of the Oriental Institute at the time, for permission to publish this piece. I would also like to acknowledge the assistance of John Larson, Dr. Raymond Tindel, and Dr. Karen Wilson in securing this permission and the photograph. The drawings of all the fragments were prepared by Jennifer R. Wegner,

Gold of Praise: Studies on Ancient Egypt in Honor of Edward F. Wente
Edited by Emily Teeter and John A. Larson
Studies in Ancient Oriental Civilization 58
Chicago: Oriental Institute, 1999

the phrase *pꜣ ỉtn,* and its appearance suggests that the carving dates to the Amarna period. The next phrase in all three lines is undoubtedly the name of the owner, *Mr-Nt,*[2] followed by the epithet *mꜣꜥ ḫrw*. It is likely that the first words, *pꜣ ỉtn,* form the end of Merneith's title. Since the goddess Neith occurs in the name, and no apparent attempt at erasure or alteration was made by Atenist revisionists, the fragment must date to the early part of the reign of Amenhotep IV.[3] Each of the three lines then continues with the same expression: *ḏd.f ỉỉ.n.ỉ m h*[*ꜣy*] "He says: I have come in jubilation ... ." The repetition of the same phrases is a feature frequently found in litanies, and this genre of text is commonly employed to record lists and is also found in hymns, recitations, and funerary literature.[4]

The exact nature of this litany is impossible to determine since the text is broken after *m h*[*ꜣy*]. A clue, however, can be found in another similar limestone fragment, now in a private collection (see Inscription II, fig. 35.2a–b). Also of limestone, it measures 43 cm × 20 cm, and it too has three surviving columns of well-detailed hieroglyphs carved in fine raised relief. The style and paleography of the hieroglyphs on the two fragments are the same, and each of the three lines on this piece also begins with (*pꜣ*) *ỉtn Mr-Nt mꜣꜥ-ḫrw*, but here, the following text is preserved: *ḏd.f ỉỉ.n.ỉ m hꜣy*. Considering the similarities in the carving, the nature of the text, and the name of the individual, it would appear that the two fragments once belonged to the same monument. I refer hereafter to the text in Inscriptions I and II as the Merneith litany. The litany carved on Inscription II duplicates the text on Inscription I in Chicago as far as *m hꜣy*, but since it preserves more text, it is possible to identify the type of litany originally carved by the sculptor. The additional text includes the name of the deity Osiris twice, suggesting a funerary hymn or text, and the undamaged condition of the hieroglyphs for Neith as well as the intact writing of the deity Osiris provide further evidence for a date in the early years of Amenhotep IV.[5]

Another late Eighteenth Dynasty official, Kheruef, had a text that bears striking similarities to our Inscriptions I and II inscribed on the walls of his tomb at Thebes. At the far end of the northern side of the passage to the court, Kheruef had fourteen columns of text carved in raised relief, detailing an address that the deceased was to make upon entering the Underworld.[6] A comparison of the Merneith and Kheruef litanies (fig. 35.3)[7] reveals that the two compositions are clearly related and suggests that perhaps they had a common source. That one is not a slavish copy of the other is clear from the many stylistic, orthographic, and paleographic distinctions. Despite the brevity of the remains of the Merneith litany, the longer lines of Inscription II suggest that the text corresponds to specific passages in the Kheruef inscription (see fig. 35.3). The texts do not appear to follow the same order, and it seems clear that lines 1, 2, and 3 of the Merneith litany (Inscription II, fig. 35.2a–b) relate to lines 8, 10, and 5 of Kheruef, respectively (fig. 35.3).

Although both litanies express essentially the same information (at least to the extent of what is preserved in the Merneith fragments), subtle distinctions exist. In the Merneith litany (figs. 35.1–3), each line has a separate introductory *ḏd.f*, whereas that expression appears only once in Kheruef (*Kheruef*, pl. 21, line 4). In Merneith the in *hꜣy* (figs. 35.1–3) is consistently reversed, as is the only appearance of the sign (Inscription II, line 1; figs. 35.2–3). The first person in *ỉỉ.n.ỉ* is always expressed in Merneith (Inscription II, figs. 35.2–3), whereas in Kheruef *ỉ* is consistently omitted in perhaps a conscious archaism. *Hꜣy* in Merneith (Inscription II, figs. 35.2–3) has the standing man with upraised arms for a determinative; in Kheruef the seated man with his hand to his mouth appears in its place. The arrangement of the three signs designating *Wsỉr* in Merneith (Inscription II, line 1, figs. 35.2–3) differs slightly from that in Kheruef (line 8). Osiris appears again in Merneith (Inscription II, line 2, figs. 35.2–3), but the apparent parallel in line 10 of Kheruef[8] has instead the epithet of Osiris, *ḥkꜣ dwꜣt* "ruler of the Duat."[9]

Keeper of the Egyptian Collection at the University of Pennsylvania Museum, with the assistance of Carole Linderman, Research Assistant.

2. Ranke (1935, p. 156.26, 28) provides references only for female examples. See below for further discussion of the name.

3. Redford (1984, p. 175) notes that such defacement began in the fifth year of the reign of Akhenaten.

4. See *LÄ* "Litanie," cols. 1062–64, and the references therein; Guglielmi 1996, pp. 474–75.

5. Redford (1984, p. 175) notes that the traditional gods survived existing outside Thebes during the first five years of the reign.

6. See *Kheruef*, pl. 21, and translation by E. F. Wente on pp. 38–40 therein. See also Fakhry 1943, pp. 464–66, wherein the whole text is referred to as "the Hymn to Osiris."

7. Note that fig. 35.3 does not include Inscription I since it contains no text that helps to identify the nature of the litany.

8. The identification is made on the basis of the appearance of *ỉnk* in both texts. It occurs in Inscription II, line 2, where it terminates with ; in line 10, the only line of Kheruef where *ỉnk* occurs, it is spelled with a stroke instead. See *Wb.* 2.2, which lists both writings.

9. See, for example, Book of the Dead 183a S1 (Allen 1974, p. 200), where the god is addressed "son of Nut, Osiris, ruler of eternity."

a

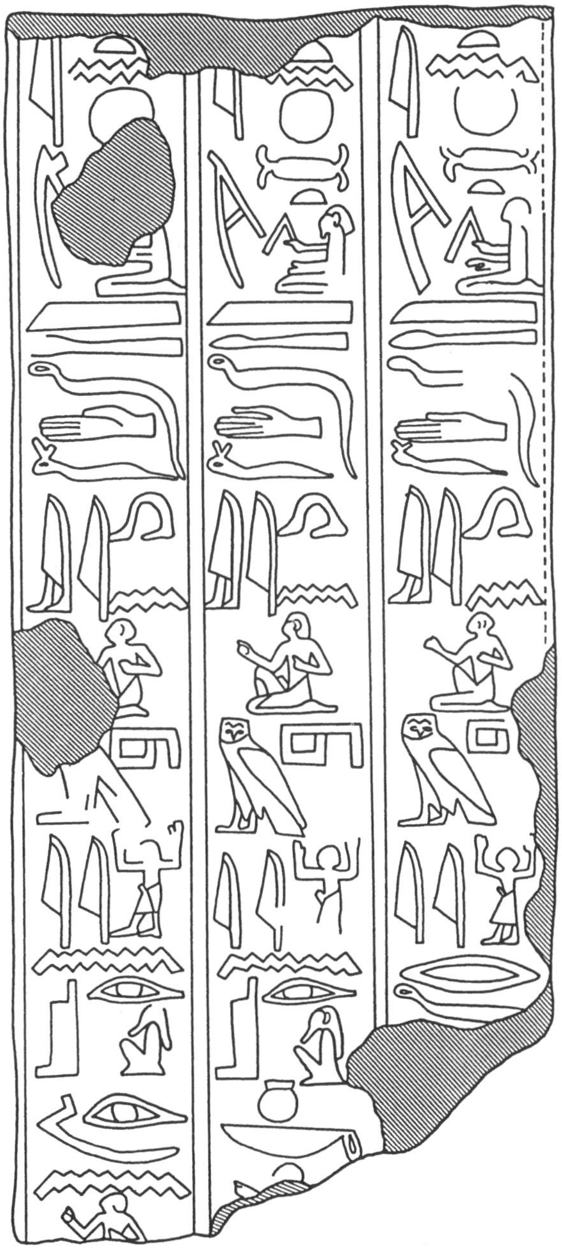

1 2 3

b

Figure 35.2. Inscription II. (*a*) Photograph and (*b*) Drawing of Relief Fragment of Merneith (Anonymous Collection). Drawing by J. R. Wegner

Despite these orthographic and paleographic differences, there exists a distinct similarity of content between the two litanies. In addition, both the Merneith and Kheruef litanies contain undamaged references to the god Osiris. All this evidence suggests that the tombs of both these officials might have been constructed within a few years of each other. The phrase *pꜣ ỉtn* in the title of Merneith with no damage to the word *ỉtn* and the intact word Osiris imply a slightly later date for Merneith[10] perhaps within the first few years of the reign of Amenhotep IV. The difference in line order as well as the distinctions in paleography and orthography suggest that while both litanies might have derived ultimately from a single source, conscious editing had occurred.

10. See Habachi in *Kheruef*, pp. 17–26 (and Nims, pp. 12–15, therein), for discussions of Kheruef's career and the dates of the effacement of some of the figures and the texts. Note that Nims (ibid., pp. 13–14) suggests that both figures and texts were altered after the tomb was abandoned. The work of the Amarna zealots can be seen in the erasure of the plural gods and the removal of the figure and the name of Amun. Some of the names and representations of other deities remain intact as does the name of Amun in the royal cartouche.

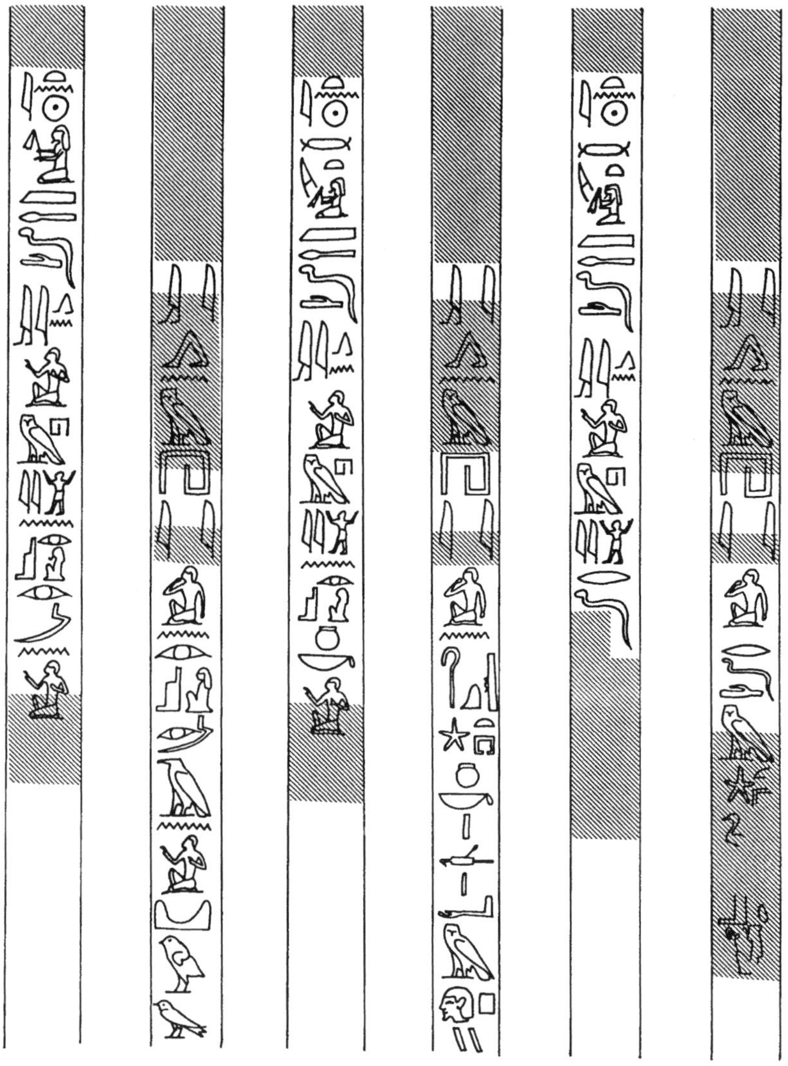

Figure 35.3. Comparison of Litanies in Tombs of Merneith and Kheruef (TT 192). Drawing by J. R. Wegner

Neither Merneith fragment has a known provenience, and it is tempting to postulate that since the litany inscribed on them resembles that in the tomb of Kheruef, the location of the tomb of Merneith might also have been Thebes. A document accompanying the Merneith fragment with Inscription II, when it was transferred to the present owner, however, notes that this piece might have originally belonged to the tomb of *Mry.ty-Nt* at Saqqara. *Mry.ty-Nt* is known from several fragments apparently deriving from his tomb (see figs. 35.4–5).[11]

In 1850, Mariette discovered three fragments of reliefs belonging to this tomb in South Saqqara, and he subsequently published them only in line drawing (fig. 35.4a–c);[12] no photograph exists today, and there is no record of the present location of the reliefs. Ranke, who lists only the name *Mry.tỉ Nt,* not Merneith, suggests that a further relief, Berlin 2070, may belong to this individual from Saqqara (fig. 35.5a–b).[13] Löhr, in her discussion of these four Saqqara fragments of *Mry.ty-Nt*,[14] proposes that this Memphite official, whose name was

11. PM 3/2, p. 666, lists the tomb as H 9 and assigns it to the area between the monastery and Sekhemhet's enclosure; note also the references therein. *LÄ* 5 "Saqqara: First Intermediate Period and Middle Kingdom," col. 409, indicates a location south of the Unas causeway.

12. Mariette (1889, p. 449) notes that the fragments were found "parmi les tombeaux de Saqqara au sud de la grande pyramide."

13. Ranke 1935, p. 162:1. I am indebted to Dr. Dietrich Wildung, Director of the State Museum of Berlin, for providing me with a photograph of this relief.

14. Löhr (1975, pp. 172–75) discusses all four pieces fully, translates the texts, and provides a full bibliography.

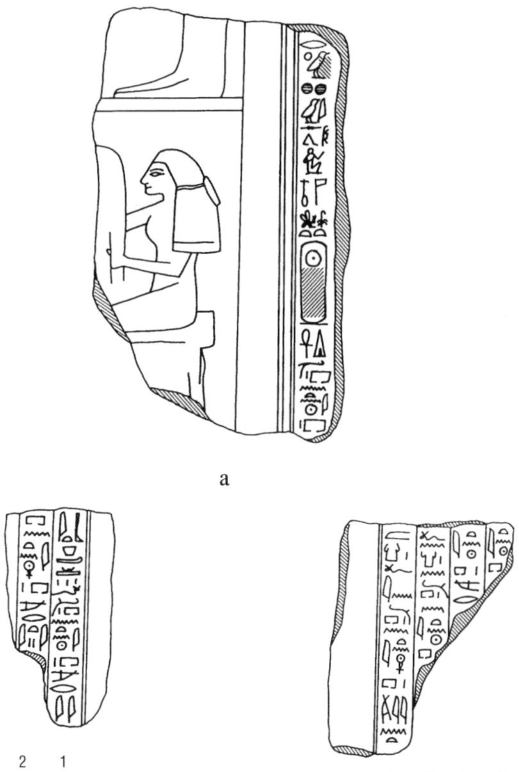

a

2 1

1 2 3 4

b c

Figure 35.4. Fragments from Tomb of *Mry.ty-Nt* Found by Mariette in Saqqara. Drawing by J. R. Wegner after Mariette 1889, p. 449

altered to *Mry.ty-R*ᶜ to reflect the emphasis of the new religion, remained in the north and was buried at Saqqara.[15]

While the style of reliefs from the Saqqara tomb is clearly pre-Amarna, the texts that record his unaltered title, steward of the House of the Aten, and show changes in the second part of his name from Neith to Ra, place this individual securely in the Amarna period. This combination of evidence, like the unmutilated writings of Neith and Osiris, suggests a date early in the reign of Amenhotep IV for the original construction of the tomb and indicates that *Mry.ty-R*ᶜ lived on into the time period when the king broke with the traditional religion.[16]

Clear evidence for the change of the name of the tomb owner occurs twice on the Berlin fragment (fig. 35.5, lines 3, 5). In each case, the traditional theophoric component Neith is replaced by the more acceptable element Ra. Interestingly, however, an unaltered form of the name also appears on the relief (fig. 35.5, lines 1–2). The original name in this instance might have remained intact because it was separated into two parts — *Mry.ty* at the bottom of line 1 and *Nt* at the top of line 2. Those charged with making the changes might not have been particularly literate and might have been working from an ostracon with the offending name written out completely, and they overlooked, therefore, the name that appears in this instance as two separate elements.

Just how the name was dealt with on the fragments found by Mariette is a bit more complicated since the name of the tomb owner is not completely intact (fig. 35.4a–c), and the orthography of what remains is inconsistent. Of the four instances where the name occurs, only one has the writing *Mry.ty* (fig. 35.4b, line 2) pre-

15. Löhr 1975, p. 172; Ranke (1935, p. 162:1) indicates that the name Ra replaced Neith. See also Fecht 1960, p. 85, and the references therein. See also Murnane 1995, pp. 53–54, #26 B, who refers to the tomb owner as Meritneith (Meritaten); Murnane does not include Löhr's Dok. III 2d (see our fig. 35.4b) in his discussion.

16. Löhr (1975, p. 175) dates the tomb early in the reign and notes that such name changes were carried out after the king had ordered the phonetic writing of Horus shortly before year 9. See the comments of Nims in *Kheruef*, pp. 14–15, for the Amarna and post-Amarna effacements in the tomb of Kheruef. Note also that the cartouche in fig. 35.4a preserves only the first element in the prenomen of Akhenaten, the remainder hacked out ostensibly during the return to orthodoxy under Horemheb.

a

b

Figure 35.5. (*a*) Photograph and (*b*) Drawing of Relief of *Mry.ty-Nt* (*Rʿ*) (Berlin 2070). Photograph Courtesy of the Staatliche Museen zu Berlin; Drawing by J. R. Wegner

served.[17] It might well have occurred earlier in the same fragment (fig. 35.4b, line 1), but only *Mry* survives.[18] In neither case does any part of the second component remain. The largest fragment (fig. 35.4a) is broken at the point where the name would appear. The third fragment has the name written twice (fig. 35.4c, lines 1, 3). In the first instance it appears to be the full writing *Mry-Nt*,[19] and in the second, only *Mr* is preserved. In the former stands without a phonetic complement,[20] but in the latter follows it.[21] Since the fragments Mariette found in Saqqara demonstrate considerable variability in the orthography of the name of the tomb owner, it may be possible to suggest that the writing Merneith, which occurs in Inscriptions I and II, represents an earlier form of the name and that these two fragments also belong to the same tomb. Thus, the original name of the tomb owner was probably *Mr-Nt* (as illustrated in Inscriptions I and II), with the latter component spelled with the ideographic sign for Neith followed by a phonetic *t*. A variant of that name, *Mry.ty-Nt,* also occurs; here the second element is written with the same ideograph, but without the phonetic *t* (as seen in Berlin 2070, fig. 35.5, line 2). A slightly later rendering may well be *Mry-Nt*, with the second element spelled out phonetically (as indicated in fig. 35.4c, line 1, and perhaps also fig. 35.4b, line 1). The latest version is clearly the altered text in the Berlin relief (fig. 35.5, lines 3, 5), *Mry.ty-Rꜥ*.

It is likely that all the pieces discussed are roughly contemporaneous, and the similarity of names, given the circumstances noted above, tends to support a common origin for all these fragments. As attractive as this solution may be, it still leaves a few questions unanswered. Why, for instance, was the name Merneith left intact in Inscriptions I and II? Perhaps the same Atenists who erred and did not change the name in one case in Berlin 2070 (fig. 35.5, lines 1–2) missed these examples because they were looking only for *Mry.ty-Nt*. (The same explanation could be put forth for the intact *Mry-Nt*; see fig. 35.4c, line 1). Another query might focus on the different styles of relief found on the fragments.[22] However, more than one style of carving in a single tomb is not unique during this period of transition; the tomb of Parennefer (TT 188) and Ramose (TT 55) are good examples of such variety.

A further question, however, may arise in regard to the titles held by Mer(*Mry.ty*)-Neith. All instances of his title in Inscriptions I and II preserve only the last part of *pꜣ ỉtn*. Such a title incorporating the definite article *pꜣ* does not appear in any other fragment. All the others, however, have titles that end with *pr ỉtn*, and many of them have the complete designation *ỉmy-r pr n(ỉ) pr-ỉtn* "steward of the House of the Aten."[23] It would not be unusual, however, to find an official with several temple-related titles.[24] Mer(*Mry.ty*)-Neith's title ending with *pꜣ ỉtn* might have associated him with a second Aten temple. Hari's (1976, pp. xiii–xxii) list of titles provides several possibilities, among which are *ỉmy-r sḥ nỉ ỉtn* [*m*] *pr ḥꜥy n pꜣ ỉtn* (72); *ỉmy-r kꜣw n pꜣ ỉtn* (96 and 332;

17. The configuration of the signs is similar to that found on Berlin 2070; see fig. 35.5, lines 1, 3, 5.

18. Another case may be that in fig. 35.4c, line 2, where only *mr* is preserved.

19. Note that the deity is spelled with phonetic elements here. The condition of the fragment precludes knowing whether the determinative followed. Merneith appears with alone on Berlin 2070 (see fig. 35.5, line 2) and with the same sign followed by in Inscriptions I and II (see figs. 35.1–2, lines 1–3). Löhr (1975, p. 175) assumes that the phonetic writing (see fig. 35.4c, line 2) is a later writing reflecting the change to the phonetic spelling of Horus, effected sometime before year 9.

20. The writing without occurs elsewhere only in Inscriptions I and II (see figs. 35.1–2).

21. The writing of *mr* with the phonetic complement occurs in all three instances on Berlin 2070 (see fig. 35.5, lines 1, 3, 5) as well as in one of the other Saqqara fragments (see fig. 35.4c, lines 1–2).

22. Inscriptions I and II (figs. 35.1–2) have only text, but the hieroglyphs on both are similarly executed in finely detailed raised relief. The Mariette fragments (fig. 35.4) were never photographed, but the available illustrations suggest a simpler style of text and a fairly classical rendering of the figure. The Berlin relief (fig. 35.5) is carved entirely in sunk relief with undetailed hieroglyphs and figures clearly indicating Amarna influence.

23. The full writing with the indirect genitive is clear in the Saqqara fragments found by Mariette (see fig. 35.4a–c), while on Berlin 2070 *n*(*ỉ*) is omitted in one case (see fig. 35.5, line 1) but included in two others; see fig. 35.5, line 3, and presumably line 5. Note that Hari (1976, p. xiii) lists only *ỉmy-r pr pr-ỉtn*, apparently basing his reading only on the example in the first line of Berlin 2070 without considering the other examples on this relief or those on the other Saqqara fragments.

24. Note that Hari (1976, p. xiii) lists under the entry for *Mry.tỉ-Nt*, in addition to *ỉmy-pr Pr-ỉtn*, *ẖry-ḥb*, *sm*, and *wꜥb snw*. Löhr (1975, p. 172) translates the text including these titles: "Rezitation für den Vorlesepriester und zweifach reinen Sem-priester, den Domänenverwalter des Jāti-Tempels … ." It is clear that the first two titles, *ẖry-ḥb* and *sm*, however, do not refer to the tomb owner, but to those officiating at the ritual. Otto (1960, p. 182, Nachtrag. 85) notes that the left side of Berlin 2070 is a combination of his scenes 36 and 39. In each of these it is the lector priest or the *sm*-priest (or the son) who performs the ritual for the deceased (ibid., pp. 96, 99). Murnane (1995, p. 53) translates: "Words spoken by the lector priest and *sm*-priest: 'Be pure, be pure … .'" Otto (1960, pp. 96–99), however, does not note any variant texts with such an introduction.

the latter adds *m ꜣḫt ỉtn*); *ỉmy-r pr n tꜣ ḥwt pꜣ ỉtn* (218); *ỉmy-r šwty m tꜣ ḥwt pꜣ ỉtn* (236); *šwy nỉ tꜣ ḥwt pꜣ ỉtn*, and *ḥry šwy nỉ tꜣ ḥwt pꜣ ỉtn* (238). Unfortunately the tops of both Merneith fragments bearing *pꜣ ỉtn* (Inscriptions I and II) provide no trace of what precedes this phrase.

If in fact all of the items discussed above do originate from the same tomb in Saqqara, it implies that both the *pr ỉtn* and the *pꜣ ỉtn* mentioned in the titles of Merneith refer to specific temples of the Aten in Saqqara. Löhr (1975, pp. 163–69) discusses the possible designations of Akhenaten's Memphite temples, and she includes both the *pr ỉtn* and the *ḥwt pꜣ ỉtn* among them. Assigning our unprovenienced fragments, with Inscriptions I and II, to the Saqqara tomb of *Mry.ty Nt/Rꜥ* would further support the suggestion[25] of a *ḥwt pꜣ ỉtn* in the Memphite area.

References

Allen, T. G.
1974 *The Book of the Dead or Going Forth by Day: Ideas of the Ancient Egyptians Concerning the Hereafter as Expressed in Their Own Terms.* Studies in Ancient Oriental Civilization 37. Chicago: University of Chicago Press.

Fakhry, A.
1943 "A Note on the Tomb of Kheruef at Thebes." *Annales du Service des antiquités de l'Égypte* 42: 447–532.

Fecht, G.
1960 "Amarna Probleme (1–2)." *Zeitschrift für ägyptische Sprache und Altertumskunde* 85: 83–118.

Guglielmi, W.
1996 "Der Gebrauch rhetorischer Stilmittel in der ägyptischen Literatur." In *Ancient Egyptian Literature: History and Forms,* edited by A. Loprieno, pp. 465–97. Probleme der Ägyptologie 10. Leiden: E. J. Brill.

Hari, R.
1976 *Repertoire onomastique amarnien.* Aegyptiaca Helvetica 4. Basel: Ägyptologisches Seminar der Universität Basel and Centre d'études orientales de l'Université de Genève.

Löhr, B.
1975 "Aḫanjāti in Memphis." *Studien zur altägyptischen Kultur* 2: 139–87.

Mariette, A.
1889 *Les mastabas de l'Ancien Empire.* Paris: F. Vieweg.

Murnane, W. J.
1995 *Texts from the Amarna Period.* Society of Biblical Literature, Writings from the Ancient World 5. Atlanta: Scholars Press.

Otto, E.
1960 *Das ägyptische Mundöffnungsritual.* Ägyptologische Abhandlungen 3. Wiesbaden: Otto Harrassowitz.

Ranke, H.
1935 *Die ägyptischen Personennamen,* Volume 1. Glückstadt: J. J. Augustin.

Redford, D.
1984 *Akhenaten, The Heretic King.* Cairo: American University.

25. See Löhr 1975, p. 163, references in notes 68–70, p. 165, reference in note 74.

36
THE NAG^c-ED-DEIR PAPYRI

WILLIAM KELLY SIMPSON

Yale University, New Haven

A long friendship with the outstanding scholar in whose honor this volume is dedicated is matched by a feeling of gratitude for the extraordinary contributions he has made to Egyptological studies in many areas: philology, grammar, history, chronology, publication of original documents, and especially his work on Egyptian letters. Although it was never my privilege to be his student, being a very slightly older contemporary, I did have the opportunity to study several texts with him on the rare occasions when we were together over the years in the same place, mainly in Cairo or at Chicago House in Luxor. In the context of this brief article on the Nagᶜ-ed-Deir papyri, which include brief Letters to the Dead, one should mention the Letter to the Dead (probably from the same site) published by Wente himself, as well as his translations of the extensive series of such letters in his *Letters from Ancient Egypt* (Wente 1975/76, pp. 595–600; Wente 1990; Parkinson 1991, p. 142, no. 55).

For a site as limited as Nagᶜ-ed-Deir, it is quite extraordinary how extensive are its cemeteries and those of the neighboring and contiguous Sheikh Farag, Mesaeed, and Mesheikh. George A. Reisner's work there for the Hearst Expedition of the University of California and the Harvard University/Museum of Fine Arts, Boston Expedition was a pioneering achievement in recording and publishing, as attested by the extensive monographs on the expedition by Reisner, Lythgoe, and Mace, and the publications of Lutz, Dunham, Peck, and Brovarski.[1]

It is perhaps due to Reisner's early career as a cuneiformist, with the extensive publication of the tablets from Tello (Reisner 1985), that he rarely undertook the detailed publication of the many texts he discovered — one exception being the *editio princeps* of the great Gebel Barkal stela of Thutmose III which he accomplished with his daughter (G. Reisner and Bronson Reisner 1933, pp. 24–39; Leprohon 1991, sheets 3.139–143; Cumming 1982, pp. 1–7).

The papyri from Nagᶜ-ed-Deir are a case in point, partly because they had been sent to Hugo Ibscher in Berlin for conservation before the Second World War. It fell to my lot to carry out the initial publication of the four rolls that I designated as the Reisner Papyri in honor of the excavator. Georges Posener brought P. Reisner I to my attention, and William Stevenson Smith, Curator of the Egyptian Department at the Museum of Fine Arts, Boston gave me permission to publish the papyri and supported their publication by the museum. Sir Alan Gardiner provided the late Paul Smither's preliminary copy of P. Reisner I, through the kindness of Mrs. Pilgrim, Smither's widow, and it proved to be of considerable use. Werner Kaiser assisted in my obtaining P. Reisner II–IV from Berlin after the war and bringing them to Boston. Later I undertook the publication of two earlier, smaller papyri with Letters to the Dead.

PAPYRUS REISNER I–IV: SOME OBSERVATIONS

When P. Reisner IV was published in 1986, I believed I had completed my own efforts on the publication of these texts, if not necessarily to their study.[2] Indices to P. Reisner I–IV were compiled by Peter Der Manuelian, as well as his palaeography to P. Reisner IV sections F and G. I also included photographs of four stelae from Abydos, across the river, of officials or families cited in the papyri, three of them dated in the reign of Sesostris I (years 13, 14, and 17), in support of my dating of the papyri to the same reign. Also included was a page of hieroglyphic corrigenda to P. Reisner I and II.

1. For a detailed account of the site with extensive notes and references to the publications, see the survey in Brovarski, *LÄ* 4 "Naga (Nagᶜ)-ed-Dêr," cols. 296–317. See also Gomaà 1986, pp. 187–222.

2. See Simpson 1963; Simpson 1965; Simpson 1969; Simpson 1973, pp. 218–20; Simpson, *LÄ* 1 "Bauwesen, Organisation des," cols. 668–72; Simpson 1986; Simpson 1988, pp. 211–12; Kemp 1989, pp. 124–26, fig. 44 ("bread ration tokens" from Uronarti) on p. 125.

Gold of Praise: Studies on Ancient Egypt in Honor of Edward F. Wente
Edited by Emily Teeter and John A. Larson
Studies in Ancient Oriental Civilization 58
Chicago: Oriental Institute, 1999

Note was taken that one of the frames of P. Reisner IV recto frame 1 = verso frame 1, was somehow lost, although good photographs were made; unfortunately it remains lost (Simpson 1986, p. 9). By rare good fortune, however, an additional frame was discovered in 1993 in the Berlin Akademie der Wissenschaften and has been united with the other frames in Boston through the good offices of Dr. Dietrich Wildung. The new frame, which can be designated for discussion purposes as P. Reisner IV frame 2/3, continues and adjoins the recto of P. Reisner IV frame 2 at its beginning and adjoins P. Reisner IV frame 3 at its end. It consists of three columns of crew lists on the recto, continuing P. Reisner IV section B with sections B 3, 4, and 5 (end) and in the last of the three columns the beginning of section C, designated as C 0 since C 1 is already so designated in P. Reisner IV. Several crew members in this new section are represented in P. Reisner I, II, and IV. On the reverse of the new sheet is the continuation of P. Reisner IV section F with a small part of the latter concluded at the beginning of the next sheet in P. Reisner IV.

The regnal years of the papyri can now be reformulated as follows:

Years 7–8	Earlier hand (earlier reign?) on the verso of P. Reisner IV section F
Year 13	P. Reisner IV heading section C 0 in new sheet (frame 2/3); possibly the preceding sections belong to year 12
Years 15–18	P. Reisner II
Years 22–23	P. Reisner III
Years 24–25	P. Reisner I

Not counting the years in the earlier hand, the archive extends over a 13 year period, from years 13 through 25 (presumably of Sesostris I). The question arises again as to the reign represented by the earlier hand. The hand is perhaps closest to that of the Heqanakht papyri, and for that reason I assumed that the clerk (Sefkhy?) who erased the recto for his reuse took over a roll originally inscribed in years 7 and 8 of an earlier reign: the end of the Eleventh Dynasty or beginning of the Twelfth Dynasty. With the perhaps controversial reassignment of the Heqanakht archive to the reign of Sesostris I by Dorothea Arnold and James Allen,[3] the P. Reisner IV verso accounts may be contemporary with the Heqanakht archive (years 5 and 8 represented there). Thus the years 7 and 8 in the earlier hand in P. Reisner IV may be assignable to the reign of Sesostris I, the archive covering 19 years. The P. Reisner IV verso accounts sections F and G are not specifically related to the content of the main P. Reisner I–IV archive.

Two officials in P. Reisner may be represented elsewhere. A steward (*ỉmy-r pr*) *Sn-mrỉ* in P. Reisner IV section F 3 (sheet 2/3) is possibly to be connected with an important official at the pyramid site of Amenemhat I at el-Lisht North (Tomb 470), although his burial equipment lacks the title of steward and provides only the rank titles of *ỉry pʿt, ḥ3ty-ʿ, ḫtmty bỉty,* and *smr wʿty*. A steward in P. Reisner II sections D and G is Hennenu's son Inyotef, the father's name previously misread by me as Hedjennenu. The corrected reading makes it conceivable to connect this man with the Inyotef of Franke's (1984, p. 111) Dossier #130 of names found in Lower Nubia (Žába 1974, p. 38, no. 9; pp. 54–55, no. 27; pp. 55–60, no. 28). The latter is the son of a Hennenu and grandson of a Djaf-Inyotef. Although he curiously bears no title, he was obviously an important man as Žába (1974, p. 111) indicates. Inyotef states that he was born in year 10 of Amenemhat I. If he came to Nubia in year 29 of the king (a year attested at the Nubian site), he would have been 19 years old then and possibly not yet a steward. If the P. Reisner II official and the official whose name was attested in Lower Nubia are the same man, he would have been 37 years old in year 17 of Sesostris I (47 years old if there was no coregency).[4]

Obviously, neither of these P. Reisner officials can be positively identified with the Lisht or Nubian officials in view of the lack of correspondence in the titles, but identifications are not impossible.

With the publication of the Reisner papyri virtually complete (except for the new sheet of P. Reisner IV), it must be stressed that the opportunity remains for continued study of the archive along various lines. A few of these are considered below.

3. Arnold 1991, pp. 5–48, esp. p. 37; see also Goedicke 1984, pp. 8–9.

4. Grimal 1995, pp. 273–80; Obsomer 1995, pp. 44–45; Fischer-Elfert 1994, pp. 195–203; Obsomer 1993, pp. 103–40.

Ledger Extents

It has always seemed to me curious that the beginnings and ends of the various daily ledgers do not coincide with the first and last days of months and/or seasons (Kadish 1993, pp. 5–6), as well as the fact that some of the ledgers seem so long. Several cases in point may be briefly considered. In P. Reisner II section K, the ledger extends from year 15 I Proyet 21 through the remaining months of Proyet, the succeeding four months of Shomu, the five epagomenal days, year 16, New Year's Day, and the second and third day of the next year, "a curious terminal point on the third day of the new year." This is an unbroken accounting for 228 days, and no "days off" or holidays seem to be indicated in any way. Obviously the laborers have to be fed even on days off and holidays, but there is no evidence I can see that such days off existed, the ledgers having principally to do with the work project(s). However in section K 5 line 46 there is the entry *ḥby* "festivals/feasts," with numerals, 3 (days) for this 228 day period. As is the case throughout the archive, the headings for the columns of figures are usually damaged or in lacuna. Nevertheless, in this case the figures evidently represent man-days and probably bread and beer units. The next entry is P. Reisner II section C in year 18 II Shomu 20, a gap of 19 months from the previous entry. The figures are recorded day by day, but with the headings generally missing, we do not know *what* is recorded.

In P. Reisner III section B, an account extends from year 22 III Shomu 9 to year 23 IIII Akhet 30, namely the last 21 days of III Shomu, all of IIII Shomu, the five epagomenal days following year 22, and the complete four months of Akhet of the next year, year 23, amounting to 178 days. In some ways this seems more logical. The following section C continues with the succeeding four months of Proyet, I Shomu, and the first 13 days of II Shomu, for an additional 176 days. This now gives us 354 consecutive days. The following section D supplies the remaining 17 days of II Shomu, for a consecutive accounting of 371 days, as well as an unspecified number of days in III Shomu in the course of a summary for III Proyet to part of III Shomu. There is a total at the end of each full month after the last (30th) day, or the day of the month on which the ledger stops, but the work projects may begin or end at a point within the month. Note an obvious feature: the epagomenal days are placed directly at the end of the year and before the next year and appear to be regular work days. Naturally the ledgers were drawn up from daily, "weekly," and monthly accounts to justify expenditures.

Work Force

The laborers are designated as *ḥsbw* or *mnyw* and are arranged, as in P. Reisner I and IV, in crews of men from 1 to 29 each, best exemplified by P. Reisner I section C. In section A the heading reads "Number of *ḥsbw* who are in Koptos, consisting of *mnyw*." In section C page 5 at the end there are three crews of a single man, the crew leader being a scribe assisted by a single laborer. Generally the crews range from 9 to 18 members and are led by men designated either as *ṯsw* "crew leader," *ẖrp* "foreman," *ỉmy-r ṯst* "overseer of a crew," *ṯst* "crew of ... ," or *sš* "scribe/clerk." The designations or titles *ẖrp* and *ṯsw* do not seem to be interchangeable. In P. Reisner I section C the leaders' names are written in red and they are not counted in the totals of members for each crew. Elsewhere there is a certain inconsistency in omitting or adding them in the crew totals, whether this means that they were separately compensated or added or omitted in error by the clerk. The crews show a certain element of consistency in their makeup, several men staying with the same crew over a period of years. Brothers, and fathers and sons and mothers and daughters, may stay in the same crew, and brothers frequently stay together. There is a case of three brothers in the same crew in P. Reisner I section F 168–170. Two sons work alongside their father in section E 1–3. Two men in section F 125–126 provide the names of four generations. Similarly, in section N, a list of women workers, three daughters work alongside their mother (N 15–18).

It is difficult to define the status of these laborers. Are they essentially "free men" hired by officials for construction and agricultural work? Or are they in forced labor gangs? The length of time they serve mitigates against their being temporary corvée laborers. The evidence is ambiguous. P. Reisner I section B has three headings for figures of man-days, translated there as (1) that which he spent on the road, (2) that which he spent on the project(?), and (3) that which he spent "fleeing." This last heading, *ỉrt.n.f wʿrw*, is perhaps better understood as "absent" or "missing" without the precise meaning of fleeing or escaping.

In the aforementioned entry for 122 days, several have perfect attendance: B 3, 4 (crew leader and scribe), as well as 6, 7, 8, 21, and 32. Others show that the days worked and days absent add up to 122; for example, B 9, 19, and 20: 97 days on the project, 25 absent; B 10: 107 days worked, 15 absent. Note B 25: 25 days on the project, 97 absent; B 15: 22 days on the project, 100 absent. Even if we allow for a "softer" reading of "absent" instead of "fleeing," one might cite the title *ỉmy-r ꜥḫnwty n ḫnrt* "chamberlain of the prison(?)," but this official appears only with a list of female workers in N 11a (Simpson 1963, p. 46). The kind of work is exemplified by the accounts of P. Reisner I relating to the construction of a temple (sections G, H, I, J, K). Presumably the men also worked in agricultural labor since they are connected with the state(?) farmlands (*ḫbsw*) of the steward Iey's son Anhur-hotep. But it is not clear whether they are assigned to or from these farmlands.

There is a slight irony in that the papyri with the list of personnel sent *to* Koptos, presumably for work on the temple of Sesostris I there, were excavated by Reisner's workmen *from* Koptos. The geographical displacement of the work force to Koptos, the unidentified Per-Kay (probably near Koptos or part of it), and possibly other regions deserves more study.

Personal Names

The large number of names of laborers forms a homogeneous group. Perhaps a statistical analysis can be attempted. These men belong to three generations (with filiation) over a birth period of perhaps fifty years and presumably from a restricted geographical area. The clerk who registered them usually found it expedient to include the name of the father and grandfather. Filiation is by the male line, whereas in the upper levels of society on memorial stelae and statuary the female line filiation frequently is the one used.

Egyptian names over a period of time vary extensively and betray geographical preferences. In view of the large number of individuals in our archive, the number of names is relatively small. As with our own society, names tend to be common to many individuals. In the archive, Nakhti is omnipresent. Theophorous names are common, but the divinities included and excluded are significant. Onuris is understandably predominant since he is the local god of the nome and is represented by Anhur-ankhu, -nakht(i), -wenu, -em-hat, and -hetep, and Dedu-Anhur and Si-Anhur. (In the contemporary chapelle blanche at Karnak, the god of the nome is Khenty-imentyw). I am surprised that so many individuals with Sobek names appear in the archive: Sobek-weser, -nefer, -nakht(i), -em-hat, and -hetep (very frequent), and Dedu-Sobek, Redi-wy-Sobek, Sankh-Sobek, Si-Sobek, and Se'n-Sobek. Two other gods figure less prominently, Montu and Min: Montu-weser and -hetep, Si-Montu and Nesu-Montu, and Min-weser, -nakht(i), and -hetep.

Even more notable is the almost complete absence of names with Ra (although a single individual in P. Reisner IV in the earlier account bears this name), Ptah, or basilophorous names like Amenemhat-ankh, Sehetepibre-ankh, Senwosret-ankh, or Kheperkare-ankh. Names that have probable connections with other geographical regions (Memphis, the Delta, Thebes) are also notably absent; for example, the absence of theophorous names with the triad of Upper Egyptian Nome 1 (Khnum, Anukis, Satis), Upper Egyptian Nome 4 (Amun, Mut, Khonsu), except Ameny, names like Ukh-hotep associated with Upper Egyptian Nome 14 (Cusae), or even names associated with the Abydene triad (Osiris, Isis, Horus), although there are a few Hor-nakhts and Shed-wy-Hors. There is a single individual named Si-Ese and a questionable Si-Ptah. On the other hand, some of the names of the officials (e.g., stewards) are missing from the names of the laborers since the officials may in part come from other regions. For example, the single Si-Sopdu is possibly a northern official.

In addition to P. Reisner I–IV there are three papyrus letters from Reisner's excavations at the site, the first two of which are clearly Letters to the Dead[5] and were initially published by me (Simpson 1966, 1970), and a fragmentary third, conceivably a real letter on the recto with a Letter to the Dead on the verso, presented below for the first time.

LETTER 1

For bibliography, see Simpson 1966, pp. 39–52. For commentary and discussion, see Szpakowska 1999, pp. 163–66; Fecht 1969, pp. 105–28; Gilula 1960, pp. 216–17. For translations, see Parkinson 1991, pp. 143–44, no. 57; Wente 1990, pp. 212–13, no. 343.

5. To the extensive account in Grieshammer, *LÄ* 1 "Briefe an Tote," cols. 864–70, can be added several recent references: Goldwasser 1995, pp. 191–205; Fischer-Elfert 1994, pp. 41–44; Frandsen 1992, pp. 31–49; Willems 1991, pp. 183–91.

LETTER 2

For bibliography, see Simpson 1970, pp. 58–64. For commentary and discussion, see Goedicke 1972, pp. 95–98; Roccati 1967, pp. 323–28; see Goedicke 1969/70, pp. 88–90, for a review of Roccati 1967. For translation, see Wente 1990, p. 213, no. 344.

LETTER 3

The third letter (figs. 36.1–2), Museum of Fine Arts, Boston accession no. 04.2059, was found folded in a straw stratum of the rubbish in front of Nagʿ-ed-Deir tomb 74, April 1903.[6] The papyrus measures 12 × 13 cm and is inscribed on both sides. The photographs used here were taken by Elbert Wall as part of his project to record all papyri in American collections. The present edition is provisional and is subject to improvement. James Allen has assisted me in examining the papyrus, made substantial suggestions, and provided the autographed text, for which I am extremely grateful. His contribution to the reading and understanding of the document is a major improvement over my own. I am particularly indebted to Allen for studying the papyrus with a microscope, whereby the dip of the brush can indicate a new thought. Dr. Rita Freed and Dr. Dorothea Arnold kindly arranged for the loan of the fragment to the Metropolitan Museum for study with the museum's equipment.

A date in the First Intermediate Period seems definite, but a closer dating is not possible. If the papyrus was from a standard sheet 16 cm high, we have 4 cm missing at the top, with a triple fold.

Transliteration and Translation of Accession No. 04.2059 Recto, Museum of Fine Arts, Boston

Recto (fig. 36.1a–b)

1. … … … … *ḫr.k nfr n ʿnḫ.(ỉ?)* …
2. …*[Ḥ]sỉ m ḏd.k ỉn s(ỉ) ḫr Ḥsỉ ỉs ỉn.k s(ỉ)*
3. … … *šdt m 2 (?) ḥnʿ snw(y).k(y) Nfr-ʾIwnw*
4. … *ḥr.s n mdt Wr snwy.f(y) ʾIṯỉ Nmtw (?)*
5. … *ỉnṯ(?).n.k q3s p3qwt dỉt.tw n mḫrwt*
6. … *ḏb3 n.k ỉnt n ḏʿbt 1 bnrt 100 ỉmỉ.k ḥm*

1. … … … … so you said (or before you). … (I) will not live …
2. … [He]si, as you said: bring it before Hesi. May you bring it
3. … which should be taken from the 2 [deben?] of[?] together with your brothers Nefer-iunu
4. … on account of it for a business matter. The older of his two brothers Itji and Nemtu(?)
5. … which you have brought. Bind the wood ladders which one should give to the *mekhrut*(?)
6. … [in order to] repay you for what was obtained for (or for what I purchased:) 1 (unit) of wood-charcoal and 100 of dates. Don't indeed …

Commentary on Recto

The nature of the letter on the recto, even in its damaged and fragmentary state, lacks any indication that it is a Letter to the Dead, although the possibility cannot be ruled out. Its find place would be suitable for such a letter. The text is written with a thick reed.

6. Information on the letter was kindly supplied by Edward J. Brovarski and Peter Der Manuelian from files in the Museum of Fine Arts, Boston, prepared by the late Caroline Nestman Peck. The papyrus is recorded on Museum of Fine Arts, Expedition negatives 9709 and 9710.

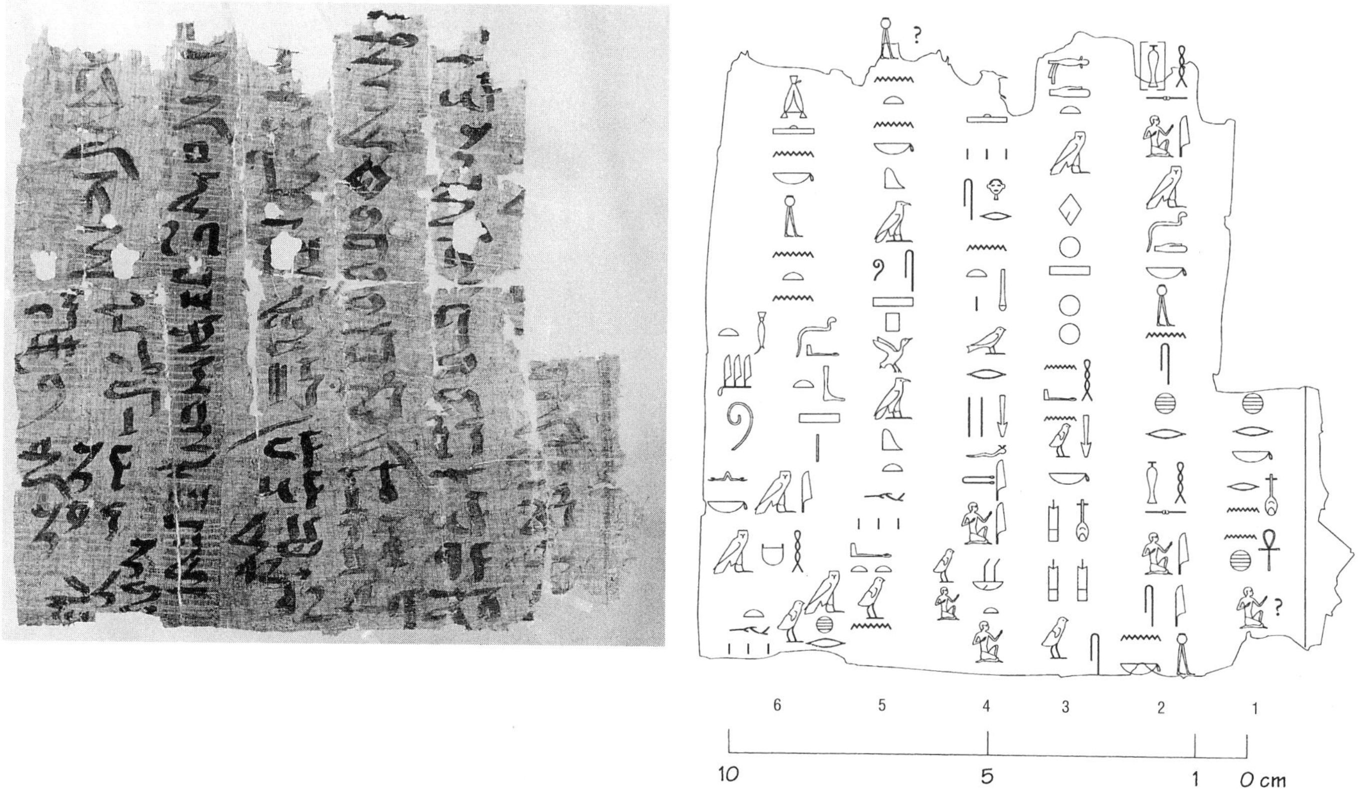

a b

Figure 36.1. (*a*) Photograph and (*b*) Drawing of Accession No. 04.2059 Recto, Museum of Fine Arts, Boston. Courtesy of the Museum of Fine Arts, Boston

Note to Column 1

The vertical line to the right of column 1 may indicate that this column is the first and the beginning of the letter. A possible reading of the first preserved text is "so you said." The next signs evidently begin a new phrase with following subject. For the construction *nfr n sḏm.f*, see Edel 1955/64, §§1130–40, a negative not used in the Pyramid Texts.

Note to Column 2

The restoration of the proper name Hesi at the top of the preserved column is virtually certain. *m ḏd.k* seems definite, although Allen (personal communication) wonders whether it might not instead be a writing of *mk*. The preposition *ḫr* instead of *n* before the name Hesi is not unusual. With this column and the following columns, it is clear that the column endings are preserved. The name Hesi is common and represented at Nagʿ-ed-Deir in Dunham 1937, pp. 54–55, no. 41 (fem.).

Note to Column 3

The signs following *šdt m* defy my competence. Compare the deben determinative(?) in Heqanakht II verso 1. Perhaps it is a term for a metal. Allen (personal communication) points out that the writing *snw* with final *w* is not a correct writing of the singular and should be read as a dual. The name Nefer-iunu is represented in Nagʿ-ed-Deir Stela N 3769 (Dunham 1937, p. 60, no. 47), possibly the same man.

Note to Column 4

The name Itji occurs in Dunham 1937, pp. 72–73, no. 60, as a feminine. Nemtu, if correctly read, is not written thus elsewhere (cf. Ranke 1935, p. 204.15); I have also considered the reading as *Nṯr.wy*. Allen (pers. comm.) suggests that the sign is possibly the two birds in a nest (cf. Gardiner 1973, Sign List G 48–50) and a possible reading *Rḫwt*. The sign also resembles the two razors in a case for the word for shaving or barber (cf. Posener-Kriéger and de Cenival 1968, pl. 12; but otherwise in P. Reisner I, E 3, 5).

a

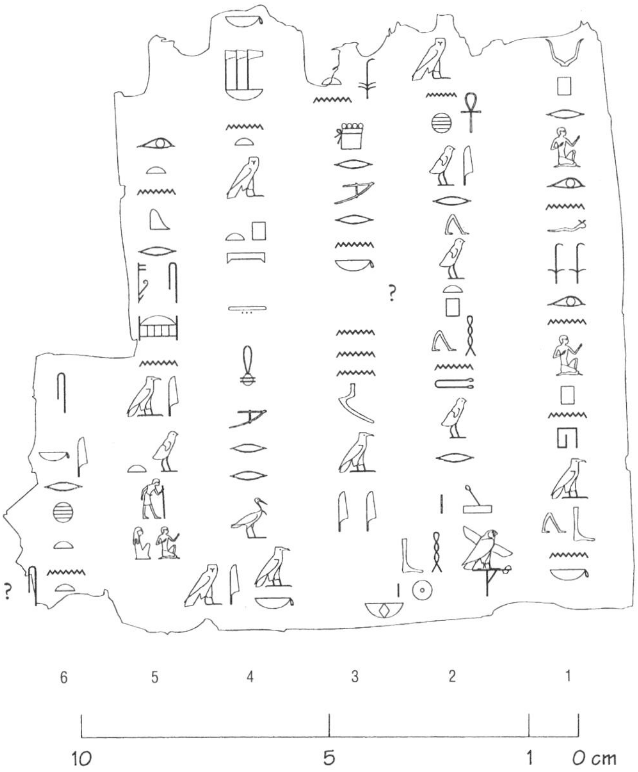

b

Figure 36.2. (*a*) Photograph and (*b*) Drawing of Accession No. 04.2059 Verso, Museum of Fine Arts, Boston. Courtesy of the Museum of Fine Arts, Boston

Note to Column 5

qꜣs pꜣqt is used of tying up a rope ladder (cf. *Wb.* 5.13:4); *qꜣs* is a term for rope ladder in Pyr. 2079. *pꜣqt* is used for rope ladder in Pyramid Text 99 (cf. *Wb.* 1.500:4). Perhaps here assembling wood ladders? *mḫrwt* is at best a guess, perhaps a term for woodsheds.

Note to Column 6

For *ḏꜥbt* as wood coals, see *Wb.* 5.536:8–17.

Transliteration and Translation of Accession No. 04.2059 Verso, Museum of Fine Arts, Boston

Verso (fig. 36.2a–b)

1. … … *wp(w)-r.ỉ ỉr n.f nn ỉr n.ỉ pn hꜣb.n.k*
2. … *m ꜥnḫ ỉw.(ỉ) r ỉwt pḥ.n.(ỉ) ṯw r-sꜣ ḥꜣb Dwn-ꜥnwy*
3. … *nswt ḏr mr.n.k* … *mꜣy*
4. … *.k nṯrw nt(y) m pt tꜣ mỉ mrr bꜣk ỉm*
5. … *ỉrt.n.(ỉ) qrs n ỉꜣwt*
6. … … … *.s ỉ(w).k rḫ.tỉ nt(t) s*

1. … except for me. Do these for him and do this for me [about which] you wrote
2. … in life. I will come. When I have reached you after the Dewen-ꜥAnwy festival
3. … king, since you desired new [a liquid, libations?]
4. … you […] the gods who are in heaven and earth, as your humble servant wishes
5. … which I did. A burial for the old
6. … … … … you know that …

Commentary on Verso

The phrases also used in the Louvre Bowl Letter to the Dead (cf. verso, columns 4 and 6 of this letter, above) perhaps indicate that the text of the verso is a Letter to the Dead. As noted above, the findspot of the papyrus also may be an indication of its nature. In the middle of column 2 the overlap of the sheet on the left on the sheet on the right can be seen in fig. 36.2a.

Note to Column 2

For *Dwn-ʿnwy,* see Kees 1923, pp. 92–101. If the sign has been correctly read, it seems curious for a festival of this god to be celebrated in the Abydene Nome.

Note to Column 3

The mention of the king (if correctly read) is also curious. Perhaps the context is something like Per-Nesut. The word determined by the water sign is not identified.

Note to Column 4

For *m wḏ nṯrw ntw m pt tꜣ* "by order of the gods who are in heaven and on earth," see Piankoff and Clère 1934, pp. 157–58, 160.

Note to Column 5

Compare *ỉw qrs.n.(ỉ) nt mwt sʿnḫ.n.(ỉ) nt ʿnḫ m ḫnt nbt ỉm m ṯsw pn* "I buried the dead and nourished the living wherever I alighted in this famine" (Černý 1961, pp. 6–7, line 9). For the first determinative of *qrs*, see Fischer 1976, pp. 104–08.

Note to Column 6

Piankoff and Clère (1934, p. 163) point out that this phrase occurs in the Louvre Bowl Letter to the Dead, the Cairo Linen Letter to the Dead, and the Chicago Jar Stand, so that it seems to be part of the epistolary formulae of Letters to the Dead, even though the phrase must have been common in all letters. Nevertheless, it might have been particularly expedient to remind the deceased ("you know that ...") of matters pertinent to the communication. For the Chicago Jar Stand, see Gardiner 1930, pp. 19–22, line 6.

References

Arnold, Do.
1991 "Amenemhat I and the Early Twelfth Dynasty at Thebes." *Metropolitan Museum Journal* 26: 5–48.

Černý, J.
1961 "The Stela of Merer in Cracow." *Journal of Egyptian Archaeology* 47: 5–9.

Cumming, B.
1982 *Egyptian Historical Records of the Later Eighteenth Dynasty,* Fascicle 1. Warminster: Aris and Phillips.

Dunham, D.
1937 *Naga-el-Dêr Stelae of the First Intermediate Period.* Boston: Museum of Fine Arts; London: Humphrey Milford.

Edel, E.
1955/64 *Altägyptische Grammatik.* Analecta Orientalia 34/39. Rome: Pontificum Institutum Biblicum.

Fecht, G.
1969 "Der Totenbrief von Nagʿ ed-Deir." *Mitteilungen des Deutschen archäologischen Instituts, Abteilung Kairo* 24: 105–28.

Fischer, H. G.
1976 *Varia: Egyptian Studies* 1. New York: Metropolitan Museum of Art.

Fischer-Elfert, H. W.
1994 "Vermischtes 3: Loyalistische Lehre und Totenbrief (Cairo Bowl) im Vergleich." *Göttinger Miszellen* 143: 41–49.

Frandsen, P. J.
1992 "The Letter to Ikhtay's Coffin: O. Louvre Inv. No. 698." In *Village Voices: Proceedings of the Symposium "Texts from Deir el-Medîna and Their Interpretation"* 1, edited by R. J. Demarée and A. Egberts, pp. 31–49. Leiden: Centre of Non-Western Studies, Leiden University.

Franke, D.
1984 *Personendaten aus dem Mittleren Reich (20.–16. Jahrhundert v. Chr.): Dossiers 1–796*. Ägyptologische Abhandlungen 41. Wiesbaden: Otto Harrassowitz.

Gardiner, A. H.
1930 "A New Letter to the Dead." *Journal of Egyptian Archaeology* 16: 19–22.
1973 *Egyptian Grammar*. Third edition revised. Oxford: Griffith Institute.

Gilula, M.
1960 "Negative Sentences in a Letter to the Dead." *Journal of Egyptian Archaeology* 55: 216–17.

Goedicke, H.
1969/70 Review of *Revista degli studi orientali*, Vol. XLII. *Journal of the American Research Center in Egypt* 8: 88–90.
1972 "The Letter to the Dead Nagᶜ ed Deir N 3500." *Journal of Egyptian Archaeology* 58: 95–98.
1984 *Studies in the Hekanakhte Papers*. Baltimore: Halgo.

Goldwasser, O.
1995 "On the Conception of the Poetic Form — A Love Letter to a Departed Wife: Ostracon Louvre 698." *Israel Oriental Studies* 15: 191–203.

Gomaà, F.
1986 *Die Besiedlung Ägyptens während des Mittleren Reiches* 1: *Oberägypten und das Fayyum*. Beihefte zum Tübinger Atlas des Vorderen Orients, Reihe B (Geisteswissenschaften) Nr. 66/1. Wiesbaden: Ludwig Reichert Verlag.

Grimal, N.
1994 "Le sage, l'eau et le roi." In *Les problèmes institutionnels de l'eau en Égypte ancienne et dans l'antiquité méditerranéenne*, edited by Bernadette Menu, pp. 195–203. Bibliothèque d'étude 110. Cairo: Institut français d'archéologie orientale.
1995 "Corégence et association au trone: L'enseignement d'Amenemhat Ier." *Bulletin de l'Institut français d'archéologie orientale* 95: 273–80.

Kadish, G. E.
1993 "Observations on Time in Ancient Egyptian Culture." In *Papers on Ancient Greek and Islamic Philosophy*, edited by P. Morewedge and A. Preus, pp. 5–6. Binghamton: State University of New York.

Kees, H.
1923 "Anubis Herr von Sepa und der 18. oberägyptische Gau." *Zeitschrift für ägyptische Sprache und Altertumskunde* 58: 79–101.

Kemp, B. J.
1989 *Ancient Egypt: Anatomy of a Civilization*. London: Routledge.

Leprohon, R.
1991 *Stelae* 2: *The New Kingdom to the Coptic Period*. Corpus Antiquitatum Aegyptiacarum, Museum of Fine Arts, Boston, Fascicle 3. Mainz am Rhein: Philipp von Zabern.

Obsomer, C.
1993 "La date de Nésou-Montou (Louvre C 1)." *Revue d'égyptologie* 44: 103–40.
1995 *Sésostris Ier: Étude chronologique et historique du règne*. Brussels: Connaissance de l'Égypte ancienne.

Parkinson, R.
1991 *Voices from Ancient Egypt: An Anthology of Middle Kingdom Writings*. London: British Museum Press.

Piankoff, A., and J. J. Clère
1934 "A Letter to the Dead on a Bowl in the Louvre." *Journal of Egyptian Archaeology* 20: 157–69.

Posener-Kriéger, P., and J.-L. de Cenival
1968 *Hieratic Papyri in the British Museum*, Fifth Series: *The Abu Sir Papyri*. London: British Museum.

Ranke, H.
1935 *Die ägyptischen Personennamen*, Volume 1. Glückstadt: J. J. Augustin.

Reisner, G. A.
1985 *Tempelurkunden aus Telloh*. Reprint, with index, of 1901 edition. Rome: Universita degli Studi di Roma "La Sapienza," Unione Accademica Nationale.

Reisner, G. A., and M. P. Bronson Reisner
1933 "Inscribed Monuments from Gebel Barkal, Part 2: The Granite Stela of Thutmosis III." *Zeitschrift für ägyptische Sprache und Altertumskunde* 69: 24–39.

Roccati, A.
1967 "Due lettere ai morti." *Revista degli studi orientali* 42: 323–28.

Simpson, W. K.
1963 *Papyrus Reisner* 1: *The Records of a Building Project in the Reign of Sesostris I* (Transcription and Commentary). Boston: Museum of Fine Arts.
1965 *Papyrus Reisner* 2: *Accounts of the Dockyard Workshops at This in the Reign of Sesostris I* (Transcription and Commentary). Boston: Museum of Fine Arts.
1966 "The Letter to the Dead from the Tomb of Meru (N. 3737)." *Journal of Egyptian Archaeology* 52: 39–52.
1969 *Papyrus Reisner* 3: *The Records of a Building Project in the Early Twelfth Dynasty* (Transcription and Commentary). Boston: Museum of Fine Arts.
1970 "A Late Old Kingdom Letter to the Dead from Nagᶜ ed Deir N 3500." *Journal of Egyptian Archaeology* 56: 58–64.
1973 "Two Lexical Notes to the Reisner Papyri: *wḫrt* and *trsst*." *Journal of Egyptian Archaeology* 59: 218–21.
1986 *Papyrus Reisner* 4: *Personnel Accounts of the Early Twelfth Dynasty* (Transcription and Commentary). Boston: Museum of Fine Arts.
1988 "Two Corrections to Papyrus Reisner IV, Sections F and G." *Journal of Egyptian Archaeology* 74: 211–12.

Szpakowska, K.
1999 "A Sign of the Times." *Lingua Aegyptia* 6: 163–66.

Wente, E. F.
1975/76 "A Misplaced Letter to the Dead." *Orientalia Lovaniensia Periodica* 6/7 (*Miscellanea in honorem Josephi Vergote*): 595–600.
1990 *Letters from Ancient Egypt*. Society of Biblical Literature, Writings from the Ancient World 1. Atlanta: Scholars Press.

Willems, H.
1991 "The End of Seankhenptah's Household (Letter to the Dead Cairo JdE 25975)." *Journal of Near Eastern Studies* 50: 183–91.

Žába, Z.
1974 *The Rock Inscriptions of Lower Nubia* (*Czechoslovak Concession*). Czechoslovak Institute of Egyptology in Prague and Cairo, Publications 1. Prague: Charles University.

37

O. HESS = O. NAVILLE = O. BM 50601: AN ELUSIVE TEXT RELOCATED

MARK J. SMITH

The Oriental Institute, Oxford

Nearly two decades ago, I published an article entitled "A New Version of a Well-known Egyptian Hymn" (Smith 1977, pp. 115–49). This was an edition of a Demotic copy of part of the hymn to the ten *ba*s of Amun, best known from the versions preserved in the Hibis temple of Darius I and the edifice of Taharqa by the Sacred Lake at Karnak.[1] The copy was inscribed on an ostracon. Although it employed the Demotic script, its language was Middle Egyptian, like that of the hieroglyphic parallels.

My edition of the text was based on a photograph which I found among the papers of Wilhelm Spiegelberg in the Research Archives of the Oriental Institute at the University of Chicago. The photograph bore the notation "Slg. J. J. Hess?" in Spiegelberg's handwriting and was one of several photographs and hand copies of Demotic ostraca in an envelope marked "Ostraca Hess, etc. (1895), Abschriften W. Sp." Enquiry revealed that all of these were now in the collection of the University of Zürich, except for the ostracon inscribed with the hymn to the *ba*s of Amun. Further efforts to trace the whereabouts of this object proved fruitless.

A few years later, while looking through Spiegelberg's *Demotische Grammatik* for a quite unrelated purpose, my eye chanced to fall upon paragraph 391, dealing with "Altertümliche Praepositionen" (Spiegelberg 1925, p. 174). Among the words listed there was an instance of *ḫft* "when" written *ẖft* and cited from what was plainly the text on the ostracon which I had been seeking. Now, however, it was identified as an "unveroffentl. Ostrakon der Slg. Naville nach Photogr. J. J. Hess." This new designation explained why the object was not in Zürich along with the other items formerly belonging to Hess. Unfortunately, it provided no clue as to the object's true location, which remained unknown.

There matters stood until September 1993, when Dr. Günter Vittmann informed me, during the course of the Fifth International Congress of Demotists in Pisa, that he had found the elusive ostracon in the collection of the British Museum. On my return to England I was able to verify this and suggested to Dr. Vittmann that he should write an article bringing the news to the attention of Egyptologists. He declined, citing lack of time, but proposed that I do so instead. This is that article, and I am very grateful to Dr. Vittmann for allowing me to publicize his discovery here.

I should like to thank the Keeper of Egyptian Antiquities in the British Museum for permission to study and publish photographs of the object in question. I am also grateful to Dr. M. L. Bierbrier for his help in tracing it in the Museum's records; and to Drs. C. A. R. Andrews and R. B. Parkinson for assistance rendered during my visits to the Museum to work on its text. When preparing my original edition of the ostracon inscribed with the hymn to the *ba*s of Amun, I received much valuable advice from Professor E. F. Wente. This article is dedicated to him with gratitude. I hope that he will find something of interest in the remarks that follow.

O. BM 50601, to give it its proper designation, is a piece of limestone measuring 33.5 cm in length and 16.2 cm in width. Its maximum thickness is 3.5 cm. According to British Museum records, the ostracon was presented as a gift in 1911 by the then Egypt Exploration Fund. A letter from the Fund's Secretary to the Director of the

1. For the former, see Davies 1953, pl. 31 (middle register); for the latter, see Parker, Leclant, and Goyon 1979, pls. 28–29. Two short extracts from the hymn are inscribed on the ceiling of the western doorway in the great pylon of the temple of Isis at Philae (Junker and Winter 1965, pp. 426–27, lines 10–12, 14–17). In addition, the ten *ba*s of Amun are represented, with accompanying legends using terminology similar to that of the hymn, on the south wall of the northern crypt in the temple of Opet at Karnak. Compare Parker, Leclant, and Goyon 1979, pp. 73, 78–79.

Gold of Praise: Studies on Ancient Egypt in Honor of Edward F. Wente
Edited by Emily Teeter and John A. Larson
Studies in Ancient Oriental Civilization 58
Chicago: Oriental Institute, 1999

Museum, Dr. F. G. Kenyon, written on 27 June of that year, announces the Egypt Exploration Fund's intention to donate a number of antiquities, among them "about 250 ostraka, hieratic, Demotic, and Coptic," from Deir el-Bahri. A report to the Museum's trustees by E. A. W. Budge, Keeper in the Department of Egyptian and Assyrian Antiquities, dated 29 June 1911, records the actual receipt of this donation. It included our ostracon, which was duly entered in the register of accessions as lot no. 574 on the tenth day of the following month.

The object was actually discovered during the Egypt Exploration Fund's excavations at Deir el-Bahri under the direction of Edouard Naville.[2] Its excavation number, 6/1/94 (= 6 January 1894), is visible on the photograph of the reverse of the ostracon reproduced in fig. 37.1b. Thus, it was found in the course of the second season of Naville's operations, which extended from 14 December 1893 to 14 March 1894. The work of this season has been described by him in some detail (Naville n.d., pp. 4–6; cf. Davies 1982, pp. 57–58). Its chief object was the clearance of the northern half of the Middle Platform of Hatshepsut's temple. This was covered with mounds of rubbish composed of debris from earlier excavations and the remains of a Coptic monastery. It had also been used as a burial ground from the Twenty-second Dynasty down to the Christian period. Presumably, it was here, among this disparate accumulation of material, that our ostracon was found.

What happened to the object between the time of its discovery in 1894 and its presentation to the British Museum in 1911 is unknown. It may have been kept in a storeroom in Egypt or, alternatively, in the offices of the Egypt Exploration Fund in London. Spiegelberg must have obtained his photograph of the ostracon from Hess during this period and wrongly assumed that its excavator was also its owner, hence his attribution of it to the "Slg. Naville."

Now that the object itself is available for study, it is possible to supplement my earlier treatment of it in two significant respects. First, on its front (fig. 37.1a), the original preserves traces of writing, in some cases entire words, which are indiscernible on the photograph found among Spiegelberg's papers. Second, the text of the hymn inscribed there actually continues on the reverse of the ostracon. The side reproduced in Spiegelberg's photograph preserves the whole of the section of the hymn addressed to the first *ba* of Amun (the sun) and a part of the section addressed to the second *ba* (the moon). The rest of the latter can now be read on the other side (figs. 37.1b, 2).

I begin with additional notes on the front of the ostracon, i.e., the portion of the text treated in my earlier publication. The line numbers used below are the same as the line numbers employed there. The comments which follow should be read in conjunction with that treatment.

Line 2

(a) Delete [*twyṯ*] before *ʾItm* in my transliteration. The surface of the stone is damaged at this point, and the expected second person singular masculine independent pronoun was never written.

(b) A trace of the dependent pronoun *sw* is visible after *ỉr*.[*n*]*=f* at the end of the line.

Line 3

The second half of this line, after *Tne ḫpr n-m-ḥ.t*, has been erased. Further erasure is apparent in the space between lines 3 and 4. The following traces can still be made out: *twyṯ nb* [....] *n-m* *ʿw*[*y=f ts=f*] *n-m* [...] .. *nb* [....]*=f*. This is clearly a rejected preliminary version of the sentence which now begins line 4: *twyṯ nb tȝy.t=f n-m ʿwy=f ts=f m ḫbr* [*nb n ȝb=f*] "You are the one who fashioned his body with his own hands in [every] form [of his desiring]." Because so little of it can now be read, it is difficult to say how radically this preliminary version differed from the final one. The most obvious difference is in the signs which stand immediately before *nb* "every." Presumably, one had here an alternative orthography of *ḫbr* "form" which occurs before *nb* in the final version, but I am unable to recognize any of the individual elements, apart from a divine determinative at the end.

Line 6

After *kȝ* "bull" at the end of the line, one has a word written *ẖ* + *n* + *m* and determined with the water sign. This is presumably an unetymological writing of the verb *ẖnm* "unite, join" with the determinative borrowed

2. For an overview of these, see Davies 1982, pp. 51–67.

from *ẖnm.t* "well." Compare the Demotic example of the latter in P. BM 10508, XXIII, 23 (Glanville 1955, pl. 23). Read *ẖnm Nꜣy.w-Ḫmnỉw n⸗f m ỉꜣw* in lines 6–7 and translate "with whom the Ogdoad unites in adoration." One probably has a play on words here between *ẖnm* and the name of the eight Hermopolitan deities.

Line 7

ḫꜥ⸗f "he rises" has been written over something else, possibly *ỉr⸗f*.

Line 8

nbe.t "flame" has been corrected from an original *nmy.t* "slaughter-house." See Erichsen 1954, p. 218, for writings of the latter with the brazier determinative as here.

Line 16

A trace of the *ḫ* of *ꜥnḫ.w* "the living" is visible just before the break at the end of the line.

Line 22

(a) The divine name in this line is *Ḥr-ꜣḫ.ṱ* "Harakhty" and not *Ḥr-m-ꜣḫ.ṱ* as I read originally. See comparable writings of the former in Smith 1993, p. 124 (s.v. *Rꜥ-Ḥr-ꜣḫ.ṱ*).

(b) The upper part of the *r* of *ṱr* "time" is visible immediately before the break at the end of the line.

Line 23

The predicative negation *nn* is actually written *n-n⸗n* and not simply *n⸗n* here.

Line 24

In my original publication, I attempted to account for the strange appearance of the initial *s* of *s-n⸗y-ntm* in this line by suggesting that part of its top had flaked away. Autopsy makes it clear, however, that no flaking has occurred here, and I am left without an explanation for the sign's curious form.

Line 25

(a) The *ꜥ* of *ḥꜥy* "rejoice" is written over an original *y*.

(b) I cannot account for the signs immediately after the divine determinative of *ḥy* "sunlight." These comprise two short vertical strokes followed by what looks like the dependent pronoun *st*. The ensuing *tw-n⸗y* (classical Egyptian *ṯnw*) is written over an original *tn*. Evidently, the scribe experimented with various ways of rendering this archaism in the Demotic script.

Line 26

I am still unable to provide a coherent translation for this line, which seems to diverge in some respects from what is preserved in the corresponding parts of the hieroglyphic parallels. Inspection of the original indicates that *n⸗s* should be read before the *ny* which stands in the middle of the line. This, in turn, is followed by a sign which could be either *s* or the man with hand to mouth determinative. Near the end, perhaps read *ḫms* (the *m* is written over an *n*). This could be the scribe's attempt at rendering the verb *ḫnms* "befriend" which occurs at roughly the same point in the parallel texts.

Line 28

A trace of the house determinative of *s.t* "seat, throne" is visible at the beginning of the line.

Line 29

The sun determinative of *nḥḥ* "eternity" can be seen at the beginning of the line, immediately before *r ḥṱy⸗f*.

a b

Figure 37.1. O. BM 50601: (*a*) Front and (*b*) Reverse. Courtesy of the British Museum

Line 30

Inspection of the original shows that my earlier suggestion to read *sp* "time" after *m* here is wrong. What I interpreted as a bolt-*s* is clearly a different sign. I am unable to suggest a more satisfactory reading.

Line 31

Contrary to what was said in my original publication, no traces of writing are preserved here. Spiegelberg's photograph is misleading in this respect. After *ỉr rʿ nb* at the end of line 30, one expects the words *nn ꜣb ʿnḫ ḏt* "without cessation, living forever." These should probably be restored in the break at the beginning of this line.

Turning now to the reverse of O. BM 50601, this is much rougher than the front. For the continuation of his text on this side, the scribe made use of a narrow flange of stone that extends vertically from the top to the bottom of the ostracon, the surface of which is somewhat smoother than those on either side of it. On this, the remainder of the section of the hymn addressed to the second *ba* of Amun is written in nine short lines. Its conclusion is marked by a large *ʿnḫ*-sign flanked by two *wꜣs*-scepters surmounting a *nb*-basket. The end of the section addressed to the first *ba* of Amun on the other side of the ostracon is similarly marked, although there the terminal marker has been inserted mistakenly below line 17 and not below line 19 where it properly belongs. That marker omits the *nb*-basket as well, possibly for lack of space.

The nine lines which constitute the remainder of the address to Amun's second *ba* are paralleled in the hieroglyphic version of the hymn preserved on the walls of the temple of Darius I at Hibis. The two versions are presented synoptically below, accompanied by a translation and comments. As in my original publication, the symbol (D) denotes the Demotic version of the hymn, and the symbol (H) the hieroglyphic parallel from Hibis.

TRANSLITERATION AND TRANSLATION

Line 1

(D) [*ʾImn by*] — (D) [Amun, *ba*]

(H) 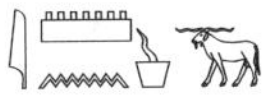

Line 2

(D) *m ꜣb=[f]* — (D) who is in [his] left eye,

(H) 

Line 3

(D) *i͗ʿḥ m grḥ* — (D) moon at night,

(H) 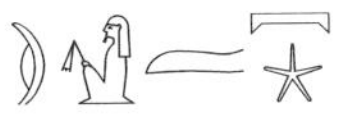

Line 4

(D) *ḥq ʿnḫ.[w]* — (D) ruler of the living [ones],

(H) 

Line 5

(D) [illegible traces] — (D) [illegible traces]

Line 6

(D) *r wpy [ṯr].w* — (D) so as to determine the [time]s,

(H) 

Line 7

(D) *wbṯ rnp.wt* — (D) months, and years.

(H) 

Line 8

(D) *i͗w=f ʿnḫ ḏt* — (D) He comes, living forever

(H) 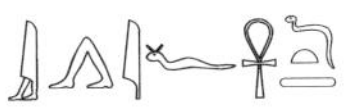

Line 9

(D) *r-ꜣh wb[n] ḥtp* — (D) ris[ing] and setting.

(H) 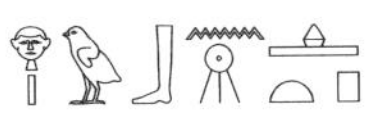

COMMENTARY

Line 1

Only a few traces of writing are visible in this line. Presumably, one had here *ˀImn by* as in (H). For the probable appearance of the words in question, see line 18 on the front of the ostracon.

Line 3

For the writing of *grḥ* "night" here, see line 21 on the front of the ostracon.

Line 4

Only the lower part of the *ḫ* of *ʿnḫ.w* is preserved. The "living ones" in this context are the stars, as is evident from the determinative of *ʿnḫ.w* in (H). Compare *Wb.* 1.204:6.

Line 5

The initial sign here is perhaps a *w*. Nothing corresponds to this line in the parallel text of (H). The traces are either of an interpolation or, as is more likely in my opinion, a rejected preliminary version of the phrase *r wpy* [*ṯr*].*w* which occurs in the following line.

Line 6

For the restoration of *ṯr* "time" here, see the parallel text of (H). The writing of the noun was probably the same as that which appears in line 22 on the front of the ostracon.

Line 7

wbṯ written without a determinative is the scribe's rendering of *ꜣbd.w* "months" which occurs at this point in (H). The writing is unparalleled elsewhere, so far as I can discover.

Line 8

For the writing of the phrase *iw⸗f ʿnḫ ḏt* here, see line 17 on the front of the ostracon.

Line 9

(a) For *r-ꜣh* as a writing of the preposition *ḥr* in the pseudoverbal construction *ḥr* + infinitive, see Smith 1978, pp. 23–25.

(b) With the traces of *wbn* "rise" here compare better preserved examples of the same verb in lines 6, 15, 17, 19, and 23 on the front of the ostracon. A blank space appears to have been left between this word and the following *ḥtp* for reasons which are obscure.

The nine lines treated above are not the only writing preserved on the reverse of O. BM 50601. To the right of and extending below the *ʿnḫ*-, *wꜣs*-, and *nb*-signs which mark the end of the section of the hymn addressed to the second *ba* of Amun there are visible traces of a further six lines of text written in the same hand (cf. figs. 37.1b, 2). These are, unfortunately, too faint to permit any coherent translation. The first line appears to begin with the noun *nṯr* "god." The third line may start with *nb* "lord." The initial signs in line 4 are *sgr*. Line 5 begins with what looks like *iw⸗s*, while line 6 preserves the phrase *nṯr ʿꜣ nb* "great god and lord."

From what little can be made of these lines, it is clear that they are not a continuation of the text written above them. Such words as are legible do not figure in the opening of the section of the hymn addressed to the third *ba* of Amun (= the wind), which is what one might have expected to begin at this point. Only the addresses to the first three *ba*s are preserved in the Hibis version of the hymn. The parallel in the edifice of Taharqa at Karnak originally included all ten, but now unfortunately the last seven of these have disappeared, except for isolated words and signs. What does survive there, however, bears no relation to the traces that appear on our ostracon.

To the left of the *ʿnḫ*-, *wꜣs*-, and *nb*-signs described earlier, and of similar proportions, are three further characters: a vertical stroke, followed by a *ḏ*-serpent above a sun disk, perhaps a writing of *ḥḏ* "white, bright."

Figure 37.2. O. BM 50601: Detail of Reverse. Courtesy of the British Museum

The significance of these characters is obscure to me. It is also possible to make out very faint traces of writing, in a hand clearly distinct from the one with which the rest of the ostracon is inscribed, along the upper left-hand edge of the reverse (fig. 37.2). There might have been as many as six or seven lines here in all. Now, however, they are so faded that only a single word can be made out with certainty, in the very last line. This is *nbyʿ* written with the evil determinative, presumably a variant of *nby*/*nbʿy* "Schaden" cited in Erichsen 1954, p. 214. The word is followed by what appears to be the third person singular feminine suffix pronoun *s*. The traces before it are perhaps those of *ḥr* "face."

In my earlier publication, I considered the question of whether the person who inscribed the first two sections of the hymn to the ten *ba*s of Amun on O. BM 50601 was also responsible for actually rendering its Middle Egyptian text into the Demotic script, or whether he simply copied an already existing Demotic version of the hymn. In other words, to what extent is the form in which the text appears on our ostracon due to him?

At the time, I felt unable to answer this question. Now, however, in the light of the additional information obtained from study of the object itself, particularly as regards the number and nature of the alterations which the scribe made in its text, I am inclined to think that he should probably be credited with having originated the Demotic version of the hymn. One can observe how he experimented with different orthographies for certain words, first trying one, then deleting it and substituting another, in one case even rewriting an entire sentence.[3] This suggests that he was actually working out the final form of the text as he wrote it down, and not simply copying what someone else had devised previously.

Another question raised in my earlier publication was that of the purpose for which our ostracon was inscribed. Various possibilities were investigated there, without any firm conclusion being reached. In view of what is now known about the provenience of the ostracon, this question merits reconsideration. As stated above,

3. See, for instance, comments above on lines 3 and 25 on the front of the ostracon.

the object was found during the clearance of the northern half of the middle platform of Hatshepsut's temple at Deir el-Bahri, an edifice originally dedicated jointly to her and the god Amun (*LÄ* 1 "Deir el-Bahari III," col. 1017). After Hatshepsut's cult was discontinued, the latter became the primary recipient of worship there (Pinch 1993, pp. 8–9; Otto 1952, pp. 15–17). By the Graeco-Roman period, most religious activity at the site was centered around the cults of the deified humans Imhotep and Amenophis the son of Hapu (Laskowska-Kusztal 1984; Karkowski and Winnicki 1983, pp. 93–102). Nevertheless, there is evidence to show that Amun had not been forgotten.[4] Since O. BM 50601 is inscribed with part of a hymn addressed to that deity, it is worth considering the possibility that it might have been deposited in the temple as a votive offering.

This can only be presented as a suggestion, inasmuch as the object was not recovered from a controlled archaeological context, but rather found amidst heaps of rubbish, including debris from earlier excavations. Nevertheless, such an explanation could, at least, account for the faint lines of writing on the reverse of the ostracon which bear no discernible relation to the hymn proper. If one has to do with a votive object, then these might have recorded the name of the dedicator and the circumstances in which his offering was made. As noted above, one of the lines in question preserves the word *nby*ᶜ "sin" and it is an established fact that votive offerings were sometimes presented in expiation of sins.[5] Perhaps desire for pardon of a transgression is what provided the motivation for the hymn on our ostracon to be inscribed.

References

Bataille, A.
1951 *Les inscriptions grecques du temple de Hatshepsout à Deir el-Bahari.* Publications de la Société Fouad I de papyrologie, textes et documents 10. Cairo: L'Institut français d'archéologie orientale.

Davies, N. de G.
1953 *The Temple of Hibis in el Khārgeh Oasis,* Part 3: *The Decoration.* Publications of the Metropolitan Museum of Art Egyptian Expedition 17. New York: Metropolitan Museum of Art.

Davies, W. V.
1982 "Thebes." In *Excavating in Egypt: The Egypt Exploration Society, 1882–1982,* edited by T. G. H. James, pp. 51–70. London: British Museum Publications.

Erichsen, W.
1954 *Demotisches Glossar.* Copenhagen: Ejnar Munksgaard.

Glanville, S. R. K.
1955 *The Instructions of ᶜOnchsheshonqy (British Museum 10508).* Catalogue of Demotic Papyri in the British Museum 2. London: British Museum.

Junker, H., and E. Winter
1965 *Das Geburtshaus des Tempels der Isis in Philä.* Österreichische Akademie der Wissenschaften, philosophisch-historische Klasse, Denkschriften - Sonderband, Philä - Publikation 2. Vienna: Böhlau Verlag.

Karkowski, J., and J. K. Winnicki
1983 "Amenhotep, Son of Hapu and Imhotep at Deir el-Bahari — Some Reconsiderations." *Mitteilungen des Deutschen archäologischen Instituts, Abteilung Kairo* 39: 93–102.

Laskowska-Kusztal, E.
1984 *La sanctuaire ptolémaïque de Deir el-Bahari.* Deir el-Bahari 3. Warsaw: PWN-Éditions Scientifiques de Pologne.

Lichtheim, M.
1976 *Ancient Egyptian Literature,* Volume 2: *The New Kingdom.* Berkeley: University of California Press.

Naville, E.
n.d. *The Temple of Deir el Bahari,* Part 2. London: Egypt Exploration Fund.

Otto, E.
1952 *Topographie des thebanischen Gaues.* Untersuchungen zur Geschichte und Altertumskunde Aegyptens 16. Berlin: Akademie-Verlag.

Parker, R. A.; J. Leclant; and J.-C. Goyon
1979 *The Edifice of Taharqa by the Sacred Lake of Karnak.* Brown Egyptological Studies 8. Providence: Brown University Press; London: Lund Humphries.

Pinch, G.
1993 *Votive Offerings to Hathor.* Oxford: Griffith Institute.

Smith, M.
1977 "A New Version of a Well-known Egyptian Hymn." *Enchoria* 7: 115–49.
1978 "Remarks on the Orthography of Some Archaisms in Demotic Religious Texts." *Enchoria* 8/2: 17–27.
1993 *The Liturgy of Opening the Mouth for Breathing.* Oxford: Griffith Institute.

Spiegelberg, W.
1925 *Demotische Grammatik.* Heidelberg: Carl Winter.

4. See, for example, Bataille 1951, pp. 27–28 (no. 44) and 79–80 (no. 116).

5. Compare the "penitential" stelae translated in Lichtheim 1976, pp. 104–10.

38

CELIBACY AND ADOPTION AMONG GOD'S WIVES OF AMUN AND SINGERS IN THE TEMPLE OF AMUN: A RE-EXAMINATION OF THE EVIDENCE

EMILY TEETER

The Oriental Institute, Chicago

Edward Wente is an exceptional scholar, and a fine teacher. As one of his many students, I benefited tremendously from his willingness to share his keen insight into Egyptian religion and culture. I present these remarks in thanks for the many years of his guidance.

The idea that the highest ranks of Egyptian priestesses of the Third Intermediate Period and early Twenty-sixth Dynasty were celibate has a long tradition in Egyptology. The earliest suggestion of such celibacy was published in 1897 by Erman who, based upon his earlier commentary on the Ankhnesneferibre stela, revised the previously held idea that the Nubian princesses were married. Erman's (1897, p. 24) thesis included the idea that because of their celibacy these priestesses had to transmit their office through adoption rather than through direct biological inheritance. Over the last 100 years there has been a tremendous amount of research on many aspects of the god's wives,[1] but very little examination of a fundamental aspect of their office, namely the assertion that they passed on their office through adoption because they were celibate.[2]

The association of celibacy with adoption among the god's wives has not been well examined,[3] nor has the existence of institutionalized celibacy among the upper ranks of priestesses. Rather, celibacy has been regarded as a distinguishing feature of the highest ranks of the priestess, the *ḥst ḫnw n ỉmn* (singer in the interior of the temple of Amun) and the *dwꜣ nṯr/ḥmt nṯr n ỉmn* (divine adoratress / god's wife of Amun).[4] Most of the rationale for institutionalized celibacy has to do with the presumed ritual purity of these women, that since they were high ranking clerics their purity was ensured by celibacy. Furthermore, the god's wives have, on the basis of their title, been supposed to be married to the god Amun and were therefore incapable of conducting an earthly union (Yoyotte 1962, p. 48; Naguib 1990, p. 225).

One might expect to find some antecedent for this assumed tradition of celibacy. However, the institution of a royal woman as god's wife of Amun,[5] which appears in the Eighteenth Dynasty with Ahmes-Nefertari (Gitton 1984, p. 28), has no previous association with sexual abstinence. To the contrary, during the Eighteenth Dynasty the god's wife was married and bore children. Indeed the title was held by some of the chief royal wives, including Ahmes-Nefertari and Hatshepsut, and it is assumed that the title was in some way associated with the transmission of the throne (Robins 1993, pp. 149–51). The title was used in the Nineteenth Dynasty (Nefertari) but only sporadically in the Twentieth Dynasty (Isis, daughter of Ramesses VI), after which time it is again attested more consistently in the Third Intermediate Period (Karomama, Tashakheper B, Shepenwepet, and the succession of Nubian women; see Kitchen 1973, table 13B). Robins (1993, pp. 153–54) states, "[the god's wives of the Third Intermediate Period] were all unmarried daughters of either kings or high priests of Amun

1. Summary in *LÄ* 2 "Gottesgemahlin," cols. 792–812.
2. Some preliminary remarks appear in Teeter 1995a; Teeter 1997. See also Ritner 1998; Ritner 1999; Graefe's (1998) response to Ritner's earlier article.
3. The entire question of the use of adoption among the god's wives, according to *LÄ* 2 "Gottesgemahlin," col. 797, is shrouded in "beaucoup d'obscurité."
4. See Yoyotte 1962, pp. 45–51; repeated by Fazzini 1988, p. 4; Naguib 1990, pp. 206–07, 224–25, 235; Niwiński 1992, p. 470.
5. The title is often combined with *dwꜣ nṯr* (divine adoratress) and *drt nṯr* (god's hand), and they seem to be virtually interchangeable; see Robins 1993, pp. 152–53. For the history of the institution, see Gitton 1976; Graefe 1981.

Gold of Praise: Studies on Ancient Egypt in Honor of Edward F. Wente
Edited by Emily Teeter and John A. Larson
Studies in Ancient Oriental Civilization 58
Chicago: Oriental Institute, 1999

who eventually [from Ramesses VI] came to select their successors by adoption."[6] The women who held the title god's wife, especially during the Twenty-fifth and Twenty-sixth Dynasties, served as the surrogate rulers of Egypt on behalf of their fathers in Napata. Since each god's wife of the Twenty-fifth and Twenty-sixth Dynasties was appointed by her father, it has been assumed that the women were forbidden from marrying to prevent the formation of a collateral dynasty in the Thebaid.

The title *ḥst ḫnw n ʾImn* is attested in inscriptions and genealogies on coffins from el-Hibeh, Thebes, Abydos, and Lahun and from funerary equipment from Medinet Habu (Hölscher 1954, pp. 30–33; Teeter 1995a). Approximately 100 women are known to have held this title (Graefe 1981), which is known from the reigns of Takelot II to the end of the Twenty-sixth Dynasty (Yoyotte 1962, p. 47). The singers are thought to be retainers of the god's wives, and indeed some of the *ḥs(w)t ḫnw n ʾImn* are buried not far from the tomb chapels of the god's wives of the Twenty-fifth and early Twenty-sixth Dynasties at Medinet Habu (Hölscher 1954, pp. 16–17); some (Ankhshepenwepet, Ankhamenirdis) compounded their name with the name of their presumed patron. It is known that some *ḥst ḫnw n ʾImn* came from elite backgrounds, such as Diesehebsed who was the daughter of the scribe of the offering table Nesptah and the sister of the fourth prophet of Amun Montuemhet. The adolescent mummy of the *ḥst ḫnw n ʾImn* Eskhonsu suggests that some assumed the title in their youth (Yoyotte 1962, p. 51).

A major influence in the idea that the *ḥst ḫnw n ʾImn* were celibate is the transcript of a lecture delivered by Jean Yoyotte in 1961 to the Académie des Inscriptions et Belles-Lettres in Paris. The transcript contains specific statements regarding the question of celibacy, yet there is virtually no documentation by which the conclusions can be traced, making the oft-quoted conclusions elusive.[7] This work has been employed by many others and it is used as the basis for statements such as the *ḥst ḫnw n ʾImn* formed a college of celibate priestesses selected when young to perpetuate the sense of cosmic regeneration (Naguib 1990, p. 225).

A re-examination of celibacy must include a discussion of the practice of adoption because it is assumed that adoption was employed to pass on high clerical titles since the priestesses were, on account of their rank, celibate and therefore unable to procreate. Certainly there is no doubt that adoption was practiced in Egypt. As stated in O. Berlin 10627, "As for him who has no child, he adopts an orphan instead [to] bring him up" (Wente 1990, p. 149, no. 206; Robins 1993, pp. 77–78). However, texts referring to adoption indicate that the practice was primarily a means of transmitting property to an individual other than the expected heir.[8] For example, the Adoption Papyrus (Eighteenth Dynasty; Gardiner 1940) refers to Nebnefer who adopted his own wife Rennefer as a means of ensuring her inheritance over other members of the family. Later, Rennefer adopted three servant children as her heirs (Gardiner 1940, pp. 23–29; Johnson 1996, p. 183). These cases were motivated by the desire to transfer property rather than by childlessness.

Although it has been assumed that the god's wives of Amun passed on their office through adoption due to celibacy, the evidence and actual motivation for the adoptions are not entirely clear because adoption among priestesses has traditionally been viewed as a function of celibacy rather than a practice that may be entirely unrelated to procreation. Indeed, the nature of the earlier adoption texts has rarely been related to the use of adoption among the priestesses. Yet the Nitocris Adoption Stela, regarding the succession of the god's wife, specifically refers to the deeding of "property given to her as a gift in towns and nomes of Upper and Lower Egypt" in conjunction with the transfer of the title god's wife of Amun from Shepenwepet II and Amunirdis II to Nitocris, daughter of Psammetichus:

> "I [Psammetichus] have heard that a king's daughter is there, ... [a daughter of Taharqa] ... , whom he gave to his sister to be her eldest daughter and who is there as Adorer of God. ... I will give her (my daughter [Nitocris]) to her (Taharqa's daughter [the current god's wife]) to be her eldest daughter, just as she (Taharqa's daughter [the current god's wife]) was made over to the sister of her father (Caminos 1964, p. 74).

Although traditionally referred to as an adoption text, the text, like the adoption texts already cited, deals with the transfer of property, which is especially evident in the terminology employed. The new god's wife is referred to as the "eldest daughter." The terms "eldest son" and "eldest daughter" are well attested as quasi-le-

6. Jacquet-Gordon (1967, p. 93) suggests that Karomama, a divine adoratress of the Twenty-second Dynasty, was also "a virgin bride of Amun."

7. See, for example, the comments of Ritner (1998, pp. 86, 89) and Graefe's (1998, pp. 110–11) response.

8. As noted also by Eyre 1992, p. 221.

gal terms that refer to a moral obligation compensated by extra inheritance.[9] The Demotic Code of Hermopolis West indicates that a son or daughter could act in the role of eldest son or daughter to undertake the responsibility of the eldest son to bury his parents.[10] O. Berlin 10627, which contains the phrase "as for him who has no children, he adopts an orphan [to] bring him up," continues "it is his responsibility to pour water onto your hands as one's own eldest son" (Wente 1990, p. 149).

Another instance of adoption among the god's wives deals with the induction of Ankhnesneferibre, the daughter of Psammetichus II as god's wife during the lifetime of Nitocris (Breasted 1906/4, §988; Leahy 1996). Unlike the Nitocris Adoption Stela that deals specifically with the transfer of property, this text deals with the formulation of the titulary of Ankhnesneferibre during the lifetime of *mwt.s* "her mother," God's Wife Nitocris. The later section of the text refers to the death of Nitocris, and the accession of Ankhnesneferibre, "her daughter ... who did for her [Nitocris] everything which is done for every beneficent king" (Leahy 1996, p. 148, lines 8–9).

What evidence do the Nitocris and Ankhnesneferibre adoptions offer to suggest that celibacy was the motivation for the adoptions? In the Ankhnesneferibre stela, Ankhnesneferibre refers to Nitocris as *mwt.s* "her mother" (Leahy 1996, pp. 146, line 2, 148) and to herself in relationship to Nitocris as *s3t.s* "her daughter." In contrast, the Nitocris Decree completely avoids the term *mwt*, referring to Nitocris merely as the *s3t.s wrt* "eldest daughter" of her predecessor (Caminos 1964, pl. 8, line 4; p. 74). The use of kinship terms in both these texts has traditionally been interpreted as an adoption,[11] yet one may question whether this adoption was undertaken merely for the passage of offices and titles, and whether it has any bearing at all on celibacy.

Genealogies of priestesses, specifically those which do not refer to a husband or children, are often cited to support the idea of celibacy. Most of the genealogies for the presumed celibate singers in the interior of the temple of Amun are recorded on their own coffins. However, this may not be the most suitable place to find a mention of a woman's husband and any children because the genealogies are usually written from the perspective of the woman herself, mentioning the names of her own mother, father, and grandparents, not her descendants. The information that is needed to establish whether a woman had children is found on the coffin or record of her child as he or she refers to parentage through the mother. In contrast to the usually accepted ideas, several genealogies indicate that these women, traditionally assumed to be celibate because of their priestly duties, indeed had children. Tafabart and Meresamenet are both daughters of *ḥst ḫnw n ʾImn* (Ritner 1999, pp. 351, 352 note 18; Ritner 1998, pp. 87–89; Teeter 1995a, pp. 200–01), and Nesptah is the son of the *ḥst ḫnw [n] ʾImn* Diesehebsed (Legrain 1912, pp. 173–74).

The assumption that priestesses were celibate has led to elaborate reconstructions of genealogies and curious uses of kinship terms. Genealogies that seem to refer to two mothers have been cited to support the practice of adoption among "celibate" priestesses. Yoyotte states that in such genealogies, one woman is the "mère charnelle," while the other the "mère spirtuelle." Yoyotte, Malinine, and Macadam, followed by Elias,[12] assert that specific kinship terms were employed to differentiate a birth mother from an adoptive mother. For example, a statue in Cairo (42198) recounts of the god's wife Amunirdis I: *dw3 nṯr ʾImn ỉr dỉ.s m3ʿ(t) ḫrw mwt.s dw3 nṯr Šp-n-wpt m3ʿ(t) ḫrw ... ms(t) n ḥmt nsw Pb3tm3* "The God's Wife Amunirdis, justified, her mother being the God's Wife Shepenwepet, justified ... born of the king's great wife Pabatma" (Legrain 1910, p. 111; Gauthier 1915, p. 11 D). This text has been interpreted as the woman referred to as *mwt.s* being the adoptive mother and the other (with *ms(t)*) the biological mother. Examples of the use of the term *mwt.s* to denote adoption cited by Yoyotte include Dimwtshepetenptah (also known as Ditankha)[13] and Meresamenet,[14] who bore the title *ḥst ḫnw n ʾImn*. The genealogies on their coffins refer to their mothers, also *ḥst ḫnw n ʾImn* as *mwt.s*, the term supposed to indicate adoption.

It is not difficult to find exceptions to this supposed clear differentiation of birth and adoptive mother designated by *mwt.s/ms n*. The genealogy of Yoyotte's primary examples of dual mothers, that of Tafabart and

9. See Eyre 1992, pp. 215 n. 50, 216–17, for further references.

10. See Mattha 1975, pp. 39–41. For examples of women functioning as eldest "son," see Johnson 1996, p. 184; Eyre 1992, p. 216, n. 56.

11. As in the case of the Ankhnesneferibre Stela; see Graefe 1998, p. 110.

12. See Yoyotte 1962, p. 46; Malinine 1953, pp. 13–14; and Macadam 1949, text 119–21; Elias (1995, p. 62) is more cautious, stating that the term *mwt.s* "may well be adoptive."

13. Cairo coffin 41061 in Gauthier 1913, pp. 365, 377.

14. Ritner 1999, p. 351: "Mere(s)amenet, whose mother [*mwt.s*] is the chantress (of) the residence (of) Amun, She(m)amen(i)mes." See his further remarks on this genealogy in Ritner 1998, pp. 88–89, and the comments of Graefe 1998, p. 111; Ritner 1999, pp. 351–52, n. 9.

Meresamenet, has been shown to be incorrectly read, and in fact the genealogy is entirely conventional.[15] The genealogy of Mutirdis at Thebes gives two different named women as her mother, both of whom are referred to by the same term of filiation (*mwt.s*) (Assmann 1977, p. 17), further suggesting that the term *mwt.s* is not diagnostic of adoption, and especially not *two* adoptive mothers.[16] Dimwtshepetenptah, who bore the title *ḥst ḫnw n ꜣImn* and who has been presumed to be celibate, refers to her mother as *mwt.s,* which has been taken as indicative of adoption. Yet the title of her mother is *nbt pr* "housewife" — a title with which celibacy has never been associated.[17] The same situation is encountered on a funerary cone of Mutirdis, where one of her mothers (*mwt.s*) bears the title *nb*(*t*) *pr* (Assmann 1977, p. 16, Abb. 4; Davies 1957, no. 387). Another use of the term *mwt* to denote other than an adoptive mother occurs on the Stèle de l'intronisation d'Aspelta,[18] where a list of six generations of the females of his family are given, each employing the term *mwt.s* in reference to her own daughter. Although Aspelta's mother is a *dwꜣ nṯr n ꜣImn Rꜥ* the other generations of women are simply *snt nsw* (king's sister) for whom there is no attested institution of celibacy; yet each generation refers to the preceding by the term *mwt.s*, the term which supposedly refers to adoption. In all these cases, the term *mwt.s* apparently refers to a normal biological relationship rather than to adoption.

Other examples that belie a clear differentiation between the two terms include a genealogy of Nitocris, the daughter of Psammetichus I, which appears in her chapel at Medinet Habu: *mwt.s ḥmt nsw Mḥt n wsḫt* "her mother is Mehtenweskhet" (Gauthier 1915, p. 81B). A similar inscription appears on an offering table from Karnak: *mwt.s ḥmt nsw wrt Mḥt n wsḫt* (Gauthier 1915, p. 82E). Both texts employ the term that has been associated with adoption; yet the coffin of Nitocris bears the inscription *ms n ḥmt nsw wrt Mḥt n wsḫt* (Gauthier 1915, p. 85 Mb), and other texts unrelated to Nitocris indicate that Mehtenweskhet was indeed the *ḥmt nsw wrt* of Psammetichus and hence was Nitocris's biological, not adoptive, mother (Gauthier 1915, p. 81A; Vittmann 1975, p. 376). A text on a doorjamb from Abydos that refers to Peksater and her mother Pabatma (wife of Takarka) likewise employs the term *mwt.s* for a woman's biological mother.[19]

Defining the meaning of kinship terms is further complicated by examples that seem to indicate two mothers for a single individual. The genealogy in the tomb of Mutirdis that refers to two different women as *mwt.s* ("her mother") was interpreted by Assmann (1977, p. 17) as an indication that the mother who shared the same title as Mutirdis was the adoptive mother, and the woman with the title *nbt pr* was the biological mother, or that the genealogy could refer to one woman with two names — an administrative name and an informal family name. As has been discussed, there is little evidence that *mwt.s* indicated adoption, and hence another, perhaps less complex solution should be explored. This solution, backed by more precedent, is that the term *mwt* could be employed to refer to a woman who bore the same title as Mutirdis (*ḥry šmst n dwꜣ-nṯr*), in reference to the fact that she stood as trainer or tutor to the younger women. Just as a mother trains a child in the ways of the world, these teachers could be referred to as "mother." The other *mwt.s*, who was simply *nbt pr* "housewife," would be her real mother.

A similar situation can be seen on a stela of Ikhernofert (BM 202) where Minhotep is credited with two fathers, Ikhernofert and Snefru, both called *it* (Simpson 1974, pl. 3; British Museum 1912, pl. 11). Although Schäfer (1904, p. 39) suggests that one was an adoptive father and the other biological, Leprohon suggests, as with the case of Mutirdis, that the title *it* could be honorary and was used with the connotation of "protector" or "patron."[20]

A third example concerns a childless couple from Deir el-Medina who apparently adopted a son (Robins 1993, p. 77). In this case, the younger man succeeded the older in his position as a scribe and he is referred to as "his son who causes his name to live," a phrase that appears in funerary formulas referring to the one responsible for the maintenance of the funerary cult or for the manufacture of a commemorative stela.[21] Again, the re-

15. Text given in Mariette 1982, p. 483, no. 1281, corrected by Ritner 1998, pp. 86–88; see the comments of Graefe 1998, pp. 109–10; Ritner 1999, pp. 351–52, n. 9.

16. Although Graefe (1998, p. 110) suggests that this may be the case.

17. Teeter 1995a, pp. 200–01. So, too, the mother of Meresamenet is *ḥst ḫnw n ꜣImn* as well as *nbt pr*; see Ritner 1998, pp. 88–89, and comments of Graefe 1998, p. 111.

18. Grimal 1981, p. 30, lines 14–16, p. 31, lines 1–3. See also the comments of Leclant and Yoyotte 1952, p. 38.

19. Daressy 1900, p. 142 (CLXXIV); Gauthier 1915, p. 10. For the actual filiation, see Kitchen 1973, p. 478 (table 2); for Pebatma as the wife of Kashta, see Gauthier 1915, p. 8. See Macadam 1949, p. 120, for the comment that it was probably an adoptive relationship.

20. Leprohon 1978, p. 34. I thank Prof. Leprohon for bringing this reference to my attention.

21. See examples in James 1974, nos. 164–65.

lationship here may not in fact be filial, but rather in the context of tutor, instructor, or one upon whom certain responsibilities fall.[22]

Attempting to determine a clear and definitive difference in the meaning of the terms *mwt.s* and *ms n* may be fruitless considering the notorious flexibility in the use of Egyptian kinship terms.[23] Further illustration of the complexity of filiation terms is the use of the term *ỉr*(*t*) *n* ("engendered of") that was more often associated with reference to a male antecedent but was also employed for women.[24] A text on the sarcophagus of Ankhnesneferibre contains the filiation *Wsỉr ꜥnḫ-n⸗s-nfr-ỉb-Rꜥ mꜣꜥt ḫrw ỉrt n ḥmt nsw wrt tp*(*t*) *n*(*t*) *ḥm.f Tꜣḫꜣwṯ* "The Osiris, Ankhnesneferibre, justified, born [literally engendered] of the great royal wife, foremost of his majesty Tikhawal."[25] Other examples of the use of *ỉrt* for female filiation are found on Late Period stelae and on statues where it has no bearing upon adoption.[26] Considering the variety of terminology used for female filiation and the variability in the use of the individual terms, it is very doubtful that the distinction between *mwt.s* and *ms n* is truly diagnostic of an adoptive relationship and thus this distinction cannot be used to prove the existence of celibacy among priestesses.

These considerations may be applied to a re-examination of the god's wives and the question whether the "adoptions" were a function of enforced celibacy. The use of *mwt* on the Nitocris Adoption Stela and even the term "daughter" on the Ankhnesneferibre Stela, the two pillars upon which the idea of celibacy among god's wives of Amun rest, may indeed be honorific titles that refer to the tutelage of the elder god's wife or the relationship of the two parties and have nothing to do with their sexuality. Since the Adoption Stela of Nitocris deals specifically with property, it can be regarded as a version of the traditional and well-attested *ỉmyt-pr* through which property was legally diverted to someone other than a direct descendant.[27] Further, the term explicitly used to refer to the new status of Nitocris is "eldest daughter," which is known to be associated with moral and financial responsibilities rather than with adoption.

Other evidence for celibacy among the god's wives might be inferred from the fact that they are never shown with a husband.[28] This omission has been taken as further evidence that these women were not married, and by extension that they were not married because they were priestesses upon whom celibacy was incumbent. However, the presence or absence of a husband in the monument of a woman is not conclusive for determining her marital status. First, there are relatively few representations of these women. The supposedly celibate and unmarried singers in the interior of Amun are known mainly from their coffins, the remains of their funerary equipment, and some fragments of reliefs, presumably from their tomb chambers (Hölscher 1954, pp. 30–33). In contrast there are a greater number of monuments of the god's wives of the Third Intermediate Period and

22. This may be the same sentiment as encountered in O. Berlin 10627: "As for him who has no children, he adopts an orphan instead [to] bring him up. It is his responsibility to pour water onto your hands as one's eldest son" (Wente 1990, p. 149). This is again the idea of a non-filial relationship being couched in common kinship terms. See also Janssen and Janssen 1990, p. 70: "Ordinary school masters are unknown from this period [the Old Kingdom]. Usually the boys will have been trained by their fathers, although some elderly men took sons of others as their pupils. In that case, they were respectfully called 'father,' a custom that persisted through all Egyptian history, so that a man could have two different 'fathers.' "

23. O'Connor 1990, pp. 8, 10–11; Whale 1989, pp. 239–49; Robins 1979. See also the comments of Allam 1972, pp. 292–94, for the rejection of *šrỉt n ḫnt* as "adoptive daughter."

24. *Wb.* 1.111:3–5; Gardiner 1973, §§361 (p. 279, nn. 12–13), 379. See the genealogy on a statue of Osiris (CG 38238) in Daressy 1894, p. 126 (CXIII), where *ỉr*(*t*) *n sꜣ*(*t*)*.s ḥs*(*t*) *ḫnw* (*n*) *ꜣImn* ... is used to describe the relationship between two sisters. Although Graefe (1998, p. 110) suggests this indicates that one sister "adopted" the other, it is less complicated and more likely that one sister trained the other in the duties of their shared temple position.

25. Gauthier 1915, p. 103 Je; Macadam 1949, p. 120, n. 2. The text continues with *mwt.s drt nṯr Nt-ỉqr mꜣꜥ*(*t*) *ḫrw* "her mother is the God's Hand Nitocris, justified." Here the term *mwt.s* is used to indicate a non-biological relationship in contrast to *ỉrt* which apparently denotes Ankhnesneferibre's actual mother.

26. Munro 1973, pl. 7, Abb. 26 (Louvre N. 3787): *Wḏꜣ-rn⸗s ỉrt n nbt pr* ...; pl. 13, Abb. 47: *Nsy-Ḫnsw* ... *ỉrt n nbt pr;* pl. 15, Abb. 53 (Field Museum, Chicago): *Tꜣkrhb ỉrt n nb*(*t*) *pr*. See also Macadam 1949, p. 120, n. 2. The Osiris statue of Diesehebsed from Medinet Habu (CG 38238) in Daressy 1894, p. 126 (CXIII), is cited by Graefe 1998, p. 110, as an example of adoption where one sister, a *ḥst n ḫnw n ꜣImn,* adopted her own sister.

27. For a re-evaluation of the *ỉmyt-pr,* see Johnson 1996, pp. 180–85. See Feucht 1997, pp. 323–24, for the resiliency of outdated ideas of the role and actors of the *ỉmyt-pr*.

28. Yet the same argument is never applied to New Kingdom and Third Intermediate Period kings whose wives are similarly omitted from their husbands' tombs. The god's wives are however shown in the company of their male majordomo or retainer: PM 2, 193 (I) (b): Chapel of Osiris-Onnophris; PM 1/1, 358 (12), (17): TT 279 (Pabasa), no doubt because of their association with the office of the god's wife.

early Twenty-sixth Dynasty,[29] and on none of them is a husband shown. Difficulties with drawing conclusions about marital status from iconographic materials in tombs have been discussed by Roth, Robins, and Russmann,[30] who suggest that men were normally never shown in a woman's tomb. Roth states that this omission is standard iconography from the reign of Snefru.[31] Since we should not expect to see a man in a high ranking woman's tomb, these materials should not be employed as evidence for marital status.

The problems in using such materials can be illustrated by the tomb of Mutirdis, who held the titles *wr ꜥꜣt n dwꜣ nṯr* "great of the divine adoratresses" and *ḥry(t) šmsw n(t) dwꜣt-nṯr* "superior of the singers of the divine adoratresses" (Assmann 1977, pp. 17–18). Considerable genealogical information is given in this tomb including the name of her father, the *ỉt-nṯr* "god's father" Pakhebw, and her mother(s). The names of her three daughters and a son are also recorded (Assmann 1977, p. 17), yet with all this genealogical information the name of her husband, who is the father of her children, is not mentioned or shown. In the context of this tomb, Mutirdis was immortalizing herself in the most egocentric way, by commemorating her role in the sacred administration, rather than her private, personal life.

An additional difficulty in using funerary iconography to determine marital status revolves around the changing themes of tomb decoration. During the Third Intermediate Period, the theme of tomb decoration generally shifted from scenes of daily life in which one might expect a couple to be shown together, to scenes of the afterlife (Assmann 1984, pp. 698–99). In such a context there is little likelihood that a woman's husband would be shown because the tomb was a commemoration of her afterlife, not her husband's.

Another argument used to assert that the higher ranks of priestesses were celibate is that because they worked in temples they must be "pure," meaning, sexually pure. This scenario ignores several basic aspects of Egyptian culture, primarily the vague separation of religion and secular life in ancient Egypt. Unlike our own Western culture where there is a definite division and separation of these spheres, in ancient Egypt religion and daily life were a more seamless whole. Theologically there is no reason to assume that priestesses were cut off from normal sexual relations and, other than the traditionally held interpretation of the god's wives and singers in the interior of the temple, no evidence whatsoever for institutionalized celibacy.[32] The association of priestesses with celibacy on account of "purity" seems completely in contrast to what can be gleaned from the Egyptians' own attitude about their cosmos and cult. Sexual imagery — ithyphallic gods, scenes of birth, love poetry — permeated their religious beliefs and daily life. To the Egyptians, sex was not, as in much of the modern world, inherently bad, but rather it was linked to the central theme of Egyptian religion: regeneration.[33] Overlaying the question of women in temples with a Judeo-Christian background has tended to equate women in temples with nuns[34] and to associate purity with the lack of sexual congress, although there is no evidence from ancient Egypt to assume this on the part of women.

The lack of connection between the ideas of chastity and purity in ancient Egypt is very evident. No lexical term for "virgin" can be identified,[35] belying the assertion that the "concern for the virginity of unmarried girls is

29. Leclant 1965; de Meulenaere 1968, pp. 183–87.

30. Roth 1999, pp. 38–45, 52–53, who discusses the omission of the wife from her husband's tomb; Robins 1994, pp. 36, 38; Russmann in paper, "Gender Segregation in Some Late Private Tombs at Thebes," delivered at the Annual Meeting of the American Research Center in Egypt, University of California, Los Angeles, April 24–26, 1998. See also the brief comments of Whale 1989, pp. 245–47.

31. Roth (1999) notes the exceptions of the tombs at Meydum and the chapels of the wives of Mentuhotep II at Deir el-Bahri.

32. See also the comments of Ritner 1998, pp. 85, 90.

33. See the comments of Jansen-Winkeln (1989, p. 203) regarding a text on the coffin of Maatkare (Twenty-first Dynasty): *nn ỉwf.s ỉrỉ.f ḏwỉ*, which he translates as "Ihr Fleisch hat nichts Böses getan." Jansen-Winkeln suggests that this is a sexual reference to "fleischliche Sünde," which as a celibate priestess she would not commit. However (as noted by Ritner 1998, p. 90 n. 40), forensic examination of the mummy of Maatkare suggests that "she died either in childbirth or very shortly hereafter" (Harris and Weeks 1973, p. 174).

34. See Caminos 1964, p. 71, in reference to Nitocris "who took the veil"; Jacquet-Gordon 1967, p. 93, for the god's wife being "a virgin bride of Amun."

35. Feucht 1997, p. 321. Janet Johnson, in the manuscript of the 1996 lecture "The Legal Status of Women" delivered at the Cincinnati Museum of Art, asserts that the terms which are often taken to mean virgin (*ꜥḏdt, rnnt, ḥnwt*) actually denote a young person. The term *ḥnwt* "clearly cannot mean 'unmarried woman' or 'virgin' since it is used in the New Kingdom inscription of Queen Hatshepsut to refer to her mother, who is already the wife of Hatshepsut's father (*Urk.* 4, pp. 218.16–219.3)." As further noted by Johnson, the phrase "not having been opened," which might be taken to refer to virginity, is more likely to refer to a woman who has not given birth rather than to a virgin. This term was applied to the wives of Horus and Seth who are referred to as *nn wp.sn* (not having been opened), when clearly they are considered to be married. The idea of *wp* "open" is therefore more likely to refer to child-

ubiquitous in the world."[36] Sexual mores in Egypt focused upon the prohibition of adultery rather than upon chastity.[37] Just as there is little evidence for a moral value placed upon virginity, there is little evidence that premarital (as opposed to extramarital) sex was considered to be impure.

There is no compelling evidence to suggest that chastity was related to ritual purity; rather it appears that the idea of purity was a transient state that could be acquired primarily through bodily cleanliness (washing[38] and purification[39]) and through priestly rank. Despite the interpretation of genealogies, terms of filiation, and iconography that have been cited as evidence for celibacy among the *ḥst ẖnw n ꜣImn* and the god's wives, there is evidence to suggest that they were not celibate. P. Louvre E. 10935, a Demotic legal text, lists property in the marriage contract of a *ḥst ẖnw n ꜣImn* (Allam 1972, p. 292, n. 51). Yoyotte attempted to dismiss this seemingly unequivocal evidence for the possibility that this rank of priestesses could marry by suggesting that such a priestess could, after reaching a certain, unspecified age, marry, or that the marriage contract referred to a marriage to the god Amun.[40]

Rare examples of the title *ḥst ẖnw n ꜣImn* held in conjunction with the title *nbt pr* (usually taken to mean "housewife" or "married woman")[41] raise further doubts about the universal celibacy of women who bore the title *ḥst ẖnw n ꜣImn*. Examples where a woman held the title *nbt pr*, the designator of an ordinary housewife or land holder (Johnson 1996, pp. 184–85), along with the priestly title may be indications of the dual role of the woman, namely that she served on a part-time basis as a priestess. It seems unlikely that a part-time clerical position would necessitate celibacy.

Additional doubts about the fact that these women were celibate are voiced by Goldberg (1994, p. 59), who suggests that Karomama G Merymut I "may very well be attested as queen herself (in spite of the usual acceptance of a celibate post-Dyn. 20 GWA-ship)." Stronger evidence comes from a fragmentary stela that recounts that God's Wife Amunirdis (II), daughter of Taharqa, was married to a vizier named Montuemhet and that they had a son named Nasalsa.[42] This evidence comes not from a monument of the god's wife, but from a stela of her husband where the rules of decorum allowed a woman of such exalted status to be shown with her husband. Further, a statue in Sydney gives Amunirdis II the title *ḥmt nsw* (Macadam 1949, p. 119, no. 3). Although Leclant makes a valiant attempt to explain how a god's wife could be married when Egyptologists had accepted the idea that they were celibate, it appears as if Amunirdis was indeed married and bore a child.

Reservations about the extent to which Amunirdis II, daughter of Taharqa, actually performed the role of god's wife[43] seem to be presented to bolster the idea of universal celibacy among the god's wives, intimating that she was not legitimate because she was not celibate. Yet Amunirdis II's legitimacy, even in her apparently married state, is attested by the text of the Nitocris Adoption Stela that clearly states: "I have heard that a king's daughter is there, (a daughter of) the Horus Lofty-of-diadems, the good god [Taharqa], justified, whom he gave

birth. Hence *wp ẖt* "to open the belly" means "to give birth." For example, in P. Westcar 9–10 the king requests women with [firm] breasts, not having yet opened up *to give birth.* I thank Professor Johnson for making her lecture notes available to me.

36. *Contra* Collins 1997; I thank Janet Johnson for bringing this reference to my attention.
37. See summary of texts in Robins 1993, pp. 67–72.
38. Gessler-Löhr 1983, pp. 3, 8, 9, 18, 22, passim.
39. Haring 1997, pp. 5–6. See inscriptions on temple doorways; for example, the southern door of the hypostyle hall at the temple of Amun at Karnak (PM 2, 58 (173) (g)): "Everyone who enters this doorway be pure four times."
40. Yoyotte 1962, p. 48. See Ritner 1998, pp. 87–88, for additional comments about this document and its lack of evidence for celibacy.
41. Shemamenimes (Third Intermediate Period) cited by Ritner 1998, p. 89.
42. From a fragmentary stela published by Habachi 1977, p. 170: "... it can be said that Taharqa, believing that his situation was safe in the Theban area with the Kushite princess occupying the important post of divine adoratrice, had his daughter married ... ." I thank Peter Dorman for bringing this reference to my attention. This son of Amunirdis, Nasalsa, is also known from the Stèle de l'intronisation d'Aspelta; see *Urk.* 3, p. 95; Grimal 1981. See also *LÄ* 1 "Amenirdas II," col. 200, for her being "mère de Ñasalsa" (quotation marks original to text) and also Goldberg's comments (1994, pp. 77–78, no. 35) about Macadam's efforts to try to explain how Amunirdis II, who was, with little supporting evidence, thought to be celibate, could have a child. See also the comments of Leahy 1996, p. 165, that certainly "not all daughters [of the Saite kings] could be kept celibate as prospective god's wives." Since there are two records of Amunirdis II being the mother of Nasalsa, it is unclear why there is such reluctance to accept the fact, other than its contradicting the assumption that the god's wives women were celibate.
43. Leclant 1965, p. 364; Lichtheim 1948, p. 164: "she never succeeded to the office ..."; *LÄ* 1 "Amenirdas II," cols. 199–200.

to his sister to be her elder daughter and who is there as Adorer of God."[44] Further, her installation is referred to in a wholly conventional way: "I [Psammetichus] will give her (my daughter) to her [Amunirdis] to be her eldest daughter just as she [Amunirdus] was made over to the sister of her father."[45] The fact that her title is not mentioned on the stela of her husband suggests that she might have been married to Montuemhet before she acceded to the office of god's wife. If so, being married was not an obstacle to becoming god's wife. The fact that her husband is not shown on her own monuments may again be a matter of decorum, much in the way that her contemporary Mutirdis' husband was excluded from her tomb.

Further doubts about the celibacy of the god's wives is raised by a single reference to Shepenwepet II being *ḥmt nsw* (king's wife) that appears on the coffin of Nitocris.[46] Rather than being accepted at face value, it has been summarily dismissed as "a mistake,"[47] presumably because it contradicts the accepted idea of celibacy.

The effort to prove that certain classes of priestesses in Egypt were celibate is based on inconclusive evidence, such as the absence of her husband in a context in which his presence would be inappropriate, an overly precise definition of filiation titles, and the imposition of western conceptions of what was considered to be appropriate behavior for a priestess.

The evidence for institutional celibacy in ancient Egypt is inconsistent and at best circumstantial. The practice of "adoption," as done by the god's wives (and by others), has no bearing upon the question of celibacy — it pertains to the transfer of property and titles in an irregular pattern or to training for a specific position. There is no evidence that celibacy or the aim of chastity — not conceiving — is related to purity and hence one should carefully look at the assertions that female priestesses were chaste. If indeed celibacy existed among some of the god's wives, such a state may better be attributed to political objectives rather than any function of cultic purity.

References

Allam, S.

1972 "De l'adoption en Égypte pharaonique." *Oriens Antiquus* 11: 277–95.

1974 "Zur Adoption im pharaonischen Ägypten." *Zeitschrift der Deutschen morgenländischen Gesellschaft, Supplement* 2 (18. Deutscher Orientalistentag vom 1. bis 5. Oktober 1972 in Lübeck: Vorträge, edited by W. Voigt), pp. 1–7.

Assmann, J.

1977 *Grabung im Asasif 1963–1970: Das Grab der Mutirdis.* Deutsches archäologisches Institut, Abteilung Kairo, Archäologische Veröffentlichungen 13. Mainz: Philipp von Zabern.

1984 "Vergeltung und Erinnerung." In *Studien zu Sprache und Religion Ägyptens,* Band 2: *Religion. Zu Ehren von Wolfhart Westendorf überreicht von seinen Freunden und Schülern,* edited by F. Junge, pp. 687–701. Göttingen: n.p.

Breasted, J. H.

1906 *Ancient Records of Egypt.* 5 volumes. Chicago: University of Chicago Press.

British Museum

1912 *Hieroglyphic Texts from Egyptian Stelae, etc., in the British Museum,* Part 3. London: British Museum.

Caminos, R.

1964 The Nitocris Adoption Stela." *Journal of Egyptian Archaeology* 50: 71–101.

Collins, J. J.

1997 "Marriage, Divorce and Family in Second Temple Judaism." In *Families in Ancient Israel,* edited by L. G. Perdue, J. Blenkinsopp, J. J. Collins, and C. Meyers, pp. 104–62. Louisville: Westminster John Knox Press.

Daressy, G.

1894 "Notes et remarques." *Recueil de travaux relatifs à la philologie et à l'archéologie égyptiennes et assyriennes* 16: 123–33.

1900 "Notes et remarques." *Recueil de travaux relatifs à la philologie et à l'archéologie égyptiennes et assyriennes* 22: 137–43.

44. Caminos 1964, p. 74 (3). The fact that her name was, unlike that of Shepenwepet II, not enclosed in a cartouche on the Nitocris Adoption Stela may suggest that she was viewed as a junior partner in the post of god's wife, rather than the omission being a reflection of her not being a legitimate holder of the office. See Kitchen 1973, p. 480, where Amunirdis is credited with thirty years as god's wife.

45. Caminos 1964, p. 74 (4). See also the comments of Caminos 1964, p. 79: "It is clearly to Amonirdis, not to Shepenwepe, that Nitocris is made over as eldest daughter or heiress by King Psammetichus I."

46. Macadam 1949, p. 119, no. 3; PM 1/2 686: Cairo temporary no. 6.2.21.1.

47. Macadam 1949, p. 119, no. 3. Admittedly, the question raised by Macadam, "had these princesses actually been the wives of kings the titles appertaining to queens would not normally have been omitted," is more difficult to dispel, unless again the conventions of decorum dictated that the role of the women vis-à-vis the god Amun was more important than that of her marriage to a mortal. Since these women are commemorated in their role as god's wife, perhaps there was a reluctance to mix the message.

Davies, N. de G.
1957 *A Corpus of Inscribed Egyptian Funerary Cones*. Edited by M. F. L. Macadam. Oxford: Griffith Institute.

Elias, J.
1995 "A Northern Member of the 'Theban' Twenty-third Dynasty." *Discussions in Egyptology* 31: 19–29.

Erman, A.
1897 "Zu den Legrain'schen Inschriften." *Zeitschrift für ägyptische Sprache und Altertumskunde* 35: 19–29.

Eyre, C.
1992 "The Adoption Papyrus in Social Context." *Journal of Egyptian Archaeology* 78: 207–21.

Fazzini, R.
1988 *Egypt Dynasty XXII–XXV*. Iconography of Religions XVI, 10. Leiden: E. J. Brill.

Feucht, E.
1997 "Women." In *The Egyptians*, edited by S. Donadoni, pp. 315–46. Chicago: University of Chicago Press.

Gardiner, A. H.
1940 "Adoption Extraordinary." *Journal of Egyptian Archaeology* 26: 23–29.
1973 *Egyptian Grammar*. Third edition revised. Oxford: Griffith Institute.

Gauthier, H.
1913 *Cercueiles anthropoïdes des prêtres de Montou*. Catalogue général des antiquités égyptiennes du Musée du Caire, nos. 41042–41072. Cairo: Institut français d'archéologie égyptienne.
1915 *Le livre des rois d'Égypte: De la XXVe dynastie à la fin des ptolémées*, volume 4. Mémoires publiés par les Membres de l'Institut français d'archéologie orientale du Caire 20. Cairo: Institut français d'archéologie orientale.

Gessler-Löhr, B.
1983 *Die heiligen Seen ägyptischer Tempel*. Hildesheimer ägyptologische Beiträge 21. Hildesheim: Gerstenberg Verlag.

Gitton, M.
1976 "Le rôle des femmes dans le clergé d'Amon à la 18e dynastie." *Bulletin de la Société français d'égyptologie* 75: 31–46.
1984 *Les divines épouses de la 18e dynastie*. Center de recherches d'histoire ancienne 61. Paris: Annales littéraires de l'Université de Besançon.

Goldberg, J.
1994 "The 23rd Dynasty Problem Revisited: Where, When and Who?" *Discussions in Egyptology* 29: 55–85.

Graefe, E.
1981 *Untersuchungen zur Verwaltung und Geschichte der Institution der Gottesgemahlin des Amun vom Beginn des neuen Reiches bis zur Spätzeit*. Ägyptologische Abhandlungen 37. Wiesbaden: Otto Harrassowitz.
1998 "Die Adoption ins Amt der *ḥzwt njwt ḫnw nj jmnw* und der *šmswt dwꜣt-nṯr* (zu Ritners Artikel in GM 164, 1998, 85 ff)." *Göttinger Miszellen* 166: 109–12.

Grimal, N.-C.
1981 *Quatre stèles napatéennes au Musée du Caire, JE 48863–48866*. Mémoires publiés par les Membres de l'Institut français d'archéologie orientale du Caire 106. Cairo: Institut français d'archéologie orientale.

Habachi, L.
1977 "Mentuhotp, the Vizier and Son-in-law of Taharqa." In *Ägypten und Kusch* (Fritz Hintze zum 60. Geburtstag), edited by E. Endesfelder, K.-H. Priese, W.-F. Reineke, and S. Wenig, pp. 165–70. Schriften zur Geschichte und Kultur des alten Orients 13. Berlin: Akademie-Verlag.

Haring, B. J. J.
1997 *Divine Households: Administrative and Economic Aspects of the New Kingdom Royal Memorial Temples in Western Thebes*. Leiden: NINO.

Harris, J. E., and K. Weeks
1973 *X-raying the Pharaohs*. New York: Scribner.

Hölscher, U.
1954 *The Excavation of Medinet Habu*, Volume 5: *Post-Ramessid Remains*. Oriental Institute Publications 66. Chicago: University of Chicago Press.

Jacquet-Gordon, H.
1967 "A Statuette of Maʿat and the Identity of the Divine Adoratress Karomama." *Zeitschrift für ägyptische Sprache und Altertumskunde* 94: 86–93.

James, T. G. H.
1974 *Corpus of Hieroglyphic Inscriptions in the Brooklyn Museum*, Volume 1. Brooklyn: Brooklyn Museum.

Jansen-Winkeln, K.
1989 "Zum Zölibat der Gottesgemahlin." *Varia Aegyptiaca* 5: 203–04.

Janssen, R., and J. Janssen
1990 *Growing Up in Ancient Egypt*. London: Rubicon Press.

Johnson, J. H.
1996 "The Legal Status of Women in Ancient Egypt." In *Mistress of the House, Mistress of Heaven*, edited by A. Capel and G. Markoe, pp. 175–86, 215–17. New York: Hudson Hills Press; Cincinnati: Cincinnati Art Museum.

Kitchen, K. A.
1973 *The Third Intermediate Period in Egypt*. Warminster: Aris and Phillips.

Leahy, A.
1996 "The Adoption of Ankhnesneferibre at Karnak." *Journal of Egyptian Archaeology* 82: 145–65.

Leclant, J.
1965 *Recherches sur les monuments thébains de la XXVe dynastie dite éthiopienne*. Bibliothèque d'étude 36. Cairo: Institut français d'archéologie orientale.

Leclant, J., and J. Yoyotte
1952 "Notes d'histoire et de civilisation éthiopiennes." *Bulletin de l'Institut français d'archéologie orientale* 51: 1–39.

Legrain, M. G.
1910 "Notes d'inspection, LXVI: Sur la mère d'Ameniritis 1re." *Annales du Service des antiquités de l'Égypte* 10: 110–13.
1912 "Researches sur la famille dont fit partie Montoemhat." *Recueil de travaux relatifs à la philologie et à l'archéologie égyptiennes et assyriennes* 34: 97–104, 168–75.

Leprohon, R. J.
1978 "The Personnel of the Middle Kingdom Funerary Stelae." *Journal of the American Research Center in Egypt* 15: 33–38.

Lichtheim, M.
1948 "The High Steward Akhamenru." *Journal of Near Eastern Studies* 7: 163–79.

Macadam, M. F. L.
1949 *The Temple of Kawa*, Volume 1: *The Inscriptions*. Oxford: Griffith Institute.

Malinine, M.
1953 "L'expression désignant l'enfant adoptif en égyptien." *Académie des inscriptions et belles-lettres, Comptes rendus du Groupe linguistique d'études chamito-semitiques, séance du 28 Mai 1952*, pp. 13–14.

Mariette, A.
1982 *Catalogue général des monuments d'Abydos découvert pendant les fouilles de cette ville*. Reprint of 1880 edition, Paris. Wiesbaden: LTR-Verlag.

Mattha, G.
1975 *The Demotic Legal Code of Hermopolis West*. Edited by George Hughes. Bibliothèque d'étude 45. Cairo: Institut français d'archéologie orientale.

Meulenaere, H. de
1968 "La famille du roi Amasis." *Journal of Egyptian Archaeology* 54: 183–87.

Munro, P.
1973 *Die spätägyptischen Totenstelen*. Ägyptologische Forschungen 25. Glückstadt: Augustin.

Naguib, S.-A.
1990 *Le clergé féminin d'Amon thébain à la 21e dynastie*. Orientalia Lovaniensia Analecta 38. Leuven: Peeters.

Niwiński, A.
1992 "Ritual Protection of the Dead or Symbolic Reflection of His Special Status in Society?" In *The Intellectual Heritage of Egypt: Studies Presented to Lászlo Kákosy by Friends and Colleagues on the Occasion of his 60th Birthday*, edited by U. Luft, pp. 457–71. Studia Aegyptiaca 14. Budapest: La Chaire d'Egyptologie.

O'Connor, D.
1990 *Ancient Egyptian Society*. Pittsburgh: Carnegie Museum.

Ritner, R. K.
1998 "Fictive Adoptions or Celibate Priestesses?" *Göttinger Miszellen* 164: 85–90.
1999 "An Oblique Reference to the Expelled High Priest Osorkon?" In *Gold of Praise: Studies on Ancient Egypt in Honor of Edward F. Wente*, edited by E. Teeter and J. A. Larson, pp. 351–60. Studies in Ancient Oriental Civilization 58. Chicago: Oriental Institute.

Robins, G.
1979 "The Relationships Specified by Egyptian Kinship Terms of the Middle and New Kingdoms." *Chronique d'Égypte* 54, no. 108: 197–217.
1993 *Women in Ancient Egypt*. London: British Museum.
1994 "Some Principles of Compositional Dominance and Gender Hierarchy in Egyptian Art." *Journal of the American Research Center in Egypt* 31: 33–40.

Roth, A. M.
1999 "The Absent Spouse: Patterns and Taboos in Egyptian Tomb Decoration." *Journal of the American Research Center in Egypt* 36: 37–53.

Schäfer, H.
1904 *Die Mysterien des Osiris in Abydos unter König Sesostris III*. Leipzig: J. C. Hinrichs.

Simpson, W. K.
1974 *The Terrace of the Great God at Abydos: The Offering Chapels of Dynasties 12 and 13*. Publications of the Pennsylvania-Yale Expedition to Egypt 5. New Haven: Peabody Museum of Natural History; Philadelphia: University Museum of the University of Pennsylvania.

Teeter, E.
1995a "Diesehebsed, a *ḥst ḫnw n ꜣImn* at Medinet Habu." *Varia Aegyptiaca* 10/2–3: 195–203.
1995b "Diasethebsed at Medinet Habu." Seventh International Congress of Egyptologists, Cambridge, 3–9 September 1995, Additional Abstracts, pp. 19–20.
1997 "Were the *ḥst ḫnw n ꜣImn* Celibate?" In American Research Center in Egypt, Forty-eighth Annual Meeting, Ann Arbor, April 11–13, 1997, Program and Abstracts, pp. 55–56.

Vittmann, G.
1975 "Die Familie der saitischen Könige." *Orientalia* 44: 375–87.

Wente, E. F.
1990 *Letters from Ancient Egypt*. Society of Biblical Literature, Writings from the Ancient World 1. Atlanta: Scholars Press.

Whale, S.
1989 *The Family in the Eighteenth Dynasty of Egypt*. Australian Centre for Egyptology, Study 1. Sydney: Australian Centre for Egyptology.

Yoyotte, J.
1962 "Les vierges consacrées d'Amon thébain." *Académie des inscriptions et belles-lettres, Comptes rendus* 1961: 43–52.

39

NEW KINGDOM TEMPLES AT ELKAB

CHARLES CORNELL VAN SICLEN III

San Antonio, Texas

Descriptions of archaeological sites often contain references to materials of various kings of the type: "There were blocks of Amenhotep I, Thutmose II, and Ramesses II," or some such statement. That we know little more can be due to the paucity of remains or to the lack of time which could be devoted to those remains by an excavator — for a myriad of understandable reasons. The brief reconstruction of the history of the city temples of Elkab during the Eighteenth and Nineteenth Dynasties, which follows, is of some interest to the scholar, teacher, and friend whom we honor with this volume.

Aside from early travelers' accounts, the bulk of the archaeological work done at Elkab has been the work of various Belgian missions, and their publications and records are the main source of documentation regarding the site (*LÄ* 1 "Elkab," cols. 1225–27). Much reused material still remains in situ, as do the foundations of the temples under discussion.

The site of Elkab — ancient Nekhbet — lies some 15 km north of modern Edfu on the east bank of the Nile. In the midst of a large mudbrick city wall are the remains of a sacred enclosure housing the city temples, in general associated with the goddess Nekhbet. The extant foundations by and large reflect alterations made to those temples during the Late Period. Still visible are walls and reused blocks from earlier stages of construction. The various changes during the Eighteenth Dynasty are shown in fig. 39.1; fig. 39.2 shows the Ramesside temple.

The earliest structure known from the site is a small chapel erected by Nebhepetre Mentuhotep. The original form and position of this structure, known from blocks later reused, are unknown, but logic would suggest that it stood on the site of the earliest New Kingdom structure. A bark chapel erected by Sobekhotep III presumably was placed in front of the Mentuhotep building.

The first New Kingdom structure was erected by Amenhotep I (fig. 39.1). Although there are no remains in situ, this sanctuary must have stood on the axis of the later temple and must have been roughly adjacent to the sanctuaries of the later Amenhotep II building. Its probable form is preserved in the plan of the sanctuary of the late temple (and the adjacent Amenhotep II building): a room with two columns fronting three smaller chambers.[1] The central chamber comprised the *st-wrt* "great place" of the goddess Nekhbet, and its central doorway was marked by a torus and cavetto. The walls of this structure were decorated in raised relief with scenes of Amenhotep I before Nekhbet. These reliefs show the repair of the Amarna period damage. This simple structure was probably fronted by a porch with four columns or pillars. Presumably the building stood within a mudbrick enclosure.

The first addition to the temple was made by Hatshepsut and Thutmose III in the form of a large rectangular pillared, or columned, court some twenty meters broad, with space for up to eight pillars on a side. Foundations of this extension are still visible on the east and south, and part of the wall itself survives on the west. The position of the north wall (and thus the front of the Amenhotep I structure) must have been between the two eastern doors in the room with two columns of the adjacent, later Amenhotep II building. The walls of the court of Hatshepsut and Thutmose III were decorated in raised relief for the most part. Some scenes, probably adjacent to the main door on the south, were in sunk relief. In addition to the main entrance, other doors probably opened onto the truncated mudbrick enclosure to the north. As might be expected, the names and images of Hatshepsut have been expunged, and there is post-Amarna period repair. Two pieces of temple furnishings survive from

1. The sanctuary's position would also have allowed it to have remained in use until the late temple sanctuary was completed, after which time the earlier building would have been pulled down, as happened at the temple of Opet at Karnak.

Gold of Praise: Studies on Ancient Egypt in Honor of Edward F. Wente
Edited by Emily Teeter and John A. Larson
Studies in Ancient Oriental Civilization 58
Chicago: Oriental Institute, 1999

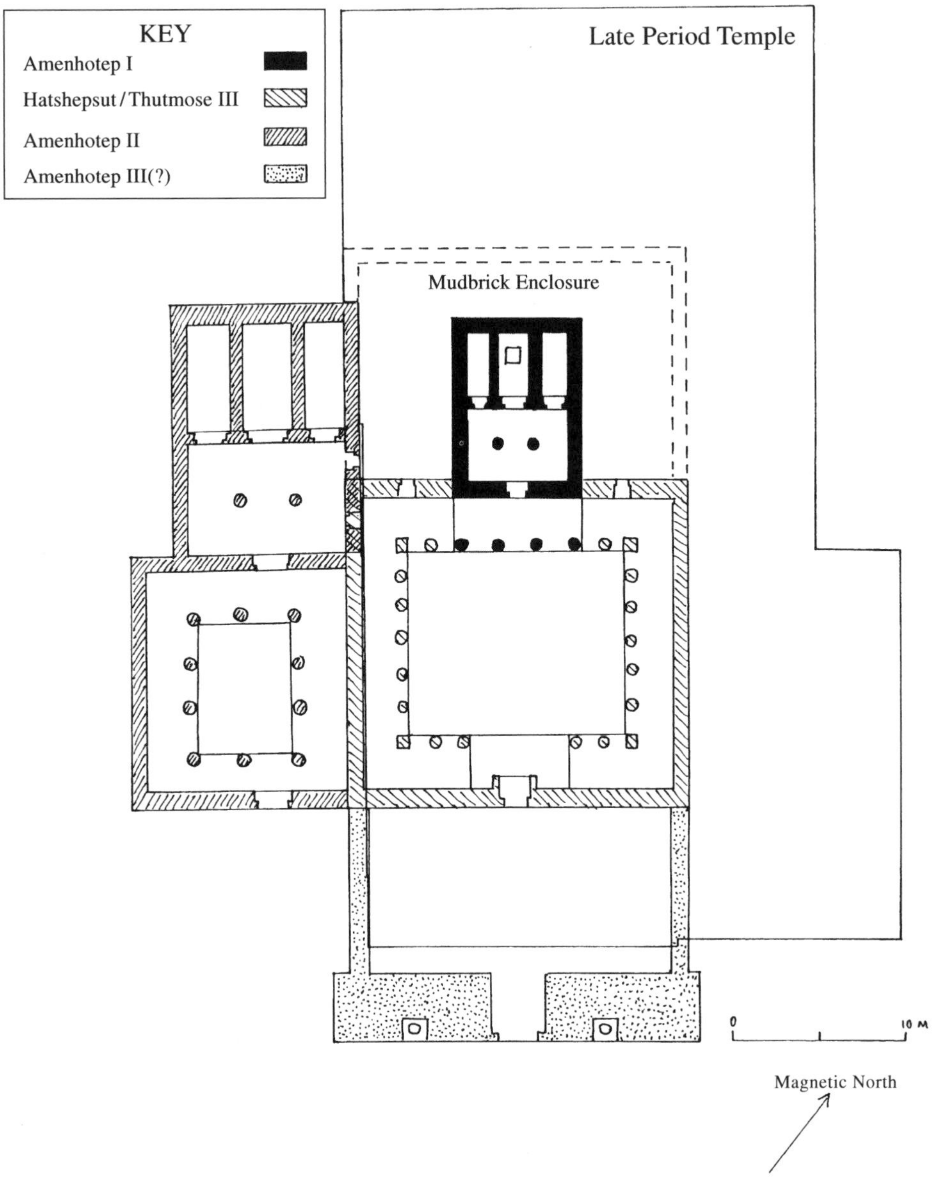

Figure 39.1. Growth of Temples of Elkab during the Eighteenth Dynasty

this period: a small obelisk of Thutmose III now divided between Brussels and Moscow, and a naos of Thutmose III now in Cambridge. This latter is of a size that it could have once stood within the *st-wrt* of the goddess.

The next stage in the development of the complex was the construction of a parallel temple by Amenhotep II. Its northern and southern walls were identified by foundation deposits naming the king and the goddess Nekhbet, and its form mimics that of the earlier temple to the east. There are three parallel chambers at the back, the central one once having had a depiction of the bark of Nekhbet and texts mentioning Amenhotep II. These chambers were fronted by a room with two columns. In its east wall were two doorways. One presumably opened onto the truncated mudbrick enclosure and the other to the court of Thutmose III. The Amenhotep II sanctuary was fronted by an open court with polygonal pillars. Its east wall reused the adjacent Thutmoside wall, and the latter's existence caused the plan of the court to be offset to the west. The function of this structure is unclear. It may be a temple for the consort of Nekhbet,[2] or it may be a spacious bark chapel for Nekhbet that is lacking in the temple proper to the east.

The next stage of the temple, which seems not to have been finished, is represented by three large pieces of granite for a doorway and perhaps two flag masts. Since the stones predate the Ramesside structures, I would suggest that they were a part of a new pylon for the temple, perhaps started late in the reign of Amenhotep III and aborted during the Amarna period.

2. At Buhen, Amenhotep II built a temple for Isis as consort of Horus, and he might have done so at Aniba as well.

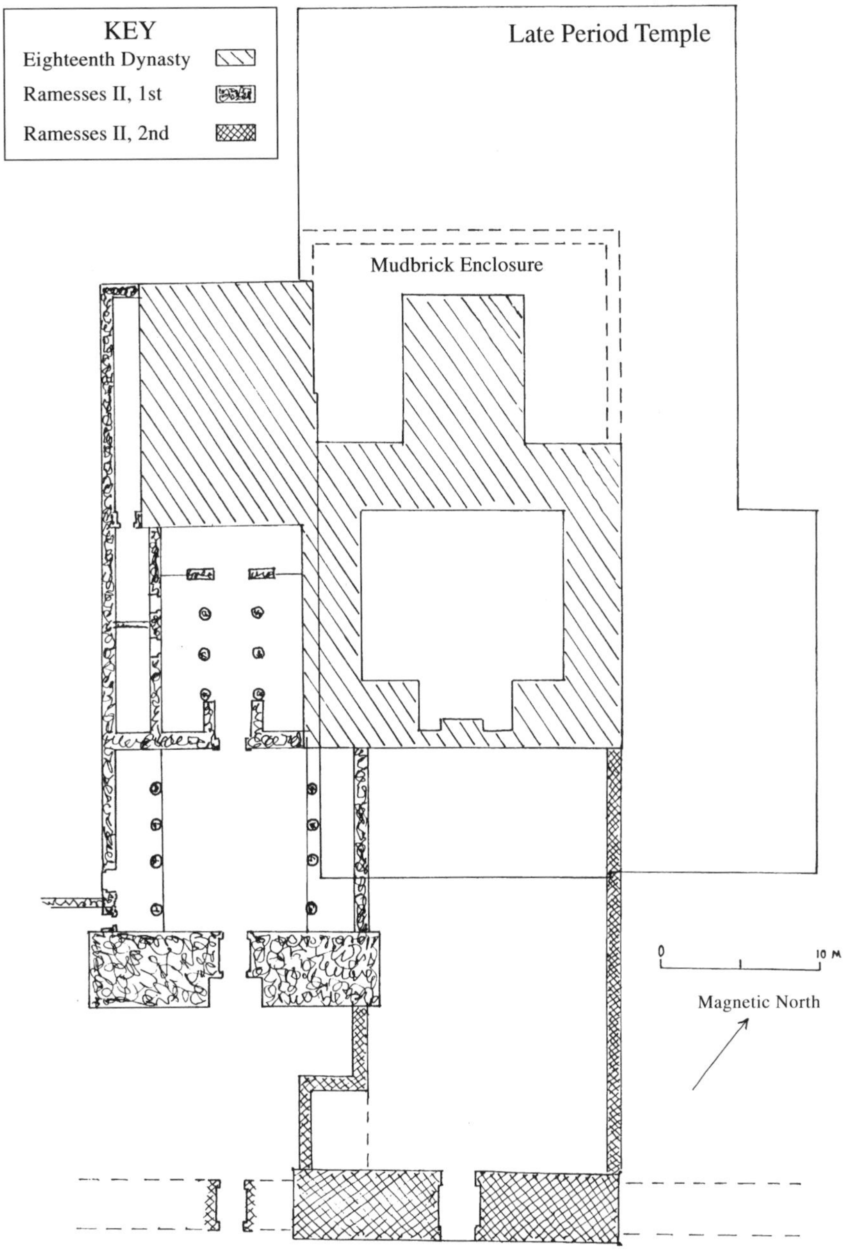

Figure 39.2. Temples of Elkab during the Ramesside Period

After the Amarna period, repairs were made to the temple reliefs. There is no evidence of immediate significant construction. It was only in the reign of Ramesses II that major changes took place (fig. 39.2). The earlier work involved the temple of Amenhotep II that was reconstructed so as to give it a more regular plan. A pylon and courtyard were added to its southern end, and the old open court was converted into a narrow, covered hall with rooms to the west. Later, but probably also in the reign of Ramesses II, a pylon was built on the axis of the main temple and on the line of the inner temple enclosure wall to provide a more fitting entry to the residence of Nekhbet. It is unclear whether or not the space between this pylon and the Thutmoside court was enclosed by walls; however, if so, the resultant plan would have been most inharmonious.[3]

This, then, is the development of the temples at Elkab during the Eighteenth and Nineteenth dynasties. With the addition of what seems to be an Ethiopian porch to the Ramesside pylon of the main temple, this was the structure that existed until the Late Period, when the great temple was partly dismantled and a new and grander temple to Nekhbet was constructed.

3. This situation is similar to that of the Third Pylon at Karnak as it connects to the Fourth Pylon on the north.

40

MENSTRUAL SYNCHRONY AND THE "PLACE OF WOMEN" IN ANCIENT EGYPT (OIM 13512)

TERRY G. WILFONG

University of Michigan, Ann Arbor

It is a great pleasure to pay tribute to Edward F. Wente in the present volume. Professor Wente was my teacher for many courses in Egyptology and a member of my dissertation committee. To him I owe many of the challenging experiences of my academic career; particularly memorable for me were a course in the cryptographic texts from the New Kingdom royal tombs and a comprehensive Coptic exam consisting (in part) of a box of unpublished and unedited Coptic ostraca. Professor Wente's generosity to his students is well known; he would often suggest potential research topics to students and then give them the benefit of his notes on the subject and his expertise. The present article is the result of one such suggestion: Professor Wente introduced me to the ostracon OIM 13512 and gave me his work on the text.[1] It is with some trepidation that I hand this text back to him in the form of an article for his festschrift since much of the basis for this article rests on his original reading of the text. The transcription of the text remains largely that of Professor Wente, although an examination of the original permitted a few refinements. However, the translation and interpretation of this text have become my own as a result of further research. I must thank Professor Wente for ceding his publication rights to me, and hope that he will find it a fitting return for his kindness and generosity. I can think of no more appropriate tribute to him than to publish a New Kingdom text that presents new problems in the social history of Ramesside Egypt. OIM 13512 not only attests to the existence of a special "place of women," but also provides us with an attestation of a group of ancient Egyptian women with synchronized menstrual cycles and a pretext for a more general discussion of menstruation in ancient Egypt.

Ostracon OIM 13512 is a piece of white limestone (discolored to greenish gray) of about 13.2 × 9.1 cm in size, acquired by purchase in Egypt along with a large group of ostraca in various scripts during the excavation of Medinet Habu by the Oriental Institute (see fig. 40.1).[2] The piece is inscribed with three lines in hieratic: both the beginning and end of the text are present, but there are small losses at the end of the first line and beginning of the second line, an uncertain amount lost at the end of the second line, and over half of the last line is broken off. The contents, style, and circumstances of acquisition lead to the conclusion that this ostracon comes from the site of Deir el-Medina or nearby. The ostracon contains a dated record of a single event; despite the short gaps in the text, its transcription and translation are fairly straightforward.

1. I would like to thank Dr. Karen Wilson, Oriental Institute Museum Curator, and Professor William M. Sumner, former Oriental Institute Director, for permission to publish ostracon OIM 13512. I am especially pleased to acknowledge the efforts of Dr. Raymond Tindel, Oriental Institute Museum Registrar, who, in the midst of major renovations, kindly arranged to keep this ostracon accessible and available for me to study on short notice. The photograph in fig. 40.1a is published courtesy of the Oriental Institute of the University of Chicago. I have greatly benefited from the insight and encouragement of the following: Ann Ellis Hanson, Remko Jas, Charles Jones, Lynn Meskell, Dominic Montserrat, Janet Richards, Jennifer Sheridan, Lauren Talalay, Emily Teeter, and, of course, Edward F. Wente.
2. Coptic ostracon OIM 19355, published in Wilfong 1992, p. 89, is from this same purchase.

Gold of Praise: Studies on Ancient Egypt in Honor of Edward F. Wente
Edited by Emily Teeter and John A. Larson
Studies in Ancient Oriental Civilization 58
Chicago: Oriental Institute, 1999

a

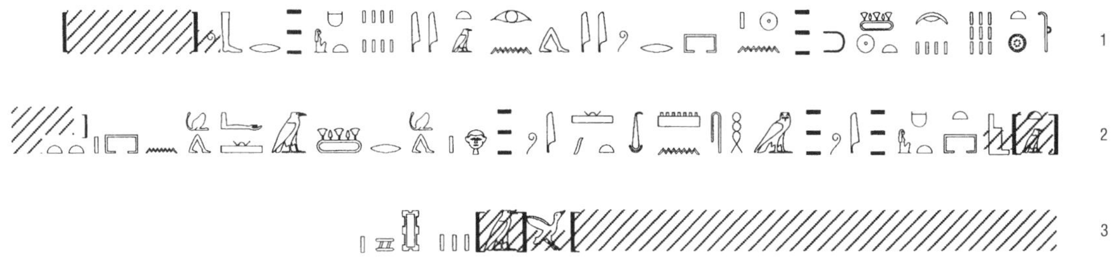

b

Figure 40.1. (*a*) Photograph and (*b*) Transcription of Hieratic Ostracon OIM 13512.
Photograph Courtesy of Oriental Institute Museum, University of Chicago

HIERATIC OSTRACON OIM 13512

Transcription and Translation

1. *Ḥꜣt-sp 9 4 ꜣḫt 13 hrw n pry ỉr.n tꜣy 8 ḥm.wt r-b*[*nr r/m*]
2. [*tꜣ*] *s.t ḥm.wt ỉw.w m ḥsmn.t ỉw.w ḥr pḥ r-šꜣꜥ pḥ*(*wy*) *n pr* [*n*]*tt* [...]
3. [...] *pꜣ 3 ỉnb*

1. Year 9, fourth month of the season of Inundation, day 13:[a] The day when these eight women came out [to/from[b]
2. the] place[c] of women while they were menstruating.[d] They got as far as the rear[e] of the house which[f] [...
3. ...] the three[g] walls.[h]

Notes

[a] Based on the palaeography, grammar, and other factors discussed below, year 9 of Merneptah seems most likely. Ramesses III is possible (the presence of *ḥr* in a pseudo-verbal construction is possible for the early

reign of Ramesses III, although largely absent by the end of his reign; see Groll 1982, p. 90) and Ramesses II unlikely with this handwriting. This would place the date of our text, following the chronology of Demarée and Janssen (1982, pp. xi–xii), at around 1204 B.C. (Merneptah) or 1173 B.C. (Ramesses III). IV *ꜣḫt* 13 would fall around late September-early October during this period.

[b] *r-b[nr r]* or *r-b[nr m]* are both possible; perhaps the former is more likely given the apparent nature of the "place of women" (see the discussion below).

[c] Top of *st*-sign is visible on the original; other alternatives (like *hw.t*) are not possible with the traces.

[d] *ḥsmn* determined with bookroll in reference to menstruation is attested in abbreviated writings in Deir el-Medina ostraca (for example, O. Cairo 25784, 17); *ḥsmn* with bookroll above *t* and stroke is otherwise unparalleled, but clear in the original; the stroke more closely resembles the diagonal stroke for abbreviating a complex character than an upright stroke (Möller 559 versus 558), in which case it would be an abbreviation for the spewing lips determinative more commonly found in *ḥsmn*. The later texts that refer to the interdiction of menstruating women in a religious context (see below) all use *ḥsmn.t* "menstruating woman."

[e] See Janssen 1982, p. 136, for *ḥr pḥwy n,* a structure, although a wall and not a house as in the present text.

[f] Two *t*-signs are clear in the original. Given the space above the *t*-signs, *ntt* for *nty* is more likely than *r-ntt.*

[g] Top of *pꜣ* sign is visible on the original; most of numeral 3 is clear.

[h] Only *ỉnb*/*ỉnb.t* is found preceded by numbers; otherwise *sbty*, as in Janssen 1982, p. 136, would be possible.

DISCUSSION

The basic sense of the text is clear: Eight women who were menstruating came out of the village on their way to or from a location called the "place of women." Something (lost in the lacuna) happened on the way after they had reached the rear of a house; the event appears to have had something to do with another place known literally as "the three walls." Despite its brevity, ostracon OIM 13512 raises a number of interesting points relevant to the lives of women in pharaonic Egypt.

Before dealing with aspects of the text that are unique, it is useful to examine the parts of the text that are paralleled. Dated records of events on ostraca from Deir el-Medina and environs are common and most were probably compiled at some later time into the well-known "journals" from that community.[3] The outlines and language of the event in the text — people coming out of the settlement and reaching a place — are paralleled elsewhere, using the same verbs *prỉ* and *pḥ*. References to "walls" are common in Deir el-Medina texts, most often in reference to guard posts rather than literal walls, and the activities of women are commonly recorded. A text that combines these elements, unfortunately fragmentary, is an entry in ostracon Cairo 25831:

> (recto 7) Further: A daughter of a widow came out in year 1, second month of the season of Inundation, day 20, she being [... (8) ...] Pharaoh gave to the captains [...] (9) together with the guardian. (verso 1) And she reached the wall [...] (2) May m[y lord] act so as to cause his agents to come [...] (3) hear her testimony.[4]

The vocabulary and phrasing are similar to those used in OIM 13512. O. Cairo 25831 has been interpreted as the report of a crime or disturbance caused by the daughter of a widow, who came and reached the wall, possibly a place she was not supposed to be (Ventura 1986, p. 141; McDowell 1990, pp. 205–06, 213). Given the great similarities to OIM 13512, though, it seems more likely that this was the report of something that happened *to* the widow's daughter on her way to or from a location in relation to one of the "walls" near Deir el-Medina. In the examples cited by Ventura (1986, pp. 121–25), this is the only text in which women are de-

3. See, for example, Valbelle 1985, pp. 47–49; Janssen 1992, p. 85. Although such ostraca sometimes record events over a longer period of time (such as the lengthy O. BM 5634 discussed below), Valbelle (1985, p. 48) notes that ostraca from the reign of Merneptah usually cover only a single day — perhaps slight additional support for the dating of OIM 13512 to year 9 of Merneptah.

4. Ostracon Cairo 25831 was published in Černý 1935, p. 119*; translation is adapted from McDowell 1990, pp. 205–06; the text is dated to a year 1 not later than the reign of Ramesses III (Ventura 1986, p. 135, n. 83), and so not far in date from OIM 13512.

scribed in relation to "walls"; most of the other examples come from the Turin Strike Papyrus and describe the actions of workmen. Given the similar actions of women in relation to "walls" in OIM 13512, the widow's daughter in O. Cairo 25831 could even be on her way to or from the "place of women."[5] The mention of locations known as the "place of women" and the "three walls" in OIM 13512, however, are otherwise unparalleled; the explicit description of a group of women menstruating at the same time is also unique.

It is this description of eight women menstruating that requires examination first. The phrase used to indicate this is *ỉw.w m ḥsmn.t* "they being *m ḥsmn.t*." *Ḥsmn* is the term traditionally associated with menstruation in Egyptian, known with this meaning from the Middle Kingdom and surviving into Demotic. *Ḥsmn.t* is usually taken as "menstruating woman";[6] thus the literal translation of the phrase in OIM 13512 would be "they being as menstruating women." The writing of *ḥsmn* usually taken to refer to menstruation is determined with the mortar and pestle ([hieroglyph]) and is also usually determined with the spewing lips ([hieroglyph]).[7] Less frequently, as in OIM 13512, *ḥsmn* for menstruation is determined with a bookroll ([hieroglyph]).[8] Shorter writings of *ḥsmn* for menstruation consist of the determinatives in various combinations.[9] So determined, these writings of *ḥsmn* are most frequently found in the prepositional phrase *m ḥsmn* or as clause subjects, most often followed by a possessive suffix pronoun *ḥsmn.s*. Enough of the sources are clear on the meaning of these examples of *ḥsmn* to leave little doubt of the translation "menstruation." Specific examples are discussed below; the most unambiguous sources are the medical texts that refer to a woman's *ḥsmn* not coming and to the blood of a woman whose *ḥsmn* has come. Less explicit are instances of workmen being absent because of the *ḥsmn* of a wife or daughter and a reference to the loincloth of a woman *m ḥsmn* in the Middle Kingdom Instruction of Khety. During the Late Period, there are references to the *ḥsmn.t* as the interdiction (*bw.t*) of particular gods in particular districts. Demotic legal texts refer to a woman's *ḥsmn* taking place in a special part of the house, while in the first story of Setna Khamwas, Ahwere (in reference to her discovery of her pregnancy) states: "When my time of menstruation arrived, I did not menstruate."[10] Although earlier Egyptologists sometimes conflated these instances of *ḥsmn* with *ḥsmn* "natron" or "purify," by the time of the compilation of the *Wörterbuch der ägyptischen Sprache,* the writings of *ḥsmn* and *ḥsmn.t* with the special determinatives had been identified as "menstruation."[11]

Still, many translators render these examples of *ḥsmn* as "purification" rather than "menstruation," even in cases where the latter is obviously more appropriate. The closeness of the *ḥsmn* for "menstruation" and the *ḥsmn* for "natron" and "purification" is usually cited as the reason, although there is the distinct possibility that "purification" becomes the Egyptological addition to a long line of euphemisms for menstruation. Indeed, it has been suggested that this usage of "purification" for "menstruation" was an ancient Egyptian euphemism, although it could also be understood as evidence of the Egyptian understanding of the function of menstruation

5. If so, the lacuna at the end of line 8 of O. Cairo 25831 would fit (and be an appropriate position for) the circumstantial statement "while she was [menstruating]" (*ỉw.s [m ḥsmn.t]*), as found in OIM 13512.

6. See *Wb.* 3.163:10; mostly late examples referring to interdictions of gods or districts, written variously [hieroglyph] and [hieroglyph], for which see discussion below.

7. As in [hieroglyph] (Papyrus Edwin Smith 20.13) — this and the following examples are discussed below, where full text information is provided.

8. As in OIM 13512 ([hieroglyph]), for which, see the philological commentary above. More problematic are a few writings that incorporate other determinatives. All published manuscripts of the Instruction of Khety give a writing [hieroglyph], which seems to refer to menstruation; see comments below. There appears to be at least one instance of *ḥsmn* determined with pellet and plural strokes — the usual writing for "natron" or "purification" — for "menstruation": [hieroglyph] in O. Deir el-Medina 230.3, noted in Janssen 1980, p. 141, n. 63, apparently cited as an instance of "purification." The text is a list of festival provisions from the reign of Ramesses II; the relevant line reads: ...] *pꜣ ỉy m ḥsmn n sꜣ.t.f Nfrw*, followed by [hieroglyph] in red, "The coming in menstruation of his daughter Nefru"(?). Unfortunately, the broken context makes the line obscure.

9. [hieroglyph] in *HO* 64.1 recto 7, verso 7; *HO* 84, 9; O. Gardiner 167, 8 (KRI 7, p. 242.9, noted Janssen 1980, p. 141, n. 62); O. Gardiner "pl. 30 Arbeiterlist 7 (110)" (unpublished, noted in *Wb. Belegstellen* 3.48); [hieroglyph] as in Papyrus Ebers 808, 832b, 833a; [hieroglyph] in O. Cairo 25784, 17 (rather than taking this as the more common abbreviation for *mn* "due," for which, see the references in Sturtewagen 1990, pp. 936–37); or just [hieroglyph] (as in *HO* 83, 4.7.9; *HO* 84, 3.4.7.9.17) or [hieroglyph] (as in O. Cairo 25782 verso 18–23; O. Turin 57388 recto 4). The latter two instances of the use of [hieroglyph] alone for *ḥsmn* in the sense of "menstruation" are unambiguous; other cases of [hieroglyph] alone are less clear and not included.

10. The full quotation is: *ḫpr pꜣy.y ss n ỉr ḥsmn, bwpw.y jr ḥsmn ʿn* (Demotic Papyrus Cairo 30646 3:7, for which, see Spiegelberg 1908, p. 88, pl. 44; with a *Normalschrift* copy and transcription in Erichsen 1937, p. 3). Lichtheim (1980, p. 128) is somewhat euphemistic, translating "When my time of purification came, I made no more purification," with a subsequent note saying "I.e., her menstruation period had failed to come" (ibid., p. 137).

11. *Wb.* 3.163; so too in von Deines and Westendorf 1962, p. 635; Faulkner 1962, p. 178. Writings of *ḥsmn* determined with spewing lips from Late Egyptian texts are not included in Lesko 1984.

(see *LÄ* 6 "Tabu," col. 138, for both possibilities). However, the exclusivity of *ḥsmn* with appropriate determinatives for cases in which "menstruation" is clearly meant indicates that the Egyptians saw these writings of *ḥsmn* as having a specific meaning. Thus, the translation "menstruation" in cases where this is appropriate reflects a distinction often made, at least in writing, by the Egyptians themselves.

In 1980, Jac. J. Janssen proposed a different meaning for some examples of the writing of *ḥsmn* usually associated with menstruation. In his study on records of absence from work at Deir el-Medina, Janssen (1980, pp. 141–43) looks at the instances in which workmen were absent for their wives' and daughters' *ḥsmn* and interprets this term as a post-childbirth purification. A number of other uses of *ḥsmn* were also included in this category. This alternative understanding of *ḥsmn* seems to have been widely accepted.[12] Janssen's main argument against taking such cases of *ḥsmn* as menstruation centers on the records of absence themselves; the study concentrated on O. British Museum 5634 (= *HO* 83–84, hereinafter O. BM 5634), a lengthy roster of absences by individual workers in year 40 of Ramesses II that lists dates and reasons for absence. In nine cases, the absence of a worker is ascribed to the *ḥsmn* of his wife or daughter (summarized in table 40.1). Absences from work due to a female relative's *ḥsmn* are infrequent compared with other reasons; in only one case in O. BM 5634 is a man absent more than once for the same woman's *ḥsmn* (O. BM 5634 verso 9) and in only one case is a man absent for the *ḥsmn* of more than one female relative (O. BM 5634 verso 4). Janssen feels that absences due to *ḥsmn* of a wife or daughter were too infrequent and irregular for *ḥsmn* to be menstruation; given the relative scarcity of absences due to childbirth, he considers that these cases of *ḥsmn* were purification after childbirth (Janssen 1980, p. 141).

There is a considerable amount of evidence for some sort of purification of women after childbirth (see Pinch 1993, pp. 219–21). The most explicit textual allusion to a post-childbirth purification comes from Papyrus Westcar 11.18–19: *ʿḥʿ.n Rwḏd.t wʿb.n.s m wʿbn hrw 15* "Rudjedet purified herself in a cleansing of fifteen days" (Blackman 1988, p. 15). But the word used for Rudjedet's postpartum purification is *wʿb*, not *ḥsmn*, which is not used at all in this context. A probable New Kingdom instance of this sort of purification after childbirth is in a list of supplies for festivals from Deir el-Medina (O. Michaelides 48 recto), where one of the festivals is called *pꜣ swʿb n tꜣy.f šr*[*ỉ.t*] "the purification (*swʿb*) of his daughter" (Goedicke and Wente 1962, pl. 71).[13] In this case, too, however, the word *ḥsmn* does not appear. Thus there is no evidence in these examples to support the contention that *ḥsmn* in these texts is a purification after childbirth.

The occurrences of *ḥsmn* in Egyptian medical texts are also noted by Janssen (1980); however, the Egyptian medical evidence actually presents a compelling case for translating the term as "menstruation." Four certain instances of this word are found in the standard medical texts.[14] Papyrus Edwin Smith 20.13 begins: *ỉr ẖꜣ.k s.t ḥr mn rꜣ jb.s n ỉỉ.n n.s* <<*m*>> *ḥsmn* … "If you examine a woman with pain in her stomach and her menstrual period does not come … ," literally "menstruation does not come for her … " (Grapow 1958, p. 466).[15] This text is apparently a reference to a case of amenorrhea, a loss of menstrual periods. Amenorrhea can be brought on by a number of factors; modern medical literature cites stress and intense physical activity as major factors in inducing amenorrhea (Golub 1992, pp. 70–78), the latter having been recognized as a cause of amenorrhea as early as the second century by the medical writer Soranus (Hanson 1990, pp. 320–21). Papyrus Ebers 832 refers to an irregularity of menstrual period, which can be caused by a number of factors: *ỉr ẖꜣ.k s.t mn.s wꜣ.t wʿ.t nt kns.s, ḏd.ḫr.k r.s: tm mꜣʿ.w.s pw ỉn ḥsmn.s* "If you examine a woman who experiences pain in one side of her vulva, you should say concerning her: It is an irregularity of her menstrual period" (Grapow 1958, p. 465). Papyrus Ebers 833 describes a woman whose menstrual periods have ceased because of age: *ỉr ẖꜣ.k s.t ỉṯ.n.s rnp.wt ʿšꜣ.w, n ỉỉ.n n.s ḥsmn.s* "If you examine a woman who is many years old and her menstrual period

12. Robins (1993, pp. 78–79), for example, comments on the general lack of sources for menstruation and seems tacitly to accept Janssen's interpretation. In Janssen and Janssen 1990, p. 3, the reference in the story of Setna I seems to be taken as indication of a purification after menstruation, though. Janssen (1997, pp. 87–98) has recently discussed the terminology for workmen's absences in these texts but does not elaborate on the interpretation of *ḥsmn*.

13. See the discussion in Montserrat 1991, p. 47, n. 16.

14. Cited from Grapow 1958. The fifth example in von Deines and Westendorf 1962, p. 635, from P. Ramesseum IV D iii 3 (not IV D 3 as cited), is determined with a pellet for "natron," as already noted by the original editor of the text (Barns 1956, p. 39). Von Deines and Westendorf translate this example as "Reinigung(?)," but include it in the same entry as *ḥsmn* for "menstruation." It is from this latter example that Janssen (1980) seems to conclude that the other cases of *ḥsmn* in the same entry, although determined with spewing lips, mean "purification" after childbirth.

15. The *m* before *ḥsmn* is a mistaken writing for the more common phrase.

does not come ..." (Grapow 1958, p. 466), i.e., a woman who has reached menopause and has ceased to menstruate. Finally, in Papyrus Ebers 808 there is a prescription for a woman's breasts: "moisten(?) them" *m snf n jw ḥsmn.s m tp* <<*m tp*>> *ỉrf* "with the blood of one whose menstruation has already come" (Grapow 1958, p. 491).[16] In none of these examples could "purification (after pregnancy)" be used as an acceptable translation for *ḥsmn*. These texts are instructive in that they (or the first three, at any rate) show that the Egyptians had an understanding of the length and predictability of the menstrual cycle and the cessation of menstruation through age. These examples conclusively point to "menstruation" as an acceptable and appropriate translation for *ḥsmn*.[17]

The evidence of the lists of workmen's absences for female relatives' *ḥsmn* also goes against the interpretation of *ḥsmn* as a post-childbirth purification. The argument that the absences are too infrequent for menstruation would be true only if workmen were absent every time their wives and daughters had their periods (which is very unlikely since it would have resulted in at least one absence per month per female relative). It makes much more sense to conclude that absence for *ḥsmn* was only permitted under certain conditions. Other cases of absence from work are for events that would have disrupted the functioning of the household (Valbelle 1985, pp. 285, 303). Thus, the Deir el-Medina workmen would have been absent from work for a female relative's menstruation only on such occasions when their wives and/or daughters were in some way absent from home or unable to do necessary work in the house. The events in OIM 13512 suggest one possibility: if menstruating wives and daughters had to go to the "place of women," this might require the presence of the husband and/or father at home. Another possibility is that the presence of the male relatives was required when the women were incapacitated by exceptional pain experienced during their menstrual periods, a condition known as dysmenorrhea. Surveys of modern populations have shown that a majority of women have some sort of physical discomfort during menstruation, while about 50% experience more severe symptoms and 5–10% "experience pain severe enough to be incapacitating for an hour to three days of each month" (Golub 1992, p. 158).[18] Estimates are not available for pre-modern populations, but conditions are likely only to have been worse. Assuming an average of one wife and one daughter per each of the 40 workmen in the absence roster and given the nine women's *ḥsmn* cited as the reason for absence, this would show just over 11% of the women as suffering from incapacitating menstrual pains. More female relatives per worker would lower the percentage of women experiencing dysmenorrhea to the levels of modern populations. Dysmenorrhea occurs with the greatest frequency in modern populations between the ages of 15 and 22, and with older women who have not experienced pregnancy (Golub 1992, pp. 159–61), possible categories for the daughters and wives of the Deir el-Medina workmen.

One woman (Simut's wife) in the O. BM 5634 absence roster is listed twice as a reason for her husband's absence, the individual occurrences happening on I *prt* 25 and IV *prt* 23, some 88 days apart. Janssen suggested this was a purification after a childbirth, followed by purification after a miscarriage on the second date (Janssen 1980, pp. 142–43). Purification after a miscarriage is unattested elsewhere in Egyptian evidence and the relatively short time elapsed makes this explanation unlikely. If the listed occurrences of Simut's *ḥsmn* are plotted on a calendar for year 40, however, the justification for translating *ḥsmn* as "menstruation" becomes completely secure: Simut's wife's *ḥsmn* on IV *prt* 23 falls exactly where one would expect her menstrual period in that month (fig. 40.2, column 5). Menstrual cycle length is normally cited as "about 28 days," but an average of 27–30 days is perhaps more realistic; in studies on modern populations, the arithmetic average tends to be 29.1 days, but drops to 28.1 days when exceptional irregularities are omitted from the sample (Golub 1992, p.

16. The second *m tp* is noted with "sic." Raven (1983, p. 10) notes the use of menstrual blood or urine as a magical ingredient for defiling a wax figure in Papyrus Bremner-Rhind (although the text appears to refer only to urine).

17. Other Egyptian medical texts appear to relate to menstruation but are less specific in their terminology. In particular, note Papyrus Ebers 828–830 (Grapow 1958, p. 481) for inducing bleeding, apparently menstrual; Riddle (1992, pp. 71–72) takes these as emmenagogues used as abortifacients. See also Papyrus BM 10059, cases 40–42 (Grapow 1958, pp. 482–83, 41–42; translated in Borghouts 1978, p. 24), for controlling women's blood flow; these are spells to be recited over knotted cloths placed inside the woman's vagina.

18. Note that this discussion is concerned with the physically incapacitating effects of dysmenorrhea, not the specious argument that menstruation itself renders women incapable of certain kinds of work. As should be clear from the discussion below, it appears that the Egyptians, at least in the pharaonic period, had a relatively realistic understanding of menstruation; this is in contrast to the post-Hippocratic Greek medical writers who considered menstruation to be an undesirable thing for women (Hanson 1990, pp. 320–22). For a discussion of the impact of misperceptions of the impact of menstruation on women, see the discussion in Cayleff 1992.

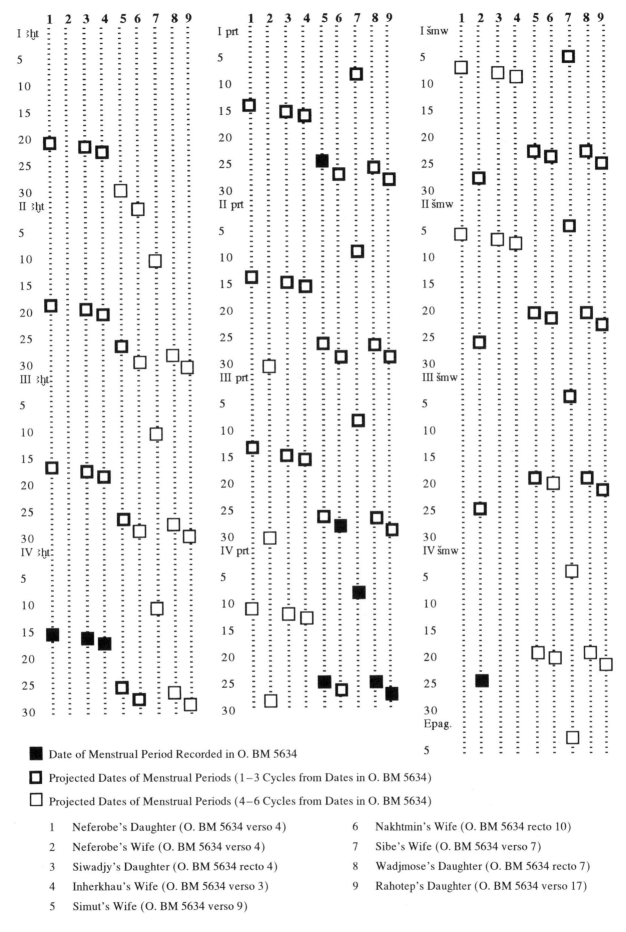

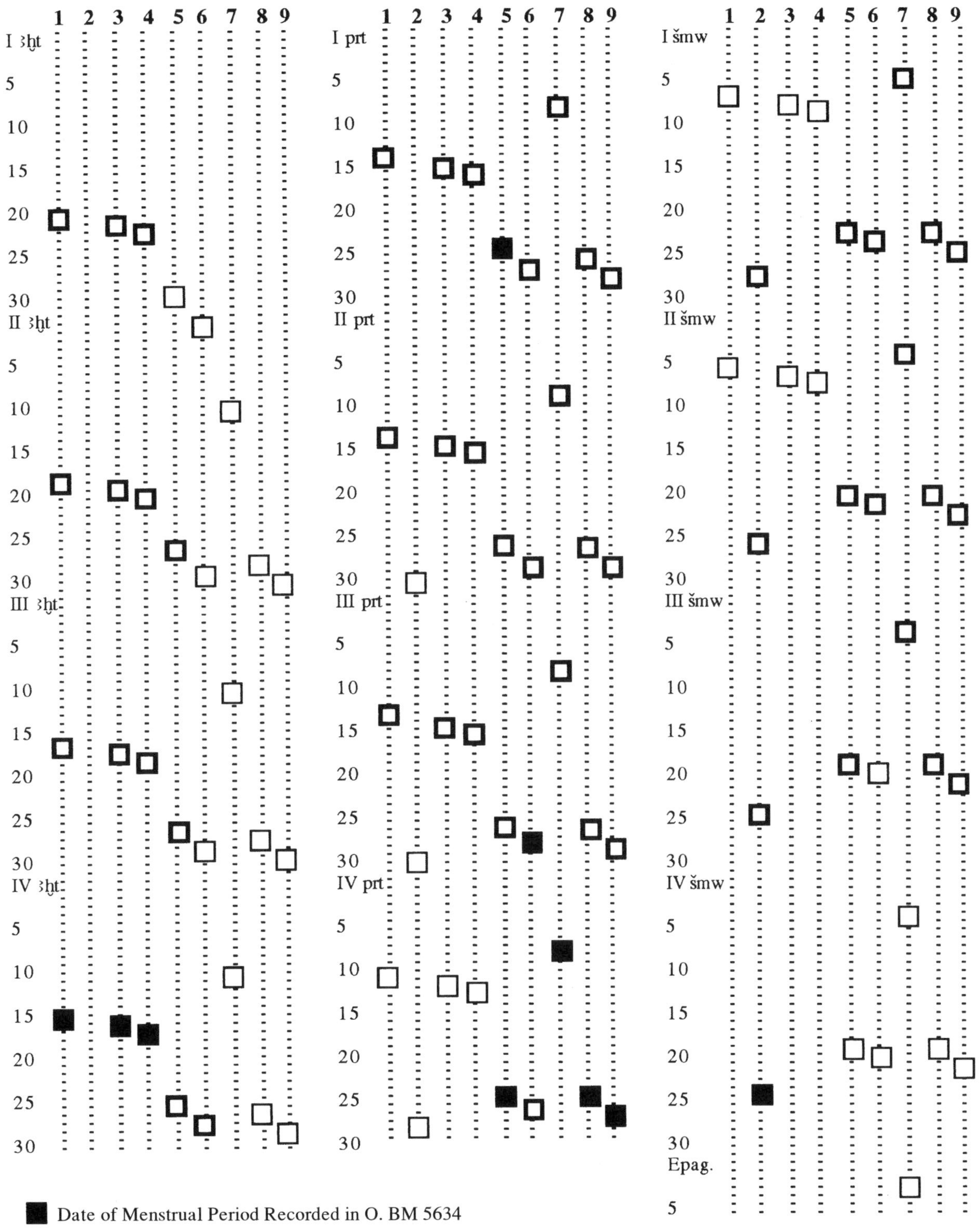

■ Date of Menstrual Period Recorded in O. BM 5634

◘ Projected Dates of Menstrual Periods (1–3 Cycles from Dates in O. BM 5634)

□ Projected Dates of Menstrual Periods (4–6 Cycles from Dates in O. BM 5634)

1 Neferobe's Daughter (O. BM 5634 verso 4)
2 Neferobe's Wife (O. BM 5634 verso 4)
3 Siwadjy's Daughter (O. BM 5634 recto 4)
4 Inherkhau's Wife (O. BM 5634 verso 3)
5 Simut's Wife (O. BM 5634 verso 9)
6 Nakhtmin's Wife (O. BM 5634 recto 10)
7 Sibe's Wife (O. BM 5634 verso 7)
8 Wadjmose's Daughter (O. BM 5634 recto 7)
9 Rahotep's Daughter (O. BM 5634 verso 17)

Figure 40.2. Dates of Women's Menstrual Periods (Recorded and Estimated) in Year 40 of Ramesses II from Ostracon BM 5634 (*HO* 83–84)

136). Between I *prt* 25 and IV *prt* 23, Simut's wife would have experienced three menstrual cycles, with an arithmetic average length of 29.33 days. Since this is the only instance from Egyptian documentation in which an average cycle length can be calculated in this manner, there is no way to tell how typical this would be for other women at Deir el-Medina. There are many factors that affect the length of a menstrual cycle, but the most important of these is age: a woman's cycle tends to get progressively longer after age thirty in modern populations (Golub 1992, pp. 137–38, fig. 6.1). Thus, the average of Simut's wife's cycles being slightly longer than the modern average need not imply any great difference in cycle length among the women at Deir el-Medina.[19]

O. BM 5634 is not unique in its records of the absence of workmen because of a female relative's menstruation. Such records are also found in briefer absence lists from the latter half of the Nineteenth Dynasty: O. Metropolitan Museum of Art 14.6.217 (*HO* 64.1, year 1 of Seti II), O. Cairo 25782 (Černý 1935, p. 103*–104*, year 3 of Amenmesse), O. Cairo 25784 (Černý 1935, p. 109*, year 4 of Amenmesse), O. Turin N. 57388 (Lopez 1982, pl. 125, Siptah-Twosret), O. Gardiner 167 (KRI 7, 242, Amenmesse), and the unpublished O. Gardiner quoted in the *Wb. Belegstellen* 3.48, for which no date is given (see table 40.1). These records are concerned primarily with the names of the workmen absent, the date and only secondarily the reason for the absence. As such, they do not discuss the women who are menstruating in any detail; in some cases (the examples in O. Cairo 25782 and 25784) the relationship of the man to the woman is not even mentioned, and even in the more extensive records the women are never named. In none of these instances is the information recorded for the woman's sake.[20] OIM 13512 contains a little more information about the women themselves because it was a record about the women's activities and not those of their male relatives. Whatever the precise reason for recording the trip of these women to the "place of women," the scribe saw fit to note that they were all menstruating at the time they went. As such, OIM 13512 is unique in its explicit description of a group of women menstruating at the same time — a rare ancient account of menstrual synchrony.

However, the absence roster O. BM 5634 does record such information implicitly and provides another attestation of menstrual synchrony among the wives and daughters of the Deir el-Medina workmen. Two groups of three women each are recorded as having had their periods near the same day: Siwadjy's daughter, Inherkhau's wife, and Neferobe's daughter at IV *ꜣḫt* 15–17 and Simut's wife, Rahotep's daughter, and Wadjmose's daughter at IV *prt* 23–25.[21] While this is striking, O. BM 5634 contains even more extensive evidence of menstrual synchrony. By plotting the attested instances of menstruation onto a calendar for year 40 and then calculating the probable succeeding and preceding dates of menstruation for each woman and plotting them on a calendar, a greater pattern emerges.[22] The periods of four of the women (Simut's wife, Nakhtmin's wife, Wadjmose's daughter, and Rahotep's daughter) fall within a few days of each other over most of the year, while the other three (Neferobe's daughter, Siwadjy's daughter, and Inherkhau's wife) have secure synchrony in the earlier part of the year. Neferobe's wife has periods near the time of the first group of four women, while Sibe's wife is the only one of the group who seems not to have synchronized. If the cycles recorded in O. BM 5634 are projected ahead through calculation, a larger possible pattern emerges. The dates of menstruation recorded in OIM 13512 (IV *ꜣḫt* 13 in year 9 of Merneptah), O. Cairo 25782 (all between I *šmw* 24–26 in year 3 of Amenmesse), and O. Cairo 25784 (III *šmw* 29 in year 4 of Amenmesse) all fall within 3–7 days of the expected dates from one of the two synchronous cycles attested in O. BM 5634. While there is far too much potential for variation to be certain, it may be possible from this correlation that the Deir el-Medina records attest to some sort of menstrual synchrony continuing among its female population for over forty years.

The synchronization of these women's menstrual cycles is not a matter of chance but is a phenomenon that is medically well documented. Although long observed and known from anecdotal evidence as early as the

19. See Dean-Jones 1994, pp. 94–96, for the opinions of the Greek medical writers on the length of menstrual cycles.

20. Compare with the Ptolemaic Greek papyrus cited in Pomeroy 1984, pp. 170–71 (P. Berol. Inv. 17942 [not 1942 as cited] = *SB* X 10209 = *BGU* X 1942), a list of female textile workers in which some of the women are described as being "sick" (*arrôstôs*), apparently recording absence. Pomeroy suggests that these absences may be due, at least in part, to "the ready excuse of menstruation" (ibid.); the remainder of the women in the list are described as "spinning" or "preparing wool" and there is no direct mention of menstruation in the text. I owe this reference to Dominic Montserrat.

21. For the discussion that follows, reference should be made to fig. 40.2. Janssen (1980, p. 143) takes the coincidence of Wadjmose's daughter and Simut's wife being cited for IV *prt* 23 as an indication that they are the same person. He cites no other evidence for this, though, and it is preferable to take the text as it stands and see Wadjmose's daughter and Simut's wife as different people.

22. Calculations are based partly on probable menstrual cycle length from the case of Simut's wife (29.33 days), but allowance was made for differing period length and alternate dates set for periods of 28–30 days. In general, the syn-

Table 40.1. Records of Women's Menstruation from Deir el-Medina (in Chronological Order)

Date	*Reference*	*Identification*	*Citation*
Year 40, Ramesses II			
O. BM 5634			
IV *ꜣḫt* 15	*sꜣ.t m ḥsmn*	*(Nfr-ꜥb.t)*	*HO* 84, 4
IV *ꜣḫt* 16	*sꜣ.t⸗f ḥsmn*	*(Sꜣ-wꜣḏy)*	*HO* 83, 4
IV *ꜣḫt* 17	*ḥm.t⸗f ḥsmn*	*(Jn-ḥr-ḫꜥ.w)*	*HO* 84, 3
I *prt* 25	*ḥm.t⸗f ḥsmn*	*(Sꜣ-Mw.t)*	*HO* 84, 9
III *prt* 27	*ḥm.t⸗f ḥsmn*	*(Nḫt-Mn.w)*	*HO* 83, 10
IV *prt* 8	*ḥm.t⸗f ḥsmn*	*(Sbꜣ)*	*HO* 84, 7
IV *prt* 23	*sꜣ.t⸗f ḥsmn*	*(Wꜣḏ-ms)*	*HO* 83, 7
IV *prt* 23	*ḥm.t⸗f ḥsmn*	*(Sꜣ-Mw.t)*	*HO* 84, 9
IV *prt* 25	*sꜣ.t⸗f ḥsmn*	*(Rꜥ-ḥtpw)*	*HO* 84, 17
IV *šmw* 26	*ḥm.t⸗f ḥsmn*	*(Nfr-ꜥb.t)*	*HO* 84, 4
Year 9, Merneptah(?)			
OIM 13512			
IV *ꜣḫt* 13	*jw⸗w m ḥsmn*	*tꜣy 8 ḥm.wt*	OIM 13512, 1–2
Year 3, Amenmesse			
O. Cairo 25782			
I *šmw* 24	*ḥsmn*	*(Nfr-ḥtp)*	O. Cairo 25782 verso 18
I šmw 24	*ḥsmn*	*(Ḥwy)*	O. Cairo 25782 verso 18
I šmw 24	*ḥsmn*	*(Nḫw-m-Mw.t)*	O. Cairo 25782 verso 19
I šmw 24	*ḥsmn*	*(Nb-nḫt)*	O. Cairo 25782 verso 19
I šmw 25	*ḥsmn*	*(Nꜣḫy)*	O. Cairo 25782 verso 20
I šmw 25	*ḥsmn*	*(Qꜣḫꜣ)*	O. Cairo 25782 verso 21
I šmw 26	*ḥsmn*	*(Ḫꜣ-m-dwꜣ)*	O. Cairo 25782 verso 23
Year 4, Amenmesse			
O. Cairo 25784			
III *šmw* 29	*ḥsmn*	*(Nḫt-sw)*	O. Cairo 25784, 17
Year ?, Amenmesse			
O. Gardiner 167			
?	*tꜣy⸗f ḥm.t ḥsmn*	?	O. Gardiner 167, 8
Year 1, Seti II			
O. Metropolitan Museum of Art 14.6.217			
III *ꜣḫt* 15	*ḥm.t⸗f ḥsmn*	*(Nb-nḫt)*	*HO* 64.1 recto 7
[? day 18]	*sꜣ[.t⸗f] ḥsmn*	([...])	*HO* 64.1 verso 6–7
Year ?, Siptah-Twosret			
O. Turin 57388			
?	*jw tꜣy⸗f ḥm.t ḥsmn*	*(ꜣny)*	O. Turin 57388 recto 4
? Date, ?			
O. Gardiner "pl. 30 Arbeiterliste 7 (110)"			
?	*ḥm.t⸗f ḥsmn*	*(Pꜣ-ḥm-nṯr pꜣ-wr)*	*Wb. Belegstellen* 3.48

Greek medical writers,[23] menstrual synchrony among humans was first described in modern scientific terms by McClintock (1971) in an investigation into the menstrual cycles of a group of 135 female residents of a dormitory at a women's college. McClintock observed the increase in synchronization of the menstrual periods in this

chrony observed strongly suggests that the average period length fell between 28 and 29 days.

23. Dean-Jones (1994, pp. 97–101) notes that the Greek medical writers often treated menstrual synchrony as a by-product of natural forces such as the phases of the moon; Knight (1991, p. 213) points out that menstrual synchrony often goes unnoticed by men in a population.

population of women from the time they entered the dormitory in the fall to the end of the academic year. In this study, McClintock concluded that the most significant factor in menstrual synchrony was that women in a group spend time together; contact with males was seen as having a possible negative impact, while the possibility of maturational and seasonal factors were largely discounted. The possibility that awareness of menstrual cycles among friends might be another source of synchrony was also considered, but the relatively low awareness among the group studied by McClintock made this unlikely. Subsequent studies have developed and refined the initial work of McClintock, leading to the conclusion that menstrual synchrony is caused by the transmission of pheromones among women in groups and is influenced by the amount of time women spend together, the sharing of sanitary facilities, as well as the use of perfumes (Golub 1992, pp. 69–70; Graham and McGrew 1992).[24] Social factors have not been definitively ruled out as a factor, but the main conditions that seem to promote menstrual synchrony are proximity and sharing of facilities, with the use of perfumes and deodorants having an inhibitory impact.

Of these conditions for menstrual synchrony, physical proximity was the most important factor at Deir el-Medina. Although there is little direct textual evidence for the amount of time spent together by the women at Deir el-Medina, the physical realities of the site would have ensured a substantial amount of proximity. The closeness and crowded nature of Deir el-Medina have been commented on frequently and a visit to the site makes this even more apparent. The area of Deir el-Medina is estimated at 5,600 square meters, of which approximately 4,900 m^2 were dwellings (Valbelle 1985, 114–17). Estimates of the population of Deir el-Medina vary widely, 100–200 being common estimates for the Nineteenth Dynasty (L. Lesko 1994, p. 133; B. Lesko 1994, p. 25).[25] Whatever the precise population, the close quarters of the village itself would force a fairly substantial amount of proximity on the inhabitants.[26] The sharing of sanitary facilities is probable but undocumented; there is, on the whole, very little evidence for elimination, sanitation, and personal hygiene at Deir el-Medina (Valbelle 1985, p. 284), or at least very little that has been identified as such. The impact of perfumes as inhibitors on menstrual synchrony at Deir el-Medina is impossible to determine with certainty, but it is certainly likely that there were no products with an effect comparable to modern deodorants, the main inhibitory factor in the studies cited above (especially in Graham and McGrew 1992). Awareness of the menstrual cycles among the group cannot be ruled out as a possible factor in synchrony at Deir el-Medina. OIM 13512 records a specific trip to the "place of women" by eight women who were known to be menstruating at least to the women themselves and the scribe writing the text; similarly, the recording of the menstruation of female relatives in the absence rosters shows awareness of women's menstrual periods outside of the home. Janssen and Janssen (1990, p. 3) make the interesting point that, in the Demotic story of Setna I, the fact of Ahwere's menstrual period *not* coming when expected (because of her pregnancy) seems to be public knowledge and is announced as such to the king. Given the active involvement of Deir el-Medina inhabitants in their neighbors' affairs and the close quarters of the town itself, public knowledge of women's menstrual cycles would not have been surprising; if trips to the "place of women" were a regular event in women's lives, it would have been impossible to be unaware of the menstrual cycle of one's relatives and neighbors.

The location of the "place of women" would have a major impact on how public the knowledge of women's menstruation would be, but this location is difficult to determine. The women get as far as the rear of a house and appear to be headed to somewhere in connection with the "three guard posts," literally the "three walls." The exact words used are *pꜣ 3 ỉnb* and appear to be a reference to a specific place. The closest parallel is "the five walls" known primarily from the Turin Strike Papyrus; this is, however, treated as feminine (*tꜣ 5 ỉnb.wt*) rather than masculine as in the case of "the three walls" of OIM 13512. "The five walls" are guard posts of some sort; Ventura (1986, pp. 120–44) gives a detailed discussion of the subject and concludes that this phrase described a specific group of five guard posts to the south of Deir el-Medina, intended to keep the workmen from leaving the village. More recent considerations of the evidence argue convincingly for a less rigid interpretation of the location of these walls and their function. In particular, it has been suggested that *tꜣ 5 ỉnb.wt* are

24. For the role of pheromones in menstrual synchrony, see now Stern and McClintock 1999.

25. These estimates are derived largely from textual evidence. Using two standard archaeological methods of estimating population (persons per individual residential structure and standard amounts of roofed floor space per person; see Meyer 1995, pp. 213–15, for references on these methods), one could arrive at somewhat higher population estimates for Deir el-Medina, from 238 to 500.

26. McClintock (1971) shows that sharing the same room was not a requirement for synchrony.

to the north of the village (Frandsen 1989, p. 121) and that they were more for the protection of the villagers than for their confinement (McDowell 1994, p. 58). Ventura makes a sharp distinction between the feminine form of the word *ỉnb.t* and the masculine form *ỉnb*, claiming that the latter is a generic term for "wall," and the former a specific term for guard post (Ventura 1986, pp. 142–43), but OIM 13512 suggests otherwise.[27] Considering the dates of the relevant entries of the Turin Strike Papyrus (year 29 of Ramesses III) and the probable date of OIM 13512 (year 9 of Merneptah), it is possible that these terms may refer to the same place, but at different stages of construction: in year 9 of Merneptah there were 3 guard posts, and in year 29 of Ramesses III there were 5 guard posts. With the uncertainty of the location of the "five guard posts" — whether south of the village according to Ventura, or north as suggested by Frandsen — even a tentative identification of the "three guard posts" with the later five does not permit the precise location of the "place of women."

The exact nature of this "place of women" at Deir el-Medina also remains unknown; OIM 13512 is the only known attestation of the term *s.t ḥm.wt* () and gives no additional information. Place-names of the same type (*s.t* X) are common in Deir el-Medina texts: *s.t mꜣꜥ.t* "Place of Truth" and its earlier name *s.t ꜥꜣ.t* "Great Place"; *s.t nfrw* "Place of Beauty" as well as *s.t ḥms* and *s.t sḏr* "Place of Rest" (for which, see Valbelle 1985, p. 254, n. 4). Some of these place-names are very specific, while others are vaguer and perhaps refer to more than one place (especially the two resting place-names); none provide an especially close parallel to *tꜣ s.t sḥm.wt* in OIM 13512. A slightly closer parallel to the "place of women" is the "place of the gate-keepers" (*tꜣ s.t n nꜣ ỉry.w-ꜥꜣ*, for which, see Ventura 1986, pp. 118–19), but the exact location and nature of this place is also uncertain. There are no obvious candidates for the "place of women" in the archaeological record, although there are a number of small structures outside of Deir el-Medina that are possibilities; Valbelle lists a number of huts and small buildings in a discussion on property at Deir el-Medina (1985, pp. 253–54). The information in OIM 13512 suggests only that the "place of women" could accommodate at least eight women and that the place had some sort of significance for women who were menstruating.

Special places for women who are menstruating are known from many cultures; these places have often been considered indicative of some sort of menstrual taboo, but more recent studies suggest that menstrual space at least began as something instituted by (and empowering for) women.[28] Many cultures have emphasized the use of what are generically called "menstrual huts," although the appearance of these "huts" differs widely in form and function across cultures. The common factor between them is a place for women to be alone at some point during their menstrual period.[29] Direct evidence for menstrual space in Egypt itself is limited to later periods. In post-pharaonic Egypt, menstrual space for women is usually found under the stairs of multistory structures. Reference to such space is most often found in agreements relating to the division or sale of houses; in Theban Ptolemaic Demotic agreements the space is given the name *ḫrr.t*[30] and is often mentioned in the clause "You/your women shall menstruate in the 'women's space.'"[31] This practice appears to continue on into the Roman, Byzantine, and even early Islamic periods, although not as explicitly stated; Coptic house divisions from seventh-eighth century A.D. Jême often cede the stairs to the woman in cases where property was split between a man and a woman, while the space was held in common in houses divided between two women.[32] In none of the references or allusions to this women's space is it expressed as a negative thing; indeed the concern

27. A seeming reference to "four guard posts" in O. Deir el-Medina 571 appears to be based on a misreading. The original editor of the text, followed by Ventura (1986, p. 123) and Frandsen (1989, p. 122), reads it as referring to people passing by "four guard posts" (*4 ỉnb.w*), but the reading has been disputed (Lopez 1988, p. 551; Janssen 1997, p. 172, n. 159). The text seems instead to be referring simply to *ỉnb.w* without a number.

28. See Young and Bacdayan 1967 for the traditional views, versus the approach of Knight 1991, pp. 354–57, 404–05; Buckley and Gottlieb 1988.

29. See Buckley and Gottlieb 1988, pp. 11–12, for discussion and references.

30. With many variants: *ḫlylꜣ.t*, *ḫlyl.t*, *ḫrḫr.t*, *ḫll*, from examples listed in Andrews 1990, p. 47. Both Zauzich (1968, pp. 19–29) and Andrews (1990, pp. 66–67) translate this word as "women's quarters." Given the consistent proximity of this word to clauses regarding the stairs of the house, the consistent identification in later documents of the stairs, and especially the space below it, with women, and the probable size of the houses described, the translation "women's quarters" probably gives a misleading impression of the size of this space. See Husson 1990, p. 126, for discussion of the evidence as it relates to houses described in Greek documents from Syene with reference to surviving examples of below-stairs space at Elephantine.

31. For a few examples, see Demotic Papyrus Louvre 2424 (= Zauzich 1968, Urkunde 11, pp. 17–21), l. 2: *mtw tꜣỉ.k sḥm.t ỉr ḥsmn n tꜣ ḫrḫr.t r ḫ tꜣ pš.t*; Demotic Papyrus Louvre 2443 (= Zauzich 1968, Urkunde 14, pp. 21–26), l. 4: *mtw.t ỉr ḥsmn n tꜣ ḫljl.t n pꜣ ꜥ.wj nty ḥrỉ r ḫ tꜣ pš.t*; Demotic Papyrus Louvre 2431 (= Zauzich 1968, Urkunde 15, pp. 26–29), l. 2: *mtw nꜣỉ.k sḥm.tw ỉr ḥsmn n tꜣ ḫrr.t r ḫ tꜣ pš.t*.

32. The Coptic evidence from Jême is discussed in Wilfong forthcoming.

over the disposition of the space in property divisions would suggest otherwise. As far as can be determined, this is not an imported (Graeco-Roman) tradition, and the "place of women" might have been located under the stairs of multistory houses in pharaonic times. The houses of Deir el-Medina, however, had little available space under the stairs and, given the tightly packed nature of the town itself, the only place to go might have been outside the settlement.

The apparent location of the "place of women" outside the village raises the question of whether the situation was symptomatic of a menstrual taboo in ancient Egyptian culture. The traditional answer to this would be affirmative, but it is instructive to examine the actual evidence for a menstrual taboo. As Frandsen (*LÄ* 6 "Tabu") points out, the term "taboo" is often used in a much looser sense within Egyptology than is customary. He notes that what are often described as taboos in ancient Egypt are more often either less specific (vague and general cultural distastes) or more specific (regional and often site-specific interdictions) than the term would imply in this context. This tendency to see a formal menstrual taboo reflected in ambiguous evidence is not exclusive to Egypt but is frequently found in studies of pre-modern cultures. Perhaps the most familiar example is the often-cited "menstrual taboo" in the Hebrew Bible, which a closer examination shows to be a more specific ritual injunction against anyone who has expelled something other than waste from their body (Cohen 1991, pp. 274–76). Anthropological literature on menstrual taboos is quite extensive but also subject to question; scholarship has begun to question the long-accepted understanding of other cultures' attitudes towards menstruation (Buckley and Gottlieb 1988).[33] Thus, it is important to examine the actual evidence usually cited when a menstrual taboo is claimed for ancient Egypt.

The earliest source traditionally taken as evidence for a menstrual taboo in Egypt is also one of the earliest to use *ḥsmn* to indicate "menstruation": the Middle Kingdom Instruction of Khety, the so-called "Satire on the Trades." In section XIX of this text (following the division of the text in Helck 1970), the disadvantages of the washerman are pointed out: in addition to working in mud, proximity to crocodiles, rejection by his son and daughter, having his food mixed with dirt, and being dirty himself all over, it is said of the washerman that "He even gives (or cleans?) the skirt of a menstruating woman."[34] Skirts or kilts (*dꜣỉw*) are well known from texts at Deir el-Medina and elsewhere (Janssen 1975, pp. 265–66), as well as from representations (Vogelsang-Eastwood 1993, pp. 53–71). Such garments are most often worn by men (these Vogelsang-Eastwood terms "kilts"), but they are also worn by women ("skirts" in Vogelsang-Eastwood); given the use of the same term in Egyptian for both, perhaps "skirt" is the better translation for *dꜣỉw*. Women in skirts are seen in a few depictions (Vogelsang-Eastwood 1993, pp. 69–71, figs 4:24–25) and Janssen notes O. Cairo 25725 in which a man gives his daughter a skirt. The "skirt of a menstruating woman," given the context, is presumably a woman's skirt stained with menstrual blood and is less likely to be a menstrual towel itself. The evidence for the latter in ancient Egypt is ambiguous. Hall (1986, p. 55) suggests that the *sḏw*/*sḏy n pḥwy* (literally "loincloth for the backside") known from Deir el-Medina documents (references in Janssen 1975, pp. 272–77) are, in Hall's words, "sanitary towels." The *sḏy*/*sḏw* are most probably cloth loincloths of the kind illustrated in Vogelsang-Eastwood 1993, pp. 10–16, pls. 1–4; these are primarily attested for men, but examples of loincloths for women are known as well (ibid., pp. 15–16, fig 2.5).[35] Whatever the precise interpretation of "the skirt of a menstruating

33. For example, the discussion in the frequently cited Young and Bacdayan 1967 is problematic since it presupposes the low status of women in cultures with taboos relating to menstruation; see Buckley and Gottlieb 1988, pp. 9–10, for a discussion of the problems of this approach.

34. The text of the entire composition is notoriously corrupt, and section XIX is not exempt from this. Helck (1970, p. 110) suggests emending initial *ḏd.f* to *twrỉ.f* "he cleans," which may make a bit more sense in the general context but cannot be considered certain. The reading of BM 29550, which seems to have a somewhat better text overall, for the second part of the sentence seems the best (*dꜣỉw n s.t wnn.t m ḥsmn.s*), but the first part is less clear (*ḏḏyw.f sw*); clearly the *m* before *dꜣỉw* found in all the other manuscripts is needed in BM 29550. The suggestion in Depla 1994, pp. 41–42 ("It is in a woman's skirt that he puts himself/and then he is in a heavy state") is unlikely: the *dꜣỉw* is worn by both men and women, and the interpretation of the group normally read as *ḥsmn* (and in a context similar to other instances of *ḥsmn* "menstruation") as an unspecified word for "heavy" is unsatisfactory. Moreover, the context of this line is a list of things that are (literally) not clean, and the skirt of a menstruating woman seems a closer parallel than the putative cross-dressing washerman suggested by Depla's translation. Helck (1970, p. 111) translates "Reinigt er doch auch das Gewand einer Frau, die menstruiert." Simpson (1973, p. 335) follows this closely ("He cleans the clothes of a woman in menstruation"), while Lichtheim (1973, p. 189) may get closer to the precise translation of the first half of the sentence ("He is given women's clothes") but shies away from the exact identification of the clothes ("...").

35. The question of whether the Isis-knot (𓎬) represents a menstrual towel is unresolved, but the evidence seems strong; see Andrews 1994, p. 44; Pinch 1994, p. 130; *LÄ* 3 "Isisknoten," col. 204. In particular, the insistent association of the Isis-knot with blood, especially in Book of the Dead

woman" in the Instruction of Khety, however, it is clear that the passage does not indicate an explicit menstrual taboo. It may be indicative of a cultural bias against men washing women's clothes and might even show a general distaste for menstrual blood, but it does not imply a formal taboo.

Another group of sources that has been interpreted as evidence of a menstrual taboo in the New Kingdom are equally ambiguous: the so-called Calendars of Lucky and Unlucky Days, now conveniently published together in a collected edition (Leitz 1994). Two places in the calendars have been associated with menstruating women in the Egyptological literature: the entries for II *ꜣḫt* 5 and I *prt* 7 (Leitz 1994, pp. 67–71 and 199–200, respectively). On II *ꜣḫt* 5, readers of the calendars are warned "you should not have sex with a woman" on this date, while on I *prt* 7 readers are cautioned "you should not have sex with any woman" — the Cairo Calendar here adding "or any man"[36] — on this date. These references have traditionally been taken as injunctions against men having sex with women while they are menstruating,[37] but this is never stated or even implied in the text of the calendars themselves. Indeed, the added phrase warning against sex with men in the Cairo Calendar for I *prt* 7 suggests strongly that this is not the case and that its injunction against sexual activity for the day was for entirely different reasons.

An explicit interdiction against menstruating women does not appear in Egyptian texts until the Graeco-Roman period, and even then only in very specific and limited religious contexts. The most basic expression of this interdiction occurs in the Tanis Geographical Papyrus, a tabular listing of various features of the religious practices of the different nomes. One row (headed "name of interdiction") lists the various principal interdictions for the gods of the individual districts, data for which is given in columns. Fragments 12 and 14 (in Griffith and Petrie 1889, pl. 10) list information about the Cynopolite and Athribite Nomes, respectively: the interdiction for the gods of both of these nomes is "the menstruating woman" (*ḥsmn.t*), with "the heart of the black bull" also listed for the Athribite Nome (Vernus 1978, pp. 263–64). That these interdictions were widely known and not just specific to the Tanis papyrus is clear from other texts. For example, the Edfu inscriptions, in which the king presents the nomes and their gods, reiterate the same points. The interdiction for the god of the Athribite Nome states *bw.t.f ḥsmn(.t)* "his interdiction is a menstruating woman" (Rochemonteix and Chassinat 1987, p. 332; Vernus 1978, pp. 261–63). The wording of the interdiction for the god of the Cynopolite Nome is different: *bwt.n.f r ḥsmn.t m nỉw.t.f* "It is against the menstruating woman that he had an interdiction in his town" (Rochemonteix and Chassinat 1987, p. 342). Similar region-specific interdictions are found in P. Jumilhac. In P. Jumilhac XII, 16–17, the phrase *bw.t.f ḥsmn.t* "his abomination is a menstruating woman" appears in a list of district interdictions, along with the howl of a certain kind of dog, the act of dreaming, the grunting of pigs, and other actions (Vandier 1961, pp. 123, 178). Later on in the same papyrus (P. Jumilhac XIX, 14) the phrase *bw.t.f tpy ḥsmn.t* "his principal abomination is a menstruating woman" is given as the sole interdiction for the god of a district.[38] The texts do not show how and to whom this interdiction was applied: whether it was temple-specific, included only temple personnel, or had a broader impact. These texts do, in many cases, reflect earlier traditions, and it may be that these interdictions against menstruating women are likewise much older than the texts in which they are found, but they are not indicative of a general menstrual taboo in Egypt.

Taking into account the Egyptian understanding of menstruation as seen through the sources examined above, it is not surprising to find no evidence for a formal, universal taboo against women in menstruation. Although recent optimistic assessments of the status of women in ancient Egypt will ultimately have to be tempered and qualified (for which, see Meskell 1994, pp. 210–12), there is no evidence to support earlier assumptions that women's menstruation was seen as a negative part of women's lives. The trip to the "place of women" made by the eight women in OIM 13512 appears, by all available evidence, not to have been an inherently negative experience for these women and might well have been a positive one. The actual "incident" be-

156 (directly referential to the Isis-knot amulet) and the description of a protective tampon in *CT* 2, 217 ff. (Spell 148), both cited in *LÄ* 3 "Isisknoten," col. 204, make the identification probable. Archaeological evidence for menstrual towels has rarely been recognized, let alone studied; for the potentials and problems of such evidence, see probable examples of menstrual napkins noted at the medieval Norwegian site of Bergen (Ehrenberg 1989, p. 35).

36. The reading of the Cairo Calendar in this instance (Leitz 1994, pp. 199–200) provides for sexual options not often found (or noticed) in Egyptian texts; it shows that the writer saw men as potential sexual partners of other men, or women as potential readers of the calendar (and having the potential to have sex with either men or women on this particular day), or some combination of these possibilities.

37. References in Leitz 1994, p. 200, n. 19.

38. Vandier (1961, pp. 131, 210) discusses whether the phrase might refer instead to "the beginning of the menstrual period."

ing recorded in OIM 13512 is uncertain because of the break in line three: either it is a simple record of the eight women's trip to the "place of women" or a record of something that happened to the women on their way.

By placing OIM 13512's single record in the broader context of the evidence for the settlement as a whole, the text provides a useful insight into the lives of women in that community. The identification of appropriately determined instances of the word *ḥsmn* with menstruation can now be taken as certain, and the other evidence for menstruation and the lack of a formal menstrual taboo in Egypt can now be better placed in its context. Similarly, explicit and implicit records of menstrual synchrony (in OIM 13512 and O. BM 5634) are now definitely identified among the Deir el-Medina documentation. The relatively limited chronological range of documentary evidence for women's menstruation at Deir el-Medina (year 40 of Ramesses II to the end of the Nineteenth Dynasty) may be due to chance preservation of the evidence but may also suggest changes either in the menstrual practice of the women of the community or in the permitted absences for men. But the location and nature of the "place of women" remain uncertain, as do the circumstances under which women went there. It seems unlikely that women went to the "place of women" for each of their menstrual periods, but the evidence suggests no criteria for determining when women went there. The study of OIM 13512, along with the related evidence, provides new insight into the social history of Ramesside Egypt but ultimately raises more questions than can be definitively answered at present.

Abbreviation

HO — *Hieratic Ostraca* 1. By J. Černý and A. H. Gardiner. Oxford: Griffith Institute, 1957.

References

Andrews, C.

1990 *Ptolemaic Legal Texts from the Theban Area*. Catalogue of Demotic Papyri in the British Museum 4. London: British Museum.

1994 *Amulets of Ancient Egypt*. London: British Museum Publications.

Barns, J. W. B.

1956 *Five Ramesseum Papyri*. Oxford: Griffith Institute.

Blackman, A. M.

1988 *The Story of King Kheops and the Magicians, Transcribed from Papyrus Westcar (Berlin Papyrus 3033)*. Edited for publication by W. V. Davies. Reading: J. V. Books.

Borghouts, J. F.

1978 *Ancient Egyptian Magical Texts*. Nisaba Religious Texts, Translation Series 9. Leiden: E. J. Brill.

Buckley, T., and A. Gottlieb

1988 "A Critical Appraisal of Theories of Menstrual Symbolism." In *Blood Magic: The Anthropology of Menstruation*, edited by T. Buckley and A. Gottlieb, pp. 3–50. Berkeley: University of California Press.

Cayleff, S. E.

1992 "She Was Rendered Incapacitated by Menstrual Difficulties: Historical Perspectives on Perceived Intellectual and Physiological Impairment among Menstruating Women." In *Menstrual Health in Women's Lives*, edited by A. J. Dan and L. L. Lewis, pp. 229–35. Urbana: University of Illinois Press.

Černý, J.

1935 *Ostraca hiératiques*. Catalogue général des antiquités égyptiennes du Musée du Caire, nos. 25501–25832. Cairo: Institut français d'archéologie orientale.

Cohen, S. J. D.

1991 "Menstruants and the Sacred in Judaism and Christianity." In *Women's History and Ancient History*, edited by S. B. Pomeroy, pp. 273–99. Chapel Hill: University of North Carolina Press.

Dean-Jones, L.

1994 *Women's Bodies in Classical Greek Science*. Oxford: Clarendon Press.

Depla, A.

1994 "Women in Ancient Egyptian Wisdom Literature." In *Women in Ancient Societies: "An Illusion of the Night,"* edited by L. J. Archer, S. Fischler, and M. Wyke, pp. 24–52. New York: Routledge.

Demarée, R. J., and J. J. Janssen

1982 *Gleanings from Deir el-Medîna*. Egyptologische Uitgaven 1. Leiden: Nederlands Instituut voor het Nabije Oosten.

Ehrenberg, M.

1989 *Women in Prehistory*. London: British Museum Publications.

Erichsen, W.

1937 *Demotische Lesestücke* 1: *Literarische Texte,* 1. Heft. Leipzig: J. C. Hinrichs.

Faulkner, R. O.
1962 *A Concise Dictionary of Middle Egyptian*. Oxford: Griffith Institute.

Frandsen, P. J.
1989 "A Word for 'Causeway' and the Location of 'The Five Walls.'" *Journal of Egyptian Archaeology* 75: 113–23.

Goedicke, H., and E. F. Wente
1962 *Ostraka Michaelides*. Wiesbaden: Otto Harrassowitz.

Golub, S.
1992 *Periods: From Menarche to Menopause*. Newbury Park: Sage Publications.

Graham, C. A., and W. C. McGrew
1992 "Social Factors and Menstrual Synchrony in a Population of Nurses." In *Menstrual Health in Women's Lives*, edited by A. J. Dan and L. L. Lewis, pp. 246–53. Urbana: University of Illinois Press.

Grapow, H.
1958 *Die medizinischen Texte in hieroglyphischer Umschreibung Autographiert*. Grundriss der Medizin der alten Ägypter 5. Berlin: Akademie-Verlag.

Griffith, F. Ll., and W. M. F. Petrie
1889 *Two Hieroglyphic Papyri from Tanis*. London: Trübner.

Groll, S. I.
1982 "Diachronic Grammar as a Means of Dating Undated Texts." *Scripta Hierosolymitana* 28: 11–104.

Hall, R.
1986 *Egyptian Textiles*. Shire Egyptology. Aylesbury: Shire Publications.

Hanson, A. E.
1990 "The Medical Writers' Woman." In *Before Sexuality: The Construction of Erotic Experience in the Ancient Greek World*, edited by D. M. Halperin, J. J. Winkler, and F. I. Zeitlin, pp. 309–38. Princeton: Princeton University Press.

Helck, W.
1970 *Die Lehre des* Dwꜣ-Ḫtjj. Kleine ägyptische Texte. Wiesbaden: Otto Harrassowitz.

Husson, G.
1990 "Houses in Syene in the Patermouthis Archives." *Bulletin of the American Society of Papyrologists* 27: 123–37.

Janssen, J. J.
1975 *Commodity Prices from the Ramessid Period: An Economic Study of the Village of Necropolis Workmen at Thebes*. Leiden: E. J. Brill.
1980 "Absence from Work by the Necropolis Workmen of Thebes." *Studien zur altägyptischen Kultur* 8: 127–50.
1982 "The Mission of the Scribe Pesiūr (O. Berlin 12654)." In *Gleanings from Deir el-Medîna*, edited by R. J. Demarée and J. J. Janssen, pp. 133–47. Egyptologische Uitgaven 1. Leiden: Nederlands Instituut voor het Nabije Oosten.
1992 "Literacy and Letters at Deir el-Medîna." In *Village Voices: Proceedings of the Symposium "Texts from Deir el-Medîna and Their Interpretation," Leiden, May 31–June 1, 1991*, edited by R. J. Demarée and A. Egberts, pp. 81–94. Centre of Non-Western Studies Publications 13. Leiden: Centre of Non-Western Studies.
1997 *Village Varia: Ten Studies on the History and Administration of Deir el-Medina*. Egyptologische Uitgaven 11. Leiden: Nederlands Instituut voor het Nabije Oosten.

Janssen, R., and J. J. Janssen
1990 *Growing Up in Ancient Egypt*. London: Rubicon Press.

Knight, C.
1991 *Blood Relations: Menstruation and the Origins of Culture*. New Haven: Yale University Press.

Leitz, C.
1994 *Tagewählerei: Das Buch* ḥꜣt nḥḥ pḥ.wy ḏt *und verwandte Texte*. Ägyptologische Abhandlungen 55. Wiesbaden: Harrassowitz Verlag.

Lesko, B. S.
1994 "Rank, Roles and Rights." In *Pharaoh's Workers: The Villagers of Deir el-Medina*, edited by L. H. Lesko, pp. 11–39, 153–56. Ithaca: Cornell University Press.

Lesko, L. H.
1984 *Dictionary of Late Egyptian*, Volume 2. Providence: B. C. Scribe Publications.
1994 "Literature, Literacy and Literati." In *Pharaoh's Workers: The Villagers of Deir el-Medina*, edited by L. H. Lesko, pp. 131–44, 185–88. Ithaca: Cornell University Press.

Lichtheim, M.
1973 *Ancient Egyptian Literature*, Volume 1: *The Old and Middle Kingdom*. Berkeley: University of California Press.
1980 *Ancient Egyptian Literature*, Volume 3: *The Late Period*. Berkeley: University of California Press.

López, J.
1982 *Ostraca ieratici n. 57320–57449*. Catalogo del Museo Egizio di Torino, serie seconda collezioni 3:3. Milan: Istituto Editoriale Cisalpino - La Goliardica.
1988 Review of *Living in a City of the Dead*, by Raphael Ventura. *Bibliotheca Orientalis* 45: 545–51.

McClintock, M. K.
1971 "Menstrual Synchrony and Suppression." *Nature* 229: 244–45.

McDowell, A. G.
1990 *Jurisdiction in the Workmen's Community of Deir el-Medîna*. Egyptologische Uitgaven 5. Leiden: Nederlands Instituut voor het Nabije Oosten.
1994 "Contact with the Outside World." In *Pharaoh's Workers: The Villagers of Deir el-Medina*, edited by L. H. Lesko, pp. 41–59, 156–62. Ithaca: Cornell University Press.

Meskell, L.
1994 "Deir el Medina in Hyperreality: Seeking the People of Pharaonic Egypt." *Journal of Mediterranean Archaeology* 7: 193–216.

Meyer, C.

1995 "A Byzantine Gold-Mining Town in the Eastern Desert of Egypt: Bir Umm Fawakhir 1992–93." *Journal of Roman Archaeology* 8: 172–224.

Montserrat, D.

1991 "Mallocouria and Therapeuteria: Rituals of Transition in a Mixed Society?" *Bulletin of the American Society of Papyrologists* 28: 43–49.

Pinch, G.

1993 *Votive Offerings to Hathor.* Oxford: Griffith Institute.

1994 *Magic in Ancient Egypt.* London: British Museum Publications.

Pomeroy, S. B.

1984 *Women in Hellenistic Egypt: From Alexander to Cleopatra.* New York: Schocken Books.

Raven, M. J.

1983 "Wax in Egyptian Magic and Symbolism." *Oudheidkundige mededelingen* 64: 7–47.

Riddle, J. M.

1992 *Contraception and Abortion from the Ancient World to the Renaissance.* Cambridge: Harvard University Press.

Robins, G.

1993 *Women in Ancient Egypt.* London: British Museum Publications.

Rochemonteix, M. de, and É. Chassinat

1987 *Le temple d'Edfou* 1/3. Second edition revised and corrected. Cairo: Institut français d'archéologie orientale.

Simpson, W. K.

1973 *The Literature of Ancient Egypt: An Anthology of Stories, Instructions, and Poetry.* New edition. New Haven: Yale University Press.

Spiegelberg, W.

1908 *Die demotischen Denkmäler 30601–31270, 50001–50022, 2: Die demotischen Papyrus.* Catalogue général des antiquités égyptiennes du Musée du Caire. Strasbourg: M. Dumont.

Stern, K., and M. K. McClintock

1999 "Regulation of Ovulation by Human Pheromones." *Nature* 392: 177–79.

Sturtewagen, C.

1990 "Studies in Ramesside Administrative Documents." In *Studies in Egyptology Presented to Miriam Lichtheim,* edited by S. I. Groll, pp. 933–42. Jerusalem: Magnes Press.

Valbelle, D.

1985 *«Les ouvriers de la tombe»: Deir el-Médineh à l'époque ramesside.* Bibliothèque d'étude 96. Cairo: Institut français d'archéologie orientale.

Vandier, J.

1961 *Le papyrus Jumilhac.* Paris: Centre national de la recherche scientifique.

Ventura, R.

1986 *Living in a City of the Dead: A Selection of Topographical and Administrative Terms in the Documents of the Theban Necropolis.* Orbis Biblicus et Orientalis 69. Freiburg: Universitätsverlag.

Vernus, P.

1978 *Athribis: Textes et documents relatifs à la géographie, aux cultes, et à l'histoire d'une ville au delta égyptien à l'époque pharaonique.* Bibliothèque d'étude 74. Cairo: Institut français d'archéologie orientale.

Vogelsang-Eastwood, G.

1993 *Pharaonic Egyptian Clothing.* Studies in Textile and Costume History 2. Leiden: E. J. Brill.

von Deines, H., and W. Westendorf

1962 *Wörterbuch der medizinischen Texte,* 2. Hälfte (h-ḏ). Grundriss der Medizin der alten Ägypter 7:2. Berlin: Akademie-Verlag.

Wilfong, T. G.

1992 "Greek and Coptic Texts from the Oriental Institute Museum Exhibition 'Another Egypt.'" *Bulletin of the American Society of Papyrologists* 29: 85–95.

NYP *Gender at Jême: Women's Lives in a Coptic Town in Late Antique Egypt.* New Texts from Ancient Cultures. Ann Arbor: University of Michigan Press.

Young, F. W., and A. A. Bacdayan

1967 "Menstrual Taboos and Social Rigidity." In *Cross-Cultural Approaches: Readings in Comparative Research,* edited by C. S. Ford, pp. 95–107. New Haven: HRAF Press.

Zauzich, K.-Th.

1968 *Die ägyptische Schreibertradition in Aufbau: Sprache und Schrift der demotischen Kaufverträge aus ptolemäischer Zeit.* Ägyptologische Abhandlungen 19. Wiesbaden: Otto Harrassowitz.

41

SERRA EAST AND THE MISSION OF MIDDLE KINGDOM FORTRESSES IN NUBIA

BRUCE BEYER WILLIAMS

The University of Chicago

The scholarly contribution of Professor Edward F. Wente has embraced language, literature, epigraphy, and history in such a way that all of these fields converge to bring the dim fragments of the ancient world into sharp focus in his work. The following paragraphs are an attempt to follow his example and show how archaeology also converges with the rest of Egyptology to amplify the reliability and detail of our picture of events.

PROBLEM OF FORTIFICATION IN NUBIA

The art of fortification reached its highest point before the Roman Empire in the strongholds maintained by pharaohs of the Twelfth Dynasty (1994–1786 B.C.) in Nubia in a chain that extended from Gebel es-Silsila to the Semna Cataract.[1] As the greatest secular constructions known from the ancient Nile Valley, they have presented an interesting enigma because their sophisticated design, large scale, and concentration give the lie to one of ancient Egypt's proudest boasts. In the days when the inhabitants of Nubia were looked upon as few in number and poor in organization, Senwosret III's pretension that Nubians would shrink from any serious offer of battle (Breasted 1906, §§656–60; Sethe 1924, pp. 83–85) could be taken at face value. Investigators could compare this statement with the careers of Old Kingdom officials (Breasted 1906, §§325–36, 350–74; *Urk.* 1, pp. 108–09, 120–40) to construct a picture of unrivaled Egyptian imperial superiority and domination. The forts were somehow made to fit this picture, however awkwardly, as guarantors of control, economic bases, or even monumental showpieces.[2]

A number of changes in the understanding of Nubian history and archaeology now call out for a re-appraisal of the fortress complex and its role. First, Senwosret's once shadowy enemy, Kush, is a shadow no more. Beginning with Hintze's realization that the great tumuli were Kushite,[3] the excavations at Kerma and Sai have revealed centuries of monumental wealth and power.[4] Osing's publication of over 175 Nubian names in late Old Kingdom execration texts has added a new dimension to the significance of Nubia in Egypt (Osing 1976, pp. 159–64).

1. Called *mnnw*, known from the Old Kingdom (Faulkner 1953, p. 36; Zibellius-Chen 1988, p. 25), both in inscriptions (Faulkner 1962, p. 109; *Urk.* 4, p. 739.16, of Thutmose III) and seals (see especially S. Smith 1990). For the term *ith*, see Faulkner 1962, p. 34; Vandier 1950, p. 198, inscription 6; Hayes 1955, pp. 41–42. For the fortress complex, see Gardiner 1916a, 1947/1, pp. 10–11; S. Smith 1991b, pp. 117–32; Zibellius-Chen 1988, pp. 186–91. For security issues generally, see Leprohon 1994.
2. For an extensive discussion, see Zibellius-Chen 1988, especially pp. 200–04; for fortresses, see ibid., pp. 186–91, especially note 316 for a list of major discussions of the purpose of the forts; for a summary of interests, see ibid., pp. 69–135. For a discussion of imperialism in Nubia, see S. Smith 1993, pp. 1–28; idem 1991a. For other interpretations, see Adams 1977, pp. 183–88; Trigger 1976, pp. 64–81; idem 1982, pp. 1–6; Adams 1984. See also S. Smith 1991b, pp. 109–15, for Askut Fortress as a center of economic activity. For general remarks on Egyptian fortifications as then known, see Lawrence 1965.
3. Hintze 1964, pp. 79–86, re-dating Reisner 1923, pp. 99–102. Compare even lesser tombs at Kerma (Bonnet 1986b, pp. 12–15) with medieval or modern royal burials in Sudan (Howell 1952, pp. 156–64; Vycichl 1958, pp. 221–22).
4. For Kerma, see Bonnet 1986a, especially pp. 27–38 for the development of the Kerma town, generally. See also Bonnet 1988, especially p. 9, and O'Connor 1984, pp. 80–107, for the development of the religious quarter; however, the deffufa structures are not Egyptian designs, as Lacovara (1986) points out. For the scale of Kush, see O'Connor 1991; Bonnet 1993, especially pp. 1–14. For Sai, see Gratien 1986, p. 441; 1978, pp. 131–221.

Gold of Praise: Studies on Ancient Egypt in Honor of Edward F. Wente
Edited by Emily Teeter and John A. Larson
Studies in Ancient Oriental Civilization 58
Chicago: Oriental Institute, 1999

If the peoples of Kush were far more formidable than supposed only a generation ago, the fortresses were much more substantial than any installation required to regulate trade on a peaceful or stable frontier. With their huge walls, cramped quarters, broad ditches, bristling fighting platforms, and carefully designed loopholes, the builders clearly did not intend these forts to be trading emporia. For thousands of years, people have been fortifying places in Nubia, and it is probable that most habitations there required some type of protective enclosure (Williams 1994, pp. 278–80; see also Ziermann 1993). However the scale, concentration, and organization of such works never approached that of the Middle Kingdom deployment. The scale was so large that the domestic economy of Nubia would have been hard put to support the large garrisons and construction crews implied.[5] Documents show that the Middle Kingdom forts indeed helped to control trade,[6] but the control applied only to a part of the routes. In addition, trade continued no matter where the frontier stood,[7] and Nubian goods were available even in Intermediate Periods. Gold, for example, was not only available, it had been re-exported to Nubia. Nubian herdsmen even brought their cattle to graze as far as Middle Egypt,[8] while Egypt had re-opened trade with Punt some time before (Breasted 1906, §§428–33; Hayes 1949, pp. 43–49). Only large blocks of Nubian stone that required specialized quarrying skills were unavailable without an Egyptian presence. The condition of Egyptian markets, and the situation along the remoter routes and at the sources of supply, probably affected the cost and availability of products more than the location and type of the Egyptian frontier.[9] The fortresses in Nubia represent a commitment of resources that trade alone cannot explain.

FOREIGNERS AND FOREIGN RELATIONS IN EGYPTIAN POLITICS

Although the Egyptian kings were wealthy and powerful, Egypt was not a complacently stable country in the Middle Kingdom. The preceding period had been one of war, disturbance, lawlessness, and famine, as every educated Egyptian was aware. The misfortunes of this turbulent age dominated much of the literature and it culminated in the assassination of the Twelfth Dynasty's founder.[10] Egypt barely managed three generations of continuity, and two of relative peace, before Senwosret III's series of campaigns and governmental upheaval.

From the end of the Old Kingdom, outsiders, especially Nubians, had played an extremely important role in the conflicts that plagued Egypt. Nubia had been intensively resettled by the Sixth Dynasty.[11] Although the Egyptian government, particularly through its governors at Aswan, dealt successfully, and sometimes high-handedly with the powers consolidating in the Nubia, its emerging political reality was one of wide-ranging dynasts and rapid consolidation (O'Connor 1986, pp. 27–39; idem 1991; Zibellius-Chen 1988, pp. 228–29).

Contemporary texts that curse the king's enemies preserve some 177 Nubian names, almost half the total (Osing 1976, pp. 159–64). The movement these names represent, as well as the development of the Nubian Nile Valley, accelerated rapidly in the following period. Nubians crossed into Egypt, mostly to serve in the armies of warring dynasts and magnates.[12] These soldiers found a place well known to us in the life of Gebelein

5. If the normal garrison of all the forts was a modest 4,000–5,000, then a supporting population would be about 400,000, if we accept one percent as a very rough maximum for an ancient standing army. The supporting hinterland of the Lower Nubian frontier was probably most of Upper Egypt.
6. The Semna dispatches report contacts with Nubians who came to trade; they display no interest in the details of the transactions, but only in the circumstances of the encounter and the disposition of the traders (Smither 1945, Despatches 1, 6, 7, 8; Wente 1990, pp. 70–72, no. 1).
7. Even when the country was divided, Merikare's predecessor noted that "You stand well with the Southern Region, for the bearers of loads come to you with produce" (Simpson 1973, p. 186; see also *LÄ* 3 "Lehre für Merikare," cols. 986–88; Helck 1977, pp. 46–47). See also Zibellius-Chen 1988, pp. 123–24, for an extensive list of products sent to Egypt during the eighteenth century A.D., when Egypt's writ hardly extended beyond its borders and much trade avoided the Nubian Nile north of Berber.
8. The so-called thin men of Meir with their deformed-horn cattle were probably from Nubia; see Williams 1983, pp. 98–99, n. 6.
9. Asiatics at Beni Hasan brought *msdmt* to trade (Newberry 1893, pls. 30, 31, 38 no. 2); see the galena mines at Gebel ez-Zeit in the Eastern Desert (Castel and Soukiassian 1989). Note Puntites already voyaging to Egypt in the Eighteenth Dynasty (Davies 1935, pp. 46–48).
10. Posener 1956, pp. 61–86; *LÄ* 3 "Lehre Amenemhets I.," cols. 967–71; Helck 1986, pp. 15–31; even an attempted assassination would indicate dangerous instability. The litany of disaster and lamentation presented in the literature contrasts the calm and order of the present and the chaos of the past. In other words, those who resent the painful exactions of the present and long for the relative freedom of the Intermediate Period should not forget its insecurity and privation.
11. Bietak 1968, pp. 132–48; see also 1987b. The events described by the tomb biographies of Aswan (O'Connor 1986, pp. 27–38; idem 1991) and the people named in the Old Kingdom execration texts (Osing 1976, pp. 159–64) date to phase IA.
12. See Fischer 1961, pp. 44–80, for immigrant soldiers; see Junker 1920, pp. 1–107, for C-Group remains in Egypt. Both the inscriptions and the archaeology indicate that the Nubians retained their identity as Nubians (Fischer 1961, p.

and they also appeared in the military establishments of Middle Egypt, particularly Asyut.[13] It is interesting that one half, or 40, of Mesekhti's model soldiers from Asyut are Nubian archers. In the armies of the day, the number of Nubians was significant, and possibly decisive.[14]

There was also some export of Egyptian goods and some Egyptian emigration. Egyptian pottery and jewelry become common in C-Group cemeteries, including necklaces of superb tiny gold and silver ring beads that look very much like official awards.[15] As a result of the interchange, Nubia learned enough about Egyptian institutions to undertake a major experiment.

Scattered on the rock faces of Lower Nubia are inscriptions of two pharaonic rulers with names typical of the First Intermediate Period. Säve-Söderbergh opined that they were a local dynasty (Säve-Söderbergh 1941, pp. 42–50; Hayes 1971, p. 486). One inscription calls a third ruler the "Son of Re, Segersenti." A relatively long inscription praises his performance in a battle to the north, probably against Egyptians (Säve-Söderbergh 1941, pp. 43–44). It is surprising to find pharaohs in Nubia at this time, but it is more remarkable that Segersenti is a name that would fit readily into the Old Kingdom lists of Nubians (Osing 1976, pp. 161–64, especially Isensenti or *Jznzntj*; Säve-Söderbergh 1941, p. 43).

When the Eleventh Dynasty managed to overcome its northern rival only after some bitter fighting (Anthes 1928, pp. 91–100, Gr. 24, pp. 54–56, for example) in which foreigners played a role, Egypt did not thereby gain stability. Apart from the representations of sieges at Beni Hasan, and possible conflicts recorded by nomarchs, the radical centralization of the country probably led to mismanagement that in turn could have created the drastic famine described by Heqanakht.[16] The vizier Amenemhat, himself part Aswani or Nubian, replaced the

---

48 above). Representations of Mentuhotep I are ambiguous, but some of the ladies at the Theban court were of Nubian origin, such as Aashayet (Winlock 1942, pl. 10 below). Sadhe, Aashayet, and Kemset are shown with complexions much darker than their servants and very tightly curled coiffures (Naville 1910, pls. 13 A, 16 A, and 20). It is likely that all of the shrines in the row at Deir el-Bahri were for Nubian women. For remarks on the Thebans of the period, see Zibellius-Chen 1988, p. 118; Winlock 1945, p. 7. For an inscription of a Nubian soldier and his career under Nebhepetre Mentuhotep, see Hayes 1971, p. 487.

13. Bietak 1985, pp. 87–98. Nubians from Wawat and Medjay are also mentioned at Hatnub serving in the same force as Asiatics. For the military significance of this incursion, see Anthes 1928, pp. 36–37, inscription 16, 6; Zibellius-Chen 1988, p. 118. In addition, the archers shown at Beni Hasan may be Nubians (Hayes 1971, p. 471). Nubians were an essential part of Egypt's military establishments.

14. Middle Kingdom expeditions ranged up to 10,000 men but could be quite small. See Breasted 1906, §442, numbering 10,000 (Vizier Amenemhat for Nebtawyre Mentuhotep), with 3,000 sailors (§453; see also *LÄ* 1 "Amenemhet I.," cols. 188–89; and Couyat and Montet 1912, no. 110, pp. 76–78, pl. 28). The 62 dead soldiers buried by Mentuhotep I (Winlock 1942, pp. 123–27; idem 1945 [on p. 7 he gives the number as 60]) appear to have been killed in assaulting a fortress. About this time, Henenu took 3,000 men into Wadi Hammamat, where at least 15 wells had to be made to support the expedition (Breasted 1906, §§430–31; Couyat and Montet 1912, no. 114, pp. 81–84, pl. 31). Amenemhat of Beni Hasan led 400 troops (to Nubia?) and then 600 troops to Coptos in the time of Senwosret I (*Urk.* 7, pp. 14.10–15.12; Breasted 1906, §§519–21). Amenemhat III dispatched armies of 2,000 to Wadi Hammamat (Couyat and Montet 1912/13, p. 42, no. 19; Breasted 1906, §710) and 734 to Sinai (Breasted 1906, §713).

15. The Royal Ornament Mayet had a string of these beads (Winlock 1942, p. 46, pl. 11 above inner ring; see also Hayes 1953, p. 229, fig. 144). Beads of this type were small rings of gold or silver on a cord of fibers that are looped at each end and bound with leather. The beads are extremely uniform, 3.0–3.5 cm in diameter, the gold beads 1.0 or even 0.5 mm (the thinnest examples were ca. 0.25 mm) in thickness. The outer surface is almost perfectly circular. See Williams 1983, pp. 92–93, pls. 116 U, W; 117 E, G–H (tombs T46 and U3); Williams 1993, pp. 51, 58, from B 73.

16. For centralization, see Hayes 1971, pp. 483–84. For Heqanakht's famine, see Hayes 1971, pp. 489–90; Baer 1963, pp. 7, 8, 14, also 16–17. Despite Baer's arguments (ibid., pp. 16–17, but see p. 14), there is really no reason to minimize the famine that was taking place, and the tone of urgency that accompanies Heqanakht's cutting of rations and mention of cannibalism is definite (also found in Ankhtify's account). Heqanakht consistently followed a strategy of accumulating food in the other transactions and took pains to point out that the reduced rations were exceptionally high; were they too low, he would not have been able to keep his employees. (Heqanakht rented rather than owned land because the land with favorable inundation varied from year to year making labor more important than land.) Despite a common preference for general Nile failure as an explanation for the First Intermediate Period famines (Bell 1971; idem 1975; Butzer 1976, pp. 40–43 [indirect]; but see Gardiner 1961, p. 111), the writers of the biographies of administrators make clear that more localized bungling, incompetence, and disorder were the causes. Ankhtify took over Edfu because it had become improperly flooded due to administrative incompetence (Vandier 1950, pp. 163–64, inscription), and he claimed to feed a large part of Upper Egypt (and Nubia) in a time of dearth (ibid., pp. 220–32, inscription 10). For other famine-relief statements, see Brunner 1937, pp. 64–65, lines 2–6; Breasted 1906, §§407–08 (Khety II of Asyut, who also undertook major irrigation schemes), §459; and Schenkel 1965, p. 57 (Ity at Gebelein), and §523, with *Urk.* 7, p. 16.9–10 (Ameny of Beni Hasan); see also Hayes 1971, p. 475. Had there been generalized Nile failure, there would have been no surplus to distribute. It is therefore more probable that disturbances and campaigns in certain areas caused the neglect or deliberate cutting of dikes, disruptions in planting, and extraordinary exactions which in turn caused laborers to flee, thus breaking down the agricultural economy in these areas. See also Hayes 1971, p. 475.

last ruler and the nomarchs of Middle Egypt resumed their prosperity and much of their power (*LÄ* 1 "Amenemhet I.," cols. 188–89; Hayes 1971, pp. 496–97).

The Eleventh Dynasty kings campaigned in Nubia (Zibellius-Chen 1988, pp. 185–86; Schenkel 1965, pp. 274–76), a policy that was continued by Amenemhat I (1991–1971/62 B.C.). However, it was only after his assassination[17] during one of his coregent and heir Senwosret I's (1971–1929/26 B.C.) campaigns that Egypt was able to complete the first real conquest of Lower Nubia.

At this time, the Egyptian government did not need to conquer Nubia to obtain its goods, but it did need to control the frontiers. Although trading interests might have encouraged Senwosret's conquest, he probably undertook this conquest, the establishment of fortresses,[18] and the stabilization of other frontiers in order to reduce the porosity of the borders. By this means, he could reduce or eliminate the foreign soldiers in the private armies of his powerful nomarchs and disaffected expatriates in the service of foreign magnates. Although records do not clearly indicate it, the existing fortresses within Egypt had probably been largely dismantled as dangerous and expensive. If left unmanned, any antagonistic noble or bandit could seize them, but manning them in peacetime would be prohibitively expensive.[19] Senwosret's motive was the most important economic motive of all, security.[20]

In this period, the strong presence of foreigners in the armies of Egypt accelerated conflict and disorder, while the permeability of the northern border allowed Asiatics to commit severe depredations, especially on agriculture.[21] These events from the recent past of civil conflict were seared into the contemporary Egyptian con-

17. This is itself interesting evidence of the perilous instability of the Egyptian state at the time. Amenemhat's revolution was apparently not quite accepted, even at court (see Simpson 1973, pp. 194–95; Posener 1956, pp. 82–85; *LÄ* 3 "Lehre Amenemhets I.," cols. 967–71). He was sufficiently prepared for an eventual attempt on his life that he had weapons immediately available when he went to rest.

18. This was an old explicit policy. Merikare's predecessor and teacher enjoined him to "build castles in the Delta ..." (Simpson 1973, p. 189; Helck 1977, pp. 66–67). He had already urged his pupil to "consolidate your frontier and your patrolled area, for it is good to work for the future" (Simpson 1973, p. 182). The Prophecies of Neferti, on the other hand, complained of the reign of Amenemhat I's predecessor: "... Asiatics have come down into Egypt, for a fortress lacks another beside it, and no guard will hear ..." (ibid., p. 237).

19. If the maximum number of the settled population that could be kept permanently under arms was about one percent, then assuming a population of 2.5 million, Senwosret would have had at most about 25,000 troops permanently under arms. If there were six major forts on the Nubian frontier and fairly elaborate complexes of walls and forts on the Delta frontiers (as described by Sinuhe), at 500 men per fort, 15–20 forts would consume 7,500–10,000 men of the maximum standing army. Given the normal wastage of military life, this would be a heavy commitment, apart from the high cost of maintenance.

    Much larger forces might be mobilized for single campaigns, if they were returned in time to resume their normal occupations. Not being peasants, the mobile peoples of the desert, and to some extent Kush, would not be as limited in the proportion of the population available to act as fighters.

20. The Nubian frontier could never be taken for granted. Nubia was a source of incursion even while nominally under Egyptian rule in the Twentieth Dynasty, and it was a feared power in the Seventeenth. Even after the Napatan period, Nubia intervened in Egypt from time to time, with varying success, down to Christian times. In the time of Mohammed Ali, the Mamelukes expected to rebuild their fortunes there. Desert peoples repeatedly re-invaded to disrupt or conquer in the country, even as late as the eighteenth century, when Maghrebi and Bedouin tribes plagued Upper Egypt. The problems caused by Asiatics in the Delta are detailed by Merikare's teacher (Simpson 1973, pp. 187–89; Helck 1977, pp. 57–61; for the later entry of Canaanites, see Bietak 1987a; for later relations with Nubia, see Bourriau 1981; idem 1991).

    This porosity worked in both directions. Not only were Nubians, Asiatics, and Libyans prominently displayed in the armies of the nomarchs, Egyptians ventured into Asia and Nubia to seek their fortunes or escape exactions. The inscriptions of Segersenti's dynasty in Nubia were written in Egyptian, and when Sinuhe fled to Asia, he was recruited by the ruler of Upper Retjenu with the promise that he would hear Egyptian. He had been recommended to that prince by the exiles already present at court, who knew Sinuhe and his reputation. Sinuhe was, in fact, a soldier (ranked as *šmsw* [Gardiner 1916b, p. 120, line 3], the rank held by Khusebek with command of sixty men), with friends and contacts among an exile community, and probably also among the assassins of Amenemhat I. He feared riot and disorder, and it is possible that some conflicts took place (Simpson 1973, pp. 60–64; for a political interpretation, see Posener 1956, pp. 87–115), although the only record is the Beni Hasan painting that shows a siege of an Egyptian-held fortress in Senwosret I's reign (fig. 41.1). Note that his furtive movements indicate a security apparatus was already in place in Egypt and that the sentries on the fortresses were known to be as alert for fugitives as for intruders (ibid., pp. 59–60). Sinuhe's precipitate flight and stealthy movements contrast with his subsequent boldness and profession as well as with the reputation that had preceded him into exile. If he were a prominent hostage held for the good behavior of the anti-royal party, it would account for his rapid escape, his reputation, and the eagerness of Amusinenshi to have him join other Egyptian expatriates in his service.

    Already in the Eleventh Dynasty, fugitives were pursued by the desert patrol to the western Oases (Dakhla?) and apprehended (Anthes 1930, pp. 108–14), so Sinuhe had good reason to fear a policy that was rigorously enforced later. He was a dangerous exile.

21. See, for example, the Prophecies of Neferti (Helck 1992, pp. 18–20; Simpson 1973, pp. 236–37; see also *LÄ* 4 "Neferti, Prophezeiung des," cols. 380–81).

sciousness and enshrined in art and a body of classical literature that served purposes of state and reflected policy.

FORTIFICATION IN STRATEGIC PLANNING AND MILITARY CAMPAIGNS

Since Senwosret I constructed the earlier complex of Nubian fortresses, the prior experience of fortresses, and related strategy and tactics as available to him, is essential for understanding the remaining physical evidence. In the First Intermediate Period, fortifications and sieges became a regular enough part of the Egyptian cultural landscape to appear in funerary art at Thebes (Jaroš-Deckert 1984, pl. 1, folding pl. 1) and Beni Hasan (see fig. 41.1 from the Twelfth Dynasty; Newberry 1893, pls. 14–16; idem 1894, pls. 5, 15). They also appear in the conventional wisdom of statecraft, and the biographies of nomarchs (Brunner 1937, pp. 18, 45, lines 16–22; Schenkel 1965, pp. 74–82).

All of these formed a body of art and literature that reflected the attitudes and policy intentions of rulers of the time, experience that would be of primary importance in the decision to build a fortress.[22] Among the most vivid are the campaign narratives of Ankhtify of Moʿalla, who apparently sought to block the rise of Thebes. His first action was to go to the aid of the army commander, possibly a warlord, of Armant whose fortresses were under attack by the forces of Thebes and Coptos. After undertaking this relief, he returned homeward, demolishing enemy fortresses (Vandier 1950, pp. 21, 42, inscription 6, pp. 198–99; Gardiner 1961, p. 111; Schenkel 1965, pp. 45–57). In a subsequent action, Ankhtify took his fleet into the Theban Nome seeking battle. In the west, no one would come out (of their fortresses) from fear of the force. On the east bank, the town of Sega shut its gates against him and his forces spread over the east and west of the nome seeking battle to no avail (Vandier 1950, pp. 202–03, inscription 7). Fortresses dominated Ankhtify's military life, and they finally frustrated his ambition.

Not long after Ankhtify's campaigns, Wahankh Inyotef consolidated Theban rule in the south, in part due to his crowning achievement of opening the fortresses of the Thinite Nome and set his boundary to the north. It is not clear whether he breached the forts (opened large gaps in the walls and gates to make them indefensible) or merely incorporated them into his defenses. However, about this time, the northern ruler recorded in his final instruction to his successor that he was able to take This "like a cloudburst," unfortunately damaging the ancient royal tombs.[23] In the same work, the ruler urged his heir Merikare to "build castles in the delta, for an enemy loves disturbance and his actions are mean" (Simpson 1973, p. 189; Helck 1977, pp. 57–67) despite the presence of 10,000 available fighters[24] and a system of protective waterworks. Merikare is advised to consolidate the frontier and the patrolled area (Simpson 1973, p. 182; Helck 1977, pp. 21–22). Not long afterward, Tefibi of Asyut defeated a Theban offensive as far as the fortress of the port of the south. Encountering a second expedition with a fleet, presumably a relief force, Tefibi claims he defeated it but nevertheless retired northward without making further progress (Brunner 1937, pp. 18, 45, lines 16–20; Schenkel 1965, pp. 16–20; Breasted 1906, §396). Within the continuous historical record available as precedent to the early Middle Kingdom, fortresses had not only been important, they had often been essential to the outcome of a campaign.

22. For early fortifications, see Williams 1994. Both fortification and siege craft appear in Egyptian art during the Old Kingdom. See, for example, Deshasha (Petrie 1898, pl. 4) and Saqqara (Quibell and Hayter 1927, frontispiece; the wall is climbed with a ladder, and men hack at it with axes, a wooden bar, and a hoe, the latter from above). These scenes are derived from a long tradition of Egyptian siege depictions.

23. The relative chronology of the events described in the Instruction for Merikare and Wahankh Inyotef's conquest of This is not certain, although the Heracleopolitan campaign has been assumed to have preceded Wahankh Inyotef. It is plausible that Wahankh Inyotef first stripped This of its usable forts, which made it easier for the northerners to overrun the nome. The latter were still not victorious.

24. Used here for any recruit or soldier. For the Egyptian term *ʿḥꜣwty* "fighter," see Smither 1945, Despatch 2, pl. IIIa, line 3, also Despatches 3 and 4 (translated "guardsman"), and Faulkner 1953, p. 40. Note that this title does not appear on seals from the Nubian forts (Gratien 1994, fig. 3), although most of the other titles in the dispatches do appear and *ʿḥꜣwty* had responsibility, sometimes leading large patrols as in Despatch 3. It may be that this group, the largest of Egyptian personnel mentioned in the dispatches, was assigned seals without names or titles. The term seems to designate an elite soldier or non-commissioned officer (Faulkner 1953, pp. 40–41). Khusebek held this rank (*ʿḥꜣ m ḫt*; Faulkner 1953, p. 39) in the royal guard, commanding seven soldiers, before he was promoted to command sixty men as a *šmsw*. Although ordinary soldiers have various designations, the privates directly below Khusebek seem to have been called *ʿnḫw* (Faulkner 1953, p. 38).

Figure 41.1. Siege at Beni Hasan from Tomb of Amenemhat. After Newberry 1893, pl. 14

It is hardly surprising that Egyptian forts figure in tomb representations as well as biographies and wisdom literature, in scenes that tell us a good deal about the way they were used (fig. 41.1). The latest of these representations, at Beni Hasan, dates to the reign of Senwosret I (Newberry 1893, p. 24, pls. 14, 16). Although, like other funerary representations, the siege scenes are probably not complete in every detail, they provide essential elements of tactics that were relatively simple. The attacking force shot arrows and sling bolts at the fortress to suppress resistance, while infantry prepared for an assault. The defenders replied, loosing arrows and casting small stone or clay missiles,[25] to disrupt the siege sufficiently for it to be abandoned, or to delay the assault long enough for a relief force to arrive. A land battle shown on the other side of the wall may depict such a relief although it may show an entirely different event, perhaps even the fall of the fortress.

The most important object in the painting is the fortress itself. A tall mudbrick structure, it has a simple gate and projecting fighting platforms, or machicolations. The lower part of the wall has a splayed base of brick or mud plaster.[26] If nothing else happened apart from the hurling of clay balls and stones, and the shooting of arrows, such a fortress would not fall until the defenders ran out of food and water. A siege might force a surrender, but it could not be carried by assault.

However, under a roofed shelter at right, two men are probing the wall with a long wooden shaft with a white point, possibly in another material. Yadin once called it a battering ram,[27] but its proportions and use indicate that it could not do serious damage to a wall several meters thick, let alone bring it down. However, the complex (probably) leather-covered testudo and probe were the actual means by which the fortress would fall, and the reason for the violent exchange of missiles on both sides.

The later fortresses in Nubia indicate that the mudbrick fortresses of Egypt were not solid constructions.[28] The mass was brick, but the curtains contained other materials and even open space. Poles and beams were often used to strengthen the walls, frequently separated by only a few courses. Beds of mats were generally included every seven to ten courses (four at Kumma), presumably to control differences in moisture. Finally, some walls had vents built into them, spaces a brick or two high and wide. Normally in Nubia, layers of mud plaster covered these features, but an attacking army would certainly know of their existence. The sappers working the probe were there to pick at the wall, finding layers of mats, vents, beams, and imperfect bricks that

25. See Newberry 1893, pl. 14. These appear as small oval white or light gray masses in the palm of the hand, which are thrown overhand, probably because the cramped conditions would make using a sling particularly hazardous. These are probably not the oval objects usually called loom weights or net sinkers found commonly in the forts of Lower Nubia that may have been weights for cords used to entangle besiegers' probes. Made of lightly fired clay, or occasionally of stone, these objects are oval, usually with one rather straight edge, generally with a hole at one or both ends for attachments, and sometimes a groove down one edge. Such a use for these objects is hypothetical since no representation shows such a countermeasure. For examples, see Emery, Smith, and Millard 1979, pls. 40–41; Dunham 1967, pls. 36c–d, 37a; Dunham and Janssen 1960, figs. 5, 28-1-53; 29, 24-1-42 (where it is called a weapon); 65, 24-2-332.

26. The fortress piers of Uronarti had plastered revetments. See Dunham 1967, p. 21, map 3, pls. 6 A, 14 A. At Mirgissa, this slope was brick (p. 154).

27. Yadin 1963, p. 159, for example. Note that this was not the only means of taking a walled place used in the Eleventh Dynasty. In the tomb of Inyotef, an Asiatic fortress is taken with the help of a siege tower with a fighting platform that reaches the wall top (Jaroš-Deckert 1984, pl. 1c, folding pl. 1).

28. For Serra East, see Knudstad 1966, p. 177; Hughes 1963, pp. 124–25. For construction techniques in other fortresses, see Dunham 1967, p. 21, pls. 6 A, 14 A (Uronarti); p. 121, pls. 50, 52 B, 53 A (Shalfak); pp. 154–57 (Mirgissa with ventilators right through the wall); Dunham and Janssen 1960, pp. 5 (Semna), 114–15 (Kumma); Žabkar 1972; idem 1975; Žabkar and Žabkar 1982 (Semna South); Smith 1993 (Askut). See also Reisner 1929 for both cataract forts.

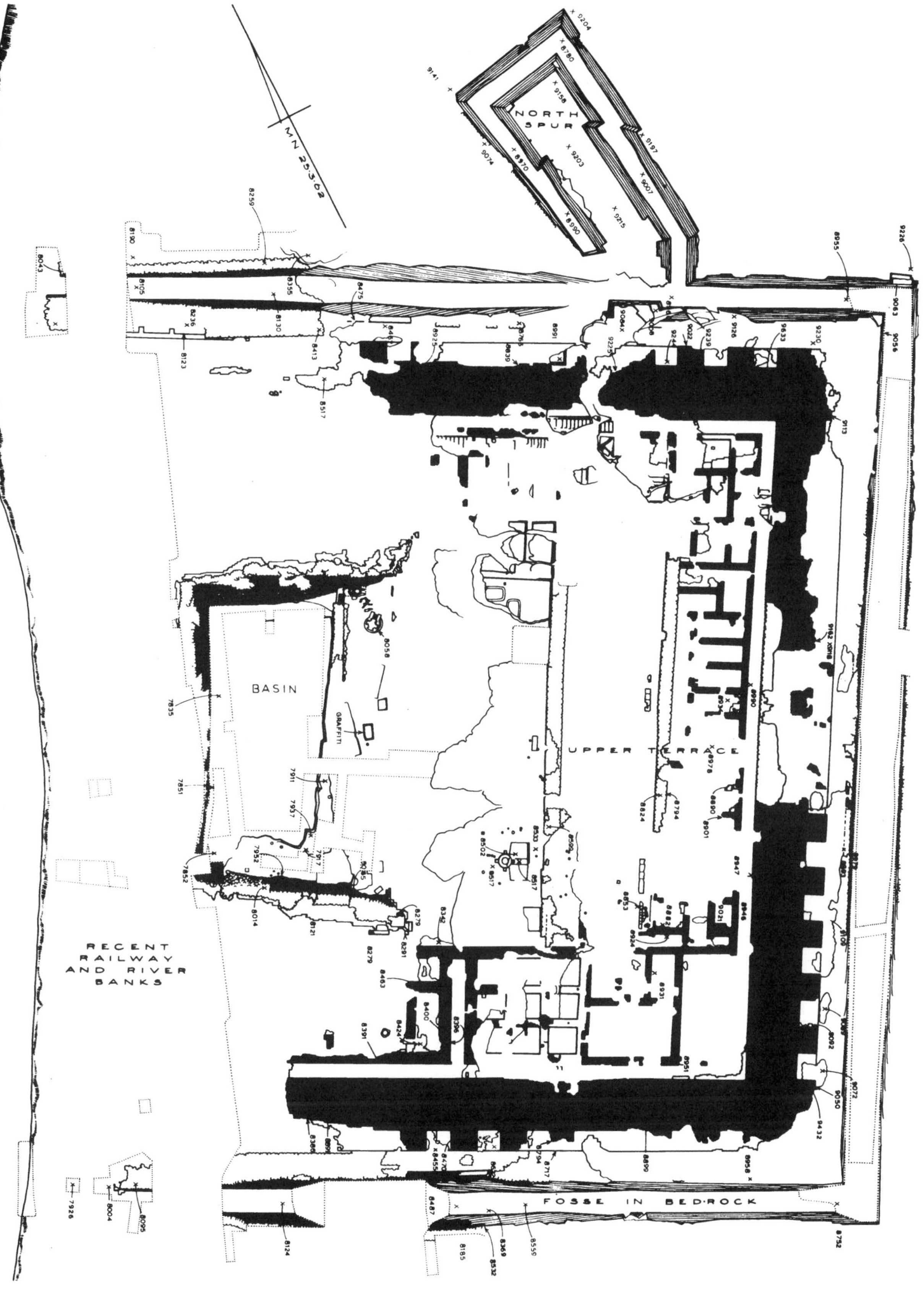

Figure 41.2. Plan of Serra East Fortress by James E. Knudstad. Courtesy of the Oriental Institute

Figure 41.3. Fortress of Serra East. Photograph Serra 399. Courtesy of the Oriental Institute

could be loosened to create a scalable set of hand- and footholds. When the sappers had made enough of these handholds, presumably at several points along the wall, an assault could begin.[29] Although besiegers might employ some additional methods, such as building large fires to weaken and crumble the brick or erecting wooden towers to overtop the wall, sappers using this simple technique could rapidly prepare most mudbrick walls for scaling. In Nubia, early fortress constructions already included countermeasures against such sapping. Wherever practicable, a stone-lined ditch some two or more meters deep surrounded the great inner curtains (see fig. 41.5). A low wall lining the inner parapet of this ditch would keep probes from the bottom of the ditch from easily picking at the curtain. This measure would not entirely prevent a besieger from filling the ditch and pulling down the parapet wall, but it would impede such action considerably. Its deterrence value was so great that most (later) forts were equipped with ditch and inner parapet wall at the cost of considerable labor.

The logic of this simple siege craft could explain Senwosret I's siting of the Lower Nubian fortresses as well as innovations in their design and the overall plan that they represent. A garrison's ability to hold territory depended on its ability to repel a force or hold it off long enough for relief to arrive. However, an attacker would have to be able to accumulate enough force to defeat any garrison in the open, confine it within walls, and overwhelm it rapidly by assault. In this earlier phase, the siting of fortresses in Nubia seems to reflect the belief that any enemy that could arise locally or infiltrate from the desert could be defeated by the garrison with any help that could be rushed from Egypt. As occurred later, the forts probably sent out armed patrols, assisted by a number of smaller posts, at least in the earliest period (Zibellius-Chen 1988, p. 187). If they were able to apprehend groups (of about 30) before they combined to become formidable, then the arrangement might succeed.

STRATEGY, SOCIAL CONDITIONS, AND DEVELOPMENT OF FORTIFICATION COMPLEXES IN NUBIA

As far as we know, the earlier fortresses were scattered from Gebel es-Silsila to the northern end of the Second Cataract. They occupied locations close to routes from the desert (Ikkur, Kuban), near important centers

29. The soldiers buried by Nebhepetre Mentuhotep seem to have perished in this type of assault (Winlock 1945, pp. 23–24). However, the corpses may not have been damaged by vultures and decomposition immediately after death. It is possible that they were damaged because they had been laid out on the high ground, as customary for their class, but retrieved for burial only later.

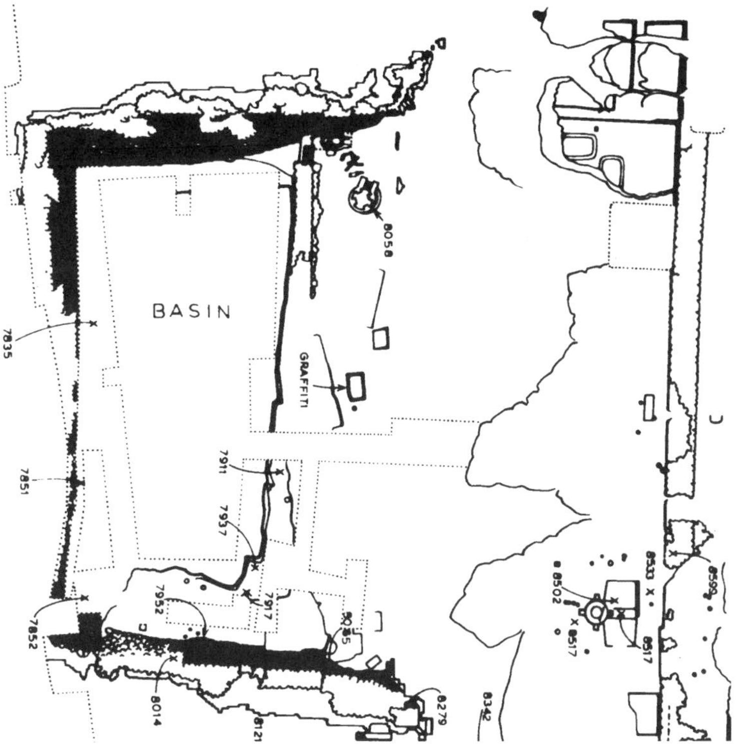

Figure 41.4. Plan of Basin at Serra East by James E. Knudstad. Courtesy of the Oriental Institute

of C-Group settlement (Aniba), and near the southern boundary (Buhen).[30] Patrol posts supplemented the forts as noted above. It is reasonable to assume that the northern forts in the list also existed and probably continued from an earlier time (see also Zibellius-Chen 1988, pp. 186–87).

Senwosret I might have put his fortresses in place to control major population centers; however, they are quite large for such a purpose. They each would have accommodated a garrison numerous enough to hold off a formidable force. Since one of the problems of strategic logistics in Nubia is assembling a force large enough to be tactically effective, the Egyptians might have deployed these forts to forestall just such an event. Small commandos of fighters could infiltrate across the desert from the Red Sea hills, Dongola, or even Abu Hamed.[31] They would arrive at the Nile, where there was water, but they would require food. As groups of commandos assembled, the larger unit would require greater resources than those available by hunting and gathering. If the local population could take refuge behind walls, or beyond the river, or active patrols could defeat the small commandos before they assembled into larger bodies, the strategy might avert a major campaign. The scattered forts deterred a kind of strategy that has been used successfully by such diverse desert fighters as the Arabs and the Apache.

30. Hayes 1971, p. 499; see also Säve-Söderbergh 1941, pp. 23, 69, 70, 88, 92, 98. A rock inscription at Semna may possibly belong to Senwosret I (Dunham and Janssen 1960, p. 132, RIS 9). Trigger (1976, pp. 64–65) credits Ikkur, Kuban, Aniba, Buhen, and, quoting H. S. Smith, Kor. His assumption of possible forts as far as Semna is not explained and may be due to the Nile mark noted above. For the early forts and reasons for the dates, see Firth 1912, pp. 22–25, pls. 34–36 (Ikkur); idem 1927, p. 43, pl. 1; Emery and Kirwan 1935, pp. 26–57 (Kuban), with the early Middle Kingdom date of the first fort pp. 26–27, pls. 11–13; Steindorff 1937, pp. 2–17 (Aniba; the fort probably does not predate Senwosret I, however). For relations with the local population, see Cohen 1992, pp. 92–101. Although some C-Group remains appear near the cataract forts, they were relatively meager and late, where they can be dated; for example, see Williams 1993, pl. 1; Säve-Söderbergh 1989, pl. 65. Serra Fort was not placed near any major C-Group settlement.

31. The largest party mentioned in the Semna dispatches consisted of thirty-two men and three asses (Smither 1945, p. 9, Despatch 4; Wente 1990, pp. 71–72, nn. 3–4). For the size of the caravan accompanied by Burckhardt through this desert and the strain it put on water resources, see Burckhardt 1822, pp. 180, 183 159 (the caravan's Ababdas fight the Bisharein). The well-known party of Asiatics depicted at Beni Hasan numbered thirty-seven. Without well-organized efforts to make wells (for example, Breasted 1906, §430–31), large bodies of troops could not pass through the desert or remain there for any length of time (for raids across the desert, see Burckhardt 1822, pp. 40, 64; along the river, p. 84). For an approximation of the range of the Pan Grave culture, see Sadr 1987, pp. 265–91; idem 1990, pp. 63–86; Bietak 1987b, pp. 113–28.

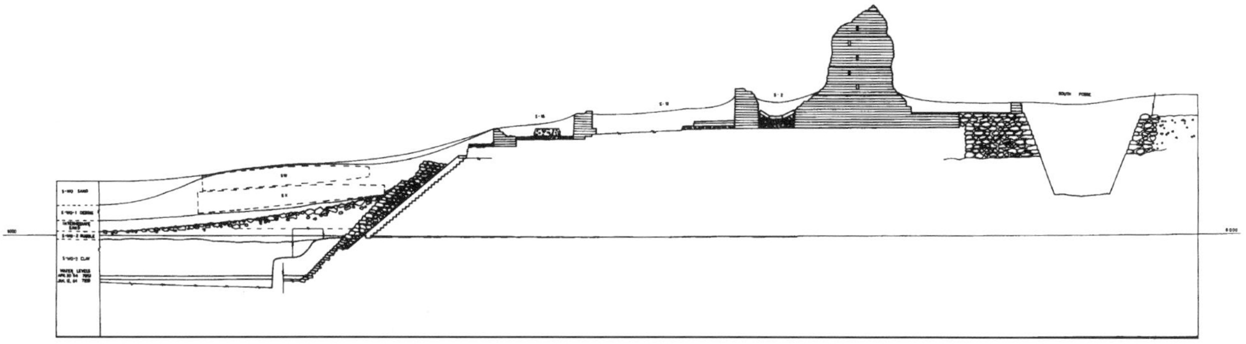

Figure 41.5. Section of Serra Fortress from South Fosse to Basin by James E. Knudstad. Courtesy of the Oriental Institute

However, the scattered fortresses of Senwosret I might not have sufficed to repel a well-organized enemy that assembled south of the frontier and advanced in force by way of the river.[32] In that case the enemy force might successfully capture fortresses or even overrun the region. To deal with such a possibility of attack from formidable Kush, Senwosret III redesigned the frontier and massively strengthened its components. The need for this change might well have emerged from some special aggressiveness on his part, which he displayed on the Asiatic as well as Nubian frontier, and which involved some of the same personnel, such as Khusebek (Sethe 1924, pp. 82–83; Breasted 1906, §§680–87). However, aggression from Kush is also a distinct possibility. The Egyptian failure at Sekmem and disruptions due to drastic constitutional and bureaucratic change could well have provided a tempting appearance of weakness.[33]

An additional factor would have been the powerful inducement for Egypt to keep foreigners as far from the population as possible. Egyptian renegades produced by the large political and administrative changes[34] and deserters from the corvée would have been available to any potential enemy for advice, encouragement, and assistance. A major dimension to this vulnerability was this large exodus of workers from their assigned labor. Egypt had long produced expatriates and had also taken pains to retrieve them. In the Eleventh Dynasty, Kay proudly recounted his successful patrol to an oasis (Dakhla?) to apprehend fugitives, while government propaganda against a life in exile was a prominent element of the literature in the early Twelfth Dynasty. If there was any change, the stream of deserters increased in the mid-nineteenth century. Many of these were apprehended and enslaved in perpetuity, but many probably remained at large, and escaped to other parts of Egypt or abroad. With a ten year total approaching 40,000 apprehended and enslaved, successful escapees probably numbered the same amount.[35] If only some of these reached upper Nubia, the rapid increase of Kushite agricultural pros-

32. The Semna stelae make clear that Senwosret expected Nubians to arrive by river (Sethe 1924, p. 84, Berlin 1157, lines 2 to end; Breasted 1906, §652), something which occurs in the Semna dispatches (Smither 1945, Despatches 1 and 7 refer to Nubians sailing upstream, while 6 does not specify the mode of transport and 8 is not well preserved). The depictions of shipping in the funerary chapels at Kerma show vessels that could be used in war fleets (Lacovara 1986, p. 54, fig 6; note that the vessels in fig. 7 are sacred barks) such as that shown in the tomb of Inyotef (TT 386; Jaroš-Deckert 1984, pl. 14, folding pl. 2; Bietak 1985, fig. 1). Some of this shipping was operated by Egyptians (see Bonnet 1991, p. 9, for a stela of two ship captains with Egyptian names).

33. Despite the triumphant phraseology, the Sekmem campaign was a retreat. Replacing the powerful nobles with an all-embracing bureaucracy is the kind of drastic change that can be expected to generate resistance. Quirke (1990, pp. 1–5), for example, accepts considerable change while noting the late date of the Qaw tombs. Nevertheless, the other nomarchs ceased to exist (Hayes 1971, p. 506).

34. Sinuhe is an example of an early Twelfth Dynasty political refugee of this type. He joined a colony of similar expatriates at the court of Amusinenshi; Gardiner (1916b, pp. 132–33 [29–30], 169) discusses his recruitment.

35. Note the processes against 76 Egyptians for desertion, which included arresting the families and enslaving either the principal or his relatives (Hayes 1955, pp. 19–60); Hayes (ibid., pp. 43–44, see also pp. 31, 56, 65) points out that this number represents three brief periods of reports in years 10, 31, and some year in between, of Amenemhat III, as much as a month, or as little as 26 days, which could be considered the general rate of desertion for the region from Akhmim to Gebel es-Silsila, perhaps including a third or a fourth of the Egyptian population. Such a rate would produce just under a thousand fugitives a year for the region, and 3,000–4,000 for the country as a whole. Considering that the bureaucratic control of the country was at its peak, this is a considerable loss, which would have been many times more severe had no means been used to stop it. In some cases, the desertions were plotted with the help of river skippers. Since these lists included only cases that resulted in permanent servitude, the actual losses were probably much larger and represented a major social hemorrhage; *LÄ* 1 "Amenemhet I.," cols. 188–89, refers to mass flight. With Egypt's population at perhaps 2.5 million, with 1.5 million or so capable adults, the loss of even a few thousand effective workers could be severely damaging. By such means, apprehended fugitives and their families could make a slave class of over 40,000 in ten years, and much more when

Figure 41.6. Basin Interior: South Wall from North. Photograph Serra 375. Courtesy of the Oriental Institute

perity and the equally dramatic improvement in every craft along Egyptian lines are thus easily explained. These developments were paralleled in western Asia, at Byblos, for example. A social hemorrhage that the state took pains to limit enriched and empowered potentially dangerous and hostile neighbors as it weakened Egypt.[36]

Although it is possible that work was done on some forts in the Batn el-Hajar before Senwosret III's great efforts, all the forts known to be complete before his time had one important feature in common, their location north of the Second Cataract. This indicates that the earlier complex was the result of a definite strategic design. If an opponent succeeded in assembling a formidable force, reinforcements could rapidly move upstream from Egypt. Because the forts were accessible to a war fleet from Egypt, any enemy without boats could easily be outmaneuvered and exhausted.[37]

The Second Cataract effectively isolated the new frontier from direct access to Egyptian support. Some serious, strategic problem must therefore have demanded the large-scale expenditure of effort and the new military

their issue and imports are considered; for the general nature of the documents, see Hayes 1955, pp. 127–29.

Weakness may have been more than apparent. If Kush was rapidly increasing in power, then the increased intensity of settlement in western Asia near the border was also a threat. Senwosret may well have had to dispossess the nobles and absorb their private forces into the national force to expand the frontier garrisons. Again, allowing for 500 men per fort, the new forts of Askut, Shalfak, Uronarti, Semna, Kumma, Semna South, and Serra East would use some 3,500 men. Even reduced this would equal the levies of five or six nomes, roughly Middle Egypt.

36. The northeast frontier was modified to accept Asiatics soon after this set of events, a move which led directly into the Hyksos age. Neither Asiatics nor Kushites nor Medjay were limited to the "one-percent rule" for available fighters. Essentially, all non-peasant adult males were available for a campaign. Thrown suddenly against forts, the Egyptians could be knocked off balance, requiring considerable time to muster and train a peasant levy to repel a large assault (see *Urk*. 7, pp. 14.10–15.12; Breasted 1906, §§519–22, for peasant levies in the period). In that case, strategic defeat was a distinct possibility for Egypt. Because of these conditions, the rise of Kush may have been a key element in the collapse of the Middle Kingdom.

Senwosret III's campaigns, four in Nubia (Hayes 1971, p. 507), foreshadow the events of the late Seventeenth and early Eighteenth Dynasties when Egypt fought enemies both in the north and south, sometimes virtually simultaneously (see Vandersleyen 1971, especially pp. 17–87; the problem did not cease with the expulsion of the Hyksos because Ahmose faced repeated revolts). At that time these enemies were in strategic communication (Habachi 1972, pp. 39–43; see also Säve-Söderbergh 1953, pp. 54–61). In this case, such a possibility might be dismissed except that Asiatics, Kushites (and other Nubians), Medjay, and Egyptians are cursed in the same group of late Middle Kingdom execration texts (Sethe 1926, pp. 33–69 [could the Egyptians, pp. 62–69, be expatriates?]; Posener 1940, pp. 47–96 [pp. 31–35 for Egyptians]). Note that contact between Medjay and Asiatics could have occurred in the Eastern Desert where both sought pasturage and mining opportunities.

37. The technique and practice of river warfare was also part of the Middle Kingdom heritage. Ankhtify of Moʿalla recounts it, as does Tefibi of Asyut, and a Nubian archer is shown at Thebes participating in a river fight (Bietak 1985).

Figure 41.7. Basin Interior: South Wall and Lower Ramp. Photograph Serra 378. Courtesy of the Oriental Institute

posture represented by the cataract forts. This change may be reflected in the deep-penetrating campaigns by Senwosret III, which needed an effective base south of the Second Cataract. It might have been due to some new exposure of Egyptian interests in Lower Nubia. Senwosret refers to Nubians arriving by river, a route that did not impose the same limitations on the deployment of enemy forces as those encountered on the desert passage.

Despite the Mirgissa slipway, the rapids of the Second Cataract proper effectively prevented the easy passage of a fleet from the north. Instead, potential opponents in the south were able to approach both from the desert and by the water, arrive in sufficient force to forage widely, and undertake a siege almost immediately. Without means of delaying the invasion, forces locally available would have to oppose any offensive without hope of rapid assistance. At the least, the patrol forces from the forts would have to be available for immediate assembly into a relief force. Since a single patrol from Iken contained 70 men plus officers, a very rough estimate of 700 to 1,000 soldiers from 10 to 15 such units might successfully oppose an attacking force sufficient to overcome a small fortified garrison of 200–250.[38] The fortresses themselves would have to remain fully manned continuously to protect the frontier. Were an enemy to seize one of them, the force might endanger the entire complex.

38. For various estimates of fortress garrisons, see S. Smith 1991b, pp. 128–30. Here I assume that the fortresses were built to have a completely defensible inner perimeter, according to the poliorcetic representations at Beni Hasan. That is, the besieger had to be prepared to pick at several stretches of wall at one time, and the defenders had to be prepared to repel an attack against the same stretches of curtain. The representations at Beni Hasan show archers and slingers attacking forts, but only archers and casters defending it, indicating that defensive practice required placing fighters too close together to permit the use of the sling. I would therefore estimate that a credible garrison required 1 or 2 fighters per meter or so of curtain (facing the land walls). If we assume that the fortresses were built to serve as bases for patrols that did not unduly deplete the garrison, Serra East might have had from 200 to 300 for wall service plus 50 for patrol. The scale is set by Mirgissa, which had at least 70 for patrol and inner land walls that could use from 400 to 500 or more fighters (S. Smith accepts 2,000 for Buhen and from 600 to 1,500 for Mirgissa, while Emery, Smith, and Millard 1979, pp. 41–42, generate a series of estimates for Buhen, of which 1,500 is the highest). Given the size of known military forces in the Middle Kingdom, from 4,000 to 5,000 would not be an unreasonable number of troops to man the walls of the forts that occupied the area from Semna South to Faras. Given the scale of the structures, this number would be quite busy repairing the forts, training, doing commissary and logistical work, and patrolling, with no other peacetime duties. Note that the outer enclosures of Mirgissa and Buhen would require large additional maintenance crews.

Using the area thought to belong to barracks, Dunham (1967, p. 118) estimates the garrison of Uronarti at 112–280, Kumma at 40–100, and the West Wing of Semna at 216–540. S. Smith (1993, p. 52) feels most would be available for service, leaving a small number to guard the walls. Since the actual dwelling space cannot be determined from ground plans, the estimate should be based on the number needed to man the perimeter against assault plus a patrol reserve. Smith

Figure 41.8. Basin Interior: North Revetment from West, Showing Kiln Area and Shelf. Photograph Serra S25 13A. Courtesy of the Oriental Institute

It is not certain that the cataract forts were strictly defensive in nature. Some of them had specialized features that could make them serve as staging areas for campaigns (Semna South, Buhen, Mirgissa)[39] or depots for supplies (Askut)[40] or administrative centers (Kor, Uronarti).[41] Even so, the areas required heavy protection, and the formidable walls indicate both that the enemy was capable of mounting a serious offensive, and that the Egyptians expected extended campaigns. In any case, like the earlier Lower Nubian forts, these were military rather than civil installations, for the latter are well known.[42]

SERRA EAST AND CATARACT COMPLEX

Like some of the other late forts Serra East might have served more than one military purpose. It was a simple rectangular fort built most probably by Senwosret III[43] so that its eastern wall was on the high desert and its western wall was along the riverbank (figs. 41.2–5), where stone piers jutting into the river protected the quay. Originally almost square (ca. 90 × 90–100 m), the walls and most of the surface installations near the river were obliterated, leaving only the upper two-thirds of the fortress,[44] which consisted of a ditch some 5 m

(ibid., p. 23) gives higher estimates for Buhen and Mirgissa of about 2,000 each, which may be a bit more than required for the inner wall of either fort.

39. See Emery, Smith, and Millard 1979, pls. 2–3; Vercoutter 1970, pp. 167–87 (discussion of the situation of Mirgissa); Žabkar and Žabkar 1982, p. 9, pl. 1a–b; a wall also ran to the vicinity of Semna South from north of Uronarti (p. 12). Neither of the low enclosure walls at Semna South were defensible.

40. S. Smith 1991b, pp. 115–17; idem 1993, pp. 58–61; Kemp 1986, pp. 123–30. For the minimum estimated ration units, see ibid., p. 133, about 8,000 for the cataract forts, maximum ca. 15,000. Kemp (ibid., p. 130) based his estimate of capacity on heights at Mirgissa and Uronarti of 3.4 m; see ibid., pp. 131–34, for the size of rations implied.

41. For the complex at Kor, see H. S. Smith 1966. Uronarti had a substantial palace (Dunham 1967, map 2, pls. 15–19, pp. 22–31). In addition to these detached buildings, the larger forts also supported enhanced administrative functions.

42. For forts and fortified settlements actually used at quarry and mining sites, see Shaw 1994, especially figs. 5–7. Note that mines in the Eastern Desert were not always in the hands of the Egyptians. The Bedja have both mined and quarried and the kohl brought to Khnumhotep, presumably from Gebel ez-Zeit, was delivered by Asiatics. For the scattered mining locations of various dates, see Castel and Soukiassian 1989, pp. 9–16.

43. Knudstad 1966, pp. 174–76. The earliest royal name found there was Senwosret III, inscribed in fine hieroglyphs on a reused block.

44. Remains of the stone piers or jetties visible early in this century were sketched by Mileham (1910, p. 40, pl. 30b). As reported to Knudstad, they later became the subject of fanciful speculation involving iron gates and, as usual, treasure.

wide and 2 m deep surrounding a great curtain. In the gebel, the ditch was rock cut, but in the alluvium, it was constructed of angled bricks with a stacked stone facing. The curtains rested on simple chip and sand foundations, consisting of a 5 m thick wall of brick laid in stretchers with some header courses. At approximately every seven to ten courses several layers of mats were put down, and transverse and longitudinal beams and poles were built into the structure, even at the surface. The wall was built in sections, which left vertical seams, and sometimes there were groups of vents in the wall one brick wide by two bricks high. At the surface, these vents seem to have been covered with mud plaster. At regular intervals along the wall, small piers were built against it. These were not bonded to the wall except by transverse beams that extended into it. Representations already noted from Beni Hasan (fig. 41.1) indicate that these piers supported machicolations or fighting platforms. At the corners, the piers were much wider. The fortress was overlooked only in one place, at the northeast corner. There the Egyptians constructed a spur with a fairly broad fighting platform that was apparently joined to the main wall by a bridge over the ditch. No gate was found, although a small postern might have existed in the eastern wall. It seems likely that the main gates faced the river. The entire exterior — walls, paving, and parapet — was repeatedly plastered and whitewashed, which was no matter of excessive military cleanliness; the plaster and wash would serve to cover up irregularities and flaws in the wall, such as beams, mats, and poles, that could be made into footholds. With the brick covered up, no precise estimate of the wall's height could be made, a common preoccupation of military intelligence in pre-modern eras.[45] Maintaining this plaster coat would probably have been a major occupation of the garrison, after patrolling.[46]

The internal structures of the fortress were deeply ruined. Nothing remains of the western structures, but remains of what may have been larger residences appear on the north. Along the east wall, on an upper terrace, relatively small rooms arranged along a corridor might have been barracks. On the south side were remains of a granary and probably storerooms and an administrative structure. On the lower terrace was a curious structure with four slabs and channels that slope inward to a central vessel, such as that which occurs in other forts. The structure was partly rock cut; nothing remains of the building in which it was located.

All of these types of buildings are well known from the Nubian forts, but the remaining structure is the most mysterious feature of any fortress: a rectangular stone-lined basin some 20 × 30 m in dimension (fig. 41.2 center). It is worth noting that Serra Fort was built in a slight declivity, which forced the construction of the terrace retaining walls; it may be that the fort was sited precisely to accommodate this feature. The basin was certainly the single largest structure in the fort, and, given the economical use of space elsewhere, it must have been the most important. Knudstad (1966, plan) originally thought it was a harbor, but there is no opening to the river.

The most obvious feature of the basin is the stone-lined sloping wall that surrounds it on three sides (figs. 41.6–8). Beginning at the eastern corners, the wall extended deeper and deeper as the rock surface on which it was founded descended. Near the western wall, the rock descended so abruptly that the base could not be found below the water table. The same was true in the middle of the basin, where workmen repeatedly probed but never found a bottom. The stone-lined wall consisted of a brick foundation with one edge carefully sloped with layers of fieldstone piled against it to make the desired angle (figs. 41.6–7). As the layers became thicker toward the top, the angle approached that used for the ditches.

This was not the only wall in the basin. To the east, Knudstad notes remains of a brick and stone wall that lined the edge of the stone slope, and he thinks that these wall remains were built as a terrace for a small group of kilns built later, but still within the Middle Kingdom. They may, however, be related to the underlying structure of the basin itself (see figs. 41.2, 4).

---

45. In estimating stone walls, an officer would usually measure a single stone, then count the stones.

46. As pointed out above, to be militarily effective walls must resist scaling and therefore be as smooth as possible. Knudstad notes repeated whitewashing and plaster layers on the forepavement of the curtain at Serra East. If the walls of Serra were 10 m high (Buhen's walls were about 11 m high; see Emery, Smith, and Millard 1979, p. 40), and the fortress were about 100 × 100 m in size, the exterior had at least 100,000 m^2 of surface to maintain on the curtains alone. If one person could plaster 5 m^2 in a day, replastering the fort would have required 20,000 man days or, at 300 days a year, about 67 man years. At this rate, a yearly plaster-whitewash would have been a full-time job for a patrol force. Even assuming incomplete maintenance, the task of keeping up the walls would have been formidable. Maintenance was probably as severe a problem as construction.

Perhaps ten million or more bricks were used in the walls at Buhen. If one bricklayer set 50 per day, 200,000 man days would be required, or 666 man years, to build Buhen. Given the size of Middle Kingdom expeditions, one or two campaign seasons would probably have made a fort defensible.

As mentioned, no bottom was found in the basin. To the east, a rough stone face appears to have been carved or quarried in the sloping rock, creating a vertical face. From the eastern corners, two sets of steps approach the slope at an angle, which has some small rock-cut cavities (including step-seats, not wall foundations). To the south, the slope was allowed to continue westward until it, too, abruptly dropped off and disappeared below the water table. This ramp-like slope had some postholes about halfway from the eastern edge to the end, and one small square depression that seems to be like an offering table. At the base of the north wall was a narrower shelf.

The Serra basin was a place difficult of access in a remote location inside a fortress. What it originally contained, the fortress guarded from people outside. The stone wall, while not sloped as abruptly as the ditches, is fairly steep, and if it were topped with a parapet wall, like the wall that closed off the eastern scarp, it would make a formidable barrier. This reconstruction would offer a reasonable explanation for an otherwise enigmatic structure: that it was intended to keep people in as much as the fortress kept them out. The people inside, being unarmed and unequipped, did not require defensive countermeasures, but they needed to be confined and to be watched and kept separate from potential friends outside. I conclude that the Serra basin was a place of confinement for dangerous military prisoners, perhaps intended for use primarily in times of unusual military activity, such as an offensive campaign.

Such a function would suit Serra's relative removal from the front line of action in the cataract region. It would also complement the forts in the group, Buhen (the rear staging area), Mirgissa (the forward staging area), Askut (the granary), and Semna South (the jump-off point, supported by Semna, Kumma, and Uronarti). These are only putative functions for a great offensive or defensive campaign. In other times the fortresses' functions and routines would be different. The frontier would be maintained in a high state of defensive readiness; desert patrols would intercept interlopers, and probably absconders. Foreigners could approach the border confidently expecting to receive correct treatment, conduct their business, and return in a highly structured procedure during which every action and statement was recorded and reviewed by responsible officials (Smither 1945, pp. 6–10).

CONCLUSION

From the Instruction to Merikare to the Semna dispatches, the policy of the Egyptians was to use fortification and patrols to control movement across frontiers where movement was expected to occur, and to repel attacks. Had there been more social cohesion in Egypt, maintaining external and internal security might not have required such a major effort. Although economic activity flourished behind these hardened frontiers, the fortresses were not outposts of trade, like those of the Portuguese so many centuries later.[47] Senwosret III said quite clearly why he built his forts (Breasted 1906, §§656–60; Sethe 1924, pp. 83–85), in a document that was as much a contract as a boast. Egypt's forts were a mudbrick curtain.

References

Adams, W. Y.

1977 *Nubia, Corridor to Africa.* Princeton: Princeton University Press.

1984 "The First Colonial Empire: Egypt in Nubia 3200–1200 B.C." *Comparative Studies in Society and History* 26: 36–71.

Anthes, R.

1928 *Die Felsinschriften von Hatnub nach den Aufnahmen Georg Möllers.* Untersuchungen zur Geschichte und Altertumskunde Aegyptens 9. Leipzig: J. C. Hinrichs.

1930 "Eine Polizeistreife des Mittleren Reiches in die westliche Oase." *Zeitschrift für ägyptische Sprache und Altertumskunde* 65: 108–14.

47. Trade is an insufficient explanation because the economic basis for a trade in luxury or ritual items in Egypt was very small. On the other hand, because the productive lifetime of a worker was short and land was more plentiful than labor, changing location to escape demands or improve one's economic situation was an attractive choice for many. For this reason, the security provided by the forts was not just political, keeping out intruders, but economic, keeping in labor.

Baer, K.

1963 "An Eleventh Dynasty Farmer's Letters to His Family." *Journal of the American Oriental Society* 83: 1–19.

Bell, B.

1971 "The Dark Ages in Ancient History 1: The First Dark Age in Egypt." *American Journal of Archaeology* 75: 2–26.

1975 "Climate and the History of Egypt: The Middle Kingdom." *American Journal of Archaeology* 79: 223–69.

Bietak, M.

1968 *Studien zur Chronologie der nubischen C-Gruppe: Ein Beitrag zur Frühgeschichte Unternubiens zwischen 2200 und 1550 vor Chr.* Berichte des Österreichischen Nationalkomitees der UNESCO-Aktion für die Rettung der Nubischen Altertümer 5. Österreichische Akademie der Wissenschaften, phil.-hist. Klasse, Denkschriften, 97. Vienna: Böhlau Verlag.

1985 "Zu den nubischen Bogenschützen aus Assiut: Ein Beitrag zur Geschichte der ersten Zwischenzeit." In *Mélanges Gamal Eddin Mokhtar,* volume 1, edited by P. Posener-Kriéger, pp. 87–97. Bibliothèque d'étude 97/1. Cairo: Institut français d'archéologie orientale.

1987a "Canaanites in the Eastern Nile Delta." In *Egypt, Israel, Sinai,* edited by A. Rainey, pp. 41–56. Tel Aviv: Tel Aviv University.

1987b "The C-Group and the Pan-Grave Culture in Nubia." In *Nubian Culture Past and Present* (Main Papers Presented at the Sixth International Conference for Nubian Studies in Uppsala, 11–16 August, 1986), edited by T. Hägg, pp. 113–28. Kungl. Vitterhets Historie och Antikvitets Akademien, Konferenser 17. Stockholm: Almqvist and Wiksell.

Bonnet, C.

1986a *Kerma: Territoire et métropole. Quatre leçons au Collège de France.* Cairo: Institut français d'archéologie orientale.

1986b "Les fouilles archéologiques de Kerma (Soudan). Rapport préliminaire sur les campagnes de 1984–1985 et 1985–1986." *Genava* n.s. 34: 5–20.

1988 "Les fouilles archéologiques de Kerma (Soudan). Rapport préliminaire sur les campagnes de 1986–1987 et 1987–1988." *Genava* n.s. 36: 5–20.

1991 "Les fouilles archéologiques de Kerma (Soudan). Rapport préliminaire sur les campagnes de 1988–1989, 1989–1990 et 1990–1991." *Genava* n.s. 39: 5–41.

1993 "Les fouilles archéologiques de Kerma (Soudan). Rapport préliminaire sur les campagnes de 1991–1992 et 1992–1993." *Genava* n.s. 43: 1–33.

Bourriau, J.

1981 "Nubians in Egypt during the Second Intermediate Period: An Interpretation Based on the Egyptian Ceramic Evidence." In *Studien zur altägyptischen Keramik,* edited by Do. Arnold, pp. 25–41. Mainz am Rhein: Philipp von Zabern.

1991 "Relations between Egypt and Kerma during the Middle and New Kingdoms." In *Egypt and Africa,* edited by W. V. Davies, pp. 129–44. London: British Museum Press.

Breasted, J. H.

1906 *Ancient Records of Egypt.* 5 volumes. Chicago: University of Chicago Press.

Brunner, H.

1937 *Die Texte aus den Gräbern der Herakleopolitenzeit von Siut mit Übersetzung und Erläuterungen.* Ägyptologische Forschungen 5. Glückstadt: J. J. Augustin.

Burckhardt, J. L.

1822 *Travels in Nubia.* Second edition. London: John Murray.

Butzer, K.

1976 *Early Hydraulic Civilization in Egypt.* Chicago: University of Chicago Press.

Castel, G., and G. Soukiassian

1989 *Gebel el-Zeit* 1: *Les Mines de galène (Égypte, IIe millénaire av. J.-C.).* Fouilles de l'Institut français d'archéologie orientale 35. Cairo: Institut français d'archéologie orientale.

Cohen, E. S.

1992 Egyptianization and the Acculturation Hypothesis: An Investigation of the Pan-Grave, Kerman and C-Group Material Cultures in Egypt and Sudan during the Second Intermediate Period and Eighteenth Dynasty. Ph.D. dissertation, Yale University.

Couyat, J., and P. Montet

1912/13 *Les inscriptions hiéroglyphiques et hiératiques du Ouâdi Hammâmât.* Mémoires de l'Institut français d'archéologie orientale 34. Cairo: Institut français d'archéologie orientale.

Davies, N. de G.

1935 "The Work of the Graphic Branch of the Expedition." In *The Egyptian Expedition 1934–1935*, edited by H. E. Winlock, pp. 46–57. Bulletin of the Metropolitan Museum of Art 30/2. New York: Metropolitan Museum of Art.

Dunham, D.

1967 *Uronarti Shalfak Mirgissa.* Second Cataract Forts 2. Boston: Museum of Fine Arts.

Dunham, D., and J. M. A. Janssen

1960 *Semna Kumma.* Second Cataract Forts 1. Boston: Museum of Fine Arts.

Emery, W. B., and L. P. Kirwan

1935 *The Excavations and Survey between Wadi es-Sebua and Adindan 1929–1931.* Service des antiquités de l'Égypte, Mission archéologique de Nubie, 1929–1934. Cairo: Government Press.

Emery, W. B.; H. S. Smith; and A. Millard

1979 *Excavations at Buhen* 1: *The Fortress of Buhen: The Archaeological Report.* Egypt Exploration Society Memoir 49. London: Egypt Exploration Society.

Faulkner, R. O.

1953 "Egyptian Military Organization." *Journal of Egyptian Archaeology* 39: 32–47.

1962 *A Concise Dictionary of Middle Egyptian.* Oxford: Griffith Institute.

Firth, C. M.

1912 *The Archaeological Survey of Nubia, Report for 1908–1909*. Cairo: Government Press.

1927 *The Archaeological Survey of Nubia, Report for 1910–1911*. Cairo: Government Press.

Fischer, H.

1961 "The Nubian Mercenaries of Gebelein during the First Intermediate Period." *Kush* 9: 44–80.

Gardiner, A. H.

1916a "An Ancient List of the Fortresses of Nubia." *Journal of Egyptian Archaeology* 3: 184–92.

1916b *Notes on the Story of Sinuhe*. Paris: Librairie Honoré Champion.

1947 *Ancient Egyptian Onomastica*. Oxford: Oxford University Press.

1961 *Egypt of the Pharaohs*. Oxford: Oxford University Press.

Gratien, B.

1978 *Les cultures Kerma: Essai de classification*. Publications de l'Université de Lille III. Lille: Université de Lille.

1986 *Saï* 1: *La nécropole Kerma*. Paris: Éditions du Centre national de la recherche scientifique.

1994 "Les institutions égyptiennes en Nubie au Moyen Empire, d'après les emprientes de sceaux." In *Nubia Thirty Years Later: Pre-publication of Main Papers* (Papers presented at Society for Nubian Studies, Eighth International Conference, Lille 11–17 September 1994), edited by F. Geus. Lille: Université Charles de Gaulle, Institut de papyrologie et d'égyptologie.

Habachi, L.

1972 *The Second Stela of Kamose and His Struggle Against the Hyksos Ruler and His Capital*. Abhandlungen des Deutschen archäologischen Instituts, Kairo, ägyptologische Reihe 8. Glückstadt: J. J. Augustin.

Hayes, W. C.

1949 "Career of the Great Steward Henenu under Nebhepetre Mentuhotpe." *Journal of Egyptian Archaeology* 35: 43–49.

1953 *The Scepter of Egypt: A Background for the Study of Egyptian Antiquities in the Metropolitan Museum of Art from the Earliest Times to the End of the Middle Kingdom*. Cambridge: Harvard University Press.

1955 *A Papyrus of the Late Middle Kingdom in the Brooklyn Museum [Papyrus Brooklyn 35.1446]*. Brooklyn: Brooklyn Museum.

1971 "The Middle Kingdom in Egypt." In *The Cambridge Ancient History*, Volume 1, Part 2: *Early History of the Middle East*, edited by I. E. S. Edwards, C. J. Gadd, and N. G. L. Hammond, pp. 464–531. Cambridge: Cambridge University Press.

Helck, W.

1977 *Die Lehre für König Merikare*. Kleine ägyptische Texte. Wiesbaden: Otto Harrassowitz.

1986 *Der Text der "Lehre Amenemhets I. für seine Sohn."* Second edition. Kleine ägyptische Texte. Wiesbaden: Otto Harrassowitz.

1992 *Die Prophezeiung des Nfr.tj*. Second edition. Kleine ägyptische Texte. Wiesbaden: Otto Harrassowitz.

Hintze, F.

1964 "Das Kerma-Problem." *Zeitschrift für ägyptische Sprache und Altertumskunde* 91: 79–86.

Howell, P. P.

1952 "Death and Burial of Reth Dak Fadier." *Sudan Notes and Records* 33: 156–64.

Hughes, G. R.

1963 "Serra East, The University of Chicago Excavations, 1961–62: A Preliminary Report on the First Season's Work." *Kush* 11: 121–30.

Jaroš-Deckert, B.

1984 *Das Grab des Jnj-jtj.f: Die Wandmalereien der XI. Dynastie*. Grabung im Asasif, 1963–1970, Band 5. Deutsches archäologisches Institut, Abteilung Kairo, archäologische Veröffentlichungen 12. Mainz am Rhein: Philipp von Zabern.

Junker, H.

1920 *Bericht über die Grabungen der Akademie der Wissenschaften in Wien auf den Friedhöfen von el-Kubanieh-Nord Winter 1910–1911*. Akademie der Wissenschaften in Wien, phil.-hist. Klasse, Denkschriften, 64/3. Vienna: Alfred Hölder.

Kemp, B.

1986 "Large Middle Kingdom Granary Buildings and the Archaeology of Administration." *Zeitschrift für ägyptische Sprache und Altertumskunde* 113: 120–36.

Knudstad, J. E.

1966 "Serra East and Dorginarti: A Preliminary Report on the 1963/64 Excavations of the University of Chicago Oriental Institute Sudan Expedition." *Kush* 14: 165–86.

Lacovara, P.

1986 "The Funerary Chapels at Kerma." *Cahier de recherches de l'Institut de papyrologie et d'égyptologie de Lille* 8: 49–58.

Lawrence, A. W.

1965 "Ancient Egyptian Fortifications." *Journal of Egyptian Archaeology* 51: 69–94.

Leprohon, R.

1994 "Maintien de l'ordre dans la Nubie au Moyen Empire." In *Hommages à Jean Leclant*, volume 2: *Nubie, Soudan, Éthiopie*, edited by C. Berger, G. Clerc, and N. Grimal, pp. 285–91. Bibliothèque d'étude 106/2. Cairo: Institut français d'archéologie orientale.

Mileham, G. S.

1910 *Churches in Lower Nubia*. Eckley B. Coxe Junior Expedition to Nubia 2. Philadelphia: University Museum.

Naville, E.

1910 *The XIth Dynasty Temple at Deir el-Bahari*, Part 2. Egypt Exploration Fund Memoir 30. London: Egypt Exploration Fund.

Newberry, P. E.

1893 *Beni Hasan*, Part 1. Archaeological Survey of Egypt 1. London: Egypt Exploration Fund.

1894 *Beni Hasan*, Part 2. Archaeological Survey of Egypt 2. London: Egypt Exploration Fund.

O'Connor, D.
1984 "Kerma and Egypt: The Significance of the Monumental Buildings, Kerma I, II, and XI." *Journal of the American Research Center in Egypt* 21: 65–108.
1986 "The Locations of Yam and Kush and Their Historical Implications." *Journal of the American Research Center in Egypt* 23: 27–50.
1991 "Early States along the Nubian Nile." In *Egypt and Africa*, edited by W. V. Davies, pp. 145–65. London: British Museum Press.

Osing, J.
1976 "Ächtungstexte aus dem Alten Reich (II)." *Mitteilungen des Deutschen archäologischen Instituts, Abteilung Kairo* 32: 133–85.

Petrie, W. M. F.
1898 *Deshasheh*. Egypt Exploration Fund Memoir 15. London: Egypt Exploration Fund.

Posener, G.
1940 *Princes et pays d'Asie et de Nubie: Textes hiératiques sur des figurines d'envoûtement du Moyen Empire*. Brussels: Fondation Égyptologique Reine Élisabeth.
1956 *Littérature et politique dans l'Égypte de la XIIe dynastie*. Bibliothèque de l'École des haute études 307. Paris: Librairie ancienne Honoré Champion.

Quibell, J. E., and A. G. K. Hayter
1927 *Teti Pyramid, North Side*. Excavations at Saqqara 8. Cairo: Institut français d'archéologie orientale.

Quirke, S.
1990 *The Administration of Egypt in the Late Middle Kingdom: The Hieratic Documents*. New Malden, Surrey: SIA Publishing.

Reisner, G. A.
1923 *Excavations at Kerma*, Parts 1–5. Harvard African Studies 5–6. Cambridge: Peabody Museum of Harvard University.
1929 "Ancient Egyptian Forts at Semna and Uronarti." *Bulletin of the Museum of Fine Arts, Boston* 27: 64–75.

Sadr, K.
1987 "The Territorial Expanse of the Pan-Grave Culture." *Archéologie du Nil Moyen* 2: 265–91.
1990 "The Medjay in Southern Atbai." *Archéologie du Nil Moyen* 4: 63–86.

Säve-Söderbergh, T.
1941 *Ägypten und Nubien: Ein Beitrag zur Geschichte altägyptischer Aussenpolitik*. Lund: Håkan Ohlssons Boktryckeri.
1953 "The Nubian Kingdom of the Second Intermediate Period." *Kush* 4: 54–61.
1989 *Middle Nubian Sites*. The Scandinavian Joint Expedition to Sudanese Nubia 4. Stockholm: Paul Åstrom Editions.

Schenkel, W.
1965 *Memphis Herakleopolis Theben: Die epigraphischen Zeugnisse der 7.–11. Dynastie Ägyptens*. Ägyptologische Abhandlungen 12. Wiesbaden: Otto Harrassowitz.

Sethe, K.
1924 *Aegyptische Lesestücke zum Gebrauch im akademische Unterricht*. Leipzig: J. C. Hinrichs.
1926 *Die Ächtung feindlicher Fürsten, Völker und Dinge auf altägyptischen Tongefässscherben des Mittleren Reiches*. Berlin: Walter de Gruyter.

Shaw, I.
1994 "Pharaonic Quarrying and Mining." *Antiquity* 68/258: 108–19.

Simpson, W. K.
1973 *The Literature of Ancient Egypt: An Anthology of Stories, Instructions, and Poetry*. New edition. New Haven: Yale University Press.

Smith, H. S.
1966 "Kor: Report on the Excavations of the Egypt Exploration Society at Kor." *Kush* 14: 187–243.

Smith, S. T.
1990 "Administration at the Egyptian Middle Kingdom Frontier: Sealings from Uronarti and Askut." In *Aegean Seals, Sealings and Administration* (Proceedings of the NEH-Dickson Conference of the Program in Aegean Scripts and Prehistory of the Department of Classics, University of Texas at Austin, 11–13 January 1989), edited by T. G. Palaima, pp. 197–216. Aegaeum 5. Liège: Université de Liège.
1991a "A Model for Egyptian Imperialism in Nubia." *Göttinger Miszellen* 122: 77–102.
1991b "Askut and the Purpose of the Second Cataract Forts." *Journal of the American Research Center in Egypt* 28: 107–32.
1993 Askut and the Changing Nature of Egyptian Imperialism in the Second Millennium BC. Ph.D. dissertation, University of Southern California.

Smither, P. C.
1945 "The Semnah Dispatches." *Journal of Egyptian Archaeology* 31: 3–10.

Steindorff, G.
1937 *Aniba*, Band 2. Glückstadt: J. J. Augustin.

Trigger, B. G.
1976 *Nubia under the Pharaohs*. Ancient Peoples and Places 85. Boulder: Westview Press.
1982 "The Reasons for the Construction of the Second Cataract Forts." *Journal of the Society for the Study of Egyptian Antiquities* 12: 1–6.

Vandersleyen, C.
1971 *Les guerres d'Amosis, fondateur de la XVIIIe dynastie*. Monographies Reine Élisabeth 1. Brussels: Fondation Égyptologique Reine Élisabeth.

Vandier, J.
1950 *Mo'alla: La tombe d'Ankhtifi et la tombe de Sébekhotep*. Bibliothèque d'étude 18. Cairo: Institut français d'archéologie orientale.

Vercoutter, J.
1970 *Mirgissa* 1. Mission archéologique française au Soudan 1. Paris: Direction général des relations culturelles, scientifiques et techniques, Ministère des

affaires étrangères avec le concours du Centre national de la recherche scientifique.

Vycichl, W.
1958 "Burial of the Sudanese Kings in the Middle Ages." *Kush* 7: 221–22.

Wente, E. F.
1990 *Letters from Ancient Egypt.* Society of Biblical Literature, Writings from the Ancient World 1. Atlanta: Scholars Press.

Williams, B. B.
1983 *Excavations Between Abu Simbel and the Sudan Frontier,* Part 5: *C-Group, Pan Grave, and Kerma Remains at Adindan Cemeteries T, K, U, and J.* Oriental Institute Nubian Expedition 5. Chicago: Oriental Institute.
1993 *Excavations at Serra East,* Parts 1–5: *A-Group, C-Group, Pan-Grave, New Kingdom, and X-Group Remains from Cemeteries A–G and Rock Shelters.* Oriental Institute Nubian Expedition 9. Chicago: Oriental Institute.
1994 "Security and the Problem of the City in the Naqada Period." In *For His Ka: Essays Offered in Memory of Klaus Baer,* edited by D. P. Silverman, pp. 267–83. Studies in Ancient Oriental Civilization 55. Chicago: Oriental Institute.

Winlock, H. E.
1942 *Excavations at Deir el Bahri, 1911–1931.* New York: MacMillan.
1945 *The Slain Soldiers of King Neb-hepet-re' Mentu-hotpe.* Publications of the Metropolitan Museum of Art Egyptian Expedition 16. New York: Metropolitan Museum of Art.

Yadin, Y.
1963 *The Art of Warfare in Biblical Lands in the Light of Archaeological Study.* New York: McGraw-Hill.

Žabkar, L. V.
1972 "The Egyptian Name of the Fortress of Semna South." *Journal of Egyptian Archaeology* 58: 83–90.
1975 "Semna South: The Southern Fortress." *Journal of Egyptian Archaeology* 61: 42–44.

Žabkar, L. V., and J. J. Žabkar
1982 "Semna South: A Preliminary Report on the 1966–68 Excavations of the University of Chicago Oriental Institute Expedition to Sudanese Nubia." *Journal of the American Research Center in Egypt* 19: 7–50.

Zibellius-Chen, K.
1988 *Die ägyptische Expansion nach Nubien.* Beihefte zum Tübinger Atlas des Vorderen Orients, Reihe B, Nr. 78. Wiesbaden: Ludwig Reichert Verlag.

Ziermann, M.
1993 *Elephantine* 16: *Befestigungsanlagen und Stadtentwicklung in der Frühzeit und im frühen Alten Reich.* Deutsches archäologisches Institut, Abteilung Kairo, archäologisches Veröffentlichungen 87. Mainz am Rhein: Philipp von Zabern.

42

END OF THE LATE BRONZE AGE AND OTHER CRISIS PERIODS: A VOLCANIC CAUSE?

FRANK J. YURCO

The Field Museum of Natural History, Chicago

The great social, economic, and political upheavals that resulted in the ending of the Late Bronze Age and brought on the onset of the Iron Age have been ascribed to many different causes and factors by scholars who have studied the period. Many agree that a major part of the initial disruption was caused by the activities of the so-called Sea Peoples, whose raids started as piratical marauding on shipping and unprotected, isolated coastal settlements; these raids are documented from the Amarna period to the time of Ramesses II (1279–1212 B.C.).[1] Their growing threat was noticed by Ramesses II, who built a line of fortresses from the western Delta edge westward to Marsah Matruh and southward to the region of Memphis (Habachi 1980; Kitchen 1982, pp. 71–72). Ramesses II fought an engagement against Sea People raiders in his 2nd regnal year (Kitchen 1982, pp. 40–41). Global climate cooling of some type may be implicated in these population movements after 1300 B.C. (Baillie 1989, p. 81).

More serious raids by the Sea Peoples began in Merneptah's reign (1212–1202 B.C.). In this period, a large body of Sea Peoples managed to land on the African coast west of the last fortress at Marsah Matruh, probably in Cyrenaica. There they armed and equipped the Libyans with bronze weapons, and with them jointly mounted an invasion into Egypt proper (Kitchen 1982, pp. 215–16). Very probably their activity also encouraged the southern Libyans, the Tjemehu, to revolt along with the Nubians. Merneptah reacted speedily and thoroughly, crushing the southern Nubian-Libyan revolt with great cruelty (Kitchen 1982, p. 215) and then met the allied Sea Peoples and Libyans as they approached Egypt, probably along the Wadi Natrun. With his archers and chariotry he inflicted a major defeat on the allied foes, slaying some 9,300 of their number (Kitchen 1982, p. 215).

Merneptah's great inscription at Karnak temple of this victory also records that he had been sending grain to the Hittites, who had stood allied with Egypt since the great peace treaty of Ramesses II's 21st regnal year (Wainwright 1960, pp. 24–28; Kitchen 1982, pp. 75–81). Additionally, the finding of a long Sea Peoples' type bronze sword, stamped with Merneptah's cartouche, at Ugarit (Schaeffer 1955, pp. 226–29; KRI 4, 24) strongly suggests that Merneptah was also sending arms aid to the Hittites and their vassal states. The sword from Ugarit may well be part of the bronze weaponry that Merneptah's forces captured from the Libyans and Sea Peoples in the great victory of his 5th regnal year because the great Karnak temple inscription mentions over 9,300 weapons seized as booty. These bits of information also suggest that the Hittites and their vassals were facing a crisis. The Egyptian grain shipments hint at crop failures in Anatolia, perhaps drought related. Schaeffer, who excavated Ugarit, thought that drought struck the Near East in this period, a view also supported by Herodotus's account of the migration of the ancestors of the Etruscans from Anatolia to Italy.[2] Though some have doubted extensive droughts (Drews 1993, pp. 77–84), glimmers of evidence do suggest that climate-induced drought might have been a factor in the troubles that the Near East was experiencing (Baillie 1989, p. 81; KRI 4, 4.14–15).

---

1. See Moran 1992, p. 111. El-Amarna letter no. 38 mentions Lukka raids on Cyprus. Ramesses II captured some Shardana who were raiding the Delta in his 2nd regnal year; see KRI 2, 290.2 (Tanis, Shardana stela); Kitchen 1982, pp. 40–41. These were the earliest piratical raids.

2. Schaeffer 1968, pp. 607–768; Grene 1987, pp. 78–79 (Herodotus I, 94); though drought is doubted by Drews 1993, pp. 79–80. The frailty of many Mediterranean environments, however, is highlighted by Sandars (1985, pp. 21–24, figs. 7–9) and Baillie (1989, pp. 80–81).

Gold of Praise: Studies on Ancient Egypt in Honor of Edward F. Wente
Edited by Emily Teeter and John A. Larson
Studies in Ancient Oriental Civilization 58
Chicago: Oriental Institute, 1999

The organized raids of the Sea Peoples were a growing menace. A second phase of Sea Peoples' marauding might also have included the Homeric assaults on Thebes and Troy recorded in the Greek epics (see Fitzgerald 1975, pp. 23–24). As Merneptah's inscription denotes, these second phase raids were not the result of migrations but rather were opportunistic raids by some of the still extant Mycenaean Bronze Age Greek and Anatolian polities. Hittite archives also indicate a long period of difficulty with their western neighbors, the Mycenaeans, and the southwest Anatolian states of Lukka and Arzawa (McQueen 1986, pp. 49–50, 55–56).

A third phase of Sea Peoples' raids came in the reign of Ramesses III (1182–1152 B.C.). This time the raids were far more serious, as they were not just raiders but in fact whole populations migrating.[3] Very different from the time of Merneptah when the Sea Peoples were bodies of armed men who approached Egypt from the west allied with the Libyans, the raid under Ramesses III during his 8th regnal year approached Egypt from the Levant (Sandars 1985, pp. 144–56; Yurco 1998). Ramesses III's inscriptions document that these Sea Peoples originated in the Aegean area, that they helped destroy the Hittites and their vassal states, and that they established an encampment in Amurru, in northern Syria, which they had also devastated. They also captured and occupied Cyprus at this stage (Sandars 1985, pp. 144–49). Next they moved by both land and sea against Egypt. Ramesses III met the sea contingent in the Delta, where the sea raiders were enticed to approach. His archers, stationed along the banks, shattered their crews, while the Egyptian naval forces capsized the enemy's ships. Many were seized as prisoners, others drowned in the Delta waterways (Nelson 1943, pp. 40–55; *MH* 1, pls. 32–34). The land contingent was confronted by the Egyptian armies somewhere in Syria-Palestine. The Medinet Habu temple reliefs of Ramesses III depict the land contingent of Sea Peoples moving together with women and children in Anatolian style wagons and carts.[4] This was then a real migration of a whole people. Ramesses III was able to deflect this land movement away from Egypt's frontier, but he was constrained to allow them to settle along the coasts of Palestine and Lebanon (Sandars 1985 pp. 157–74; Dothan and Dothan 1992; Redford 1992, pp. 250–56, 289–93). Ramesses III also faced two additional attacks from the Libyans during his 5th and 11th regnal years. Though Ramesses III defeated them, especially after the second war, some were settled inside Egypt as prisoners (Kitchen 1986, p. 245; KRI 5, 91.5–7). These major Libyan attacks suggest that some pressures were impelling the Libyans towards Egypt.

This same period of migrations by the last Sea Peoples also marks the era of the collapse of the Hittite imperial state, the northern Syrian states, the Kassite state in Babylon, and the Mycenaean Bronze Age kingdoms. Various causes have been proposed for this broad-ranging series of societal collapses, from the Dorian invasions, to a revolt of the subject peoples of the Mycenaeans, the introduction of a new style of weaponry for infantry and tactics that crippled the sole dependence on chariotry practiced by many Late Bronze Age states (McQueen 1986, pp. 50–52; Drews 1993). Certainly all these elements could be possible causes, among others, for the collapses, but was any one of them enough to cause the wide-ranging collapses and difficulties that marked the end of the Late Bronze Age, especially the widespread migrations, attested by the Medinet Habu reliefs and texts, of Libyans and Sea Peoples who settled in coastal Palestine and Lebanon, and the movement of the survivors of the Hittite state into northern Syria? There also are many legends and traditions about migrations that arose at this time, including the great Aramaean migrations into the settled areas of the Near East. So, it seems that some global scale disturbance was at work to account for such widespread collapses and migrations, and Egypt may provide the clue to that.

Ramesses III (1182–1152 B.C.) started facing difficulties in supplying grain rations to the state-employed Deir el-Medina community in the later years of his reign (Edgerton 1951, pp. 137–45). Slightly later, under Ramesses VI–VIII (1141–1127 B.C.), the grain prices of emmer wheat and barley rose very sharply to a peak before declining, while the prices for cattle, sheep, pigs, goats, and slaves remained quite constant and stable (Janssen 1975, pp. 112–16, 119–22; Trigger et al. 1983, pp. 228–29). Hitherto, no reasonable cause of this distinctive economic crisis in Egypt has been established; bureaucratic corruption, Libyan marauding, and low Nile floods have been proposed as causes (Trigger et al. 1983, pp. 226–29), but they either do not coincide chronologically or they are not documented countrywide. A possible cause to be considered here is a mega-volcanic eruption and its impact on the global climate, in particular, regarding this crisis, the 1159–1140 B.C. extended

3. Edgerton and Wilson 1936, pp. 30–39, 41–42; *MH* 1, pls. 32–34; Yurco 1998.

4. Sandars 1985, pp. 120–24, pls. 76–78; also *MH* 1, pls. 32–34, that clearly depict and describe the migrations; contra Drews (1993, pp. 48–72) who doubts the migrations in this period.

eruption of Mount Hekla in Iceland.[5] The study of mega-volcanic eruptions and their impact on history is a relatively recent field of research, one propelled by ongoing research in volcanology and supplemented by ice-core analysis and dendrochronology, which have advanced dramatically in recent decades. The effects of these volcanic eruptions have left evidence across many cultures worldwide.

Briefly assessed, mega-volcanic eruptions of certain volcanoes eject vast quantities of ash and other erupted materials high into the stratosphere. Especially violent eruptions of volcanoes that spew out ash high in silica and sulfur often have a major impact on the climate, as the ejecta rise into global circulating winds and jet streams, causing the volcanic matter to circle around the globe (Rampino and Self 1984, pp. 677–79). This volcanic matter in the stratosphere can cause a lowering of global temperatures by means of the globe circling ejecta reflecting solar radiation back out into space.[6] The lowering of global temperatures may be severe enough to cause aborted growing seasons, crop failures, and major dislocations near the erupting volcano and hemispherically or globally after a large-scale eruption. Trees have narrowed or missing growth rings following such eruptions. Long and deep records of tree rings from Irish and German oaks, American bristlecone pines, and now Aegean and Mediterranean trees can, independent of carbon 14 dating, even more precisely date a historic eruption (Baillie 1995, pp. 73–90, 108–21; Baillie 1989, pp. 78–81). Such massive eruptions, termed Plinian-Krakatauan, may be so great that their world-circling ejecta is deposited in the ice forming on the polar regions of the world, and if the eruption is high in sulfur and silica emissions, the ejecta that falls on the polar ice leaves an acidic signature in the forming ice. The study of ice cores extracted from the polar ice can pinpoint such acidic traces and then using carbon 14 dating establish a historical date for the eruption.

In modern times, the best example of such a mega-eruption is the 1815 eruption of Mount Tambora on Sumbuwa Island in the East Indies (Foden 1986; Stothers 1984, pp. 1194–98; Rampino and Self 1982, pp. 127–43). After that enormous eruption which was reflected in ash and acidic deposits in the ice caps of both polar regions, major climatic disturbances were documented in 1816/17 in the northern hemisphere (Scandinavia, Europe, Canada, and New England). All these areas experienced snow and frosts in midsummer, causing crop failures. In autumn 1816, grain prices rose sharply, but animal and meat prices stayed level, as farmers unable to feed their stock on hay butchered their animals and thus saturated the meat market (Post 1977; Stommel and Stommel 1979, pp. 176–86, especially pp. 180–82; Stothers 1984, pp. 1191–98). This very same price and economic pattern is recorded for the reigns of Ramesses VI–VIII, when grain prices rose sharply, while prices for animals stayed quite stable. Scandinavia was aided in 1816/17 by Egypt, as Muhammad Ali, the khedive, exported Egyptian grain in exchange for pig iron (Marsot 1988, pp. 144, 167). New England suffered far more, as farms failed, people suffered privation, and some finally migrated out of the region (Stommel and Stommel 1979, pp. 176–86). Other great eruptions in modern times have been Krakatau in the Sunda Strait, Indonesia, 1883; Mount Katmai-Novarupta, Alaska, 1912; Mount Agung, Indonesia, 1963; and most recently, Mount Pinatubo, Philippines, 1991/92. All these volcanic eruptions have been high in silica and sulfur ejecta and have left distinctive signatures in the polar ice, in tree rings, and in ash fall over widespread regions.[7] Each also cooled the global climate, but not on the scale that Tambora did in 1816/17, as none approached Tambora in the sheer volume of ejecta. Thus, it can be demonstrated from the modern era volcanic eruptions of large enough scale that ice cores and tree rings reflect such an eruption and yield an exact dating of it.

Hekla volcano's massive, extended eruption is now dated from 1159 B.C. to about 1140 B.C. by Greenland ice cores, shrunken tree rings in California bristlecones, Irish and German oaks, and tephra (ash) recovered from Irish peat bogs. The eruption is labeled Hekla III.[8] The central Icelandic volcanoes, of which Mount Hekla is one, have extended basaltic lava eruptions, but they also eject highly acidic and sulfuric material into the stratosphere (Gudmundsson 1995, pp. 5–6). Ancient Zhou Dynasty Chinese chronicles of the same date as the

5. Baillie 1995, p. 82, fig. 5.3; Baillie 1994, p. 216, table 1; Baillie 1989, pp. 78–81; Stothers and Rampino 1983, pp. 411–13; Hammer, Claussen, and Dansgaard 1980, p. 231, table 1, p. 233.

6. Stothers et al. 1989, pp. 3–9; Lamb 1971, pp. 203–30; Rampino, Stothers, and Self 1985, p. 272; Rampino, Self, and Stothers 1988, pp. 82–89; Handler 1989, pp. 233–49.

7. For the ice-core data, see Hammer, Claussen, and Dansgaard 1980, pp. 230–35. For tree-ring evidence, see Baillie 1989, pp. 78–79; LaMarche and Hirschboek 1984, pp. 121–26; also Baillie and Munro 1988, pp. 344–46. For tephra (ash) falls, see Watkins et al. 1978, pp. 122–26; Rampino and Self 1982, pp. 127–43; Stothers and Rampino 1983, pp. 411–13.

8. Baillie 1995, p. 82, fig. 5.3; Baillie 1989, pp. 78–81; Hammer, Claussen, and Dansgaard 1980, pp. 230–35; Baillie and Munro 1988, pp. 344–46; Bernal 1991, pp. 281–83.

eruption of Hekla III mention ash fall and snow in summer, crop failures, and governmental collapse.[9] To judge by the tephra in the Irish peat bogs, the tree-ring evidence, and also ice-core data, as well as the Chinese historic documentation, the impact of the Hekla III eruption was worldwide, and its effects appear, like those of Tambora in 1816/17, to have had serious economic effects (Baillie 1995, pp. 88–89; Baillie 1989, pp. 80–81).

The date of the eruption of Hekla III, 1159 B.C., falls seven years before the end of Ramesses III's reign, precisely at the time that he began to face difficulty in supplying grain rations to Deir el-Medina's workers (Edgerton 1951, pp. 139–45). According to the tree-ring analysis especially, Hekla III continued to have climatic impact until about 1140 B.C. (Baillie 1989, pp. 79–81); thus, the same volcanic event may also be echoed in the mid-Twentieth Dynasty price inflation under Ramesses VI–VIII. The Egyptian crisis again exactly parallels the 1816/17 crisis after Mount Tambora's eruption of 1815. Egypt normally stocked grain adequate to weather one or two bad crops caused by low Nile floods, but the prolonged effect of Hekla III's eruption might have exhausted even these reserves. The Icelandic volcanoes differ from explosive volcanoes, such as those in the East Indies, or Thera-Santorini; they are more akin to hot-spot volcanoes such as those in Hawaii, as Iceland is in fact an outcrop of land built off the ocean floor and the mid-Atlantic rift. Such volcanoes can have much longer extended eruption cycles and that may explain Hekla III's extended eruption documented by the tree rings from 1159 to 1140 B.C. Exactly as the situation in Europe and North America documents the aftermath of the Tambora 1815 eruption in 1816/17, during mid-Twentieth Dynasty Egypt grain prices rose sharply and peaked while the prices of animals stayed level (Janssen 1975, pp. 112–16, 119–22; Trigger et al. 1983, pp. 228–29). So, the Ramesses III/mid-Twentieth Dynasty crisis in Egypt's economy seems to be the result of the global impact of the eruption on an extended scale of the volcano, Hekla III, and its 1159–1140 B.C. eruption cycle (Baillie 1995, pp. 82–83, 89).

If the impact of the extended eruption cycle and its effects were indeed thusly reflected on Egypt's economic life, the impact on Greece, Anatolia, and the Levantine lands could only have been worse, as those regions normally did not produce grain surpluses that could be set aside in a reserve, as Egypt normally did (Sandars 1985, pp. 77–79; Baillie 1989, p. 81). The effect over desert regions might have been even worse, leading such people as the Libyans and the Aramaeans to migrate toward the settled areas (Sandars 1985, pp. 21–24, figs. 7–9; Baillie 1989, p. 81; KRI 4, 4.14–15). In Merneptah's reign, indeed, the Egyptians had been able to ship surplus grain to the Hittites, but in the mid-Twentieth Dynasty, when Egypt itself felt the crisis, there could be no relief for foreign lands. Further, Egypt might have faced additional Libyan inroads from migrations and internal strife during Ramesses VI's reign (Amer 1985, pp. 67–68; Baillie 1989, p. 81), probably driven by the volcanically disturbed climate (Baillie 1995, pp. 82–90). So, the Hekla III global climate impact seems to have been responsible for setting in motion some of the large population migrations that caused empires and nations to collapse. All these events occurred between 1150 and 1100 B.C. (Baillie 1995, pp. 82–83, 129).

Some notes about the mega-eruption of Santorini-Thera in the Aegean and its effect on the climate and other impacts are in order. Tree ring data, calibrated carbon 14 readings from Thera itself, and again Chinese oracle bones have dated the Minoan era eruption to 1628 B.C.[10] These fresh data certainly disassociate the eruption from the early Eighteenth Dynasty events claimed by some scholars.[11] Rather, the fresh data place this eruption squarely in the reigns of the later Hyksos rulers of Egypt, ca. 1674–1567 B.C. Whatever impact this Minoan eruption had on Egypt, including ash fall,[12] it would have impacted most heavily on the Delta-based Hyksos rulers, rather than on Upper Egypt. Additionally, tsunami waves from the eruption might have seriously damaged Hyksos shipping in the Mediterranean. Perhaps, in fact, the eruption sufficiently disrupted the Hyksos rulers that the Thebans were enabled to initiate their revolt against the Hyksos. With the Santorini-Thera eruption now securely dated 1628 B.C., how can one explain the cataclysm mentioned in Ahmose I's stela that some would identify with Thera's eruption?[13] Ritner and Foster (1996, pp. 5–12) demonstrate clearly that this cataclysm was a countrywide event that was felt equally in both Upper and Lower Egypt. On the other hand, the ef-

9. Pang and Chou 1984, p. 846; Pang 1985, p. 816; Weisburd 1985, pp. 91–94; Baillie 1995, pp. 80–81.

10. Baillie 1995, pp. 108–21; Baillie 1990, pp. 160–66; also Kuniholm 1990, pp. 13–18; Baillie 1989, pp. 78–79; LaMarche and Hirschboek 1984, pp. 121–26; Baillie and Munro 1988, pp. 332–46; Hammer et al. 1987, pp. 517–19; Druitt and Francaviglia 1992, pp. 487–93; Pang 1985, p. 816 (abstract); Bernal 1991, pp. 291–93; Kuniholm et al. 1996, pp. 780–83.

11. Goedicke 1985, pp. 37–47; Davis 1990, pp. 232–35; Ritner and Foster 1996, pp. 5–12.

12. Stanley and Sheng 1986, pp. 733–35; Bernal 1991, pp. 291–93; Goedicke 1985, pp. 37–47.

13. Goedicke 1985, pp. 37–44; Ritner and Foster 1996, pp. 1–12.

fects of Thera's eruption were felt most strongly in the Egyptian Delta, and in Upper Egypt, hardly or not at all. While Thera's ash has been found in Delta lake sediments, and perhaps pumice also (Bietak 1992, p. 28), nothing like these traces have been found in Upper Egypt, nor do any projections of the eruption cloud extend so far south (Watkins et al. 1978, pp. 122–26, fig. 1). Also, the date 1628 B.C. for the eruption does not accord with the chronology of the reign of Ahmose I. The pumice found by Bietak at Tell ed-Dabʿa was described as well rounded (Bietak 1992, p. 28; Hankey 1993, pp. 28–29). Deposition of the pumice in a stratum dated to Ahmose I/Thutmose III at Tell ed-Dabʿa hence need not be of that period because it might have been quite weathered, or perhaps it originated from a disturbed Hyksos-era deposit. Alternatively, pumice has long been known to have had an economic use in Egypt (Lucas 1962, p. 73), and given that pumice was commonly found in Greece, but not in Egypt, perhaps this was a shipment of pumice exported from Greece to Egypt. Thus this deposit need not have any bearing on the dating of the eruption of Thera-Santorini, and until it is subjected to further chemical analysis, it cannot be certain that it originated from Thera-Santorini.

Accordingly, the Ahmose I cataclysm probably represents some other large-scale event. The October/November 1994 storms that struck Egypt offer a possible parallel for the Ahmose I cataclysm. These storms were countrywide and caused serious damage in Upper and Middle Egypt, as well as in Cairo and the Delta, and they included lightning, thunder, and hail — weather phenomena very rarely experienced in Egypt but all mentioned in the Ahmose I stela (Ritner and Foster 1996, pp. 11–12; *Middle East News* 32, no. 46, 15 November 1994, p. 2).

To quantify such mega-eruptions as Hekla III, from 1159 to 1140 B.C., and Thera-Santorini, from 1628 B.C., volcanologists have developed the VEI, Volcanic Explosivity Index, which grades such mega-eruptions according to the solid matter ejected and the height reached by the eruption column (Newhall and Self 1982, pp. 1231–38; Simkin et al. 1981). The Minoan eruption of Santorini had a VEI of 6.9 (Decker 1990, p. 451). Hekla III's eruption came from a rift type volcano, but one that ejected much sulfur-laden material over an extended period of time.[14] These are the two largest volcanic events of the first and second millennia B.C., as shown by tree rings, acidity peaks in the polar ice, and climate effects of hemispheric or global extent.[15] Thera-Santorini's eruption in 1628 B.C. was only slightly less in VEI than Tambora's eruption of 1815, with a VEI of 7.0, the largest-known eruption of recent times. Tambora is well attested to have had dramatic climatic impact in both hemispheres. Such enormous eruptions are quite rare, happening once every 300 years or so (Decker 1990, p. 451), and there is no trace of any other volcanic event of such magnitude in the fifteenth and sixteenth centuries B.C. either in tree rings or in ice cores (Baillie 1994, p. 216, table 1). One reason not all great eruptions leave acidity traces in the polar ice is that only the eruptions highest in sulfur content create the climatic acid fallout that leaves traces in the polar ice (Rose et al. 1995, pp. 477–79). Still, Thera-Santorini may be reflected in the polar ice since as the ice-core dating depends on carbon 14 dating it may disagree slightly with the tree-ring dates. Narrowed or absent tree rings are caused directly by the intensity of the eruption and its climatic effects, and that is reflected in the same year or the year after the eruption.[16] Hence, tree rings are inherently more precise in their dating of an eruption. Secondarily, high northern or far southern latitude eruptions, such as Katmai-Novarupta (1912) or Hekla, almost always leave acidic traces in the polar ice because of their geographic location close to the polar regions (Sigurdsson, Carey, and Divine 1990, pp. 110–12). By contrast, Thera-Santorini's 1628 B.C. Minoan eruption, some theorize, was a sulfur depleted eruption,[17] which may account for its absence from the polar ice-core records, although there is an acid peak in the ice cores dated 1645+/-7 B.C., and another that has been dated 1597+/-30 B.C.[18] The second date is barely within the carbon 14 variability range if the eruption came late in 1628 B.C. So, as ice-core dates are carbon dated and carbon 14 has an acknowledged error factor, one of these ice cores may indeed reflect Thera-Santorini's eruption also dated to 1628 B.C. by tree rings (Baillie 1995, pp. 117–21). An alternate possibility is that either the 1597 B.C. or the 1645 B.C. ice-core dates may reflect another high northern latitude, hitherto unidentified, volcanic eruption (Baillie 1995, pp. 115–21). Nonetheless, the magnitude of the eruption of Thera-Santorini was immense, much greater than Krakatau (1883), and closer in scale to Tambora (1815), as judged by the VEI index, and its sulfur output has recently

14. Stothers and Rampino 1983, pp. 411–13; Baillie 1989, pp. 78–81; Baillie and Munro 1988, p. 346; Hammer, Claussen, and Dansgaard 1980, pp. 230–35.

15. Decker 1990, pp. 446–47; Baillie 1995, pp. 82–83, 108–21; Baillie 1993, pp. 68–69; Baillie 1994, p. 216, table 1; Baillie 1989, pp. 78–81, Pang and Chou 1984, p. 846; Pang 1985, p. 816.

16. Baillie 1994, pp. 213, 216, table 1; Baillie 1995, pp. 111, 117–21; Baillie 1989, pp. 78–79.

17. Rose et al. 1995, p. 479; but see Baillie 1995, pp. 113–14, for an upward estimate of Thera's sulfur output.

18. Baillie 1994, p. 216, table 1; but again see Baillie 1995, pp. 117–21.

been revised upwards (Baillie 1995, pp. 113–14, 118–21). Were there in fact another high northern latitude eruption a few years earlier or later than 1628 B.C., it could only have compounded the effects on the climate of the Thera-Santorini 1628 B.C. eruption (Baillie 1995, pp. 114–16). If, however, the tree rings do not reflect another such eruption, it is probably the variability of the carbon 14 dates that is reflected by the divergent ice-core dates. Recent assessment, however, demonstrates how even a mid-scale eruption such as that of Mount Pinatubo in the Philippines and other eruptions of recent times have produced significant cooling of the climate in the Middle East (Genin, Lazar, and Brenner 1995, pp. 507–10), and sulfur output is subject to serious underestimates (Baillie 1995, p. 121).

In conclusion, the tree-ring data from multiple locations, ash traces in the Irish peat bogs, and the ice-core acidity peaks concur on the extended 1159–1140 B.C. range for the eruption of Hekla III in Iceland, with the tree rings in particular indicating the extended eruption cycle and its long-lived impact on climate. This date also synchronizes with recorded ash fall and unusually cold summers in China; and now, it has been shown to synchronize also with the hitherto inadequately explained economic problems that Egypt confronted in the mid-Twentieth Dynasty. The Egyptian crisis also matches exactly that experienced by Europe and North America after the Tambora eruption of 1815. This Hekla eruption probably produced the climatic effects that came as the concluding blow in the sequence of disasters that marked the end of the Late Bronze Age and the start of the Iron Age. Many empires and states are documented to have disappeared, and great migrations of peoples out of marginal habitation zones are attested in Egyptian and Assyrian records.

The Minoan era eruption of Thera-Santorini is quite securely dated to 1628 B.C., especially by the tree rings from widespread areas, by new high precision carbon 14 data from the island of Thera itself, and possibly also by ice-core data. The assessments by geologists and volcanologists at the 1990 Thera III conference indicate that it was a very massive eruption, much exceeding Krakatau (1883) and closer in scale (VEI) to Tambora (1815). The effects of Thera-Santorini's 1628 B.C. eruption in the Mediterranean area were highly dramatic, with widespread ashfall, perhaps pumice deposits attested from Egypt, the Levant, and Anatolia, and a high probability that tsunami waves also devastated the eastern Mediterranean coasts; worldwide it is echoed in tree rings and in Chinese oracle bones.

Chronologically, the extended eruption of Hekla III (1159–1140 B.C.) is securely fixed in the reigns of Ramesses III to Ramesses VI–VIII in the twelfth century B.C. with solid scientifically based data. Thus it utterly refutes attempts to lower the chronology of Ramesses II and III's reigns.[19] Dating the eruption of Thera-Santorini to 1628 B.C. indirectly might support the higher chronology for the start of the Eighteenth Dynasty, if the idea holds that the eruption so dislocated the Hyksos that the Seventeenth Dynasty at Thebes was able to initiate the revolt against the Hyksos. Accordingly, this fresh evidence from the ability to date two volcanic eruptions of antiquity, evidence of their impact on the ancient climate, and other impacts of Thera-Santorini in the Mediterranean and Near East make a most fitting tribute for Professor Edward F. Wente because it supports in some measure the Wente and Van Siclen (1977, pp. 217–18) chronology of the New Kingdom. It also supports the Memphite observation of the Sothic date from Papyrus Ebers. Lastly the re-analysis of the cataclysm mentioned in the Ahmose I stela, a very powerful storm that affected both Upper and Lower Egypt (Ritner and Foster 1996, pp. 5–12), provides the strongest evidence for disassociating that storm from the eruption of Thera-Santorini because the eruption and its effects were felt most strongly in the Delta and not at all in Upper Egypt, where neither ash nor projections of the eruption cloud extended.

References

Amer, A. A. M. A.

1985 "Reflections on the Reign of Ramesses VI." *Journal of Egyptian Archaeology* 71: 66–70.

Baillie, M. G. L.

1988 "Irish Oaks Record Volcanic Dust Veils Drama." *Archaeology Ireland* 2/2: 71–74.

1989 "Hekla 3: How Big Was It?" *Endeavor* n.s. 13/2: 78–81.

1990 "Irish Tree Rings and an Event in 1628 B.C." In *Thera and the Aegean World,* Volume 3: *Chronology* (Proceedings of the Third International Congress at Santorini, Greece, 3–9 September 1989), edited by

19. James et al. 1991; Rohl 1995; also see reviews in Leonard 1993; Forbes 1995.

D. A. Hardy and A. C. Renfrew, pp. 160–66. London: Thera Foundation.

1993 "Using Tephra to Date the Past." *Current Archaeology* 134, Volume 12, No. 2: 68–69.

1994 "Dendrochronology Raises Questions about the Nature of the A.D. 536 Dust-Veil Event." *The Holocene* 4/1: 212–17.

1995 *A Slice through Time: Dendrochronology and Precision Dating*. London: Batsford.

Baillie, M. G. L., and M. A. R. Munro

1988 "Irish Tree-Rings, Santorini, and Volcanic Dust Veils." *Nature* 332: 344–46.

Bernal, M.

1991 *Black Athena: The Afroasiatic Roots of Classical Civilization,* Volume 2. New Brunswick: Rutgers University Press.

Bietak, M.

1992 "Minoan Wall Paintings Unearthed at Ancient Avaris." *Bulletin of the Egypt Exploration Society* 2: 26–28.

Davis, E. N.

1990 "A Storm in Egypt during the Reign of Ahmose." In *Thera and the Aegean World,* Volume 3: *Chronology* (Proceedings of the Third International Congress at Santorini, Greece, 3–9 September 1989), edited by D. A. Hardy and A. C. Renfrew, pp. 232–35. London: Thera Foundation.

Decker, R. W.

1990 "How Often Does a Minoan Eruption Occur?" In *Thera and the Aegean World,* Volume 3: *Chronology* (Proceedings of the Third International Congress at Santorini, Greece, 3–9 September 1989), edited by D. A. Hardy and A. C. Renfrew, pp. 446–51. London: Thera Foundation.

Dothan, T., and M. Dothan

1992 *People of the Sea: The Search for the Philistines*. New York: Macmillan.

Drews, R.

1993 *The End of the Bronze Age, ca. 1200 B.C.* Princeton: Princeton University Press.

Druitt, T. H., and V. Francaviglia

1992 "Caldera Formation on Santorini and the Physiography of the Islands in the Late Bronze Age." *Journal of Volcanology* 54: 484–93.

Edgerton, W. F.

1951 "The Strikes in Ramses III's Twenty-Ninth Year." *Journal of Near Eastern Studies* 10: 137–45.

Edgerton, W. F., and J. A. Wilson

1936 *Historical Records of Ramses III: The Texts in Medinet Habu, Volumes 1 and 2*. Studies in Ancient Oriental Civilization 12. Chicago: University of Chicago Press.

Fitzgerald, R., translator

1975 *Homer, The Iliad*. New York: Anchor Books.

Foden, J.

1986 "The Petrology of Tambora Volcano, Indonesia: A Model for the 1815 Eruption." *Journal of Volcanology and Geothermal Research* 27: 1–41.

Forbes, D.

1995/96 Review of *A Test of Time,* by David M. Rohl. *KMT* 6, no. 4: 83–87.

Genin, A.; B. Lazar; and S. Brenner

1995 "Vertical Mixing and Coral Death in the Red Sea Following the Eruption of Mount Pinatubo." *Nature* 377: 507–10.

Goedicke, H.

1985 "The End of the Hyksos in Egypt." In *Egyptological Studies in Honor of Richard A. Parker,* edited by L. Lesko, pp. 37–47. Hanover: Brown University Press.

Grene, D., translator

1987 *Herodotus, The History*. Chicago: University of Chicago Press.

Gudmundsson, A.

1995 "Infrastructure and Mechanics of Volcanic Systems in Iceland." *Journal of Volcanology and Geothermal Research* 64: 1–22.

Habachi, L.

1980 "The Military Posts of Ramesses II on the Coastal Road and the Western Part of the Delta." *Bulletin de l'Institut français d'archéologie orientale* 80: 13–30.

Hammer, C. U.; H. B. Claussen; and W. Dansgaard

1980 "Greenland Ice Sheet Evidence of Post-Glacial Volcanism and Its Climatic Impact." *Nature* 288: 230–35.

Hammer, C. U.; H. B. Claussen; W. L. Friedrich; and H. Tauber

1987 "The Minoan Eruption of Santorini in Greece Dated to 1645 B.C.?" *Nature* 328: 517–18.

Handler, P.

1989 "The Effect of Volcanic Aerosols on Global Climate." *Journal of Volcanology and Geothermal Research* 37: 233–49.

Hankey, V.

1993 "Egypt, the Aegean, and the Levant." *Bulletin of the Egypt Exploration Society* 3: 28–29.

James, P.; I. J. Thorpe; N. Kokkonos; R. Morkot; and J. Frankish

1991 *Centuries of Darkness*. London: Jonathan Cape.

Janssen, J. J.

1975 *Commodity Prices from the Ramessid Period*. Leiden: E. J. Brill.

Kitchen, K. A.

1982 *Pharaoh Triumphant: The Life and Times of Ramesses II*. Mississauga: Benben.

1986 *The Third Intermediate Period in Egypt*. Second edition. Warminster: Aris and Phillips.

Kuniholm, P. I.

1990 "An Overview of the Evidence for the Date of the Eruption of Thera." In *Thera and the Aegean World,* Volume 3: *Chronology* (Proceedings of the Third International Congress at Santorini, Greece, 3–9 September 1989), edited by D. A. Hardy and A. C. Renfrew, pp. 13–18. London: Thera Foundation.

Kuniholm, P. I.; B. Kromer; S. W. Manning; M. Newton; C. Latini; and M. J. Bruce
1996 "Anatolian Tree-Rings and the Absolute Chronology of the Eastern Mediterranean 2220–718 B.C." *Nature* 381: 780–83.

LaMarche, V. C., and K. K. Hirschboek
1984 "Frost Rings in Trees as Records of Major Volcanic Eruptions." *Nature* 307: 121–26.

Lamb, H. H.
1971 "Volcanic Activity and Climate." *Palaeogeography, Palaeoclimatology, and Palaeoecology* 10/2–3: 203–30.

Leonard, A., Jr., ed.
1993 Review of *Centuries of Darkness: A Challenge to the Conventional Chronology of Old World Archaeology*, by P. James et al. *Colloquenda Mediterranea* A/2. Bradford: Loid Publishing.

Lucas, A.
1962 *Ancient Egyptian Materials and Industries*. Fourth edition revised and enlarged by J. R. Harris. London: Edward Arnold.

Marsot, A. L. al-Sayid
1988 *Egypt in the Reign of Muhammad Ali*. Cambridge: Cambridge University Press.

McQueen, J. G.
1986 *The Hittites and Their Contemporaries in Asia Minor*. Revised and enlarged edition. London: Thames and Hudson.

Moran, W. L.
1992 *The Amarna Letters*. Baltimore: Johns Hopkins Press.

Nelson, H. H.
1943 "The Naval Battle Pictured at Medinet Habu." *Journal of Near Eastern Studies* 2: 40–55.

Newhall, G. G., and S. Self
1982 "The Volcanic Explosivity Index (VEI): An Estimate of Explosive Magnitude of Historic Eruptions." *Journal of Geophysical Research* 87: 1231–38.

Pang, K. D.
1985 "Three Very Large Volcanic Eruptions in Antiquity and Their Effects on the Climate of the Ancient World." *EOS, Transactions of the American Geophysical Union* 66: 816 (abstract).

Pang, K. D., and H. H. Chou
1984 "A Correlation between Greenland Ice Climatic Horizons and Ancient Oriental Meteorological Records." *EOS, Transactions of the American Geophysical Union* 65: 846 (abstract).

Post, J. D.
1977 *The Last Great Subsistence Crisis in the Western World*. Baltimore: Johns Hopkins University Press.

Rampino, M. R., and S. Self
1982 "Historic Eruptions of Tambora (1815), Krakatau (1883), and Agung (1963), and Their Stratospheric Aerosols and Climate Impact." *Quaternary Research* 18: 127–43.
1984 "Sulfur-rich Volcanic Eruptions." *Nature* 310: 677–79.

Rampino, M. R.; S. Self; and R. B. Stothers
1988 "Volcanic Winters." *Annual Review of Earth and Planetary Sciences* 16: 73–99.

Rampino, M. R.; R. B. Stothers; and S. Self
1985 "Climatic Effects of Volcanic Eruptions." *Nature* 313: 272.

Redford, D. B.
1992 *Egypt, Canaan and Israel in Ancient Times*. Princeton: Princeton University Press.

Ritner, R., and K. P. Foster
1996 "Texts, Storms, and the Thera Eruption." *Journal of Near Eastern Studies* 55: 1–12.

Rohl, D. M.
1995 *A Test of Time: The Bible from Myth to History*. London: Century.

Rose, W. I.; D. J. Delene; D. J. Schneider; G. J. S. Bluth; A. J. Krueger; I. Sprod; C. McKee; H. L. Davies; and G. G. J. Ernst
1995 "Ice in the 1994 Rabaul Eruption Cloud: Implications for Volcano Hazard and Atmospheric Effects." *Nature* 375: 477–79.

Sandars, N. K.
1985 *The Sea Peoples: Warriors of the Ancient Mediterranean, 1250–1150 BC*. Revised edition. London: Thames and Hudson.

Schaeffer, C.
1955 "A Bronze Sword from Ugarit with Cartouche of Mineptah." *Antiquity* 29: 226–29.
1968 "Commentaires sur les lettres et documents trouvés dans les bibliothèques privées d'Ugarit." *Ugaritica* 5: 607–768.

Sigurdsson, H.; S. Carey; and J. D. Divine
1990 "Assessment of Mass, Dynamics, and Environmental Effects of Santorini Volcano." In *Thera and the Aegean World*, Volume 3 (Proceedings of the Third International Congress at Santorini, Greece, 3–9 September 1989), edited by D. A. Hardy and A. C. Renfrew, pp. 100–12. London: Thera Foundation.

Simkin, T.; L. Siebert; L. McClelland; D. Bridge; C. Newhall; and J. H. Latter
1981 *Volcanoes of the World*. Stroudsberg: Hutchinson-Ross.

Simpson, W. K.
1973 *The Literature of Ancient Egypt: An Anthology of Stories, Instructions, and Poetry*. New edition. New Haven: Yale University Press.

Stanley, D. J., and H. Sheng
1986 "Volcanic Shards from Santorini (Upper Minoan Ash) in the Nile Delta." *Nature* 320: 733–35.

Stommel, H., and D. Stommel
1979 "The Year without a Summer." *Scientific American* 240/6: 176–86.

Stothers, R. B.
1984 "The Great Tambora Eruption of 1815 and Its Aftermath." *Science* 224: 1191–98.

Stothers, R. B., and M. R. Rampino
1983 "Historic Volcanism, European Dry Fogs, and Greenland Acid Precipitation, 1500 B.C. to A.D. 1500." *Science* 222: 411–13.

Stothers, R. B.; M. R. Rampino; S. Self; and J. A. Wolff
1989 "'Volcanic Winter?' Climate Effects of the Largest Volcanic Eruptions." In *Volcanic Hazards*, edited by J. H. Latter, pp. 3–9. Berlin and Heidelberg: Springer Verlag.

Trigger, B. G.; B. J. Kemp; D. O'Connor; and A. B. Lloyd
1983 *Ancient Egypt: A Social History*. Cambridge: Cambridge University Press.

Wainwright, G. A.
1960 "Meneptaḥ's Aid to the Hittites." *Journal of Egyptian Archaeology* 46: 24–28.

Watkins, N. D.; R. S. J. Sparks; H. Sigurdsson; T. C. Huang; A. Federman; S. Carey; and D. Ninkovich
1978 "Volume and Extent of the Minoan Tephra from Santorini Volcano: New Evidence from Deep-Sea Sediment Cores." *Nature* 271: 122–26.

Weisburd, S.
1985 "Excavating Words: A Geological Tool." *Science News* 127/6: 91–94.

Wente, E. F., and C. C. Van Siclen
1977 "A Chronology of the New Kingdom." In *Studies in Honor of George R. Hughes, January 12, 1977*, edited by J. H. Johnson and E. F. Wente, pp. 217–61. Studies in Ancient Oriental Civilization 39. Chicago: Oriental Institute.

Yurco, F. J.
1998 "Merenptah's Wars, the 'Sea Peoples,' and Israel's Origins." In *Ancient Egypt, the Aegean, and the Near East: Studies in Honour of Martha Rhoads Bell*, Volume 1, edited by J. Phillips, pp. 497–506. San Antonio: Van Siclen Books.

INDICES

GENERAL INDEX

INDEX OF COPTIC WORDS DISCUSSED

INDEX OF EGYPTIAN NAMES IN TRANSLITERATION DISCUSSED

PERSONAL NAMES

ROYAL NAMES

INDEX OF EGYPTIAN WORDS IN TRANSLITERATION DISCUSSED

INDEX OF GREEK WORDS DISCUSSED

INDEX OF MISCELLANEOUS CITATIONS

GIZA TOMBS

HELWAN TOMBS

KARNAK NORTH: EXCAVATIONS IN THE TREASURY AREA

INDEX OF NAMED AND MISCELLANEOUS PAPYRI

INDEX OF NAMED OSTRACA

INDEX OF REGISTERED OBJECTS BY CITY

INDEX OF SELECTED MODERN TEXT CITATIONS